THE OXFORD HANDBOOK OF

ECCLESIOLOGY

THE OXFORD HANDBOOK OF
ECCLESIOLOGY

Edited by
PAUL AVIS

Great Clarendon Street, Oxford, OX2 6DP,
United Kingdom

Oxford University Press is a department of the University of Oxford.
It furthers the University's objective of excellence in research, scholarship,
and education by publishing worldwide. Oxford is a registered trade mark of
Oxford University Press in the UK and in certain other countries

© Oxford University Press 2018

The moral rights of the authors have been asserted

First Edition published in 2018

All rights reserved. No part of this publication may be reproduced, stored in
a retrieval system, or transmitted, in any for2m or by any means, without the
prior permission in writing of Oxford University Press, or as expressly permitted
by law, by licence or under terms agreed with the appropriate reprographics
rights organization. Enquiries concerning reproduction outside the scope of the
above should be sent to the Rights Department, Oxford University Press, at the
address above

You must not circulate this work in any other form
and you must impose this same condition on any acquirer

Published in the United States of America by Oxford University Press
198 Madison Avenue, New York, NY 10016, United States of America

British Library Cataloguing in Publication Data

Data available

Library of Congress Control Number: 2018937419

ISBN 978-0-19-964583-1

Links to third party websites are provided by Oxford in good faith and
for information only. Oxford disclaims any responsibility for the materials
contained in any third party website referenced in this work.

PREFACE

THIS *Oxford Handbook of Ecclesiology* is a unique academic resource for the study of the Christian church. It brings out the continuities and discontinuities in the changing understanding of the church in the Bible, church history, and contemporary theology. Ecclesiology is a vibrant discipline within the spectrum of Christian theology. As the scholarly study of the self-understanding of the church, its identity, ecclesiology is at the centre of contemporary theological research, reflection, and debate. Because understandings of the church differ in interesting ways from one Christian tradition to another over time, notwithstanding substantial common ground, ecclesiology has to be a critical discipline. It not only takes an objective, critical approach to its sources and history, but also remains self-critical, constantly vigilant, revising and reforming its major paradigms accordingly. Ecclesiology is carried forward by research, dialogue, debate, publication, and controversy on the part of many persons, from various Christian traditions and sometimes from none, in many academic centres and beyond them, around the world.

Ecclesiology is also the theological heart of the ecumenical movement. Ecclesiology has been the main focus of the intense ecumenical engagement, study, and dialogue of the past century. While significant convergences have been achieved, it is in ecclesiology that the most intractable differences remain to be resolved. So ecclesiology today is largely carried forward in an ecumenical context. It remains an exploratory and critical discipline, but is now undertaken in a more irenic and dialogical way.

Ecclesiology investigates the church's manifold self-understanding in relation to a number of research fields, including the origins, structures of authority and governance, doctrine, ministry and sacraments, unity and diversity, and mission of the church, not forgetting its relation to the state, to civil society, and to culture. The main sources of ecclesiological reflection are the Bible (interpreted in the light of scholarly research), church history and the wealth of the Christian theological tradition, the experience and practice of the church today, together with the information and insights that can be gleaned from other relevant academic disciplines.

This *Oxford Handbook of Ecclesiology* covers the biblical resources, historical development, and contemporary initiatives in ecclesiology. In particular, generous space is allocated to the New Testament sources of ecclesiology and to some of the most influential shapers of modern understandings of the church. It aims to be a widely useful, comprehensive guide to understanding the church and the ways that the church has been understood in history and is understood today.

It has been rather a long haul to bring this book to birth, as is almost unavoidable in a work with nearly thirty contributions. So I am immensely grateful to all my distinguished authors, especially those who were very prompt with their assignments and have had to exercise considerable patience while the portfolio was completed. However, they have had an opportunity recently to check, revise, and update their chapters.

I also wish to thank the editorial team of Oxford University Press, especially Tom Perridge for initiating the invitation to me to edit such a volume, and Karen Raith who has seen it through editorially in recent times. Their kindness, understanding, and patience has made a big difference. I am grateful also to various members of the production team, who have seen a complex operation through to a successful conclusion.

Paul Avis
University of Durham
University of Exeter
October 2017

CONTENTS

List of Contributors	xi
1. Introduction to Ecclesiology Paul Avis	1

PART I BIBLICAL FOUNDATIONS

2. The Ecclesiology of Israel's Scriptures R. W. L. Moberly	33
3. The Church in the Synoptic Gospels and the Acts of the Apostles Loveday C. A. Alexander	55
4. The Johannine Vision of the Church Andrew T. Lincoln	99
5. The Shape of the Pauline Churches Edward Adams	119
6. The Church in the General Epistles Gerald O'Collins SJ	147

PART II RESOURCES FROM THE TRADITION

7. Early Ecclesiology in the West Mark Edwards	163
8. The Eastern Orthodox Tradition Andrew Louth	183
9. Medieval Ecclesiology and the Conciliar Movement Norman Tanner SJ	199

viii CONTENTS

10. The Church in the Magisterial Reformers 217
DOROTHEA WENDEBOURG

11. Anglican Ecclesiology 239
PAUL AVIS

12. Roman Catholic Ecclesiology from the Council of Trent
to Vatican II and Beyond 263
ORMOND RUSH

13. Baptist Concepts of the Church and their Antecedents 293
PAUL S. FIDDES

14. Methodism and the Church 317
DAVID M. CHAPMAN

15. Pentecostal Ecclesiologies 335
AMOS YONG

PART III MAJOR MODERN ECCLESIOLOGISTS

16. Karl Barth 361
KIMLYN J. BENDER

17. Yves Congar 383
GABRIEL FLYNN

18. Henri de Lubac 409
GABRIEL FLYNN

19. Karl Rahner 431
RICHARD LENNAN

20. Joseph Ratzinger 449
THEODOR DIETER

21. John Zizioulas 467
PAUL MCPARTLAN

22. Wolfhart Pannenberg 487
FRIEDERIKE NÜSSEL

23. Rowan Williams 505
MIKE HIGTON

PART IV CONTEMPORARY MOVEMENTS IN ECCLESIOLOGY

24. Feminist Critiques, Visions, and Models of the Church   527
    ELAINE GRAHAM

25. Social Science and Ideological Critiques of Ecclesiology   553
    NEIL ORMEROD

26. Liberation Ecclesiologies with Special Reference
    to Latin America   573
    MICHELLE A. GONZALEZ

27. Asian Ecclesiologies   595
    SIMON CHAN

28. African Ecclesiologies   615
    STAN CHU ILO

Index of Names   639
Index of Subjects   645

List of Contributors

···

Edward Adams is Professor of New Testament at King's College London. He is the author of several books including, *The Earliest Christian Meeting Places: Almost Exclusively Houses?* (Revised Edition, Bloomsbury T&T Clark, 2015). He is also the co-editor, with David G. Horrell, of *Christianity at Corinth: The Quest for the Pauline Church* (Louisville, KY: Westminster John Knox Press, 2004).

Loveday C. A. Alexander is Emeritus Professor of Biblical Studies at the University of Sheffield, former Canon-Theologian at Chester Cathedral, and a parish priest in the diocese of Chester. She edited *Images of Empire* (1991), and is the author of *The Preface to Luke's Gospel* (1993), *The People's Bible: Acts* (2006), and *Acts in its Ancient Literary Context: A Classicist Looks at the Acts of the Apostles* (2006). She serves on the Church of England's Ministry Council and Faith and Order Commission (FAOC). She co-edited *Faithful Improvisation? Theological Reflections on Church Leadership* (2016). She was President of the British New Testament Society (2012–15), and has served on the Council of the Society of Biblical Literature, and on the editorial boards of several academic journals (currently *New Testament Studies).* She is currently working on commentaries on the Acts of the Apostles and on the Epistle to the Hebrews.

Paul Avis, the editor of this *Handbook*, served in full-time parish ministry in the Diocese of Exeter, 1975–98, as the General Secretary of the Council for Christian Unity of the Church of England, 1998–2011, as Theological Consultant to the Anglican Communion Office, London, 2011–12, and as Canon Theologian of Exeter Cathedral, 2008–13. He is currently Honorary Professor in the Department of Theology and Religion at the University of Durham, UK, and Honorary Research Fellow in the Department of Theology and Religion at the University of Exeter, UK, and Editor-in-Chief of *Ecclesiology.* His recent publications include *The Vocation of Anglicanism* (2016), *Becoming a Bishop: A Theological Handbook of Episcopal Ministry* (2015), *In Search of Authority: Anglican Theological Method from the Reformation to the Enlightenment* (2014), *Reshaping Ecumenical Theology* (2010), *The Identity of Anglicanism: Essentials of Anglican Ecclesiology* (2008), *Beyond the Reformation? Authority, Primacy and Unity in the Conciliar Tradition* (2006), and *Anglicanism and the Christian Church: Theological Resources in Historical Perspective* (2nd edn, 2002). He is joint editor with Benjamin Guyer of *The Lambeth Conference: Theology, History, Polity and Purpose* (2017). He is also editor of the series *Anglican-Episcopal Theology and History.*

xii   LIST OF CONTRIBUTORS

Kimlyn J. Bender is Professor of Christian Theology at George W. Truett Theological Seminary, Baylor University, Texas, USA. He is the author of *Karl Barth's Christological Ecclesiology* (2005) and *Confessing Christ for Church and World: Studies in Modern Theology* (2014) as well as works in numerous journals and collections.

Simon Chan was the Earnest Lau Professor of Systematic Theology at Trinity Theological College, Singapore, and currently serves as lecturer and spiritual director at the college. His recent books include *Grassroots Asian Theology: Thinking the Faith from the Ground Up* and *Pentecostal Ecclesiology: An Essay on the Development of Doctrine*.

David M. Chapman is Methodist District Chair for Bedfordshire, Essex, and Hertfordshire, England. He serves on the British Methodist Faith and Order Committee with a special interest in ecclesiology and ecumenism. He is a member of the World Methodist Council and co-chair of the international Methodist–Roman Catholic Dialogue Commission. The author of three books on Methodist theology and history, he has contributed to several edited volumes and published numerous articles and reviews.

Theodor Dieter has been Research Professor at the Institute for Ecumenical Research in Strasbourg since 1994 and its Director since 1997. He studied Protestant theology and philosophy in Heidelberg and Tübingen and gained his theological doctorate from the Faculty for Protestant Theology in Tübingen in 1991 ('Die philosophischen Thesen der "Heidelberger Disputation" Luthers und ihre Probationen. Ein kritischer Kommentar') and his Habilitation there in 1998 ('Der junge Luther und Aristoteles'). He is a pastor of the Württembergische Landeskirche. He has served as consultant to the international Lutheran/Roman Catholic dialogue and the Lutheran/Mennonite dialogue. Together with Prof. Thönissen from the Catholic Johann-Adam-Möhler-Institut in Paderborn (Germany) he is the leader of a working group of fourteen Roman Catholic and Protestant theologians reconstructing the debate on Luther's 95 Theses on Indulgences. Dieter's publications include *Der junge Luther und Aristoteles* (2001) and many articles on Luther's theology and social ethics and on Lutheran ecumenical relations.

Mark Edwards has been University Lecturer in Patristics in the Faculty of Theology (now Theology and Religion) at the University of Oxford, and tutor in Theology at Christ Church, Oxford, since 1993. Since 2014 he has held the title Professor of Early Christian Studies. His books include *Optatus: Against the Donatists* (1997), *Constantine and Christendom* (2004), *Catholicity and Heresy in the Early Church* (2009), and *Religions of the Constantinian Empire* (2015).

Paul S. Fiddes is an ordained minister of the Baptist Union of Great Britain and Professor of Systematic Theology in the University of Oxford. Formerly Tutorial Fellow of Regent's Park College, University of Oxford (1975–89) and Principal (1989–2007), he is currently Director of Research at Regent's Park College. He is a Doctor of Divinity of the University of Oxford, Honorary Fellow of St Peter's College, Oxford, and an Ecumenical Honorary Canon of Christ Church Cathedral, Oxford. He is an editor of *Ecclesiology* and *Ecclesial Practices*. His publications include: *The Creative Suffering of God* (1989); *Past*

Event and Present Salvation (1989); *Freedom and Limit: A Dialogue Between Literature and Christian Doctrine* (1991); *The Promised End: Eschatology in Theology and Literature* (2000); *Tracks and Traces: Baptist Identity in Church and Theology* (2003); *Seeing the World and Knowing God: Hebrew Wisdom and Christian Doctrine in a Late-Modern Context* (2013).

Gabriel Flynn is Associate Professor of Theology at Dublin City University. He has written *Yves Congar's Vision of the Church in a World of Unbelief* (2004), edited *Yves Congar: Theologian of the Church* (2005), and co-edited (with Paul D. Murray) *Ressourcement: A Movement for Renewal in Twentieth-Century Catholic Theology* (2014). He has published scholarly articles in *Louvain Studies, Concilium, New Blackfriars, La Vie spirituelle, Irish Theological Quarterly, Journal of Business Ethics*, and *Ecclesiology*.

Michelle A. Gonzalez is Professor of Religious Studies and Assistant Provost of Undergraduate Education at the University of Miami. She received her PhD in Systematic and Philosophical Theology at the Graduate Theological Union in Berkeley, California, in 2001. Her research and teaching interests include Latino/a, Latin American, and Feminist Theologies, as well as inter-disciplinary work in Afro-Caribbean Studies. She is the author of: *Sor Juana: Beauty and Justice in the Americas* (2003); *Afro-Cuban Theology: Religion, Race, Culture and Identity* (2006); *Created in God's Image: An Introduction to Feminist Theological Anthropology* (2007); *Embracing Latina Spirituality: A Woman's Perspective* (2009); *Caribbean Religious History* (co-authored with Ennis Edmonds, 2010); *Shopping: Christian Explorations of Daily Living* (2010); and *A Critical Introduction to Religion in the Americas: Bridging the Liberation Theology and Religious Studies Divide* (2014).

Elaine Graham is the Grosvenor Research Professor at the University of Chester and was until October 2009 the Samuel Ferguson Professor of Social and Pastoral Theology at the University of Manchester. She is the author of *Making the Difference: Gender, Personhood and Theology* (1995), *Transforming Practice: Pastoral Theology in an Age of Uncertainty* (1996), *Representations of the Post/Human: Monsters, Aliens and Others in Popular Culture* (2002), and *Words Made Flesh: Writings in Pastoral and Practical Theology* (2009), and co-author, with Heather Walton and Frances Ward, of *Theological Reflection: Methods* (2005). She was a member of the Archbishops' Commission for Urban Life and Faith (2004–6) and wrote, with Stephen Lowe, *What Makes a Good City? Public Theology and the Urban Church* (2009). Her most recent book, *Apologetics without Apology: Speaking of God in a World Troubled by Religion* (2017), explores the relationship between public theology and Christian apologetics.

Mike Higton is Professor of Theology and Ministry at Durham University. He previously worked at the Cambridge Inter-faith Programme, and in the Department of Theology and Religion at the University of Exeter. His publications include *A Theology of Higher Education* (2012), *The Text in Play: Experiments in Reading Scripture* (with Rachel Muers, 2012), and *Difficult Gospel: The Theology of Rowan Williams* (2004). He also edited *Wrestling with Angels: Conversations in Modern Theology*, a collection of Rowan Williams's essays (2007).

Stan Chu Ilo is Research Professor of African Studies at the Center for World Catholicism and Inter-Cultural Studies, Department of Catholic Studies, Faculty of Liberal Arts and Social Sciences, DePaul University, Chicago, Illinois, USA. He is the founder and President of the Canadian Samaritans for Africa, author of many books and articles, editor of the *African Christian Studies* series with Pickwick Publications, and recipient of the 2017 Afroglobal Television Excellence Award for Global Impact.

Richard Lennan is Professor of Systematic Theology in the School of Theology and Ministry at Boston College, where he focuses his research and teaching on the theology of church, the theology of ministry, fundamental theology, and the theology of Karl Rahner. He is the author of *The Ecclesiology of Karl Rahner* (1995), contributed to *The Cambridge Companion to Karl Rahner* (2005), and has published numerous articles on Rahner's work. In addition, he has published *Risking the Church: The Challenges of Catholic Faith* (2004) and edited various books, the latest of which (co-edited with Nancy Pineda-Madrid) is *The Holy Spirit: Setting the World on Fire* (2017). He has also served as President of the Australian Catholic Theological Association and currently chairs the Steering Committee of the Karl Rahner Society.

Andrew T. Lincoln is Emeritus Professor of New Testament at the University of Gloucestershire. He previously taught in the University of Sheffield and the University of Toronto. Among his publications are *Paradise Now and Not Yet* (1981), *Ephesians* (1990), *Colossians* (2000), *Truth on Trial: The Lawsuit Motif in the Fourth Gospel* (2000), *The Gospel According to St. John* (2005), *Hebrews: A Guide* (2006), and *Born of a Virgin? Reconceiving Jesus in the Bible, Tradition and Theology* (2013). He has served as President of the British New Testament Society (2006–9) and has present research interests in the area of the Bible and spirituality.

Andrew Louth is a graduate of Cambridge and Edinburgh Universities. He taught at the Universities of Oxford and London (Goldsmiths College). He is now Professor Emeritus of Patristic and Byzantine Studies, University of Durham, UK, and Visiting Professor of Eastern Orthodox Theology (2010–14) at the Amsterdam Centre of Eastern Orthodox Theology, Vrije Universiteit, Amsterdam. He is Archpriest of the Diocese of Sourozh, Moscow Patriarchate. He is the author of many articles and several books including *The Origins of the Christian Mystical Tradition: From Plato to Denys* (1981, second revised edition 2007), *St John Damascene: Tradition and Originality in Byzantine Theology* (2002), *Greek East and Latin West: The Church AD 681–1071* (2007), *Introducing Eastern Orthodox Theology* (2013), and *Modern Orthodox Thinkers: From the* Philokalia *to the present* (2015).

Paul McPartlan is a Roman Catholic priest of the Archdiocese of Westminster (UK) and Carl J. Peter Professor of Systematic Theology and Ecumenism at The Catholic University of America, Washington DC. After degrees in mathematics at Cambridge and philosophy and theology in Rome, he completed his doctorate at Oxford in 1989 and then served in a London parish for several years and on the faculty of Heythrop College in the University of London 1995–2005. He has been a member of the Joint International Commission for Theological Dialogue between the Roman Catholic Church and the Orthodox Church since 2005, and is also a member of the North American Orthodox–Catholic Theological Consultation. He served for ten years on the Catholic Church's International Theological Commission and also as a member of the International Commission for Theological Dialogue between the Roman Catholic Church and the World Methodist Council. He is the author of *The Eucharist Makes the Church: Henri de Lubac and John Zizioulas in Dialogue* (1993, 2006), *Sacrament of Salvation: An Introduction to Eucharistic Ecclesiology* (1995), *A Service of Love: Papal Primacy, the Eucharist, and Church Unity* (2013, 2016), and many articles on ecclesiology and ecumenism. He edited John Zizioulas, *Communion and Otherness: Further Studies in Personhood and the Church* (2006), and is the co-editor with Geoffrey Wainwright of *The Oxford Handbook of Ecumenical Studies*.

R. W. L. Moberly is an Anglican priest and is Professor of Theology and Biblical Interpretation at Durham University, UK, where he has been teaching since 1985. His scholarly research centres on the responsible understanding and use of the Old Testament as Christian Scripture for today. He has written *The Bible, Theology, and Faith: A Study of Abraham and Jesus* (2000), *Prophecy and Discernment* (2006), *The Theology of the Book of Genesis* (2009), *Old Testament Theology: Reading the Hebrew Bible as Christian Scripture* (2013), and *The Bible in a Disenchanted Age: The Enduring Possibility of Christian Faith* (2018).

Friederike Nüssel studied theology and philosophy of religion at Tübingen, Göttingen, London, and Munich. She did her theological dissertation at the University of Munich with Wolfhart Pannenberg in 1994, followed by the habilitation in 1998. From 2001 to 2006 she was full professor of Systematic Theology at the University of Muenster. In 2006 she became full professor of Systematic Theology and the director of the Ecumenical Institute of Heidelberg University (Germany). She has been involved in many ecumenical, faith, and order dialogues and commissions.

Gerald O'Collins SJ was born in Melbourne, Australia, and took his PhD at the University of Cambridge, where he was a research fellow of Pembroke College. From 1973 to 2006 he taught at the Pontifical Gregorian University in Rome, where he was also Dean of Theology (1985–91). Author or co-author of seventy published books and hundreds of articles in professional and popular journals, he is now Adjunct Professor of the Australian Catholic University and a Fellow of the University of Divinity (Melbourne). His recent publications include *Saint Augustine on the Resurrection of Christ* (2017), *Revelation: Towards a Christian Interpretation of God's Self-Revelation in Christ* (2016), and *Christology: Origins, Developments, Debates* (2015).

Neil Ormerod is Research Professor of Theology at Australian Catholic University. He is widely published in journals such as *Theological Studies, Irish Theological*

Quarterly, and *Gregorianum* in areas such as ecclesiology, Trinitarian theology, natural theology, Christian anthropology, and Lonergan studies. He is the author of *Re-Visioning the Church: An Experiment in Systematic-Historical Ecclesiology* (2014) and *A Public God: Natural Theology Reconsidered* (2014). In 2013 he was made a Fellow of the Australian Catholic Theological Association, the first lay theologian to be so honoured.

Ormond Rush is a priest of the Roman Catholic diocese of Townsville, Australia, with a doctorate from the Gregorian University, Rome. He taught theology at the former Pius XII Provincial Seminary in Banyo, Australia (1991–2000), was Dean of the ecumenical consortium, the Brisbane College of Theology (1998–2001) and President of St Paul's Theological College, Banyo (2001–6). He was elected President of the Australian Catholic Theological Association for three terms from 2007. His publications include *Still Interpreting Vatican II: Some Hermeneutical Principles* (2004), *The Eyes of Faith: The Sense of the Faithful and the Church's Reception of Revelation* (2009), and *The Vision of Vatican II: Principles for Ongoing Reception* (2019). He is currently Associate Professor and Reader at the Australian Catholic University, Banyo campus.

Norman Tanner SJ was Professor of Church History at the Gregorian University, Rome. Born in England in 1943, he was educated at Ampleforth College, entered the Society of Jesus in 1961, and was ordained priest in 1976. For many years he taught in the History and Theology faculties at Oxford University, while also giving short courses on church history and councils in many countries. He moved to Rome in 2003 and in 2015, on becoming emeritus, returned to England where he now lives with the Jesuit community in Bournemouth. His publications include *Decrees of the Ecumenical Councils* (2 vols, 1990), *The Councils of the Church: A Short History* (2001), *Was the Church too Democratic?* (2003), and *New Short History of the Catholic Church* (2011 and 2014).

Dorothea Wendebourg is Chair of Early Modern and Modern Church History and Reformation at the Theologische Fakültaet Humboldt Üniversitaet, Berlin. She received her Dr theol and Dr theol habil from Munich University and formerly held chairs at Göttingen University and Tübingen University. She was a member of the Standing Commission of Faith and Order of the World Council of Churches and of the Joint Roman-Catholic/Evangelical-Lutheran Commission. She also served as Chair of the Theological Commission of the Vereinigte Evangelisch-Lutherische Kirche in Deutschland (VELKD) and as Co-chair of the Theological Commission of the Evangelische Kirche in Deutschland (EKD) and as a member of the Meissen Theological Conferences with the Church of England. Her recent publications include: *So viele Luthers: Die Lutherjubiläen des 19. und 20. Jahrhunderts* (2017); 'A Teacher Requiring a Discriminating Approach: The Jews in Martin Luther's Theology', *Reformation & Renaissance Review*, 19 (2017); *Protestantismus, Antijudaismus, Antisemitismus*, ed. D. Wendebourg, A. Stegmann, and M. Ohst (2017); 'Die weltweite Ausbreitung des Protestantismus', *Weltwirkung der Reformation*, ed. U. Di Fabio and J. Schilling (2017), pp. 114–40; 'Freiheit des Glaubens—Freiheit der Welt', *Reformation und Säkularisierung*.

Zur Kontroverse um die Genese der Moderne aus dem Geist der Reformation, ed. Ingolf Dalferth (2017), pp. 57–89; 'Reformation und Gottesdienst', *ZThK* 113 (2016), pp. 323–65.

Amos Yong is Professor of Theology and Mission at Fuller Theological Seminary, Pasadena, California. His graduate education includes degrees in theology, history, and religious studies from Western Evangelical Seminary and Portland State University, Oregon, and Boston University, Massachusetts, and an undergraduate degree from Bethany University of the Assemblies of God. He has authored or edited almost four dozen books. Recent titles include *The Kerygmatic Spirit: Apostolic Preaching in the 21st Century* (2018), *Tracking the Spirit: A Primer for Young Theologians* (2018), and *The Hermeneutical Spirit: Theological Interpretation and the Scriptural Imagination for the 21st Century* (2017).

CHAPTER 1

INTRODUCTION
TO ECCLESIOLOGY

PAUL AVIS

THE purpose of this introductory chapter is to provide the reader with an overview of the theological discipline of ecclesiology and a basic orientation to its questions and methods. I will begin shortly with an attempt to describe and define this area of theological study. But, first, we should note that ecclesiology is a comparatively late arrival on the scene as a distinct theological discipline. As we shall see, systematic reflection on the nature and purpose of the church took many centuries to emerge and belongs entirely to the era of modernity. Why that should have been the case will, I trust, become clear in the subsequent chapters of this *Handbook*. However, during the past couple of centuries, ecclesiology became a major theological discipline; today, at the beginning of the twenty-first century of the Christian era, it is at the heart of theological research and debate.

WHAT IS 'ECCLESIOLOGY'?

Since the Second World War ecclesiology has undergone a renaissance, thanks to the impetus of three main factors. (1) The significantly titled multi-volume *Church Dogmatics* of Karl Barth (the first volume of the English translation appeared in 1936) which elaborated a vast field of Christian doctrine from the exclusive standpoint of commitment to the Christian church. In the preface to the first part of the first volume (published in German in 1932 during Adolf Hitler's rise to power), Barth lamented that in 'modern Protestantism the very authorities of the Church seem to have no more urgent wish than to give as little heed as possible to the doctrine of the Church'. But Barth insisted that 'from the very outset dogmatics is not a free science. It is bound to the sphere of the Church, where alone it is possible and meaningful.' For Barth, anything less was mere dilettantism (Barth 1975–, I/1: xv, xiii, xvi). (2) The revolution in the official attitude of the Roman Catholic Church to the ecumenical movement and therefore to other churches that took place at the Second Vatican Council (1962–5), especially in the Decree on Ecumenism *Unitatis Redintegratio* (1964)—though the ground had been prepared by theologians well before the council—and the manifold bilateral dialogues with other Christian world communions that followed the council and continue to the present day (Kasper 2009). And (3) the ecumenical movement itself with its stimulus to multilateral theological dialogue on faith and order questions between all the major Christian churches. The ecumenical movement had got under way well before the Second World War, from at least the beginning of the twentieth century in fact, as signalled by the Edinburgh International Missionary Conference of 1910, but reached its peak of activity and success following the formation of the World Council of Churches (WCC) in 1948 and the involvement of the Roman Catholic Church in the Faith and Order Commission (though not in the WCC itself) following the reversal of Roman Catholic policy at Vatican II (Avis 2010).

Ecclesiology remains one of the most challenging and creative areas of theological endeavour today. It has a direct relevance to church life and Christian practices and penetrates several other areas of theological enquiry, just as they in turn impact on ecclesiology. As a major department of the overall theological enterprise, ecclesiology relates particularly to fundamental theology (the study of the methods, norms, and sources of theology), systematic theology, and practical theology and interacts all along the line with them. A significant example of such interaction is the Radical Orthodoxy school or tendency. It combines doing theology from the standpoint of commitment to the church—its dogmas, sacraments, order, and tradition—while speaking into the perplexities and incoherencies of the (post)modern world, intellectual, social, political, and economic (e.g. Milbank 2006; Milbank, Pickstock, and Ward 1998).

The term 'ecclesiology' derives from the Latinized forms of two Greek words: *ekklēsia*, assembly, congregation, church; and *logos*, word, speech, discourse. Just as the term 'theology' is made up of *theos*, God, and *logos*, reasoned discourse, to make 'reasoned discourse about God', ecclesiology is 'reasoned discourse concerning the church'. *Ekklēsia* is a 'secular' Greek word for an assembly of persons and is derived from the verb to call. It was used by the translators of the Greek Bible (Old Testament), the Septuagint (LXX), to render the Hebrew *qahal*, assembly, which in turn stems from the Hebrew word for voice (*qol*). (The LXX also used *sunagōge* to translate *qol*.) In both the main biblical languages, Hebrew and Greek, then, the church is the assembly of those who are *called*—called together to worship and serve the Lord. It is worth noting in passing that the English word 'church' actually comes from a different source: the Greek *kyriake* (cf. the Scottish 'kirk'), belonging to the Lord (*kurios*).

The transition from the political meaning 'assembly' to the theological meaning 'church' is made in the New Testament itself. *Ekklēsia* is found in only one of the Four Gospels—Matthew—where it occurs three times. On two occasions it denotes an assembly (Matt. 18:17), but the third instance has a broader sense: ' . . . on this rock I [Jesus] will build my *ekklēsia*' (Matt. 16:18). In the Epistles *ekklēsia* occurs frequently and three main meanings can be discerned. First, *ekklēsia* refers to the local Christian assembly: 'all the churches of Christ greet you' (Rom. 16:16). Secondly, it refers to the church as a whole, the universal church: 'I persecuted the church of God' (Gal. 1:13). Thirdly, in the later, probably pseudo-Pauline epistles, *ekklēsia* refers to what we might call the cosmic, transcendent or mystical church, which is the body of Christ (Eph. 1:22–3; Col. 1:18). Clearly, these are three interrelated, not three separate, meanings. They feed into the scope of ecclesiology, as it reflects on particular churches, the universal church on earth, and the one, holy, catholic, and apostolic church in earth and heaven, the 'communion of saints', *sanctorum communio*.

Ecclesiology may be defined as the discipline that is concerned with *comparative, critical, and constructive reflection on the dominant paradigms of the identity of the church*. Ecclesiology will normally start from the church's own understanding of its identity, 'the faith of the Church concerning itself' (as *The New Catholic Encyclopedia* puts it). However, the *identity* of the church refers not only to how it sees itself on the basis of Scripture and tradition (its self-understanding), but also to how it is perceived and understood by those who stand outside the church, looking in. In other words its identity refers also to its *locus* in culture and society, the prevailing image of the church. Hans Küng defines ecclesiology as 'the theological expression of the church's image' (Küng 1971: 6). Situating the church 'in the eye of the beholder' in this way gives ecclesiology an open and public dimension; 'public theology' requires 'public ecclesiology' and that can only be healthy.

In a further, secondary and derivative sense, ecclesiology includes the comparative and critical study of the identities of the various particular churches, often called 'denominations'—how they see themselves and how other churches see them. The bewildering plurality of ecclesial bodies, defying the credal affirmation that the church is 'one', constitutes one of the most searching of ecclesiological problems (Avis 2002, 2011). (We should also perhaps note that 'ecclesiology' formerly referred, though this usage is now archaic, to the science of the building and decoration of churches, promoted by the Cambridge Camden Society in the nineteenth century and its journal *The Ecclesiologist*.)

This reflexive aspect of the church's identity and image relates ecclesiology to the project of apologetics (the defence and confirmation of the gospel by building bridges with the assumptions and positions of contemporary culture and non-theological disciplines) and brings it into an alliance with missiology, a parallel and complementary discipline to ecclesiology—they are in fact two sides of a coin. It also gives ecclesiology its reforming cutting edge because those outside are often the ones who are most acutely aware of the church's shortcomings and of where it needs to change. Clearly one cannot commend the Christian faith to enquirers and doubters in apologetics without explaining the nature and mission of the church which is not only an article of the faith itself, but is also the vehicle for the transmission and communication of that faith, the matrix of its elaboration and articulation; Christian belief is 'the faith of the church'. Similarly, one cannot—with theological integrity—engage in missiology except by keeping in close *rapport* with ecclesiology, because mission is the essential work of the church and indeed its *raison d'être*. And the whole business of reform and renewal concerns the church because the church is both the subject (the actor) and the object (the sphere) of renewal and reform. Ecclesiology is pivotal, then, to three key areas of contemporary theological activity: apologetics, missiology, and reform.

THE SCOPE AND SOURCES OF ECCLESIOLOGY

Ecclesiology investigates the church's manifold identity in relation to a wide range of research areas: the origins, mission, ministry, governance, authority, liturgy, sacraments, unity, and diversity of the church, including its relation to the state and to civil society. The title of a report of the Faith and Order Commission of the WCC, *The Nature and Mission of the Church*, typifies the scope or approach of ecclesiology today: what the church is in the purposes of God, how it is constituted, and what its role is in relation to its social, cultural, and political environment. Study of the *shape and structure* of the church, including governance, order, and office, is the discipline of ecclesiastical polity, a subsidiary study of ecclesiology; in every age the church necessarily takes *form* (Avis 2016a). Ecclesiology may also study the church as an institution, an enduring, structured socio-political phenomenon, and when it does so it will need to draw on collateral academic approaches, including sociology, statistics, and political science. But to keep our topic within reasonable bounds, ecclesiology in this *Handbook* will be taken in the previously mentioned sense of *the comparative, critical, and constructive study of the dominant paradigms of the church's identity*.

The sources of that many-faceted reflection are first the Bible (interpreted in the light of modern biblical scholarship and criticism), alongside and together with the history and present experience and practice of the church and the wealth of the Christian theological tradition (historical theology), including its worship and liturgy, together with the information, insights, and challenges that are thrown up by the church's engagement with the surrounding culture and society and with relevant 'non-theological' disciplines. Ecclesiology, like other key aspects of doctrinal theology, seeks, in an attitude of humility and receptiveness, to hear the word and revelation of God made known through the Scriptures and focused most intensively and definitively in the person and work of Jesus Christ (see generally Fahey 1991).

The roots of the theology of the church lie of course in the New Testament writings: the Four Gospels, the Acts of the Apostles, the letters of Paul and others (chapters in this *Handbook* are referenced here by *, so for this area see *Alexander, *Lincoln, *O'Collins, and *Adams). But the New Testament presupposes the Old: the Hebrew Bible contains an implicit ecclesiology—or more than one—in the form of prophetic reflection on the covenantal calling, beliefs, worship, and governance of ancient Israel (*Moberly). The biblical material in both Testaments is a rich quarry for the theology of the church and has been interpreted, of course, in different and sometimes contradictory ways. But what also needs to be elucidated is the sense in which biblical patterns and precepts are regarded as normative in the various traditions; there is a spectrum of positions from literal to symbolic readings, both between and within the churches. All

Christian traditions claim to be faithful to Scripture and to the early church in their worship, teaching, and governance. But it is not plausible to think that all of them, in their extreme diversity, could be equally faithful to the New Testament. A notable feature of this *Handbook* is the substantial treatment of the biblical sources of ecclesiology.

Above all, ecclesiology discovers and reveals the mystery of the church, 'hidden with Christ in God' (Col. 3:3). The church is, as Martin Luther said, 'a high deep hidden thing'. As the mystical body of Christ, the nature of the church cannot be plumbed by our puny human intellectual efforts. Its depths are unfathomable (Congar 1960). In modern ecclesiology the church is often called the sacrament of salvation—an outward visible sign of the mysterious working of grace—and the sacramentality of the church is not confined to Roman Catholic theology (Kasper 1989: chapter VI). The human, worldly, institutional, political dimension of the church is 'too much with us' and often its mystery escapes us, so that we 'have the experience and miss the meaning' (to slightly paraphrase T. S. Eliot). That is the overriding reason why ecclesiology finds in liturgy its true matrix, for the liturgy lifts up our studies into prayer where we join with 'angels and archangels and all the company of heaven'.

THE BIRTH OF ECCLESIOLOGY

There is an abundance of 'raw' ecclesiological material in the New Testament; most of it is of an 'occasional' nature, provoked by practical issues in the life of the early Christian communities (Bockmuehl and Thompson, eds, 1997). Like all biblical theology, none of it is cast in a systematic form. A doctrine of the church cannot simply be 'read off' the pages of the New Testament. An arduous and tangled process of interpretation has taken place through the Christian centuries to arrive at a spectrum of ecclesiologies. Although there is certainly a massive central area of agreement on the nature and mission of the church, as ecumenical dialogue has shown, there is also much diversity nearer to the edges of this variegated tradition (for this whole section see Kelly 1965: 189–93, 200–7, 401–6, 409–17; Pelikan 1983: 73–80, 98–109; Tavard 1992: 7–13; Pannenberg 1998: 21–7; Avis 2018).

The Apostolic Fathers, especially Ignatius of Antioch, certainly held the rudiments of an ecclesiology—a working doctrine of the church—but without methodical or systematic reflection. The patristic period generated more coherent, structured ecclesiological reflection in the work of the Western Fathers: Tertullian, Cyprian, Ambrose, and Augustine (Evans 1972). The Apostles' Creed and the creed of the Councils of Nicea-Constantinople (the 'Nicene Creed') affirm belief in the church under the rubric of faith in the Holy Spirit and the latter creed speaks of the church as 'one, holy, catholic, and apostolic', which is certainly the kernel of an ecclesiology. But neither the creed nor the council that produced it elaborate a doctrine of the church as such. The church was 'not a dogmatic concept' (Harnack) in the Eastern Roman Empire, which was the locus of the early councils. But certain Eastern Fathers, especially Basil the Great, with his implicit Trinitarian ecclesiology centred on the motif of the church as 'a fellowship of love', have much to say about the church as they expound other areas of Christian doctrine (*Louth; Druzhinina 2016). The idea that dominated much patristic thinking on the church was of the Christian community as the mystical body of Christ, but the problems and dilemmas that this key idea generates, as we compare the church as we know it with the theological ideal, were not fully addressed (*Edwards).

Following the Constantinian establishment of Christianity in the early fourth century, the church gradually came to pervade European society, progressively enveloping the life of all people. Whether because of this fact or in spite of it, a separate treatise on the church was not included in the great medieval theological syntheses, e.g. Peter Lombard's *Sentences* or Thomas Aquinas' *Summa Theologiae*, though the sacraments were extensively discussed. The *Rationale divinorum officiorum* of William Durandus the elder, which appeared in the last decade of the thirteenth century, perpetuated a spiritual approach to the theology of the church, drawing on the mystical interpretation of Scripture and the symbolism of the church building and its worship (Holmes 2011). But a more polemical ecclesiology, weighted towards political and institutional aspects, was generated by the enhanced papal claims of Boniface VIII in the bull *Unam Sanctam* (1302). Intense reflection on the church and the need for its reform 'in head and members' was sparked by weaknesses and failures on the part of the papacy, the linchpin of the unity of Christendom, in the late Middle Ages, particularly the papal 'captivity' across the French border in Avignon, and the Great Schism of the West when in 1378 the papacy split and Europe was divided into two halves, each following a different pope and the hierarchy that was loyal to him. The ecclesiological ferment, seeking to restore the unity of the Western church, that this trauma generated helped to resource the Councils of Pisa, Constance, and Basel that successfully attempted to reunite the papacy and, less successfully, to reform the church in the early fifteenth century (Avis 2006). Ecclesiological work had earlier belonged with the canon lawyers and with the 'publicists' debating the respective powers of the pope and the emperor (e.g. James of Viterbo, Giles of Rome, John of Paris—all early fourteenth century). The great political theorists, especially William of Ockham and Marsilius of Padua, and the conciliarist writers, such as Dietrich of Niem, Pierre d'Ailly, Jean Gerson, and Nicholas of Cusa, were the inheritors of this work. A century later, the sixteenth-century Reformers inherited the legacy of Conciliarism, and were caught up in its momentum, without being full blown conciliarists themselves (*Tanner).

Martin Luther had a dynamic, eschatological ecclesiology and wrote a great deal on the church that was highly polemical but not systematic (*Wendebourg; Avis 1981/2002). Philipp Melanchthon included a section on the church in his *Loci Communes* (Commonplaces, 2nd edition, 1535) and John Calvin devoted Book IV of the final (1559) edition of his *Institutes of the Christian Religion* to an extensive treatment of the church. In the post-Reformation period, a more systematic, indeed scholastic Protestant ecclesiology emerged, largely devoted to the defence of the Reformation churches and to intra-Protestant polemics between Lutheran and Reformed. But right up to very modern times Protestant ecclesiology tended to treat the salvation of the individual prior to, if not apart from, consideration of the church, in a way that could not happen today, except among extreme evangelicals. The two greatest English theologians of the sixteenth century, Thomas Cranmer and Richard Hooker, made huge contributions to the evolution of Anglican ecclesiology, the former through its expression in liturgy in his two Prayer Books (1549 and 1552) and the latter in *Of the Lawes of Ecclesiastical Politie*, whose title belies the fact that it is not merely devoted to the structure and governance of the church, but is in fact a major treatise on ecclesiology, supported by the twin pillars of law, divine and human, and Christology (*Avis).

Thus the late fourteenth- and early fifteenth-century Conciliar Movement and the sixteenth-century Protestant Reformation saw the 'birth' of ecclesiology in its modern sense. Its emergence in the Roman Catholic Church was triggered by the Reformation and responded to it defensively and aggressively. But the ecclesiological work of this period did not need or intend to start from scratch; it returned to the biblical and patristic sources and, particularly in the case of the Conciliarists, it built also on the canon law tradition. The main lines of ecclesiological development are amply expounded in the chapters of this *Handbook*, but it is already abundantly clear that ecclesiology tends to assume added urgency at times of conflict and crisis in the life of the church.

ECCLESIOGY AS A PROBLEM

However, this way of looking at ecclesiology—as the comparative, critical, and constructive discipline of reflection on the identity of the church—poses an immediate theological problem. The church believes, as a matter of faith and thus in a completely non-negotiable way, that it has received its essential identity from God. Its identity is not self-generated and cannot be. Its self-understanding is given to it, not produced from its own resources. We may express this principle thus: the church neither creates, nor shapes, nor governs itself, but is dependent on and subject to the power and rule of the Holy Spirit in all three respects. (We may compare this threefold schema—creating, shaping, and governing the church—with Barth's fourfold schema: the upbuilding, growing, upholding, and ordering of the community (Barth 1975– IV/2: §67).)

(1) The church holds that it does not *create* itself. It did not bring itself into being and does not and cannot maintain itself in existence. The church has no bootstraps! It is the creation of the Holy Spirit through the ministry of word and sacrament. The Second Vatican Council (1962–5) stated that Jesus Christ 'founded' and 'inaugurated' the church by proclaiming the gospel of God's coming Kingdom (which equates to the ministry of the word) (Flannery 1992: *Lumen Gentium* 5). Henri de Lubac coined the mantra, 'the Eucharist makes the Church' (which equates to the ministry of the sacraments) (de Lubac 1954: 129ff; McPartlan 1993). It is the

preaching of the gospel and the teaching of the faith, combined with the celebration of the two sacraments explicitly instituted by Christ in the New Testament, baptism and the Eucharist, that bring the church into being and maintain it in existence—all underpinned by compassionate pastoral care. The church does not *make* itself; it can only *find* itself as an already given reality that comes from the hand of God.

(2) If the church does not create itself, it does not *shape* itself either. The church does not believe that it has the freedom to devise its organizational shape and function—its polity in the broadest sense—according to human wisdom or insight, except in those areas where discretion is given to it by God through the fact that Scripture is silent on the details of worship or organization. But fundamentally, the structure and purpose (or mission) of the church—for example: its ordained ministry (normally bishops, priests, and deacons); its conciliar nature and functions; its mandate to preach and teach, to celebrate the sacraments, and to provide pastoral care and oversight for its members and to serve the needs of all—is derived from Scripture as it has been understood and interpreted in the course of the church's history.

(3) To complete the picture of the church's absolute dependence on the God who both creates and shapes the church, we need to add—as a doctrinal and even dogmatic statement—that the church does not *govern* itself either. The church's governance takes place as those of its members who have responsibility for that aspect of the church's life—which means ultimately all of them, at least through their elected or appointed representatives—come together in council to wait upon the Holy Spirit and to gather around the Scriptures, seeking God's purpose for the flourishing of the whole community and the greater effectiveness of its mission. Christ is the only head of the church, his body, and he rules, guides and governs it through the presence of the Holy Spirit—provided that the church is willing to listen in humility and receptiveness to the Spirit speaking through the Scriptures and through the spiritual discernment of those with oversight.

It may seem absurdly—indeed provocatively—naive to say that the church is created, shaped, and governed by God—a crass example of self-deception, of false consciousness. A quick glance at the Christian church in any of its many manifestations, both in history and today, will show us how profoundly, how ineradicably, the church has been and continues to be affected by contingent forces and influences, social, political, economic, geographical, and cultural. None of these influences and forces can be or ought to be played down. Theology cannot be 'in denial' about the major contingent elements in its make-up. Ecclesiology is not in the business of fantasizing about the object of its study, the church, or of dreaming up ideal images of the church, at the expense of the utterly real and inescapable contingent factors—that is to say, factors that could have been different from what they were and are—that have moulded the church through the centuries and continue to do so. Ecclesiology is not interested in a purely Platonic church, one that has no real existence in this world. The concern of ecclesiology is with the real church. It is patently obvious that the Christian church in its historical form has not simply come down from heaven, perfect and entire! So what follows?

We are addressing a theological problem about the identity, in the sense of the self-understanding, of the church. The nub of the problem is this: if, as the church holds as a matter of faith, its essential identity is given to it by God and its self-understanding is something to be discovered and explored as a 'given', rather than constructed from purely human resources, what possible role can there be for ecclesiology, the discipline that is devoted to constructive and critical reflection on precisely those matters of identity and self-understanding?

The answer to our question lies in the brute fact of massive contingency in the life of the church (and the churches). Why is contingency so significant? Contingency ('It could always have been otherwise than it is now—and it could be different again') brings with it change—change over time and from place to place—and change generates difference—difference within the one church. Difference creates oppositions and conflicts. Oppositions and conflict bring the possibility of error, when we define ourselves over against the other and when we engage in power struggles within our own church. When what I have called, in a neutral term, 'error' is unpacked a bit, it can be found to involve not only theological mistakes (inevitable) and wrong official teaching (serious), but also moral failure and sin (perhaps worst of all). Some sins within the church are crimes in civil law, crimes of abuse or corruption, for example. So contingency brings with it the reality of an ever-increasing diversity and it entails the need for continual reform of abuses and corruption.

So how does ecclesiology respond to the reality of contingency in the church—the fact that it could have turned out differently—and to the ensuing realities both of radical difference, opposition, and conflict, on the one hand, and of error, sin, and crime, on the other? The answer must be this: the more rigorously we recognize the contingency, diversity, and sheer difference, combined with moral failure, in the church as we see it, the more imperative it becomes to affirm that the church is created, shaped, and governed by the Holy Spirit. To so affirm is not self-deception or a cry of despair; it is not spitting into the wind. For ecclesiology it is also an affirmation of faith to say that the church, on the analogy of the person of Jesus Christ, is *incarnational* in its nature. Although it comes from God and depends on God, it is fully embedded in creaturely reality, in all the changes and chances, the risks and dilemmas of this world. It is bound up with the historical, the political, and the social complexion of human life in the world. Unlike the person of Jesus Christ, however, the church is also contaminated by human sin and crime. But in spite of all that, the divine origin and divine upholding of the church do shine through—the more so as the church continually reminds itself, through the work of theologians, specifically ecclesiologists, that it is created, shaped, and governed by the Holy Spirit working through the word of God in the Scriptures.

Contingency and Reform

How does the diversity of the church affect ecclesiology? Because the church is radically and essentially embodied in the human, worldly context, it is radically and essentially varied and diverse in its manifestations and expressions. To put it at its very lowest, churches are *not the same*; they are not identical in their teaching, worship, discipline, polity, self-definition, views of each other, and many other aspects of their practice. (The churches also have a great deal in common, as ecumenical dialogue has brought out and emphasized during the past 100 years—they are far from being incommensurable—but that is not our concern at this precise point.) The fact of difference between the churches—that is to say within the one church—is a major ecclesiological problem and challenge.

Because the practices of the churches are different in so many ways, their understandings of the church—their ecclesiologies—differ from one Christian tradition to another. There are many variants of ecclesiology in Christianity. Some are certainly complementary in many ways, but others are contradictory in some respects. Therefore, ecclesiology cannot be a purely descriptive discipline; it must be analytical also and it must make value judgements. It is compelled to be a critical, indeed self-critical discipline, one that can only be carried forward by deep research, challenging dialogue, intense debate, and endless controversy! That is the nature of the beast. If ecclesiology seems bland, idealistic, and irrelevant, that must indicate that our engagement with it has been superficial hitherto! The past century has witnessed intense and creative ecumenical engagement and theological dialogue; the main focus of all that has been ecclesiological and this is the area where the most intractable differences between the churches remain to be tackled. Ecclesiology today is, therefore, necessarily an exploratory, critical, dialogical, and constructive discipline—but more than that.

The human, mundane, political complexion of the church, incarnated as it is in the world, plunges it into the arena of *power*. Before we shy away from this truth, holding up our hands in horror and pleading, as some misguided people do, that the church has no business wielding power, but should rejoice in powerlessness (whatever that may be), let me say that the involvement of the church (and churches) with power is unavoidable, completely inescapable. All human relations, individual and social, involve an element of power, which is usually defined as the capacity to effect the result that others should do as we wish, should accede to our will. Whether this result is achieved by manipulation, persuasion, or brute force, it matters not, for these are all forms of power. Power equals leverage. The business of the church is relationships, social and individual, with one another and above all with God the Holy Trinity. So the church is inescapably implicated in power-play (Avis 1992; 2015b; Sykes 2006; Percy 1998). But the inevitability of power-play immediately gives scope for abuse, corruption, and oppression, the very sins and crimes that continually rear their ugly heads within the church. This factor also determines the nature of ecclesiology—it must be concerned with the reform and purification of the church. Ecclesiology is not merely descriptive, painting a portrait of the churches as they are, without making value judgements. It is also prescriptive, showing how the churches need to change, by reforming themselves in the light of the searching judgements of the word of God, in order to conform more closely to the nature of the church of Jesus Christ, which it confesses in the Nicene Creed to be one, holy, catholic, and apostolic. To be faithful to its calling, ecclesiology must be replete with value judgements. It has a prophetic, reforming purpose and agenda and this intensifies its critical and constructive nature. If we do not deceive ourselves about the kind of reality that the church is—human as well as divine, sinful as well as holy—we can see at once, I trust, that ecclesiology is an intrinsically reforming or reformational discipline.

RECENT AND CURRENT DEVELOPMENTS

The twentieth century was called 'the century of the Church'. The ecumenical movement, the liturgical movement, and the biblical theology movement all made their contribution to the revival of ecclesiology—and there is little sign of a slackening of ecclesiological energy so far in the twenty-first century. One straw in the wind is the fact that the only journal, in the English language, devoted purely to ecclesiology, began in 2004: *Ecclesiology*, edited by the editor of this *Handbook*, together with an international, ecumenical team of colleagues, and published by Brill. (We might also note that *The International Journal for the Study of the Christian Church*, published by Routledge, has a wider remit than *Ecclesiology*, but does include strictly ecclesiological material.) Other journals that major on ecclesiological questions, such as the Roman Catholic organs *Concilium* and *Communio*, were generated by the energy produced by the Second Vatican Council (1962–5), the greatest ecclesiological event of the twentieth century. In America the journal *Pro Ecclesia* includes Lutheran and Roman Catholic contributions to theological reflection across a broader front.

A major forum for ecclesiological work, initiated and chaired by Gerard Mannion, is the Ecclesiological Investigations International Research Network, with its prolific publications, frequent conferences, and regular seminar at the American Academy of Religion conference. Mannion is also the joint editor of a major ecclesiological resource, *The Routledge Companion to the Christian Church* (Mannion and Mudge, eds, 2008).

A remarkable recent achievement in the sphere of ecclesiology is the *Christian Community in History* trilogy by Roger Haight SJ. The first two volumes provide a scholarly, insightful survey of understandings of the church through the centuries—a valuable resource for students of ecclesiology. The third volume *Ecclesial Existence* is synthetic in character and offers what Haight calls a 'transdenominational' (and I would probably call an 'ecumenical') ecclesiology. Such an ecclesiology stands alongside denominational ecclesiologies, running parallel to them. It is avowedly pluralist, but not relativist. It looks for the authentic experience of life in the church that the many churches have in common in spite of their differences. The method of discerning this shared ecclesial existence is the 'analogical imagination' searching the comparative phenomenology of the churches. The process of discernment is guided by four criteria: 1. connection with Scripture; 2. continuity with the church in history; 3. coherence and intelligibility; 4. ability to empower the Christian life and, by its language, to awaken a common, shared experience. Haight's work has been criticized for methodological weaknesses (Ormerod 2008; 2014: 24–6; but see Mannion 2008; 2009), but it has highlighted for us, in tune with what certain ecumenical dialogues have aspired to, that the goal of ecumenical theology must be the faith of the church today in continuity with the faith of the church in Scripture and tradition, and that this is the heart of the ecclesiological task (Haight 2004; 2005; 2008a; 2008b).

The Second Vatican Council (1962–5) itself prioritized ecclesiological questions, seeing them as foundational, and placing its Dogmatic Constitution on the Church (*Lumen Gentium*) at the head of the series of documents that it promulgated. The council set the tone of contemporary ecclesiology by rejecting a draft prepared in advance by Vatican officials and insisting that what the council said about the church should be deeply biblical, spiritual, and pastoral and should draw on the most vital elements in the tradition. The legacy of Vatican II is now a battleground where theologians fight over the proportions of continuity and discontinuity in the council's teaching—though Ormerod has shown how complex and elusive those concepts are (Avis 2015a; Ormerod 2014: Postscript). The impetus that Vatican II gave to ecclesiology, and the vexed question of the 'reception' of the council, are fully brought out in this *Handbook* (*Rush).

In addition, there is a number of modern theologians—some still living—of various traditions, whose contribution and influence in the sphere of ecclesiology is such that they merit specific studies in their own right. One salient feature of the *Handbook* is a series of essays on the work of seminal modern ecclesiologists: Barth, Ratzinger, de Lubac, Congar, Rowan Williams, Rahner, Zizioulas, Pannenberg (*Bender, *Dieter, **Flynn, *Higton, *Lennan, *McPartlan, *Nüssell).

In addition to the major traditions of ecclesiology that go back for centuries— Eastern Orthodox, Roman Catholic, Anglican, Lutheran, Reformed, and Baptist—this *Handbook* takes account of the more modern Methodist (*Chapman) and Pentecostal (*Yong) ecclesiologies. In the past few decades, fresh critiques of traditional ecclesiology have appeared in the form of Liberation Theology (*Gonzales) and Feminist Theology (*Graham and see below) and the theologies that have emerged in East Asia (*Chan) and Africa (*Ilo).

In my view, though not everyone would agree, the contributions and perspectives of the social sciences and of critical theory need to be taken on board, though discriminatingly, and this volume includes a chapter on this area. To have integrity, ecclesiology should include the ideological critique of Christianity and the church. The post-modernist, deconstructive challenge to the standard ecclesiological ingredients of form, structure, continuity, tradition, consensus, essence, etc. needs to be grappled with by those working in the field of ecclesiology (*Ormerod; 2014: chapter 2; Mannion 2007). But one of the most crucial areas of contemporary ecclesiology is its connection with mission and missiology.

MISSIOLOGICAL ECCLESIOLOGY

The connection between ecclesiology and missiology—the study of the principles and practice of Christian mission, including evangelization—is an intimate one. It is arguable—though missiologists might not like it—that missiology is a subdivision of ecclesiology, since it is the church that is mandated to the task of mission and it is the members of the church, ordained and lay, who engage in it. Theologically speaking, mission cannot be an activity of freelance individuals who accept no accountability to the church (though mission in the form of evangelism or social reform has sometimes been exactly that). Mission is an action of the church as such and is therefore an ecclesial matter. On the other hand, in one sense mission is greater than the church because it arises from the *missio dei* and therefore springs from God's eternal being and purpose. The church plays its assigned part as the privileged instrument—but by no means the sole instrument—of a great purpose that transcends it, the mission of God. That foundational classic of modern missiology, David Bosch's *Transforming Mission: Paradigm Shifts in Theology of Mission*, is a solidly ecclesiological work and as such it is a model of how missiology should be done (Bosch 1991/2011). While missiology is a major theological discipline in its own right, it should always go hand in hand with ecclesiology. A theology of the church that is not orientated to mission will tend to be inward-looking, uncritical, and sterile. On the other hand, theological reflection on mission that is not geared to the worship, ministry, and oversight of the church is likely to be rather freewheeling, individualistic, and unaccountable. So an ecclesiology for the twenty-first century—an age of pluralism in faith, confident atheism, openly proclaimed agnosticism, and consumer materialism, as well as spiritual searching and New Age syncretism—will be infused with and permeated by missiological concerns and insights. Given the decline of Christianity in the West and the need to re-evangelize 'Christendom', it seems likely that ecclesiology will take its bearings from missiology more strongly in the immediate future and that the two approaches will increasingly be seen as two sides of a coin.

ECUMENICAL ECCLESIOLOGY

Ecclesiology today can only be undertaken with integrity and validity in an ecumenical context and in an ecumenical spirit; the days of strictly confessional ecclesiologies are over (Avis 2010). Thanks to the ecumenical movement during the past century and more, the major churches now stand in a relationship of unprecedented amity and trust to each other, though there remains a residue of suspicion and resentment based on historic and also recent failures in charity and understanding (and there are numerous Evangelical and Pentecostal churches, especially in the developing world, that have hardly been touched by the new climate and stand outside the ecumenical movement, regarding it with suspicion). Through their membership of the World Council of Churches and national councils of churches (or the equivalent) the historic churches (and many more recent arrivals) have been able to recognize, to one degree or another, the one church of Jesus Christ in each other. Their relationship is one of mutual reception (drawing from each other's theology and practice) and even mutual accountability, in the sense that no church can pretend that its actions affect only itself and will have no impact on other churches globally.

The terms 'recognition' and 'reconciliation' are key to defining the relationship in which churches stand to each other. They are concerned with degrees of communion (*koinōnia, communio*), ranging from mutual recognition of baptism (or Christian initiation), to acknowledgement of the authenticity of one another's ordained ministries, to full interchangeability of ordained ministers (interchangeable Eucharistic presidency and appointments), the collegial practice of oversight, and a shared life as far as is practicable (Zizioulas 1985; Anglican–Roman Catholic International Commission 1990; Fuchs 2008; Lim 2017). Although ecumenism is largely a grass-roots phenomenon, few expressions of Christian unity would be possible without the high-level theological dialogue that seeks, with some success, to discover common ground, clear up misunderstandings, isolate unresolved problems, and find fresh ways of expressing a common faith. The ecumenical movement has been well served by ecclesiology and has made a massive contribution to it through its dialogue reports; they are now among the most important resources of ecclesiological reflection.

Ecumenism has effectively modified the character of ecclesiology within the churches. Because ecclesiology is compelled to recognize the new situation that pertains between churches—the degrees of communion—it cannot go on being merely confessional. Confessional ecclesiology is defunct. In the confessional mode of ecclesiology we tend to define our own church over against other churches, as though they were inferior specimens of 'church' or were not equally 'church' at all. But to do ecclesiology in an ecumenical way avoids invidious comparisons and hostile value judgements. It invites a range of diverse voices to the table and is compelled to formulate its conclusions in a way that is sensitive and respectful to ecumenical partners. While this approach should characterize all ecclesiology, its fullest expression is found in the work of the Faith and Order Commission of the World Council of Churches and its most fruitful outcomes so far have been the reports *Baptism, Eucharist and Ministry* (1982), *The Nature and Mission of the Church* (2005), and *The Church: Towards a Common Vision* (2013) (Faith and Order Commission 1982, 2005, 2013).

One of the most fruitful expressions of ecumenical ecclesiology is the initiative known as 'Receptive Ecumenism'. Emanating from the University of Durham, UK, Receptive Ecumenism can be seen as a particular form of 'spiritual ecumenism' (an alternative, favoured by Cardinal Walter Kasper as President of the Pontifical Council for Promoting Christian Unity, to a supposedly institutional ecumenism—though ecumenism has never been merely that). Receptive Ecumenism's distinctive method focuses *not* on what one church can teach another, showing it where it has gone wrong (because it is different), but on what one church can *learn* from another in order to redress its own weaknesses and so serve the mission of God more effectively. We could say that Receptive Ecumenism is the antithesis of the confessional ecclesiology of the past. Its approach is intrinsically marked not by competitiveness and judgementalism, but by charity and humility; these are its ethical methodological criteria. Receptive Ecumenism is all the more remarkable for being a project brought to birth by a Roman Catholic (lay) theologian, Paul Murray, who clearly believes that it has a special relevance to his own church (Murray 2008; Avis 2012).

FEMINIST ECCLESIOLOGY?

The feminist theologians of the past few decades have not been particularly drawn to specifically ecclesiological work, with the main exception of Natalie Watson (Watson 2002; 2008). But they have inevitably been engaged in ecclesiological reflection in an indirect and oblique way (Loades 1987; Hampson, ed., 1996). Those Christian feminist theologians who have remained within the church have tended to be ambivalent about ordination and about involvement in church structures, though there are some in England and America who are priests. Sarah Coakley is a shining transatlantic example of commitment without compromise in church affairs, as well as providing deep conceptual foundations for a theological reconstruction that has passed through the feminist revolution and assimilated its insights (Coakley 2002; 2013; 2015). Other feminist theologians are either lay Anglicans (e.g. Anne Loades, Elaine Graham, Natalie Watson) or Roman Catholic women who do not have the option of being ordained, even if they had wished to seek it (e.g. Mary Grey, Janet Martin Soskice, Karen Kilby). But the still prevalent male-dominated paradigms of biblical and historical Christianity—andocentric, patriarchal, and sexist—continue to provoke a sense of alienation from the institutional church among many reflecting women (*Graham; Daly 1973; Ruether 1983; Hampson 1990; 1996).

Feminist versions of ecclesiology are often marked by a radical alternative vision of the church, one shaped by women for women and centred on intimate, supportive forms of community. However, feminist theologians who have hung on within the historic churches point out that the church has given women much, as well as denying them much. What we might call 'ecclesial feminist theology' does not despair of the church, but aims to reshape its identity and self-understanding in a non-hierarchical, democratic, participatory, and gender-equal or gender-neutral direction and to remodel the church's practices of worship, teaching, and governance accordingly. This may well involve a critique of traditional expressions of Christology by emphasizing that what the Logos united with at the Incarnation was not some specifically male version of human nature (whatever that might be), but human nature as such, created in the image of God and shared by women and men equally (which happens to be orthodox doctrine anyway). Ecclesial feminist ecclesiology then proceeds to deconstruct the oppressive implications of the biblical and traditional images of the church as the body and bride of Christ, before setting about reconstructing ecclesial imagery along gender-neutral and psychologically androgynous lines as far as possible, stressing the equality and mutuality of women and men, recovering the significant roles that women played in the early church, discovering female role models in church history, and altogether putting forward a vision of the church as modelling the true community of the sexes (Fiorenza 1983; Avis 1989; Loades 2001; Watson 2002; 2008). Feminist ecclesiology seeks to purge and reform the church of all that demeans women. It is indeed a new reformation, with far-reaching implications.

A REALISTIC ECCLESIOLOGY

Although, as I have already pointed out, ecumenism has never been merely institutional, fixated on committees, structural mergers, and so on, it is undeniable that the ecclesiology of the mid-twentieth century reflected and embodied the culture of modernity. Thus it was programmatic, optimistic, expansive, even grandiose. Self-criticism and theological humility were not always among its most obvious characteristics. It did indeed think that structural, institutional mergers were the goal of ecumenism. Ecumenical ecclesiology has often been conducted up in the theological stratosphere, dreaming of ideal models of the church, especially of a future united church ('the coming great church'), without being sufficiently aware of the ambiguities of the concept of unity or 'oneness' itself or of the rather intractable difficulties of realizing in practice a strongly organizational vision of unity. Modern ecclesiology was not adequately grounded in empirical reality. It did not take sufficiently seriously the hard-won convictions and well-winnowed practices that are among the building blocks of the identity and self-understanding of the historic churches as moral communities.

After high modernity, in the melting pot of post-modernity, a more realistic, modest, and somewhat chastened ecclesiology seems more appropriate. This will be an ecclesiology that is undertaken in a more tentative, exploratory, realistic, and even empirical way. As it takes form in ecumenical ecclesiology, it will need to find a voice that is persuasive, yet practical; visionary, yet not utopian. It will prove its worth when it can point to incremental steps forward to greater unity—unity in mission—pursuing the method that has been found serviceable in ecumenical dialogue, that of 'unity by stages' (Healy 2000; Avis 1986; 2010).

PRACTICAL ECCLESIOLOGY

To be intentionally realistic in our ecclesiology (including our ecumenical theology)—to do ecclesiology in the real world—must mean to take the concrete forms of the church and the actual expressions of church life into our purview and to adapt our method accordingly. It must entail that we eschew 'blueprint' ecclesiologies (Healy 2000) that fix their gaze on the ideal church, the church (as we suppose) as it exists in the mind of God. By the same token, ecclesiological realism means shunning 'Rolls-Royce' ecclesiologies—that glide smoothly and effortlessly forward, so that, cocooned and cosseted by the comforting luxury of dreams and fantasies about the church, we remain oblivious to the faults and failings that compromise its witness, and to the sins and crimes that are being committed in its name, all around us (see 'The Imperfect Church' herein). If we are to avoid those pitfalls, our ecclesiology must be critical, pastoral, and practical. Within practical theology, the social-science discipline of ethnography can play a role.

(a) *Critical.* It will not do for ecclesiology to be merely descriptive or phenomenological—even less, celebratory—of the church. It must always have an ethical cutting edge. If it is true that 'the time has come for judgement to begin with the household of God' (1 Peter 4:17), then theology should be mindful of the judgement that is now 'at hand' and seek to anticipate it as best it can, unworthily indeed in its poor human way. Just as the eighth-century prophets of the Hebrew Bible brought an ethical searchlight to bear on the waywardness and idolatry of Israel, so ecclesiology should be pursued in the spirit of the prophets, exposing the moral failings of the institution, not least the abuse of power and the exploitation of the vulnerable by those in the church who have some kind of authority. In this respect ecclesiology needs to be informed by the Critical Theory developed by the Frankfurt School and by the Sociology of Knowledge and other forms of ideological critique (e.g. Arato and Gebhardt 1978; Mannheim 1936; Eagleton 1991). Ecclesiology has a prophetic dimension; ethical and ideological critique belong to its vocation (see also Hinze 2016).

(b) *Pastoral.* Of course, Pastoral Theology is a theological discipline in its own right and ecclesiology will want to respect its integrity as such and not trespass on its territory. Nevertheless, in order to be real, ecclesiology must be infused with a pastoral awareness—which it will be if it keeps in close contact with missiology, for the pastoral mode of mission is particularly effective (Avis 2003). Ecclesiology can serve pastoral practitioners—who, after all, do their work in the name of the church—by providing them with an orientation to the church, an understanding of its mission and unity, and a critical awareness both of the winning strengths of the church and of its debilitating weaknesses. Pastors of all kinds and those who teach them their pastoral wisdom and skills certainly need to know their ecclesiology. In return, ecclesiology can be helped to keep its feet on the ground by being attuned to the pastoral. Like the clergy, ecclesiologists need to know (in Pope Francis's famous phrase) 'the smell of the sheep'.

(c) *Practical.* Practical theology has also become a distinct discipline in recent years and is closely related to Pastoral Theology—indeed in some cases it is another name for it (Graham 1996). Ecclesiology will want to listen to exponents of Practical Theology and to learn from their work. Ecclesiology would fail in its task if it were to be a purely theoretical discipline, abstracted from the practice of the Christian life in the community of the church. Ecclesiology can become *praxis*, that is, practice that is informed, shaped, and enlightened by theology (*theoria*)—or, to look at it another way, a lived or performed theology (C. Boff 1987). Ecclesiology understood as *praxis* will not only be orientated to working for social and political justice and flourishing, in the way that Liberation Theology has pioneered (*Gonzales), but will also address other areas of embodied church life, such as the outworking of pastoral ministry, Christian initiation, worship and liturgy, authority and power, and issues of gender and sexuality. So ecclesiology will seek to become a critical, pastoral, practical, and applied theology with an intentionality towards the freedom and flourishing of individuals in the community of the church (Pattison 1997).

A mandate and an agenda for practical ecclesiology has been clearly set out by Clare Watkins in conversation with others (Watkins 2012). I agree with her that ecclesiology will only be 'authentic' when it is able to 'speak truthfully about concrete realities' and that 'actual practices' need to be given their rightful place in theological talk about the church. Practices are indeed 'bearers of theology' and potentially 'a theological voice ... spoken from the heart of the church' which has 'authority'. To attend to them is 'to listen to works of theology'. Obviously, theory and practice, theology and life, are not identical; they need to be distinguished in our thinking about them and our doing of them. But they belong together and need each other; an enlightened ecclesiology will be geared to effect their interaction at all times.

(d) *Ethnography and ecclesiology.* The church is unquestionably a historical-social-cultural reality, as well as a theological reality. In fact it is also an economic and political reality—hence the need for ecclesiology to be informed by ideological critique. If ecclesiology is to take the historical, social, cultural, economic, and political dimensions of the church seriously—if it is to be 'grounded' in the actual life of Christian communities at various levels and to be relevant to them—it will need to be instructed by empirical or 'field' work, as well as by the study of its standard textual sources, primarily Scripture, historical and systematic theology, philosophy, and so on. Such an earthing of ecclesiology can be secured by bringing ethnographical researches to bear on ecclesiological reflection and incorporating ethnographic approaches into our method. Ethnography is understood here in a broad sense as the empirical-conceptual study of the life of communities as it is lived and experienced. Ethnography uses qualitative—that is to say in-depth, exploratory, hermeneutical, analytical—empirical methods to understand the life of social groups and what it means to its members to belong to the group. In conjunction with ecclesiology, ethnography is concerned with the life of a congregation or parish (Hopewell 1987), aiming for a 'thick description' of the life and practice of that community by means of participative observation and evaluation. Ethnography provides no escape from theology more narrowly and traditionally conceived (nor do its leading exponents claim that it does). Like every science, it has a theoretical, heuristic, hermeneutical dimension. And like every other science it cannot avoid engaging in explanation. It asks not only 'What?', but also 'Why?' and 'How?' Ethnography has its limits. Like any empirical discipline, it is necessarily selective in its data, interpretative in its method, and limited in its application to wider questions. So ecclesiology cannot be confined to—or reduced to—ethnography and no one to my knowledge is suggesting that it should be. But, given those caveats, we may say that ethnography deserves to be recognized as a vital aspect of ecclesiology—indeed as a partner in a common enterprise (Ward 2012; Scharen 2012; Jenkins 1999).

Questions to Wrestle with

There are certain perennial questions in ecclesiology that go to the root of the integrity of the church and touch on the validity and coherence of ecclesiology as a theological discipline. They are uncomfortable, possibly insoluble, questions that we continually wrestle with in ecclesiology. In this section I very briefly highlight a few of them, without much referencing or attempting to provide an adequate answer, even if that were possible, so that readers can, if they wish, revolve them in their minds in reading further in this *Handbook*.

Did Jesus Found the Church?

As mentioned above, Vatican II spoke of Jesus Christ 'founding' and 'inaugurating' the church by preaching the gospel of the Kingdom or Reign of God. All Christian traditions assume that Christ founded the church (and presumably also that he particularly approves of their brand of it). The presupposition of ecclesiology is that we are talking about the church of Christ. But did Jesus of Nazareth *intend* there to be a church in ongoing institutional form? I do not say, 'the church as we know it' (though that way of putting it does point in the right direction), because it can hardly be denied that the church as it now is—visibly fragmented, morally compromised, often dysfunctional— could not possibly have been intended by Jesus, whatever else he may have hoped for. But I can put the question like this: Did Jesus foresee that the community of disciples/ apostles, which he undoubtedly gathered around him to continue his mission in the 'last days', would endure through the centuries, spreading to all nations and taking vastly different—sometimes incompatible—forms? This question needs to be answered both historically and theologically, not in one way or the other: the history must count and the theology must make sense. It is a question that has been frequently discussed and is in fact inescapable, for obvious reasons. If Jesus did not found the church, at least in the sense of explicitly intending it, what business do we have working for it, promoting it, and defending it? Why then does the church matter and what is the point of ecclesiology?

The overwhelming consensus of modern New Testament scholarship is that it is highly unlikely that Jesus envisaged or intended the church as it turned out to be. His mission and message were eschatological through and through. The last days of decision and judgement in the face of the coming Kingdom or Reign of God precluded any such thoughts and plans. Divine intervention was imminent. If that is the case, what are the consequences for the Christian doctrine of the church ('I believe . . . one holy, catholic, and apostolic church') and for the theology of the church (ecclesiology)?

First we may ask whether we can soften the challenge to received Christian, ecclesial claims by proposing that the church is founded *on* Christ—taking him as its one foundation (1 Cor. 3:11)—even though it was not founded *by* him, historically speaking? The church is indeed founded on Christ, but that might be a colossal delusion if it was not in tune with his intentions or even contrary to them; it would be one of the biggest confidence tricks in history. The fact of the *church* would be in intolerable tension with the fact of *Jesus of Nazareth*. It would also be insufferably patronizing: 'Never mind what *he* wanted; we see things differently now', or 'The church is what Jesus *would* have wanted if he could have thought that far ahead.' So the problem with that gambit is that it is in danger of making the church into a human construction, the result of human initiative, and more than initiative—arrogance. That is the exact antithesis of what the New Testament *does* say about the church: in essence that it was and is *founded* and founded by God: 'the household of God, built upon the foundation of the apostles and prophets, with Jesus Christ himself as the corner stone' (Eph. 2:20; cf. 1 Cor. 3:11). That statement is both theological and historical.

On the other hand, we should note that 'institutional' elements are not absent from the New Testament picture of the church. The historical Jesus saw his mission as being to recall Israel, by repentance, to its true vocation as the people of God, serving God's Kingdom in the world. As the renewed and re-gathered Israel, such 'political' concepts as order, office, and the transmission of authority were not foreign to the community of disciples, even when the emphasis was more on spiritual gifts (*charismata*) than on an institution. The first Palestinian Christians worshipped in the temple and Christians of the Jewish *diaspora* modelled their communities and their worship on the synagogue. They did this not because they had nowhere else to go, but because they saw themselves as standing in continuity with Israel and its institutions. The significance of the New Testament writers naming twelve apostles, for the twelve tribes of Israel (even though there are many more than twelve who are called 'apostles'), can hardly be overestimated. Although the letter to the Hebrews shows that the sacrificial system of the Jerusalem temple was now superseded (probably the temple had by now been destroyed, in AD 70), so that one thread of continuity was cut, this letter might be said to excel all others in its sense of the fulfilment of types and shadows in Christ, and its depiction of the suffering early Christians as continuing the roll call of the heroes and heroines of faith in ancient Israel (chapter 11).

The New Testament itself begins a *trajectory* that has continued, with many twists and turns and some blind alleys, to the present day. Whatever the truth about the dominical founding of the church, it is patently clear that it has evolved through history and continues to do so. In his *Essay on the Development of Christian Doctrine*, Newman wrestled with the tension of continuity and discontinuity (Newman 1974). Does continuity outweigh discontinuity? That will be a matter of judgement, provided that it is informed by profound scholarship, though it is a judgement that it is almost impossible to make, even very tentatively, because no one scholar can hold all the necessary information. However, the uncomfortable fact remains that much in the church's teaching and practice throughout history cannot be legitimized by appealing to Christ's overt intentions in the Scriptures. He said little about the shape of his community and left no blueprint. But the church has the teaching and practice of the New Testament church to guide it and where that teaching and practice do not answer our questions—it is occasional and therefore incomplete—we have the spirit and character of Christ to point the way (see further Avis 2019).

The Imperfect Church

This second question generates as much heart-searching as the first, if not more so. Even if we cannot claim with any assurance that Jesus founded or intended the church as an ongoing, structured society, and if we have to admit that he almost certainly did not envisage the church as it turned out to be, the fact remains that the self-understanding of the church as it now exists pivots on its faith about itself, what it holds dear about its place in the mission of God. The church confesses in the creed what it believes in faith about itself: that it is 'one, holy, catholic, and apostolic'. The church believes that it has been called and commissioned by God to worship and serve God, to proclaim the gospel, to celebrate the sacraments (which it believes to have been instituted by Christ), and to minister in Christ's name to the sick, the sorrowful, and the poor. It holds that it is mandated by God to do precisely those things. St Paul presents the church as the new humanity in Christ, the paradigm of human being, so the church should be able to model to the world what it means to be truly human, living in true community, as God intended (Hardy in Gunton and Hardy, eds, 1989: 34).

How is that precious sense of identity and that high calling compatible with the blatant failures, stupidities, sins, errors, and even crimes of the church as an institution throughout the ages? Does not that deplorable part of its record undermine our faith in the church as in a definite sense 'God's Church'? Is it credible that God would choose to own and use such a body and to persevere with it through the ages—a body for which the word 'imperfect' is seriously, even ludicrously, understating the matter? This is the challenge of what I call 'ecclesial theodicy'—the problem of explaining (without excusing) evil in the Church, the problem of the Church gone wrong. The task of theodicy, if we choose to engage in it, is 'to justify the ways of God to man', as John Milton put it in the opening lines of *Paradise Lost*. So the task of 'ecclesial theodicy' is to attempt to defend or justify the Christian claim that God owns and uses the Church as an instrument—even the 'privileged instrument'—of the *missio dei*.

One possible response to the challenge of ecclesial theodicy is to claim, as some modern popes have done, that these sins and crimes (e.g., topically, the sexual abuse of minors and vulnerable adults and the concealing of these sins and crimes by some of those in authority) should not be attributed to the church, but are solely the responsibility of certain individuals within it. Individual Christians, even priests and bishops, it is admitted, can go dreadfully wrong, but the church itself somehow remains unscathed, uncontaminated. But can the whole be distinguished from its constituent parts as easily, especially when serious misdemeanours have been committed or condoned by senior officials in the hierarchy? The church is, theologically, a body, an organic whole, to which, therefore, some kind of collective responsibility must belong. If the 'wrongs' of its representatives cannot be attributed to the church as such, neither can its 'rights', the lives of holiness and acts of charity of the saints and of many ordinary dedicated Christian people. I think that that corollary would not be welcomed by those who insist that the church as such cannot sin (Radner 2012: chapters 1–3).

On the other hand, we might ask whether, given all its faults and worse, there are moments or actions in the life of the church when the truth of the Christian faith and the presence of God, the divine love, mercy, and goodness, shine through—moments of transparency to the divine. Where is it, in the whole complex phenomenon of the church, that people find help, comfort, guidance, and healing—in other words, encounter grace—as they surely do? Where is it that the shortcomings and worse of the church as an institution are eclipsed or overcome or transcended? Perhaps that happens when the church, in the persons of its clergy particularly, but also of its lay members, ministers compassionately and selflessly to the poor, the oppressed, and the heartbroken; when Christians keep faith with Christ even unto death; when the Eucharist is celebrated and Holy Communion is received; when Christians pray fervently for the needs of the world; when love and forgiveness bring reconciliation and healing to tortured relationships between individuals, families, and communities. I think that I am speaking of those activities of the church that most reflect the character of Christ. Are such moments as these windows through which we glimpse the divine purpose and presence that lies behind the chequered historical career of the Christian church and which help to restore and maintain our faith in the church's credal identity? Certainly, that faith is maintained for many millions of faithful Christians who are not blind to the faults and sins of the church, over which they continually grieve, yet do not lose hope that the church can be reformed and restored to its true holiness.

Division in the One Church

In 'The Imperfect Church' we have taken one of the credal marks or notes of the church, that of holiness, and wrestled with the glaring discrepancy between the church of faith ('I believe . . .') and the empirical church, the church as we see and experience it. We have portrayed the church as, in the title of the English translation of one of Thomas Mann's novels, 'The Holy Sinner'. We have asked how this contradiction can be overcome, if at all. It is often said that the notes of the church (*notae ecclesiae*) are not empirical but eschatological, not so much descriptive as prescriptive, pointing to what the church is in the purposes of God and to what it will be when those purposes are perfectly fulfilled, in the *eschaton*. There is much truth in that tactic: everything in the Christian faith and therefore everything about the church has to be understood eschatologically. But if the empirical correlative of the eschatological hope is nugatory—if we cannot see any evidence now, any foretaste of what is to come—we have a serious problem of credibility, a major plausibility gap. That is why it is important to show that there is not a vacuum where the empirical holiness of the church should be; and I think it is clear that there is certainly not a vacuum—though how to adjust the balance sheet, the loss and gain, remains problematic. I think that, as ecclesiologists, we need to believe that the church has been more productive of good than harm, that faith, hope, and charity are its true *métier*, and that its moral failures are an aberration. How we resolve the equation 'good:bad' partly depends on how we understand the church, whether our focus is mainly on its political aspect—the doings of the hierarchy and clergy—or on its popular aspect: the lives, prayers, love, and charitable deeds of all the faithful.

Each of the credal notes of the church could be examined in this way. *Catholicity* raises the question of the discrepancy between the all-embracing welcome that should characterize the church's gospel invitation to all people and the fact that some groups of persons feel excluded because they have been condemned for the way that they live their lives with what seems to them sufficient integrity. *Apostolicity* suggests the tension or discrepancy between the church as it is today and the church of the apostles. It raises the question: How far does the church faithfully emulate the apostolic teaching and continue the apostolic mission (without *per impossibile* attempting to replicate the situation and circumstances of the first-century Roman Empire)? But, along with holiness, the credal note of the church that most invites troubled reflection is the note of *unity*.

The church that is presented in the New Testament writings knows itself to be one church but is already struggling against the odds to preserve its unity. The many apostolic appeals for unity, harmony, and unanimity betray the seriousness of threats to those attributes of the community (e.g. 1 Cor. 1:10; Phil. 2:1–5). Unity is threatened and Christians are urged to make 'every effort to maintain the unity of the Spirit in the bond of peace' (Eph. 4: 3). But the author of Ephesians is emphatic that 'there is one body and one Spirit . . . one hope of your calling, one Lord, one faith, one baptism, one God and Father of all' (Eph. 4:4–6). That is the ultimate, albeit concealed, reality which the appearance of disunity cannot destroy. However, it is much harder to hold on to that hidden reality after two millennia of division, schism, and mutual excommunication and anathemas. The ecumenical movement has transformed the climate of inter-church relations, but it has made little impact on the structural divisions of the church and in fact new denominations are being formed every day, infinitely outstripping our hesitant, half-hearted moves towards unity.

In John 17:21–3 Jesus' last prayer before his passion is a prayer for the unity of his disciples both then and in the future. 'That they may be one' has been the watchword of the ecumenical movement and motivates those who work tirelessly for greater unity. But we have to admit that it is a prayer that has not been fully answered to date, to say the least. And it raises troubling questions about prayer if even the High-Priestly prayer of Jesus has not been answered. But such questions rebound on those who ask them: Christians are compelled to ask themselves to what extent, if at all, the prayer of Christ has been answered in and through them and in and through their own particular church (Avis 2010: chapter 10).

Ecclesiology wrestles with the truth that the church is *at one and the same time both united and divided*. It knows itself to be united in Christ; its unity is part of its confession; but it also knows itself to be lamentably divided, above all at the altar and the communion rail because a common Eucharist is the most difficult expression of unity to achieve. So the Eucharist, the 'sacrament of unity', becomes in practice the 'sacrament of separation'. The fact of the fragmentation of the one church is the almost unbearable paradox that confronts ecclesiology.

Local versus Universal Church

In this chapter I have spelled 'church' always with a lower case 'c'. Why is this? Common practice is to write 'the church' or 'a church' when we mean a neighbourhood church, but 'Church' when we are referring to the universal 'Church', the 'Christian Church', the 'one, holy, catholic, and apostolic Church' of the creed, or for the name of a church (e.g. 'the United Reformed Church'). But modern ecumenical theology, drawing on the 'Eucharistic ecclesiology' of some Orthodox and Roman Catholic theologians, has taught us to see that the community gathered around its bishop, where word and sacrament are ministered, is just as much 'the church' as is the universal church. The one church is embodied in local and universal forms. So it is arguable that it is invidious to distinguish between 'church' and 'Church' by sometimes capitalizing the first letter and that, to do so, unhelpfully prioritizes the universal over the local. In my opinion, that argument is finely balanced. But let us explore the symmetry of local and universal forms of the church a little further.

All Christian traditions acknowledge at least two basic expressions of the church: the church in a parish or neighbourhood and the church throughout the world, the catholic church. In some traditions the national expression of the church is also theologically significant ('the Church of England'; 'the Church of Greece'; 'the Church of Sweden'). The sixteenth-century Reformers emphasized the notion of 'particular' churches, which were coterminous with nations, countries, or cities (the Church of France, the Church of Geneva, the Church of Rome), while of course they also acknowledged the universal church, which was made up of these 'particular' churches. The Reformers claimed that such churches had the authority and duty to reform themselves, when the universal church could not act as one, or when one church (that of Rome) sought to inhibit other churches from acting unilaterally. The notion of particular churches was needed to support the Reformation principle of legitimate diversity in traditions and practices (as opposed to Roman Catholic uniformity). In modern terms, the autonomy of particular churches (where this is the case) promotes the diverse inculturation of the gospel: the churches are free to respond to their cultural context in taking forward their mission.

The Roman Catholic Church is a globally organized church with its administrative and symbolic centre in Rome. It is made up of dioceses, governed and led by their bishops, and referred to as 'local churches'. This usage points up the fact that episcopally ordered churches understand the concept of the diocese in an ecclesiological way, not merely functionally; they see it as an authentic expression of the church. This principle has given rise to an unresolved debate, in fact an argument, within the Roman Catholic Church's magisterium (teaching authority) as to whether the universal church or the local church (diocese) is theologically primary, with Cardinal Joseph Ratzinger (later Pope Benedict XVI) defending the former view and Cardinal Walter Kasper the latter. The question is: does the local church exist because there is already a universal church, or is the universal church only possible because it is constituted by dioceses? If the Ratzinger doctrine is right, dioceses and their bishops are regarded as dependent on and beholden to a universal authority, the papacy. If Kasper's view is correct, dioceses and their bishops have more freedom to adapt to local circumstances and challenges. However, to some, this polarization seems to create a false dichotomy: local and universal expressions or instantiations of the church are necessarily coinherent and mutually constitutive; they cannot exist without each other (McPartlan 2004; Zizioulas 2001; Kasper 2015).

In today's post-modern culture the ecclesial centre of gravity is located in practice in the very local or neighbourhood church and it is difficult to persuade church people to invest ecclesial value in more remote structures which do not have the same emotional purchase (except perhaps for the papacy for Roman Catholics). The notion of the 'gathered church' derives from the Radical Reformation (Anabaptists) and belongs within the congregational strand of church polity, being found today mainly among Baptists and Pentecostals (*Fiddes; *Yong; *Chan; *Gonzales). It is perhaps the image of the church that is most appealing to our post-modern culture which looks for an eclectic coming together of the likeminded. Christians today find it hard to see that it is important to be part of something on a regional, national, or global scale or that their parish or congregation could be in any sense dependent on or even accountable to a higher level of pastoral oversight. The territorial aspect of the church's mission, based on the parish and the diocese, which remains significant to the historic national churches of Europe, is an opaque concept to many modern Christians. Its mission potential, involving extending the offer of the ministry of word, sacrament, and pastoral care to all in the community who are willing to receive it, is not always appreciated. So there remains a tension between the universal and the more local expressions or instantiations of the church which sometimes flares up into controversy, especially over the limits of legitimate adaptation to local cultural norms and mores. Ecclesiology has to grapple with this challenge also.

ECCLESIOLOGY AS A VOCATION?

Anyone, whether they are a professing Christian or not, is free to become involved in the work of ecclesiology or in any other aspect of theology, for that matter. But it does make a difference to our approach if we see ourselves as working within the church and for the church. Karl Rahner spoke of doing theology 'in the bosom of the church', but that imagery sounds a little quaint today. However, it remains true that it makes a huge difference if one loves the church—and one's own particular branch of it too, though without arrogance, triumphalism, invidious comparisons, or even complacency. Christians sometimes need to be given permission to love the church in spite of all its deficiencies and therefore to serve it (or rather to serve God in and through it) willingly and gladly. Then the work of ecclesiology becomes not a chore, but a joy and privilege—we may say a calling, a vocation (Avis 2016b: chapter 1).

Theologians, including ecclesiologists, sometimes have a love–hate relationship with the church. If they are believers, they are dependent on it for their spiritual life, yet are provoked to kick against it. There are many Christians, including theologians, who have been hurt or damaged by 'the church', by which they usually mean the clergy, the apparently impersonal structures of oversight, or fellow parishioners. Then the temptation is to hit back, to allow oneself to be driven by (understandable) negative impulses, so that destructive, hyper-critical elements creep in to the work. It is better if such persons can contribute as 'wounded healers' of the church, making their contribution in an irenic and constructive spirit as far as is humanly possible, but without being bland and the ecclesiastical equivalent of politically correct. Only occasionally, when the need is to uphold vital truths against ideological distortion, should ecclesiology be fiercely polemical, in the spirit of the Fathers, the Conciliarists, the Reformers (and their antagonists), and in fact theologians operating at times of tension and crisis throughout history.

REFERENCES

Anglican–Roman Catholic International Commission (1990). *Church as Communion.* London: CTS/SPCK. <http://www.vatican.va/roman_curia/pontifical_councils/chrstuni/angl-comm- docs/rc_pc_chrstuni_doc_19900906_church-communion_en.html>.

Arato, Andrew and Eike Gebhardt (1978). *The Essential Frankfurt School Reader.* Oxford: Blackwell.

Avis, Paul (P. D. L.) (1981, 2002). *The Church in the Theology of the Reformers.* London: Marshall, Morgan & Scott; Atlanta, GA: John Knox Press; reprinted Eugene, OR: Wipf & Stock, 2002.

Avis, Paul (1986). *Ecumenical Theology and the Elusiveness of Doctrine.* London: SPCK; Cambridge, MA: Cowley Press (as *Truth Beyond Words*).

Avis, Paul (1989). *Eros and the Sacred.* London: SPCK.

Avis, Paul (1992). *Authority, Leadership and Conflict in the Church.* London: Mowbray.

Avis, Paul (ed.) (2002). *The Christian Church: An Introduction to the Major Traditions.* London: SPCK.

Avis, Paul (2003). *A Church Drawing Near: Spirituality and Mission in a Post-Christian Culture*. London and New York: T&T Clark.

Avis, Paul (2006). *Beyond the Reformation? Authority, Primacy and Unity in the Conciliar Tradition*. London and New York: T&T Clark.

Avis, Paul (2010). *Reshaping Ecumenical Theology: The Church Made Whole?* London and New York: T&T Clark.

Avis, Paul (2011). 'Denomination: An Anglican Appraisal'. In Paul M. Collins and Barry Ensign George (eds), *Denomination: Assessing an Ecclesiological Category*. London and New York: T&T Clark, chapter 2.

Avis, Paul (2012). 'Are we receiving "Receptive Ecumenism"?' *Ecclesiology* 8.2: 223–34.

Avis, Paul (2015a). 'Contested Legacy: An Anglican Looks at Vatican II'. *Theology* 118.3 (May–June): 188–95.

Avis, Paul (2015b). *Becoming a Bishop: A Theological Handbook of Episcopal Ministry*. London and New York: Bloomsbury T&T Clark.

Avis, Paul (2016a). 'Polity and Polemics: The Function of Ecclesiastical Polity in Theology and Practice'. *Ecclesiastical Law Journal* 18.1: 2–13.

Avis, Paul (2016b). *The Vocation of Anglicanism*. London and New York: Bloomsbury T&T Clark.

Avis, Paul (2019). *The Church's One Foundation*. London and New York: Bloomsbury T&T Clark.

Barth, Karl (1975–). *Church Dogmatics*. Ed. Geoffrey W. Bromiley and Thomas F. Torrance. London and New York: Bloomsbury T&T Clark.

Bockmuehl, Marcus and Thompson, Michael B. (eds) (1997). *A Vision for the Church: Studies in Early Christian Ecclesiology in Honour of J. P. M. Sweet*. Edinburgh: T&T Clark.

Boff, Clodovis (1987). *Theology and Praxis: Epistemological Foundations*. Trans. Robert R. Barr. Maryknoll, NY: Orbis.

Bosch, David J. (1991, 2011). *Transforming Mission: Paradigm Shifts in Theology of Mission*. New York: Orbis (additional material by others in the 2011 edition).

Coakley, Sarah (2002). *Powers and Submissions: Spirituality, Philosophy, and Gender*. Oxford: Blackwell.

Coakley, Sarah (2013). *God, Sexuality and the Self: An Essay 'On the Trinity'*. Cambridge and New York: Cambridge University Press.

Coakley, Sarah (2015). *The New Asceticism: Sexuality, Gender and the Quest for God*. London: Bloomsbury Continuum.

Congar, Yves (1960). *The Mystery of the Church*. Trans. A. V. Littledale. Baltimore, ML: Helicon Press.

Daly, Mary (1973). *Beyond God the Father: Toward a Philosophy of Women's Liberation*. London: The Women's Press.

de Lubac, Henri (1954). *Meditation sur l'Église*. 3rd edn. Paris: Aubier.

Druzhinina, Olga A. (2016). *The Ecclesiology of St Basil the Great*. Eugene, OR: Pickwick Publications.

Eagleton, Terry (1991). *Ideology: An Introduction*. London and New York: Verso.

Evans, Robert F. (1972). *One and Holy: The Church in Latin Patristic Thought*. London: SPCK.

Fahey, Michael A. (1991). 'Church'. In Francis Schlüssler Fiorenza and John P. Galvin (eds), *Systematic Theology: Roman Catholic Perspectives*. Vol. 2. Minneapolis: Fortress Press.

Faith and Order Commission (1982). *Baptism, Eucharist and Ministry*. Geneva: World Council of Churches.

Faith and Order Commission (2005). *The Nature and Mission of the Church*. Geneva: World Council of Churches.

Faith and Order Commission (2013). *The Church: Towards a Common Vision*. Geneva: World Council of Churches.

Fiorenza, Elizabeth S. (1983). *In Memory of Her: A Feminist Theological Reconstruction of Christian Origins*. London: SCM Press.

Flannery, Austin (1992). *Vatican Council II: The Conciliar and Post Conciliar Documents*. Rev. edn. Northport, NY: Costello; Dublin: Dominican Publications.

Fuchs, Lorelei F. (2008). *Koinonia and the Quest for an Ecumenical Ecclesiology*. Grand Rapids, MI: Eerdmans.

Graham, Elaine L. (1996). *Transforming Practice: Pastoral Theology in an Age of Uncertainty*. London: Mowbray.

Gunton, Colin E. and Hardy, Daniel W. (eds) (1989). *On Being the Church: Essays on the Christian Community*. Edinburgh: T&T Clark.

Haight, Roger (2004, 2005, 2008a). *Christian Community in History*. 3 vols. London and New York: Bloomsbury T&T Clark.

Haight, Roger (2008b). 'The Promise of Constructive, Comparative Ecclesiology: Partial Communion'. *Ecclesiology* 4.2: 183–203.

Hampson, Daphne (1990). *Theology and Feminism*. Oxford: Blackwell.

Hampson, Daphne (1996). *After Christianity*. London: SCM Press.

Hampson, Daphne (ed.) (1996). *Swallowing a Fishbone? Feminist Theologians Debate Christianity*. London: SPCK.

Healy, Nicholas M. (2000). *Church, World and the Christian Life: Practical-Prophetic Ecclesiology*. Cambridge: Cambridge University Press.

Hinze, Bradford E. (2016). *Prophetic Obedience: Ecclesiology for a Dialogical Church*. Maryknoll, NY: Orbis.

Holmes, Stephen Mark (2011). 'Reading the Church: William Durandus and a New Approach to the History of Ecclesiology'. *Ecclesiology* 7.1: 29–49.

Hopewell, James F. (1987). *Congregation: Stories and Structures*. Minneapolis: Fortress; London: SCM Press.

Jenkins, Timothy (1999). *Religion in English Everday Life: An Ethnographic Approach*. New York and Oxford: Berghahn.

Kasper, Walter (1989). *Theology and Church*. Trans. Margaret Kohl. London: SCM Press.

Kasper, Walter (2009). *Harvesting the Fruits: Basic Aspects of Christian Faith in Ecumenical Dialogue*. London and New York: Continuum.

Kasper, Walter (2015). *The Catholic Church: Nature, Reality and Mission*. London and New York: Bloomsbury T&T Clark.

Kelley, J. N. D. (1965). *Early Christian Doctrines*. 3rd edn. London: A. & C. Black.

Küng, Hans (1971). *The Church*. London: Search Press.

Lim, Timothy T. N. (2017). *Ecclesial Recognition with Hegelian Philosophy, Social Psychology & Continental Political Theory*. Theology and Mission in World Christianity series, Volume 6. Leiden: Brill.

Loades, Ann (1987). *Searching for Lost Coins: Explorations in Christianity and Feminism*. London: SPCK.

Loades, Ann (2001). *Feminist Theological Voices from the Past*. Cambridge: Polity Press.

McPartlan, Paul (1993). *The Eucharist Makes the Church: Henri de Lubac and John Zizioulas in Dialogue*. Edinburgh: T&T Clark; new edn Fairfax, VA: Eastern Christian Publications, 2006.

McPartlan, Paul (2004). 'The Local Church and the Universal Church: Zizioulas and the Ratzinger–Kasper Debate'. *International Journal for the Study of the Christian Church* 4.1: 21–33.

Mannheim, Karl (1936). *Ideology and Utopia: An Introduction to the Sociology of Knowledge*. New York: Harcourt, Brace and World.

Mannion, Gerard (2007). *Ecclesiology and Postmodernity—Questions for the Church in our Times*. Collegeville, MN: Liturgical Press.

Mannion, Gerard (ed.) (2008). *Comparative Ecclesiology: Critical Investigations*. London and New York: T&T Clark.

Mannion, Gerard (2009). 'Constructive Comparative Ecclesiology: The Pioneering Work of Roger Haight'. *Ecclesiology* 5: 161–91.

Mannion, Gerard and Mudge, Lewis S. (eds) (2008). *The Routledge Companion to the Christian Church*. New York and London: Routledge.

Milbank, John (2006). *Theology and Social Theory: Beyond Secular Reason*. 2nd edn. Oxford: Blackwell [1990].

Milbank, John, Pickstock, Catherine, and Ward, Graham (eds) (1998). *Radical Orthodoxy: A New Theology*. London: Routledge.

Murray, Paul (ed.) (2008). *Receptive Ecumenism and the Call to Catholic Learning*. Oxford: Oxford University Press.

Newman, John Henry (1974). *An Essay on the Development of Christian Doctrine*. Ed. and introd. J. M. Cameron. Harmondsworth: Penguin.

Ormerod, Neil (2008). 'Ecclesiology and the Social Sciences'. In Mannion and Mudge (eds), *The Routledge Companion to the Christian Church*, chapter 37.

Ormerod, Neil (2014). *Re-Visioning the Church: An Experiment in Systematic-Historical Ecclesiology*. Minneapolis: Fortress Press.

Pannenberg, Wolfhart (1998). *Systematic Theology, Vol. 3*. Grand Rapids, MI: Eerdmans.

Pattison, Stephen (1997). *Pastoral Care and Liberation Theology*. London: SPCK.

Percy, Martyn (1998). *Power and the Church*. London: Cassell.

Pelikan, Jaroslav (1983). *The Christian Tradition, Vol. IV: Reformation of Church and Dogma (1300–1700)*. Chicago and London: University of Chicago Press.

Radner, Ephraim (2012). *A Brutal Unity: The Spiritual Politics of the Christian Church*. Waco, TX: Baylor University Press.

Ruether, Rosemary R. (1983). *Sexism and God-Talk: Toward a Feminist Theology*. Boston: Beacon Press; London: SCM Press.

Scharen, Christian B. (ed.) (2012). *Explorations in Ecclesiology and Ethnography*. Grand Rapids, MI: Eerdmans.

Sykes, Stephen (2006). *Power and Christian Theology*. London and New York: Continuum.

Tavard, George (1992). *The Church: Community of Salvation*. Collegeville, MN: Liturgical Press.

Ward, Pete (ed.) (2012). *Perspectives on Ecclesiology and Ethnography*. Grand Rapids, MI: Eerdmans.

Watkins, Clare (2012). 'Practical Ecclesiology: What Counts as Theology in Studying the Church?' In Pete Ward (ed.), *Perspectives on Ecclesiology and Ethnography*. Grand Rapids, MI: Eerdmans, chapter 9.

Watson, Natalie K. (2002). *Introducing Feminist Ecclesiology*. London: Sheffield Academic Press.

Watson, Natalie K. (2008). 'Feminist Ecclesiology'. In Mannion and Mudge (eds), *The Routledge Companion to the Christian Church*, chapter 25.

Zizioulas, John (1985). *Being as Communion: Studies in Personhood and the Church*. New York: St Vladimir Seminary Press; London: Darton, Longman & Todd.

Zizioulas, John (2001). *Eucharist, Bishop, Church: The Unity of the Church in the Divine Eucharist and the Bishop during the First Three Centuries*. Trans. E. Theokritoff. 2nd edn. Brookline, MA: Holy Cross Orthodox Press.

SUGGESTED READING

Avis, Paul (ed.) (2002). *The Christian Church: An Introduction to the Major Traditions*. London: SPCK.

Bosch, David J. (1991, 2011). *Transforming Mission: Paradigm Shifts in Theology of Mission*. New York: Orbis.

Haight, Roger (2004, 2005, 2008a). *Christian Community in History*. 3 vols. London and New York: Bloomsbury T&T Clark.

Healy, Nicholas M. (2000). *Church, World and the Christian Life: Practical-Prophetic Ecclesiology*. Cambridge: Cambridge University Press.

Küng, Hans (1971). *The Church*. London: Search Press.

Mannion, Gerard and Mudge, Lewis S. (eds) (2008). *The Routledge Companion to the Christian Church*. New York and London: Routledge.

Watson, Natalie K. (2002). *Introducing Feminist Ecclesiology*. London: Sheffield Academic Press.

Zizioulas, John (1985). *Being as Communion: Studies in Personhood and the Church*. New York: St Vladimir Seminary Press; London: Darton, Longman & Todd.

PART I

BIBLICAL FOUNDATIONS

CHAPTER 2

THE ECCLESIOLOGY OF ISRAEL'S SCRIPTURES

R. W. L. MOBERLY

To discuss ecclesiology in relation to the Hebrew Bible/Old Testament might seem like a category mistake. For if there is not yet a church (*ecclēsia* in both Greek and Latin) in a pre-Christian context, how is there scope for ecclesiology? Or, to put the point slightly differently, there are some preliminary methodological issues to raise in relation to thinking about the Christian church in relation to Israel's Scriptures before substantive discussion of our topic can get under way.

ESTABLISHING A FRAME OF REFERENCE

One approach could be to say that if there is no church in Israel's Scriptures the issue must be entirely one of looking for historical antecedents: What preceded the church and gave rise to it? But although there must be such a historical dimension to any discussion, Christianity has characteristically regarded the Old Testament not only as prehistory but also as an enduring source and norm for Christian thought and practice. Christian realities may not yet have existed in the original frame of reference of these pre-Christian documents, yet Christian faith can still be shaped by Israel's Scriptures when they are read as the Christian Old Testament.

Alternatively, one might say that there *is* a church in Israel's Scriptures. For a common Hebrew term to depict the 'assembly' of Israel is *qāhāl*, which the Greek translators of the Septuagint generally rendered by *ekklēsia*. Might one then, like some older writers, refer to 'The Church of Israel' (Kennett 1933 [2011])? Yet at the present time, when many Christians are freshly appreciating the importance of Judaism as a living and enduring religious reality, such terminology can feel insensitive and inappropriate. After all, *qāhāl* could also be rendered in Greek by *synagōgē*, and Jewish gatherings are synagogue rather than church.

Rather than lingering on such preliminary puzzles, it may be best directly to set out the premises and frame of reference for this discussion. Central to the Old Testament is Israel as a people called by God to be his people. The New Testament presents a self-understanding of early Christian faith in terms of Jesus' followers still being Israel, but Israel as redefined and reconstituted by the crucified and risen Jesus (thus Galatians 6: 14–16 should probably be read as such a redefinition of 'the Israel of God'). However, although both Jesus and all the first Christians were Jews, the church was soon predominantly made up of Gentiles. The Jewish people for the most part did not recognize Jesus as Messiah/Saviour, and went on to develop their own forms of religious life and thought which are related to their Scriptures and in which they continue to be Israel. That is, rabbinic Judaism developed in terms of the 'oral law', which is expressed in Mishnah and Talmud—and in these works Jesus plays no part. There are thus senses in which the church both is, and is not, Israel.

Israel's Scriptures have given rise to two enduring religious faiths, Judaism and Christianity, synagogue and church. Although each faith takes these Scriptures seriously, for neither of them does it function independently of its recontextualization and appropriation, as Tanakh for Jews and Old Testament for Christians. This means that Jews and Christians read the material differently—not so much at the level of philology or particular literary or historical settings, but rather in terms of which larger frame of reference these texts are set in, which specific texts are appealed to, and which further texts and practices contribute to the task of articulating the enduring meaning and function of the biblical material.

Within a Christian frame of reference, even for Gentiles the story of Israel becomes 'our story', as believers come to recognize that they are incorporated into an antecedent people of God through their response to Jesus Christ. Israel in some sense becomes church. How then might Christians best think of Israel's Scriptures in a way that both illumines the nature and purpose of the church and is able to respect Jewish self-understanding and use of the same Scriptures? The task entails moving beyond the historic Christian hostility to Jews—as classically expressed in the reception of Tertullian's and St John Chrysostom's polemical writings (*Adversus Judaeos*; for a nuanced account of Chrysostom in his context see Wilken 2004)—which has often disfigured Christian history.

DIFFERENT WAYS OF INTERPRETING THE OLD TESTAMENT IN RELATION TO ECCLESIOLOGY

Scholarly literature on the nature of Israel as people of God in Israel's Scriptures abounds. However, the distinctive character of the biblical literature gives rise to continuing methodological debates about the best way of handling the literature. This needs some discussion as the nature of the approach adopted can make a significant difference to one's findings.

Historical Approaches: Hanson and Goldingay

Much modern study of the Old Testament has been conceived as an attempt to reconstruct the history of Israel and its religion, with all its diverse and disparate voices, via the critical analysis and dating of its literature in relation to a wider ancient Near Eastern context (an approach which is driven in part by the recognition that the likely course of Israel's religious development differed, to a greater or lesser extent, from the form it has in the canonical portrayal). Such an approach to the Old Testament, carried out constructively and from a Christian perspective that presumes the enduring significance of the biblical material, is well exemplified in the most weighty discussion of our topic in recent years, Paul Hanson's *The People Called: The Growth of Community in the Bible* (Hanson 1986). Hanson looks also at Christian community in the New Testament, though is uninterested in Judaism's appropriation of its Scriptures.

Another example, somewhat comparable to Hanson but briefer and more theologically synthetic in approach, is offered by John Goldingay in his discussion of 'The People of God' in the Old Testament (Goldingay 1987: 59–96). Goldingay finds five primary images or modes of being for Israel in the Old Testament, for each of which there are particular Hebrew terms. First is a family (Heb. *mišpāhâ*), which Goldingay speaks of as The Wandering Clan (i.e. Abraham, Isaac, and Jacob). This pre-political form of existence 'speaks of being a people on the way, between promise and fulfilment, and dependent on the one who brought it into being by his will'. Second is a nation (*'am*) or people (*gōy*), that is The Theocratic Nation (i.e. Moses and Joshua). This 'speaks of living in the world and of learning from it, but of standing over against the world and its religion'. Third is a royal state, a kingdom (*mamlākâ*), which Goldingay depicts as The Institutional State (i.e. the period of Monarchy). This 'speaks of an openness to learn from the world, to let the world provide the vehicles for expressing the faith, and to attract the world to that faith'. Fourth is the remnant (*še'erît*), about which Goldingay speaks as The Afflicted Remnant (i.e. Israel/Judah in exile). This 'means recognizing that the final purpose of God cannot be effected in the regular course of human history, because of the waywardness both of God's people and of other nations. It means that God's people are subject to his judgment, but that all is not lost when God cuts his people down to size.' Fifth is a religious community (*qāhāl*), which Goldingay depicts as The Community of the Promise (i.e. Postexilic Israel). This indicates 'a people that . . . recognizes that even when history ceases to be the sphere in which God fulfils his ultimate purpose through them, it does not cease to be the sphere in which they actually have to live; that is honest about what they can believe yet pledged to making sense of the old faith; that is committed to personal discipleship if the corporate seems to lapse; that lives as a people dedicated to the praise of Yahweh for what he has done yet to hope in him for what he is yet to do'. Alongside these positive implications Goldingay also recognizes the distinct temptations and perils to which each mode of being is exposed, so that there is always a 'this, yet not this' quality to the discussion, in keeping with the Christian theology's classic mode of combining affirmation and denial in its understanding of God and of life in God's world.

Goldingay is also suggestive about the enduring theological insights that should be found by those seeking to appropriate the Old Testament. For example:

> Israel's story suggests that the relationship between life in the Spirit and life in the world is insoluble. The people of God cannot live as a political theocracy ruling the world in Yahweh's name, but neither can they take the way of separation which evades life in the world. Nor is there any way of living in obedience to God and being organized for existence in history. History, politics, and statehood, though inevitable, make it difficult to live as the people of God. The NT has little to add to this OT picture, and church history confirms it. (1987: 88–9)

Goldingay's is a fine example of a synthesis of historical and theological insight.

Canonical and Figural Approaches: Lindbeck and Radner

In recent years, however, there has been a renewed engagement with methodological questions about how best to approach Israel's Scriptures, especially when they are regarded as a continuing source and norm for thought and practice in a contemporary context. Particularly notable has been the work of Brevard Childs, who has articulated a 'canonical approach' (Childs 1992; Driver 2010). Instead of regarding the received, canonical form of the Old Testament as needing a greater or lesser amount of rearrangement, and separating out of voices, in the service of a more accurately historical account of Israel's religion (as in Hanson), Childs has proposed that Israel's traditions in their received form should be the focal point for purposes of theological thinking. He proposes that the familiar texts should be seen as the fruit of a lengthy process of sifting and discerning Israel's traditions, with a view to making their mature understanding of God, Israel, and the world accessible to generations to come, who would thereby be enabled, in their different situations, to enter into the enduring wisdom and truth of Israel's encounter with God. Childs does not deny the likely complexity of the processes that have led to the familiar texts, and indeed argues that some understanding of these processes can nuance one's reading of the text in beneficial ways. But if one focuses on the biblical texts in their received form one is potentially reconnecting both with the concerns of those who edited, preserved, and canonized the texts (so that the fruit of Israel's wisdom would continue to function in new contexts) and with the concerns of those Jews and Christians who articulated the normative forms of Judaism and Christianity in the ancient world. Jews and Christians in antiquity, amidst all the variety of interpretative moves that they made, built their construals of God, Israel, and the world on the texts in their received form.

This approach also means that one need not solely trace historical developments from old to new, from ancient Israel to the church, but one can move dialectically between the two testaments as literary collections that are intertexually related. Such an approach to the text does not attempt to put the clock back or deny the insights of modern scholarship, but rather seeks to embody, in Paul Ricoeur's famous phrase, a 'second naiveté': the recovery of a certain kind of simplicity on the other side of working through issues of great complexity, an ability to take the world of the biblical text with full imaginative and existential seriousness, even as one recognizes that its content does not conform to our modern category of 'history'.

If one adopts this frame of reference, it is still not self-evident how best to work with the biblical text, and more than one approach is possible. One notable example has been the work of Childs's colleague at Yale, George Lindbeck, who from the perspective of contemporary theology has sought a renewed engagement with the biblical text. Lindbeck has proposed that ecclesiology could usefully be thought of as 'Israelology' (Lindbeck 1997 [1987]: 45). Lindbeck draws on the resources of recent narrative theology (which is a way of working with the world of the biblical text as meaningful in itself) to propose a post-modern recovery of classic pre-modern approaches to the biblical text, especially with regard to a typological or figural reading of the Old Testament in the light of Christ:

> The most succinct scriptural warrant for the retrieval of the practice of viewing the church in the mirror of Israel is the text in 1 Corinthians . . . [where] Paul tells us that *all* the things that happened to 'our fathers . . . were written down for our instruction . . .' (10:1, 11). These instructions remain verbally the same as when first recorded, but they are multiple in meaning. God's scriptural word, so Paul believes, fits every conceivable context, and from this follows the possibility that seeing the church as Israel is a biblically mandated universal; it applies in the twenty-first century just as much as in the first. (Lindbeck 2003: 90–1)

The correlation of the church with Israel is, of course, a classic pre-modern Christian approach, but Lindbeck sees it to have been historically disfigured by two questionable moves. On the one hand, Christians considered the church to have superseded historic Israel, and so disparaged Jews. On the other hand, Christians tended to ignore Paul's 'all' and so appealed to the Old Testament selectively: 'They have focused selectively on the favourable prefigurations Paul mentions—on Christ the rock, on manna as type of the Eucharist, on baptism under the cloud—and have neglected his more numerous warnings of the punishments for disobedience to which Christians are liable' (Lindbeck 2003: 91). Indeed, 'the more unsavoury aspects of the history of Israel were no longer genuinely portions of the history of the Church, but were projected exclusively on the synagogue' (Lindbeck 1997 [1987]: 47). So Lindbeck seeks to retrieve the classic notion in a fresh form:

> [T]he relation of Israel's history to that of the church in the New Testament is not one of shadow to reality, or promise to fulfilment, or type to antitype. Rather, the kingdom already present in Christ alone is the antitype, and both Israel and the

Church are types. The people of God existing in both the old and new ages are typologically related to Jesus Christ, and through Christ, Israel is prototypical for the Church in much the same way that the exodus story, for example, is seen as prototypical for all later Israelite history by such prophets as Ezekiel. Christ is depicted as the embodiment of Israel . . . and the Church is the body of Christ. Thus, in being shaped by the story of Christ, the Church shares (rather than fulfils) the story of Israel. The communal fulfilment will take place in God's kingdom which, though already actualized in the crucified, resurrected, and ascended Lord, is only anticipated in the communities that witness to him before and after his first coming. (Lindbeck 1997 [1987]: 43)

Thus a positive approach to Jews and Judaism (appreciatively outlined and analysed from a Jewish perspective in Ochs 2011), together with a more humble and ecumenical ecclesial self-understanding, becomes central to Lindbeck's vision; and it represents a handling of the biblical text markedly different from that of Hanson.

A striking development of aspects of Lindbeck's approach can be found in the work of Ephraim Radner. Radner's *The End of the Church* (Radner 1998) propounds an astringent and controversial thesis that the condition of the divided churches of the contemporary world is such that the Holy Spirit is, in an important sense, absent from them. One of Radner's moves is to construe the divided churches scripturally in terms of divided Israel:

According to the scriptural pattern of divine 'abandonment' in sin, divided Israel was left to encounter its shattered life on its own. This fact determines how we are to view the topic at hand: partitioned Israel is 'abandoned' Israel; and this Israel, separated among its members, is separated too from the Holy Spirit . . . In Ezekiel's terms, the restoration of the Holy Spirit upon the divinely abandoned people of Israel must coincide with their return as a united body (Ezek. 39:25–9). In this way, the prophets make clear that a firm connection exists between the condition of division and the experience of pneumatic deprivation. (Radner 1998: 37–8)

Moreover Radner, like Lindbeck, seeks to move beyond the partisan and self-serving nature of many past appeals to this material, because all churches are implicated:

From the time of Jeroboam's rebellion and the rending of Israel into northern and southern kingdoms (1 Kings 12), the people of Israel were dragged down into a steady decline marked by internal apostasy and external victimization. Although there were respites and brief reversals to this pattern—for example, Hezekiah's or Josiah's reigns—both kingdoms eventually succumbed to almost total annihilation at the hands of Assyria and Babylon . . .

But while the polemicists of Christian division have tended to apply this story one-sidedly, choosing to identify their particular communities with various righteous 'remnants' alluded to in the course of the narrative, it should be stressed that the narrative as a whole forbids such distinguishing of actors within the history. Both kingdoms are ultimately destroyed; the peoples of both are murdered and enslaved; and only the reunion of both as having come through this common ordeal embodies the restoration of Israel in the public arena of time (cf. Jer. 50:2–4). That there was to be a 'remnant' for whom this restoration was ordered is not in question . . . [b]ut . . . [t]he restoration of the remnant is not the unveiling, let alone the vindication, of the 'true church' from amid its travails, but rather the gracious action of recreating a united people out of the dust of their past obliteration (cf. Ezek. 11:14–21). (Radner 1998: 36)

One can of course argue about the specifics of Radner's construal of the divided kingdoms, and note the absence of any close reading of the biblical texts. He says nothing, for example, about the fact that, although for the writers of Kings the northern kingdom is schismatic and more problematic than the southern kingdom, remarkable space (most of 1 Kings 17–2 Kings 13) is given to Elijah and Elisha, whose prophetic ministries are exercised at God's behest in the northern kingdom. The content of Radner's ecclesiological appeal to the Old Testament is also strikingly different from that of Lindbeck, despite their common methodology. But whatever one makes of Radner's overall thesis, it is illuminating as an example of a kind of fresh theological thinking that works with the Old Testament in its received form and in important ways replicates, even while correcting, classic Christian engagement with the material.

I propose in the remainder of this chapter to offer a close reading of selected Old Testament passages, working with the material in its received, canonical form, and making the theological assumption that one should imaginatively bring together Israel and the church—in historical terms, by analogy, and in literary terms, by figuration. Readings of the biblical text will be accompanied, or followed by, reflections on their theological and ecclesiological implications.

THE MISSION OF ISRAEL: GOD'S CALL OF ABRAHAM

A well-known passage of prime importance is Genesis 12:1–3:

> [1] Now the LORD said to Abram, 'Go from your country and your kindred and your father's house to the land that I will show you. [2] I will make of you a great nation, and I will bless you, and make your name great, so that you will be a blessing. [3] I will bless those who bless you, and the one who curses you I will curse; and in you all the families of the earth shall be blessed [*or* by you all the families of the earth shall bless themselves]. (NRSV)

In canonical context, this divine call of Abraham (I use the familiar form of the name, though in Genesis 12–17 the name is Abram) is central to the transition between the universal primeval history (Genesis 1–11) and the particular history of Israel's ancestors

(Genesis 12–50). It implicitly raises the question of the relationship between Abraham and his descendants (Israel, church) and the world as a whole.

In terms of its classic interpretation, Paul sees the depiction of the families of the earth being blessed in Abraham as anticipating justification of all nations through their believing as Abraham believed (see Galatians 3:6–9 where Paul cites Genesis 12:3b together with Genesis 15:6). We thereby have an Old Testament basis for the mission of the church and its universal proclamation of the gospel. Moreover Gerhard von Rad, probably the most significant Old Testament theologian of the twentieth century, interpreted Genesis 12:1–3 in a way that in effect (*mutatis mutandis*) reformulated Paul's understanding of its significance:

> From the multitude of nations God chooses a man, looses him from tribal ties, and makes him the beginner of a new nation and the recipient of great promises of salvation. What is promised to Abraham reaches far beyond Israel; indeed, it has universal meaning for all generations on earth . . . Truly flesh and blood did not inspire this view beyond Israel and its saving relation to God! With this firm linking of primeval history and sacred history the Yahwist indicates something of the final meaning and purpose of the saving relation that God has vouchsafed to Israel. (von Rad 1972: 152–4, 159–61 [154])

Von Rad has influenced numerous subsequent theologians in seeing God's promise of the blessing of the nations in Abraham and his descendants as the Old Testament basis for the mission of the church. So, for example, Christopher Wright argues:

> So the Gentile mission, Paul argued, far from being a betrayal of the Scriptures, was rather the fulfilment of them. The ingathering of the nations was the very thing Israel existed for in the purpose of God; it was the fulfilment of the bottom line of God's promise to Abraham. Since Jesus was the Messiah of Israel and since the Messiah embodied in his own person the identity and mission of Israel, then to belong to the Messiah through faith was to belong to Israel . . . The words of Jesus to his disciples in Matthew 28:18–20, the so-called Great Commission, could be seen as a christological mutation of the original Abraham commission—'Go . . . and be a blessing . . . and all the nations of the earth will be blessed through you.' (Wright 2006: 194, 213)

Both Israel and the church as Israel are called and blessed by God, and they are commissioned to be agents of enabling that blessing to come to others.

The interpretation of Genesis 12:1–3 is, however, not quite so straightforward (Moberly 2009: 141–61). For example, many interpreters take the divine words to Abraham to 'be a blessing' in the same idiomatic sense that the phrase 'be a blessing' has in contemporary English, that is to embody and mediate benefit or help to another person. Yet such an idiomatic sense is in fact nowhere attested in the Old Testament (Grüneberg 2003: 121), for 'blessing' in such contexts (like 'curse') always means a paradigm of being blessed (or cursed), a paradigm which is invoked as a desired destiny, either good or bad, for someone. Thus Jacob says of Joseph and his sons: 'By you Israel will invoke blessings, saying, "God make you like Ephraim and Manasseh"' (Genesis 48:20). Alternatively Jeremiah says of two false prophets, Ahab and Zedekiah: '[O]n account of them this curse shall be used by all the exiles from Judah in Babylon: "The LORD make you like Zedekiah and Ahab, whom the king of Babylon roasted in the fire"' (Jeremiah 29:22). Thus the likely sense of Abraham's 'being a blessing' is that Abraham will be so blessed by God that others will aspire to his condition for themselves and those they favour, and so say, 'May you be like Abraham.' Abraham is a model, rather than a medium, of being blessed; it is not that others are to receive blessing through him and his descendants, but rather that they will aspire to be blessed like him and his descendants.

Although God's promise of blessing in Genesis 12:1–3 is often reckoned to be for the benefit of the nations, it is more likely that it is primarily for the benefit of Abraham himself and his descendants. When told to leave everything behind (12:1) he might readily fear swift oblivion, and so God reassures him that, far from experiencing oblivion, he will become a great nation, well regarded by others (12:2). God will defend Abraham and his descendants against their enemies, with the result that they will be universally admired and esteemed, a paradigm of being blessed to which others will aspire (12:3, where the disputed sense of the verb in 3b—'be blessed' or 'bless themselves'?—is probably the latter, with NRSV margin). In the midst of a large, and sometimes hostile, world, God will uphold Abraham and his descendants.

To be sure, if the primary sense of Genesis 12:1–3 is that Abraham and his descendants are to be blessed *in spite of*, rather than *for the sake of*, the nations, this does not exclude the possibility that this blessing could in due course come to be understood as being also *for the sake of* other nations. Elsewhere in the Old Testament such an understanding seems to be attested in the words of YHWH to his servant who in some way embodies Israel (Isaiah 49:3). The LORD says:

> It is too light a thing that you should be my servant
> to raise up the tribes of Jacob
> and to restore the survivors of Israel;
> I will give you as a light to the nations,
> that my salvation may reach to the end of the earth.
> (Isaiah 49:6)

It can thus become natural to re-read Genesis 12:1–3 with a view to seeing a blessing for the nations as already adumbrated at the outset of Israel's story. Arguably this is what is happening in Paul's reading of Genesis, which, Francis Watson argues, 'can justly claim to realize something of the semantic potential of a complex and polysemic text' (Watson 2004: 183). Paul reads the biblical text in the Septuagint, where the verb in Genesis 12:3b is passive, 'in you will all the tribes of the earth be blessed', which makes it natural to read the text as envisaging Abraham and his descendants not just modelling but bringing blessing to the whole world.

Moreover, this interpretative move (Israel's call is for the sake of the world) is not just a characteristic of Christian faith, for many Jews have also historically understood their vocation as Israel to be in some way for the sake of the world, even though neither the Hebrew Scriptures nor Jewish tradition envisage the world in general as actually adopting, or being expected to adopt, Israel's religion (even though a few people might do so). For example, the Jewish Renaissance philosopher and biblical scholar Abravanel said, 'All the families of the earth will be blessed, provided for and benefitted on his account, for the world will become aware of God through Abraham and his offspring. Blessing and providence will adhere to any people that adopt his discipline and his faith' (Greenberg 1995: 240). More recently Yoram Hazony, in the course of arguing that the Hebrew Bible is a work of moral and political philosophy that is of universal significance because 'the Israelite cause is the cause of all mankind', appeals to Genesis 12:1–3 as the prime biblical statement of his thesis. After citing 12:1–3 (with the rendering '... be blessed' in v. 3b) he comments: '[T]he father of the Jewish people is introduced to us as a man who will somehow be a "blessing" to all the peoples on the earth, with the implication that Abraham's people will somehow bear this blessing with them for all nations' (Hazony 2012: 59, 111).

Genesis 12:1–3 thus provides a good example of how historic Jewish and Christian faiths can encourage a re-reading of the biblical text so as to find in it a fuller sense than was perhaps initially envisaged. The divine commitment to uphold Abraham and his descendants is clear on any reckoning, and an extension to others of that blessing which Israel enjoys becomes an intuitive way of reading the text within a Jewish or Christian frame of reference. For Christians Abraham becomes paradigmatic of faith/trust in God as a transformative reality for all humanity, an exemplar of divine blessing upon human life that is made accessible in principle through the mission of the church.

THE PROPHETIC CRITIQUE OF ISRAEL: THREE TEMPLE SERMONS

The life of Israel, as portrayed in the Old Testament, focuses on the worship of God, an activity which should, in principle (from the perspective of the canonical writers), take place in the temple in Jerusalem. The temple is a place of enormous symbolic significance, a place where YHWH is in some way specially present. The Psalms in particular often celebrate Zion as the focus of YHWH's delight, the place where his people can expect to meet with him and receive his blessing. Here Israel sings, 'God is in the midst of the city; it shall not be moved . . . The LORD of hosts is with us; the God of Jacob is our refuge' (Psalm 46:5, 7 [Heb. vv. 6, 8]; compare Psalm 48).

However, a basic understanding that is widely shared among Israel's prophets is concisely articulated by Amos: 'You only have I known of all the families of the earth; therefore I will punish you for all your iniquities' (3:2). Being called and chosen by God brings with it special responsibility (as Jesus puts it, where much is given, there much is expected, Luke 12:48). A recurrent failure on the part of Israel/Judah to live up to those expectations and conduct themselves in a way commensurate with the presence of God

THE ECCLESIOLOGY OF ISRAEL'S SCRIPTURES   43

in their midst is a prime concern in the prophetic literature, and can be instructively focused on three famous 'temple sermons' (cf. Moberly 2008). I will first read these three sermons, and then reflect upon them.

Amos's Temple Sermon (Amos 5:18–27)

The first passage, Amos 5:18–27, is a direct address to people engaged in the practices of temple worship, and so is in that sense a temple sermon, whether or not the reader should imagine Amos speaking the words in a temple (perhaps, in Amos's context, the temple of the northern kingdom at Bethel, as in Amos 7:10–13). Amos says:

> [18] Alas for you who desire the day of the LORD!
>> Why do you want the day of the LORD?
> It is darkness, not light;
> [19]   as if someone fled from a lion,
>> and was met by a bear;
> or went into the house and rested a hand against the wall,
>> and was bitten by a snake.
> [20] Is not the day of the LORD darkness, not light,
>> and gloom with no brightness in it?

The people Amos addresses have a confident expectation associated with God, an expectation depicted as 'the day of YHWH' (v. 18). The precise nature of this day is assumed to be known, and although present-day readers no longer share that assumption, it seems to have entailed some kind of celebration within the temple. This day could be expected to be 'light' (vv. 18, 20), which would presumably mean a time of joy for God's people. But Amos inverts this: 'darkness, not light' is how the day of YHWH will be (v. 20). It is illustrated by a picture of a man trying to escape deadly animals, but escaping one danger only to be met by another (v. 19); the day of YHWH will confound hopeful expectation.

Why should this be? A reason (additional to those found earlier in the text of Amos) is immediately given.

> [21] I hate, I despise your festivals,
>> and I take no delight in your solemn assemblies.
> [22] Even though you offer me your burnt-offerings and grain-offerings,
>> I will not accept them;
> and the offerings of well-being of your fatted animals
>> I will not look upon.
> [23] Take away from me the noise of your songs;
>> I will not listen to the melody of your harps.
> [24] But let justice roll down like waters,
>> and righteousness like an ever-flowing stream.

This text focuses on YHWH's priorities, both what he seeks and what he rejects, in relation to what the people are doing in their temple worship. The point is emphatic: worship without a concomitant practice of justice and righteousness is not merely worthless but actively affronts YHWH and is even an object of loathing to him. The imagery of rolling, ever-flowing waters (v. 24) suggests that the practice of justice and righteousness should be both strong and constant, an integral aspect of Israel's life. Integrity in public life is the *sine qua non* of true worship.

> [25] Did you bring to me sacrifices and offerings the forty years in the wilderness, O house of Israel? [26] You shall take up Sakkuth your king, and Kaiwan your star-god, your images that you made for yourselves; [27] therefore I will take you into exile beyond Damascus, says the LORD, whose name is the God of hosts.

In this difficult section Israel's worship is seen as too readily directed to recipients other than YHWH (vv. 25, 26), such that YHWH is not the 'one and only' focus of Israel's acts of devotion (as Israel is to recite daily in the Shema, Deuteronomy 6:4–9). Consequently, Israel will not only lose temple and land by going into exile, but YHWH himself will be the instigator of that loss (v. 27), presumably through the agency of one of Israel's enemies. The 'day of YHWH' will be darkness, and the form that the darkness will take will be the loss of home through defeat and deportation. YHWH becomes, as it were, the enemy of his chosen people.

Micah's Temple Sermon (Micah 3:9–12)

No narrative context is given for this material, but again its content qualifies it as a temple sermon. Moreover, the appeal to Micah's words as a precedent for Jeremiah in the narrative account of Jeremiah's temple sermon (Jeremiah 26, especially vv. 17–19) implicitly locates Micah within Jerusalem, and the text of Micah is imaginatively open to such a location. Micah says:

> [9] Hear this, you rulers of the house of Jacob
> and chiefs of the house of Israel,
> who abhor justice
> and pervert all equity,
> [10] who build Zion with blood
> and Jerusalem with wrong!
> [11] Its rulers give judgement for a bribe,
> its priests teach for a price,
> its prophets give oracles for money;
> yet they lean upon the LORD and say,
> 'Surely the LORD is with us!
> No harm shall come upon us.'

Micah's address is blunt. He speaks to the leaders of Israel, those with responsibility for its common life (3:9a), and portrays them as corrupt, failing in their obligations for just dealings in public (3:9b), and maltreating those labouring on public and/or private building projects with a harshness that is careless of life (3:10). The leadership in its various forms—both 'secular' (rulers) and 'spiritual' (priests, prophets)—is venal; the justice and guidance that should enable healthy communal life have become commodities, to be had only for a price (3:11a). Yet apparently these leaders do not see their conduct as incompatible with strong religious claims; they acknowledge their dependence upon Yhwh, and claim Yhwh's presence in their midst, which is clearly a reference to the Jerusalem temple as the focal point of Yhwh's presence with Israel/Judah; and they regard Yhwh's presence in the temple as a guarantee of security from their enemies (as celebrated in, for example, Psalms 46 and 48).

Micah continues:

> [12] Therefore because of you
> Zion shall be ploughed as a field;
> Jerusalem shall become a heap of ruins,
> and the mountain of the house a wooded height.

Micah brusquely draws out the implications of the mismatch between the leaders' practice and their religious claims. It is precisely because of their complacent corruption that the disaster that they are confident cannot happen will happen: city and temple together will be reduced to ruins overgrown by vegetation. What will happen to the people is not specified; though insofar as the site of city and temple returns to the wild, the implication is that its inhabitants will not be there to rebuild, and so will either be dead or deported into exile.

Jeremiah's Temple Sermon (Jeremiah 7:1–15)

Jeremiah's words are a temple sermon because of their explicit narrative setting. Their content is similar to that of those passages just considered.

> [1] The word that came to Jeremiah from the LORD: [2] Stand in the gate of the LORD's house, and proclaim there this word, and say, Hear the word of the LORD, all you people of Judah, you that enter these gates to worship the LORD. [3] Thus says the LORD of hosts, the God of Israel: Amend your ways and your doings, and I will let you dwell [following NRSV margin, in preference to 'let me dwell with you'] in this place. [4] Do not trust in these deceptive words: 'This is the temple of the LORD, the temple of the LORD, the temple of the LORD.'

Jeremiah is to position himself and speak in a place of maximal exposure to temple worshippers. First, he challenges temple worshippers to change the way they are living

(v. 3a). Secondly, he holds out a positive consequence of such turning, which is that YHWH will let the people of Judah stay in their land and not (by implication) be defeated by their enemies with consequent deportation for the survivors (v. 3b). (The NRSV margin, which follows the MT vocalization, is the better text because the threat of exile is the note on which the primary section of the sermon ends (v. 15), and so the possibility of averting exile is appropriate to the introduction of the message.) Thirdly, he warns against a deceptive thought, a false presumption, that is the (implicit) assumption that YHWH's presence in the temple means security for Judah from its enemies (v. 4).

The rest of Jeremiah's address expands these three points.

> [5] For if you truly amend your ways and your doings, if you truly act justly one with another, [6] if you do not oppress the alien, the orphan, and the widow, or shed innocent blood in this place, and if you do not go after other gods to your own hurt, [7] then I will let you dwell [as in v. 3] in this place, in the land that I gave to your ancestors for ever and ever.

First, Jeremiah gives fuller content to the initial challenge to amendment, and spells out what is involved. The basic requirement is to practise justice, the same keyword as in Amos (5:24) and Micah (3:9). This is specified in terms of not taking advantage of those of whom advantage might most easily be taken—the resident foreigner, the orphan, the widow—because they lacked normal social security as embodied in kin or head of the house. As so often in Israel's Scriptures, the assumption is that if justice is given to those who are most easily denied it, then justice is most likely to be practised elsewhere too. The 'shedding of innocent blood' could envisage either the oppressive maltreatment of labourers (as in Micah 3: 10), or the manipulation of legal procedure (as against Naboth, 1 Kings 21), or possibly some other malpractice; whichever way it is understood, exploitation and violence are seen as the denial of justice. Going after other gods represents fundamental disloyalty to YHWH (a denial of the first of the Ten Commandments and of the Shema), and would also entail Judah's undoing ('to your own hurt'). In all these ways, Jeremiah's hearers are challenged to change for the better.

Also, YHWH's gift to Israel/Judah of its land in perpetuity ('for ever and ever') is implied to be no guarantee against YHWH's depriving them of that gift. The prophetic understanding is that gift implies expectation, and so failure to live up to expectation can imperil the gift. Jeremiah's account of what that expectation entails now leads into his speaking further about how the people of Judah's belief in their security with YHWH, because of his presence in the temple, has in fact become false, and so idolatrous.

> [8] Here you are, trusting in deceptive words to no avail. [9] Will you steal, murder, commit adultery, swear falsely, make offerings to Baal, and go after other gods that you have not known, [10] and then come and stand before me in this house, which is called by my name, and say 'We are safe!'—only to go on doing all these abominations? [11] Has this house, which is called by my name, become a den of robbers in your sight? You know, I too am watching, says the LORD.

Just as vv. 5–7 expanded v. 3, so now vv. 8–11 expand v. 4. The people's mantra, their 'deceptive words', 'This is the temple of the LORD', is now resumed and clarified by the claim 'We are safe', which makes explicit the belief that YHWH's presence in the temple means the deliverance of Jerusalem from its enemies. Yet Jeremiah sees self-contradiction here. In essence, Jeremiah's point is that the claim to YHWH's presence and protection is self-involving language, language that implies a human way of living commensurate with the divine presence that is invoked. But Judah is living in flagrant disregard of YHWH's priorities, and their specified transgressions read like a summary of disobedience to the Ten Commandments. To suppose that one can use the language of YHWH's presence and protection and yet detach oneself from the intrinsic moral and spiritual requirements of YHWH's will is to misunderstand one's language, to empty it of content, and to abuse it. This is what turns the claims about YHWH's temple, which on one level are factually true—the building *was* the temple of YHWH—into something deceptive, a falsehood.

Jeremiah next develops further the issue mentioned in v. 3b, only casting it now not as hopeful possibility but as pure warning of disaster, where the possibility of hope can only be realized if the warning is heeded and acted upon:

> [12] Go now to my place that was in Shiloh, where I made my name dwell at first, and see what I did to it for the wickedness of my people Israel. [13] And now, because you have done all these things, says the LORD, and when I spoke to you persistently, you did not listen, and when I called you, you did not answer, [14] therefore I will do to the house that is called by my name, in which you trust, and to the place that I gave to you and to your ancestors, just what I did to Shiloh. [15] And I will cast you out of my sight, just as I cast out all your kinsfolk, all the offspring of Ephraim.

The warning is backed by appeal to a precedent—the temple of YHWH at Shiloh which by Jeremiah's time had been reduced to ruins and had been abandoned (i.e. Shiloh exemplified Micah's depiction of Jerusalem: Micah 3:12). If the corruption of Israel led to the overthrow of Shiloh, then the heedless and unresponsive corruption of Judah can similarly lead to Jerusalem's overthrow at the hands of an enemy, operating at YHWH's behest. The consequence will be the familiar fate of the vanquished, already experienced by the northern kingdom—deportation into exile. The tragic irony is that YHWH himself, to whose divine presence in the temple the people of Judah complacently appeal as protection against disaster, will be the primary cause and agent of that disaster.

SOME IMPLICATIONS
OF THE TEMPLE SERMONS

The common concerns in these three temple sermons should be clear. Each criticizes corrupt practice in temple worship, which could be summarized as a failure concomitantly to practise justice; each criticizes spurious trust in YHWH, focused in some way upon his presence in the temple; each sees the trust as spurious because it is complacent and has become detached from an obedience commensurate with the trust; each warns of a coming destruction of the temple and/or a deportation into exile; and each sees the destruction and/or exile as the act of YHWH (albeit through human agency). Put differently, although the people claim to trust their God, they show by their actions that they do not know him and his ways; arguably, in an important sense they do not really want to be his covenant people; but this is to deny their basic identity, and leads only to calamity.

In reflecting on this material it is important to resist oversimplifying shorthand formulations, such as 'ethics trumps ritual'. It is one thing to say that the rituals of worship without appropriate moral practice are empty, indeed offensive; it is another to denigrate ritual as such in relation to moral practice. To be sure, it is sometimes suggested that Amos genuinely proposes abolishing animal and cereal sacrifice altogether (as also other prophets when they criticize Israel's sacrificial worship) (Barton 2012: 84–92, 197), perhaps in favour of faithful moral practice as the 'true sacrifice'. Of course, such a metaphorical move is indeed made in the New Testament, as in Romans 12:1–2, and it has an important role in Christian thought and practice. But in terms of Amos himself this suggestion surely depends on too wooden a reading of the prophetic rhetoric. So startling a religious innovation would require much more to be said about it than Amos or any other prophet actually says.

Similarly, it is probably unhelpful to see the critiques of presumed security in and through the temple as representing rejection of 'Zion theology' as expressed in Isaiah and the Psalms (e.g. Bright 1977, Sweeney 2003). This in effect transposes the existential issues that intrinsically surround the implications of trust and obedience in relation to God into a conflictual history of ideas. It is not that the latter may not have existed. But we have no hard evidence, only the varying plausibility of inferences from a biblical corpus which never mentions such a conflict but is open in places to be read as implying it. The real challenge that the canonical material presents is to be able to hold together a confidence in God's presence and protection, as in Isaiah and the Psalms, with a clear-eyed recognition of how easily that confidence can be corrupted in self-serving ways.

Within a Christian context two prime symbols of confidence in God are the Bible and the Eucharist. In many and various ways these are understood to be vehicles of the divine presence, and as such become focal points of hope and expectation, and also of assurance that God is with his people. Yet contemporary Christians no less than ancient Israelites may live in ways that conflict with the implications of their symbols, and fundamentally misunderstand God's nature and ways. As such the prophetic censure of religious practices emptied of their real meaning loses none of its significance.

THE FUTURE OF ISRAEL: EXILE AND HOPE

The category of Israel/Judah in exile has become central to much recent scholarship. On any reckoning, the fall of Jerusalem to the Babylonians and the subsequent exile of many of its inhabitants receive much space within the Old Testament, and are seen as a major turning-point in biblical history. In historical-critical approaches, the exile has increasingly been seen as the catalyst for the formation and preservation of many of the documents that comprise Israel's Scriptures. Among ideological critics the category of 'exile' has become problematic, insofar as it privileges one particular perspective, that of the canonical writers and compilers, over other possible perspectives on the historical realities of the period (though it is a time about which we know all too little). Among some contemporary theologians the category of 'exile' has seemed fruitful as a way of depicting the situation of the churches in a post-Christendom and increasingly secularized Western culture.

Towards Theological Thinking about the Exile

The prime theological issue that exile poses is that of God's ultimate purposes for his people. Does there come a point when their failures lead to God's casting them off and having done with them? Or is God's commitment to his people irrevocable, such that he will always make a new future possible for them? This is a recurrent issue that takes many forms both within the Old Testament and within historic Christian thought—not only in terms of whether or not Christians have replaced Jews as God's people, but also whether or not the contemporary church can properly hope for a future as well as a past.

Numerous interpretative debates revolve around this issue. For example, Martin Noth famously proposed that the primary history of Israel that ends with the Babylonian exile at the end of the books of Kings (the 'Deuteronomistic History') was written as an account of human failure which envisaged the end of Israel and Judah: 'Clearly he [the deuteronomistic author] saw the divine judgement which was acted out in his account of the external collapse of Israel as a nation as something final and definitive and he expressed no hope for the future' (Noth 1981 [1943]: 97). Numerous other scholars, from von Rad onwards (von Rad 1953 [1948]), have proposed more hopeful readings of the material, usually with reference to God's promises to the house of David (2 Samuel 7) and perhaps also the release of the Davidic king from prison as the very last scene (2 Kings 25:27–30). Since the text is open to be read in more than one way, overall interpretations are not unlikely to be indebted to the interpreter's larger theological sense of 'how things go' in the purposes of God.

Alternatively, there is the question of whether Amos, for example, when he said, 'The end has come upon my people Israel' (Amos 8:2) and other comparable things, really meant what he said. Did he really mean that God's election of, and covenant with, Israel was now terminated? Some interpreters insist that such a reading is the plain sense of the text, and that to suppose otherwise is to evade a hard message. Since the book as it stands contains more hopeful notes also, and finishes with a picture of Israel wonderfully restored (9:11–15), they assume that these other passages must be the work of later writers who saw things differently from Amos (Barton 2012: 70–132). This interpretation is, of course, possible, though we will never actually know. It provides a good example of the modern scholarly tendency to transpose theological tensions within the biblical text into a developing history of ideas. But even if one grants the likelihood of the proposed history of thought on its own terms, there remains the question of how best to read the text in its received form, and whether there may be an integrity to the whole that is more than the sum of its parts. As the book of Amos stands, perhaps the greatest interpretative challenge is to attend to the promised hope that frames its message without allowing that hope in any way to trivialize the awfulness of the divine judgement upon Israel's complacency and corruption. In other words, how can one articulate ultimate hope in God in a way that does not diminish or undercut the seriousness of the call to heed God's moral challenge in the here and now (an undercutting famously represented by the words ascribed to Heinrich Heine on his deathbed, 'Dieu me pardonnera. C'est son métier')?

The Concept of a Remnant

One of the prime ways in which the Old Testament articulates hope for the future beyond disaster is through the idea of a remnant (Hebrew *še'ār*)—a faithful few who will constitute the core of a renewed people. Probably the idea of a remnant is best known in relation to famous prophetic texts: for example, Isaiah's son Shear-jashub, whose name means 'a remnant will return' (Isaiah 7:3–9); or YHWH's words to Elijah that, despite a coming bloodbath, 'I will leave [verbal form of *še'ār*] seven thousand in Israel, all the knees that have not bowed to Baal' (1 Kings 19:18). But arguably the Flood narrative in Genesis should be read as the paradigmatic portrayal of the faithful remnant—in the person of Noah (and his somewhat faceless family)—who survive disaster and enable a fresh beginning subsequently. The key term *še'ār* is used in verbal form of Noah and his family just at the point when the flood waters have wiped out all other life on earth and the story is at its nadir (Genesis 7:23b). The location of the Flood narrative at the outset of Israel's Scriptures, which gives it a framing function in relation to all that follows, makes its portrayal of disaster through divine judgement, yet with a purpose of preserving a remnant so that there can be a new beginning, an archetypal resource for thinking about the prophetic portrayal of divine judgement and disaster in the course of history for Israel and Judah—and by extension for the Church also.

Israel and the Golden Calf

Another paradigmatic Old Testament narrative in this context is the story of the golden calf and covenant renewal at Mount Sinai (Exodus 32–4). To utilize this story for thinking about exile and hope does not depend on supposing the story to have been written or edited around the time of the exile—which it may, or may not, have been.

In itself, it is a story set at the outset of Israel's life as Yhwh's covenant people, which poses in archetypal form the issue that recurs through Israel's history: Does Israel's breaking of the covenant terminate the covenant? Does Israel's faithlessness nullify God's faithfulness?

The context of the story makes it as weighty as could be (Moberly 1983). The people of Israel are still at Sinai, the mountain of God, where they have just entered into their covenant with Yhwh. But as soon as Moses' back is turned (while he is on the mountain with God to receive the tablets of stone on which God's way for Israel is recorded), Israel make a calf and proclaim it as their deity (Exodus 32:1–6). This act is seen as fundamental apostasy, in other words a kind of equivalent to committing adultery on one's wedding night. But although Yhwh proposes to terminate Israel and make a fresh start with Moses (32:7–10), Moses shows his greatness in declining the offer and imploring Yhwh to keep his commitment to the Israel that currently exists; to which Yhwh accedes (32:11–14). This sets up the basic dynamic of the story—the judgement and mercy of Yhwh, mediated through the faithful intercession of Moses (who arguably represents God to God; see Anderson 2008: 216–24, 229–31)—which the rest of the narrative develops.

After further depictions of divine anger and judgement towards Israel, which brings death to some, the turning point comes when Yhwh 'speaks face to face with Moses, as one speaks to a friend' (33:11). Thereafter Moses intercedes at length in such a way that Yhwh promises, 'I will make all my goodness pass before you, and will proclaim before you the name, "The Lord" ' (33:19). This episode paves the way for the divine self-revelation in the following chapter, the most extended depiction of the name and nature of God in the Old Testament—though not without a further qualification, that Moses will see only Yhwh's back and not his face, which preserves the divine mystery, since the fullest self-depiction of God by God is said to be like seeing God only from behind and not face to face (33:20–3). God then reveals himself:

> The Lord passed before him, and proclaimed,
> 'The Lord, the Lord,
> a God merciful and gracious,
> slow to anger,
> and abounding in steadfast love and faithfulness,
> keeping steadfast love for the thousandth generation,
> forgiving iniquity and transgression and sin,
> yet by no means clearing the guilty,
> but visiting the iniquity of the parents
> upon the children
> and the children's children,
> to the third and fourth generation.' (34:6–7)

Israel has been fundamentally faithless. Yet the emphasis in the divine words is strongly on the divine mercy. There remains a note of judgement ('by no means clearing the guilty...'), which conveys that the divine mercy is not leniency and that right and wrong still matter. But the point is that, if there is to be a future for Israel, then that future depends on divine mercy to the undeserving. On this basis Moses prays a final prayer (34:9) and the covenant is renewed, with an emphasis on the awesome nature of such a renewal of relationship in this context (34:10).

The wording of Moses' final prayer is also striking, for he mentions that Israel 'is a stiff-necked people' (34:9b), even though Israel's being a stiff-necked people has been mentioned three times previously, each time on God's lips as a reason for God's anger towards, and distancing himself from, Israel (32:9; 33:3, 5). This paradoxically makes the point that Israel has not changed, and is still as stiff-necked when the covenant is renewed as when they broke it; so the renewal and hope for the future emphatically lie in God.

A similar feature can be found also in the Flood narrative (Moberly 2009: 118–20), where the corruption of the human heart, which YHWH mentions as a reason for sending the Flood (Genesis 6:5), is mentioned again in the context of YHWH's responding to Noah's sacrifice by promising never again to send a flood (8:21). Again, the point appears to be that humanity is no more deserving after the Flood than before, and that therefore if there is hope for the future that hope is located in the mercy of God. There is thus a direct analogy between how God deals with the world as a whole (in the Flood narrative) and how he deals with his chosen people (in the golden calf narrative). In each context people are unchanging, but God, who indeed judges sin, is nonetheless merciful, and this mercy is, as it were, the bottom line.

It is thus apparent that the issues about Israel's possible future, which are posed by the prophets in relation to Israel's history in the promised land—after faithlessness, judgement, and exile, is there hope for the future?—are raised archetypally at the outset of Israel's story in its canonical presentation. When similar things are said in the book of Jeremiah, the reader should hardly be surprised:

> Thus says the LORD,
> who gives the sun for light by day
>   and the fixed order of the moon and the stars for light by night,
> who stirs up the sea so that its waves roar—
>   the LORD of hosts is his name:
> If this fixed order were ever to cease
>   from my presence, says the LORD,
> then also the offspring of Israel would cease
>   to be a nation before me for ever.
> Thus says the LORD:
> If the heavens above can be measured,
>   and the foundations of the earth below can be explored,
> then I will reject all the offspring of Israel
>   because of all they have done,
> says the LORD. (Jeremiah 31:35–7)

CONCLUSION

If one is to utilize the portrayal of the people of God in the Old Testament for constructive ecclesiological thought and practice in a Christian context, it is important to look at the canonical portrayal as a whole. Although the focus here has been on three core areas—vocation and assurance, warning and challenge, failure and hope—there is of course much else in the Old Testament that could also be used.

Perhaps the appropriate note on which to conclude is that a Christian refusal to see God's covenant with the Jews as revoked, whatever their failures, gives grounds for the churches also to hope that, whatever their failures, the God whose character and purposes they discern in Scripture, and whom they know in Jesus Christ, will yet have a future for them in his service.

REFERENCES

Anderson, Gary (2008). 'Moses and Jonah in Gethsemane: Representation and Impassibility in their Old Testament Inflections'. In Beverly Roberts Gaventa and Richard B. Hays (eds), *Seeking the Identity of Jesus: A Pilgrimage*. Grand Rapids, MI: Eerdmans, 215–31.

Barton, John (2012). *The Theology of the Book of Amos*. Old Testament Theology. Cambridge: Cambridge University Press.

Bright, John (1977). *Covenant and Promise*. London: SCM.

Childs, Brevard S. (1992). *Biblical Theology of the Old and New Testaments: Theological Reflection on the Christian Bible*. London: SCM.

Driver, Daniel R. (2010). *Brevard Childs, Biblical Theologian*. FAT 2nd series 46, Tübingen: Mohr Siebeck.

Goldingay, John (1987). *Theological Diversity and the Authority of the Old Testament*. Grand Rapids, MI: Eerdmans.

Greenberg, Moshe (1995). 'To Whom and for What Should a Bible Commentator Be Responsible?' In Greenberg, *Studies in the Bible and Jewish Thought*. Philadelphia and Jerusalem: Jewish Publication Society, 235–43.

Grüneberg, Keith N. (2003). *Abraham, Blessing and the Nations: A Philological and Exegetical Study of Genesis 12:3 in its Narrative Context*. BZAW 332, Berlin and New York: de Gruyter.

Hanson, Paul D. (1987). *The People Called: The Growth of Community in the Bible*. New York: Harper & Row. New edition, Louisville, KY, and London: Westminster John Knox Press, 2001.

Hazony, Yoram (2012). *The Philosophy of Hebrew Scripture*. Cambridge: Cambridge University Press.

Kennett, Robert Hatch (1933 [reissued 2011]). *The Church of Israel*. Cambridge: Cambridge University Press.

Lindbeck, George (1997). 'The Story-Shaped Church: Critical Exegesis and Theological Interpretation'. In Stephen E. Fowl (ed.), *The Theological Interpretation of Scripture: Classic and Contemporary Readings*, Oxford: Blackwell, 39–52 (reprinted from Garrett Green (ed.) 1987, *Scriptural Authority and Narrative Interpretation*, Philadelphia: Fortress).

Lindbeck, George (2003). 'The Church as Israel: Ecclesiology and Ecumenism'. In Carl E. Braaten and Robert W. Jenson (eds), *Jews and Christians: People of God*. Grand Rapids, MI: Eerdmans, 78–94.

Moberly, R. W. L. (1983). *At the Mountain of God: Story and Theology in Exodus 32–34*. JSOTSS 22, Sheffield: JSOT Press.

Moberly, R. W. L. (2008). '"In God We Trust"? The Challenge of the Prophets'. *Ex Auditu* 24: 18–33.

Moberly, R. W. L. (2009). *The Theology of the Book of Genesis*. OTT, Cambridge: Cambridge University Press.

Noth, Martin (1981). *The Deuteronomistic History*. JSOTSS 15, Sheffield: JSOT Press (ET of 3rd German edition (1967) of original of 1943).

Ochs, Peter (2011). 'George Lindbeck and the Church as Israel'. In Ochs, *Another Reformation: Postliberal Christianity and the Jews*. Grand Rapids, MI: Baker Academic, 35–62.

Radner, Ephraim (1998). *The End of the Church: A Pneumatology of Christian Division in the West*. Grand Rapids, MI: Eerdmans.

Sweeney, Marvin (2003). 'The Truth in True and False Prophecy'. In Christine Helmer and Kristin de Troyer, with Katie Goetz (eds), *Truth: Interdisciplinary Dialogues in a Pluralist Age*. Leuven: Peeters, 9–26.

Von Rad, Gerhard (1953). 'The Deuteronomistic Theology of History in the Book of Kings'. In von Rad, *Studies in Deuteronomy*. SBT 9, London: SCM, 74–91 (ET from German of 1948).

Von Rad, Gerhard (1972). *Genesis*. 3rd edition, London: SCM Press (ET from 9th German edition of 1972).

Watson, Francis (2004). *Paul and the Hermeneutics of Faith*. London and New York: T&T Clark.

Wilken, Robert Louis (2004). *John Chrysostom and the Jews: Rhetoric and Reality in the Late 4th Century*. Eugene, OR: Wipf & Stock.

Wright, Christopher J. H. (2006). *The Mission of God: Unlocking the Bible's Grand Narrative*. Nottingham: InterVarsity Press.

SUGGESTED READING

Childs, Brevard S. (1992). 6:III, 'Covenant, Election, People of God'. In Childs, *Biblical Theology of the Old and New Testaments: Theological Reflection on the Christian Bible*. London: SCM, 413–51.

Goldingay (1987). 'A Contextualizing Study of "The People of God" in the Old Testament'. In Goldingay, *Theological Diversity and the Authority of the Old Testament*. Grand Rapids, MI: Eerdmans, 59–96.

Hanson, Paul D. (1987). *The People Called: The Growth of Community in the Bible*. New York: Harper & Row. New edition, Louisville, KY, and London: Westminster John Knox Press, 2001.

Lindbeck, George (2003). 'The Church as Israel: Ecclesiology and Ecumenism'. In Carl E. Braaten and Robert W. Jenson (eds), *Jews and Christians: People of God*. Grand Rapids, MI: Eerdmans, 78–94.

Lohfink, Gerhard (1999). *Does God Need the Church? Towards a Theology of the People of God*. Collegeville: Liturgical Press (ET by Linda Maloney from 1998 German edition).

CHAPTER 3

THE CHURCH IN THE SYNOPTIC GOSPELS AND THE ACTS OF THE APOSTLES

LOVEDAY C. A. ALEXANDER

THE three Synoptic Gospels (SG), Matthew (Mt), Mark (Mk) and Luke (Lk), are biographical narratives about Jesus and his disciples. They offer three individual perspectives on the same story: the life, death, and resurrection of the Galilean teacher and wonder-worker Jesus of Nazareth, the story that Mark identifies as 'the good news (*euangelion*, 'gospel') of Jesus Christ, the Son of God' (Mk 1.1). They are not—as numerous critics have rightly insisted—narratives about the church: they are narratives about Jesus (Burridge 1992). Thus by their very nature, they contain very few explicit statements on the nature of the *ekklēsia* (indeed, few statements of propositional theology of any kind). Yet their underlying narrative shape both reflects and creates a profoundly ecclesiological sub-structure, and this is foundational for the self-understanding of the emergent life of the church. In the words of Rudolf Schnackenburg:

> The Church is everywhere present in the New Testament even when it is not manifest in concepts and imagery. The Church gave birth to the New Testament writings and they all bear witness to its existence and life . . . Consequently, an exposition of the teaching of the New Testament regarding the Church will not only have to take into account the explicit statements regarding the *ecclēsia,* but must also ponder and judge the New Testament documents themselves as expressions of the Church's life and as speaking testimony to the way the Church viewed itself.
>
> (Schnackenburg 1974: 9–10)

THE GOSPELS AND THE CHURCH

For many NT critics, looking for the ecclesiology of the Gospels is like looking for oranges in an apple orchard: it is simply asking the wrong kind of question. Many would argue that there is a profound discordance between the Jesus of the Gospels and the ideas we associate with 'the church'. The discomfort is well expressed in Paul Minear's classic study (originally published in 1960), *Images of the Church in the New Testament* (Minear 2007: 16): 'some find it most difficult to recognize any kinship whatever to the wandering band of Jesus' disciples in the modern church as a powerful and prosperous social institution.' Others are disturbed by a perceived contrast between the 'power politics' of the modern churches and the 'radical pacifism of the Sermon on the Mount', or between the 'leadership of laymen' and the 'priestly hierarchy', or between Jesus' 'rejection of cant, cloth and custom' and the ceremonies and rituals of the church. The whole thing is summed up in a famous quotation from Alfred Loisy: 'Jesus foretold the Kingdom, and it was the Church that came' (cited from Barrett 1985: 23).

The dilemma may be illustrated neatly in the debate over the one unambiguous reference to the future church in the Gospels. The word *ekklēsia* only occurs on two occasions in the Gospels, both in Matthew. At Mt 18:18, a passage referring to discipline within the congregation, the word could plausibly be read as 'congregation' or 'assembly', in line with current Jewish and Greek usage. But at Mt 16:18 the word has a clear future reference. Jesus says, 'You are Peter, and on this rock I will build my church (*ekklēsia*), and the powers of death (Hades) shall not prevail over it.' Ecclesiologically, interpretation of this famous passage is almost completely divided along confessional lines. For Roman Catholic exegesis (at least since the Reformation) it has played a central role in the affirmation of the primacy of the Roman See. Protestant exegesis has almost without exception either denied its authenticity (chiefly on the a priori grounds that Jesus did not found a 'church') or denied that it has anything to say about Roman primacy. (We discuss this passage more fully under 'Confessing the Christ, Carrying the Cross'; for a survey of the exegetical tradition, see Cullmann 1962; Luz 2005: 165–82.) Behind these positions lie two fundamentally divergent approaches to the ecclesiology of the Gospels: the Roman Catholic tradition, which takes the disciples as types for the ordained ministry and reads the ecclesiology of the Gospels as fundamentally hierarchical (e.g. Schnackenburg 1974: 126–8); and the Protestant tradition, which emphasizes the anti-hierarchical features of the Gospels and takes the disciples as types for all believers, that is for the church as a whole (e.g. Schweizer 1961: 28–33; Carlston and Evans 2014: 315–25). And the simple fact is that Matthew is the only Gospel to contain this saying: Mark and Luke tell the same story, but without the crucial *ekklēsia* saying. Does this mean that Mark and Luke were not interested in the church, or did not believe that Jesus founded it? Does the saying refer to the future church at all? Without a secure understanding of the narrative framework of the Gospels—and the thought-world to which they belong—we have no means of discriminating between apparently limitless interpretative possibilities.

So where should we look to find the 'ecclesiology' of the Gospels? Vocabulary studies (as we have seen) will not help us much: the word *ekklēsia* occurs twenty-three times in Acts, but only twice in the Gospels. Minear's approach via the 'images' of the church is at first sight more promising. He points out the distance that separates the thought-world of the New Testament from 'the modern thought-world where priority is given to prosaic, apodictic, propositional definitions and where other forms of speech (parable, riddle, picture, images, allegories) circulate only under a heavy discount'. In the thought-world of the New Testament, as Minear points out, the priorities are reversed: so 'the church must perennially open its imagination to the wide panorama of NT imagery . . . not as tools for rhetorical ingenuity or as mirrors for self-preening, or as weapons in ecclesiastical warfare, but as modes of perceiving afresh that mystery of eternal life which God shares with his people' (Minear 2007: 24–6).

Yet (despite its richness in detail) there is something strangely unsatisfactory about Minear's thematic approach to the NT images of the church. The clue may lie in a perceptive remark on Jesus' saying, 'You are the salt of the earth' (Mt 5:13):

> Does this saying have an ecclesiological connotation? Almost certainly we must say yes . . . Many undoubtedly ecclesiological statements tend to take this form: Jesus, the Lord of the community of disciples, speaking directly to them, not as separate individuals but as a band of followers, says, 'You are . . .' This second person plural reminds us that the congregations that preserved and utilized this saying heard themselves being addressed by him who had called the church into being. . . . This kind of formula ('You are . . .'), therefore, is an important characteristic of many ecclesiological images. (Minear 2007: 29)

There is an important insight here: but who is being addressed? Is it the disciples (Mt 5:1)—or the crowds (Mt 7:28)? We cannot evaluate the ecclesiological significance of individual sayings without a more coherent analysis of the narrative roles of speaker and audience. If we are to understand the theological import of the Gospels, we have to understand their generic structure: we have to read them first and foremost *as narratives*. Thus in what follows (like much contemporary NT scholarship) we adopt a broadly narrative-critical approach, which draws attention to 'the integral connection between narrative, identity, and way of life whereby narratives constitute identity, interpret behaviour, and determine action . . . I can only answer the question, "What am I to do?" if I can answer the prior question, "Of what stories do I find myself a part?"' (Carter 1994: 190–209, citing Alasdair Macintyre). The search for the ecclesiology of the Gospels is not a search for propositional statements as such but a quest to understand the shape of a narrative and the impact or effects of that narrative on its audience(s). We are seeking to discover not the community (or communities) behind this narrative, but rather 'the question of the identity and way of life that might emerge in an audience's interaction with [the Gospel] narrative' (Carter 1994: 204). What I propose to do in this chapter, therefore, is to analyse the narrative structures of the SG themselves to see how they build bridges between the story of Jesus (as told in the Gospels) and the story of the church (as told in Acts). We begin with the opening chapter of Acts.

MAKING CONNECTIONS: THE APOSTLES AND THE RISEN CHRIST

The opening chapters of Acts encapsulates the moment of transition from the story of Jesus to the story of the church, embodying a very Lukan ecclesiology. First, the eleven disciples receive Jesus' instruction in 'the things concerning himself', in the forty days immediately after the resurrection, as described in Luke 24:44–9 and Acts 1:1–8. Then after Pentecost, the apostles (now augmented to twelve) receive the Spirit, preside over the life of the church, and preach the gospel, as described in Acts chapters 2–4. Luke's narrative is deliberately constructed to provide a narrative bridge, creating continuity between the story of Jesus in the Gospels and the story of the church in Acts. The beginning of Acts is at once the final scene of the Gospel ('all that Jesus began both to do and to teach') and the opening scene in the unfolding story of the church: it looks simultaneously forward to the mission of the church and backward to the story of Jesus.

In human terms, the disciples are the key characters who link the two narratives. They are described as the apostles 'whom he [Jesus] had chosen' (Acts 1:2)—a reference back to the call narratives of the Gospel (a link reinforced by the listing of their names at 1:13, echoing the original list at Lk 6:14–16). This is not just a chance group of friends but an intentional community—and the intention is Jesus'. *Sunalizomenos* ('sharing meals together', Acts 1:4) evokes the table-fellowship which has been such a significant part of their lives together—especially, perhaps, the Emmaus meal where the risen Christ was 'made known to them in the breaking of bread' (Lk 24:35). Jesus' next words provide a further link with the opening of the Gospel: the apostles are to 'wait for the promise of the Father, which (he said) you heard from me, for John baptized with water, but before many days you shall be baptized with the Holy Spirit' (Acts 1:5). This sends us back to the very beginning of Jesus' own story and the climactic moment of his own anointing with the Holy Spirit (Lk 3:22). John had predicted that in time Jesus would himself baptize his followers 'with the Holy Spirit and with fire' (Lk 3:16): and that promise is about to be fulfilled. Now, as Jesus is taken up to heaven, it is his followers who need the Spirit's anointing for the task ahead of them, a task to which they are solemnly commissioned (Acts 1:8). The disciples' question about the kingdom (Acts 1:6) provides a further link back with the gospel narrative. The kingdom of God is a constant theme of Jesus' preaching throughout the Gospel (Lk 4:43, 8:1); it is both imminent and future, both warning and promise. The question reveals an element of uncertainty: 'waiting', it seems, is still going to be part of the experience of discipleship.

At the same time, Acts 1 provides a series of forward links into the unfolding story of the church. The disciples receive their commission as Jesus' witnesses (Acts 1:8): the word's forensic connotations (cf. 'proofs' in Acts 1:3) remind us that the resurrection of Jesus is a contested fact in a hostile or agonistic environment. They are chosen as transmitters of memory (Acts 1:21–2), the future bearers of the memory of Jesus in the life of the church. They are trained as interpreters of Scripture (Lk 24:25–7, 44–9), in a foreshadowing of the crucial role that the interpretation of Scripture will play in the apostolic preaching: the Christ-event is the key to unlock the Scriptures. Their geographical horizons are enlarged: their mission will take them 'to the ends of the earth' (Acts 1:8). And the promise of the Spirit is also a promise of power (Acts 1:8), a foretaste of the words and deeds of power that will characterize the apostolic mission. There are glimpses too of the unfolding inner life of the church. The apostles are not the only followers of Jesus waiting for Pentecost: 120 believers, including 'the women' and Jesus' family, are waiting together (Acts 1:14–15) in a life characterized by focused prayer and attentiveness. Peter begins to assume the mantle of leadership. There are hints of the supernaturally validated transmission of office: Judas has 'turned aside', but 'this ministry' will continue (Acts 1:20, 24–5). All this takes place in a private location (Acts 1:13), away from the public centres of power. None of this is yet called 'the church': but it holds the ingredients (to borrow C. K. Barrett's term) of what will become the church in the Acts of the Apostles.

All of this looks distinctively Lukan. Luke is the only evangelist to describe the Ascension as a narrative event, and the only one to gather the apostles in Jerusalem immediately after the resurrection. The Jerusalem setting serves an important apologetic function for Luke's construction of Christian origins—even though it leaves open obvious questions (e.g. What happened to Jesus' followers in Galilee?) which are never really answered in Acts. By contrast, Mark has Jesus instruct his disciples to meet him *in Galilee* after the resurrection, and that is where Matthew and John set their final scenes. But the underlying ecclesiology is by no means unique to Luke. The other Synoptic Gospels use different narrative techniques to create a similar effect. If we look more closely, we discover that the ecclesiological clues that enable Luke to create an organic connection between the story of Jesus and the story of the church are not Lukan peculiarities but integral to the core gospel narrative. Many of them are also shared with John (even though his narrative has its own distinctive shape: see Chapter 4).

To summarize: Luke identifies a number of connecting points which forge a link between the story of Jesus and the story of the church: the call of the disciples and their table-fellowship with Jesus; the preaching of the kingdom; the baptism of John and the promise of the Holy Spirit; the commissioning and empowering of the apostles to a future mission after Jesus' death and resurrection. Far from being Lukan peculiarities, all of these key points belong to the deep structure of the gospel narrative. All the Synoptic Gospels agree that Jesus' mission to Israel involved proclaiming a message of repentance and the coming of the kingdom of God, a mission that begins with the baptism of John and the promise of the Holy Spirit. As part of this mission, Jesus creates a community of disciples, and expects this messianic community to play a part in the coming of the kingdom, both during his lifetime and beyond. Jesus' relationship with this group includes promises and instructions that are unfulfilled in the gospel narrative and point beyond it. In order to understand the ecclesiological significance of all this, we need to look at the individual gospel narratives in more detail, starting with Mark.

THE CHURCH IN MARK

Mark's Gospel is the story of Jesus the Messiah, anointed with the Holy Spirit, proclaiming God's Kingdom in word and deed, calling God's people to repentance, calling disciples to follow him, dying on the cross. But it is also the story of the messianic community: a story that begins with baptism and repentance, hearing the call of Jesus, listening to the word of the kingdom, and watching the kingdom in action. The community is made up of individuals who have come to Jesus in faith and found salvation in the encounter. So this Gospel tells three stories at once: the story of Jesus: the story of the messianic community; and the story of the individual encounter with Jesus and its results. I follow here the dominant scholarly consensus that Mark is the earliest of the SG, and that his underlying narrative structure has been taken over and expanded in different ways by Matthew and Luke.

Preaching the Kingdom

Mark's church—that is, the church that reads Mark's Gospel—tells the story of its origins as the story of the messianic community founded by Jesus of Nazareth. The key to Mark's ecclesiology lies in his summary of Jesus' mission at 1:14–15: Jesus 'came into Galilee, preaching the gospel of God and saying, "The time is fulfilled and the kingdom of God is at hand: repent and believe in the gospel"'. The kingdom of God provides the link between the emergent self-understanding of the church and the historical matrix of Second Temple Judaism in which the church was born. It is integrally linked to Jesus' messianic identity, and has both an individual and a communal dimension. The kingdom in the gospel narratives is both imminent and future: it belongs to the time of Jesus, but simultaneously points beyond itself to a fulfilment outside the text. For Mark, this is the core of the 'good news' (*euangelion*) that Jesus proclaimed (1:15). It is a message not for the chosen few but for the whole people. Jesus teaches it in synagogues, in houses, and on the sea-shore, travelling on from town to town and village to village, 'for that is why I came out' (1:38). Its mysteries are revealed to the disciples in parables (4:11, 26, 30), and to children (10:14–15), while the rich find it difficult to enter (10:23–5). The imminence of the kingdom looms over Jesus' ministry from start to finish (11:10), yet at the end it is still in the future (14:25).

The concept of the kingdom was familiar to Jesus' hearers and draws on a long tradition of development in the Hebrew Scriptures and in Second Temple Judaism. In his classic study of *The Teaching of Jesus*, T. W. Manson identifies three interdependent strands in the concept of the kingdom: the eternal sovereignty of God; its present manifestation in those who recognize God's sovereignty in the world; and its perfect consummation at some indeterminate future point, which may be either utopian (on earth) or paradisal (in heaven). These three aspects of the kingdom 'are not peculiar to the teaching of Jesus, but are present in the OT, in rabbinic theology, and in the documents of the primitive Christian community' (Manson 1935: 141).

The kingdom or 'reign' of God is present on earth wherever God finds a community of people who are willing to 'take upon themselves the yoke of the Kingdom' and acknowledge God as king. When Israel proves faithless, a faithful remnant emerges as the spiritual kernel of the nation who continue to recognize God's kingship and show their loyalty by obedience to his commands. Post-exilic Judaism knows a succession of such movements, from the Hasidim of the Maccabean period to the Pharisaic movement and the sectaries of Qumran. Jesus' mission to Israel (like John's) belongs within a spectrum of renewal movements seeking to restore the kingdom by re-awakening God's people to a repentant acknowledgement of God's sovereignty. Jesus' preaching of the kingdom, then, already has strong communal (as well as personal) implications: it is an impassioned call to Israel to re-awaken her vocation as 'a kingdom of priests and a holy nation,' living out in the world the loyalty, trust, and obedience that characterize God's kingdom.

Baptized in the Spirit

Mark's story begins with the mission of John the Baptist (1:1). The baptism of John marks the opening of a new era in salvation-history for the people of God, offering a new start for God's people and 'preparing the way' for the one whom Mark knows as 'Jesus Christ, the Son of God'. This is a movement of divine initiative: the prophetic voice crying in the wilderness is a voice that comes from God (1:1–3). In preparation for this divine visitation, John offers a simple ritual of 'repentance for the forgiveness of sins'. The people who flocked to John from Jerusalem and the surrounding countryside were seeking *metanoia*, a complete transformation of mind and heart, symbolically enacted by dipping in the River Jordan.

When Jesus appears, this simple cleansing ritual takes on a new and surprising significance. It opens a direct channel of access between heaven and earth (1:10), marking the point where Jesus is anointed with God's Spirit and hears the divine accolade: 'You are my beloved Son, with you I am well pleased'. Baptism thus marks a new beginning for Jesus too: it affirms his identity as God's Son, and marks the inauguration of his messianic ministry. John wears the distinctive garb of the prophet Elijah, forerunner of the Messiah (Malachi 4:5–6), and recognizes that Jesus is 'mightier than I'. And John prophesies that Jesus will offer a new kind of baptism 'with Holy Spirit' (1:9). This promise is not fulfilled within the gospel narrative: it opens out the horizons of the text to something that will only make sense within the life of the church.

Called to Discipleship

The opening chapters of Mark's Gospel also depict the gathering of the messianic community at the start of Jesus' mission. Jesus' first action is the call of the fishermen, with the promise that he will make them 'fish' for people (1:16–20). Jesus sets out very deliberately to found a gathered messianic community to act as an agent of the kingdom and to realize in itself, by its very existence, the values of the kingdom. Thus the priestly destiny of Israel-within-the-world is replicated by the priestly role of the messianic community-within-Israel, the seed that grows secretly within the field (4:26–9), the grain of mustard seed that becomes a tree (4:30–2), the lamp whose light cannot be concealed (4:21–2). This community of 'those around Jesus' (*hoi peri auton* is one of Mark's distinctive terms for the disciple-group) becomes a new family, more important than parents or siblings (3:31–5). Drawn from those marginalized by the religious elite, fishermen, tax-collectors, and 'sinners' (2:15–17), Jesus' followers share table-fellowship with him and experience a foretaste of the joy of the eschatological kingdom (2:18–22). This is a group to whom the mysteries of the kingdom of heaven have been revealed (4:11), a group demarcated from 'those outside'.

Within the larger group, Mark names an inner circle of twelve who have a dual role: 'to be with him, and to be sent out' (3:14). As disciples (*mathetai*), their primary task is 'being around' Jesus, studying and memorizing his words, acting as his apprentices. *Imitatio*, learning by imitation, as always in ancient society, is central to the role of the disciple: at its heart is a disciplined process of internalizing the kingdom values embodied by their teacher (Burridge 2007; Alexander 2009). But the Twelve are also apostles (*apostoloi*), 'sent out' as Jesus' delegates with authority to preach and cast out demons in his name (3:14–15), and specifically instructed to report back to him (6:7–13, 30). The key factor here that distinguishes the Twelve from the wider circle of disciples is their readiness to leave home and 'follow' Jesus, that is to adopt his itinerant lifestyle.

The apostolic mission probably gives us an accurate glimpse into Jesus' Galilean mission. These are not foreign missionaries imposing an alien creed, but neighbours and guests, reliant on traditional patterns of village hospitality (9:41). As Jesus' delegates, the disciples are carrying out Jesus' mission, a mission described in a series of metaphors (fishing, harvesting, shepherding) which are all well-established scriptural images for the eschatological gathering-in of God's people (see also Chapter 4). They are a community within a community, a gathered and intentional sub-group that exists for the sake of the wider community to which they also belong.

What is the structural relationship between this inner circle of followers and the wider community? The nature of our sources makes it impossible to maintain clear-cut lines of demarcation between the Twelve, the wider circle of disciples, supporters, and followers, and the 'crowds' addressed by Jesus. It is better to think in terms of intersecting 'circles of discipleship' (Dunn 2003: 540). This means that when we ask, 'Who is the *you* of this passage?' (Minear 2007: 29), we have to avoid being too dogmatic in our answers. This has important implications for the way that later Christian communities hear themselves being addressed in the gospel narratives. Sometimes the disciples act as intermediaries between Jesus and the crowds (6:37–41), sometimes they get in the way (10:13). Frequently and dramatically in Mark the disciples fail to get the point of Jesus' teaching (8:14– 21; 8:32–3; 9:18–19). Some interpreters read this feature as a transparent attack on church leaders, but within the narrative it makes more sense to read them as representative disciples with whom all readers (hearers) will identify: Peter in Mark functions above all as the representative (and fallible) disciple (Malbon 2000: 70–99; Luz 2005: 176).

The Work of the Kingdom

Thus the dominant image of the church in the first part of Mark's Gospel is the disciple-group gathered around Jesus as he carries out the work of the kingdom in word and deed. They are there to watch and listen, to record and remember, sometimes to help, sometimes just to avoid getting in the way. But what they are watching—and this is crucial to their apprenticeship role—is God's kingdom at work in the world. For Mark, Jesus' ministry of healing and exorcism signifies the 'binding' of Satan and the 'plundering' of his kingdom (3:22–7). This mission is actualized in the saving encounters that crowd the earliest chapters of Mark, in which Jesus brings cleansing, forgiveness, healing, and salvation. These stories relate what happens when God's kingdom is present: they highlight the central messianic agency of Jesus, his authority in the physical and the spiritual realms, and his compassion for needy and damaged individuals.

In ecclesiological terms, this is the template for the future work of the church. Jesus challenges the disciples to match his own compassion with action, and gives them authority to cast out demons and to heal (6:7, 13). Yet despite their privileged position, the Gospels underline the disparity between the disciples' role and that of Jesus (Klutz 2004). Mighty works can only be performed 'in the name of Jesus' (9:38–41). The disciples themselves are lost without Jesus' saving power (6:45–52). In Mark's story of the feeding of the 5,000, it is Jesus who feels compassion for the crowd and challenges the disciples to give them something to eat (6:34–7). But only Jesus has the power to satisfy the world's physical and spiritual hunger; in a foretaste of the Eucharist, the role of the disciples is to distribute the food their master has provided (6:41). Left to themselves, they still do not have the necessary faith to act on Jesus' behalf (9:14–29).

But we must not lose sight of the ecclesiological significance of the individual's encounter with Jesus. The Greek word for 'salvation' also means 'healing' (3:4; 5:23, 28, 34; 6:56; 10:52), and it has both a personal and a communal dimension in the Gospels. At the narrative level, marginalized individuals are healed in order to be re-integrated into the community: the leper is instructed to report to the priest (1:44); the Gerasene demoniac is told to go back to his friends (5:18–20); Peter's mother-in-law is healed in order to serve her guests (*diakonein*: 1:31). And on a symbolic level these healing encounters provide vividly dramatic type-scenes of the importance of faith (*pistis*) and the effects of encountering Jesus at a person-to-person level (Malbon 2000: 198–202; Cotter 2010). Key words like *katharismos* (cleansing); forgiveness; *soteria* (healing, wholeness, salvation); and resurrection (*talitha cumi*) operate on both the physical and the spiritual plane—whence the popularity of these episodes in early Christian iconography (Jensen 2005: 146–53).

We should be wary, therefore, of translating these narrative roles into a firm ecclesiologial distinction between apostles (clergy) and 'those who are saved' (ordinary believers)—a tendency already visible in the iconography of fourth-century sarcophagi—or between disciples (the church) and 'outsiders'. Rather, these stories (which make up a large proportion of the synoptic tradition) underline the fundamental ecclesiological importance of personal faith in the saving encounter with Christ. 'Those who are saved' (a group that includes women) represent a proper response to Jesus' saving power, a response of faith, worship, and service that facilitates the entry of the kingdom into the world. The church is called to carry out Jesus' mission by continuing the work of the kingdom in the world—the work of liberation, restoration, and jubilee, reaching out to the damaged and broken and making space for God's work of healing and forgiveness. But in order to do that, she must first understand and accept Jesus' saving power in her own life.

The Word of the Kingdom

Equally fundamental to Jesus' mission is the preaching of the Word. Mark tells us repeatedly that Jesus 'taught with authority' and that the people listened gladly to his teaching. The disciples are sent out on mission to preach that people should repent (6:12, 30). The parable of the Sower in Mark 4 underlines the church's primary task of *listening* to the Word of God, seeking to *understand* it (cf. 7:14, 8:17–21), and letting it bear fruit in transformed lives. But the underlying allegory of the seed, repeated in the parables of the mustard seed and the seed growing by itself, is making an even more fundamental point, one that is crucial for understanding Jesus' vision of the kingdom. This is a kingdom that grows secretly and invisibly—it is small but irresistible.

The seed parable also underlines the diversity of response, and the limits of the preacher's responsibility. The Word can be rejected: only one seed in four will take root and bear fruit. The disciples' question and the interpretation that it elicits (4:10–20) reflect a concern of the early church about the relative lack of response to Jesus' message. The quotation from Isa. 6:9–10 (4:12) was an important apologetic text in early Christian debate about Israel's failure to respond to the message of Jesus (Evans 1989). This polemical context shapes Mark's relatively sparse account of the content of Jesus' teaching. Jesus 'taught them as one who had authority, and not as the scribes' (1:22). The contrast runs right the way through Mark's Gospel, from the Galilean disputes over fasting, Sabbath-keeping, and hand-washing (2.18–27; 3:1–6; 7:1–23), to the Judaean debates over divorce (10:2–12), taxation, resurrection, and the commandments (12:13–34). The cumulative effect is of a teacher who has the confidence to offer his own interpretation of the Law, upholding the fundamental principles of love of God and neighbour, but sitting light to restrictive practices and coming down hard on religious pretension (12:38–40) or tradition for its own sake (7:6–13). The fundamental challenge for hearers of the gospel is to *pay attention* to the word that is being spoken in the person and actions of Jesus himself: it is impossible to make a correct response to the word of the kingdom without recognizing that something new is happening here, something as disruptive as new wine in old wineskins (3:22).

Confessing the Christ, Carrying the Cross

Caesarea Philippi marks a watershed in Mark's narrative: 'At this point the atmosphere of the gospel changes dramatically: from now on the dominant theme is that of the Cross' (Hooker 1991: 204). The second half of Mark's Gospel sees a marked change of tone, with a gradually intensified focus on the inner life of the messianic community. The catalyst for this new focus is Peter's confession that Jesus is 'the Christ' (8:29). This point signals Peter's recognition that in Jesus, the kingdom of God has really 'broken in' and is fully present: and this is confirmed by the Transfiguration (9:2–8). The confession of Jesus as the Christ is foundational to the life of the church: it marks the point at which the disciple-group begins to realize its identity as a messianic community. But the confession is followed immediately by intensified and repeated teaching on the necessity of the cross, not only for Jesus himself but for his disciples. Confession and cross are integrally linked: Peter's attempt to turn Jesus aside from the path of the cross is roughly dismissed as a satanic attempt to deflect Jesus from his chosen path as a suffering Messiah. It is not enough to identify Jesus as Messiah: equally if not more important is the slow and painful realization of the nature of his Messiahship—which is also the nature of the messianic community. Only those who share Peter's confession of Jesus' messianic identity will share in the ultimate glory of the Son of Man (8:38).

As the shadow of the cross looms over the narrative, Jesus' instructions become more future-oriented; the focus shifts from public teaching to private instruction of the disciples, setting out the demands of discipleship as a distinctive way of life (9:30–2). 'Following Jesus' demands a higher level of commitment, whether in chastity in marriage (10:10–12), or in giving to the poor (10:17–22; cf. 12:41–4). Among Jesus' followers, the exercise of authority must conform to the pattern of self-giving love exhibited in Jesus' own relationship with his Father and with the world (9:33–7; 10:42–5). Looking into the future, Jesus foresees that his disciples will discover that the only way to the kingdom lies through the path of suffering—'The cup that I drink you shall drink, and with the baptism with which I am baptized, you shall be baptized' (10:38–40)—another unfulfilled prophecy that points to a world beyond the gospel narrative.

Israel and the Kingdom

But the kingdom is never identified solely and simply with the messianic community. Discipleship is a private commitment with public consequences. Jesus' preaching of the kingdom (as we have seen) implies from the outset a prophetic mission to Israel, focused on recalling Israel to her vocation as 'a kingdom of priests and a holy nation'. Yet there are certain contradictory elements built into this mission from the start. Jesus' concept of holiness is more dynamic than that of many of his contemporaries. He makes a point of associating with those whom other holiness movements regarded as 'sinners', like prostitutes and tax-collectors (2:15–17), and there are hints that the benefits of the kingdom may extend beyond the borders of ethnic Israel (7:24–8:10). And (partly because of this), there is an element of conflict woven right through Mark's story, rapidly intensifying after Caesarea Philippi. Whatever Jesus' own aims may have been, the SG show Israel's leaders constantly challenging—and ultimately rejecting—Jesus' mission to his own people.

The early church was constantly on the defensive about the highly problematic (but undeniable) fact that Jesus had been rejected by his own people. There is an apologetic agenda here (already evident in Paul's impassioned discussion in Rom. 9–11) which colours the construction of the gospel narratives, all seeking different ways to deal with an acute *ecclesiological* question about the relation of the church to Israel—and of the kingdom of God to both. Mark deals with these questions both through narrative and through parable. The final chapters show a very deliberate testing of the boundaries of Jesus' authority. His journey to Jerusalem brings him into direct confrontation both with the temple authorities and with the sectarian politics of his day (chapters 10–12). Following a recognizable messianic template, he rides into the city as Zechariah's prince of peace (11:1–11), cleanses the temple, and reclaims its biblical status as a house of prayer for all nations (11:15–19). In a series of polemical encounters, Jesus demonstrates his authority to speak on issues that touch on the ordering of civil society and its relations with the wider world: marriage, resurrection, taxation (11:27–12:44). However we interpret these enigmatic sayings, they implicitly assert the messianic claim to speak and act in the public domain (while retaining the prophetic distinction between Caesar's realm and God's).

The parable of the vineyard (12:1–12) provides Mark's readers with a hermeneutical key to the unfolding debate (Kloppenborg 2006). Using a familiar metaphor from Israel's Scriptures (Isa. 5:1–7), the parable demonstrates both continuity and discontinuity in the church's relation with Israel: the rejection of the beloved son is simply the last in a series of rebuffs by the tenants who fail to produce the fruit that is rightly due to the vineyard's owner. The parable sets out with chilling clarity a salvation-history divided into epochs (rejection of the prophets; rejection of the Son), and points to a future of destruction and redistribution to 'others'. The linked proof-text of the Rejected Stone (12:10–11) is widely cited in early Christian apologetic as an allegory for the contested status of Jesus as simultaneously 'cornerstone' for the church and 'stone of stumbling' for unbelieving Israel (Lindars 1961). But whereas Isaiah's parable was a challenge to God's people as a whole, for Mark the vineyard parable is directed at Israel's leaders (12:12).

Waiting in Hope

The Markan apocalypse (chapter 13), the longest concerted piece of teaching in Mark, deals with the question, '*When* will these things be?' (13:4). The expectation of the imminent coming of the kingdom, so pervasive in the early part of Mark's Gospel, is so integral to the self-understanding of the church that it must be sustained despite the constant raising and dashing of apocalyptic hopes. Despite the Gospel's pervasive sense of the imminence of the kingdom, Jesus impresses on his disciples (here a small inner group) that 'the End is not yet'. The discourse discourages its readers from getting fixated on calculations of the end-time, while at the same time encouraging them to maintain an attitude of expectancy and faithfulness: 'Take heed! Watch!' The image of the household of faithful servants, waiting for the return of an absent master, was to become one of the definitive images of the church (13:32–7). *Not knowing when* the master will return defines a state of mind: faithful, expectant—and accountable.

This eschatological framework enlarges the scope of the gospel narrative, placing the outwardly small and insignificant messianic community on a worldwide stage. It is a reminder that the sovereignty of God is not restricted to Israel but controls the rise and fall of empires. For the disciples, it is both warning and promise: warning of the need for faithful endurance in a time of persecution and tribulation, promise of the help of the Holy Spirit at some unspecified future time when 'you shall be brought before governors and kings for my sake' (13:9). Jesus' words affirm a future for the church beyond the time-frame of the narrative, a future that contains both tribulation and worldwide mission: 'This gospel must first be preached to all nations' (13:10). The mission of the church takes place 'between the times'—between the in-breaking of the kingdom in Jesus' ministry and the return of the Son of Man (14:62; cf. Dan. 7:13).

Remembering Jesus

The passion of the Christ—from Palm Sunday to Easter Day—takes up more than a third of the gospel narrative and forms its climax. In narrative terms, the final chapters of Mark's Gospel signal a change of tempo and a change of subjectivity. While the figure of Jesus has been the focus of action all through the narrative (Burridge 1992), we have always seen him (as it were) through the eyes of the disciple-group who surround him. In these final chapters, shepherd and sheep are separated: the disciples fall away in confusion, and the spotlight falls on Jesus alone.

Thus we have effectively two parallel storylines in Mark's spare and brutal passion narrative. At one level, this is the story of the failure and disintegration of the messianic community. Jesus' mission to Israel has failed: her leaders decisively reject his messianic claim (14:53–65; 15:1–15). Even the disciple-group begins to disintegrate and fall apart: its failure is acted out in the individual tragedies of Judas' betrayal and Peter's denial, while the rest of the disciples sleep, then flee (with Mark's 'young man' perhaps emphasizing the moral and spiritual nakedness of the disciples: 14:10–11, 17–21; 14:51; 14:66–72). Only the women remain faithful, still gathered around Jesus on the cross; but they are powerless, watching from a distance (15:40–2). Jesus goes forward alone to taste the full cost of obedience to the Father's will. With stunning dramatic irony, Mark leaves it to an outsider, the Roman centurion, to recognize in death the innate truth of Jesus' life: 'Truly, this man was the Son of God' (15:39).

Christologically speaking, the focal point of this narrative is the cross: this is the point (ironically) where Jesus' true identity is revealed (cf. 15:19), while the tearing of the temple veil hints at the sacrificial significance of his death (15:38). But to understand its ecclesiological significance, we have to pay particular attention to the points in the narrative where the messianic community gathers around its Lord, before and after the saving acts which he carries out alone. Mark's passion narrative begins with two scenes of table-fellowship, both (implicitly) pointing to the table-fellowship of the Eucharist. The anointing at Bethany (14:3–9) in Mark is not a scene of penitence but a coronation: the woman who breaks a jar of costly ointment over Jesus' head is recognizing his kingship. In accepting this wasteful act of devotion as a pointer to his burial, Jesus accepts the sacrificial nature of his messianic calling (crown = cross). But he also points forward to a future beyond the cross: 'Wherever the gospel is preached in the whole world, what she has done will be told in memory of her' (14:9). Jesus' death is not the end of the gospel: the story will continue to be told in unexpected places, and it will go on being good news.

The Last Supper in Mark is a Passover feast to which Jesus invites his disciples (14:12–16). Here Jesus is both host and feast. The four acts of taking, blessing, breaking, and giving recall the miraculous feeding of the 5,000 (6:41), but here what Jesus offers his disciples is himself: 'Take; this is my body . . . this is my blood' (14:22–4). Mark's minimalist wording lacks the liturgical richness of Paul and the other evangelists; but it provides the necessary coordinates to anchor the events of the coming passion within salvation history, both past and future, recalling both Israel's foundation as a covenant community at Sinai (Exodus 24:8) and the self-offering of the suffering servant (Isa. 53:11–12, cf. Mk 10:45). Whatever their origins, the sayings over the bread and the cup show that 'by the time of Mark the Christian community is looking back on the death of Jesus in a way similar to that in which the Jews looked back to the Exodus. The Eucharist has become a celebration of God's saving activity, centred on the death of Jesus. His self-sacrifice is seen as the new act of redemption, establishing a covenant between God and his people' (Hooker 1991: 340). And like the Passover meal, the meal has an eschatological framework: it looks beyond the cross to the messianic banquet 'in the Kingdom of God' (14:25).

Being Sent Out

Mark's story ends enigmatically with the moment of *anagnorisis* at the empty tomb, where the angel instructs the women to 'tell his disciples (and Peter): He is risen: he is not here: he goes before you to Galilee' (16:6–7). Mark's narrative stops there, with the women departing in fear and silence, leaving it to second-century readers to add a collage of resurrection appearances drawn from gospel tradition. These 'longer endings' (16:9–20) clearly point to a future role for the disciples, preaching the gospel 'to the whole creation', and performing 'signs' in Jesus' name: casting out demons, speaking in tongues, laying hands on the sick, and handling poisonous snakes with impunity

(16:15–18; 16:8b). But even the enigmatic 'shorter' ending envisages a future for the messianic community in Galilee, reunited with its risen Lord—a future to which he had already pointed them (14:28). And (as we have seen), the whole of Mark's narrative is structured to point beyond itself to a future in which those who follow Jesus will be baptized in the Spirit (1:8), become fishers of men (1:17), receive kindness because they bear the name of Christ (9:41), drink the cup that Jesus drinks (10:39), bear testimony and suffer for Jesus' sake (13:9–13), and receive hundredfold compensation for what they have given up 'for my sake and the gospel' (10:29–30)—a future in which the stories will be told and the gospel will be preached in the whole world (14:9).

Summary: The Core Synoptic Ecclesiology

Thus we may sum up the deep structure of Mark's ecclesiology as a sequence of narrative images, clustered around two key ecclesiological themes: the gathering-in of the people of God, and the formation of a messianic community of disciples. Both have enormous potential as ecclesiological symbols.

The opening chapters of the Gospel are dominated by a 'people of God' ecclesiology, chronicling Jesus' mission to Israel and the restoration of God's people as a messianic community. Crucial to this process are:

- The proclamation of the imminence of God's kingdom;
- the baptism of John, the call to repentance, and the promise of a future baptism with the Holy Spirit;
- the call of the disciples as agents of the kingdom;
- the preaching of the word; and
- the performance of deeds of power in which the coming of the kingdom is made visible in transformed lives and restored community.

From chapter 9 onwards, Mark shifts towards a 'discipleship' ecclesiology, with Jesus focusing his attention on the instruction and formation of the disciples as a messianic community, living out the kingdom in its internal and external life, and based on:

- the confession of Jesus as the Christ;
- the call to follow him on the way of the cross, *imitatio Christi*;
- costly and courageous engagement with the public life of the people of God;
- an attitude of expectancy generated by a consciousness of 'living between the times';
- table-fellowship built around the remembrance of Jesus;
- the commissioning and empowering of the apostles to a future mission to the nations.

The key ecclesiological question is: what is the relationship between the two parts? How does the formation of a messianic community of disciples relate to the gathering-in of the people of God? For Mark, the role of the disciples is ambivalent. They are called and commissioned to act as messianic agents of the kingdom, like fishermen gathering in the harvest of the sea, preaching the same message as Jesus and performing the same mighty deeds. But they are also called to demonstrate a foretaste of the coming of God's kingdom within their own lives: and here they show a signal lack of comprehension of what it means to accept the reign of God at a personal or communal level. Hence the darker tone of the second half of Mark's narrative, with a more inward focus on teaching the disciples to understand the real meaning of discipleship. What holds the two together is the person of Jesus, the messianic agent who undertakes in his own person (and alone) the saving act of losing his own life as a ransom for many: that is, as a redemptive act which constitutes the base of a new covenant.

THE CHURCH IN MATTHEW

Matthew is widely regarded as the most 'ecclesiastical' of the Gospels. It is the only Gospel to use the word *ekklēsia*: most famously at 16:18 where Jesus tells Peter 'You are Peter; and on this rock I will build my church'; and again at 18:17, in a passage dealing with church discipline. Like Luke, Matthew ends his Gospel with a scene where the risen Christ directly commissions his disciples to 'go into all the world, and preach the gospel to every creature' (Mt 28:20). Matthew is also both the most 'Jewish' and the most 'anti-Jewish' of the Gospels, with a strong focus on the Law, counterbalanced by bitter polemic against the leaders of the Jewish community. Most scholars believe that Matthew comes from a Jewish-Christian community (likely in Syria) engaged in bitter sectarian disputes with the local Jewish community. Accepted in tradition as the first of the Synoptic Gospels (and the only one with an apostolic author), Matthew has been hugely influential on the ecclesiology of the Western church, and its influence can be felt across the iconography of Western art.

How do we determine Matthew's ecclesiological focus? We start with the fact that (apart from a few verses) Matthew incorporates the whole of Mark's Gospel in his narrative: in other words, Matthew implicitly embraces the deep structure of the core synoptic ecclesiology that we have seen in Mark, with the same ambivalence between the restoration of the people of God and the creation of a new messianic community. Matthew's story, like Mark's, is the story of Jesus' proclamation of the Kingdom in word and deed, a prophetic mission to gather 'the lost sheep of the house of Israel' (Mt 10:6, 15:24), and the formation of a messianic community of disciples to act as agents of the kingdom both now and in the future. Matthew's abbreviations and additions serve to highlight significant aspects of this underlying story and give it its distinctive shape.

The Baptist narrative (Mt 3:1–17) confirms the importance of the preaching of the kingdom on a national scale. The Baptist is a prophetic figure who calls Israel's leaders to account, calling for 'fruits worthy of repentance' and warning them to 'flee from the wrath to come' (Mt 3:7–10). But Matthew's narrative also shows a degree of embarrassment about the relation between Jesus and the Baptist (3:14–15).

The kingdom ('Kingdom of heaven' in Matthew) remains a central feature, with heightened focus both on the moral demands of the kingdom and on the eschatological judgement in store for those who fail to fulfil them. The Lord's Prayer places the prayer 'Thy Kingdom come on earth'—with its radical demand for forgiveness—at the heart of the worship of the messianic community (Mt 6:10). If the kingdom is the place where God's kingship is fully acknowledged, for Matthew this is both a kingdom of righteousness and a kingdom of judgement. The dual theme of 'fruit' and 'wrath' runs right through Matthew, culminating in 21:43 where the 'chief priests and Pharisees' are warned that 'the kingdom of God will be taken away from you and given to a people (*ethnos*) who will produce its fruit'.

The call to discipleship is also a call to bear fruit, by living out the heightened standards of righteousness demanded by the kingdom. But Matthew is acutely aware of the multifarious opportunities for failure and deception within the church; the false prophets and miracle-workers of 7:15–23 are Christian teachers who are to be judged 'by their fruits'; and the warning about building a house on sand has to be taken seriously by all Jesus' followers. The words of Jesus offer the only safe foundation for the life of the kingdom (7:24–7)—and it is these words that will form the basis for the future life of the church (Mt 28:19).

Matthew's presentation of Jesus' teaching in five discourses (chs 5 –7; ch. 10; ch. 13; ch. 18; chs 21–5) highlights the importance of the preaching of the word in Jesus' mission. By placing the Sermon on the Mount (chs 5–7) right at the beginning of the narrative, Matthew sets out what is in effect a moral manifesto for the messianic community. The audience for this is clearly wider than the four disciples who have already been called (Mt 4:18–22): cf. the interplay of 'crowds' and 'disciples' at the beginning and end of the 'Sermon' (Mt 5:1; 7:28–9). Far from relaxing the demands of the Torah, Jesus calls his followers to a 'better righteousness' that 'exceeds that of the scribes and Pharisees', a Torah-true life lived out from the heart (without hypocrisy), whose ultimate aim is perfection (Mt 5:48). By framing his teaching as a series of antitheses ('You have heard that it has been said . . . but I say to you': 5:17–48; 'do not be like the hypocrites': 6:1–18), Matthew presents Jesus as setting out a new law for a new people of God (Allison 1993).

Thus for Matthew (as for Mark), the messianic community shares in Jesus' mission of proclaiming an eschatological message of repentance, restoration, and renewal for the people of God. Matthew is more conscious than Mark of the different time-frames that contextualize this mission. During Jesus' earthly life, this mission is strictly limited to Israel. The apostles are instructed not to go to the Gentiles or to the Samaritans, but to 'the lost sheep of the house of Israel' (Mt 10:6, 23; cf. 15:24); 10:23 implies that they will still be occupied with this primary apostolic mission to 'the towns of Israel' when 'the Son of Man comes'. But Matthew's closing scene points unequivocally towards a world-wide mission to 'all nations' as the culmination of Jesus' whole mission (Mt 28:16–20); and there are hints of this earlier in the narrative: cf. the Syro-phoenician woman (15:21–8) and the centurion ('I have not found such faith in anyone in Israel!' Mt 8:5–13).

The apostolic mission follows the pattern of Jesus' proclamation of the kingdom in word and deed, a combination of preaching and healing (Mt 10:7–8). Despite the uncompromising demands of his teaching, Matthew stresses that Jesus' mission is based on 'compassion' for sick and weary souls (cf. esp. the summaries: 4:23–5; 9:33–8; 10:2–6; 12:15–21, 28; 14:14, 34–6; 15:24–32; 19:1; 21:14–16). The kingdom belongs to the poor in spirit, the hungry and thirsty, those who mourn—and to the children (Mt 5:3–10; 18:1–6). Jesus shares table-fellowship with sinners, and offers rest to the heavy-laden (Mt 9:9–13; 11:16–19; 11:28–30; 21:1–4). The life of the kingdom is marked by healing and forgiveness (Mt 6:12; 9:1–8; 18:15–35). Prophetic citations highlight the importance of the theme of mercy: Hosea's 'I desire mercy and not sacrifice' is quoted twice by Jesus (Hos. 6:6; cf. Mt 9:13; 12:7), and Mt inserts a long quotation from Isaiah 42: 1–4, pointing to the Servant who 'will not break a bruised reed' as a role-model for Jesus' messianic ministry (Mt 12:15–21).

There is a subtle but perceptible shift in focus in Matthew's depiction of the work of the kingdom, cutting out individual detail in the miracle stories and shifting the focus to Jesus' spiritual authority and the awe and wonder of the crowds. One effect of this is to heighten the Christology of the Gospel: Jesus is presented as one who dispenses divine mercy to a needy world, and one worthy of worship. But Matthew is also careful to make the connection between receiving mercy and offering mercy to others (Mt 18:23–35), and thus spotlights the call to carry out Jesus' work of 'mercy' in the world (cf. Mt 5:7) through almsgiving (cf. Mt 6:1–4) and acts of practical charity (Mt 25:31–46). Matthew's church has already begun to make the move to identifying the work of the kingdom with charitable 'acts of mercy' (Rhee 2012).

Eschatology forms one of the most prominent themes in Matthew's Gospel, but with a change of tone from Mark. For Matthew, the coming of the kingdom is always shadowed by the prospect of divine judgement, described in graphic imagery drawn from the apocalyptic tradition, and this shadow theme runs all the way through the narrative. The unquenchable hell-fire and the 'wailing and gnashing of teeth' so vividly depicted in medieval church art are much more prominent in Matthew than in the other Gospels (cf. e.g. 8:12, 13:50, 22:13, 24:51); and Matthew constantly stresses the eternal significance of the moral choices we make (7:13–14; 7:24–7; 21:28–32; 25:1–13; 25:31–46). While many of the parables evoke the traditional messianic images of feasting and joy (Mt 22:1–14; 25:1–2), there is a pervasive undertow of judgement, most vividly in the parable of the wedding guest who gains access to the feast only to be thrown out for wearing the wrong garment (Mt 22:11–14). Perhaps the dominant eschatological image of the final chapters of Matthew is the return of the absent Lord of the household, whose servants are called to await his coming in a state of constant readiness, fidelity, and expectancy, and whose reward is to 'enter into the joy of your Lord' (Mt 25:21; cf. Mt 24:45–51; 25:1–13; 25:14–30).

This sense of impending judgement, which looms as heavily over the church as over the unbelieving world, has a significant effect on Matthew's ecclesiology. The gospel must be preached to all nations (Mt 24:14) in the interval before the apocalyptic coming of the Son of Man (ch. 24): the master may be absent, but his servants have work to do

(Mt 25:14–30). The mission is presented as the 'gathering-in' of God's people into the kingdom, but the harvest gathered has a strangely provisional character: the field is a mixture of wheat and weeds, the fishing-net is a mixed bag of edible and inedible fish (Mt 13:24–30, 36–43, 47–50). Eternal destinies will not be allocated until the final gathering-in of the eschatological harvest (Mt 13; Mt 25). Matthew strongly resists any attempt to pre-empt this divine judgement: 'Let both grow together until the harvest' (Mt 13:30). In other words, *because* he has a strong sense of eschatological judgement, Matthew can be comparatively relaxed about maintaining firm ecclesial boundaries in the here and now. The church is called to perfection (Mt 5: 45); but as an earthly institution, it is not a perfect society but is a *corpus mixtum* 'on the way to holiness' (Schnackenburg 1974: 132–5).

What, finally, can we say about church structures, ministry, and primacy? The 'Great Commission' at the very end of the Gospel projects a very clear image of the church as the disciple-group gathered around the Risen Lord, a group united in worship—though still with 'some' doubters (Mt 28:16–20). This scene enlarges the church's horizons both in time and space, as Jesus gives the disciples their marching-orders: 'Go and make disciples of all nations, baptizing them . . . and teaching them to observe all that I have commanded you.' Being a disciple is not an end in itself: its object is to make more disciples—that is, more followers of Jesus—down to the end of time. Jesus is not going away: he will continue to be the focal point of the church's life, and 'all authority' belongs to him. Whatever the church does, it does 'in his name' and with the assurance of his continued presence. 'Discipleship'—that is, being a follower of Jesus—is a relational term for Matthew: it encompasses both the past (the eleven historic disciples who have heard his teaching and witnessed his resurrection) and the future (those who will become disciples through their teaching).

This climactic ending provides a hermeneutical key for rereading the way Matthew has constructed the story of Jesus and his interactions with the historic disciples. Matthew's church is both a school and a cultic community, gathered in worship around the risen Lord and learning to live out the life of the kingdom as taught by Jesus. The apostolic task is both didactic and sacramental. The teaching contained in Matthew's Gospel is intended to form the basis for the ongoing task of 'making disciples' in Jesus' name: the future of the church is already implicit within the Gospel text. In this sense, Matthew highlights the continuities between the future church and the historic disciples.

Inevitably, then, there is a degree of leakage (or 'transparency': Luz 2005, ch. 8) between the future and the past, between Matthew's own church and the messianic community at the time of Jesus. This is why Matthew does not distinguish clearly between teaching addressed to 'the crowds' and teaching addressed to 'the disciples': for him, *all* of Jesus' words are foundational for the life of the messianic community, present and future (7:24–7). The teaching of the kingdom is not a distinct message for historic Israel alone. It is Jesus' message to the entire world; and ultimately the whole world is a legitimate fishing-ground for the gathering-in of God's people. Hence there is a certain ambivalence in Matthew's portrayal of the Twelve. Unlike Luke, Matthew does not use the term 'disciple' in the broad sense of Jesus' followers: it is more or less restricted to the Twelve. Jesus' teaching and healing mission is directed to the people of God, with the Twelve as his agents. So within the framework of Matthew's 'people of God' ecclesiology, the disciples function as prototypical church leaders, ministering in Jesus' name and with his authority to the 'people of God' (the *laos*).

This 'transparency' is evident in the mission discourse of ch. 10, where Jesus commissions the Twelve and sends them out as apostles. This is directly linked with Jesus' compassion for the crowds who are 'like sheep without a shepherd', a harvest ripe for gathering (Mt 9:35–8). As in Mark, the mission charge (Mt ch. 10) portrays the disciples as itinerant agents of Jesus' mission to Israel, dependent on local hospitality and a positive response from the local community (with a very Matthean warning of judgement for those who fail to respond: Mt 10:15, 40–2; cf. 11:20–4). Matthew however (unlike Mark and Luke) does not link this discourse to an actual mission of the Twelve: like all the Matthean discourses, it is (in Ulrich Luz's phrase) addressed 'out of the window' to the post-Easter church and 'goes far beyond instructions for a specific commissioning'. Thus Luz reads the discourse as 'a Matthean manifesto for a dynamic ecclesiology', identifying in it four *notae ecclesiae* or 'constitutive marks' for all future discipleship: mission, itinerancy, poverty, and suffering, adding up to 'a discourse on the way of life of the disciples which corresponds to that of the master' (Luz 2005).

A similar 'leakage' between the time of the narrative and the time of the future church is also evident in the fourth teaching discourse in ch. 18. Starting with a question from the disciples ('Who is the greatest in the kingdom of heaven?'), the discourse moves seamlessly from children to 'little ones', from scandals (causes of offence) to church discipline, and finally to the need for forgiveness. The parable of the lost sheep (Mt 18:10–14) is told here from the perspective of the shepherd rather than the sheep: it becomes a message for pastors, going out to seek the 'little ones' who have strayed from their flock. (There may be an allusion here to local pastors, perhaps the Christian 'prophets, sages and scribes' who appear elsewhere in Matthew (Schnackenburg 1974: 75).) Disputes between 'brothers' are to be settled by appeal to 'the church' (*ekklēsia*: 18: 15–20): the word here seems to point to a local congregation or 'assembly' acting as a civil court (much as in 1 Cor. 5:1–4/6:1–6). As in the 'Great Commission', the point of continuity is the presence of Jesus 'in the midst' of the community gathered in his name (18:20). It is his presence that makes the disciple-group a 'church' and gives them (the verbs are plural here) authority to 'bind and loose' (18:18), that is to exercise discipline and to make authoritative and binding legal decisions (the context is juridical rather than liturgical). As Luz observes, there is a tension in this discourse (and within the Gospel) between the image of the church as a 'pure community' with clear boundaries, able to 'excommunicate' offenders, and the parable's injunction to apparently unlimited forgiveness and care for the 'little ones' (Luz 1993: 104–8; Carlston and Evans 2014: 307 + n. 67).

Matthew's image of the church, then, readily accommodates both leadership roles within the church (pastoral responsibility for the 'little ones') and the exercise of authority ('binding and loosing') by the community (or its leaders) acting as a body. The fact that something akin to 'excommunication' is a possibility should not surprise us, since we already have evidence for such a procedure in 1 Cor. 5:1–4. Elsewhere he speaks of 'prophets' within the church (false and true) and of 'prophets, scribes and sages' sent by Jesus as messengers to his people (23:34: cf. Carlston and Evans 2014: 309–15). The household parables, like the parable of the talents (Mt 25: 14–30) and the parable of the faithful steward (Mt 24:45–51), set over his fellow servants 'to give them their food in due season', also suggest differentiated roles within the household of God and recall Paul's use of the same metaphor in 1 Cor. 4:1–5.

Do these images imply that the structures of the church are inherently hierarchical? What is the role of the Twelve (the historic disciples) in all this and how does Peter fit in? Protestant and Roman Catholic exegetes read Matthew very differently here. Both read Matthew in terms of a 'people of God' ecclesiology, with the church as the *laos*, the restored people of God (Schnackenburg 1974: 69–73; Schweizer 1961: 4b–e/52–8). In a traditional Roman Catholic ecclesiology, the natural corollary is a hierarchical view of ministry, with the disciples representing the ordained ministry, with Peter at their head. Thus Schnackenburg notes the authoritative power of 'binding and loosing' given to Peter at 16:19 (singular verbs), and deduces from this that 18:18 must refer to the disciples, not to the community as such: 'In the Church there is an authority conferred by God and concerning salvation which . . . can hardly repose in the community as such, but is rather made over to certain persons. . . . The authority of the *ekklesia* [in 18:17] rests not only on its dignity as representative of the people of God, but also on its guidance by those empowered by God' (Schnackenburg 1974: 74–5). The Protestant Schweizer, on the other hand, starting with the undoubted fact that Matthew contains some of the strongest anti-hierarchical statements of any of the Gospels (23:8–12), argues that since the time of Peter this authority belongs to the whole church: 'Matthew makes it clear that he regards the demands and bestowal of authority on the apostles as valid for all the believers of his time. . . . The whole Church is called to on to listen to Jesus' exposition of the law, mediated by Peter, to follow the way of Jesus through lowliness, and to carry out the binding and loosing that will one day be confirmed in heaven' (Schweizer 1961: 4f./ 58–60). Behind these positions (as we have seen) lie two fundamentally divergent approaches to the ecclesiology of the Gospels.

These issues come to the fore in the exegesis of Peter's confession at Caesarea Philippi (16:13–28), one of the most contentious passages in the Gospel. Matthew broadly follows Mark's narrative structure here, following Peter's confession with Jesus' warning of future suffering, and his rebuke of Peter as a 'stumbling-block' ('Get behind me, Satan!'). Matthew's version, however, is unique in including Jesus' affirmation of Peter (16:18–19):

> Blessed are you, Simon bar-Jona! For flesh and blood has not revealed this to you, but my Father who is in heaven. You are Peter, and on this rock [*petra*] I will build my church [*ekklēsia*], and the powers of death [lit, 'gates of hades'] shall not prevail against it. I will give you the keys of the kingdom of heaven, and whatever you bind on earth shall be bound in heaven, and whatever you loose on earth shall be loosed in heaven.

Ecclesiologically interpretation of this passage is almost completely divided along confessional lines. Luz identifies four classic types in the exegesis of this passage: the 'papal' (which only becomes dominant in the wake of the Reformation); the 'typological' (cf.

Origen's interpretation of Peter as the 'prototype' of the pneumatic person founded on faith); the 'Eastern', which became dominant in the Greek and Syrian churches (Peter as the guarantor of genuine and public apostolic tradition); and the 'Augustinian', which looks at other 'rock' sayings in the canon and concludes that the only rock on which the church is founded must be Christ himself (Luz 2005: 168–72). Is it possible to get behind the confessional interpretations of this saying?

Three points from Matthew's portrayal of the disciples suggest a way forward: transparency; itinerancy; Christology. (1) The 'transparency' of the disciples in Mt means that the historic disciples (the Twelve) function *both* as types for all future disciples *and* as authoritative bearers of the Jesus tradition. Both functions are visible in 28:16–20, and this duality runs all the way through the Gospel. (2) The mission charges point to a distinctive dual structure of itinerant, mendicant 'apostles' working alongside local community leaders (Luz 2005: 151–3). This duality is a recurrent feature of the life of the early church (as exemplified in the *Didache,* a text with which Matthew has strong associations). The interplay between travelling apostles and settled communities need not be understood as a hierarchical relationship but as complementary loci of authority. There is no sign in Matthew of the *transmission* of authority from the Twelve to prophets or local community leaders: on the contrary, 23:34 implies that the latter (like the apostles) are 'sent' by Jesus himself. But there are also very clear warnings against seeking primacy (18:4; 20:26–7; 23:11–12), coupled with an explicit prohibition (unique to Matthew) of usurping the role of Jesus 'the only teacher' (23:8–12; Byrskog 1994). (3) Thus the controlling hermeneutic for *all* discipleship (including leadership) has to be Christological (Luz 2005: 136–7; Carlston and Evans 2014: 325–9). Within the church *all* leadership has to be refracted through the lens of *imitatio Christi*: this is the point of 10:24–5 ('the disciple is not above his master'), and of all the leadership paraenesis in Matthew (and indeed in the NT in general).

These insights may help us to make more sense of the particular problem of Peter's position in Matthew's ecclesiology. (1) First, what is true of the disciples in general is supremely true of Peter, who functions as the 'prototype disciple' within Matthew's narrative. 'Peter is both first among equals and no better than the other disciples. As "spokesperson," he brings to Jesus the questions of all the disciples—in some instances, of any disciple of any time. He probably also prefigures in a unique way the possibilities and temptations of church leaders. He is truly a paradigm of what disciples, even at their best, always seem to be' (Carlston and Evans 2014: 321–3). Within the narrative, Jesus' affirmation of Peter in 16:17 is balanced by his rebuke in the following verses (16:21–3): both are consistent with Peter's role as the primary spokesman and representative for the group of disciples, something attested right across the synoptic tradition.

(2) Nevertheless, it is striking how much Peter eclipses all the other disciples in Matthew's narrative: and 16:18–20 offers a remarkable affirmation of Peter's individual authority to 'bind and loose' which is not paralleled in any other Gospel. Both Luke and John, in different ways, affirm Peter's leading pastoral role in the future church, but neither of them assigns him quite this level of personal authority. John, in particular, while,

acknowledging Peter's pre-eminence, shows signs of 'competition' with the Beloved Disciple (Cullmann 1962: 25–33). Paul clearly deprecates such apostolic competitiveness, but his letters provide concrete evidence that it existed in the early church (1 Cor. 1–3). The importance of itinerancy in the early concept of the apostolate may allow us to suggest a historically plausible context for Matthew's championing of Peter's authority. Peter's traditional association with Antioch may be a factor in this: but it is important to remember that in the NT the apostles are associated not so much with territories as with travel networks: cf. 1 Peter 1:1–2 (Alexander 2003). Matthew seems to reflect a community (or a network of communities) for whom Peter is the disciple *par eminence*, much as the Beloved Disciple is for John.

(3) Which leaves us with the question: in what sense is Peter's confession 'foundational' for Matthew's ecclesiology? The first point to note is that it is Jesus himself who will 'build my church'. For Matthew, Jesus himself is the architect and builder of the church—a church that is still in the future at this point in the gospel narrative, but is built onto and shows continuity with something that already exists. Though exegetes are almost unanimous in agreeing that this saying cannot go back to Jesus himself (see the section 'Jesus and the Church'), it is entirely consistent with Matthew's own ecclesiology. But what is the 'foundation' on which the church is built? Ephesians can speak of the 'apostles and prophets' as the foundation of the church, 'with Christ Jesus himself as the cornerstone' (Eph 2:10)—whereas Paul speaks of himself as the *architecton* or master builder and insists that 'no one can lay any other foundation than that which is laid, which is Jesus Christ' (1 Cor. 3:10–17). Scripture consistently shows a freedom and flexibility in its use of metaphors that is distressing to more tidy-minded interpreters. Elsewhere in Matthew, Jesus states firmly that 'my words' are the rock (*petra*) which provide the only safe foundation on which to build (7:24–7): which does leave us with a prima facie issue of intra-textual consistency.

The solution, I would suggest, is to return to Mark's account of Peter's confession. For Mark, Peter's confession ('You are the Christ') plays a pivotal role in the narrative, marking the point at which the disciple-group properly becomes (or begins to become) a messianic community: that is, in the recognition of Jesus as Messiah. Matthew's 'rock' saying can be seen as a legitimate interpretation of this Markan scene. What is foundational to the church is not Peter's 'faith' as an inner, personal attribute, nor even as an intellectual assent, but his *confession:* that is, the public, verbal articulation of a foundational truth which can only be received from God. This is the public 'confession' (*homologia*) of the martyrs (10:23; cf. John 9:22; 1 Tim. 6:12–13), the confession 'with the mouth' that leads to salvation (Rom 10:9–10). A similarly brief confession that 'Jesus is Lord' was foundational for the Pauline churches; Matthew adds 'the son of the living God' to Mark's 'You are the Christ' (while Lk 9:20 has 'the Christ of God'), perhaps because *Christos* was beginning to lose its full messianic force for his readers. But that some form of this confession is foundational to the life of the church is widely evident from the NT and early Christian history. Augustine's Christological interpretation needs to be held together with Matthew's other insight that it is Jesus' *words* that are foundational. Peter's importance to the church (especially to Matthew, who takes over Mark's Petrine

Gospel and incorporates it wholesale into his own) lies not simply in this flashing moment of insight in the past (almost immediately annulled by his *faux pas* over the Cross), but in his role as guarantor of the authentic tradition of Jesus' teaching. In other words, Peter's confession is foundational because it is a pointer to the true and only foundation of the messianic community, Jesus the Christ.

THE CHURCH IN LUKE

If Matthew is the Dostoyevsky of the evangelists, Luke is their Tolstoy: compassionate and humane, with a wide-ranging and inclusive vision of humanity and the church. Known to tradition as the patron saint of artists, Luke paints unforgettable portraits of the women in his Gospel, especially of the Virgin Mary and her circle. He gives us some of the Gospels' most vivid and compassionate parables (the prodigal son; the good Samaritan) as well as some of the most challenging (the rich fool; the crafty steward). Luke's narrative is liturgically rich: it is the source of the Gospel canticles (*Benedictus, Magnificat, Nunc Dimittis*), the infancy feasts (Christmas, Candlemas, the Annunciation, the Visitation), the Ascension and Pentecost, and the birth of John the Baptist. Luke frames the core Markan gospel story with vivid narratives of Jesus' birth (chapters 1–2) and resurrection (chapter 24). He shares some of Matthew's teaching material, but arranges it differently and with a different focus (whether Luke derives this material from Matthew or from a common source ('Q') is for our purposes immaterial). He omits two chapters of Mark (Mk 6:45–8:26), but adds a considerable amount of unique material ('L'), especially in the so-called 'Travel narrative' in chapters 10–19 (Moessner 1989). Above all, Luke gives us the book of Acts: our only canonical narrative of the church's origins and early development. This means that in some respects Luke's Gospel is *less* ecclesial than Matthew's, because Luke can save the story of the church (and the Gentile mission) for his second volume. Luke's ecclesiology, therefore, must be studied over the whole two-volume work.

Nevertheless, Luke's Gospel is not simply there to provide a back-story for the story of Acts: it is 'good news' in its own right. Like Matthew, Luke represents not an entirely different gospel but a new performance of the same gospel, reflecting the particular concerns of a new and later context and audience. In choosing to hang his unique material on to a broadly Markan narrative thread, Luke (like Matthew) implicitly embraces the deep structure of the core synoptic ecclesiology. The outline of this core structure is reflected in the apostolic preaching in Acts: it begins with the baptism of John (Acts 1:22), and tells of Jesus going about 'doing good and healing all who were oppressed by the devil, for God was with him', of his crucifixion, resurrection, and exaltation to heaven, and the command to preach 'forgiveness of sins through his name' (Acts 10:38–43). Thus the Gospel is 'Part One' of Luke's story of the church, the beginning of 'all that Jesus began both to do and to teach' (Acts 1:1); everything in the book of Acts presupposes this story and builds on it. The Ascension scene at the Mount of Olives, with the disciples gathered around the risen Lord, forms the centre-point of the whole work: this is both the end-point of the Gospel (Luke 24) and the beginning of the story of the church (Acts 1). Everything in the Gospel moves towards 'the fulfilment of the days of his lifting up', right from 9:51 where the journey to Jerusalem begins; and everything in Acts' story of the church flows from this point.

Once again we find that the mission to Israel is the key to understanding Luke's portrayal of Jesus. Preaching 'the good news of the Kingdom' is the underlying theme both of Jesus' mission (4:43; 8:1) and of the mission he entrusts to his disciples (9:2, 60; 10:9, 11). The language of judgement is muted in comparison with Matthew (cf. Lk 3:9, 17); Luke's emphasis is much more strongly on forgiveness and inclusion. But this is first and foremost about the gathering in and restoration of God's people. Israel for Luke means the twelve tribes, including the lost ten tribes: hence a persistent interest in the Samaritans (9:52–6; 10:25–37; 17:19; Acts 1:8; 8:5–25). Luke anchors the birth stories firmly in the history of the covenant people through liberal use of scriptural typology and language. The heavenly messengers (angels) who announce the births emphasize the divine initiative underpinning the entire narrative, and the canticles reiterate the fulfilment of the ancient scriptural promises to Abraham, David, and Isaiah (1:54–5, 70–3; 2:32). Zechariah and Elizabeth, Simeon and Anna evoke the prophetic 'remnant' of faithful Israelites 'looking for the consolation of Israel' (1:6; 2:25, 38). The birth of John the Baptist heralds redemption for God's people through the forgiveness of sins (1:67–80); his task is 'to make ready for the Lord a people prepared' (1:17). The canticles point forward to a restored community in which the humble will be exalted and the strong will be cast down from their thrones (1:46–55)—a community carefully defined in terms not of land but of worship, salvation, and forgiveness (1:73–4, 79).

These themes come to prominence in the baptism narrative (3:1–32), which is planted with clues anticipating the narrative of Acts. Luke extends the quotation from Isaiah to include the promise that 'all flesh shall see the salvation of our God' (3:6). He portrays John as a prophet, calling the people of God (*laos*) to repentance, warning of judgement, and helping them to work out the practical consequences of living in God's kingdom ('What are we to do?': 3:10–14). Luke is careful to tidy away John's ministry before Jesus' begins, but also acknowledges the importance of John's baptism in preparing 'the people' to recognize 'the righteousness of God' (7:29–30). And it is to this expectant people that John declares that 'the one who comes after me' will 'baptize you with the Holy Spirit and with fire' (3:16). Luke knows of followers of the Baptist who continue to practise water baptism (Acts 19:1–7), and he is careful to distance this practice from Christian baptism 'with the Holy Spirit'. The Holy Spirit is much more prominent in Luke's Gospel than in Mark or Matthew. Already present at Jesus' birth and in the prophetic speech of those who acclaim him (1:35, 41, 67; 2:25, 27), the Holy Spirit is active throughout Jesus' ministry, both in his exercise of healing power (5:17, 6:19), and in his inner life of prayer and joy in the Spirit (3:21; 10:21–2).

Thus, for Luke, Jesus' mission is the proclamation of an eschatological message of repentance, restoration, and renewal for the people of God, a combination of preaching, healing, and exorcism. Luke highlights the community-forming potential of the work of the kingdom (cf. the crowd's perception that 'a great prophet has come among us!' 7:11–17); the bent woman healed on the Sabbath who is 'a daughter of Abraham' (13:10–17); the ten lepers, only one of whom—a Samaritan—returns to give thanks to God (17:11–19). The 'people' (*laos*) in Luke are almost uniformly supportive of Jesus: it is their leaders who fail to recognize that 'the Kingdom of God is come upon you' (11:20). For Luke, this work of healing and exorcism is not just a demonstration of supernatural power but the proper work of God's anointed one, bringing salvation and restoration for God's people, as predicted in the great post-exilic prophecies of restoration from Isaiah 61 (4:16–30; 7:18–23).

Equally important to Jesus' mission is the word of the kingdom, the prophetic task of bringing the good news of salvation to the whole people, but especially to the poor and marginalized (4:18, 7:22; cf. 6:20). For Luke, the whole story begins with the prophetic Word of God, an active subject in its own right and the subject of the only proper dating in the New Testament (3:1–2). Luke gives us many opportunities to hear this word as preached by Jesus and to see its effect in changed lives. The Lukan parables depict God as a shepherd gathering his flock, a woman seeking her lost coin, a father reconciled with an errant son (chapter 15). But they also offer pungent criticism of wealth and social pretension, and advocate a practical charity and a responsible stewardship that looks ahead to the benefactors of the future church (e.g. 10:25–37; 12:13–21; 16:1–13, 19–31) (Johnson 1977). Jesus brings salvation to the community as well as to the individual: his mission culminates with the story of Zacchaeus, who fulfils the Baptist's call to 'show fruits worthy of repentance': when Zacchaeus announces the restoration of his ill-gotten gains, Jesus' comment is: 'Today salvation has come to this household, because he too is a son of Abraham. For the Son of Man came to seek and to save the lost' (19:1–10).

Discipleship also plays a crucial role in Luke's ecclesiology. It is the disciples who provide a bridge to the story of Acts, for example in the repeated list of names and the election of Mathias to replace the traitor Judas at Acts 1:15–26. In Luke's Gospel, the call of the disciples comes very deliberately second to the gathering of Israel, *after* the initial healings and Jesus' announcement of his mission at the synagogue in Nazareth (4:16–44). The call of Simon Peter in 5:1–11 is a theophanic 'encounter' story, enhanced with a miraculous draft of fishes and Peter's awe-struck falling at Jesus' feet. This has the effect of blurring Mark's distinction between 'discipleship' and 'encounter', and makes the point that all discipleship begins with repentance and worship (cf. Lk 5:32). The twelve apostles are named at 6:12–16, and sent out on mission 'to proclaim the kingdom of God and to heal the sick' at 9:1–10, armed with 'power and authority' from Jesus over all demons and diseases. The number twelve clearly relates their appointment to the historic people of God, and (as in Matthew) they are promised an eschatological role, 'seated on thrones judging the twelve tribes of Israel' (22:30; cf. Mt 19:28). Among the Twelve, the leadership role of Peter is highlighted at the Last Supper (22:31–2). As spokesman and leader of the group, Peter has both a particular vulnerability to Satanic attack and a particular responsibility for the welfare of his brothers ('When you have turned, strengthen your brothers')—a responsibility that can only be exercised with the support of Jesus' prayer. Luke points ahead here to the role that Peter will play in the opening chapters of Acts.

But Luke never allows us to identify discipleship solely with the Twelve (9:49–50). He speaks of a 'crowd' of disciples (6:13), and constantly blurs the distinction between disciples and the wider audience. Jesus' followers include the women supporters (Mary Magdalene, Joanna, Susanna, and 'many others') who travel with Jesus and the Twelve around the towns and villages and provide for them out of their resources (8:1–3); the sisters Mary and Martha, offering hospitality from their village home (10:38–42); the anonymous 'woman who was a sinner' who anoints Jesus' feet in the house of Simon the Pharisee and provides a paradigm of saving faith (7:36–50). They also include Cleopas and the other disciple who meet the risen Lord on the road to Emmaus (24:32–5), Matthias and his fellow witnesses (Acts 1:21–3) as well as the group of 120 gathered in the upper room immediately after the resurrection (Acts 1:15). Most important, they include the group of 70 (or 72: the mss differ) sent out on mission in 10:1–20, to whom Jesus addresses his second and longer mission charge. Like the Twelve, the seventy are given authority to heal the sick and proclaim the kingdom (and to tread on snakes and scorpions); they too speak in Jesus' name and with his delegated authority. This second mission is traditionally seen as a foreshadowing of the Gentile mission in Acts: the number 70/72 is the symbolic number of the nations of the world in Jewish tradition. It represents the culmination of prophecy and the gathering-in of the eschatological harvest, and marks the fall of Satan from heaven (10:18, 23–4). But it is hard to miss a double allusion to the seventy elders of Numbers 11:16–25, pointing forward to the local elders who, in Luke's church, were gradually beginning to assume authority with the passing of the apostolic generation. Thematic links with Paul's farewell address to the Ephesian elders in Acts 20:17–36 suggest that the whole of Luke's travel narrative (chapters 10–19), with its focus on prayer, hospitality, stewardship, and the correct use of wealth, is a treatise on discipleship, and opens a window into the needs of the post-apostolic church (Kim 1998). So, already in the Gospel Luke is preparing his readers for a world in which the twelve apostles are not the only disciples, and not the only ones who bear Jesus' authority and speak in his name. But—as with the scribes of Mt 23:34—we must note that it is Jesus himself who appoints the seventy and sends them out, with full apostolic authority. It is the seventy (not the Twelve) to whom Jesus says: 'The one who listens to you listens to me, and the one who rejects you rejects me, and the one who rejects me rejects the one who sent me' (Lk 10:16). There is no trace of any 'apostolic succession' here.

But the prophetic word does not enter the world without encountering resistance. Jesus makes it clear that his disciples can expect the same opposition that he experiences in the preaching of the kingdom (Lk 4:23–30; 10:10–16; 21:12–19). As in Mark, Peter's confession is followed immediately by a call to 'take up the cross' and stand firm in the face of persecution (9:18–27). Many of Jesus' parables are addressed to those who reject his message, or object to Jesus' mission to the marginalized (15:3ff). Luke is aware of the apologetic issues raised by Jesus' ultimate failure to win over his own people, and deploys an argument from Scripture to demonstrate *both* that 'it was necessary that the messiah should suffer' *and* that 'repentance for the forgiveness of sins would be proclaimed in his name to all nations, beginning from Jerusalem' (18:31–4; 24:46–8). Mark

4:12 had already quoted Isaiah 6:9–10, which played a key role in this debate in early Christian apologetic. Luke holds this quotation over to the very end of Acts, an indication that the theme of the preaching of the Word and its varied reception is one that runs right through the two volumes (Alexander 2005: 207–29).

Crucial to this theme is the prophetic template that Luke deploys as a hermeneutical key to understanding Jesus' mission and its ultimate rejection. Both John and Jesus are described as prophets, bearers of a prophetic word from God and facing God's people with the fateful choice of rejection or acceptance. This prophetic paradigm draws on a rich interplay of themes from the Hebrew Bible and Jewish tradition: the prophet Elijah; the anointed 'servant' of Isaiah 61; the 'prophet like Moses' of Deuteronomy 18:15–22 (cf. Acts 3:22–6); and the post-biblical tradition of the prophet as martyr, travelling to Jerusalem to die and grieving over the city like a mother hen grieving over her chicks (13:34–5; cf. especially Johnson 2011). Johnson argues that this prophetic theme has significant implications for Luke's ecclesiology, moving beyond prediction to 'prophecy-as-a-way-of-being-in-the-world', being characterized by responsiveness to the Spirit of God, and an embodiment of God's vision for the world. It also provides a clue as to Luke's eschatology and the fate of Israel. Most scholars agree that Luke is writing after the Jewish War and the destruction of the temple in 70 CE. Jesus' lament over the city appears to allude quite specifically to these events: 'If only you had known the things that make for your peace! The days will come upon you when your enemies will build an embankment against you and surround you and close in on you from every side . . . because you did not recognize the time of your visitation' (19:42–4). Unlike Matthew, Luke does not blame all Jews everywhere for the rejection of the Messiah: the responsibility lies specifically with 'the people of Jerusalem and their leaders' (Acts 13:27)—and even so the events of the passion were part of 'the determinate plan and foreknowledge of God', foreseen by the prophets (Acts 2:23; cf. Acts 4:28). The rejection of the prophetic word carries a penalty (Lk 10:13–16), a penalty already laid down in Scripture (Deut. 18:19). This is not the end of the story, however. The eschatological discourse of Lk 21 places the siege of Jerusalem ('Jerusalem surrounded by armies', 21:20) in a broader eschatological context: it is not the end (indeed, for Luke and his readers it is already in the past), but it marks the beginning of the 'times of the Gentiles' which have to be fulfilled before the fullness of God's redemption is revealed (21:24). Luke's vision of salvation is always 'both-and' rather than 'either-or': the infant Christ is *both* 'a light of revelation to the Gentiles' *and* 'the glory of your people Israel' (2:32).

THE CHURCH IN THE ACTS OF THE APOSTLES

We are now in a position to return to the opening chapters of Acts and understand better how Luke's narrative constructs a bridge between the core synoptic ecclesiology and the developing history of the church. The deep structure of synoptic ecclesiology, we have suggested, is built around a sequence of narrative images. These narrative images are linked with a series of unfulfilled predictions and commands that point to a future beyond the text. If the narrative of Acts is structured to show continuity with the ecclesiology of the Gospels, we would expect it to share some or all of these features; and this in fact is what we find.

Proclaiming the kingdom 'now'	Proclaiming the kingdom 'not yet'
The baptism of John	Baptism with the Holy Spirit
The call of the disciples	Apostles as 'fishers'
Jesus' words of power	Apostolic ministry of the word
Jesus' deeds of power	Apostolic deeds of power
Confessing the Christ, carrying the cross	Being hated for the name of Christ
Courageous engagement with the public life of the people of God	Testimony before governors and kings
Living 'between the times'	Living in expectancy
Table-fellowship with Jesus	Life in community
Mission to the world	Preaching to the Gentiles

Luke's portrayal of the church in Acts exhibits both *continuity* with the ecclesiology of his Gospel and *adaptation* to fit the changing circumstances of the growing church.

The Ascension and the Coming of the Kingdom

'Lord, is this the time that you will restore the Kingdom to Israel?' (Acts 1:6). The disciples' question puts the question of the kingdom on the agenda right at the beginning of Acts. It's a reasonable question: Jesus had promised his disciples, 'It is the Father's good pleasure to give you the Kingdom' (Lk 12:32). In answer, the eschatological energy behind the question is not denied but redirected. Jesus will return, but his disciples are not to waste their energies on speculation about 'times and seasons': they have a job to do (Acts 1:8, 11). The nature of the task gradually unfolds through the first chapter of Acts: a promise of receiving 'power from on high' when the Holy Spirit comes; a commission to be Jesus' 'witnesses' to the ends of the earth; persevering prayer with the 120 disciples gathered in the upper room; and the reconstitution of the Twelve.

The redirection of eschatological questions is familiar from the Gospel (Lk 17:20–1). Jesus never encouraged end-time speculation for its own sake. Future eschatology (interest in the final manifestation of God's reign on earth) in fact all but disappears from Acts. Acts is remarkably free of apocalyptic language—though the final judgement is still part of the underlying framework of thought (3:21; 17:31). The preaching of the kingdom, however, does not disappear: Lk describes the mission of both Philip and Paul as 'preaching the kingdom of God', and the final scene of Acts has Paul 'teaching about the Kingdom' in the Jewish community in Rome (8:12; 14:22; 19:8; 20:25; 28:23, 31). Much more important to the ecclesiology of Acts is the sense of living in the end-times, seeing the breaking-in of God's reign in the here and now and an unbroken continuity between

Jesus' preaching of the Kingdom and the apostolic mission to Israel. It is precisely *because* the era of the church is the time between Jesus' Ascension and his return (1:11) that the church's consciousness is formed by living 'in the last days' (2:16–21), watching for the signs of God's kingdom at work.

Moreover, the apostles are conscious that Jesus is in heaven *now*. By placing the Ascension at the beginning of his narrative, Luke effectively establishes the heavenly realm (the 'up' dimension of eschatology) as a crucial 'third space' in all that follows (Sleeman 2009). The church is 'the domain ruled by the exalted Christ and is his instrument in the world until his coming in glory' (Schnackenburg 1974: 66). The focus is now not so much on the *future* coming of the Son of Man (Lk 21:27) as on the *present* fact that he is 'standing at the right hand of God' (Acts 7:55–6): Jesus is now part of the eternal truth about God. The theological implications are enormous: the kingdom cannot in future be understood without reference to the crucified-and-exalted Christ. Luke does not spell out this theme as propositional theology, but he uses the opening speeches of Acts to explore it in exegetical terms. Just as there is an integral link between passion and exaltation (Lk 24:25–6, 46–7), so there is an integral link between the exaltation of the Messiah and the release of the blessings of the last days—specifically, the outpouring of the Spirit (Acts 2:32–6; 3:19–21). So the Ascension also refocuses the disciples' eschatological energy outward to the immediate task of learning what it means to be the messianic community living in the last days but with their messianic leader (*archegos*, Acts 3:15, 5:31) now in heaven.

The Eschatological Gathering-in of the People of God

It is no accident that the eschatological gathering-in of the people of God dominates the beginning of Acts just as it dominates Luke's Gospel. The Twelve are in some indefinable way apostles *to and for Israel* (Lk 22:28–30): hence the need to fill up the gap caused by the defection of Judas (Acts 1:15–26). The location in Jerusalem confirms the privileged position of Israel in the apostolic mission: the gospel has to be preached 'first' to the Jewish people (3:26; 13:46), and Jerusalem is its spiritual heartland and symbolic centre. Jerusalem is a significant place for the gathering-in of the scattered Jewish people of the Diaspora, coming to worship and to receive the revelation of God's law (2:9–11); and there is an ancient prophetic tradition that in the last days, the Gentiles too will be gathered in to Jerusalem (Lohfink 1984: 17–20; 137–41). The apostolic mission to the people of Jerusalem and the gathered diaspora in Acts chapters 1–7 is in direct continuity with Jesus' mission of the gathering-in and restoration of the people of God (Ravens 1995; Scott 2001). In Luke's geographical scheme, it is only *after* the mission to greater Israel (first Jerusalem, then the lost ten tribes of Samaria, then a proselyte from Ethiopia) that the mission to the Gentiles can really begin (chapters 8–10). And even then, the pattern 'to the Jew first, then also to the Greek' (Rom. 1:16, 2:9–10) continues to dominate the narrative construction of Acts. In terms of narrative time, Paul spends as much time talking to Jews as he does to Gentiles: he always goes first to the synagogue when he visits a new city, the 'turn to the Gentiles' can only be justified by Jewish rejection of the message (13:46–7), and the final scene of the book is a dialogue within the Jewish community of Rome.

But the message of the Kingdom is not just for Israel. Luke's language suggests that the metaphor of 'gathering in' God's scattered people underlies the missions of both Peter and Paul. Peter's Pentecost sermon quotes the prophecy of Joel that 'all who call on the name of the Lord will be saved' (2:21), and Peter declares that 'the promise is to you, and your children, and to those that are afar off, as many as the Lord our God will call to himself' (2:39). This is precisely what Cornelius is (chapter 10): a Gentile whom God 'calls to himself'. He is carefully described (in terms that echo the centurion of Lk 7:4–5) as a devout God-fearer, one who prays and gives alms and is open to God's revelation: hence Peter's reaction: 'Now I perceive that God is no respecter of persons: for in every nation the person who fears him and does what is right is welcomed before him' (10:34–5). Even more boldly, Paul's Areopagus sermon in Athens redefines pagans as those who worship the unknown God: so that preaching to pagans becomes simply making known the hidden God who is already worshipped (17:22–31). This theology underlies James's interpretation of the key text from Amos 9:11–12 (LXX) at Acts 15:13–18: 'the restoration of Israel occurs in order that the Gentiles also seek the Lord (cf. Acts 15:17). After all, his name has been invoked over them, which means that they have long since stood under his rule. Yet they can find God and enter the reign of God only if Israel is rebuilt' (Lohfink 1984: 140).

If the kingdom is the key to understanding the ecclesiology of the Gospels, the key to understanding the ecclesiology of Acts is the Holy Spirit. The importance of John's baptism is reinforced repeatedly in Acts: it marks the beginning point of the story to which the apostles are to bear witness (1:22), and Peter refers back to it in his own testimony (10:37). The outpouring of the Spirit at Pentecost is a direct fulfilment of the promise made by John the Baptist (cf. 1:5): the tongues of flame echo the language of biblical theophany, but also perhaps the 'fire' predicted by John (2:3, 19; Lk 3:16). So the beginning of the church in Acts is marked by a dramatic 'baptism in the Spirit' to match the anointing of Jesus at the start of his ministry: other 'Pentecost' experiences mark significant points in the narrative (4:31; 10:44; 19:6). This experience is eschatological: it is a sign of the last days (2:17); it is inclusive and far-ranging, embracing not only 'you and your children' (gathered Israel, symbolized by the assembled crowds from Jerusalem, Judaea, and the diaspora) but also 'those who are far off' (2:39). It is important for Luke to explain that this is not a new story but the continuation of the old: as Peter explains, the outpouring of the Spirit is a direct result of Jesus' Ascension to heaven (2:33). The gift promised by the prophets to all Israel is now freely available to all: but only in the name of (and through the work of) the crucified-and-exalted Messiah.

So the Holy Spirit is first and foremost the eschatological sign of God's presence with his people, a sign of the restoration of the people of God, of the 'times of refreshing' promised by the prophets (3:19, cf. Ezek. 37). The accusation of being 'drunk with new wine' echoes the intoxicating effects of Jesus' presence at the beginning of his ministry (2:13, cf. Lk 5:37–8). The Spirit continues to play an important role as a sign of God's presence in the life of the church: in the discernment and equipping of those selected for mission and ministry in the life of the church (6:3, 5; 13:1–3; 20:28); in guidance for specific occasions (8:39; 10:19; 16:6, 7). The Spirit is the guardian of the church's holiness and protector of its fragile fellowship (5:1–11). The Spirit 'bears witness' to the presence of God (5:32) through signs and wonders and especially through prophetic speech—which in Acts includes glossolalia, understood as divine speech miraculously understood in diverse tongues (2:7–11). Above all, the Spirit is connected with baptism. Repentance and baptism, combining the cleansing ritual of immersion in water (cf. 8:37–8) with the gift of the Spirit (2:38)—though not in any fixed order—are the necessary preliminary to the restoration of the people of God and the fulfilment of promise, including the promise that through Abraham's seed, God's blessing will be channelled to the whole of humanity (3:20–6).

Following Jesus: From Disciples to Church

But it is the messianic community of disciples, rather than the 'people of God' as a whole, that forms the nucleus of the emergent church in Acts. Discipleship forms the narrative bridge between the Gospel and Acts, beginning with the naming of the apostles chosen by Jesus (1:13). These in turn form the nucleus of a larger group of 120 'brothers' (the group includes the women and the family of Jesus: 1:14–15), which soon grows to several thousand (2:30; 4:4). Luke uses a surprising variety of terms to describe this growing community. 'Disciples' and 'brothers' are used throughout the narrative, more or less interchangeably with Luke's favourite term 'believers' (e.g. 4:32). The Pauline 'saints' appears occasionally, as does the Lucan term 'The Way' (9:2; 18:26; 19:9, 23; 22:4; 24:14, 22). *Christianoi* does not appear until 11:25, at the point where Gentiles are beginning to join the church in Antioch, and seems to be a term used by outsiders (cf. 26:26), as is 'sect [of the Nazarenes]' (*hairesis:* 24:5, 14; 28:22). Luke is at some pains to stress that the group includes both men and women (5:14; 8:3, 12; 9:2; 22:4; cf. the rare feminized form of 'disciple' at 9:36).

These terms might suggest that Luke thinks of the church primarily as a collection of individual 'names' (*onomata* Acts 1:15) or 'souls' (*psuchai* 2:41, 43). The narrative of Acts, like the Gospel, is built around a series of personal encounters, highlighting the choices made by individuals to 'receive' or 'hear' the Word of God (2:40; 4:4; 8:14; 15:7; 16:14), to be 'persuaded' to 'follow' or 'join up with' Paul (13:43; 17:4, 34), to 'turn to God' (26:20), to 'believe' in the Lord Jesus (10:43; 16:31) and to 'call on his name' (22:16). However, Luke is also careful to stress that the work of faith is a 'grace' of God (18:27) and (in one place) implies it is only given 'to such as were ordained to eternal life' (13:48). To be a believer is 'to turn from darkness to light and from the power of Satan to God', to receive 'forgiveness of sins and a place among those who are being sanctified by faith' in Christ (26:18, cf. 20:32): believers are 'those who are being saved' (2:47), with the emphasis on salvation as a future event dependent on 'the grace of the Lord Jesus' (15:11; 16:31). To become a disciple is to enter a process of sanctification whose horizon is the future judgement: it is quite possible for disciples to be drawn away by false teaching (20:30), or to continue in mistaken practices or beliefs (19:1–7, 18–19)—or indeed to disagree quite profoundly about major issues (21:20, 25). Hence the importance of the apostolic task of 'strengthening the souls of the disciples' (14:22) and of commending them 'to the Lord in whom they had come to believe' (14:23; 20:32).

But to focus exclusively on the individual aspect of discipleship would be to miss an essential element of Luke's portrayal of the messianic community. Right from the outset, Luke is at pains to show how this group of 'brothers' functions as a real community. The term 'church' itself (*ekklēsia*) does not appear until Acts 5:11: but other collective nouns (*ochlos, plethos*) are used to highlight the group's capacity for concerted action right from the outset (exemplified in the orderly process of the election of Matthias and the Seven: 1:23–6; 6:1–7). The whole narrative is structured to portray a unified body of believers, operating with 'one heart and one soul', under a unified leadership, from a single place of origin (2:43–7; 4:32–7). Luke's geographical focus on Jerusalem means that even Galilee is marginalized, or rather subsumed under an overarching unity: the first hint we get of continuing Christ-followers in Galilee is at 9:31: 'The church throughout all Judea and Galilee and Samaria had peace and was built up; and walking in the fear of the Lord and in the comfort of the Holy Spirit it was multiplied.'

What is the significance of Luke's use of the word *ekklēsia*? Paul already uses this phrase of the Jerusalem church (1 Cor. 15:29; Gal. 1:13). 'There is no doubt that here, with a look at the people of God in the OT, it refers to the whole company of Christians, though at this time the whole company of Christians is the local church of Jerusalem' (Barrett 1994, vol. 1: 271). The language echoes the biblical description of the assembly of the people of God in the wilderness as the *ekklēsia tou theou* (Hebrew *qahal*)—a usage found in Stephen's speech (Acts 7:38, cf. Deut. 23:1–8 LXX). Luke, like Paul, uses *ekklēsia* primarily of the body of God's people in a given place. 'The Church is grounded in the being of God *in a particular place*: we might almost say, *the* church is a form of local incarnation of what it means (ontologically, historically, and universally) to be God's people' (cf. Acts 20:28; Alexander 2008: 52–3).

Structures and Ministry

Luke also uses *ekklēsia* to distinguish the body of believers (cf. *to plethos* in Acts 6:1–3) from the apostles and elders (15:4, 22): and from a literary point of view, it is the apostles who form the narrative focus of Acts. Luke is not writing a 'history of the church', and his narrative provides much less information than we would like on the structures and ministry of the early communities. The twelve apostles clearly have a special and unique role in the mission to Israel. They were 'chosen' by Jesus (1:2), and their ministry (*diakonia*) is an 'office' (*episcope*) which can only be filled under the guidance of God (1:15–26). With Peter as their spokesman, they take a leading role within the assembled community, act as focal point for the community's charitable donations (4:35, 37), and exercise spiritual discipline (5:1–11; 8:14–17; 11:1–3). As the church grows, however, the apostles gradually distance themselves from the day-to-day running of the community's affairs (6:1–4) and assume a more itinerant oversight of 'the church throughout Judea, Galilee and Samaria' (9:31). When the church spreads to Antioch, they send down Barnabas in their place (11:19–26), and it is Barnabas and Paul who become this church's 'apostles' on the first Gentile mission (14:4, 14).

But leadership is not confined to the apostles. Just as in the Gospel (Lk 10) Luke makes it clear that the Holy Spirit equips other leaders too: the Seven 'deacons', evangelists, prophets and teachers, elders—and Paul. Luke's lack of interest in structural precision makes it hard to establish a consistent pattern of ministry, but over the course of the narrative we find a variety of ministries being exercised in different churches. The Seven are appointed by the Greek-speaking portion of the Jerusalem church to ensure the fair distribution of charitable aid within the community—though two of them, Stephen and Philip, also exercise a 'ministry of the word' in Jerusalem and Samaria (chapters 6–8). The 'elders' (*presbuteroi*), led by James the Lord's brother, appear without explanation as leaders of the Jerusalem church (chapters 11 and 15). The church in Antioch is led by 'prophets and teachers', guided by the Holy Spirit (13:1–3); and Paul and Barnabas appoint elders for the new churches founded on their first Gentile mission (14:23).

Towering over all is the figure of Saul/Paul, persecutor, convert, teacher, and travelling evangelist, called and appointed by Jesus himself as 'my chosen instrument to carry my name before Gentiles and kings and the people of Israel' (Acts 9:15). Luke is reluctant to give Paul the title 'apostle': but he dominates the second part of the Acts narrative, and the role he adopts (under the guidance of the Spirit: 13:3, 16:6–10)—preaching the gospel, planting churches, appointing elders, offering guidance and encouragement—is clearly apostolic. Central to Luke's presentation of Paul (and indeed to the whole narrative) is the Miletus speech at 20:17–35. To an audience of Ephesian 'elders', local church leaders, Paul speaks movingly of his own itinerant ministry as a commission (*diakonia*) 'received from the Lord Jesus, to testify to the good news of God's grace', carried out with tears and tribulations, 'teaching publicly and from house to house' (20:18–24). But—and this is the point—the local elders too have a God-given ministry: 'Watch out for yourselves, and for all of the flock of which the Holy Spirit has made you overseers (*episkopoi*), to shepherd the church of God that he obtained with the blood of his own [Son]' (20:28). The speech serves part as farewell (Paul is nearing the end of his ministry), part as warning (beware of false teachers), part as exemplar: the apostolic image is itself part of the encouragement (*paraklesis*) that Luke wants to pass on to the next generation of leaders as the apostolic generation passes away. For Luke and his readers, the apostles too are in the past: all the more important to stress that the local leaders, like the itinerant apostles, are called and inspired by the Holy Spirit.

What are the Distinguishing Characteristics of this Community?

The distinguishing features of the growing messianic community in Acts show a remarkable continuity with the essential discipleship paradigm of the Gospels.

1. Central to the activity of the church is the ministry of the word. The preaching of the word (or 'preaching the gospel') takes up a significant amount of narrative space in Acts, both in Jerusalem and in the diaspora, and must be counted one of its most prominent features: indeed 'the Word' functions as a narrative subject more frequently than 'the church' in Acts (6:7; 12:24; 19:20). But its content is quickly and quietly redefined as 'preaching the good news *of Jesus Christ*' (5:42; 8:35; 10:36; 11:20; 17:18). Peter's Jerusalem sermons accuse his hearers of responsibility for the crucifixion of Jesus (2:23, 36; 3:14–18; 4:10). But the charge is always linked with the premise of acting 'in ignorance', and with the offer of forgiveness, and thus becomes part of the tight nexus already seen in Luke's Gospel, tying together repentance, forgiveness, salvation, cleansing, and faith (2:38–9; 3:19–20). As 'witnesses' appointed by Jesus (1:8), the apostles are the prime bearers of the community's teaching tradition (2:42)—equipped for this role not only by their status as 'eyewitnesses' (Lk 1:2; Acts 1:21–2) but by their post-Easter training in the Christological interpretation of Scripture (Lk 24:44–9; Acts 1:3). Interpreting God's present action in the light of God's revelation in Scripture plays a central role in the apostolic preaching in Acts: cf. chapters 2, 3, 4, 13, and 15. The apostolic preaching of the word is rhetorically effective: those who hear it are 'cut to the heart' (2:37), and its result is spectacular growth in numbers, a further proof that 'the hand of the Lord was with them,' (2:41, 47; 4:4, 33). And even where it does not convince, this public act of 'bearing witness' is significant in itself: Luke depicts the 'boldness' (*parrhesia*) of the apostles and their willingness to suffer for the name of Jesus as making a powerful impression on rulers and people alike (4:10–17; 5:41; 13:31).

2. The work of the kingdom is also expressed in deeds of power (Acts 2:43; 5:12–16). As in the Gospels, the community is a fellowship of individuals who have experienced the saving effects of encountering Jesus in their own lives (3:1–10; 9:32–43). The apostles continue the work of healing and exorcism entrusted to them by Jesus, demonstrating his messianic authority over the kingdom of Satan. Thus the healing of the lame man at the Gate Beautiful in Acts chapter 3 is cited as proof of Jesus' exaltation to heaven (3:11–16; 4:7–12). These healings are always carried out 'in the name of Jesus' (3:6; 9:34): any attempt to set up a rival source of spiritual power is doomed to failure (19:11–17: Klutz 2004). The power to heal is not limited to the Twelve; it includes Philip (8:5–8) and Paul, who has his own series of healings and exorcisms in parallel to Peter (13:4–12; 14:3, 8–10; 16:16–18; 19:11–17; 28:8). Luke is careful to differentiate this ongoing apostolic work from magic or

sorcery: it is a gift of the Holy Spirit, and it cannot be bought (8:18–24; 13:6–12; 19:11–20). But the church as a whole begins very quickly to practise new forms of 'good news to the poor' through the sharing of goods and the performance of charitable works. Luke portrays these good works as integral to the fellowship of the church (2:44–5; 4:32–7; 6:1; 9:36; 20:33–5). This practical work of *koinōnia* is the work of the Holy Spirit, and any attempt to defraud it is an offence against the Holy Spirit and receives summary punishment (5:1–11): the church as a body of fallible believers is both 'made holy and pursuing holiness' (Schnackenburg 1974: 132).

3. The link between confessing the Name and carrying the cross is a prominent feature of the Acts narrative. Jesus' prediction that his disciples will be hated for the name of Christ is amply fulfilled in the experiences of Peter and John, Stephen, James, and Paul. Their suffering is not meaningless: it is welcomed as 'suffering for the Name' (Acts 5:41), and is directly linked with the profession of the name of Jesus (4:7–18, 30; 9:13–16). Paul's Damascus Road vision (repeated three times) makes the identification even closer: in persecuting the church, Saul is persecuting Jesus himself (9:5; 22:7; 26:15). Peter and John, Stephen and Paul are celebrated as heroic exemplars of steadfastness and endurance. Inevitably this means that their stories also exemplify the gospel theme of courageous engagement with the public life of the people of God, fulfilling Jesus' prediction that his followers will bear testimony before governors and kings and receive inspiration from the Spirit—a prediction already foreshadowed in Scripture (4:23–32). This theme is vividly portrayed in the narratives of Peter and John in Acts 3–5, and in Paul's *apologia* in chapters 21–6, which plays it out on a world stage. Paul's appeal to Caesar implies willingness to testify to the gospel before the highest tribunal in the empire: this never happens in the narrative, but perhaps gives a clue to the rhetorical setting of Acts (cf. Philippians 1:12–14). Paul's trial speeches show a conflation of apologetic with personal testimony, with the ultimate object of persuading his exalted hearers to 'become Christian' (26:28–9, and already Phil. 1:7; cf. Alexander 2005: 183–206).

4. The inner life of the community—especially its worship—figures less prominently in Luke's narrative than we might like. The narrative image of the disciples gathered in table-fellowship around Jesus dominates the final chapters of the Gospel and the beginning of Acts. Like John, Luke incorporates a great deal of discipleship instruction into his Last Supper narrative, including leadership paraenesis and the (unique) instruction to Peter to 'strengthen' his brethren (Lk 22:24–32). It is Luke who lays particular stress on the fact that this table-fellowship continued after the resurrection, and that Jesus made himself known to the two disciples at Emmaus 'in the breaking of the bread' (Lk 24:305: note the emphasis on the physicality of 'eating and drinking' at Lk 24:36–43 and Acts 10:41). All of this implies that the passing references to 'the breaking of bread' in the life of the community in Acts should be given full weight (2:42, 46; 20:7; and perhaps 27:33–5). This is one of the four 'marks of the church' (*notae ecclesiae*) at 2:42–7, which should be taken as indicative of general community practice: 'They devoted themselves to the apostles' teaching and to fellowship, to the breaking of bread and to the prayers.' The apostles' teaching,

if the speeches in Acts are indicative, implies brief formulaic summaries of the key events of Jesus' life, death, and resurrection, rooted in extensive exegesis of scriptural *testimonia*. 'Fellowship' (*koinōnia*) suggests an intentional focus on building and cementing community, expressed above all in the community of goods (2:44–5; 4:32–7; cf. 11:27–30). Luke seems to take it for granted that such practices would be readily understood by his readers. The worship of the community ('the prayers') takes place both in the temple and 'from house to house' (2:46). Luke consistently shows his protagonists as connected to the ongoing liturgical life of the people of God, both in synagogue and temple (Lk 1:8–23; 2:22–38, 41–52; 4:16; Acts 3:1–11; 5:12; 13:14–15; 14:1; 16:13–16; 17:1:4, 10; 19:8; 21:26).

5. Much more prominent (indeed central to Acts) is the theme of mission to the Gentiles. The open-ended conclusion to the book is emblematic: it shows Paul the prisoner, in a hired lodging in Rome, preaching the kingdom to all comers 'and teaching about the Lord Jesus Christ, with complete boldness'; its last word is 'unhindered' (28:30–1). The mission to the Gentiles is one of the major themes of Acts, prefigured in Peter's encounter with Cornelius in chapter 10. It is part of Paul's particular calling, an aspect of his conversion experience (9:15; 22:14–15, 21; 26:16–18). To the attentive reader, the mission 'to all nations' has been foreshadowed from the start of the Gospel (Lk 2:31–2), and is explicit in Jesus' mission charge at Lk 24:47 and Acts 1:8. Luke is too good a dramatist, however, to make this a narrative in which the apostles are simply following a pre-determined programme. It is easy to forget that the commission to go 'to the ends of the earth' (1:8) echoes words from the prophet Isaiah which in their original context refer to the gathering-in of the scattered people of God (Isa. 43:6); and by dramatizing the apostles' puzzlement and reluctance to take this step (cf. Peter in chapter 10; the apostolic council in chapter 15), Luke allows us to see that it takes time, listening, and debate to find out where God is leading the church. The whole narrative is held together by the central episode of Peter's visit to Cornelius (chapter 10), Paul's first Gentile mission (chapters 13–14), and the apostolic council (chapter 15), a dramatic exemplification of the ecclesiological insight that the catholicity of the church cannot simply be assumed (or imposed) but demands fidelity to the leading of the Spirit and a commitment to mutual listening (Alexander 2008: 67–77). Luke portrays the church in Acts as a church that is both 'united and pursuing unity' (Schnackenburg 1974: 128).

This raises the question of the ultimate fate of unbelieving Israel in Acts (for the debate see Marguerat 2002: 129–54). The prophetic theme of Israel as a 'light to the nations' (Isa. 49:5–6) is an important one for Luke (Lk 2:32), and is especially associated with the mission of Paul (Acts 13:47; 26:18). This was widely interpreted in terms of an eschatological gathering in of the Gentiles as the natural sequel to the restoration of Israel. In Rom. 9–11, however, Paul is faced with the dreadful paradox that it is not Israel's faith but Israel's (temporary) rejection of the gospel that opens the door for the gathering-in of the Gentiles (Lohfink 1984: 142). This seems to be something close to Luke's view.

Luke is careful to establish that Paul's 'turn to the Gentiles' comes *after* the rejection of the gospel by Jews (Acts 13:44–8), and there is no corresponding rejection of the mission to Israel, even by Paul. On this reading the 'tragic' ending of Acts is deliberately open-ended: Paul expresses the hope that the Gentiles 'will listen' (28:28), but there is no closure on discussion and debate with the ancient people of God (Tannehill 2005: 105–68). The messianic community still exists in and for the people of God: it has simply enlarged its understanding of the boundaries.

JESUS AND THE CHURCH

> 'The question of the founding of the Church by Jesus Himself is really the question of His Messiahship' (Schmidt 1965: 521–2)

The deep structure of synoptic ecclesiology, we have suggested, is built around a sequence of narrative images:

- Jesus' proclamation of the kingdom;
- the baptism of John;
- the call of the disciples;
- the preaching of the word;
- the performance of deeds of power;
- the confession of Jesus as the Christ and the call to follow him on the way of the cross;
- courageous engagement with the public life of the people of God;
- a consciousness of 'living between the times';
- table-fellowship built around the remembrance of Jesus;
- the sending out of the apostles on a mission to the nations.

These are the key elements in the narrative that the church tells of its own origins, the story that gives the church its distinctive structures. It is the underlying coral reef that supports and shapes a myriad forms of ecclesial life: its commitment to proclaiming the kingdom in word and action; its sacraments; its valorization of order and its suspicion of autocracy; its sense of vocation and commitment to following the way of the cross; its determination to engage with public life; its eschatology, both realized and future; its sense of mission. This is the story that brings the church back, time and again, to its fundamental commitment to the person of Christ and the gift of the Spirit. It is not an institutional blueprint but a *narrative*, an invitation to inhabit a narrative world that can be heard in different ways in different times and places.

Beneath this sequence lie two intertwined ecclesiological models: a 'people of God' ecclesiology and a 'discipleship' ecclesiology. John's call to repentance and baptism, and the promise of the Spirit, marks the inauguration of the eschatological gathering-in of the people of God. The process continues in Jesus' proclamation of the kingdom in words of authority and deeds of power. This is an inclusive ecclesiology of good news offered to the poor and marginalized, in which individuals who respond to Jesus in faith receive cleansing, forgiveness, salvation, new life, and reintegration into the community. Jesus issues a radical challenge to the whole nation (including the religious authorities) to recognize the demands of the incoming kingdom of God by responding positively to his own messianic claims. The call of the disciples marks the inauguration of a messianic community, called to follow Jesus, to confess him as Messiah, and to follow him on the way of the cross. This is a radical call to *imitatio Christi*, a call to courageous engagement with the public life of the people of God and the wider world; to a lifestyle based on an attitude of eschatological expectancy; to table-fellowship built around the remembered presence of Jesus; and to a commissioning and empowering for a future mission to the world. These two ecclesiological themes (which interweave throughout the gospel narratives) are distinct but not disconnected: the messianic community always exists in and for the larger community of which it forms a part. They have continued to interweave throughout the history of the church, and have enormous implications for its ecclesiology. The gospel ecclesiology of the gathering-in of the people of God leads naturally to a parish-based or 'national' church, which sees itself as 'salt and light' within the larger community but may not see the need for 'mission' as such. The gospel ecclesiology of 'discipleship' leads naturally to a more inward-focused, bounded church, a 'contrast-society' with a focus on holiness and separation from a hostile world (Lohfink 1984: 132–8). Both belong to the gospel narrative: a healthy ecclesiology, we might say, is one that holds the two together, with all their tensions.

Where does that leave us in relation to the historical question? Can we draw any conclusions about Jesus himself—the 'historical' Jesus—from this material? I think (with proper caution) we can. First, the material we have assembled passes the criterion of multiple attestation. The narrative images we have identified do not belong to an individual redactional layer of this or that Gospel—they are part of the bony structure of the Gospel story, the pillars and beams that hold the whole thing together. Unlike Mt 16:18, they can't be dismissed as 'solitary' or 'editorial'. They are spread right across the synoptic tradition (and across John too)—especially the three foundational elements: the baptism of John, the preaching of the kingdom, and the call of the disciples.

Second, they also pass the criterion of dissimilarity—or, as we should perhaps call it, the criterion of embarrassment. John the Baptist, the kingdom of God, discipleship: none of these are Pauline terms, though they surface occasionally in Paul's letters (Rom. 14:17; 1 Cor. 4:20, 6:9–10, 15:24, 50; Gal. 5:21; Eph. 5:5; Col. 4:11; 2 Thess. 15). 'Disciples' is a term Luke continues to use for the followers of Jesus throughout Acts, alongside (and eventually superseded by) more 'Pauline' terms like 'brothers' or 'saints'. The Baptist is perhaps the most interesting and puzzling of all. *Why* do the evangelists insist that John's baptism is 'the beginning of the good news'? Why does Luke continue to insist on this in Acts (and why does he enhance John's importance by giving him a birth story in Lk 1)? This is usually attributed to some lingering polemic against 'Baptist circles' (though the later we place Luke–Acts, the odder this becomes).

But surely it would have been easier to drop John altogether? Matthew shows already the embarrassment caused by the fact that Jesus apparently accepted John's baptism 'for the forgiveness of sins' (Mt 3:14–15), and Luke is careful to get John off the scene before the start of Jesus' ministry (Lk 3:18–20)—but why mention him at all? Why not start Jesus' story with the heavenly voice and the anointing of the Spirit, like the pagan prophet Apollonius of Tyana? The Baptist makes sense as an ineradicable item of tradition—but not as an invention. And even as part of the tradition, he clearly has an importance which, while puzzling in Christological terms, is readily explicable ecclesiologically. John's mission is integral to the ecclesiology of the gospel because it links Jesus to a divine initiative directed at the restoration and renewal of the people of God: Luke's insight that John was sent 'to prepare a people' (Lk 1:16–17) is precisely the point.

This still does not prove that this structure has any *historical* value—in fact (as the form critics would have said), that's part of the problem. It's *because* of their ecclesial nature that we have to be wary of using the evidence of the Gospels to get back to Jesus himself. But for historians of early Christianity, the deeply ecclesial substructure of the Gospels which we have uncovered is itself a remarkable and potentially significant historical fact—a fact about *the Gospels* (as historical artefacts), if nothing else. It is especially remarkable if we begin with Mark, which is widely recognized as the *least* ecclesial of the canonical Gospels (and is often read as anti-ecclesial). We expect to find more 'transparency' towards the later church in Matthew and Luke—but in fact they are often simply making explicit what is already implicit in Mark.

But can we use this material to get back to the historical Jesus—or have the Gospels simply got Jesus all wrong? That brings me to my final point, which is to argue that the narrative images that we have identified are thoroughly *congruent* with the thought-world of first-century Jewish messianism. Jesus' mission to Israel (like John's) can readily be understood within a spectrum of renewal movements seeking to restore the kingdom by re-awakening God's people to a repentant acknowledgement of God's sovereignty. The foundation of Jesus' teaching is his own submission to the will of God, his acceptance of the yoke of the kingdom in his own person. This teaching is expressed in the Lord's Prayer, dramatized in the Temptation narrative (Mt 4:1–11; Lk 4:1–13) and ultimately in the prayer of Gethsemane (Mk 14:36). But Jesus did not operate alone. Right from the start, his mission had an irreducible dimension of *community*, both in the address to the people of God and in the call of the disciples. To say that Jesus founded a messianic community, to assist him in his mission and to act as 'sign, instrument and foretaste' of the kingdom in its own being—that seems to me not only well attested by the tradition but, in historical terms, intrinsically plausible.

In other words, I would suggest, the bare bones of the gospel narratives are sufficiently robust (and show sufficient discontinuity with developed catholic theology) to allow us to glimpse a world of ideas that is entirely congruent with other messianic movements in late Second Temple Judaism. Interestingly, this is the burden of T. W. Manson's argument in *The Teaching of Jesus* (Manson 1935: 136–41; 171–90); but Manson could not have known how strikingly his conclusions would be vindicated by the discovery of the Dead Sea Scrolls in 1947. Obviously the evangelists are writing from within the history of the later church: they are reading backwards—even Mark—from the perspective of a more developed ecclesiology and a more developed Christology. Especially, and crucially, they are reading back from a post-crucifixion perspective: they know what is going to happen to Jesus—and they know (at least Matthew and Luke do) what is going to happen to Jerusalem in 70 CE. Luke knows too of the further rejection of the gospel message by the religious authorities in Jerusalem (as described in the first seven chapters of Acts). Nevertheless, though this knowledge overshadows their narratives and at times leaches into them, the evangelists preserve a memory of an original messianic mission to Israel which could have turned out very differently: and it is to their credit (or perhaps we should say, it is a testimony to the tenacity of the gospel tradition) that the Gospels are so strongly marked with the story of a messianic mission to Israel, of a gathering of the people of God and the intentional formation of a messianic community, not to replace or supplant Israel as God's chosen people, but to act as agents for the coming of God's kingdom and the restoration of God's people— which itself is a necessary prerequisite for the prophetic vision of the gathering-in of the Gentiles.

We need to beware the fallacy of confusing *causality* with *predictability*. Of course we do not want to argue that everything that the church has become down the centuries can be predicted from the Gospels. But that Jesus was (whatever else he might be) a first-century Jew with a strong messianic consciousness; that he started his messianic mission, spurred on by John's baptism, preaching the kingdom of God in Galilee, and performing healings and exorcisms as signs of the kingdom's imminence; that, as an integral part of that mission, he formed a messianic community to act as agents of the kingdom; that, as opposition increased, he turned his attention more to the community's inner life, teaching and inspiring them to embody the values of the kingdom in a counter-cultural lifestyle (a 'saving remnant' rather than a 'saved remnant', to use Manson's terms: Manson 1935: 179, 181); that he foresaw his own death and made provision for the messianic community to continue the work of the kingdom after his death—all that is entirely within the bounds of historical plausibility. Whatever its discontinuities and adaptations, we can at least say with a degree of historical confidence that the foundation of the church lies in the messianic community founded by Jesus as 'sign, instrument and foretaste' of the kingdom of God.

REFERENCES

Alexander, Loveday (2003). 'Mapping Early Christianity: Acts and the Shape of Early Church History'. *Interpretation*, April 2003: 163–73.

Alexander, Loveday (2005). *Acts in its Ancient Literary Context*. LNTS 298. London: T & T Clark.

Alexander, Loveday (2008). 'Community and Canon: Reflections on the Ecclesiology of Acts'. In Anatoly A. Alexeev, Christos Karakolis, Ulrich Luz, and Karl-Wilhelm Niebuhr (eds), *Einheit der Kirche im Neuen Testament*. Tübingen: Mohr Siebeck, 45–78.

Alexander, Loveday (2009). 'Memory and Tradition in the Hellenistic Schools'. In Samuel Byrskog and Werner Kelber (eds), *Jesus in Memory*. Waco, TX: Baylor University Press, 113–53.

Allison, Dale (1993). *The New Moses: A Matthean Typology*. Minneapolis: Fortress Press.

Barrett, C. K. (1985). *Church, Ministry & Sacraments in the New Testament*. Exeter: Paternoster Press.

Barrett, C. K. (1994). *The Acts of the Apostles* (ICC). Vol. 1. Edinburgh: T & T Clark.

Burridge, Richard (1992). *What are the Gospels? A Comparison with Graeco-Roman Biography*. SNTSMS 70. Cambridge: Cambridge University Press.

Burridge, Richard (2007). *Imitating Jesus: An Inclusive Approach to NT Ethics*. Grand Rapids, MI: Eerdmans.

Byrskog, Samuel (1994). *Jesus the Only Teacher. Coniectanea Biblica NTS 24*. Stockholm: Almqvist & Wiksell.

Carlston, Charles and Evans, Craig (2014). *From Synagogue to Ecclesia*. WUNT 334. Tübingen: Mohr Siebeck.

Carter, Warren (1994). *Households and Discipleship: A Study of Matthew 19–20*. JSNTSS 103. Sheffield: JSOT.

Cotter, Wendy (2010). *The Christ of the Miracle Stories: Portrait Through Encounter*. Grand Rapids, MI: Baker Academic.

Cullmann, Oscar (1962). *Peter: Disciple, Apostle, Martyr*. 2nd expanded edition. London: SCM.

Dunn, James (2003). *Christianity in the Making, Vol. 1: Jesus Remembered*. Grand Rapids, MI: Eerdmans.

Evans, Craig (1989). *To See and not Perceive: Isaiah 6.9–10 in early Jewish and Christian Interpretation*. Sheffield: JSOT.

Hooker, Morna (1991). *The Gospel According to Mark (Black's New Testament Commentaries)*. London: A & C Black.

Jensen, Robin (2005). *Face to Face: Portraits of the Divine in Early Christianity*. Minneapolis: Fortress.

Johnson, Luke Timothy (1977). *The Literary Function of Possessions in Luke–Acts*. Missoula, MT: Scholars Press.

Johnson, Luke Timothy (2011). *Prophetic Jesus, Prophetic Church*. Grand Rapids, MI: Eerdmans.

Kim, Kyoung-Jin (1998). *Stewardship and Almsgiving in Luke's Theology*. JSNTSS 155. Sheffield: SAP.

Kloppenborg, John (2006). *The Tenants in the Vineyard: Ideology, Economics, and Agrarian Conflict in Jewish Palestine*. Tübingen: Mohr Siebeck.

Klutz, Todd (2004). *The Exorcism Stories in Luke–Acts: A Sociostylistic Reading*. Cambridge: Cambridge University Press.

Lindars, Barnabas (1961). *New Testament Apologetic*. London: SCM.

Lohfink, Gerhard (1984). *Jesus and Community*. Philadelphia: Fortress.

Luz, Ulrich (1993). *Theology of the Gospel of Matthew*. Cambridge: Cambridge University Press.

Luz, Ulrich (2005). *Studies in Matthew*. Grand Rapids, MI: Eerdmans.

Malbon, Elizabeth (2000). *In the Company of Jesus*. Louisville, KY: Westminster John Knox.

Manson, T. W. (1935). *The Teaching of Jesus*. 2nd edition. Cambridge: Cambridge University Press.

Marguerat, Daniel (2002). *The First Christian Historian: Writing the Acts of the Apostles*. SNTSMS 121. Cambridge: Cambridge University Press.

Minear, Paul (2007). *Images of the Church in the New Testament*. Cambridge: James Clarke [1960].

Moessner, David (1989). *Lord of the Banquet: The Literary Significance of the Lukan Travel Narrative*. Harrisburg, PA: Trinity Press International.

Ravens, David (1995). *Luke and the Restoration of Israel*. JSNTSS 119. Sheffield: SAP.

Rhee, Helen (2012). *Loving the Poor, Saving the Rich: Wealth, Poverty, and Early Christian Formation*. Grand Rapids, MI: Baker Academic.

Schmidt, Karl Ludwig (1965). Article *Ekklēsia. Theological Dictionary of the New Testament* (TDNT). Ed. G. Kittel. Vol. 3, pp. 501–36. Grand Rapids, MI: Eerdmans.

Schnackenburg, Rudolf (1974). *The Church in the New Testament*. London: Burns & Oates.

Schweizer, Eduard (1961). *Church Order in the New Testament*. Studies in Biblical Theology 32. London: SCM.

Scott, James, ed. (2001). *Restoration: Old Testament. Jewish, and Christian Perspectives*. Leiden: Brill.

Sleeman, Matthew (2009). *Geography and the Ascension Narrative in Acts*. Cambridge: Cambridge University Press.

Tannehill, Robert (2005). *The Shape of Luke's Story: Essays on Luke–Acts*. Eugene, OR: Wipf & Stock.

SUGGESTED READING

Alexander, Loveday (2008). 'Community and Canon: Reflections on the Ecclesiology of Acts'. In Anatoly A. Alexeev, Christos Karakolis, Ulrich Luz, and Karl-Wilhelm Niebuhr (eds), *Einheit der Kirche im Neuen Testament*. Tübingen: Mohr Siebeck, 45–78.

Barrett, C. K. (1985). *Church, Ministry & Sacraments in the New Testament*. Exeter: Paternoster Press.

Cullmann, Oscar (1962). *Peter: Disciple, Apostle, Martyr*. 2nd expanded edition. London: SCM.

Johnson, Luke Timothy (2011). *Prophetic Jesus, Prophetic Church*. Grand Rapids, MI: Eerdmans.

Lohfink, Gerhard (1984). *Jesus and Community*. Philadelphia: Fortress.

Luz, Ulrich (2005). *Studies in Matthew*. Grand Rapids, MI: Eerdmans.

Minear, Paul (2007). *Images of the Church in the New Testament*. Cambridge: James Clarke [1960].

Schnackenburg, Rudolf (1974). *The Church in the New Testament*. London: Burns & Oates.

Schweizer, Eduard (1961). *Church Order in the New Testament*. Studies in Biblical Theology 32. London: SCM.

CHAPTER 4

THE JOHANNINE VISION
OF THE CHURCH

ANDREW T. LINCOLN

READERS of the Gospel of John (GJ) have their attention directed towards the identity of Jesus in relation to God. Indeed this Gospel's stated purpose is to establish and reinforce commitment to Jesus as Messiah and Son of God (cf. 20:31). To that extent its subject matter is Christological rather than ecclesiological. Yet, if it is a truism to state that without the person of Jesus the church would not exist, it is also the case that a Christology would not be operative without those who hold it. In the dialectic between Christ and community, GJ's consistent stress is that the members of the latter are entirely dependent for their existence on the identity and mission of the former. It should not be surprising that the appropriate interpretation of that identity and mission is also a major issue in the Johannine Epistles (JE) addressed to local churches associated with the Gospel.

INTRODUCTION

Before pursuing how these writings set out the church's role, it is important to clarify the scope of this chapter's title. 'Johannine' will be taken to mean both the Gospel and the Epistles, but with a primary focus on the more extensive and profound Gospel. The 'Johannine vision' refers to how the identity and life of the believing community are envisaged in these writings themselves. This means that, while this chapter is certainly aware of the most plausible settings that are proposed for these documents and from which the vision emerges, it is not concerned with engaging in the contested enterprises of reconstructing the literary relationship among the writings or the nature of actual communities and the various stages of their development behind them. It presupposes, for example, that the narrative of GJ reflects and is to some extent shaped by an earlier traumatic break between Jewish followers of Jesus and their local synagogue but that it expresses a vision of the church's future now that that break is in the past and that Gentile believers are also fully included among its members. A different essay could also have been written that takes account of the use and abuse of these writings' view of the church in their reception history. While acknowledging that this later reception cannot be neatly separated from questions of interpretation and that GJ's fulfilment themes have been taken to support the type of supersessionism or anti-Judaism that finds no further place for Israel in God's purposes, these issues, about which there is a substantial body of scholarly literature (see esp. Bieringer et al. 2001; Kierspel 2006), are not the focus of this chapter. It presupposes, for example, that the accounts of Jesus' public mission reflect the conventions of fierce intra-Jewish debate and that the invective against the opponents in JE is part of the usual polemic of the time and that both are therefore particular cultural expressions of these documents' pursuit of religious truth. The approach here, however, will be more literary and theological than historical and social, as it asks, in the light of its potential contribution to discussions of Christian ecclesiology, how the Johannine writings envisage the relation of Jesus' followers to God, one another, and the world.

The third term in the title that requires explanation is 'church'. As is frequently observed, the term *ekklēsia* (church, assembly) does not occur at all in the Gospel and is employed only in 3 Jn 6, 9, 10 with reference to a local assembly. To talk of 'the church' with general reference to the community of all followers of Jesus is therefore, at least to some extent, to impose a category that the Johannine literature does not use. Provided that one is aware of this and that its use does not import a variety of assumptions about the church derived from elsewhere, such talk need not have a distorting effect but can simply serve as a convenient category for describing what the texts have in view through a variety of functional equivalents for the believing community. The actual word *ekklēsia* may be absent from the Gospel but an extensive section, the farewell discourses in chapters 13–17, is devoted in major part to addressing the situation of Jesus' followers and their communal life after his departure, and JE, in which the term *ekklēsia* does occur briefly, reflect more directly the life of specific local communities with which the Gospel was associated.

A COMMUNITY THAT PARTICIPATES IN THE DIVINE MISSION TO THE WORLD

The most appropriate starting point for appreciating GJ's perspective is with the function of the believing community in the overall flow of its narrative. The prologue provides a preview. Though that prologue is justly celebrated for the way it introduces the central character, Jesus, as the Logos in relation to God, its latter section also depicts the relationship of God and the Logos eventuating in the formation of a community that receives the Logos (1:12, 13) and makes its confession about his glory (1:14–18). In fact, as the children of God (1:12), this community is now enabled to participate in the prior familial relationship between God as Father and the Logos as unique Son (1:14, 18). Participating in their relationship also entails being part of their mission in the world. Those who have received the Logos by believing are represented in the Gospel's main storyline primarily by the disciples, not simply the twelve but an indeterminate group of Jesus' followers, who are also the characters in the narrative with whom readers are likely to identify most readily. At the end of that storyline, after the account about Jesus himself has reached its climax in the glorification of his death and resurrection, the risen Jesus appears for the first time in the midst of a gathering of these still fearful followers and commissions them with the words, 'Peace be with you. As the Father has sent me, so I send you' (20:21). Jesus' mission has been that of the uniquely authorized agent of the Father and now his followers are sent on an analogous mission as the authorized agents of the Son.

Repeatedly in this narrative Jesus has described himself as sent by God or the Father and spoken of God as the one who sent him. In the context of Jewish and Graeco-Roman conventions about envoys, the language of sending conveyed notions of both commissioning and authorized representation. What Jesus has been commissioned to do is expressed in a variety of ways, some of which are formulated explicitly as mission statements: 'I have come to . . .'. These include making known God or God's name (e.g. 1:18; 17:6, 26), bearing witness to the truth (e.g. 3:32, 33; 8:14; 18:36), judging (e.g. 5:22, 27; 8:15, 16; 9:39), bringing life (e.g. 3:16; 10:10; 17:2), and simultaneously glorifying God and being glorified (e.g. 13:31, 32; 17:1, 4). The work for which Jesus has been commissioned is, however, opposed by other characters in the narrative who include the chief priests and Pharisees, Judas, Pilate, 'the Jews' in the sense of those unbelieving Jews who reject Jesus' witness, 'the world' in its negative connotation of humanity hostile to God, and the ruler of this world or the devil. Paradoxically, the apparent success of the opposing world in bringing Jesus' mission to an end by his death turns out to be the means by which his mission is accomplished, as is made clear by his final words on the cross—'It is finished' (19:30)—and their anticipation in the earlier prayer—'I glorified you on earth by finishing the work that you gave me to do' (17:4).

That prayer also indicates that the commissioning of the disciples by the risen Jesus is not simply an afterthought or addition to the storyline. A significant aspect of the mission that Jesus has now completed had been the gathering of a group of disciples, preserving them, and bringing them to appropriate belief in preparation for their being sent into the world. In interceding for their mission, Jesus states that he has made God's name known to them (17:6), given them the words God gave him so that they have believed that God sent him (17:8, 14), protected them in God's name that has been given to him, and guarded them (17:12). Because he has completed this task, Jesus can tell his Father, anticipating the formulation of his later actual commissioning of the disciples, 'As you have sent me into the world, so I have sent them into the world' (17:18).

This is not the first time that Jesus, as the one who has been sent, speaks of his sending others. As early in the narrative as his encounter with the Samaritan woman Jesus employs the image of harvesting to depict his own mission. Harvesting was a figure of eschatological consummation with its elements of blessing or judgement (cf. e.g. Amos 9:13–15; Isa. 41:14–16; Hos. 6:11–7:1; Joel 3:13; Mic. 4:12, 13). Jesus tells his disciples that they too have their part to play in the harvesting that has already been inaugurated: 'I sent you to reap that for which you did not labour' (4:38). Later, in order to emphasize that his washing of the disciples' feet is a model for them to follow, Jesus tells them that the one who is sent is not greater than the one who sent him (13:16) and that whoever receives anyone he sends receives him and whoever receives him receives the one who sent him (13:20). Again the links in the chain of the divine mission are apparent. Disciples are sent as the authorized agents of Jesus, representing Jesus and all that he stands for, just as Jesus fully and uniquely represents the Father who sent him.

The epilogue of GJ, usually held to be an addition to the main narrative by its final editor, is in continuity with the preceding ecclesiological vision, confirming the centrality of mission for understanding the believing community's role. Its account of the miraculous catch of fish (21:1–14) points beyond itself to the disciples' mission, as readers are reminded both of the synoptic call narratives, in which Jesus talks of making the disciples those who fish for people (cf. Mark 1:17; Matt. 4:19; Luke 5:10), and of fishing as a metaphor, like harvesting, for God's eschatological judgement (cf. e.g. Jer. 16:16; Ezek. 29:4, 5). The number of the fish (153) in all probability signifies completeness, and dependence on the risen Christ and his word is shown to be necessary for the disciples' mission to be fruitful in harvesting the full amount of fish.

In order to appreciate what continuation of God's mission to the world through Jesus involves, something more needs to be said about the nature and scope of that mission. The various descriptions of Jesus' mission are linked by their juridical connotations to an overall metaphor in which, through Jesus, God is judging the world or putting it on trial (Lincoln 2000). In Jewish scriptural thought, of course, judgement is not primarily a negative concept. For God to act as judge was to establish justice and restore well-being and therefore frequently also involved rescue of Israel from its plight. Similarly in GJ the process of divine judgement is primarily a salvific one. Jesus acts as witness and judge in a trial where the issues at stake are the divine identity or name and the divine glory or reputation, now inseparable from the identity and glory of Jesus, and where the outcome is either eternal life or condemnation. The intended verdict is the positive one of life whereby God's action in Jesus' life and death establishes his glory, deals with the world's plight of death through alienation, and restores conditions of well-being. To experience this positive saving verdict rather than condemnation humans need to respond appropriately to Jesus. A summary of the mission of this loving God is found also in JE (Johannine Epistles) where God's purpose in sending the Son into the world is for him to be the world's Saviour and the atoning sacrifice for sin, 'so that we might live through him' (1 Jn 4:9, 10, 14).

In line with the narrative's overarching juridical metaphor and in continuity with one of the main aspects of Jesus' role, followers of Jesus participate in the divine mission primarily as witnesses to the salvific verdict in the cosmic lawsuit and to the identity of the one through whom it is accomplished. This is made explicit when Jesus states, 'You also are to testify because you have been with me from the beginning' (15:27). The vantage point of Jesus' first followers, being able to supply first-hand knowledge of Jesus' mission as a whole, is foundational for the witness of future followers to the significance of that mission. But the believing community is not alone in its task. In fulfilment of the Deuteronomic injunction about the validity of two witnesses (8:17, cf. Deut. 17:6), they are accompanied by a third divine agent, the Spirit, who is sent from the Father, just as Jesus has been sent, and who will, after Jesus' departure, testify on his behalf (15:26; cf. also 1 Jn 5:6). The Spirit is designated here as the Paraclete (*paraklētos*; cf. also 14:16, 26; 16:7). The term could have a broad meaning of a mediator in a patron–client relationship but in a forensic context this mediating function becomes one of advocacy. The term had become a loan word in Hebrew and Aramaic with this particular force, referring to a person of influence who could be called into court to speak on behalf of defendants. Jesus had called the Spirit 'another Advocate', underlining that his own mission involved advocating both God's and his own cause and that the Spirit would be his successor in such a role (14:16). Like that of Jesus, the Spirit's advocacy includes both witnessing and prosecuting, as he presses home the divine verdict, convicting the world about the issues in the trial and exposing the false values operative as its criteria for judgement (16:7–11). The witness of the Spirit and that of Jesus' followers are not, however, simply distinct roles. The former takes place primarily in and through the latter, since at their commissioning the disciples receive the Spirit (20:22) and have been told that this Advocate has been sent to them and will be in them (14:17; 15:26; 16:7). In the continuation of the divine mission, the community's witness to Jesus as Messiah and Son of God and to the salvific judgement accomplished in him depends for its impetus, sustainability, and effectiveness on the presence of the divine Spirit.

The Identity of the Community

Believers

In a number of places so far, those involved in the continuation of the divine mission have already been described in passing as the believing community. It would be a mistake, however, to take the latter phrase casually. GJ's ancient biographical narrative explicitly calls for belief in the subject whose life it relates (20:31). Correspondingly, the key term that serves as its functional equivalent to 'church' is 'believers' (Trebilco 2012: 114–17). The verb 'to believe' occurs ninety-eight times in GJ and in twenty-one of those occurrences its participial form serves as a substantive, as Jesus talks of 'the one(s) who believe(s) in me'. In JE the verb is found nine times, while the participial form as a substantive accounts for five of these. In the Johannine writings as a whole, the participial form occurs in the singular nineteen times and in the plural seven times. In the former case it is preceded on six occasions by *pas*, 'everyone'. These statistics reflect that, though believing is mediated through others and brings a person into a relationship with others who believe, it is an act primarily exercised by individuals. The participle is employed by itself or absolutely in four of its twenty-six uses, but mostly occurs with the preposition 'in/into' (*eis*) and an object, which is in nearly every instance, Jesus. Those for whom this Gospel was seen as authoritative and who comprised the groups to whom the letters were sent could be expected to identify themselves as faith communities. But while such parlance has become common to designate adherents of any religion and to treat belief as a characteristic that they have in common, the Johannine literature is unmistakably clear that belief always has a specific object and that believers' identity is dependent not on some generic ability to believe but on their faith's particular object, Jesus as the Messiah and Son of God. Though there are occasional blurrings of the sharp distinction, Jesus' mission produces either belief or unbelief. Clearly, it is those who have believed who constitute the new community. So, for example, as early as the prologue, the group within Israel who receive the Logos are designated as 'those who believe in his name' (1:12). After the first sign at Cana the disciples are said to have believed in him (2:11). When asked by the Galilean crowd what to do to perform the works of God, Jesus replies, 'This is the work of God, that you believe in him whom he has sent' (6:28, 29). The message in Jerusalem is similar, 'You will die in your sins, unless you believe that I Am' (8:24). The ones for whom Jesus prays in their task of mission are those who 'have believed that you sent me' (17:8) and 'those who will believe in me through their word', and the goal of their unity and their relation to God and Jesus is 'that the world may believe that you have sent me' (17:20, 21), a vision in which the believing community extends to include those at present alienated from God and Jesus.

Witness or testimony plays a crucial role both for those who have come to believe and for those who will believe. To believe is to receive or accept such testimony. Whether it is the witness of John, the baptizer (1:6, 32–4), leading to his disciples following Jesus, of the Samaritan woman, leading to the belief of those from her city (4:39), or of the Beloved Disciple, leading to the potential belief of readers (19:35; 20:31; 21:24), testimony to Jesus is that which on the human level underlies the faith of the community. This is made clear in the post-resurrection appearance to Thomas, who is exhorted by Jesus not to be disbelieving. His problem is not the wish to see and touch the risen Jesus but the setting of his own conditions for believing by his adamant prior refusal to accept the testimony of the other disciples. The incident leads into the saying, 'Blessed are those who have not seen and yet have believed', indicating that future followers will need to believe on the basis of earlier testimony, particularly that of the Beloved Disciple, which is incorporated in this Gospel's narrative (20:25, 27, 29).

There are also a number of terms that function as metaphorical equivalents of 'to believe', such as 'to come', 'to see', 'to eat', and 'to drink'. All indicate that believing involves a personal relationship of entrusting oneself to Jesus in reliance on who he is and what he does. At the same time such believing clearly involves commitment to propositions about his identity and mission, such as believing that he is the Christ, the Son of Man, the Son of God, the one who bears the divine name, 'I Am', or that he takes away the sin of the world and has given his flesh for the life of the world.

The identity of the believing community needs to be maintained and readers are made aware that not all who claim to believe are authentic believers, that genuine belief requires remaining in Jesus' teaching and will involve growth in knowledge and understanding, and that lapses in discipleship need not be obstacles to continuing in belief. JE underline the necessity of the believing community abiding in the truth in their talk of those who seceded from the community because they did not confess that Jesus is the Christ who has come in the flesh, thereby revealing that they never really belonged and showing themselves to be antichrists (1 Jn 2:18–24; 4:2, 3; 2 Jn 7–11).

In the Johannine vision the belief exercised by the community is not simply self-generated. It entails both a positive human decision-making and God bringing this about for those who have previously been alienated in the death and slavery of sin. Divine election and human responsibility both operate fully without one detracting from the other. The Father draws those who come to Jesus and gives them to him (6:36, 37, 44, 65), and his disciples have not chosen him but he has chosen them (15:16).

FAMILY

In terms of community identity this emphasis on God's role leads to characterizing believers through familial imagery (van der Watt 2000). The prologue indicates that, in believing, humans are given authority to become children of God and emphasizes that this results from birth by God, which has nothing to do with ordinary human procreation, thus distinguishing it from defining God's family ethnically (1:12, 13; cf. also 1 Jn 5:1). This birth into God's family is elaborated in the discourse with Nicodemus in terms of being born from above or being born of water and the Spirit and again distinguished from birth within the natural human order, 'the flesh' (3:3–6). The legitimacy of the claim to be children of God is debated in 8:41–7, where Jesus insists that those who genuinely have God as their Father will love him because he came from God. The designation 'children of God' for those who share such an origin is employed again in 11:52 and the diminutive form, 'little children', occurs in 13:33. 'Children' for members of the community is employed more frequently in JE: 'See what love the Father has given us, that we should be called the children of God, and that is what we are' (1 Jn 3:1; cf. also 3:2, 10; 5:2), as is the diminutive 'little children' (1 Jn 2:1, 12, 28; 3:7, 18; 4:4; 5:21).

The corollary of being children who have God as Father is that other believers are seen as brothers and sisters in this family. It is significant that the narrator can describe the community for whom the Beloved Disciple is an authoritative figure as 'the brothers and sisters' (*adelphoi*—21:23). This usage proliferates in JE, where the term is found sixteen times (ten times in the singular and six times in the plural) as the designation for a member of the community (Trebilco 2012: 62–4). Nearly all the references are to members of one's own local community, as is indicated, for example, by 1 Jn 3:10, 11, in which loving one's brothers and sisters is in parallel to loving one another, that is, others within one's community. The referent is extended somewhat in 3 Jn 5, where itinerant visiting believers are brothers and sisters because they belong to a broader group of house churches that share the same faith, even though they are unknown in a particular local assembly.

Two further features of the family relationship are worth noting. First, the incident at the cross, in which Jesus announces a new son–mother relationship for the Beloved Disciple and Jesus' mother (19:26, 27) can be seen both as the completion of Jesus' mission of ensuring a group of followers and as inaugurating them as the new family (cf. 'from that hour'). The Beloved Disciple is to be Jesus' human successor and Jesus hands over his mother, representing those who are receptive to the salvation he brings (cf. 2:3–5), to the former's care, that is, to the witness to revelation he provides. Secondly, the risen Jesus is depicted as part of the new family, as he talks of the disciples as his brothers but does so in a way that also maintains a distinction between himself and them—'my Father and your Father' (20:17). The combination of his unique relation to the Father and his solidarity with his brothers and sisters makes available for believers a participation in the intimacy between the divine Father and Son.

The People of God Reconfigured Christologically

The believing community is also depicted in terms that reconfigure portrayals of the people of God in the Jewish Scriptures. The notion of Israel or Israelites having God as Father and therefore being God's children or sons and daughters is itself one that is present in Scripture (cf. e.g. Exod. 4:22; Deut. 14:1; Isa. 1:2, 4; Jer. 31:9; Hos. 1:10; 11:10) and that is now given a new twist in relation to believers in Christ. Similarly, the imagery of God as bridegroom and God's people as bride is taken up with Christ exercising God's role and believers in him, represented by various female characters, as the new bride (cf. esp. McWhirter 2006).

There are, however, two major scriptural images for the corporate people of God that are elaborated more extensively in GJ. In a number of places the nation without effective leadership is pictured as 'sheep without a shepherd' (e.g. Num. 27:12–23; 1 Kgs 22:17). While God is Israel's ultimate shepherd (e.g. Gen. 48:15; Ps. 23:1; 74:1; 95:7; Isa. 40:11; Jer. 23:1–4), a variety of leaders can be depicted as shepherds and in particular David serves as the model for the future messianic shepherd-king (Ezek. 37:24; Mic. 5:2–4). One extended passage, Ezekiel 34, brings these themes together, as it talks of the judgement of unfaithful shepherds, of God as shepherd rescuing, feeding, caring for, and judging between the sheep, and of God appointing one shepherd, a Davidic king, who will provide peace, security, and abundance for God's sheep. In GJ's creative reconfiguring of such notions in 10:1–18 Jesus is the fulfilment of expectations both about Israel's faithful leaders, especially the promised Davidic king, and about God as the divine shepherd, and the sheep are now those who listen to Jesus, gain access to the sheepfold through him, and in doing so find pasture, salvation, and abundant life

(10:7–10). These benefits are made possible because what identifies Jesus as the good or noble shepherd is that, quite distinctively, he lays down his life for the sake of the sheep (10:11, 15). What identifies the members of this shepherd's flock is that they are known and called by him, recognize and hear his voice, and follow him (10:3–5, 14–16, 26, 27). The mutual knowledge meant to characterize the relation between God and Israel is to be found in the recognition and love between Jesus and his own, which is grounded in and modelled on the relationship between Jesus and the Father. Promises that Israel will again be one nation under one future Davidic shepherd-king (Ezek. 34:23; 37:22, 24) are seen to be fulfilled in the coming into being of one flock and one shepherd (10:16). Those who belong to this one flock also have the assurance that their shepherd will not allow them to perish or be snatched from his or the Father's hand (10:28, 29).

The second major corporate image for believers is that of branches rooted in the true vine, Jesus (15:1–11). The extent to which this is a corporate image might be questioned, since the emphasis is on the relationship of the individual branches to the vine rather than to each other. Nevertheless, in the imagery Jesus himself is here the corporate representative of the people of God, fulfilling the role of Israel, the vine that God had planted (cf. Ps. 80:8–18; Jer. 2:21; 6:9; 8:13; Hos. 10:1), and so believers exist as part of the new community centred in him. The main scriptural background for Jesus' discourse on the vine, however, is the cluster of passages in Ezek. 15:1–8; 17:1–10; and 19:10–14, where, as here, there is talk of the vine bearing fruit, a distinction between the vine and its branches, and mention of branches that are good for nothing, that wither, and that are thrown into the fire to be burned. In the new community God remains the owner of the vineyard, the vine-grower (15:1) who will either prune and cleanse branches to enable fruit-bearing or cut away and burn branches that fail to be fruitful (15:2, 3, 6). In this reminder that initial faith is not enough, the key requirement is to abide or remain in Jesus (15:4–7). The figure of the vine and the branches enables Jesus, in a narrative setting of preparation for his departure, to talk not of his separation from believers but of continued connection and union. Staying connected to Jesus means remaining in his love and keeping his commandments to love others (15:9, 10, 12, 17). Here a further corporate aspect of the imagery comes into play, as the fruit-bearing that results from remaining in the vine entails believers' love for one another. Not surprisingly, given the connotations of the fruit of the vine as the wine of gladness (cf. e.g. Ps. 104:15; Eccl. 10:19; Jer. 48:33), the lives of those who remain in Jesus will also be characterized by joy (15:11).

There can be little doubt that GJ extensively reworks images and, more broadly, themes such as election, mutual knowledge, love, obeying commandments, and abiding that were used in the Jewish Scriptures to characterize the covenantal relationship between God and God's people. Yet the absence of the term 'covenant' may suggest that caution is needed in relation to the claims of some scholars (e.g. Malatesta 1978, Chennattu 2006) that the Johannine writings make the concept of covenant as such a major concern or that believers in Jesus can in an unqualified fashion simply be seen as the new covenant community.

DISCIPLES

In the discourse on the vine fruit-bearing is linked to the notion of becoming Jesus' disciples (15:8). The term 'disciple' (*mathētēs*) is used seventy-eight times in this Gospel (cf. Matt. 73 times; Mark 46 times; Luke 37 times). The existence of the twelve as a core inner group of disciples is assumed but this group is mentioned explicitly only twice (6:67; 20:24) and there is no list of their names. Some of the individuals who encounter Jesus are disciples who have names that would have been familiar from the synoptic tradition, such as Peter, Andrew, and Philip, and they, as well as other characters in the narrative, have representative features that allow believing readers to identify with them or treat them as positive or negative models (cf. Bennema 2009; Farelly 2010; Skinner 2013; Hunt 2013). Usually, however, when 'the disciples' are mentioned, they constitute a larger indeterminate group whose depiction, especially their uneven growth in faith and knowledge, frequently enables the later believing community to see itself as addressed by their situation.

Disciples, of course, followed and were instructed by a rabbi or teacher and this is how they address Jesus (1:38, 49; 4:31). The identity of a group is marked by the one whom it follows, as becomes clear when the designation 'disciple' is employed in the contrast between those Jews who believe in Jesus and those who reject their claims. The man born blind who now sees because of Jesus' healing power is told, 'You are his disciple, but we are disciples of Moses' (9:28). From GJ's perspective the religious authorities, in line with their decision about excommunication (9:22), are forcing an unnecessary choice between these two identities. One need not exclude the other. Once Torah is read in the light of God's present speaking in Jesus, disciples of Moses should also be disciples of Jesus, because in Jesus' own words, 'If you believed Moses, you would believe me, for he wrote about me' (5:46).

Jesus' disciples are not only followers of a teacher but also servants of a master (cf. 13:13). Yet this servant–master relationship also includes friendship (15:14). Disciples' obedience has a new level of intimacy because they are made privy to Jesus' own relationship with the Father: 'I have called you friends, because I have made known to you everything that I have heard from my Father' (15:15). In the JE 'the friends' has become one of the ways in which believers can talk about each other (cf. 3 Jn 15).

The account of Jesus washing the disciples' feet illustrates graphically that 'servants are not greater than their masters' and that disciples need to follow Jesus' example of self-giving (cf. esp. 13:14–17). His stripping down to the garb of a slave in order to carry out the act anticipates the laying down of his life in death and the act itself exemplifies the reversal of traditional values of honour and shame. Acceptance of Jesus' alternative set of values is necessary for those who wish to maintain solidarity with Jesus in his mission (13:8) and appropriation of those values takes place in disciples' washing one another's feet, demonstrating the humble service that also includes a readiness to give one's life for others (cf. 15:13).

The metaphors attached to discipleship include, paradoxically, not only being on the move by following Jesus but also staying put by abiding with or, even more intimately, in him. 'To abide' or 'to remain' (*menein*) is another distinctive term in the Johannine writings (40 times in GJ, 27 times in JE in comparison with 45 times in the rest of the NT) for disciples' relationship with Jesus and, through him, with God. The qualities of permanence and rootedness in this relationship are of particular concern in the Johannine vision (cf. e.g. 6:56; 8:31). As has been noted, in the discourse about the vine the necessity of abiding in Jesus, just as branches need to remain in the vine to be fruitful, is a dominant emphasis (15:4–7, 9, 10). In JE also there are exhortations to abide (cf. 1 Jn 2:27, 28), but because this way of viewing one's identity as a believer appears to have become common (e.g. 1 Jn 2:6—'whoever says, "I abide in him"'), the claim needs to be tested both ethically and Christologically. Genuine abiding in Jesus will be characterized by living as Jesus lived, by not sinning, by keeping Jesus' commandments and, in doing so, by loving one's brothers and sisters (cf. e.g. 1 Jn 2:6; 3:6, 23, 24). Those who truly abide in Jesus will have abiding in them the message about Jesus as the Christ and Son of God that they have heard from the beginning and that is taught by his 'anointing'—most probably a reference to the gift of the Spirit in initiation (cf. 1 Jn 2:24, 27; 4:13–15). For believers, then, to abide in Jesus is to inhabit continually the sphere of influence that the person of Jesus represents in his relation of love to God and humanity.

CHARACTERISTICS
OF THE COMMUNITY'S LIFE

Experience of the Spirit

The disciples' abiding in Jesus is one side of a mutual relationship with God and Christ who in turn abide in believers or the community through the Spirit. Again, the discourse about the vine has both sides of the relationship in view: 'those who abide in me and I in them bear much fruit' (15:4, 5, 7). Believers' experience of Jesus being in them is illuminated in the preceding teaching. Jesus' future physical absence will in fact be advantageous to the disciples because, in a relationship of love, both the Father and Jesus will come to them and make their home (*monē*) with them (14:23). The other advantage of the period of Jesus' physical absence—the giving of the Advocate—clarifies the nature of this divine indwelling: 'the Spirit of truth . . . abides with you, and he will be in you' (14:17). The Spirit is the mediator of the presence of Jesus and God to believers and the 'you' here is plural, allowing that the Spirit is not only in individuals but also among believers as a group. This perspective is reiterated in JE where it is the gift of the Spirit that provides the knowledge that Christ abides in believers (cf. 1 Jn 3:24; 4:13). If earlier in GJ's narrative the incarnate Logos, Jesus, was the location of God's presence as the new temple, in the period after Jesus' departure the believing community becomes the location of God's and Jesus' presence as the temple of God in the Spirit.

The Spirit not only enables the experience of the presence of Jesus in the community but also mediates between the past, present, and future of Jesus' cause. The Spirit 'will teach you everything and remind you of all that I have said to you' (14:26), 'will guide you into all the truth', 'will declare to you the things that are to come', and 'will glorify me because he will take what is mine and declare it to you' (16:13, 14). The Spirit's teaching keeps the believing community centred on Jesus and opens up new insights into the significance of his earthly mission, ensuring that it continues to be applicable to his followers' changing circumstances.

Worship, Structures, and Rites

In the Johannine vision worship is no longer attached to particular sacred places. When Jesus says, 'Destroy this temple, and in three days I will raise it up' (2: 19), the narrator makes sure that readers understand that he was speaking of the new temple of his crucified and risen body (2:21, 22). Jesus embodies both the divine presence, whose locus on earth had previously been the Jerusalem temple, and the significance of the festivals that were celebrated in the temple. Implications emerge in Jesus' exchange with the Samaritan woman when he first predicts that the time is coming when people will worship the Father neither on Mt Gerizim nor in Jerusalem and then announces the arrival of that time 'when the true worshippers will worship the Father in spirit and in truth'. Worship in the time of eschatological fulfilment has as its focus the relationship not to a place but to the one who declares himself to be the Messiah and employs the formula of divine self-disclosure, 'I Am' (4:21–6). Worship in Spirit and in truth therefore has in view the divine Spirit (cf. 4:24a: 'God is Spirit'), who makes such worship possible, and the truth, revealed in Jesus' person and mission by the Spirit of truth, namely, that God is known in him and that he is one with God.

This perspective affects praying. In GJ no instruction about prayer is given to the disciples during Jesus' public mission. Instead what is said about prayer is clustered in the farewell discourse section—two sayings in each of its three main units (14:13–14; 15:7–8, 16b; 16:23–4, 26–7)—underlining that this is an activity that will be especially important for disciples in the physical absence of Jesus. In these sayings there is a relentless focus on Jesus' promise that whatever they ask in his name they will receive. The repeated phrase 'in my name' indicates both that believers can pray to God as Father because Jesus as Son has already mediated this relationship and that such praying is an activity carried out by the disciples as the authorized representatives of Jesus. The farewell discourses are structured in such a way that, having been told about their need to pray in Jesus' name, the disciples are then given a model for such prayer in Jesus' own prayer that follows (17:1–26). He enacts what is entailed in the confident asking of the Father that the disciples have been told will be their privilege after his glorification (cf. also 1 Jn 5:14, 15). It can now be seen that 'whatever you ask' in the promises in effect means whatever is requested in line with Jesus' prayer, because this represents his name, what he stands for, and what his mission in the world entails. The topics of his prayer—concern for the Father's name to be glorified, believers being kept in that name, their protection from the evil one, their being set apart in the truth, their mission of love and unity in relation to the world—become those of believers' prayers.

In the Johannine vision very little is communicated about how the believing community is meant to be structured or what rites it is meant to practise. The lack of emphasis on such matters has led some scholars to speculate that the actual communities associated with the writings were radically egalitarian and non-hierarchical or that they were anti-sacramental. Staying with the world projected in the texts, however, permits only more cautious and general observations about these aspects of their ecclesiological vision. The commissioning of the original group of disciples, who are representatives of future believers, includes the authority to forgive and retain sins (20:23). This appears to be a reference to what will occur as part of their missionary proclamation rather than to an office or function exercised by leaders in relation to other believers. If it is thought that post-baptismal sins should not be excluded from this reference, then it is significant that praying about such sins is an activity to which all believers are exhorted (1 Jn 5:16, 17). From within the original group of disciples Peter and the Beloved Disciple are singled out for special roles that carry authority. The two appear together in a number of episodes, in which it is possible to detect a certain tension between their roles, particularly since the Beloved Disciple is consistently the one who has the privileged information or prior insight. Again, however, it would be speculative to read the narrative as illustrating a major rivalry between the Johannine community, represented by the Beloved Disciple, and the broader apostolic church, represented by Peter. In the epilogue of John 21, while the Beloved Disciple again communicates his prior recognition of the risen Jesus to Peter (21:7), their two roles are seen as complementary. Peter is commissioned to be an under-shepherd in Jesus' flock who will care for his sheep and die a martyr's death (21:15–19) and the Beloved Disciple is the one whose witness in its written form guarantees the truth of this Gospel and ensures its continuing authoritative role in the believing community (21:24). In the JE leadership is exercised by the elder who cares for and exercises authority in more than one church (2 Jn 13) and other leaders are mentioned, including Diotrephes who appears to be abusing that role (3 Jn 9, 10). In JE, though local churches can be personified as female (cf. 'the elect lady' and her 'elect sister' in 2 Jn 1, 13), we learn nothing about women's actual roles within them. They do, however, play a prominent role in GJ's narrative. The mother of Jesus, the Samaritan woman, Mary and Martha, and Mary Magdalene can be depicted in similar ways to male characters in terms of misunderstanding, believing, and making confessions of faith. Mary Magdalene's commission to tell the disciples of the ascent of the risen Jesus enables her to be seen as 'an apostle to the apostles' (Brown 1979: 170), the encounter with the Samaritan woman demonstrates that Jesus' mission was seen as cutting across both gender and ethnic divisions, and women are treated as full members of the believing community and participants in its mission of witness alongside men. Whether or not there was actually a further subversion of patriarchal culture with women exercising leadership and authority in the Johannine churches, the ecclesiological vision of GJ contains that potential.

It is similarly difficult to discover how prominent a place the sacraments are meant to have in the community's life. As is well known, Jesus' last meal with the disciples is not designated a Passover meal in GJ and there are no words of institution over bread and wine. Instead Jesus' washing of the disciples' feet becomes the central feature of the meal and three times Jesus indicates that the disciples are to do for one another what he has just done for them (13:14, 15, 17). In the light of this stress it would be strange if actual foot-washing were not part of the vision for churches' practice. There is no warrant, however, for deducing from the account that such a rite was meant to replace the Eucharist or Lord's Supper. Instead GJ apparently presupposes the Eucharist and gives it a distinctive interpretation. As the discourse on the bread of life moves from Jesus' assertion that he, as the one who descended from heaven, is the source of life for those who believe to the accompanying assertion that the bread that he gives for the life of the world is his flesh, the language employed for believing this claim also becomes more graphic. The talk is now of the necessity of eating Jesus' flesh and drinking his blood (6:51–8), indicating belief in an incarnate Christ who gives up his life in a violent death. It is hard to escape the conclusions that the words of institution from 1 Cor. 11:23–6 and the synoptic accounts (particularly Matt. 26:26–8 with its explicit commands to eat and drink) have influenced this formulation, that acceptance of Eucharistic practice and language on the part of readers is assumed, and that, in line with its incarnational language of the Logos becoming flesh (cf. 1:14), 'body' now becomes 'flesh' in GJ's version.

There is no post-resurrection commission for Jesus' disciples to baptize in his name in GJ and no mention of this rite in JE, but the Gospel is unique in depicting Jesus and/or the disciples baptizing during his mission (cf. 3:22, 26 with 4:1, 2). Rather than this being seen as simply carrying on John's baptism and its significance, it may be intended to show that Christian initiation was not an innovation but had its antecedent in Jesus' own mission. In addition, it would be surprising if the language of 'born of water' (3:5), which occurs just prior to the references to baptizing, was not meant to recall this initiatory rite, although the emphasis in the dialogue with Nicodemus is clearly on the Spirit's agency in the birth that provides access to the kingdom of God. In the Johannine vision the background function of baptism and the Eucharist need not mean that these sacraments are deliberately being downplayed but rather that their practice is taken for granted and their significance in relation to the Spirit and to faith is being highlighted.

Life, Love, and Unity

Salvation is designated as the gift of eternal life (*zōē aiōnios*) and so the experience of this life is central for members of the believing community. They have been put back in relationship with the source of life through Jesus who embodies life and are able to enjoy the life of the ages in the present ahead of the end-times. Not surprisingly, it is the Spirit who is the agent of this present enjoyment. When Jesus, taking up temple imagery (cf.

Ezek. 47:1–12; Zech. 14:8), talks about living water flowing out from himself, the narrator then adds, 'Now he said this about the Spirit, which believers in him were to receive, for as yet there was no Spirit, because Jesus was not yet glorified' (7:37–9). Just as in the creation account God breathed life into humans, after his glorification Jesus breathes into his followers the new life of the Spirit, equipping them for their mission as witnesses to this life (20:22).

Earlier in the narrative Jesus' prayer asserted, 'This is eternal life that they may know you, the only true God, and Jesus Christ whom you have sent' (17:3), and this knowledge of God and Christ that is at the heart of eternal life affects all of human living. Eternal life is not simply the same as present creaturely existence, because such existence is caught up in the cycle of death, but nor is it divorced from created physical life and to be found in some immaterial sphere. Any such notions are subverted by the conviction that the Logos, the source of life, became flesh (cf. 1:3, 4, 14; cf. also 1 Jn 1:1, 2) and by the signs of life that he performed affecting human bodies and the material elements that sustain them. Jesus' claim to be the resurrection and the life (1:25) is dramatically demonstrated in the account of the raising of Lazarus that, in its connection with Jesus' own resurrection, indicates that physical death does not have the last word. 'Those who believe in me, even though they die, will live, and everyone who lives and believes in me will never die' (11:25b, 26). Believers remain a community of life, even in the midst of the anguish and mourning of death, as they are sustained by their present experience of eternal life and their trust in the fulfilment of Jesus' promise of resurrection.

While the emphasis on eternal life dominates the public mission of Jesus, it is noticeable that in the farewell discourse the language of love is to the fore. Eternal life has the quality of love and love is what is to characterize the witnessing community of Jesus' followers. Jesus leaves them with a new commandment that they are to love one another as he has loved them (13:34; 15:12). What is new here is not the command to love itself but its role in the new situation that will be brought about by Jesus' glorification and the distinctive quality of the love displayed in that event: 'as I have loved you' (cf. also 13:1b; 1 Jn 3:16). This is a love that entails giving oneself away generously for the sake of others, even to the point of laying down one's life (15:13), and exhibiting such love is essential for the credibility of the community's continuing witness in the world: 'By this everyone will know that you are my disciples, if you have love for one another' (13: 35). The command focuses on the relationship between members of the believing community, but this need not be thought to be exclusive of or contradictory to love of neighbour or enemy. After all, the love of God and Jesus on whom believers' love is patterned is love for a world of humanity that is hostile to God's purposes, and believers were at one time themselves part of such a world (3:16; cf. 1 Jn 4:9–11). Participation in the divine mission of love to the world requires love for those who are at present outsiders and the quality of love within the community is crucial to a witness intended to draw others into the relationship of love between Father and Son, in which believers already participate. In JE the love commandment is repeatedly invoked. Yet here it is said to be an old commandment, that is, not an innovation in Johannine teaching but part of its gospel proclamation from the beginning (1 Jn 2:7; 3:11; 2 Jn 5, 6). Nevertheless, it can also be said to be new because it has now been made real and become operative within the community (1 Jn 2:8). Indeed, talk of love is not enough; it has to be real and to be displayed in such practices as giving of one's possessions to those who are in need (1 Jn 3:17, 18). Over against the secessionists, who appear to have thought that it was enough to declare their love for God and saw no ethical implications in such an avowal, there is an insistence that, because God is love and those who abide in God abide in love, those who do not love the brothers and sisters whom they see cannot possibly love the God whom they have not seen (1 Jn 4:7–21).

A community characterized by love, concerned for the diversity of its members and their needs, will also be a united one. The good shepherd discourse, while mentioning other sheep not of this fold that will be drawn into the flock (probably a reference to Gentile believers), is clear that all will be one flock under one shepherd (10:16). Three times in his farewell prayer Jesus petitions for the unity of the believing community (17:11, 21, 23). This unity is crucial to its witness to the identity of Jesus, the issue that has been at stake in his mission. The oneness of the witnesses is to reflect the oneness of Jesus as the Son with the Father and has as its goal that the world may believe and know 'that you have sent me'. At the same time the relationship between the divine unity and the community's unity is even closer, since the latter actually participates in the former ('As you, Father, are in me and I am in you, may they also be in us'), thereby not simply mirroring but also embodying in its unified witness the oneness of the relationship between the Son and the Father.

Here it is important to emphasize again that what has been described is the Johannine *vision*. There is awareness in GJ of disciples who are offended by Jesus' teaching and who leave his company (6:60–6) and JE confront readers with the reality of a schism that has taken place in the community concerning the appropriate confession of Jesus and its ethical implications (1 Jn 2:18, 19; 4:2, 3; 2 Jn 7–11) and the consequences of this in each of the two resulting groups withholding hospitality from the other (2 Jn 10, 11; 3 Jn 10). From the elder's perspective the onus for the division is on the opponents, who left the church and thereby showed that they had never truly belonged. However, once this has taken place and the schismatics' true colours have been shown, they are no longer to be welcomed. If hospitality is a sign of love, this appears to narrow love to those within what is considered to be the true circle of believers. Jesus' prayer had already indicated that the call to unity was not at the expense of truth and holiness, since he also petitions both that the disciples be kept in God's name that he has given to Jesus, that is, that they be preserved as a community shaped by Jesus' disclosure of who God is, and that they be sanctified in the truth (17:11, 12, 17). Indeed, it is assumed that those for whom Jesus prays for unity are those who have believed the truth about Jesus' identity (17:6–8). What is seen in JE is not only that there is a tension between unity and truth but also that the attempt by fallible followers to maintain and discern the truth about Jesus and the gospel message in changing circumstances can result in fractured communities and relationships. Whether or not John 17 was composed with an awareness of the problems of division, the juxtaposition in the Johannine writings as a whole between, on the one hand, Jesus' prayer and the command to love and, on the other, the schism in the churches, indicates the necessity of keeping paramount the vision

of unity, the difficulties of living it out in the midst of the messy and fragmented circumstances of contested truth and holiness, and the self-sacrificial quality of the love
required to make it a reality.

Witness in the World

One major scholarly debate concerns whether the Johannine community was an isola-
tionist sect, hostile to the surrounding world, concerned only with its own inner life and
employing its own idioms in an 'anti-language' meant to be inaccessible to outsiders (for
various representations of this view, see e.g. Meeks 1972, Malina and Rohrbaugh 1998,
Gundry 2002) or whether each aspect of such a depiction is a flawed evaluation (see
e.g. Fuglseth 2005, Volf 2005, Klink 2010, Lamb 2014). The categories in this important
discussion are, however, somewhat tangential to the focus of this essay on the vision
conveyed in the Johannine writings rather than on actual communities behind the writings. Asking how they envisage the witness of the community in relation to the world
still does not produce a simple answer, not least because the actual term 'world' (*kosmos*)
is employed with a variety of shades of meaning, ranging from the positive (the created
world), through the more neutral (the world of humanity in general), to the negative
(the world of humans who reject God's purposes), to the most negative (the world as
the systematically evil sphere of opposition to God). Different shades of meaning can
be juxtaposed in the same context. In the prologue, for example, the Logos as the light
is in the world that came into being through him and yet the world does not know him
(1:10). In the latter clause the world already begins to shade over from the created world,
including humans (cf.1:3), to the world of humanity that in its failure to respond appropriately reveals its alienation from and hostility to its Creator. The world in which Jesus
and then his followers carry out their missions is not then inherently alien territory.
They are representatives of the God to whom the world belongs by virtue of creation
and who now rightfully subjects it to salvific judgement. Those who reject the claims of
this judgement constitute the world in its negative sense. Jesus' followers do not belong
to the world in this sense but have been chosen or given to him out of it and thus have
become the object of its hatred (15:18–25; 17:6, 9, 14, 16). They are not a community that
is hostile to the rest of the world of humanity, but, like Jesus previously, are on the receiving end of hostility.

When JE tell believers not to love the world, the sense of world is spelled out in terms
of the attractions of an evil system that is passing away: falsely oriented desires and pride
(1 Jn 2:15–17). This is the world 'that lies under the power of the evil one' (1 Jn 5:19). While
not belonging to the world, believers are to remain in it and indeed are sent into it on
their mission of witness (17:11, 15, 18), but will be in need of protection from the evil one,
the personification of the world's evil, who is also portrayed as its ruler (17:15; cf. 12:31;
14:30; 16:11). The rule, to which the community bears witness, that of Jesus' kingship, is
also not of this world and yet operates effectively within it. At his trial before Pilate and
in the midst of a political power struggle between the Roman prefect and the Jewish

religious authorities, Jesus asserts that his kingdom is not from this world but has its source elsewhere: from above, from God (18:36; cf. 8:23). It is a power that will not be co-opted by this world's cycle of violence, since, if it were, his followers would be fighting for him. Instead Peter's wielding the sword in order to resist arrest has already been rebuked (18:10, 11) and Jesus in fact subordinates the whole matter of royal power to that of truth: 'You say that I am a king. For this I was born, and for this I came into the world, to testify to the truth' (18:37). The truth to which Jesus bears witness subverts normal human assumptions about power and confronts both Pilate and the Jewish leaders with a choice between his claims and allegiance to Caesar's rule. The believing community's non-violent witness to this truth embodied in Jesus, who has absorbed the violence of death by crucifixion in order to bring life, will also expose the ultimate values behind the world's hostility and may lead to social ostracism, persecution, and martyrdom (9:34, 35; 16:2; 21:18, 19). Yet from the paradigm of Jesus' death as a witness this community knows that it is through the weakness of self-giving love that the power of God's salvific judgement is at work. For this reason its stance towards the world is to be ultimately positive: 'In the world you face persecution. But take courage; I have conquered the world!' (16:33; cf. 1 Jn 5:4, 5). This ringing announcement that Jesus has already decisively reclaimed the world that was rightfully his gives his followers confidence about the final outcome of their own mission of witness to the one who 'is truly the Saviour of the world' (4:42).

Conclusion

The Johannine vision of the church is of a community whose existence is shaped by God, Christ, and the Spirit. It is caught up in God's mission of providing life for the world. Within the context of the divine mission its *raison d'être* is to bear witness to Jesus in whom this life is embodied and through whose own mission, death, and resurrection it is restored for humanity. This witness is accompanied and empowered by the Spirit who mediates eternal life and the presence of God and Christ to the community and draws out the truth of God's verdict in Christ for the community's changing circumstances in the world. The church of the Johannine writings is a community identified by its believing in Jesus as the sort of Messiah who is the Son of God and the Logos become flesh, by its discipleship of following him and remaining in him, and by the solidarity of its family relationships. Its present experience of eternal life constitutes an embodied witness of love, service, and unity. By bearing this witness the believing community both confronts this world's values by pointing to glory or honour displayed in humiliation, the power of truth effected through weakness, and life brought about through death and provides a bridgehead for God's continuing saving judgement of the world. In its place within the church's canon, the Johannine vision draws believing readers and their communities into a transformative engagement requiring critical appropriation and the ongoing guidance of the Spirit in discerning how what was seen and heard from the beginning can come to new expression in different times and under changed cultural settings.

References

Bennema, Cornelis (2009). *Encountering Jesus: Character Studies in the Gospel of John*. Milton Keynes: Paternoster.

Bieringer, Reimund, Pollefeyt, Didier, and Vandecasteele-Vanneuville, Frederique (eds) (2001). *Anti-Judaism and the Fourth Gospel: Papers of the Leuven Colloquium, 2000*. Assen: Royal van Gorcum.

Brown, Raymond E. (1979). *The Community of the Beloved Disciple: The Life, Loves, and Hates of a New Testament Church in New Testament Times*. New York: Paulist.

Chennattu, Rekha M. (2006). *Johannine Discipleship as a Covenant Relationship*. Peabody, MA: Hendrickson.

Farelly, Nicolas (2010). *The Disciples in the Fourth Gospel: A Narrative Analysis of their Faith and Understanding*. Tübingen: Mohr Siebeck.

Fuglseth, Kåre S. (2005). *Johannine Sectarianism in Perspective: A Sociological, Historical, and Comparative Analysis of Temple and Social Relationships in the Gospel of John, Philo, and Qumran*. Leiden: E. J. Brill.

Gundry, Robert M. (2002). *Jesus the Word according to John the Sectarian*. Grand Rapids, MI: Eerdmans.

Hunt, Steven A., Tolmie, D. Francois, and Zimmermann, Ruben (eds) (2013). *Character Studies in the Fourth Gospel: Narrative Approaches to Seventy Figures in John*. Tübingen: Mohr Siebeck.

Kierspel, Lars (2006). *The Jews and the World in the Gospel of John: Parallelism, Function, and Context*. Tübingen: Mohr Siebeck.

Klink, Edward W. III (2010). *The Sheep of the Fold: The Audience and Origin of the Gospel of John*. Cambridge: Cambridge University Press.

Lamb, David (2014). *Text, Context and the Johannine Community*. London: Bloomsbury/T&T Clark.

Lincoln, Andrew T. (2000). *Truth on Trial: The Lawsuit Motif in the Gospel of John*. Grand Rapids, MI: Baker Academic.

Malatesta, Edward (1978). *Interiority and Covenant: A Study of 'einai en' and 'menein en' in the First Letter of St. John*. Rome: Biblical Institute Press.

Malina, Bruce J. and Rohrbaugh, Richard L. (1998). *Social-Science Commentary on the Gospel of John*. Minneapolis: Fortress.

McWhirter, Jocelyn (2006). *The Bridegroom Messiah and the People of God: Marriage in the Gospel of John*. Cambridge: Cambridge University Press.

Meeks, Wayne A. (1972). 'The Man from Heaven in Johannine Sectarianism'. *Journal of Biblical Literature* 91: 44–72.

Skinner, Christopher W. (ed.) (2013). *Characters and Characterization in the Gospel of John*. London: Bloomsbury/ T&T Clark.

Trebilco, Paul R. (2012). *Self-Designations and Group Identity in the New Testament*. Cambridge: Cambridge University Press.

Van der Watt, Jan G. (2000). *Family of the King: Dynamics of Metaphor in the Gospel according to John*. Leiden: Brill.

Volf, Miroslav (2008). 'Johannine Dualism and Contemporary Pluralism'. In Richard Bauckham and Carl Mosser (eds), *The Gospel of John and Christian Theology*. Grand Rapids, MI: Eerdmans, 19–50.

SUGGESTED READING

Barton, Stephen C. (2000). 'Christian Community in the Light of the Gospel of John'. In David G. Horrell and Christopher M. Tuckett (eds), *Christology, Controversy and Community: New Testament Essays in Honour of David R. Catchpole*. Leiden: E. J. Brill, 279–301.

Black, C. Clifton (1990). 'Christian Ministry in Johannine Perspective'. *Interpretation* 44: 29–41.

Burge, Gary M. (1987). *The Anointed Community: The Holy Spirit in the Johannine Tradition*. Grand Rapids, MI: Eerdmans.

Byers, Andrew J. (2017). *Ecclesiology and Theosis in the Gospel of John*. Cambridge: Cambridge University Press.

Culpepper, R. Alan (2009). 'The Quest for the Church in the Gospel of John'. *Interpretation* 63: 341–54.

Dahl, Nils A. (1962). 'The Johannine Church and History'. In William Klassen and Graydon F. Snyder (eds), *Current Issues in New Testament Interpretation: Essays in Honor of Otto Piper*. New York: Harper and Row, 124–42.

Ferreira, Johan (1998). *Johannine Ecclesiology*. Sheffield: Sheffield Academic Press.

Hengel, Martin (1995). 'The Kingdom of Christ in John'. In Martin Hengel, *Studies in Early Christology*. Edinburgh: T&T Clark, 333–57.

Koester, Craig R. (2008). *The Word of Life: A Theology of John's Gospel*. Grand Rapids, MI: Eerdmans, 187–214.

Köstenberger, Andreas J. (2009). *A Theology of John's Gospel and Letters*. Grand Rapids, MI: Zondervan, 457–508.

Lincoln, Andrew T. (2000). *Truth on Trial: The Lawsuit Motif in the Gospel of John*. Grand Rapids, MI: Baker Academic.

Moloney, Francis J. (2013). *Love in the Gospel of John: An Exegetical, Theological, and Literary Study*. Grand Rapids, MI: Baker Academic.

Rensberger, David (1988). *Johannine Faith and Liberating Community*. Philadelphia: Westminster.

Schnelle, Udo (1991). 'Johanneische Ekklesiologie'. *New Testament Studies* 37: 37–50.

Van der Watt, Jan G. (2000). *Family of the King: Dynamics of Metaphor in the Gospel according to John*. Leiden: Brill.

CHAPTER 5

THE SHAPE OF
THE PAULINE CHURCHES

EDWARD ADAMS

THE Pauline epistles constitute the primary biblical source of constructive ecclesiology. A treatment of ecclesiologically relevant data in the Pauline writings is thus a sine qua non of the kind of project embodied in the present volume. This chapter discusses what the Pauline letters reveal about the shape of the Pauline churches. By 'Pauline churches' I mean groups of Christ-believers founded by Paul (and/or his associates), addressed by him or otherwise represented in the Pauline letters. The term is standard within scholarship, though it can be misleading, suggesting that these groups formed an autonomous branch of early Christianity, a scenario for which there is no evidence (Horrell 2008). I focus on a number of key questions. What sort of groups were the Pauline churches? How were they formed? Of what kind of people were they composed? How does Paul define the identity of his communities? How were they governed? What do we know about their rituals and meetings? In what kinds of places did they meet?

The Pauline churches have been intensively researched over recent decades. Pioneering work was done by Theissen, Malherbe, and Meeks in the 1970s and early 1980s, and since then there has developed a massive scholarship in the area, which I am representing in this essay. My aim, though, is not simply to reflect the contemporary scholarly consensus but also to challenge and move beyond it, specifically by pushing back on the dominant household/'house-church' model of the Pauline groups and arguing for a more diversified picture (building on and developing Adams 2015). Thus, while the chapter is intended as an orientation to the subfield of the Pauline communities, it also seeks to make a fresh contribution to our understanding of the shape of the Pauline *ekklēsiai*.

I would like to thank the editor of this volume Prof. Paul Avis, Prof. Joan Taylor, and Prof. David Horrell for their comments on earlier versions of this chapter, which have helped to improve the quality of my work.

The chapter works with the division, conventional within Pauline studies, between the undisputed letters (Romans, 1 and 2 Corinthians, Galatians, Philippians, 1 Thessalonians, Philemon) and the disputed letters, and so distinguishes the evidence of Colossians, Ephesians, and the Pastoral Epistles (1 and 2 Timothy and Titus) from the data in the uncontested letters. It is clear that Colossians and Ephesians, taken together, and the Pastorals, exhibit developments in ecclesiology beyond what we find in the undisputed epistles. These developments, particularly those in the Pastorals, are widely regarded as post-dating Paul. MacDonald (1988: 3–4), for example, sees Colossians and Ephesians as reflecting the situation in the Pauline movement shortly after Paul's death, and the Pastorals as evincing the state of affairs around the time of the Apostolic Fathers (100–40 CE). I do not myself push a line on the authorship and dating of Colossians, Ephesians, and the Pastorals, leaving readers to take their own position on these matters. We begin, then, by considering the genus of the Pauline churches.

SOCIAL COMPARISONS

What kind of groups were the Pauline churches? Scholars have sought to answer this question by means of social comparisons. The Pauline congregations have been set alongside other first-century groups and institutions for the purpose of illumination. Households, associations, synagogues, and philosophical schools have all been found to offer some measure of analogy to Paul's communities (Meeks 1983: 75–84; Adams 2009; Ascough 1998), and more recently parallels with the civic assembly have been explored (Van Kooten 2012; Park 2015).

The household has been deemed especially important for understanding the nature of Paul's churches. It is generally accepted that the household was the 'basic context' in which the Pauline groups were set, with the household unit supplying the social core of an *ekklēsia* and the house providing its physical meeting space (Meeks 1983: 75–6). The household context is seen as having a significant bearing on the shape of the Pauline churches, influencing their composition, identity, government, rituals, and meetings. The Pauline churches are regularly referred to as 'house churches' (Banks 2012; Branick 1989; Gehring 2004), anachronistically suggesting an affinity with the house-church movement of recent times. (When I place 'house church/churches' in quotation marks, it is to indicate that I regard the phrase as an inappropriate one for the Pauline groups: Adams 2015: 201–2.) Yet, as will be seen as the chapter proceeds, the household, both as social unit and as material space, may have been rather less influential on the Pauline congregations in general than commonly thought.

As well as seeking analogies from contemporary social groups, scholars have gone to the social sciences for comparative models. A frequently employed sociological model has been that of the 'sect'. The sect-model has been found useful for investigating the boundaries between the Pauline groups and their wider social world (Meeks 1983: 84–110). The early Pauline movement as a whole has been classified and interpreted as a sect of the 'conversionist' type, which sees human society as evil and thus to be eschewed, and yet seeks its evangelization, for which some degree of ongoing contact with outsiders is necessary (MacDonald 1988; Wilson 1973: 22–3). The use of social-scientific comparisons to elucidate the Pauline churches raises issues of historical and cross-cultural applicability, which are particularly acute in the case of the sect-model (Holmberg 1990: 110–13). Another problem with the sect-model is its lack of analytical power. It does not do justice to 'the complex relations between Pauline communities and their multifaceted environment' (Barclay 2011: 6); nor does it show up social diversity within the Pauline movement (the Corinthian community, I have argued elsewhere, resists classification as a sect in any meaningful sense: Adams 2000: 99–100; cf. Barclay 2011: 187–201).

Insight may be gained into the nature of the Pauline churches through social comparisons, using both ancient analogies and modern social-scientific models. Comparison with ancient associations, of which there were many varieties and forms (Ascough, Harland, and Kloppenborg 2012), may be singled out as a particularly fruitful line of research at present (Ascough 2003; Harland 2003; 2009; Last 2016a) with much still to offer. It is important, though, that no single model, whether ancient or modern, is used in a totalizing way, since different models offer different lines of illumination (though the surest points of comparison tend to be those that all social groups have in common: Adams 2009: 77–8). Moreover, the comparative exercise must leave sufficient room for distinctive features of the Pauline groups to be registered and affirmed (on early Christian distinctiveness in the Graeco-Roman world, see Hurtado 2016).

Social Formation

The leading view of the formation of Paul's churches is that they were, as a rule, created from existing household units, which converted to the faith. Some think that Paul's evangelistic strategy was to target and win over heads of households, knowing that if the (normally male) householder converted then the rest of the household would most likely convert along with them (Gehring 2004: 227–8; MacDonald 1988: 58). According to Meeks (1983: 75), a converted household would form the core of what Paul calls a 'church at the home', a *kat' oikon ekklēsia* (Rom. 16:5; 1 Cor. 16:19; Col. 4:15; Philem. 2). Since households were extended units, consisting not only of close family members but also slaves, freedmen, freedwomen, and other dependants, a 'church at the home' could be a group of sizeable proportions, and it had the potential to expand through the wider 'network of relationships' in which the household was located (Meeks 1983: 76; on the strategic importance of the household to the Pauline mission, see Gehring 2004). It is held that there were normally multiple household assemblies in each city (Meeks 1983: 76). Together these household groups would make up a local *ekklēsia*, such as the church at Corinth. On the basis of the greetings in Romans 16, at least five distinct 'house churches' (Rom. 16:5, 10, 11, 14, 15) have been deduced for Rome (Lampe 2003: 359–60 posits the existence of at least seven house communities at Rome). Around six 'house churches' have been conjectured for Corinth (e.g. White 1990: 105–6).

The phenomenon of household conversion is certainly attested in the Pauline letters. Paul tells us that the household of Stephanas were his first converts in the province around Corinth (1 Cor. 1:16; 16:15), and we read of several household conversions in Luke's account of Paul's mission in Acts (16:14–15, 31–3; 18:8; cf. 11:13–14). It is also clear, though, that conversion did not always embrace households (e.g. Mark 10:29–30; 13:12; Matt. 8:21–2; Luke 9:61–2; cf. Barclay 1997: 73–5). Paul indicates that some members of his churches had unbelieving spouses (1 Cor. 7:12–16; cf. 1 Pet. 3:1–6). Household instructions envisage believing slaves serving under non-Christian masters (Col. 3:22–5; 1 Tim. 6:1–2) and apparently Christian masters having non-believing slaves (Eph. 6:9; Col. 4:1; cf. Philem. 8–16). Even when household conversion did take place, we cannot assume that it produced a sizeable group of believers. Although it was long held within classical scholarship that Roman families were of the extended kind, more recent research has established that many households would have been quite small (the seminal work in this regard is Saller and Shaw 1984, though see now Huebner 2013 on varied family patterns in Roman Egypt), and even small families could own a slave or two (Meggitt 1998: 129–31). The household of Stephanas, even if it included the two individuals, Fortunatus and Achaicus, mentioned alongside Stephanas in 1 Cor. 16:17, need not have been a large unit.

While the 'church at the home' of Philemon (Philem. 2) may have been formed through household conversion (though this is less certain than is usually assumed, Horrell 2016: 60–2), this does not seem to have been the case with the *ekklēsia* in the home of Prisca and Aquila in or near Ephesus, mentioned in 1 Cor. 16:19, and the church in their dwelling in Rome referred to in Rom. 16:5. Prisca and Aquila appear in the Pauline letters (2 Tim. 4:19) and the book of Acts (18:2, 18, 26) as a peripatetic Christian couple (Murphy-O'Connor 1992). There is no indication that they had children or slaves or travelled with a retinue of any kind (Lampe 2003: 193). Thus, the 'church at their home', both in/near Ephesus and at Rome, probably consisted of local converts made by them as they plied their trade and evangelized in these places. None of the other four groups indicated in Romans 16 conforms exactly to the model of a church formed around a converted household. The two groups mentioned in vv. 10–11, 'those who belong to the family of Aristobulus' and 'those in the Lord who belong to the family of Narcissus', were apparently groups of believers operating within wider households (of the extended type) headed by non-believers. The formulation in v. 11 makes a clear distinction between those members of Narcissus' household who are believers and those who are not (Jewett 2007: 967). The various individuals named in v. 14 (Asyncritus, Phlegon, Hermes, Patrobas, and Hermas) do not appear to be linked to each other by household ties. Of the people mentioned in v. 15, only Nereus and his sister are said to be related.

That household conversion was an important means of ecclesial formation in the Pauline mission there is no doubt, but it should not be assumed that all the Pauline groups came into existence in this way. More consideration needs to be given to other ways in which community formation could have occurred. One new direction for research, recently proposed by Last (2016b), would be to explore the street or neighbourhood as a network for expansion.

Romans 16 clearly bears witnesses to the existence of multiple assemblies in Rome, but, as we have seen, it is less clear from this passage that the Roman groups can be branded 'house churches': only one is identified as a 'church at the home', and apart from probably not being a household-based assembly, the dwelling in question was probably not a 'house' (see herein the section 'Meeting Places'). Paul's reference in 1 Cor. 14:23 to 'the whole church' at Corinth coming together has been taken to imply that members of the church would also, and perhaps more frequently, gather in smaller groups. It is not necessary, though, to conclude that such smaller groups must have been 'house churches'. It is striking that Paul never speaks of a 'church at the home' at Corinth, not even in connection with Stephanas. Moreover, that 1 Cor. 14:23 implies smaller meetings is open to question. This interpretation builds a great deal on the word 'whole', which may simply be rhetorical, supporting the use of the word 'all' in vv. 23–4 (Gielen 1986: 117; Last 2016a: 59).

It is sometimes claimed that the formulation 'church at the home' itself implies the existence of multiple 'house churches' at a given location. For example, Button and Van Rensberg (2003: 3–11) argue that the prepositional phrase *kat' oikon* within the expression, *kat' oikon ekklēsia*, functions distributively (as in Acts 2:46; 5:42), so making the larger expression convey the idea of a local church distributed into various houses. But a distributive meaning is not possible when *kat' oikon* is qualified by a personal pronoun (different to Acts 2:46; 5:42), indicating that a specific home is in view (Gielen 1986: 122–4)—and this is the case in each instance of the formulation in the Pauline letters.

Although the picture of a local Pauline church consisting of multiple 'house churches' is a firmly ingrained one within Pauline studies, it is not as firmly grounded as might be thought.

COMPOSITION

Consideration of the formation of Paul's churches leads to the question of their composition. In terms of ethnic composition, Paul's churches consisted primarily of Gentiles (e.g. 1 Cor. 12:2; Gal. 4:8–9; 1 Thess. 1:9; 4:5), which accords with his self-representation as 'apostle to the Gentiles' (Rom. 11:13; cf. Gal. 2:9). In the Corinthian church, there were at least some Jews (7:18; 12:13). The community at Rome, though again mainly Gentile (Rom. 1:5, 13; 11:13), also included a number of Jewish believers (Rom 16:7, 11, 21). Although some think that Paul's Gentile converts were often former 'God-fearers' who had been attending the synagogues and had already accepted aspects of the Jewish faith, Paul tends to portray them as having converted directly from 'paganism' (1 Cor. 12:2; 1 Thess. 1:9; 4:5).

The Pauline communities included both men and women. The presence of women in the churches is indicated in the Pauline letters by both general references to women

(1 Cor. 7:11; Gal. 3:28) and references to named women (Rom. 16; 1 Cor 16:19; Phil 2:4; Col. 4: 15; Philem. 2). In the list of greetings in Romans 16, nine women belonging to the Roman Christian community are singled out for mention. Interestingly, seven of these nine are commended, while only five of the seventeen named men receive praise (Finger 2007: 7–8; cf. Lampe 2003: 165).

Paul's statement in 1 Cor. 1:26 ('Consider your own call, brothers and sisters: not many of you were wise by human standards, not many were powerful, not many were of noble birth') seems to suggest that while the majority of the Corinthian congregation came from the lower strata of society, a minority belonged to the upper classes (taking 'not many' to mean, more positively, 'some'). This verse is thus a key text for the 'New Consensus' view of the socio-economic composition of Paul's churches (see especially Theissen 1982), on which the Pauline groups embraced a wide socio-economic spectrum. According to Meeks (1983: 51–73), the Pauline communities in general contained a reasonable cross-section of the urban population, with only the top-most and bottom-most echelons missing.

The 'New Consensus', however, has been challenged by Meggitt (1998), who maintains that the Pauline communities were composed of the poor: those living close to subsistence level and who constituted the vast majority (99%) of the population of the Roman Empire. Meggitt argues (1998: 105–6) that Paul's comment in 1 Cor. 1:26 'can tell us nothing about the social constituency of the congregation he addresses except that a small number were more fortunate than the others'. Assessing the alleged evidence for affluent individuals in the Pauline churches, Meggitt comes to the conclusion that no Pauline Christian can be located among the elite. Friessen (2004) also sets the Pauline churches among the poor. Unlike Meggitt, Friessen recognizes gradations of economic impoverishment in the Roman world, and he endeavours to plot named Pauline Christians against a 'poverty scale'. Most lived on the breadline, but there were a few that had surplus resources.

The presence of well-to-do individuals in the Pauline churches has been thought to be necessitated by the household setting of the congregations: wealthy church members with sufficiently large houses would have been required for the hosting of church meetings, and one especially wealthy householder with an especially commodious house would have been needed to accommodate 'the whole church' in a given city (Branick 1989: 91). However, recent reconsideration of the kinds of spaces—both house spaces and non-house spaces—in which the early Christians could have gathered has significantly undermined that assumption (see 'Meeting Places' herein).

In truth, we know too little about Paul's converts to be able to determine their socio-economic statuses with any degree of accuracy (Barclay 2004). Following an emerging trend within scholarship (Smith 2012: 7; Oakes 2009: 46–80), it seems fair to locate the Pauline groups generally among the non-elite (with the possible exception of Erastus, mentioned in Rom 16: 23, though precisely what social level is indicated by the descriptor 'city treasurer' remains hotly debated), especially if they tended to be small traders and craftspeople (Meeks 1983: 73). At any rate, there was probably some degree of socio-economic diversity within these communities (Horrell 2015: 156; Longenecker 2010).

IDENTITY

Paul uses various terms and images to define and configure the identity of his congregations. He can greet local believing communities to which he writes as the 'saints' or 'holy ones' (*hagioi*) in a particular location (Rom. 1:7; 1 Cor. 1:2; Phil. 1:1; cf. Eph. 1:1; Col. 1:2). The term 'brothers' can also serve as a group designator in the Pauline letters (Rom. 16:14; Col. 1:2). The word *ekklēsia*, though, is 'the single most frequent term used by Paul to refer to the groups of those who met in the name of Christ' (Dunn 1998: 537). We will look at Paul's use of this term and then consider his images of community.

Ekklēsia

Paul uses the word *ekklēsia* for specific local congregations. Thus, he writes to 'the *ekklēsia* of God at Corinth' (1 Cor. 1:2; 2 Cor. 1:1), and 'the *ekklēsia* of the Thessalonians' (1 Thess. 1:1; cf. 2 Thess. 1:1). He can also use the plural *ekklēsiai* for multiple groups either within a geographical region (e.g. the *ekklēsiai* of Galatia, Gal. 1:2; the *ekklēsiai* of Macedonia) or more widely spread, as when he speaks generally 'the *ekklēsiai*' (e.g. 1 Cor. 14:34; 2 Cor. 8:19) or 'all the *ekklēsiai*' (e.g. Rom. 16:4, 16; 1 Cor. 7:17). It is unlikely that the use of *ekklēsia* as a group designation for Christ-believers was Paul's innovation, since we find it in other New Testament writings too (Acts, the Johannine Epistles, and Revelation). Most think that it was probably part of the sociolect of Greek-speaking Jewish-Christians, from whom Paul adopted it (but note the objections of Van Kooten 2012: 524–6).

   Although it is sometimes claimed that the word *ekklēsia* means 'called out people' on the basis of the word's formation from *ek*, meaning 'out of', and *kaleo*, meaning 'call', there is no evidence that the etymology of the word plays any role in its meaning in the Pauline epistles (so rightly Dunn 1998: 537). (The descriptor 'saints', *hagioi*, though, conveys a sense of social distinction: Horrell 2005: 133–4.) The conventional Greek meaning of *ekklēsia* was 'assembly', 'gathering'. The word was applied to the civic assembly, the formal meeting of the city's citizens (cf. Acts 19:39). In the Septuagint (LXX) *ekklēsia* is characteristically used of the 'assembly' of Israel, for example the assembly of God's people at Sinai (Deut. 4:10; 9:10; 18:16), translating the Hebrew word *qahal*. That the sense 'assembly', 'gathering', is basic for Paul is clear from several passages in 1 Corinthians, in which he uses *ekklēsia* for the actual 'assembly' of the Corinthian believers (1 Cor. 11:18; 14:19, 28, 34–5). It is by extension that he uses of the word of the group that gathers (Trebilco 2011: 172). The use of *ekklēsia* as a group designation is very clear in 1 Cor. 1:1 and 2:1, where Paul speaks of 'the *ekklēsia* of God that *is* in Corinth' (the Greek present participle translated 'is' signalling 'an ongoing existence': Button and Van Rensburg 2003: 4). For Paul, an *ekklēsia* is thus both 'an assembly in which its members come together, and . . . a community or group whose members are bound together even outside their actual meetings through reciprocal social interaction' (Stegemann and

Stegemann 1999: 264). In some instances of *ekklēsia* (e.g. 1 Thess. 1:1; 2 Thess. 1:1), it is difficult to decide whether a gathering or group is in view. But even as a group designation, the thought is always of 'a regularly gathering community' (Banks 2012: 29). The fact that the believing community at Rome is not addressed as an *ekklēsia* is often taken to mean that Roman Christians did not gather as an ensemble but only as distinct groups.

There is some evidence that the term *ekklēsia* was used for club meetings (Harland 2003: 106, 182) and also for Jewish synagogue gatherings (Korner 2015). Yet, the sparseness of this evidence seems to indicate that *ekklēsia* did not serve as a group designator within other circles in the way, or at least to the extent, that it did for the early Christians.

On a number of occasions, Paul speaks of the 'church of God' or 'churches of God' (e.g. 1 Cor. 1:2; 10:32; 11:16; 2 Cor. 1:1; Gal. 1:13). The phrase is often taken as a deliberate echo of the Old Testament expression 'the assembly of the Lord' (e.g. Deut. 23:2, 3, 4, 9; so Dunn 1998: 538; Trebilco 2011: 173–4), and thus as indicating continuity between Christ-believing assemblies, or the Christ-believing movement more generally, and the assembly of Israel. It is worth noting, however, that Paul does not use the exact Old Testament expression, 'the assembly of the Lord'. The phrase 'assembly of God' is actually very rare in the Old Testament, occurring only once (Neh. 13:1). The Hebrew equivalent of Paul's expression occurs in texts from Qumran (e.g. 1QM 4:10), but we cannot be certain that these occurrences would have been known to Paul or have had any indirect influence on him. In certain instances, such as 1 Cor. 1:2 and 2 Cor. 1:1, Paul may be using the phrase 'church of God' to distinguish the Christian *ekklēsia* from the civic assembly (as argued by van Kooten 2012).

The Pauline expression, 'church at the home', discussed here, has received a lot of attention in recent years. The formulation has been taken as indicative of the 'house-church' nature of the Pauline movement (the church constituted in a household manner: Klauck 1981: 12, 21). Yet, the phrase occurs only four times in the whole Pauline corpus (the word *ekklēsia* appears 62 times in total), and accounts for less than 7 per cent of occurrences of *ekklēsia* in Pauline literature. Therefore, it should not be given a disproportionate emphasis in scholarly reconstructions of the Pauline communities.

In Colossians (Col. 1:18, 24) and especially Ephesians (Eph. 1:22; 3:10, 21; etc.) *ekklēsia* is used in the singular for the worldwide community of believers, the 'universal church'. Whether Paul in the undisputed letters can use *ekklēsia* with this meaning is debated (the debated texts are Rom. 16:23; 1 Cor. 10:32; 12:28; 15:9; Gal. 1:13; Phil. 3:6). Dunn (1998: 540), for example, thinks that Paul 'does not seem to have thought of "the church" as something worldwide or universal'. However, a universal meaning seems difficult to escape in 1 Cor. 10:32. Here, Paul divides the whole of human society into three groups: 'Jews', 'Greeks', and 'the *ekklēsia* of God' (Hurtado 2016: 99; cf. Gehring 2004: 161; as an aside, the way that Paul uses the phrase '*ekklēsia* of God' here to signify a *distinct* group identity makes it unlikely that he is insinuating continuity with the 'assembly of the Lord', a phrase which is never used in the Old Testament to denote Israel as a people). Also, a universal interpretation seems called for in 1 Cor. 12:28, where Paul says that 'God has appointed in the *ekklēsia* first apostles, second prophets, third teachers.' Assuming that 'apostles' here means church-founding apostles as Dunn (1998: 540–1) thinks, a local reference to the church at Corinth would seem highly unlikely, since Paul regards himself as the *sole* (human) founder of that church (1 Cor. 3:6, 10; 4:15). This is not to deny, of course, that the idea of the church as a universal body is significantly developed in Colossians and Ephesians. The cosmic significance accorded to the worldwide church in these letters (Col. 1:18; Eph. 1:22; 3:10) clearly goes beyond what is said about the universal *ekklēsia* in the undisputed letters. When used of the worldwide church, in both the undisputed letters and Colossians and Ephesians, *ekklēsia* would seem to have moved away from its basic meaning 'assembly' or 'gathering' (toward denoting a people). Perhaps, though, the thought is of an extensive body of people, which, though currently existing in geographically dispersed groups, will ultimately assemble together in one place.

Images of Community

Turning now to Paul's images of community, the apostle's best-known image of the church is that of the body (the classic treatment is Best 1955). Another key set of metaphors for the church is building/temple imagery (Gärtner 1965: 47–71, comparing Pauline temple imagery with temple symbolism in the Qumran writings). According to Banks (2012: 49), Paul's most fundamental image of the Christian community is that of the family. Banks and others take family imagery as including household metaphors, but the household should be treated as a distinct metaphorical field, since household units could include slaves and others who were not 'natural' family members (see further Horrell 2001).

Body

The body metaphor is prominent in 1 Corinthians, appearing in 1 Cor. 6:15 (implicitly), 10:17 and 11:29, before being developed in detail in 12:12–27. It also occurs in Rom. 12:4–5 and in passages in Colossians and Ephesians. The comparison of the human body to a social form, such as the city or the state, was long established (Dunn 1998: 550). A famous instance of the metaphor is the fable of Menenius Agrippa recorded by the Roman historian Livy (2.32.9–12). It has often been suggested that Paul is deliberately alluding to this fable in 1 Cor. 12:12–27 (like Menenius Agrippa, Paul personifies body parts and imagines them acting inharmoniously). The function of the body metaphor in 1 Cor. 12:12–27 'is to affirm the variety of gifts and the oneness of the body, neither at the expense of the other' (Witherington 1995: 258). The combination of diversity and unity is asserted in v. 20: 'there are many members [i.e. body parts], yet one body.' In vv. 14–19, the emphasis falls on diversity: the body requires a variety of parts; it cannot consist of a single organ. Unity is stressed in vv. 21–6: the multiple parts of a complex body are effective only when they are coordinated. The point made in vv. 22–4 about seemingly 'weaker' and 'less honourable' body parts (genitalia?) being worthy of 'greater respect' is no doubt aimed at the mistreatment of 'weaker' Corinthian Christians by others in the congregation (cf. 1 Cor. 8). Paul's deployment of the body metaphor thus differs from more conventional uses of it, as in Menenius Agrippa's fable: instead of supporting hegemony, Paul challenges it (Witherington 1995: 259).

Although the image of the body is clearly applied in 1 Cor. 12:12–27 to the local congregation (at Corinth), a more universal application is evident in v. 13, where Paul states that 'we were all baptized into one body' (i.e. not the Corinthian believers only but the Corinthians in solidarity with other Christians). A universal conception of the 'one body' also seems to be present in 1 Cor. 10:17 ('we who are many are one body, for we all partake of the one bread') and perhaps also in Rom. 12:4–5. That Paul can apply the body metaphor to believers generally shows that the idea of universal church as Christ's body in Colossians and Ephesians is not a new development, although it is more strongly emphasized in these two letters (Col. 1:18, 24; 2:19; 3:15; Eph. 1:23; 2:16; 3:6; etc.). What is new, though, is the depiction of Christ as the head from whom the other parts of the body receive nourishment and vitality (Col. 2:19; Eph. 4:16). In 1 Cor. 12:12–27, the head is just one of many parts of the body.

Building/Temple

Paul's talk of 'building up' fellow church members (1 Cor. 14:4; 1 Thess. 5:11) conveys the idea of the local congregation as a building. In 1 Cor. 3:9–10, Paul expressly speaks of the Corinthians as 'God's building' and compares himself to 'a skilled master builder', laying the foundation, which is Christ alone. A few verses later, vv. 16–17, he refers to the congregation as 'God's temple', perhaps giving specificity to the structure of which he has just spoken. As God's sanctuary, the community embodies God's presence (in 1 Cor. 6:19, the body of the individual believer is said to be a temple of God's Spirit). Paul warns that anyone who harms the congregation will face divine punishment (1 Cor. 3:17). The image of temple is used again in 2 Cor. 6:16 (perhaps of Christians generally). The emphasis is on the purity of the temple people (2 Cor. 7:1), which means that believers must not enter into compromising relations with unbelievers (2 Cor. 6:14–15).

In Eph. 2:20–2, the universal church is pictured as God's temple, built on the foundation of the apostles and prophets, with Christ as the cornerstone (or perhaps keystone, but cornerstone is to be preferred: Muddiman 2001: 142–3). The expansion of the foundation to include the apostles and prophets is certainly a development of the figure from 1 Cor. 3:9–10, but only a strict literalist would see a contradiction between the two passages. The structural significance of Christ is not weakened by the inclusion of the apostles and prophets but rather made more specific by the attribution to him of the role of cornerstone. The idea of the church as temple may be present in 1 Tim. 3:15 where the local *ekklēsia* is described as 'the pillar and bulwark of the truth', which recalls the pillar that formed part of Solomon's temple (1 Kings 7:15–22; cf. Knight 1992: 181).

Family

The idea of the community as a family comes across in Paul's use of kinship language in connection with local groups of believers. The apostle can depict himself as 'father' (1 Cor. 4:15; 1 Thess. 2: 11) of *ekklēsiai* founded by him. He can also picture himself as mother of his converts (Gal. 4:19). He calls members of the communities his 'children' (1

Cor. 4:14; 2 Cor. 6:13; 12:14; Gal. 4:19). Above all, he addresses them as 'brothers', *adelphoi* (plural of *adelphos*). The use of 'brothers' as a term of address is spread across the undisputed epistles (with the exception of the letter to Philemon, though even Philemon is directly addressed as 'my brother', Philem. 7). Since Paul's churches included both men and women, and he writes to 'all' members of his communities (Rom. 1:7; 1 Cor. 1:10; 2 Cor. 2:3; Gal. 3:28; Phil. 1:1; 1 Thess. 1:2), it follows that *adelphoi* is meant as an inclusive form of address. The inclusive application of 'brothers' is particularly clear in passages such as Phil. 4:1–2, where Paul first addresses church members generally as 'brothers' and then immediately appeals to the two women Euodia and Synteche specifically (Trebilco 2011: 24). Modern Bible translations such as the NRSV thus legitimately render the address *adelphoi* as 'brothers and sisters'; 'siblings' would be another appropriate translation. Paul can also refer to an individual member of a congregation as a 'brother' or 'sister' (Rom. 14:10, 15, 21; 1 Cor. 7:15; 1 Thess. 4:6). Paul's labelling of his readers as 'brothers and sisters' is clearly meant to convey a sense of 'familial solidarity' (Horrell 2005: 115) at the level of the local congregation. Horrell (2005: 114–15) observes that sibling language is used in a particularly concentrated way in contexts where there is some kind of community conflict (Rom. 14:10–21; 1 Cor. 6:5–8; 8:11–13) and underpins an appeal for unity and mutual regard. The sibling bond reaches beyond the immediate congregation 'to encompass believers elsewhere' (Horrell 2005: 315; on siblingship in Paul, see Aasgaard 2004).

For Banks (2012: 56), Paul's use of family language to describe relations between community members coheres with the household context of his churches (so also Branick 1989: 17). However, the image of family hardly demands a household setting and is not evidence for it. Family metaphors were common among associations (Harland 2009: 63–96), only a portion of which were household based. For Paul, the identity of believers as siblings in Christ is grounded primarily in the theological conviction that they are children of God (Rom. 8:14–17, 19–21, 29).

Household

Household imagery (properly defined) is not conspicuous in the undisputed letters (Horrell 2001; Adams 2015: 21–4). In Gal. 6:10, Paul urges his readers to do good to all, and especially to 'household members (*oikeioi*) of (the) faith', which is a way of talking about Christians generally rather than fellow congregants specifically (Dunn 1993: 333; Oakes 2015: 184). In Rom. 14:4, the believer is depicted as a 'household slave', but with reference to their *individual* relation to the Lord not in relation to other church members. In neither passage is the idea of the local congregation as God's household developed.

In Eph. 2:19, readers are called 'members of the household of God' (the Greek word used is *oikeioi*, as Gal. 6:10). Here, the household image applies to the worldwide church. The image is not sustained, though, and the figure of the church as building and temple takes over (vv. 20–2).

The household is widely regarded as the dominant image of the believing community in the Pastorals (see esp. Verner 1983; cf. Gehring 2004: 260–8). In 1 Tim. 3:15, the local church is explicitly called 'the household of God', though the possibility that *oikos theou* means 'house of God' and alludes to the Jerusalem temple (cf. 2 Chron. 5:1, 14; 7:5) should not be entirely discounted (Gärtner 1965: 66–71). The metaphor of the household or house is also present in 1 Tim. 3:5 and 2 Tim. 2:20–1. According to Gehring (2004: 260), in the Pastoral Epistles, the household is 'the model for responsible behavior as well as for church order and leadership structures'. Certainly, there is teaching about the need for church members to treat each other with familial respect (1 Tim. 5:1–2). Also, being a good household manager is among the qualifications for church leadership (1 Tim. 3:4). But whether household leadership is being invoked as the template for church leadership is less certain. The rhetorical question of 1 Tim. 3:4 ('for if someone does not know how to manage his own household, how can he take care of God's church?') makes the household a proving ground for church leadership, but it does not necessarily set forth household management as the pattern for church government (see the section 'Governance'). The government of the local church under overseer, elders (or overseers/elders), and deacons does not obviously look like the rule of the household under the paterfamilias.

For Gehring (2004: 264), the household language and imagery of the Pastorals points to a 'house-church' setting, in which private houses belonging to wealthy church members served as meeting places for the congregations. However, the household or house metaphor no more implies a 'house-church' setting than the image of the community as a temple demands actual temples as gathering sites (cf. Adams 2015: 39). The Pastorals indicate the existence of Christian households (2 Tim. 1:16; 3:6; 4:19; Tit. 1:11), but at no point is it indicated that any of them is a 'house church'. The phrase 'church at the home' (which does not in any case necessarily equate to what is normally meant by 'house church') occurs nowhere in these letters.

Governance

Having touched on the issue of church governance, we now take up this topic directly. From the apparent lack of evidence for church offices in the undisputed letters, scholars of an earlier generation frequently concluded that Paul's churches were without leadership (see the summary of Clarke 1993: 2–3). The 'charismatic' nature of the early Pauline congregations was often contrasted with the 'institutionalized' church that meets us in the Pastoral Epistles: whereas in the early Pauline churches, all church members participated in ministry, exercising their Spirit-endowed gifts (prophecy, speaking in tongues, the interpretation of tongues, the working of miracles, etc.: 1 Cor. 12:4–12), the Pastorals reflect a situation in which power and ministry are concentrated in the hands of designated ecclesiastical officials.

That the early Pauline groups were totally leaderless, as Johnson (2003: 207) points out, runs against 'sociological logic'. More recent study has thus emphasized the extent to which authority structures were present within the early Christian movement from the outset (Holmberg 1978). The 'apostles' constituted a level of leadership across the movement as a whole (1 Cor. 12:28; Eph. 2:20). Paul, 'apostle to the Gentiles', occupied a position of authority over the assemblies he founded and 'fathered', exercising it through visitation and missives. His missionary associates bore his delegated authority, as they visited and worked with the churches on his behalf. Also, within the Pauline churches themselves there were evidently individuals who functioned as leaders.

Local Leadership in the Earlier Pauline Letters

In 1 Thess. 5:12, within what is probably the earliest of his letters, the apostle refers to 'those who labour among you, and have charge of (lit. "stand before", *proistemi*) you in the Lord and admonish you'. He gives them no title and describes them by their activities, but they were apparently performing a leadership role within the congregation addressed. He instructs the Thessalonians to 'esteem them very highly' (v. 13), using a Greek verb (*hegeomai*) implying the recognition of authority. In 1 Cor. 12:8 'forms of leadership' are included among the gifts of the Spirit. The underlying Greek word *kubernesis* was a common word for leadership (Thiselton 2000: 1021), carrying the nuance of steering a ship. Towards the end of 1 Corinthians, Paul urges his readers to (lit.) 'be subject' to the household of Stephanas (1 Cor. 16:15–18), seemingly according this household some kind of governing role in the church. In Rom. 12:6–8, another list of gift ministries, Paul mentions 'the leader' (lit. 'the one standing before'; the Greek verb used is *proistemi*, as in 1 Thess. 5:12). Finally, in Phil. 1:1, Paul greets the saints together with the 'overseers', *episcopoi* (singular, *episcopos*), and 'deacons', *diakonoi* (singular: *diakonos*; the word simply means 'servant', but here it is taking on a more specialized sense, as perhaps also in Rom. 16:1, where Phoebe is called the *diakonos* of the church at Cenchreae). These are two of the three leadership titles found in the Pastorals. Although Paul does not prioritize the overseers and deacons over the other members of the church, and makes no mention of them elsewhere in the letter, there is little doubt that they constituted a definite group within the congregation addressed, exercising 'a ministry of supervision and care' (Bockmuehl 1997: 55).

The undisputed letters thus indicate the existence of at least a functional form of local leadership in the Pauline churches (distinct from the external leadership given by Paul and his missionary co-workers), with Philippians, traditionally dated to the early 60s CE, bearing witness to titled local-leadership positions. This shows that a bald contrast between the charismatic form of church life in the earlier epistles and the institutional church of the Pastorals is erroneous (cf. Towner 2006: 243–4). As MacDonald (1988: 31–84) has argued, incipient institutionalization is evident in the earlier letters. Also, the charismatic dimension is not entirely absent from the Pastorals (1 Tim. 4:14; 2 Tim. 1:16; though gift ministries are mediated by others through the laying on of hands).

On the standard household/'house-church' model of Paul's communities, governance was provided by the householders, in whose homes *ekklēsiai* were based (Gehring 2004: 196–210). As Campbell (1994: 126) puts it, 'The church in the house came with its leadership so to speak "built in." The church that met in someone's house met under that person's presidency.' In towns and cities where there were multiple 'house churches', the householder-patrons would together form a plural local leadership. Thus, Gehring understands the group indicated in 1 Thess. 5:12 as household heads who made their homes available as gathering places in Thessalonica (2004: 201), and takes the 'overseers' referred to in Phil. 1:1 to be 'householders' and 'hosts of the house churches' (2004: 207) in Philippi.

It is entirely reasonable to suppose that the host of a 'church at the home'—who (as noted) was not necessarily the head of a household—would exert some degree of influence and authority over that group. But as has been observed, not all Pauline groups fit the pattern of a 'church at the home' of a believer. Neither of the two household-based groups in Rom. 16:10–11 could have been led by the householder since, in both cases, he was apparently not a believer, and a householder-patron is not indicated for either of the two groups in Rom. 16:14–15. The language of leadership in 1 Thess. 5:12–13, 1 Cor. 12:8 and Rom. 12:6–8 is quite general and by no means applies exclusively to household heads. In 1 Cor. 16:15–16, it is significant that Paul urges the Corinthians to submit to the household of Stephanas and not to Stephanas specifically as household head. Apparently other members of Stephanas' household (perhaps Fortunatus and Achaicus, who may have been Stephanas' slaves or ex-slaves) exercised church leadership along with him. There is no exegetical evidence for householders acting as a collective leadership group at Corinth. In both 1 Thess. 5:12–13 and 1 Cor. 16:15–18, the basis of congregational recognition is the individuals' hard work (Thompson 2014: 186). If hard work on behalf of the congregation amounts to a criterion for leadership in Paul's churches (Dunn 1998: 585), it is not one that could only be met by householder-patrons.

Local Leadership in the Pastoral Epistles

In the Pastorals, we read of 'overseer' (*episcopos*, 1 Tim. 3:2; Tit. 1:7), 'elders' (*presbuteroi*, 1 Tim. 5:17, 19; Tit. 1:5), and 'deacons' (1 Tim. 3:8, 12). It has often been claimed (e.g. Burtchaell 1992: 292–9) that the appearance of the term 'elders' (used widely in Acts for church leadership: 11:30; 14:23; 15:2–23; etc.) reflects the influence of the synagogues, where the term denoted a definite office. Campbell (1994: 28–65), however, has argued that there was no office of eldership in the synagogues; the term 'elders' was rather a general one in early Judaism for collective community leadership. The ecclesiastical duties attaching to the three titles are not specified in the Pastorals; emphasis falls on the attributes that aspirants to these roles should possess (1 Tim. 3:1–13; Tit. 1:5–9). The lists of qualifications focus on moral qualities, reputation, and proven leadership ability. The elaboration on what makes someone suitable for church office goes considerably beyond what is implied or hinted at in the undisputed letters, though the earlier emphasis on hard work has not disappeared (1 Tim. 5:17). It is clear that the role of 'deacon' is distinct from that of overseer and/or elders. Whereas the overseer and elders are expected to teach (1 Tim. 3:2; 5:17; Tit. 1:9), deacons are not required to do so; nor are they called upon to 'take care of God's church' (which is a duty of the overseer, 1 Tim. 3:5). Moreover, unlike elders, deacons are not remunerated (1 Tim. 5:17; the remuneration of local teachers seems to be indicated in Gal. 6:6). Whether the offices of 'overseer' and 'elder' are separate or identical (or overlapping) is of course keenly debated (for a summary of different views on the relation of overseer and elders, see Merkle 181–2; see also the discussion in Clarke 2008: 42–78). On the one hand, the fact that the term 'overseer' is always singular while 'elders' is plural (except in 1 Tim. 5:19) seems to point to a distinction between the two titles. On the other, the sudden switch from 'elders' to 'overseer' at v. 7 of Tit. 1:5–9 seems to suggest that the two terms denote the same office.

According to Campbell (1994), the Pastorals were written 'to commend and legitimate' the recognition of a single 'overseer' in a town or city from among those who were individually leaders of their own 'house churches' and who were previously collectively known as 'overseers' (Phil. 1:1). However, the fact that no reference is made to being a good leader of the 'church at his home' in the lists of qualifications for the office of overseer renders Campbell's view doubtful. An aspiring overseer is expected to run his household well (1 Tim. 3:4–5), but there is no hint that his household functions as an ecclesial unit. In fact, 1 Tim. 3:5 makes an emphatic distinction between household and *ekklēsia*. Campbell's theory presupposes a 'house-church' setting for the congregations, which, as we have seen, is not directly indicated in the Pastorals.

That good management of one's household is a qualification for the offices of both overseer and deacon (1 Tim. 3:4, 12) seems now—in contrast to the earlier letters—to restrict church leadership to householders (though it is not certain that non-householders are definitely excluded). The emphasis on the aspirant's household leadership fits with the strong approbation of the household institution in the Pastorals (esp. 1 Tim. 5:8). Yet, the emphasis may also be pragmatically motivated: would-be church leaders should already possess leadership skills, and the household is the most immediate environment in which to demonstrate them. It is important to note that being a household head does not automatically make a person a church leader. The Pastorals do not support the dominant model of the Pauline churches according to which household heads were de facto church leaders.

The qualifications for overseer in 1 Tim. 3:1–7 and overseer/elders in Tit. 1:5–9 presume that the officeholder/s will be male (though 1 Tim. 3:11 seems to indicate that women may hold the office of 'deacon' (cf. Rom. 16:1); alternatively, this verse may be about deacons' wives). In 2 Tim. 2:11–12, women are prohibited from teaching men in the church (they may teach other women, Tit. 2:3–5). Most think that the evidence of the earlier Pauline letters supports the view that women were involved in local church leadership. The references to Prisca co-hosting *ekklēsiai* (Rom. 16:5; 1 Cor. 16:19) probably imply that she exercised co-leadership of these groups. In Romans 16, four women are commended for their hard work—Mary, Tryphaena, Tryphosa, and Persis (Rom. 16:6, 12)—which as we have seen, is a quality that Paul looked for in church leaders. One woman, Junia, is even accorded the status of apostle (Rom. 16:7). The Pastorals would thus seem to introduce a more restrictive perspective. Whether the restrictive outlook is due to growing patriarchalism in the Pauline churches and early Christianity more generally (Fiorenza 1983) or relates to specific local issues (in Ephesus and Crete; cf. 1 Tim. 1:3; 2 Tim. 1:18; 4:12; Tit. 1:5) is a matter of debate.

RITUALS

Turning our attention to rituals, baptism and the Lord's Supper were plainly the two main rites of the Pauline communities. Meeks (1983: 150–7) defines baptism as a 'ritual of initiation', signifying a dramatic break from the convert's former sphere of life and their incorporation into a new community, and the Lord's Supper as a 'ritual of solidarity', an action that expresses and promotes group unity (Meeks 1983: 157–62). Other rituals—the weekly collection (1 Cor. 16:2), the kiss greeting (Rom. 16:16; 1 Cor. 16:20; 2 Cor. 13:12; 1 Thess. 5:26)—are also indicated in the letters, but baptism and the Lord's Supper were clearly the most symbolically significant.

Baptism

All members of Paul's churches were baptized (Rom. 6:3; 1 Cor. 1:13; Gal. 3:27). From the stinging rhetorical question in 1 Cor. 1:13, aimed at Corinthian factionalism ('were you baptized in the name of Paul?' Cf. v. 15), it may be deduced that baptism was regularly conducted 'in the name of Christ'. Although the form of the rite is nowhere described in the Pauline literature, Paul's talk of being 'buried' with Christ in baptism (Rom. 6:4) seems to fit with immersion under water (Ferguson 2009: 157). The correspondence drawn between passing through the sea and the Christian rite of baptism in 1 Cor. 10:1–2 also points to immersion.

When Paul says in 1 Cor. 1:17 that Christ did not commission him to baptize but to preach the gospel, he is reacting to an excessive importance that some Corinthians were attaching to the role and identity of the baptizer (1 Cor. 1:13–16); he is not denying the importance of the act of baptism itself.

In Rom. 6:3–11, Paul teaches that baptism acts out the death, burial, and resurrection of Jesus and expresses the baptizand's identification with Christ's experience. The introductory formula, 'Do you not know …?', seems to suggest that this view of the significance of baptism was widely known and accepted, at least among his communities.

Galatians 3:27–8 is commonly regarded as incorporating an early Christian baptismal formula. Paul declares that believers 'baptized into Christ' have been brought into a new oneness in which 'There is no longer Jew or Greek, there is no longer slave or free, there is no longer male and female.' Baptism thus 'provides a radically new foundation for communities freed from hierarchical systems of distinction' (Barclay 2015: 397). The extent to which the radical communal effects of baptism were realized in any given congregation is another question.

According to Banks (2012: 79), 'baptism was often a family occasion, signaling the introduction of a whole household into the Christian way of life'. However, the Pauline letters give us only one case of household baptism, and it would be somewhat injudicious to build a general pattern from it. Uncertainty about the commonness of household baptisms renders shaky any attempt to derive from them a practice of infant baptism in the Pauline mission. In the single case of household baptism we have, we can say with some confidence that it did not involve infants, since, as we have seen, Paul accords to the household of Stephanas some kind of leadership status within the church (1 Cor. 16:16).

Although the house is widely accepted as the setting of assembly and church life generally within the Pauline movement, it is noteworthy that even strong proponents of the 'house-church' model of the Pauline church agree that 'most houses did not have a built-in facility for baptism' (Gehring 2004: 290; cf. Branick 1989: 112) and that the baptismal act would have been conducted elsewhere (on early baptismal locations, see Adams 2015: 187–8; Jensen 2010: 129–32).

The Lord's Supper

Our knowledge of the Lord's Supper as a ritual within the Pauline movement is entirely dependent on a couple of passages in 1 Corinthians: 10:16–17 and 11:17–34. As has often been pointed out, had there not been abuses of it at Corinth (on account of which, according to Paul, some people had suffered divine judgement, 1 Cor. 11:30), we might have known very little about the rite. Despite the silence of the other Pauline letters on the Lord's Supper, that it was commonly practised in the Pauline churches is not in doubt. As part of his corrective teaching, Paul reminds the Corinthians of the tradition concerning the Lord's Supper that he had previously given to them, and the language he uses for passing on this tradition is the same technical language that he uses for the transmission of the essential truths of the gospel (1 Cor. 15:3–5), which would indicate that he established the ordinance of the Lord's Supper in every church he founded as a matter of basic missionary practice. Also, the fact that the tradition of 1 Cor. 11:23–6 contains the commandment of the Lord to 'Do this in remembrance of me' surely means that Paul would have regarded it as an obligation to set up the ritual in all his churches (so Marshall 1993: 570).

It is clear that 'the Lord's Supper' as described in 1 Cor. 11:17–34 was a full meal and not just a piece of bread and a sip of wine. That the main worship ritual of the Pauline churches was a meal is viewed by some as an effect of meeting in a house, but cultic meals could be eaten in various contexts (such as temples, restaurants, and outdoor locations) and not only in houses with a *triclinium* (dining room). The Corinthian abuses that so outrage Paul relate to the prandial aspect of the rite. Some had a plentiful supply of food and drink and were able to eat and drink to indulgence, while others went hungry (vv. 21–2). Those who had plenty to eat and drink were almost certainly the better-off members of the congregation. The meal thus accentuated socio-economic differences within the church. In humiliating their fellow congregants 'who have nothing', the better-off church members were, in the apostle's view, showing 'contempt' for God's church (v. 22). Paul issues a grave warning that 'all who eat and drink without discerning the body, eat and drink judgment against themselves'. While 'discerning the body' may mean discerning that the bread represents (or constitutes) the body of Christ, more likely it means recognizing that the community of believers gathered together at the Lord's Supper is the body of Christ (cf. 10:17; 12). Paul's directive, 'If you are hungry, eat at home', might be seen as a step towards separating the meal from the cultic partaking of bread and wine (cf. Barclay 2001: 1126; on the later separation between the communal meal and the Eucharist see McGowan 2014: 47–52), but his intent seems rather to put a stop to overindulgence at the meal and its deleterious effects. The Lord's Supper is still to be a meal but one with modest provisions evenly distributed.

The cultic aspect of the meal comes out in the tradition that Paul cites (vv. 23–6). The tradition recalls Jesus' Last Supper with his disciples, which establishes a pattern for churches to follow. Verses 23–5 show substantial agreement with the synoptic accounts of the words of institution at the Last Supper and with Luke's version (Luke 22:17–20) in particular (it is important to remember that Paul's account pre-dates the Gospel accounts). The tradition tells how Jesus took and distributed the bread and the cup and explained their significance in terms of his body and the new covenant in his blood; he commanded that his actions be repeated as a memorial, not of the Last Supper but of his actual death. Verse 26 is generally taken as Paul's addendum to the tradition: by partaking of the bread and wine, believers 'proclaim' Jesus' death until he returns. In 1 Cor. 10:16–17, Paul indicates that the Lord's Supper expresses, or perhaps *is*, a collective participation (*koinōnia*) in the body and blood of Christ, that is his death. The fact that believers partake of 'one bread' at the supper symbolizes that they are 'one body'.

MEETINGS

Since it was the act of gathering that constituted an *ekklēsia*, meeting together was absolutely central to church life. Paul's first letter to the Corinthians is our main source of information about church meetings in Pauline circles. In 1 Cor. 11:17–34 Paul speaks of 'coming together' (vv. 17, 18, 20, 33, 34) in order to 'eat the Lord's Supper' (v. 20). In 1 Corinthians 14, he again speaks of 'coming together' (vv. 23, 26) but with wider communal worship in view. What was the relationship between these comings together? According to some, they were two different meetings. Dunn (1998: 618–19), for example, thinks that the 'coming together' of 1 Corinthians 11 was for the shared meal, which was of an exclusive nature, while the 'coming together' of 1 Corinthians 14 was for communal worship, which was open to outsiders (1 Cor. 14:16, 23–5). An alternative view, which I would cautiously favour, is that they were a single 'coming together' with two stages. It was standard in Graeco-Roman dinner parties for the main meal to be followed by learned conversation (a symposium) or entertainments (Smith 2003: 188–214).

The order of a meal followed by various worship activities would fit the pattern. It was possible for additional guests who had not been present at the earlier part to attend the second stage (Lampe 1994: 38). Thus, the Lord's Supper could be reserved for community members, while non-believers might be allowed to attend the activities that followed.

1 Corinthians 14:26 is a golden nugget of information about the pattern of corporate worship in the Pauline churches, or at least the pattern of worship that Paul prescribes for his churches. He states: 'When you come together, each one has a hymn, a lesson, a revelation, a tongue, or an interpretation.' The pattern indicated is one of open worship, involving the participation, at least potentially, of everyone present, exercising their spiritual gifts. As Witherington (1995: 290) points out, 'Paul says nothing about a sermon being part of early Christian worship.' The mention of a 'lesson' (*didache*) indicates the inclusion of teaching, perhaps accompanied by the reading of Scripture, but Paul 'definitely does not assume the support of a preacher or a service dominated by preaching' (Witherington 1995: 290).

In response to Corinthian excesses, particularly with regard to speaking in tongues, Paul gives instructions in 1 Cor. 14:27–40 about how communal worship should be conducted. He restricts the number of glossolalic contributions to two or three, one glossolalist speaking at a time, and insists that someone should interpret (as Witherington (1995: 285) notes, this may mean either that two or three glossolalists may speak in the whole meeting or that only two or three may speak before an interpretation is given). If there is no interpreter, glossolalists should refrain from contributing orally and pray silently (v. 28), since what takes place in the meeting must be intelligible both to church members and also to outsiders (vv. 9, 16). If a revelation comes to someone while another person is speaking, the latter should stop speaking so as to let the former communicate the revelation to the whole company (v. 30). Paul's instructions are governed by two basic principles (Barclay 2001: 1129): contributions to worship must 'build up' (vv. 3, 4, 5, 12, 17, 26); conduct at the meeting should be decent and 'orderly' (v. 40). MacDonald (1988: 65) rightly sees in Paul's instructions a form of 'institutionalization of ritual behaviour'. It should be emphasized, though, that in effectively establishing a 'code of conduct' for communal worship, Paul is not striving to repress freedom in worship but to facilitate it by preventing the domination of one person or group, and allowing each member to make a contribution.

Given Paul's concern that 'each' and 'all' should be able to participate vocally in the meeting, it is baffling that in vv. 34–5 he should seemingly ban women (or wives) from speaking in the assembly. The instruction in these verses is also inconsistent with his allowance of women's audible participation in worship in 1 Cor. 11:2–16 (despite his insistence that they should have their heads covered). Branick (1989: 103) suggests that 1 Cor. 11:2–16 concerns activities in the 'private house church', whereas the instruction in 1 Cor. 14:34–5 relates to the city-wide gathering (also house-based), for which different rules apply, but there is no indication in 1 Cor. 11:2–16 that only a small household gathering is here envisaged. Some regard 1 Cor. 14:34–5 as a later interpolation, reflecting the more restrictive perspective of 1 Tim. 2:12–14 (Fee 1987: 705; Horrell 1996: 184–95). There is some text-critical support for this suggestion (several manuscripts have vv. 34–5 at the end of the chapter rather than in their present location), and so it merits consideration. Others think that Paul is not calling for absolute silence but prohibiting a certain kind of speech, such as the asking of questions, which was having a disruptive effect on the meeting. Dunn (1998: 592) opines that married women were questioning prophecies uttered by their husbands, thereby undermining 'the good order of the household', which Paul is keen to protect because of the church's dependence on the household as its social base. But the passage actually distinguishes between household convention and what is proper in the church: speech that is somehow shameful in the *ekklēsia* is perfectly acceptable at home. If the text shows deference to a cultural institution, it is to the civic assembly rather than the household (Van Kooten 2012: 546). However this passage is handled (and on 1 Cor. 11:2–16 and 14:34–5, see now Peppiatt 2015), it should not override the picture we otherwise get in the earlier Pauline letters of women's full participation in the life of the church.

As to the frequency of meetings, we are given no secure information. Whether the instruction in 1 Cor. 16:2 to church members to set aside some money 'on the first day of every week' points to a weekly Sunday meeting is debated. On the 'house-church' model of Paul's churches, believers met frequently in household gatherings and less often, perhaps once a month, as a 'whole church' (Banks 2012: 34), but there is no hard evidence in the Pauline letters to support this reconstruction. If the Corinthians did meet as a whole church on the first day of every week, there may have been little need for smaller gatherings.

Estimations of the size of church meetings depend on the assumption of the house as meeting place. Banks (2012: 35) thinks that whole-church meetings averaged thirty to thirty-five persons (the number of people meeting in individual 'house churches' would have been much smaller). Murphy-O'Connor (2002: 182) estimates that Corinthian Christians numbered 'between forty and fifty persons' and envisions them meeting together in a large villa. Meetings of around 100 people have been conjectured by some (e.g. Gehring 2004: 290) but on the basis of improbably grand houses as meeting locales. If non-house venues are admitted, larger meetings (of more than thirty persons) are more easily conceivable (for example, in a large storage building or an outdoor setting). This brings us, then, at last, to the question of meeting places.

MEETING PLACES

The house as meeting place is part and parcel of the household/'house-church' model of the Pauline churches. According to Branick (1989: 13–14), the house functioned for the early Christians on two levels: 'It formed the environment for house churches strictly speaking, gatherings of Christians around one family in the home of that family'; it also 'formed the environment for gatherings of the local church, the assembly of all the Christian households and individuals of a city'. Scholars have traditionally imagined a large Roman *domus*, or atrium-house (a house structured around an open-roofed central court), as the house setting of early church gatherings. In an oft-cited reconstruction, Murphy-O'Connor (2002: 178–85) draws on large Pompeian domestic buildings of this type along with the luxurious Anaploga Villa at Corinth to visualize the house of Gaius, which he takes, on the basis of Rom. 16:23, to be the setting of the Corinthian common meal. Murphy-O'Connor argues that since the whole company could not be accommodated in the *triclinium*, there would be a spillover into the atrium. Gaius would invite the more socially prominent members of the congregation into the *triclinium*, which could hold up to nine guests, while relegating the others to the atrium, which was open to the air and much less comfortable, thus making a spatial discrimination reinforcing the social division that so appalls the apostle in 1 Cor. 11:17–34.

The established, *domus*-centred view of the context of Pauline assembly, however, has come under question in more recent scholarship, as doubts have increased about the 'New Consensus' picture of Paul's churches as elite-sponsored groups. Smith (2012: 7), for example, has stated that in the light of the recent emphasis on the extent to which early Christianity was a non-elite movement, 'examples of more modest houses should be identified and brought into the discussion'. Research on Roman housing in recent years, much of it based on the archaeology of Pompeii and Herculaneum (Wallace-Hadrill 1994), has greatly increased our knowledge of the variety of urban housing patterns and heightened our awareness of non-elite habitations.

As an alternative to the villa setting of the Corinthian sacred meal proposed by Murphy-O'Connor, Horrell (2004) envisions the meal taking place in non-elite domestic space above a shop, such as the conjectured upper-level accommodations in shops excavated east of the theatre in Corinth. Jewett (1993) argues that in large cities such as Rome and Thessalonica, non-elite groups of believers, which he labels 'tenement churches', would have met in flats in apartment blocks. Oakes, who stresses that early Christian groups 'will not generally have met in elite houses' (Oakes 2009: 70), identifies a modest craftworker's house in Pompeii as an example of a more plausible kind of setting (Oakes 2009: 15–33, 80–9). The house is a small atrium-house within a large block known as the Insula of the Menander. The craftsman used his house as a workplace as well as a residence, and Oakes imagines him as the host of 'craftworker house church'. If the same craftsman lived and worked in Rome, Oakes reasons, he would probably have rented a workshop on the ground floor of a tenement building and modest residential quarters either higher up in the same building or in another block (Oakes 2009: 94). His 'house church' would have met in the workshop, which, though spartan, dark, filled with materials and tools, and noisy outside, would have allowed around thirty people or so to assemble (Oakes 2009: 95). Shops and workshops have been mooted as likely 'house-church' locales by other scholars, including Murphy-O'Connor (2002: 192–8), who posits a workshop as the setting of one of the smaller 'house churches' (specifically the 'house church' hosted by Prisca and Aquila) in Corinth, as opposed to 'the whole church', which met in the house of Gaius. Shops and small workshops, *tabernae* (singular: *taberna*) in the technical parlance of Roman archaeologists, often doubled up as living (or at least sleeping) space for those who worked in them. Yet, they were not 'houses' strictly speaking, and so to postulate them as 'house-church' settings is somewhat anomalous.

But what is the evidence in the Pauline letters for the use of houses as meeting places? As I have shown elsewhere (Adams 2015: 17–40), much of the claimed Pauline evidence—references to actual households, family and household metaphors of community, etc.—is indirect and inconclusive (the evidence in Acts is stronger, yet even Acts does not support the view that meeting places were almost exclusively houses: Adams 2015: 51–66). Although it has often been deduced from Rom. 16:23 that Gaius hosted 'the whole church' at Corinth in his house (and must therefore have had a residential property of considerable proportions), as Last (2016a: 62–5) has now shown, the word rendered 'host' (*zenos*) is never used for the host of a private cult group. Paul's reference to Gaius as 'host' to 'the whole church' (as well as to Paul himself) most likely relates to Gaius's provision of food and shelter to Christians visiting Corinth from other places, understood as a service to the worldwide church (see Adams 2015: 27–8; for an alternative explanation, according to which Gaius was the 'guest' of Paul and the church at Corinth, see Last 2016a: 62–71). There is nothing in 1 Cor. 11:17–34 (or 1 Cor. 14) that demands a setting in the house of a believer. Indeed, Paul's remark in 1 Cor. 11:22 ('Do you not have homes to eat and drink in?') seems to tell against such a scenario. In terms of hard exegetical evidence in the Pauline literature for the use of houses as meeting places all we have are the four references to the 'church at the home', which scarcely constitute proof of a pervasive practice of meeting in homes. Moreover, although the phrase is commonly translated 'church in [someone's] house' (e.g. NRSV), the Greek word *oikos* when used of an accommodation simply means 'dwelling'; it could apply to any type of dwelling place, including an apartment or shop, and does not necessarily imply a 'house' in the strict sense. The *oikos* in which Prisca and Aquila hosted their *ekklēsiai* (at Ephesus, at Rome) was probably a rented workshop or *taberna*. The couple were tent makers who worked to support their missionary activity (Acts 18:3; Lampe 2003: 192–3), and a *taberna* is the kind of environment in would they would have most likely carried out their craft (Murphy-O'Connor 1992).

The exegetical evidence, therefore, does not compel us to focus only on houses when considering the meeting spaces of the Pauline churches. Indeed, it gives us some encouragement to think more widely. Prisca and Aquila's probable deployment of their *taberna* as an ecclesial meeting place may not have been unique in the Pauline movement. *Tabernae* were typical working and living spaces for small traders and craftspeople, which, as we have seen, is often taken to be the demographic profile of Pauline Christians. The *taberna*, whose main architectural feature was a wide front leading into a large rectilinear room, constituted 'the most ubiquitous and dominant architectural form in Rome and throughout the Roman world' (MacMahon 2003: 9). Around 800 *tabernae* have been discovered in Pompeii alone (Holleran 2012: 112). Many had upper areas and/or additional rooms to the side or back of the open-fronted room, which would have functioned as domestic quarters. A *taberna* would have been a basic yet adequate place for assembly. The large open-fronted room, which could be closed at night with shutters, would have offered a reasonable amount of space for meeting, though some rearrangement of the room would no doubt have been necessary. It is by no means unrealistic to imagine a meal meeting in such surroundings (on *tabernae* and other workshops as Christian meeting places, see Adams 2015: 138–46).

A *taberna* is only one of a host of non-house possibilities for meeting. Modest associations that could not afford their own clubhouse could assemble in a variety of places including inns, restaurants, storehouses, and stables (Adams 2015: 119–24; Last 2016a: 107–8); Pauline groups could well have utilized such spaces, as well as houses of various types (I am certainly not suggesting houses should be discounted as Pauline meeting places!). The groups indicated in Rom. 16:10–11 may have gathered in workshops or storehouses owned by their non-Christian masters, and the companies of believers mentioned in Rom. 16:14–15 may have met in inns or warehouse space among other options. The Corinthians may have assembled (as a whole church) in a rented dining hall (Adams 2015: 203–6), or, in warmer months, a garden or other outdoor venue.

Defocusing the traditional approach to Pauline meeting places away from the *domus* and houses generally opens up new possibilities for exploring the influence of the physical environment of gathering on early Christian gatherings and groups (for suggestive work along this line, see Oakes 2016).

CONCLUSION

The Pauline *ekklēsiai* are the New Testament churches about which we are best informed. They are thus of enormous and enduring ecclesiological importance. In this chapter, I have sought to give an orientation to the Pauline churches as a subject of scholarly enquiry. The discussion has taken in a range of issues—the genus of the churches, their social formation, their composition, etc.—and I have tried to cover as much of the data and scholarship as seemed possible within present confines. As well as giving an overview of the subject, I have endeavoured here to advance it, specifically by critiquing—over the course of the chapter—the dominant household/ 'house-church' model of the Pauline communities and arguing for a more variegated approach. There has been an excessive emphasis on the household (understood in a certain way) as the context in which the Pauline churches were located and shaped; more attention now needs to be given to other possible modes of ecclesial formation and other physical settings for gathering.

The Pauline assemblies are an ancient-historical phenomenon, which cannot authentically be reproduced in our time. Nevertheless, Paul's vision for his churches, as expressed in his images of community and other aspects of his teaching, is abiding, and serves as an 'indispensable guide' (Thompson 2014: 19) to being the church today.

References

Abbreviations used in References

JBL	*Journal of Biblical Literature*
JJMJS	*Journal of the Jesus Movement in its Jewish Setting*
JSNT	*Journal for the Study of the New Testament*
JSNTSup	Journal for the Study of the New Testament Supplement Series
LNTS	Library of New Testament Studies
NICNT	New International Commentary on the New Testament
NIGTC	The New International Greek Testament Commentary
NTS	*New Testament Studies*
SBS	Stuttgarter Bibelstudien
SNTSMS	Society of New Testament Studies Monograph Series
SNTW	Studies of the New Testament in its World
WUNT	Wissenschaftliche Untersuchungen Zum Neuen Testament
ZNW	*Zeitschrift für die neutestamentliche Wissenschaft*

Aasgaard, R. (2004). *'My Beloved Brothers and Sisters!' Christian Siblingship in Paul.* JSNTSup 265; London: T&T Clark.

Adams, E. (2000). *Constructing the World: A Study in Paul's Cosmological Language.* SNTW. Edinburgh: T&T Clark.

Adams, E. (2009). 'First-Century Models for Paul's Churches: Selected Scholarly Developments since Meeks'. In Still and Horrell 2009: 60–78.

Adams, E. (2015). *The Earliest Christian Meeting Places: Almost Exclusively Houses?* Revised Edition. LNTS 450. London: Bloomsbury T&T Clark.

Alexeev, A. A., Karakolis, C., and Luz, U. (eds) (2008). *Einheit der Kirche in Neuen Testament.* WUNT I/218. Tübingen: Mohr Siebeck.

Ascough, R. S. (1998). *What are They Saying About the Formation of the Pauline Churches?* New York/Mahwah, NJ: Paulist Press.

Ascough, R. S. (2003). *Paul's Macedonian Associations: The Social Context of Philippians and 1 Thessalonians.* WUNT II/161. Tübingen: Mohr Siebeck.

Ascough, R. S, Harland, P. A. and Kloppenborg, J. S. (2012). *Associations in the Greco-Roman World: A Sourcebook.* Waco, TX: Baylor University Press.

Banks, R. (2012, orig. 1994). *Paul's Idea of Community: The Early House Churches in their Cultural Setting.* Revised Edition. Grand Rapids, MI: Baker Academic.

Barclay J. M. G. (1997). 'The Family as Bearer of Religion in Judaism and Early Christianity'. In Moxnes 1997: 66–80.

Barclay, J. M. G. (2001). '1 Corinthians', in Barton and Muddiman 2001: 1108–33.

Barclay, J. M. G. (2004). 'Poverty in Pauline Studies: A Response to Steven Friesen'. *JSNT* 26.3: 363–6.

Barclay, J. M. G. (2011). *Pauline Churches and Diaspora Jews.* WUNT I/275; Tübingen: Mohr Siebeck.

Barclay, J. M. G. (2015). *Paul & the Gift.* Grand Rapids, MI: Eerdmans.

Barton, J. and Muddiman, J. (eds) (2001). *The Oxford Bible Commentary.* Oxford: Oxford University Press.

Best, E. (1955). *One Body in Christ: A Study in the Relationship of the Church to Christ in the Epistles of the Apostle Paul.* London: SPCK.

Bockmuehl, M. (1997). *The Epistle to the Philippians*. Black's New Testament Commentary. London: A&C Black.

Branick, V. (1989). *The House Church in the Writings of Paul*. Wilmington, DE: Michael Glazier.

Burtchaell, J. T. (1992). *From Synagogue to Church: Public Services and Offices in the Earliest Christian Communities*. Cambridge: Cambridge University Press.

Button, M. B. and Van Rensburg, F. J. (2003). 'The "House Churches" in Corinth'. *Neotestamentica* 37.1: 1–28.

Campbell, R. A. (1994). *The Elders: Seniority within Earliest Christianity*. SNTW. Edinburgh: T&T Clark.

Cissé, A. and Osiek, C. (eds) (2012). *Text, Image and Christians in the Graeco-Roman World: A Festschrift in Honor of David Lee Balch*. Princeton Theological Monograph Series. Eugene, OR: Pickwick.

Clarke, A. D. (1993). *Secular and Christian Leadership in Corinth: A Socio-Historical and Exegetical Study of 1 Corinthians 1–6*. Leiden: Brill.

Clarke, A. D. (2008). *A Pauline Theology of Church Leadership*. LNTS 362. London/New York: T&T Clark International.

Dunn, J. D. G. (1993). *The Epistle to the Galatians*. Black's New Testament Commentary. London: A&C Black.

Dunn, J. D. G. (1998). *The Theology of Paul The Apostle*. Grand Rapids, MI: Eerdmans.

Dunn, J. D. G. (ed.) (2003). *The Cambridge Companion to St Paul*. Cambridge: Cambridge University Press.

Fee, G. D. (1987). *The First Epistle to the Corinthians*. NICNT. Grand Rapids, MI: Eerdmans.

Ferguson, E. (2009). *Baptism in the Early Church: History, Theology, and Liturgy in the First Five Centuries*. Grand Rapids, MI: Eerdmans.

Finger, R. H. (2007). *Roman House Churches Today: A Practical Guide for Small Groups*. Grand Rapids, MI: Eerdmans.

Fiorenza, E. S. (1983). *In Memory of Her: A Feminist Theological Reconstruction of Christian Origins*. New York: Crossroads.

Friesen, S. J. (2004). 'Poverty in Pauline Studies: Beyond the So-called New Consensus'. *JSNT* 26.3: 323–61.

Gärtner, B. (1965). *The Temple and the Community in Qumran and the New Testament*. SNTSMS 1. Cambridge: Cambridge University Press.

Gehring, R. W. (2004). *House Church and Mission: The Importance of Household Structures in Early Christianity*. Peabody, MA: Hendrickson.

Gielen, M. (1986). 'Zur Interpretation der paulinischen Formel h9 kat' κατ' οἶκον ἐκκλησία'. *ZNW* 77: 109–25.

Harland, P. A. (2003). *Associations, Synagogues, and Congregations: Claiming a Place in Ancient Mediterranean Society*. Minneapolis, MN: Fortress Press.

Harland, P. A. (2009). *Dynamics of Identity in the World of the Early Christians*. New York/London: T&T Clark.

Hawthorne, G. F., Martin, R. P., and Reid, D. G. (1993). *Dictionary of Paul and his Letters*. Downers Grove, IL/Leicester, UK: IVP.

Holleran, C. (2012). *Shopping in Ancient Rome: The Retail Trade in the Late Republic and the Principate*. Oxford: Oxford University Press.

Holmberg, B. (1978). *Paul and Power: The Structure of Authority in the Primitive Church as Reflected in the Pauline Epistles*. Coniectanea Biblica, NTS 11. Lund: Gleerup.

Holmberg, B. (1990). *Sociology and the New Testament: An Appraisal*. Minneapolis, MN: Fortress Press.

Horrell, D. G. (1996). *The Social Ethos of the Corinthian Correspondence: Interests and Ideology from 1 Corinthians to 1 Clement*. SNTW. Edinburgh: T. and T. Clark.

Horrell, D. G. (2001). 'From ἀδελφοί to οἶκος θεοῦ: Social Transformation in Pauline Christianity'. *JBL* 120.2: 293–311.

Horrell, D. G. (2004). 'Domestic Space and Christian Meetings at Corinth: Imagining New Contexts and the Buildings East of the Theatre'. *NTS* 50: 349–69.

Horrell, D. G. (2005). *Solidarity and Difference: A Contemporary Reading of Paul's Ethics*. London/New York: T&T Clark.

Horrell, D. G. (2008). 'Pauline Churches or Early Christian Churches? Unity, Disagreement, and the Eucharist'. In Alexeev, Karakolis, and Luz 2008: 185–203.

Horrell, D. G. (2015). *An Introduction to the Study of Paul*. 3rd edition. T&T Clark Approaches to Biblical Studies; London: Bloomsbury T&T Clark.

Horrell, D. G. (2016). 'Farewell To Another Wealthy Patron? Reassessing Philemon in the Light of Recent Scholarly Discussion of Socio-Economic Level and Domestic Space'. In Marguerat 2016: 51–74.

Huebner, S. R. (2013). *The Family in Roman Egypt: A Comparative Approach to Intergenerational Solidarity and Conflict*. Cambridge/New York: Cambridge University Press.

Hurtado, L. W. (2016). *Destroyer of the gods: Early Christian Distinctiveness in the Roman World*. Waco, TX: Baylor University Press.

Jensen, R. M. (2010). *Living Water: Images, Symbols, and Settings of Early Christian Baptism*. Supplements to Vigiliae Christianae 105. Leiden: Brill.

Jewett, R. (1993). 'Tenement Churches and Communal Meals in the Early Church'. *Biblical Research* 38: 23–43.

Jewett, R. (2007). *Romans*: Hermeneia. Minneapolis, MN: Fortress Press.

Johnson, L. T. (2003). 'Paul's Ecclesiology'. In Dunn 2003: 199–211.

Klauck, H. J. (1981). *Hausgemeinde und Hauskirche im frühen Christentum*. SBS 103. Stuttgart: Katholische Bibelwerk.

Knight, G. W. III (1992). *Commentary on the Pastoral Epistles*. NIGTC. Grand Rapids, MI: Eerdmans.

Korner, R. J. (2015). 'Ekklēsia as a Jewish Synagogue Term: Some Implications for Paul's Socio-Religious Location'. *JJMJS* 2: 53–78.

Köstenberger, A. and Wilder, T. L. (eds) (2010). *Entrusted with the Gospel*. Nashville: B&H Publishing Group.

Lampe, P. (1994). 'The Eucharist: Identifying with Christ on the Cross'. *Interpretation* 48: 136–49.

Lampe, P. (2003). *From Paul to Valentinus: Christians at Rome in the First Two Centuries*. Trans. M. Steinhauser. Minneapolis, MN: Fortress Press.

Last, R. (2016a). *The Pauline Church and the Corinthian Ekklēsia: Greco-Roman Associations in Comparative Context*. SNTSMS 164. Cambridge: Cambridge University Press.

Last, R. (2016b). 'The Neighborhood (vicus) of the Corinthian Ekklēsia: Beyond Family-Based Descriptions of the First Urban Christ-Believers'. *JSNT* 38.4: 399–425.

Longenecker, B. W. (2010). *Remember the Poor: Paul, Poverty, and the Greco-Roman World*. Grand Rapids, MI: Eerdmans.

Longenecker, B. W. (ed.) (2016). *Early Christianity in Pompeian Light: People, Texts, Situations*. Minneapolis, MN: Fortress Press.

Macdonald, M. Y. (1988). *The Pauline Churches: A Socio-Historical Study of Institutionalization in the Pauline and Deutero-Pauline Writings*. SNTSMS 60. Cambridge: Cambridge University Press.

McGowan, A. B. (2014). *Ancient Christian Worship: Early Church Practices in Social, Historical, and Theological Perspective.* Grand Rapids, MI: Baker Academic.

MacMahon, A. (2003). *The Taberna Structures of Roman Britain* (British Archaeological Reports, British Series 356. Oxford: BAR Publishing).

Malherbe, A. J. (1977). *Social Aspects of Early Christianity.* Baton Rouge: Louisiana State University Press.

Marguerat, D. (ed.) (2016). *La Lettre à Philémon et l'ecclésiologie Paulinienne/Philemon and Pauline Ecclesiology.* Colloquium Oecumenicum Paulinum 22. Leuven: Peeters.

Marshall, I. H (1993). 'Lord's Supper'. In Hawthorne, Martin, and Reid 1993: 569–75.

Meeks, W. A. (1983). *The First Urban Christians: The Social World of the Apostle Paul.* New Haven, CT: Yale University Press.

Meggitt, J. J. (1998). *Paul, Poverty and Survival.* SNTW. Edinburgh: T&T Clark.

Merkle, B. L. (2010). 'Ecclesiology in the Pastoral Epistles'. In Köstenberger and Wilder 2010: 199–218.

Moxnes, H. (ed.) (1997). *Constructing Early Christian Families: Family as Social Reality and Metaphor.* London: Routledge.

Muddiman, J. (2004). *The Epistle to the Ephesians.* Black's New Testament Commentary. London and New York: Continuum.

Murphy-O'Connor, J. (1992). 'Prisca and Aquila Traveling Tentmakers and Church Builders'. *Bible Review* 8.6: 40–51, 62.

Murphy-O'Connor, J. (2002). *St. Paul's Corinth: Texts and Archaeology.* 3rd revised and expanded edition. Collegeville, MN: Liturgical Press.

Oakes, P. (2009). *Reading Romans in Pompeii.* Minneapolis, MN: Fortress Press.

Oakes, P. (2015). *Galatians.* Paideia Commentaries on the New Testament. Grand Rapids, MI: Baker Academic.

Oakes, P. (2016). 'Nine Types of Church in Nine Types of Space in the Insula of Menander'. In Longenecker 2016: 23–58.

Park, Y.-H. (2015). *Paul's Ekklēsia as a Civic Assembly: Understanding the People of God in their Politico-Social World.* WUNT II/393. Tübingen: Mohr Siebeck.

Peppiatt, L. (2015). *Women and Worship at Corinth: Paul's Rhetorical Arguments in 1 Corinthians.* Eugene, OR: Cascade.

Saller, R. P. and Shaw, B. D. (1984). 'Tombstones and Family Relations in the Principate: Civilians, Soldiers and Slaves'. *Journal of Roman Studies* 74: 124–56.

Smith, D. E. (2003). *From Symposium to Eucharist: The Banquet in the Early Christian World.* Minneapolis, MN: Fortress Press.

Smith, D. E. (2012). 'The House Church as Social Environment'. In Cissé and Osiek 2012: 3–21.

Stegemann, E. and Stegemann, W. (1999). *The Jesus Movement: A Social History of its First Century.* Edinburgh: T&T Clark.

Still, T. D. and Horrell, D. G. (eds) (2009). *After The First Urban Christians: The Social-Scientific Study of Pauline Christianity Twenty-Five Years Later.* London: T&T Clark.

Theissen, G. (1982). *The Social Setting of Pauline Christianity: Essays on Corinth.* Edinburgh: T&T Clark.

Thiselton, A. C. (2000). *The First Epistle to the Corinthians.* NIGTC. Grand Rapids, MI: Eerdmans; Carlisle: Paternoster.

Thompson, J. W. (2014). *The Church According to Paul: Rediscovering the Community Conformed to Christ.* Grand Rapids, MI: Baker Academic.

Towner, P. H. (2006). *The Letters to Timothy and Titus.* NICNT. Grand Rapids, MI: Eerdmans.

Trebilco, P. (2011). *Self-Designations and Group Identity in the New Testament.* Cambridge: Cambridge University Press.

Van Kooten, G. H. (2012). Ἐκκλησία τοῦ θεοῦ: The "Church of God" and the Civic Assemblies (ἐκκλησίαι) of the Greek Cities in the Roman Empire: A Response to Paul Trebilco and Richard A. Horsley'. *NTS* 58.4: 522–48.

Verner, D. C. (1983). *The Household of God: The Social World of the Pastoral Epistles.* Chico, CA: Scholars Press.

Wallace-Hadrill, A. (1994). *Houses and Society in Pompeii and Herculaneum.* Princeton: Princeton University Press.

White, L. M. (1990). *The Social Origins of Christian Architecture.* Vol. 1: *Building God's House in the Roman World: Architectural Adaptation among Pagans, Jews, and Christians.* Harvard Theological Studies 42. Valley Forge, PA: Trinity Press International.

Wilson, B. R. (1973). *Magic and the Millennium: A Sociological Study of Religious Movements of Protest Among Tribal and Third-World Peoples.* London: Heinemann.

Witherington, B. (1995). *Conflict and Community in Corinth: A Socio- Rhetorical Commentary on 1 and 2 Corinthians.* Grand Rapids, MI: Eerdmans.

Suggested Reading

Adams, E. (2015). *The Earliest Christian Meeting Places: Almost Exclusively Houses?* Revised Edition. LNTS 450. London: Bloomsbury T&T Clark.

Ascough, R. S. (1998). *What are They Saying About the Formation of the Pauline Churches?* New York/Mahwah, NJ: Paulist Press.

Banks, R. (2012, orig. 1994). *Paul's Idea of Community: The Early House Churches in their Cultural Setting.* Revised Edition. Grand Rapids, MI: Baker Academic.

Macdonald, M. Y. (1988). *The Pauline Churches: A Socio- Historical Study of Institutionalization in the Pauline and Deutero-Pauline Writings.* SNTSMS 60. Cambridge: Cambridge University Press.

Meeks, W. A. (1983). *The First Urban Christians: The Social World of the Apostle Paul.* New Haven, CT: Yale University Press.

Still, T. D. and Horrell, D. G. (eds) (2009). *After The First Urban Christians: The Social-Scientific Study of Pauline Christianity Twenty-Five Years Later.* London: T&T Clark.

Thompson, J. W. (2014). *The Church According to Paul: Rediscovering the Community Conformed to Christ.* Grand Rapids, MI: Baker Academic.

CHAPTER 6

THE CHURCH IN
THE GENERAL EPISTLES

GERALD O'COLLINS SJ

AT first glance, James, 1 Peter, Hebrews, Jude, and 2 Peter (known as the General Epistles) do not promise to yield much for those who study the ecclesiology of early Christianity. Only 1 Peter and Hebrews clearly mention baptism, and there may be a reference to the Eucharist in Hebrews 13:10. Otherwise nothing seems to be said about the sacramental life of the church. When Hebrews twice speaks of the *ekklēsia* (Heb. 2:12; 12:23), as does James 5:14, most scholars do not render the word as 'the church' (as NRSV does for Jas. 5:14), but in all three cases they accept the translation 'assembly' (Hartin 2009: 267; NRSV for Heb. 12:23) or 'congregation' (NRSV for Heb. 2:12). Otherwise *ekklēsia* never occurs in these five 'books' of the New Testament. Apart from passing references to 'leaders' (Heb. 13:7, 17, 24), 'teachers' (Jas. 3:1), and 'elders' (Jas. 5:14; 1 Pet. 5:1), these texts seemingly indicate nothing about leadership roles in the Christian communities. They do not say much about the Holy Spirit, who gives life to the whole church and her mission—in the vision of Luke–Acts, John, and Paul.

Further central beliefs can fail to surface. For instance, James never refers to the crucifixion and resurrection, and explicitly mentions Jesus only twice (1:1; 2:1); the letter comes across as more 'theological' than 'Christological'. Nevertheless, in his opening words the writer presents himself as 'a slave of God and of the Lord Jesus Christ', and proceeds to echo Jesus' teaching: for example, the Sermon on the Mount and, in particular, the beatitudes (2:5, 13; 3:18). James 2:11 joins Jesus (Mark 10:19) in upholding the Decalogue.

There are notorious difficulties about assigning even approximate dates to these five texts and/or about identifying their authors. Add to that, while St Athanasius of Alexandria in his *Festal Epistle* for 367 finally listed all twenty-seven books of the New Testament, James, Hebrews, Jude, and 2 Peter had struggled to win a place in the emerging Christian canon. James eventually came to head the third major section of the New Testament writings, 'the General Epistles', but this letter had not featured on the

Muratorian Fragment (most probably of the late second century) and seemingly owed its canonical recognition to Origen and others in the school of Alexandria.

Nevertheless, these five texts disclose a diversity of church life in early Christianity. While some themes hold Jude and 2 Peter together, James, 1 Peter, and Hebrews reveal a distinctive (but not separate or opposed) theory and practice of church life. We would be the poorer if we lacked their particular ecclesiological material, emphases, and implications.

JAMES

Without proving knock-down arguments, the reasons for holding that the Letter of James originated from James of Jerusalem, who belonged to the same family network as Jesus and wrote the letter in the 60s (Hartin 2009: 16–25; Johnson 1995: 89–123), seem plausible. Coming from the Jewish milieu of early Christianity, this circular letter or encyclical was addressed with a tone of moral authority to 'the twelve tribes in the Dispersion', communities of Jewish Christians living outside the homeland of Israel/Palestine and scattered around Asia Minor and elsewhere. Permeated with the Jewish heritage of Christianity and belonging to the general category of wisdom literature, James proves quite Jewish in the ecclesiological material and implications it offers. Significantly the place where Christians meet is called a *sunagōgē* ('assembly' NRSV); at times, or even often, it may have been a Jewish synagogue (Oropeza 2012: 72). The letter includes six themes for the life of the church and for ecclesiological reflection that should be retrieved. They converge in depicting the church as an egalitarian, wisdom community of courageous disciples who follow Jesus in facing the trials of life.

First, the letter is primarily directed to communities rather than to their 'teachers' or 'elders' (3:1; 5:14). Over and over again, James addresses 'my brothers [and sisters]' (1:2; 2:1, 14; 3:1; 4:11; 5:7, 12, 19) and, three times, 'my beloved brothers [and sisters]'(1:16, 19; 2:5). His primary audience is the whole local church rather than some leading figure, like Timothy or Titus (as in the Pastoral Epistles). The communities as such enjoy precedence over those who have founded them and/or who, from time to time, have leadership functions within them.

Second, the letter understands Christian identity to call for moral integrity and loving action that involve keeping oneself 'pure and undefiled before God' and 'unstained by the world' (1:27). It exhorts the community of the faithful to maintain an identity that distinguishes them from the society in which they live—in other words, to nourish friendship with God rather than friendship with the world (4: 4). What James prescribes for the scattered Christian communities parallels what Jesus had said about the impossibility of serving both God and wealth (Luke 16:11, 13). In the third millennium, James, along with Jesus, continues to raise for churches tough questions about the counter-cultural nature of their calling.

Third, the values proposed to those who belong to 'the twelve tribes in the Dispersion', the new society that is the church, include equality between the rich and the poor (2:1–7). Privileging the rich members of communities over the poorer ones betrays faith in 'the glorious Lord Jesus Christ' (2:1). Challenging the Christian communities to care for the 'naked and those who lack daily food' (2:15–16) and for others in serious need, like widows and orphans (1:27), the letter takes a firm stand *for* 'social services' as essential to church life and *against* showing special favours to rich Christians.

Fourth, James stresses the responsibility that all members of each Christian community share vis-à-vis those who may have 'wandered' away: 'Whoever brings back a sinner who has been wandering' will be specially blessed (5:19–20). The letter repeatedly recognizes how sin disfigures the life of the early churches and even leads some of the baptized to abandon the practice of their faith. But, rather than reflecting theologically on 'the church constantly needing to be reformed (*ecclesia semper reformanda*)', the letter emphasizes the mutual responsibility of Christians for one another and for public 'apostates' (Oropeza 2012: 94–7).

Fifth, James includes some hints about the sacramental life of the church communities. A diatribe against class prejudice leads him to denounce rich people who 'drag' Christians into court and 'blaspheme the excellent name that was invoked over you' (2:7). This 'excellent name' seems to be that of Jesus, the name invoked at the time of their baptism. The letter closes with several pastoral or 'sacramental' concerns. The elders should anoint the sick with oil and pray over them 'in the name of the Lord' (evidently the Lord Jesus Christ). Christians should 'confess their sins to one another and pray for one another', so that they might be 'healed' (5:16). Roman Catholics and some other Christians have found here a scriptural basis for the anointing of the sick. These verses, however, while providing grounds for later sacramental practice, encourage readers to look back to the anointing with oil practised by the twelve when sent by Jesus on a trial mission (Mark 6:13) and to the healing and forgiveness that characterized Jesus' own ministry (e.g. Matt. 11:2–6; Mark 2:1–12).

Sixth, James draws heavily on the Jewish wisdom tradition (e.g. 1:5–8; 3:13, 17–18) and, even more, on the preaching of Jesus. The letter's emphasis on the power of prayer (e.g. Jas. 5:16) retrieves Jesus' confident announcement, 'ask and you shall receive' (Matt. 7:7–11). The call to moral integrity in speech (Jas. 5:12) aligns itself closely with what Jesus had said (Matt. 5:33–7). Jesus' 'woe to you rich' (Luke 6:24) stands behind James's warnings to the unjust rich (1:9–11; 5:1–6). James calls loving one's neighbour 'the royal law' (Jas. 2:8); this precept had featured strongly in the teaching of Jesus (e.g. Mark 12:31; Luke 10:27). Right through the Letter of James one hears the voice of Jesus denouncing as insufficient and even false an allegedly 'orthodox' faith that fails to bear fruit in the moral life (e.g. Matt. 7:21–3). Here we find the appropriate response to the classical objection made by Martin Luther against James (esp. 2:14–26) for being in conflict with justification by faith alone and not by works (St Paul). Modern New Testament scholars have pointed out that James and Paul have different concerns and that the conflict is more apparent than real (Johnson 1995: 58–65, 140–5; Oropeza 2012: 91–4). James persistently echoes the prophetic ethics of Jesus in constructing a church order that should distinguish 'servants of God and the Lord Jesus Christ' (1:1).

1 PETER

Like the Letter of James, the First Letter of Peter presents itself as a circular letter aimed at meeting pastoral problems experienced by 'exiles of the Dispersion', albeit in this case the communities are specifically located in five Roman provinces of Asia Minor (Pontus, Galatia, Cappadocia, Asia, and Bithynia) (1 Pet. 1:1). The former letter originated from the mother church in Jerusalem, the latter came from 'your sister church in Babylon' (1 Pet. 5:13), a code name for Rome. James writes to communities of Jewish Christians, whereas 1 Peter addresses Gentile Christians, who have formerly lived sinful, idolatrous lives (1:14, 18, 21; 2:1, 9–11, 25; 4:3). In both cases, however, a major church community aims to maintain communion with scattered Christian churches, and to fulfil a perceived responsibility towards those who face serious difficulties in living out their faith as tiny minorities surrounded by a general population indifferent or even actively hostile to their faith. While James is more 'theological', 1 Peter is much more 'Christological', and prescribes the kind of life the followers of Jesus should live in the time between his resurrection and return at the end of history.

While some scholars continue to hold that Simon Peter (with secretarial help) authored this letter shortly before his martyrdom around AD 64, many argue that it drew its authority from the name of the great apostle, expressed key elements in the Petrine legacy, showed influence from the Pauline tradition, and was composed at some point between the early 70s and the early 90s (Elliott 2000: 118–38). 1 Peter takes its authority from three names: Sylvanus or Silas (5:12), Mark (5:13), and, above all, the apostle Peter himself (1:1).

The letter may imply baptism when speaking about 'being called out of darkness into his [God's] marvellous light' (2:9); it clearly points to the spiritual transformation of baptism (3:21), and the personal charisms to be exercised by the baptized for the glory of God (4:10–11). For many years it was popular to think of this letter as a baptismal homily to which further material had been added. But this theory has been widely abandoned. Yes, 1 Peter explicitly refers to baptism (3:21), but it is a genuine letter and not a liturgical homily (Elliott 2000: 7–11).

1 Peter invokes some leadership roles: Peter himself as 'apostle of Jesus Christ' (1:1), evangelists who have converted to Christian faith those who are being addressed (1:12), and the elders who 'tend the flock of God' (5:1–5). As regards ecclesiological material and implications, three particular themes invite attention.

First, the letter yields early intimations of the challenges that will be brought by 'church–state' relations down through the centuries. The Christians in Roman provinces of Asia Minor suffer for 'the name of Christ' (4:12–14), but it seems that they are enduring only verbal abuse (3:9–12, 16). They are encouraged to honour the emperor and accept the authority of the governors he has appointed (2:13–17). They are not yet facing persecution and even martyrdom. In the current situation they should show themselves exemplary citizens. A few years later (around AD 112), Pliny, the emperor's legate in Pontus, scorned Christianity as 'a depraved superstition', but even then there was no question of their being proscribed and systematically hunted down (Elliott 2000: 97–103, 767–808).

Second, 'by reaching across the waters to the communities of Asia Minor, the letter establishes a bridge between the Church at the heart of the Roman Empire and the heaviest concentration of Christians anywhere in the Roman world'. As John Elliott adds, 'it represents the first of many efforts on the part of the Church of Rome to support and influence Christian communities abroad' (Elliott 2000: 134). Before the first century ends, 1 Clement will provide another example (concerned in this case with Corinth) of the Roman Church reaching out with pastoral responsibility to other Christian communities. Beyond question, the Gospels, the Acts of the Apostles, some letters of Paul, traditions about the martyrdom of Peter and Paul in Rome, and further early witness must come into play when examining the ministry of Peter along with its subsequent role, claimed and exercised by the church and bishop of Rome. 1 Peter has its special place for those examining the emergence of the specific Petrine ministry.

Third, 1 Peter signals a seismic change that will reverberate at the time of the Reformation, and in the teaching of the Second Vatican Council (1962–5) when it develops the theme of the priestly calling of the people of God. Like Paul (Rom. 12:1), 1 Peter applies priestly, sacrificial language to the baptized faithful. But their priesthood is not only 'royal', but also prompts their prophetic calling to 'proclaim the mighty acts of God' (2:9). We can detect an early pointer to baptism as sharing in the *munus triplex* of Christ as priest, prophet, and king—a theme developed by John Calvin, Blessed John Henry Newman, and Vatican II (O'Collins and Jones 2010: 206–38). Let me attend here to the holy priesthood of the baptized.

This letter calls Christ the 'living Stone' (2:4), a seeming contradiction, since stones are normally lifeless and dead. Yet the 'Stone rejected by the builders' (2:7) has been made 'alive' and 'raised' (to life) by God (1:3; 3:22), chosen to be the 'precious Cornerstone' (2:7) for God's new, 'spiritual house' (2:5), and is paradoxically not only the living Stone but also, by implication, *the* life-giving Stone. Freed from the perishable and dead existence of contemporary paganism, believers have been transformed into 'living stones', who share in the existence of the living Stone and are built together into one 'spiritual house'. The implied agent of this 'construction' is God, who brings the living stones together into a single unit that is joined together and supported by Christ, the foundation of the whole structure.

A 'spiritual house' (or 'household') seems to be 'a metaphor for the community where the Spirit of God dwells, although 1 Peter's intention is not to call attention to the Holy Spirit per se' (Michaels 1988: 100), nor to apply unambiguously temple imagery to the Christian community (1 Cor. 3:16–17; 2 Cor. 6:16) and to the individual believer (1 Cor. 6:19). By defining this 'spiritual house' as the place for 'a holy priesthood' (1 Pet. 2:5) or a 'royal priesthood' (1 Pet. 2:9), the letter implies that it is some kind of temple. A 'spiritual house' defined by priesthood should be a place where sacrifices are offered; after all, the work of priesthood is to offer sacrifices (Michaels 1988: 101). Hence, not surprisingly, 1 Peter talks of 'offering spiritual sacrifices acceptable to God through Jesus Christ' (2:5). Yet this image of the Christian community as a building (made up of 'living stones') embodies metaphorical or extended use of language. In the literal sense, a community is not a building. Furthermore, to write of 'spiritual sacrifices' offered by a holy priesthood is also an extended use of language. Literally speaking, sacrifices are offered by priests (see Heb. 5:1; 8:3) through ritual ceremonies conducted in temples. What then are the 'spiritual sacrifices', which are presumably sacrifices prompted by the Holy Spirit through whom believers have been sanctified (1:2)?

The Hebrew Scriptures, which provide in a covenant formula (Exod. 19:6) the term 'priesthood' to express the privileged and holy character of God's chosen people, had long used sacrificial language in an extended, metaphorical sense to describe prayer, repentance, and good works (e.g. Ps. 50:13–14, 23; 51:17; 141:2). 1 Peter follows suit by proposing a royal priesthood of Christians that involves prayer (in particular, proclaiming the 'saving acts' of God), holy conduct, and effective witness in their daily lives (1 Pet. 2:9, 11–12). Motivated by the Spirit, such sacrifices mean praising God and living a saintly way of life to the glory of God. The theme of the Christian community's 'spiritual sacrifices' 'acceptable to God through Jesus Christ' (2:5) evokes what we find in Romans 12:1 and in Hebrews 13:15–16, where such 'sacrifices' involve praising God and performing good deeds for those in need (Elliott 2000: 423).

1 Peter offers then a priestly, sacrificial vision of the whole church. Priestly/sacrificial language, in an extended, metaphorical way, portrays the chosen, covenant people called to a life of holiness (1:14–15). The priestly property of holiness applies to the entire community, as it did in Exodus 19:6 and Isaiah 61:6. Besides being the living Stone, who communicates life to those who as a royal priesthood constitute together a 'spiritual household', Christ might have been called a priest (as he is in Hebrews). But 1 Peter never gives him this title. Yet the letter goes beyond Hebrews by picturing the believing community as God's 'covenant people, whose intimate relation to God is like that of holy priests' (Elliott 2000: 437). Hebrews differs from 1 Peter by not deploying this notion of the church as God's holy, *priestly* community.

Two metaphors mark the verses we have examined in 1 Peter: the metaphors of growth and construction. While the metaphor of construction describes her corporate existence (2:4–5), the church is not called 'the body of Christ'. Unlike Ephesians 2:12–16, 5:21–32, 1 Corinthians 12:12–26, and Colossians 1:18, 1 Peter does not introduce the image of the church as a body, of which Christ is the living head. In short, we do not find in this letter the images of the church as the Body of Christ and the temple of his Holy Spirit. Finally, Christ is called the Cornerstone of a new 'spiritual household', but 1 Peter does not press on to develop any such 'structural' or spatial image, as Hebrews does when talking about Christ entering the heavenly sanctuary and ministering there eternally from the right hand of God.

HEBREWS

Written some time between AD 60 and 95 (perhaps more plausibly before 70), produced by a priestly milieu, and sent, not from Rome to Asia Minor (as was 1 Peter), but to Italy (Rome?) probably from Ephesus (Heb. 13:23–4), Hebrews is an anonymous sermon aimed at encouraging a community, which had earlier suffered considerable hardships (10:32–4), to maintain their faith and hope. They may be facing further persecution (13:3). Some of them could already be 'slipping away' (2:1), in danger of letting their hearts become 'hardened by sin' (3:13), being threatened by 'strange teaching' (13:9), and even abandoning faith in Christ (3:12; 6:4–6; 12:25). Certain individuals are already staying away from the liturgical meetings of the community (10:25). Hebrews maintains that apostates cannot repent and be restored to the grace of Christ (Oropeza 2012: 37–41).

It is the responsibility of 'the leaders' to speak the word of God, give a shining example in living their Christian faith, and watch over those whose faith may be eroded by strange teaching (13:7, 15). The community addressed by Hebrews is being 'served by a group of leaders rather than by one leading individual' (Koester 2001: 75). How they have become leaders is not made clear, nor does Hebrews clarify the situation by relating them to the elders (*presbyteroi*), overseers (*episcopoi*), and deacons (*diakonoi*) mentioned variously in Acts, the Pastoral Epistles, and elsewhere in the New Testament (e.g. the 'elders' in Jas. 5:14 and 1 Pet. 5:1; and the 'overseers' and 'deacons' in Phil. 1:1). At all events, the writer of Hebrews urges the community to 'obey' their leaders, who themselves are accountable to God (Heb. 13:17).

Hebrews stands apart by containing the best-known biblical narrative of Christ as priest and portraying him extensively in the exercise of his high priesthood. The vision of Christ as eternal High Priest makes its first appearance in Hebrews and seems a self-consciously avant-garde interpretation of Christ's death and exaltation. This exposition of Christ almost inevitably involves introducing the most complete theology of worship in the New Testament. As a 'word of encouragement' (13:22), the letter is to be presented orally to an audience gathered as a worshipping community.

Hebrews summons its audience to glorify God and 'approach' the divine presence through the Son, who has entered the heavenly sanctuary and is himself 'a most worthy and appropriate object of worship' (Heil 2011: 28). God's angels, spirits ministering through heavenly worship (1:6–7, 14), assist the faithful who meet 'today' (1:5; 4:7) in their liturgical assembly on earth and who open their hearts to hear the 'living word' of God (4:12). Christians, by faithfully taking part in the earthly liturgy, are already entering the future 'rest' (Heb. 3:11) in the heavenly Jerusalem, where they will share forever with 'innumerable angels' in the celestial worship (Heb. 12:22).

Somewhat like Hebrews, the Book of Revelation shows an interest in the worship for which Christians meet (1:3, 9–10). The church on earth can model its worship on the heavenly liturgy and the worship of the Lamb. Scenes of heavenly liturgy are woven seamlessly into the text (e.g. chs 4–5; 7:9–12; 11:15–19; 15:2–8). The 'lamp stands' (1:12–13,

20) lead on to the angels and saints who worship in the heavenly temple. Not surprisingly, liturgical hymns play an important role in Revelation (from 5:9 through to 19:1–10), and are sung by a choir that comprises angels, the elect, and all possible voices in the cosmos (14:1–3; 15:2–4). But such modelling of the church's earthly worship on heavenly worship is not a theme taken up by Hebrews, which is interested above all in the once-and-for-all high-priestly sacrifice of Christ, only partly prefigured by the repeated Yom Kippur sacrifices.

Like Revelation, Hebrews associates angels with the human worship of God. But, unlike Revelation, Hebrews explicitly mentions baptism, along with 'laying on of hands' (probably a ritual of commissioning) (Heb. 6:2), and adds to its picture of the church's sacramental life by probably referring to the Eucharist in which Christians share on a weekly basis: 'we have an altar (*thusiastērion*) from which those who officiate in the tent [= the Jewish priests] have no right to eat' (13:10). Something similar to what Paul wrote in 1 Corinthians 10 (about communal participation through the Eucharist in the sacrificial death of Christ) seems to be intended (O'Collins and Jones 2010: 28–9). As the spiritual food available on an altar, the Eucharist commemorates and sacramentally perpetuates for Christians the bloody death of Christ on the cross (Heb. 13:12). Through Eucharistic eating, believers share in the covenant established by Christ's death, and find 'the altar' where they can offer to him the sacrifice of their daily lives (Heb. 13:10).

What catches attention in Hebrews is not so much what we might call the liturgical 'specifics' but rather the cultic-priestly language which describes Christian access to God through prayer and worship. John Scholer has illustrated in much detail how three verbs, already used in the Septuagint with cultic-priestly meaning (*proserchesthai, eiserchesthai*, and *teleioun*), are applied to the audience that Hebrews addresses (Scholer 1991).

Without expressly saying that they share in Christ's own priesthood, Hebrews uses cultic, sacrificial language to depict the appropriate lifestyle of members of the church, and has more to convey along these lines than Paul (Rom. 12:1). Exhorting his addressees, the author of Hebrews says: 'through him [Christ] let us continually offer a sacrifice (*thusian*) of praise to God: that is the fruit (*karpon*) of lips that confess his name. Do not neglect to do good and to share what you have, for God is pleased (*euaresteitai*) with such sacrifices (*thusiais*)' (Heb. 13:15–16). Christians are to offer in sacrifice not the fruit of the fields, but the 'fruit' of their lips in confessing and praising God.

The priestly existence to which members of the church are called involves ongoing sacrifice, 'offered' not only through their prayers of praise and confession of faith but also through 'doing good' and generously sharing with others. A previous chapter has made it clear that it is obedience, expressed in praise of God and service of others (rather than e.g. animal sacrifices), that 'pleases' God (Heb. 10:5, 8). Such 'doing good' has also been clarified only a few verses earlier: it involves mutual love, hospitality to strangers, service to those in prison, fidelity in marriage, and avoiding avarice (13:1–5). One should also recall the exhortation at the end of the penultimate chapter to 'offer God a pleasing worship (*latreuōmen euarestōs*)' (12:28). What the closing chapter of Hebrews says about the daily sacrifice of Christian life fills out what such 'pleasing worship' entails. For the baptized faithful, Hebrews echoes the Old Testament's conviction about what is meant by a true 'sacrifice of thanksgiving' (Ps. 50:14, 23).

JUDE

Along with the Letter of James, Jude offered some of the last echoes in the New Testament of Jewish Christianity. But, unlike James and like 1 Peter, Hebrews, and 2 Peter, it frequently mentioned Jesus himself. As we shall see, 2 Peter drew on Jude, but that does not necessarily mean that Jude was written late in the first century; 2 Peter could have used a text composed decades before. In fact, some scholars date Jude as early as AD 50. Jude, while not referring to the fall of Jerusalem (AD 70) or any of the calamities connected with that traumatic tragedy, nevertheless, recalled 'the predictions of the apostles' (v. 17), as if they were a well-known group belonging to the past (the Twelve plus Paul, or an even wider group). It likewise spoke of 'the faith that was once and for all entrusted to the saints' (v. 3), giving an impression of looking back to an earlier generation of Christians to whom was delivered a body of faith and practice, the foundational revelation that came through the life, death, and resurrection of Jesus, together with the outpouring of the Holy Spirit.

The Letter of Jude may have been written in Palestine by Jude, one of the Twelve (Luke 6:16; John 14:22; Acts 1:13), who could have been a kinsman of Jesus (Mark 6:3) and a brother of James, the leader of the Jerusalem church (v.1) (Davids 2006: 8–12). But, for two reasons, Jude does not provide much help towards glimpsing life in any of the early Christian churches. First, at twenty-five verses, it is the shortest New Testament letter after Philemon and the Second and Third Letters of John. Second, the Letter of Jude does not develop any teaching about the church (or other such theological topic) but simply meets an emergency facing an unknown community (apparently in the Eastern Mediterranean) threatened by ungodly 'intruders' (v. 4), who present themselves as travelling teachers or prophets (a feature of early Christianity), but are not legitimate members of the community. They somehow 'pervert the grace of our God' (v. 4), 'indulge their own lusts, are bombastic in speech, and flatter people to their own advantage' (v. 16). Firmly opposed to their erroneous and dangerous teaching, the writer of the letter wants to help the community, who are 'called, are beloved in God the Father, and kept safe for Jesus Christ' (v. 1). But it is not made clear what his relationship to them is and why, apart from his being a 'servant' of Christ and 'brother' of James, they should respect the authority of his letter.

What themes could we glean from Jude about the practice and theory of church life? Three points suggest themselves. First, the injunction to 'contend for the faith that was once and for all entrusted to the saints' (v. 3) might be translated into later language: 'remain faithful to the faith that comes to us from the apostles'. In other words, we could recognize here an early, albeit implicit, attention to the need to maintain the church as 'apostolic' in her teaching.

Unnamed opponents threaten this foundational, apostolic faith. Hence Jude announces that 'these dreamers' will suffer judgement as did the Israelites (Num. 14:20–3), the angels who went astray (Gen. 6:1–4), and the people of Sodom and Gomorrah (Gen. 19). The opponents reject authority and are guilty of slander (Jude 8–10); they will be severely judged as happened to Cain the murderer (Gen. 4:9), Balaam who prophesied for profit (Num. 22), and Korah who rebelled (Num. 16) (Oropeza 2012: 165–7). Jude concludes his condemnation of the 'intruders' by citing against them a prophecy of judgement from 1 Enoch, a collection of apocalyptic sayings (vv. 14–16). Jude is obviously convinced that their errors lead the community towards death (see Cain), that they are acting for their own gain (see Balaam), and that they rebel against apostolic authority in the church (see Korah). It is then in strong language that Jude condemns the intruders (see Matt. 7:23). But the precise nature of their false teaching is left unspecified, apart from the general statement that 'they deny our only Master and Lord, Jesus Christ' (v. 4). Jude clearly insists that the health of church life depends on upholding what would later be called 'sound teaching', but spends more time denouncing those who threaten to pervert such teaching and harm the members of the community. Their doctrinal errors lead to immoral behaviour.

Nevertheless, one might understand the letter to unfold at the end what it understands to be the heart of 'the faith entrusted to the saints'. Jude beautifully connects the moral life of Christians to their faith in the Spirit, God [the Father], and 'the Lord Jesus Christ' (in that order): 'beloved, build yourselves up on your most holy faith, pray in the Holy Spirit; keep yourselves in the love of God; look forward to the mercy of our Lord Jesus Christ that leads to eternal life' (20–1). This Trinitarian confession leads Jude to exhort the members of the church to show mercy towards sinners: 'have mercy on some who are wavering, save others by snatching them out of the fire'. In the spirit of 'love the sinner but hate the sin', the letter adds something about concern for those who apparently commit sexual sins: 'have mercy on still others with fear, hating even the tunic defiled by their bodies' (22–3).

To conclude his letter, Jude adds a beautiful doxology, inspired by and elaborating 'the faith entrusted to the saints': 'to him who is able to keep you from falling, and to make you stand without blemish in the presence of his glory with rejoicing, to the only God our Saviour, through Jesus Christ our Lord, be glory, majesty, power, and authority, before all time, and now and forever. Amen' (24). Hardly any books in the New Testament have a theologically richer ending; it moves from acknowledging the primacy of divine grace (which 'keeps us from falling' and 'makes us stand') to praising and glorifying God through 'Jesus Christ our Lord'. Jude closes with a prayer that exemplifies how the community of the church should express the heart of their apostolic faith.

A second theme, which touches the core of church life and has been developed in modern times by such theologians as Henri de Lubac, Hans Boersma, and a number of Orthodox thinkers, shows up, almost in passing, when Jude refers to the Christian 'love feasts (*agapais*)'. In denouncing the activity of the intruders, Jude calls them 'blemishes on your love feasts, while they feast with you without fear, feeding themselves' (12). He manifests here a concern for what can happen when Christians meet to celebrate the Lord's Supper and eat together at an *agapē* or love feast. Paul shows a similar worry when writing to the Corinthians: instead of such common meals building up the community, some go hungry and others drink too much (1 Cor. 11:20–1). What should be a Eucharistic occasion building up the church can lose its communal purpose.

Admittedly, what Jude and, for that matter, Paul say is brief and as such negatively expressed. Yet, taking up in a positive way what they have in mind, we find here an early hint of the principle 'the Eucharist makes the church'. Jude, like Paul, hopes and expects that the celebration of the Lord's Supper and the meal that accompanies it should build up the church as a truly holy, loving, and undivided community. Those assemblies should make, rather than unmake, the church.

Thirdly and more broadly, Jude illustrates a lasting concern for the healthy life of scattered Christian communities: they should be concerned for the well-being of each other and, in particular, for their willingness to heed the Holy Spirit and maintain deep unity with one another. Beyond question, this kind of 'catholic' concern for other churches shows up most emphatically in the letters of St Paul. But we can spot it also in what Jude writes. The intruders, whom he dismisses as 'worldly people, devoid of the Spirit, are causing divisions' in the community which he addresses (19). Putting positively what he says, those led by the Holy Spirit will remain deeply united with each other. In his less famous way, Jude reveals something of Paul's 'anxiety for all the churches' (2 Cor. 11:28).

For material, or at least implications, involving church life, we can glean three pointers from Jude: the apostolic nature of Christian faith; the principle of the Eucharist making and uniting the church; and a 'catholic' spirit that cares about and wants to help other ecclesial communities. In short, this letter wants the church founded by Christ to be truly 'apostolic', 'one', and 'catholic'. To this we can add the commitment to true holiness that underpins Jude's campaign against the ungodly intruders, who threaten to lead Christians not only away from their true faith but also towards immorality. In short, Jude aspires to uphold a church that is one, holy, catholic, and apostolic.

2 PETER

Many scholars date 2 Peter to around AD 100 or even later, often holding it to be the very last New Testament book to be composed, and hence placing it after the other four texts that we have already examined. It draws extensively from Jude, being the only New Testament letter to incorporate so much material from another letter. Yet 2 Peter differs from Jude: for instance, by explaining what it opposes. Where Jude never specifies clearly the false teaching of the 'intruders', 2 Peter denounces those who reject the final coming of Christ and the last judgement (3:1–13).

What ecclesiological material might we glean from 2 Peter? What specific emphases does it offer for the theory and practice of church life? First, the warnings against false teachers (2:1–22) witness to a deep concern that the members of the community should be guided by true teaching. Accusing the false teachers of moral corruption implies that failure in orthodox belief will corrupt the church and lead to sinful and even vicious misdeeds. Down the centuries many Christians endorsed a similar conviction: ortho-doxy and orthopraxy go hand in hand, or, at least, failures in orthodoxy will issue in be-haviour unworthy of a follower of Christ. Second, the letter upholds the central function of the Scriptures, inspired by the Holy Spirit, for church life. The 'prophetic message' of the Scripture will guide believers like a 'lamp shining in a dark place until the day dawns' (1:19–21).

Perhaps the most significant contribution of 2 Peter to ecclesiology comes in the spe-cific 'twist' it gives to belief in the apostolic (see 3:2) foundation and nature of the church. It does so by linking the figures and functions of Peter and Paul. Here 2 Peter clarifies and continues a trajectory initiated by 1 Peter. Let me explain.

1 Peter not only adopts the Pauline letter form (for instance, in its opening salutation) but also refers to Silvanus and Mark (5:12–13), known companions of Paul (1 Thess. 1:1; Philemon 24), and develops Pauline themes in presenting the new identity of the people of God (1:13–2:10), their conduct (2:11–3:12), and the suffering they endure (3:13–5:11). While never mentioned by name, Paul remains a kind of subtext in a letter which pictures Peter exercising a pastoral oversight towards Christians in five Roman provinces of Asia Minor.

Some or even many years later, 2 Peter explicitly introduces Paul and, referring to 'all his letters', implies that they had already been collected and are associated with 'the other scriptures'. While 'some things' in these letters may be 'hard to understand', their scrip-tural authority is unchallenged and their correct interpretation remains a life-and-death matter (3:15–16). This brief allusion to Paul's letters, provided that they are rightly inter-preted, being authoritative for church life prefigures the role of Paul in Christian history. To a greater or lesser extent, Christian faith and practice has been shaped by these let-ters, their interpretation, and their application. Thus 2 Peter signals a point of arrival, the collection of Paul's letters, and a point of departure, their revealing and saving impact as the further story of Christianity begins to unfold in its post-apostolic history.

Thus 2 Peter, by continuing a trajectory already initiated by 1 Peter, suggests that, taken together, these two letters offer an early intimation not only of a Petrine role of pastoral oversight, but also of a Pauline role in teaching the whole church (and not simply those communities founded by Paul). Drawing such an ecclesial vision from 1 Peter and 2 Peter interprets the apostolic character of the church as called to be both Petrine and Pauline. Within the wider group who, being sent by Christ, established the apostolic origin and character of Christianity, Peter and Paul stand out as apostles with special and lasting roles for the church.

SUMMING UP THE ECCLESIOLOGY
OF THE FIVE TEXTS

What themes deserve to be recalled and emphasized from James, Hebrews, Jude, and 1 and 2 Peter? In their somewhat distinctive ways, these four letters and a homily

(Hebrews) express and promote the four 'marks' of the church (as one, holy, catholic, and apostolic). All five texts are concerned with the healthy and unified life of individual Christian communities that face suffering. Two of them (James and 1 Peter) address various, scattered communities in a desire to maintain a worldwide, catholic communion. All five books promote an ecclesiology based on their inherited Scriptures, and in one case (2 Peter) scriptural authority is understood to distinguish the letters of the apostle Paul. Both 1 and 2 Peter open by appealing to the apostolic authority of Peter.

James suggests the role of teachers and elders in the dispersed communities. 1 Peter addresses the elders in the communities of Asia Minor. With what it says about 'leaders' in its closing chapter, Hebrews gives that name to a group called to speak the word of God and nourish the genuine faith of their community.

To conclude. The Letter of James portrays a counter-cultural, wisdom ecclesiology for suffering communities. 1 Peter envisions church members as royal and prophetic priests who worship God through their sacrificial living, and, albeit briefly, points to all the baptized as being priests, prophets, and kings. Hebrews proposes an ecclesiology of worship which exhorts Christians to praise God and serve others. Jude highlights the apostolic faith on which the church's life is based. Finally, 2 Peter suggests, once again briefly, an ecclesiology that combines a Petrine and a Pauline trajectory. We could sum up significant elements in the five approaches by saying that the church should be wise (James), priestly (1 Peter), worshipping (Hebrews), faithful (Jude), and both Petrine and Pauline (2 Peter).

References

Davids, P. H. (2006). *The Letters of 2 Peter and Jude*. Grand Rapids, MI: Eerdmans.
Elliott, J. H. (2000). *1 Peter*. New York: Doubleday.
Hartin, P. J. (2009). *James*. Collegeville, MN: Liturgical Press.
Heil, J. P. (2011). *Worship in the Letter to the Hebrews*. Eugene, OR: Wipf and Stock.
Johnson, L. T. (1995). *The Letter of James*. New York: Doubleday.
Koester, C. R. (2001). *Hebrews*. New York: Doubleday.
Michaels, J. R. (1988). *1 Peter*. Waco, TX: Word Books.
O'Collins, G. and Jones, M. K. (2010). *Jesus our Priest: A Christian Approach to the Priesthood of Christ*. Oxford: Oxford University Press.
Oropeza, B. J. (2012). *Churches under Siege of Persecution and Assimilation: The General Epistles and Revelation*. Eugene, OR: Cascade Books.
Scholer, J. M. (1991). *Proleptic Priests: Priesthood in the Epistle to the Hebrews*. Sheffield: Sheffield Academic Press.

Suggested Reading

Allison, Dale C. (2013). *The Epistle of James* (*ICC*). New York/London: Bloomsbury.
Bauckham, R. (1999). *James: Wisdom of James, Disciple of Jesus the Sage*. London: Routledge.

Bauckham, R. J. (ed.) (2009). *The Epistle to the Hebrews and Christian Theology*. Grand Rapids, MI: Eerdmans.

Bockmuehl, M. (2010). *The Remembered Peter in Ancient Reception and Modern Debate*. Tübingen: Mohr Siebeck.

Chilton, B. and Evans, C. A. (eds) (1999). *James the Just and Christian Origins*. Leiden: Brill.

Edgar, D. H. (2001). *Has not God Chosen the Poor? The Social Setting of the Epistle of James*. Sheffield: Sheffield Academic Press.

Mason, E. F. and McCruden, K. B. (eds) (2011). *Reading the Epistle to the Hebrews: A Resource for Students*. Atlanta: Society of Biblical Literature.

Neyrey, J. H. (1993). *2 Peter, Jude*. New York: Doubleday.

Niebuhr, K.-W. and Wall, R. W. (eds) (2009). *The Catholic Epistles and Apostolic Tradition*. Waco, TX: Baylor University Press.

Nienhuis, D. R. and R. W. Wall (2013). *Reading the Epistles of James, Peter, John & Jude as Scripture*. Grand Rapids, MI: Eerdmans.

O'Collins, G. (2012). 'Peter as Witness to Easter', *Theological Studies* 73: 263–85.

Wachob, W. H. (2000). *The Voice of Jesus in the Social Rhetoric of James*. Cambridge: Cambridge University Press.

Watson, D. F. and Callan, T. (2012). *First and Second Peter*. Grand Rapids, MI: Baker Academic.

PART II

RESOURCES FROM THE TRADITION

CHAPTER 7

EARLY ECCLESIOLOGY IN THE WEST

MARK EDWARDS

ECCLESIOLOGY is one of the youngest of the theological sciences, and it would arguably be an abuse of language to bring any ancient work under that description. This is not to say that the church was of no consequence to the Fathers; on the contrary, its existence—with the notes of unity, catholicity, and apostolicity which the creeds accorded to it—was an ineluctable presupposition of all dogmatic reasoning and scriptural exegesis. Whereas exegesis could be a medium of instruction or contemplation in the absence of any heretical interlocutor, a defence of the church was never undertaken without an apologetic motive. Accordingly, we cannot separate ecclesiology from ecclesiastical history: the occasion prescribes the content of the work, and it is often the case that ecclesiological principles can be inferred only from the legal manoeuvres which resolved or exasperated the original cause of estrangement. These facts account for the presence in this chapter of more narrative material than might appear to be warranted by the title; on the other hand, limits of space and the bias of evidence entail that the adjective 'western' must be understood with reference primarily to Africa and Rome.

GREEK PROLEGOMENON

The epistle of Paul to the Romans makes no mention of a Eucharist or any order of ministers. Those who deduce that the city had no bishop are required by their own logic to conclude that its church possessed no organization of any kind. The community was diverse in composition, if the apostrophe 'I speak to you Gentiles' (Romans 11:13) is correctly taken to imply that Jews are addressed in other portions of the letter. This, however, is a weak foundation for what has now become a dogma in some quarters, that there was not one congregation in Rome, but a loose ensemble, each receiving a different communication from the apostle (cf. Minear 1971: 7–8). Reliable gleanings from

Ignatius' letter to the Romans are even scantier. His proem is a string of adulatory epithets, not because he accorded any precedence to the Roman church but because he is addressing it in the posture of a suppliant. On the other hand, the absence of any reference to a bishop signifies only that he was ignorant of the structure of this church, or that no schism had been brought to his attention, or simply that he could not speak to the children of Peter and Paul with the authority that he assumed when answering delegations from the churches of Asia (Romans 3; cf. Streeter 1929: 223). It is from the inhabitants of the city, not from their correspondents, that we must hope to learn what can be learned about the structure of the Roman church in the first two centuries, and about the principles by which it was underwritten.

The first document to emerge from the Roman communion is a long epistle, attributed in Greek and Latin versions to Clement, one of the earliest bishops of the city, though in a Coptic text the superscription is simply 'from the Romans' (Turner 1912: 257). Scholars have dated the letter to a time of persecution on the strength of the author's allusion to a series of calamities (*First Clement* 1); nevertheless it was certainly written after Peter and Paul had died to cover the sins of Nero, and Domitian's persecution of AD 95 is generally believed to have been fictitious, or at least exaggerated (cf. Lampe 2003: 198–205). Since Pliny's confession that he had never been present at the trial of a Christian (Letter 96) indicates that such trials were not rare in the later first century, it is useless to seek a more accurate date for the letter. It is equally impossible to discover from the letter what authority the writer supposed himself to possess in the church at Corinth, to which it is addressed. The occasion, to use his own word, is 'sedition' (*First Clement* 3)—that is, refusal of deference to *episkopoi*, or overseers; the antidotes are repentance (7) and humility (13). Embellishing Paul's comparison of the church to a body (and intimating, perhaps, that he regards himself as heir to the apostle), the author exhorts the Corinthians to submit to their rulers, just as the members of the imperial army submit to those who are placed at the head (37). This is a plea for order, not a summons to militancy in the publication of the gospel. Similarly, the subsequent comparison of the *diakonoi* (deacons or servitors) to the Levites who performed inferior functions in Jerusalem (42) is designed to inculcate obedience, not to confer a sacerdotal function on the *episkopoi*. The inference that the temple had not yet fallen would be unwarranted, since Jewish survivors of this event assumed that the priesthood was only temporarily suspended. Nor can we surmise that the author recognized only two ministries, for he later commends those presbyters who have 'obtained a fruitful departure from this world' (44).

The dissemination of the visions of Hermas, another Greek-speaking author of the Roman church, were also entrusted to a certain Clement (*Shepherd*, vision 2.4). This cannot be the bishop if, as the author of the Muratorian canon affirms, the *Shepherd* of Hermas was written 'in our times, during the episcopate of Pius'. This dating of Hermas (*pace* Hahneman 1992: 51–61) is corroborated by the Liberian Catalogue of Roman bishops (Turner 1912: 149). Once we have uncoupled the Clement of Hermas from his namesake, the conjecture that the bishop of Rome was merely a secretary loses all credit (cf. Brent 2011: 284). The seer receives his vision not from any officer but from the church herself, who appears to him at Cumae first as an aged woman whom he mistakes for the Sibyl (vision 1.2 and 2.4) and then in the forms of two younger women (vision 3.10). Whereas the first epiphany reveals that the church has existed from the beginning, and that all was made for her, the rejuvenation of the old woman betokens the renewal of life in the repentant sinner (vision 3.11–13). The church is shown to Hermas as a tower of polished stones, reinforced by others 'dragged up from the depths', while others again are discarded with contempt, and a further quarry of unhewn or disfigured stones lies around the tower awaiting the hand of the mason (vision 3.2–9). Hermas is informed that the edifice represents the church, that the polished stones are the apostles, *episkopoi*, teachers, and *diakonoi*, that the stones from the depths are martyrs, the discarded stones the hypocrites, and the rough materials Christians who have lapsed and cannot be restored to the church without penance. It is not clear, any more than at 1 Corinthians 12:28, whether the apostles are current members of the church, or whether the teachers correspond to the presbyters of *First Clement*. The purpose of the *Shepherd* is to persuade the church that the lapsed are not lost for ever, but the means of reconciliation are not described with liturgical precision. He himself is chastised not by a minister but by an angel (vision 5; similitude 7); teaching appears to be the task of prophets (similitude 9), while the presbyters figure as governors or patrons rather than sacred functionaries (vision 2.4; cf. Stewart-Sykes 2001: 41).

We learn more of the ceremonial practices of the Roman congregation from Justin Martyr, whose *First Apology* was written in the years preceding the death of the Emperor Antoninus Pius in 161. In order to dispel false accusations and deprive the pagan cults of their claim to precedence, he explains that baptism is a bath of regeneration, the candidate being escorted to the waters by a sponsor and immersed with a threefold blessing in the name of the Father, the Son, and the Holy Spirit (*First Apology* 61). He does not tell us how the sponsor is nominated or who administers the blessing. The 'illuminated' neophyte is admitted to the assembly of the brethren, where the man who presides at the Eucharist utters a prayer of thanks for the gifts of bread and wine which are then distributed by the deacons and received by the men and women of the flock as the body and blood of Christ in accordance with his own promise at the Last Supper (65). We are not told whether the president is appointed for each meeting or exercises a permanent office.

Now we come to a crux of interpretation in Irenaeus. He writes:

> *Ad hanc enim ecclesiam propter potentiorem principalitatem necesse est omnem convenire ecclesiam, hoc est eos qui sunt undique fideles, in qua simper ab his qui sunt undique conservata est ea quae est ab apostolis traditio.* (Irenaeus, *Against Heresies* 3.3.2)

Roman Catholic polemicists have been apt to take the words *necesse est convenire* (literally, 'it is necessary to come together') to mean that every church has a duty of submission to Rome. Their Protestant counterparts, dwelling on the appeal to *eos qui sunt undique fideles* ('the faithful who are from everywhere'), have argued that *necesse est convenire* signifies only that, since everyone's business takes him to Rome at some stage, this city has more right than any other to be regarded as a microcosm of the church universal (Beaven 1841: 64–7, citing Gregory Nazianzen, *Oration* 32). Neither the Roman nor the Protestant reading, however, has done perfect justice to the syntax of the Latin which is our only witness to the Greek original. It was only to be foreseen that when a more adequate translation was proposed by Pierre Nautin (1957: 59), it turned the scale for neither party, since the subject of the sentence proved to be not the church at Rome but any church that fulfilled the generic definition of orthodoxy:

> For the church to which, on account of its greater potency, it is necessary that every church—that is, the faithful from everywhere—should be united, is the one in which people from everywhere have always conserved the tradition which comes from the apostle. (Cf. Abramowski 1977)

The context shows that this description applies to Rome, but only because she meets the conditions that would vindicate the doctrine of any other church. She is at best an amanuensis, not the arbiter, of catholicity; the sundial, not the sun.

The list of bishops supplied by Irenaeus (*Against Heresies* 3.3.3), concurring roughly with that of Hegesippus (Eusebius, *Church History* 4.22), shows that he was writing in the episcopate of Eleutherus (d. 185). His dealings with the successor of Eleutherus—the Latin-speaking Victor, sometimes said to have been an African—have been cited to prove that Gaul had no conception of papal primacy in this epoch, and even that Rome herself did not yet possess a monarchical episcopate. Once more, the facts do not justify all that has been deduced from them. According to Eusebius (*Church History* 5.23.2), Irenaeus had been party to an agreement with the bishop of Rome and prelates in Asia Minor which required the Asiatics in Rome to renounce the 'Quartodeciman' rule for the calculation of Easter which they had brought with them from the east. When they proved refractory, Victor pronounced them excommunicated; when Polycrates, bishop of Ephesus, tried to intercede, the irascible Roman applied the same sentence to him. At this point Irenaeus wrote a letter of remonstrance; at no point, however, does he suggest that Victor was claiming more than his right or deny that Rome was under the jurisdiction of a single bishop. On the contrary, he implies that it has always been a monarchy when he enumerates the predecessors of Victor to show that, while they had powers as absolute as his, they employed them with a more Christian lenity (*Church History* 5.24.14). If we had other evidence for a doctrine of papal primacy, this letter would not count against it, since a subject is not forbidden to advise his sovereign, least of all when he has such a manifest advantage in age, in scholarship, and in knowledge of affairs.

The Age of Callistus

At the beginning of the third century, we find another autocrat in Rome, and on the other hand, a fierce proponent of a less arbitrary (though in this case not a less rigorous) mode of governance. Whether the *Refutation of all Heresies* is the work of Hippolytus the commentator or of a disciple, its author asserts the right to excommunicate those whom he has convicted of heresy and to give lessons in orthodoxy to the present incumbent of the Roman see. That there is such an office, and that Callistus holds it, he does not deny, though he thinks the man quite unworthy of his position. Callistus, we are told, owed his elevation to his predecessor Zephyrinus, who rescued him from the penalties of a long career of lechery and imposture (*Refutation* 9.11). This report, whether true or false, is evidence of what could be done in Rome by episcopal fiat; Callistus made an equally tyrannical use of his status when he published a decree readmitting murderers, adulterers, and apostates to communion in defiance of his fellow churchmen in Rome and other provinces. He compounded this offence by permitting the ordination of men who had been twice married, by sanctioning marital unions (not recognized in Roman law) between free women and slaves, and by administering second baptisms to penitent schismatics who had already been duly baptized (9.12.22–6). At the same time, he had connived at heresy, even propagating one of his own, and had overruled the excommunications which the author of this invective had imposed on other heretics (9.12–13). Defamation in the ancient world was not restrained by legal sanction or any canon of verisimilitude, but it is obvious that unless such acts were generally agreed to be illicit they would not have served the polemical intention of the author. We may be confident, therefore, that the church of Rome had hitherto refused ordination to digamists, denied its blessing to marriages not recognized in Roman law, acknowledged any baptism duly administered, withheld its pardon from the most heinous sinners, and regarded the sentence passed by a suffragan as irreversible. The term 'suffragan' here is conjectural (tradition makes Hippolytus, perhaps anachronistically, bishop of Portus), but the author of the refutation is certainly not to be characterized as an antipope or as an opponent of episcopal monarchy (cf. Döllinger 1876: 68–100; Brent 2011: 305). The quarrel is not between monarchists and republicans but between absolute and constitutional notions of the bishop's prerogative.

Among Hippolytus' writings was a manual of church order, entitled *The Apostolic Tradition* (Dix and Chadwick 1992; Stewart-Sykes 2001). Robert Connolly identified this with his reconstruction of a third-century ordinal from its surviving variants in Coptic, Arabic, Ethiopic, and Latin (Dix and Chadwick 1992: d). The marks of a tortuous history of redaction are visible even in this reconstructed archetype, and the ascription to Hippolytus, or even to a Hippolytean school, is not universally accepted. It requires some ingenuity to detect in it any evidence of a desire to curtail the pretensions of Callistus (*pace* Hennecke 1921). We cannot be sure, for example, that when Zephyrinus ordained Callistus he flouted the ordinance that this rite should be performed in the presence of other bishops and presbyters (Dix and Chadwick 1992: 3); a popular election is mandatory (2), but this need not be incompatible with nomination by the last incumbent. The powers of a monarchical bishop would not be abridged by the clause which requires that other presbyters should lay hands on a candidate whom the bishop is admitting to their college (13). The canon bestowing the honours of the presbyterate on all confessors may in some eyes have compromised the dignity of that office (18), but it was not inimical to episcopal monarchy, since other qualifications were required of the confessor before he could be installed as a bishop. Both presbyters and bishops could perform baptismal immersion, but the recitation of the subsequent prayer was reserved for the bishop, as were the ordination of deacons and the appointment of readers (20–1 and 30–9). Whether we understand the term 'bishop' to signify the president of the entire church or a suffragan, Callistus would have no reason to take offence at the consecratory prayer which accords to the bishop the function of a high priest who remits the sins of the laity (5). In any case, no sound history can be based upon a document that is merely the precipitate of scholarly rumination on other texts.

ROME AND AFRICA

Tertullian, an African contemporary of Hippolytus, wrote a caustic tract against one whom he styles ironically 'bishop of bishops' and Pontifex Maximus—surely the first application to the bishop of Rome of a title that he could not accept so long as it was still borne by the emperor as the chief dignitary of the civic cult (*On Modesty* 1.6). The sin of the pontifex is that of Callistus, the readmission of sinners whom the ordinances of Christ and his apostles had cut off from the church for ever. We should not conclude, for all that, that Tertullian was an opponent of the papacy. Having espoused the new prophecy of Montanus, he was at odds with the majority of Christians, shunning them as psychics because they failed to observe the austerities which the Spirit had now enjoined on the elect (*On Modesty* 1.10; *On Fasting*). There is only one morality, he avers, for clergy and laity; the church itself is the Spirit (*On Modesty* 21.16) and two or three gathered in the name of Christ are a congregation (*On Flight* 14.1). Nevertheless, Tertullian neither rejects the existing ministry nor proposes to set up a new one for his own sect (Rankin 1995: 27–52). While he can appeal to the visions of 'sisters' to decide a question of discipline or philosophy (*On the Soul* 9), he admits to the clerical rank neither women nor men who have contracted a second marriage (*Veiling of Virgins* 9; *Exhortation to Chastity* 7). His admonitions to virgins who refused the veil and his opposition to the baptism of infants who were incapable of penance (*On Baptism* 18.5) show that he was no friend to the passive Christianity which hopes to be saved by mere adherence to an institution. But rigorism is not secession (at least not in the third century), and his complaint that Zephyrinus had failed to bring peace to the churches of Asia suggests that he ascribed to the Roman see a higher authority than such a tenant as Zephyrinus was capable of wielding (*Against Praxeas* 1). It also reveals that what we call Montanism was to him an internal movement of reform, not yet a conventicle outside the Asian church.

While Carthage was never a patriarchate, its most illustrious bishop was often known to posterity as Papa Cyprian. By birth a pagan of high rank, he did not share the reluctance of the New Testament to use the term 'priest' (*sacerdos*) of the bishop as celebrant of the Eucharist (Seagraves 1993: 86). He was accused, however, of putting his life before his duty when he went into hiding in 251 to escape an edict requiring universal sacrifice.

Those who remained had a choice between compliance and imprisonment on capital charges. Cyprian was scandalized to hear that these confessors were being credited with the power of absolution, and that indulgences were being granted in the names of martyrs. From his asylum he denounced these practices. Resuming his office after the persecution, he decreed that those who had compromised their faith should perform strict penance before they could be restored to communion. Many preferred to listen to the confessors who embraced a more lenient policy, and a cabal of five presbyters urged that the bishop had forfeited his position by his flight. Only after Rome had examined the case and endorsed his tenure was he secure.

This dispute inspired the first ecclesiological treatises in Latin. In *On the Lapsed* Cyprian argues, against those who believed that his prerogative could be overruled by the charismatic authority of the confessors, that those who wilfully court persecution are tempting Christ and flouting his command to the disciples. In *On the Unity of the Church* he insists that there is but 'one dove' whom the bridegroom calls his own in the Song of Songs (4). The church has many branches but one root; her numerous streams have issued from a single font (5). Some of those who mouth the slogan that the church is where two or three are gathered together (12) are joining ranks with Korah, Dathan, and Abiram (18). Christ's seamless robe cannot be rent (7); he who tries to part it will find himself outside the church, like one who swims outside the ark (6). Though Christ vouchsafed the keys to all the apostles, it was to Peter alone that he said 'upon this rock I shall build my church', in order to teach us that the church and the episcopate that governs it must be one (4). His precept is that brethren should live in unity, and the malcontent, even when he claims the dignity of a confessor, is no longer confessing Christ (20). Neither in the short version of this treatise nor in letters which adduce the same words of Christ is there any reference to Peter's sojourn in Rome or to his episcopal successors. Some manuscripts, however, contain a longer form of chapter 4 of the treatise, in which agreement with the Roman church is said to be a condition of the true faith. Anglicans have argued that the short text is the more original, Roman Catholics either that the longer is more authentic or that one is Cyprian's own revision of the other for a new occasion (Bevenot 1938). The controversy that darkened the later years of Cyprian shows that, whichever text he preferred, he did not hold the understanding of Roman primacy that was fostered in his time by at least one occupant of that see.

Carthage was obliged to intervene in Roman affairs when the election of Cornelius was challenged by the first antipope, Novatian, on the grounds that a man who was willing to readmit the lapsed to communion was no fit successor to the martyred Fabian. Cornelius, in a letter to the bishop of the East, protested that the clandestine election of Novatian gave him no right to assume the charge of the forty-six presbyters, seven deacons, seven sub-deacons, forty-two acolytes, fifty-two exorcists, numerous readers and doorkeepers, and 1,500 widows who were under the tutelage of the Roman see (Eusebius, *Church History* 6.43.11). Cyprian wrote to corroborate his argument that the suffrage of the people was a necessary prerequisite of episcopal tenure (Letter 42), and characterized his own detractors, now Novatian's allies, as false bishops ordained outside the church and therefore unknown to God (Letter 40). He and Cornelius, therefore, were at one in their doctrine of penance and in their belief that the voice of the populace cannot be countermanded by an appeal to the primitive usage of the church.

Cornelius, dying after a brief episcopate, was succeeded by Stephen, who, finding it prudent to make friends where he could, confirmed the tenure of a Novatianist in Gaul and of two Spanish bishops who had lapsed under persecution. Members of both congregations appealed to Cyprian, who in taking up their cause revealed that he, like his plaintiffs, recognized no duty of submission to Roman mandates. He and Stephen also differed as to the necessity of rebaptizing those who joined the catholic fold after baptism at the hands of Novatianist ministers. In letters to his own sympathizers (70, 73), Cyprian averred that only one baptism can prepare the church as a spotless bride for Christ, and that no one who holds a false notion of Christ's relation to the Father can be said to have baptized in the name of Father, Son, and Spirit. No distinction is acknowledged here between schism and heresy, as in Cyprian's eyes the paramount commandment is that all Christians should be one. Stephen, it would appear, replied with a menacing rattle of the keys that he had inherited from Peter. Cyprian forwarded this response to Bishop Firmilian of Cappadocia, who indignantly accused Stephen of usurpation and of making common cause with the most notorious dividers of the church in the second century (Letter 75). It is evident that, although the moral pre-eminence of Rome had been admitted by Greek Christians, they did not concede an unqualified power of legislation to the heirs of Peter. Cyprian died before the quarrel could be resolved, and long before the Council of Nicaea had vindicated Stephen's principle that even schismatic baptisms could be valid if administered in due form.

Steps in the Ascent of Rome

We have seen that it was as common to appeal from Rome to Carthage as from Carthage to Rome in this era. Roman law permitted the appointment of any arbiter who was acceptable to all parties, with the proviso that there should be no further appeal from the judgement given on that occasion (Harries 2001: 177–8). It is possible, therefore, that when, around the year 260, subordinates of Bishop Dionysius of Alexandria denounced him as a heretic to his namesake Dionysius of Rome, they chose this referee because they could be assured of his neutrality and not because they thought him a more authoritative judge of orthodoxy than any prelate of the east (Athanasius, *On the Opinion of Dionysius*). On the other hand, a deliberate marriage of temporal and spiritual authority may have been envisaged by the pagan emperor Aurelian in 270 when, at the instance of the eighty eastern bishops who had deposed their Antiochene colleague Paul of Samosata, he forced the condemned man to accept his sentence and entrusted the nomination of his successor to the 'bishops of Rome and Italy' (Eusebius, *Church History* 7.30.19). In 313, after intrigues that are now obscure, a tribunal of twelve Italian and three Gallic bishops met under the presidency of Miltiades, bishop of Rome, to judge the case of Felix of Abthugni, who was accused of having handed over copies of the Scriptures during the Great Persecution under Diocletian (Optatus, *Against the Donatists* 1.23–4). Felix was also one of the consecrators of Caecilian as successor to Mensurius, bishop of Carthage. His accusers, soon to be the 'party of Donatus' (Optatus, 1.22), had declared the election invalid and set up a rival bishopric. Much has been written of the primitive mentality of the Donatists and of their supposed conviction that the true church is the church of martyrs. Be that as it may, to catholic observers this was nothing but a new Novatianist schism, an appeal from popular suffrage to a private canon of rectitude. The synod of 313 had only to judge whether Felix was innocent; when they pronounced him to be so, the matter might have rested, had the trial not taken place within a year of Constantine's occupation of Rome. The Christian emperor was soon persuaded not to accept the position later enunciated by Augustine: 'Rome has spoken; the case is done.' Instead, and at the instance of the Donatists, he brought the case before the Council of Arles which he convened in 314. This was not the first council in the West: an earlier assembly of Spanish bishops at Elvira had republished a 'Hippolytan' list of prohibited occupations and excluded from clerical office those who had fallen into heinous sin after baptism (Jonkers 1954: 5–23). It was, however, the first such event in which a Christian sovereign had acted in conjunction with the anointed representatives of the church.

Silvester, the successor to Miltiades, did not attend the council, on the plea, as it appears, that he could not desert the place in which the blood of the apostles daily testified to God. Hereafter Rome's claim to be the apostolic see par excellence was always to rest on the fact that she was the city in which two apostles had won the crown of martyrdom. The council's letter to him is a study in irony, returning his own words to him with mock solemnity as a preface to a list of resolutions which they had issued in his absence (Optatus, appendix 4). It is not clear whether the emperor was present; if he was, he was not content with the decision to confirm Caecilian in the see of Carthage and acquiesced only after subjecting him to a private interrogation. Despite his exclamation that a prince who awaited judgement was not fit to judge the affairs of bishops, the role of the imperial voice in clerical deliberation had yet to be defined.

Nicaea as Canon

At the Council of Nicaea in 325, Silvester was the one bishop to be represented solely by his legates. It is a measure of Rome's pre-eminence that their names stand first in a list of over 200 signatories; so too is the sixth canon, which in ratifying Alexandria's primacy in Egypt cites as a parallel the position of Rome in the western provinces. Fifteen years after Nicaea, Rome was drawn by overtures from both sides into the quarrel between Athanasius of Alexandria and a party of eastern prelates. Pope Julius, having reviewed the charges against Athanasius, unilaterally pronounced him innocent and summoned the easterners to account for their machinations at a Roman inquest (Athanasius, *Defence against the Arians* 20–36). They refused, and took no part in the Western Council of Sardica in 343. At the instance of Hosius of Cordova (Julius once again being absent), the council agreed by acclamation to forbid the installation of bishops by a single presbyter or in a place with few inhabitants (Turner 1930: 500–1); to prescribe that none should be made a bishop until he had held the offices of reader, deacon, and presbyter (514–15); to forbid the translation of bishops from one see to another (490–1); to restrain the use of bribery in securing popular suffrage (492–3); to provide for appeals by aggrieved defendants to their metropolitans (524–5), while discouraging overtures to the secular powers (512–13); and to arrange for the security of the possessions that a bishop left behind in his see when visiting one of his properties elsewhere (520–1). The most notable resolution granted the bishop of Rome the privilege of reopening a case that had been tried in another province and of being represented on a tribunal appointed under his supervision (494–5). It does not expressly confer on him the privilege, lately assumed by Julius, of summoning to his own court those who had already judged the matter. This canon can thus be seen either as a supplement to or as an abridgement of the powers to which he had laid claim on that occasion (Puller 1893: 151 versus Chapman 1928: 66–8). Subsequent bishops of Rome gave an appearance of oecumenical authority to these canons by annexing them to those of Nicaea (Hess 2002: 56–7). Although the historical falsehood was unmasked when they were invoked in a dispute between Rome and Africa, it was possible in the ninth century for the learned patriarch Photius to assert that Silvester and Julian had jointly presided at the Nicene Council (Epistle 1, p. 4 (Laourdas and Westerink)).

Under Constantius II, who ruled with less tact than his father Constantine, a series of councils rendered the Nicene Creed untenable. After Pope Liberius had first submitted to the Council of Sirmium in 357 and then refused to accept the ratification of its decrees at Ariminium in 359, the antipope Felix (set up by the emperor in 355) acquired a larger following. After the deaths of both, the vacancy was filled by Damasus, but not without a bloody riot which showed that, whatever had been the electoral custom hitherto, no aspirant could now hope to prevail unless he commanded an active majority of the people. Damasus used his power as imperiously as he had won it. His own voluminous name at the beginning of a letter to eastern bishops, which announces a synodical resolution in favour of strict adherence to the Nicene doctrine, could almost have been taken for that of the emperor whose rescript convened the synod (Schwartz 1936: 19–20). The superiority of the Nicene Council of 325 to that of Ariminum, which met in 359 under the auspices of Constantius, lies in the fact that only the former was attended by representatives of Rome. Against Rome the 600 delegates at Ariminum count for nothing, though this (questionable) number was later adduced by the Vandals in Africa as proof that the Nicene creed did not express the true mind of the church (Victor of Vita, *Vandal Persecution* 3.5).

Further Aggrandizement of the Papacy

Among the most zealous advocates of the papacy was the foremost scholar and satirist of the epoch, Jerome of Stridon. Himself a presbyter, he held that the primitive church had recognized only two orders of ministry; it was only to forestall schism that Peter

EARLY ECCLESIOLOGY IN THE WEST   173

was set above the eleven, and so long as schism threatens the church her unity is preserved by our paying honour to the high priest (*Against the Luciferians* 9). Clerics in Rome who argued that diaconal and episcopal orders were equal could derive no support from Jerome (Chapman 1928: 106). Shocked and perplexed by the rivalries that had troubled the see of Antioch for three decades, he exclaimed to Damasus, 'I know not Vitalis; I spurn Meletius and disown Paulinus. He who does not gather with you scatters; that is, whoever is not of Christ is of antichrist' (Letter 15.2.2). He appeals to the practice of the bishop of Rome against Vigilantius, who had slighted the cult of relics: does the Roman bishop do wrong when he prays upon the relics of the two apostolic martyrs (*Against Vigiliantius* 8)? Scholars have remembered that the walls of the capital had been cemented by the blood of Remus, brother to Romulus (Knight 1936: 97). It can be argued that, in Rome and elsewhere, the church ascribed the same tutelary function to its martyrs that the city had once accorded to its founder (but cf. Brown 1982: 6). To Jerome, however, Rome is not so much a place as an instrument of ecclesiastical unity. He turned his acidulous pen against the orthodox but schismatic sect of Lucifer of Cagliari, who had severed themselves from other Nicene bishops after the latter restored communion with bishops whom they considered heterodox. Treating the Luciferians as latter-day Novatianists, he accepted on Nicene principles that their baptisms remained valid. The Luciferians challenged this logic. An Arian, they protested, cannot baptize, since he denies the Nicene teaching on the Trinity. We show as much by requiring one who has been baptized as an Arian to do penance before he rejoins the true fold; a bishop who is required to do penance, however, cannot retain his office, since the role of a bishop is to confer forgiveness, not to be forgiven. Jerome retorts that one of two alternatives must be granted: either an Arian baptism confers the Holy Spirit or an Arian cannot baptize. If the latter is true, the Luciferians ought to rebaptize the penitent Arian; if they do not rebaptize, they admit that an Arian can confer the Spirit, and that is possible only if he who baptizes has the Spirit, which is to say that he has been validly ordained (*Against the Luciferians* 6–9). These sentiments would have seemed liberal to Cyprian, but in questions of clerical discipline it was impossible to be more austere than Jerome. Denouncing Jovinian, who urged that ministers should be allowed to marry, he retorted that the verse which allows a bishop to have one wife does not permit the begetting of offspring during his tenure of the episcopate. As it is now universally agreed (he goes on) that a bishop who begets offspring betrays his office, it is better that he should have no wife and leave the task of populating the world to the less continent among the laity (*Against Jovinian* 34). Although the titles 'bishop', 'deacon', and 'presbyter' signify office rather than merit (34), those who hold them are required to maintain a higher standard of chastity than the priests of the elder covenant, which was a shadow of things to come (39).

What was the emperor doing meanwhile? Whenever there were two sovereigns, the one who ruled the West was the junior partner, and in this era his realm was more exposed to usurpation and to encroachment from without. He often resided elsewhere than Rome, where he had to contend both with the real power of the bishop and with the antiquated pretensions of the senate. In consequence the bishop of Rome enjoyed a far greater measure of autonomy than his brother in Constantinople; nor was there any other patriarch in the adjoining provinces to contest his seniority. In 378 a council sought a decree from the Emperor Gratian making those bishops who defied provincial synods subject to discipline at Rome. The decree that was issued granted to Rome this hegemony over bishops of every province, and also extended to clerics in every province the right of appeal against episcopal decisions. The Roman bishop's right to play the autocrat thus appeared to have been sanctioned from above, and the immediate heirs of Damasus—Siricius and Xystus—adopted a magisterial tone when writing to lesser prelates which bespeaks a sense of having received not merely the papal chair but the dignity of a 'great potentate' (Puller 1893: 162). Yet while the imperial mandate gave a louder voice to the bishop of Rome, it did not confer any new powers of coercion on him or his allies. Ambrose was obliged to secure the favour of Gratian in 379 by the public catechization of his adversary Palladius (McLynn 1994: 124–37), and when Priscillian of Avila had the honour to be the first Christian burned for heresy in 395, it was not a mitred churchman but the tyrant Maximus Magnus who ordered the kindling of the fire.

Ecclesiology Outside Rome

Thus we learn from the canons of Sardica that a bishop could be wealthy and that the office was now coveted; from Jerome we learn that continence (if not celibacy) had now become a norm. The duties and perquisites of Christian ministers are set out in treatises longer than those of Cyprian by two contemporaries of Damasus. Ambrose, however, is less concerned, in his manual *On the Duties of the Clergy*, to define the liturgical functions of the bishop than to inculcate the humility that ought to accompany his teaching office and to illustrate the practice of holiness, charity, and virtue in daily intercourse with the people. His brief text *On the Mysteries* informs the catechumen at the outset that the presbyter is a priest and the bishop an arch-priest (2.6); these titles pertain to them not because they perform a sacrifice but because they preside over rites that incorporate the believer into the body of Christ. It is the priest's invocation of Christ that renders baptism efficacious, not his merits as a man (5.27), and it is the Spirit, not the man, who imparts the blessing (4.19). As we purge the sin of the first man in the footwashing after baptism (4.32: perhaps an innovation of the Milanese church), so when we receive the flesh and blood of Christ in the Eucharist, we are not receiving life in the present world but anticipating the imperishable joy of the life to come (8.49). As Hilary of Poitiers had already intimated (*On the Mysteries* 13), the church is an ark for those not yet delivered from the flood.

The Donatist controversy forced an undistinguished stylist, Bishop Optatus of Milevis, into a prolix work on the formal desiderata of catholicity. The true church, he declares, is represented in every province, and its unity is sustained by the exchange of episcopal letters or *formatae* (*Against the Donatists* 2.3). Membership of this church is conferred by a single baptism in the name of the Holy Trinity: to repeat this is to forget that the circumcision which prefigures it can be performed but once and was ordained for all time by a single promise to Abraham (5.1). The sacraments are holy in themselves; it is God who cleanses, ministers being but God's executives (5.4). Even if the catholic succession in Carthage were tainted by apostasy, the example of Peter shows that the penitent can be reconciled (7.3). Christ pronounced a blessing on the peacemakers (4.2), remembering the Psalmist's exclamation, 'Behold, how good it is for brethren to dwell in unity' (3.6 and 4.4; Ps. 32:1). The Donatists who have wilfully torn apart the body of Christ are worse than apostates: they are imitating the sin of Dathan, Abiram, and the sons of Korah, who set up unhallowed altars in the wilderness against those whom God had anointed for his service (1.21). Few Christians of this period would have questioned the assumption that the church inherits the sacramental and sacerdotal dispensations of Israel; Optatus is, however, the earliest writer outside Italy to make communion with Rome the test of a valid priesthood. Six notes define the true church: the throne of Peter, the angel in baptism, the Holy Spirit, the keys, the font, and the priesthood (Ratzinger 1954: 106). The Donatists who have set up their own conventicle near the city (2.4) are not only flouting the judgement of Miltiades but despising the authority that Christ vested in Peter, the first incumbent of the Roman see (2.3; cf. Eno 1993).

The mantle of Optatus passed to Augustine. Posthumously refuting the same opponent, the Donatist bishop Parmenianus, he urged again that a church cannot exist only in one province. The discovery of his aphorism *securus judicat orbis terrarum* ('the world is a secure judge') was recalled by John Henry Newman as one of the accidents that prompted his own conversion to Roman Catholicism (*Against Parmenianus* 3.25; Newman, 2008: 228). The new element in the treatise—new to the controversy, though it is the life-giving sap of Augustine's theology in all its branches—is his doctrine that the efficacy, as opposed to the mere validity, of the sacrament is determined by the ability of the church that administers it to imbue the neophyte with a faith that works by love (Galatians 5:6). As fallen beings, we cannot find love in ourselves without the infusion of the same Spirit that descended on Christ at his baptism and raised him from the dead. The catholic church is the body on earth of him who was love incarnate; since his death and our baptism were ordained for the remission of sins, the Donatists too must learn to tolerate sin if they would call themselves a church (*On Baptism* 1.9.12; 3.16.21, etc.). If sinlessness in the minster is a prerequisite, the layman cannot know whether he is receiving a valid sacrament (*Against Cresconius* 3.11.13); and who would accept the sacrament from a man who, being convinced of his own impeccability, cannot comply with the Lord's injunction to pray each day that his sins may be forgiven (*Against the Letters of Petilian* 2.104.237)? Schism is the one vice that deprives the font of its power to effect the remission of sins (*On Baptism* 5.22.30).

The Donatists assert that they alone are the heirs of Cyprian, but those who hold that saint in higher reverence will not forget that he never divided himself from other catholics, but maintained communion for the sake of charity with those who differed from him in their readiness to accept baptisms administered by schismatics (*On Baptism* 2.15.20, etc.). It was Cyprian, after all, who said that to leave the church is to swim outside the ark (5.28.39). The Donatists have been obliged to excommunicate their greatest scholar Tyconius because he maintained that the true church must be universal (*Against the Letter of Parmenianius* 1.1). Furthermore he took Matthew 13:40, as catholics also do, to mean that the wheat in the church will not be separated from the tares until the last day (*On Christian Teaching* 3.37.55 cf. *Against Petilian* 3.3.4). Augustine thus acknowledges, like Ambrose, that the church as we see it is only the provisional, and therefore imperfect, tenement in which we await the day when our corrupt flesh will be clothed in incorruption. The true number of the saints, as Augustine demonstrates at length in the *City of God* (O'Daly 1999: 211–17), will remain unknown until the last day.

So much Calvin might have said; there are, however, passages in Augustine's writings, such as his protestation to the Manichees that he would not believe the gospel if the church did not commend it, which would sit more happily now with a Roman Catholic ecclesiology (*Against the Fundamental Letter* 5.6). In his essay *On Christian Teaching*, which holds up love as a hermeneutic prism to the Scriptures, Augustine declares that the reader need not be troubled about the authorship of a biblical text so long as the church admits it to the canon (2.8.12–13). Yet here a provincial note intrudes, for the canon stipulated by the African church encompasses the whole of the Septuagint, and is therefore wider than those laid down by the most illustrious of his Greek precursors, Athanasius and Cyril of Jerusalem. It seems that he could impute error to the Greeks without compromising the principle of catholicity: thus, when he heard that the Eastern Council of Sardica in 343 had recognized Donatus, he retorted that this had been an assembly of heretics (Letter 44.3.6). Since this council upheld the deposition of Athanasius, he was speaking for every knowledgeable catholic; but he did not so easily find friends outside Africa when he argued that the synod of Diospolis would not have acquitted Pelagius of heresy had they known how to construe his evasive answers. When Pope Zosimus, also a Greek, endorsed this exculpation of Pelagius, he was obliged to change his ruling by a storm of remonstrance from Africa (Merdinger 1997: 128–30). Only in an early poem against the Donatists does Augustine equate catholicity with adherence to Rome (Batiffol 1920), and the Pelagian controversy appears to have taught him that it was possible for a single province to be more catholic than the church at large.

LEO TO GREGORY

Nevertheless appeals to Rome from Africa grew more frequent—so frequent that the popes refused a hearing to plaintiffs who had not first laid their grievances before the primate of Africa (Merdinger 1997: 63–110). This rule was often breached, as we learn from Augustine's strictures on Antony of Fussala (Letter 20; Munier 1983). While the position of Rome was thus aggrandized from below, it was Pope Celestine who in 431 extended Rome's writ beyond the Roman Empire by commissioning Palladius to preach the gospel in Ireland. In the same year, by ordering his legates to regard Cyril of Alexandria as his own deputy, he ensured that he and Cyril, not the Emperor

Theodosius II, would be remembered as the presidents of the Third Oecumenical Council held in Ephesus. In 449 Celestine's successor Leo received a letter from Flavian of Constantinople, which announced that the local synod had condemned the archimandrite Eutyches for his misconstruction of Cyril's doctrine. Leo's *Tome to Flavian*, which reaffirms the headship of Peter and upbraids the synod for its failure to stigmatize all the defendant's errors, was designed for public reading at a new council, convened once again in Ephesus to hear the appeal of Eutyches. When his legates were silenced and Eutyches acquitted, Leo would not rest until the insult to Rome and the faith had been expiated by an oecumenical council. The Council of Chalcedon in 451 complied, saluting Rome as the apostolic see and adding words from the *Tome* to its definition of the two natures in Christ. It also decreed, however, that Constantinople, as the New Rome, should enjoy the same prerogatives in the East that already pertained to Rome in the West. Leo expressly refused to endorse this canon when assenting to the Definition, and hinted that the Definition itself was an otiose supplement to the Nicene Creed, which he himself had already vindicated in the *Tome* (Grillmeier 2002: 120–48). Here he implies, more clearly than in the *Tome* itself, that the creed of the Roman church was that of Nicaea, and no longer the so-called Apostles' Creed, hitherto the only one to receive a Latin commentary. Leo failed to deter his brothers in Constantinople from employing the title 'Oecumenical Patriarch', which survived even the eloquent reprimand of Gregory the Great (Letters 5.18).

A rupture between Constantinople and Rome in the late fifth century inspired the famous letter of Pope Gelasius in which he defined two sovereignties, that of the pope as vicar of Peter and that of the emperor as vicar of God. It followed, as he fearlessly informed his nominal overlord Anastasius that an emperor was bound to submit his conscience to the prelates who were bound to honour him in temporal matters (Barmby 1880: 619). Rome at this time was under the dominion of Theodoric, who, as an Arian (more properly, Ariminian), was perhaps the first Christian sovereign to tolerate two churches without partiality. Only when he was asked in 498 to adjudicate between rival claimants to the Roman see did he lay his hand on catholic affairs. He had reason to regret his choice of Symmachus, who suffered more than one impeachment during his pontificate. His plea that only a pope can judge a pope secured his immunity; when his accusers scoffed, his bellicose champion Ennodius of Pavia declared that if a man's merits did not fit him for the chair of Peter the chair bestowed its merits on the man (*Libellus* 24 at Caspar 1931: 36).

The catholic church in Africa had fallen under the Vandal yoke in 430, but was liberated in 534 by the strategy of Belisarius and the statesmanship of his master Justinian. Determined to return as subjects, not as slaves, the African bishops told Vigilius of Rome, after unctuous flattery of his office, that the royal condemnation of Cyril's antagonists Theodore, Ibas, and Theodoret was unacceptable to them because the dead had no opportunity to recant (Price 2012: 111). Justinian, who had also reconquered Rome through Belisarius, had just enough reverence for the see of Peter to kidnap Vigilius, detain him in Constantinople, and browbeat him into signing the acts of the Fifth Oecumenical Council in 553 (Price 2012: 42–59). Italian bishops outside the sway of

Byzantium lost no time in excommunicating Vigilius, since he had forfeited his primacy by anathematizing three men whom the Council of Chalcedon had acquitted or ignored with the approbation of Pope Leo. From this nadir the papacy was rescued by the atrophy of Byzantine power in Italy and by the elevation of Gregory, the second bishop of Rome to be styled 'the Great'.

The 'servant of the servants of God', as Gregory preferred to be known, reunited almost the whole of the former Western Empire under Roman primacy in the space of fourteen years (590–604). It was during his pontificate that the Visigoths of Spain, traducing their former selves as Arians, adopted the faith of the subjugated Catholics. It was Gregory who sent Augustine to evangelize the Kentish king who had married a Frankish princess, and thus inaugurated the reconversion of southern Britain. To judge by his *Pastoral Rule* and his letters, however, nothing was further from his thoughts than ecclesiastical despotism. The first quality required of any ruler, he asseverates in the former work, is humility (1.6); he must covet pre-eminence (*Pastoral Rule* 1.8), but regard all righteous members of the church as his fellow workers (2.6). His virtues must be fortified by study and maintained by sedulous practice, so that his mind will not be driven to and fro by the fluctuation of worldly affairs (1.2; 1.4). He must learn to temper his preaching to his audience, to be stern with the rich offender while giving solace to the poor, to set the hope of heaven before the sad and the fear of hell before the joyful (3.3). In accordance with his own principles, he weighed the case before he returned an answer when he was consulted (as he desired to be) on questions of ecclesiastical discipline. In Spain he sanctioned the use of baptism in the name of Jesus alone when he learned that immersion in the threefold name had been the usage of the Goths when they were Arians (Letters 1.43). Writing to Augustine, his missionary in Kent, he relaxed the law excommunicating persons who had married their second cousins because a neophyte would be unable to bear such an alteration to his hereditary custom (Bede, *Ecclesiastical History* 1.27). It was by this acquiescence in diversity that Gregory was to become the most absolute ruler that western Christendom had known (cf. Meyvaert 1963).

Epilogue

After Gregory's death the papacy wrestled with the shadow of Byzantium, truckled to the Lombards, and was forced at length to clasp the mailed fist of Charlemagne. Rome's pretensions grew as her power declined, and the forged Donation of Constantine awarded to her both temporal and spiritual dominion over all the patriarchates of the obsolete Roman Empire. This document, however, could be ignored, overruled by *force majeure*, or bent to the will of those who professed to be Charlemagne's successors. When the papacy once again reached the height to which Gregory had raised it, it was under Cardinal Hildebrand, who as Gregory VII was the sixth pope to avail himself of the lustre of that name.

REFERENCES

Primary Sources

Translations are cited where possible. The abbreviations ANF and NPNF denote respectively *A Select Library of the ante-Nicene Fathers* and *Nicene and Post-Nicene Fathers*, both published by Eerdmans (Grand Rapids, MI) and often reprinted.

Ambrose. *Select Works.* NPNF 2–10.

Athanasius. *Select Works.* NPNF 2–4.

Augustine. *Writings against the Manichaeans and Donatists.* NPNF 1–4.

Augustine (1997). *On Christian Teaching.* Trans. R. P. Green. Oxford: Oxford University Press.

Bede (1969). *Ecclesiastical History of the English People.* Ed. and trans. B. Colgrave and R. Mynors. 2 vols. Oxford: Clarendon Press.

Clement of Rome (2007). In M. W. Holmes (ed. and trans.), *The Apostolic Fathers.* Grand Rapids, MI: Baker.

Cyprian (1971). *De Lapsis* and *De Unitate Ecclesiae.* Ed. and trans. M. Bevenot. Oxford: Clarendon Press.

Cyprian (1984–9). *Letters.* Trans. G. W. Clarke. 4 vols. New York: Paulist Press.

Ennodius. *Libellus pro synodo.* See Caspar (1931).

Eusebius (1926). *Ecclesiastical History.* Ed. and trans. Kirsopp Lake and others. 2 vols. Cambridge, MA: Harvard University Press.

Hermas (2007). *The Shepherd.* In M. W. Holmes (ed. and trans.), *The Apostolic Fathers.* Grand Rapids, MI: Baker.

Hilary of Poitiers (1947). *Traité des mystères.* Ed. and trans. J-P. Brisson. Paris: Cerf.

Hippolytus. *Refutation of all Heresies.* ANF 5.

Ignatius of Antioch (2007). In M. W. Holmes (ed. and trans.), *The Apostolic Fathers.* Grand Rapids, MI: Baker.

Irenaeus (2012). *Against the Heresies.* Book 3. Trans. M. Steenberg. New York: Paulist Press.

Jerome. *Principal Works.* NPNF 6.

Justin Martyr (2009). *Apologies.* Ed. and trans. D. Minns and P. Parvis. Oxford: Clarendon Press.

Leo the Great (1899). *Tome to Flavian.* Ed. and trans. T. H. Bindley. *The Oecumenical Documents of the Faith.* London: Methuen, 279–91.

Optatus (1997). *Against the Donatists.* Trans. M. J. Edwards. Liverpool: Liverpool University Press.

Photius (1983). *Epistulae.* Vol. 1. Ed. B. Laourdas and L. G. Westerink. Leipzig: Teubner.

Pliny the Younger (1969). *Letters and Panegyric.* Ed. and trans. B. Radice. 2 vols. Cambridge, MA: Harvard University Press.

Victor of Vita (1992). *History of the Vandal Persecution.* Trans. J. Moorhead. Liverpool: Liverpool University Press.

Scholarly Literature

Abramowski, L. (1977). 'Irenaeus, *Adv. Haer.* 3.3.2: Ecclesia Romana and Omnis Ecclesia; and ibid. 3.3.: Anacletus of Rome'. *Journal of Theological Studies* 28: 101–8.

Barmby, J. (1880). 'Gelasius, Pope'. In W. Smith and H. Wace (eds), *Dictionary of Christian Biography.* Vol. 2. London: John Murray, 617–25.

Batiffol, P. (1920). *Le Catholicisme de saint Augustin.* Paris: Lecoffre.

Beaven, J. (1841). *An Account of the Life and Writings of St Irenaeus, Bishop of Lyons and Martyr*. London: Rivington.

Bevenot, M. (1938). *St Cyprian's* De Unitate *Chap. 4 in the Light of the Manuscripts*. London: Burns, Oates and Washbrooke.

Brent, A. (2011). 'The Identification of Christian Communities in Rome', in E. Norelli (ed.), *Des évêques, des écoles et des hérétiques*. Prahins: Zèbre, 275–315.

Brown, P. (1982). *The Cult of Saints*. Chicago: Chicago University Press.

Caspar. E. (1931). *Theoderich der Grosse und das Papstum*. Berlin: De Gruyter.

Chapman, J. (1928). *Studies on the Early Papacy*. London: Sheed and Ward.

Dix, G. and H. Chadwick (trans.) (1992). *The Treatise on the Apostolic Tradition of Hippolytus of Rome*. London: Alban Press.

Döllinger, I. Von (1876). *Hippolytus and Callistus: The Church of Rome in the Early Third Century*. London: T. and T. Clark.

Eno, R. B. (1993). 'The Significance of the Lists of Roman Bishops in the Anti-Donatist Polemic'. *Vigiliae Christianae* 47: 157–70.

Grillmeier, A. (2002). *Christ in Christian Tradition*. Vol. 2, part 1. London and New York: T&T Clark.

Hahneman, G. M. (1992). *The Muratorian Fragment and the Development of the Canon*. Oxford: Clarendon Press.

Harries, J. (2001). *Law and Empire in Late Antiquity*. Cambridge: Cambridge University Press.

Hennecke, E. (1921). 'Hippolyts schrift "apostolichen Überlieferung über Gnadengaben"'. *Harnackc-Ehrung*. Leipzig: Hinrichs, 159–82.

Hess, H. (2002). *The Early Development of Canon Law and the Council of Sardica*. Oxford: Clarendon Press.

Jonkers, E. (1954). *Acta et symbola Conciliorum quae saeculo quarto habita sunt*. Leiden: Brill.

Knight, W. Jackson (1936). *Cumaean Gates*. Oxford: Blackwell.

Lampe, P. (2003). *From Paul to Valentinus*. London and New York: T&T Clark.

McLynn, N. (1994). *Ambrose of Milan*. Berkeley: University of California Press.

Merdinger, M. (1997). *Rome and the African Church in the Time of Augustine*. New Haven: Yale University Press.

Meyvaert, P. (1963). 'Diversity within Unity: A Gregorian Theme'. *Heythrop Journal* 4: 141–62.

Minear, P. S. (1971). *The Obedience of Faith*. London: SCM Press.

Munier, C. (1983). 'La Question des appels à Rome d'après la Lettre 20e d'Augustin'. In *Études augustiniennes* (special volume): *Les Lettres de saints Augustin découverts par Johannes Divjak*. Paris, 287–99.

Nautin, P. (1957). 'Irénée, *Adv. Haer.* III.3.2: église de Rome ou église universelle?'. *Revue de l'histoire des religions* 151: 36–76.

Newman, J. H. (2008), *Apologia pro Vita Sua*. New Haven: Yale University Press.

O'Daly, G. (1999). *Augustine's City of God: A Reader's Guide*. Oxford: Clarendon Press.

Price, R. (2012). *The Acts of the Council of Constantinople of 553*. Liverpool: Liverpool University Press.

Puller, R. (1893). *The Primitive Saints and the See of Rome*. London: Longman.

Rankin, D. (1995). *Tertullian and the Church*. Cambridge: Cambridge University Press.

Ratzinger, J. (1954). *Volk und Haus Gottes in Augustins Lehre von der Kirche*. Munich dissertation.

Seagraves, R. (1993). *Pascentes cum disciplina: A Lexical Study of the Clergy in the Cyprianic Correspondence*. Fribourg: Éditions universitaires.

Schwartz, E. (1936). 'Über die Sammlung des Cod. Veronensis LX'. *Zeitschrift für die Neutestamentliche Wissenschaft* 35:1–24.

Stewart-Sykes, A. (2001). *Hippolytus on the Apostolic Tradition*. English Version with Introduction and Commentary. New York: St Vladimir's Seminary.

Streeter, B. H. (1929). *The Primitive Church*. London: Macmillan.

Streeter, B. H. (1930). *Ecclesiae Occidentalis Mounmenta Iuris Antiquissima*. Vol. 1, fascicle 2, part 3. Oxford: Clarendon Press.

Turner, C. H. (1912). *Studies in Early Church History*. Oxford: Clarendon Press.

SUGGESTED READING

Brent, A. (1995). *Hippolytus and the Roman Church in the Third Century*. Leiden: Brill.

Brown, P. (2012). *Through the Eye of a Needle: Wealth, the Fall of Rome and the Making of Christianity in the West*. Princeton: Princeton University Press.

Humfress, C. (2007). *Orthodoxy and the Courts in Late Antiquity*. Oxford: Oxford University Press.

Jalland, T. (1941). *The Life and Times of St Leo the Great*. London: SPCK.

Markus, R. (1976). *Saeculum: History and Society in the Theology of St Augustine*. Cambridge: Cambridge University Press.

Markus, R. (1997). *Gregory the Great and his World*. Cambridge: Cambridge University Press.

Pietri, C. (1976). *Roma Christiana*. 2 vols. Rome: École Française de Rome.

Van Dam, R. (1992). *Leadership and Community in Late Antique Gaul*. Berkeley: University of California Press.

CHAPTER 8

THE EASTERN ORTHODOX TRADITION

ANDREW LOUTH

ECCLESIOLOGY in the Eastern Orthodox Tradition is deeply problematic. On the one hand, there is a beautiful and inspiring ecclesiology expressed in the Divine Liturgy and the liturgical texts, which might be summarized as 'the church: the Body of Christ, Virgin Mother of Christians, and the Bride of the Lamb slain from the Foundation of the World'. On the other hand, there is a history of ways of understanding the church in the world, in which the church has largely accepted the consequences of the conversion of the Roman Empire in the course of the fourth century, namely, its incorporation into the structures of the Roman Empire as part of the ideal of *symphonia*, harmony, between the church and the Empire: an ideal passed on to the Slav nations that accepted Byzantine Christianity towards the end of the first millennium, first in Bulgaria, and then among the Rus' in Kiev, finally providing the ideology for the Russian Empire with its capital in Moscow. This ideal of *symphonia* was embraced again by the Orthodox nations that emerged from under the Ottoman yoke in the nineteenth and early twentieth centuries; most of these nations soon passed under the Communist yoke, causing further problems for the ideal of *symphonia*. In the diaspora, the notion of Eucharistic Ecclesiology became popular as an alternative to what had become the tradition of *symphonia*. Orthodox ecclesiology is further complicated by the fact, common to the West, that there was little direct reflection on ecclesiology in the early period (indeed hardly at all, even in the West, until the later Middle Ages), so there is no patristic doctrine to give a steer to modern Orthodox reflection on the Church.

This chapter will consist of three parts. First, an exposition of the, largely poetic and symbolic, understanding of the church that we can glean from the early centuries, which underlies the liturgical experience of ecclesiality in the Orthodox tradition. Second, an exposition of the Orthodox understanding of the four notes of the church, confessed in the Nicene (or Niceno-Constantinopolitan) Creed: namely, unity, holiness, catholicity, and apostolicity. Finally, we shall turn to the practical working-out of ecclesiology, both in the history of the church and today.

The Church as Body of Christ, Virgin Mother of Christians, and Bride of the Lamb, Slain from the Foundation of the World

The earliest reflection on the church was bound up with understanding how God had been at work in Christ. In order to make sense of this the apostles and evangelists turned to the Scriptures. Especially important for understanding the person and the passion of Christ were what scholars nowadays call the songs of the Suffering Servant, especially the last (Isa. 52:13–53:12), which speaks of the suffering of the servant, bruised for our iniquities and pouring out his soul unto death. Modern scholars reckon this song to close with verse 12; the apostle Paul, however, in his allegory of the two sons of Abraham (Gal. 4:22–31), takes the following verse as the conclusion of the song, followed in this by the liturgical practice of the Orthodox Church, where this passage is read once a year, at Vespers on Good Friday, which commemorates the entombment of Christ: 'Sing, O Barren One, who did not bear; break forth into singing and cry aloud, you who have not been in travail! For the children of the desolate one will be more than the children of her that is married, says the Lord' (Isa. 54:1).

Thus the proclamation of the Suffering Servant concludes with the joyful exclamation that the barren one will give birth, for it is, after all, into Christ's death and resurrection that Christians are baptized, being born again of the water and the Spirit, putting on Christ, and living in him by the grace of the Spirit as sons and daughters of God (Rom. 6, etc.). Paul calls the Barren Woman the heavenly Jerusalem, the church, in whom, as a result of Christ's passion, Christians are born as children of the promise, children of God. The placing of Christ in the tomb prepares the way for the womb to become fertile. A verse recited as the Holy Gifts are placed on the holy table at the Great Entrance says: 'As life-bearing, as truly more beautiful than paradise, your tomb, O Christ, has been shown to be more radiant that any royal wedding chamber, for it is the source of our resurrection.'

Numerous texts from the early centuries, and beyond, continue to reflect on the church as Mother or the Virgin Mother, the barren Woman who as a result of Christ's passion conceives children of God. There are two particularly relevant texts from the second century. The first is *The Shepherd of Hermas*, the first part of which recounts various visions, in which a woman, identified as the church, appears to Hermas. In the first vision, chiding Hermas for his sin of desiring his mistress as a wife, she appears as an old woman, 'clothed in shining garments and holding a book in her hand' (*Vision* 1.2.1). Later, Hermas has another vision:

> And a revelation was made to me, brethren, while I slept, by a very beautiful young man, who said to me, 'Who do you think that the ancient lady was from whom you

received the little book?' I said, 'The Sibyl.' 'You are wrong,' he said, 'she is not.' 'Who is she, then?' I said. 'The Church,' he said. I said to him, 'Why then is she old?' 'Because,' he said, 'she was created the first of all things. For this reason she is old; and for her sake the world was established [ὅτι, φησίν, πάντων πρώτη ἐκτίσθη· διὰ τοῦτο πρεσβυτέρας καὶ διὰ ταύτην ὁ κόσμος κατηρτίσθη]'. (*Vision* 2.4.1)

In a still later vision, the old woman shows Hermas a tower being built out of stones that had been prepared for the task. The stones that were cracked, rotten, or of the wrong shape were rejected, while the stones that were used fitted together so well that the tower seemed to be built out of a single stone. When he asked for an explanation, Hermas was told by the woman: 'The tower which you see being built is myself, the Church, who have appeared to you both now and formerly' (*Vision* 3.3.3).

The church is personified as a female figure, not so much in terms of a mother giving birth, but as a mother who nourishes her children, preparing them to become the building of the church, which is herself. This formative process is paralleled by the changing appearance of the woman in successive visions: she begins as an old woman, older than all creation, and then in every successive vision, she appears younger each time, until, in the fourth vision, she appears as a maiden ' "adorned as if coming forth from the bridal chamber" (Ps. 19:5), all in white and with white sandals, veiled to her forehead, and a turban for a head-dress, but her hair was white' (*Vision* 4.2.1). The church is at once older than the rest of creation—she is created first of all things, and all things are created for her—and yet, as the revelation continues, she becomes a pure virgin, for it is as a spotless virgin that the apostle Paul says that he *will* present his communities to Christ (1 Cor. 11:2–4): this is something to be achieved, lying in the future.

The idea that the church pre-exists creation is also found in the second text, the *Second Epistle of Clement*: 'Brethren, if we do the will of our Father God, we shall belong to the first Church, the spiritual one which was created before the sun and moon.' The *Epistle* continues by interpreting the statement that 'God made man male and female' as referring to Christ and the church, and claims:

> Now I imagine that you are not ignorant that the living Church is the Body of Christ. For the scripture says, 'God made the human male and female'; the male is Christ, the female is the Church. And moreover the books and the apostles indicate that the Church belongs not to the present, but has existed from the beginning [τὴν ἐκκλησία οὐ νῦν εἶναι, ἀλλὰ ἄνωθεν]; for she was spiritual, as was also our Jesus, but he was made manifest in the last days that he might save us; and the Church, which is spiritual, was made manifest in the flesh of Christ, showing us that any of us who guards her in the flesh without corruption will receive her back again in the Holy Spirit. (*II Clement* 14)

The manifestation of Jesus is also the manifestation of the church, his body, which is to be preserved in the flesh in purity, so that those belonging to the church might receive the Spirit—becoming truly spiritual.

Although *II Clement* draws only on Genesis 1 for the analogy between male/female and Christ/church, other writers would also draw it out of Genesis 2. Here, when God presents the Woman, built up from the rib (or side) taken from the sleeping Adam, Adam exclaims, with a concluding explanation: ' "This at last is bone of my bones and flesh of my flesh; she shall be called Woman, because she was taken out of Man." Therefore a man leaves his father and his mother and cleaves to his wife, and they become one flesh. And the man and his wife were both naked, and were not ashamed' (Gen. 2:23–5). These are striking words for scarcely, if ever, has this been practised in human history: in most cultures, from the earliest times into modern times, it is the bride who is brought into the husband's home and family, adopting his name. Not surprisingly, then, this passage was taken by Paul as referring to Christ and the church: the Son who leaves his Father's side in heaven to join his spouse (Eph. 5:31–2). This image is developed by Tertullian: 'As Adam was a figure of Christ, Adam's sleep provided a shadow of the death of Christ, who was to sleep a mortal slumber, that from the wound inflicted on his side might be figured the true Mother of the living, the Church' (*On the Soul* 43.10). The church, which came from the side of the crucified Christ (referring to the blood and the water: John 19: 34), is foreshadowed by the formation of Eve from the side of Adam when he was asleep, the sleep which foreshadowed Christ's own sleep in death. While Eve was certainly called the mother of the living (Gen. 3:20), it is really the church that is this.

The figure of the Virgin Mother of the living appears frequently in martyrdom literature. Most striking is the description in the letter, probably by Irenaeus of Lyons, addressed to the Christians in Asia Minor and Phrygia, reporting on a violent pogrom that had taken place in Lyons around AD 177 (*HE* 5.1–3). The heroine of the letter is Blandina, who, as a young slave girl—the epitome of weakness in the ancient world—personifies Christ's words to Paul: 'My strength is made perfect in weakness' (2 Cor. 12:9). She was so 'weak in body' that the others were fearful lest she not be able to make a good confession. Yet, she 'was filled with such power that even those who were taking turns to torture her in every way, from dawn until dusk, were weary and beaten. They, themselves, admitted that they were beaten . . . astonished at her endurance, as her entire body was mangled and broken' (*HE* 5.1.18). Not only is she, in her weakness, filled with divine power by her confession, but she also becomes fully identified with the one whose body was broken on Golgotha:

> Blandina, hung on a stake (ἐπὶ ξύλου), was offered as food for the wild beasts that were let in. She, by being seen hanging in the form of a cross, by her vigorous prayer, caused great zeal in the contestants, as, in their struggle, they beheld with their outward eyes, through the sister, him who was crucified for them, that he might persuade those who believe in him that everyone who suffers for the glory of Christ has for ever communion with the living God . . . the small and weak and despised woman had put on the great and invincible athlete, Christ, routing the adversary in many bouts, and, through the struggle, being crowned with the crown of incorruptibility. (*HE* 5.1.41–2)

Through her suffering, Blandina becomes identified with Christ: she no longer lives, but Christ lives in her (cf. Gal. 2:20). Blandina's passage out of this world is Christ's entry into this world. After describing her suffering, and that of another Christian called Attalus, the letter continues:

> Through their continued life the dead were made alive, and the martyrs showed favour to those who had failed to witness. And there was great joy for the Virgin Mother in receiving back alive those who she had miscarried as dead. For through them the majority of those who had denied were again brought to birth and again conceived and again brought to life and learned to confess; and now living and strengthened, they went to the judgment seat. (*HE* 5.1.45–6)

Life and death are here reversed: those who turned away from making their confession are simply dead; their lack of preparation has meant that they are stillborn children of the Virgin Mother. But now, strengthened by the witness of others, they also are able to go to their death, and so the Virgin Mother receives them back alive, finally giving birth to living children of God. The death of the martyr is their 'new birth', and the death of the martyr is celebrated as their true birthday (*HE* 5.1.63).

Life, as ζωή, lives, when life, as ψυχή, animation, no longer lives for itself but rather lays itself down for others, as did Christ and the martyrs after him. And it is this life that Christ brings to the Virgin, so that others may be born to life through her and in him. As the Sunday (Resurrection) troparion in tone six proclaims: 'Angelic Powers were at your grave, and those who guarded it became as dead, and Mary stood by the tomb, seeking your most pure Body. You despoiled Hell and emerged unscathed; you met the Virgin and granted life. Lord, risen from the dead, glory to you.' Mary here is clearly Mary Magdalene (unless the later tradition that the risen Lord appeared first to his mother has overshadowed the biblical evidence), and just as clearly 'the Virgin' is not! Rather, the Virgin to whom the risen Christ comes granting life is the church, the Virgin who now becomes a virginal mother, granting new life to her children as the Mediatrix of Life.

How does the reflection that we have seen so far, developed by reflecting upon the Scriptures (the Old Testament) in the light of the passion, relate to the Virgin Mary presented in the Gospels? Generally speaking, the typological relationship in which Mary is understood in the first centuries is as the New Eve, undoing by her obedience the disobedience of Eve. However, from the fourth century, Mary is increasingly brought into relationship with the church. Ephrem the Syrian, whose poetic writings lend themselves most readily to such associations of images, develops this point extensively. For example: 'The Virgin Mary is a symbol of the Church, when she receives the first announcement of the gospel. And, it is in the name of the Church that Mary sees the risen Jesus. Blessed be God, who filled Mary and the Church with joy. We call the Church by the name of Mary, for she deserves a double name' (Gambero 1999: 115; for the development of these themes in modern Orthodox theology, see Bulgakov 2002: 379–526).

Ephrem here identifies the Mary that saw the risen Jesus with Mary the Mother of Jesus, maybe on the basis of a tradition that the risen Christ appeared first to his mother, maybe because both Marys received the gospel, the proclamation about passion, the former at the Annunciation, the latter by seeing the risen Jesus in the Garden, and in so doing she is a 'symbol of the Church', the Barren Woman become Virgin Mother through the passion of Christ. So strong is this connection between the church and her symbol, Mary (when seen in this light), that Ephrem can simply call the church 'Mary'.

This is not the place to expound what this means for understanding the birth of Christ. Suffice it to say that Mary is understood to give birth to the crucified one, whose birth is effected in those who follow the lead of 'the Firstborn of many brethren' (Rom. 8:29), 'the Firstborn of all creation' (Col. 1:15) and 'the beginning, the Firstborn of the dead' (Col. 1:18). It is, even more directly, through his preaching that Paul 'is in travail, until Christ be formed in you!' (Gal. 4:19), till his converts can say, like him, that 'I have been crucified with Christ: it is no longer I who live, but Christ who lives in me' (Gal. 2:20). As 'the head of the body, the Church' (Col. 1:18), Christ cannot in fact be born, as Ignatius points out, without his body (*Ad Trall*. 11). As he is made known through 'the exodus' that he accomplishes in Jerusalem (Luke 9:31, where he discusses this with Moses and Elijah, the Law and the Prophets), he is made known, incarnate even, in those who follow him in this exodus, such as Blandina, returning in them to transform their lowly bodies to be like his glorious body (cf. Phil. 3:21).

Finally, to return to the Theologian, and his depiction of the crucifixion: here Christ is not abandoned, as in the other Gospels, but is crucified with his mother and the beloved disciple standing by at the foot of the cross (the Gospel also mentions two other women, both called Mary: his mother's sister, Mary the wife of Cleopas, and Mary Magdalene— but they recede into the background on the icon, if there at all). And the words spoken by Christ from the cross pertain, once again, to motherhood: 'Woman, behold your son'; and to the disciple, 'Behold your mother' (John 19:26–7). By Christ's own words, his mother is now the mother of the beloved disciple, and this disciple is himself identified with Christ. As Origen points out, Christ does not say, 'Woman, behold another son for you in my place', but, 'Behold your son', or, as Origen paraphrases it, 'this is Jesus whom you bore' (*Comm. John* 19:28). Those who stand by the cross, and are not ashamed of it, receive as their mother the one who embodies this fertile, generative faithfulness, and they themselves become sons and daughters of God, for they have Christ, the Son of God, living in them. This concludes our brief sketch of the ideas about the church as Mother of those reborn in Christ, as found in the early centuries of the church, which informs the liturgical tradition of the Orthodox Church.

THE FOUR TRADITIONAL NOTES
OF THE CHURCH

What we have looked at so far is the divine aspect of the church, expressed in the notion of the church as Mother of Christians born through baptism, and Bride of Christ, in whom they are reborn. In this aspect, the church partakes in some way of the divinity of Christ, whose body she is; she is older than creation. It is this aspect of the church that is most obviously celebrated in the services and liturgical poetry of the church. The four notes of the church, as confessed in the Creed—that she is One, Holy, Catholic, and Apostolic—mediate in some way between the divine reality of the church and her earthly—often, all too earthly—expression.

The Church is One

The Church is One is the title of a short treatise on the church that the Slavophil philosopher and theologian Alexei Khomiakov wrote for William Palmer, an Anglican deacon, who visited Russia in the nineteenth century in the vain hope that he would be received as a deacon as a step towards recovering the unity of the church. Khomiakov begins his treatise with these words:

> The Church is one. Her unity follows of necessity from the unity of God; for the Church is not a multitude of persons in their separate individuality, but a unity of the grace of God, living in a multitude of rational creatures, submitting themselves willingly to grace. Grace, indeed, is also given to those who resist it, and to those who do not make us of it (who hide their talent in the earth), but these are not in the Church. In fact, the unity of the Church is not imaginary or allegorical, but a true and substantial unity, such as is the unity of many members in a living body.

Khomiakov continues:

> The Church is one, notwithstanding her division, as it appears to a man who is still alive on earth. It is only in relation to man that it is possible to recognize a division of the Church into visible and invisible; her unity is, in reality, true and absolute. Those who are alive on earth, those who have finished their earthly course, those who, like the angels, were not created for a life on earth, those in future generations who have not yet begun their earthly course, are all united together in one Church, in one and the same grace of God; for the creation of God which has not yet been manifested is manifest to Him; and God hears the prayers and knows the faith of those whom He has not yet called out of non-existence into existence. Indeed the Church, the Body of Christ, is manifesting forth and fulfilling herself in time, without changing her essential unity or inward life of grace. And therefore, when we speak of 'the Church visible and invisible', we so speak only in relation to man. (Khomiakov 1968: 18)

The unity of the church is a fact, resting on the unity of the Triune Godhead; the divisions in the church—between angels and human kind, between those yet unborn, those now dead, and those alive—are only 'in relation to man', they are not ultimate. The unity of the church is a unity in diversity, a notion expressed with great beauty by St Maximos the Confessor in a passage from his *Mystagogia*:

> It is in this way that the holy Church of God will be shown to be active among us in the same way as God, as an image reflects its archetype. For many and of nearly

boundless number are the men, women and children who are distinct from one another and vastly different by birth and appearance, by race and language, by way of life and age, by opinions and skills, by manners and customs, by pursuits and studies, and still again by reputation, fortune, characteristics and habits: all are born into the Church and through it are reborn and recreated in the Spirit. To all in equal measures it gives and bestows one divine form and designation: to be Christ's and to bear his name. In accordance with faith it gives to all a single, simple, whole and indivisible condition—which does not allow us to bring to mind the existence of the myriads of differences among them, even if they do exist—through the universal relationship and union of all things with it. It is through it that absolutely no one at all is in himself separated from the community since everyone converges with all the rest and joins together with them through the one, simple, and indivisible grace and power of faith. 'For all,' it is said, 'had but one heart and one mind' (Acts 4:32). Thus to be and to appear as one body formed of different members is really worthy of Christ himself, our true head, in whom says the divine Apostle, 'there is neither male nor female, neither Jew nor Greek, neither circumcision nor uncircumcision, neither barbarian nor Scythian, neither slave nor free, but he is all and in all' (Col. 3:11). It is he who encloses in himself all beings by the unique, simple and infinitely wise power of his goodness. (*Mystagogia*, 1 in Maximus Confessor 2011: 12–13)

Like Khomiakov, Maximos derives the unity of the church from the unity of God, but explores the nature of this unity in a different way: the church unites all people of every kind, of every language, race, way of life, age, and so on. It is a unity that underlies the very real diversity found among its members. Unity in diversity is something for which the members of the church need continually to strive, for after the Fall, such unity is something precious, easily threatened. That is why among the prayers that the church offers at the Eucharist, there has always been—and in the Byzantine rite repeatedly—prayer for unity: 'for the peace of the whole world, the welfare of the Churches of God, and the union of all, let us pray ... ', in the litany of peace (Τὰ Εἰρηνικά). This was not prayer for the unity of Christians, as we think of it nowadays, but prayer for the unity of Christians within the one church of the Roman Empire: the deepening of an acknowledged unity. The idea that the church could be separated into different communities, not at unity with each other, would have seemed bizarre to Christians in the patristic period: separation was separation from the church, not within the church (for the way this is developed by St Maximos, see Louth 2013). This is still the position of the Orthodox Church, though the status of Christians outside the communion of the Orthodox Churches is not defined. It is a unity expressed in a common profession of the Faith: expressed initially through the rules of faith that formed the basis for the baptismal profession of faith, later (though not as quickly as many think), the Creeds (or Symbols) of Œcumenical Councils (in practice the creed agreed by the Fathers of the Second Œcumenical Council, held at Constantinople in 381, as confirming and slightly expanding the Symbol of Faith affirmed at Nicaea in 325). The creeds, however, are secondary, even if in practice binding, for they are intended to safeguard faith in Christ, rather than being exhaustive expressions of faith of Christians (for example, neither the creed of Nicaea nor that of Constantinople affirms explicitly the death of Christ, unlike the so-called Apostles' Creed, which became popular in the West).

This unity has a local dimension—the unity of the Christians worshipping together in a particular place—and a universal dimension—the unity of the churches in different places throughout the world: the former is expressed through gathering together to celebrate the Eucharist together in mutual love, the latter also expressed through the common Eucharist, but articulated, too, through the Episcopal hierarchy. Most fundamentally, this unity is expressed in and fostered by prayer. To quote Khomiakov again:

> We know that when any one of us falls, he falls alone; but no one is saved alone. He who is saved is saved in the Church, as a member of her, and in unity with all her other members. If anyone believes, he is in the communion of faith; if he loves, he is in the communion of love; if he prays, he is in the communion of prayer. Wherefore no one can rest his hope on his own prayers, and every one who prays asks the whole Church for intercession, not as if he had any doubts of the intercession of Christ, the one Advocate, but in the assurance that the whole Church ever prays for all her members. All the angels pray for us, the apostles, the martyrs, and patriarchs, and above all, the Mother of our Lord, and this holy unity is the true life of the Church. (Khomiakov 1968: 39)

The Church is Holy

On the credal note of holiness let us quote Khomiakov again:

> The Church, even upon earth, lives, not an earthly human life, but a life which is divine, and of grace. Wherefore not only each of her members, but she herself as a whole solemnly calls herself 'Holy'. Her visible manifestation is contained in the Sacraments; but her inward life in the gifts of the Holy Spirit, in faith, hope, and love. Oppressed and persecuted by enemies without, at times agitated and lacerated within by the evil passions of her children, she has been and ever will be preserved without wavering or change wherever the Sacraments and spiritual holiness are preserved. (Khomiakov 1968: 34)

Holiness is not primarily a matter of moral virtue, but of participation in the holiness of God. Holiness characterizes the church as a whole, and also each member of it, for the church and its members are set apart (one of the root meanings of holiness) by God to witness to his presence in the world. The Apostle Paul therefore refers to the members of any local church as the 'saints of' that place. This sanctity, or holiness, is nourished by participation in the Holy Gifts at the Eucharist; in the Byzantine Rite, the priest begins the rite of Holy Communion by exclaiming, 'The holy things for the holy ones.' The church professes in its Creed the 'communion of Saints', which has layers of meaning: *communio sanctorum*, κοινωνία τῶν ἁγίων, can mean communion in the holy things (gifts), or it can mean the communion of the Saints, depending on whether *sanctorum*, ἁγίων, is regarded as masculine (or feminine) or neuter. The two meanings are bound up with one another: the communion of holy people is maintained and nourished by communion in the holy gifts (see Stăniloae 2012). There is also a specialized use of the word saint, *sanctus*, ἅγιος: to refer to those who have truly been 'perfected in the faith'. To begin with, this specialized use was applied to the martyrs, those witnesses who had borne testimony to their faith in Christ with their lives. After the end of persecution in the Roman Empire at the beginning of the fourth century, the term was applied more widely: to those who had lived lives of heroic love, and especially to those who had embraced the ascetic life, monks and nuns. Sanctity, thus formally acknowledged, is less to do with their providing examples for Christian living, but rather expresses the conviction that, as friends who are now close to the heavenly throne, they have become faithful intercessors, friends to whom we can turn for help. Devotion to the saints began, as a rule, locally (and still does), and many saints remained (and remain) of special interest to the descendants of those among whom they lived; devotion to them is focused on their mortal remains, their relics, which are believed in some way to participate in the future resurrection, and therefore even now to be sources of healing. Devotion to the saints is also focused on images depicting them, their icons.

The Church is Catholic

The Greek word καθολικός is generally translated 'universal', and in this sense means that the church is not bound up with any particular locality but is universal; it also means, however, that the truth the church proclaims is truth that is the same for all, universal. How, then, to ensure that the church is one in its profession of the truth, the truth of the gospel? Without catholicity, as Vladimir Lossky explains, we would have 'the Church without Truth, without the assured knowledge of the data of revelation, without conscious and infallible experience of the divine mysteries'. Lossky continues:

> If she keeps her unity, it will be a unity of many opinions, products of diverse human mentalities and cultures, a unity having as its basis administrative constraint or relativistic indifference. If she—this Church deprived of assurance of the Truth—keeps her holiness, it will be an unconscious holiness, a lightless path towards sanctification, in the darkness of not knowing what grace is. If she keeps her apostolicity, it will be only blind fidelity to an abstract principle, void of meaning. (Lossky 1974: 172)

The Greek word καθολικός derives from καθ' ὅλου, meaning something like to take as a whole. Sometime in the Middle Ages, the Slavonic translation of the Creed changed the transliteration of καθολικός to a translation, *soborny*, from *sobrat'*, meaning precisely to take as a whole, or to gather together. The church is *soborny*, embracing wholeness, both as a whole and in each of its members. This means, as Florovsky put it, that

The commandment to be catholic is given to every Christian. The measure of his spiritual manhood is the measure of his catholicity. The Church is catholic is every one of its members, because a catholic whole cannot be built up or composed otherwise than through the catholicity of its members . . . Union can become possible only through the mutual brotherly love of all the separate brethren. (Florovsky 1972: 42–3)

The truth is neither ensured by some central authority nor lost in a cacophony of voices dissenting from one another, but discovered in the mutual love of the catholic members of the catholic community; as the deacon exclaims before the singing of the Creed: 'Let us love one another that with one mind we may confess,' to which the people respond, 'Father, Son, and Holy Spirit, Trinity consubstantial and undivided,' before embarking on the Creed. The Slavonic word for a synod, or council, is also derived from *sobrat'*—*sobor*—so that *soborny* conveys the sense of conciliar, with the suggestion that Christian truth is found in mutual agreement in love. One expression of catholicity, or *sobornost'*, is found in the synodical structure of the church, culminating in œcumenical synods or councils, called originally by the emperors and named 'œcumenical' because they spoke for, or concerned, the whole *œcumene*, the 'inhabited world', as the Romans regarded their empire (though the original reason for the use of οἰκουμενικός in relation to a church council may have had to do with the bishops being able to use the imperial postal network for travelling). The Orthodox Church recognizes seven Œcumenical Councils—from the first, held in Nicaea in 325, to the last, also held in Nicaea in 787—which were concerned, so far as doctrine is concerned, with fundamental issues of Trinitarian and Christological doctrine (the question of icons, settled at Nicaea II, was regarded as a matter of Christology); they also issued canons, which provide the basis for Orthodox ecclesiastical law.

The Church is Apostolic

The band of the twelve apostles chosen by Christ formed the core of the early Christian church. The identity of the church with that original community is ensured by means called apostolic: the apostolic faith, the apostolic witness gathered together in what came to be called the New Testament, and the designated successors of the Apostles themselves, the bishops—and also the sacraments established by the Lord himself, Baptism and the Eucharist. All of these are necessary; all of them in some way depend on each other. Although the details of the process are lost in the mists of history, the agreement on the books of the New Testament involved judgement that they were apostolic, faithful to the apostles' witness, and this judgement involved those who were successors of the apostles (though maybe not exclusively). The apostolic faith was maintained in apostolic sees that could demonstrate a line of succession through their bishops back to the original apostolic band; the authority of the successors to the apostles, the bishops, depended on their faithfulness to the apostolic faith, witnessed to in the rule of faith, or the rule of truth. Later on, in the West, apostolicity came to be defined more narrowly: *the* apostolic see was that of Rome, founded by St Peter, and sanctified by his blood and that of the apostle Paul, as well as many other martyrs. No such narrowing of the notion of apostolicity took place in the Eastern Church, not least because there were so many sees that could claim apostolic foundation, whereas in the West Rome could claim what seemed like a plausible monopoly on apostolicity.

THE CHURCH IN THE WORLD

From the beginning, the church in the Roman Empire reflected the structures of that world in her own structures. By the end of the second century, the local church came be regarded as the Christian community in a city, ruled by a single bishop, for the city, the successor of the ancient city state, was, with its surrounding territory, its χώρα, the basic unit in the Roman Empire. Already during the days of persecution by the Roman Empire, the way in which the church modelled itself after the structure of the Empire went further: cities were grouped together in provinces, and the bishop of the metropolis, or mother-city of the province, was called a metropolitan bishop, with duties to all the Christians of the province, which he exercised through an assembly, a synod, consisting of his fellow bishops with some participation by the laity. At the first Œcumenical Synod, held at Nicaea in 325, a further level of modelling on the administrative structures of the Roman Empire was acknowledged: the rights of what would later be called 'patriarchs' over groups of provinces, corresponding to the dioceses of the Empire, as it emerged from the extensive administrative reform, begun by Diocletian and continued by Constantine (see Canon 6 of Nicaea I). With Constantine's conversion, there emerged a sense that the unity of the church was reflected in (and maybe constitutive of) the unity of the Roman Empire under the imperial office. Eusebius (in his *Life of Constantine* and *Encomia*) presents a picture in which the imperial rule extends over both the Empire and the church: the emperor supports the church, in return the church prays for the emperor. By the end of the century, Christianity had become the religion of the Empire, and this model of harmony, συμφωνία, between the Empire and the church found its fullest expression in Justinian's idea of a Christian Roman Empire, expressed in *Novella* 6 (535):

> The greatest blessings of mankind are the gifts of God which have been granted us by the mercy on high—the priesthood and the imperial authority. The priesthood ministers to things divine, the imperial authority is set over, and shows diligence in, things human; but both proceed from one and the same source, and both adorn the life of man. Nothing, therefore, will be a greater matter of concern to the emperor than the dignity and honour (*honestas*) of the clergy; the more as they offer prayers to God without ceasing on his behalf. For if the priesthood be in all respects without blame, and full of faith before God, and if the imperial authority rightly and duly adorn the commonwealth committed to its charge, there will ensue a happy concord,

which will bring forth all good things for mankind. We therefore have the greatest concern for the true doctrines of the God-head and the dignity and honour of the clergy; and we believe that if they maintain that dignity and honour we shall gain thereby the greatest of gifts, holding fast what we already have and laying hold on what is yet to come. 'All things', it is said, 'are done well and truly if they start from a beginning that is worthy and pleasing in the sight of God.' We believe that this will come to pass, if observance be paid to the holy rules [canons] which have been handed down by the Apostles—those righteous guardians and ministers of the Word of God, who are ever to be praised and adored—and have since been preserved and interpreted by the holy Fathers. (Preface to *Novella* 6: Barker 1957: 75–6)

There are different ways of understanding what is involved in this assimilation of the church to the Roman Empire: it could be regarded as purely provisional—the church, in its earthly pilgrimage, adapts itself to the society in which it lives, but that could well change—or the structures of the Empire could be endowed with some lasting significance through this ideal of συμφωνία. In practice, as history has borne out, this model of συμφωνία came to be regarded as possessing some kind of eternal sanction. In the Roman Empire itself, the ideal was expressed in terms of a graded hierarchy of patriarchs–metropolitans–bishops, with the church ruled through synods: local synods under bishops, metropolitan and patriarchal synods, culminating in 'œcumenical' synods, called by the emperor and possessing final authority, when acknowledged by the whole church. The five patriarchates—of Rome, Constantinople, Alexandria, Antioch, and Jerusalem—became known as the 'Pentarchy'. Rome was conceded a primacy of honour, which Constantinople, as New Rome, shared, though in second place. This understanding of authority, as modelled on the structures of the Empire, was never accepted by Rome, and became a bone of contention within the church. When other nations embraced Christianity of the Byzantine rite—first Bulgaria in the ninth century, and then the Rus' of Kiev in the tenth—this model of συμφωνία was borrowed and took the form of emperor (or prince)–patriarch–church–nation. In the process, the (admittedly threadbare) justification which matched the universal mission of the church with the claims of the Roman Empire to govern the whole inhabited world (οἰκουμένη, *œcumene*) was, perforce, abandoned, and the notion of autocephalous churches, that is, churches that were self-ruling and not dependent on a hierarch outside the autocephalous church, such as the patriarch of Constantinople, emerged. This process took place very gradually: the Russian church only became completely independent of Constantinople after the Union Council of Florence (1437–9) and the fall of Constantinople (1453). The idea of autocephaly, expressed in the pattern of king–patriarch–church–nation, was adopted by the Orthodox nations emerging from the Ottoman Yoke in the nineteenth and early twentieth centuries, despite the warning issued by the synod of Constantinople in 1872, when it condemned the heresy of 'ethno-phyletism'. There is general agreement among Orthodox about the heresy of ethno-phyletism, though the synod of 1872 was largely motivated by self-interest on the part of the patriarch (Louth 2010).

The Bolshevik revolution and the exile of many Russian intellectuals to the West led to much heart-searching about the nature of the church. In Russia itself the ideal of συμφωνία seemed unrealistic with a Bolshevik régime bent on the extermination of the church, though the hierarchy, under the patriarchal *locum tenens*, Metropolitan Sergii, appeared to act as if συμφωνία still made sense. In the diaspora, the experience of ecclesiality in small émigré communities led to an attempt to reach back beyond the notion of a Christian Empire, ushered in by Constantine's conversion, to the experience of the early church, persecuted by the state. There emerged from this the notion of 'Eucharistic Ecclesiology', associated especially with the name of Nikolai Afanasiev, one of the professors at the Institut Saint-Serge in Paris: it is the Eucharist celebrated by the bishop that makes of the local community the church (Afanasiev 2007; though his article in Afanassieff 1960 has been far more influential). Such Eucharistic Ecclesiology was immensely influential in the twentieth century, not only among the Orthodox, but also on reflection on the church at Vatican II, as well as within the ecumenical movement. It has also been roundly criticized, not least by Metropolitan John Zizioulas, who has devised his own form of Eucharistic Ecclesiology (Zizioulas 1985; 2006; 2010; McPartlan 1993).

However popular Eucharistic Ecclesiology is among the Orthodox and elsewhere, little attempt has been made to work out what the structures of the church would be on such a model (save for Zizioulas whose revised Eucharistic Ecclesiology could be thought to make too much of the bishop: see Bathrellos in Knight 2007: 133–45). In the diaspora, there is ecclesiological chaos, the Orthodox community being divided up among the jurisdictions of national hierarchies (with the partial exception of the Orthodox Church in America). Hankering after the model of συμφωνία makes it difficult for Orthodox to think out the implications of living in a modern, multicultural, democratic society (for a brave attempt to engage in such thinking, see Papanikolaou 2012). Perhaps the notion of 'diaspora' should be taken absolutely seriously, and ecclesial structures sought to express the sense of Christians, who, as the *Epistle to Diognetos* put it, 'live in their own countries, but as foreigners; they share in everything as citizens, but dwell everywhere as strangers; every foreign country is theirs and every country foreign' (*Diog.* 5.5).

REFERENCES

(I am indebted to some unpublished papers by Fr John Behr, and to conversations with him. I have used his unpublished papers with permission.)

Texts

The Apostolic Fathers (1970 [1913]). 2 vols. Ed. and trans. Kirsopp Lake. Loeb Classical Library; Cambridge, MA: Harvard University Press.
Eusebius (1965 [1926]). *Ecclesiastical History.* 2 vols. Ed. and trans. Kirsopp Lake. Loeb Classical Library; Cambridge, MA: Harvard University Press [= *HE*].

Gambero, L. (1999). *Mary and the Fathers of the Church: The Blessed Virgin Mary in Patristic Thought.* ET T. Buffer. San Francisco: Ignatius Press.

Maximus Confessor (2011). *Mystagogia.* Ed. C. Boudignon. *Corpus Christianorum Series Graeca 69.* Turnhout: Brepols Publishers.

Origen (1982). *Commentary on the Gospel of John.* Ed. and French trans. C. Blanc. Sources Chrétiennes 290; Paris: Cerf. ET R. E. Heine, *Fathers of the Church 89*, Washington DC: The Catholic University of America Press, 1993.

Modern Literature

Afanassieff, N., et al. (1960). *La Primauté de Pierre dans l'Église orthodoxe.* Neuchatel: Delachaux et Niestlé. ET Leighton Buzzard: Faith Press, 1963.

Afanasiev, Nicholas (2007). *The Church of the Holy Spirit.* ET Vitaly Permiakov. Notre Dame, IN: University of Notre Dame Press.

Barker, Ernest (1957). Ed. and trans. *Social and Political Thought in Byzantium, from Justinian I to the last Palaeologus.* Oxford: Clarendon Press.

Behr, John (2013). *Becoming Human: Meditations on Christian Anthropology in Word and Image.* Crestwood, NY: Saint Vladimir Seminary Press.

Bobrinskoy, Boris (2003). *Le Mystère de l'Église: cours de théologie dogmatique.* Paris: Le Cerf. ET Michael Breck, Yonkers, NY: Saint Vladimir Seminary Press, 2012.

Bulgakov, Sergius (2002). *The Bride of the Lamb.* ET Boris Jakim. Grand Rapids, MI: Eerdmans/ Edinburgh: T. & T. Clark.

Florovsky, Georges (1972). *Bible, Church, Tradition: An Eastern Orthodox View.* Vol. 1 of the *Collected Works of Georges Florovsky.* Belmont, MA: Nordland.

Khomiakov, Alexy Stepanovich (1968 [1863]). *The Church is One.* ET William Palmer; revised Nicolas Zernov. London: Fellowship of St Alban and St Sergius.

Knight, Douglas H. (ed.) (2007). *The Theology of John Zizioulas: Personhood and the Church.* Aldershot: Ashgate.

Lossky, Vladimir (1967). *À l'image et à la resemblance de Dieu.* Paris: Aubier-Montaigne; ET Crestwood, NY: Saint Vladimir Seminary Press, 1974.

Louth, Andrew (2010). 'Ignatios or Eusebios: Two Models of Patristic Ecclesiology'. *International Journal for the Study of the Christian Church* 10: 46–56.

Louth, Andrew (2013). 'The Views of St Maximus the Confessor on the Institutional Church'. In Bp Maxim (Vasiljević) (ed.), *Knowing the Purpose of Creation through the Resurrection: Proceedings of the Symposium of St Maximus the Confessor, Belgrade, October 18–22, 2012.* Alhambra, CA: Sebastian Press, 347–55.

McPartlan, Paul (1993). *The Eucharist Makes the Church: Henri de Lubac and John Zizioulas in Dialogue.* Edinburgh: T. & T. Clark.

Papanikolaou, Aristotle (2012). *The Mystical as Political: Democracy and Non-Radical Orthodoxy.* Notre Dame, IN: University of Notre Dame Press.

Scouteris, Constantine (2006). *Ecclesial Being: Contributions to Theological Dialogue.* South Canaan, PA: Mount Thabor Publishing.

Stăniloae, Dumitru (2012). *The Experience of God: Orthodox Dogmatic Theology.* Vol. 4: *The Church: Communion in the Holy Spirit.* Brookline, MA: Holy Cross Orthodox Press.

Zizioulas, John D. (1985). *Being as Communion.* London: Darton, Longman & Todd.

Zizioulas, John D. (2006). *Communion and Otherness.* London: T&T Clark.

Zizioulas, John D. (2010). *The One and the Many: Studies on God, Man, the Church, and the World Today*. Ed. Gregory Edwards. Alhambra, CA: Sebastian Press.

SUGGESTED READING

Afanasiev, Nicholas (2007). *The Church of the Holy Spirit*. ET Vitaly Permiakov. Notre Dame, IN: University of Notre Dame Press.

Behr, John (2013). *Becoming Human: Meditations on Christian Anthropology in Word and Image*. Crestwood, NY: Saint Vladimir Seminary Press.

Bobrinskoy, Boris (2003). *Le Mystère de l'Église: cours de théologie dogmatique*. Paris: Le Cerf. ET Michael Breck, Yonkers, NY: Saint Vladimir Seminary Press, 2012.

Khomiakov, Alexy Stepanovich (1968 [1863]). *The Church is One*. ET William Palmer; revised Nicolas Zernov. London: Fellowship of St Alban and St Sergius.

Papanikolaou, Aristotle (2012). *The Mystical as Political: Democracy and Non-Radical Orthodoxy*. Notre Dame, IN: University of Notre Dame Press.

Zizioulas, John D. (2010). *The One and the Many: Studies on God, Man, the Church, and the World Today*. Ed. Gregory Edwards. Alhambra, CA: Sebastian Press.

CHAPTER 9

MEDIEVAL ECCLESIOLOGY AND THE CONCILIAR MOVEMENT

NORMAN TANNER SJ

INTRODUCTION

ECCLESIOLOGY remained a contentious issue within the Christian community throughout the Middle Ages and long after. It was the most important issue in the schism between the churches of East and West—between Rome and Constantinople— beginning in 1054. This schism was accompanied by the strongly papal ecclesiology which much influenced the Roman church in the second half of the eleventh century and which lay at the heart of the Gregorian reform, the movement named after its foremost proponent pope Gregory VII (1073–84). However, within the Western church there was unease at some of the extreme claims made for the papacy during the Gregorian reform. Unease and opposition came from the clergy as well as from the laity throughout the Middle Ages. An alternative ecclesiology within the Western church reached its zenith during the councils of Constance (1414–18) and Basel (1431–7) but it was outmanoeuvred by the revived Renaissance papacy.

Ecclesiology was fundamental to the divisions between Catholics and Reformers after 1517, but it also remained a contested issue within the Catholic Church. Fear that the 'conciliar ghost'—the conciliarism of Constance and Basel—might reappear convinced the Council of Trent (1545–63) to avoid discussion of the topic. Ecclesiology was scheduled to be treated properly at the First Vatican Council (1869–70). However, curtailment of the council, due to the imminent invasion of Rome (by troops seeking the reunification of Italy), meant its programme was drastically reduced. Only the papacy was treated; coverage of the rest of the church was left to a future council. This task was finally completed at the Second Vatican Council (1962–5), in the long and comprehensive decree on the Church entitled *Lumen Gentium*.

The period from 1050 to the beginning of the Reformation in 1517, the focus of this chapter, therefore forms a crucial epoch in the development of ecclesiology within the Catholic Church—important too for the entire Christian community—even though it left as many loose ends as resolutions. The chapter must be seen within its wider context: principally Andrew Louth's chapter on Eastern Orthodox tradition; but also the ecclesiologies that emerged during the Reformation and Counter-Reformation, which were much influenced by medieval developments—whether mainly in reaction against them (Reformation) or more favourably (Counter-Reformation).

THE GREGORIAN REFORM
AND ITS AFTERMATH

Pope Leo IX (1049–55) was the first in a line of reforming popes in the second half of the eleventh century. He sent Cardinal Humbert of Silva Candida to Constantinople to treat with Patriarch Cerularius, but the result was the mutual exchange of excommunications initiating the schism between the two churches, which has never been properly healed. The schism had profound ecclesiological implications for relations between the two churches. Nevertheless, while efforts at reunion persisted throughout the medieval period, the reformed papacy turned its attention principally towards relations between clergy and laity within the Western church. The papacy regarded the Western church of the time as too much controlled by the laity and needing, therefore, to be freed from this secular domination.

The *Dictatus Papae* of Pope Gregory VII is a key document, very revealing about the ecclesiology of the reformed papacy. Although it was never promulgated, it was copied into the pope's Register as an official document. Here is the text:

1. The Roman church was founded by God alone.
2. The Roman pontiff (pope) alone is rightly called universal.
3. He alone can depose or reinstate bishops.
4. His legate, even if of lower grade, takes precedence in a council over all the bishops and may render a sentence of deposition against them.
5. The pope may depose the absent.
6. People ought not to stay in the same house with those excommunicated by him.
7. For him alone is it lawful to enact new laws according to the needs of the time ...
8. He alone may use the imperial insignia.
9. The pope is the only person whose feet are to be kissed by all princes.
10. His name alone is to be recited in churches.
11. His title is unique in the world.
12. He may depose emperors.
13. He may transfer bishops, if necessary, from one see to another.

14. He has the power to ordain a cleric of any church he may wish.
15. The person ordained by him may rule over another church ...
16. No council may be regarded as a general council without his order.
17. No chapter or book may be regarded as canonical without his authority.
18. No sentence of his may be retracted by anyone: he alone can retract it.
19. He himself may be judged by nobody.
20. Nobody shall dare to condemn a person who appeals to the apostolic see (papacy).
21. To this see the more important cases of every church should be submitted.
22. The Roman church has never erred, nor shall, by the witness of Scripture, ever err to all eternity.
23. The Roman pontiff, if canonically elected, is undoubtedly sanctified by the merits of saint Peter.
24. By his order and with his permission, subordinate persons may bring accusations.
25. Without convening a synod, he can depose and reinstate bishops.
26. Nobody should be considered as Catholic who is not in conformity with the Roman church.
27. The pope may absolve subjects of unjust men from their fealty (loyalty). (Tierney 1964: 49–50)

The teaching of Pope Gregory VII, encapsulated in *Dictatus Papae*, dominated papal policy for the remainder of the eleventh century. Various of the twenty-seven propositions, especially the more extreme ones, were not fully accepted by most civil rulers: many ecclesiastics, too, had their reservations.

The early twelfth century brought more conciliatory popes. The new mood of realism and compromise is best illustrated by the Concordat of Worms, which was concluded between Pope Callixtus II and the German Emperor Henry V in September 1122. The issues were not church–state relations in the modern sense, whereby the state is quite distinct from the Christian church. At stake, rather, was the relationship between two authorities within the one Christian society, regarding the appointment of bishops and abbots. The emperor saw himself as an integral part of Christian society, alongside the pope. According to the Concordat, on the one hand:

> I, Callixtus, servant of the servants of God, do grant to you, beloved son, Henry—by the grace of God Emperor of the Romans, Augustus—that the elections of bishops and abbots of the German kingdom, who belong to that kingdom, shall take place in your presence ... The one elected shall receive the regalia from you and shall perform his lawful duties to you on that account ...

On the other hand:

> In the name of the holy and indivisible Trinity I, Henry by the grace of God Emperor of the Romans, Augustus, for the love of God and of the holy Roman church and of

our lord pope Callixtus, and for the salvation of my soul, do surrender to God ... and to the holy Catholic Church, all investiture through ring and staff; and do grant that in all the churches that are in my kingdom or empire there may be canonical election and consecration ... (Bettenson 1963: 111–12)

The most famous clash in the twelfth century, regarding the competing jurisdictions of lay and clerical authority within the church, occurred between King Henry II of England and the archbishop of Canterbury, Thomas Becket. The conflict culminated in 1170 with the murder of Becket in his cathedral, at the instigation of the king. Henry did public penance for the crime and Becket's tomb in Canterbury cathedral became the most popular pilgrimage shrine in the country. Nevertheless the extreme claims put forward by Becket for the immunity of the church from royal authority were shared by few outside his immediate circle. Pope Alexander III lived through the conflict and its aftermath during his long reign from 1159 to 1181. He canonized Becket as a saint and martyr in 1173, just three years after his death. But for long the pope had urged Becket to be more cautious, partly because he wanted Henry's support in his struggle against a succession of antipopes who threatened his hold on Rome. Most of the English bishops, too, were uneasy with or openly opposed to Becket's provocative stances, most notably Gilbert Foliot, bishop of London, and Robert of Pont l'Evêque, archbishop of York.

THE 'LONG' THIRTEENTH CENTURY: WIDER CONSIDERATIONS

So far our attention has been upon the higher reaches of Christian society: relations of popes and senior ecclesiastics with secular rulers, principally emperors and kings. This dimension of ecclesiology remained important throughout the thirteenth century and it will be treated first in this section. Thereafter other important developments affecting ecclesiology within the Western church during this century—taken in the 'long' sense of the late twelfth to the early fourteenth century—will be discussed: the new orders of friars; universities and schools; developments within the laity.

Ecclesiology at the Top

The strong papal claims characteristic of the Gregorian reform movement remained with the papacy throughout the thirteenth century, though with some differences. In the first half of the century they were proclaimed more suavely, less abrasively, than under Gregory VII. In the second half of the century reality became more divorced from theory, culminating with the humiliation of Pope Boniface VIII in 1303.

Innocent III (1198–1216) was the most effective pope in the first half of the century. His reign culminated with his summoning and presiding over the general council of the Western church which was held in St John Lateran basilica, the cathedral church of Rome: the fourth Lateran council of 1215. Its seventy-one decrees provided a programme of reform and renewal at all levels of Catholic life, while reinforcing the position of the papacy at the top. Its first decree 'On the catholic faith' contained this strong statement which would influence the ecclesiology of the Catholic Church for many centuries: 'There is indeed one universal church of the faithful, outside of which nobody at all is saved.'

Pope Innocent was determined in asserting the supremacy of the clergy over the laity within Christian society: the approach that had been enunciated so clearly by Pope Gregory VII. In this vein he intervened actively in German politics, favouring and taking under his tutelage the young emperor Frederick II; he persuaded Philip Augustus, king of France, to be reconciled with his estranged wife Ingebord of Denmark, and he was active in the politics of the country; he made his political authority felt as far afield as Scandinavia, Spain, the Balkans, Cyprus, and Armenia. In England, too, King John, beset by difficulties with his barons, did homage to the pope and 'donated' the kingdom to him. As a result, soon afterwards, Innocent annulled Magna Carta, the famous charter of rights which the barons had imposed on the king, on the grounds that it had been concluded without papal permission. But Innocent's interventionist policy was dangerous. Its success depended much upon the weakness or compromising situations of major European monarchs of the time. When stronger monarchs emerged, such interventions would not be possible and the ecclesiology behind them would partly disintegrate.

Robert Grosseteste, bishop of Lincoln in England from 1235 until his death in 1253, was noted for his learning, holiness, and pastoral zeal. But he was also a fierce critic of some papal policies. In 1250 he travelled to Lyons in France, where Pope Innocent IV was residing, in order to confront the pope with his anxieties. He brought with him a written denunciation of what he saw as the abuses of power by papal officials and by the pope himself, particularly their sale of church offices and the promotion of their families. His speech reached a climax:

> The papal see, the throne of God, the sun of the whole world . . . which should, like the sun, give light, life, nutrition, growth, preservation and beauty to the earth, has lost its proper functions, the reasons for its existence. It has been perverted and it has become a source of perdition and destruction. He who bears the *persona* of Christ has divested himself of this *persona* and taken that of his earthly relatives and of his own flesh and blood.

Bishop Grosseteste went on almost to identify the pope with Antichrist, the 'Son of Perdition', and then outlined his own pastoral vision with a further side-swipe at the pope and his curia.

> The most divine and absolutely overriding art of saving souls must be given to those who understand the gospel of Christ as set forth in the Old and New Testaments, without the interference of those who understand only the subordinate arts of secular administration. (Gieben 1971: 359–63)

Pope Innocent, to his credit, listened to Bishop Grosseteste though he was annoyed and he does not seem to have changed his behaviour. The two men soon clashed again when the pope appointed his nephew to a canonry in Lincoln cathedral, an appointment which the bishop resisted fiercely. Grosseteste shows the extent to which robust criticism was acceptable in that age: how concern for the papacy could be combined with outspoken remarks. In other respects, moreover, Innocent IV was notable as a reforming pope. He summoned and presided over the Council of Lyons in 1245, a reforming council in much the same vein as Lateran IV, and just as Innocent III had been responsible for confirming the new orders of Franciscans and Dominicans, so Innocent IV was responsible for giving papal approval to the orders of Carmelite and Augustinian friars.

Pope Boniface VIII, at the end of the century, gave even stronger emphasis to the papacy in his ecclesiology. But strong secular rulers made its implementation much more problematic. This ecclesiology was expressed most forcefully in *Unam Sanctam*, the bull which Boniface promulgated in 1302:

> We are obliged by faith to believe and hold that there is one holy catholic and apostolic Church and outside this Church there is neither salvation nor remission of sins . . . Of this one and only Church there is one body and one head, namely Christ, and Christ's vicar is Peter and Peter's successor . . . And we learn from the words of the Gospel that in this Church and in her power are two swords, the spiritual and the temporal . . . Both (swords) are in the power of the Church, but the latter is to be used for the Church, the former by her; the former by the priest, the latter by kings and captains but at the will and by the permission of the priest. The one sword, then, should be under the other, and temporal authority subject to spiritual . . . Furthermore we declare, state, define and pronounce that it is altogether necessary to salvation for every human creature to be subject to the Roman pontiff. (Bettenson 1963: 115–16)

Pope Boniface was confronted by an equally determined monarch, King Philip IV 'le Bel' of France. Angered by the pope's intransigence and his threat to forbid the king to tax the French clergy, he sent troops to Anagni, south of Rome, who arrested and imprisoned the pope in September 1303. Although he was soon freed from prison by Italian troops, Boniface died a broken man in Rome a month later.

Friars

The approval of the four main orders of friars—Franciscans, Dominicans, Carmelites, and Augustinians—by Popes Innocent III and IV has been mentioned. The ecclesiological effects of these new religious orders were profound for the Western church, though they are difficult to pin down. The numbers of friars are very impressive. At the peak of the population around 1300, Christians in Western Christendom may be estimated at some 60 million (the Black Death plague of 1348–50 and its recurrences brought a notable reduction in the overall population, which by 1500 had still not regained the 1300 figure). Of the adult men in 1300 (around 20 million) we may estimate the number of parish clergy and men in religious orders at around half a million, divided fairly equally between the two groups: huge figures for an overall population similar to that of the United Kingdom today. Of male religious, approaching half were members of the four orders of friars: some 50,000 Franciscans, 30,000 Dominicans, and together some 25,000 Carmelites and Augustinians. All four orders had much smaller associated orders of women as well as large 'third orders' comprising 'tertiaries' who bound themselves to a mitigated observance of the Rule.

The new orders of friars crossed the boundaries of lay and clerical which had dominated many controversies of the earlier period. They crossed, too, some of the boundaries between male and female. Francis of Assisi declined priesthood on the grounds of his unworthiness, accepting only the diaconate. In the early years the Franciscan order regarded itself as more lay than clerical, though gradually the clerical group gained control of the order. Dominicans were more openly clerical, but the Augustinians and Carmelites regarded themselves as hermits as much as friars. Relations between the friars and women were more obvious and open than they had been in the older monastic orders. Clare of Assisi saw herself as directly inspired by Francis; Dominic founded convents for Dominican nuns even before the male order was canonically established. Catherine of Siena, Dominican tertiary in the fourteenth century, was the best known of the many tertiaries of the friars. Raymond Lull, the brilliant linguist and missionary into North Africa, Angela of Foligno, mother of seven children and mystic, Margaret of Cortina, and Pier Pettinaio the comb-maker of Siena recorded by Dante, were all Franciscan tertiaries in the thirteenth century.

The energy and diversity of the new orders of friars—there were other orders besides the four best known—brought corresponding energy and diversity to medieval ecclesiology. Most of the friaries were established in towns though friars sometimes preached and ministered in the countryside too. Their apostolate in the universities will be discussed in the section on Universities and Schools. Among writers on mysticism, particularly notable were three German Dominicans of the early fourteenth century: Meister Eckhart, Henry Suso, and Johann Tauler. Remarkable among missionaries in the thirteenth century were John of Piano Carpini, who led a group of Franciscan friars to Mongolia; Ricoldus da Monte Croce, the Dominican friar who laboured in Persia; and Hyacinth, the Dominican friar who established the Polish province of his order and laboured in Ukraine. The friars produced, too, popes and many bishops during this remarkable 'long' century: the short-lived Dominican popes Innocent V (1276) and Benedict XI (1303–4); the Franciscan pope Nicholas IV (1288–92); and two archbishops of Canterbury in succession, the Dominican Robert Kilwardby (1273–8) followed by the Franciscan John Peckham (1278–92).

The loyalty of the friars to the institutional church—despite some exceptions, mainly due to the creativity of the Franciscans—and their success meant that ecclesiology in the Western church developed notably during the thirteenth century. Altogether ecclesiology became more inventive and broad-based. The older orders, principally Benedictines, Carthusians, and Cistercians, continued to make an important contribution, alongside many other smaller and more recent orders, but it was the four main orders of friars—especially the Franciscans and Dominicans—that made the most significant and enduring contribution to ecclesiology during this period.

Universities and Schools

The first three universities in Western Christendom began in the second half of the twelfth century (they grew out of schools and are without precise dates of foundation): Bologna, Paris, and Oxford, in that order. There were fifteen further foundations in the thirteenth century, some twenty-three in the fourteenth century and thirty-four in the fifteenth century (the exact figures are debatable because of mergers and changes of location). They varied greatly in size, from Paris with several thousand students and Oxford with a peak of some 1,500 around the year 1300, to much smaller institutions with a hundred or so students. By the fifteenth century universities were to be found in most countries of Western Christendom.

Philosophy and Theology were the principal faculties, but Canon Law was important too and a few universities—such as Montpellier in France and Salerno in Italy—had faculties of Medicine. Laymen studied medicine and the attendance of Héloise at Abelard's lectures in Paris (at the 'school' there, before it became a university) indicates the presence of some women at the universities. But the principal function of the universities was the education of priests: young men either preparing for the priesthood or recently ordained. However, only a select few went to university: at most one in ten of the clergy.

Bologna, Paris, and Oxford were all founded by the diocesan clergy and this remained the normal pattern throughout the Middle Ages, though sometimes royal or other lay patronage was involved. The three medieval universities in Scotland, for example, were founded by the local bishop in conjunction with the reigning pope: St Andrews in 1413, Glasgow in 1451, and Aberdeen in 1494/5. Members of the diocesan clergy were prominent among the teachers: Abelard and Peter Lombard at Paris (in its pre-university days); later, John Wyclif at Oxford, and John Hus at Prague. But the religious orders, especially the friars, soon came to play an important—almost dominant—role. Their large houses and numerous students—some 300 friars in the four friaries in Oxford by 1300 alongside sizeable communities of Benedictines and other religious orders—were conspicuous. They produced, too, many of the most famous teachers: the Dominicans Albertus Magnus and Thomas Aquinas who taught at Paris university; the Franciscans Bonaventure who taught at Paris, William of Ockham who taught at Oxford, and Duns Scotus who taught at both Paris and Oxford and (possibly) Cambridge. Gratian, the most famous teacher of canon law at Bologna, is thought to have been a Camaldolese monk.

Universities exercised much influence upon learning and ecclesiology, though perhaps this influence has been exaggerated. Most modern historians studied at university and so tend to emphasize—perhaps exaggerate—the importance of these institutions in the Middle Ages. Certainly we should not forget schools, which could be similar to universities except in formal status. Monasteries often contained a school for boys as well as providing education for their own monks; friars received formal education within specified friaries, outside the universities; important too were parish schools, either situated within the parish church or in a separate building. Convents gave education to nuns and young women: as at the abbey of Bingen in German during the time of Hildegard; or at Helfta, also in Germany, during the time of Gertrude 'the Great', Mechtild of Magdeburg, and Mechtild of Hackeborn.

How did this learning and schooling impact upon ecclesiology? Latin as the common language of university learning, and mostly of schools, had an important cohesive factor. It had long been the common academic language of Western Christendom, but its currency in the universities raised its importance to a new level. University students and teachers thought and communicated in a common language. Some felt this university learning, commonly called Scholasticism, was becoming too abstract, too divorced from the practical concerns and needs of Christians. Yet it fostered an academic probing and excellence that had not been seen in Western Christendom since the early church.

Latin as the common language of the schools and universities also helped to preserve the ecclesial unity of Western Christendom during the medieval period. This unity was fostered, too, by the international nature of the religious orders, especially the friars. There was plenty of lively and creative debate, both philosophical and theological, but there was also a shared forum for this debate, principally through the universities and works written in Latin. There were tensions, of course, but this was expected, almost taken for granted. Most of the major academic personalities mentioned above ran into trouble at some time. Abelard was condemned at the Council of Soissons in 1121; the teaching of Aquinas was censured as too favourable to Aristotle by the archbishop of Paris both before and after his death; William of Ockham was summoned to Avignon to answer various charges and he died excommunicated, though principally for his political stances. Nevertheless the basic theological unity of Western Christendom held together until the late fourteenth century. Then more serious fissures appeared with John Wyclif and the Lollards in England and John Hus and the Hussites in Bohemia. Their dissent more obviously anticipated the sixteenth-century Reformation. With the development of vernacular languages, the divisions of Europe into Catholic and Reformed countries, and the accompanying development of nation states, many of the ecclesiological assumptions of the medieval era would disappear.

Universities were regarded as an integral part of the ecclesial *magisterium*, the teaching authority of the church. Recently there has been a move in the Catholic Church to restrict this *magisterium* to the pope and bishops. But in the Middle Ages *magisterium* was interpreted more widely, including teachers and other authorities in the universities.

Developments Regarding the Laity

The canonist Gratian, writing in the early twelfth century, stated clearly, allegedly quoting St Jerome, that Christians are distinguished into two categories: clergy and laity (*Decretum* II.12.1.7). This basic distinction was underlined by Pope Boniface VIII in his bull *Clericis laicos* of 1296 in which he pointed to inherent tension between the two groups:

> History relates that laymen have been very hostile to the clergy; and this is clearly proved by the experiences of the present time. For not content with what is their own, the laity strive for what is forbidden and loose the reins for things unlawful . . . They impose heavy burdens on prelates of churches and ecclesiastics . . . and they tax them and impose collections . . . (Bettenson 1963: 113)

Nevertheless we have already seen major developments during the thirteenth century which tended to blur the sharp distinction between clergy and laity, resulting especially from the friars. More than this, the century brought more appreciation of the laity in their own right, preparing the way for further developments in the late Middle Ages. This section will focus on two examples of this more positive appreciation and their ecclesial implications: King Louis IX of France and the beguines.

France lay at the heart of Western Christendom in the thirteenth century and King Louis IX's long reign dominated the middle of the century. Born in 1214, he succeeded as king of France in 1226, initially as a minor under the tutelage of his mother, and he reigned until his death in 1270. He was happily married to Margaret of Provence at the age of 20 and they had ten children. He was an able ruler, warding off attempts by King Henry III of England to regain lost territories in France and active in expanding the authority of the French monarchy throughout the kingdom and beyond, into Flanders and Aragon.

He was a devout Christian as well as a loyal friend and good companion. He was, too, a man of his age with many of its limitations. King Louis was notable for his promotion of justice and his defence of the rights of the poor and vulnerable. He actively promoted church life in many ways, including his support for the new orders of Dominicans and Franciscans, for the beguines, and for the university of Paris. At the same time he maintained the royal prerogative, both in his relations with the papacy and in his dealings with the clergy of his realm. In terms of church building, he is chiefly remembered for the exquisite Sainte-Chapelle in Paris, which he had constructed to house Christ's supposed Crown of Thorns, having acquired the relic from the emperor of Constantinople. Twice he led crusades to regain the Holy Land, though without success: in 1248–50 when he was captured and had to be ransomed, and in 1270 when he died at Tunis. His holiness and good sense are well summed up in the written advice which he left for his son and heir in his *Testament*:

> My dear son, in the first place I teach you that you must love the Lord, your God, with all your heart and all your strength . . . Be compassionate towards the poor, the destitute and the afflicted . . . Towards your subjects, act with such justice that you may steer a middle course, swerving neither to the right nor to the left, but lean more to the side of the poor than of the rich until such time as you are certain about the truth. Do your utmost to ensure peace and justice for all your subjects but especially for clergy and religious. Devotedly obey our mother, the Roman Church, and revere the Supreme Pontiff as your spiritual father. Endeavour to banish all sin, especially blasphemy and heresy, from your kingdom . . . (*Divine Office* 1974, 25 August, Saint Louis)

Louis was canonized as a saint by Pope Boniface VIII in 1297. The acerbic side of Boniface has been noted as well as his promotion of extreme claims for the papacy and the Catholic Church. So his canonization of Louis reminds us of another side of the pope's character and policy, as well as the fundamental point that Western ecclesiology of the time always recognized the vital role of monarchy and civil authority within Christian society, even when ecclesiastics felt obliged to rebuke secular rulers for their erring ways.

Beguines provided the most innovative movement within religious life for women during this period. The origin of the word 'beguine' is obscure: it may derive from the simple cloth habit (*béguin* = hood, *beige* = cloth in natural colour) which the women wore. The description was not used consistently either by the women themselves or by others describing them. Mary of Oignies (1177–1213), who lived a devout life in Flanders and inspired other women, is widely considered the founder of the movement. Rather than enter convents, beguines chose to live together, in small groups, in houses and apartments in towns: the communities were called beguinages. The movement received early ecclesiastical backing. Pope Honorius III granted it verbal permission in 1216 and Pope Gregory IX gave further authorization in the bull *Gloriam Virginalem* of 1233. Matthew Paris (1200–59), the English chronicler and Benedictine monk, described the movement in his *Chronica Majora* for the year 1243. Despite the somewhat hostile tone, the description provides precious early evidence of the lifestyle and its attraction for women:

> At this time, especially in Germany, certain . . . women have adopted a religious profession though it is a light one. They call themselves 'religious' and take a private vow of continence and simplicity of life, though they do not follow the Rule of any saint, nor are they as yet confined within a cloister. They have so multiplied within a short time that two thousand have been reported in Cologne and the neighbouring cities.

The movement received important secular patronage when King Louis IX of France founded a beguinage in Paris in 1264. Beguines were largely confined to the Rhineland, northern France, and the Low Countries; though there were similar initiatives in other countries that went under other names. In a provocative talk to the student Franciscans in Oxford, Robert Grosseteste, the outspoken bishop of Lincoln who had confronted Pope Innocent IV, praised the beguine way of life even above that of the friars because they practised poverty while 'living by their own labour'. Beguines are well known for their mystical writings. Mary of Oignies was one such writer; another was Juliana of Liège, who inspired Pope Urban IV to establish the feast of Corpus Christi. The mystic Mechtild of Magdeburg lived for some time as a beguine before becoming a Cistercian nun; Hadewijch, from Flanders, is noted for the 'mysticism of love' which she developed in her writings.

In the early fourteenth century, however, the movement fell under a cloud. Margarete Porete, a beguine originally from Flanders, was burnt at the stake in Paris in 1310 for her allegedly heterodox views on the soul's union with God through mystical prayer. In the following year the Council of Vienne, a general council of the Western church convoked by Pope Clement V, issued a wide ranging censure of beguines, influenced by the case of Margarete Porete:

> The women commonly known as beguines, since they promise obedience to nobody, nor renounce possessions, nor profess any approved rule, are not religious at all, although they wear the special dress of beguines . . . We (the pope) therefore, with the approval of the council, perpetually forbid their mode of life and remove it completely from the church of God. (Tanner 1990, vol. 1: 374)

The decree of the Council of Vienne ended with a saving clause: 'Of course we in no way intend to forbid any faithful women, whether they promise chastity or not, from living uprightly in their hospices, wishing to live a life of penance and serving the Lord of hosts in a spirit of humility.' Beguinages survived but in sharply diminished numbers. Records of property transactions in Cologne indicate 169 beguinages in the city in 1310, 62 in 1320, and only two in 1400 (Southern 1970: 279–80). Much of the original inspiration was lost. From small apartments and houses, beguinages developed into the much larger complexes of houses that can be seen today, mostly dating from the sixteenth century onwards, in various cities in Belgium and the Netherlands.

THE LATE MIDDLE AGES

The late Middle Ages, until the beginning of the Reformation in 1517, may be divided into three periods: the Avignon papacy from 1309 to 1377; the papal schism and conciliar movement from 1378 to 1440; and the early Renaissance. Each period brought distinctive challenges and responses for ecclesiology in the Western church.

The Avignon Papacy

The difficulties and death of Pope Boniface VIII have been mentioned. His successor, Benedict XI, reigned less than a year. The cardinals who met in Perugia in northern Italy to elect the next pope were divided between those who supported the firm policies of Boniface and those who wanted rapprochement with the French King Philip IV, who was the most powerful monarch in Christendom. Eventually after eleven months of bitter debate, the latter group emerged triumphant. Bernard de Got, who was archbishop of Bordeaux in southern France and on relatively good terms with King Philip, gained the necessary two-thirds majority and chose the name Clement V. Almost immediately he moved to France and was crowned pope at Lyons in November 1305. After stays in various places in southern France, he settled with the papal curia, at King Philip's request, in Avignon in 1309.

Avignon made some sense. The city was a papal 'fief' (property owned by the papacy, outside the Papal States in Italy) and was more secure—helped by the protection of the king of France—than the unruly city of Rome. With the Muslim conquest of the eastern Mediterranean world and North Africa, Rome lay on the edges of Western Christendom while Avignon was geographically more central. Exaltation of papal authority from Gregory VII onwards had emphasized the pope's role as head of the church, somewhat at the expense of his title of bishop of Rome. So an important new question arose. Could this primary role be equally well carried out, perhaps even better in the circumstances, away from Rome? From the mid-thirteenth century onward various popes had spent long sojourns in southern France. Pope Innocent IV (1243–54) had fled from Rome in 1244 and spent the next seven years in southern France, where he presided over the first Council of Lyons in 1245. Pope Gregory X came to the same city in 1274 to preside over the second Council of Lyons. Several popes of the second half of the thirteenth century were Frenchmen: Urban IV (1261–4), Clement IV (1265–8), and Martin IV (1281–5). Others had studied at Paris university. Altogether the papacy had acquired a French air, interrupted by Boniface VIII, so the move to Avignon was in continuity with this trend.

The papacy soon became firmly established in Avignon. A huge palace was built, which can still be seen today remarkably intact, to accommodate the pope and his curia. All seven of the Avignon popes were Frenchmen, more precisely from southern France, and most of the cardinals and other curial officials were from the same country. The overtly French atmosphere gave some offence. Criticism came notably from England, which was in the early stages of the Hundred Years War with France. Several of the popes, however, strove to mediate in the war and to bring it to an end. The papal curia became a model of efficiency, though there was criticism of its greed regarding the payment of fees and favouritism in the appointment to offices.

Many good initiatives came from the Avignon papacy, particularly regarding the promotion of learning. Urban V (1362–70) was noted for holiness and was beatified by Pope Pius IX in 1870. Nevertheless, there was widespread feeling that the pope ought to return to his proper city, Rome. Pope Urban was partly of this mind. He journeyed to Rome in 1367 and remained there for three years, before returning to Avignon in September 1370 where he died two months later. His successor, Gregory XI, was of a similar mind. Urged on by Catherine of Siena, who visited him in Avignon, he reached Rome in January 1377 but died there later in the same year.

Papal Schism and the Conciliar Movement

The disputed election that followed the death of Gregory XI resulted in the longest papal schism in the history of the church. There was pressure from the Roman populace upon the electing cardinals to choose an Italian as pope, lest if another Frenchman were chosen he would return to Avignon. But was the pressure from the crowd so great as to invalidate the election? The archbishop of Bari in Italy was eventually chosen and he took the name Urban VI. At first he was recognized as pope both by his electors and by various secular authorities. However, his difficult character soon became apparent. According to many accounts, he was rude and insulting towards both the cardinals who had elected him and various lay dignitaries who came to visit him. At least arrogance and imbalance of mind were evident. To the issue of the possible invalidity of Urban's election, due to pressure from the Roman crowd, was now added that of his 'incapacity' for the papal office.

Within a few months almost all the cardinals had deserted Urban, declared his election invalid, and elected in his place Cardinal Robert of Geneva, who took the name Clement VII. Urban managed to hold Rome and Clement was obliged to retire to Avignon, where he established an alternative curia. The resulting schism lasted for nearly forty years. Europe was almost equally divided in its loyalties. France, most of Spain, and Scotland were the principal supporters of the Avignon popes; Italy from Rome northwards, England, Germany, central Europe, and Scandinavia sided with the Roman popes; some countries were divided or switched loyalties. Eventually, in 1409, the two groups of cardinals, with widespread support, deserted their respective popes and called a council at Pisa in northern Italy, to attempt a resolution. The result, however, only aggravated the situation further. Another claimant to the papacy was elected, Alexander V, while the other two popes retained a measure of support.

The deadlock was finally resolved by the Council of Constance, which met from 1414 to 1417. The German emperor Sigismund was the principal initiator of the council—thereby reviving the practice of the early ecumenical councils which had been summoned by the eastern emperors. The summons had widespread approval in Western Christendom, including the support of most secular rulers, and the council was well attended. John XXIII, who had succeeded Alexander V in the Pisan line, initially supported the summons, expecting the council to confirm him as the true pope. But when he realized the council was expecting his resignation along with those of the other two candidates, he fled from the council and threatened to dissolve it.

In this situation of emergency, the council promulgated the decree *Haec Sancta* (sometimes called *Sacrosancta*, due to different initial words in some manuscripts), which asserted the council's superiority over the pope and therefore its right to proceed in the present delicate situation. This famous decree had major implications for ecclesiology inasmuch as it involved the crucial issue of the relationship between pope and council, between the papacy and conciliarism. The key passage of the decree, which was approved on 6 April 1415, reads as follows:

> This holy synod of Constance . . . declares that, legitimately assembled in the holy Spirit, constituting a general council and representing the catholic church militant, it has power immediately from Christ; and that everyone of whatever state or dignity, even papal, is bound to obey it in those matters which pertain to the faith, the eradication of the present schism and the general reform of the church of God in head and members. (Tanner 1990: vol. 1, 409)

Pope Gregory XII, of the Roman line, was persuaded to resign in July. John XXIII also abdicated, under pressure. Benedict XIII, of the Avignon line, adamantly refused to resign and was eventually deposed by the council. Thereby the path was cleared for a fresh election. Oddo Colonna was duly elected by the council in November 1417 and took the name Martin V. Opposition to his legitimacy was restricted to Benedict XIII, now residing in the castle of Peniscola on the Mediterranean coast of Spain, and a small band of his supporters.

The main focus of the Council of Constance was on resolving the papal schism, but it treated quite a wide range of other issues. The council's condemnations of John Wyclif and John Hus, and their teachings, have been mentioned—conciliarism, at least in these cases, did not mean liberalism in theology or mild treatment for the condemned. Towards the end of the council, Constance sought to institutionalize conciliarism through its decree *Frequens*, which ordered the regular holding of general councils; the next after five years, another seven years later, and thereafter every ten years.

Following the requirements of *Frequens*, a thinly attended council met first at Pavia and then Siena in 1423/4. Seven years later a much more substantial council met at Basel in Switzerland. However, the newly elected Pope Eugenius IV immediately showed himself hostile to the council at Basel. A long struggle ensued and eventually Eugenius ordered the transferral of the council to Florence. The majority at Basel refused to recognize the move and so there resulted two rival councils in session at the same time, one at Basel and the other at Florence.

Muslim advances were threatening the city of Constantinople and there was renewed desire within the leadership of the Orthodox church for reunion with Rome, partly in the hope that reunion might lead to Western aid for the defence of Constantinople. To discuss this reunion, the Orthodox Church decided to send its delegation to Florence rather than to Basel. Although the resulting decree of reunion *Laetentur Caeli* was soon rejected by the Orthodox Church, within Western Christendom it was considered a triumph for Pope Eugenius and it helped to take the initiative away from the Council of Basel. This council elected in 1439 a rival pope, the pious duke of Savoy, a widower and father of five children, who took the name Felix V. This risky move reopened the prospect of papal schism, which few welcomed. The Council of Basel lingered on until 1449, when, now transferred to Lausanne in Switzerland, it finally dissolved itself and Felix V formally resigned his claims to the papacy.

Thereafter the papacy became more openly hostile to the decrees *Haec Sancta* and *Frequens*. No further general council was called until Lateran V in the early sixteenth century and Pope Pius II, in the bull *Execrabilis* of 1462, condemned appeals from the pope to a general council. The papacy, however, never attempted formally to rescind the two decrees.

Early Renaissance and Conclusion

The decades from 1440 to the beginning of the Reformation in 1517 brought various developments in ecclesiology but also uncertainties. Altogether the period combines well with the Conclusion of this chapter, so they are taken together.

The papacy regained confidence during this time. The Council of Basel petered out. The decree *Frequens* fell into abeyance. Claiming observance of this decree, some French and Italian cardinals, supported by King Louis XII of France, called a general council which met at Pisa in 1511. It was to outmanoeuvre this council, rather than enthusiasm for councils, that persuaded Pope Julius II to summon to Rome a general council of the Western church. Lateran V duly met, somewhat sporadically, from 1512 to 1517, ending a few months before Martin Luther nailed his 95 theses to the door of the castle church at Wittenberg. The council's final decree concluded thus, with eerie unawareness of what would soon follow.

> Finally, it was reported to us (pope Leo X, who had succeeded Julius II) on several occasions, through the cardinals and prelates of the three committees (of the council), that no topics remained for them to discuss and that over several months nothing at all had been brought before them by anyone. [Tanner 1990: vol. 1, 652–3]

The popes became secure in the city of Rome. There were no serious calls for a return to Avignon. A succession of popes from Nicholas V (1447–54) onwards became identified with the Renaissance, though caution is needed here: the identification was emphasized by later historians and to some extent was their construction. The popes in question had many concerns and interests besides the promotion of art, architecture, and scholarship. In many respects they were more medieval than modern or Renaissance figures. Nevertheless, most of them devoted considerable attention, for a variety of motives, to rebuilding the city of Rome and to the patronage of art and scholarship. St Peter's church was rebuilt on a grand scale by the finest architects and artists of the period. The Sistine chapel in the Vatican and its Sistine choir are named after their principal patron, Pope Sixtus IV (1471–84). The threat to the city of Constantinople, and its eventual capture by the Turkish army in 1453, led to the partial transfer of Greek scholarship—in terms of both scholars and manuscripts—from Constantinople to Rome.

The Spaniard Rodrigo Borgia, who took the name Alexander VI (1492–1503), is the most notorious of the Renaissance popes, indeed perhaps of all popes. He kept a string of mistresses and fathered through them at least ten illegitimate children, including two who were borne by Giulia Farnese while he was pope. Promotion of family interests, and of his illegitimate offspring, and the accumulation of wealth, dominated much of his reign. Yet he was active in other areas too. By the Treaty of Tordesillas in 1494, he assigned the 'New World' of the Americas to the authority of Spain and Portugal, reaching an agreement with the monarchs of the two countries regarding the line of demarcation between the two zones. He was co-founder, together with the local bishop William Elphinstone, of the university of Aberdeen in Scotland in 1494/5. For all the enigmas of his personal life, he was devout after a fashion and defended orthodoxy. He celebrated the Jubilee year of 1500 in style and by granting many indulgences. His quarrels with Girolamo Savanarola, the famous Dominican preacher, ended tragically with Savanarola's condemnation and execution by burning at the stake in Florence. Alexander was an important patron of Renaissance artists and he engaged Michelangelo to draw up plans for the rebuilding of St Peter's church. He died suddenly in August 1503 when, it seems, a poisoned cup of wine, intended for a guest, was given to him by mistake.

The Reformation came, nevertheless, somewhat unexpectedly. Alongside elements of decadence, as portrayed by Pope Alexander VI, there was creativity and harmony too. Most of the Renaissance artists were laymen as were many of the scholars. Writers of genius, led by Dante and Chaucer, had been developing vernacular languages, which were to prove so important in the Reformation. In many ways the Reformation must be seen as springing out of the late medieval church even more than as a reaction against it.

Finally, it is important to remember wider concerns and interests. The focus of the professional church historian is often too narrow. A fascinating glimpse of the wider ecclesiology of the late medieval laity is provided by the decree 'On Jews and Neophytes' which was promulgated by the Council of Basel in 1434. The decree sought to outlaw close relations between Christians on the one hand, and Jews and 'other infidels' (principally Muslims) on the other hand. Yet implicitly and revealingly, it recognizes that such familiarity and mutual appreciation was widespread:

> Renewing the sacred canons, we command both diocesan bishops and secular powers to prohibit in every way Jews and other infidels from having Christians, male or female, in their households, or as nurses of their children; and Christians from joining them in festivities, marriages, banquets or baths, or in much conversation, and from taking them as doctors or agents of marriages or officially appointed mediators of other contracts. (Tanner vol. 1: 483)

REFERENCES

Note: Quotations are provided in English translation rather than in their (mostly) Latin original, following the translation in the publication indicated, though sometimes with minor adjustments.

Bettenson, H. (1963). *Documents of the Christian Church*. Oxford: Oxford University Press.

Divine Office (1974). *The Divine Office: The Liturgy of the Hours According to the Roman Rite*. London: HarperCollins.

Gieben, S. (1971). 'Robert Grosseteste at the Papal Curia, Lyons 1250: Edition of the Documents'. *Collectanea Francescana* 41: 340–93.

Southern, R. (1970). *Western Society and the Church in the Middle Ages*. Grand Rapids, MI: Eerdmans.

Tanner, N. (1990). *Decrees of the Ecumenical Councils*. 2 vols. London and New York: Sheed & Ward and Georgetown University Press.

Tierney, B. (1964). *The Crisis of Church and State 1050–1300: With Selected Documents*. Englewood Cliffs, NJ: Prentice-Hall.

SUGGESTED READING

Bettenson (1963), Tanner (1990), and Tierney (1964), listed under 'References', provide extensive collections of relevant documents together with some commentary. Also very useful in this regard are: Heinrich Denzinger and Peter Hünermann (eds), *Enchiridion symbolorum definitionum et declarationum de rebus fidei et morum: Compendium of Creeds, Definitions and Declarations on Matters of Faith and Morals*, 43rd edn (San Francisco: Ignatius Press, 2012); Colman J. Barry (ed.), *Readings in Church History* (Westminster, MD: Christian Classics, 1985); Jacques Dupuis (ed.), *The Christian Faith in the Doctrinal Documents of the Catholic Church*, 7th edition (New York: Alba House, 2001). A. Friedberg (ed.), *Corpus Iuris Canonici*, 2 vols (Leipzig: Bernhard Tauchnitz, 1879) is the standard edition of the canons of church law which were in force throughout Western Christendom. Vols 2 to 5 of *English Historical Documents*, general editor David C. Douglas (Eyre & Spottiswoode: London, 1968–96) provide an invaluable collection of documents, focused on England but many with wider relevance. Norman Tanner, *New Short History of the Catholic Church* (London and New York: Burns & Oates/ Continuum/Bloomsbury, 2011 and 2014), chapter 3 'Central and Late Middle Ages', provides an overall survey of the period and situates ecclesiology within its wider context.

CHAPTER 10

THE CHURCH IN THE MAGISTERIAL REFORMERS

DOROTHEA WENDEBOURG

THE ecclesiological concepts of the Magisterial Reformers were not monolithic. Yet, although they differed from each other and each had its own characteristic traits, there were undeniably kindred and shared basic theological presuppositions. The historical reason for this kinship is the theology of Martin Luther which deeply influenced all other Reformers, Magisterial and Radical. Therefore the ecclesiology of Luther will not only take up the first part of this chapter, but will also occupy more space than that of Philipp Melanchthon and Jean Calvin, the other most important and influential Magisterial Reformers on whom the chapter will then concentrate. A relatively broad picture of Luther's ecclesiological conception will allow us to see which convictions Melanchthon and Calvin shared with him, as well as where they took their own road.

MARTIN LUTHER (1483–1546)

The church did not stand at the centre of Martin Luther's interest; neither was ecclesiology the main object of his theological passion, nor were his reflection and activity focused on the reform of the church, the much discussed *reformatio ecclesiae*. The centre was rather justification, the gift of salvation through the gospel of Jesus Christ by faith alone. It was only from this angle that the church came into the picture: Luther asked what the right understanding of justification meant for the definition, the shape, and the life of the church. However, from this angle the church certainly did come into the picture. For in his eyes it went without saying that without the church there is no justification, salvation, and Christian faith. Only through the church can a human being hear the gospel. And when he trusts the gospel he becomes a member of the church. Thus the same Luther for whom the church never came first, but always second, wrote emphatically: '*Ecclesia* shall be my fortress, my palace, my chamber' (44, 713, 1).[1] Outside the church 'there is no truth, no Christ, no salvation' (10/1/1, 140, 17).

This background explains how Luther dealt with the church in his writings. There is a host of statements about this subject from his pen, but very few of his works are explicitly ecclesiological. In most cases he dealt with the church in the context of other issues or discussed practical questions which were important for the establishment of an evangelical ecclesial body. Besides, the concerns prevalent in his statements on the church vary according to the state of the theological debates and the historical situations. Thus he never laid down a systematic ecclesiology. However, the basic lines which governed whatever he said and wrote about the church remained the same since the evangelical doctrine of justification had found its final shape. Thus while the lack of a comprehensive and systematical ecclesiological treatise makes it necessary to look for statements on the church in all kinds of works written by him in the course of his life, it is also perfectly possible to do so because of their theological coherence.

In his early years Luther mentioned the church only rarely and marginally. He went into the subject more broadly only when he criticized the church of his time, which he did less for individual grievances than for severe spiritual defects. After Rome's conflict with the Saxon monk had begun (1518), his criticism was directed sharply against the church authorities, first of all the papacy. This led to his first ecclesiological treatise *On the papacy in Rome against the most celebrated Romanist in Leipzig* (1520) (6, 285–324). As soon as it became necessary to reform the church in the territories where the Reformation had taken hold according to evangelical insights, Luther complemented his critical arguments with constructive writings on various questions of the institutional structure of the church which included implicit or explicit ecclesiological statements. The first of these writings was *That a Christian assembly has the right and power to judge all teaching and to call, appoint, and dismiss teachers* from 1523 (11, 408–16); then followed treatises on the reform of worship in the middle of the 1520s (particularly 12, 35–7.205–20; 19, 73–113) and the Wittenberg liturgy of ordination in 1535 (38, 423–33, commented upon in 41, 457, 33–459, 11; 762, 18–763, 18), finally the *Model for the consecration of a true Christian bishop* (53, 231–60), written in 1542 in the context of the endeavour to create a genuine evangelical episcopacy. In his later years Luther also produced several treatises which were largely dedicated to the theological understanding of the church, called forth not least by the ever more evident reality of two antagonistic church bodies side by side. Of particular weight were *The private mass and*

---

[1] All references are to the Weimar edition (WA) of Martin Luther's works: *D. Martin Luthers Werke. Kritische Gesamtausgabe* (Weimar: Hermann Böhlau, 1883–), following the convention of referring to volume, page, and line. It is therefore not necessary to add WA before the volume numbers, except in the cases of WADB (Deutsche Bibel/German Bible), WAT (Tischreden/Tabletalk), and WAB (Briefe/Letters). Those writings by Luther which became part of the Lutheran Confessions (Small and Large Catechism, Smalcald Articles), appear with their official abbreviations (Small Cat., Large Cat., ASm) and numbers of articles. Latin titles are given as such; German or French titles are translated into English. The standard English translation of most of Luther's works is: *Luther's Works*, ed. Jaroslav Pelikan and Helmut T. Lehmann. Minneapolis/St. Louis: Fortress Press/ Concordia Publishing House, 1957–.

the consecration of priests (1533) (38, 195–256), his most important ecclesiological work *On the councils and the church* (1539) (50, 509–653), and *Against Hanswurst* (1541) (51, 469–572).

There is one *cantus firmus* which runs through all of Luther's statements about the church from his early period right to the end. It is the declaration that the One, Holy, Catholic, and Apostolic Church is the communion of those who hear the gospel and believe in it. This declaration is nothing short of a definition as the *Smalcald Articles* say: 'Thank God, a seven-year-old child knows what the Church is, namely the holy believers and "sheep who listen to the voice of their shepherd". For thus pray the children: I believe one holy Christian Church' (ASm III, art. 12; cf. 50, 624, 14–18).

This definition means first: The church in its essence is communion—'gathering', 'people', 'Christendom', etc., as Luther wrote in ever new variations (e.g. Large Cat., Creed art. 3; Small Cat., Creed art. 3; 7, 219, 3; 7, 712, 39; b 26, 506, 31.35; 26, 507, 7; 50, 624, 17.29). Throughout his translation of the New Testament, Luther consequently rendered the Greek word ἐκκλησία by 'communion' or 'congregation' ('Gemeine'), which is at times to be understood in the sense of 'local congregation' and in other instances means the whole of Christendom. In other words, the church is first of all the totality of the persons who belong to it, not an institution. It is not bound to a certain place or a single church but is catholic, living 'in all the world' (26, 506, 31); as in Wittenberg so also 'under the pope, the Turks, the Persians, the Tartars, and all over' (26, 506, 38f).

The definition quoted means secondly: The church is a specific communion, namely the communion of those who believe in Christ (50, 624, 29; cf. 6, 300, 35f). It is such not by its own strength but thanks to the power of the Holy Spirit. The Spirit 'calls, gathers, illuminates, sanctifies . . . Christendom . . . and keeps it united to Christ in the true, one faith' (Small Cat., Creed art. 3). Thus, like all works of the Holy Spirit, the church is not an entity evident to anybody, but a hidden reality (18, 652, 23). This does not mean that the church is not an empirical reality in space and time (cf. 7, 683, 8–26)—a misunderstanding because of which Luther prefers the wording 'hidden church' (*ecclesia abscondita*) to the traditional Augustinian formula 'invisible church' (*ecclesia invisiblis*). As a communion of physical, visible and audible human beings, the church is indeed visible and audible. But its essence, that which makes the church the church, is not accessible to human senses. This is true because as the communion of believers it is manifest only to God, since only he can see into the heart of human beings (17/2, 501, 32–5; cf. 21, 332, 37–333, 2) and diagnose who is part of the believers and thereby of the church (6, 298, 2f; 17/2, 510, 37f). But this is also true because the church on earth is miserable, powerless, foolish, and scandalous, often exposed to derision and persecution—thus its real life is hidden 'under the opposite' (*contrarium*) like that of its crucified Lord, until it shall be manifest splendidly in heaven (4, 450, 39–451, 27; cf. 5, 285, 35f; 42, 187, 14–16). What is more, it is also hidden under sin, which sticks to the church while it is in this world, since as the communion of the faithful it is the communion of the justified who on earth are at the same time still sinners. Thus the church hides its spiritual reality by its own failure, abuses, scandals, divisions, under which only the eyes of faith are able nevertheless to identify the church of Jesus Christ (WADB 7, 418, 9–13; 418, 36–420, 4; cf.

WA 7, 710, 1f). This sin can seize the doctrine, the form, and the life of the church to such a degree and set them in such opposition to its essence that what comes to the fore is a false church. In that case the Antichrist is at work about whom the Bible not accidentally says that he is active *within* the church of Christ.

All these statements about the church's hiddenness imply nevertheless that the visible reality under which it is hidden has something to do with the church itself, since otherwise it would be impossible to say that the church is hidden precisely *here* and that what is hidden here is precisely *the church*. Thus the church has also a visible side, it is also 'bodily, external' church (1, 639, 3; 6, 297, 2). It presents itself as an identifiable number of human beings whose unity has an institutional shape, who profess one common faith, and do certain things together.

The number of the church's marks which Luther puts together varies: at times it is larger, at times smaller (cf. 50, 628, 29–642, 4; 51, 479, 4–487, 2). However, only one feature of the church is an unequivocal mark in the sense of allowing us to say with certainty that wherever it is, there is the Christian church. This feature is the third implication of the definition in the *Smalcald Articles* cited above: The church is wherever the Word of God, more precisely, wherever the gospel can be heard. In saying this, it is vital for the function of the Word as a mark of the church that 'to be heard' means real, sensuous audibility, external 'sound and words' (56, 426, 1), proclaimed by human mouths (50, 629, 16–20; 11, 408, 8–10). What is true of the gospel proclaimed orally is also valid for the other sensual forms of the Word of God, the sacraments. Thus it can be said as a summary: 'The marks by which one can recognize externally where in the world is the Church are baptism, sacrament [i.e. the Lord's Supper], and the gospel' (6, 301, 3f). In the precise, unequivocal sense only these are *notae ecclesiae*. For where the gospel is preached, where baptism takes place and the Lord's Supper is held, it cannot be otherwise. Human beings come to have faith or are being kept in faith; the communion of the faithful comes into existence or continues to exist: 'God's Word cannot be without God's people' (50, 629, 34f) as God himself has promised (Isa. 55, 11): 'My Word shall not come back empty' (11, 408, 13; 50, 629, 31). Hence it follows: 'Wherever you hear such a Word or see it preached, believed, confessed, and obeyed, do not doubt that there must certainly be a true *Ecclesia sancta Catholica*, a Christian holy people, even if there are but very few. For God's Word does not go forth void' (50, 629, 28–31). In short, the Word of God in its different forms is the unequivocal external mark of the church because it creates the church, and it creates the church because it creates faith and thus also the communion of the faithful.

The affirmation that God's Word creates the church does not compete with the statement that the church is the work of the Holy Spirit. Rather the Spirit achieves his hidden work of creating and preserving the communion of the faithful only in such a way that human beings 'hear the voice of the shepherd', that they come to faith in the external, audible gospel: I have been 'brought here by the Holy Spirit and incorporated into the Church through having heard God's Word and still hearing it' (Large Cat., Creed art. 3). Conversely it is true that 'wherever Christ is not preached there is no Holy Spirit who creates, calls, and gathers the Christian Church' (Large Cat., Creed art. 3). More than anything else Luther urged upon his hearers and readers this dependency of the church on the Word of God: The church is 'creature of the Gospel' (2, 430, 6f.; cf. 7, 721, 10–12). It is such not in the sense that it has been created once by the Word of God and since then continues thanks to a strength that is now its own intrinsic life, but it remains dependent on being incessantly filled with life by God through the gospel: 'The whole life and essence of the Church is in the Word of God' (7, 721, 12f). Which means nothing else but that the church in its essence is the communion of believers who become and remain believers through the very Word in which they believe.

The first place of the gospel cannot be outstripped. This holds true although it is the church that proclaims the gospel and human beings come to faith only under the condition that the church does so. Luther can emphasize this aspect under which the church precedes faith with strong words. Thus he calls the Christian communion 'the mother that begets and bears every Christian through the Word of God' (Large Cat., Creed art. 3). But he outlines the church's role very precisely: First of all its motherly function is restricted to passing on the—external—Word in oral proclamation and distribution of the sacraments. To 'reveal' this Word to the hearers in such a way that their hearts are kindled and they become and remain faithful and members of the communion of the faithful is the work of God the Holy Spirit himself (Large Cat., Creed art. 3). Secondly, the church, also when passing on the Word of God, is subject to it both regarding its being and regarding the norm of its actions: It *is able* to pass on God's Word because, being the 'creature of the gospel', it owes its very existence to it; although being mother of the faithful, in relation to the Word it is 'not mother', but 'daughter', 'born from the Word' (42, 334, 12; cf. 6, 560, 33–561, 2). And the church can only *pass on* God's Word, without additions of its own making or alterations, obedient to the revelation of Christ which has preceded it (38, 239, 1–7). The yardstick of the church's obedience is the testimony of the Holy Scriptures. Thus the obedient passing on of the gospel by the church is carried out in the faithful explication of the Scriptures and in the distribution of the sacraments according to the Scriptures (51, 481, 7f.; 50, 630, 22f.; 631, 7f.).

The audible and the visible Word as the external means and marks of the church are the pivot by which the visibility and the hiddenness of the church are connected. What corresponds to the external means in the first instance is the communion which uses them equally externally, the communion of the hearers, the baptized, the communicants. But this 'bodily', visible church is not a second church besides the hidden one. After all, the members of the hidden church, the believers, having become and remaining such only through the Word of God, are themselves part of the visible communion of the hearers, baptized, and communicants. Thus visible and hidden church are two dimensions of the same thing (cf. 1, 639, 2–4). At the same time they differ from each other: in the visible church there are distinctions which do not exist in the hidden one, the distinction between believers and non-believers, the distinction between ministers and the other Christians, and the distinction between true and false church.

Concerning the first distinction, not all members of the visible church are part of the communion of believers. Both dimensions are not coextensive. For not all who hear the gospel and receive the sacraments thereby become or are believers. Among them there are also human beings who are not touched internally by these external means. Yet both are part of the visible church. Where exactly in the visible church the dividing line runs between them is known by God alone who knows the human heart (21, 332, 31–39). The Christian will, according to the 'yardstick of love', which means assuming the best about everybody, consider every member of the visible church also as part of the communion of believers (18, 651, 34–652, 4).

Among the members of the visible church there are—secondly—holders of ministry vis-à-vis the other Christians. In the communion of believers, however, there is no such distinction, here all are equal, namely 'truly of Christian estate' (6, 407, 13f); that is, they all equally have immediate communion with God, which means they all are priests since a stance of such immediacy with God is a characteristic feature of priesthood (41, 153, 30f). Thus they participate in Christ's own priesthood (12, 179, 15–21; 41, 207, 20f; 45, 683, 20f). Indeed all of them do—'all Christian men are priests, all women priestesses, be they old or young, lord or servant, mistress or maid, learned or lay' (6, 370, 25–7). As the basis of this common priestly estate of the Christians Luther names baptism (6, 408, 11f.; 17/2, 6, 33–5) as well as faith (6, 370, 24f.; 7, 27, 18f.; 28, 18f.:10/III, 398, 24–9), both statements meaning two sides of the same reality, since faith as a person's most intimate union with Christ presupposes the Holy Spirit given in baptism, and baptism reaches its goal only in faith (cf. 17/2, 6, 13). However, the priests receive their new estate not only for themselves. Just as Christ became priest for others, so are they; thanks to their union with Christ they stand vis-à-vis their fellow human beings in Christ's own name, that is with his authority (49, 139, 3–7) and with his priestly power (10/3, 394, 32–395, 6), aimed at helping other human beings to get in and live in the same relation with God they enjoy (45, 540, 17–19). It is the power to hand on the means by which he brings about this relation. In other words: Those who are 'all equally priests' also all have 'the same power regarding the Word and every sacrament' (6, 566, 27f; cf. 8, 273, 12f; 10/3, 395, 3–9), namely the same power to teach, 'to preach and proclaim the Word, to baptize, to consecrate or hold the Lord's Supper, to administer the keys, to intercede for others, to sacrifice, and to judge all doctrine and spirits' (12, 180, 2–4).

Insofar as the priestly activities consist in the distribution of the external means of grace they take place within the visible church. This, however, happens in a certain order which generates a differentiation between the priests. Therefore Luther, as much as he underlines the commonness of the priesthood of the Christians and as extensively as he defines the powers entailed in this priesthood, often adds a qualification: 'Although we are all equally priests, nevertheless we cannot all . . . preach' (7, 28, 34f). Or: All Christians are 'truly of a spiritual estate' with all the implications stated, there is no difference between them—'except only regarding the ministry' (6, 407, 14f). Under the aspect of ministry it must be said: 'One alone has to preach, baptize, absolve, and distribute the Lord's Supper, the others have to be content with this and consent' (50, 633, 8–10). That is, as much as all spiritual powers implied in the participation in Christ's priesthood are common to all baptized believers, the right to *use* them is not in every case. The reason for this restriction is that the proclamation of the gospel commanded by Christ takes place in two different contexts: It is a matter 'between brother and brother', but it is also an affair which encompasses the individual level in space and time, a 'public' affair directed at the whole congregation and realized in the name of the whole congregation. Such public proclamation of the gospel has to be done by individual Christians entrusted with this special ministry, in other words, it has to be done in an institutionalized way: 'It is necessary to have bishops, pastors, or preachers who publicly and exclusively give, distribute, and exercise the four pieces or sacred things named above [sc. preaching, baptism, Lord's Supper, absolution] for the sake and in the name of the congregations and moreover because of Christ's institution, as St. Paul says in Eph. 4: . . . He has instituted some as apostles, prophets, evangelists, teachers, governors etc.' (50, 632, 36–633, 5).

As this citation shows, Luther presents two seemingly contradictory reasons for the tie of public proclamation to holders of a special ministry: the priesthood of all believers or of the baptized and the institution by Christ. Thus he says on the one hand: it is 'because of and in the name of' the church (cf. also 49, 600, 12f.) that individual Christians entrusted with this task have to perform the public proclamation of the Word of God, precisely because all Christians possess the power of proclaiming. For this very reason there must be 'one person [. . .] who speaks and does the talking because of the command and permission of the others' (49, 600, 13f; cf. 38, 227, 20ff; 38, 247, 10–31; 50, 633, 4–6; 54, 251, 31–4). Otherwise there would be a scandalous 'chaos' in the church (12, 189, 23; cf. 50, 633, 6–8). Or some individuals would arrogate the proclamation in the church to themselves although they do not own more power than their fellow Christians (12, 189, 17–23). Then both would be damaged: God's Word would not come across any more as the Word spoken—to all—by God but as the word of human individuals, and the priesthood of all would cease to be common to all. Only when the public proclamation, oral as well as sacramental, is entrusted to individual Christians by the entire communion, for which and to which they are to speak, can this damage be avoided. Therefore the church is not free to undertake such entrusting or not, but it 'must have bishops, pastors, or preachers' (50, 633, 1). At this point Luther's other argument for the ministry of public proclamation comes into play: 'Moreover', it is necessary to have such ministers 'because of Christ's institution' (50, 633, 3; cf. 6, 441, 24f.). Luther does not speak of the institution of the ministry in the same sense as he speaks of the institution of the oral proclamation of the gospel or of the sacraments, namely as a commandment of Christ which can be found as such in the Gospels. Nevertheless, by having a ministry, the church is obedient to an institution by Christ. For what is done through the ministry, 'public' proclamation, is a necessary implication of Christ's commandment to propagate the gospel. Therefore 'apostles, evangelists, prophets who do God's Word and work must always be, however they want to be named or can be named' (50, 634, 13–15; cf. 11, 411, 22–4). To have such ministers, the church has to entrust the ministry of public proclamation to individual priests by way of ordination, which is the calling (*vocatio*) exclusively to fulfil this task, but not the conferment of special spiritual qualities or powers for which there is no place beyond those given with the participation in Christ's priesthood common to all (38, 228, 27–9).

The primary place of the ministry is where the preaching of the gospel and the distribution of the sacraments take place: the congregation assembled around one pulpit, one baptismal font, and one table. Its primary holder is the pastor of such a congregation whom Luther, because of the identity of his task with the original episcopacy, programmatically called 'bishop' (e.g. 6, 440, 21f; 12, 205, 3f). Nevertheless Luther was not a Congregationalist who advocated the complete independence of the individual congregation. He rather maintained that the essential oneness of the church across the borders of the local congregations should find expression also in the visible church. Thus he provided for regular visitations of the congregations and worked for the establishment of a continuous ecclesial institution above the parish level. Which concrete form this institution would take—synodal or personal—was for him a question not of ecclesial necessity, but of tradition and historical context. Personally he would have preferred an evangelical diocesan episcopacy whereby this office after having degenerated into a mainly political function was to become genuinely spiritual again. Whereas the Wittenberg Reformation was able to establish such an episcopal office on the regional level, the so-called office of superintendent, for mainly political reasons it succeeded in so doing on the level of the former dioceses only outside the Holy Roman Empire. What within the Empire came into being instead, the church government of the princes, he viewed with undisguised mistrust (cf. WAB 10, 436).

As regards the worldwide unity of the church, Luther rarely addressed the question whether, and if so, how it should be expressed in the visible church. Where he did, he favoured a conciliar form: the bishops, all vested with equal authority, should lead the church together, as was the case with the apostles and in the beginning with the bishops in the Ancient Church (ASm II, art. 4). Above them there is only the one Head who does not himself belong to the visible church, Jesus Christ (ASm II, art. 4; 51, 494, 10f). Thus the claim of the pope to be the visible head of the church is rejected. He owns no superiority according to divine right whatsoever; to declare that he does is an expression of anti-Christian presumption. Yet Luther also rejects a superiority of the pope over the church according to human law as neither feasible nor useful (ASm II, art. 4). What the Christian church needs is not the exercise of ecclesial power, but a regime of spiritual concordance in which 'we all live under one head Christ and the bishops all equal according to their office, hold eagerly together in unanimous doctrine, faith, sacraments, prayers, and works of love, etc.' (ASm II, art. 4).

Finally there is yet a third difference within the visible church which does not exist in the hidden church, the difference between the 'true' and the 'false church' already mentioned. This difference is rooted in the fact that the means of grace are handed on by human beings who, even when they are Christians, are not immune to error and sin. Thus it is not only the case that preaching and distribution of the sacraments are performed by ministers who are sinners, at times even unbelieving—a situation Luther countered with the classical anti-Donatist argument that the effectiveness of the means of grace does not depend on the dignity of the person who passes them on (e.g. 38, 241, 6–23). What is worse, it also happens that the gospel is proclaimed and taught and the sacraments are distributed in a way which is not in accordance with Holy Scripture.

In fact, the perversity can reach such a degree that the opposition to the gospel is not restricted to individual cases but becomes customary and systemic and takes on even the form of official ecclesial doctrine and practice. Then one must conclude: Here is the 'false church'. Behind such ecclesial opposition to the gospel Luther saw not only the human beings involved, but a demoniac perversion triggered by none other than the antagonist of Jesus Christ announced in the Scriptures, the Antichrist (26, 147, 27f; 38, 232, 15–17; 51, 505, 11f). All the more urgent it is to have a criterion which allows us to diagnose where the church is to which one has to hold on. The criterion is the mark whereby the church can be recognized: the proclamation of the gospel in Word and Sacraments. In short: The marks of the church are by definition the marks of the true church (43, 388, 7–9; 51, 479, 1ff.).

For Luther the church in opposition to the gospel was realized particularly in the papal church: This is 'not the true church' (43, 386, 21), but the 'false' church (42, 193, 4), indeed, the church of the Antichrist (26, 28f; 50, 217, 23–31), which in its doctrine (51, 493, 8–16) and its use of the sacraments (6, 501, 35f.; 527, 25f; 543, 12f; 39/2, 160, 13f), as well as in the claims of the hierarchy and especially the papacy (51, 494, 24–6), contradicts the gospel and therefore cannot claim to be truly the church (43, 157, 9f, 34). Rather the evangelical congregations, which have turned to the right proclamation of the gospel and administration of the sacraments and have done away with the perversions in this field, thereby show that they are the true church (43, 387, 21–4; cf. WAT 4, 179, 9–11). However, what is true and false church cannot simply be distributed among two ecclesial institutions. The same papal church which Luther characterized as the church of the Antichrist in another passage is described by him with these words: 'Although the city of Rome is worse than Sodom and Gomorrha, in it remain baptism, the Lords Supper, the proclamation and text of the gospel, Holy Scripture, offices, the name of Christ, the name of God' (40/1, 69, 23–6; cf. 38, 221, 18–31). And 'where these things have remained there certainly have remained the Church and several saints' (40/1, 69, 31f). Moreover, Luther freely admitted that he and the other Reformers, as well as the evangelical congregations themselves, owed all those goods to the church under the pope (51, 501, 23–5; cf. 26, 147, 13–15). If both lines of statements are equally correct that means that the true church is entwined with the false one; the 'holy Church is the holy place of the abomination' (38, 221, 18), the Antichrist is a phenomenon *within* the church (51, 505, 10–12; cf. 26, 147, 29–35) and with his perversion of the gospel deprives *Christians* of salvation (51, 505, 16–506, 1). If the church in which he sits nevertheless remains the church and if within it the gospel and the sacraments continue to be passed on and Christians to exist, then it is Christ himself who takes care of that: Christ 'has had with all his might to preserve' the means of grace, and equally 'with his might he has had to preserve the hearts so that they have not lost nor forgotten their baptism, Gospel, etc. in spite of so much scandalous ado' (38, 222, 1–6).

Although Luther developed these thoughts in his altercation with the papacy, the interwovenness of true and false church, the battle between Christ and Antichrist was not restricted to this institution. The Antichrist was, in his eyes, at work also in the groups of the Radical Reformation (50, 646, 27–647, 5). And Luther warned the evangelical congregations not to become the field of the Antichrist themselves. The true church, after having barely survived under the official government of the false church, was now embodied in an institution in which the official doctrine and practice corresponded to the criteria of true proclamation of the gospel and right administration of the sacraments. Yet the followers of the Reformation must not 'presume' and flatter themselves that the Antichrist was 'far from us' (50, 468, 10–469, 5; cf. 43, 428, 42). The battle between true and false church, between Christ and the Antichrist, is not an occasional happening. Rather it accompanies Christendom from its beginnings until the Last Judgement. Thus it forces the faithful to exercise constant vigilance and incessant prayer (50, 468, 10–469, 1).

However fierce the battle, there can be no doubt who will finally end up victorious: the true church, which carries 'the victory until doomsday' (51, 291, 20f; cf. 5, 493, 12f). In itself weak (51, 291, 1–5), the church owes this perspective to Christ alone, the 'victor over the world' (WAB 5, 412, 38). He 'remains with his Church until the consummation of the world' (18, 649, 31–650, 1). He does so by preserving Word and sacrament and through them by the Holy Spirit the communion of the believers. Thus he keeps the church in unity although its members find themselves across the world and in different institutional churches (26, 506, 38f). Thus he keeps it inerrant in the truth (51, 515, 30), though its doctrine often enough is not pure (42, 423, 30f). And thus he keeps it in unbroken spiritual continuity (50, 593, 7–14.628, 16–19), although its outward, institutional continuity, for example the succession of its representatives, far from keeping the church in the continuity of the gospel (43, 387, 14–19), again and again ran counter to it (43, 157, 9.14) so that Christ had to make new beginnings with the church and preserve its continuity through external breaks—and might have to do it again (42, 332, 35–7; 333, 30–4). This is so until, at his second coming, its hiddenness will come to an end and the church, free from sin, frailty, and suppression, will in its very essence be manifest (30/1, 191).

As fundamental as Martin Luther's ecclesiological thought was for all Reformers, Magisterial or Radical, his resolute approach to the understanding of the church from the angle of the doctrine of justification and the intricate distinction as well as connection of the spiritual and the external dimensions which, as they characterized his concept of justification also marked his ecclesiology, were not always upheld. The so-called spiritualists and Radical Reformers left it in favour of a more spiritual vision of the church. The principal theologian of the Reformed Reformation, Jean Calvin, gave a more independent weight to its external, institutional side, and so did in the end also Philipp Melanchthon.

PHILIPP MELANCHTHON (1497–1560)

To outline the ecclesiological position of Philipp Melanchthon is both easier and more complicated than in Luther's case. It is more complicated because Melanchthon's thoughts on the church went through different stages, whereas Luther's—after his fundamental theological insights had emerged—remained the same with changes in accents only. It is easier, because Melanchthon, unlike his older colleague, left a series of comprehensive theological works, among them the first Protestant dogmatics, the *Loci Communes*, and several summaries of the doctrines of the Wittenberg Reformation, first of all the *Confessio Augustana* (1530) (Augsburg Confession, *CA*) and the *Apologia Augustanae Confessionis* (1530) (*Apol*), supplemented by the *Tractatus de potestate et primatu papae* (1537) (*Tract*). However, in the first version (*aetas*) of the *Loci* published in 1521 (21, 81–228),[2] which was modelled as a commentary on the Epistle to the Romans, Melanchthon mentioned the church very rarely and only in passing, which remained true in his writings throughout the 1520s. Only in the second version of the *Loci* from 1535 (21, 253–558), after his overview over the whole range of central theological issues including the church in *CA* and *Apol*, Melanchthon changed to a comprehensive dogmatic order of theological themes where the church was a topic treated on its own. In the final version of the *Loci* (1559, 21, 601–1106) the ecclesiological part gained even more weight. Yet before the composition of the Confessions of 1530 Melanchthon became engaged with the institutional side of the church when he took part in the evangelical reordering of the church through visitations which he provided with a set of instructions in the *Instructions for the visitors of parish pastors in Electoral Saxony* (1528, 26, 49–96/WA 26, 195–240). His participation in the religious negotiations with the non-evangelical estates of the Empire (Worms, Ratisbon) and with the king of England occasioned the treatise *De ecclesia et de autoritate verbi Dei* (1539, 23, 595–642) that clarified the relation of the Reformation with the ancient church. Besides the later *Loci*, Melanchthon published several other comprehensive works which included ecclesiological parts, namely the *Confessio doctrinae Saxonicarum ecclesiarum* (1551, 28, 369–468) composed for the Council of Trent, the *Examen ordinandorum* (1553, XXXV–CX), and the *Responsiones . . . ad impios articulos Bavaricae Inquisitionis* (1558, StA 6, 285–364). These writings show the context in which Melanchthon's ecclesiological reasoning intensified: his key responsibility, especially after Luther's death, for the development of the evangelical churches in the face of an increasingly threatening Counter-Reformation.

In the few and scattered remarks on the church uttered during the 1520s Melanchthon repeated basic insights of Luther's like the understanding of the church as the communion of believers brought into being and upheld by the gospel (1, 329; 410), the priesthood of all believers or of the baptized with its implication of equal ecclesial power (21, 222;

---

[2] Apart from the Lutheran Confessions written by Melanchthon which appear with their official abbreviations (see n. 1) and numbers of paragraph, all references to his works are given according to *Corpus Reformatorum* (CR): *Philippi Melanthonis [sic] Opera quae supersunt omnia*, vols 1–28, ed. Carl Gottlieb Bretschneider and Heinrich Ernst Bindseil (Halle/Braunschweig, 1834–60 = Frankfurt/Main, 1963). The one Exception are the *Responsiones . . . ad impios articulos Bavaricae Inquisitionis* which cannot be found in CR. They are therefore referred to in the selective *Studienausgabe* (StA): *Melanchthons Werke in Auswahl*, ed. Robert Stupperich, vol. VI (Gütersloh: Bertelsmann, 1955). In this case there are letters (StA) before the numbers of volume and page, all references with numbers only are to CR. English translations are sparse, but C. L. Manschreck (ed.), *Melanchthon on Christian Doctrine: Loci Communes 1555* (New York: Oxford University Press, 1965) has material on the church.

1, 126), the public use of which was, however, to be assigned to called individuals (21, 222), and the denial of any claim of ecclesial hierarchs to be immune from error in matters of faith and to have a special authority by divine right (1, 126; 21, 132), particularly on the part of the pope, whose regime was characterized as that of the Antichrist predicted by the Scriptures (1, 326; 408).

In *CA* and *Apol* with *Tract* Melanchthon for the first time presented an ecclesiological outline—an outline which gained official status in the Lutheran churches since these writings became part of their Confessions. He again took up Luther's definition of the church as the 'communion of the faithful', created and sustained as well as recognizable by Word and sacraments. Thus he stated that the church which would exist until the end of time 'is the communion of the saints/faithful in which the Gospel is preached purely and the sacraments are administered in the right manner/according to the Gospel' (*CA* 7, Latin/German; cf. *Apol* 7, 5). *CA* concluded that because the Church is created and upheld by no other means, for its unity 'it is enough' (*satis est*) to agree about the right preaching and correct administration of the sacraments. However, since the oral and sacramental proclamation of the gospel does not always and automatically create faith and the communion of the faithful, but only when the Holy Spirit uses this action (*CA* 5), the church, besides being such 'in the proper sense', has a visible social dimension as the congregation of all who hear the Word and receive the sacraments. In this respect the church also includes sinners, even sinful clergy (*CA* 8; *Apol* 7/8, 3). In *CA* Melanchthon did not mention the priesthood of all baptized (believers). His line of thoughts, however, very much followed Luther's arguments. In the context of the doctrine of justification (*CA* 4–6) *CA* states that, in order to make faith possible, God has 'instituted' the 'ministry' (*ministerium/Amt*) of proclaiming the gospel and administering the sacraments, 'ministry' here having only the functional sense of task or service; no specification is given as to who has to fulfil this task (*CA* 5). This is done later when, in the context of ecclesiology, *CA* speaks about the institutional form of that service. Here the necessity of a special calling (*vocatio*) is stressed, but it is a necessity for the sake of *public* proclamation and administration of sacraments (*CA* 14). *Apol* specified this with regard to who would be the one to perform the calling: the traditional right of the bishops to ordain was called a regulation based on human authority which the churches who stood behind *CA* were nevertheless prepared to respect as the existing order, but only if the bishops did not reject the Reformation (*Apol* 14). The principal legitimacy of diocesan bishops was, in spite of everything, upheld and certain of their rights were even classified as rights 'by divine law' (*iure divino*), yet they were those which were the rights of the ordained ministry in general (*CA* 28, 30): the purely spiritual and not political rights of teaching, preaching, administering the sacraments, absolving and denying absolution (*CA* 28, 21), though performed on a wider scale than that of a parish. In *Tract* Melanchthon affirmed even more strongly the theological identity of the ministry of the diocesan bishop and the local pastor, the difference between them being based on 'human law' (*ius humanum*; *Tract* 63–5). It followed that, however the church was ordered in a given historical context, the spiritual power (*potestas*) of bishop and local minister was the same (*Tract* 61.63), including the power to ordain (*Tract* 64–5). That this principal statement in Melanchthon's eyes did not preclude an office of oversight in the churches which opted for the Reformation is evident from his *Instructions for the visitors* which requires the installation of 'overseers' (*superattendentes*) (26, 90/WA 26, 235). In *Tract* Melanchthon also addressed the question of the papacy which he had left out in *CA* and *Apol*: He rejected any papal claim of superiority 'by divine law' (*Tract* 7) as well as the idea that the church was bound in a special way to particular places or persons (*Tract* 26). Yet, in spite of these objections and the classification of the pope as Antichrist which he confirmed (*Tract* 39–41; cf. WA 11, 373–9), Melanchthon in his subscription to the *Smalcald Articles* declared himself prepared for the sake of peace to concede to the pope a superiority over the bishops 'by human law' if he admitted the proclamation of the gospel; according to an earlier remark Melanchthon understood this superiority in the sense that the pope under such circumstances could preside among the bishops and attend to the doctrinal consensus among the nations (2, 744ff.).

CA understood itself as a presentation of the doctrine that safeguarded the pure preaching of the Word and the right administration of the sacraments which according to its own statement were the basis of the church and made it possible to recognize where the church is. It claimed thereby to say nothing new but to reaffirm the consensus of the *ecclesia catholica*, including that of the Roman church, at least as far as its patristic writers were concerned, the centre of the consensus being the ancient Creeds (*CA*, end of part I). In the following decades Melanchthon meditated more intensely on the question of the doctrinal continuity of the church. He affirmed that there had always been Christians who upheld the basic 'articles of faith', which meant the central doctrines about God, Christ, and salvation (3, 601), especially in the ancient church which was still close to the New Testament era. At the same time there had been nearly from the beginning 'false opinions' in the church (23, 600), even in the great church fathers and in the ancient synods which must therefore be read selectively, always with the yardstick of the apostolic gospel (23, 609f.; 21, 837f.). As long as the basic truths about Christ and salvation were upheld, such aberrations did not alter the situation fundamentally (28, 411; StA 6, 292). Yet, as soon as the majority of the church leaders opposed themselves to central truths of the gospel or even persecuted the adherants of the gospel, they and their followers ceased to be the church. The church then consisted only of the few who held fast to the 'articles of faith' (23, 601; 21, 843)—a situation which was more often than not the case ever since Old Testament times (21, 827sq. 836.846; 23, LXXVIsq.). Melanchthon identified this loss of being the church particularly in the Roman church (23, 639; StA 6, 288.291.292), regardless of the preservation of baptism (21, 843) and of individual members of the church under the pope (23, 602; StA 6, 288.292). Whoever wanted to belong to the church therefore had to leave the flock of the pope (21, 843; StA 6, 291–3). The churches of the Wittenberg Reformation, on the other hand, belonged to the church. Moreover, in the present times they were the church because they upheld the true doctrine of the gospel and administered the sacraments accordingly (23, 640sq.; StA 6, 292.288), minor errors and weaknesses that existed also here notwithstanding (StA 6, 292; 28, 411). Thus, being the church, they were in accordance with the church Catholic of all times (23, 641; StA 6, 290–2), with the Creeds, with the 'better' church fathers (23, 634), and with those Christians who often against the official course of the hierarchy and theology had remained faithful to the gospel.

The 1550s saw a conspicuous shift in Melanchthon's ecclesiology: his understanding of the church became more institutional. Thus he no longer defined the church proper as the communion of the believers with visible marks, but as 'the visible assembly of those who uphold the Gospel of Christ and use the sacraments in the right manner, in which God through the ministry of the Gospel (*ministerium Evangelii*) is at work and regenerates many to eternal life, in which assembly, however, there are many who are not born again, but agree in the true doctrine' (21, 826; cf. 23, LXXV; StA 6, 285). In other words, the church continued to be defined as a group of people, yet these were not characterized by their faith, but by their institutional and thus visible behaviour, the preservation of the doctrine and administration of the sacraments which corresponded to the gospel, regardless of whether they believed in it or not. Thus now being a 'mixed body' which includes sinners was not a secondary dimension of the church, but part of its essence. The believers or saints were not more truly part of the church than the non-believers or 'dead members' (StA 6, 285), except that only the former realized what the proclamation of the gospel was for and would be saved. True proclamation of the gospel and right administration of the sacraments continued to be considered the marks that allowed one to identify which group of people was the church. Yet as this group came into focus as the subject of institutionalized behaviour, the proclamation of the gospel, too, appeared in a more institutional form, and that in two respects: first, Melanchthon added the church's confession, that is the ancient Creeds, to the biblical Word of God as a criterion for the true proclamation of the gospel (21, 836). This criterion was clearly secondary and itself subordinate to the biblical Word (21, 837), but an element of tradition had gained a place in Melanchthon's ecclesiology which at least explicitly it had not possessed before. Second, although Melanchthon, when speaking of the 'ministry of the Gospel' as a basic element of the church, continued to underline the functional sense of 'transmission of the Gospel' (21, 834), in most instances he now had in view the office of certain individuals who were particularly responsible for this transmission. This office he did not derive any more from the logic implied in the proclamation of the Word, but directly from biblical prooftexts like John 20:21 or, most of all, Eph. 4:11 (23, XXXVIsq.; 21, 834). It had to be conferred by God through a special call of the church, that is ordination, after he had in former times called prophets or apostles directly (28, 412). As a consequence of the special responsibility of the holders of the ministry for the transmission of the gospel the other Christians were obliged 'by divine law' to obey them wherever the gospel was concerned (21, 838sq.; 28, 413), an obedience which was occasionally even numbered among the marks of the church (StA 6, 286; 23, LXXV). However, essentially this obedience was directed to the gospel itself by which also the ordained must be judged (21, 837). Melanchthon underlined as strongly as before that the church was not 'tied' to certain office holders, to their line of succession, or to certain places, let alone to a pope (21, 835.839). Such a vision of the church would adapt it to a political reign which was not a model for the church (21, 835). Rather the church resembled an academic community where the truth would prevail without a formal authority or exercise of power (21, 835).

For God wanted the church to be an assembly which relied solely on him and trusted that he would keep his Word alive and effective (21, 836f. 846), if only as a minority and in the midst of enemies and persecutors (21, 836.839f.), as befitted the church under the cross until the end of the world (23, LXXVIff.).

JEAN CALVIN (1509–64)

Jean Calvin was a Reformer of the second generation. Thus the beginning of his evangelical career did not only, like Melanchthon's—or those of other contemporaries not treated here, like Andreas Karlstadt, Huldrych Zwingli, or Martin Butzer (Bucer)—presuppose that certain evangelical insights had been developed and certain public steps taken by Martin Luther, but he was able to look back at fully formed evangelical doctrines and largely formed evangelical institutions. He could therefore from the start take the central thoughts of the Reformation as a systematic whole and systematize them further along his own lines. This is true also for the field of ecclesiology. Unlike Melanchthon, Calvin paid attention to the understanding of the church already in the first version of his dogmatics, the *Christianae Religionis Institutio* from 1536 (I, 19–283)[3] which since it followed the order of the catechism dealt with the church in the explication of the Apostolic Creed, but characteristically added a much longer passage on the 'power of the church' (*potestas ecclesiastica*) in the final chapter on Christian freedom. The *Genevan Catechism* (I, 378–417) which appeared one year later likewise had its ecclesiological passage in the explication of the Creed, and so did the second *Genevan Catechism* from 1542 (II, 72–150 [ed. 1545]). Calvin's two *Genevan Church Orders* (*Ordonnances Ecclésiastiques*) (I, 369–377; II, 328–385), published 1537 and 1541 (several revisions until 1561) as legal and disciplinary counterparts of the catechisms, concentrated on the evangelical reshaping of church life. Two years later ecclesiology was the main subject in Calvin's polemical *Responsio ad Cardinalem Sadoletum* (1539) (I, 457–89). In the restructured *Institutio* of the years 1539, 1543, and 1550 the respective chapters grew considerably, not least because Calvin's pastoral work at Strasbourg under Butzer's wing, 1538–41, as well as his participation in the religious negotiations with the non-evangelical estates of the Empire (Worms, Ratisbon) during the same period, caused him to treat more ecclesiological issues than before and to increase the extent of patristic references. In the final version of the *Institutio* of 1559 (III–V), which divided the further augmented theological material into four books, half of the fourth one is dedicated to the church, which together with the sacraments is counted

---

[3] All references to Calvin's works are to *Joannis Calvini Opera Selecta* (OS), ed. Petrus Barth and Guilelmus Niesel, vols I–V. 3rd edn. Munich: Chr. Kaiser, 1974. Arabic numbers after the Roman numbers refer to pages in this edition unless stated otherwise. In English see J. Calvin, *Institutes of the Christian Religion*, trans. H. Beveridge. London: James Clarke, 1962; *Institutes of the Christian Religion*, ed. J. T. McNeill; trans. F. L. Battles. 2 vols (*Library of Christian Classics* 20–1). London: SCM Press, 1961.

among God's 'external means or devices' for our communion with Christ (title of the fourth book).

Calvin's ecclesiological thought started with the invisible church. In fact, in the first *Institutio* he defined the question of the church's visibility or invisibility as the cardinal difference between the Reformation and Rome (I, 31). The church could exist without a visible institutional shape; after all, the people of God before as well as after Christ had more often than not lived in the situation of a hidden minority, at times even hidden by the splendour of an Antichristian ecclesial institution, and only God had known who belonged to him (I, 31). It had but one mark (*nota*) by which it could be recognized unequivocally, namely the 'pure preaching of the word of God and the lawful administration of the sacraments' (I, 31; cf.I, 464). For, according to Christ's promise, where these are to be found there must needs be 'some church of God' (I, 91), Calvin wrote in line with the Wittenbergians.

However, there were already in Calvin's early writings three distinctive features in the future Genevan Reformer's ecclesiological thinking which would characterize it throughout all future developments.

The first was its intimate connection with the doctrine of predestination. In the first *Institutio* predestination was indeed discussed within the chapter on the church: the church itself was defined not as the communion of the faithful, but as the 'whole number of the elect' (I, 86). Yet, as the definition in the *Genevan Catechism* of 1542, according to which the church is 'the body and society of the faithful whom God has predestined to eternal life' (Q. 93) shows, being the communion of the elect for Calvin did not exclude being the communion of the faithful. Rather both statements had in view two aspects of the church which were related to each other in a certain order: what is fundamental is God's eternal decision to elect certain human beings for salvation. Their faith in Christ and membership in the church is only the way in which God carries through and makes manifest their election (I, 86f.). On the other hand this soteriological path is the sole way in which God realizes his eternal decree of election; in other words, there are no elect outside the communion of the faithful. Following this soteriological order, whoever believes in Christ is, by the same token, certain to be a member of the communion of the elect (I, 87; cf. I, 401). Yet only he himself is certain, not his fellow Christians. Calvin stressed that nobody is able to diagnose whether somebody else has enduring faith and thus belongs to the 'number of the elect' (I, 88). Still he added that there are 'certain marks in a sense' which allow one to state, albeit not with surety but 'with a certain judgement of love', who are members of the church and elect: those 'who by their confession of faith, the example of their lives, and the participation in the sacraments profess the same God and Christ with us', whereas those who do not have the same faith or deny it in their lives thereby show that they are, at least 'for now', outside the church (I, 98).

These people have to be excommunicated in order that they do not damage the church by bringing it into disrepute or by setting a bad example to its members and that they themselves repent and still reach the aim of their possible election; for except in the case that someone is actively opposed to the truth of the gospel, one can never be sure whether God in his mercy has not decided finally to save a seemingly rejected person after all (I, 89f.). The concern for the issue of discipline, notably of excommunication, was the second feature which, although not absent in Luther and Melanchthon, from the start had a distinctive weight for Calvin's ecclesiology: 'the integrity of the Church particularly consists in and rests on doctrine, discipline, and the sacraments' (I, 467), a statement confirmed by his Church Orders.

This concern for discipline, which affects Christians as an empirical group of people, is all the more conspicuous in a phase of Calvin's theology in which he defined the church exclusively as an invisible communion. The same tension holds true for the third specific feature which characterized Calvin's ecclesiology from the start: his interest in the diversity between the members of the church. Whereas Luther's and at least the early Melanchthon's primary concern was the equality of all Christians as expressed in the concept of the priesthood of all believers or of the baptized, Calvin who mentioned the Christians' priesthood only in passing (I, 82) stressed the difference between their gifts and tasks (I, 91f.243.401). Among them were various ministries which on the basis of Ephesians 4 were presented as institutions given as such by Christ (I, 243). However, Calvin underlined that the authority and inerrancy of the holders of such ministries as well as of their conciliar assemblies only went so far as their fidelity to the Word of God (I, 244–7). To demand that the church was to be obeyed as such as if it could think and speak only the truth, to claim that its possession of the Spirit made any verification superfluous, meant nothing less than to say that it did not need the Word of God (I, 244; cf. 464f.)—an attitude which according to Calvin was equally to be seen in two seemingly opposite 'sects': the Roman church and the Anabaptists (I, 465).

Although Calvin had started from a definition of the church as 'invisible church' only, the development of his ecclesiology took him to revaluate that dimension of the church's life in which he had always been so keenly interested, but which in his early years he had not integrated theologically. He envisaged the church also as 'visible church' and concentrated more and more on this dimension—a development which reflected his involvement in the building up of evangelical churches as well as the increasing altercations with radical groups who contested any institutional character of the church. Calvin never came to the point, like Melanchthon in his late years, only to define the church as 'visible church'. In the *Institutio* of 1559 he still insisted that according to Holy Scripture the church 'which is in truth the Church before God' is the 'band of the elect' (V, 4; cf. 12) which is as such One and Catholic (V, 4). He repeated that God alone is able to perceive it (V, 12; cf. V, 3f.) and that for the elect themselves this church, as well as their membership in it, is a matter of faith (V, 6). Yet he added that the Scriptures use the word 'church' also in another sense, namely for an entity which is visible also to human eyes (V, 12.7). In this sense the church is 'the whole worldwide multitude which professes to worship one God and Christ, is introduced into the faith in him through baptism, bears witness to the unity in the true doctrine and love through the participation in the Lord's Supper, has agreement regarding the word of the Lord, and for the preaching of it preserves the ministry which is instituted by Christ' (V, 12). It is this aspect in which the *Institutio* of 1559 is mainly interested. The principal ecclesiological questions take up only a small fraction of its fourth book, whereas most chapters are dedicated to the ordering of ministries and the authority of the church in matters of teaching, legislation, jurisdiction, and discipline. These issues now comprise a coherent unfolding of an ecclesiology focused on the notion of 'visible' or 'external church' (V, 4.7).

This visible church is the 'mother of all the pious' (title of book 4, ch. 1). For it is only within the visible church that human beings are born and nourished as Christians through the gospel and educated to lead a Christian life through the order which corresponds to it (V, 7–10). Outside the external church salvation cannot be found (V, 7). The reason for this exclusivity is the same as Calvin had given in the *Institutio* of 1536 for the exclusive linkage of salvation and faith: the basis of salvation is God's eternal election, but this election is realized in a certain way, that is by human beings becoming and remaining believers in Christ and members of the invisible church (V, 4). Yet since God inspires faith exclusively through the 'instrument of his Gospel', which can be heard only in the visible church (V, 8–10), the membership in the 'visible church' is the necessary condition for membership in the 'invisible church' and thus for being saved, whereas separation from it means separation from Christ (V, 15). It is not a *sufficient* condition, however, because among those who belong to the external church there are 'hypocrites' who are members only outwardly (V, 12).

As in 1536, Calvin states that the church can be recognized by two marks (*notae, symbola*), the pure proclamation of the Word and the administration of the sacraments according to their institution by Christ (V, 13.14.15). He repeats that these are the marks of the church because where they are found there must needs be believers (V, 13), that is the invisible church. But he adds that they are also the marks of the visible church, because they enable us 'with certainty' 'to embrace a society in which both [marks] exist as the Church' (V, 16). Therefore a 'society' where they exist must never be rejected (V, 16).

Although the church has only the two unequivocal marks just mentioned, its visible life takes place in the frame of an institutional structure which is based on the ecclesial ministries. Under the influence of Butzer, Calvin had come to envisage four such ministries, which were not different grades of one, but distinct offices, namely pastor, teacher, elder, and deacon (V, 45–51; II, 335–43). Entailed in the New Testament (Rom. 12:8; 1 Cor. 12:7f.28; Eph. 4:11, etc.) they were instituted by Christ himself (V, 45.57f.) who alone leads and preserves the church with his Word, but does so through the service (*ministerium*) of human beings (V, 42.44). Thus the pastor, who can also, as in certain parts of the New Testament, be called 'bishop', 'minister', or 'presbyter' (V, 50), is responsible for preaching the Word of God and administering the sacraments (V, 48)—and in a way for everything which goes on in the church, his ministry being the most important one and comprising all other functions (V, 46). The teacher is responsible for explicating the Scriptures (V, 46). The elders are the guardians of discipline and, together with the pastor, govern the congregation (V, 50), not least in deciding about excommunication (V, 213). The deacons take care of charity (V, 50f.). All these ministries which traditionally are conferred by acting pastors (V, 57) have their place within the local congregation. However, Calvin in no way opted for an ecclesial model of congregational independence. Yet as he envisaged not a monarchical, but a collegial government on the level of the congregation, so he did for the level of the wider church. All congregations were integrated into and accountable to a system of synods from the regional to the national level in which they were represented by delegates of their parish councils (*Discipline ecclésiastique*, 1559, composed on the basis of a draft by Calvin). Where this ideal could not be realized, Calvin admitted the less perfect episcopal structure, provided that doctrine and sacramental practice corresponded to the evangelical norm.

However strongly Calvin in the *Institutio* of 1559 underlined the authority of the ministers as governors of the visible church, he continued to insist that the Word of God was not necessarily tied to them (IV, 33f.) and that neither they nor their conciliar assemblies could guarantee the church's preservation in the truth (V, 152.155f.). In fact, for centuries the ministers had more often than not betrayed the gospel, and the worst perversions were brought about in the church by them (V, 153f.). Thus from the earliest times the Word had to assert itself against the ministers (V, 152–156). Where this was evident, the faithful could not have communion with them any more (V, 39). Calvin was careful not to diagnose such a necessity lightly. In his eyes it could not be justified by moral failure in the church which had to be met with discipline but would never be overcome completely since the believers, though holy, would on earth always also be sinners (V, 26.145), apart from the fact that the visible church is a mixture of believers and 'hypocrites' anyway (V, 1, 12.18). Even in the field of doctrine and administration of the sacraments a certain level of mistakes has to be tolerated since not all issues of the faith are of equal importance and everyone suffers from 'some little cloud of ignorance' (V, 16). However, when 'lie has entered the bulwark of religion, when the main points of the necessary doctrine are overthrown and the use of the sacraments has broken down' the situation is different: the marks of the church are themselves affected and the church has perished (V, 31; cf. 129). What remains is the 'false church' (V, 30). Whoever leaves it in the name of Christ, far from being a heretic and splitting the church, rather restores its unity which is based in the faith in the one gospel (V, 36). Calvin diagnosed this ecclesial downfall in the church of the pope, the 'leader and commander' of the Antichrist's reign 'with us' (V, 41; cf. 129), with which church therefore no communion was possible (V, 31–42). Nevertheless he conceded, even there God had preserved some 'remainders' and 'traces of the Church', e.g. baptism, and true Christians, even Christian congregations (V, 41f.). The church under Rome had not been levelled to the ground completely, but had remained as a 'half-collapsed edifice' (V, 41). It was the task of the Reformation to build up an integral edifice again so that the visible church would once more be the 'true Church with whom we have to keep unity' (title of book 4, cap.1).

CONCLUSION

Obviously the ecclesiologies presented by Philipp Melanchthon and Jean Calvin were distinct from the concept of the church laid down by Martin Luther and among themselves. The reasons were, on the one hand, that the Reformation meanwhile had taken on a more institutional shape than when Luther developed his ecclesiological insights, and, on the other hand, that the two younger Reformers developed specific accents in their ecclesiological reasoning. Therefore the two—Melanchthon only in his later years, Calvin from the beginning—attributed a weight on its own to the institutional side of the church not to be found in Luther who always took the starting point for his ecclesiological thoughts—like the early and middle Melanchthon and the Lutheran Confessions—from the understanding of the church as communion of the faithful. At the same time all three Reformers, who in spite of this difference unanimously stressed that the church has a visible, institutional dimension, agreed in how they defined its function, namely as having to fulfil in a public, institutional way that exterior task without which faith and thus also the communion of the faithful could not come about and by which this communion can be identified: the proclamation of the gospel in its audible and sacramental forms. As regards the concrete realization of the institutional dimension of the church, the three Reformers were flexible, which allowed—and allows to the churches standing in the tradition of the Magisterial Reformation—for a broad range of ecumenical bridges as long as it was—and is—clear that a church and its ministers as the agents of the public proclamation truly serve the gospel.

The total dependence of the church on the proclamation of the gospel and the corresponding relativity of its institutional shape at the same time have an implication which for the Reformers of all camps was a fundamental lesson that their own ecclesial experience had taught them: No ecclesial structure is able to guarantee that the church remains faithful to the gospel and thus remains the—One, Holy, Catholic, and Apostolic—church. Rather the visible church may turn into false church against which the faithful cannot but resist. The positive side of this lesson was that even under such circumstances Christ finds ways to keep up the proclamation of the gospel and to preserve communions of the faithful, the true church, against and within the anti-evangelical framework. Resistance in the name of the gospel then aims at embodying the true church again institutionally. Thus by breaking with the existing institution such resistance paradoxically serves the unity, and by breaking with tradition it serves the apostolic continuity of the church which are the unity and the continuity of the gospel creating and sustaining the church. The experience of the sixteenth century has become the ecclesiological legacy of that part of Christendom which has gone through the Reformation: a particular awareness of the dependence of the church on the gospel; the call for watchfulness to remain true to the gospel in proclamation, practice, and structures, and the consciousness of how much the church is always in danger of failing in this respect, even to the point of making necessary ruptures with existing institutions; finally the confidence that it is Christ himself who carries the church through after all.

Suggested Reading

Althaus, P. (1966). *The Theology of Martin Luther*. Trans. R. C. Schultz. Philadelphia: Fortress Press, 287–344.

Avis, P. (1981). *The Church in the Theology of the Reformers*. London: Marshall, Morgan & Scott. Reprinted Eugene, OR: Wipf & Stock, 2002. Parts 1 and 2.

Avis, P. (2012). 'The Church and Ministry'. In David M. Whitford (ed.), *T&T Clark Companion to Reformation Theology*. London and New York: T&T Clark, 143–56.

Haight, R. (2005). *Christian Community in History (Comparative Ecclesiology*, Vol. 2). New York and London: Continuum.

Locher, G. (2004). *Sign of the Advent: A Study in Protestant Ecclesiology*. Fribourg: Academic Press.

Lohse, B. (1999). *Martin Luther's Theology: Its Historical and Systematic Development*. Trans. and ed. R. Harrisville. Minneapolis: Fortress Press, 277–97.

Milner, B. C. (1970). *Calvin's Doctrine of the Church*. Leiden: Brill.

Oberman, H. (1982). *Luther: Man between God and the Devil*. New Haven: Yale University Press, 246–71.

Pelikan, J. (1968). *Spirit Versus Structure: Luther and the Institutions of the Church*. London: Collins.

Spitz, L. W. (1953). 'Luther's Ecclesiology and his Concept of the Church as Notbischof'. *Church History* 22: 113–41.

Wendebourg, D. (2003). 'The One Ministry of the One Church'. In Ingolf U. Dalferth and Paul Oppenheim (eds), *Einheit bezeugen. Zehn Jahre nach der Meissener Erklärung/Witnessing to Unity. Ten Years after Meissen Declaration*. Frankfurt/Main: Lembeck, 300–23.

Wendebourg, D. (2010). 'The Use of Scripture by the Reformers and by the Confessions of the Reformation in their Theology of the Ministry'. In Christopher Hill, Christoph Schwöbel, et al. (eds), *Bereits erreichte Gemeinschaft und weitere Schritte. 20 Jahre nach der Meissener Erklärung/Communion Already Shared and Further Steps. 20 Years after the Meissen Declaration*. ii. Frankfurt/Main: Lembeck, 308–30.

Wendel, F. (1963). *Calvin: The Origins and Development of his Thought*. Trans. P. Mairet. London: Collins, chapter 5.

Wengert, T. (2010), *Philip Melanchthon, Speaker of the Reformation: Wittenberg's Other Reformer*. Farnham and Burlington, VT: Ashgate.

CHAPTER 11

ANGLICAN ECCLESIOLOGY

PAUL AVIS

THE ANGLICAN DIFFERENCE?

ANGLICAN theologians, interpreting their own tradition, have sometimes struggled to identify what makes Anglicanism different from other major Christian traditions. Some of these interpreters, including distinguished scholars and prelates of the twentieth century, such as Michael Ramsey, Stephen Neill, and Henry McAdoo, denied that Anglicanism stood for any distinctive teaching. They insisted that it had no special doctrines of its own, but simply upheld the catholic faith of the (so-called) undivided church (Ramsey 1945; Neill 1958: 417; McAdoo 1965: 1). These writers certainly did not mean by this that there was not a flourishing and impressive tradition of Anglican *theology*. Ramsey made the stimulating suggestion that, while Anglicanism lacked any special doctrines of its own, its unique contribution to Christian theology was 'a method, a use and a direction' and McAdoo concurred (Ramsey 1945; McAdoo 1965: 1, 6). That the distinctiveness of Anglican theology is essentially methodological is a thesis that invites deeper exploration (Avis 2014).

But, for our present purposes, we may ask: if pursuing a particular, perhaps unique, theological method merely arrives at the same doctrines as are held by everyone else, what is the point of it? Bizarrely, the theological method followed would be unrelated to the theological content affirmed at the end of the journey. It does not make sense to suggest that a distinctive method simply leads to common content. The 'no special doctrines' school of thought appeared to hold that Anglicanism is simply a particular local and temporal expression of essential Christianity. As such it has its own existence, with integrity, in time and place. But because Anglicanism holds to the ecumenical creeds and councils and stands by the consensus of the teaching of the fathers, it cannot (according to this view) take up a distinctive doctrinal position among the churches of Christendom. It is simply catholic Christianity, once that has been detached from papal autocracy and distanced from the excesses and abuses of the late medieval Western church. The only identity that it is left with is therefore historical and cultural.

Thus Anglican identity becomes purely contingent, in the sense that it has no doctrinal contribution of lasting value to make to the wider Christian church. I do not think that we would say that of any other major doctrinally orthodox tradition. Sykes pertinently asked why it is thought impossible for a church both to be catholic (or orthodox) in its teaching *and* to state its doctrine in a distinctive, albeit not necessarily unique, way (Sykes 1978).

The 'no special doctrines' stance no doubt lay behind the puzzling Anglican rhetoric of the second half of the twentieth century, articulated by the American Bishop Stephen Bayne (the first executive officer of the Anglican Communion) and promoted by Archbishop Robert Runcie at the 1988 Lambeth Conference, that Anglicanism was a provisional expression of the church, destined to be re-absorbed one day, through ecumenical rapprochement, into the greater church (Runcie 1988: 13). This 'provisionality' gambit needs careful teasing out. If by 'provisional' we mean that Anglicans do not see their churches as the whole church (a point made by Archbishop Runcie in that address), then it points to an important truth about Anglicanism. Anglicans believe that their church is a 'true church' in the Reformation sense of the phrase: a church identifiable by the divinely instituted means of grace, the ministry of word and sacrament, and therefore a church where grace and salvation are to be obtained (Avis 1981). The Anglican Communion is the only world family of churches, universally maintaining the apostolic succession of the episcopate, that does not believe, when push comes to shove, that it is *the one true Church*, the whole church, the only church. The Eastern Orthodox Churches explicitly claim this and in practice the Roman Catholic Church still seems to maintain this historical claim about itself, in spite of qualifying it somewhat at the Second Vatican Council (1962–5). In sharp contrast to those two major Christian traditions, it is an article of faith—a doctrine—for Anglicans that their churches (as the Church of England puts it: Canons A 1 and C 15 [Preface to the Declaration of Assent]) 'belong to' or are 'part of' the one, holy, catholic, and apostolic church. It is certainly a catholic and apostolic church, a manifestation or expression of the one church, but it is not the whole church, nor is it the only church that can be so described. But if that is how Anglicans understand their church, that church cannot be more provisional than other churches—other parts of the one church. It cannot have as its distinctive cachet that it is provisional, while others are not, or that all churches are provisional, but some are more provisional than others. All empirical manifestations of the church of Jesus Christ must be provisional *sub specie aeternitatis*. Not one of them is destined to remain unchanged and, in the *eschaton*, simply to be vindicated for what it is, as it is. All will be purified by fire and transformed at the judgement seat of Christ (1 Cor. 3:12–15). If Anglicans acknowledge the truth that all churches (not merely their own) are provisional, eschatologically speaking, then that also is to be accounted an Anglican doctrine.

Sykes (1995) and Avis (2008) have challenged, on the basis of first principles, what Sykes dubbed the 'no special doctrines' account of Anglican identity. Taking our cue from Sykes, we need to ask: What *is* this Anglicanism that 'has no special doctrines'? What sort of entity is making the claim? How can we identify it, if not by its doctrine, since other aspects, such as worship, governance, and spirituality—even historical events—presuppose certain doctrines? In any case, is it not precisely a doctrinal claim—a claim precisely about your teachings—to say that you have no special doctrines? As a phenomenon, Anglicanism is readily identifiable in history and in the ecumenical landscape. It is something particular, something different. What makes it stand out? Is it not precisely that it upholds certain teachings about itself and that these teachings therefore and necessarily concern the church? Could it be that the distinctiveness of Anglicanism lies largely in its ecclesiology? To support that hypothesis, we must sketch the outlines of Anglican ecclesiology, illustrating the argument from history.

A Protestant Ecclesiology?

Why should Anglican ecclesiology have a chapter to itself in this *Handbook*? Is not Anglicanism simply a particular instance of Protestantism and therefore already covered by what has been said in Chapter 10 about the Reformation on the Continent of Europe? Much theological polemic, especially in older Roman Catholic theology, found it useful to lump Anglicans in with Protestants as equally heretical. Without the polemical edge, that allocation of Anglicanism by Roman Catholics is by no means a thing of the past. Even the former President of the Pontifical Council for Promoting Christian Unity, Cardinal Walter Kasper, a true ecumenist, nevertheless includes the Anglican Communion among the 'churches of the Reformation' in a book published in 2015 (Kasper 2015: 28–9). That description entails several disputable claims: that what later evolved into Anglicanism was invented in the sixteenth century and that the Church of England was a new church that came into being because King Henry VIII wanted to get rid of one wife and marry another and the pope would not allow him to do so. Furthermore, an exclusively Reformation or Protestant provenance for Anglicanism implies not only that Anglicanism rejects the universal jurisdiction and infallibility of the pope (which it does), but it also implies that Anglicanism has an essentially different understanding of the Eucharist and of Holy Orders from that of the Roman Catholic Church and that it does not believe in the visible church and its visible unity—prejudices that are all too commonly met with even today, but which are not borne out either by the Anglican historic formularies and modern liturgies or by recent ecumenical dialogue such as that of the Anglican–Roman Catholic International Commission (ARCIC) in its work on Eucharistic doctrine, ministry, and ordination, the church as *communio*, and the relation between salvation and the church (ARCIC 1982, 1987, 1991).

However, there is more than a grain of truth in the notion that Anglicanism is Protestantism by any other name. The Church of England and consequently the churches of the worldwide Anglican Communion have been indelibly shaped by the Reformation. Although the English Reformers generally did not regard themselves as disciples of Luther or Calvin and were critical of their personal or theological foibles, they followed the major continental Reformers in their doctrine of the true church, identifiable by the authentic ministry of word and sacrament, in their rejection of the jurisdiction of the pope, and in their alliance with the civil authority ('the magistrate') (Avis 1981; 2012). The Church of England under Edward VI and Elizabeth I embraced (though not uncritically or all at once) the doctrines of the European Reformation. These included: justification by grace through faith; the royal priesthood of all the baptized; Holy Communion in both kinds; the supreme doctrinal authority of Scripture and the right of the laity to read it in the vernacular; the imperative of a vernacular liturgy that the laity could understand and participate in; the right of the clergy to marry; and the role of the laity, especially the sovereign, in church governance. The worship, devotional practice, and spirituality of the reformed Church of England from Edward VI to James I generally savoured of Protestantism and regarded Roman Catholic Counter-Reformation forms of piety as toxic (Tyacke 1987, 1998; Lake 1988; Collinson 1967, 1982; Ryrie 2013).

For several centuries Anglicans, even High Churchmen, did not disdain the name 'Protestant'. John Cosin, the 'High Church' bishop of Durham in the latter part of the seventeenth century and a significant liturgist, described the Church of England as 'Protestant and Reformed according to the ancient Catholic Church' and similar expressions were used by the Tractarians in the 1830s (McAdoo 1992: 108; *Tracts for the Times*, no. 27), and there are many Anglican clergy and laity today who would cheerfully identify themselves as Protestant. Some Anglican ecclesiologists wish to stress the essentially Protestant and Reformed character of Anglicanism. Kenneth Locke wrote: 'The evidence clearly shows that the Anglican Evangelical Protestant understanding of the Church is historically and theologically a legitimate and respectable option within Anglicanism' (Locke 2009: 43; cf. Bradshaw 1992). In the reigns of Elizabeth I (1558–1603) and James I (1603–25) the default theology of English bishops and divines was Calvinism—not of course Reformed presbyterian polity, for they were wedded to episcopacy (at least pragmatically), but the 'doctrines of grace', the theological analysis of the path to salvation. In 1618–19 the Church of England had a senior delegation, appointed by King James I, at the (Reformed) Synod of Dort (Dordrecht, The Netherlands). Although the liberal theologian John Hales, among the delegates, was disaffected and famously 'bid John Calvin goodnight', the delegation officially subscribed to the doctrinal decrees, though not those relating to polity (Peters 1971). Although Anglo-Catholic scholars have not liked to admit it, the Church of England belonged securely among the reformed churches of Europe at that time. Anthony Milton poses the issue nicely:

> The presence of the English divines at perhaps the most important Reformed synod to meet before modern times has often raised eyebrows and temperatures in the Church of England, provoking constant and sometimes agonized debate among Anglican scholars and church historians ever since. It has, perhaps inevitably, become a significant issue in the perennial debates about how close the Church of England should consider itself to continental protestantism, and one that is perhaps all the more striking in that the synod occurred, not in the early stages of England's Reformation, but several generations further on, when any 'Anglican' identity might have been assumed to have come to full fruition. (Milton 2005: xviii)

In recent years Anglican churches across the world have entered into ecumenical agreements with confessedly Protestant churches, recognizing their ecclesial credentials. The Church of England and the Evangelische Kirche in Deutschland (EKD, a federation of Lutheran, Reformed and United *Landeskirchen*) signed the Meissen Agreement in 1991. The four British and Irish Anglican churches entered into ecclesial communion with the Nordic and Baltic Lutheran churches through the Porvoo Agreement in 1996. In 2001 The Episcopal Church (then the Episcopal Church of the USA, ECUSA) entered into 'full communion' through *Called to Common Mission* with the Evangelical Lutheran Church in America (ELCA) and has since taken a similar step with the two North American provinces of the Moravian Church. The Anglican Church of Canada and the Evangelican Lutheran Church in Canada (ELCC) made their own agreement for full communion in the Waterloo Declaration (2001). The Anglican–Methodist Covenant between the Church of England and the Methodist Church of Great Britain was signed in 2003. In February 2012 the Church of England and the United Reformed Church took a new step in their relationship in a service of 'Reconciliation, Healing of Memories and Mutual Commitment' in Westminster Abbey. There is a Meissen-type agreement (2016) between the Church of England and the (Reformed, Presbyterian) Church of Scotland, as two established churches with a territorial ministry. Anglican churches belong to the national, regional, and global councils of churches or 'churches together', thus having Protestant churches as close ecumenical partners. The formal agreements, whether for ecclesial communion with an interchangeable ordained ministry on the basis of the historic episcopate (as in Porvoo, *Called to Common Mission*, and Waterloo), or for a more limited relationship where there is not full agreement on episcopacy (as in Meissen and the Anglican–Methodist Covenant), tend to be premised on the dual approach of mutual recognition and mutual commitment that was pioneered in the Meissen Agreement.

Like the Lutherans and the Reformed, Anglicans have historically 'protested', both in official texts and in the voluminous works of individual divines, against several Roman Catholic teachings and practices: the infallibility and universal jurisdiction of the pope; purgatory and with it indulgences; compulsory private or sacramental confession and clerical celibacy; the mass understood as a propitiatory sacrifice, together with transubstantiation; the invocation of the saints in heaven for their intercession and the modern dogmas concerning the Blessed Virgin Mary, together with unchecked popular forms of Marian devotion; and the claim that ecumenical councils need to be called, convened, and ratified by the pope. In spite of notable convergence in ecumenical dialogue with the Roman Catholic Church in some disputed areas of theology, and private opinions among Anglicans who may entertain some of the tenets mentioned above, they are still resisted by official Anglican teaching. There is a consistency of Anglican witness to biblical truth and of 'protest' against error, from the Reformation to the present day. It is a foolish fancy and a canard that Anglicanism does not stand for anything in particular, or that one can believe whatever one chooses and yet remain a loyal Anglican.

The extent of Protestant influence on Anglicanism can be seen particularly in the history of the Puritan movement within the Church of England. A formidable 'Puritan' constituency had been gathering momentum within the Church of England since the late sixteenth century (Collinson 1967; Brachlow 1988). 'Puritanism' is notoriously difficult to define and its edges are blurred. It would be invidious to say that Puritans were more ardent in their faith and devotion than other Anglicans; some of the most devout Christians of that time were not Puritan, were indeed anti-Puritan. But what did mark out individuals as Puritan is that they were zealous for further reform of the English church in its polity and worship, tending to take the Swiss Reformation, particularly that of Geneva under Calvin and his successor Beza, as their model. Ecclesiology was unquestionably the focal point of discontent with the established church among left-wing Puritans and radicals (Brachlow 1988: 4). Partly for this reason, some scholars eschew the term 'Puritan', which sounds pejorative and dismissive, and prefer 'reformist' (as opposed to 'conformist') (Prior 2005). But the term 'Puritan' retains its relevance, because those so labelled sought a 'pure' church as well as a 'pure' life, as they understood those ideals. But black and white, binary oppositions are unhelpful in interpreting internal Anglican conflict in the seventeenth century. In truth there were many gradations of 'purity' and it was not always clear in advance which way individuals would jump when they were compelled to make a choice, above all at the outbreak of the Civil War.

Puritanism was hostile to overt ceremonial and to the repertoire of sacred signs, such as the sign of the cross at baptism, the ring in marriage, and wearing the surplice, that had been taken over from the pre-Reformation church. Puritan theology and practice was weak as far as sacramentality was concerned. Puritans favoured the local expression of the church and were suspicious of bishops ('prelates'). They exalted the ministry of the word—the word preached, not read—over the ministry of the sacraments, stressing plainness, simplicity, and austerity in life and worship. They tended to be legalistic about Sunday ('the Sabbath') observance, especially opposed to Sunday sports, and were strait-laced when it came to entertainment generally. The Puritans preferred to work through their own networks of 'the godly', rather than through diocesan and parochial structures where, they felt, the half-converted lowered the spiritual tone. The Puritans were constantly and obsessively taking their spiritual temperature (though they were not the only ones to do this) and developed a culture and a literature of religious introspection, coupled with an often censorious attitude to those who did not conform to Puritan standards and conventions.

In the late sixteenth century, especially through the work of Thomas Cartwright (1535–1603), a section of Puritanism embraced presbyterian polity, which had been pioneered in Geneva by Beza on the basis of Calvin's somewhat sketchy ideas. For these presbyterians, church polity was laid down *de iure* (by the law of God) in Scripture, and it was necessary to salvation to have the one and only correct polity (Brachlow 1988: 268–9). Puritanism thus became doubly subversive, a threat not only to the liturgy of the Church of England, but also to the hierarchical structures of authority in the realm. As James I told the Hampton Court Conference in 1604, his Scottish upbringing had taught him, 'No bishop, no king.' Suppressed towards the end of the sixteenth century by the strong-arm tactics of Archbishops Whitgift and Bancroft and held at bay throughout James I's reign, Puritanism became resurgent in the 1630s and 1640s as a result of the high-handed, provocative High Church policies of King Charles I and his archbishop of Canterbury, William Laud, neither of whom was capable of compromise (Davies 1992; Sharpe 1992; Fincham, ed. 1993). During the 1630s the Long Parliament steadily demolished the Church of England, abolishing bishops, the Prayer Book, and the Christian Year with its feasts and fasts (the former, especially Christmas, being the more missed). Laud and Charles paid for their inflexibility with their lives, being executed in 1645 and 1649 respectively. In the Civil War, churches and cathedrals were damaged by both sides and desecrated by Oliver Cromwell's troops. The Prayer Book was used only surreptitiously and the episcopal succession was precariously continued by underground methods.

Following the Restoration of the monarchy in the person of Charles II in 1660, the Church of England, with its episcopate, cathedrals, episcopally ordained clergy, and Prayer Book, was also restored (Usher 1910; Bosher 1951; Spurr 1991). The bishops, who had suffered deprivation and exile and seen their king—the Lord's Anointed—and their archbishop executed, were in no mood for compromise. The revised Book of Common Prayer 1662, enforced by an Act of Uniformity, ensured that those (mainly presbyterian) ministers, usually not episcopally ordained, who had taken over parsonages and pulpits during the Commonwealth period and now refused to conform to the Prayer Book with its Ordinal, were ejected at this time and probably over 1,000 of them went out into the wilderness (Keeble, ed. 2014). Puritanism—whether Presbyterian or Independent in polity—had led to social instability, political insecurity, religious sectarianism, and general lack of merriment. From this point, while 'evangelical' and Calvinist groups continued to exist and indeed to flourish within the Church of England (Hampton 2008), those Puritans who were opposed to bishops, the prescribed liturgy, and modest ceremonial continued their existence outside the established church, forming the dissenting communities of Baptists, Congregationalists, and Quakers.

A CATHOLIC ECCLESIOLOGY?

The watershed of the restoration of Crown and Church in 1660–2 and the departure of nonconforming Puritans did not mean that the Church of England had become any less anti-Roman than before or significantly less reformed in its theology. However, the opposition to Roman Catholic overweening authority that has typified the Anglican tradition in all its strands (except for a small group of Anglo-Catholic Papalists in the early twentieth century: Yelton 2005) since the Reformation and which continues today needs to be balanced by other factors. At the same time as Anglicans, from the Reformation onwards, rejected what they regarded as Roman Catholic errors and abuses, they affirmed what they believed to be the uncorrupted form of the faith and order of the early church. Scripture and the 'Primitive [pristine, uncorrupted] Church' was the platform of the Reformers, both on the Continent of Europe and in England. Early apologists for the Church of England, from John Jewel (1522–71) to Richard Field (1561–1616) claimed that the English church had returned to the early, authentic, apostolic form of Christianity, while the Roman church, especially at the Council of Trent, had not only rejected essential reforms, but had condemned the churches that had reformed themselves in the light of Scripture. In one important sense, the Reformation was a manifestation of the Renaissance impulse, 'Back to the sources!' (*Ad fontes!*). It became a standard gambit of Anglican apologetic to claim that, of all the churches in the world, the Church of England was the closest approximation to the church of the apostles because it honoured and emulated the fathers and their teaching.

While it is easy to detect the elements of defensiveness, special pleading, and complacency in such a claim, we should not forget that, as literate sixteenth-century Christians, clerical and lay, read both the Scriptures and the fathers in the new texts edited by humanist scholars and produced on the new technology of the printing presses, many were troubled in conscience by the disparity between the picture of the 'Primitive Church' that they found there and the widespread corruption and abuse of the late medieval Western church centred in Rome, notwithstanding flourishing popular piety. The two pictures did not match up. It seemed self-evident that the reform in 'head and members'—from the papacy downwards—that had been demanded for centuries was imperative. All such claims are infected with ideology (theories and arguments that serve vested interests and are dictated by power play), but it does not necessarily follow that there is no truth in them. Of course, there is more than one way of reforming the church. Erasmus, the pre-eminent humanist (exponent of the Renaissance recovery of the humane literature of Christian and pagan antiquity) of his age, was courageously outspoken and outrageously subversive, but he would not condone a split in Christendom. Modern Anglicans do not attempt to defend Henry VIII's bloodthirsty methods of achieving his aims, nor do they think that his dissolution of all religious foundations was the best way of reforming the monastic life. Anglican apologists—including the 'judicious' Richard Hooker—need to be critiqued when they attempt to defend the indefensible.

Anglicans stoutly affirm the catholicity of their churches and have always done so. They believe—and always have believed—that they have genuine catholic sacraments and ordinations (Holy Orders) and that they have preserved the apostolic succession of ministries and teaching (the 'historic episcopate') from apostolic times. Saints' days were drastically pruned from the liturgical calendar in the English Reformation, but biblical saints were retained. While prayer to the saints in heaven for their intercession has never been part of Anglican teaching, Anglican liturgies have acknowledged that, as the Book of Common Prayer 1662 puts it, the church offers worship to God 'with angels and archangels and with all the company of heaven'. Many post-biblical saints, martyrs, and teachers of the faith are now commemorated in Anglican calendars. While transubstantiation is condemned in the Thirty-Nine Articles (Article XXVIII), a doctrine of the real presence and real reception of the body and blood of Christ in Holy Communion has been expressed in the Anglican liturgies from the very first.

Anglicans reject any suggestion—beloved by the media and uncritically regaled by uninformed church persons, many of whom should know better—that the Church of England came into being in the sixteenth century at the whim of Henry VIII. They know that a church started by an individual and invented at some date *Anno Domini* cannot be the church of Christ. Anglican apologists trace the English church back through the Reformation, through medieval Christendom, to the fathers and the apostles themselves. When Matthew Parker, Elizabeth I's first archbishop of Canterbury, fancifully claimed that the English church was established by St Joseph of Arimathea, he was following a sound instinct, though bad history, in his attempt to ground the English church in the apostolic era. In the sixteenth century English divines went through all sorts of intellectual contortions to maintain the antiquity and apostolicity of their church, without conceding that it owed its pre-Reformation form to the initiative of a pope, Gregory I, in 596 in sending Augustine and his fellow monks to England (Avis 2002: ch. 1).

Furthermore, the basic structures of the medieval church—the dioceses and parishes—were retained when the English church was reformed in the sixteenth century. Uniquely in Europe, cathedral foundations in England were preserved, though religious orders and their houses were dissolved by Henry VIII. Much medieval canon law was incorporated into the canons of the Church of England from the first, from the draft Henrician Canons of 1535–6, through the abortive *Reformatio Legum Ecclesiasticarum*, compiled by Cranmer, to the first published Canons of 1603 (Bray 2000: lxiv). The ministry of bishops, priests, and deacons was perpetuated, though the minor orders were quietly suppressed. The authority of the monarch was, in effect, substituted (by the monarch with the agreement of Parliament and the somewhat reluctant acceptance by the Convocations) for that of the pope.

So to describe the churches of the Anglican Communion today as 'Protestant', without qualification, would be to distort their identity. They acknowledge without apology their debt to the Reformation and continue to reject certain aspects of Roman Catholicism. But, as we have noted, they also affirm and rejoice in aspects of 'catholicism'. Anglicans are not unique in this; the catholicity of some other mainstream, historic churches that were also shaped by the Reformation, most notably perhaps the (Lutheran) Church of Sweden and the Evangelical Lutheran Church of Finland, to look no further, is manifest. The Church of England began to move in a more 'catholic' direction, though without compromising its reformed identity, in the late sixteenth and early seventeenth centuries in the work of Richard Hooker (1554–1600) and Lancelot Andrewes (1555–1626), with their strong sacramental theology, their sense of historical continuity, their debt to medieval writers, and their love of beauty and decorum in worship. Hooker provided the paradigm of Anglican theology that is both classic and enduring; and the heart of it is methodological, for though Hooker did not write a systematic theology, he was 'the first great systematic Anglican theologian' (Barry 1877: 3). It is true of Hooker (and the phrase is significant given Ramsey's view, quoted at the start of this chapter, that Anglicanism stands for 'a method, a use and a direction') that 'perhaps more than any other single writer' he gave to Anglican theology 'a tone and a direction which it has never lost' (Barry 1877: 59, endorsed by Shirley 1949: 36).

The Church of England swung further into balance as a reformed catholic church thanks to the Caroline divines of the middle decades of the seventeenth century. The trend was pushed further, in a radical way, by the Tractarian or Oxford Movement, led by John Keble (1792–1866), John Henry Newman (1801–90), Richard Hurrell Froude (1803–36) and Edward Bouverie Pusey (1800–82), from its inception in 1833. This 'catholic movement' in the Church of England was part of a wider high church trend that affected not only the Episcopal Church (then the Protestant Episcopal Church of the USA) and other Anglican churches around the world, but also Lutheran churches in Scandinavia and, paradoxically, even the Roman Catholic Church (Franklin 1987; Morris 2016).

In the second half of the nineteenth century catholic-minded Anglicans fought to be allowed to use certain practices that they associated with the medieval church and with the Roman Catholic tradition in Western Europe since then: the reservation of the consecrated elements, first for the sick and then for devotional purposes; the eastward position of the priest at Holy Communion; wafers and the mixed chalice; Eucharistic vestments and robed choirs; private confession and absolution; crucifixes and the sign of the cross; stone altars; incense. Against intense opposition, the Catholic movement gradually and painfully gained the right to use these practices and by the mid-twentieth century they had become normal and uncontroversial in most of the churches of the Anglican Communion, though certainly not all Anglican clergy and parish churches go in for all of them. The sixteenth-century abolition of the religious vocation, religious communities, and religious houses began to be reversed in the mid-nineteenth century, especially through the efforts of E. B. Pusey and the sisterhoods that he promoted.

CATHOLIC AND REFORMED: A MIDDLE WAY?

While Anglicans did not disdain the description 'Protestant' right up until the nineteenth century (and some still glory in it today), they insisted at the same time on the term 'Catholic'. Queen Elizabeth I told the Spanish Ambassador, 'We only differ from other Catholics in things of small importance' (McAdoo 1992: 107). The point is not the bizarre implication that the papacy and the Council of Trent, both of which Elizabeth repudiated, were of little importance, but her desire to identify herself and her church as Catholic. 'I am such a CATHOLIC CHRISTIAN', wrote her successor King James I, 'as believeth the three Creeds, that of the Apostles, that of the Council of Nice, and that of Athanasius . . . And I believe them in that sense as the ancient Fathers and Councils that made them did understand them . . . I reverence and admit the Four First General Councils as Catholic and Orthodox ...' (More and Cross 1935: 3). The combination 'catholic and reformed' or 'reformed catholic' or 'Protestant Catholic' were the favoured slogans for Anglican apologists. In the mid-nineteenth century F. D. Maurice claimed that the Anglican synthesis was not formed from fragments of other people's systems, nor was it a system itself. 'Our faith', Maurice insisted, 'is not formed by a union of Protestant systems with the Romish system, nor of certain elements taken from the one and of certain elements taken from the others. So far as it is represented in our liturgy and our articles, it is the faith of a Church and has nothing to do with any system at all' (Maurice

1958: 343). The Anglican platform, articulated in worship and hedged by the boundary markers of the Thirty-Nine Articles, had an integrity of its own. A recent writer has updated this combination of elements to reflect the ecumenical cross-fertilization of the twentieth century: McMichael describes Anglicanism as a 'hybrid' of Protestantism and Roman Catholicism, 'with a little Eastern Orthodoxy thrown in for good measure' (McMichael 2014: xi). Some might respond that, in that case, Anglicanism has the best of all worlds!

The famous Anglican 'middle way' (*via media*) requires further examination. It is not plausible to claim, as nineteenth-century interpreters of Anglicanism sometimes did, that the English Reformation sought to plot a middle course, to set up a halfway house, between the Protestantism of the Continental Reformation, on the one hand, and the Roman Catholic Church, especially after the Council of Trent, on the other. The English Reformation under Edward VI, Elizabeth I, and James I was fully Protestant, not halfway to being Protestant (Tyacke 1987; Lake 1988, 2006). The notion of the 'middle way' owed much to the principle of moderation, based on the Aristotelian avoidance of extremes and pursuit of 'the golden mean', according to the old adage, 'Nothing too much.' In church order, especially worship, it meant shunning both what was seen as Roman Catholic 'gaudiness' and supposed Protestant 'slovenliness'. George Herbert's poem 'The British Church' engages in extreme stereotyping, though Herbert was hardly a fanatic. It contrasts both the painted harlot on the seven hills of Rome, and the slovenly Protestant wench in the valley, in her state of undress, with 'the mean' of the Anglican way: 'A fine aspect in fit array, | Neither too mean [in another sense], nor yet too gay' (More and Cross 1935: 11–12). 'We are freed,' claimed Joseph Glanville in the 1660s, 'from the idolatries, superstition, and other corruptions of the Roman Church on the one hand; and clear from the vanities and enthusiasms that have overspread some Protestant churches on the other.' 'Our church,' Glanville continued complacently, 'hath rejected the painted bravery of the one and provided against the sordid slovenliness of the other' (Walsh, Haydon, and Taylor 1993: 58).

These were, of course, invidious ideological stereotypes (Shagan 2011). The middle way certainly did not mean that the Church of England disowned or denied Reformation principles, only Reformed plainness and meanness when it came to the ordering of the church and its worship (such plainness or meanness could hardly have been attributed to the Lutheran churches of Germany and Scandinavia). The metaphor of the golden mean comes into clearer focus when Simon Patrick exuberantly describes 'that virtuous mediocrity which our Church observes between the meretricious gaudiness of the Church of Rome and the squalid sluttery of fanatic conventicles' (More and Cross 1935: 12). The lurid phrase 'squalid sluttery of fanatic conventicles' fits the sectaries of the Civil War and Commonwealth period better than the sober demeanour of the Lutheran and Reformed churches of the Continent, the products of the magisterial Reformation. More constructively, the *via media* meant positioning the English church where it could recognize its affinity with the medieval, catholic tradition, on the one hand, and with the enduring legacy of the Reformation, on the other: catholic *and* reformed; both-and, not either-or.

The stress on 'balance, restraint, moderation, measure' (P. E. More in More and Cross 1935: xxii) becomes intensified as we move towards the Enlightenment. It was always ideological and selective. The ejected Puritan ministers of 1662 would have been hard pressed to recognize the spirit of moderation and restraint in the bishops who returned from their exile during the Commonwealth and rejected the idea of a comprehensive national church. Under the influence of the Romantic movement, Anglican theologians, inspired by the poet, philosopher, and Anglican lay divine Samuel Taylor Coleridge (1772–1834), attempted to hold the polarity of catholic and reformed elements in a passionate unifying embrace (Sanders 1942; Wright 2010). Thus Frederick Denison Maurice (1805–72) insisted with dizzying paradox that the church is most Catholic when she is most Protestant (Maurice 1842: 13). One possible interpretation of Anglicanism is that it is an enduring experiment to see whether this dual allegiance can work in practice over time.

An Anglican Ecclesiology?

It only makes sense to speak about an identifiably *Anglican* ecclesiology from a point somewhere in the first third of the seventeenth century. Where exactly that point should be located is debatable. The ecclesiology of the English Reformation of the previous century, though not completely identical with either Luther's or Calvin's understanding of the church, was nevertheless not essentially different from the mainstream European Reformation. It thought in terms of national or 'particular' churches, insisting on their right to reform themselves and to re-Christianize the population and the national institutions, in accordance with biblical, evangelical principles, under the firm guidance of the 'magistrate' (civil ruler). While the doctrine of the 'godly prince' could claim strong biblical and historical precedent, it was essentially an appeal from the political power of the pope, who was seen as a great temporal prince, to the political protection (and therefore dominance) of the magistrate (Avis 1981, part 2; Cross 1969). The Church of England under Henry VIII, Elizabeth I, and James I was under the thumb of the sovereign. It was an Erastian church, in which outward governance was dictated by the sovereign. Parliament, and the Convocations (which overlapped in membership because of the bishops in the House of Lords) were unable to put up much resistance. When Charles I attempted, through Archbishop Laud, to replicate his predecessors' methods and to shape the church to his own design—and moreover attempted to impose that design on the recalcitrant Scots—it brought about his downfall. He lacked the ruthless power of Henry and the subtlety of Elizabeth. The same fate befell Charles I's second son, the Roman Catholic James II, who was, in effect, forced to abdicate. The 'divine right of kings', together with 'passive resistance' to oppressive regimes, were once Anglican (though not only Anglican) doctrines. They did not long survive the 'Glorious Revolution' of 1688 ('glorious' because bloodless in England, though not in Ireland or Scotland) when the Protestant (Calvinist) William of Orange was invited to take the throne, jointly with Mary, the daughter of James II.

A substantial measure of self-government for the Church of England arrived in 1919, with the Church of England Assembly (Powers) Act (known as the Enabling Act) that provided for representative institutions, and was progressively enlarged after the Second World War, the General Synod coming into being in 1970, until the point has been reached today when the Church of England controls its doctrine, liturgy, and discipline, and nominates its bishops. Interestingly, in view of those freedoms, it remains the established church in England, though no longer Erastian, or in any meaningful sense a 'state church'. It is the only fully established church in the Anglican Communion, which consists mainly of churches that have never been established together with some that have been disestablished in the past (in some American and Australian states, New Zealand, Ireland, Wales: Doe 1998; Avis 2001).

As we have seen, continental Protestant influences were dominant in the reformed English church in the sixteenth century and beyond (Ha and Collinson 2010). John Jewel (the first apologist for the reformed English church), Thomas Cranmer (its first archbishop of Canterbury), and John Whitgift (archbishop of Canterbury towards the end of the century, defender of the Church of England against radical, Puritan reformists), and perhaps even Richard Field (1561–1616, author of a multi-volume work *The Church*), can be seen to belong within a Protestant milieu and to fall on the Reformation side of any hypothetical division between the Reformation and a later distinctive Anglican identity. In Reformation ecclesiology, the continuity of the reformed church with the continuum of Christian history was a moot point. It was difficult to affirm the church of previous centuries without feeling sucked back into what were regarded as the abuses and superstitions of the late medieval Roman church. For the Reformers, therefore, the continuity of Christian history was a dotted line, with some sizeable breaks in it.

But with the work of Richard Hooker (1554–1600) and Lancelot Andrewes (1555–1626) at the end of the sixteenth century and the beginning of the seventeenth, a new spirit begins to stir in the English church (Lake 2003: 119; 1988: 225–30). For although Hooker and Andrews made no compromise whatsoever with Roman Catholic claims, they had no qualms about drawing on the theology, the canon law, the spirituality, and the devotional practices of the medieval period. A sense of living continuity re-emerged in their thought—and a sense of continuity is a vital ingredient of catholicity. Their theology was more incarnational and more sacramental than that of their Reformation predecessors. Identifiable elements of later 'Anglicanism', especially an emphasis on episcopacy and priesthood, the sanctity of the church building and its furnishings, and 'the beauty of holiness' in decorous worship, are apparent in the writings of Hooker and Andrewes and we should add—not as a heavyweight theologian but as a scholar-priest and poet—George Herbert. These themes came to vigorous and rigorous expression in the archiepiscopate of William Laud who was the entirely sympathetic instrument of the inflexible, insensitive policy of his king, Charles I. After the Commonwealth period, when the Church of England was suppressed, 'Anglicanism' came back with a vengeance. The 'Caroline divines', though sometimes located in the reign of Charles I, may be said to span the reigns of both King Charles, in other words, the periods on either side of the Civil War and Commonwealth, the latter phase showing a distinct hardening of approach, especially in the requirement for episcopal ordination which is reflected in the 1662 additions to the Preface to the Ordinal, enforced by the Act of Uniformity. But a recognizable Anglicanism had emerged, marked by a sense of continuity from the apostles and fathers, through the early Christian presence in Britain, and continuing through the upheavals of the Reformation—one English church, 'catholic and reformed' (Avis 2008; 2016).

'Anglican' and 'Anglicanism'

The terms 'Anglican' and 'Anglicanism' are derived from the Latin *Anglicanus*, 'English'. Pope Gregory the Great referred to the *Ecclesia Anglorum*, 'the church of the English people', in the early seventh century. The Latin equivalent of 'Church of England' (*Ecclesia Angliae*) is used by St Anselm, archbishop of Canterbury, at the end of the eleventh century and the beginning of the twelfth, and *ecclesia Anglicana* had become common by the mid-twelfth century, while *Anglicana ecclesia* occurs in Magna Carta, 1215. The English church already consisted of the two Provinces of Canterbury and York which were then integral parts of the greater Western church. At the Reformation similar Latin terms began to take on different connotations—connotations of national integrity and of independence from Roman jurisdiction. The term 'the Anglican Communion' first appears in 1847 and the first Lambeth Conference endorsed it twenty years later (Podmore 2005: 26–41; Wright 1998: 477–82; Avis 2008: 19–21).

Today the term 'Anglicanism' has overtones of an ideological movement of thought and practice, analogous to 'Catholicism', 'Marxism', 'Modernism', 'Capitalism', and so on. It is an abstraction, a form of shorthand for a diverse, dynamic phenomenon. As such, Anglicanism is (rightly) exposed to an ideological critique, a hermeneutic of suspicion, that employs the methods of the social sciences, particularly that of critical theory and the sociology of knowledge. 'Anglicanism' can then be seen as what it is: a portmanteau word, an umbrella term, an elastic concept that embraces a considerable variety of theology, worship, and ethical conviction, even within a single Anglican church, let alone the worldwide Communion. But it would not be right to let the argument rest there.

As this chapter shows, there are certain fundamental ecclesiological principles that all Anglican churches profess and stand by: that the church was founded by or at least *on* Jesus Christ by the will of the Father and that its existence reflects Christ's intention; that it is his body and is thus constituted as a unity; that because this unity has been damaged by human sin and frailty, there is a divine imperative to heal the wounds of division; that the church is inspired, sanctified, and guided by the Holy Spirit; that it enjoys fellowship with God the Holy Trinity and with the saints in heaven and therefore has a mystical as well as a visible dimension; that the visible church is continuous in history and geography, time and space; that it takes parochial, diocesan, national, and universal forms (the diocesan and universal expressions of the church being ecclesiologically fundamental); that it is constituted and sustained by word and sacrament, ministered by the successors of the apostles and those ordained by them; that the people of God (*laos*) is an ordered community with differentiated callings; that the church is entrusted with a mission from God, to proclaim the gospel in word and sacrament, underpinned by pastoral care and compassionate action, to every person and at every level of society; that the whole body shares responsibility for its life and mission and acts representatively in council and synod to implement this; that the church can err in its teaching and has done so and can go badly wrong in its behaviour and actions; that the church is therefore continually in need both of reform in the light of Scripture and of spiritual renewal by the power of the Holy Spirit. The list could easily be filled out and augmented, but it is a start, a core Anglican ecclesiology and one that is by no means negligible (Avis 2013).

A Communion of Churches?

Anglicanism is now a global Christian family, a Communion of thirty-nine member churches, often (and ambiguously) called 'provinces', plus a few non-provincial dioceses, with a total of about 80 million adherents. Anglican ecclesiology today must take into account the various ways that Anglican identity is perceived and understood in diverse global contexts and the degree of inculturation (which is encouraged, especially in worship matters) therein. It is fashionable to celebrate cultural diversity or multiculturalism in a rather uncritical way. While affirming inculturation, Anglicans cannot be uncritical of it—it has given rise to intractable tensions and divisions within the Anglican Communion: in particular, the sex and gender norms of one culture may be an abomination in another.

Having said that about the global diversity of Anglicanism today, it remains true that the early, formative history of Anglican ecclesiology mainly concerns the Church of England. Anglicanism came to maturity in the seventeenth century and continues to evolve. We should not forget, however, the antiquity of the Church of Ireland, whose Primatial See of Armagh pre-dates that of Canterbury, and its scholarly luminaries like Archbishops John Bramhall and James Ussher and Bishop Jeremy Taylor and the lay theologian Alexander Knox. Nor should we overlook the witness of the small but historic Scottish Episcopal Church to a high liturgical, sacramental, and episcopalian (i.e. episcopal on principle) ecclesiology. Nevertheless, the centre of gravity of Anglicanism, in terms of church population, number of dioceses, cathedrals and parishes, and weight of theological scholarship, lay with the Church of England until recent times, and in some respects still does. But the balance has shifted hugely. There are now more Anglicans in Nigeria than in England, where allegiance is often nominal. There are considerably more Anglican bishops in America and in Nigeria than in England—and they are the two member churches that represent opposite poles of theological and ethical development and inculturation within the Communion. In a limited sense, however, the Church of England remains the mother-church of Anglicanism, not because all Anglican churches sprang from England (they did not, though most did, directly or indirectly), but because the archbishop of Canterbury is recognized, both de facto and constitutionally, as the first among equals within the Anglican episcopate, and it is the archbishop who calls the ten-yearly Lambeth Conference of all Anglican bishops and presides not only at that conference, but also at meetings of the primates and gatherings of the Anglican Consultative Council, the only one of the four Instruments of Communion to involve elected priests and laity (Avis 2017).

There is an ecclesiology of each individual Anglican church (or 'province') as a national or regional church that maintains the faith and order of the Church Catholic and remains in communion with the See of Canterbury (Lambeth Conference 1930, Resolution 49; Coleman 1992: 83–4). But there is also an ecclesiology of the Anglican Communion as a whole, and the key to that is that it describes itself as a communion or fellowship of churches. The Anglican Communion is not a single global church, like the Roman Catholic Church. It does not have a unified system of oversight, a single liturgical template, or a common body of canon law. There is no way that one church can enforce its will on any other, or that the Communion as a whole can insist that any individual church should toe the common line. The archbishop of Canterbury has jurisdiction only in the Province of Canterbury (with an exceptional visitatorial role in the Province of York). The four Instruments of Communion lack any juridical authority, but work by theological teaching and moral persuasion. Where member churches decline to heed advice from the Instruments, there is nothing that can be done, except to keep talking (though the Anglican Covenant, recently under consideration throughout the Communion, proposes some sanctions as a last resort, when efforts at mediation fail). It is, therefore, inappropriate to refer to 'the Anglican Church' when the worldwide Communion is meant. Like the Eastern Orthodox Churches, the Anglican Communion is a family of churches. These churches are in communion with one another and with the See of Canterbury—and this is a doctrinal tenet of Anglicanism.

In describing itself as a 'fellowship' or 'communion' of churches, the Anglican Communion is consciously tapping into the New Testament Greek term *koinōnia*, which refers to common participation in a reality of value that is greater than ourselves, and is translated in English-language Bibles as 'communion', 'fellowship', 'participation', or 'sharing'. The word 'communion' speaks of an intimate relationship of indwelling— the indwelling of the believer in God the Holy Trinity and at the same time the union or fellowship of Christians with each other in God. It points to the community of life with God and with one another in the church. The word 'communion' resonates immediately with the sacrament of 'Holy Communion', the Eucharist, the sacrament of unity with God and with all the faithful in the body of Christ. The Collect for All Saints' Day in the Book of Common Prayer, 1662, begins, 'O Almighty God, who hast knit together thine elect in one communion and fellowship, in the mystical body of thy Son Christ our Lord ...'. The name of the Anglican family thus evokes a twofold relationship, just as the New Testament language does: with God the Holy Trinity and with all the baptized people of God.

Two sets of issues, both of which came to a head in 2003, tested Anglican 'communion' and Anglican cohesion to breaking point. First, issues concerning human sexuality: the election and consecration to the episcopate of a priest living in a same-gender union in the Episcopal Church of the USA (Gene Robinson), and public rites of blessing of such unions in the Diocese of New Westminster in the Anglican Church of Canada. Second, issues concerning cross-border interventions by bishops of Anglican churches in the global South in dioceses where some parishes or congregations were alienated by these developments of church policy in the area of human sexuality and were looking for outside support. The phenomenon of intrusion into another bishop's jurisdiction was not new in 2003, but it was intensified by the issues concerning human sexuality that became critical at that time. So in summary we may say that in the first quarter of the twenty-first century the cohesion of the Anglican Communion is threatened by passionate disagreements about Christian morals and equally passionate disagreements about what kind of mutual obligation is involved in membership of the Communion.

The Anglican Communion's response to the crisis caused by these two sets of developments—in the areas of human sexuality and pastoral intervention—was the Lambeth Commission, which produced *The Windsor Report* (*Windsor Report* 2004). The report made two main recommendations: first, a moratorium on the consecration of bishops in same gender partnerships, public rites of blessing, and episcopal interventions; second, a Covenant for the Anglican Communion (the definitive text is at <http://www.anglicancommunion.org/identity/doctrine/covenant.aspx>; accessed 090516). Though regarded with suspicion by some critics as a penal measure designed to exclude the Episcopal Church from the Communion, the Covenant's real focus is on reconciliation through consultation and mediation. The sanctions ('consequences') take the form of restricted participation in the Instruments, but it seems that these have to be agreed by (a) the Standing Committee (b) the Instruments affected, and (c) all the churches of the Communion, before they can take effect—so they will probably peter out into the sand before they can be applied. But the most important element of the Covenant is not the sanctions but the procedures for ensuring that the Communion remains in conversation with itself, or rather that divergent parts of it are brought into a mediated dialogue. The three moratoria have been only partly observed and the future of the Covenant is unclear at the time of writing—having lost momentum when the Church of England's synodical process failed to deliver a decision—though to date more churches have accepted it than have rejected it. The Anglican Communion is well described as a family, combining deep mutual loyalty and affection with tensions, arguments, and even episodes of mutual estrangement (see further Avis 2016).

'HOLY ORDER'

The threefold ministry of bishops, priests, and deacons in visible historical continuity is a key element of Anglican ecclesiology. It provides common ground with the Roman Catholic and Orthodox Churches—though the former do not recognize Anglican orders and the latter in practice do not, though there has been some sporadic recognition in the past. The Preface to Cranmer's Ordinal of 1550, which continued in the 1662 revision (with some additional clauses), makes a high claim for the threefold order as upheld by Anglican churches. 'It is evident unto all men, diligently reading Holy Scripture and ancient Authors, that from the Apostles' time there have been these orders in Christ's Church; Bishops, Priests, and Deacons.' It is not plausible to maintain the claim today that the threefold order goes back to the apostles, and modern Anglican ordinals tend to weaken it, merely stating, as the Church of England's *Common Worship Ordinal* does, that the church maintains the historic threefold pattern of ordained ministry. Modern historical scholarship has made it more difficult than in the past to appeal to the Bible or the early church for a template of church government. It is generally agreed among scholars that the New Testament does not reveal a single pattern of polity, that nomenclature for various offices varies within the New Testament, and that there was a process of development in the apostolic and post-apostolic communities. The Liberal-Protestant antithesis, associated with F. C. Baur and A. von Harnack, between the charismatic Corinthian community and the proto-catholic structures of the Pastoral Epistles, was exaggerated, but had a point. This relaxation of ecclesiological claims grounded in Scripture weakens the case for differences of polity becoming causes of serious division between the churches. It also generates a search for the deeper ecclesiological principles that inform the structure of the church in the New Testament. Both of these factors are at work in ecumenical theology. The Anglican–Roman Catholic International Commission (ARCIC) renounced a direct appeal to the Petrine texts of the Gospel according to St Matthew in support of the universal primacy of the bishop of Rome, and looked instead to a providentially guided process of development in history (ARCIC 1982). The Lima multilateral ecumenical text (*Baptism, Eucharist and Ministry* 1982) discerned three dimensions of ministry—personal, collegial, and communal—in the New Testament, and urged that they be reflected at every level of the churches' life (<http://www.oikoumene.org/en/resources/documents/commissions/faith-and-order/i-unity-the-church-and-its-mission/baptism-eucharist-and-ministry-faith-and-order-paper-no-111-the-lima-text>; accessed 090516).

By the mid-second century, a threefold ministry of bishop, presbyter, and deacon was firmly and widely, but not universally established, as appears in Ignatius of Antioch (*c.*115) and in Polycarp (mid-first–mid-second century). Irenaeus and Tertullian give no inkling that they were aware of a time when there were no bishops. Advocates of episcopacy point to the transitional roles of James, who had a presiding role at the Council of Jerusalem, and to Timothy and Titus, who had a more than presbyteral authority, as apostolic delegates. Bishops are seen as successors of the apostles, not in the latter's unique role as witnesses to the resurrection, but as carrying on their ministry of proclaiming the gospel, teaching the faith, overseeing the celebration of the sacraments, and exercising discipline in the community, especially with regard to other ministers.

However, while some apostles (notably Paul) were itinerant, bishops were normally localized (Barrett 1996; Brown 1971; Sullivan 2001; Stewart 2014).

The late nineteenth-century Anglican scholar, later bishop of Durham, J. B. Lightfoot (Lightfoot 1885) held that the episcopate was derived from the presbyterate, as Jerome had stated with regard to the church in Alexandria, while Edwin Hatch (Hatch 1881) argued that the emergent episcopacy reflected the structure of Hellenistic societies and their senior administrator of funds (*episkopos*). But Charles Gore, later a bishop, attacked both views, which he regarded as reductionist, maintaining that bishops were the lineal descendants of the apostles (Gore 1886). The contemporary Jesuit scholar Francis Sullivan believes that both the 'Lightfoot' and the 'Gore' scenarios are plausible for different regions (Sullivan 2001). Thankfully, Anglican formularies do not take sides on this historical question, but identify the ministry of bishops with that of the apostles in an oblique and functional way. The Roman Catholic Church has decided the historical questions by dogma, holding that the episcopal college, with the pope at its head, is the literal continuation of the apostolic college, in which Peter presided (both parts of this statement are questioned by modern Roman Catholic scholars such as Brown and Sullivan).

Related to the question of origins is the question of necessity: why bishops? A significant medieval view was that a bishop is a priest with wider jurisdiction. There was no higher calling or authority than to celebrate Mass and perform the miracle of transubstantiation as a priest. On that basis, the episcopate could not be the crown of orders. Consequently, the English Reformers generally saw episcopacy as an inherited, expedient form of church government, one that had the support of 'the magistrate' (the civil ruler). Only after the early presbyterians had claimed divine right for their favoured system did some Anglicans begin to match that claim with regard to episcopacy. Richard Hooker (d. 1600), however, did not go that far. While holding in Book VII of his *Of the Lawes of Ecclesiasticall Politie* that bishops were 'apostolical' and God-given, he recognized that divine positive laws could be changed by the consent of the church if circumstances altered and he went as far as to envisage that, if the episcopate were to be abolished, it could be reconstituted (presumably from the presbyterate) (Hooker 1977–98; cf. Avis 2002: 45–8). The High Church divines of the seventeenth- and eighteenth-century Church of England did not regard episcopacy as absolutely of the being (*esse*) of the church, because they refused to unchurch the non-episcopal reformed churches on mainland Europe and recognized their superintendents (Greek: *episkopoi*) as de facto bishops. The Non-Jurors, who saw themselves as the continuing Church of England, and then the more extreme among the Tractarians, began to make episcopacy necessary to the existence of the church (Avis 2002). Charles Gore believed that the abolition of episcopacy by certain churches at the Reformation was a breach of the divinely ordained church order (Gore 1909: 183–4; Avis 1988: 25–6, 97–100).

However, the stance adopted by the Non-Jurors, the Tractarians, and Anglo-Catholics such as Gore has not determined the Church of England's ecumenical policy, nor that of other churches of the Anglican Communion. Anglican churches have entered into agreements of mutual ecclesial recognition with several churches that do not have bishops in the historic succession, though the traditional Anglican concern to affirm episcopacy without absolutizing it is reflected in the fact that these agreements do not bring about the interchangeability of ordained ministries: for that to be possible, episcopal ordination in intended visible historical continuity from the apostles is required. In episcopally ordered churches, presbyters lay on hands with the bishop at the ordination of presbyters: some theologians understand this action as a gesture of solidarity, an acceptance into the college of presbyters; others believe that the presbyters are actually sharing with the bishop in conferring the power of order.

Episcopacy belongs in the context of the threefold ministry as a whole. A bishop is first a deacon and then a priest and retains these orders and what they signify on being made bishop. Anglican churches involve non-episcopal clergy and the laity in synodical structures of church government. They are conciliar as well as episcopal—though not quite 'episcopally led and synodically governed' (as the facile mantra has it), because there are lay people who lead and bishops have a special role in governance. For Anglicans, the phrase 'the bishop in synod' is an apt summary of the role of the episcopate in relation to the whole church with respect to its governance. Anglicanism is best seen as an expression of conciliar, reformed catholicism. The conciliar tradition gives a high place to the church gathering in council through its representatives. It holds that authority should be constitutionally defined and that the assent of the governed is required for legitimate authority (Avis 2006; Oakley 2003; Valliere 2012). There is now an ecumenical consensus, one that Anglicans have been involved in shaping, that the visible unity (or communion) that the churches seek to attain will involve episcopacy. In this area, as in others, Anglican ecclesiology and polity, has been steadily evolving, in response to internal controversy and external challenges, over the past five centuries and no doubt will continue to do so (Chapman 2012). Does this fact detract from what it has to teach us? Does it undermine the theological integrity of Anglican polity? I think not, because in this respect, it is no different from the ecclesiology and polity of the other major Christian traditions: they are all continually undergoing development, whether they admit it or not.

References

ARCIC (Anglican–Roman Catholic International Commission) (1982, 1987, 1991). *The Final Report*. London: Catholic Truth Society/SPCK; *Salvation and the Church*; *Church as Communion*; see all ARCIC reports at <http://www.anglicancommunion.org/ministry/ecumenical/dialoguhttp://www.anglicancommunion.org/ministry/ecumenical/dialogues/catholic/arcic/es/catholic/arcic/>.

Avis, Paul (P. D. L.) (1981). *The Church in the Theology of the Reformers*. London: Marshall, Morgan & Scott. Reprinted Eugene, OR: Wipf and Stock, 2002.

Avis, Paul (1988). *Gore: Construction and Conflict*. Worthing: Churchman.

Avis, Paul (2001). *Church, State and Establishment*. London: SPCK.

Avis, Paul (2002). *Anglicanism and the Christian Church: Theological Resources in Historical Perspective*. Revised edition. London: T&T Clark.

Avis, Paul (2006). *Beyond the Reformation? Authority, Primacy and Unity in the Conciliar Tradition*. London and New York: T&T Clark.

Avis, Paul (2008). *The Identity of Anglicanism: Essentials of Anglican Ecclesiology*. London and New York: T&T Clark.

Avis, Paul (2012). 'The Church and Ministry'. In David M. Whitford (ed.), *T&T Clark Companion to Reformation Theology*. London and New York: T&T Clark, chapter 9.

Avis, Paul (2013). *The Anglican Understanding of the Church: An Introduction*. 2nd edn. London: SPCK.

Avis, Paul (2014). *In Search of Authority: Anglican Theological Method from the Reformation to the Enlightenment*. London and New York: Bloomsbury T&T Clark.

Avis, Paul (2016). *The Vocation of Anglicanism*. London and New York: Bloomsbury T&T Clark.

Avis, Paul (2017). 'The Archbishop of Canterbury and the Lambeth Conference'. In Paul Avis and Benjamin E. Guyer (eds), *The Lambeth Conference: Theology, History, Polity and Purpose* (London and New York: Bloomsbury T&T Clark), chapter 2.

Baptism, Eucharist and Ministry (1982). Geneva: World Council of Churches.

Barrett, C. K. (1996). *The Signs of an Apostle: The Cato Lecture 1969* (2nd edn, Carlisle: Paternoster Press [1st edn, London: Epworth Press, 1970]).

Barry, Alfred (1877). *Masters in English Theology*. London: Murray.

Bosher, Robert S. (1951). *The Making of the Restoration Settlement*. Westminster: Dacre Press.

Brachlow, Stephen (1988). *The Communion of Saints: Radical Puritan and Separatist Ecclesiology 1570–1625*. Oxford: Oxford University Press.

Bradshaw, Timothy (1992). *The Olive Branch: An Evangelical Anglican Doctrine of the Church*. Carlisle: Paternoster.

Bray, Gerald (2000). *Tudor Church Reform: The Henrican Canons of 1535 and the* Reformatio Legum Ecclesiasticarum. Woodbridge; Rochester, NY: The Boydell Press for the Church of England Record Society.

Brown, Raymond E. (1971). *Priest and Bishop: Biblical Reflections*. London: Geoffrey Chapman.

Chapman, Mark (2012). *Anglican Theology*. London and New York: T&T Clark.

Coleman, Roger (1992). *Resolutions of the Twelve Lambeth Conferences 1867–1988*. Toronto: Anglican Book Centre.

Collinson, Patrick (1967). *The Elizabethan Puritan Movement*. London: Cape.

Collinson, Patrick (1982). *The Religion of Protestants: The Church in English Society 1559–1625*. Oxford: Clarendon Press.

Cross, Claire (1969). *The Royal Supremacy in the Elizabethan Church*. London: Allen and Unwin.

Davies, Julian (1992). *The Caroline Captivity of the Church: Charles I and the Remoulding of Anglicanism 1625–1641*. Oxford: The Clarendon Press.

Doe, Norman (1998). *Canon Law in the Anglican Communion*. Oxford: Clarendon Press.

Fincham, Kenneth (ed.) (1993). *The Early Stuart Church, 1603–1642*. Basingstoke and London: Macmillan.

Franklin, R. William (1987). *Nineteenth-Century Churches: The History of a New Catholicism in Württemberg, England, and France*. New York and London: Garland Publishing Inc.

Gore, Charles (1886). *The Ministry of the Christian Church*. London: Rivingtons.

Gore, Charles (1909). *Orders and Unity*. London: John Murray.

Ha, Polly and Collinson, Patrick (eds) (2010). *The Reception of the Continental Reformation in Britain*. Oxford: Oxford University Press for the British Academy.

Hampton, Stephen (2008). *Anti-Arminians: The Anglican Reformed Tradition from Charles II to George I*. Oxford: Oxford University Press.

Hatch, Edwin (1881). *The Organization of the Early Christian Churches*. London: Rivingtons.

Hooker, Richard (1977–98). *The Folger Library Edition of the Works of Richard Hooker*. Ed. W. Speed Hill. 7 vols (vols 1–5, Cambridge, MA and London: The Belknap Press of Harvard University Press, 1977–90; vol. 6, Binghampton, NY: Medieval and Renaissance Texts & Studies, 1993; vol. 7, Tempe, AZ: Medieval and Renaissance Texts and Studies, 1998).

Kasper, Walter (2015). *The Catholic Church: Nature, Reality and Mission*. London and New York: Bloomsbury T&T Clark.

Keeble, N. H. (ed.) (2014). *Settling the Peace of the Church: 1662 Revisited*. Oxford: Oxford University Press.

Lake, Peter (1988). *Anglicans and Puritans: Presbyterian and English Conformist Thought from Whitgift to Hooker*. London: Unwin Hyman.

Lake, Peter (2003). 'The Anglican Moment'. In Stephen Platten (ed.), *Anglicanism and the Western Christian Tradition*. Norwich: Canterbury Press.

Lake, Peter (2006). 'Introduction: Puritanism, Arminianism and Nicholas Tyacke'. In Kenneth Fincham and Peter Lake (eds), *Religious Politics in Post-Reformation England: Essays in Honour of Nicholas Tyacke*. Studies in Modern British Religious History, vol. 13. Rochester, NY: The Boydell Press.

Lightfoot, J. B. (1885). *Saint Paul's Epistle to the Philippians* [with appended dissertation on 'The Christian Ministry']. London: Macmillan.

Locke, Kenneth (2009). *The Church in Anglican Theology: A Historical and Ecumenical Exploration*. Farnham and Burlington, VT: Ashgate.

McAdoo, H. R. (1965). *The Spirit of Anglicanism: A Survey of Anglican Theological Method in the Seventeenth Century*. London: A & C Black.

McAdoo, H. R. (1992). 'Richard Hooker'. In Rowell 1992.

McMichael, Ralph (ed.) (2014). *The Vocation of Anglican Theology*. London: SCM Press.

Maurice, Frederick Denison (1842). *Three Letters to the Rev. W. Palmer*. London: Parker.

Maurice, Frederick Denison (1958). *The Kingdom of Christ or Hints to a Quaker respecting the Principles, Constitution and Ordinances of the Catholic Church*. Based on the 2nd edition of 1842. Ed. Alec R. Vidler. 2 vols. London: SCM Press.

Milton, Anthony (2005). *Catholic and Reformed: The Roman and Protestant Churches in English Protestant Thought 1600–1640*. Cambridge: Cambridge University Press.

Milton, Anthony (ed.) (2005). *The British Delegation and the Synod of Dort (1618–1619)*. Woodbridge: The Boydell Press (Church of England Record Society 13).

More, P. E. and Cross, F. L. (1935). *Anglicanism: The Thought and Practice of the Church of England, Illustrated from the Religious Literature of the Seventeenth Century*. London: SPCK.

Morris, Jeremy (2016). *The High Church Revival in the Church of England*. Leiden: Brill.

Neill, Stephen (1958). *Anglicanism*. Harmondsworth: Penguin.

Oakley, Francis (2003). *The Conciliarist Tradition: Constitutionalism in the Catholic Church 1300–1870*. Oxford: Oxford University Press.

Peters, R. (1971). 'John Hales and the Synod of Dort'. In G. J. Cuming and D. Baker (eds), *Studies in Church History, 7: Councils and Assemblies*. Cambridge: Cambridge University Press.

Podmore, Colin (2005). *Aspects of Anglican Identity*. London: Church House Publishing.

Prior, Charles W. A. (2005). *Defining the Jacobean Church*. Cambridge: Cambridge University Press.

Ramsey, A. M. (1945). 'What is Anglican Theology?' *Theology* 48: 2–6.

Rowell, Geoffrey (ed.) (1992). *The English Religious Tradition and the Genius of Anglicanism*. Wantage: Ikon.

Runcie, Robert (1988). 'Opening Address'. In *The Truth Shall Make You Free: The Lambeth Conference 1988; The Reports, Resolutions and Pastoral Letters from the Bishops*. London: Anglican Consultative Council.

Ryrie, Alec (2013). *Being Protestant in Reformation Britain*. Oxford: Oxford University Press.

Sanders, C. R. (1942). *Coleridge and the Broad Church Movement*. Durham, NC: Duke University Press.

Shagan, Ethan, H. (2011). *The Rule of Moderation: Violence, Religion and the Politics of Restraint in Early Modern England*. Cambridge: Cambridge University Press.

Sharpe, K. (1992). *The Personal Rule of Charles I*. New Haven and London: Yale University Press.

Shirley, F. J. (1949). *Richard Hooker and Contemporary Political Ideas*. London: SPCK.

Spurr, John (1991). *The Restoration Church of England, 1646–1689*. New Haven and London: Yale University Press.

Stewart, Alistair C. (2014). *The Original Bishops: Office and Order in the First Christian Communities*. Grand Rapids, MI: Baker Academic.

Sullivan, Francis A., SJ (2001). *From Apostles to Bishops: The Development of the Episcopacy in the Early Church*. New York/Mahwah, NJ: The Newman Press.

Sykes, Stephen (1978). *The Integrity of Anglicanism*. London: Mowbray.

Sykes, Stephen (1995). *Unashamed Anglicanism*. London: Darton, Longman & Todd.

Sykes, Stephen, Booty, John, and Knight, Jonathan (eds) (1998). *The Study of Anglicanism*. 2nd edn. London: SPCK; Minneapolis: Fortress Press.

Tracts for the Times. <http://anglicanhistory.org/tracts/tract27.html>.

Tyacke, Nicholas (1987). *Anti-Calvinists: The Rise of English Arminianism, c.1590–1640*. Oxford: Clarendon Press.

Tyacke, Nicholas (ed.) (1998). *England's Long Reformation 1500–1800*. London: University College London Press.

Usher, Roland G. (1910). *The Reconstruction of the English Church*. 2 vols. London and New York: Appleton.

Valliere, Paul (2012). *Conciliarism: A History of Decision-Making in the Church*. Cambridge: Cambridge University Press.

Walsh, J., Haydon, C., and Taylor, S. (eds) (1993). *The Church of England c.1689–c.1833: From Toleration to Tractarianism*. Cambridge: Cambridge University Press.

Windsor Report, The (2004). London: Anglican Communion Office.

Wright, J. Robert (1998). 'Anglicanism, *Ecclesia Anglicana*, and Anglican: An Essay on Terminology'. In Sykes, Booty, and Knight 1998: 477–83.

Wright, Luke Savin Herrick (2010). *Samuel Taylor Coleridge and the Anglican Church*. Notre Dame, IN: University of Notre Dame Press.

Yelton, Michael (2005). *Anglican Papalism: An Illustrated History 1900–1960*. Norwich: Canterbury Press.

SUGGESTED READING

Avis, Paul (2002). *Anglicanism and the Christian Church: Theological Resources in Historical Perspective*. Revised edition. London: T&T Clark.

Avis, Paul (2008). *The Identity of Anglicanism: Essentials of Anglican Ecclesiology*. London and New York: T&T Clark.

Avis, Paul (2016). *The Vocation of Anglicanism*. London and New York: Bloomsbury T&T Clark.

Chapman, Mark (2012). *Anglican Theology*. London and New York: T&T Clark.

Sykes, Stephen (1978). *The Integrity of Anglicanism*. London: Mowbray.

Sykes, Stephen (1995). *Unashamed Anglicanism*. London: Darton, Longman & Todd.

Sykes, Stephen, Booty, John, and Knight, Jonathan (eds) (1998). *The Study of Anglicanism*. 2nd edn. London: SPCK; Minneapolis: Fortress Press.

CHAPTER 12

ROMAN CATHOLIC ECCLESIOLOGY FROM THE COUNCIL OF TRENT TO VATICAN II AND BEYOND

ORMOND RUSH

NARRATING a history requires of the narrator some choice of perspective for making sense of the story. This account of the history of Roman Catholic ecclesiology from the Council of Trent up until the Second Vatican Council and beyond attempts to show—retrospectively, through the lens of Vatican II—the pre-history of the dramatic shifts in ecclesiology undertaken at that council. It is only one way of telling the story.

Three factors constitute a 'theology of the church' at a particular time throughout church history: (1) the lived sense of being the church experienced by the faithful within their society's worldview and historical circumstance; (2) how theologians articulated that lived faith according to particular models and background theories of the time; and (3) how the official teaching authority in the church may have either appropriated or rejected those perceptions through the formulations of ecumenical councils and popes. Of course, these three factors exist in a complex relationship that is not always interactive.

Accordingly, while 'the history of the church', 'the history of theology', and 'the history of doctrine' need to be distinguished, they are overlapping stories. Within the history of the church, historical forces and events impact the Christian community within the particular culture and society in which it lives its faith. Also, as the following narrative shows, throughout church history there is potentially an interactive relationship between theology and official doctrine: not all theology becomes doctrine, but all doctrine is expressed in theological frameworks. Moreover, doctrine—once formally promulgated—undergoes a history of reception, in which spiritual appropriation by the faithful and theologians' further interpretation and application of the doctrine in new circumstances play important ecclesial roles in the church's evangelizing mission. The history of ecclesiology, furthermore, is entwined with the broader history of theology itself. This history involves shifting theological methods, engagement with relevant background theories such as philosophy, as well as responses to 'external' historical forces and answers to new questions posed to the tradition.

'Ecclesiology,' in the more narrow sense of the specific discipline of scholarly theology regarding the church, has been an explicit part of theological treatises only in the last few centuries. Of course, themes related to the nature and mission of the church were certainly addressed in the New Testament and later patristic writings, but not in any way that treats the church as its central focus, with an explicit analysis of its nature and mission. For example, in the works of medieval scholastics including Thomas Aquinas there was no tract dealing specifically with the church. It was only in the nineteenth century that the first 'systematic' ecclesiologies emerge. Michael Himes defines 'systematic ecclesiology', in this sense, as 'an ecclesiology which considered the connections between the Church and the central doctrinal areas of the Christian faith, such as Trinity, incarnation, Holy Spirit, creation, grace, eschatology, etc.' (Himes 2000: 45).

Trent and 'Tridentine' Ecclesiology

Pope Paul III (b. 1468; pope 1534–49) convoked an ecumenical council to address the crises arising from the Protestant Reformations. Centred on the town of Trent, the council met in three periods over eighteen years, from 1545 to 1563. The documents it produced treated a broad range of issues related to doctrine and church discipline (Tanner 1990: vol. 2: 660–799). Four points can be made about the 'ecclesiology' reflected throughout the council and in its documents.

First, the council did not attempt a comprehensive treatment of the church. Trent deliberately set out to highlight, thirty years after the start of the Lutheran Reformation, the differences between the conceptions of the Protestants and those of the Roman Catholic Church. Areas of significant agreement, for example concerning the Triune God and Jesus Christ, and indeed the nature and mission of the church, were not discussed. Therefore, the vision of the council, as expressed in the conciliar debates and in its promulgated documents, is deliberately narrow in scope. This narrowness conditions the ecclesiology that emerges in the centuries following the council, both in the minds of Catholics and in the writings of theologians.

Secondly, the issue of how to label this historical period beginning with Trent reveals something of the ecclesiology of the council and the period of its reception over the next century: it is both negatively polemical and positively reformative. On the one hand, the term 'Counter-Reformation' is used by historians to capture the narrowness of the ecclesiological vision that followed the council's focus only on *differences* with Protestant ecclesiology, as well as its desire to counter the advances of Protestantism in Europe. On the other hand, the term 'Catholic Reformation' is used to capture the genuine efforts on the part of the council to address calls for institutional reform coming from within the church long before the Reformation, as well as the council's genuine efforts to bring about a more cogent proclamation and living of the gospel in the new situation in which the church now found itself. Reception of the latter impulse can be seen in the Baroque art, spiritual renewal movements, and missionary outreach in the century following Trent. Some historians prefer the broader term 'Early Modern Catholicism' as a better term for naming both of these reactive and proactive dimensions, as well for capturing other aspects of the complex reception of the Council of Trent (O'Malley 2000). 'Responding to the Protestant challenge was at the forefront of Catholicism for a long time [after Trent], but much else was happening within the Catholic church' (Tanner 2011: 165).

Thirdly, the Protestant Reformation is not the only context within which the ecclesiology of Trent is to be understood. In his pre-history of the Council of Trent, the historian John O'Malley points out that issues such as 'Gallicanism' and 'conciliarism' are not far from the surface during the conciliar debates (O'Malley 2013: 23–48). Ever since the Council of Constance (1414–17), there had lingered a papal suspicion of councils. Not surprisingly, at Trent the popes maintained a tight control on the agenda of the council and a tension between pope and council was ever present. Therefore, the ecclesiology of Trent is evident as much in the 'body language' of the council as in its decrees.

The council promulgated its decrees sequentially in pairs: one clarifying doctrine and another proposing reform in some area of discipline. The doctrinal 'chapters' were accompanied by a series of 'canons' that judged those who held certain doctrinal positions to be declared 'out' (*anathema sit*). A particular 'style' is evident in its discourse (O'Malley 2006).

Theologians played an important role at the council (Minnich 1998: 431–4). In clarifying official Catholic doctrine, these theologians drew on the current Catholic theological approach, that of scholasticism, dominant since the early Middle Ages (Schüssler Fiorenza 2011: 13–26). As evident in the decrees of the council, scholastic theology—whatever its achievements—betrayed two major weaknesses: a proof-texting approach to Scripture and an underdeveloped historical sense (O'Malley 2013: 249–50).

The words 'Tridentine' and 'Tridentinism' (from the Latin name of the town Trent, *Tridentum*) have come to describe post-Trent Roman Catholicism right up to the eve of Vatican II. However, analysing the history of the reception of the Council of Trent reveals that, in the centuries after the council, both the lived Catholicism on the ground and the dominant ecclesiology among theologians have features that cannot be grounded in the council and its documents (O'Malley 2013: 248–75). The Tridentine vision of the church that soon emerged 'saw a Roman version of Trent becoming the norm for Church life; it looked for the center of the Church only in Rome rather than being also in the local Church; it exalted the papacy at the expense of the episcopate, and it revered the clerical over the lay state; it displaced medieval canon law and became almost the sole source for legislation and the practical running of the Church; it led to a static ecclesiology' (O'Donnell 1996: 451; Prodi 2010).

Within a year of the council's close, the pope of the council's third and final period, Pius IV, followed the mandate of the council and promulgated a Profession of Faith which all bishops and pastors were from then on required to profess (a disciplinary requirement lasting until the twentieth century). However, its summary statements failed to capture the nuances of the council's position. Likewise, the Catechism of the Council of Trent, published in 1566, incorporated the council's teachings into a virtual summa of official church teaching (on the ecclesiology of the catechism, see Haight 2004: 266–75).

An equally influential factor in the emergence of Tridentinism came from one of the most enthusiastic promoters of the council's reforms, the archbishop of Milan, Cardinal Charles Borromeo (1538–84). Secretary to his papal uncle Pius IV during the council's third period, Borromeo immediately after the council set about introducing one of the major stipulations of the council, that bishops set up diocesan synods to implement the council's reforms. However, the eleven diocesan (and six provincial synods) of Milan went beyond the general stipulations of the council and introduced requirements that Trent had not required, such as a 'confessional' in every church and a 'tabernacle' for the reserved sacrament to be situated in the middle of the main altar. These and other innovations were published in a collection of the 'Acts of the Church of Milan', which became a publishing phenomenon, being read throughout the Catholic world. Soon the Catholic world was imitating Milan. With these and other factors, 'within a year of the council's closing, the Catholic body-social was thus moving into *Tridentinismo*, that is, into phenomena claiming origin in the council but in fact taking a step beyond it' (O'Malley 2013: 263).

Another highly significant factor in the rise of Tridentinism involved a theologian who is arguably the most influential ecclesiologist in the 400 years from Trent to Vatican II—the Jesuit Robert Bellarmine (1542–1621), born three years before the opening of the council's first period and ordained a priest in 1570, seven years after the close of the council. His major work was the three-volume apologetical *Disputations on the Controversies of the Christian Faith*, published between 1586 and 1593 (for a summary of Bellarmine's ecclesiology, see Hardon 1966). Bellarmine's ecclesiology focused on external and institutional aspects of the church. The true church, he claimed, is not—as the Protestants proposed—something hidden, with its membership to be revealed only at the end of time. Rather, the church in the present is clearly recognizable by visible characteristics that can be used as criteria for judging genuine membership. Accordingly, Bellarmine defined the church as: 'the group of men brought together by (1) the profession of the same Christian faith and by (2) communion in the same sacraments (3) under the governance of legitimate pastors, especially of the one vicar of Christ on earth, the Roman Pontiff.' Bellarmine goes on to state that internal characteristics, such as virtue, are not necessarily required for membership: 'we do not think that any internal virtue is required, but only the external profession of faith and communion in the sacraments, which can be perceived by the senses themselves. For the Church is a group of men as visible and palpable as is the group of the Roman people or the Kingdom of France or the Republic of Venice' (Bellarmino 1586–93: 4 III 2; 3 II; trans. J. Komonchak 1995: 322, numbering added).

According to Avery Dulles, 'By applying these criteria, Bellarmine is able to exclude all persons who in his opinion do not belong to the true Church. The first criterion rules out pagans, Moslems, Jews, heretics, and apostates; the second rules out catechumens and excommunicated persons; the third rules out schismatics. Thus only Roman Catholics remain' (Dulles 2002: 8). Only the Roman Catholic Church, so defined, is the one, true church. A corollary of Bellarmine's definition is that the church is a society like the emerging post-feudal nation states of Europe, such as France. The pope is therefore conceived as an absolute monarch who rules over a society where governing authority is exercised in a pyramidal way from top to bottom. Bellarmine did give a fuller conception of the church when he spoke of not only the body of the church but also the soul of the church, which is the Holy Spirit. This more balanced conception, however, was lost to further generations.

Implicit, although not explicit, in Bellarmine's ecclesiology is the notion of the church as a *societas perfecta* ('perfect society'), which becomes more explicit in those who expand on Bellarmine's framework over the following centuries (Granfield 1982). The notion has its roots in Greek political thought and is a notion which Thomas Aquinas in the thirteenth century, in the context of debate regarding spiritual and temporal powers, had applied to the political 'State', of which the church was understood to be an integral part (Thomas Aquinas 1966: 12–15 [*ST* 1–2ae, q90, a3 AD 3]). Applied to a political society, the notion meant that a society possesses all that it needs to achieve its purpose. Increasingly applied to the Roman Catholic Church, the notion of *societas perfecta* held that the church contains all it needs for its mission and can be free from control by secular authorities; as the church develops, it becomes 'perfect' in both a moral sense and in its entitlement to dictate its norms to society (O'Donnell 1996: 359).

The reception history of Bellarmine's ecclesiology is central to our story because it was the official ecclesiology of the Roman Catholic Church right up till the eve of Vatican II. Canon lawyers in the eighteenth century and then ecclesiologists in the nineteenth century took up Bellarmine's thought, making even more explicit the notion of the church as a perfect society. This soon became the reigning model in official Catholic ecclesial self-understanding. For example, in the nineteenth century, the notion of *societas perfecta* appeared as a major theme in the first draft of the document on the church *Supremi pastoris* for the First Vatican Council (1869–70), and then in its revised form as *Tametsi Deus*. Although this second draft was never debated on the floor of Vatican I, these two schemata reveal of the importance of the notion at the time (Granfield 1979; Mansi 1960: 51: 543). In the following decades, Pope Leo XIII (b. 1810; pope 1878–1903) frequently mentioned the notion in his encyclicals, for example, *Satis cognitum* (Carlen 1981: 2: 396). In the twentieth century, the 1943 encyclical *Mystici corporis* of Pope Pius XII (b. 1876; pope 1939–58), while emphasizing the spiritual dimensions of the church as Christ's mystical body, nevertheless continued to emphasize that the church is a perfect society (e.g. Carlen 1981: 49 [no. 63]). The neo-scholastic manuals on the eve of the Second Vatican Council (1962–5) highlighted this primary model of the church (e.g. Ott 1954: 275–6). The draft schema *De Ecclesia* prepared for Vatican II is testimony to the resilience of both Bellarmine's ecclesiology and in particular to the juridical notion of the Roman Catholic Church as a perfect society, with the pope understood in terms of a reigning monarch of a kingdom.

The role of the papacy within such a view of the church was given greater and greater importance in ecclesial life and ecclesiological reflection across the four centuries under review here (Schatz 1996). However, there were always attempts to limit over-inflated views of papal primacy (Oakley 2003). The Council of Trent had gathered with memories of Gallicanism and conciliarism causing tension between the popes of the time and the conciliar assembly. The tension came to the fore in various ways in the centuries after Trent. For example, conflicts in the relationships between the French state, the French bishops, and the bishop of Rome gave rise to various attitudes regarding their appropriate relationship, such as 'royal Gallicanism' and 'episcopal Gallicanism'; similar issues were at play in German-speaking areas in the controversies of Febronianism and Josephinism (Himes 2000: 50–4). Often, political and ecclesial ideologies operated side by side in these debates. French 'Gallicans' referred derogatorily to proponents of papal maximalism as 'ultramontane', that is always deferring to papal authority 'beyond the Alps' down in Rome. Ultramontanists saw their maximalist views of the papacy vindicated in the definition of papal primacy and infallibility by the First Vatican Council (1869–70).

'THE LONG NINETEENTH CENTURY'

By the beginning of 'the long nineteenth century' (O'Malley 2008: 53–92), a new worldview had emerged in Europe. The French and American revolutions had disrupted the social and political fabric of a monarchical European society. 'Romanticism' in the arts valued 'emotion' and 'spirit' in reaction to what was felt to be the Enlightenment's one-dimensional rational view of human existence. Notions such as 'evolution' and 'development' characterized the emerging life sciences such as biology and the emerging human sciences such as psychology and history. The evolutionary theory of Charles Darwin (1809–92) outlined in his *On the Origin of Species* (1859), and the psychological theories of Sigmund Freud (1856–1939) focusing on the origins of human personality, shaped the worldview of the times. This spirit of the age touched Roman Catholic life and theology and soon a flowering of 'Romanticism' in Catholic theology occurred, particularly at the Roman Catholic theology faculty in Tübingen, Germany.

Johann Sebastian Drey (1777–1853), considered the 'founder' of the Catholic Tübingen school, wrote no specific treatise on the church, and gave no explicit place to such a treatise in his outline of topics to be treated by theology considered in his *Brief Introduction to the Study of Theology* (Drey 1994). Nevertheless, Drey presented the church as the living embodiment of revelation and indeed the realization of the reign of God in history (Fehr 1981: 239–44). Drey's student Johann Adam Möhler (1796–1838) is arguably the first Roman Catholic theologian to write systematic works of ecclesiology. Möhler's ecclesiology shifted throughout his relatively brief writing period. Attempting to balance the outer and the inner dimensions of the church, his early 1825 work *Die Einheit in der Kirche* (Möhler 1996) emphasized the Holy Spirit as the unifying life-principle among the community of believers. For Möhler 'tradition' is an organic, dynamic process of development guided by the Holy Spirit: 'Tradition is the expression of the Holy Spirit giving life to the totality of believers . . . Scripture was created out of the living tradition, not vice versa' (Möhler 1996: 117). In 1836, dissatisfied with *Die Einheit*, and in dialogue with the positions of his colleagues in the Protestant theology faculty at Tübingen, Möhler published his second major ecclesiological work *Symbolik* (Möhler 1997), which attempted to balance his earlier pneumatological approach with one that emphasized the church as the body of Christ in history; analogically, he proposed, the church continues the Incarnation in time. In an oft-quoted passage, he stated, 'Thus, the visible Church, from the point of view here taken, is the Son of God himself, everlastingly manifesting himself among men in a human form, perpetually renovated, and eternally young—the permanent incarnation of the same, as in Holy Writ, even the faithful are called "the body of Christ." Hence it is evident that the Church, though composed of men, is yet not purely human' (Möhler 1997: 259).

When Möhler's ecclesiology is taken as a whole, several themes stand out: his focus on the role of the Spirit; the value of the analogy of the Incarnation for exploring the visible and invisible dimensions of the church; and his notion of living tradition (Himes 1997). Möhler 'paved the way for a truly theological study of the Church which, with its Trinitarian dimension, was incalculably richer than the more polemic and apologetic ecclesiology of previous and following generations' (O'Donnell 1996: 310).

After Möhler, the work of Catholic canonists during the nineteenth century became important, particularly for their appropriation from Protestant ecclesiology of the notion of Christ's three offices in the church: the prophetic, the priestly, and the kingly offices (see Rush 2003: 140–3). Following on from Ferdinand Walter (1794–1879), George Phillips (1804–72) identified the church with the kingdom of God and understood its governance in terms of monarchical authority. Phillips portrayed the triad of *magisterium, ministerium*, and *regimen* in terms of Christ's prophetic (teaching), priestly (sanctifying), and kingly (governing) offices (Fuchs 1969).

This motif also figured prominently in the work of John Henry Newman (1801–90), both as an Anglican and as a Roman Catholic. Although Newman wrote no specific work on the church, several ecclesiological themes dominated his sermons and writings: the rubric of the three ecclesial offices of Christ as Prophet, Priest, and King (Newman 1911; Dulles 1990); the organic development of doctrine in the life of the church (Newman 1989; McCarren 2009); the importance of the laity in the church and the authority of the *consensus fidelium* (Newman 1962; Dulles 2009). Also characterizing his vision of the church were the themes of the church as the people of God, the mystical body of Christ, the temple of the Holy Spirit, and as a communion of the faithful (Ker 2009). Unable to attend the First Vatican Council, Newman ultimately defended the council's teachings on papal primacy and papal infallibility (Sullivan 2009).

A significant stage in the reception history of Möhler's ecclesiology was his appropriation by what has been called 'the Roman School' of theology (Antón 1987: 287–317; Congar 1971: 92–6). The work of the Roman School falls within the pontificates of three popes: Gregory XVI (b. 1765; pope 1831–46), Pius IX (b. 1792; pope 1846–78), and Leo XIII (b. 1810; pope 1878–1903). Most of this group were lecturers at the Jesuit Roman College (later the Gregorian University) in Rome. Their work was written according to the approach of the scholasticism of their day. But what distinguished their method from that scholasticism was their desire to incorporate biblical and patristic themes into their theology, leading to a greater balance in their ecclesiology between the visible-institutional and the invisible-spiritual dimensions of the church. An important factor in that greater balance was also their reception of the Tübingen School's notion of 'living tradition' (Kasper 1962). Nevertheless, the overall tenor of their work remained 'ultramontane'.

The leading figure in the early period of the Roman School was Giovanni Perrone (1794–1876). However, the more creative ecclesiological thinkers in the group throughout the second half of the nineteenth century included Joseph Kleutgen (1811–83), Carlo Passaglia (1812–87), Johannes Baptist Franzelin (1816–86), and Clemens Schrader (1820–75). Passaglia and Franzelin were students of Perrone. Unlike most of the Roman School who taught at the Jesuit Roman College, Kleutgen taught at the Germanicum College in Rome. Matthias Joseph Scheeben (1835–88), while not strictly a member of the Roman School, was a student of many of its members at the Roman College, and his creative theological writing while teaching at the seminary of Cologne can be considered alongside theirs (O'Donnell 1996: 419).

Although most theological manuals of the time, in the tradition of medieval scholasticism, did not have a specific treatise on the church, Passaglia and Schrader wrote a two-volume book specifically on the church, *De ecclesia Christi*. While certainly written in the prevailing neo-scholastic style, it did go beyond the ecclesiologies of the day by highlighting themes such as the church as the Body of Christ, the role of the Holy Spirit in the church, and the importance of the invisible as well as the visible dimensions of the church. The brilliant Passaglia, however, soon left the Jesuits and the church, partly in reaction to the ultramontanism of the day.

Franzelin's ecclesiology is noteworthy, first for his reception of Möhler's theology of the church as the mystical body of Christ, and secondly, and consequently, for expanding the notion of *communio* beyond the reigning ecclesiology of the time, that of Robert Bellarmine (Komonchak 1995). Franzelin's unfinished *Theses de Ecclesia Christi* was published in 1887, a year after his death. According to Joseph Komonchak, 'within the manual tradition [Franzelin's *Theses*] is one of the most serious efforts to restore some theological and spiritual substance to the treatise on the church [and] illustrates the difficulty Catholic ecclesiology, down through *Mystici Corporis*, experiences in breaking the narrow Bellarminian mould' (Komonchak 1995: 326).

In the face of perceived threats to Catholic ecclesial identity in a revolutionary Europe, Pope Pius IX convoked an ecumenical council, which met in St Peter's Basilica from 1869 to 1870. The major theologians involved in the preparation of documents for the bishops' consideration came from the Roman School. Fifty-six draft schemas on various topics were prepared. Schrader was involved in drafting a schema on the church, titled *Supremi pastoris* (Mansi 50: 539–636). It spoke of the church as a perfect society, but also in terms of its being the Mystical Body of Christ and in terms of the three offices of Christ. In their written responses to the document, the bishops did not give it a positive reception. So Kleutgen was entrusted with redrafting the constitution, now with a new title *Tametsi Deus* (Mansi 53: 308–17). Significantly it depicted the fullness of supreme power in the church as lying in two subjects, the pope and the body of bishops united to him (Tagle 2004: 33–5). However the council never discussed the text. If it had indeed debated and received Kleutgen's text, then Vatican I might perhaps have presented a richer ecclesiological vision overall. Certainly, the council had intended to give a broader treatment of the pope's relationship with the rest of the bishops, but the premature closure of the council, owing to the onset of the Franco-Prussian war, prevented such discussion.

In the time available, Vatican I promulgated only two documents: *Dei Filius*, the Dogmatic Constitution on the Catholic Faith (Tanner 1990: 2: 804–11), and *Pastor Aeternus*, The Dogmatic Constitution on the Church of Christ, with a focus on papal infallibility and papal primacy (Tanner 1990: 2: 811–16). As the *Relatio* of Bishop Vinzenz Gasser (1809–79) made clear, the doctrine of papal infallibility is grounded on the church's infallibility (Gasser 2008). In the reception of the council's teaching regarding papal primacy, a significant clarification of the council's meaning was made five years later in a statement by the German hierarchy, reacting to the German Chancellor Bismarck's implication that Vatican I had reduced the world's bishops to mere functionaries of an all powerful pontiff (Denzinger 2012: 3112–17).

After Pius IX, Leo XIII's 1896 encyclical *Satis cognitum* (Carlen 1981: 2: 387–404) not only emphasized Vatican I's teaching regarding papal primacy, but also can be taken as an exemplar of the persistent reiteration of an ecclesiology of the church as a perfect society. Also in this period, Leo XIII gave further energy to an already growing neo-scholastic revival through his 1879 encyclical *Aeterni Patris* (Carlen 1981: 2:17–27), calling for a return to the 'perennial philosophy' of St Thomas. Kleutgen was responsible for drafting the encyclical. Leo XIII also began a shift in papal teaching towards addressing what would later be called 'the social mission of the church' when in 1891 he published the encyclical *Rerum Novarum* on the conditions and rights of workers (Carlen 1981: 2: 241–61).

The ecclesiology of Vatican I, focusing primarily on papal authority in governance and teaching, was particularly embodied in the style of the pontificate of Pope Pius X (b. 1835; pope 1903–14). The so-called 'modernist crisis' during his pontificate raised several issues directly related to ecclesiology, as well as others that had indirect implications for ecclesiology. Centred mainly in France, England, and Italy, this disparate 'movement' was an amalgam of approaches, which nevertheless had the common aim of bringing historical-critical reflection to the study of theology, doctrine, and the church.

The writings of two figures in particular treat specifically ecclesiological topics. In France, Alfred Loisy (1857–1940) applied historically conscious biblical criticism to the origins of the church in his 1902 *L'Évangile et L'Église* (Loisy 1988). Intended as a polemical work directed against the Protestant Adolf von Harnack, it attempted to defend Catholicism by showing its hierarchical and sacramental structure to be an organic development of the seed which Jesus had planted: 'Jesus did not systematize beforehand the constitution of the Church as that of a government established on earth and destined to endure for a long series of centuries' (Loisy 1988). However, the Holy Office considered his defence heretical and the following year it was added to the Index of Forbidden Books. In England, the Jesuit George Tyrrell (1861–1909) argued that historical criticism inevitably undermined accepted beliefs such as the authority of Scripture, the ahistorical truth of dogma, and any hierarchical claim to infallibility. In 1903 he published *The Church and the Future* under the pseudonym Hilaire Bourdon (Bourdon 1903). It presented the church as a community of believers through whom the Holy Spirit spoke authoritatively; dogmas were mere expressions of religious experience; and the role of the hierarchy was to guide the church democratically (Gratsch 1975: 196).

In 1907, both the Holy Office decree *Lamentabili* (Denzinger 2012: 3401–66) and the papal encyclical *Pascendi Dominici Gregis* (Carlen 1981: 3: 71–98) artificially grouped together and condemned positions that could not be attributed to any one scholar; however, Loisy and Tyrell were clearly among the intended targets. A core issue in the whole affair was the historicity of human knowing: 'Here, it seems, in clashing theories of knowledge, lay the central quarrel of the Modernist crisis' (O'Connell 1994: 344). *Pascendi,* to the contrary, defended a metaphysical realism and a realist epistemology (O'Connell 1994: 344). The response to *Pascendi* of the French philosopher Maurice Blondel (1861–1949) captures the feeling of many Roman Catholic scholars at the time: 'I am suffering deeply. It almost makes one cry out, Happy are those who are dead in the Lord! . . . I have read the encyclical, and I am in a stupor. Is it possible? What attitude should one take? Internal attitude, I mean, as well as external. And, above all, how does one prevent so many souls from just giving up, just doubting the *goodness* of the church?' (quoted in O'Connell 1994: 348). In 1910, the *motu proprio Sacrorum Antistitum* prescribed that all office-holders take an Oath against Modernism (Daly 1980: 235–6). A period of vigilantism followed throughout the Roman Catholic world. The 'sinister' procedures of Monsignor Umberto Benigni (1862–1934) from the Roman curia set the tone (O'Connell 1994: 361–5, at 61), especially with his *Sodalitium Pianum*—'the chilling parody of a secret service' (Daly 1980: 218).

Pius X died in 1914, just a few weeks after the outbreak of the First World War. The new pope Benedict XV (b. 1854; pope 1914–22) soon issued his first encyclical *Ad Beatissimi* (Carlen 1981: 3: 143–51), which somewhat softened Pius' aggressive policy regarding tracking down people with 'modernist' views. While surveillance and threat of censorship still continued to create a climate of repression, new shoots, nevertheless, began to appear in Catholic ecclesiology.

Renewal Movements

'The nineteenth century ended on August 1, 1914', Paul Tillich would often state to his students (Hall 1999: 3). The utter devastation wrought by the First World War brought forth a desire in European society for community and solidarity beyond national borders; the great symbol of this desire was the birth of the League of Nations in 1920. In a war-weary Germany, there flowered a greater emphasis on the importance of the *Volk* ('the People') and its traditions, and a deep-felt need for *Gemeinschaft* ('community'). A particularly significant phenomenon was the grass-roots emergence of youth movements. These societal shifts were mirrored within ecclesial communities and came to be reflected in the ecclesiologies of the time, which soon began to give greater emphasis to the church as a community (Schoof 1970: 76–81). These sentiments for unity likewise gave greater impetus to efforts for Christian unity, through the ecumenical movement, leading to greater openness by some individual theologians to the ecclesiological riches of other Christian traditions.

Another stimulus for deeper reflection within Roman Catholic ecclesiology in the decades between the wars was a growing dissatisfaction with the official ecclesiology, still bound to Bellarmine's model emphasizing visibility, perfect society, and juridical structures of organization and authority. Moreover, scholars came to believe, the whole neo-scholastic style of theology—by the way it separated the divine from human affairs—was the very cause of the contemporary secularism and loss of a sense of the sacred evident throughout Europe (Komonchak 1990: 582–4).

Over the next four decades, in response to these challenges and attentive to the grass-roots desire for a deeper sense of the church, Roman Catholic scholars from different theological disciplines turned to the scriptural, liturgical, philosophical, and theological sources of the tradition, especially in the biblical, patristic, and medieval periods. Furthermore, these studies were conducted in an increasingly ecumenical climate in which the traditions of Eastern Orthodoxy, long ignored by Western Catholicism, as well as traditions growing out of the Reformations of the sixteenth century, became sources for a richer Roman Catholic ecclesiology. The result was a greater appreciation of the rich diversity of the Catholic tradition, beyond the then dominant Tridentinism. In France, the poet and essayist Charles Péguy would later be the first to use the term *ressourcement* ('back to the sources') to name this return especially to the biblical and patristic writings. It was a term embraced by the scholars themselves—unlike the polemical term *nouvelle théologie*, which nevertheless became a common way to name this scholarship within France.

Thus, from the end of the First World War up to the convocation of Vatican II, renewal movements within Roman Catholicism blossomed in a range of areas of study and activity: the biblical movement, the liturgical movement, the lay apostolate movement, the ecumenical movement, the social action movement, etc. (Iserloh 1981). Rather than constituting separate streams in the life of the church, these movements influenced each other. For example, the biblical movement brought forth greater interest in personal reading and study of Scripture, a Christ-centred spirituality, and a focus on the personal call to discipleship, which in turn supported the lay apostolate movement. Similarly, 'the liturgical movement was an expression of a new awareness of the Church, just as, conversely, the celebration of the liturgy permitted an entirely new experience of the Church as a community' (Iserloh 1981: 305). All the major shifts in ecclesiology over these decades find their origins in these renewal movements (O'Donnell 1996: 409–10), eventually bearing fruit in the ecclesiological vision of Vatican II (Rousseau 1965). 'All these formed parallel currents that would converge in Vatican II's [*Lumen Gentium*]' (Moeller 1966: 124).

In Germany, two writers were particularly significant in the post-war renewal of Catholic ecclesiology: Romano Guardini (1885–1968) and Karl Adam (1876–1966). The Italian-born Guardini grew up in Germany and taught in Berlin, Tübingen, and Munich. In the wake of the grass-roots phenomenon of youth movements across Germany, Guardini became involved in the Catholic youth movement 'Quickborn'. Influenced by phenomenology, existentialism, and personalism in contemporary philosophy, his writings ranged over the disciplines of liturgy, Christology, and ecclesiology. Alert to the post-war desire for more meaningful community, away from inflated individualism and subjectivism (Krieg 1997: 47–51), Guardini began his 1922 work *Vom Sinn der Kirche* with a reference to the renewal of the sense of the church occurring at that time: 'A religious process of incalculable importance has begun—the Church is awakening in the souls of men [Die Kirche erwacht in den Seelen]' (Guardini 1935: 11). His 1935 *Vom Leben des Glaubens* emphasized a communal, ecclesial notion of faith over against an individualistic conception, highlighting the importance of *sentire cum Ecclesia* ('thinking with the church'). As a consequence of his critical essay against National Socialism, he was dismissed from his teaching role at the university of Berlin (Krieg 1997: 115–36). After the Nazi era and the end of the Second World War, in works such as the 1950 *Das Ende der Neuzeit* (Guardini 2001), Guardini proposed that a greater sense of evil in the world and of the delusions of the Enlightenment were ushering in the end of modernity's reign, and challenging the church to greater engagement with the world.

In 1919, Karl Adam was appointed to the Catholic theological faculty at Tübingen and soon followed in the tradition of his predecessors. His inaugural lecture was critical of the reigning neo-scholastic theology and proposed an approach that was based on historical studies, nevertheless to be interpreted through the lens of contemporary problems. Despite the severity of his critics' reactions to the lecture, he was widely supported. 'He became, almost overnight, the most discussed Catholic theologian in Germany' (Schoof 1970: 85). In 1924, Adam published *Das Wesen des Katholizismus*, on the 'spirit' or 'essence' of Catholicism (Adam 1997), a work very much influenced by one of Adam's predecessors at the Tübingen Catholic faculty, Möhler. In the spirit of Germany's post-war search for the meaning or essence (*Wesen*) of life, particularly as expressed in the phenomenology of Max Scheler (1874–1928) and the 'life-philosophies' of the time, Adam set out to present the *Wesen* of Catholicism in terms of the living presence of Christ, the life principle of the church. He understood the church primarily as Christ's Body. Adam's book became a best seller and a major reference point in Catholic ecclesiology for the next forty years (Krieg 1992: 29–56).

In France, a similar dual emphasis—on historical studies and attention to contemporary problems—was emerging, in two centres in particular: Le Saulchoir and Lyon-Fourvière. From 1935 to 1942 the Dominican faculties of Le Saulchoir were significant in the *ressourcement* of Thomism. Founded in Belgium in 1934, and from 1937 located in the town of Étiolles outside Paris, the centre fostered a historical-critical approach to interpreting the sources of theology, and, particularly after the atrocities of the Second World War, a theological method grounded not only in the sources of the past but also in addressing the pressing issues of the day. Under the leadership of Marie Dominique Chenu (1895–1990), its leading theologians included Yves Congar (1904–95).

Early on, Chenu published what became a manifesto, *Une école de théologie: Le Saulchoir*, outlining the school's historical approach (Chenu 1937). Chenu believed that historical scholarship should ground theology; but such *ressourcement* was less some abstract 'returning' to the riches of the past than a 'sourcing' of the wisdom of the past for the sake of answering the urgent questions of today (Gray 2011). Chenu's approach was exemplified in the life work of his junior colleague, Congar, who was heavily influenced by the early pneumatological ecclesiology of Johann Adam Möhler and shaped by his own broad ecumenical contacts and research. In 1935 Congar was involved in launching the ecumenical series of studies *Unam Sanctam*, which was to become an important vehicle for disseminating the historically grounded biblical, liturgical, patristic, and ecumenical research that Le Saulchoir promoted.

The work of Congar is particularly significant in the history of twentieth-century ecclesiology for many reasons, especially his detailed historical research into the riches of the tradition, his pneumatologically balanced approach to the church, his theology of the laity, his ecumenical studies of other Christian traditions, and his calls for reform of the Roman Catholic Church. 'By the mid-twentieth century Yves Congar had replaced Bellarmine as the Church's premier ecclesiologist' (McBrien 1995: 448). Four works in particular represent Congar's major contributions to ecclesiology before the early 1960s. In 1937, he published *Chrétiens désunis* (Congar 1939), with a vision for 'communion' among the Body of Christ. His 1950 work *Vraie et fausse réforme dans l'Église* (Congar 2011) set out a criteriology for genuine reform in the Roman Catholic Church. In 1953, he published *Jalons pour une théologie du laïcat* (Congar 1965a) where, in outlining the fundamental role of the laity in the mission of the church, he employs as his structuring principle the rubric of the three offices of Christ as prophet, priest, and king. Finally, his 1958 work *Le Mystère du Temple* (Congar 1962), while biblical in its focus, nevertheless brings to the fore the role of Holy Spirit as the co-animator of the church, a pneumatological theme that would come to feature more and more in Congar's later works (Hanvey 2005).

The second centre of *ressourcement* scholarship in France was focused around the Jesuit faculty in Lyon-Fourvière. Its outstanding representative was Henri de Lubac (1896–1991). Although not teaching at the Lyon-Fourvière faculty, de Lubac became associated with this group and was one of the co-founders of its *Sources chrétiennes*, a series of critical translations of patristic works. His first book, published in 1938, was *Catholicisme: les aspects sociaux du dogme* (de Lubac 1988) in which he set out to show that contemporary scholastic theology had dualistically severed the divine from human affairs, making Catholicism irrelevant to people's lives. Through erudite quotation of authors throughout the tradition, de Lubac presented Catholicism as truly 'catholic', inclusive of all that is genuinely human (Komonchak 1990: 591–2). His 1944 work *Corpus Mysticum* (de Lubac 2006) presented a series of historical studies on the church and the Eucharist where he set out to retrieve the rich tradition of Eucharistic ecclesiology (McPartlan 1993). In his 1953 work *Méditation sur l'Église* (de Lubac 1999) he treats themes such as the church as mystery, the church as a sacrament, and develops further the notion that it is the Eucharist that makes the church.

This diverse group of *ressourcement* theologians came to be associated with the initially derogatory term *nouvelle théologie* (Boersma 2009; Flynn and Murray 2011; Mettepenningen 2010). The first to use the term *nouvelle théologie* was one of the opponents of the *ressourcement* scholars, Chenu's doctoral supervisor, the French Dominican Réginald Garrigou-Lagrange (1877–1964), then teaching at the Angelicum College in Rome. He was a leading exponent of the manualist tradition and a consultor to the Roman curia. In a 1946 article, Garrigou-Lagrange posed the question: 'La nouvelle théologie où va-t-elle?' ('The new theology, where is it going?'). His answer is that it leads to a new form of Modernism and he goes on to propose that the methods used to suppress Modernism should now be applied to these theologians (Garrigou-Lagrange 1946). Four years later, Pius XII's encyclical *Humani Generis* in 1950 directly addressed the methods and conclusions of *nouvelle théologie* scholarship (Carlen 1981: 4: 175–84).

Throughout these decades of work within the various renewal movements, several major themes came to the fore that attempted to give a vision of the nature and mission of the church grounded on the diversity of a broader and longer Catholic tradition. The first was the biblical and patristic motif of the church as the Mystical Body of Christ. Möhler had been one of the first to retrieve the theme, particularly in his later work *Symbolik*. The Roman School then developed the motif and it found expression in the first draft of the schema on the church prepared for Vatican I: 'The Church is the mystical body of Christ' (Mansi 1960: 51: 539; trans. Hamer 1964: 13). Encyclicals of Leo XIII used the theme, and it was echoed in the writings of Guardini and Adam (Hahnenberg 2005: 7–11). In the 1930s, the theme was brought to greater prominence through the work of the Jesuit theologian Émile Mersch (1890–1940), especially in his 1936 biblical and patristic study *Le Corps mystique du Christ* (Mersch 1938). The following year, the Dutch Jesuit Sebastian Tromp (1899–1975) published the first of his four-volume *Corpus Christi quod est ecclesia* (Tromp 1937–1972), in which he attempted to balance the visible, institutional, and juridical dimension of the church with that of the invisible dimension, captured in the notion of the mystical body.

By the end of the 1930s, after exploration over the previous three decades, Mystical Body ecclesiology had become dominant (for an extensive bibliography of works in that period see Bluett 1942). However, ecclesiologies centred on the theme soon had their critics. One of the most prominent was the German Dominican scholar Mannes Dominikus Koster (1901–81) who became controversial in Germany by proposing that the mystical body notion was too vague for structuring an ecclesiology. As a counterproposal, Koster employed the theme of 'the people of God' as the most suitable integrating motif in his book *Ekklesiologie im Werden* (Koster 1940); he would later develop this theology further in a book on the church's *sensus fidei* (Koster 1948).

In 1943, after decades of maturing theology on the theme, Pope Pius XII published the encyclical *Mystici Corporis Christi* (Carlen 1981: 4: 37–63), partly as a deliberate response to the controversy in Germany ignited by Koster's challenge. The Gregorian University theologian Tromp had been chosen to be the principal drafter of the encyclical. It had strong echoes of Tromp's earlier work on the theme, presenting however a juridical slant to the biblical doctrine. The encyclical blurred the distinction between Christ and his church, and identified the mystical body of Christ exclusively with the Roman Catholic Church (Carlen 1981: 4: 39–40 [no. 13]). Nevertheless, while the encyclical did go somewhat beyond the Bellarminian exclusive focus on visible and institutional elements of the church, strong echoes of Bellarmine remained: 'Actually only those are to be included as members of the Church who have been baptized and profess the true faith, and who have not been so unfortunate as to separate themselves from the unity of the Body, or have been excluded by legitimate authority for grave faults committed' (Carlen 1981: 4: 41 [no. 22]).

The imbalance in the encyclical's vision of the church was soon noted. Karl Rahner (1904–84), for example, aligned the encyclical's overemphasis on the visible and juridical dimensions of the church with 'ecclesiological Nestorianism' (Rahner 1962: 70; Lennan 1995: 16–18). Nevertheless, in the end, the encyclical can rightly be considered to be 'the most important ecclesiological document to appear in the period between the anti-Modernist campaign of Pius X in the early twentieth century and the beginning of the Second Vatican Council in 1962. The encyclical represented the first significant shift in ecclesiology since the Counter-Reformation of the late sixteenth and early seventeenth centuries' (McBrien 2008: 121–2). However, while the encyclical marks the official reception of theological work on the mystical body motif, theological interest in the theme as an integrating category began to wane within a few years. Biblical and patristic studies had already been highlighting other themes, which were now proposed as necessary complements to overcoming the perceived limitations of the mystical body theme.

Since Trent the favoured Protestant theme of the 'People of God' had received little attention in Roman Catholic ecclesiology. In the nineteenth century, in ecclesiologies centred on the church as a perfect society, the notion of the People of God had certainly been employed, but merely to designate the laity over against the hierarchy. In the middle decades of the twentieth century, the theme was receiving greater attention from Roman Catholic biblical scholars and ecclesiologists, through a cross fertilization between biblical, patristic, liturgical, and ecumenical studies (Hahnenberg 2005: 14). Scholars highlighted the way that the notion brings to the fore the nature of the church as a community, and noted its overlap with other biblical themes such as the church within salvation history and the church's relationship with the reign of God.

One of the first to bring the theme of the church as the people of God to greater prominence in the twentieth century was the Benedictine Anscar Vonier (1875–1938), Abbot of Buckfast Abbey, with his 1937 theological study, *The People of God* (Vonier 1937). In 1940, as noted above, Mannes Dominikus Koster, in a deliberate attempt to highlight the inadequacies of a Mystical Body ecclesiology, used the rubric of the People of God as an integrating principle for his 'salvation history' oriented ecclesiology. In 1947 the Belgian biblical scholar Lucien Cerfaux published *La Théologie de l'Église suivant saint Paul* in which he outlined how 'the Jewish idea of "God's people" is basic to Paul's theology of the church' (Cerfaux 1959: 7). Cerfaux's work therefore showed 'that the concept of the (Mystical) Body was not, for St Paul, the *fundamental* concept to be used in *defining* the church' (Congar 1965b: 9; italics original). Likewise, liturgical studies were highlighting the frequency of 'People of God' language in liturgical texts (Schaut 1949), while patristic scholars were showing the importance of the theme in the ecclesiology of writers such as Ambrose of Milan (Eger 1947). Furthermore, studies on the notion of the People of God as a *pilgrim* people brought to the fore the eschatological dimension of the church throughout history (Grosche 1938). Parallel to this focus was greater attention to 'salvation history' and the journey of God's people through time. The Protestant biblical scholar Oscar Cullmann's 1946 work *Christus und die Zeit* (Cullmann 1964) was very influential on Catholic ecclesiologists in this regard.

Alongside the development of Mystical Body ecclesiology a related notion, that of the church as a sacrament, emerged. If the weakness of the former is that it can tend to blur the distinction between Christ and the church, then the strength of the latter is that it holds the two in tension: a sacrament is a symbol of something other than itself, even while it makes the other truly present. According to the analogy of the Incarnation, the model of 'church as sacrament' asserts that just as Christ is the sacrament of God, so the church is a sacrament of Christ. Once again, the reception of Möhler in this development is evident (O'Donnell 1996: 414). In his 1938 work *Catholicisme* de Lubac wrote: 'If Christ is the sacrament of God, the Church is for us the sacrament of Christ' (de Lubac 1988: 76); he would develop this further in his 1953 book *Méditation* (de Lubac 1999: 202–35). In the same year his fellow Jesuit Otto Semmelroth (1932–79) published a book on the church as 'the primordial sacrament', *Kirche als Ursakrament* (Semmelroth 1953). The previous year the Le Saulchoir Dominican student Edward Schillebeeckx (1914–2009) had published the first part of his dissertation *De sacramentele Heilseconomie* in which he delineated a notion of the sacraments in terms of the church itself as a sacrament of encounter with God. In 1960 Schillebeeckx published a summary of his thesis in German and French, later translated in English as *Christ, the Sacrament of Encounter with God* (Schillebeeckx 1963). Likewise, Karl Rahner wrote in 1942 of the church as 'the historico-sacramental permanent presence of the salvation reality of Christ' (Rahner 1967: 248). In 1960 he took up the theme in terms of his 1959 work on the theology of symbol: 'The Church is the abiding presence of that primal sacramental word of definitive grace, which Christ is in the world, effecting what is uttered by uttering it in sign. By the very fact of being in that way the enduring presence of Christ in the world, the Church is truly the fundamental sacrament, the well-spring of the sacraments in the strict sense' (Rahner 1963: 18; Rahner 1966).

Related to these developments concerning the church as Mystical Body and the church as sacrament is the related development of two other ecclesiological emphases: 'eucharistic ecclesiology' and 'communion ecclesiology'. De Lubac's *Corpus Mysticum*, first published in 1949, traced the terminological shift of the phrase 'mystical body' in reference first to the Eucharistic body and then to the ecclesial body. As he later noted in his 1953 *Méditation*: 'the relation between the Church and the Eucharist [is] as cause to each other. Each has been entrusted to the other, so to speak, by Christ; the

Church produces the Eucharist, but the Eucharist also produces the Church' (de Lubac 1999: 133). In 1962, on the eve of Vatican II, the Belgian Dominican scholar from Le Saulchoir, Jérôme Hamer (1916–96) published a study of the notion of 'communion' in ecclesiology, *L'Église est une communion*, using Pius XII's 1943 encyclical as his starting point: 'The principal effect of *Mystici Corporis* . . . was to give a new and decisive orientation to ecclesiology. With the weight of authority, it revived the great traditional idea of communion' (Hamer 1964: 13).

VATICAN II AND BEYOND

By the time Pope John XXIII called for an ecumenical council in 1959 many of these developments in ecclesiology had reached mature formulation. Nonetheless, under the supervision of the Holy Office, the draft schemas prepared for discussion at the council were still couched in the language and frameworks of neo-scholastic theology of the manualist tradition. Sebastian Tromp, as a member of the Preparatory Theological Commission, was a major drafter of the schema that was prepared on the church, *De Ecclesia*. This document is not only representative of the official ecclesiology of the Roman Catholic Church on the eve of the council, but it can be used to contrast the shifts made during the council, as traced in the various commentaries on the final documents: 'In many of these redactional histories, the differences between the texts officially prepared and the final texts are great enough for one to be able to speak at times of "break" or "discontinuity"' (Komonchak 2007: 32).

Like the exemplars of the manualist tradition, such as Louis Billot's *De Ecclesia Christi*, the draft *De Ecclesia* was apologetic in tone, defined the church as a perfect society, emphasized the visible nature of the church, and concentrated on aspects of ecclesial governance in terms of the model of monarchy, giving heightened importance to the papacy (Hastings 1968–9: 1: 28–34). The notion of *societas perfecta* shaped the mindsets of the bishops who came to the council. For example, the future Pope John Paul II, Bishop Karol Wojtyla of Krakow, would state in a speech to the council assembly during the second session: 'Although the notion "People of God" is in itself best for explaining the social nature of the Church, it does not seem best for describing the Church *in actu*, because it does not explicitly convey the idea of *societas perfecta* . . . The Church is a *societas perfecta* in the supernatural order, that is, disposing all the means necessary to attain the supernatural end' (Acta synodalia II, 3, 155–6; quoted in Granfield 1982: 3). However, in the final documents of Vatican II, the term *societas perfecta* is not to be found.

In the lead up to the council, Pope John's call for an *aggiornamento* ('updating') in the life of the Catholic Church raised expectations of what the council might achieve. In 1960 the Swiss theologian Hans Küng (1928–) published *Konzil und Wiedervereinigung* (*The Council and Reunion*, Küng 1961), 'perhaps the single most influential book in Vatican II's preparatory phase, because it alerted so many in the Catholic world to the possibilities for renewal and reform through the medium of the forthcoming council' (McBrien 2008: 138).

The council met in the European autumn for an average of two months each year from 1962 to 1965. Out of the approximately seventy draft schemas prepared for the bishops' consideration, the council assembly accepted for further discussion only the document on the Liturgy. All the others were basically rejected. By the close of the council, sixteen documents had been promulgated. Although two of these were devoted specifically to the church's life *ad intra* and *ad extra* (*Lumen Gentium* and *Gaudium et Spes*), all of the documents treat ecclesial themes in some way. While interpretation of the council over the last half-century has been controversial, often portrayed one-dimensionally either in terms of continuity or discontinuity, most commentators agree that Vatican II marks a significant shift in the Roman Catholic Church's self-understanding of its nature and mission, in terms very different from the juridical vision presented in the draft schemas that were originally presented to it.

One major factor at work in this dramatic shift was the creative dynamic between *aggiornamento* and *ressourcement* that soon became evident in the council's procedures. A collaborative relationship developed between the bishops and the theologians participating in the council, either as theological consultants to individual bishops or as experts (*periti*) serving on the commissions and sub-commissions entrusted with incorporating the bishops' wishes into drafting of the documents. Throughout the months that the council was sitting each year, many of the official *periti* from various theological disciplines would give talks around Rome to groups of bishops on matters related to the documents currently under discussion (Rush 2012a: 13–14). While some bishops would have already read widely translated books such as Adam's *Das Wesen des Katholizismus*, Guardini's *Vom Sinn der Kirche*, Congar's *Jalons pour une théologie du laïcat*, and de Lubac's *Méditation*, many were eager to learn more about the scholarship of recent decades to inform their deliberations on the council floor. Most of them had been educated in the shadow of the Modernist crisis and in a climate where 'Trent' was the norm for all things ecclesiological. Now, with exposure to the diversity of the Catholic tradition through the riches of *ressourcement* theology, the appeal to Trent's authority, which had so dominated the period of 'Tridentine Catholicism', was now recontextualized, as Joseph Komonchak notes: at Vatican II, 'the tradition was no longer read in the light of Trent; Trent was read in the light of the tradition' (Komonchak 2006: 76).

It is simplistic and inaccurate to state: 'Theologians were the engineers of the massive reforms that were initiated at Vatican II . . . In essence the theologians wrote the Vatican II documents that the bishops voted on and signed' (Swidler 1987: 189–90). The crucial leadership on many levels by the bishops and popes in the conciliar proceedings (especially key figures from northern Europe) show how the council was far from being 'engineered' by the theologians (Kobler 1989). Nevertheless, the theologians did play a critical and decisive role. Vatican II was, in the end, the result of 'an intense and fruitful collaboration between the church's teaching office, especially the bishops who were members of the Council, and theologians who served as experts (*periti*) at Vatican II' (Wicks 2009: 187).

Theologians were present at the council, in two senses. First, there were those significant figures from the history of theology who hovered over the discussions on particular topics, for instance Augustine, Aquinas, Bellarmine, Newman, Möhler, Mersch, Adam, Guardini, Teilhard de Chardin, to name just a few. Second, there were those who were actually there as *periti*, on drafting commissions or as advisers to individual bishops or national episcopal conferences. These scholars mediated to the bishops the decades of *ressourcement* theology of the preceding four decades. According to Leo Scheffczyk, 'the council was determined by the spirit and content of the theology preceding it. Therefore, in relation to the dogmatic motive, the question "Who determined the theology of the council?" can be answered by a competent representative of the theology following the First World War [Yves Congar]: "An intensive work . . . for a good thirty years." But it may also be added that in dogma the council neither would nor could go beyond the results of this work' (Scheffczyk 1981: 271).

Many of the significant figures over the previous decades now participated as *periti*: Chenu, Congar, de Lubac, Rahner, Semmelroth, Cerfaux, Schillebeeckx. Histories of the council and commentaries list the *periti* on the various drafting commissions and subcommissions (Vorgrimler 1967; Alberigo and Komonchak 1996–2004; Hünermann et al. 2004). One critically important theologian involved in the drafting of *Lumen Gentium* was the Belgian Gérard Philips (1899–1972), who from 1963 held the key role of vice-secretary for the conciliar Doctrinal Commission, where 'it was his particular genius to be able to find a way forward amid conflicting views to a consensus which was in no way a compromise' (O'Donnell 1996: 362). Given that role, and the fact that he was often directly involved in the drafting of text, his commentary on *Lumen Gentium* became especially authoritative (Philips 1967).

The particular contributions of key scholars could well be explored in greater detail— for example, that of Congar (Congar 2012) or Rahner (Vorgrimler 1986). However, the contribution of Henry de Lubac can be selected as an example. According to Karl-Heinz Neufeld, the influence of de Lubac (like that of others such as Congar and Rahner) went beyond his work on subcommissions; his reputation had gone before him.

> At the beginning of the Council, he was often mentioned. However, the other *periti* soon moved much more strongly into the limelight, and his work remained largely hidden, only rarely attracting attention. He influenced the Council [above all] by his works, which had long since been available in printed form. Many Fathers of the Council had studied books by him, from which they had adopted ideas that, during debates, were repeatedly referred to, positively or negatively. (Neufeld 1988: 90)

His 1953 work *Méditation sur l'Eglise* was particularly familiar to the bishops. The content of its chapter four—summed up in the axiom 'The Church makes the eucharist, but the eucharist makes the Church'—is echoed in the Eucharistic ecclesiology of *Sacrosanctum Concilium*. The title of the first chapter of that same book, 'The Church as Mystery', is echoed in the title of the first chapter of *Lumen Gentium*, 'The Mystery of the Church', a theme that de Lubac had developed in his earlier works *Catholicisme* and

Corpus Mysticum. The sixth chapter of *Méditation*, 'The Sacrament of Christ', found expression in *Lumen Gentium*'s notion of church as 'a kind of sacrament' (LG 1), 'the universal sacrament of salvation' (LG 48; GS 45).

While all the council's sixteen documents address ecclesiological themes in some way, they do not present a systematic treatise on the church. Oftentimes, some ecclesiological treatments contain statements that deftly juxtapose the juridical 'Bellarminian' ecclesiology with perspectives from the ecclesiologies of more recent decades. Accordingly, some interpreters propose that, in the end, *Lumen Gentium*, for example, contains two ecclesiologies, one juridical, the other a communion ecclesiology (Acerbi 1975). However, an intra-textual reading of *Lumen Gentium* reveals a richer interplay of elements. Furthermore, in reconstructing 'the ecclesiology' of the council, interpreters should not only interpret *Lumen Gentium* in terms of *Gaudium et Spes*—and vice versa—they should read all sixteen documents in the light of each other and each's particular compositional history. While the four constitutions (*Dei Verbum, Lumen Gentium, Gaudium et Spes,* and *Sacrosanctum Concilium*) function as the core, all sixteen documents must be interpreted as a corpus; they are to be interpreted *inter*textually (Rush 2004, 2012b).

The council and its documents propose a vision for the pastoral reform of the Roman Catholic Church in all areas of its life, worship, and doctrine (Antón 1987: 835–951; Baraúna 1965; Kloppenburg 1974; Komonchak 2000). Over the four years of its deliberations, the bishops of the council made their own many of the insights proposed by scholars in the first half of the twentieth century: a desire for communion among Christians and among the whole human race; a dialogic opening to ecumenical and interreligious perspectives and relationships, as well as to 'the world' and to the signs of God working in history; a historical-critical approach to biblical and theological research; a balancing of the visible and the invisible dimensions of the church by highlighting the church as mystery, sacrament, *communio*, and as the People of God, the Body of Christ, and the Temple of the Holy Spirit; a foregrounding of baptismal identity and the fundamental role of the laity in the mission of the church; the significance of local churches in Eucharistic *communio* constituting the one universal church; episcopal ordination and collegial communion of bishops with the bishop of Rome; participation in the three offices of Christ by all the faithful, not just the bishops; the significance of the *sensus fidelium* in ensuring the church's infallibility in believing; and so on.

Many of these elements are captured in two of the more influential interpretations of Vatican II's fundamental vision for reform. Karl Rahner interprets the council as initiating a shift from a Hellenistic model of church, which had reigned since the time of Constantine, to a truly catholic 'world-church' (Rahner 1981). The historian John O'Malley interprets the council as fundamentally a shift in ecclesial 'style'—from a top-down authoritarian, juridical style, to one that is dialogic in its relationships within the church and without (O'Malley 2008). Certainly Vatican II's vision of the church could well be described as 'a corrective to Bellarmine' (McBrien 1995: 448).

Already in the latter stages before the council's closure, portents of diverse trajectories in the council's later reception emerged, even among the so-called 'progressives'.

This tension was characterized in an encounter during Vatican II between the two *periti* Henri de Lubac and Hans Küng in St Peter's Basilica, after Küng had delivered a paper on 'Truthfulness in the Church'. De Lubac came up to him: 'One does not talk like that about the church. *Elle est quand-même notre mere*: after all, she's our mother!' (Küng 1995: 4).

The reception of the council has been variously evaluated. Writing twenty years after the council, Hermann Pottmeyer saw two phases in the council's reception: an initial phase of 'excitement', and a second phase (depending on one's point of view) either of 'disillusionment' or of 'truth and realism' (Pottmeyer 1987: 33–4; similarly, Kasper 1989: 166–7). De Lubac certainly saw an almost-immediate phase of 'decomposition' and 'crisis' (de Lubac 1969). Not insignificant in this reception is the fact that the half-century since Vatican II has been stamped by the twenty-six-year pontificate of Pope John Paul II (b. 1920; pope 1978–2005) and the eight-year pontificate of Benedict XVI (b. 1927; pope 2005–2013), both participants at Vatican II as bishop and as *peritus* respectively. Massimo Faggioli portrays the narrative of the council's reception in these years in terms of a 'battle' (Faggioli 2012). According to Richard Lennan, one reason for this problematic reception has been precisely the 400-year dominance of an unchanging, monolithic Catholicism: 'Contributing to this mixed character of the Council's reception was the fact that the church's history . . . left Catholics unskilled in discerning and negotiating possibilities for change. More specifically, there was no lived memory of how the dynamics of the *sensus fidei* might operate as the Council had advocated. Since descending models of authority had been so prominent, there was little awareness of either the theory or practice needed to nurture a communion of faith, including dealing with differences' (Lennan 2008: 243).

Twenty years after the council's close, John Paul II convoked a special sitting of the Synod of Bishops to consider the reception of Vatican II over that time. Its Final Report proposed a key for interpreting the council's documents: 'The ecclesiology of communion is the central and fundamental idea of the Council's documents' (Extraordinary Synod of Bishops 1986: C.1). However, despite this choice of a single hermeneutical key, the synod was not singular in its composition and theology. Avery Dulles saw among the attending bishops, and within the Synod's Final Report, three 'schools' of theology at work: a neo-Augustinian school with an eschatological and other-worldly viewpoint; a communitarian school, with an incarnational and this-worldly viewpoint; and a liberationist school, with a socio-economic-political albeit biblical viewpoint (Dulles 1987). The first was concerned to give priority to the transcendent and sacral emphases of the Augustinian stream of the Catholic tradition; the second, to the immanent and secular emphases of the Thomist and humanist streams; the third, to the social engagement and critical impulse of the biblical-prophetic stream. Since the 1985 Synod of Bishops the same typology could well be used heuristically to characterize the diversity and tensions within Roman Catholic ecclesiology, constituting, as it were, three models of church in the contemporary Roman Catholic Church.

It would seem that the election of the Argentinian Jorge Bergoglio (b. 1936) as Pope Francis in March 2013 has ushered in what could be called a third phase in the reception of Vatican II, bringing together in a new form the phases of 'excitement' and 'disappointment'/'realism'. Here, however, the 'realism' is the plight of the poor and the tenderness of God's mercy for moral failures. This new phase also seems to be marking a shift in balance in church life by giving a different weighting to the various streams of the Catholic tradition. If the neo-Augustinian school's emphasis on divine transcendence and suspicion of the world characterized the pontificates of John Paul II and Benedict XVI, then the incarnational and social justice emphases of the neo-Thomist and prophetic traditions are now being given greater emphasis by Francis. Determined to make the vision of Vatican II his benchmark, Francis has spoken of the dangers of over-intellectualizing the faith and of the church being too self-referential, that is, focusing too much on itself, rather than being missionary. Attempting to balance *communio* and *ad intra* concerns, Francis is equally *ad extra* and mission oriented, with a particular priority given to those who are physically and spiritually poor and marginalized. He has a strong focus on the pneumatological dimensions of the church and on a baptism ecclesiology: the church is 'the Temple of the Holy Spirit, the Temple in which God works, the Temple in which, with the gift of Baptism, each one of us is a living stone. This tells us that no one in the Church is useless ... we are all necessary for building this Temple! No one is secondary. No one is the most important person in the Church, we are all equal in God's eyes. Some of you might say "Listen, Mr Pope, you are not our equal". Yes, I am like each one of you, we are all equal, we are brothers and sisters!' (Pope Francis 3 July 2013).

As this third phase of Vatican II's reception unfolds, at least ten issues remain on the ecclesiological agenda. They could be set out as ten ecclesial relationships, *ad intra* and *ad extra*. Each relationship is between two ecclesial terms, groups, or roles in the church—which Vatican II wished to hold in dynamic tension, often in an innovative way (in the light of previous church teaching). All of these relationships were given a new orientation at Vatican II. The relationships: between the dignity and conscience of the individual baptized believer and the whole community of believers; between the interrelated centripetal and centrifugal forces of *communio* and *missio*; between the church *ad intra* (in its inner life) and the church *ad extra* (the church engaging with other Christians, believers of other religions, non-believers, and ultimately with a suffering world); between the local church and the universal church; between legitimate plurality in the faith and unity in the faith; between the whole People of God and the hierarchy; between lay people and the ordained; between the college of bishops and the bishop of Rome (and his administrative arm, the Roman curia); between the *sensus fidelium* and the magisterium; and between theologians and the magisterium (as modelled within Vatican II itself).

The history of Roman Catholic ecclesiology since Vatican II has seen many of these issues addressed (Antón 1987: 952–1180; 1988). In all of them, however, the balance—as the council envisaged them—has yet to be realized, whether it be as the faithful experience it in the church's daily ecclesial life, or in the ecclesiological syntheses of theologians, or in the hierarchy's implicit and explicit promotion (or otherwise) and official teaching regarding all these issues.

More than a half-century after the council, new questions continue to be posed to the tradition regarding the church's nature, mission, structures, and ministries—questions that Vatican II did not address, nor could even have envisaged at that time. In an interview soon after the close of Vatican II, Yves Congar stated: 'The danger now is that we shall cease to search and simply go on drawing on the inexhaustible reserves of Vatican II . . . It would be a betrayal of the *aggiornamento* if this were regarded as permanently fixed in the texts of Vatican II' (quoted in Schoof 1970: 265). The same spirit of *ressourcement* and *aggiornamento* that the bishops embraced at Vatican II continues to challenge the church, demanding that it address these new questions with similar fidelity and creativity.

REFERENCES

Acerbi, Antonio (1975). *Due ecclesiologie: Ecclesiologia guiridica ed ecclesiologia di comunione nella 'Lumen Gentium'*. Bologna: Edizioni Dehoniane.

Adam, Karl (1997). *The Spirit of Catholicism*. New York: Crossroad.

Alberigo, Giuseppe and Komonchak, Joseph A. (eds) (1996–2004). *History of Vatican II*. 5 vols. Maryknoll: Orbis.

Antón, Angel (1987). *El misterio de la Iglesia: Evolución histórica de las ideas eclesiológicas, II. De la apologética de la Iglesia-Sociedad a la teología de la Iglesia-misterio en el Vaticano II y en el posconcilio*. Madrid: La Editorial Católica.

Antón, Angel (1988). 'Postconciliar Ecclesiology: Expectations, Results, and Prospects for the Future'. In René Latourelle (ed.), *Vatican II: Assessment and Perspectives. Twenty-Five Years After (1962–1987). Volume 1*. New York: Paulist, 407–38.

Aquinas, Thomas (1966). *Summa Theologiae. Latin Text and English Translation, Introductions, Notes, Appendices, and Glossaries*. Volume 28. New York: Blackfriars and McGraw-Hill.

Baraúna, Guilherme (ed.) (1965). *La Chiesa del Vaticano II: Studi e commenti intorno alla Costituzione dommatica 'Lumen Gentium'*. Firenze: Vallecchi Editore.

Bellarmino, Roberto (1586–93). *Disputationes de controversiis Christianae fidei adversus huius temporis haereticos*, 3 vols. Ingolstadt.

Bluett, J. J. (1942). 'The Mystical Body of Christ: 1890–1940'. *Theological Studies* 3: 261–89.

Boersma, Hans (2009). *Nouvelle Théologie and Sacramental Ontology: A Return to Mystery*. Oxford: Oxford University Press.

Bourdon, Hilaire (1903). *The Church and the Future: l'Eglise et l'avenir*. Abridged and re-arranged. Edinburgh: Turnbull and Spears.

Carlen, Claudia (ed.) (1981). *The Papal Encyclicals*. 5 vols. Wilmington, NC: McGrath.

Cerfaux, Lucien (1959). *The Church in the Theology of St Paul*. 2nd edn. Edinburgh: Thomas Nelson.

Chenu, Marie-Dominique (1937). *Une école de théologie: Le Saulchoir*. Kain-lez-Tournai: Le Saulchoir.

Congar, Yves (1939). *Divided Christendom: A Catholic Study of the Problem of Reunion*. London: G. Bles.

Congar, Yves (1962). *The Mystery of the Temple: or, The Manner of God's Presence to his Creatures from Genesis to the Apocalypse*. Westminster, MD: Newman.

Congar, Yves (1965a). *Lay People in the Church: A Study for a Theology of Laity*. Trans. Donald Attwater. 2nd rev. edn. Westminster, MD: Newman.

Congar, Yves (1965b). 'The Church: The People of God'. *Concilium* 1.1: 7–19.

Congar, Yves (1971). *Die Lehre von der Kirche: Vom abendländischen Schisma bis zur Gegenwart*. Trans. Hans Sayer. *Handbuch der Dogmengeschichte*. Bd 3, Faszikel 3d. Freiburg: Herder.

Congar, Yves (2011). *True and False Reform in the Church*. Rev. edn. Collegeville, MN: Liturgical.

Congar, Yves (2012). *My Journal of the Council*. Collegeville, MN: Liturgical.

Cullmann, Oscar (1964). *Christ and Time: The Primitive Christian Conception of Time and History*. Rev. edn. Philadelphia: Westminster (German original 1946).

Daly, Gabriel (1980). *Transcendence and Immanence: A Study in Catholic Modernism and Integralism*. Oxford: Oxford University Press.

de Lubac, Henri (1969). 'The Church in Crisis'. *Theology Digest* 17: 312–25.

de Lubac, Henri (1988). *Catholicism: Christ and the Common Destiny of Man*. San Francisco: Ignatius.

de Lubac, Henri (1999). *The Splendor of the Church*. San Francisco: Ignatius.

de Lubac, Henri (2006). *Corpus Mysticum: The Eucharist and the Church in the Middle Ages. Historical Survey*. Ed. Laurence Paul Hemming and Susan Frank Parsons. London: SCM.

Denzinger, Heinrich (2012). *Compendium of Creeds, Definitions, and Declarations on Matters of Faith and Morals*. Peter Hünermann et al. (eds), 43rd, rev. and enl. edn. San Francisco: Ignatius.

Drey, Johann Sebastian (1994). *Brief Introduction to the Study of Theology with Reference to the Scientific Standpoint and the Catholic System*. Notre Dame, IN: University of Notre Dame Press.

Dulles, Avery (1987). 'The Reception of Vatican II at the Extraordinary Synod of 1985'. In Giuseppe Alberigo, Jean Pierre Jossua, and Joseph A. Komonchak (eds), *The Reception of Vatican II*. Washington, DC: Catholic University of America Press, 349–63.

Dulles, Avery (1990). 'The Threefold Office in Newman's Ecclesiology'. In Ian T. Ker and Alan G. Hill (eds), *Newman after a Hundred Years*. Oxford: Clarendon, 375–99.

Dulles, Avery (2002). *Models of the Church*. Expanded edn. New York: Image Books Doubleday.

Dulles, Avery (2009). 'Authority in the Church'. In Ian Ker and Terrence Merrigan (eds), *The Cambridge Companion to John Henry Newman*. Cambridge: Cambridge University Press, 170–88.

Eger, J. (1947). *Salus gentium*. University of Munich: Unpublished dissertation.

Extraordinary Synod of Bishops (1986). 'Final Report'. *Documents of the Extraordinary Synod of Bishops November 28–December 8, 1985*. Homebush, Australia: St Paul, 17–51.

Faggioli, Massimo (2012). *Vatican II: The Battle for Meaning*. New York: Paulist.

Fehr, Wayne L. (1981). *The Birth of the Catholic Tübingen School: The Dogmatics of Johann Sebastian Drey*. Chico, CA: Scholars.

Flynn, Gabriel and Murray, Paul D. (eds) (2011). *Ressourcement: A Movement for Renewal in Twentieth-Century Catholic Theology*. Oxford: Oxford University Press.

Fuchs, J. (1969). 'Origines d'une Trilogie ecclésiologique à l'epoque rationaliste de la Theologie'. *Revue de sciences philosophiques et théologiques* 53: 186–211.

Garrigou-Lagrange, Réginald (1946). 'La Nouvelle Théologie où va-t-elle?' *Angelicum* 23: 126–45.

Gasser, Vinzenz (2008). *The Gift of Infallibility: The Official Relatio on Infallibility of Bishop Vincent Gasser at Vatican Council I*. Ed. James T. O'Connor. 2nd updated edn. San Francisco: Ignatius.

Granfield, Patrick (1979). 'The Church as *Societas Perfecta* in the Schemata of Vatican I'. *Church History* 48: 431–46.

Granfield, Patrick (1982). 'The Rise and Fall of *Societas Perfecta*'. *Concilium* 157: 3–8.

Gratsch, Edward J. (1975). *Where Peter Is: A Survey of Ecclesiology*. New York: Alba House.

Gray, Janette (2011). 'Marie-Dominique Chenu and Le Saulchoir: A Stream of Catholic Renewal'. In Gabriel Flynn and Paul D. Murray (eds), *Ressourcement: A Movement for Renewal in Twentieth-Century Catholic Theology*. Oxford: Oxford University Press, 205–18.

Grosche, Robert (1938). *Pilgernde Kirche*. Freiburg im Breisgau: Herder.

Guardini, Romano (1935). *The Church and the Catholic, and The Spirit of the Liturgy*. London: Sheed & Ward.

Guardini, Romano (2001). *The End of the Modern World*. 2nd edn. Wilmington, DE: ISI Books.

Hahnenberg, Edward P. (2005). 'The Mystical Body of Christ and Communion Ecclesiology: Historical Parallels'. *Irish Theological Quarterly* 70: 3–30.

Haight, Roger (2004). *Christian Community in History. Volume 2: Comparative Ecclesiology*. New York: Continuum.

Hall, Douglas John (1999). '"The Great War" and the Theologians'. In Gregory Baum (ed.), *The Twentieth Century: A Theological Overview*. Maryknoll, NY: Orbis, 3–13.

Hamer, Jérôme (1964). *The Church is a Communion*. London: Geoffrey Chapman.

Hanvey, James (2005). 'In the Presence of Love: The Pneumatological Realization of the Economy: Yves Congar's *Le Mystère du Temple*'. *International Journal of Systematic Theology* 7.4: 383–98.

Hardon, John A. (1966). 'Robert Bellarmine's Concept of the Church'. In John R. Sommerfeldt (ed.), *Studies in Medieval Culture*. Kalamazoo, MI: Western Michigan University. Vol. 2: 120–7.

Hastings, Adrian (1968–9). *A Concise Guide to the Documents of the Second Vatican Council*. 2 vols. London: Darton Longman & Todd.

Himes, Michael J. (1997). *Ongoing Incarnation: Johann Adam Möhler and the Beginnings of Modern Ecclesiology*. New York: Crossroad.

Himes, Michael J. (2000). 'The Development of Ecclesiology: Modernity to the Twentieth Century'. In Peter C. Phan (ed.), *The Gift of the Church: A Textbook on Ecclesiology in Honor of Patrick Granfield, O.S.B.* Collegeville, MN: Liturgical, 45–67.

Hünermann, Peter, Hilberath, Bernd Jochen, and Bausenhart, Guido (2004). *Herders theologischer Kommentar zum Zweiten Vatikanischen Konzil*. 5 vols. Freiburg: Herder.

Iserloh, Erwin (1981). 'Movements within the Church and their Spirituality'. In Hubert Jedin, Konrad Repgen, and John Dolan (eds), *The Church in the Modern Age: History of the Church*. New York: Crossroad, vol. 10, 299–336.

Kasper, Walter (1962). *Die Lehre von der Tradition in der römischen Schule: Giovanni Perrone, Carlo Passaglia, Clemens Schrader*. Freiburg: Herder.

Kasper, Walter (1989). 'The Continuing Challenge of the Second Vatican Council: The Hermeneutics of the Conciliar Statements'. *Theology and Church*. New York: Crossroad, 166–76.

Ker, Ian (2009). 'The Church as Communion'. In Ian Ker and Terrence Merrigan (eds), *The Cambridge Companion to John Henry Newman*. Cambridge: Cambridge University Press, 137–55.

Kloppenburg, Bonaventure (1974). *The Ecclesiology of Vatican II*. Chicago: Franciscan Herald Press.

Kobler, J. F. (1989). 'Were Theologians the Engineers of Vatican II?' *Gregorianum* 70: 233–50.

Komonchak, Joseph A. (1990). 'Theology and Culture at Mid-Century: The Example of Henri de Lubac'. *Theological Studies* 51: 579–602.

Komonchak, Joseph A. (1995). 'Concepts of Communion: Past and Present'. *Cristianesimo nella Storia* 16: 321–40.

Komonchak, Joseph A. (2000). 'The Significance of Vatican Council II for Ecclesiology'. In Peter C. Phan (ed.), *The Gift of the Church: A Textbook on Ecclesiology in Honor of Patrick Granfield, O.S.B.* Collegeville, MN: Liturgical, 69–92.

Komonchak, Joseph A. (2006). 'The Council of Trent at the Second Vatican Council'. In Raymond F. Bulman and Frederick J. Parrella (eds), *From Trent to Vatican II: Historical and Theological Investigations*. New York: Oxford University Press, 61–80.

Komonchak, Joseph A. (2007). 'Vatican II as an "Event"'. In David G. Schultenover (ed.), *Vatican II: Did Anything Happen?* New York: Continuum, 24–51.

Koster, Mannes Dominikus (1940). *Ekklesiologie im Werden*. Paderborn: Bonifacius-Druckerei.

Koster, Mannes Dominikus (1948). *Die Firmung im Glaubenssinn der Kirche*. Regensberg.

Krieg, Robert A. (1992). *Karl Adam: Catholicism in German Culture*. London: University of Notre Dame Press.

Krieg, Robert A. (1997). *Romano Guardini: A Precursor of Vatican II*. Notre Dame, IN: University of Notre Dame Press.

Küng, Hans (1961). *The Council and Reunion*. London: Sheed and Ward.

Küng, Hans (1995). *Christianity: Its Essence and History*. London: SCM.

Lennan, Richard (1995). *The Ecclesiology of Karl Rahner*. New York: Oxford University Press.

Lennan, Richard (2008). 'Roman Catholic Ecclesiology'. In Gerard Mannion and Lewis S. Mudge (eds), *The Routledge Companion to the Christian Church*. New York: Routledge, 234–50.

Loisy, Alfred (1988). *The Gospel and the Church*. Buffalo, NY: Prometheus.

McBrien, Richard P. (2008). *The Church: The Evolution of Catholicism*. New York: HarperOne.

McCarren, Gerard H. (2009). 'Development of Doctrine'. In Ian Ker and Terrence Merrigan (eds), *The Cambridge Companion to John Henry Newman*. Cambridge: Cambridge University Press, 118–36.

McPartlan, Paul (1993). *The Eucharist Makes the Church: Henri de Lubac and John Zizioulas in Dialogue*. Edinburgh: T. & T. Clark.

Mansi, Giovanni Domenico (1960). *Sacrorum conciliorum, nova et amplissima collectio*. 54 vols. Graz: Akademische Druck-u. Verlagsanstalt.

Mersch, Emile (1938). *The Whole Christ: The Historical Development of the Doctrine of the Mystical Body in Scripture and Tradition*. Trans. John R. Kelly. Milwaukee, WI: The Bruce Publishing Company.

Mettepenningen, Jürgen (2010). *Nouvelle Théologie—New Theology: Inheritor of Modernism, Precursor of Vatican II*. London: T & T Clark.

Minnich, Nelson H. (1998). 'The Voice of Theologians in General Councils from Pisa to Trent'. *Theological Studies* 59: 420–41.

Moeller, Charles (1966). 'History of *Lumen Gentium*'s Structure and Ideas'. In John H. Miller (ed.), *Vatican II: An Interfaith Appraisal*. Notre Dame, IN: University of Notre Dame Press, 123–52.

Möhler, Johann Adam (1996). *Unity in the Church or the Principle of Catholicism: Presented in the Spirit of the Church Fathers of the First Three Centuries*. Washington, DC: The Catholic University of America Press.

Möhler, Johann Adam (1997). *Symbolism: Exposition of the Doctrinal Differences between Catholics and Protestants as Evidenced by Their Symbolical Writings*. New York: Crossroad.

Neufeld, Karl-Heinz (1988). 'In the Service of the Council: Bishops and Theologians at the Second Vatican Council (for Cardinal Henri de Lubac on His Ninetieth Birthday)'. In René Latourelle (ed.), *Vatican II: Assessment and Perspectives. Twenty-Five Years After (1962–1987)*. Vol. 1. New York: Paulist, 74–105.

Newman, John Henry (1911). 'Preface to the Third Edition'. *The Via Media of the Anglican Church: Illustrated in Lectures, Letters, and Tracts Written between 1830 and 1841. Volume 1: Lectures on the Prophetical Office of the Church Viewed Relatively to Romanism and Popular Protestantism*. London: Longmans, Green, and Co., xv–xciv.

Newman, John Henry (1962). *On Consulting the Faithful in Matters of Doctrine*. New York: Sheed & Ward.

Newman, John Henry (1989). *An Essay on the Development of Christian Doctrine*. 6th edn. Notre Dame, IN: University of Notre Dame Press.

O'Connell, Marvin R. (1994). *Critics on Trial: An Introduction to the Catholic Modernist Crisis*. Washington, DC: The Catholic University of America Press.

O'Donnell, Christopher (1996). *Ecclesia: A Theological Encyclopedia of the Church*. Collegeville, MN: Liturgical.

O'Malley, John W. (2000). *Trent and All That: Renaming Catholicism in the Early Modern Era*. Cambridge, MA: Harvard University Press.

O'Malley, John W. (2006). 'Trent and Vatican II: Two Styles of Church'. In Raymond F. Bulman and Frederick J. Parrella (eds), *From Trent to Vatican II: Historical and Theological Investigations*. New York: Oxford University Press, 301–20.

O'Malley, John W. (2008). *What Happened at Vatican II*. Cambridge, MA: Belknap Press of Harvard University Press.

O'Malley, John W. (2013). *Trent: What Happened at the Council*. Cambridge, MA: Belknap Press of Harvard University Press.

Oakley, Francis (2003). *The Conciliarist Tradition: Constitutionalism in the Catholic Church, 1300–1870*. Oxford: Oxford University Press.

Ott, Ludwig (1954). *Fundamentals of Catholic Dogma*. St. Louis, MO: Herder.

Philips, Gérard (1967). *L'Église et son mystère au II Concile du Vatican: histoire, texte et commentaire de la Constitution Lumen Gentium*. Paris: Desclée.

Pope Francis (3 July 2013). 'Where We Are All Equal and No One Is Useless'. *L'Osservatore Romano*: 3.

Pottmeyer, Hermann J. (1987). 'A New Phase in the Reception of Vatican II: Twenty Years of Interpretation of the Council'. In Giuseppe Alberigo, Jean Pierre Jossua, and Joseph A. Komonchak (eds), *The Reception of Vatican II*. Washington, DC: The Catholic University of America Press, 27–43.

Prodi, Paolo (2010). *Il paradigma tridentino: un'epoca della storia della Chiesa*. Brescia: Morcelliana.

Rahner, Karl (1962). 'Membership of the Church According to the Teaching of Pius XII's Encyclical "Mystici Corporis Christi" '. *Theological Investigations*. Vol. 2. Baltimore: Helicon, 1–88.

Rahner, Karl (1963). *The Church and the Sacraments*. Freiburg: Herder.

Rahner, Karl (1966). 'The Theology of the Symbol'. *Theological Investigations*. Vol. 4. London: Darton, Longman & Todd, 221–52.

Rahner, Karl (1967). 'Priestly Existence'. *Theological Investigations*. Vol. 3. London: Darton, Longman and Todd, 239–62.

Rahner, Karl (1981). 'Basic Theological Interpretation of the Second Vatican Council'. *Theological Investigations*. Vol. 20. London: Darton, Longman & Todd, 77–89.

Rousseau, Olivier (1965). 'La costituzione nel quadro dei movimenti rinnovatori di teologia e di pastorale degli ultimi decenni'. In Guilherme Baraúna (ed.), *La Chiesa del Vaticano II: Studi e commenti intorno alla Costituzione dommatica 'Lumen Gentium'*. Firenze: Vallecchi Editore, 111–30.

Rush, Ormond (2003). 'The Offices of Christ, *Lumen Gentium* and the People's Sense of the Faith'. *Pacifica*, 16: 137–52.

Rush, Ormond (2004). *Still Interpreting Vatican II: Some Hermeneutical Principles*. New York: Paulist Press.

Rush, Ormond (2012a). 'The Australian Bishops of Vatican II: Participation and Reception'. In Neil Ormerod, Ormond Rush, et al. (eds), *Vatican II: The Reception and Implementation in the Australian Church*. Melbourne: John Garrett, 4–19.

Rush, Ormond (2012b). 'Toward a Comprehensive Interpretation of the Council and its Documents', *Theological Studies* 73: 547–69.

Schatz, Klaus (1996). *Papal Primacy: From Its Origins to the Present*. Collegeville, MN: Liturgical.

Schaut, A. (1949). 'Die Kirche als Volk Gottes: Selbstaussagen der Kirche im römischen Messbuch'. *Benediktinische Monatsschrift* 25: 187–95.

Scheffczyk, Leo (1981). 'Main Lines of the Development of Theology between the First World War and the Second Vatican Council'. In Hubert Jedin, Konrad Repgen, and John Dolan (eds), *The Church in the Modern Age. History of the Church*. Vol. 10. New York: Crossroad, 260–98.

Schillebeeckx, Edward (1963). *Christ, the Sacrament of Encounter with God*. London: Sheed and Ward.

Schoof, Mark (1970). *A Survey of Catholic Theology 1800–1970*. New York: Paulist.

Schüssler Fiorenza, Francis (2011). 'Systematic Theology: Task and Methods'. In Francis Schüssler Fiorenza and John P. Galvin (eds), *Systematic Theology: Roman Catholic Perspectives*. 2nd and revised edn. Minneapolis: Fortress, 1–78.

Semmelroth, Otto (1953). *Die Kirche als Ursakrament*. Frankfurt a.M.: Knecht.

Sullivan, Francis A. (2009). 'Infallibility'. In Ian Ker and Terrence Merrigan (eds), *The Cambridge Companion to John Henry Newman*. Cambridge: Cambridge University Press, 156–69.

Swidler, Leonard (1987). 'The Context: Breaking Reform by Breaking Theologians and Religious'. In Hans Küng and Leonard Swidler (eds), *The Church in Anguish: Has the Vatican Betrayed Vatican II?* San Francisco: Harper & Row, 189–92.

Tagle, Luis Antonio (2004). *Episcopal Collegiality and Vatican II: The Influence of Paul VI*. Manila, Philippines: Loyola School of Theology.

Tanner, Norman P. (1990). *Decrees of the Ecumenical Councils*. 2 vols. Washington, DC: Georgetown University Press.

Tanner, Norman (2011). *New Short History of the Catholic Church*. Tunbridge Wells: Burns & Oates.

Tromp, Sebastian (1937–1972). *Corpus Christi quod est Ecclesia*. 4 vols. Romae: Universitas Gregoriana.

Vonier, Anscar (1937). *The People of God*. London: Burns, Oates & Washburn.

Vorgrimler, Herbert (ed.) (1967). *Commentary on the Documents of Vatican II*. 5 vols. London: Burns & Oates.

Vorgrimler, Herbert (1986). 'Karl Rahner: The Theologian's Contribution'. In Alberic Stacpoole (ed.), *Vatican II: By Those Who Were There*. London: Geoffrey Chapman, 32–46.

Wicks, Jared (2009). 'Theologians at Vatican Council II'. *Doing Theology*. New York: Paulist Press, 187–223.

SUGGESTED READING

Antón, Angel (1987). *El misterio de la Iglesia: Evolución histórica de las ideas eclesiológicas, II. De la apologética de la Iglesia-Sociedad a la teología de la Iglesia-misterio en el Vaticano II y en el posconcilio*. Madrid: La Editorial Católica.

Baraúna, Guilherme (ed.) (1965). *La Chiesa del Vaticano II: Studi e commenti intorno alla Costituzione dommatica 'Lumen Gentium'*. Firenze: Vallecchi Editore.

Bulman, Raymond F. and Parrella, Frederick J. (eds) (2006). *From Trent to Vatican II: Historical and Theological Investigations*. New York: Oxford University Press.

Congar, Yves (1970). *L'Église: De saint Augustin à l'époque moderne*. Paris: Éditions du Cerf. German translation: (1971). *Die Lehre von der Kirche: Vom abendländischen Schisma bis zur Gegenwart* Trans. Hans Sayer, *Handbuch der Dogmengeschichte*. Bd 3, Faszikel 3d. Freiburg: Herder.

Cooke, Bernard J. (1976). *Ministry to Word and Sacraments: History and Theology*. Philadelphia: Fortress.

Doyle, Dennis M. (2000). *Communion Ecclesiology: Vision and Versions*. Maryknoll, NY: Orbis.

Dulles, Avery (1989). 'A Half Century of Ecclesiology'. *Theological Studies* 50: 419–42.

Dulles, Avery (2002). *Models of the Church*. Expanded edn. New York: Image Books Doubleday.

Flynn, Gabriel and Murray, Paul D. (eds) (2011). *Ressourcement: A Movement for Renewal in Twentieth-Century Catholic Theology*. Oxford: Oxford University Press.

Gaillardetz, Richard (2006). *The Church in the Making: Lumen Gentium, Christus Dominus, Orientalium Ecclesiarum*. New York: Paulist.

Gratsch, Edward J. (1975). *Where Peter Is: A Survey of Ecclesiology*. New York: Alba House.

Haight, Roger (2004). *Christian Community in History. Volume 2: Comparative Ecclesiology*. New York: Continuum.

Hinze, Bradford (2010). 'Roman Catholic Theology: Tübingen'. In David Fergusson (ed.), *The Blackwell Companion to Nineteenth-Century Theology*. Chichester; Malden, MA: Wiley-Blackwell, 187–213.

Kloppenburg, Bonaventure (1974). *The Ecclesiology of Vatican II*. Chicago: Franciscan Herald Press.

Lennan, Richard (2004). *Risking the Church: The Challenges of Catholic Faith*. New York: Oxford University Press.

McBrien, Richard P. (2008). *The Church: The Evolution of Catholicism*. New York: HarperOne.

O'Donnell, Christopher (1996). *Ecclesia: A Theological Encyclopedia of the Church*. Collegeville, MN: Liturgical.

Phan, Peter C. (ed.) (2000). *The Gift of the Church: A Textbook on Ecclesiology in Honor of Patrick Granfield, OSB*. Collegeville, MN: Liturgical.

Prusak, Bernard P. (2004). *The Church Unfinished: Ecclesiology through the Centuries*. New York: Paulist.

Ratzinger, Joseph (1988). 'The Ecclesiology of the Second Vatican Council'. *Church, Ecumenism and Politics: New Essays in Ecclesiology*. Slough: St Paul, 3–28.

Ratzinger, Joseph (2009). *Theological Highlights of Vatican II*. New York: Paulist.

Schüssler Fiorenza, Francis (2000). 'Vatican II and the *Aggiornamento* of Roman Catholic Theology'. In James C. Livingston et al. (eds), *Modern Christian Thought. Volume 2: The Twentieth Century.* 2nd edn. Upper Saddle River, NJ: Prentice Hall, 233–71.

Wood, Susan (2011). 'Continuity and Development in Roman Catholic Ecclesiology'. *Ecclesiology* 7/2: 147–72.

CHAPTER 13

BAPTIST CONCEPTS OF THE CHURCH AND THEIR ANTECEDENTS

PAUL S. FIDDES

BAPTIST ecclesiology shows a substantial heritage from the English Separatist tradition. Its debt to the continental Anabaptist tradition is more contested, and is certainly more limited. Both forms of ecclesiology, however, are clearly *antecedents* to a Baptist ecclesiology that has played a prominent part in the life of dissent and nonconformity in England and Wales since the early seventeenth century; this in turn has had a formative role in the shape of Baptist churches existing in 124 countries throughout the world today, which are linked through the Baptist World Alliance into a major Christian global communion. There is no doubt that the Separatist tradition is a direct influence on the development of Baptist ecclesiology, and that Baptist life is also more widely an heir of the radical Puritan tradition following the English Reformation. How far the Anabaptist tradition is a shaping force on Baptist thought, or whether there is merely an illuminating parallel or analogue between groups who similarly wished to restore what they regarded as a biblical pattern of the church, is a matter of dispute. This chapter intends to bring three ecclesiologies into conversation with each other—Anabaptist, Separatist, Baptist—not so much to resolve the question of genealogy, as to discover what further light might be shed on each of them through this interaction. The place to begin to stage the conversation is with a sketch of what might be meant by 'Baptist ecclesiology'.

COVENANT AND THE RULE OF CHRIST

To get to the heart of Baptist ecclesiology, we need only look to a Baptist confession of 1644, the so-called 'London Confession' to which seven Particular Baptist churches in the city subscribed. 'Particular' Baptists restricted the scope of Christ's atonement to those elected by God 'in particular', while 'General' Baptists believed that it was 'generally' effective for all human persons. The two streams of Baptist life in England, Wales, and Ireland were united in 1891 into the present Baptist Union of Great Britain (now without Northern Irish Baptists). This confession contains two tensions in authority which have been characteristic of Baptist ecclesiology since the time of the congregation led by John Smyth and Thomas Helwys in 1609, and which still persist today. The first is a tension between the pastoral oversight exercised by the whole church community and the oversight committed to its 'officers' or spiritual leaders. As article 44 expresses it:

> And as Christ for the keeping of this Church in holy and orderly Communion, placeth some special men over the Church, who by their office are to govern, oversee, visit, watch; so likewise for the better keeping thereof in all places, by all the members, he hath given authority, and laid duty upon all, to watch over one another. (*Confession* 1644: 168)

Spiritual discipline, called variously 'overseeing' or 'watching over' the congregation, was regarded by Baptists in the first century of their life (along with more radical Puritans in the Church of England) as a mark of the church to be placed alongside the two Reformation marks of true preaching of the word and administration of the sacraments. It included admission to membership, the calling of ministers, pastoral care, rebuke of error, suspension from sharing in the Lord's Table due to behaviour unbecoming of a disciple, and excommunication in severe cases. Its perceived absence in the Church of England was seen as evidence of the decline of the established church and a reason for separation from it. Article 44 describes a dynamic view of authority in the community, in which oversight flows to and fro between the personal and the communal; the responsibility of 'watching over' the church belongs both to *all* the members gathered in a church meeting to find the mind or purpose of Christ, and to the spiritual leader(s). The London Confession expresses this duality without any apparent sense of strain: while all members agree to 'watch over' (oversee) each other spiritually, they also recognize that Christ has called some to an office in which they have a special responsibility for oversight. But this tension is not resolved by any rule or formula defining the limits of oversight in each case. The two kinds of oversight are left fluid and open, requiring a relationship of trust. While 'discipline' among Baptists of modern times has modulated into general pastoral care, the general tension in authority remains between ministers and congregation and gives a Baptist congregation its recognizable tone.

The second ecclesial tension discernible in the London Confession is between the local congregation and the associating of churches together. The seven churches, scattered throughout London, confess in article 47 that

> ... although the particular Congregations be distinct and severall Bodies, every one a compact and knit Citie in it selfe; yet are they all to walk by one and the same Rule, and by all meanes convenient to have the counsell and help of one another in all

needfull affaires of the Church, as members of one body in the common faith under Christ their onely head. (*Confession* 1644: 168–9)

Each congregation makes decisions for its own faith and life, and yet together they are members of 'one body', observing 'one and the same Rule'. The Rule is that of Christ, not an ecclesial rule or canon law defining areas of authority, and is discerned on the basis of Scripture by assembling together. Like authority within the local congregation, this tension can only be lived within by trust. Both tensions are in fact held within a framework of 'covenant', or an agreement made between members of the church, and between those members and God in Christ. As the minister of the first Baptist congregation gathered in Amsterdam, John Smyth, defined it: 'A visible communion of Saincts is of two, three or more Saincts joyned together by covenant with God & themselves …' (Smyth 1607: 252). Separate congregations could also be envisaged as being in covenant with each other. While the London Confession does not explicitly use the word 'covenant' it applies the covenant language of 'walking together' for the associating of the congregations in 'one body' and 'one rule'.

The two characteristic tensions of authority, in congregation and association, could (and still can) issue in a lapsing towards one side of the polarity or the other—for example towards the autonomy of the local church, to the authoritarianism of leaders, or to the tyranny of the majority of the congregation. If, however, the tensions are held in bonds of trust, they can be truly creative, and they have been worked out in ways which are contextual for each age in which Baptists have lived.

We can identify two basic dimensions of this Baptist covenant ecclesiology in a local church. First and central to the idea of covenant is the rule of Christ, who calls a church into covenant. Though it is essential that faith be voluntary, in response to the initiating grace of God, the church is not regarded as a merely voluntary society, since it gathers in obedience to Christ as the covenant-maker; it is 'gathered' in the sense of *being* gathered by Christ. According to the Second London Confession, Christ is 'the Head of the Church in whom by the appointment of the Father, all power for the calling, institution, order, or Government of the Church is invested in a supreme & soveraigne manner', and he 'calleth out of the world unto himself … those that are given him by the Father' (*Confession* 1677: 286 [ch. 26]). As in the sacrament of believers' baptism among Baptists, there is an encounter here of divine grace with personally owned faith. Taking up the Reformation stress on Christ as 'prophet, priest, and king', and faced by the claims of a state-sanctioned ecclesiastical authority, the early Baptists claimed that it was the risen Christ, present in the midst of the congregation in the authority of his threefold office, who gave his people the 'seal' of the covenant, and so the right to celebrate the sacraments (as priests), to call some to the ministry of the word (as prophets), and to exercise a mutual discipline among each other (so sharing the kingly role of Christ) (*Declaration* 1611: 119 [art. 9]; *Confession* 1644: 159–60, 166 [arts. 10, 13]; *Confession* 1677: 260 [ch. 8]).

The plea that Baptists made from the beginning of their life for freedom of conscience with regard to the beliefs and practice of religion was founded precisely in the rule of Christ. The monarch and parliament certainly must be honoured for their commission from God to keep order in the state and rebuke evil, but to appoint spiritual leaders in the church (bishops) and to require a certain form of worship (the prayer book) was to infringe the sole headship of Christ in the church (Helwys 1612: 61–4; *Brief Confession* 1660: 233 [art. 25]). It could not be that membership in the church was simply identical with membership of the commonwealth, as the Anglican apologist Richard Hooker had argued. Further, Baptists urged, it was not the business of the state to punish anyone for their beliefs, whether—as Thomas Helwys put it—they 'be heretikes, Turcks [i.e. Muslims], Jewes, or whatsoever' (Helwys 1612: 69), since all were responsible to the one to whom God alone had committed judgement in spiritual matters, that is, Christ. The Baptist view of state–church relations and freedom of religion was, and is, based first in the 'vertical' dimension of covenant, although in the eighteenth and nineteenth centuries Baptists added to this basis an appeal to 'the rights of man' made in the image of God (Hall 1831a: 125–38).

Intersecting with the 'vertical' dimension of covenant with God in Christ is the 'horizontal dimension' of the members' commitment to each other. It was historically a pact undertaken and signed when a particular local church was founded, and subsequently made by new members on entering it. They promised both to 'give themselves up to God' *and* to 'give themselves up to each other'; to 'walk in the ways of the Lord' *and* 'to walk together'; to obey the 'rules of Christ' *and* to 'watch over each other'. The horizontal dimension is well expressed by the covenant made at Gainsborough near Lincoln in 1606 or 1607 by the congregation of English Separatists who were shortly to travel into religious exile in Amsterdam and in 1609 to adopt the practice of believers' baptism and form the first ('General') Baptist church. As William Bradford recalled the event years later in America, the members 'joyned them selves (by a covenant of the Lord) into a Church estate, in the fellowship of the gospell, to walke in all his wayes, made known, or to be made known unto them, according to their best endeavours, whatsoever it should cost them, the Lord assisting them' (Bradford 1912: I, 20–2).

These covenants were not only common among the believer-baptist descendants of the Separatists from the early decades of the seventeenth century onwards, but also (and perhaps more consistently) among paedobaptist descendants beginning with the Southwark congregation of Henry Jacob, gathered by covenant in 1616, often called 'semi-separatist', whose covenant promise was 'to walk in all Gods Ways as he had revealed or should make known to them' (Burrage 1904: 21). Geoffrey Nuttall well expresses the advantages in this Independent (Congregationalist) tradition of what was a physical as well as spiritual act: 'The drawing up of a covenant and the committing of it to writing added to its solemnity; while the appending of the signatures (or marks) of those who entered into it both underlined its binding character and satisfied their self-consciousness as individuals' (Nuttall 1957: 78). That John Smyth is envisaging a literal act of covenant-making is clear from his assertion that 'the outward part of the true forme of the true visible church is a vowe, promise, oath, or covenant betwixt God and the Saints' (Smyth 1607: 254).

When the term 'covenant' referred to an agreement which God makes with his church, or with particular churches, writers tended to appeal to the covenant formula of God with Israel, 'I will be their God and they shall be my people', together with forms of the formula in the New Testament referring to the church (e.g. 2 Cor. 6:16–18; Heb. 8:10; Smyth 1609a: 386–7). But this covenant in the local congregation also had a wider theological context in the seventeenth century. In the first place, 'covenant' referred to an eternal 'covenant of grace' which God had made with human beings and angels for their salvation in Jesus Christ. Calvin was influential in developing this idea (*Institutes* 2.6.1–4; 3.21.6–7; McNeill 1960: 340–8, 929–32), and again from Calvin is the belief that there is only one eternal covenant, but that it takes a different form of application or dispensation in the two eras of the Old Testament and the New Testament. Under either Testament the covenant is made through Christ as mediator, but under the old Christ is present in shadowy types whereas he is fully manifested in the new, as the Particular Baptist theologian John Gill affirmed (Gill 1839: I, 308; cf. Calvin, *Institutes*, 2.10.23, 2.11.4–10; McNeill 1960: 448–9, 453–61). Second, the divine covenant could refer to an agreement between the persons of the triune God, in which the Son is envisaged as consenting to the will of the Father to undertake the work of salvation. This idea is embodied in the Westminster Confession, and its influence is seen in the Particular Baptist Second London Confession of 1677, which specifies the eternal covenant as a being 'a transaction between the Father and the Son about the Redemption of the Elect' (*Confession* 1677: 260 [ch. 7]). In a treatise on the Covenant, the Particular Baptist minister Benjamin Keach regards the 'federal' agreement between the Father and the Son as the primary meaning of the covenant of grace (Keach 1698: 285). In the 'Holy Covenant' between the Father and Son, 'Jesus Christ struck hands with God the Father, in behalfe of all God's Elect' (Keach 1698: 243; see Arnold 2013: 141–59). While there was a danger that this idea might degenerate into a mere cosmic bargain, or what Matthew Arnold later criticized as the 'mechanical dogma' of nonconformists (Arnold 1873: 200, 306–10), it expressed the truth that God was fully committed to involvement in the world since it was impossible to think about the relationships in the Trinity without the covenant established with humanity.

The idea of covenant became definitive for Baptists in the thought of John Smyth. The Baptist historian B. R. White finds a stroke of originality in Smyth's fusing together the eternal covenant of God with a covenant made by a particular church here and now, maintaining that 'it seems that for him, in the covenant promise of the local congregation the eternal covenant of grace became contemporary and man's acceptance of it was actualized in history' (White 1971: 128). White further points out that the relation between the local covenant bond and the eternal covenant offered to all humankind will be analogous to the relation between a particular local congregation and the invisible company of all God's elect. This means that a Baptist ecclesiology built on the concept of covenant should take a strong view of the church universal. As Baptists have agreed in recent conversations with the Roman Catholic Church, the universal church cannot be merely a multiplication of many local communities (*Word of God* 2012: 37 [art. 12]). Rather, there is a universal reality which exists *simultaneously* with any local manifestation of it, just as God's eternal covenant with humankind is simultaneous with the local covenant bond.

Baptists reflected from their earliest days on the relation between the 'invisible church' and 'visible saints'. They *did* think that there was an invisible church here and now on earth as well as in heaven, but they did not use this concept as a justification for rejecting wider visible structures of the church beyond the local congregation. Early Baptists understood the 'invisible church' to be the total company of all the redeemed, whether they were inside or outside the visible church, and whether they lived in the past, present, or future. However, the positive affirmation of the local congregation as making the invisible catholic church visible did not imply the negative—that there was no visibility of structures or social organization anywhere else. We have already seen this exemplified in the 1644 Particular Baptist confession of a larger 'body' of local churches in relation with each other, and it is interestingly expressed in the General Baptist *Orthodox Creed* of 1679. After an article headed 'Of the invisible catholick Church of Christ', the accompanying article on 'Of the catholick Church as visible' is careful to place in apposition 'church' (singular) and '*several* distinct congregations' (plural). It is clear that the body of Christ becomes visible, not only in *each* congregation, but in the gathering of congregations together (*Orthodox Creed* 1679: 319 [art. 29]). As the eighteenth-century Particular Baptist ecclesiologist Daniel Turner makes clear, there is a 'visible Catholic Church' as well as an 'invisible Catholic Church' and a visible local church (Turner 1778: 2–4). Turner also presents the Lord's Supper as a necessary sign of the 'visible' unity of the whole church of Christ 'in the bonds of peace and love'. Though the Christian church is, 'because of the great numbers of its members', dispersed into 'many distinct societies', since these are all under Christ as one head 'they are to be considered but as parts of the same whole; composing one intire spiritual body', and the Lord's Supper signifies this reality (Turner 1778: 119–20; cf. Hall 1831b: 9–14). This affirmation has resonances with more recent ecumenical theology about the church as a 'eucharistic community'.

When a section of the new Baptist congregation returned to London under Thomas Helwys in 1612, baptism among General Baptists gradually became not only the occasion for making the covenant but a replacement for it. During the course of the seventeenth century it seems that the actual act of covenant-making dropped out of practice in some congregations as receiving baptism as a believer was deemed sufficient for church membership (see e.g. Knollys 1645: 13–14), but the theology of the church as a covenant community persisted. The covenantal language of 'walking together' regularly appears in early Baptist confessions, including the Second London Confession of 1677 which echoes the wording of covenant promises when it states that members of the church 'do willingly consent to walk together according to the appointment of Christ, giving up themselves, to the Lord & one to another' (*Confession* 1677: 286 [ch. 26]; cf. *Confession* 1644: 69 [art. 47]; *Faith and Practise* 1651: 183 [art. 52]; *Sixteen Articles* 1655: 199 [art. 15]; *Confession* 1656: 209 [art. 24]). In the last years of the seventeenth century the publication of their church covenants by both Benjamin and Elias Keach (father and son) exercised a considerable influence on the revival of covenant-making among Baptists. These covenants were often copied or modified, and the popularity of making church covenants among both General and Particular Baptists increased to the extent that when the church at Downton, Wiltshire, was re-established in 1793 it assumed that the making of a covenant was 'the usage of all organized Churches of the faith of Jesus Christ' (Anon. 1935: 213).

The stress on church discipline meant that the covenant was understood to be mutual and conditional upon human obedience. This had already been the firm view of Separatists such as Robert Browne, Henry Barrow, and Francis Johnson. For them, therefore, the covenant relationship between God and the national English church was broken and void. Radical Puritans who remained within the establishment could certainly take a conditional view when it suited their argument in urging internal reforms within the church. William Perkins, for example, could define covenant as '[God's] contract with man concerning the obtaining of life eternal, upon a certain condition' (Perkins 1591: 31). But Puritans such as Perkins could equally lay stress upon the unconditional aspect of the covenant when opposing separation from the established church, and especially when seeking to counter the case for believers' baptism. In general, those maintaining the established church appealed to the unconditional nature of the covenant; it is not quite correct to say that this was 'Calvinist', since many passages can be found in Calvin that set out the mutuality of the covenant, and its conditionality from the human side on faith and obedience. For Calvin, the covenant from God's vantage point is absolutely unconditional. God's absolute goodness means that God cannot deny divine promises to the people of God; but from the human vantage point the covenant is conditional. At any point in human history God's people can 'break' the covenant, 'violate' it, even 'destroy' it. The result is the removal of God's blessings, things that are 'accessories to the covenant'. Disobedient people are 'deprived, like covenant-breakers, of all the advantage derived from the covenant' (Lillback 2001: 170, 175–6). Calvin frequently uses the term 'condition' in the context of the covenant, and describes it as a 'free agreement'. In light of this account, it is clear how Particular (Calvinistic) as well as General (Armenian) Baptists could maintain that the Church of England had broken a conditional covenant, and that God's blessing had been withdrawn from it.

For two centuries, then, Baptists thought of the gathering of the local church in covenantal terms, even if they did not always have the 'outward form'. As the Particular Baptist minister John Fawcett wrote in 1797, 'it is the custom in many of our churches to express this [covenant or mutual compact] in writing . . . though this circumstance cannot be thought essentially necessary to the constitution of a church . . .' (Fawcett 1797: 12). Although the theology and practice of covenant was widely lost among Baptists during the nineteenth century, when it was felt to be too inward-looking in an age of interdenominational societies (Briggs 1994: 15–20) and there was a tendency instead to stress the 'voluntary' character of Baptist churches (e.g. Angus 1839: 191–3), there are signs that it is being recovered today, and being understood as central to Baptist identity (see Fiddes 2003: 21–47; Grenz 1994: 603–21; Haymes 2008: 201–11). Among churches of the Baptist Union of Great Britain, many use a service which marks a covenant both within the local church and with the association of churches (Baptist Union 2000), and on the global scene the Baptist World Alliance has introduced a Covenant on Intra-Baptist Relations (Baptist World Alliance 2013), thereby giving an ecclesial tone to the international communion of national unions and conventions. Baptist theologians have increasingly emphasized that 'covenant' need not be an introspective or sectarian concept, but can embrace the relations between the triune God, all human society, and even the natural world.

TWO CREATIVE TENSIONS OF COVENANT

If we return to the two ecclesial tensions identified earlier, we can now see how they belong within the perspective of the 'Rule of Christ' which is characteristic of covenant. First, fluidity in *episkope* flows from participation in the rule of Christ which is shared by church and officers. The direct presence of Christ as covenant-maker in the midst of the congregation means that as the gathered disciples find his mind for them, they share in his rule ('kingship') as well as in his priestly and prophetic offices. Thus they have the power to exercise church disciple in 'watching over' each other. Deeply rooted in Baptist tradition is the conviction that the church is constituted by the presence of Christ. For Baptists, a key text for the nature of the gathered congregation has been Matthew 18: 20: 'where two or three are gathered together in my name, there am I in the midst of them.' Every congregation, confessed the English Baptists at Amsterdam in 1611, 'though they be but two or three have Christ given them' (*Declaration* 1611: 120 [art. 11]; cf. *Confession* 1644: 165 [art. 33]). The aphorism of Ignatius, *ubi Christus, ibi ecclesia* ('where Christ is, there is the church'), echoing the dominical promise, has been often quoted, but the idea took on particular force in the situation of a movement of dissent from the established church. In its context this promise, Baptists noted, validated the instructions about discipline ('tell it to the church', v. 17) and the giving of the power to 'bind and loose' (v. 18). As part of its responsibility for *episkope*, the congregation also has the duty of recognizing whether someone has been called by Christ to embody this oversight in a personal way, and whether this calling has come to an end.

In Baptist ecclesiology, offices of leadership are thus established by the call of Christ and the recognizing of that call by the body of Christ on earth, the Christian community. Without such offices the church is not 'complete' (*Confession* 1677: 287 [ch. 26]). Since they focus and sum up the ministry of the community, they must be set aside by it; but at the same time they have been raised up by an act of divine grace to challenge the community with the Word of the risen Lord. They thus receive their appointment both 'from above' and 'from below'. As a Baptist report in modern times stresses, since '*episkope* flows back and forth between individual leaders and community', what is required is 'the gaining and giving of trust' (Baptist Union of Great Britain 1994: 26).

It has been characteristic of Baptist understanding of New Testament passages about church leadership to hold to a twofold rather than threefold ministry: the pattern has been pastor—otherwise named 'bishop' (*episkopos*), elder (*presbuteros*), or minister—and deacon (*diakonos*). In the words of the Second London Confession: 'A particular Church gathered, and completely Organized, according to the mind of Christ, consists of Officers, and Members; And the Officers appointed by Christ to be chosen and set apart by the Church . . . to be continued to the end of the World, are Bishops or Elders and Deacons' (*Confession* 1677: 287 [ch. 26]).

Trans-local ministries have generally fitted into this pattern as forms of the same pastoral *episkope* but with an inter-church scope, not as a third kind of office.[1] In Baptist practice, a person holding the office of *diakonia* is set aside by the local church acting on its own, and a person holding the office of *episkope* is usually only set aside in the context of fellowship with the wider church. If a minister is to represent the church as a whole, he or she must have the call from Christ to this ministry recognized by as wide a section of the church universal as is appropriate and possible, beyond the local scene. From early days of Baptist life there was a coming together of ministers from a wide area around the local church to share in the act of ordination. In accord with this, the General Baptist Assembly of 1702 held that 'the ordination of Elders by Elders [is] of Divine Institution' (Whitley 1909: I, 70; so Gill 1839: II, 265). In modern times this has been accompanied (and sometimes replaced) by the involvement of a representative figure from the national Baptist union or convention or from a regional association. The practice of ordination of a minister by other ministers was sometimes justified simply by appeal to instructions about laying on of hands in the Pastoral Epistles (*Confession* 1677: 287 [art. 26.9]; *Orthodox Creed* 1679: 320 [art. 31]) or by the need to control the quality of ministry and to safeguard the local church from powerful personalities who might want to abuse it. But we may also see in this practice an expression of the link of the *episkopos* with the church beyond the local scene; as Daniel Turner put it in the eighteenth century, 'a minister of a particular church . . . is a minister of the church in general' (Turner 1778: 60; so Baptist Union 1994: 43–4).

The second kind of ecclesial tension identified above is a fluidity in ecclesial authority between local congregation and the assembling of church representatives together in 'association'. This derives from the standing of both local church and assembly of churches under the same rule of Christ, and the responsibility of seeking the 'mind of Christ' at every level of socialization. The freedom of a local church from external ecclesiastical authority is therefore not based in Enlightenment concepts of the freedom of the individual, or in the self-regulation of a voluntary society, but in the lordship of Christ. The local church meeting cannot be imposed upon because it stands under the direct rule of Christ; at the same time it must pay seriously attention to the resolutions of the wider church in seeking to find Christ's mind for itself. It will not have all the resources for finding the mind of Christ in some issues without listening to the insights of others, but it always remains responsible for testing wider decisions as to whether they do indeed embody the purpose of Christ. This is the Baptist contribution to the idea of 'reception' of synodical decisions, which is central to the notion of authority in all Christian communions.

---

[1] There was an exception to this principle among the General Baptist churches which subscribed to the *Orthodox Creed*, for whom the 'bishop' or 'messenger' was a distinct office; see art. 31: 319–20.

If a local church is under the direct rule of Christ in his office as 'king', then it is necessarily drawn into fellowship with all those who are under Christ's rule and so part of his body. Thus the 'Somerset Confession' drawn up in Bridgewater in 1656 asserts that it is 'the duty of the members of Christ . . . *although* in several congregations and assemblies (being one in the head) if occasion be, to communicate each to other in things spiritual and things temporal' (*Confession* 1656: 211 [art. 28]). We note in both this confession and the London Confession that the separateness of the congregations is regarded as a matter of concession ('although'). The latter confession even goes so far as to describe this situation as being a matter of simple practical necessity, stating that 'though wee be distinct in respect of our particular bodies, for conveniency sake, being as many as can well meete together in one place, yet are all one in Communion, holding Jesus Christ to be our head and Lord; under whose government wee desire alone to walk' (*Confession* 1644: 155).

In the record of the first general meeting of the Abingdon Association (Particular Baptist) in 1652 there is an interesting theological argument advanced for the churches to hold 'a firm communion with each other': that is, there is the same relation between the particular churches as there is between the particular members of one church. The record adds, 'For the churches of Christ doe all make up one body or church in generall under Christ their head' (White 1974: 126). From the General Baptists, we have already noted that the *Orthodox Creed* (1679) affirms that the 'visible church of Christ on earth is made up of several distinct congregations, which make up that one catholick church, or mystical body of Christ' (319 [art. 30]). In line with this it refers to the representatives to general councils or assemblies of churches as making 'but one church' (327 [art. 29]), although it must be said to be unusual among Baptists in using the word 'church' to refer directly to a gathering of churches.

It is not just that the terms 'body' and 'Christ as head' are used in these examples to *describe* wider assemblies than the local congregation. The point is being made that local churches are therefore under a *necessity* 'to hold communion among themselves for their peace, increase of love and mutual edification' (*Confession* 1677: 289 [ch. 26]), just as members in any congregation are called by Christ to gather together. In modern times, a report of the Faith and Unity Committee of the Baptist Union of Great Britain declares: 'It follows from a biblical understanding of Church as covenant, fellowship and body that there is . . . no option about local churches being part of a wider fellowship of churches. They are gathered together by Christ' (Baptist Union 1994: 8). The distinctive Baptist view has not been that associating is only an option, but that these wider assemblies cannot *impose* their decisions on the local church meeting. This report thus advises that the local congregation 'must have good reason for going against the consensus of the wider community' and notes that the tension in authority thus arising requires that it have 'trust that churches in covenant together have genuinely been searching for the mind of Christ' (Baptist Union 1994: 12).

It follows that whether covenant is an exclusive or inclusive idea depends upon how the rule of Christ in the church and the world is to be understood. In the turmoil following the English Reformation it was inevitable that Baptists understood the scope of

Christ's rule to run in a fairly narrow way, but some recent English Baptist writing has taken up a wider vision of the rule of Christ in reviving the covenant concept: it has urged that if the local church meeting aims to find the mind of Christ for its life and mission, it should be anxious to discover how assemblies of other denominations, gathering under the same rule, discern the mission of God and their place in it. It is apt that a number of Baptist churches in Wales (though not the Union itself) have been able to participate in the ecumenical 'Covenanted Churches in Wales'. Unlike a similar but unsuccessful attempt at covenanting between denominations in England in the mid-1970s (Churches' Unity Commission 1976) the Welsh Covenant avoided both the language of 'organic union' and the setting of a date for structural unity; instead it declared that 'we do not yet know the form union will take' and echoed earlier covenant documents in expecting that 'God will guide his Church into ways of truth and peace' (British Council of Churches 1989: 74–6). This openness in walking together was also the spirit of the 'Inter-Church Process' or 'Churches Together in Pilgrimage' in Great Britain as a whole, in which the Baptist Union of Great Britain was a partner (British Council of Churches 1989: 9–15). The language of covenant was, however, strangely not used in the foundation document for the ecumenical instruments of the ensuing 'Churches Together'.

COVENANT AND SEPARATIST PREDECESSORS

The same two ecclesial tensions that we have identified can be found in an influential Separatist confession of 1596. In fact, the compilers of the 1644 Baptist confession took the two passages in articles 44 and 47 cited above verbatim from articles 26 and 38 of the 1596 confession (*True Confession* 1596: 90, 94), as well as modelling their whole confession on the earlier one, demonstrating their heritage from English Separatism. This 'True Confession' was written for the Separatist congregation which was split between London and Amsterdam, and whose pastors from 1585 had been Henry Barrow and John Greenwood (both executed in 1593). The main author of the confession was probably the pastor of the congregation in Amsterdam, Henry Ainsworth, with advice from the London pastor Francis Johnson, who was imprisoned at the time. The covenant framework of these tensions is also characteristic of Separatism: article 33 of the confession notes the desire of church members 'to joyne together in christian communion and orderly covenant' (92). There is some earlier indication of the practice of covenant in one of the London Separatist congregations, probably pastored by Robert Fitz (from about 1570), where it appears that members made a promise beginning 'I have now joined myself to the Church of Christ wherein I have yielded myself subject to the discipline of God's word ...' (White 1971: 27). This congregation also in 1571 made a supplication to Queen Elizabeth I, citing in their defence Matthew 18:15–20, verses concerning both the presence of Christ in the congregation (v. 20) and the exercise of pastoral discipline (vv. 15–18), confessing that they have organized themselves in 'separation' from the parish churches (White 1971: 30). Affirmation of the rule of Christ alone in the congregation is central to Separatism from the beginning, as voiced in 1567 by one member of a London congregation, Robert Hawkins, complaining that 'You preach Christ to be priest and prophet, but you preach him not to be king, neither will you suffer him to reign with the sceptre of his word in his church alone; but the Pope's canon law and the will of the prince must have the first place ...' (White 1971: 25). Calvin had expressed this sole rule of Christ theologically (*Institutes* 4.6.8–10; McNeill 1960: 1109–1111) but did not work it out in the form of a congregation which exercised its own authority in church discipline.

The concept of covenant was developed most thoroughly in the Separatism practised by Robert Browne in the Separatist congregations he led at Middelburgh and Norwich from 1581 onwards, in intermittent periods between conformity to the Church of England in what can only be called an inconsistent career. He explicitly linked the practice of covenant-making with the rule of Christ, formally organizing the congregation by 'their consent to join themselves to the Lord, in one covenant and fellowship together, and to keep and seek agreement under his laws and government' (Peel and Carlson 1953: 422). He affirmed that 'when we make and hold the covenant of the Lord to be under his government ... we have the power of the Lord amongst us, and the sceptre of Christ amongst us' (Peel and Carlson 1953: 421). The two dimensions of covenant, vertical and horizontal, are thus clearly linked. Finally, the covenant between Christ and his church is understood to be conditional and mutual, a departure from most contemporary Puritan thinking, although it was, as we have seen, present within the Genevan (and also the Rhinelander) tradition of Reformation:

> First, by a couenant and condicion, made on God's behalfe. Secondlie by a couenant and condicion made on our behalfe ... The couenant on Gods behalf is his agreement or partaking of condicions with us that if we keepe his lawes, not forsaking his gouernment, hee will take vs for his people, & blesse vs accordingly ... What is the covenant or condicion on our behalfe? We must offer and geve vp our selues to be of the church and people of God. (Peel and Carlson 1953: 254–6)

Within this account of covenant we are not surprised to discern the two ecclesial tensions we have already identified. First, the rule of Christ is shared by all members of the congregation, each of whom 'is made a king, a priest and a prophet' so that 'the kingdom of all Christians is their office of guiding and ruling with Christ, to subdue the wicked, and make one another obedient to Christ' (Peel and Carlson 1953: 276–7). But Browne also declares that 'church' is 'the whole people, guided by the elders and forwardest' (Peel and Carlson 1953: 399). There is a tension left unresolved here: every person has the office of guiding another, but guidance is also apparently committed to the elders (*presbuteroi*). Second, the local church has freedom to make decisions about its own life, under the rule of Christ. But he also envisages the need for the meeting of a synod as 'a joining or partaking of the authority of many Churches met together in peace, for redress and deciding of matters which cannot well otherwise be taken up' (Peel and Carlson 1953: 271). In the context of his time, these two tensions owe much to a fusion of the presbyterian or radical Puritan pattern of presbyteral leadership with a stress on finding the mind of Christ by the whole community. But the tensions are also endemic to a covenantal pattern itself.

Browne's influence in developing a covenant theology among Separatists in general may not have been as strong as scholars have previously supposed. Barrow and Greenwood in leading their London congregation had a similar covenant theology to Browne, but they always denied any contact with him, regarding him as vacillating in faithfulness to the truth. We may suppose that they reached their position first because there was probably a tradition of covenant before Browne (Browne himself may indeed have gleaned his ideas from association with the London Separatist groups), and second because they believed the covenant of God with the Church of England was broken, so that it was now being remade with Separatist congregations (Carlson 1962a: 163–4; Carlson 1966: 338–40). They held, then, a similar view of the mutuality and conditionality of the covenant as did Browne. They also showed the same ecclesial tensions as were expressed by Browne and which were to be expressed in articles 26 and 38 of the 1596 Confession. First, following the injunction of Christ to 'tell the church' (Matt. 18:15), according to Barrow the whole congregation had power 'both to receive into and cast out their fellowship' (Carlson 1962a: 318), but at the same time, for the people to act without 'their governors and guides, those most fit members that God hath given them', would be an act of rebellion against the rule of Christ (Carlson 1966: 219). Ministry was still a 'holy order' commanded by Christ and necessary also for administration of sacraments. When the congregation had enquired the will of God, 'they all walk by the same rule, and with one consent do the will of God accordingly', yet 'though all members have received of this spirit of God, yet have not all received in like measure' (Carlson 1966: 146). There is an unresolved tension here, described by Greenwood as a mutual covenant between pastor and congregation (Carlson 1962b: 161). There is a similar tension, second, in the relation of churches together. Every congregation could choose its own pastor, each member declaring assent or dissent, but it collaborated with the elders of other churches in the ordination of those chosen.

In the early writings of Johnson and Ainsworth, covenant does not take such a high profile, despite the wording of the 1596 confession. But Johnson in a later work approves—at least implicitly—Browne's view of the covenant (Johnson 1606: 13–14), and Ainsworth's highly influential book *The Communion of Saincts* (first printed 1607) contains a version of the covenant promise which is reminiscent of Browne's: a true Christian will promise 'to walk in all [God's] ways, and to keep his ordinances, and his commandments and his laws, and . . . to walk in the paths of God as he shall teach them' (Ainsworth 1615: 343). This is the tradition in which the first Baptist minister John Smyth stood, and from which he received the form of the covenant administered at Gainsborough in 1607. Johnson indeed had been his tutor at the University of Cambridge before either became Separatists.

However, in the English Separatist congregation in Amsterdam we perceive a tendency to try and resolve the two ecclesial tensions of covenant we have identified. With regard to the first, Johnson controversially came to understand 'tell the church' as 'tell the elders' and made the whole church subordinate to the leadership of elders

(Johnson 1611: Preface), thereby prompting a split with his colleague Ainsworth and a section of the congregation. In a related modification of covenant theology he defended infant baptism against the Mennonites and the new Baptist congregation by affirming that the divine covenant was unconditional, so that both the Church of Rome and the Church of England, while corrupt, were 'on God's part, yet a church' (Clifton 1610: 109). Nevertheless, with regard to the second tension, Johnson asserted the independent judgement of the local congregation to the detriment of fellowship with other churches, even where they were recognized as true churches (Johnson 1606: 70). Ministers of the English 'congregational classis' in the Netherlands between 1621 and 1625 showed similar polarizations, though in varying directions: William Bradshaw followed Johnson in insisting on the autonomy of a local church in which members delegated government to the elders, while the minister Robert Parker was a member of the Dutch Presbyterian Classis and gave the synod the decisive judgement over the local church (Nuttall 1957: 10). Although John Smyth himself made the elders subordinate to the whole congregation (Smyth 1609a: 389), it might be argued that as Baptist ecclesiology developed in the following century on English soil, it retained the creative tensions of *earlier* Separatism without the same sectarianism.

COVENANT AND ANABAPTIST ANTECEDENTS

Another antecedent of Baptist ecclesiology was that of the continental Anabaptists, the radical wing of the European Reformation which was concerned less with reformation than with the *restitution* of the 'true church' (Littell 1958: 1). Aiming to restore the New Testament pattern of the church, in 1526 at Augsburg Anabaptist leaders made a confession in which the baptism of believing disciples was declared to be the only sign of membership in the churches, entailing re-baptism of those baptized as infants. They held to a rigid 'separation' from a church regarded as 'fallen', whether this was Catholic or newly Protestant. Anabaptists were a collection of diverse groups, distributed mainly in north and south Germany, Switzerland, Moravia, the Netherlands, and Poland. They took 'quietist', 'spiritualist', and 'revolutionary' forms, and in the last manifestation (*Schwärmer*) were responsible for the violent seizure of Münster, thereby acquiring a reputation which unjustly guaranteed oppression, as well as disavowal of the name by Baptists in England. Savagely persecuted in Switzerland and Germany, they took time to reach any common identity. However, in general analogies can be discerned with the later Separatist and Baptist traditions.

First, they confessed that the congregation stands under the direct rule of Christ. In the words of the Netherlander Dietrich Philips, 'God rules over the congregation of the first born . . . the congregation of God' of which Christ is 'the head' and 'the mediator of the new covenant' (Williams 1957: 229), and according to the confession of the Waterlander Mennonites, who were based around Amsterdam, Christ is 'Lord and Master' in the church (Lumpkin 1959: 57 [art. 24]). This gives the congregation freedom from external ecclesiastical constraints and from compulsion in matters of religion by the state. Among south German Anabaptists Pilgram Marpeck declared, 'All outward power may not command . . . in the kingdom of Christ' (Wenger 1938: 171) and Hans Denck anticipated the Baptist Thomas Helwys in affirming that the rule of Christ meant that 'each will let the other move and dwell in peace—be he Turk or heathen believing what he will . . . in the name of his God' (Littell 1958: 66). Unlike later Separatists and Baptists, however, being a member of the 'spiritual kingdom' of Christ also required complete withdrawal from involvement in any of the offices of state such as that of the magistrate, as they were seen to be tainted with the use of force that Christ had disavowed in his own spreading of the gospel in the golden age at the beginning of the church. Second, for Anabaptists the rule of Christ was at the heart of a strong covenant theology. As with the Reformers and Separatists, baptism was a 'sign of the covenant', but like later Baptists this was confined to the baptism of believing disciples. Hans Hut declared (1527) that 'your baptism is a sign of covenant and surrender of will towards God and the Christian church' (Burrage 1904: 17), and Balthasar Hubmaier affirmed that 'the meaning of this sign and symbol is a pledge' (Williams 1975: 135). The formative Schleitheim Confession of the Swiss Brethren in 1527, largely shaped by Michael Sattler, uses typical covenant language in referring to those baptized into the body of Christ as 'those who have given themselves to the Lord, to walk in his commandments' (Lumpkin 1959: 25 [art. 2]), but there is very little indication that there was actually a ceremony of covenant-making or covenant-subscribing anywhere among Anabaptists. Indeed, the examination of Jakob Kautzen and Wilhelm Reublin (1529) at Strasbourg reports these Anabaptists as referring to the act of water baptism as the occasion when 'we made a covenant (*Bund*) with God in our hearts' (Burrage 1904: 19).

The Anabaptists were in agreement with both the Reformers and the Separatists that there was a link between the old and new covenants, while the new fulfilled the old (see Dietrich Philips in Williams 1957: 232). We must dismiss the proposal that the Anabaptists' assertion of covenant continuity between Israel and the church was simply adopted by the Reformers (Schrenk 1923: 37), but it seems that dispute with the Anabaptists did lead the Reformers to use covenant continuity as an argument in defence of infant baptism (so Lillback 2001: 81–97). The argument of Zwingli was that the point of the baptismal sign was not to confirm faith, but to be a sign of God's 'contract' with children of the covenant community in both eras (Bromiley 1953: 138–9). For the Anabaptists the personal faith of the baptizand was essential to make the 'pledge', and Melchior Hofman underlined this with his theology of covenant as betrothal to Christ, drawing on sexual imagery from the Old Testament, declaring that 'the bride of the Lord Jesus Christ has given herself over to the Bridegroom in baptism, which is the sign of the covenant' (Williams 1957: 193).

Again, the Anabaptist stress on the conditional nature of the covenant, later to be affirmed by Separatists and Baptists, was not different in principle from the theology of the Rhineland Reformers who followed Calvin in this respect. Oecolampadius, for example, finds the covenant to be a mutual relationship which can be 'violated', and Bullinger echoes this (Lillback 2001: 85–7, 163). However, the Anabaptists drew the conclusion that the Church, Catholic and Reformed, was 'fallen' (Williams 1957: 229, 254; Littell 1958: 46–78), a judgement comparable to the view of the Separatists that the Church of England had broken the covenant.

A third analogue with later Separatists and Baptists was the Anabaptist concern for discipline in the church. The rule of Christ, they believed, had been committed to the congregation in the use of the 'ban', or the power to 'bind and loose', and the key passage—as later—was Matthew 18:15–20. So representatives from Mennonite churches who formulated the *Concept of Cologne* (1591) claimed that 'This community of the saints has the power through the keys of the kingdom of heaven to bind and to loose, and in this manner, the rule of Matthew 18 is to be observed, when a sin is committed between brother and brother' (*Concept* 1591: art. 7). The Schleitheim Confession earlier agreed on the use of the ban, and urged that the discipline of admonishing and banning shall be applied before the breaking of bread so that members may eat and drink 'with one mind and in one love' (Lumpkin 1959: 25 [art. 2]). This attitude is echoed by the *Concept of Cologne* which urges that its subscribers 'shall at all times be reconciled with one another in love, listening to each other's views in the spirit of love, without strife and quarreling' (*Concept* 1591: art. 7). Dietrich Philips makes clear the centrality of discipline to ecclesiology when he calls it 'evangelical separation, without which the congregation of God cannot stand or be maintained' (Williams 1957: 246–7).

It is likely that 'on the ground' a similar tension existed in Anabaptist thinking and practice about the relation between the oversight of the minister and the whole congregation as was later to be characteristic of both Separatists and Baptists, although the evidence is not as available. Among the Moravian Hutterites, Peter Riedemann is emphatic that the power of the ban is given to the whole congregation 'and not to individual persons' (Lumpkin 1959: 40 [art. 1]), but elsewhere there appears to be an ambiguity about what it might mean for elders to exercise discipline and to confirm calls to ministry (as pastors, elders, and 'helpers') with the consent of the church. It seems that initiatives were taken and proposals made by the elders (*Vorsteheren*) in both cases, but the authority of the congregation in response is not clear. According to the Schleitheim Confession, the pastor holds the power of discipline and ban, but provision is also made for him to be disciplined by the congregation (Lumpkin 1959: 27 [art. 5]). In a meeting near Strasbourg in 1557 persons accused of persistent quarrelling were questioned by the elders in front of the congregation, every member of which then gave their verdict (Clasen 1972: 107–8). In the Waterland Confession, however, the 'exercise of fraternal admonition' and 'removal' is assigned to a distinct ministry in the church, and confirmation of the call to office of ministry is to be by elders 'in the presence' of the church (Lumpkin 1959: 58–9 [arts. 25, 28]). We have an account of meetings held near Strasbourg in 1545 and 1557 between elders and pastors, 'at a distance from the assembled believers' (Clasen 1972: 54–5), but when John Smyth's congregation applied for membership in the Waterlander association of Mennonite churches in 1610, the elders polled their members on the issue, evidently feeling that they must be consulted (Coggins 1991: 82).

With regard to the second ecclesial tension that we have identified in the practice of covenant, between local church and the wider church, there seems to be a similar ill-defined area in Anabaptism. There was no hierarchy above the level of the local congregation, but congregational leaders gathered occasionally to discuss doctrinal and practical issues. For example, leaders of the Swiss Brethren met at Schleitheim in 1527, Anabaptist leaders from South Germany met at Strasbourg in 1555, 1557, and 1568, and south and north German leaders met with some from the Netherlands at Cologne in 1591. Confessions or declarations were sometimes drawn up which were nominally binding on those churches whose representatives participated in them, but one social historian comments that 'it is uncertain to what extent the congregations really complied with them' (Clasen 1972: 51). Congregations were, however, tied together by the practice of believers' baptism, in that baptized members were able to transfer from one congregation to another. Elders also had authority in all the churches in their association, and it is possible that, despite the doctrinal assertion that a congregation under the rule of Christ could choose its own leaders, in some Anabaptist groups the elders were in fact elected by an assembly of brethren (not just elders) from various congregations, as appears to have happened at Heilbronn in 1539 (Clasen 1972: 53). All this made for a greater sense of associating than was often present among Separatists, despite the theory of the 'one rule' of the 1596 confession, and it may have been the adoption of believers' baptism that later gave Baptists a greater sense of the wider church than existed in late Separatism.

Given these analogues between Anabaptists, Separatists, and Baptists, the question obviously arises about any direct influence of Anabaptism on the covenant ecclesiology of the others. There were certainly Anabaptists in exile in Britain in the later sixteenth century, and we must always reckon with the fact that—as E. A. Payne put it—'ideas had legs' (Payne 1956: 340). However, there is no evidence of any *direct* contact between any individual Separatists and Anabaptists (White 1971: 163). The Separatist, and later Baptist, stress on the use of discipline, as in Matt. 18:15–17, matches the continental radicals' use of 'the ban', but insisting on this mark of a true church probably derives from the theology of Martin Bucer mediated through Calvin (Brachlow 1988: 28–9). There is, further, no evidence that Separatists were influenced by Anabaptist teaching on believers' baptism before the residence of one Separatist congregation—Smyth's—in Amsterdam, and nor is there evidence of adoption of a Melchiorite Christology of 'heavenly flesh' which was typical of Anabaptists in England.

The covenant ecclesiology of Separatism is explicable—as B. R. White has argued (White 1971: 160–4)—by the modification of the general covenantal theology of the period by two factors. First, a pattern of separation had been developed in the Protestant withdrawal from the Catholic Church in the reign of Mary Tudor, as popularized in the highly influential *Acts and Monuments of the English Martyrs* by John Foxe. Indeed, William Bradford and John Smyth both claim a continuity with the Marian Martyrs, whom they name a separated church (Colonial Society 1920: 132–3; Smyth 1609a: 386). Second, the radical Puritan conviction that a local congregation should be able to choose its own ministers, as expressed in the debates over the *Admonitions to Parliament* in

1571–2, was easily expandable into a more extensive view of the powers of congregation under the rule of Christ.

There must, however, have been some influence of Anabaptism in the form of Waterlander Mennonites on the congregation of Smyth and Helwys in Amsterdam. Perhaps (although there is no evidence) their witness had some effect on the conversion of this paedobaptist Separatist group to believers' baptism. It probably prompted the Baptist rejection of the power of the magistrate to promote and enforce 'true religion', which was allowed by the Separatists. And it most probably helped to move the theology of the group from the strict Calvinism of the Separatists to moderate Armenianism and a belief in 'general atonement'. This theology was thereafter characteristic of the 'General Baptists' who were descended from the group led by Helwys which separated from Smyth over his union with the Waterlanders and returned to England. The other main strand of English Baptists, 'Particular Baptists', emerged from radical Puritans in the 1630s, and held to a stricter Calvinism, without contact with Mennonites in their history.

CONCLUSION:
BAPTISTS AND A FREE CHURCH

If we place the ecclesiologies of Baptists and their antecedents side by side, we can see what happens when a covenant ecclesiology is located in different contexts of time and place. We notice that in both Anabaptism and Separatism covenant generally expresses a closure of community to those 'outside', an attitude which becomes most acute in the identifying of baptism with a covenant of suffering (Littell 1958: 101). In contrast to Anabaptism, covenant theology among Separatists did not prevent magistrates from being church members, although magistrates had to be subject to the rule of Christ within church discipline on churchly matters. However, Separatist ecclesiology absolutely excluded any communion with churches that had not themselves separated from communion with the Church of England.

While early Baptists imbibed much of this Separatist spirit, the situation in England after the Act of Uniformity and other associated Acts to suppress worship outside the parish church from 1662 onwards was one in which Baptists sought to make common cause with other dissenting Protestant groups (notably Presbyterian and Independent) who were suffering the same oppression from the state and the established church. The Particular Baptist Confession of 1677 and the General Baptist *Orthodox Creed* of 1679 both show a reaching out to common ground, especially with their debt to the Presbyterian Westminster Confession (Fiddes 2013: 202–4). Ernst Troelsch, a sociologist of religion who popularized the distinction between 'sect' and 'church', regarded Baptists from this period onwards not as a sect but as a mixture of the two types in a new species of 'free church', and saw the Baptist movement as a major driver in creating this form of church. The free church, he thought, combines churchly and sectarian tendencies, as a voluntary group that still maintains a church-like relation to society, aiming to be deeply involved in it and to serve it as a whole in all its diversity (Troeltsch 1950: 807–8, 819). While in continuity with the church-type, the free church differs profoundly from the earlier church-type which showed its fully developed form in medieval Catholicism, since a free church accepts religious toleration and relinquishes a claim to exclusiveness (Troeltsch 1950: 671). While Baptists, with other Dissenters, were excluded from public office until 1828, they protested against this discrimination and wanted to take their place in the service of society, as they seek to do today.

All this is within the logic of a covenant ecclesiology, contextualized in its time and place. The rule of Christ takes priority over the making of a covenant promise, and so if this rule can be discerned elsewhere, either in other churches or in civil society, the concept of covenant has to make room for it. It is the rule of Christ that gathers the church, and this accounts for what may seem a bewildering diversity of Baptist practice over membership and communion at the Lord's Supper throughout the world. Those Baptists who have adopted 'closed' membership and communion, confining it to baptized believers, root this not in a preference for one form of baptism over another but in obedience to the command of Christ to baptize in this form, as they discern it (Booth 1778: 73–7, 85–7). Those Baptists—in the overwhelming majority today in the UK—who have adopted 'open' membership, accepting believers who have been baptized as infants to their membership and table, do so for a number of reasons which stem equally from obedience to Christ. Some, like John Bunyan in the seventeenth century, find that the church is 'constituted' by faith *rather than* baptism, but faith which is response to the rule of Christ among them (Bunyan 1673: 28–30; cf. Robinson 1781: 29–31). Others, like Daniel Turner in the eighteenth century, think that entrance into the church is always by baptism, but that Christian disciples must be allowed freedom of conscience over what they consider to be true baptism, as responsible to Christ who alone bears the rule of God and will be the final judge of truth (Turner 1772: 6–10; Turner 1778: 124–7, 138).

While Troeltsch detected a move from sect to 'free church' in the mid-seventeenth century, we may find at least the spirit of the latter in a confession issued by Smyth's congregation after his death (drafted by Smyth, modifying a Mennonite confession): article 69 affirms 'that all penitent and faithful Christians are brethren in the communion of the outward church, wheresoever they live, by what name soever they are known, which in truth and zeal follow repentance and faith, though compassed with never so many ignorances and infirmities' (*Propositions and Conclusions* 1612: 137). Smyth himself, we may say, opened the way for this more catholic vision of the church by his understanding of the 'seal' of the covenant. Anabaptists and Separatists both regarded baptism itself as the 'seal', and so were committed to endless arguments about whether the seal could be applied to a young infant without faith of its own, the first group denying this and the second asserting it. Smyth took the view that the seal of the covenant was the Holy Spirit, and baptism was the sign and occasion of sealing by the Spirit. His argument was that 'sealing' must involve transformation of the person by the Spirit, and so the ability to confess this change by the word of mouth (Smyth 1609b: 567, 582–7). The advantage of Smyth's approach over Anabaptism is that it has room both for faith as *declaring* the work of the Spirit, and for the grace of God as the actual *working* of the Spirit in baptism. It was consistent with this view of a 'baptism of the Spirit' for later General Baptists to affirm that baptism was 'the new Testament-way of bringing in Members, into the Church by regeneration' (*Brief Confession* 1660: 228). Smyth's main concern is admittedly with defending the restriction of baptism to believing and confessing disciples, but today we can see that his theology has the potential for recognizing the work of God's Spirit beyond the borders of any particular Christian group, in line with the dynamic of covenant itself.

This dynamism is expressed through the two tensions identified in this chapter as typical of a covenant ecclesiology—a fluidity of authority *within* the local church, and *between* local and wider manifestations of church. These tensions have had the potential for the shipwreck of the ark of God, and with John Smyth's congregation we may be 'heartily grieved that we which follow after one faith, and one spirit, one Lord and one God, one body, and one baptism, should be rent into so many sects and schisms' (art. 69). But these tensions have also been highly creative in Baptist ecclesiology and its antecedents, and may still be so in our ecumenical age, calling as they do for trust in each other.

References

Ainsworth, Henry (1615). *The Communion of Saincts.* Amsterdam.

Angus, Joseph (1839). *The Voluntary System.* London: Jackson and Walford.

Anon. (1935). 'Church Covenants'. *Baptist Quarterly* 7.5: 227–34.

Arnold, Jonathan W. (2013). 'The Reformed Theology of Benjamin Keach (1640–1704)'. Oxford: Regent's Park College.

Arnold, Matthew (1873). *Literature and Dogma.* 2nd edn. London: Smith, Elder & Co.

Baptist Union of Great Britain (1994). *Forms of Ministry among Baptists: Towards an Understanding of Spiritual Leadership.* Faith and Unity Executive Committee. London: BUGB.

Baptist Union of Great Britain (1994). *The Nature of the Assembly and the Council of the Baptist Union of Great Britain.* Faith and Unity Executive Committee. London: BUGB.

Baptist Union of Great Britain (2000). *Covenant 21: Covenant for a Gospel People.* London: BUGB.

Baptist World Alliance (2013). *Covenant on Intra-Baptist Relations.* Available at <http://www.bwanet.org/2013-08-14-13-07-48>.

Booth, Abraham (1778). *An Apology for the Baptists.* London: Dilly, Keith, Johnson.

Brachlow, Stephen (1988). *The Communion of Saints: Radical Puritan and Separatist Ecclesiology 1570–1625.* Oxford: Oxford University Press.

Bradford, William (1912). *History of Plymouth Plantation, 1620–1647.* Ed. W. C. Ford. 2 vols. Boston: Massachusetts Historical Society.

Brief Confession or Declaration of Faith, A (1660). Repr. in Lumpkin 1959: 224–35.

Briggs, John H. Y. (1994). *The English Baptists of the Nineteenth Century.* London: Baptist Historical Society.

British Council of Churches (1989). *Not Strangers but Pilgrims: The Next Steps for Churches Together in Pilgrimage*. London: British Council of Churches and Catholic Truth Society.

Bromiley, G. W. (ed.) (1953). *Zwingli and Bullinger: Selected Translations with Introductions and Notes. Library of Christian Classics* XXIV. London: SCM.

Bunyan, John (1673). *Differences in Judgment about Water-Baptism No Bar to Communion*. London: John Wilkins.

Burrage, Champlin (1904). *The Church Covenant Idea: Its Origin and its Development*. Philadelphia: American Baptist Historical Society.

Carlson, Leland H. (ed.) (1962a). *The Writings of Henry Barrow 1578–90*. London: Allen and Unwin.

Carlson, Leland H. (ed.) (1962b). *The Writings of John Greenwood 1587–1590*. London: Allen and Unwin.

Carlson, Leland H. (ed.) (1966). *The Writings of Henry Barrow 1590–91*. London: Allen and Unwin.

Churches' Unity Commission (1976). *Visible Unity: Ten Propositions*. London.

Clasen, Claus-Peter (1972). *Anabaptism: A Social History, 1525–1618, Switzerland, Austria, Moravia, and South and Central Germany*. Ithaca, NY: Cornell University Press.

Clifton, R. (1610). *An Advertisement Concerning a Booke Published by C. Lawne*. ?Amsterdam.

Coggins, James R. (1991). *John Smyth's Congregation: English Separatism, Menonnite Influence, and the Elect Nation*. Waterloo, Ontario: Herald Press.

Colonial Society of Massachusetts (1920). *Plymouth Church Records 1620-1859*. Vol. 22. Boston.

Concept of Cologne (1591). Available at: <http://www.anabaptistwiki.org/mediawiki/index.php?title=Concept_of_Cologne_(Anabaptists,_1591)&oldid=10489>.

Confession of Faith Put Forth by the Elders and Brethren of Many Congregations (1677). Repr. in Lumpkin 1959: 241–95.

Confession of Faith, of those Churches which are commonly (though falsly) called Anabaptists, The (1644). Repr. in Lumpkin 1959: 156–71.

Confession of the Faith of Several Churches of Christ in the County of Somerset, and of some Churches in the Counties neer adjacent (1656). Repr. in Lumpkin 1959: 203–16.

Declaration of Faith of English People Remaining at Amsterdam in Holland (1611). Repr. in Lumpkin 1959: 116–23.

Faith and Practise of Thirty Congregations, Gathered According to the Primitive Pattern (1651). Repr. in Lumpkin 1959: 174–87.

Fawcett, John (1797). *The Constitution and Order of a Gospel Church Considered*. Halifax.

Fiddes, Paul S. (2003). *Tracks and Traces: Baptist Identity in Church and Theology*. Milton Keynes: Paternoster.

Fiddes, Paul S. (2013). 'Baptists and 1662: The Effect of the Act of Uniformity on Baptists and its Ecumenical Significance for Baptists Today'. *Ecclesiology* 9.2: 183–202.

Gill, John (1839). *Complete Body of Doctrinal and Practical Divinity (1769). A New Edition in Two Volumes*. London: Tegg & Co.

Gregory, Olinthus (ed.) (1831). *The Entire Works of the Rev. Robert Hall*. 6 vols. London: Holdsworth and Ball.

Grenz, Stanley J. (1994). *Theology for the Community of God*. Nashville: Broadman & Holman.

Hall, Robert (1831a). *An Apology for the Freedom of the Press (1793)*. Repr. in Gregory 1831: Vol. III, 61–174.

Hall, Robert (1831b). *On Terms of Communion*. Repr. in Gregory 1831: Vol. II, 9–174.

Haymes, Brian, Gouldbourne, Ruth, and Cross, Anthony R. (2008). *On Being the Church: Revisioning Baptist Identity*. Milton Keynes: Paternoster.

Helwys, Thomas (1612). *A Short Declaration of the Mistery of Iniquity*. Amsterdam.

Johnson, Francis (1606). *An Inquirie and Answer of T. White. ?*Amsterdam.

Johnson, Francis (1611). *A Short Treatise Concerning the Words of Christ, Tell the Church*. Amsterdam.

Keach, Benjamin (1698). *The Display of Glorious Grace. Or, The Covenant of Peace Opened. In Fourteen Sermons*. London.

Knollys, Hanserd (1645). *A Moderate Answer unto Dr. Bastwick's Book; Called, Independency not Gods Ordinance*. London.

Lillback, Peter A. (2001). *The Binding of God: Calvin's Role in the Development of Covenant Theology*. Grand Rapids, MI: Baker Academic.

Littell, Franklin Hamlin (1958). *The Anabaptist View of the Church*. 2nd edn. Boston: Starr King Press.

Lumpkin, William L. (ed.) (1959). *Baptist Confessions of Faith*. Chicago: Judson Press.

McNeill, John T. (ed.) (1960). *Calvin: Institutes of the Christian Religion*. Library of Christian Classics, Vols XX, XXI. London: SCM Press.

Nuttall, Geoffrey F. (1957). *Visible Saints: The Congregational Way 1640-1660*. Oxford: Basil Blackwell.

Payne, Ernest A. (1956). 'Who were the Baptists'? *Baptist Quarterly* 16.8: 339-42.

Peel, A. and Carlson, L. (eds) (1953). *The Writings of Robert Harrison and Robert Browne*. London: Allen and Unwin.

Perkins, William (1591). *A Golden Chaine*. Cambridge.

Propositions and Conclusions Concerning True Christian Religion (1612). Repr. in Lumpkin 1959: 124-42.

Robinson, Robert (1781). *The General Doctrine of Toleration Applied to the Particular Case of Free Communion*. Cambridge: Francis Hodson.

Schrenk, Gottlob (1923). *Gottesreich und Bund im alteren Protestantismus*. Gutersloh: Bertelsmann.

Sixteen Articles of Faith and Order Unanimously Assented To by the Messengers Met at Warwick (1655). Repr. in Lumpkin 1959: 198-200.

Smyth, John (1607). 'Principles and Inferences Concerning the Visible Church'. Repr. in Whitley 1915: I, pp. 249-68.

Smyth, John (1609a). *Paralleles, Censures, Observations*. Repr. in Whitley 1915: II, 327-546.

Smyth, John (1609b). *The Character of the Beast*. Repr. in Whitley 1915: II, 563-680.

Troeltsch, Ernst (1950). *The Social Teaching of the Christian Churches*. 2 vols, trans. Olive Wyon. London: George Allen & Unwin.

Turner, Daniel (1772). *A Modest Plea for Free Communion at the Lord's Table*. London.

Turner, Daniel (1778). *A Compendium of Social Religion*. 2nd edn. London: John Ward.

Wenger, John C. (1938). 'Pilgram Marpeck: Confession of Faith Composed at Strasburg'. *Mennnonite Quarterly Review* 12.3: 167-202.

White, B. R. (1971). *The English Separatist Tradition: From the Marian Martyrs to the Pilgrim Fathers*. Oxford: Oxford University Press.

White, B. R. (ed.) (1974). *Association Records of the Particular Baptists of England, Wales and Ireland to 1660*. 3 parts. Part 3. The Abingdon Association. London: Baptist Historical Society.

Whitley, W. T. (ed.) (1915). *The Works of John Smyth*. 2 vols. Cambridge: Cambridge University Press.

Williams, George Hunstan and Mergal, Angel M. (eds) (1957). *Spiritual and Anabaptist Writers: Documents Illustrative of the Radical Reformation*. Library of Christian Classics. Volume XXV. London: SCM Press.

Williams, George H. (1975). *The Radical Reformation*. Philadelphia: Westminster Press.

Word of God in the Life of the Church, The (2012). *A Report of International Conversations Between the Catholic Church and the Baptist World Alliance 2006–2010*. Repr. in *American Baptist Quarterly* 31.1: 28–122.

SUGGESTED READING

Bebbington, David (2010). *Baptists Through the Centuries: A History of a Global People*. Waco, TX: Baylor University.

Clasen, Claus-Peter (1972). *Anabaptism: A Social History, 1525-1618, Switzerland, Austria, Moravia, and South and Central Germany*. Ithaca, NY: Cornell University Press.

Fiddes, Paul S. (2003). *Tracks and Traces: Baptist Identity in Church and Theology*. Milton Keynes: Paternoster.

Harmon, Steven R. (2016). *Baptist Identity and the Ecumenical Future. Story, Tradition, and the Recovery of Community*. Waco, TX: Baylor University.

Lillback, Peter A. (2001). *The Binding of God: Calvin's Role in the Development of Covenant Theology*. Grand Rapids, MI: Baker Academic.

Sell, Alan (2012). *The Great Ejectment of 1662: Its Antecedents, Aftermath and Ecumenical Significance*. Eugene, OR: Pickwick.

Watts, Michael R. (1978). *The Dissenters: From the Reformation to the French Revolution*. Oxford: Oxford University Press.

White, B. R. (1971). *The English Separatist Tradition: From the Marian Martyrs to the Pilgrim Fathers*. Oxford: Oxford University Press.

Williams, George Hunstan and Mergal, Angel M. (eds) (1957). *Spiritual and Anabaptist Writers: Documents Illustrative of the Radical Reformation*. Library of Christian Classics. Volume XXV. London: SCM Press.

CHAPTER 14

METHODISM AND THE CHURCH

DAVID M. CHAPMAN

METHODIST reflection on the nature and location of the Church has been shaped by Methodism's origins in the Church of England as a holiness movement with universal missionary horizons and by a series of practical developments in response to its cultural context. Forged in the crucible of the eighteenth-century English Evangelical Revival, John Wesley's Methodism successfully harnessed a volatile combination of elements that fuelled its expansion into a global 'Empire of the Spirit' (Hempton 2005), conscious of occupying an independent, if disputed, place in the Holy Catholic Church.

Marshalled by the preaching and formidable organization of the Wesley brothers, together with their band of itinerant lay preachers, Methodism operated in the dialectical tension between Enlightenment and 'enthusiasm' (Hempton 2005: 52). Its hallmark polarities were: discipline and spiritual freedom; rational piety and enthusiasm; sobriety and ecstasy. The network or 'connexion' of Methodist societies, held together by an emerging polity enforced by the preachers, constituted a disciplined community at the service of God's mission in the world, interpreted as the proclamation of the evangelical faith and the spread of scriptural holiness.

While Methodism has come to acquire many of the elements commonly associated with the church, its ecclesiology mostly reflects the suppositions and priorities of a holiness movement (Kissack 1964; Carter 2002; Richey 2009; Chapman 2011). The present chapter investigates Methodist ecclesiology under six headings: Wesleyan foundations; methods, sources, and norms; credal marks of the church; ordained ministry; the means of grace and authority; future agenda.

WESLEYAN FOUNDATIONS

At first, since the Methodist economy of society meetings, preaching services, vigils, and fasting was (in theory) auxiliary to religious observance in Anglican parishes, John

Wesley insisted that Methodism was not 'the Church' and refused to separate from the Church of England, despite appeals by many of his itinerant preachers (Baker 1970). Eventually, in 1784, the elderly Wesley, regarding himself as apostle to the Methodists and concerned for their spiritual welfare in North America now that they were without access to Anglican sacraments following the War of Independence, personally endowed Methodism in the United States with the principal elements of a church—an ordained ministry, a liturgy adapted from the 1662 Book of Common Prayer, and Articles of Religion based on the Thirty-Nine Articles of the Church of England. 'The Doctrines and Discipline of the Methodist Episcopal Church in America' (1792) expanded the Wesleyan foundations into a comprehensive polity but said little about the nature of the church. When American Methodism fractured in the nineteenth century along the fault lines of race, slavery, and authority, the separate Methodist denominations generally retained these same ecclesial elements.

In Britain, following John Wesley's death in 1791, recurring power struggles produced rival Methodist denominations. The largest, the Wesleyan Methodist Connexion, only gradually came to describe itself as a church, strategically positioning itself in reaction to resurgent Anglo-Catholicism in the Church of England. But if Wesleyan hopes for reunion with Anglicans were never completely extinguished, the transition from holiness movement to independent Protestant church had already effectively been achieved by the close of the eighteenth century as a result of the sacramental self-sufficiency of the Methodist societies under the itinerant preachers.

What did John Wesley mean by the term 'church' and how has this influenced its current use in Methodism? Abandoning the Cyprianic concept of his youth, Wesley came to adopt a minimalist definition that considerably widened the visible boundaries of the church (Oh 2008). For instance, as a young Anglican priest, Wesley had maintained that only an episcopally ordained minister could validly administer baptism. Later, he came to distinguish between the outer call of the church, as confirmed by public ordination, and the inner call of the Spirit—a distinction that he used to justify irregular ministries, especially lay preaching, which manifestly brought people to salvation. What he did not foresee, however, was that later generations of Methodists would employ this distinction to distance the Holy Spirit from authorized forms of ministry, with enduring consequences for their understanding of the church.

The clearest statement of Wesley's mature ecclesiology is found in his sermon 'Of the Church' (Wesley 1784) and his Articles of Religion. Article XIII is lifted from Anglican Article XIX, which was based on Article VII of the Lutheran Augsburg Confession (1530): 'The visible Church of Christ is a Congregation of faithful men, in which the pure Word of God is preached, and the Sacraments be duly administered' (Wesley 1784: 51). This concise definition is both ontological and functional—what the church *is* and *does*—but offers no criteria for identifying where the church is concretely located.

Wesley's distinctive contribution to the study of the church, subsequently enshrined in Methodist ecclesiology, lies in his inclusive definition. For Wesley, 'the pure Word of God' denoted the minimum core of evangelical doctrines (which he assumed can be universally agreed), irrespective of accompanying errors and theological 'opinions' concerning non-essential aspects of the faith (Wesley 1784: 52). Reluctant to un-church even Roman Catholics, despite holding views that were conventionally anti-Catholic by the standards of the day, he omitted the second part of Anglican Article XIX that condemned the errors of the church of Rome.

To Wesley's way of thinking, which is still espoused by Methodists, the church is present wherever a faithful community gathers in response to the preaching of the gospel and the celebration of the sacraments under an authorized ministry. Accordingly,

> The catholic or universal church is all the persons in the universe whom God hath so called out of the world as to entitle them to the preceding character; as to be 'one body', united by 'one spirit'; having 'one faith, one hope, one baptism; one God and Father of all, who is above all, and through all, and in them all'. (Wesley 1784: 50)

The universal church, already a rather abstract entity in Wesley's ecclesiology, becomes even more formless when Methodists emphasize his apparent ambivalence towards ecclesial structures, overlooking the stabilizing effect of his solidly Anglican theology of ordained ministry. Wesley asks rhetorically:

> What is the end of all *ecclesiastical order*? Is it not to bring souls from the power of Satan to God? And to build them up in his fear and love? *Order*, then, is so far valuable as it answers these ends; and if it answers them not it is nothing worth. (Wesley 1746: 206)

This polemical retort to critics of irregular ministries makes the moderate point that an obsessive concern for ecclesiastical order obscures the salvific purpose of the church and restricts the freedom of the Spirit. However, the strong teleological orientation of Methodist ecclesiology tends to overemphasize the freedom of the Spirit in such a way that it undermines ecclesiastical order as a received means of giving stable, visible shape to the church.

Being 'called out of the world' as a result of Methodist preaching entailed a commitment to holy living. 'The Nature, Design, and General Rules of the United Societies' (1743) required Methodists to demonstrate the fruits of holy living: 'By doing no harm, by avoiding evil in every kind'; 'By doing good'; 'By attending upon all the ordinances of God' (Wesley 1743). Yet, for all its apparent rigour, Methodism was never intended to be an exclusive holy club for the spiritual elite but an inclusive holiness movement for the spiritually awakened, who manifested 'a desire to flee from the wrath to come'. Practical support came from a Methodist society exercising mutual oversight, 'watching over one another in love', as a way of helping one another on towards full salvation. Methodism, not being the church, could exclude backsliders from membership without implying excommunication.

Contemporary Methodism's ingrained societal understanding of church membership reflects the clear intention in Scripture that the baptized will always practise their faith. However, it fails to acknowledge that the church is a *corpus permixtum* (Matt. 13:24–30).

A societal model of membership sits uncomfortably with Methodism's status de facto as a church and its recently acquired custom, in many places, of admitting into membership through rites of confirmation into the church.

Central to the Christian life in Methodism is a strong affirmation of the baptismal vocation of all the faithful. Grudgingly at first, John Wesley came to believe that lay people possess spiritual gifts for building up the church. Those displaying the requisite 'gifts and graces' (including women) were accepted as itinerant preachers, though the Wesley brothers often quarrelled about the suitability of individuals—John being content with evidence of religious experience, a reluctant Charles demanding proof of technical and doctrinal competence. The ecclesiological legacy of this failure to reconcile the exercise of personal *charisms* with the desiderata of public authorization by the community (essentially what was at stake in these disputes) is evident in contemporary Methodism's inability to distinguish theologically and practically between ministry and discipleship which thus obscures both the distinctive nature of ordained ministry and the worldly orientation of the baptismal vocation.

The Wesley brothers' contrasting priorities with regard to innovation typifies the ecclesiological dilemma at the heart of Methodism. When it came to choosing between Methodism and the Church of England, the Wesleys came down on opposite sides. John, despite insisting that he lived and would die as a member of the Church of England, encouraged the very forces that threatened to unstitch the patchwork of Methodist societies from the Anglican fabric, leaving Charles to lament, 'All the difference between my brother and me was that my brother's first object was the Methodists and then the Church: mine was first the Church and then the Methodists' (Telford 1931: 8: 267). Reconciling the freedom of a holiness movement with the church's duty to preserve its apostolic character remains unfinished business in Methodist ecclesiology.

The writings of John Wesley are foundational for Methodist reflection on the church, though they contain a variety of competing theological convictions that are difficult to systematize. Moreover, their precise influence on contemporary Methodist theology is debatable, since they are often quoted out of context to support preconceived positions. Besides, select quotations from occasional pieces seldom capture the complexity of Wesley's thought. Nevertheless, the principal features of Methodist ecclesiology can all be traced directly to Wesley: an inclusiveness that recognizes the church in diverse Christian communities; the soteriological criterion of ecclesial structures; the baptismal vocation of lay people; the connexional nature of the church; holy living; and Christian conference (see the section 'The Means of Grace and Authority').

METHODS, SOURCES, AND NORMS

'Methodists affirm the Holy Scriptures of the Old and New Testaments as the primary rule of faith and practice and the centre of theological reflection' (World Methodist

Council (hereafter WMC) 2006: 151). This is a formula that grounds the doctrine of the church in the Bible but is susceptible to anachronistic attempts at replicating the earliest Christian community. The hermeneutical matrix in which Methodists read the Scriptures comprises the historic creeds, unspecified Reformation principles, and John Wesley's Articles of Religion, 'Sermons on Several Occasions' and 'Explanatory Notes on the New Testament', as well as current Methodist experience. Hence Methodist ecclesiology draws on an eclectic assortment of Roman Catholic, Protestant, Wesleyan, contemporary, and ecumenical sources.

Concerning method, 'Methodists acknowledge that scriptural reflection is influenced by the processes of reason, tradition and experience, while aware that Scripture is the primary source and criteria [sic] of Christian doctrine' (WMC 2006: 151). In practice, theological method in Methodism fluctuates according to the importance attached to each of these elements of the misleadingly termed 'Wesleyan Quadrilateral', the present tendency being to give priority to contemporary experience. Positively, this allows fresh insights to be applied to classical and Wesleyan authorities in the reading of Scripture. For instance, in 1970 the General Conference of the United Methodist Church in the United States (hereafter UMC) resolved to interpret its doctrinal standards—some of which perpetuate anti-Roman Catholic sentiments of the sixteenth century—in accordance with its best ecumenical insights and judgement (Oden 2008: 124). On the other hand, theological method in Methodism is susceptible to transient theological tastes.

Methodist polity, as the juridical embodiment of accumulated experience, provides an additional, if underused, source of official teaching on the church, despite the presence of competing ecclesiological convictions. While such inconsistencies further complicate attempts to produce a systematic doctrine of the church, their presence in Methodist polity says a great deal about theological method in Methodism. Essentially, Methodist ecclesiology is a form of practical, rather than speculative, theology: flexible and adaptable in response to changing circumstances, culture, and missionary needs as it seeks to articulate an authentically Methodist way of being the church in a particular time and place.

Theoretical reflection on the church in Methodism has therefore never been a priority. Even substantial surveys of Methodist theology (Abraham and Kirby 2009) do not devote a chapter specifically to the doctrine of the church. Addressing the question 'Do Methodists have a doctrine of the Church?', Albert Outler concluded: 'The answer "yes" says too much; "no" says too little' (Outler 1964: 11). In fact, Methodists have a working doctrine, which, though it suits the priorities of a holiness movement, pays insufficient attention to the need for structures that safeguard the apostolic tradition. Instead, Methodists have tended to assume that Christian communities will instinctively recognize in one another the presence of those core doctrines and authentic forms of Christian living that minimally constitute the church. This is neither a safe assumption in a pluralistic age nor one that is shared by Methodism's principal dialogue partners.

The doctrinal standards of Methodist churches (Oden 2008) continue to cite the Augsburg formula to define the church, though the centre of Methodist ecclesiology lies in the Wesleyan idea that the church is known primarily by its work of salvation. According to the UMC, for instance,

> The Church is a community of all true believers under the Lordship of Christ. It is the redeemed and redeeming fellowship in which the Word of God is preached by persons divinely called, and the Sacraments are duly administered according to Christ's own appointment. (UMC 2012: 23)

That the church can be defined as 'the redeemed and redeeming fellowship' denotes a minimal soteriological criterion: the church is constituted by its salvific work and not by the presence of any specific structures such as the historic episcopate.

While this definition emphasizes the salvific purpose of Christianity, it is heavily existential, narrowly conceiving the work of the church in terms of individual salvation ('all true believers'), to the neglect of the corporate and prior activity of the Holy Spirit as embodied in ecclesial structures. Moreover, it appears to leave open the question of whether the sacraments are strictly necessary to the church (even though Methodists uphold baptism and the Lord's Supper as instituted by Christ and of perpetual obligation), thereby implying that any ecclesial community in which saving grace is present is, by that alone, a church.

In a polemical age, a minimal soteriological criterion for identifying the church was an effective retort to those who un-churched Methodists, but at a cost of impairing the marks of catholicity and apostolicity. The Second Vatican Council, modifying the exclusive claims of Counter-Reformation ecclesiology, adopted a more nuanced approach to identifying the location of the church, the implications of which have yet to be fully embraced in ecumenical dialogue. Roman Catholics now affirm that the one church of Christ may be 'effectively present' in a particular ecclesial community (making it a means of salvation), without necessarily recognizing that community as a church in the 'proper' sense of the term (John Paul II 1995: 14–16). Rather than engage in controversy as to what minimally constitutes the *esse* of the church, Methodists might usefully consider whether 'being the Church' is not all or nothing but a matter of degree. Reflection on what properly belongs to the *plene esse* of the church in God's providence would be consistent with Methodism's theological method.

Methodists maintain that the church is 'connexional': each part is connected to every other so that all are affected by any one. This 'connexional principle . . . has been intrinsic to Methodism since its origins . . . it enshrines a vital truth about the nature of the Church. It witnesses to mutuality and interdependence which derive from the participation of all Christians through Christ in the very life of God' (Methodist Church of Great Britain 1999: §4.6.1). By accepting John Wesley's authority, the itinerant preachers were 'in connexion' with him (subsequently with the Conference); Methodism itself was a connexion of religious societies. Nowadays, connexionalism, the antithesis of congregationalism, is realized in structures of communion, governance, oversight, and consultation that bind Methodists at every level of ecclesial existence, replicating the mutual oversight that lies at the heart of Methodism. Yet, despite its historic importance in Methodism, only recently have Methodists begun to reflect critically on connexionalism, concluding that connexion and *koinōnia* are complementary ways of describing the juridical, sacramental, and spiritual unity of the church (Beck 1998; Chapman 1999; 2005).

Credal Marks of the Church

'Methodists profess the ancient ecumenical creeds, the Apostles' and Nicene Creed' (WMC 2006: 151), but have developed their own interpretation of what it means to believe in one holy catholic and apostolic church.

The unity of the church is necessarily visible in common structures of ministry and oversight, as well as being invisible (as a spiritual and sacramental reality). Visible unity expresses the social reality of a gospel of reconciliation, anticipating the final recapitulation of all things in Christ. Methodists regard the church as existing everywhere in a state of impaired unity and thus reject an ecumenism of return to the historic churches. For Methodists, the goal of ecumenism is nothing less than full visible unity, rather than reconciled diversity, which merely tolerates division (Chapman 2009, 2015). Unity will be achieved through mutual recognition (where possible) or an act of reconciliation that involves an exchange of ecclesial gifts, though Methodists are wary of receiving anything that could be construed as conferring legitimacy or remedying deficiencies in their ordained ministry.

The church is holy in the sense that its members are called from the world to live and grow in fellowship with God and one another. Holy living is doxological and not deontological, a life not of obligation but of beatitude, through participation in the means of grace and by showing forth the fruit of the Spirit in acts of faith and love that are transformative of self and human society. The Church is the communion of saints on the way to the perfection that is proper to redeemed humans united with Christ, though Methodists are deeply conscious of the institutional imperfections of the church, its capacity for error and structural sin. Nevertheless, Methodists affirm that, through God's gracious gift of holiness, the church is the realization and foretaste of the kingdom that awaits its final consummation.

Classically, holy living centred on the Methodist society, whose regular pattern of devotional and social activities provided an edifying alternative to worldly pursuits and a ready outlet for natural talents. Holy living beyond the Methodist society produced model citizens and employees, which often led to social advancement, thereby widening the gulf between Methodism's revivalist culture, exemplified in the nineteenth-century religious camp meetings, and the aesthetic tastes of a significant number of Methodists. Despite being socially conservative, Methodists were noted for moral earnestness bordering on the radical, a trait that prompted them to challenge injustice in the workplace (not least through the promotion of trade unions) and to alleviate social problems caused by gambling and alcohol, but which sometimes exhibited a puritanical streak that frowned upon frivolity and idle leisure. That Methodists no longer look on secular culture with suspicion stems in part from a changing perception that the church is not a fortress against a fallen world, but also from a weakening sense of ecclesial identity and religious subculture, with corresponding gains and losses on both counts. Nevertheless, Methodists still exhibit an identifiable commitment to Christian community and holy living.

As a result of Puritan influence, Methodists are reluctant to associate the Holy Spirit with material objects, notably buildings and devotional items, in a way that marks them as sacred, blessed, or holy. Methodist architectural styles encompass a broad spectrum from Puritan plainness to Renaissance extravagance, though simplicity and neatness of style is generally favoured. For missionary reasons, Methodists have sometimes built centres of worship and evangelism to look as little like conventional religious buildings as possible; whereas Methodist neo-Gothic architecture of the nineteenth century mirrored the ecclesiastical and social aspirations of affluent congregations, even if there was little sense of a correlation between a heavenly liturgy and the liturgical drama centred on earthly altars. While Methodists have not embraced any particular theology of sacred space, typically a Methodist place of worship is predominantly functional, a *domus ecclesiae* rather than a *domus dei*.

The growing sophistication in Methodist architecture, liturgy, theology, and devotional practice in the course of the past 200 years indicates that the ecclesial location of Methodism has continued to shift under the influence of those forces that generally affect the lifecycle of renewal movements of all shades. The changing architectural symbolism in Methodist worship (notably the reconfiguration of space to make the altar-table, instead of the pulpit, the central focus) and the increasing use of liturgical colour and vestments constitutes a rediscovery of traditional Western Catholic iconography, though many Methodists continue to prefer the beauty of holiness to the holiness of beauty. To be true to its origins, Methodism must somehow hold together in dialectical tension these modern spatial expressions of rational piety and enthusiasm which would pull it in opposite directions.

Methodists interpret catholicity quantitatively as denoting the universality of the church. Following Wesley's lead, the Holy Catholic Church is perceived to be the sum total of Christians living and departed, a universal community in which Methodism claims and cherishes its place. Methodists do not normally think of catholicity in the qualitative sense of denoting the fullness of the gospel or Christian truth. For Methodists, such fullness is an eschatological reality—the fullness of truth into which the Holy Spirit guides the church (John 16:13) rather than the fullness of the deposit of faith once delivered to the saints (Jude 1:3). Though the relationship between history and eschatology has yet to be worked out in Methodist ecclesiology, the church is seen more as a community of hope than of memory, a perspective that is matched by an eschatological orientation of the Eucharist as foretaste of the heavenly banquet. Nevertheless, in affirming their catholicity, Methodists increasingly seek to reconnect with the Christian past (Wainwright 2007).

Apostolicity denotes the church's continuity with the apostles. 'Methodists seek to confess, to interpret, and to live the apostolic faith, the faith once delivered to the saints' (WMC 2006: 151), but do not regard continuity in ministry as a guarantee of apostolicity. Methodists interpret apostolicity as continuity in the apostolic *mission* and so affirm the ecumenical consensus that

> apostolic tradition in the Church means continuity in the permanent characteristics of the Church of the apostles: witness to the apostolic faith, proclamation and fresh interpretation of the Gospel, celebration of baptism and the eucharist, the transmission of ministerial responsibilities, communion in prayer, love, joy and suffering, service to the sick and the needy, unity among the local churches and sharing the gifts which the Lord has given to each. (World Council of Churches 1982: §M34)

This multifaceted approach may yet lead to further ecumenical convergence, though much depends on what theological account is given of the relationship between these elements of apostolicity.

Ordained Ministry

Methodists have consistently rejected the idea that the New Testament contains a blueprint for the church and that the threefold ministry of bishop, priest/presbyter, and deacon belongs to the *esse* of the church. They maintain that no single pattern of ministry is prescribed in Scripture and that missionary needs may give rise to different forms of order. Still, Wesley regarded the threefold ministry as scriptural and belonging to the *bene esse* of the church, while his reading of Edward Stillingfleet and Peter King convinced him that 'bishops and presbyters are (essentially) of one order' (*Journal*, 20 January 1746; Wesley 1975: xx: 112) and thus equally possessed of the power to ordain, if circumstances required.

By laying hands on Thomas Coke (a fellow Church of England priest) for 'superintendency' in America, Wesley created a threefold ministry of bishop, elder/presbyter, and deacon. However, Methodist bishops do not exercise exactly the same ministry as their counterparts in other churches, nor do they claim to belong to the historic episcopate (Frank 2002: 229–53). Eschewing the diocesan model of episcopacy, they constitute a 'general, itinerant superintendency' for the vast majority of the Methodist people. The relentless itinerancy of bishops, elders, and lay preachers was a key factor in the rapid growth of American Methodism in the early nineteenth century as the frontier pushed westwards, though the later development of a settled pastoral ministry of elders (and even bishops) reflects the transition of Methodism from holiness movement to church.

Today, the status and role of Methodist bishops suggests continuing uncertainty about the threefold ministry. They do not belong to a distinct order of ministry but hold a permanent office within the eldership, though the liturgical order for the episcopal consecration of UMC bishops constitutes ordination into a distinct ministerial order in all but name. As spiritual leaders, Methodist bishops wield considerable influence but have few executive or legislative functions. Nor do they have a specific place in worship, beyond presiding at the ordination of candidates selected by Conference. Being officeholders, UMC bishops are constitutionally subordinate to the General Conference; yet the council of bishops gives them a distinct episcopal voice.

The interface between episcopal oversight and that of the General Conference has long been a source of tension (Kirby 2000). Asbury, appointed by Wesley to joint superintendency with Coke, thought it prudent to submit to election by the Conference of preachers. The rival claims of bishops and General Conference to exercise supreme authority were an underlying cause of the separation between Northern and Southern Methodism in 1844, and even today tensions remain between the two forms of oversight. In 1992, UMC bishops acquired responsibility 'To guard, transmit, teach, and proclaim, corporately and individually, the apostolic faith', as well as 'To teach and uphold the theological traditions' of the UMC (UMC 2012: 330). While this appears to strengthen episcopal oversight, bishops may not ordain on their own authority, and other developments in UMC polity blur the distinction between lay and ordained ministries.

That Wesley made no provision for ordained ministry in British Methodism can be attributed to his reluctance to precipitate a break with the Church of England in territory where episcopal oversight was firmly established. Proposals for a threefold ministry were rejected by the Conference in 1794, leaving the itinerant preachers (regarded by Wesley as extraordinary messengers of the gospel) to assimilate the status and functions of an ordained ministry. The Conference in 1795 allowed the itinerant preachers to celebrate the sacraments in Methodist societies where a majority of leaders were in favour. Canonical reception into 'full connexion' with the Wesleyan Conference came to be regarded as 'virtual ordination', though a liturgical form of ordination by prayer and the imposition of hands was introduced from 1836, probably in response to the Oxford Movement (George 1978: 154). To avoid creating a personal ministerial succession, no one ordained by Wesley was permitted to participate in the laying on of hands; instead the (ministerial) President of the Wesleyan Conference ordained candidates on its behalf—a personal expression of an essentially corporate *episkope* which remains the practice today.

In Britain and the United States, later developments in Methodism's ordained ministry reflect general trends among Protestants. The 'pastoral office' of the ordained ministry was held in high esteem until the levelling idea of 'the priesthood of all believers' made heavy inroads into Methodism in the latter part of the nineteenth century. Membership of the Conference was reserved to ministers until lay people were finally admitted in the 1870s under the influence of democratizing trends in secular society. In the twentieth century, changing social attitudes eventually resulted in the ordination of women, their pioneering role as itinerant preachers having long since been forfeit to Methodism's social conservatism. Since Methodists have little sense of their movement's history, these pragmatic developments are now popularly regarded as foundational principles of Methodist ecclesiology.

Probably the most significant development in the structure of ordained ministry in Methodism concerns the diaconate. Until recently, the diaconate in American Methodism was a transitional order constituting a period of probation prior to ordination into the presbyterate. In the 1990s the UMC opened the diaconate as a permanent order (Frank 2002: 204–6), and British Methodists instituted a permanent diaconate in parallel with the presbyterate. In neither case has the nature of the diaconate and its relationship with the other order(s) of ministry been fully defined. Direct ordination into the presbyterate, reflecting deep-seated antipathy towards ministerial hierarchy, introduces a false dichotomy between the ministry of service and that of word and sacrament.

While Methodist ordinals boldly assert an intention to ordain bishops, presbyters/elders, and deacons into the ministry of the one, holy, catholic, and apostolic church, there is little evidence to suggest that ecumenical considerations inform the development of the ordained ministry in Methodism. Driven by perceived missionary needs, the ordained ministry has continued to develop in ways that sometimes diverge from the classical threefold pattern. Even if such divergence can be defended, it raises questions about the nature of the ordained ministry and the process by which the church reforms itself. Lacking a long historical perspective, Methodism exhibits the impatience for reform characteristic of a renewal movement, relying on the processes of Christian Conference (see the section 'The Means of Grace and Authority'), with their inbuilt checks and balances, in order to discern the guidance of the Holy Spirit. One of the challenges facing Methodist ecclesiology is to state the conditions for authoritative discernment in the light of the Holy Spirit's past providence.

Ordinarily, presidency at the Lord's Supper in Methodism is reserved to bishops and elders/presbyters, though other individuals—typically lay pastors—may be authorized to preside in situations where Methodists would otherwise be deprived of receiving the sacrament. While there is no doctrinal basis in Methodism for the increasingly voiced suggestion that individuals are qualified to preside at the Eucharist solely by virtue of their baptism, appeal to the principle of *necessity* is impeccably Wesleyan, though Wesley would have strongly objected to the present tendency in some quarters of Methodism to confuse convenience with necessity.

Ecumenical partners are entitled to ask Methodists whether the practice of lay presidency, however circumscribed, is consistent with an intention to ordain into the ministry of the universal church in which bishops and presbyters are generally understood to be sacramentally configured to Christ as head and shepherd of the church and thereby uniquely qualified to represent him before the church by presiding at the Eucharist. Despite references in official Methodist texts to ordained ministers as representing Christ before his people, the emphasis is heavily on the ordained minister as the authorized representative of the church in a way that obscures the sense of a ministerial office possessed of a distinctive vocation and corresponding spiritual gifts for its exercise.

The reluctance to associate ordained ministry with the possession of spiritual gifts conferred at ordination has a long history in Methodism, an unintended consequence of Wesley's distinction between the inner call of the Spirit and the outer call of the church. This quasi-Donatist tendency to dissociate the Holy Spirit from authorized ministries undoubtedly contributed to the fissiparity of Methodism in the nineteenth century and is evident today in the erosion of theological distinctions between lay and ordained and in the widespread distrust of ministerial authority. Altogether, the relationship between ordained ministry and the ministry of the whole people of God requires further investigation in Methodism.

THE MEANS OF GRACE AND AUTHORITY

Since 'Methodists believe in the centrality of grace; prevenient, justifying, and sanctifying' (WMC 2006: 151) holy living involves what Wesley called 'pressing on towards full salvation'. His doctrine of Christian perfection or entire sanctification, whatever its defects, attests the power of saving grace at work in the baptized. For Wesley, the instituted means of grace comprise those repeatable actions appointed by God as ordinary channels of grace: prayer (public and private); 'Searching the Scripture'; the Lord's Supper; fasting; 'Christian Conference'. Supplementing these are 'prudential' means initiated within the church from time to time to meet particular needs, including society meetings, love-feasts, and watch-nights (Wesley 1975: x: 855–7), which are still valued in some parts of Methodism. Since baptism is unrepeatable, Wesley did not rank it among the regular means of grace, though he regarded it as one of two dominically instituted sacraments conferring saving grace (the other being the Lord's Supper) and the normal means of entry into the church.

That Methodists have dutifully continued to baptize infants reflects their theological roots in the Church of England and an intuitive sense that baptism is the prevenient gateway into the new covenant in Christ, even if they have not always been sure that its benefits include regeneration. Sympathetic to Puritan belief that reliance upon the efficacy of baptism led to spiritual complacency, Wesley revised the baptismal liturgy for Methodist use to remove explicit references to regeneration as being among its sacramental effects. To Wesley's way of thinking, this was a modest concession to Puritan sensitivities. However, by weakening the link between the gift of the Holy Spirit and its sacramental sign, he started a trend that saw later generations of Methodists distance the 'new birth' from the sacrament of baptism. Modern Methodist baptismal liturgies go some way towards restoring the link between baptism and the washing of original sin.

Early Methodism aspired to produce a Eucharistic revival in the Church of England, at least in the mind of Wesley, who impressed upon Methodists the duty of 'constant communion'. For Methodists in the United States, he envisaged a celebration of the Eucharist every Sunday using his revision of the Book of Common Prayer. The evident desire of Methodists to receive the sacrament from their own pastors was a crucial factor in their separation from the Church of England and incidentally confirms the importance of the Lord's Supper in early Methodism. But whereas Methodists have always valued Holy Communion, for various reasons, including an insufficient number of presbyters, they have never established a weekly celebration. In the United States, frontier culture proved impervious to the literary ethos necessary for the appreciation of liturgical texts. Here extempore forms of worship quickly became the norm, with quarterly celebrations of the Lord's Supper coinciding with a visit from the travelling elder. In Britain, the preaching service became normative, though (Anglican) Morning Prayer was the preferred form of worship for a minority of Wesleyan Methodists well into the twentieth century.

While the Lord's Supper remains a cherished ordinance among Methodists, regular spiritual nourishment is supplied by services of the Word, supplemented by the cycle of denominational festivals. The style of Methodist worship has adapted over the years in response to changing spiritual needs, though evangelical and revivalist forms remain popular in many places. Elsewhere, Methodist worship has mostly settled into a pattern little different from other mainstream Protestant churches, though the past forty years have also witnessed a resurgence of sacramental worship, partly encouraged by liturgical reforms (Tucker 1996). At the same time, Pentecostal influences on Methodist worship, especially in South America and Asia, ensure a diverse global picture.

For much of Methodism's history, admission to the Lord's Supper was limited to holders of the ticket of membership, a restriction equivalent in intention to the Book of Common Prayer's invitation to 'draw near with faith' all those 'that do truly and earnestly repent' of their sins and are 'in love and charity' with their neighbours. Recently, however, the historical fiction of an 'open' communion table in Methodism has become firmly embedded in popular Methodist self-understanding—suggesting that the principle of inclusion is currently the preferred hermeneutical key to the New Testament. That Wesley could describe the Eucharist as a 'converting ordinance' is often cited as sufficient justification for admitting even the non-baptized to the Lord's Supper, ignoring the very precise way in which he thought of 'conversion' in relation to the life of the baptized. Whether theological method in Methodism will be able to restore a more holistic reading of the Wesleyan corpus remains to be seen.

The question of whether the church itself is a means of grace is controversial in Methodism. Methodists have generally taken the view that the Holy Spirit confers grace upon the individual directly, without the church's mediation. To this way of thinking, the church is not the sacrament, but the herald, of salvation. However, recent Methodist statements seek to combine the two ideas: 'The Church is both the creation of the Word of God, and also the "mystery" or "sacrament" of God's love for the world' (Methodist Church of Great Britain 1999: §3.1.10). But whether the two concepts can be integrated without one occluding the other requires further investigation. A possible theological framework might be the Joint Declaration on the Doctrine of Justification between the Roman Catholic Church and the Lutheran World Federation, which the WMC formally became associated with in 2006 (WMC 2006: 210). It is also worth noting that Methodists have not been impervious to the development of Eucharistic ecclesiology. If Methodists are not yet ready to affirm that 'the Eucharist makes the Church', they have a greater sense than ever before that the church is most fully itself when the people of God gather to celebrate the Lord's Supper.

Methodists take the view that authoritative discernment is properly exercised corporately and open to revision. At first, John Wesley's personal oversight of Methodism was absolute, extending even to Methodist missions overseas. However, from 1744 onwards he met annually with a number of invited itinerant preachers to confer about issues of concern to the Methodist societies, though in his lifetime the Conference was consultative and advisory, the final decision resting with him. The succinct agenda of the first Conference went beyond the horizons of a holiness movement to touch upon the life of the church itself: '(1) What to teach; (2) How to teach; and (3) What to do, that is how to regulate our doctrine, discipline and practice' (Wesley 1975 x: 120).

In Wesleyan perspective, 'Christian Conference' is an instituted means of grace enabling authoritative discernment sufficient for the people of God to continue in their providential way. In the United States, the Methodist Episcopal Church developed a quadrennial General Conference, with annual Conferences of preachers organized regionally. In Britain, Wesley provided for the pastoral oversight of Methodism to be transferred to the corporate *episkope* of an annual Conference of preachers upon his death. Nowadays fully inclusive of lay people, the various autonomous Conferences within World Methodism continue to exercise authoritative discernment, combining the roles of spiritual leader, legislator, regulator, and *Magisterium*.

The extensive consultative processes of Christian Conference provide a reasonably reliable means of discerning the *consensus fidelium* among Methodists, though concerns have long been expressed that spiritual discernment is too easily confused with the views of a democratic majority. As Methodists become increasingly conscious of their intentional catholicity, the question is whether and how Christian Conference might be better informed by the teaching of ecumenical partners. In Christian Conference, as with so much else in Methodism, the challenge is to balance the freedom of a holiness movement with the responsibilities of being the church.

Methodists readily affirm that the exercise of authority in the church is personal, collegial, and communal (World Council of Churches 1982). Authority in Methodism is exercised personally by bishops and others, collegially by ministerial synods, and communally by church councils, representative synods, and Conferences elected from among the Methodist people. Together, Methodist structures of oversight constitute a consensual and consultative form of ecclesiastical government, with the Conference as the supreme agent of authoritative discernment. Methodist ecclesiology has yet to describe the contribution of personal *episkope* to authoritative discernment. However, Methodist experience suggests that theoretical definitions of the exercise of authority in the church fail to take account of the tensions that can arise between its personal, collegial, and communal forms.

Future Agenda

As an exercise in practical theology, Methodist ecclesiology remains a work in progress. A number of issues requiring further study have already been identified. The chapter concludes with an overview of the future agenda in terms of method and priority issues.

Concerning method, a number of influences on Methodist ecclesiology can be identified as requiring investigation. One such influence is the growing ecumenical consensus on the nature of the church. Methodists gave the World Council of Churches' Faith and Order Commission's report *Baptism, Eucharist and Ministry* (1982) a cautious welcome (Thurian 1986) and have since incorporated many of its themes and ideas into their teaching documents. They also identify with much of what is contained in the follow-up convergence statements *The Nature and Mission of the Church* (WCC 2005) and *The Church: Towards a Common Vision* (WCC 2013). However, current Methodist ecclesiology describes the church primarily in instrumental terms and has yet to exploit fully the ecumenical consensus that the church is also sign and foretaste of God's kingdom.

The influence of missiology on ecclesiological method also requires investigation. In practice, Wesley's soteriological criterion for the church has been replaced by a missiological norm without consideration of the theological and practical consequences. That the purpose of ecclesiastical order in Methodism is normally thought of as being to facilitate mission, and not to save souls, reinforces an instrumental definition of the church as the *redeeming* community, at the cost of minimizing the role of those ministries that strengthen the church as a *redeemed* community committed to holy living as sign and foretaste of God's kingdom.

What is more, the appeal to 'missionary needs', which caused Wesley much soul-searching before acting *ultra vires* to establish a threefold ministry for Methodists in North America, is now so frequently heard that it risks compromising Methodism's ecclesial integrity. The problem is compounded by the language of crisis, which is employed to add leverage to proposed changes in polity irrespective of the ecclesiological implications. At some point, Methodists will have to decide whether and how their understanding of the nature of the church should determine mission strategy, or whether ecclesiology is a chapter of missiology. Calls for a 'missional ecclesiology' obscure the theological difference between these approaches. A fresh vision of the church is necessary for the proper orientation of Methodism's historic mission to spread scriptural holiness.

For all its inconsistencies, Methodist polity, as an implicit carrier of belief concerning the nature of the church, is a potentially rich, if still largely untapped, resource for continuing ecclesiological reflection. For instance, it is theologically significant that Methodist polity has consistently affirmed the lifelong vocation of ordained ministers and specifically prohibited re-ordination in cases of reinstatement to ministry, even though Methodists have no teaching about indelible sacramental character. Many other liturgical and constitutional reforms in Methodism in the past fifty years (including the gradual replacement of societal language by references to the church) implicitly express ecclesiological convictions that have yet to be fully developed.

Lastly, two specific issues would seem to be priorities for any future agenda. Probably the most urgent issue, because of its implications for relations with Anglicans, concerns whether and how sufficient theological and practical convergence can be achieved to enable Methodist bishops to be incorporated into what Anglicans term 'the historic episcopate' as the effective means of achieving the reconciliation and interchangeability of ordained ministries. In the United States, practical convergence between the UM and Episcopal (Anglican) churches has led to proposals for the establishment of 'full communion' and the interchangeability of ordained ministries on the basis of a mutual recognition of episcopal ministries (UMC 2017). In Britain, theological agreement in principle concerning *episkope* has led to proposals for British Methodism to receive the gift of the historic episcopate from the Church of England as the effective means of achieving the reconciliation and interchangeability of ordained ministries (Methodist Church of Great Britain 2017). In both cases, it remains to be seen whether these convergences establish sufficient common ground for such proposals to gain the necessary support in Anglican Synods and Methodist Conferences given the contrasting concerns of 'High Church' Anglicans and 'Low Church' Methodists. The second, related, issue is the pressing need to develop a theological account of the means by which Methodism seeks to define and safeguard the specific content of the church's apostolicity and catholicity.

If ecclesiology as a form of practical theology, as typically found in Methodism, has certain weaknesses, notably its systematic inconsistencies, an undoubted strength is its focus on the actual life of the people of God rather than on abstract (and thus potentially idealized) theory. Drawing on the accumulated experience of 275 years of spreading scriptural holiness, Methodists are more confident than ever before that they have theological insights into the nature of the church and rich ecclesial endowments to offer ecumenical partners in an exchange of gifts (Chapman 2008). Equally, Methodist ecclesiology is open to reorientation as horizons develop. 'In effect, Methodists rule out no development compatible with our ethos which strengthens the unity and effectiveness in mission of the Church' (Methodist Church of Great Britain 1999: §4.6.11).

The key strategic decision affecting the development of Methodist ecclesiology relates to the question of where Methodism intends to be located in the ecclesial spectrum. A shared understanding of the doctrine of grace and sanctification brings Methodists closer to Roman Catholics (WMC 2016), whereas current Methodist trends in describing the status of the ordained ministry suggests an affinity with Protestants. Given the competing theological convictions and trends in the melting pot of Methodism, as well as the different contexts in which Methodists operate, it remains to be seen how Methodist ecclesiology will develop. The question is whether being 'at full liberty, simply to follow the scriptures and the primitive church' (as Wesley advised Methodists in North America) will result in Methodism moving closer to its Anglican parent or more in the direction of its spiritual heir in the shape of Pentecostalism. At present, Methodist ecclesiology continues to display the hallmarks of a holiness movement in search of the church.

References

Abraham, William J. and Kirby, James E. (eds) (2009). *The Oxford Handbook of Methodist Studies*. Oxford: Oxford University Press.
Baker, Frank (1970). *John Wesley and the Church of England*. London: Epworth.

Beck, Brian E. (1998). 'Connexion and Koinonia: Wesley's Legacy and the Ecumenical Ideal'. In Randy L. Maddox (ed.), *Rethinking Wesley's Theology for Contemporary Methodism*. Nashville: Kingswood, 129–41.

Carter, David (2002). *Love bade me welcome: A British Methodist Perspective on the Church*. Peterborough: Epworth.

Chapman, David M. (1999). 'Koinonia and Connexionalism'. *Epworth Review* 26: 82–7.

Chapman, David M. (2005). 'Koinonia, Connexion and Episcope: Methodist Ecclesiology in the Twentieth Century'. In Richard Sykes (ed.), *Methodism across the Pond: Perspectives Past and Present on the Church in Britain and America*. Oxford: Applied Theology Press, 4–10.

Chapman, David M. (2008). 'The Exchange of Gifts: A Methodist Perspective'. In Paul D. Murray (ed.), *Receptive Ecumenism and the Call to Catholic Learning*. Oxford: Oxford University Press, 449–67.

Chapman, David M. (2009). 'Methodism and the Future of Ecumenism'. In William J. Abraham and James Kirby (eds), *The Oxford Handbook of Methodist Studies*. Oxford: Oxford University Press, 449–67.

Chapman, David M. (2011). 'Holiness and Order: British Methodism's Search for the Holy Catholic Church'. *Ecclesiology* 7: 71–96.

Chapman, David M. (2015). 'Ecumenism and the Visible Unity of the Church: Organic Union or Reconciled Diversity?' *Ecclesiology* 11: 350–69.

Frank, Thomas Edward (2002). *Polity, Practice, and the Mission of the United Methodist Church*. Nashville: Abingdon.

George, A. Raymond (1978). 'Ordination'. In Rupert Davies, A. Raymond George, and Gordon Rupp (eds), *A History of the Methodist Church in Great Britain*. London: Epworth, vol. 2, 143–60.

Hempton, David (2005). *Methodism: Empire of the Spirit*. New Haven: Yale University Press.

John Paul II, Pope (1995). *Ut Unum Sint: Encyclical Letter of the Holy Father John Paul II on Commitment to Ecumenism*. London: Catholic Truth Society.

Kirby, James E. (2000). *The Episcopacy in American Methodism*. Nashville: Kingswood.

Kissack, Reginald (1964). *Church or No Church? A Study of the Development of the Concept of Church in British Methodism*. London: Epworth.

Methodist Church of Great Britain (1999). *Called to Love and Praise: The Nature of the Church in Methodist Experience and Practice*. Peterborough: Methodist Publishing.

Methodist Church of Great Britain (2017). *Mission and Ministry in Covenant: Report from the Faith and Order Bodies of the Church of England and the Methodist Church*.

Oden, Thomas C. (2008). *Doctrinal Standards in the Wesleyan Tradition*. Nashville: Abingdon.

Oh, Gwang Seok (2008). *John Wesley's Ecclesiology: A Study in its Sources and Development*. Lanham, MD: Scarecrow Press.

Outler, Albert C. (1964). 'Do Methodists have a Doctrine of the Church?' In Dow Kirkpatrick (ed.), *The Doctrine of the Church*. London: Epworth, 11–28.

Richey, Russell E. (2009). *Doctrine in Experience: A Methodist Theology of Church and Ministry*. Nashville: Kingswood.

Telford, John (1931). *The Letters of John Wesley AM*. 8 vols. London: Epworth.

Thurian, Max (ed.) (1986). *Churches Respond to BEM*. vol. 2. Geneva: World Council of Churches.

Tucker, Karen Westerfield (1996). *The Sunday Service of the Methodists: Twentieth-Century Worship in Worldwide Methodism*. Nashville: Kingswood.

United Methodist Church (2012). *The Book of Discipline of the United Methodist Church.* Nashville: United Methodist Publishing House.

United Methodist Church (2017). *A Gift to the World: Co-Laborers for the Healing of Brokenness. The Episcopal Church and The United Methodist Church. A Proposal for Full Communion.* <https://www.episcopalchurch.org/library/document/gift-world-co-laborers-healing-brokenness>.

Wainwright, Geoffrey (2007). *Embracing Purpose: Essays on God, the World and the Church.* Peterborough: Epworth.

Wesley, John (1743). 'The Nature, Design and General Rules of the United Societies'. In Wesley 1975–: vol. ix, 69–73.

Wesley, John (1746), 'To "John Smith"'. In Wesley 1975–: vol. xxvi, 197–207.

Wesley, John (1784). 'Sermon 74: Of the Church'. In Wesley 1975–: vol. iii, 45–57.

Wesley, John (1975–). *The Works of John Wesley.* 34 vols projected. Oxford: Clarendon; Nashville: Abingdon.

World Council of Churches (1982). *Baptism, Eucharist and Ministry.* Geneva.

World Council of Churches (2005). *The Nature and Mission of the Church: A Stage on the Way to a Common Statement.* Geneva: World Council of Churches.

World Council of Churches (2013). *The Church: Towards a Common Vision.* Geneva: World Council of Churches.

World Methodist Council (2006). 'Wesleyan Essentials of the Faith'. *Proceedings of the Nineteenth World Methodist Conference Seoul, Korea 2006,* 151–3.

World Methodist Council (2016). *The Call to Holiness: From Glory to Glory, Report of the Joint International Commission for Dialogue between the World Methodist Council and the Roman Catholic Church.* <http://worldmethodistcouncil.org/wp-content/uploads/2016/09/The-Call-to-Holiness-Final-copy-28062016.pdf>.

Suggested Reading

Anglican–Methodist International Commission for Unity in Mission (AMICUM) (2014). *Into all the World: Being and Becoming Apostolic Churches. A Report to the Anglican Consultative Council and the World Methodist Council.* London: Anglican Consultative Council.

Carter, David (2002). *Love bade me welcome: A British Methodist Perspective on the Church.* Peterborough: Epworth.

Chapman, David M. (2013). '"Social Holiness"—Antidote to "Solitary Religion": Recovering a Theology of Church as Community'. In Peter de Mey (ed.), *Believing in Community: Ecumenical Reflections on the Church.* Leuven: Leuven University Press, 29–40.

Field, David N. (2017). *Bid our Jarring Conflicts Cease: A Wesleyan Theology and Praxis of Church Unity.* Nashville: Foundery.

Outler, Albert C. (1964). 'Do Methodists have a Doctrine of the Church?' In Dow Kirkpatrick (ed.), *The Doctrine of the Church.* London: Epworth, 11–28.

Richey, Russell E. (2009). *Doctrine in Experience: A Methodist Theology of Church and Ministry.* Nashville: Kingswood.

CHAPTER 15

PENTECOSTAL ECCLESIOLOGIES

AMOS YONG

INTRODUCTION

AT the present time, there are a number of emerging pentecostal ecclesiological constructions, but there is no dominant pentecostal ecclesiology (Kärkkäinen 2002a: ch. 6).[1] It is not that there are no discussions of ecclesiology in pentecostal theological textbooks or systematic theological treatises (Duffield and Van Cleave 1983: ch. 8; Williams 1992: part I; Dusing 1995; Warrington 2008: ch. 4), but that these by and large reflect more evangelical rather than distinctively pentecostal ways of thinking about the nature of the church. Further, pentecostal theology as a scholarly enterprise is itself a relatively recent development (Yong 2007a), so there is also the question of what, if any, is a unique pentecostal theological methodology. More important, as will be clear from discussion to come, like many other Christian movements, there is a variety of ecclesiological views among Pentecostals in part due to the fact that there are many different ecclesiological forms and structures across the pentecostal world. And given the dynamic, improvisational, and experimental nature of the pentecostal-charismatic spirituality, it is as improbable to expect theological, much less ecclesiological, consensus, as it is unlikely that the proliferating trends long associated with this phenomenon will dissipate. So if the main lines of ecclesiological reflection in the Christian tradition have been guided in substantive measure by considerations of the four marks of the church—the church as one, holy, catholic, and apostolic (cf. Yong 2002)—what then might provide coherence for thinking about pentecostal, charismatic, and renewal ecclesiology across its diverse landscape?

[1] Thanks to my (by now graduated) doctoral student Timothy Lim Teck Ngern for his feedback on a previous version of this chapter. Unless otherwise noted, all Scripture references will be from the New Revised Standard Version.

This chapter can do no more than scratch the surface of pentecostal ecclesiological thinking. The first, longest, section provides some historical perspective on the classical pentecostal movement, its dominant ecclesiological forms, and the burgeoning contemporary setting. The second and third sections are in part cartographic and in part constructive. I will argue that pentecostal ecclesiological dynamism is inspired largely by its pneumatic spirituality; hence the two sections map emerging ecclesiological tendencies under the rubrics 'the church as the charismatic fellowship of the Spirit' and 'the church as the people of God, the body of Christ, and the temple of the Holy Spirit'. While the former will reflect, or so I will suggest, some of what is distinctive about pentecostal ecclesiological self-understanding, the latter will situate that self-understanding within the mainstream of ecclesiological developments. Throughout both sections, however, we will trace both the opportunities and challenges opened up by such a pneumatologically oriented set of ecclesiological sensibilities.

A few definitional clarifications are in order before proceeding. In this chapter, while our focus will be on classical pentecostal churches (to be described immediately), their histories cannot be strictly separated from later developments such as the charismatic renewal in mainline Protestantism, Roman Catholicism, and the Orthodox stream. Thus the designation 'pentecostal-charismatic' will include this wider set of movements and usage of 'charismatic' will similarly refer to this broader spectrum. At various points, the terminology of 'renewal' (Yong 2007b) will be the all-inclusive nomenclature utilized for pentecostal, charismatic, and related movements and their self-understandings. Further, as readers will have observed, these labels appear in lower case when used adjectivally; capitalization will be used when referring to Pentecostalism as a noun, to Pentecostals as a group, or to churches that have the words Pentecostal or Charismatic as part of their proper name.

Pentecostal Churches: A Historical and Phenomenological Sketch

It is difficult to understand pentecostal ecclesiological diversity without first getting a good sense of its historical manifestations and trajectories. The following unfolds across three horizons: a brief historical sketch, a survey of classical pentecostal ecclesial forms, and an overview of contemporary renewal expressions. Our goal here is to get a sense of why it is difficult to talk about any dominant pentecostal ecclesiology, but at the same time to lay the groundwork for how and why an overarching pneumatological theology of the church may yet provide a way forward for constructive reflection.

Modern Pentecostalisms: Historical Contours

While there is plenty of vigorous scholarly debate about the origins of what is called 'modern Pentecostalism', most agree that it is a set of twentieth-century movements—hence, 'Pentecostalisms'. To be sure, there are—and these are disputed terms—'pre-pentecostal' or 'proto-pentecostal' movements that some scholars identify back as far as the first part of the nineteenth century, even as there are other revivals which relationships to Pentecostalism are not easily classified. The standard account is that the modern pentecostal movement can be dated back to the Azusa Street revival in Los Angeles, California, from 1906 to 1908. Those associated with the so-called 'Birmingham School'—led by Walter Hollenweger (1997), the doyen of pentecostal studies (Price 2002), and his successor at the University of Birmingham, Allan Anderson (2004), among others who have studied under both of these scholars—consider such an America-centric narrative simplistic and have long argued that there were multiple revivals around the world during the first decade of the twentieth century which together catalysed what is now called modern Pentecostalism. Yet even those who call for recognition of the global provenance of Pentecostalism acknowledge the key role played by missionaries stemming from Azusa Street in establishing networks of pentecostal churches, organizations, and initiatives around the world (Anderson 2007).

To be sure, the Azusa Street revival not only launched missionaries to the ends of the earth but also precipitated the founding of pentecostal churches across North America. (Note: there is some debate also about whether Pentecostalism in Canada pre-dated or was dependent on the Azusa Street mission; Stewart 2010.) Initially many of these were self-identified 'movements' or 'fellowships' of churches. Their members were 'come-outers' from the established Protestant churches who considered these routinized ecclesial environments to be bereft of spiritual vitality at best and even inimical to what they considered to be the 'higher Christian life' (a more deeply committed Christian calling and vocation) at worst. Hence they, like other restorationist movements of the nineteenth century such as the Disciples of Christ, were not necessarily seeking to establish alternative denominations, but to be a part of something more dynamic and organic, less ritualized and bureaucratized. Thus they began associations, voluntary cooperative fellowships, as such have since come to be known, through which they could experience spiritual renewal and revitalization, and participate in collaborative evangelistic and missionary ventures, among other undertakings.

In due course, these associations organized themselves variously. Over the next generation, some became de facto denominations even while the come-outers among them have resisted the denominational label since that is what they thought they had left behind. Yet the institutionalization process rolled on. Groups like the Assemblies of God, the Church of God (Cleveland, Tennessee), the Church of God in Christ, and the International Church of the Foursquare Gospel, among many others, became denominationalized, all the while insisting that they were more organic 'fellowships' of ministers. As we shall see in a moment, these groups of churches embraced a wide range of ecclesiastical structures and forms which have not only persisted but also multiplied. However, they all have come to be classified together by historians and sociologists as 'classical pentecostal churches' due primarily to their originating in North America in the first quarter of the twentieth century, almost always by groups of ministers who had connections to the Azusa Street revival in some way.

Moving into the second half of the twentieth century, many of these pentecostal churches and gradually developing denominations remained at the margins of North American society. By the early 1940s, however, some of their leading groups had become accepted by sister conservative Protestant organizations like the National Association of Evangelicals. Yet by and large, Pentecostals were viewed suspiciously, in part because of their own sectarian habits and rhetoric and in part because the established churches had long distanced themselves from such 'enthusiastic' practices and spiritualities. All of this would change, however, with the appearance of charismatic renewal in mainline Protestant circles starting in the late 1950s.

Henry Pitt Van Dusen, President of Princeton Theological Seminary, had predicted as much when, in an article in *Life* magazine in 1958, he observed that Pentecostalism was arising as what he then called 'the third force in Christendom', after the ancient Catholic synthesis and then the later Protestant reformation. Shortly thereafter, during the Easter service in 1960, the rector of St Mark's Episcopal church in Van Nuys, California, Dennis Bennett, announced to the congregation his own pentecostal experience and journey. Charismatic renewal then began to spread across the various mainline Protestant denominations, and continued almost unabated for at least the next two decades (Hunt 2009: ch. 5; Hummel 1994). In 1967 the renewal broke out among Roman Catholics at Duquesne University in Pittsburgh, Pennsylvania, and spread in short order across the Roman Catholic world into South America (Hanna 2006; Maurer 2010). By the end of the century, one Roman Catholic scholar argued that the charismatic renewal had saved the Roman Catholic Church from losing ground to Protestantism in general and Pentecostalism specifically, especially in the Latin American hemisphere (Stoll 1991; Cleary 2009, 2011).

Charismatic renewal across the Christian spectrum set off numerous chain-reactions. While some Protestants and Catholics left their churches and joined up with pentecostal groups and denominations, many did not. Those who remained within their familiar contexts contributed variously to the renewal and revitalization of their churches. Such 'neo-pentecostal' streams swelled within the ranks of especially mainline Protestant churches leading to the formation of offices to manage, facilitate, and even integrate such expressions into denominational and ecclesial life. In hindsight after more than fifty years, these efforts appear to have been more or less successful when assessed globally. Mainline Protestant denominations in North America have in many cases continued to suffer numerical losses. On the other hand, across Asia, Africa, and Latin America, more often than not these same denominations and churches have embraced a pentecostal or charismatic identity, or at least set of expressions. Some scholars have thus begun talking about the gradual pentecostalization or charismatization of global Christianity, even among historic traditions and churches, now fifty plus years into the renewal movement (Omenyo 2002; Asamoah-Gyadu 2004).

In the North American scene, such pentecostalization and charismatization has also been occurring, but recently amidst more evangelically oriented churches. Some charismatics who refrained from joining pentecostal churches or who did not remain within their historic denominations themselves converged among what one author has called a 'third wave' of the Holy Spirit—after the Azusa Street revival and the charismatic renewal in the mainline churches—across the twentieth century (Wagner 1988). Others within this overarching trajectory have included those fed up with denominationalism altogether and committed either to local church autonomy (thus preferring non-denominational or independent congregational formats) or to non-hierarchically and informally organized relational networks. I will return toward the end of the section 'The Church as a Charismatic and Missionary Fellowship of the Spirit' to further discuss some of the unfolding ecclesiastical forms as this so-called 'third wave' has continued to roll onto the global renewal shoreline of the twenty-first century.

Diversity of Historic Ecclesial Forms and Practices

At this point I want to comment on the diversity relevant to ecclesiologically specific matters. In particular, we will focus on structural forms that pentecostal churches have taken, and on central practices, including baptism and the Lord's Supper, as these have developed in pentecostal contexts. As will be clear, pentecostal ecclesial intuitions are not monolithic. And if theological and doctrinal beliefs either presume or are informed by concrete practices, then the heterogeneity of the latter is suggestive for why there is no single or dominant pentecostal theology of the church. The following discussion thus prompts a question that will percolate throughout the remainder of this chapter: what, if anything, can provide lucidity for any discussion of pentecostal ecclesiology?

With regard to forms of ministry, pentecostal churches can be found across the spectrum. The largest pentecostal denomination in the world, the Assemblies of God, has consistently operated with a presbyterian or representative form of government. Regional clusters of churches come together to form a district, and the combined districts within a country form a general council. Churches send elected representatives to participate in their district councils and districts do the same at the national or general council. Within this framework, local congregations by and large retain their autonomy. This latter feature reflects the congregationalist impulse bequeathed by Radical Reformation traditions which resonated with pentecostal intuitions concerning the freedom of individuals to follow the leading of the Spirit as they discerned it.

Other classical pentecostal churches, however, have grown out of Holiness soil and appropriated, from that nineteenth-century milieu, more episcopal forms of ecclesial governance handed down by their Methodist ancestors and cousins. The Church of God, Cleveland, Tennessee (predominantly white), and the Church of God in Christ (largely African American) are two of the largest denominations that have bishops and elders. Both churches (denominations) have general assemblies/convocations that elect their presiding bishops (or general overseers, as is known in the Church of God), who in turn through various established processes appoint jurisdictional or other bishops (state overseers, in the Church of God). This latter group for their part appoints local church pastors, more often in recent times in consultation with and even after getting the consent of local congregations. The intricacies through which such processes unfold indicate that an 'episcopal bishopric, presbyterian general assembly, congregational autonomy, and charismatic-founder led churches' (Pitt 2012: 27) are all evidenced in both churches. Yet within these dynamic structures, episcopal appointments are subject to re-election, with the difference that in the Church of God, there are official term limits (even if after their terms of service bishops retain various forms of influence), while in the Church of God in Christ, many are typically lifetime appointments. Both churches, however, do not allow women to serve in episcopal roles. On the other hand, the episcopacy of a number of other African American pentecostal churches—for example the Church of the Living God and Mt Sinai Holy Church of America—has been erected within matriarchal rather than patriarchal frames of reference.

By and large, however, smaller pentecostal churches have arisen and not a few have faded away. Many independent congregations have come and gone—those of the storefront variety or at strip malls, schools, private homes, and other rented premises—and others continue to bubble up. Those that grow and persist often get connected to one or another group of churches with compatible values. There are presbyterian, episcopal, and congregational types of pentecostal churches, among other forms. And new structures are appearing, which we will examine in a moment.

If the full range of historic ecclesial polities exists among pentecostal churches, there is generally speaking more consensus about historic ecclesial practices, especially those related to what the tradition has called sacraments. Aside from charismatics who have remained in mainline Protestant, Roman Catholic, and Orthodox communions that have a sacramental understanding, most pentecostals have followed the line of the Radical Reformation in embracing 'ordinance' rather than 'sacramental' language (Bicknell 1998). The difference is that, as historically understood, the sacraments—at least baptism in water and the celebration of the Lord's Table, also known as the Eucharist—are ritual means through which the saving grace of God is imparted to and received by believers, while ordinances are generally no more than outward expressions of faith in obedience to the instructions of Christ. If for many Protestant traditions, along with most pentecostals in this train, the seven sacraments of the medieval church were reduced to two (usually water baptism and Eucharist), a few pentecostal churches include the rite of footwashing as a third ordinance instituted by Christ (Tomberlin 2010: ch. 8).

Yet even if the 'ordinance' terminology is fairly widespread across pentecostal circles, there is some latitude about what actually transpires during these events. Some pentecostals, following a more Zwinglian interpretation, understand the ordinances to be not much more than symbolic re-enactments of the primordial rites established by Christ. In this view, Christ's presence at the Supper or Holy Communion, for instance, is merely memorial, following his words of institution, 'Do this in remembrance of me' (Luke 22:19; cf. 1 Cor. 11:24–5). The majority of others, following their pentecostal instincts, take a more spiritualized perspective, albeit one that insists that there are not only spiritual benefits, but also physical ones, available through these rites. Yet these benefits are not sacramentally mediated, as in one strand of the classical understanding which argues that divine grace follows the promises of the gospel as pronounced by the priest or pastoral agent. Instead, within the Protestant paradigm, the efficacy of the ordinances depends not on their mere ritual performance but on both the posture of faith and the sovereignty of God. Physical healing that is expected by some pentecostals to accompany the Lord's Supper, hence, is predicated less on enactment of the ordinances (after all, God can and does heal on many other occasions and at many other times) than upon the atoning work of Christ (see Kärkkäinen 2002b: 142–4). Nevertheless it remains the case that the pentecostal concern to avoid 'dead ritual' inspires a spiritual intensity and expectation that on these occasions the faithful will encounter God and experience the Holy Spirit in transformative ways.

There is one more feature of pentecostal baptismal praxis that deserves comment. 'Oneness' pentecostal believers who reject the classical doctrine of the Trinity (because this is for them comprehensible only in the tri-theistic terms that are at odds with the scriptural witness to the unity of the Godhead) also follow the apostolic baptismal formula repeated in the book of Acts ('in Jesus' name'; e.g. Acts 8:16, 10:48, 19:5), rather than that otherwise more universally practised as recorded in the Matthean Great Commission passage ('in the name of the Father and of the Son and of the Holy Spirit': Matt. 28:19). Beyond this, however, Oneness Christians insist that full Christian initiation involves a sequence detailed by Peter: 'Repent, and be baptized every one of you in the name of Jesus Christ so that your sins may be forgiven; and you will receive the gift of the Holy Spirit' (Acts 2:38). As most Oneness are classically pentecostal and hold to the doctrine that the evidential sign of the reception of the gift of the Spirit is speaking in tongues, the manifestation of glossolalia comes to represent the culmination of the order of salvation delineated in this verse. More interestingly for our purposes, however, a not inconsequential segment of the Oneness movement embraces, because of its soteriology, the connection between water baptism and the forgiveness of sins central to more classical understandings of the sacrament of initiation as involving the regeneration of sinners (Reed 2008: ch. 9). To be sure, these Oneness do not generally resort to sacramental explications of this relationship, insisting only that according to the apostolic pattern and doctrine, the combination of repentance, baptism, and reception of the Holy Spirit suffices to ensure cleansing from sin and the new birth (Bernard 1984). Nevertheless this Oneness doctrine and correlative baptismal practice is suggestive of how, despite the use of 'ordinance' nomenclature, there are arguably sacramental benefits (the forgiveness of sins) effected by apostolic practices.

An Abbreviated Phenomenology of Renewal Movements

If classical pentecostal churches exhibit a range of ecclesial forms and practices, the variations abound even more when considered across the full scope of the global renewal movement. In this final portion of our descriptive orientation to pentecostal ecclesiology, we expand our lens to include historic and especially more recent developments across global renewal Christianity. We shall see the central roles of prophet-healers in the African context, charismatic leadership across the Pacific Rim, and apostolic networks in the contemporary transnational domain. These observations, however curtailed (there is no hope within the space constraints of this chapter of providing any exhaustive phenomenological account), highlight the prophetic dimension of global renewal Christianity and prompt consideration about what some have called the church—a 'prophethood of believers' (Stronstad 1999).

We begin with the African scene in part because it is here that charismatic leaders have long made key contributions to an indigenous sub-Saharan Christianity. A good number emerged as far back as the early twentieth century—parallel to when the Azusa Street revival was occurring in North America—and established or initiated independent movements and churches that met the spiritual needs of African Christians in ways that were largely absent in the mission churches. These prophet-healers exercised charismatic leadership styles as precursors of the pentecostal movement in the African context (Anderson 2001: part II; Amanor 2004).

Although pentecostal missionaries arrived early on the African continent, it was not until the 1970s that growth and then massive expansion began to occur. Similar to the African instituted churches, however, charismatic leaders have been at the forefront of pentecostal explosion (Kalu 2008). Pentecostal megachurches and indigenously founded denominations have been evolving at a remarkable rate, led by spiritually and organizationally gifted and visionary individuals. In certain contexts these have been intentionally competitive with the earlier African prophetic type churches; yet even when not so engaged, these newer pentecostal megachurches offer similar services: prayer and praise in matchless African style; healing services to address physical ailments; prophetic sessions to provide guidance to the masses; and deliverance ministries through exorcistic rituals, etc. In a few cases, these ministries are part of established pentecostal denominations; by and large, however, they have begun their own churches—many blossoming into networks of churches—that have in turn launched new church planting, missionary, and other initiatives.

In the Chinese context, the pentecostal explosion has taken place primarily in the last generation since the end of the Cultural Revolution period, so far as researchers have been able to determine. The difference has been that, given the persisting presence of the Three-Self Church that has official governmental recognition as representing Christianity for the people, much of the renewal movement remains intentionally at the grass-roots level. Any form of official relationship is thus seen as potentially domesticating revival fires and generally avoided. Hence the predominant expressions of pentecostal-charismatic Christianity in China have been in the form of house churches. In this context, then, there are fewer leaders that build institutionalized versions of the church and more organic networks of churches clustered around common values, practices, and beliefs (Wesley 2004).

To be sure, there are certainly leaders within these house-church networks across the Chinese scene. Yet these function less institutionally than charismatically and relationally in providing oversight and leadership from city to city or province to province. House churches, however, are congregational centres, nodes within their networks, so to speak, that influence and impact the ongoing shapes of these movements. Historically, sacramental functions in these environments are presided over by laity in many cases, or by pastoral leaders that come to their position through a variety of means (rather than through any institutionalized process). Itinerant preachers are also common, whose credentials are validated not through educational, episcopal, or other formal procedures but often through charismatic giftings as received by network and local congregational authorities. In this fluid and vibrant field, we have a range of ecclesiological practices and characteristics, but it is difficult to talk about any ecclesiological doctrine that could possibly reflect or be prescriptive of what is happening on the ground.

If what is occurring in China is relatively self-contained nationally (although even this is an overstatement given the size of the country and the effusive and dynamic nature of the renewal movement there), there are similar developments in the Anglo-American world, albeit with transnational dimensions. While some scholars have gathered these new ecclesial movements together under the rubric of 'apostolic networks' (Kay 2007) they are arguably of a more disparate character. To be sure, there are extensive developments of apostolic organizations from what in classical pentecostalism was called the 'fivefold ministry' paradigm—derived from the gifts of apostles, prophets, evangelists, pastors, and teachers in Ephesians 4:11—and these have spread around the world in various guises. But whereas some conservative evangelical (especially Reformed and dispensational) theological traditions would downplay the apostolic role after the end of the early Christian period (believing thereby that only the other four offices of ministries extend through the history of Christianity to the present time), many pentecostal movements insist that this fivefold ministry has never been abrogated and continues to be manifest through the empowering of the Holy Spirit. The difference is that whereas the other ministries contribute to the establishment (through evangelism) or maturation of congregations (via prophesying, pastoring, teaching), the apostolic ministry is uniquely gifted to found, launch, and initiate new churches and movements in various regions or even across regions (not to say continents). Contemporary apostles are thus those who, following the New Testament model of ecclesial mission and church formation, especially those sketched of the earliest disciples in the Acts of the Apostles and in St Paul's ministry, facilitate the growth and development of local congregations in distinct locales by providing oversight and by empowering and equipping local leadership. In that sense, these apostolic networks are part of a restorationist paradigm that sees certain aspects of contemporary Christian leadership as exemplified in the early church's apostolic practices (Lee 2005).

Yet as we have hinted, what goes under the label of apostolic networks is rather heterogeneous. To be sure, there are numerous apostolic-type leaders whose charismatic gifts and abilities have mobilized followings that have developed into relational networks of churches. Many of these have roots in the independent (post- and non-denominational) streams flowing out of the charismatic renewal in especially the mainline Protestant churches such as the house-church movement (Walker 1985), as well as other similar exploratory ventures. Others have been connected to higher-impact revivals that have spawned global presence (like the so-called 'Toronto Blessing') or emerged out of the interface between innovative music and worship trends and contemporary culture (Poloma 2003; Evans 2006; Ingalls and Yong 2015). What links them together is not the older denominational forms, episcopal hierarchies, or ecclesiastical structures, but liminal dynamics and processes (Vondey 2011). These are charismatically endowed authorities whose capacity to mobilize, direct, and influence followers has produced not necessarily congregations first and foremost but networks of ministry and mission that intersect with local churches through various media and cultural venues, marketplace domains, and socio-political, economic, and communal initiatives. Those with staying capacity are globalizing at a phenomenal rate, which means that apostolic networks, if we were to retain this terminology, are increasingly transnational, certainly with media capacities, charismatic personalities (leaders), and organizational resources for a wider reach than could be readily imagined.

In other words, pentecostal Christianity is now—and perhaps has always been—phenomenologically multifarious. On the one hand, Christian ideas, thinking, and even beliefs are rooted in or flow out of Christian practices; on the other hand, the case has also been made that Christian doctrines are grammars that structure Christian behaviours. As variegated as are pentecostal movements, arguably there is insufficient doctrinal unity for the latter claim to structure the remainder of this chapter's argument. Yet this ought not to be taken then as presuming the exclusive truthfulness of the former assertion. What we will do in the following pages, however tentatively, is suggest how the preceding sketch might still be generative for thinking about pentecostal ecclesiology. Along the way, we will be attentive to the normative implications and also applications of our proposal.

The Church as a Charismatic and Missionary Fellowship of the Spirit

The preceding phenomenology of pentecostal-charismatic Christianity invites, I suggest, the development of what I have elsewhere called a pneumatological ecclesiology (Yong 2005: ch. 3). There are at least three elements to such a proposal that I see as rooted in the pentecostal modality of ecclesial life: the diversity of its forms, the charismatic nature of its expressions, and the missional orientation of its commitments. I want to argue in what follows that this putative pentecostal ecclesiology is not only empirically informed but also has normative force. In the last part of this chapter, we will return to assess the plausibility of this pneumato-ecclesiological construct against other theological factors and issues.

The Classical Pentecostal Fivefold Paradigm

Those who have stayed with the discussion so far cannot deny the palpable diversity that characterizes pentecostal-charismatic Christianity. This pertains not only to ecclesial forms but also to the practices, relationships, and activities of pentecostal churches. Amidst this pluralism of manifestations and expressions does or can the centre hold, and if so, how?

The earliest modern pentecostals, called classical pentecostals in this chapter, did not even try to develop any ecclesiological doctrine but rather talked about the four- (for those more oriented toward Keswickian pietist traditions) and fivefold (for Holiness pentecostal believers) gospel: Jesus as saviour, healer, sanctifier (this was the Holiness addition), Spirit-baptizer, and coming king. In another place, I have argued at length that this can be understood as registering pentecostal instincts and has methodological implications for how to handle and understand pentecostal spirituality and even theology (Yong 2010: ch. 3 and *passim*). What I mean is that while classical pentecostals did not formulate a neat or systematic theological construct, they did preach and proclaim this four/fivefold gospel, and this reflected their intuitive sense that the Jesus they worshipped met them on multiple fronts of their lives. This was precisely 'good news' (*evangelion*) for human beings who had a range of real needs, hopes, and desires.

Other classical pentecostal theologians have proposed, concurrently with my own project, an alternative fivefold ecclesiological paradigm (Thomas 2010). Previous, more preliminary articulations suggested viewing the church through a fivefold lens as the Redeemed, Healing, Holy, Empowering, and Eschatological community, or translating these into a range of ecclesial practices: Jesus' saving is marked by baptism in water, his healing by the practice of anointing with oil, his sanctifying by footwashing, his baptizing in the Spirit by the experience of Spirit-infilling (marked by glossolalia), and his return by the Lord's Supper which anticipates the day of the Lord (Thomas 1998: 18–19). Updated and expanded, such a fivefold ecclesiology now maps on also to the fivefold functionality of the church's ministries and offices (Archer 2010: 40).

One ought to proceed cautiously along these lines. Any rigid equation between the fivefold Christology and any ecclesial or ecclesiological scheme will no doubt appear haphazard, arbitrary, and even tendentious from other vantage points (Kärkkäinen 2010: 267). My claim, however, is not that the pentecostal fivefold gospel provides a normative ecclesiological template, but that it represents the classical pentecostal insight into the multiplicity of ways that encounter with Jesus was experienced. It is this pluralism which, I suggest, provides clues into the plurivocity of pentecostal ecclesial forms. In effect, then, the pentecostal fivefold gospel underwrites not necessarily the details of any of the ecclesiological proposals suggested above—not even my own—but the plausibility conditions for their consideration. One result is that those reflecting on such matters will be inclined to think about a plurality of pentecostal ecclesiologies as a general rule of thumb, rather than insisting on any single or authoritative pentecostal ecclesiological formulation. And this is in itself also consistent with the foundational pentecostal imagination rooted in the multiplicity of tongues spoken on the Day of Pentecost.

The Church as Charismatic Fellowship

My proposal for a pneumatological ecclesiology has begun on the pentecostal ecclesiological ground in all its variegatedness and moved through the pentecostal fivefold gospel in order to secure a pluralistic ecclesiological vision commensurate with the implications and applications of the Day of Pentecost narrative. Many tongues, many ecclesial practices, many ecclesial forms—this is one possible mantra for a pentecostal and pneumatological ecclesiology. Relatedly, others have seen fit to move from the fivefold Christology through a Spirit-Christology to a pneumatological ecclesiology. In this construal, not only is Jesus saviour, sanctifier, Spirit baptizer, and healer, but the Spirit also empowers believers to live into the vocation of Christ by 'birthing them into the kingdom, sanctifying them, healing them, baptizing them in the Spirit, and engaging in all the charisms that actualize Jesus's identity' (Coulter 2010: 331). In other words, the Spirit's charismatic giftings are not against structure but extend the vocation of Jesus and establish both structures of charismatic giftings and charismatically discerned structures like the episcopacy so that there are others now, apostles for instance, who extend the forgiveness of sins offered by Jesus through his ministry, life, death, and resurrection.

Such a proposal is constant with and complementary to the broader pentecostal aspiration for a pneumatological ecclesiology (see Kärkkäinen 2002: part II). There are a number of elements to this understanding, including a Trinitarian view of the church as the communion of the Spirit, a pneumatically oriented perspective on the sacraments and the ministry of the church, and a notion of the church as a charismatic fellowship of and in the Holy Spirit. These are embedded within the ecclesiological sentiments of more ecumenical streams touched by charismatic renewal (Bittlinger 1981). In this forum, there is widespread embrace of the idea that the church is the church precisely as constituted by and constantly renewed through the Holy Spirit.

My own approach has been to suggest, as indicated, how the fivefold gospel opens up to multiple modes of being the church in the various historical contexts within which it is found and that this happens only pneumatically, through the Spirit of Jesus, who gives diverse gifts to the body appropriate for their differentiated evangelical witness in various missional contexts (Yong 2011: ch. 4). Such a pneumatological ecclesiology is rooted not only in the Lukan corpus but also in the Pauline witness, in particular the extensive discussion of the charismatic ministry of the Spirit in and through the church in 1 Corinthians (12–14). There are at least three aspects to be emphasized in thus speaking of the church as the charismatic fellowship of the Spirit. First, this highlights the role of the Spirit in ways that fulfil the Trinitarian character of the church that is left out in other New Testament metaphors such as the 'body of Christ'. Second, the fellowship of the people of God exists in and through the Spirit similarly to how the perichoretic fellowship of the Godhead is not binitarianly but Trinitarianly formed in and through the Spirit. Last but not least, the fellowship of the Spirit is established charismatically by the Spirit, 'who allots to each one individually just as the Spirit chooses' (1 Cor. 12:11).

Remember, though, that according to Pauline principles, the Spirit's gifts are never for the aggrandizement of the one so gifted but are for the edification of the whole. Further, the fact that the gifts of the Spirit are distributed to those 'members of the body that seem to be weaker' (1 Cor. 11:22) indicates that, as the Lucan Pentecost narrative puts it, the Spirit of God is truly poured out upon all flesh, even upon those like women, youth, or the impoverished or enslaved who may have been thought to be excluded from such divine operations (Acts 2:17–19). Finally, for our purposes, such a charismatic ecclesiology is suggestive for understanding how church movements, denominations, and even whole ecclesial traditions have their own charisms, their own distinctive witness and contribution to the church catholic, even if only for specific times and places. None are to be despised since each bears particular testimony to 'God's deeds of power' (Acts 2:11) in its own language.

Network Church: A Missional Ecclesiology

In the end, however, a pentecostal and pneumatological ecclesiology must clarify the *So what for?* question. Here we connect the notion of the church as charismatic fellowship of the Spirit with the church as the mission of the Spirit, sent and empowered by the Spirit to declare and manifest the works of Christ for the redemption of all creation to the glory of the Father. Towards this end, charismatic theologian Andy Lord's (2012) 'network church' model highlights especially the missional character of the Spirit-empowered and inspired people of God.

Lord's intuitions about a network-ecclesiology derive from the phenomenology of charismatic movements. Networks, for Lord, are relational media that facilitate multi-directional interactions between individuals, congregations, churches, organizations, denominations, and even whole ecclesial traditions, in particular between hierarchically situated entities. In pentecostal environments, they are the charismatically inspired ministers and ministries, their organized conferences, and published periodicals and journals (both print and electronic) which most concretely manifest network dynamics. Networks thus function as neither spatially nor geographically limited connectors that enable the missionary task of the church, especially but not limited to evangelism, church planting and growth, and social activity.

In Lord's account, the network model is also illuminative of the early apostolic church. To be sure, the claim is not that modern sociological network theory should be naively applied to the New Testament texts, but that the ecclesial relations reflected in the early Christian writings can be comprehended, at least in part, as network connections unfolded in and through the missional work of the first believers. Beyond this scriptural horizon, there are theological and Trinitarian reasons to consider a network ecclesiology that correspond to, if they are not also both foundational to and expressive of pentecostal intuitions. The relationality, multi-dimensionality, and reciprocity characterizing pentecostal ecclesial phenomena can also, arguably, be mapped, at least in part, onto the divine nature understood according to the ancient notion of perichoresis. Within this framework, the network church is theologically and metaphorically analogous to, if not also imagistic of, the triune God (Volf 1998).

Such an ecclesiology, articulated in pneumatological, charismatic, and missional terms, is a natural extension of pentecostal evangelistic impulses (Goff 1988; McGee 2010). Pentecostal 'pragmatism' (Wacker 2003) has never been merely about getting something done, but has perennially been missionally focused. The text of Acts 1:8, 'But you will receive power when the Holy Spirit has come upon you; and you will be my witnesses in Jerusalem, in all Judea and Samaria, and to the ends of the earth', has always been at the heart of pentecostal spirituality. Hence the pentecostal emphasis on the prophethood rather than on the priesthood of all believers highlights not merely the primacy of prophetic manifestations that are central to pentecostal spirituality, but also its activist, evangelical, and missional thrust. Prophecy in the pentecostal paradigm includes not merely the charisms of forth- and fore-telling through which the Spirit reproves, encourages, and directs believers in the present and prepares them for what is coming, but also the ways in which Spirit-filled Christians build up one another, challenge injustice in the world, and engage critically, creatively, and transformatively in the mission of God. It is this kind of practical-prophetic sensibility (Morgan 2010) that underwrites the pentecostal way of being the missionary and charismatic fellowship of the Spirit.

THE PEOPLE OF GOD, THE BODY OF CHRIST, THE TEMPLE OF THE HOLY SPIRIT

This section of the chapter will look briefly at the opportunities and challenges attending such a pentecostal and pneumatological ecclesiology. We will explore what it means to think about the church as a charismatic and missionary fellowship of the Spirit, by taking up three sets of questions: the first looking backward, in a sense, to understand the relationship between the church and ancient Israel as the people of God; the second looking ecumenically, to comprehend the catholic and sacramental dimensions of the church as the body of Christ; and the last looking forward, effectively, to clarify what difference a pneumatological perspective makes for a more systematic theological understanding of the biblical drama of redemption, particularly as related to the notion of the church viewed as the temple of the Holy Spirit. These by no means exhaust the critical issues attendant to the preceding sketch. However, interaction along these lines will chart trajectories for possible development vis-à-vis the broader Christian theological tradition.

Israel, Covenant, and the People of God: Toward a Pentecostal-Charismatic Ecclesiology

The major issue that emerges for the project of shifting ecclesiology in a pneumato-logical direction has to do with the historical nature of what it means to be the people of God. Pentecostal rhetoric that tends to spiritualize the essence of the church to begin with similarly spiritualizes the elect of God, especially in what is understood as a present dispensation separate from that described in the Old Testament. While the implications of such a line of thinking are innumerable, a few more ecclesiologically relevant notions can be specified. First, such a dispensationalist theology of history and eschatology in-volves a supersessionist view of Israel with its covenantal benefits being transferred to the church. On the flip side, second, such a theology of Israel unfolds in unanticipated political directions, even as efforts expanded in the evangelization and proselytization of Jews stresses contemporary Jewish-Christian relationships. Last but not least, such a spiritualized ecclesiology tends toward an eschatological other-worldliness that in turn often undermines the concrete Christian witness in the real world.

There is no denying the very real differences between Israel and the church, both in the past, beginning with what is registered in the New Testament documents, and in the present. Yet such a recognition also ought not to foreclose discussion on the histor-ical nature of the one people of God revealed in ancient Israel and the church. If that is agreed upon, then yes, there are discontinuities between Israel and the church, but there are also important continuities. The question of course extends to what, if any, those continuities may be in the present time between the first and second coming of Christ. Part of what complicates the matter is the dispensationalist cast within which the rela-tionship between Israel and the church is parsed in pentecostal circles. The irony is that dispensationalism is incidental rather than essential to pentecostal spirituality (Yong 2010: ch. 8), and even antagonistic to pentecostal intuitions and sensibilities in the way that it cordons off the time of the apostles from the rest of the age of the church via a pre-supposed cessationism (that the charismatic work of the Spirit in the early church has subsided, if not stopped, since the canon of Scripture was completed and closed).

A pneumatological ecclesiology, however, need not be either ahistorical or merely ideal/spiritual. Instead, recognition of the work of the Spirit as being central to and constitutive of what it means to be the people of God potentially leads to a more dy-namic theology of divine election. If ancient Israel was empowered by the Spirit of God to bear witness to the God of Abraham, Isaac, and Jacob, so does the Spirit-filled church now testify to God's wondrous works in Christ. As important, the Spirit's ongoing re-newal of ancient Israel—that is, through the Davidic kingdom, the Solomonic expan-sions, the reforms of Josiah, the post-exilic renewal (Spawn 2008)—can be understood as prototypical of the Spirit's perpetual renewal of the church. From a pentecostal perspective, Christians can do no less than bear witness to Christ in the power of his Spirit, and if Jews in the present time are prompted thereby to give allegiance instead to Christ, they are certainly within their prerogative to explore what it means to live this out faithfully, perhaps as Jews. On the other side, there is also no reason to think that the Spirit's renewing work begun in ancient Israel does not continue somehow among the Jewish community and, if so, then there is also no denying the possibility that the Jewish witness to the God of Abraham has ceased and that Christians might also come to new perspective and even appreciation of what this witness requires of their own lives and faith. In either case, any authentic work of the Spirit will anticipate the coming reign of God when all things, including contemporary Judaism and the church, will be made new.

Sacramentality, Spirituality, and the Body of Christ: Toward a Renewal Ecclesiology

As indicated in the earlier part of this chapter, Pentecostals were 'come-outers' from historic church traditions and they came out for various reasons. Many of these were related to their sense that formalized ritual had displaced the vibrancy, vitality, and spontaneity of the Spirit's present work. Further, their instincts and practices regarding both the priesthood and prophethood of *all* believers were inconsistent with, in their own experience, a more hierarchically organized clergy who retained authority to preside over the sacraments. The sacraments were, generally speaking, not mediators of supernatural and redeeming grace but rather outward signs, memorials in the case of the Lord's Supper, of grace already really present inwardly in believing hearts and lives. In many respects, these various rationales for 'coming out' were related to their sense that the body of Christ as they had experienced it was burdened by formalism, hierarchicalism, and ritualism.

Yet there may not be such a stark antagonism between classical Christian notions of sacramentality and pentecostal spirituality as popularly understood. Pentecostal ministry understood in terms of the prophethood of all believers—male and female, young and old, slave and free, as referenced by Peter's Day of Pentecost sermon (Acts 2:18–19)—is not necessarily opposed to some kind of hierarchical or organizational formation, especially as reflected in the early church (Coulter 2007). Furthermore, pentecostal spontaneity also does not operate in an entirely unstructured environment even as Christian ritual in general is not inflexible (Albrecht 1999). In fact, pentecostal spirituality itself, while often considered as the wellspring of improvisation, innovation, and spontaneity, is, when phenomenologically examined, thoroughly embodied. Healing of the body, speaking in tongues, the dance, the shout, the lifting up of hands, being 'slain in the Spirit'—all of these are embodied modalities through which the Holy Spirit is believed to interact with and, finally, build up the people of God. In other words, the work of the Spirit is being mediated through the concrete particularities of human bodies. If the central claim of sacramental theologies was that grace was mediated through created elements, then is not pentecostal spirituality also sacramental in these respects (Macchia 1993)? Might then the one body of Christ find sustenance through the Spirit whether given through the historic sacraments and the priesthood on the one hand, or through the prophets or the material bodies of the laity on the other hand?

Pentecostal theologians and pastors are hence gradually rethinking their theology of the sacraments or ordinances (Vondey 2010: chs 4–5; Stephenson 2012: ch. 5). They are also finding that historically, sacramental theology and practice has always recognized the central role of the Holy Spirit, whether it be to heal, to build up, to bring about encounter with the divine presence, or to revive the church (DeArteaga 2002). Hence the sacraments or ordinances are effective precisely because they are the means through which the people of God are constituted as the body of Christ: they enable the celebrations of Christ, obedience to Christ, and anticipation of his soon-return (Green 2012).

More precisely, however, if the sacraments or ordinances foster encounter with the living Christ, they do so only through the Spirit of the resurrected Christ. Hence, not just pentecostal sacramentality in particular, but any Christian theology of the sacraments must be thoroughly pneumatological. In this case, the body of Christ is what it is through the regular and ongoing celebration of the sacraments precisely as the fellowship of the Holy Spirit. Christ is head of his church, his body, only as the Spirit is pervasively present, giving life organically to the body. Thus also are the many members sustained, through the Spirit, even as each member contributes something vital apart from which the body suffers, is impoverished, and is less healthy. Herein lies the possibility of the continual renewal of the body of Christ, through the ever-present activity of the Holy Spirit.

The Spirit, Creation, and Pentecost: Toward a Pneumatological Ecclesiology

A final question, however, must be briefly attended to. If the church is to be understood pneumatologically, what if anything is the difference between the Spirit of creation and the Spirit of Pentecost? While this is in some respects a twist on the prior question regarding the continuities and differences between the church and ancient Israel, it is also a discrete query. The concern here is that a pneumatological ecclesiology does not enable recognition of the uniqueness of the biblical drama of redemption and its salvation-historical arc. If that is the case, then the incomparable mission and witness of the church is compromised as the work of the Spirit of Pentecost is not distinguishable from that of the work of the Spirit of creation (Chan 2011: ch. 1).

This is a valid concern that invites further systematic clarification of a pneumatological ecclesiology. On the one hand, a pneumatological approach to the nature and work of the church emphasizes the redemptive character of the church's mission to respond to the fallen character of creation. Hence, the church as the charismatic fellowship of the Spirit has inimitable theological and pneumatological resources to bring to bear on ecclesial responses to ecological challenges and could potentially complement environmental stewardship theologies with a more robust missional approach to creation-care (Swoboda 2013). These developments would address further some of the escapism in renewal and other Christian circles impacted by certain strands of dispensationalist rapture-theologies.

On the other hand, any pneumatological ecclesiology will be only as robust as its Christological credentials. The Holy Spirit is no more or less than the Spirit of Jesus Christ. It is Jesus who pours out the Spirit from the right hand of the Father, according to the Lukan witness (Acts 2:33). Hence the church as the charismatic fellowship of the Spirit is also the body of Christ, with Christ as its head and as its Spirit-baptizer (Macchia 2006: chs 4–5). Towards this end, then, any pneumatological ecclesiology cannot be creation-centred, although it will address how creation is redeemed in Christ by the Spirit, and be suggestive for ways in which the church participates in this redemptive work of the triune God.

But Christ pours out the Spirit in order that the Spirit who has formerly resided *upon* creation can now take up residence *within* creatures. Thus if a pneumatological theology of creation emphasizes that the wind or breath of God 'swept over the face of the waters' (Gen. 1:2) so that God can be enthroned above the world (Walton 2009), a pneumatological ecclesiology maintains that the Spirit of Christ is poured out on all flesh (Acts 2:17) so that creation can become the dwelling place of God. So the Most High no longer 'dwell[s] in houses made by human hand' (Acts 7:48), but rather within the bodies of Jesus-followers, now understood individually and aggregately as the temple of the divine Spirit (1 Cor. 3:16, 6:19). If God was enthroned upon the primordial creation, the eschatological redemption of the world ought to be nothing less than its Spirit-infilling (Macchia 2010). In that case, the church bears present witness as the charismatic fellowship of the Spirit to this ultimate vision of a Spirit-baptized creation and heralds this eschatological vision as the temple of the Holy Spirit.

CONCLUSION:
RENEWED AND ALWAYS RENEWING

This chapter began with some phenomenological observations on the variety of pentecostal ecclesiologies, went on to propose a view of the church as the charismatic fellowship of the Spirit as one way to think coherently about a topic shot through with diversity, and concluded with recognition of some of the parameters as well as possibilities inherent in such a pneumatological approach. If the Reformed tradition has emphasized the church as reformed and always reforming (*Ecclesia reformata semper reformanda*; Olson 2007), pentecostal movements might well want to suggest a pneumatological ecclesiology in which the church is being renewed and always renewing. Renewal, however, is not only retroactively directed; pentecostal restorationism should be focused not only on re-establishing what the apostles did but on doing what they did, which was to adapt their understanding and practice in light of the new realities of the resurrected

Christ and the pentecostal outpouring of the Spirit. In this case, then, the renewal of the church both captures something important about the past and brings that forward in new ways appropriate to the present novel context, and hence anticipates the coming reign of God which is not merely a reversal to a primordial Eden. Instead, according to multiple apostolic witnesses, 'For now we see in a mirror, dimly, but then we will see face to face. Now I know only in part; then I will know fully, even as I have been fully known' (1 Cor. 13:12); and 'What we do know is this: when he is revealed, we will be like him, for we will see him as he is' (1 John 3:2b). And given the ongoing 'pentecostalization' and 'charismatization' of Christianity as a whole, even across the majority world, such a renewal ecclesiology will perhaps also in the future contribute to the transformation of other churches as well, including their ecclesiological doctrines and theologies.

References

Albrecht, Daniel E. (1999). *Rites in the Spirit: A Ritual Approach to Pentecostal/Charismatic Spirituality.* Journal of Pentecostal Theology Supplement Series 17. Sheffield: Sheffield Academic Press.

Amanor, Jones Darkwa (2004). 'Pentecostalism in Ghana: An African Reformation.' *Cyberjournal for Pentecostal-Charismatic Research* 13 <http://www.pctii.org/cyberj/cyber13.html>.

Anderson, Allan (2001). *African Reformation: African Initiated Christianity in the 20th Century.* Trenton, NJ: Africa World Press.

Anderson, Allan (2004). *An Introduction to Pentecostalism: Global Charismatic Christianity.* Cambridge: Cambridge University Press.

Anderson, Allan (2007). *Spreading Fires: The Missionary Nature of Early Pentecostalism.* London: SCM, and Maryknoll, NY: Orbis Books.

Archer, Kenneth J. (2010). 'The Fivefold Gospel and the Mission of the Church: Ecclesiastical Implications and Opportunities'. In John Christopher Thomas (ed.), *Toward a Pentecostal Ecclesiology: The Church and the Fivefold Gospel.* Cleveland, TN: CPT Press, 7–43.

Asamoah-Gyadu, J. Kwabena (2004). *African Charismatics: Current Developments within Independent Indigenous Pentecostalism in Ghana.* Studies of Religion in Africa 27. Leiden and Boston: Brill.

Bernard, David K. (1984). *The New Birth.* Hazelwood, MO: Word Aflame Press.

Bicknell, Richard (1998). 'The Ordinances: The Marginalised Aspects of Pentecostalism'. In Keith Warrington (ed.), *Pentecostal Perspectives.* Carlisle: Paternoster Press, 204–22.

Bittlinger, Arnold (ed.) (1981). *The Church is Charismatic.* Geneva: World Council of Churches.

Chan, Simon (2011). *Pentecostal Ecclesiology: An Essay on the Development of Doctrine.* Journal of Pentecostal Theology Supplement Series 38. Sheffield: Deo Publishing.

Cleary, Edward L. (2009). *How Latin America Saved the Soul of the Catholic Church.* New York and Mahwah, NJ: Paulist Press.

Cleary, Edward L. (2011). *The Rise of Charismatic Catholicism in Latin America.* Gainesville, FL: University Press of Florida.

Coulter, Dale M. (2007). 'The Development of Ecclesiology in the Church of God (Cleveland, TN): A Forgotten Contribution?' *Pneuma: The Journal of the Society for Pentecostal Studies* 29.1: 59–85.

Coulter, Dale M. (2010). 'Christ, the Spirit, and Vocation: Initial Reflections on a Pentecostal Ecclesiology'. *Pro Ecclesia* 19.3: 318–39.

De Arteaga, William L. (2002). *Forgotten Power: The Significance of the Lord's Supper in Revival*. Grand Rapids, MI: Zondervan.

Duffield, Guy P., and Van Cleave, Nathaniel M. (1983). *Foundations of Pentecostal Theology*. Los Angeles: LIFE Bible College.

Dusing, Michael L. (1995). 'The New Testament Church'. In Stanley M. Horton (ed.), *Systematic Theology*. Stanley M. Horton, Rev. edn. Springfield, MO: Logion Press, 567–96.

Evans, Mark (2006). *Open Up the Doors: Music in the Modern Church*. Sheffield: Equinox Publishing.

Goff, James R., Jr (1988). *Fields White unto Harvest: Charles F. Parham and the Missionary Origins of Pentecostalism*. Fayetteville, AR: University of Arkansas Press.

Green, Chris (2012). *Toward a Pentecostal Theology of the Lord's Supper: Foretasting the Kingdom*. Cleveland, TN: CPT Press.

Hanna, Tony (2006). *New Ecclesial Movements: Communion and Liberation, Neo-catechumenal Way, Charismatic Renewal*. Staten Island, NY: Alba House.

Hollenweger, Walter J. (1997). *Pentecostalism: Origins and Developments Worldwide*. Peabody, MA: Hendrickson.

Hummel, Charles E. (1994). *Fire in the Fireplace: Charismatic Renewal in the Nineties*. Downers Grove, IL: InterVarsity Press.

Hunt, Stephen (2009). *A History of the Charismatic Movement in Britain and the United States of America: The Pentecostal Transformation of Christianity*. Book 1. Lewiston, NY: The Edwin Mellen Press.

Ingalls, Monique, and Yong, Amos (eds) (2015). *The Spirit of Praise: Music and Worship in Global Pentecostal-Charismatic Christianity*. University Park, PA: Penn State University Press.

Kalu, Ogbu U. (2008). *African Pentecostalism: An Introduction*. Oxford: Oxford University Press.

Kärkkäinen, Veli-Matti (2002a). *An Introduction to Ecclesiology: Ecumenical, Historical & Global Perspectives*. Downers Grove, IL: InterVarsity Press.

Kärkkäinen, Veli-Matti (2002b). *Toward a Pneumatological Theology: Pentecostal and Ecumenical Perspectives on Ecclesiology, Soteriology, and Theology of Mission*. Ed. Amos Yong. Lanham, MD: University Press of America.

Kärkkäinen, Veli-Matti (2010). ' "The Leaning Tower of Pentecostal Ecclesiology": Reflections on the Doctrine of the Church on the Way'. In John Christopher Thomas (ed.), *Toward a Pentecostal Ecclesiology: The Church and the Fivefold Gospel*. Cleveland, TN: CPT Press, 261–71.

Kay, William K. (2007). *Apostolic Networks of Britain: New Ways of Being Church*. Milton Keynes and Waynesboro, GA: Paternoster Press.

Lee, Edgar R. (ed.) (2005). *He Gave Apostles: Apostolic Ministry in the 21st Century*. Springfield, MO: Assemblies of God Theological Seminary.

Lord, Andy (2012). *Network Church: A Pentecostal Ecclesiology Shaped by Mission*. Global Pentecostal and Charismatic Studies 11. Leiden and Boston: Brill.

Macchia, Frank D. (1993). 'Tongues as a Sign: Toward a Sacramental Understanding of Pentecostal Experience'. *Pneuma: The Journal of the Society for Pentecostal Studies* 15: 61–76.

Macchia, Frank D. (2006). *Baptized in the Spirit: A Global Pentecostal Theology*. Grand Rapids, MI: Zondervan.

Macchia, Frank D. (2010). *Justified in the Spirit: Creation, Redemption, and the Triune God.* Grand Rapids, MI, and Cambridge: Eerdmans.

McGee, Gary B. (2010). *Miracles, Missions and American Pentecostalism.* Maryknoll, NY: Orbis Books.

Maurer, Susan A. (2010). *The Spirit of Enthusiasm: A History of the Catholic Charismatic Renewal, 1967–2000.* Lanham, MD: University Press of America.

Morgan, David (2010). *Priesthood, Prophethood and Spirit-Led Community: A Practical-Prophetic Pentecostal Ecclesiology.* Saarbrücken: Lambert Academic Publishing.

Olson, Roger E. (2007). *Reformed and Always Reforming: The Postconservative Approach to Evangelical Theology.* Grand Rapids, MI: Baker Academic.

Omenyo, Cephas N. (2002). *Pentecost Outside Pentecostalism: A Study of the Development of Charismatic Renewal in the Mainline Churches in Ghana.* Mission Studies 32. Zoetermeer: Boekencentrum.

Pitt, Richard N. (2012). *Divine Callings: Understanding the Call to Ministry in Black Pentecostalism.* New York and London: New York University Press.

Poloma, Margaret M. (2003). *Main Street Mystics: The Toronto Blessing and Reviving Pentecostalism.* Walnut Creek, CA: Altamira Press.

Price, Lynne (2002). *Theology Out of Place: A Theological Biography of Walter J. Hollenweger.* Journal of Pentecostal Theology Supplement Series 23. London: Sheffield Academic Press.

Reed David A. (2008). *'In Jesus Name': The History and Beliefs of Oneness Pentecostals.* Journal of Pentecostal Theology Supplement Series 31. Blandford Forum: Deo Publishing.

Spawn, Kevin L. (2008). 'Sacred Song and God's Presence in 2 Chronicles 5: The Renewal Community of Judah and Beyond'. *Journal of Pentecostal Theology* 16: 51–68.

Stephenson, Christopher A. (2012). *Types of Pentecostal Theology: Method, System, Spirit.* Oxford: Oxford University Press.

Stewart, Adam (2010). 'A Canadian Azusa? The Implications of the Hebden Mission for Pentecostal Historiography'. In Michael Wilkinson and Peter Althouse (eds), *Winds from the North: Canadian Contributions to the Pentecostal Movement.* Religion in the Americas 10. Leiden and Boston: Brill, 17–37.

Stoll, David E. (1991). *Is Latin America Turning Protestant? The Politics of Evangelical Growth.* Berkeley, CA: University of California Press.

Stronstad, Roger (1999). *The Prophethood of All Believers: A Study in Luke's Charismatic Theology.* Journal of Pentecostal Theology Supplement Series 16. Sheffield: Sheffield Academic Press.

Swoboda, A. J. (2013). *Tongues and Trees: Towards a Pentecostal Ecological Theology.* Journal of Pentecostal Theology Supplement Series 40. Blandford Forum: Deo Publishing.

Thomas, John Christopher (1998). 'Pentecostal Theology in the Twenty-First Century'. *Pneuma: The Journal of the Society for Pentecostal Studies* 10.1: 3–19.

Thomas, John Christopher (ed.) (2010). *Toward a Pentecostal Ecclesiology: The Church and the Fivefold Gospel.* Cleveland, TN: CPT Press.

Tomberlin, Daniel (2010). *Pentecostal Sacraments: Encountering God at the Altar.* Cleveland, TN: Center for Pentecostal Leadership and Care.

Van Dusen, Henry Pitt (1958). 'The Third Force in Christendom'. *Life* 9 June: 113–24.

Volf, Miroslav (1998). *After our Likeness: The Church as the Image of the Trinity.* Grand Rapids, MI, and Cambridge: Eerdmans.

Vondey, Wolfgang (2010). *Beyond Pentecostalism: The Crisis of Global Christianity and the Renewal of the Theological Agenda.* Pentecostal Manifestos series. Grand Rapids, MI, and Cambridge: Eerdmans.

Vondey, Wolfgang (2011). 'The Denomination in Classical and Global Pentecostal Ecclesiology: A Historical and Theological Contribution'. In Paul M. Collins and Barry Ensign-George (eds), *Denomination: Assessing an Ecclesiological Category*. Ecclesiological Investigations 11. New York and London: T&T Clark, 99–116.

Wacker, Grant (2003). *Heaven Below: Early Pentecostals and American Culture*. Cambridge, MA: Harvard University Press.

Wagner, C. Peter (1988). *The Third Wave of the Holy Spirit: Encountering the Power of Signs and Wonders Today*. Ann Arbor, MI: Vine Books.

Walker, Andrew (1985). *Restoring the Kingdom: The Radical Christianity of the House Church Movement*. London: Hodder and Stoughton.

Walton, John H. (2009). *The Lost World of Genesis One: Ancient Cosmology and the Origins Debate*. Downers Grove, IL: IVP Academic.

Warrington, Keith (2008). *Pentecostal Theology: A Theology of Encounter*. London and New York: T&T Clark.

Wesley, Luke (2004). *The Church in China: Persecuted, Pentecostal, and Powerful*. Baguio City, Philippines: AJPS Books.

Williams, J. Rodman (1992). *Renewal Theology: Systematic Theology in Charismatic Perspective*. Vol. 3: *The Church, the Kingdom, and Last Things*. Grand Rapids, MI: Zondervan.

Yong, Amos (2002). 'The Marks of the Church: A Pentecostal Re-Reading'. *Evangelical Review of Theology* 26.1: 45–67.

Yong, Amos (2005). *The Spirit Poured Out on All Flesh: Pentecostalism and the Possibility of Global Theology*. Grand Rapids, MI: Baker Academic.

Yong, Amos (2007a). 'Pentecostalism and the Theological Academy'. *Theology Today* 64.2: 244–50.

Yong, Amos (2007b). 'Poured Out on All Flesh: The Spirit, World Pentecostalism, and the Performance of Renewal Theology'. *PentecoStudies: An Interdisciplinary Journal for Research on the Pentecostal and Charismatic Movements* 6.1: 16–46 (<http://www.glopent.net/pentecostudies>).

Yong, Amos (2010). *In the Days of Caesar: Pentecostalism and Political Theology—The Cadbury Lectures 2009*. Sacra Doctrina: Christian Theology for a Postmodern Age series. Grand Rapids, MI, and Cambridge: Eerdmans.

Yong, Amos (2011). *The Bible, Disability, and the Church: A New Vision of the People of God*. Grand Rapids, MI, and Cambridge: Eerdmans.

SUGGESTED READING

Chan, Simon (2000). *Pentecostal Theology and the Christian Spiritual Tradition*. Journal of Pentecostal Theology Supplement Series 21. Sheffield: Sheffield Academic Press.

Clifton, Shane (2009). *Pentecostal Churches in Transition: Analysing the Developing Ecclesiology of the Assemblies of God in Australia*. Global Pentecostal and Charismatic Studies 3. Leiden and Boston: Brill.

Crowe, Terrence (1993). *Pentecostal Unity: Recurring Hope and Enduring Frustrations*. Chicago: Loyola University Press.

Moore, S. David (2003). *The Shepherding Movement: Controversy and Charismatic Ecclesiology*. Journal of Pentecostal Theology Supplement Series 27. London: T&T Clark.

Peterson, Cheryl M. (2013). *Who Is the Church? An Ecclesiology for the Twenty-First Century*. Minneapolis: Fortress Press.

Robson, Robert Brian (2012). 'The Temple, the Spirit and the People of the Presence of God: Examining Critical Options for a Pentecostal Ecclesiology'. PhD thesis, Toronto School of Theology.

Stephenson, Lisa P. (2012). *Dismantling the Dualisms for American Pentecostal Women in Ministry: A Feminist-Pneumatological Approach*. Global Pentecostal and Charismatic Studies 9. Leiden and Boston: Brill.

Suurmond, Jean-Jacques (1994). *Word and Spirit at Play: Towards a Charismatic Theology*. Trans. John Bowden. Grand Rapids, MI: Eerdmans.

Vondey, Wolfgang (2004). *Heribert Mühlen: His Theology and Praxis—a New Profile of the Church*. Lanham, MD: University Press of America.

Vondey, Wolfgang (2008). *People of Bread: Rediscovering Ecclesiology*. New York and Mahwah, NJ: Paulist Press.

Vondey, Wolfgang (ed.) (2010–13). *Pentecostalism and Christian Unity*. 2 vols. Eugene, OR: Wipf & Stock.

PART III

MAJOR MODERN ECCLESIOLOGISTS

CHAPTER 16

KARL BARTH

KIMLYN J. BENDER

KARL BARTH stands as a pre-eminent figure of twentieth-century theology, and while better known for questions of theological method and revelation, as well as for his revival of the doctrine of the Trinity and reformulation of election, his understanding of the church deserves its own attention and marks a watershed in Protestant ecclesiology. The centrality of the church for Barth is evident in the title of his most famous work, the *Church Dogmatics* (hereafter cited as *CD* with volume number). Barth there attempts to provide a comprehensive ecclesiology in the Protestant tradition centred within a Christological and Trinitarian framework. Before Barth formulated this mature ecclesiology, however, he travelled a road that began with a quite negative view of the church.

BARTH'S EARLY REFLECTION ON THE CHURCH

Barth's initial theological reflection on the church coincided with his famous break from Protestant liberalism and was marked by a critical evaluation of both (Busch 1994: ch. 3; McCormack 1995: ch. 2). In a 1920 essay outlining his new theological path, Barth could declare that the church was more harmful than beneficial with regard to the question of the knowledge of God (Barth 2011: 76). The high point of this critical phase was the second edition of the *Romans* commentary appearing in 1922. Already in the first edition Barth could state: 'The church has crucified Christ. The way of Christ and the way of the church are from now on two separate ways' (Barth 1985: 361). Barth would reiterate this judgement in the second edition of the commentary, and such criticisms would not lessen but intensify in that later volume (Barth 2010). In the second edition Barth emphasized (against the optimism and cultural religiosity of nineteenth-century Europe) that all human achievements, including religion and the church, stood under the judgement of a 'Wholly Other' God who opposed them as sinful works of hubris.

Barth's criticisms of the church corresponded to his general indictment of a theology of culture that sought to domesticate God by attempting to claim divine revelation as the justification for its own desires, aspirations, and programmes. In Barth's estimation, both the church and the prevailing culture thus set up idols in place of God so that God's judgement falls upon both, with no strong distinction made between the church and the world, both falling under the umbrella of human sin. Even as the high point of human achievement, the church still falls on this side of the chasm separating the world from God. The gospel is therefore set over against the church itself, for in Barth's judgement, 'Here it is clear that the opposition between the Gospel and the church is fundamental and infinite all along the line. Here one standpoint stands against another. Here one is in the right and another in the wrong. The Gospel is the abolition [*Aufhebung*] of the church, as the church is the abolition [*Aufhebung*] of the Gospel' (Barth 2010: 455, English translation [ET] 333; here author's own translation).

It would be easy to conclude in light of such statements that Barth's view of the church was solely negative in this commentary, but this would be to overlook the highly dialectical nature of his argument. Even as the gospel stands in judgement over against the church, the church is nevertheless the place where the question of God is asked with seriousness. Barth calls not for an abandonment of the church in an attempt to achieve moral purity or escape its sin, but an acceptance of divine judgement as a member of the church: 'We must not, because we are fully aware of the eternal opposition between the Gospel and the Church, hold ourselves aloof from the Church or break up its solidarity; but rather, participating in its responsibility and sharing the guilt of its inevitable failure, we should accept it and cling to it' (Barth 2010: 457, ET 334). Even in his strongest criticisms, Barth never advocated abandoning the church (Barth 2010: 459–60, ET 336; cf. 503, ET 371). As Barth wrote to his friend Eduard Thurneysen three years after the appearance of the second edition of the commentary, this harsh criticism of the church during the *Romans* period was given from within the church itself for its renewal (Smart 1964: 216).

Though Barth strongly criticized a compromised and accommodated church within an optimistic and complacent social order, what is also overlooked in estimations of the *Romans* commentary is that he spoke not only of the church's tribulation (Barth 2010: ch. 9) and its guilt (ch. 10), but also of its hope (ch. 11). Even in his strong condemnation of the church and its sin and guilt, Barth esteemed the church the one place where such guilt could be heard and accepted, and insofar as this occurred the very sinfulness and hopelessness of the church could, by God's grace, serve as a sign pointing to the hope and salvation that God alone could give. Barth's negation of all attempts at ecclesial self-justification was thus intended only to make room for God's own salvation. This salvation is the hope of the church because the church is the place where the gospel is proclaimed. In Barth's highly dialectical thinking, however, such human proclamation and divine revelation could not be simply equated, for the first belonged to the side of humanity and time, the second to the divine eternity. Yet in and through the inadequate human speech of the church about God, God himself could choose to speak, the human word taken up as a vehicle for God's own Self-disclosure, so that the infinite chasm between God and the world could be overcome from God's side. Such divine proclamation not only judged and condemned the church but also established and enlivened it.

The church is therefore the locus of God's saving action precisely because, and not in spite of, its being the locus of divine judgement. In earlier parlance, the Lord kills to make alive. The church is the site of the event of divine revelation, the meeting place of the contact between eternity and time. Already here in this early commentary, Barth's understanding of the divine 'No' was one that was subsumed under the divine 'Yes,' God's rejection occurring for the sake of God's election, God's judgment serving a divine mercy (Barth 2010: ch. 9). This dialectical theme would run through all of Barth's later thinking on election, reconciliation, and the church. He would in time leave this critical stage behind but would never rescind his criticisms of ecclesiastical triumphalism or cultural Christianity. He could revive them in the face of the threat of growing nationalism and self-congratulation in the lead up to the Second World War in Germany (Barth 1961: 27–32; 33–57).

The stark time–eternity dialectic that governed Barth's thinking during this period protected against any direct identification or confusion of the church and the kingdom of God or of church proclamation and revelation. This consistent eschatology therefore served an important critical function in staving off and censuring any domestication of revelation, all ecclesial triumphalism, and the assimilation of gospel to culture (McCormack 1995: 282–90). Yet it did not provide the means for a sustainable and substantive ecclesiology in any formal or material sense. Barth himself would later esteem the *Romans* commentary as having been a necessary step of theological and ecclesial criticism but ultimately insufficient due to its lack of a developed Christology and its inadequate appreciation for the church (Barth 1960: 37–65). What is missing in the *Romans* commentary and in Barth's other writings of this period is any affirmative account of the church as God's new people within the world or any constructive and appreciative description of the church's worship, doctrine, and practices. Indeed, there is no positive sense of the church's historical duration at all, but rather simply a moment of divine disclosure that touches history only as a 'tangent touching a circle', in Barth's language of *Romans*. Barth emphasized the division between the kingdom and the church during this period but failed to provide any adequate account of their relation, such that the visibility and historicity of the church are simply equated with its sin and failure. This made any positive and constructive ecclesiology impossible (Bender 2005: ch. 2).

As the 1920s progressed, Barth became more interested in Roman Catholicism than Protestant liberalism as a dialogue partner for ecclesiological thinking, but he would be as critical of the former as he had been of the latter. Moreover, his arguments against Roman Catholic theology and its ecclesiology were interestingly not different but in fact related to these earlier criticisms of liberalism. As witnessed in a number of significant essays on Roman Catholic theology from Barth's time in Münster between 1925 and 1930, he saw in Tridentine Roman Catholic ecclesiology another infringement upon the sovereign freedom and transcendent otherness of God in its direct identification of divine revelation and grace with the visible church and its dogmas and sacraments (Barth 1962: chs 9–11). For Barth, this historicizing of revelation entailed that revelation, grace, and the Spirit are identified and equated with their historical mediation and therefore are understood to be permanent possessions of the church passed on through apostolic succession, tradition, and sacramental elements and action. This assimilation of revelation into history again led to a danger of revelation's domestication and of a loss of divine transcendence and sovereignty, such that divine and ecclesial subjectivity and agency were confused, with the second overtaking the first. Correspondingly, the agency of Christ was subsumed into and replaced by the church, which itself took the place of Christ in the world. In sum, Barth saw in Catholicism a relation of the church with Christ that was reversible, such that the former was an extension of the incarnation of the latter. Barth therefore saw in both Protestant liberalism (traced back to Schleiermacher) and the Roman Catholicism of his day a sacrificing of divine freedom and an abrogating of the 'infinite qualitative difference' between God and the world, and correspondingly an annulment of the absolute distinction between Christ and the church and between the Spirit and the church's visible means of grace. Against such synergistic identifications, Barth stressed the irreversibility of the relation of God and world as well as that of Christ and the church. He emphasized the distinction and discontinuity between them in order to protect the divine lordship and to preserve grace as *grace* (Barth 1962: 281; 294–6; 315–16; etc.). For Barth, there was an *indirect* (i.e. dialectical), rather than *direct*, relation between Christ and the church, one marked by permanent differentiation and irreversible subordination of the church to Christ, the relation between them mediated by Scripture. Scripture thus stands as the bridge between Christ and the church, the presence of his living and active voice not only *within* but *over* the church (Barth 1962: 292–6). These early criticisms of both liberal Neo-Protestant and Roman Catholic conceptions of the church were not so much revoked as taken up and subsumed into a richer and more positive and constructive ecclesiology in the *Church Dogmatics*.

Barth would continue such lines of thinking as he set his own developing ecclesiological reflection in contrast to these two dialogue partners of Roman Catholicism and Protestant liberalism. These early engagements need to be taken into account in order to understand that Barth's mature ecclesiology is always formulated in opposition to and in conversation with these two positions, one on the right and one on the left (see *CD I/ 1*: 36–41; 61–71; etc.; cf. Barth 1957: 166–7, ET 20–2). At the heart of Barth's argument with both are their respective understandings of Christ and the church. For Barth, the key is to understand that the relation between Christ and the church is irreversible, and this is precisely what he found transgressed both in Protestant liberalism (i.e. Schleiermacher and his legacy), where Christ was subsumed into the religious experience or moral message of the community, and in the Roman Catholic thought of his day, in which revelation and the agency of Christ were subsumed into the history and activity of the church in its infallible dogmas, sacramental mediation, and juridical view of apostolic succession (see Bender 2005: chs 2–3).

Barth's Turn from Critical to Constructive Ecclesiology

The *Romans* commentary marked the turning point in Barth's thinking from a predominantly critical ecclesiology to a more positive one, from emphasizing the church as the locus of judgement to emphasizing it as the locus of revelation and proclamation, witnessed in his 1922 lecture 'The Tribulation and Promise of Christian Preaching' (Barth 2011: ch. 5). This development marked a shift in emphasis, not a renunciation of the former critical concerns, a shift from stress upon divine judgement to an accent upon the divine promise in speaking of the church (Bender 2005: 79–80). What did not change, however, was that in Barth's theology of this period the church continued to serve a purely formal function as the site of divine revelation in the act of proclamation, and the church was almost entirely treated as a question of theological method and revelation.

During the early years of his teaching career in Göttingen (1921–5), Barth's eschatological time–eternity dialectic would give way to a Christological dialectic rooted in Chalcedonian Christology understood along Reformed lines as he recovered this early patristic heritage and his own Protestant one (see McCormack 1995: ch. 8). This discovery of a more adequate Christology allowed him to speak not only of the differentiation but also of the relation of God and the world, and specifically of divinity and humanity in Christ. This Christological development in turn had a profound effect upon his ecclesiological thought, and with it comes a further progression from a critical to a constructive emphasis in ecclesiology. This Christological dialectic of unity and differentiation, asymmetry and irreversibility, thus became for Barth a paradigm for other relations between divine and human agency, though none of these relations stands on the same plane as the unique and singular relation of divine and human activity in the incarnation (Bender 2005: 59–65; 75–82). Correspondingly, the general problem of the relation of revelation and history as addressed in *Romans* was now translated into the specific one of the relation of revelation and the church. Trutz Rendtorff has noted that a central concern of ecclesiology can be framed by the question: 'How can revelation enter into relationship with human reality without losing its proper distinctiveness?' (Rendtorff 1971: 181). This question was central to Barth's ecclesiological thought, and the specific answer to this general problem that he addressed in the *Romans* commentary was found in a Reformed understanding of Chalcedonian Christology. In turn, Barth's ecclesiology followed his Christological development. Just as Barth rejected an *identification* of revelation and history (which he associated with liberals like Adolf von Harnack and with Roman Catholicism), and likewise repudiated a *divorce* of revelation and history (which he associated with Paul Tillich and later with Rudolf Bultmann), so he refused both triumphalistic and positivistic direct identifications of the visible church with the Spirit's action in the church on the one side, and a flight from the visible church on the other. Barth's ecclesiology remained dialectical even as he gained a more positive appreciation for the church in time and history, for the divine action that calls the church into existence and empowers it cannot be equated with the practices of the church itself—divine and ecclesial action exist in an irreversible relation in which they are united but not confused. In other words, the church as divine event precedes the church as human institution.

Barth's early eschatological concerns were thus preserved in this later ecclesiological thought, and he did not retract his earlier convictions and criticisms, though they were now taken up into a more positive and constructive ecclesiological programme. It was therefore during the years of 1924–6, within a cycle of dogmatic lectures, that he first attempted to address the church not simply as a question of theological prolegomena and method, but as a material doctrine of dogmatics, and thus to articulate an ecclesiology proper (Barth 2003b: 349–77). It was precisely the Trinitarian and Christological framework that Barth discovered and developed during this lecture cycle that in turn shaped his ecclesiology outlined there.

Barth's chapter on the church in this set of lectures (now commonly known as the *Göttingen Dogmatics*) is undeveloped and thin in light of the richness of the later ecclesiology of the *Church Dogmatics*, but a number of significant themes developed there would continue to shape all of his future ecclesiological thinking. As in the later work, Barth places the doctrine of the church in the context of the doctrine of reconciliation. His ongoing concern for a proper understanding of the general relation of revelation and history, now seen in the specific one of revelation and the church, is evident throughout his discussion. Barth maintains that the origin of the church comes not from a power or principle within history, but from the particular action of God in calling the church into existence, a calling itself grounded in an eternal decision. The church thus exists within history but is not of history, for the church exists like other communities in the world yet lives by a power that is not of this world. Therefore, in spite of the imperfection of the church and its sin as witnessed throughout history, it lives not only in contradiction to the will of God, but, because of the divine work within it that both calls it into existence and preserves it, it lives in correspondence to the divine will as well. The church's true existence as divinely constituted is known only to faith, for it is *invisible*, yet this invisible power of the Spirit calls the church into *visible* existence—the church is therefore both invisible and visible, the invisible-becoming-visible (Barth 2003b: 353; 359–66). Here Barth's dialectical thinking on the church is again on full display, for one must believe in the church's visibility despite its invisible nature [*Wesen*] and in its invisibility despite its visible appearance [*Erscheinung*]. In language again reflecting his Christology developed earlier in the lecture cycle, Barth states: 'The true church exists everywhere and at all times only in a veil, just as its true members are what they are only in the hiddenness of a veil' (Barth 2003b: 359–60). Just as Jesus Christ is the Word that becomes human in the veil of flesh, so the true church is the invisible that becomes visible in the ambiguities of history (Barth 2003b: 361–2). The ecclesiological doctrine of the invisible-becoming-visible in the church is thus an analogy (neither more nor less) to the Christological doctrine of the Word-becoming-flesh in the person of Christ, God's work and power coming to visibility in human history through the power of the Spirit (Barth 2003b: 366). Here Barth has grounded ecclesiology within Christology and Trinitarian thought, and this will remain a hallmark of his mature ecclesiology.

The constructive ecclesiology of the *Göttingen Dogmatics* retains the dialectical tensions in Barth's understanding of the church witnessed in his earlier critical period. On the one hand, the visible church in history is marked by spiritual and moral failure, by sin and guilt. Yet on the other, the visible church cannot be abandoned because it is the visible manifestation of God's decision to give the mystical body of Christ a concrete and historical existence within a people elect and called to be a visible and historical body. There cannot be an invisible church without a visible one that exists in particular confessions and individual churches (Barth 2003b: 363–4). The church thus not only stands under God's judgement due to its failure and sin, but also stands under his promise, for it lives by the will and grace of God. Drawing upon his Reformed heritage, Barth goes on to state that the church, even in its visibility, is thus to strive to demonstrate marks of obedience that witness to the true source of the church, the most important of these being the right and proper proclamation of the Word and celebration of the sacraments, as well as the responsible practice of church discipline (Barth 2003b: 366–72). Barth can even speak of the church as the *ecclesia mater fidelium*, the mother of faith, for it is the place where the relation between God and humanity is realized and enacted: 'This place is the church, the *communion sanctorum*' (Barth 2003b: 358–9).

As such a communion, the church is a place where the task of witness must be taken up by *all* Christians, and Barth entirely eschews strong distinctions between clergy and laity (a conviction he forever held, and terms he never embraced). Moreover, he rejects all hierarchical conceptions of church offices, for the only office is held by Christ, the threefold office of prophet, priest, and king. Barth does acknowledge that, though the ministry of witness belongs to all, there may be persons who are set apart for the ministry of the Word within the church. Nevertheless, there is no vicar or substitute for Christ's office upon earth, for Christ cannot be replaced by others within the church, nor by the church itself (Barth 2003b: 372–7). What is central in Barth's thought here, and will remain so, is that Christ is distinct from the church, though he is not absent from, but present to, the church even in this time following the ascension, this presence determining the shape of the church's life and ministry. Barth's ecclesiology in the *Göttingen Dogmatics* is a marked development over his thought in the *Romans* period and displays Trinitarian and Christological patterns of thought and construction that would be further and more fully developed in his abandoned *Die christliche Dogmatik* of 1927 (Barth 1982) and in his mature *Church Dogmatics* (see Bender 2005: 75–82).

BARTH'S FORMAL ECCLESIOLOGY IN THE *CHURCH DOGMATICS*

The Church as the Locus of Revelation and Authority

These themes of Barth's earlier theology find their full and final expression in Barth's magnum opus, the *Church Dogmatics*. In the first volume of that work, on the Word of

God, Barth develops his earlier topic of the church as a question of theological method and locus of revelation and authority (*CD I/1 & I/2*). Barth's emphasis here is upon formal and methodological questions, but it is not without important material implications as well (Currie 2015: ch. 3). Theology is described as a discipline of the church, for theology takes place within the sphere of the church as a testing of the church's own proclamation in light of its norm and standard, the revelation of God in Jesus Christ as attested in Holy Scripture (*CD I/1*: 4; 11). The church thereby provides the *context* for theological reflection in its life and the *content* of that reflection in its speech, as well as its *purpose*, as theology exists in service to the church and its task of witness. There is in fact no possibility of dogmatics outside of the church, for dogmatics is a function of the church itself (*CD I/1*: 17). The church is the place where proclamation occurs, and its reflection upon such proclamation in the form of doctrine provides the church and its teaching with a relative authority. It is a relative rather than absolute authority because all of the church's doctrine falls under the absolute authority of Holy Scripture, the direct witness to God's revelation in Christ and thus the standard by which the church's proclamation and doctrine are judged. For Barth, the authority of Scripture thus stands over, and not only within, the church (*CD I/2*: §§19–21; esp. 574–85). Having heard God's Word in Scripture, the church offers its own proclamation that, like the revelation in Christ and Holy Scripture, is the Word of God insofar as it is based on Scripture and is taken up by God for the purpose of his own Self-revelation (*CD I/2*: §§22–4). Scripture is nothing less than the living voice of Christ within and over the church, the expression of Christ's sovereign lordship for the church in the present, the time between Christ's ascension and second coming: 'To say that Jesus Christ rules the Church is equivalent to saying that Holy Scripture rules the Church' (*CD I/2*: 693). As persons thus proclaim Scripture, proclamation itself (in Word and sacrament, with the second dependent upon the first for its intelligibility and meaning) becomes Christ's word for the church today: 'Jesus Christ in the power of His resurrection is present wherever men really speak really of God' (*CD I/2*: 752).

As the church reads and interprets and teaches Scripture, it produces a tradition of interpretation (confessions and doctrine) that possesses a relative authority. Though its authority is relative rather than absolute, neither infallible nor equal to Scripture, it nevertheless provides real guidance for the church and its life. The church's past confessions provide direction for its current confession because they are a primary commentary on Scripture, though never replacing Scripture itself and themselves ever open to its correction (*CD I/2*: 586–7; 649). The teaching church is on this account always first the hearing church, and Barth rejects strong distinctions between them, similar to his consistent rejections of sacerdotalism and strong clergy–laity distinctions (*CD I/2*: 844). As the church listens to Holy Scripture, and does so in respectful acknowledgement of its past interpreters foremost exemplified in prior confessions, it then teaches and confesses. To serve and teach this Word is the church's greatest joy and privilege, for 'it is the whole meaning of the Church's existence' (*CD I/2*: 852–3). As it teaches, the church stands between Christ and the individual believer. In this placement the church possesses a real authority, for it is only within the context of the church that the believer hears the Word of God and is a member of the body of Christ (*CD I/2*: 703).

The Doctrine of Election—The Basis of the Church

In the second volume of the *Church Dogmatics*, on the doctrine of God, Barth now turns to more substantive claims for the church. In light of the doctrine of election that Barth elaborates there, the existence of the church is grounded in an eternal decree, its own election standing between that of Christ and the individual Christian (*CD II/2*: §34, 'The Election of the Community'). Election reveals that God has chosen to be for the world in Jesus Christ and is itself the ground and basis for the claim that God's relation to the world is one of grace, love, and mercy. This election of grace is 'the eternal beginning of all the ways and works of God in Jesus Christ' in which God determines to be God for the world and to bear away humanity's sin in Christ (*CD II/2*: 94). Election is consequently first concerned with the particular person of Jesus Christ, who in Barth's understanding is both the elect and rejected one, and secondarily with those joined to him, the 'community of God' [*Gemeinde*], a term chosen because it can include both Israel and the church (*CD II/2*: 196). Only then is it concerned with individual persons. The church's election is thus a 'mediate and mediating election', one in which the church is appointed for a particular service of witness to God's reconciliation of the world in Christ (*CD II/2*: 196–7; also 205–6). Though for Barth Israel represents the rejection of election while the church represents the believing response to it, both together form the one elect community, for 'the bow of the one covenant arches over both' (*CD II/2*: 200). Here again, judgement and rejection serve the larger goal of mercy and inclusion, Israel and the church united under one covenant, and both belonging to Christ (*CD II/2*: 199–201; 204; 224–7). Barth's highly nuanced and dialectical understanding of this relationship of Israel and the church has been, not surprisingly, the subject of controversy and criticism (see Bender 2005: 121–7).

Because Barth grounds the church within the doctrine of election (itself taken up within the doctrine of God), the church is no longer to be seen solely as an aspect of redemptive history, but as a part of God's eternal intention for covenant with humanity. As such, the church cannot be considered simply as a collective of individuals sharing theological convictions, beliefs, or religious experiences. It is, rather, rooted in eternity in God's free decision of grace and comes into existence in time as a work of the Spirit, the invisible work of God bringing about a visible people in the world in analogous relation to the unique and unsubstitutable Word taking on flesh through the miracle of the Spirit. The church does not exist as a second incarnation or replace Christ within this world. Nevertheless, it does stand in qualified correspondence and as a witness to the unique divine and human relation that exists in the person of Jesus Christ and the enacted reconciliation he accomplished. As Barth will state in the fourth volume of the *Church Dogmatics*, the church is Christ's 'earthly-historical form of existence' (*irdisch-geschichtliche Existenzform*) in the world today (*CD IV/1*: 643; *passim*).

Here once again, Barth's Christological logic governs his ecclesiological thought, preserving the divine and human distinction while speaking of their relation, now in a new key as forged in a reformulated doctrine of election. By grounding the church in an eternal act of divine decision, Barth has now placed the church not against the gospel and the purposes of God, as stressed in his earlier critical period, but at their centre as joined with Christ. Now the church is portrayed by Barth not in contradiction to the will of God (though in its sinfulness it retains such judgement), but in correspondence to it, a divinely and eternally appointed witness to God's reconciliation of the world in Jesus Christ. Barth can write: 'It is in virtue of this self-determination that God wills to be God solely in Jesus Christ. And it is as such that He is the Lord of Israel and the Church, and as such, and not otherwise, that He is the Creator, Reconciler and Redeemer of the universe and man. But it is with this primal decision of God that the doctrine of election deals' (*CD II/2*: 91). For this reason, and following Barth's already outlined commitments, all statements concerning the church and humanity are true only insofar as they are determined by Christology (*CD II/1*: 148–9; cf. *CD I/2*: 123; 883). From this point onward, Barth's ecclesiology remains from first to last rooted in the doctrines of Christology, Trinity, and election. The church therefore must be understood theologically before it is understood sociologically, for the basis of its existence is not simply the sum of human decisions within history, but a divine decision grounded in eternity. Barth's description of the church within his doctrine of election witnesses how far he has travelled beyond the *Romans* commentary. Yet the discussion of the church even in the doctrine of election of *CD II/2* falls short of providing concrete description of the church as a social entity with distinct practices enduring through history. In other words, the church is portrayed primarily as a formal medium for the gospel rather than as a historical and concrete embodied reflection of the gospel in the world. Further, Barth maintains that the church has 'no history in the strict sense but only . . . a status of continual self-renewal' (*CD II/2*: 342). Lacking such historical duration, the church could not be described in rich and concrete terms, and a developed material ecclesiology remained for later volumes of the *Church Dogmatics*, as we see in the next section.

BARTH'S MATERIAL ECCLESIOLOGY IN THE *CHURCH DOGMATICS*

The Doctrine of Reconciliation—The Context of the Church

Barth began to provide such thick concrete descriptions in an often overlooked brief discussion of the church in the ethical section 'The Active Life' of the third volume of the *Church Dogmatics*, concerning the doctrine of creation (see *CD III/4*: §55.3 'Freedom for Life', 470–564). There, he addresses the particular shape and form of life that the Christian community takes within the world as well as the particular practices and dispositions that mark its commissioned service and activity. Nevertheless, Barth would develop a dedicated ecclesiology in the proper and full sense only in the fourth volume of the *Church Dogmatics* under the rubric of the doctrine of reconciliation (the proposed fifth and final volume on redemption remaining unattempted and unfinished at the end of his lifetime). He does this in three distinctive sections: 'The Holy Spirit and the Gathering of the Christian Community' (*CD IV/1*: §62); 'The Holy Spirit and the Upbuilding of the Christian Community' (*CD IV/2*: §67); and 'The Holy Spirit and the Sending of the Christian Community' (*CD IV/3.2*: §72). While distinct themes are prominent in each of the sections, these themes span across the sections, not limited to a single discussion.

The Church and the Holy Spirit—The Nature and Origin of the Church

In the first of these sections, 'The Holy Spirit and the Gathering of the Christian Community', Barth focuses upon the *nature and origin* of the church. He can now speak of the church not only as an event but also as a history that endures through time, itself a work of the Holy Spirit that falls within a larger Christological framework. In the geometric language of the *Romans* commentary, but now in a greatly enriched and expanded key, Barth states:

> The Christology is like a vertical line meeting a horizontal. The doctrine of the sin of man is the horizontal line as such. The doctrine of justification is the intersection of the horizontal line by the vertical. The remaining doctrine, that of the Church and of faith, is again the horizontal line, but this time seen as intersected by the vertical. The vertical line is the atoning work of God in Jesus Christ. The horizontal is the object of that work; man and humanity. (*CD IV/1*: 643)

Barth now speaks of the church not only in the language of event but as a history that exists through time. The church is that horizontal history transformed by the intersection of the vertical in justification, a history taken up into and assumed by the history of Jesus Christ: 'The history which we consider when we speak of the Christian community and Christian faith is enclosed and exemplified in the history of Jesus Christ' (*CD IV/1*: 644; cf. 151). It thus comes into real and visible existence 'in the form of a sequence and nexus of definite human activities' (*CD IV/1*: 652). As such, it can be perceived as one phenomenal reality among others and can be described in 'historical and psychological and sociological terms like any other' (*CD IV/1*: 652).

But to know the church in this (natural) way is not to discern its true identity and nature, for the church is not simply one community among others, one institution among a host of institutions enduring through time. The church is a community that is called into existence and continues to exist by the Spirit and that therefore exists within history but is not the product of historical forces. It is both divinely established and historically constituted (*CD IV/1*: 647). This is the basis of Barth's understanding in this section of the church as both invisible and visible and as both event and institution (as witnessed earlier in the *Göttingen Dogmatics*). In each of these pairings, the former term precedes and gives reality to the second, each term united in an irreversible ordering, where the second exists only by means of the first. In other words, before the church comes to exist as a visible institution in history, it is grounded in a divine event of the Spirit that calls it into being and sustains its existence. The church is ever dependent upon this work of the Spirit for its life and identity. To know the church as both invisible and visible, and thus in its *true* reality, is to understand the church as a *mystery* known only to faith, and not simply as a sociological entity known through historical investigation. In this regard, to know the church as a mystery is akin to knowing the mysteries of incarnation and creation (*CD IV/1*: 645; cf. 653–4). To see the church only as invisible *or* visible, then, is to fall into corresponding docetic and ebionitic ecclesiological heresies (*CD IV/1*: 653–5; cf. *CD IV/3.2*: 726). Once again, Barth's very early eschatological concerns are preserved even as developed now along established Christological and pneumatological lines of thought (Bender 2005: ch. 6). The church is in short the body of Christ called into existence by the Spirit that exists in the particular time given to it between the first *parousia* of Christ and the second (*CD IV/1*: 725–39). As he writes: 'The Christian community, the true Church, arises and is only as the Holy Spirit works—the quickening power of the living Lord Jesus Christ' (*CD IV/2*: 617). For this reason, the church's spiritual growth cannot be confused with its external numerical increase, nor can the Nicene marks of the church be directly attributed to the church in its simple visibility, but must themselves be understood dialectically and as Christologically grounded, for the church in time is both one and many, holy and profane, catholic and contested, apostolic and in constant need of having its message authenticated (*CD IV/2*: 644–8; *CD IV/1*: 668–725).

The Church and Christ—The Form and Order of the Church

In the second major section on the church, 'The Holy Spirit and the Upbuilding of the Christian Community', Barth continues to emphasize that it is the work of the Spirit, and not the church's institutions, traditions, or practices, which guarantees its true character. But now he turns to elaborate its particular *form and order* as the body of Christ in the world. The church is 'the living community of the living Lord Jesus Christ', a phrase which Barth also used as the title to his address to the World Council of Churches Assembly in Amsterdam in 1948 (*CD IV/2*: 681; see also Barth 2003a: 75–104). The unrelenting focus upon the church as the true and real body of Christ in the world, along with Barth's strictly ordered understanding of the relation between and differentiation of Christ, church, and world, are perhaps his most singular contributions to ecclesiology. In this time between Christ's first and second Advents, the time of the ascension, the church is the particular form that Christ's body takes within the world, though he exists not only united to but distinct from this earthly body and remains the Head of it. Christ is present to the church and thus to the world even in his ascended bodily absence: 'Where this community lives by the Holy Spirit, Jesus Christ Himself lives on earth, in the world and in history' (*CD IV/1*: 353). This tension between Christ's presence in the world through the power of his Word and Spirit, and his absence such that the church is his body within the world between his ascension and final return, is a consistent theme in Barth's mature ecclesiology. The emphasis, however, is upon Christ's presence through the power of the Holy Spirit, rather than upon his absence (*CD IV/2*: 652). Barth can go so far as to say that the Holy Spirit is 'Jesus Christ Himself in the power of His resurrection' (*CD IV/3.1*: 352; cf. *CD IV/3.2*: 503).

Because he is present as a speaking Lord to the church, and because the salvation he accomplishes is a finished work, there is no need for the church to make him present through some form of sacramental mediation or to supply vicars to represent him. Nor can he be subsumed into (or be replaced by) the church or its activity (*CD IV/3.1*: 349–50). Barth brings these themes together in a major passage on his understanding of the church as Christ's body, one that displays his understanding also of the relation of Christ and the church in all of its dialectical and analogical richness, a relation fully predicated on Chalecedonian logic of unity and differentiation, asymmetry and irreversibility:

> This people, this community, is the form of His body in which Jesus Christ, its one heavenly Head, also exists and has therefore His earthly-historical form of existence. It is of human essence—for the Church is not of divine essence like its Head. But it does not exist in independence of Him. It is not itself the Head, nor does it become such. But it exists (ἀνυπόστατος and ἐνυπόστατος) in and in virtue of His existence. It lives because and as He lives, elected and awakened and called and gathered as a people by Him. It is His work, and it exists as His work takes place. Not for a single moment or in any respect can it be His body without Him, its Head. Indeed, it cannot be at all without Him. It does not exist apart from Him. It exists only as the body which serves Him the Head. For this reason—for otherwise it would have a separate and autonomous existence—it cannot even be His likeness or analogy. We cannot speak, then, of a repetition or extension of the incarnation taking place in it. But He, the one Jesus Christ Himself, exists as man. He exists not only in heavenly form, but also in earthly-historical form. To His heavenly form of existence as Son of God and Son of Man He has assumed this earthly-historical—the community as His one body which also has this form. He carries and maintains it in this unity with Himself as the people which not merely belongs to Him but is part of Himself. In God's eternal counsel, in His epiphany, and finally in His revelation at the end of the age, He was and is and will be this *totus Christus*—Christ and Christians. And these two elements of His one being are not merely related to one another *as* He Himself as Son of God is related to His human nature. But, in this second form, His relationship to His body, the community, *is* the relationship of God and man as it takes place in this one being as Head and body. Thus the community of Jesus Christ can be that which the human nature of its Lord and Head is. It cannot and must not be more than this. There can, therefore, be no question of a reversal in which either the community or the individual Christian equates himself with Jesus Christ, becoming the subject where He is only the predicate. There can be no question of a divinisation of the Church or the individual Christian which Jesus Christ has only to serve as a vehicle or redemptive agency. All this is cut away at the root and made quite impossible by the fact that He Himself is the Subject present and active and operative in His community. 'Christ liveth in me.' He Himself lives in this His earthly-historical form of existence, in the community as this form of His body. (*CD IV/2*: 59–60; cf. *CD IV/1*: 661–8; *CD IV/3.1*: 207; 278–9; *CD IV/3.2*: 754–5)

The importance of this passage (and the related parallel passages) cannot be over-emphasized in understanding Barth's highly dialectical and paradoxical conception of the church (Bender 2005: chapters 5 and 7). The image of the church as the 'earthly-historical form of existence (*irdisch-geschichtliche Existenzform*) of Jesus Christ Himself', the body of Christ 'created and continually renewed by the awakening power of the Holy Spirit', was the central image and governing concept that shaped all of Barth's mature ecclesiology (*CD IV/1*: 661). To say that the church is Christ's body does not, however, entail that it be seen as an extension of his incarnation and history, of his person, life, or work. The relation of Christ and the church is one of unity as the *totus Christus*, but this relation is also one of 'indissoluble differentiation and irreversible order' (*CD IV/3.2*: 594). Barth consistently from his earliest reflection onward denied any direct identification of Christ and the church. He can rather state regarding the church and Christians within it:

> They have not to assist or add to the being and work of their living Savior who is the Lord of the world, let alone to replace it by their own work. The community is not a prolongation of His incarnation, His death and resurrection, the acts of God and their revelation. It has not to do these things. It has to witness to them. It is its con-solation that it can do this. Its marching-orders are to do it. (*CD IV/1*: 317–18; cf. *CD IV/3.2*: 729)

It is this ministry of witness and correspondence that forms the heart of Barth's under-standing of what the church is ordained to do (rather than notions of mediation or cooper-ation). The church witnesses to the finished work of Christ and lives in correspondence to his own life of obedience. It stands in the present as the provisional representation of the salvation that Christ has accomplished for all (*CD IV/1*: 661–2). To live in correspondence and as a witness to the reconciliation of the world completed in Christ is the church's (and the Christian's) primary purpose and task, its own particular form of obedience (*CD IV/1*: 149–53; *CD IV/3.2*: 573–6). When the church seeks to do something more or other than this, it becomes, paradoxically, not something greater but something less, for the glory of the church belongs in giving God alone the glory (*CD IV/1*: 657). Yet it does have this real form of obedience and service because the church (and Christians within it) exists in a real union with Christ and 'in proximity to Him and therefore in analogy to what He is ...' (*CD IV/3.2*: 532–3). The relationship between Christ and the Christian community is 'indirectly identical to the relationship between Himself as the eternal Son of God and His being as man' (*CD IV/2*: 59). Just as the Spirit alone calls the church into existence and gives it life, so also the church exists only insofar as it is taken up and hidden in the life of its Lord (*CD IV/2*: 655). It is the Spirit that unites this Lord with the church in a bond of unity analogous to the relations of God in the inner-Trinitarian life itself (*CD IV/2*: 336–48).

The church as Christ's body takes a particular form and concrete instantiation in the world, and thus one with a particular order. Even though no church order can be absolutized, the fact that the church exists in space and time requires that it be given structure and shape. The upbuilding of the community hence entails the existence of a definite order and law for the church that oppose lawlessness, amorphousness, and chaos. Barth states that 'the christologic-ecclesiological concept of the community is such that by its very nature it speaks of law and order, thus impelling and summoning us to take up this question' (*CD IV/2*: 680). This order and law concerns not only worship but also every aspect of the church's life and activity, though worship stands indisputably at its centre. The specifics of these details belong to canon law and practical theology, but the presuppositions and general criteria behind them are predicated upon Christology and outlined in dogmatic theology (*CD IV/2*: 677–8; 698). Such law is neither to be rigid nor non-existent, and Barth's understanding of church law mirrors his conception of church doctrine: it provides guidance but can itself be corrected and revised in the light of Holy Scripture. It is neither revelation itself nor intrinsically opposed to revelation, and its guidance is real and necessary yet its authority remains relative rather than absolute. Church law is provisional law. Barth thereby opposes both ecclesiastical antinomianism and indifference on the one side and an inflexible and infallible jurisprudence and legalism on the other. He allows for great diversity and flexibility with regard to the specific shape, order, and activities a particular community embraces in light of its embodiment in a particular geographical and temporal location, but also maintains that Christological presuppositions regulate and place limits upon the specific type and shape they can take. These presuppositions dictate that all church law must demonstrate and be characterized by service, worship, dynamic life with definite form, and a nature worthy of emulation so that it be exemplary in character, a model for the world, and a pattern for civil law (see *CD IV/2*: 689–726).

The Church as God's People in the World—The Witness and Ordination of the Church

In the final section on the church, 'The Holy Spirit and the Sending of the Christian Community', Barth focuses on the *witness and ordination* of the church as the people of God in the world (language of course reminiscent of *Lumen Gentium* of Vatican II, though preceding it in time). In this, his longest sustained discussion of the church, he turns to the church's unique life and task in relation to the world, the 'people of God in world-occurrence' (*CD IV/3.2*: 681, *passim*). Barth emphasizes throughout that the church, grounded in an eternal election of God, is sent by divine commission into the world as a witness to it and for its benefit. The vocation of the church is nothing other than to bear witness to God's reconciliation of the world in Jesus Christ (*CD IV/3.2*: 681–3). The Christian community lives to serve God's purposes and the world's need. It is set apart from the world, yet set apart in order to serve in and to the world (*CD IV/3.2*: 762–4). The church has no existence or reality apart from this special ordained task and ministry entrusted to it by Christ (*CD IV/3.2*: 795–6; 830–1). There is thus a parallel between the Father's sending of the Son and the Son's sending of the community into the world (*CD IV/3.2*: 768–9).

Barth's actualistic ontology is reflected in his ecclesiology in that it is determined and defined by a teleological concern: the church does not exist in or for itself but in order to serve the world. The identity of the church is therefore defined by means of its existence as mission, a central element of his ecclesiological thought that he admitted to have discovered not in the magisterial Reformers but in Anabaptism and Pietism (*CD IV/3.1*: 11–38). As in prior sections, Barth here emphasizes that the church's mission does not augment or supplement, but witnesses to, Christ's unique, irreplaceable, and completed work (*CD IV/3.2*: 834–8). This limitation that circumscribes and defines the church's proper activity and task is not a denigration of the church and its ministry, but an establishment of its proper charge and thus an affirmation of its true dignity. This particular vocation is limited and subordinate to Christ's own, but it is nevertheless ennobled and also empowered and sustained by the Spirit of God and the Word of Christ himself (*CD IV/3.2*: 838–43). In that the church undertakes this mission of witness and lives in correspondence to the ministry of its Lord, it is itself a 'likeness' (*Gleichnis*) or 'subsequent and provisional representation' (*nachträgliche und vorläufige Darstellung*) of the kingdom of God in the present world (*CD IV/3.2*: 792). The church can reflect the kingdom but is never equated with it, for in Christ alone is the presence of the kingdom manifest in all its perfection (*CD IV/3.2*: 792).

The particular task of the church's witness hinges first on the declaration of the gospel in the church's verbal proclamation and its provisional (if imperfect) representation of the kingdom of God within world history. Secondly, the church also expounds the inner meaning and logic of the gospel as it proclaims it (*CD IV/3.2*: 844–7). This explication of the gospel and its meaning and significance is done through nothing more nor less than narrating the history of God's relation with and reconciliation of the world in Christ (*CD IV/3.2*: 849). The church does this as it lives in analogy to this divine redemption in the sphere of human history. Beyond the proclamation and explication of the gospel, the church thirdly addresses the world as it appeals to the world for its reception (*CD IV/3.2*: 850–3).

For the church to live in such a way it must take up a particular life that incorporates specific practices within this life. Barth broadly outlines these practices, which he designates forms of ministry, in the final and most extensive discussion of the church's mission in this section. He argues that the church's unity is not threatened, but strengthened, by this diversity and multiplicity of ministries. In a section often overlooked by critics who claim he lacks concrete description of church practices, he specifically names and discusses twelve concrete forms of ministry. He chooses these forms of ministry because they exist across space and time and endure in every age and context of the church. They are lasting forms of ministry that endure through the necessary changes that the church's specific practices may undergo throughout history. The ultimate criterion for their choice lies in the fact that they appear in the historic ministry of Christ.

Barth categorizes these twelve ministries under the two headings of the church's speech and its action (prioritizing the first over the second in a manner parallel to Barth's prioritizing of the ministry of the Word over that of sacraments earlier noted). He thus provides two lists of six forms each. The first list of the church's speech includes: (1) the praise of God; (2) the proclamation of the Gospel; (3) instruction in Scripture and faith; (4) evangelization to the surrounding culture; (5) mission to the nations of the world; and (6) the discipline of theology. The second list of the church's action includes: (1) prayer;

(2) the cure of souls (pastoral care); (3) the production of exemplars of the Christian life; (4) the rendering of service (diaconal ministries that address physical needs and that include within them a place for social criticism); (5) the prophetic action of the community in light of current events; and (6) the establishment of fellowship between persons (*CD IV/3.2*: 865–901). At the heart of Christian practice are baptism and the Lord's Supper, which serve not only as proclamations of the gospel, but as the most eloquent means of the church's witness to the world, 'the witness of peace on earth among the men in whom God is well-pleased' (*CD IV/3.2*: 901). They are not 'empty signs' but the means by which such peace and unity are effected through the action of the triune God. Barth's full discussion of baptism (in which he embraced believer's baptism and repudiated infant baptism) occurred in an incomplete fragment of the *Dogmatics* (*CD IV/4*) and his dedicated discussion of the Lord's Supper was never completed.

In this last section on the church in *CD IV/3*, the primary relation of Barth's investigation has shifted from that between Christ and the church to that between the church and the world. Whereas his understanding of the relation between Christ and the church is always strictly ordered and irreversible, his understanding of the relation of the church and the world is less so. While the church and its law and life are paradigmatic for the world, the relation of the church and the world allows for mutual and reciprocal influence. For instance, the church borrows the language, thought forms, and social structures of the world to communicate its message and form its communal life in the present and is free to do so (*CD IV/3.2*: 735–41). The distinction between the church and the world (as that between the Christian and the non-Christian) is less sharp and strictly demarcated as that between Christ and the church, nor is the relation strictly irreversible (*CD IV/3.2*: 809–12). Yet this does not mean that important distinctions do not exist between them, for whereas the church knows the meaning of its history, the world cannot know its own meaning apart from the witness of the Christian community (*CD III/3*: 203–10). The Christian community is thus the place where the true nature of the world is revealed to the world itself:

> The world does not know itself. It does not know God, nor man, nor the relationship and covenant between God and man. Hence it does not know its own origin, state nor goal . . . The community of Jesus Christ exists for and is sent into the world in the first basic sense that it is given to it, in its knowledge of God and man and the covenant set up between them, to know the world as it is. We may well say that, itself belonging also to the world, it is the point in the world where its eyes are opened to itself and an end is put to its ignorance about itself. (*CD IV/3.2*: 769; see also 769–73; 801–12)

The church exists, as joined to Christ, as the inner circle of the world, which forms its periphery, in analogous manner as Christ stands at the center of the *totus Christus* with the church his periphery. On this account, the history of the world even in its rebellion falls under the rule of Christ, so that its history, while distinct, is inseparable from the history of the Christian community (*CD IV/3.2*: 687–8). Once again, patterns of unity in distinction govern Barth's thought on the relation of church and world, but there is no strict irreversibility or asymmetry here as in the other ecclesiological relationships, for in this one, church and world stand on the same created plane (Bender 2005: ch. 8). The line between church and world is one of acknowledgement of the lordship of Christ and correspondence to that lordship; it is not one of absolute difference, for both church and world find their ultimate meaning in the universal atonement of Jesus Christ:

> This knowledge of the new heaven and the new earth already given in relation to Him distinguishes it [the church], for all the restriction of its vision, from the rest of humanity which does not yet participate in the knowledge of Jesus Christ and what has taken place in Him. And it is this distinction which capacitates it for witness to the world, and commits it to this witness. (*CD* IV/3.2: 715; cf. 793–5)

What Barth here provides is a theological description of the identity of the world in light of Christ and the community joined to him. The church provides the world with nothing other than an alternative community of peace in contrast to a world of strife and enmity, a community that lives in and is transformed by the truth of the atonement of Christ (*CD* IV/3.2: 899–901).

Whether for good or ill, Barth does not allow for strong distinctions between the church and the world, for both fall under the common lordship of Jesus Christ. The church thus lives not in separation from, but in solidarity with, the world. While emphasizing the distinctiveness of the church and its life over against the world, he also simultaneously emphasizes such solidarity over against any type of sectarian separation. This solidarity retains a place for critical and prophetic witness against the world that lives in rebellion to the lordship of Christ. Yet even the church's 'No' to the fallen practices and life of the world must serve the larger affirmation of its 'Yes' (*CD* IV/3.2: 773; 797–8). Barth thus steers a course between sectarian isolation and cultural accommodation, and opposes, in his terms, both the 'sacralization' and 'secularization' of the church, both a self-exalted church ('the church in excess') and a church that does not take itself seriously ('the church in defect') (*CD* IV/2: 667–71; Barth 1981: 132–42). He develops his political thought of the relation of the church and the civil order (the state) along similar Christological and affirmative (if critical) lines, placing the state, like the world at large, in a divinely determined relation to the church and to Christ. He moreover situates this theological discussion of the state not under the order of creation (where it is most often placed), but within the order of reconciliation. Though of interest in itself, this political thought extends beyond what can here be addressed (see *CD* IV/2: 719–26; also the essays in Barth 1968).

The church in the end stands between the world and its Lord, calling the world to faith and obedience in light of the atonement and reconciliation that God has perfectly accomplished through Jesus Christ. The church's *mission* therefore not only flows out of, but also conditions and defines, its *nature* and *form*, such that the church's being is defined in its act (Bender 2005: 243–4). The church is a missionary church because God is a missionary God (Flett 2010: ch. 6). The greatest service the church can perform for the world (and thus the state) is simply to be the church (*CD* IV/2: 721). Two quotations nicely summarize Barth's understanding of the relation between the church and the world and bring this discussion to a close:

> As God exists for it [the world] in His divine way, and Jesus Christ in His divine-human, so the Christian community exists for it in its own purely human. All

ecclesiology is grounded, critically limited, but also positively determined by Christology; and this applies in respect of the particular statement which here concerns us, namely, that the Church exists for the world. The community neither can nor should believe in itself. Even in this particular respect, there can be no *credo in ecclesiam*. Yet as it believes in God the Father, the Son and the Holy Ghost, it can and should believe and confess its own reality: *credo ecclesiam*, and therefore the reality rather than the mere ideal that it exists for the world. (*CD IV/3.2: 786*)

The purpose of its [the church's] existence is the subsequent and provisional representation of the calling of all humanity and all creatures to the service of God as it has gone forth in Jesus Christ. The origin and goal of the ways of God, which took place initially but perfectly in the resurrection of Jesus Christ, and which will take place definitively and no less perfectly in His final appearing, is the calling of every man and indeed of all creation to the service of God. The function of the community is to follow and yet at the same time to precede His universal call. (*CD IV/3.2: 793; cf. 729–30*)

FINAL REFLECTIONS

This chapter has taken a developmental view of Barth's ecclesiology for two reasons. First, Barth's mature ecclesiology in the *Church Dogmatics* is best understood and appreciated in light of the progression of his thought. Barth's mature ecclesiology did not arise out of a vacuum, but at the end of a long period of dialogue, reflection, and struggle. Second, misunderstandings of Barth's ecclesiology often occur when this development is overlooked, either judging Barth's thought on the church only in the context of its early critical period, or failing to see the continuity of themes throughout his thought. Barth's theology and hence ecclesiology must be seen in light of the tension between real continuity in development, and real innovation in the context of consistently held convictions. Its ecumenical promise must also be evaluated in light of its historical context, one before the Second Vatican Council. Nonetheless, Barth's theology did in fact exert an influence upon a number of significant figures of mid-twentieth-century Roman Catholicism and the Second Vatican Council who were both appreciative yet critical of it, such as Hans Urs von Balthasar, Henri Bouillard, Hans Küng, and Yves Congar. Barth's ecclesiology has not been without its share of criticism, of course. His theology has been accused of subsuming the Holy Spirit into Christ such that the distinctive person and work of the Spirit in the church is lost. Correspondingly, some have charged that Barth fails to make the church a necessary part of God's salvation, thus ignoring and sacrificing its place in the salvific economy—his notion of 'witness' being deemed inadequate to describe the church's work, the church's own agency thus slighted. He has also been criticized for refusing to identify the concrete activity of the church with the Spirit's work and in turn failing to give full consideration to the historicity of the church, thus providing an abstract and de-historicized ecclesiology (for these and other criticisms, as well as re-evaluations of them, see the works of Buckley, Hauer was, Healy, Hütter, Mangina, McFarland, and O'Grady listed in the References). Whether such criticisms are sustainable and fair to Barth's ecclesiology, or can themselves be sufficiently answered, is a matter of ongoing debate (see Bender 2005: ch. 9; Bender 2014: chs 1 and 4; Hawksley 2011; Healy 2004; McCormack 2011).

In the end, Barth's ecclesiology deserves more attention than it has historically received, if for no other reason than because of its unique perspective and comprehensive intention and vision. It provides a richly theological understanding of the church, but one in a decidedly evangelical (i.e. Protestant) key, while overcoming traditional Protestant deficiencies such as setting soteriology against ecclesiology and a penchant for providing thin accounts of the church. It is a consistently evangelical ecclesiology with catholic implications and aspirations, yet one with distinctive free church elements (Bender 2005: 284–7; Carter 1995). It stands as an alternative to both organic and sociological approaches in ecclesiology, incorporating the church into the economy of salvation without making it a steward of grace. It emphasizes the church as a concrete congregation in a specific place and time (hence Barth's penchant for the term *Gemeinde* [community] rather than *Kirche* [church]) while also acknowledging its universal character. It favours a 'bottom-up' rather than 'top-down' approach to ecumenical relations. While Barth does not provide a specific discussion of ordained ministry, he does provide a (non-hierarchical) picture of the church in which every member is called to be a witness to Jesus Christ and to share in ministry to one another and to the world in a radical embrace of the doctrine of the priesthood of all believers. It is an ecclesiology that has left all remnants of the *corpus Christianum* far behind and may thus appear strange and disorienting, but may also be prophetic and promising.

REFERENCES

Primary Texts

Barth, Karl (1981). *The Christian Life: Church Dogmatics IV/4 Lecture Fragments*. Trans. Geoffrey W. Bromiley. Grand Rapids, MI: Eerdmans.

Barth, Karl (1982). *Die christliche Dogmatik im Entwurf*. Ed. Gerhard Sauter. Zurich: Theologischer Verlag Zurich.

Barth, Karl (1936–77). *Church Dogmatics*. Ed. G. W. Bromiley and T. F. Torrance. Edinburgh: T & T Clark.

Barth, Karl (1968). *Community, State, and Church*. Gloucester: Peter Smith. Reissued Eugene, OR: Wipf & Stock Publishers, 2004.

Barth, Karl (2003a). *God Here and Now*. Trans. Paul M. van Buren. London: Routledge.

Barth, Karl (1961). *Der Götze Wackelt*. Ed. Karl Kupisch. Berlin: Käthe Vogt Verlag.

Barth, Karl (1966). *How I Changed my Mind*. Richmond: John Knox Press.

Barth, Karl (1960). *The Humanity of God*. Trans. John N. Thomas and Thomas Wieser. Westminster, NC: John Knox Press.

Barth, Karl (1985). *Der Römerbrief [Erste Fassung] 1919*. Ed. Hermann Schmidt. Zurich: Theologischer Verlag Zurich.

Barth, Karl (2010). *Der Römerbrief [Zweite Fassung] 1922*. Ed. Cornelis van der Kooi and Katja Tolstaja. Zurich: Theologischer Verlag Zürich. English translation: *The Epistle to the Romans*. Trans. Edwyn C. Hoskyns. Oxford: Oxford University Press, 1968.

Barth, Karl (1957). *Theologische Fragen und Antworten*. Zollikon: Evangelischer Verlag AG Zollikon. English translation of selected texts: *God in Action: Theological Addresses*. Trans.

E. G. Homrighausen and Karl J. Ernst. New York: Round Table Press, 1936. Reissued Eugene, OR: Wipf & Stock Publishers, 2005.

Barth, Karl (1962). *Theology and Church: Shorter Writings 1920–1928*. Translated Louise Pettibone Smith. New York: Harper & Row.

Barth, Karl (2003b). *Unterricht in der christlichen Religion, III: Die Lehre von der Versöhnung/ Die Lehre von der Erlösung, 1925/1926*. Zurich: Theologischer Verlag Zurich.

Barth, Karl (2011). *The Word of God and Theology*. Trans. Amy Marga. London and New York: T & T Clark/Continuum.

Smart, James D. (1964). *Revolutionary Theology in the Making: Barth–Thurneysen Correspondence 1914–1925*. Trans. James D. Smart. Richmond: John Knox Press.

Secondary Studies

Bender, Kimlyn (2005). *Karl Barth's Christological Ecclesiology*. Aldershot: Ashgate Publishing. Reissued Eugene, OR: Cascade Books, 2013.

Bender, Kimlyn (2014). *Confessing Christ for Church and World: Studies in Modern Theology*. Downers Grove, IL: InterVarsity Press.

Buckley, James J. (1994). 'A Field of Living Fire: Karl Barth on the Spirit and the Church'. *Modern Theology* 10: 81–102.

Busch, Eberhard (1990). 'Karl Barth's Understanding of the Church as Witness'. *St. Luke's Journal of Theology* 33: 87–101.

Busch, Eberhard (1994). *Karl Barth: His Life from Letters and Autobiographical Texts*. Trans. John Bowden. Grand Rapids, MI: Eerdmans. Reissued by Eugene: Wipf and Stock, 2005.

Carter, Craig (1995). 'Karl Barth's Revision of Protestant Ecclesiology'. *Perspectives in Religious Studies* 22: 35–44.

Currie, Thomas (2015). *The Only Sacrament Left to Us: The Threefold Word of God in the Theology and Ecclesiology of Karl Barth*. Eugene, OR: Pickwick.

Flett, John (2010). *The Witness of God: The Trinity, Missio Dei, Karl Barth, and the Nature of Christian Community*. Grand Rapids, MI: Eerdmans.

Hauerwas, Stanley (2001). *With the Grain of the Universe: The Church's Witness and Natural Theology*. Grand Rapids, MI: Brazos Press.

Hawksley, Theodora (2011). 'The Freedom of the Spirit: The Pneumatological Point of Barth's Ecclesiological Minimalism'. *Scottish Journal of Theology* 64: 180–94.

Healy, Nicholas M. (1994). 'The Logic of Karl Barth's Ecclesiology: Analysis, Assessment and Proposed Modifications'. *Modern Theology* 10: 253–70.

Healy, Nicholas M. (2004). 'Karl Barth's Ecclesiology Reconsidered'. *Scottish Journal of Theology* 57: 287–99.

Hütter, Reinhard (1994). 'The Church as Public: Dogma, Practice and the Holy Spirit'. *Pro Ecclesia* 3: 334–61.

Hütter, Reinhard (2000a). 'Karl Barth's "Dialectical Catholicity": Sic et Non'. *Modern Theology* 16: 137–57.

Hütter, Reinhard (2000b). *Suffering Divine Things: Theology as Church Practice*. Grand Rapids, MI: Eerdmans Publishing Co.

McCormack, Bruce (1995). *Karl Barth's Critically Realistic Dialectical Theology: Its Genesis and Development 1909–1936*. Oxford: Clarendon Press.

McCormack, Bruce (2011). 'Witness to the Word: A Barthian Engagement with Reinhard Hütter's Ontology of the Church'. *Zeitschrift für Dialektische Theologie* 5: 59–77.

McFarland, Ian (2005). 'The Body of Christ: Rethinking a Classic Ecclesiological Model'. *International Journal of Systematic Theology* 7: 225–45.

Mangina, Joseph L. (1999a). 'Bearing the Marks of Jesus: The Church in the Economy of Salvation in Barth and Hauerwas'. *Scottish Journal of Theology* 52: 269–305.

Mangina, Joseph L. (1999b). 'The Stranger as Sacrament: Karl Barth and the Ethics of Ecclesial Practice'. *International Journal of Systematic Theology* 1: 322–39.

O'Grady, Colm (1969a). *The Church in Catholic Theology: Dialogue with Karl Barth.* Washington-Cleveland: Corpus Books.

O'Grady, Colm (1969b). *The Church in the Theology of Karl Barth.* Washington-Cleveland: Corpus Books.

Rendtorff, Trutz (1971). *Church and Theology: The Systematic Function of the Church Concept in Modern Theology.* Trans. Reginald H. Fuller. Philadelphia: Westminster Press.

SUGGESTED READING

Barth, Karl (1936–77). *Church Dogmatics.* Ed. G. W. Bromiley and T. F. Torrance. Edinburgh: T & T Clark, §§3; 20–2; 34; 62; 67; 72.

Barth, Karl (1968). *Community, State, and Church.* Gloucester: Peter Smith. Reissued Eugene, OR: Wipf & Stock Publishers, 2004.

Barth, Karl (2003a). *God Here and Now.* Trans. Paul M. van Buren. London: Routledge, 75–104.

Bender, Kimlyn (2005). *Karl Barth's Christological Ecclesiology.* Aldershot: Ashgate Publishing, chs 1 and 4. Reissued Eugene, OR: Cascade Books, 2013.

Busch, Eberhard (1990). 'Karl Barth's Understanding of the Church as Witness'. *St. Luke's Journal of Theology* 33: 87–101.

Currie, Thomas (2015). *The Only Sacrament Left to Us: The Threefold Word of God in the Theology and Ecclesiology of Karl Barth.* Eugene, OR: Pickwick.

Flett, John (2010). *The Witness of God: The Trinity, Missio Dei, Karl Barth, and the Nature of Christian Community.* Grand Rapids, MI: Eerdmans.

Healy, Nicholas M. (2004). 'Karl Barth's Ecclesiology Reconsidered'. *Scottish Journal of Theology* 57: 287–99.

Hütter, Reinhard (1994). 'The Church as Public: Dogma, Practice and the Holy Spirit'. *Pro Ecclesia* 3: 334–61.

Hütter, Reinhard (2000a). 'Karl Barth's "Dialectical Catholicity": Sic et Non'. *Modern Theology* 16: 137–57.

Hütter, Reinhard (2000b). *Suffering Divine Things: Theology as Church Practice.* Grand Rapids, MI: Eerdmans Publishing Co.

McCormack, Bruce (2011). 'Witness to the Word: A Barthian Engagement with Reinhard Hütter's Ontology of the Church'. *Zeitschrift für Dialektische Theologie* 5: 59–77.

Mangina, Joseph L. (1999a). 'Bearing the Marks of Jesus: The Church in the Economy of Salvation in Barth and Hauerwas'. *Scottish Journal of Theology* 52: 269–305.

Mangina, Joseph L. (1999b). 'The Stranger as Sacrament: Karl Barth and the Ethics of Ecclesial Practice'. *International Journal of Systematic Theology* 1: 322–39.

O'Grady, Colm (1969a). *The Church in Catholic Theology: Dialogue with Karl Barth.* Washington-Cleveland: Corpus Books.

O'Grady, Colm (1969b). *The Church in the Theology of Karl Barth.* Washington-Cleveland: Corpus Books.

CHAPTER 17

YVES CONGAR

GABRIEL FLYNN

Yves M.-J. Congar (1904–95) was the foremost French theologian of his lifetime. From the outset, he regarded his vocation as being Dominican and Thomist, ecumenical and ecclesiological. The key elements of his theology include the restoration of the genuine value of ecclesiology; ecumenism; a fresh consideration of the person and mission of the Holy Spirit; reform; the laity; a return to the sources; and the application of the rich resources of tradition to the current problems of the church. His theological corpus has been lauded for its breadth, brilliance, and lucidity. He considered himself as a man of ideas (Congar 2000: 215), but it is his idea of reform, viewed in the context of the return to the sources, that dominates his entire oeuvre and constitutes his most important and original contribution to theology. He was one of the chief architects of an exceptional renewal in Roman Catholic ecclesiology in the twentieth century.

RETURN TO THE SOURCES

The place of the church in Congar's theology is best understood in relation to his utter dedication to its service and to the pursuit of truth. He writes: '[I decided] to dedicate myself particularly to the Church and ecumenism. . . . I've consecrated my life to the service of truth. I've loved it and still love it in the way one loves a person' (Congar 1981: 405). He contributed to the recovery of the biblical images of the church, which emphasize its mystical nature rather than the hierarchical and societal aspects that had been given such prominence in the previously dominant post-Tridentine ecclesiology. Congar's vision for renewal led to a profound transformation of the church, its relationship with the other Christian churches, and with the world. The Second Vatican Council (1962–5) became the catalyst for this change, and his prodigious ecclesiological programme was translated directly into its documents. 'All the things to which I gave quite special attention issued in the Council: ecclesiology, ecumenism, reform of the Church, the lay state, mission, ministries, collegiality, return to sources and Tradition' (1981: 405). Further, the importance and continued relevance of Congar's historical works (1968a; 1970a) has been acknowledged by historians and should assist in the formulation of a more adequate response to the most complex disagreements and challenges confronting the institutional church (O'Malley 2005).

The present chapter examines how Congar's comprehensive theology of the church, synthesized in the notion of a 'total ecclesiology' (Congar 1985a: xvi; 1953a: 13), was formulated in response to particular problems within the church which, in his view, contributed to unbelief. In support of this claim, I look at the principal findings of his 1935 study, 'The Reasons for the Unbelief of our Time: A Theological Conclusion'. In addition, I refer to later writings by him in which he says plainly that this essay, published as a theological conclusion to a three-year investigation by the journal *La Vie intellectuelle* into the causes of unbelief, provides the inspiration for his major works on the church and motivated him to institute a new series on the church called *Unam Sanctam* (Congar 1962a; 1961a). Congar notes that the results of the survey on unbelief conducted by *La Vie intellectuelle* are valid only for France (1938a: 13; 1935: 215). The findings of his 'Theological Conclusion' to that study, however, as well as his subsequent deliberations on unbelief and other related issues in an article published shortly before the Second Vatican Council, 'The Council in the Age of Dialogue', are clearly relevant to the entire church. Essentially, Congar held that certain ideas of God and faith, together with a 'wholly juridico-hierarchical' image of the church, were largely to blame for unbelief (1985b: 213). He was convinced that the countenance (*visage*) presented by the Roman Catholic Church was crucial for the evangelization of the modern world and would determine, to a large degree, the chances for the reunion of the Christian churches (Congar 1962a: 146, 149–50; 1961a: 694, 697–9). In order to transcend the juridical idea of the church, Congar, together with his colleagues Marie-Dominique Chenu (1895–1990) and Henri-Marie Féret (1904–92), embarked on an enterprise to eliminate 'baroque theology' (Puyo 1975: 45–6), a term which they coined to describe the theology of the Catholic Reformation (Congar 1983: 79). The accomplishment of this goal was an important reason for his founding of the *Unam Sanctam* collection in November 1935, which was destined to become a highly influential ecclesiological and ecumenical library running to almost eighty volumes.

What follows seeks to provide an interpretative framework for understanding Congar's ecclesiology. The section 'Return to the Sources' shows that a renewed ecclesiology forms an essential theological basis for church renewal. 'The Vision of the Church in Congar's Theology' investigates the vision of the renewed church, with particular attention to the principal means proposed by Congar for its renewal. 'The Shape of the Church in Congar's Theology' assesses his idea of true reform, based on a recognition of the indefectibility of the church's visible institution and adherence to its tradition.

A preliminary matter to be considered is the series of profound changes in the French church in the period 1930–60. During this time, a broad intellectual and spiritual movement arose within Roman Catholicism, largely in response to an atheistic secularism which lay at the heart of the crisis in European society. This movement for a return to the sources encompassed Belgium and Germany, but was most powerful in France, where it was led primarily by Jesuits and Dominicans. The foremost exponents of *ressourcement* were principally, though not exclusively, leading French Dominicans and Jesuits of the faculties of the Saulchoir (Paris) and Lyon-Fourvière, respectively. They included Congar and his Dominican *confrères* Chenu, Féret, and Dominique Dubarle (1907–87), and the Jesuits Jean Daniélou (1905–74), Henri de Lubac (1896–1991), Henri Bouillard (1908–81), and Hans Urs von Balthasar (1905–88) who, under the influence of Adrienne von Speyr, left the Society of Jesus in 1950 in order to found a 'secular institute' for lay people. This renowned generation of French *ressourcement* theologians inspired a renaissance in twentieth-century Roman Catholic thought and initiated a movement for renewal that made a decisive contribution to the reforms of Vatican II.

A host of new initiatives emerged in the French church during and after the Second World War as a spirit of hope, creativity, and originality pervaded the period. These projects included the movement for the reform of the liturgy, *Centre de Pastorale Liturgique*, the return to biblical and patristic sources, exemplified especially in the foundation of the *Sources chrétiennes* series, the renewal of ecclesiology, demonstrated by the establishment of the *Unam Sanctam* series, and the realization of the church's missionary task. According to Congar, this was 'one of the finest moments in the history of French Catholicism' as the church sought to regain evangelical contact with the world (1966a: 32; 1964a: xliii).

The *ressourcement* passed through various stages of development (Congar 1948; Daniélou 1946; Aubert 1954). The biblical renewal, which began in Germany during the inter-war period, spread progressively to the rest of the Roman Catholic world. The liturgical renewal is older than the biblical renewal. Although known in France from before the First World War, its first intense period of activity was linked with the name of Dom Lambert Beauduin (1873–1960), the Belgian liturgist and founder of Chevetogne, who was condemned by a Roman tribunal in 1930 following the publication of his view that the 'Anglican Church' should be 'united to Rome, not absorbed' ('unie non absorbée'). But it was in Germany during the inter-war period that the liturgical renewal blossomed when the church was forced, especially during the Nazi era, to renounce social action and to focus instead on the lively celebration of the divine mysteries. The biblical renewal and the liturgical movement were completed by a patristic rejuvenation (Bouyer 1947; Pottier 2012). The *ressourcement* reached a dramatic high point in French theology in the period during and following the Second World War. There were new missionary strategies, including the Young Christian Worker/Young Christian Student movements, which developed during the inter-war period, and, during the World War, Godin and Daniel's *La France: Pays de mission?* (Godin and Daniel 1950).

Ressourcement engendered controversy from its inception and attracted considerable attention beyond those directly concerned with it. An inevitable part of that controversy related to the vexed question of terminology. The word *ressourcement* was coined by the poet and social critic Charles Péguy (1873–1914). According to Congar, Péguy was a great influence in favour of *ressourcement*, though in his view Péguy's understanding of the Christocentric dimension of the faith was weak. The liturgical changes inaugurated by Pope Pius X (1835–1914) were also an inspiration for *ressourcement* (Congar 1939: 11). Protestant theologians, most notably Karl Barth (1886–1968), contributed to the Catholic *ressourcement* by showing Catholics that it is possible to read the Bible in ways which are faithful both to the historic faith and to the methods of historical criticism. The power of the movement for a return to the sources was, however, most evident on the Catholic side, with Congar as its pre-eminent practitioner. He outlines his commitment succinctly: 'In everything I have always been concerned to recover the sources, the roots. I am firmly convinced: a tree strikes deep roots and cannot rise to heaven except to the extent those roots hold firmly to the soil of the earth' (Congar 1985b: 215). Congar adopted *ressourcement* as the standard for church reform understood as an urgent call to move from 'a less profound to a more profound tradition; a discovery of the most profound resources' (1950a: 601–2). Much later, he would restate this original emphasis in the context of a glowing tribute to Chenu. 'What would a little later be called "*ressourcement*" was then at the heart of our efforts' (1985c: 499; 1990: 242). The combination of *ressourcement* and *recentrement* was important in Congar's ecclesiology. It provided the insight which enabled him to deal with the important though difficult question of the relationship between the church and the world—a relationship that Congar defined in such a way as to avoid the dangerous error of either being subordinate to the other.

The *ressourcement* project was severely criticized by M.-Michel Labourdette (1946a; 1946b), as well as by Réginald Garrigou-Lagrange (1946c), who seems to have borrowed the phrase *la nouvelle théologie* to describe it (see Flynn 2012: 5). This controversial term was first used by Pietro Parente, Secretary to the Holy Office, in an article entitled 'Nuove tendenze teologiche' which appeared in *L'Osservatore Romano*, 9–10 February 1942. The epithet *nouvelle théologie* in fact corresponds to a theology that is concerned to know the tradition, as opposed to a purely scholastic and repetitive theology. The view of tradition proposed by the *nouvelle théologie*, far from being traditionalist, in the sense of a repetition of the recent past, was concerned rather with the unity of the ever-living tradition. This was precisely Congar's position (1964b: 146; 1984: 118–19). In an atmosphere of suspicion and controversy, *Humani Generis* was published on 12 August 1950. Here Pius XII warned against the dangerous tendencies of the 'new theology', attacking the historical contextualization of dogma as leading inevitably to relativism, and also warning against a 'false eirenicism' towards the other Christian denominations, thus compromising the fundamental tenets of the faith. In the wake of the controversial encyclical, it is hardly surprising that Congar as well as de Lubac, both astute political analysts, rejected the term *nouvelle théologie*. In 1950, Congar compared *nouvelle théologie* to the 'tarasque', a legendary monster of Provence (see Puyo 1975: 99).

Although no names had been mentioned in *Humani Generis*, the Jesuit and Dominican superiors felt compelled to act. Congar read *Humani Generis* attentively, having been advised by Emmanuel Suárez OP, the then Master of the Dominican Order, that there were things in it which concerned himself. He denied, however, that either he or anyone in his ecumenical milieu had ever practised a bad 'eirenicism' (see Puyo: 106–13). In February 1954, he was summoned to Paris and, together with his *confrères* Chenu,

Féret, and Pierre Boisselot, was dismissed from his post at the Saulchoir. Going first to Jerusalem, then assigned to Cambridge, he returned to France in 1955 through the kind offices of the bishop of Strasbourg to continue his work, which he describes as 'that of an inner renewal, ecclesiological, anthropological and pastoral' (1966a: 44; 1964a: lvi).

Turning to Congar's new vision of the church—the most enduring element of his theological legacy—we consider its central elements in order to reconstruct it. An understanding of his unique contribution to the renewal of ecclesiology; a consideration of his role at Vatican II; and an analysis of his view of the church as a cause of unbelief constitute the principal areas of concern.

The Vision of the Church in Congar's Theology

Congar's life's work concerned the articulation of a complete theology, through the study of the totality of Catholic doctrine, for the advancement of the church's mission in the world. A clear idea of his rich hopes for the church may be found in a short essay written in 1937, entitled 'Pour une théologie de l'Église': 'Everywhere we get a sense that it would be of great profit in our pastoral ministry and would allow Christianity to spread to a far greater extent throughout the world, if the concept of the Church were to recover the broad, rich, vital meaning it once had, a meaning deriving wholly from the Bible and Tradition' (Congar 1937: 98). Clearly the development of a comprehensive theology of the church was one of the most important concerns of Congar's theological career. *Église et papauté: regards historiques* is a later and valuable collection of Congar's historical writings which he chose for this volume for their decisive importance in understanding the ecclesiological renewal of the twentieth century (Congar 1994). Commenting on this work, Étienne Fouilloux affirms a clear consistency of purpose in Congar's theology, namely, 'to elucidate the course of the Church across history' (1995: 404).

Congar is careful to draw attention to certain serious difficulties for the church that would ensue from a failure to formulate the principles of a full ecclesiology: 'Without those principles, we should have, confronting a laicized world, only a clerical Church, which would not be the people of God in the fullness of its truth. At bottom there can be only one sound and sufficient theology of laity, and that is a "total ecclesiology"' (1985a, xvi; 1953a: 13). It is clear that, for Congar, church and laity cannot be understood in isolation from each other. A study of the concept of the church in Congar's theology is, then, a necessary prerequisite to an analysis of his theology of the laity.

Congar's notion of the church is multifaceted. His ecclesiology is markedly disparate, being made up of many different images or models. However, he did not produce a systematic theology. His theology is occasional in the sense that it was written in response to requests, but also charismatic, since these requests emanated from within the heart of the church. Although he never produced a complete ecclesiology, the church is none-theless the major theme of his theological corpus.

Congar's Affective Ecclesiology

Congar loved the church and this informed and inspired all his theological projects. In every question regarding the church, its mission in the world, and its reform, the guiding principle is, so to speak, love. As he remarks: 'But this [reform] must be done in love, not in indifferent disinterestedness neither in cold criticism, nor in latent re-volt' (1970b: 30). A defining feature of Congar's theology of the church is its orienta-tion towards the world. His ecclesiology, far from being ecclesio-centric, is for the world and at the service of all. Even a cursory reading of his works shows that Congar was not prepared to ignore the modern world or its history. Such a course would have had the inevitable consequence of rendering the church, as presented in his theology, irrelevant to modern society. Congar's was a prophetic voice speaking as much for the benefit of the world and humanity as for the sake of the church. His view of the relationship between the church and the world is one of dependency: 'At bottom, the Church and the world need one another. The Church means salvation for the world, but the world means health for the Church: without the world there would be danger [sic] of her becoming wrapped up in her own sacredness and uniqueness' (1961b: 23; 1959: 34).

The goals of Congar's ecclesiological programme referred to above do not stand in isolation from each other. He indicates that the interior renewal of the church and the realization of Christian unity, for which he worked untiringly, are only attainable through action inspired by prayer. 'When it is a matter of the renewal of the Church and the conversion of heart, prayer for unity, especially when made in common, and when it attains a certain level of sincerity and depth—as it is generally the case—makes us aware of the exigencies of Jesus Christ, and the indifference of the rest. It invites us to go inside ourselves and not to harden our hearts' (1969: 115; 1968b: 121).

Congar may be numbered among those outstanding Roman Catholic theologians whose efforts contributed to the transformation of theology in the decades preceding the Second Vatican Council. He provides an outline of some of the reasons for the renewal of the sense of the church: 'One does not have to deny the general influ-ence exercised on the work of theologians by the development of sociological studies and the rebirth of the social sense. We have rediscovered, in social philosophy, the notion of wholeness (*tout*)' (1939: 9–10). Congar believed, however, that the true causes of the renewal in ecclesiology were to be found in the religious domain. He was convinced that the most decisive element in the ecclesiological renewal in the period before the council was a deepening in the interior life of the church, especially with regard to the person of Christ. Congar was concerned that the Roman Catholic Church could be for many a cause of unbelief, as it was often perceived as a harsh and condemning judge.

The Church: A Cause of Unbelief?

Congar's 1935 study on unbelief, 'The Reasons for the Unbelief of our Time: A Theological Conclusion', is important for a correct understanding of his most significant projects in ecclesiology. It was precisely his findings regarding the causes of unbelief that moved him to initiate the *Unam Sanctam* collection, dedicated to the renewal of ecclesiology, and to write his most important works on the church. The topics considered in these works are among the most significant in Congar's theology, namely, a renewal in ecclesiology, the reform of the church, ecumenism, the role of the laity, and the place of Mary in the church. In an article written shortly before the opening of Vatican II, Congar shows that these issues are still uppermost in his mind:

> It seemed to me that *since the belief or unbelief of men depended so much on us*, the effort to be made was a renovation (*rénovation*) of ecclesiology. . . . This conclusion led to the *Unam Sanctam* collection (37 volumes to date) and the books which I have written myself: *Divided Christendom, Vraie et fausse réforme dans l'Église, Lay People in the Church, Christ, Mary and the Church, The Mystery of the Temple*. (1962a: 147–8; 1961a: 695)

Congar's study on unbelief provides the *raison d'être* for his entire programme of ecclesiological reform. In order to address the current causes of unbelief, Congar recognizes the need to rediscover the true face of the church in Scripture and tradition, thereby effecting a renewal in ecclesiology. It is possible, on the basis of Congar's remarks, to identify an overall unity in his entire theological programme. In 1967 he described the basic findings of his 'Theological Conclusion' in a way that brings us to the heart of the matter: 'This led to the conclusion that as far as this unbelief depended on *us*, it was caused by a poor presentation of the Church. At that time, the Church was presented in a completely juridical way and sometimes even somewhat political' (Granfield 1967: 251).

In his 'Theological Conclusion', Congar identified two causes of contemporary unbelief. First, the replacement of a Christian way of life by a purely human spirituality. This was part of the movement towards secularization that began in the fourteenth century with the passing of culture into the hands of the laity, and spread inexorably affecting the professions and social life. All human activities were gradually reconstituted outside of the church and independent of the Christian faith. The second reason for contemporary unbelief concerns the response of the church to secularization and its own changed status. In the face of the new, secular-human spirituality, the church was reduced to a fenced-off, special, and anti-progressive group. 'The separation which exists between faith and life appears to us to be at once the most specific reason for the present state of unbelief and a fact which, in the most literal meaning of the words, does violence to the nature of faith and constitutes a mortal poison, the worst of abortifacients for it' (1938a: 14; 1935: 216). The failure or inability of the church to respond positively to the problem of the separation between faith and life is an important factor in explaining the phenomenon of continued widespread unbelief in contemporary society. It is not a question of power or even of influence with those in positions of power. Rather, it is a question of the church creating ways of making the Christian faith meaningful for people. The challenge for the church is to unite faith and life and to show that faith offers the possibility of attaining a degree of understanding of the true meaning of life. This is precisely what Congar was attempting to achieve by linking faith in Christ to the human search for happiness and meaning in life.

The movement towards secularization was sustained and animated by a certain human, or what Congar prefers to describe as 'humanitarian', mysticism. It was precisely this mysticism which, in his view, made the transfer from one spiritual whole to another possible. Congar depicts it in this way: 'This mysticism is characterized by the principle of immanence implying the sufficiency of reason and the possibility of an indefinite progress within the world. . . . It is a feeling of the perfect mastery of man in a world whose key he can possess' (1938b: 13–14; 1935: 230–1). Congar identifies the construction of a spiritual whole, outside and independent of Christianity, and the church's defensive reaction, as the main reasons for the hiatus between faith and life in the world, the principal cause of unbelief.

Vatican II: 'Congar's Council'?

When Pope John XXIII (1958–63) summoned an ecumenical council in January 1959, it was recognized that a new climate was stirring in the Vatican (Daniel-Rops 1962: 12). The announcement was greeted with excitement in the world at large. But most of the Roman curia thought a council unnecessary. Even the Italian bishops distrusted what the pope had decided to do (Chadwick 1992: 116). The Second Vatican Council, arguably the most important event in the history of the Roman Catholic Church since the Protestant Reformation, is certainly at the zenith of twentieth-century Catholic ecclesiology. The great movements of renewal that emerged at the turn of the twentieth century in biblical studies, liturgy, early Christian literature, and the apostolate of the laity all exercised an influence on the conciliar documents with the greatest innovators coming from German- and French-speaking countries. The reforms of Vatican II, while not excluding doctrine, were essentially pastoral and missionary (see Komonchak 1995: 179). Congar captures something of the profound hopes of the church after Vatican II in a brief description of its achievement: 'The Second Vatican Council was a council of reform: Karl Barth proclaimed that not without a certain emotion. One could also say, very rightly, that it marked the end of the Counter-Reformation' (1983: 79). Congar was also well aware that the conciliar *aggiornamento* gave rise to a feeling of insecurity and incertitude for many Catholics. In 1967, less than two years after the close of the council, he expressed his reservations plainly: 'Where are we to go from here? Where shall we be in twenty years? I, too, feel almost every day a temptation of uneasiness (*inquiétude*) in the face of all that has changed or is being called into question' (Congar 1968c: 50; 1968d: 19).

The council marked the beginning of a new and important phase in Congar's theological career. According to Avery Dulles, 'Vatican II could almost be called Congar's Council' (1995: 6). The success of his ecclesiological programme is nowhere more apparent than in its impact on the teaching of the church at Vatican II. The far-reaching programme of ecclesial reform executed at the council is the de facto consummation of Congar's whole previous theological oeuvre. Without his contribution, the process of renewal initiated there would have been seriously impeded, and the battle for a real council capable of substantial reform might not have been fully realized (Congar 2012: 4; 2002: vol. 1, 4). The story of that battle is recounted in Congar's diary *My Journal of the Council*.

Congar placed himself entirely at the disposition of the council in which he saw the possibility of the achievement of one of his dearest wishes, a reform of the church without injury to its unity which would facilitate a presentation of the true face of the church to the people of the twentieth century. Gradually, he became deeply engaged in the preparation of some of the most important council documents. In his diary, Congar provides a precise description of his part in what was undoubtedly the most important aspect of the council's entire enterprise (2012: 871; 2002: vol. 2, 511). He says that he worked on *Lumen Gentium*, especially the first draft of many numbers of chapter I, and on numbers 9, 13, 16, and 17 of chapter II, as well as on some specific passages. In *De Revelatione*, he worked on chapter II, and on number 21 which came from a first draft by him. In *De Oecumenismo*, the preamble and the conclusion are, he says, more or less by him. Likewise, in the *Declaration on Non-Christian Religions*, the introduction and the conclusion are, he says, more or less his. In *Schema XIII* (a working text that led to *Gaudium et Spes*), he worked on chapters I and IV. He wrote all of chapter I of *De Missionibus*, while Joseph Ratzinger contributed to number 8. In *De Libertate Religiosa*, Congar says that he cooperated with the entire project, and most particularly with the numbers of the theological part, and on the preamble which was entirely his own. Congar notes that the drafting of *De Presbyteris* was undertaken by three scholars: Joseph Lécuyer, a professor at the Lateran University and subsequently head of the Holy Ghost Congregation; Willy Onclin, a priest of the diocese of Liège and professor of canon law at the University of Louvain; and, of course, Congar himself. Congar indicates that he reworked the preamble of *De Presbyteris*, as well as numbers 2–3, while also writing the first draft of numbers 4–6, and revising numbers 7–9, 12–14 and the conclusion, of which he compiled the second paragraph.

In an appendix to *My Journal of the Council* (2012: 919–28; 2002: vol. 2, 561–71), the editor presents a series of valuable recapitulative chronological tables indicating, in full, Congar's substantial role in the elaboration of conciliar schemata during the preparatory phase, and at the sessions of the council. Included in the appendix are precise details of his participation in official meetings of various commissions and sub-commissions during the preparatory period and at the council itself, as well as the involvement of Congar and of other experts in workshops organized by the French bishops during the conciliar sessions. Congar's presence at a certain number of informal meetings of bishops and of experts, or of experts alone, is also outlined. The diary provides an original contribution to the knowledge of the history and proceedings of Vatican II. It gives particular insights into the thought and hopes of the popes and bishops, the theologians and observers of the council; describes the politics and the spirituality of individuals, as well as of powerful groupings of bishops and of theologians at the council; and supplies a profoundly personal account of the most important period of Congar's life, a kind of soliloquy with God, but also a dialogue with the church and the modern world. The council, as a matter of fact, was a catalyst that facilitated a reunion of the church and the world, the former having rather a lot of catching up to do with the latter, in a relatively short period of time.

That Congar considered himself a servant of the church is clear from the guiding principle he adopted to govern his work at the council: 'As a pragmatic rule, I have taken this one: to do nothing except that solicited by the bishops. IT IS THEY who are the Council. If, however, an initiative bore the mark of a call of God, I would be open to it' (2012: 141; 2002: vol. 1, 177). This important principle demonstrates that the office of teaching is the domain of bishops rather than of theologians. Congar's adoption of such a modus operandi does not mean that he failed to pursue creative initiatives at the council, or that he lacked political astuteness. Congar's political adroitness—immediately evident to readers of the diary—may be illustrated by the following points. First, and perhaps most important, his close association with the Belgian deputation and, above all, with Monsignor Gérard Philips who became assistant secretary to the Doctrinal Commission in December 1963, indicates a shrewd political acumen. Since Congar's contribution to the council lay primarily in the theological domain, cooperation with the Belgian deputation was essential, because of their theological pre-eminence, their political dexterity, and their militancy in council debates (2012: 506–11; 2002: vol. 2, 50–6), factors which gave them a position of unparalleled dominance at Vatican II. Second, Congar's decision to reside at the Belgian College during the meetings of the Theological Commission, when that college was the centre of work for that commission, is further evidence of his political dextrousness. It is worth noting that Congar was unable to reside at the Belgian College during the three conciliar sessions of the council because, as he points out, the only available rooms there were occupied by Belgian bishops. He, nonetheless, maintained a close liaison with the Belgians throughout the entire period of the council referred to as 'the first Council of Louvain held in Rome' (2012: 508; 2002: vol. 2, 53), and in particular during the second session, when the Belgian College was once again the centre of theological work. Finally, Congar's assiduous commitment to a spirit of *rapprochement* between bishops and theologians at the council indicates a level of political acuity above many of his contemporaries (2012: 82; 2002: vol. 1, 101–2). Conservative though he was in doctrine and theology, he focused the council's aspirations for reform. By a combination of courage and wisdom, and with the aid of his Belgian friends, Congar prepared the way, step by step, for the return at the council, after centuries of defensive isolationism, of the dynamic of openness in the church's relations with the world.

If, along with his obvious political astuteness, we bear in mind Congar's willingness to take risks, his commitment to truth, and his abiding concern to construct an essentially pastoral ecclesiology, we can understand how he came to be regarded in his day as an innovator. The diary, in fact, reveals the thought and work of a modern, advanced thinker, who patiently pursued realizable goals at Vatican II. It is worth noting how, in the portrayal of his work as a Consultor at the council, truth is resplendent: 'After all, I have nothing to lose, and I must do my duty. One must always say what one knows or believes to be true. So I shall be frank and will try to be evangelical' (2012: 17; 2002: vol. 1, 20). Similarly, Congar's real gift of patience, his innate optimism, and a remarkable capacity for work, meant that he was ideally suited to the role he assumed at the council.

While Congar was not without powerful adversaries at the council, he and his Belgian allies were, nonetheless, a formidable force in the battle for the Second Vatican Council (Flynn 2003; Scarisbrick 2005). The Belgians' strategy was as simple as it was effective. They would meet in advance, decide on a course of action, and then work together to win support for it, by effectively neutralizing objectors. Their influence pervaded the whole council. They came to occupy important positions on the Theological Commission and exercised a commanding role in the Biblical Sub-Commission, where they effectively dominated everything. Since this Sub-Commission controlled biblical citations, it also exercised ultimate control on the texts, with the power to modify, and even to reintroduce something. As Congar comments, 'In any case, there is a monitoring of all the work. Sometimes this monitoring is not even done in Rome, but in Louvain. It is a final means by which the Belgians, closely linked in solidarity, influence the content of the texts' (2012: 510; 2002: vol. 2, 56). According to Klaus Wittstadt, many of the council fathers were indebted to Congar for a broadening of their notion of the church (1995: 459). Further, it is to Congar, among others, that credit must also be given for one of the most important achievements of the council, namely, the transition from a predominantly juridical conception of the church to a more eschatological vision of the church as the People of God.

THE SHAPE OF THE CHURCH
IN CONGAR'S THEOLOGY

Study of the vision of the church in Congar's theology shows the importance of his contribution to the renewal of ecclesiology, to which Vatican II is the clearest testimony. His carefully formulated vision forms the essential foundation on which to construct a renewed church. The use of the term 'shape' is based primarily on Congar's application of two verbs to the church, namely, *construire* and *se réaliser*. Shape, in his thought, may then be applied to the construction of the church and brings us to the centre of his ecclesiology. The heavenly church will be a pure temple, a communion with God, whereas the church on earth, the means of obtaining that communion, is referred to as a scaffolding (*échafaudage*) thus indicating its contingent nature. Congar outlines the precise parameters for a theological treatise on the church in order to realize a true reform. An analysis of the means he proposes for such a reform will be undertaken in three steps. The first is a study of the images or models which Congar says we must rediscover in order to restore the true nature of the church as expressed in the gospel and in the Christian tradition: People of God, Body of Christ, and Temple of the Holy Spirit. Second, a consideration of the theology of the laity, in which Congar was such a dominant and pioneering figure, constitutes a key element in the analysis of the shape of the church in his theology. A study of Congar's original and transformative contribution to the emergence of the ecumenical movement in the Catholic Church is the third major task in this survey of the shape of the church in his theology. A preliminary question is a consideration of the definition of the church proposed by Congar.

The question of defining the church is intricate because the church is a divine mystery and because of the variety of senses in which the word church is used in Scripture and theology. Congar rejected the medieval notion of the church defined principally in terms of the clergy. In his view, chapter II of *Lumen Gentium* on the People of God is clear evidence that the excessively clerical medieval church belongs to the past. He worked assiduously for the restoration of the true conception of the church as a communion of persons sharing equally in the life of God. His description of this endeavour is noteworthy: 'There remains a great deal to do to restore, theoretically and practically, the true conception of the Church. I mean the conception of the Church as a communion of persons who all participate in the same goods of the Covenant and are all fully first-class citizens of this Holy City, this family of God' (1968e: 150; 1967a: 96). For Congar, the church is primarily the church of love. The most important and frequently posed question in his writings concerns the meaning attributed to the church, a question that can only be answered by reference to the biblical images of the church.

In order to realize the ideal of 'a Church less *of* the world and more *for* the world', then the institution must be renewed and de-clericalized (Congar 1964c: 210). Although Congar does not construct a Christian anthropology similar to that of the Fathers, he nonetheless insists indefatigably on the need for an anthropological theology of the church in which the person and not the ecclesiastical institution is the essential reference point. In order, therefore, to correct an obviously false and deleterious view of the church, Congar proposes 'a de-clericalisation of the idea of the Church', which is too often viewed as a powerful institution (Congar 1964c: 213). He wished to centre the church's life once again on Christ and on the pure spiritual message of the gospel. It is by reference to this profusion of images of the church that theologians attempt to arrive at a clearer understanding of the church's identity. The full knowledge of the mystery of that identity is, however, only attainable if the current situation of the church is also taken into consideration. A critical assessment of Congar's proposals for the shape of the Christian church of the future must, then, be examined in conjunction with an analysis of his use of biblical images.

Congar's examination of the biblical images of the church was in fact as a result of his commitment to a renewed church. In order to contribute to its actualization, he worked on a revitalized *De ecclesia* tract which, without eclipsing the essential juridical nature of the church, stresses the element of mystery realized in the biblical images Body of Christ and People of God.

Biblical Images in Congar's Ecclesiology

A striking feature of Congar's analysis of the biblical images of the church is its impartiality. Though he may favour certain images, Congar's objective approach enables him to extract what is best from the totality of biblical images for the renewal of the church. The idea of the People of God, by placing the church at the service of the world, helps to overcome a predominantly hierarchical, juridical view of the church, and an ecclesiology reduced to a system of public law. Vatican II, without prejudice to the notion of the Mystical Body, put special emphasis on the concept of the People of God, which was seen by him as offering the richest prospect for ecclesiology.

Congar viewed the decision of the coordinating commission of Vatican II to insert a chapter on the People of God in the Constitution *De Ecclesia* between the first and third chapters, which were concerned with the mystery of the church and the hierarchy, as a momentous contribution towards the elimination of juridicism. He evaluated the importance of this initiative not only in terms of the content of the new chapter but also by reference to its title and its place in the Constitution (Congar 1966b: 200). The many advantages of the People of God motif are clearly outlined by Congar. In his opinion, its strong emphasis on the historical nature of the church introduces a dynamic element into the church. The view of the church as the People of God also expresses continuity with Israel and has helped the church to regain an awareness of its messianic character, thus enabling it to offer the hope of ultimate fulfilment in Christ to an irreligious world. Congar observes that the neglect of the church's message of hope for the world served as a preparation for godless interpretations of history and of the world in the modern era (Marx and Hegel). As he remarks: 'Confronted by religion without a world, men formulated the idea of a world without religion. We are now emerging from this wretched situation; the People of God is rediscovering once again that it possesses a messianic character and that it bears the hope of a fulfilment of the world in Jesus Christ' (1965a: 10; 1965b: 21). Congar considers eschatology to be one of the great rediscoveries of contemporary Catholic theology. He stresses that the kingdom is the ultimate destiny of God's people and points to an essential, dialectical tension between its present reality (the *already*) and its future expectation (the *not yet*) in the concept of the church as the People of God.

Congar's contribution to the understanding of the church as the People of God has been criticized by various Protestant commentators as lacking a full awareness of the church's historicity, because of its apparent failure to acknowledge that the church is actually subject to fallibility and error (Hoffmann 1968: 201; Skydsgaard 1965: 161). Skydsgaard's imputation that Congar's ecclesiology leads inevitably to a theology of glory cannot be sustained, as a consideration of the place of reform in his theology will show. Congar was, of course, aware of the ecumenical significance of the view of the church as People of God, especially among Protestants. Notwithstanding his deep commitment to the idea of the People of God he is, nonetheless, aware of its shortcomings and of the need to relate it to other images of the church. Congar views the People of God motif as insufficiently Christological and pneumatological and, therefore, incapable of expressing the reality of the church by itself.

Congar, like Ratzinger, while recognizing the notion of the People of God, considers the church to be essentially the Body of Christ, thus pointing to the latter as the more fundamental image of the church. In order to indicate a permanent distance between Christ and the church, Congar, in common with Ratzinger and de Lubac, insists on a distinction between the Body of Christ and the People of God, thereby avoiding an unacceptable self-identification of the church with Christ. This is important, as an inordinate assimilation of the church with Christ risks placing the church above legitimate criticism and opening it to a renewed charge of triumphalism. In Congar's treatment of the Mystical Body, he stresses the oneness of the church as well as its essentially penultimate nature. The view of the church as Mystical Body helps to unite the notions of People of God and society. Nevertheless, the understanding of the church based on these images is still incomplete, which leads Congar to another image, that of the church as the universal sacrament of salvation. A major advantage of Congar's understanding of the church as sacrament is that it takes into account the visibility of the church as well as its indispensable missionary nature. The non-people of God can become the People of God only through union with Christ which, in turn, depends on the sacramental activity of the church. Vatican II, by giving prominence to the church as sacrament of salvation alongside the People of God motif, makes this point clearly. The elements of the programme for the renewal of the church which Congar articulates through various biblical images form part of his original contribution to communion ecclesiology.

Communion Ecclesiology

The origins of communion ecclesiology cannot be understood without reference to the influence of Johann Adam Möhler (1796–1838), the German ecclesiastical historian and theologian of the church. Möhler and the Catholic School of Tübingen introduced a principle of renewal into nineteenth-century theology with a concept of faith which integrates its historical, psychological, and pastoral dimensions. Chenu, perhaps the single most significant influence on Congar and his *confrères* at the Saulchoir, states that he and Congar effected a rediscovery of Möhler. Chenu suggested the work of Möhler as a possible model for a Catholic contribution to ecumenism and, accordingly, Congar embarked on a study of church unity for his lectorate, an internal Dominican degree equivalent to a licentiate. Möhler awakened in him an awareness of the historical dimension of reality, and also provided the motivation for some of his most important theological endeavours (Congar 1966a: 3; 1964a: xi–xii). Congar notes that Vatican II set aside the concept of the church as 'societas inaequalis, societas perfecta' in favour of a vision of the church as communion (1977: 150; 1995a: 238). This change effected a vertical decentralization oriented towards Christ and a horizontal decentralization towards the local church, the People of God. With de Lubac, Congar worked assiduously for a reform of the hierarchical and centralized church that had been dominant from medieval times and in particular from the Council of Trent (1545–63). The most effective solution for this was the revival of what Congar called the 'ecclesiology of communion and holiness' (1967b: 261). Some of the major expressions of communion ecclesiology include conciliarity, collegiality, and reception.

It is precisely in the view of the church as communion that Congar locates the New Testament notion of *koinōnia* which shows clearly that 'there is no union with God without fraternal relations, sharing and community' (1988: 91; 1985d: 98). Congar was engaged in ground-breaking work immediately prior to and during Vatican II in order to develop a more properly theological ecclesiology by appropriating the idea of *communio*. He recognized in this notion a key for the renewal of ecclesiology (Congar 1950b). The principal elements in his communion ecclesiology include solidarity in love and service accomplished in the sacraments, particularly the Eucharist; the communion of bishops, who form the linchpin between the local churches and the universal church; and the place of the pope as guardian of the unity of the church (Congar 1962b).

Congar contributed to the formulation of an organic concept of the church that is conciliar, collegial, Christological, pneumatological, and ecumenical. Pneumatology in fact played a decisive role in his communion ecclesiology and helped to restore balance to the church. In this way, the local and the catholic dimensions, far from being contradictory, are, in fact, suggestive of each other. As he remarks: '[P]neumatology is an essential ecclesiological datum. The total Church only enjoys the fullness of the Spirit's gifts by welcoming and integrating the contributions brought from all sides, both from the grass roots and the summit' (1973: 17–18; 1972a: 547; Groppe 2004).

While the notion of *communio* has proved to be a fruitful starting point for ecumenism, the results have been rather disappointing. Some commentators have criticized Congar's communion ecclesiology for not going far enough in terms of church reform and practical ecumenism. Pope Paul VI (1963–78) alluded to the work that de Lubac, Congar, and others had done in his first encyclical, *Ecclesiam Suam*, which was commended for its perceptive and highly influential treatment of dialogue. Perhaps the clearest testimony to the success of communion theology as articulated by Congar and other leading *ressourcement* theologians is the *Final Report* of the 1985 Assembly of the Synod of Bishops, on the theme of the Second Vatican Council, in which communion is hailed as 'the central and fundamental idea of the documents of the Council' (Synod of Bishops 1986: 15).

Congar's ecclesiology is also sensitive to the perennial need of humanity to experience a sense of belonging. In his reflections on what it means to belong to the church in the radically changed post-Vatican II period, Congar, while carefully avoiding an ever-decreasing ghettoized church or the status quo based on religious observance but without much emphasis on personalized faith, proposed a third solution, namely, a threshold church. In effect, the threshold church aims 'to support the spiritual life of those whose faith is unsure and, above all, of those who are unable to participate fully in the sacramental life' (1977: 158; 1995a: 245–6). Congar makes a clear-cut distinction between the proposed threshold structures and the church in its fullness. The legitimacy of the former cannot be determined except by reference to the latter. This point brings out the fact that the proposed threshold church for catechumens is essentially transitional. Thus, while the church is the gathering of catechumens before being a sacramental assembly, Congar, nonetheless, considers that the church itself is fully realized only in communion with the Trinity.

The realization of the renewal in ecclesiology that inspired Congar's contribution to the recovery of the biblical images can only occur insofar as those images are implemented by clergy and laity. This brings us to a consideration of the theology of the laity which can best be understood in the context of Congar's communion ecclesiology, since both are formed from the same source of a renewal of the church's true nature as expressed in Scripture and tradition.

Theology of Ministry

The formulation of a theology of ministry, of which the laity is a part, reflects Congar's dual concern for wholeness in theology and for redressing the causes of unbelief. He was in fact one of the few theologians to address the question of the role of the laity and to create the conditions for its flourishing. Nonetheless, a theology of the laity is problematic. It can be criticized as presenting a clerical and canonical view of the church that is untenable because it necessarily restricts the vocation of the laity to a limited aspect of the church's mission. It was precisely in order to overcome a restricted, clerical view of the church and to outline the doctrinal elements of a theology of the laity that Congar wrote *Jalons pour une théologie du laïcat* (ET *Laypeople in the Church*). In the original edition of the work, Congar, on the basis of the essential distinction between clergy and laity, refers to three states or conditions: lay, clerical, and monastic. In the 1964 revised edition of the book, however, he states that the present movement of ideas, surpassing the classification of the layperson in relation to the cleric, moves to the organic notion of the People of God. Although Congar's original and modest intention for *Laypeople in the Church* was merely to offer 'signposts' or 'material for further research', he nonetheless attributes permanent significance to the description of laity articulated there (1985b: 214).

Congar's insistence that a diverse range of services within the church be recognized as ministries constitutes an important contribution to the formulation of an adequate theology of ministry (see 1972b: 175; 1995b: 129). A clear evolution may be observed in his theology of the laity. In 1970, he acknowledged a departure from his original formulation of the question: 'As to terminology, it is worth noticing that the decisive coupling is not "priesthood/laity" (*sacerdoce-laïcat*), as I used it in *Jalons*, but rather "ministries/modes of community service" (*ministères ou services-communauté*)' (1972b: 176; 1995b: 130). The advantage of the 'ministries/modes of community service' terminology is that it contributes towards a more inclusive view of ministry that acknowledges, not only the contribution of the ordained priesthood to the mission of the church, but also those services performed by the laity which, Congar insists, must also be recognized as ministries.

In *Ministères et communion ecclésiale* (1971), Congar provides a perspicuous synthesis of developments in lay theology almost two decades after the publication of *Laypeople in the Church*. He notes that, following Vatican II's recentring on Christ and the Holy Spirit along with the decentralization of the church's pastorate into more collegial structures, the previously dominant hierarchy-faithful terminology was replaced by that of the priesthood of Christ enveloping the priesthood of the faithful and of ministers. In maintaining that God builds the church not only through institutional ministries but also by many other initiatives, Congar, in fact, proposes a threefold distinction within ministry: occasional, for instance visitation of the sick; habitual, for instance catechesis; and the ordained ministries of diaconate, priesthood, and episcopate. In the final analysis, he views the church as the People of God. This places a major new emphasis on baptism in a more developed theology of ministry enlivened by the Holy Spirit.

An important and original aspect of Congar's initial contribution to the theology of the laity concerns his claim that 'there can be only one sound and sufficient theology of laity and that is a "total ecclesiology"' (1985a: xvi; 1953a: 13). In an authentic search for wholeness within the theology of the laity, he outlines the place of anthropology, Christology, and a theology of creation. In view of the importance attributed to wholeness in his theology of the laity, it is not surprising that, in Congar's view, the root cause of all depreciation of the laity is attributable to 'a deficiency in ecclesiology and a deficiency in anthropology' (1967c: 249; 1962c: 277). In order to rectify this insufficiency, he worked for a restoration of the concept of the church made of the faithful through a return to the sources.

Congar's communitarian model of church and worship places the ministerial priesthood at the service of the priesthood of all believers. He sees the priesthood of the faithful as profoundly sacramental (Augustine), associated particularly with baptism and Eucharist. An important element for the theologies of laity and liturgy is the cosmic dimension of the Eucharist. Congar emphasizes the offering of the faithful from below (*sacrificium laudis*); an aspect of liturgy which had been neglected owing to a much decreased consideration of the part of the laity in the church's worship (1985a: 221–2; 1953a: 292). The vision of ministry articulated by Congar represents an important contribution to communion ecclesiology by encompassing in a dialectical relationship the authoritative concept, which stresses respect for church structures, and the participative concept, which is primarily communitarian and emphasizes co-responsibility and partnership in the church.

Congar: Father of Roman Catholic Ecumenism

Congar, who is perhaps best known for his contribution to the ecumenical movement, views the Roman Catholic principles of ecumenical dialogue in the context of *ressourcement* and a revitalized *communio*. In his *Memoirs*, W. A. Visser't Hooft (1900–85), first General Secretary of the World Council of Churches, described Congar as 'the father of Roman Catholic ecumenism'. Congar viewed his involvement in the ecumenical movement in terms of vocation and grace and was indefatigable in his commitment to its advancement. In 1937, he published *Chrétiens désunis*, translated into English as *Divided Christendom*, the chief advantage of which, in his view, was that 'for the first time it attempted to define "ecumenism" theologically or at least to put it in that context' (1966a: 25; 1964a: xxxvi). Immediately after the announcement of the council, which was to give official status to his ecumenism, Congar commented: 'For the first time in history, the Catholic Church is entering into the structure of dialogue' (1962a: 151; 1961a: 699). The development in Congar's ecumenism from the original emphasis on Catholicity in *Divided Christendom* to his qualified acceptance of 'reconciled diversities' in *Diversity in Communion* (1982) has been carefully documented by scholars. Ultimately, Congar places the ecumenical reality in an eschatological context, the absence of which in pre-conciliar ecclesiology he viewed as a hindrance to ecumenism.

Congar's overriding concern was to construct a living church in which all its members could participate actively as subjects. The renewed church in his theology and the socially orientated vision on which it stands have a common origin, namely, a return to the sources. This indicates that his theological programme for church renewal forms a unified whole pastorally and theologically. In order to realize his programme, Congar engaged in nothing less than a reform of, or rather in, the church.

CONGAR'S PRINCIPLES FOR TRUE REFORM IN THE CHURCH

Congar's contribution in this field makes him an architect of the contemporary church. Looking at the matter historically, he stands out as one of the great champions of church reform in the twentieth century. His notion of reform is founded on the dialectical principle of Catholic fidelity, that is, a dual fidelity to the tradition and, by the eventual overtaking of certain concrete historical forms of its life, to the future realization of the church's 'missionary function, its programme of Catholicity, of belief and of adaptation' (Congar 1950a: 601). This dual fidelity is, in Congar's view, at the heart of his vision for church reform. While there is tension between its two aspects, there must also be 'a communication, indeed a continuity, and thus a harmony' (Congar 1950a: 599). The precise relation between reform and tradition is pivotal in Congar's ecclesiology and shows an awareness of what has become an unfortunate consequence of reform in the post-conciliar period, namely, a certain polarization within the church between reformers and those who see themselves as defenders of tradition. Congar was fully cognizant of such problems, the preservation and restoration of the church's unity being the pre-eminent concern of his ecclesiology.

Congar's approach to reform facilitates an openness to change and development while exercising a profound fidelity to the tradition. Reform and tradition cannot, then, be considered in isolation. In *True and False Reform in the Church*, his *magnum opus* on reform and one of his most influential works, Congar describes the conditions for a true reform of the church, which he says can be reduced to four principles:

(i) 'The Primacy of Charity and the Pastoral'. In the first principle of reform, defined by charity and pastoral sensitivity, Congar insists on respect for the reality of the church and on a willingness to work within it.

(ii) 'To Remain within the Communion of All'. The second principle of reform is a precision of the idea of communion. The concern for communion with the whole, so brilliantly articulated by St Augustine in his controversies with the Donatists, is indispensable for a true reform. Congar holds as indisputable the belief that the understanding of the full truth of Scripture depends on communion with the one, holy, catholic, and apostolic church.

(iii) 'Patience; Respect for Delays'. Movements of reform which do not have patience as a constitutive feature are a source of danger for the church. Congar notes that the lack of patience, which he sees as a failure to respect the delays of God, the church, and life, contributes towards turning a reform into a schism.

(iv) 'A True Renewal by a Return to the Principle of the Tradition'. A true Catholic and Christian reform must be based on the authentic principles given in the gospel and tradition. In an expression of his concern for the unity and catholicity of the church, Congar proposes an examination of the tradition, a return to the sources, as the cardinal rule for reform (2011: 199–307; 1950a: 229–352).

It is important to recognize that Congar, while admitting the need for a reform of the church, did not write *True and False Reform in the Church* as a negative appraisal of the church. It is, rather, a work of 'love and confidence'. The aim of *True and False Reform in the Church* is not to propose a programme of reforms for the church, but to study the place of reforms in the life of the church, the reasons which eventually make reform necessary, and, most importantly, how to carry out a reform without injury to the unity of the church. 'Reform *of* the Church', in Congar's view, must then be 'reform *in* the Church' (Puyo 1975: 117). He had already shown in 1938 that a reform ceases to be authentic if it moves outside the church (Congar 1965c: 104, note 1; 1953b: 126, note 2). A true reform of the church, in fact, requires such a demanding form of fidelity that its essential reference point can only be love. In order to avoid what he identifies as an inherent danger in every reformist undertaking, namely, a tendency to deviation and schism, Congar indicates, by reference to an important lesson of history, that the best milieu for reform is a council of the church. In an article written eight years after the close of Vatican II, Congar displays his consistent concern to achieve reform without schism: 'History shows that a reform requires the commitment of all the forces of the Church. This is one of the main reasons why, historically, reforms and councils have so often been linked with one another' (1972c: 46; 1972d: 42).

It is within the context of a return to the sources that Congar approaches the difficult question of the reform of church structures that no longer respond to the present situation of the church or of the world. A consideration of the question of the structure and the life of the church is important in order to clarify the differences between a Protestant understanding of reform and Congar's proposals for a true Catholic reform which rests on a fundamentally different notion of the church. At the centre of his theology of reform, Congar acknowledges that there is an element of the church which is irreformable.

It is within the framework of a critique of the Protestant *Ecclesia semper reformanda* that Congar refers to two crucial differences between the Protestant and Catholic perceptions of the church and of reform. He expresses three objections to the concept of *Ecclesia semper reformanda*: First, he asserts that the apostolic church did not have either the atmosphere or the mystique of a church engaged in a permanent reform understood in the Protestant sense. Second, the idea of a permanent reform is somewhat theoretical. Congar refers to Luther who, having achieved the reform called for by God, did not recognize the need for another reform. Third, he expresses his fear that this notion of reform, by a declaration of total penitence, actually engenders pride, thus rendering a concrete, effective penitence impossible. True penitence, on the other hand, is inspired by the Holy Spirit (John 16:8) and so is more discreet and less general.

Although doubts have been raised about the validity of Congar's elucidation of the dialectic of structure and life, an authentic reform of the church is, in fact, only possible if there is a clear acknowledgement of the irreformability of its structure which he defines by reference to the presence of the Spirit in the church. By making the Holy Spirit the fundamental criterion for reform, Congar gives his most adequate statement of what is required for a legitimate church reform. Still, his claim that the church cannot err in its secular and general practice is remarkable. Further, Congar distinguishes between the structure of the church, that is its dogma, sacraments, and hierarchical constitution, on the one hand, and the ecclesial structures, that is the organization of parishes, catechesis, preaching, and other such matters, all of which may be changed because they pertain to the life of the church, rather than its essential structure, which is always irreformable. The differentiation between structure and structures is an important element of precision in Congar's thought which contributes to a fuller understanding of the parameters within which a true reform of the church is possible. Congar also recognizes the possibility of new structures or forms for the transmission of the Christian message, a position which, far from being anti-institutional, is concerned to ensure that the institution is at the service of the gospel.

Congar's conception of a true reform of the church is based on the Catholic perception of the church, which recognizes the indefectibility of the visible institution and affords a full appreciation to the role of tradition. Without reform, tradition is reduced to a mere tract on apologetics, while reform without tradition is flawed and so thwarts the course of true ecclesial renewal. The church, in order to conform more closely to Christ, must engage in perpetual self-reform. This is actualized by means of a return to the sources which provided the inspiration for *True and False Reform in the Church* (Flynn 2005: 99–134).

Space does not permit analysis of Congar's contribution to inter-religious dialogue, a topic on which scholars continue to reflect (Merrigan 2005: 427–57). These considerations leave us with the following recognitions. The Second Vatican Council is Congar's greatest legacy and its continued fruitful reception would be his most fitting monument. Above all, however, Congar was a scholar of integrity and moral courage. The writers and intellectuals of the French Enlightenment challenged what they perceived as an intolerant and authoritarian church thus contributing to religious freedom. Influenced perhaps by the Enlightenment, Congar's stance for intellectual freedom and ecclesiological renewal laid the foundation for a true reform of the church.

References

Aubert, Roger (1954). *La Théologie Catholique au milieu du XXe siècle*. Tournai: Casterman.

Bouyer, Louis (1947). 'Le Renouveau des études patristiques'. *La Vie intellectuelle* 15: 6–25.

Chadwick, Owen (1992). *The Christian Church in the Cold War*. Owen Chadwick (ed.), *The Penguin History of the Church*, 7. London: Penguin.

Congar, Yves (1935). 'Une conclusion théologique à l'enquête sur les raisons actuelles de l'incroyance'. *La Vie intellectuelle* 37: 214–49.

Congar, Yves (1937). 'Pour une théologie de l'Église'. *La Vie spirituelle* 52: 97–9.

Congar, Yves (1938a). 'The Reasons for the Unbelief of our Time: A Theological Conclusion'. Part I. *Integration*, 13–21; ET of Congar (1935).

Congar, Yves (1938b). 'The Reasons for the Unbelief of our Time: A Theological Conclusion'. Part II. *Integration*, 10–26.

Congar, Yves (1939). 'Autour du renouveau de l'ecclésiologie: la collection "Unam Sanctam"'. *La Vie intellectuelle* 51: 9–32.

Congar, Yves (1948). 'Tendances actuelles de la pensée religieuse'. *Cahiers du monde nouveau* 4: 33–50.

Congar, Yves (1950a). *Vraie et fausse réforme dans l'Église. Unam Sanctam* 20. Paris: Cerf.

Congar, Yves (1950b). 'Notes sur les mots "Confession", "Église" et "Communion"'. *Irénikon* 23: 3–36.

Congar, Yves (1953a). *Jalons pour une théologie du laïcat. Unam Sanctam* 23. Paris: Cerf.

Congar, Yves (1953b). *Esquisses du mystère de l'Église*. 2 vols. New edn. *Unam Sanctam* 8. Paris: Cerf.

Congar, Yves (1959). *Vaste monde ma paroisse: vérité et dimensions du salut*. Paris: Témoignage Chrétien.

Congar, Yves (1961a). 'Voeux pour le concile: enquête parmi les chrétiens'. *Esprit* 29: 691–700.

Congar, Yves (1961b). *The Wide World my Parish: Salvation and its Problems*. Trans. Donald Attwater. London: Darton, Longman & Todd. ET of Congar (1959).

Congar, Yves (1962a). 'The Council in the Age of Dialogue'. Trans. Barry N. Rigney. *Cross Currents* 12: 144–51; ET of Congar (1961a).

Congar, Yves (1962b). 'De la communion des Églises à une ecclésiologie de l'Église universelle'. In Congar and B.-D. Dupuy (eds), *L'Épiscopat et l'Église universelle*. Paris: Cerf. *Unam Sanctam* 39: 227–60.

Congar, Yves (1962c). *Sacerdoce et laïcat devant leurs tâches d'évangélisation et de civilisation*. Paris: Cerf.

Congar, Yves (1964a). *Chrétiens en dialogue: contributions catholiques à l'oecuménisme. Unam Sanctam* 50. Paris: Cerf.

Congar, Yves (1964b). *Tradition and the Life of the Church.* Trans. A. N. Woodrow. *Faith and Fact Books* 3. London: Burns & Oates. ET of Congar (1984).

Congar, Yves (1964c). 'L'Avenir de l'Église'. In M. Olivier Lacombe et al (eds), *L'Avenir: semaine des intellectuels catholiques (6 au 12 novembre 1963).* Paris: Fayard, 207–21.

Congar, Yves (1965a). 'The Church: The People of God'. Trans. Kathryn Sullivan, *Concilium* 1: 7–19. ET of Congar (1965b).

Congar, Yves (1965b). 'L'Église comme peuple de Dieu'. *Concilium* 1: 15–32.

Congar, Yves (1965c). *The Mystery of the Church: Studies by Yves Congar.* Trans. A. V. Littledale. 2nd edn, rev. London: Geoffrey Chapman. ET of Congar (1953b).

Congar, Yves (1966a). *Dialogue between Christians: Catholic Contributions to Ecumenism.* Trans. Philip Loretz. London: Geoffrey Chapman. ET of Congar (1964a).

Congar, Yves (1966b). 'The People of God'. In John H. Miller (ed.), *Vatican II: An Interfaith Appraisal.* Notre Dame, IN: University of Notre Dame Press, 197–207.

Congar, Yves (1967a). 'Religion et institution'. In T. Patrick Burke (ed.), *Théologie d'aujourd'hui et de demain.* Paris: Cerf, 81–97.

Congar, Yves (1967b). 'L'"Ecclesia" ou communauté chrétienne, sujet intégral de l'action liturgique'. In J.-P. Jossua and Y. Congar (eds), *La Liturgie après Vatican II.* Paris: Cerf, 241–80.

Congar, Yves (1967c). Priest and Layman. Trans. P. F. Hepburne-Scott. London: Darton, Longman & Todd. ET of Congar (1962c).

Congar, Yves (1968a). *L'Ecclésiologie du haut moyen âge: de saint Grégoire le grand à la désunion entre Byzance et Rome.* Paris: Cerf.

Congar, Yves (1968b). *Cette Église que j'aime. Foi Vivante* 70. Paris: Cerf.

Congar, Yves (1968c). 'Theology's Tasks after Vatican II'. In Laurence K. Shook (ed.), *Renewal of Religious Thought.* 2 vols. New York: Herder and Herder, I, 47–65. ET of Congar (1968d).

Congar, Yves (1968d). 'Les Tâches de la théologie après Vatican II'. In L. K. Shook and Guy-M. Bertrand (eds), *La Théologie du renouveau.* 2 vols. *Cogitatio Fidei* 27. Montreal: Fides; Paris: Cerf, II, 17–31.

Congar, Yves (1968e). 'Institutionalised Religion'. In T. Patrick Burke (ed.), *The Word in History: The St. Xavier Symposium.* London: Collins, 133–53. ET of Congar (1967a).

Congar, Yves (1969). *This Church That I Love.* Trans. Lucien Delafuente. Denville, NJ: Dimension Books. ET of Congar (1968b).

Congar, Yves (1970a). *L'Église de saint Augustin à l'époque moderne. Histoire des dogmes* 20. Paris: Cerf.

Congar, Yves (1970b). 'Pourquoi j'aime l'Église'. *Communion: Verbum Caro* 24: 23–30.

Congar, Yves (1971). *Ministères et communion ecclésiale.* Paris: Cerf.

Congar, Yves (1972a). 'Actualité renouvelée du Saint Esprit'. *Lumen Vitae* 27: 543–60.

Congar, Yves (1972b). 'My Path-Findings in the Theology of Laity and Ministries'. *Jurist* 32: 169–88. ET of Congar (1995b).

Congar, Yves (1972c). 'Renewal of the Spirit and Reform of the Institution'. Trans. John Griffiths. *Concilium* 3: 39–49. ET of Congar (1972d).

Congar, Yves (1972d). 'Renouvellement de l'esprit et réforme de l'institution'. *Concilium* 3: 37–45.

Congar, Yves (1973). 'Renewed Actuality of the Holy Spirit'. Trans. Olga Prendergast. *Lumen Vitae* 28: 13–30. ET of Congar (1972a).

Congar, Yves (1977). 'What Belonging to the Church has Come to Mean'. Trans. Frances M. Chew. *Communio* 4: 146–60. ET of Congar (1995a).

Congar, Yves (1981). 'Reflections on Being a Theologian'. Trans. Marcus Lefébure. *New Blackfriars* 62: 405–9.

Congar, Yves (1983). *Martin Luther sa foi, sa réforme: études de théologie historique. Cogitatio Fidei* 119. Paris: Cerf.

Congar, Yves (1984). *La Tradition et la vie de l'Église*. 2nd edn. *Traditions chrétiennes* 18. Paris: Cerf.

Congar, Yves (1985a). *Lay People in the Church: A Study for a Theology of Laity*. Trans. Donald Attwater. Rev. edn with additions. London: Geoffrey Chapman; Westminster, MD: *Christian Classics*. ET of Congar (1953a).

Congar, Yves (1985b). 'Letter from Father Yves Congar, O.P.'. Trans. Ronald John Zawilla. *Theology Digest* 32: 213–16.

Congar, Yves (1985c). 'The Brother I have Known'. Trans. Boniface Ramsey OP. *The Thomist* 49: 495–503. ET of Congar (1990).

Congar, Yves (1985d). *Appelés à la vie*. Paris: Cerf.

Congar, Yves (1988). *Called to Life*. Slough: St Paul; New York: Crossroad Publishing. ET of Congar (1985d).

Congar, Yves (1990). 'Le Frère que j'ai connu'. In Claude Geffré et al., *L'Hommage différé au Père Chenu*. Paris: Cerf, 239–45.

Congar, Yves (1994). *Église et papauté: regards historiques. Cogitatio Fidei* 184. Paris: Cerf.

Congar, Yves (1995a). 'Sur la transformation du sens de l'appartenance à l'Église'. In J.-P. Jossua (ed.), *Cardinal Yves Congar, O.P.: écrits réformateurs*, 235–47.

Congar, Yves (1995b). 'Mon cheminement dans la théologie du laïcat et des ministères'. In J.-P. Jossua (ed.), *Cardinal Yves Congar, O.P.: écrits réformateurs*. Paris: Cerf, 123–40.

Congar, Yves (2000). 'Loving Openness Toward Every Truth: A Letter from Thomas Aquinas to Karl Rahner'. *Philosophy and Theology* 12: 213–19.

Congar, Yves (2002). *Mon journal du Concile*. Ed. with notes Éric Mahieu. 2 vols. Paris: Cerf.

Congar, Yves (2011). *True and False Reform in the Church*. Trans. Paul Philibert OP. Collegeville, MN: Liturgical Press. ET of Congar (1950a).

Congar, Yves (2012). *My Journal of the Council*. Trans. Mary John Ronayne OP and Mary Cecily Boulding OP. Collegeville, MN: Liturgical Press. ET of Congar (2002).

Daniel-Rops, Henri (1962). *The Second Vatican Council: The Story Behind the Ecumenical Council of Pope John XXIII*. Trans. Alastair Guinan. London: Harrap; New York: Hawthorn.

Daniélou, Jean (1946). 'Les Orientations présentes de la pensée religieuse'. *Études* 249: 5–21.

Dulles, Avery (1995). 'Yves Congar: In Appreciation'. *America* 173: 6–7.

Flynn, Gabriel (2003). '*Mon Journal du Concile*: Yves Congar and the Battle for a Renewed Ecclesiology at the Second Vatican Council'. *Louvain Studies* 28: 48–70.

Flynn, Gabriel (2005). 'Yves Congar and Catholic Church Reform: A Renewal of the Spirit'. In Gabriel Flynn (ed.), *Yves Congar: Theologian of the Church*. Louvain: Peeters; Dubley, MA: Eerdmans, 99–134.

Flynn, Gabriel (2012). 'Introduction: The Twentieth-Century Renaissance in Catholic Theology'. In Gabriel Flynn and Paul D. Murray (eds), *Ressourcement: A Movement for Renewal in Twentieth-Century Catholic Theology*. Oxford: Oxford University Press, 1–22.

Fouilloux, Étienne (1995). 'Frère Yves, Cardinal Congar, Dominicain: itinéraire d'un théologien'. *Revue des sciences philosophiques et théologiques* 79: 379–404.

Garrigou-Lagrange, Réginald (1946c). 'La Nouvelle Théologie où va-t-elle'. *Angelicum* 23: 126–45.

Godin, Henri and Daniel, Yvan (1950). *La France: pays de mission?* 7th edn. Paris: Cerf.

Granfield, Patrick (1967). *Theologians at Work*. New York: Macmillan; London: Collier-Macmillan.

Groppe, Elizabeth Teresa (2004). *Yves Congar's Theology of the Holy Spirit*. Oxford: Oxford University Press.

Hoffmann, Manfred (1968). 'Church and History in Vatican II's Constitution on the Church: A Protestant Perspective'. *Theological Studies* 29: 191–214.

Komonchak, Joseph A. (1995). 'The Struggle for the Council during the Preparation of Vatican II (1960–1962)'. In Giuseppe Alberigo (ed.), *History of Vatican II: Announcing and Preparing Vatican Council II*. Joseph A. Komonchak English version (ed.). 5 vols. Maryknoll: Orbis; Louvain: Peeters. I, 167–356.

Labourdette, M.-Michel (1946a). 'La Théologie et ses sources'. *Revue Thomiste* 46: 353–71.

Labourdette, M.-Michel (1946b). 'La Théologie, intelligence de la foi'. *Revue Thomiste* 46: 5–44.

Merrigan, Terrence (2005). 'The Appeal to Yves Congar in Recent Catholic Theology of Religions: The Case of Jacques Dupuis'. In Gabriel Flynn (ed.), *Yves Congar: Theologian of the Church*. Louvain: Peeters; Dubley, MA: Eerdmans, 427–57.

O'Malley, John W. (2005). 'Yves Congar as Historian of Ecclesiology'. In Gabriel Flynn (ed.), *Yves Congar: Theologian of the Church*. Louvain: Peeters; Dubley, MA: Eerdmans, 229–48.

Pottier, Bernard, SJ (2012). 'Daniélou and the Twentieth-Century Patristic Renewal'. In Gabriel Flynn and Paul D. Murray (eds), *Ressourcement: A Movement for Renewal in Twentieth-Century Catholic Theology*. Oxford: Oxford University Press, 250–77.

Puyo, Jean (1975). *Jean Puyo interroge le Père Congar: 'une vie pour la vérité'*. Paris: Centurion.

Scarisbrick, J. J. (2005). 'An Historian's Reflections on Yves Congar's *Mon Journal du Concile*'. In Gabriel Flynn (ed.), *Yves Congar: Theologian of the Church*. Louvain: Peeters; Dubley, MA: Eerdmans, 249–75.

Skydsgaard, Kristen E. (1965). 'The Church as Mystery and as People of God'. In George Lindbeck (ed.), *Dialogue on the Way: Protestants Report from Rome on the Vatican Council*. Minneapolis: Augsburg, 145–74.

Synod of Bishops (1986). *The Final Report on the theme: The Second Vatican Council*. London: Catholic Truth Society.

Wittstadt, Klaus (1995). 'On the Eve of the Second Vatican Council (July 1–October 10, 1962)'. In Giuseppe Alberigo (ed.), *History of Vatican II: Announcing and Preparing Vatican Council II*, I, 405–500.

SUGGESTED READING

Aubert, Roger (1954). *La Théologie Catholique au milieu du XXe siècle*. Tournai: Casterman.

Congar, Yves (1938). 'The Reasons for the Unbelief of our Time: A Theological Conclusion'. Part I. *Integration*, 13–21. ET of Congar. 'Une conclusion théologique à l'enquête sur les raisons actuelles de l'incroyance'. *La Vie intellectuelle* 37: 214–49.

Congar, Yves (1939). *Divided Christendom: A Study of the Problem of Reunion*. Trans. M. A. Bousfield. London: Geoffrey Bles.

Congar, Yves (1962). 'The Council in the Age of Dialogue'. Trans. Barry N. Rigney. *Cross Currents* 12: 144–51. ET of Congar (1961). 'Voeux pour le concile: enquête parmi les chrétiens'. *Esprit* 29: 691–700.

Congar, Yves (1965). 'The Church: The People of God'. Trans. Kathryn Sullivan, *Concilium* 1: 7–19. ET of Congar (1965). 'L'Église comme peuple de Dieu'. *Concilium* 1: 15–32.

Congar, Yves (1966). *Dialogue between Christians: Catholic Contributions to Ecumenism*. Trans. Philip Loretz. London: Geoffrey Chapman. ET of Congar (1964). *Chrétiens en dialogue: contributions catholiques à l'oecuménisme. Unam Sanctam* 50. Paris: Cerf.

Congar, Yves (1969). *This Church That I Love*. Trans. Lucien Delafuente. Denville, NJ: Dimension Books. ET of Congar (1968). *Cette Église que j'aime. Foi Vivante* 70. Paris: Cerf.

Congar, Yves (1972). 'My Path-Findings in the Theology of Laity and Ministries'. *Jurist* 32: 169–88. ET of Congar (1995). 'Mon cheminement dans la théologie du laïcat et des ministères'. In J.-P. Jossua (ed.), *Cardinal Yves Congar, O.P.: écrits réformateurs*. Paris: Cerf, 123–40.

Congar, Yves (1977). 'What Belonging to the Church has Come to Mean'. Trans. Frances M. Chew. *Communio* 4: 146-60. ET of Congar (1995). 'Sur la transformation du sens de l'appartenance à l'Église'. In J.-P. Jossua (ed.), *Cardinal Yves Congar, O.P.: écrits réformateurs*, 235–47.

Congar, Yves (1985). *Lay People in the Church: A Study for a Theology of Laity*. Trans. Donald Attwater. Rev. edn with additions. London: Geoffrey Chapman; Westminster, MD: Christian Classics. ET of Congar (1953). *Jalons pour une théologie du laïcat. Unam Sanctam* 23. Paris: Cerf.

Congar, Yves (2000). 'Loving Openness Toward Every Truth: A Letter from Thomas Aquinas to Karl Rahner'. *Philosophy and Theology* 12: 213–19.

Congar, Yves (2011). *True and False Reform in the Church*. Trans. Paul Philibert OP. Collegeville, MN: Liturgical Press. ET of Congar (1950). *Vraie et fausse réforme dans l'Église. Unam Sanctam* 20. Paris: Cerf.

Congar, Yves (2012). *My Journal of the Council*. Trans. Mary John Ronayne OP and Mary Cecily Boulding OP. Collegeville, MN: Liturgical Press. ET of Congar (2002). *Mon journal du Concile*. Ed. with notes Éric Mahieu. 2 vols. Paris: Cerf.

Famerée, Joseph and Gilles Routhier (2008). *Yves Congar*. Les Éditions du Cerf, Paris.

Flynn, Gabriel (2004). *Yves Congar's Vision of the Church in a World of Unbelief*. Farnham and Burlington, VT: Ashgate.

Flynn, Gabriel (ed.) (2005). *Yves Congar: Theologian of the Church*. Louvain: Peeters; Dubley, MA: Eerdmans.

Flynn, Gabriel (2012). 'Introduction: The Twentieth-Century Renaissance in Catholic Theology'. In Gabriel Flynn and Paul D. Murray (eds), *Ressourcement: A Movement for Renewal in Twentieth-Century Catholic Theology*. Oxford: Oxford University Press, 1–22.

Fouilloux, Étienne (1995). 'Frère Yves, Cardinal Congar, Dominicain: itinéraire d'un théologien'. *Revue des sciences philosophiques et théologiques* 79: 379-404.

Groppe, Elizabeth Teresa (2004). *Yves Congar's Theology of the Holy Spirit*. Oxford: Oxford University Press.

Jossua, Jean-Pierre (1967). *Le Père Congar: la théologie au service du peuple de Dieu. Chrétiens De Tous Les Temps* 20. Paris: Cerf.

Merrigan, Terrence (2005). 'The Appeal to Yves Congar in Recent Catholic Theology of Religions: The Case of Jacques Dupuis'. In Gabriel Flynn (ed.), *Yves Congar: Theologian of the Church*. Louvain: Peeters; Dubley, MA: Eerdmans, 427-57.

Webster, John (2005). 'Purity and Plenitude: Evangelical Reflections on Congar's *Tradition and Traditions*'. In Gabriel Flynn (ed.), *Yves Congar: Theologian of the Church*. Louvain: Peeters; Dubley, MA: Eerdmans, 43-65.

CHAPTER 18

HENRI DE LUBAC

GABRIEL FLYNN

Henri Marie-Joseph Sonier de Lubac (1896–1991) was born during a time of increased hostility between church and state in France. The *laïc*/secular republican government of Pierre Waldeck-Rousseau (1846–1904) launched an attack on the influential regular clergy that reached its zenith during the term of office of the next government (June 1902–January 1905) when, under the premiership of Émile Combes (1835–1921), up to 10,000 religious-run schools were closed in the course of 1903–4. Combes enacted legislation for the strict separation of church and state, which resulted in the expulsion from France of some 20,000 religious (Mayeur 1966; Ravitch 1990: 104–12). These grave difficulties were compounded by the modernist crisis of the *fin de siècle* and subsequently by the bitter controversy engendered by the *nouvelle théologie* in the late 1940s and 1950s. In the face of these complexities, the church in France, and, in particular, the religious orders, displayed a remarkable capacity for innovation and adaptation as a host of new movements, journals, and highly successful publishing initiatives emerged as part of a Catholic intellectual *Aufklärung*.

INTRODUCTION

The dual aim of this chapter is to document the indispensable relationship between Eucharist, church, and world in de Lubac's thought and to situate it within his overarching view of a 'total' ecclesiology. De Lubac's triadic vision of 'totality' in fact provides a hermeneutical key to interpret his thought on the church and will be considered in the context of his contribution to the renewed theology of the 'mystical body', the fruits of which have been garnered since Vatican II under the appellation 'communion ecclesiology'. The lens of sacrament in fact provides what is perhaps the most helpful point of entry into the vision of church articulated by de Lubac who, along with Yves Congar (1904–94), is ranked among the primary authors of communion ecclesiology (see Boersma 2009, Doyle 2000, Flynn 2004, Pelchat 1988). This chapter first considers de Lubac's understanding of the relationship between the church and the Eucharist, since he viewed that relationship as crucial to his entire ecclesiology: 'Thus everything points to a study of the relation between the Church and the Eucharist, which we may describe as standing as cause each to other' (1986: 92; 1954: 113). Second, it outlines the links between the church and the world, something de Lubac perceived as being at once paradoxical and conflictual:

> Again paradox; the mystical Bride, the Church with the hidden heart, is also a being very much visible among the beings of this world . . . There is—disastrously—a rivalry between the two and a more or less unceasing struggle, each complaining of the encroachments of the other: 'Nothing is more unstable and precarious than their equilibrium.' (1986: 114; 1954: 139)

De Lubac extends his ecclesial vision beyond the normally fractious relationship between the church and the world to the domain of humanity and to each person individually. He outlines his hypothesis in eschatological terms but without denying its essential this-worldly character:

> To remind man what constitutes his final end is not to tell him something that substantially fails to interest him . . . It is rather to illuminate the total meaning of his being by helping him to find and then to interpret the inscription written into his heart by his Creator. (2008: 613)

What follows attempts to provide an interpretative framework for understanding de Lubac's ecclesiology. 'De Lubac's Vision for the Church' reconstructs key elements in his ecclesiological vision. It assesses, first, his important contribution to reform at Vatican II and shows that Eucharist and communion are his dominant ideas for ecclesial renewal. Second, it analyses the mission of the church since, as de Lubac insists emphatically, '[t]here is no "private Christianity"' (1986: 231; 1954: 265). 'Church and Eucharist in the World: A Spiritual Vision for Civilization' endeavours to demonstrate how de Lubac's profoundly Eucharistic ecclesiology provides a spiritual and social vision for the contemporary world.

A preliminary matter to be considered concerns de Lubac's early life and education; he was born into a *bourgeois* family in Cambrai, northern France, and entered the Society of Jesus in 1913. He was drafted into the French army in 1915, was wounded in action at Éparges near Verdun in 1917, and was decorated for his service to France at this time with the *Croix de Guerre* (Guillet 1992). He studied humanities in Canterbury (1919–20), philosophy in Jersey (1920–3), and theology in Hastings (1924–6) and at Lyon-Fourvière (1926–8). During his philosophical studies, he came under the influence of the writings of Maurice Blondel (1861–1949) and Pierre Rousselot (1878–1915) (see Russo 1990; McDermott 1997). He was ordained priest in 1927 and appointed Professor of Fundamental Theology at the Catholic Theology Faculty of Lyon in September 1929 (de Lubac 1993: 15–16; 2006a: 11–12), where he remained until June 1950 when he was forbidden to teach or publish by his religious superiors and was transferred to the Jesuit residence on Rue de Sèvres in Paris (1993: 16; 2006a: 12–13). During the German, Nazi occupation of France (1941–4), he emerged as a firm opponent of anti-Semitism, most notably in his role as co-editor of the clandestine *Cahiers du Témoignage chrétien* (de Lubac 1992: 67–82).

Although de Lubac's literary legacy is looked upon as historical scholarship rather than as a precise speculative system (Milbank 2005: 106–8; Voderholzer 2008: 107–21; Coffele 1996: 757), his major concerns were not formulated randomly, as may be seen from his earliest works *Catholicisme: les aspects sociaux du dogme* (1938), *Corpus Mysticum* (1944), and *Surnaturel* (1946a). While de Lubac rejected the idea of a 'synthesis' in his writings (Voderholzer 2008: 107), he nonetheless asserted that there was a unity: 'In this multi-colored fabric gradually formed according to teaching assignments, ministries, situations and appeals of all kinds, it nevertheless seems possible to me to discern a certain texture that, come what may, creates a unity' (1993: 143; 2006a: 147). Von Balthasar (1905–88) identifies an 'organic whole' in his theology (1991: 24), while Dulles (1918–2008) asserts that 'de Lubac's work possesses a remarkable inner coherence' (1991a: 334). Tilliette argues that de Lubac 'displays a profound coherence, one may even say an organic structure' (1992: 334). Nichols shows that unity constitutes 'the key to de Lubac's entire enterprise'. He points out that de Lubac's preferred formula to express his love of unities was 'unir pour distinguer'. In order to bolster his 'proposal', Nichols cites de Lubac's letter to Blondel in which he refers to the latter's philosophical journey: 'It is in fact when one does not know how to unite things well that one particularly fears confusing them' (Nichols 2012: 32).

Commentators place the church at the centre of de Lubac's late work (von Balthasar 1991: 105; O'Sullivan 2009: 413). Careful analysis of his oeuvre shows that his ecclesiology, formulated in response to the problems of his day, is of relevance to the Christian churches confronted with an array of complex difficulties in the post-modern period. His vast corpus is both dynamic, in the sense of striving for a spiritual goal, and charismatic, in the sense of responding to the requests and demands of others, and must be viewed in the dual context of place and time. As he remarks, '[N]early everything I have written has been as a result of circumstances that were often unforeseen, in scattered order and without technical preparation' (1993: 143; 2006a: 146). It is important to note that while de Lubac did not see himself as an original thinker, still less did he view his work as mere systematization or naive hankering after the glories of a lost past. His aim was to make the tradition known, loved, and efficacious for the present. In constructing a 'return to the sources', de Lubac was careful to avoid the twin dangers of antiquarianism and any rejection of progress in later developments.

> Without claiming to open up new avenues of thought, I have sought rather, without any antiquarianism, to make known some of the great common areas of Catholic tradition. I wanted to make it loved, to show its ever-present fruitfulness . . . So I have never been tempted by any kind of 'return to the sources' that would scorn

later developments and represent the history of Christian thought as a stream of decadences (1993: 143–4; 2006a: 147).

De Lubac's career spans one of the most complex, controversial, and divisive periods in the history of the French church and may be divided into two phases; first, the period from the Modernist crisis (1910) to the publication of *Humani Generis* (1950), and second, from the decade prior to the Second Vatican Council (1962–5) to the tumultuous post-conciliar period. The first phase represents a significant period in de Lubac's theological career, not least because the censures of *Humani Generis* were generally thought to be directed against his positions and those of the other prominent *ressourcement* theologians. De Lubac was linked by his theological opponents with the anti-Thomistic Blondel. An important question, therefore, concerns his view of philosophy and its role in his theology. In this regard, the significance of Blondel's challenge to the kind of Catholic apologetics which prevailed down to the 1960s and his influence on de Lubac's conception of philosophy, and consequently his view of nature and grace, are paramount (Conway 2012: 65–82). Taking de Lubac's *Surnaturel: études historiques* as his fundamental text, this study considers the implications of its theses for his ecclesiology (Cholvy 2011: 797–827).

Along with his *confrères* Jean Daniélou (1905–74), Henri Bouillard (1908–81) and von Balthasar, de Lubac was part of the renowned generation of European *ressourcement* theologians who made an outstanding contribution to the twentieth-century renaissance in Catholic theology (von Balthasar 1991; Flynn 2011: 323–38; Wagner 2007, 1997; Milbank 2005; Chantraine 2008; McPartlan 2006). The epithet *nouvelle théologie* corresponds to a theology that is concerned to know the tradition, as opposed to a purely scholastic and repetitive theology. The view of tradition proposed by the *nouvelle théologie*, far from being traditionalist, in the sense of a repetition of the recent past, was concerned rather with the unity of the ever-living tradition. The *ressourcement* project was severely criticized by Labourdette (1946a; 1946b; Aubert 1954) as well as by Garrigou-Lagrange who seems to have borrowed the phrase *la nouvelle théologie* to describe it (1946). The controversial term was first used by Pietro Parente, Secretary to the Holy Office, in an article entitled 'Nuove tendenze teologiche' which appeared in *L'Osservatore Romano*, 9–10 February 1942. Parente saw this *nouvelle théologie* as a crude attempt to demolish the by then classical system of the schools.

In an atmosphere of suspicion and controversy, Pius XII (Pope 1939–58) published *Humani Generis* on 12 August 1950, which condemned philosophical relativism and other perceived errors in Roman Catholic theology and philosophy. The controversial encyclical had traumatic consequences for the Lyon Jesuits (de Lubac 1993: 71, 74; 2006a: 72, 75; also Pius XII 1950; Guelluy 1986). It marked the beginning of a period of isolationism and hostility, as well as a time of fecund intellectual work in the midst of seemingly unending difficulties for the beleaguered de Lubac. As *Humani Generis* was strictly enforced by the ecclesiastical authorities in France, it is hardly surprising that de Lubac, an astute political analyst, rejected the term *nouvelle théologie* (1993: 361; 2006a: 362; also de Lubac 2007a/1985: 12; Chantraine 2007, 2009). The draconian censures imposed by his superiors resulted in the withdrawal from Jesuit libraries of some of de Lubac's key texts as well as his removal from all lecturing duties, effectively ending his academic career (1993: 71, 74; 2006a: 72, 75).

In the wake of *Humani Generis*, de Lubac points out that Pius XII wrote to him, through the kind offices of Cardinal Augustin Bea (1881–1968), in order to thank him for his work and to encourage him to undertake a future study that would yield rich fruit for the church (de Lubac 2007a/1985: 14). De Lubac was instrumental, with others, in the foundation of the *Théologie* series, a project of the Fourvière Jesuits, dedicated to the 'renewal of the church'. He launched the series before the end of the Second World War with Henri Bouillard, who became the project's first secretary. Bouillard said that the twofold objective of the project was 'to go to the sources of Christian doctrine, to find in it the truth of our life' (de Lubac 1993: 31; 2006a: 29). But it was *Sources chrétiennes*, the bilingual collection published by Éditions du Cerf, under the general editorship of de Lubac and Daniélou, which was the crowning glory of the Fourvière Jesuits, as well as their greatest and most enduring contribution to *ressourcement*. Fouilloux notes that one of the aims of *Sources chrétiennes*, from its beginnings, was a *rapprochement* between separated Christians of East and West (1995: 219; Aubert 1954: 84–6; Fédou 2011; De Lubac 1993: 95–6; 2006a: 96).

The profound influence of de Lubac's theology is perhaps nowhere more evident than at Vatican II where it affected such questions as the nature of the church and its mission, revelation, the relationship between the church and the world, and the church's response to atheistic humanism (de Lubac 2007b; 2007a/1985, chs 2–5). De Lubac, in fact, made a decisive contribution to the reforms of the Second Vatican Council. As Joseph Ratzinger (1927–) remarks: '[I]n all its comments about the Church [Vatican II] was moving precisely in the direction of de Lubac's thought' (Ratzinger 1987: 50). This pertinent remark prompts a closer consideration of his role at Vatican II. The publication of *Carnets du Concile* (2007b) and *Entretien autour de Vatican II* (2007a/1985) provides a clear representation of de Lubac's contribution to Vatican II, as well as his mature reflections on critical issues for the church. These important works will be analysed in the section 'De Lubac's Vision for the Church', which presents his vision for a renewed church.

DE LUBAC'S VISION FOR THE CHURCH

In *Méditation sur l'Église* (1954) translated into English as *The Splendour of the Church* (1986), an infelicitous title that was always vexatious to him, de Lubac sought to formulate a 'total' vision of the church. His notion of totality has its origins in Scripture and the Fathers of East and West, as may be understood from his 1944 study *Corpus Mysticum*. This concern was replicated in other *ressourcement* thinkers, including Congar and von Balthasar. Drawing on St Irenaeus, de Lubac argued that the church is 'one total reality', a 'unique body' in which all the members are engaged in continual interaction (1986: 7; 1954: 16–17). It should be noted, however, that his attempt to furnish a comprehensive ecclesiology is constrained, since 'the Church is not a this-worldly reality such as lends itself to exact measurement and analysis' (1986: 4; 1954: 12). In some respects, his idea of 'totality' resembles a complex series of crenellations on a medieval fortress, the precise objective of which is to protect and defend the church and its members. It may be suggested that de Lubac had not succeeded in fully extricating himself from the old defensive model of the church, as may be seen from his clearly pre-critical view of obedience in *Méditation sur l'Église*.

The first element of de Lubac's 'total' ecclesiology on which some general remarks may be made concerns the controversial doctrine on the necessity of the church for salvation. He notes that the confession of faith is an act of the 'whole Church'. Citing St Augustine, he maintains that the person who voluntarily separates himself/herself from the church no longer has a valid faith (1986: 24; 1954: 35). He argues forcibly for the necessary role of the church in salvation and asserts that '[t]he entire process of salvation is worked out in her; indeed, it is identified with her' (1986: 24; 1954: 35). He envisages the church as an all-embracing receptacle of Christ's love for the world. 'It lays hold on the whole of us and surrounds us; for it is in His Church that God looks upon us and loves us, in her that He desires us and we encounter Him, and in her that we cleave to Him and are made blessed' (1986: 24–5; 1954: 36).

Following St Paul, de Lubac views the church as a communion founded on love that provides a total vista where 'Christ loves us individually but not separately, saying to each of us, as He did to Moses, "I know thee by name" [Exod. 33:12]; He loves us in His Church, for which He shed His blood' (1986: 24; 1954: 35). De Lubac stresses the 'total' character of God's gratuitousness: 'The gratuitousness of the supernatural order is true individually and totally' (1998a: 236; 2009: 289). Furthermore, he insists on the indispensable link between Christology and ecclesiology. As he writes in his 'Spiritual Testament': 'Without Jesus-Christ, who leads us to God, the Church would be nothing.' Fundamental to his entire vision of the church is the notion of mystery in the New Testament, particularly in the Pauline corpus. For de Lubac, the church is the mysterious spring from which flows the gift of salvation. 'The Church is a mystery because, coming from God and entirely at the service of his plan, she is an organism of salvation, precisely because she relates wholly to Christ and apart from him has no existence, value or efficacy' (1969: 15; 1967: 34). Jacques Dupuis (1923–2004) provides an incisive *précis* of de Lubac's explication of the relationship between Christianity and the world religions, one that includes the vexed question of 'anonymous Christianity':

> According to the fulfillment theory which de Lubac makes his own, the mystery of Christ reaches the members of other religious traditions as the divine response to the human aspiration for union with the Divine, but the religious traditions themselves play no role in this mystery of salvation. Henri de Lubac explains that to attribute positive salvific value to them would be tantamount to setting them in competition with Christianity thus obscuring the latter's uniqueness. . . . According to Henri de Lubac, while it is legitimate to speak of 'anonymous Christians,' the expression 'anonymous Christianity' is, on the contrary, seriously misleading, for it fails to do justice to the newness of Christianity and its singular character as the way to salvation. (Dupuis 2001: 138–40; 147–8)

Second, we consider de Lubac's view of 'orthodoxy'. This concerns, above all, the church in times of crisis or growth and is, therefore, as important as it is controversial. In moments of error or indecision in past debates, whether on the Trinity, Christology, or grace, one particular mystery inevitably became the standard around which was fought the crucial battle for orthodoxy (1986: 8; 1954: 17; also 2002: 118; 1994: 146). In this context, de Lubac, citing St Hilary of Poitiers (*De Trinitate*, 1. bk iv, ch. vii), points out that doctrinal formulas undergo necessary revision and are re-cast 'for the greater security of the faith' (1986: 8; 1954: 17). While he maintains that 'truth finds its own equilibrium' in such crises, it is noteworthy that he situates the 'crucial battle for orthodoxy' in the context of 'the total Christian mystery'. Indeed, it is within the 'one total reality' of the church's life that he sees a sure safeguard against the threats of 'subjectivism', 'individualism', and 'formal schism' (1986: 5–9; 1954: 13–17).

Turning to the relationship between the church and the world, one arrives at the high point of de Lubac's design for a 'total' ecclesiology. Along with Congar, he locates the church at the heart of human life and activity (1986: 6; 1954: 14) where it acts as a standard bearer of Christ, a source of peace as well as of ferment. De Lubac proceeds to articulate a vision for social justice with acuity: 'The Church is in the world, and by the effect of her presence alone she communicates to it an unrest which cannot be soothed away. She is a perpetual witness of the Christ who came "to shake human life to its foundations", as Guardini puts it, and it is a fact that she appears in the world as a "great ferment of discord"' (1986: 133; 1954: 159). De Lubac's all-encompassing vision of the church in the modern world resonates with von Balthasar's who views the church as being active everywhere (1991: 46).

De Lubac, without denying the apparently 'irresolvable conflicts' inherent in all church–state relations, proposes a framework of mutuality based on the principle of perpetual 'reciprocal embarrassment'. Fully cognizant of the dangers in every form of separation and union of church and state, he was only able to resolve the dilemma by recognizing in the church a 'sign of divine wisdom', while also seeing in the human person, a duality between 'animal' and 'spirit', that is, between the terrestrial and the eternal. De Lubac was resolute in his opposition to any form of absolutism of state or culture in order to avoid any future repetition of totalitarianism and a concomitant quiescence by the Christian churches before the forces of evil. He constructed an integrated spirituality for a 'militant' church at the heart of the world (1986: 107–10; 1954: 129–33; von Balthasar 1991: 107), which will be considered in the section 'Church and Eucharist in the World: A Spiritual Vision for Civilization'.

De Lubac at Vatican II

The preparations for Vatican II proceeded in two phases. The first was the appointment of the Ante-Preparatory Commission (May 1959) under the direction of Cardinal Domenico Tardini (1888–1961). Its task was to gather the opinions of bishops and others on issues requiring action. On 5 June 1960 John XXIII closed the ante-preparatory phase and commenced the proximate preparations for the council. Ten preparatory commissions were set up which, with the exception of the Commission on the Apostolate of the Laity, were presided over by cardinals who were prefects of the various curia Congregations. A Central Preparatory Commission oversaw the work of the others. It was the task of the preparatory commissions to collate the results of the worldwide consultation among bishops and to draw up drafts (*schemata*) for the council. The pope also established a Secretariat for Christian Unity, with a limited mandate.

On 20 July 1960 John XXIII nominated de Lubac and Congar as consultors to the Preparatory Theological Commission. The Commission's President Cardinal Alfredo Ottaviani (1890–1979) was a veritable opponent of the *nouvelle théologie* and did not share the pope's confidence in de Lubac, while the Commission's Secretary Sebastian Tromp (1889–1975), a Jesuit, could hardly be considered a friend of de Lubac or Congar. De Lubac later commented poignantly on the historical significance of the pope's nominees: 'These were two symbolic names. John XXIII had undoubtedly wanted to make everyone understand that the difficulties that had occurred under the previous pontificate between Rome and the Jesuit and Dominican orders in France were to be forgotten' (1993: 116; 2006a: 117–18). De Lubac in fact viewed the Commission as an annex of the Holy Office and quickly became disenchanted with it, not least because consultors were unable to contribute except by invitation of a member. Although de Lubac considered resigning from the Preparatory Theological Commission, he ultimately recorded two notable achievements. First, he successfully defended his friend Pierre Teilhard de Chardin (1881–1955) from an explicit condemnation by the council, based on serious misinterpretations of his thought by certain individuals. Second, he defended the orthodoxy and integrity of his own writings against false readings.

De Lubac's membership of the Preparatory Theological Commission brought him 'almost automatically to the Council' and on 28 September 1962 he was appointed a *peritus* (expert) on the Doctrinal Commission. In an entry in his Council Diary of 6 October 1962, he remarks:

> On 28 September, *La Croix* published a list of 'experts' nominated by the pope for the Council; my name figured on the list. The following day, the 29th, we read in the papers that John XXIII had nominated me as an expert at the Council, to show his unhappiness at the *Monitum* [warning] of the Holy Office on Teilhard and the anonymous article in *L'Osservatore Romano* which explained the *Monitum* as an action against my book on *The Religious Thought of Father Pierre Teilhard de Chardin*, which certain individuals had wished to place on the Index. (de Lubac 2007b: vol. 1, 89)

De Lubac's influence as a conciliar theologian has been aptly described as follows: 'Within the throng of *periti* at Vatican II, Henri de Lubac was one of the best-known and most outstanding from the very beginning' (Neufeld 1988: 88). He was destined to play a central role in the deliberations of the council that provided him with a unique opportunity to realize his vision of the church on a global stage (de Lubac 2007b: vol. 1, 7).

De Lubac placed his considerable spiritual, psychological, and intellectual talents at the disposal of the council. In the face of divisions in French Catholicism in the post-war period and of the continued reverberations from *Humani Generis*, he worked tirelessly at the council to ensure that the vision of `the 'Fourvière School' for a renewed church at the service of the world came to fruition. He influenced the council first by his works that had been widely read. Second, his patient and reserved response to the injunctions placed on him prior to the council significantly enhanced his reputation. Third, he exercised an indirect but powerful influence on the council debates through the bishops who drew on his works. Unlike other *periti*, de Lubac did not offer regular reports on the council nor did he seek, much less accept, opportunities for publicity.

De Lubac's influence on *Lumen Gentium* and *Gaudium et Spes* has been carefully delineated by scholars. The following elements of *Lumen Gentium* are attributed to him: (i) the duty of the church to proclaim the gospel to all peoples as explained in *Le Fondement théologique des missions* (de Lubac 1946b); (ii) the idea of Mary as a type of the church and (iii) the use of the term 'the mystery of the church' both of which are expounded in his *Méditation sur l'Église*. Karl Heinz Neufeld provides a precise account of de Lubac's influence on *Lumen Gentium*:

> *Lumen gentium* also shows signs of de Lubac's influence. In 1963 he had already described the Church as the sacrament of Jesus Christ, just as Jesus Christ as man is for us the sacrament of God. This is the expression of one of the principles of the Council's view of the Church. De Lubac developed this from his idea of the Church as mystery, which he had used as a title in his *Méditation sur l'Eglise* and which he was to discuss in detail after the Council in his *Paradoxe et Mystère de l'Eglise*. But *Catholicisme* and *Corpus Mysticum* had already taken important preparatory steps in this direction. However, it was above all the *Méditation sur l'Eglise* with which the Council Fathers were familiar as a source of theological ideas and as inspiration for the spiritual life. (Neufeld 1988: 94)

De Lubac's influence at the council was also evident on the question of the relation of the church to non-Christian religions, drawing on *Catholicisme* and his works on Buddhism. Then, during the debates on divine revelation, his name was mentioned explicitly in the Council Hall and, through his direct collaboration on *Dei Verbum*, he was able to counter criticism of his thought on Revelation. De Lubac considered this text the most important document of Vatican II (see Neufeld 1988: 103, note 56). He wrote a commentary on the Preamble and first chapter of *Dei Verbum* in 1966 and again in a larger work published in 1968. De Lubac was a member of the sub-commission that produced the first chapter of *Gaudium et Spes* which reflects his vision of the place of the church in the modern world, as outlined in *Catholicisme*. He was also invited to write an Introduction to *Gaudium et Spes*. Further, de Lubac exercised a profound influence on the treatment of atheism in the Pastoral Constitution through his work *Le Drame de l'Humanisme athée*.

De Lubac's contribution to Vatican II cannot be properly understood without noting his claim, expressed from a certain point of view, that there are two types of theologians with radically divergent methodologies, namely, those guided by the sources and those guided exclusively by 'ecclesiastical texts' (see de Lubac 2007b: vol. 1, 53). On 4 December 1962 de Lubac records in full a momentous intervention of Cardinal Leon-Joseph Suenens (1904–96) on the church, as a result of which important progress was made: 'The Church must enter into dialogue with its faithful,—with our brothers "not yet in unity with us",—with the world of today' (de Lubac 2007b: vol. 1, 464). What resulted was of fundamental importance for the remainder of the council. Suenens, in the context of inviting all to a collective examination of conscience, articulated an important conclusion: '1. That the programme of the remainder of the Council be determined by the Council itself, in the sense already expressed . . . ; 2. That the commissions, without delay, reconsider their schemes according to this decision' (de Lubac 2007b: vol. 1, 464).

A Return to the Sources for a 'New Church'

De Lubac held that the most decisive sign that the council would effect a 'return to the living sources of the Catholic tradition' was the decision of 28 November 1962 to reformulate the initial curia version of *Lumen Gentium*. He praised Gérard Philips (1899–1972) who, as the Assistant-Secretary of the Doctrinal Commission, was the principal editor of *Lumen Gentium* and the author of its most authoritative commentary (De Lubac 2007a/1985: 21). According to de Lubac, the council inaugurated a 'new church' by placing the laity as the foundation of *Lumen Gentium*. He expressed his admiration for the document's order of chapters and its focus on mystery as 'a decisive reminder of the authentic Tradition thus blocking secularization, politicization and democratization' (2007a/1985: 22). In patristic theology, it became usual to designate Christ, Scripture, the liturgical rites and the church as *mysterion* or *sacramentum*. The Second Vatican Council took up again this ancient usage in order to ascribe to the church the value of a sacramental symbolism and instrumentality in the economy of salvation for all humankind (*LG* 1, 8, 17, 48). De Lubac's dual focus on sacrament and mystery was translated directly into the documents of Vatican II. Not a few commentators have noted that the first chapter of *Méditation sur l'Église*, 'The Church as Mystery', foreshadowed *Lumen Gentium*, chapter one, while the notion of church as 'sacrament' occurs in three of the council's four constitutions: *Sacrosanctum Concilium* which refers to the church as the 'sacrament of unity', n. 26; *Lumen Gentium*, nn. 1, 9, and 48 which refers to the church as the 'universal sacrament of salvation'; also *Gaudium et Spes*, nn. 42, 45. De Lubac worked assiduously to reform the excessively patriarchal structure of the church and expressed agreement with the remarkably perceptive view that 'as the Church lost the working class in the nineteenth century, it will lose women in the twentieth' (de Lubac 2007b: vol. 1, 73).

The Principal Conciliar Texts

De Lubac viewed the *ensemble* of conciliar texts as important and insisted that 'no document may be neglected' (2007a/1985: 41–2). He was part of the sub-commission that drew up Schema 13 which served as the foundation of *Gaudium et Spes*. He acknowledges the important role of Karol Józef Wojtyła (Pope John Paul II, 1978–2005) in its preparation and composition, which he notes were long and laborious. Although de Lubac was involved only in the later stages, he responds, in passing, to a controversial point regarding *Gaudium et Spes*: 'It is not as naïvely optimistic as is sometimes maintained' (2007a/1985: 46). He viewed *Lumen Gentium* as an essentially doctrinal text that contributes richly to collegiality.

According to de Lubac, Friday 8 November 1963 was a historic day at the council. He outlines his reasons for this assertion with particular reference to Cardinal Joseph Frings, archbishop of Cologne:

> Cardinal Frings, with a polite, clear voice and an ever-calm, moderate expression but without detours, approached the question of the reform of the Holy-Office. Then came the vehement . . . response of Cardinal Ottaviani: 'I protest in the strongest possible manner . . .' Ottaviani was applauded by his partisans. Between the two came the intervention of Cardinal [Giacomo] Lecarto, outlining a plan, supposedly inspired by Paul VI: 'a special commission would be created to study the essential point'. (de Lubac 2007b: vol. 2, 15)

The present-day efforts at reform of the curia are reminiscent of those forthright conciliar exchanges, a half-century ago. In a subsequent entry on 30 November 1963 de Lubac criticized those bishops who, as members of the Theological Commission, failed 'to denounce before the council the obstructionist methods of their president' (de Lubac 2007b: vol. 2, 53). In a similar vein, on 12 October 1964 he refers to 'curial manoeuvres' of some of the council participants. Furthermore, in response to three French bishops who referred to Msgr Marcel Lefebvre (1905–91), the controversial founder of the Society of St Pius X in Econe, Switzerland, as a 'challenge to the French episcopate', de Lubac replied: 'Say rather: a challenge to the Council' (de Lubac 2007b: vol. 2, 200).

Although ecumenism was not a dominant theme in de Lubac's ecclesiology, he nonetheless displayed remarkable ecumenical sensitivity and innovativeness. Fully cognizant that cooperation between the churches had been elevated to a higher plane by Vatican II, he requested that more attention should be given to the patriarchates of the East. Aware of the complexity of this question and in order not to miss a unique opportunity in the history of the church, he wisely suggested asking the advice of the Orthodox. He also advocated the creation of additional patriarchates in the Latin church as a remedy for 'excessive centralisation' (de Lubac 2007b: vol. 2, 225). In the closing entry of his council Diary, de Lubac makes an important point for the ultimate success of the council, one that has not yet been fully exploited: 'I spoke on the period after the Council, on the example given by John XXIII and Paul VI, on the necessity to found the aggiornamento on the two great dogmatic constitutions [*Lumen Gentium* and *Dei Verbum*]' (de Lubac 2007b: vol. 2, 483).

De Lubac's disenchantment with the manner of the reception and enactment of the reforms of Vatican II is well known. He insisted on a true and historically accurate understanding of the council and rejected the idea of 'the Church of Vatican II' as an 'abuse of language' and 'a way of emphasizing discontinuities, of exaggerating them, indeed, of imagining ruptures, of making too much of contingent, secondary traits to the detriment of the essential, which endures'. He insists that those in authority in the church are only 'the servants of the Christian tradition' and concludes unambiguously, 'I know only one Church, the Church of all time, the Church of Jesus Christ.' For de Lubac, the preservation of the unity of the church was paramount. As he writes, '[I]t is a betrayal (*trahir*) of the Council to consider it like an open door to something else and virtually to repudiate it in both letter and spirit on the pretext, as is sometimes said, of "going farther"' (de Lubac 2002: 38–9; 1994: 46–7).

It is well known that de Lubac was critical of the post-conciliar church. He believed that the crisis at the heart of the church after the council was a reflection of the crisis at the heart of Western society originating from a refusal to acknowledge the transcendent, a kind of modern Gnosticism that he referred to as 'a global repugnance to admitting the idea of a divine revelation'. This refusal to believe resulted inevitably in a spiritual decline and a corresponding growth in secularization. De Lubac was nonetheless critical of the fundamental misinterpretation of the council (Walsh 1992).

De Lubac's ecclesiology constitutes a grand plan for salvation and evangelization based on a dynamic view of the Eucharist actively engaged with the world. While he had a tendency towards amorphousness, his discussion of 'totality' in the context of the Eucharist provides a key to understanding this aspect of his thought, as will be considered in the section 'Church and Eucharist in the World: A Spiritual Vision for Civilization'.

Church and Eucharist in the World: A Spiritual Vision for Civilization

The precise concern of this section is to demonstrate how de Lubac's essentially Eucharistic ecclesiology provides a spiritual and social vision for the contemporary world. This vision comprises the following three elements: first, a spirituality of the church articulated in *Méditation sur l'Église*; second, his treatment of 'Western Atheism', a crucial element in the Catholic engagement with modern unbelief; and third, his proposals for dialogue with atheists and non-Christian religions.

Any attempt to delineate de Lubac's spiritual vision for civilization should refer to his most acclaimed and controversial work *Surnaturel: études historiques*. Fully aware of the ferocity of the debate that followed the publication of this work, our aim is to note its implications for de Lubac's vision of the church (see Neufeld 1988: 92). In short, *Surnaturel* gave rise to the most acrimonious controversy in twentieth-century Catholic thought, and, by challenging the standard neo-scholastic theology of nature and grace, de Lubac laid bare the error and ignorance of esteemed Thomist commentators in their reading of the tradition. 'De Lubac soon realized', von Balthasar shows, 'that his position moved into a suspended middle in which he could not practice any philosophy without its transcendence into theology, but also no theology without its essential inner substructure of philosophy' (1991: 15; also Milbank 2005: ch. 2; Kerr 2007: ch. 5; 2002: ch. 8).

Beginning with de Lubac's forceful response to atheism, we note that he viewed *Le Drame de l'humanisme athée* as a composite study similar to *Catholicisme*. In this book, de Lubac worked for a rediscovery of the true '*spirit* of Christianity', viewed as nothing other than a return to the sources of Christianity. As he writes, 'In order to do so we must be plunged once more in its wellsprings, and above all in the Gospel. The Gospel that the Church unvaryingly offers us is enough for us. Only, always new, it always needs to be rediscovered' (1998b: 127; 1945: 106). Christianity is perceived as 'the religion of love', a contention he seeks to defend by reference to Dostoevsky's profession of faith: 'I declare that love for mankind is something completely inconceivable, incomprehensible and even impossible without faith in the immortality of the human soul' (1998b: 128, 283; 1945: 106, 234). De Lubac advocated a heroic love that would be capable of resisting the corruption of Christian values in the world. His ambitious plan of social action is founded on charity: 'Christianity will never have any real efficacy, it will never have any real existence or make any real conquests, except by the strength of its own spirit, *by the strength of charity*' (1998b: 129; 1945: 108). For de Lubac, as for Dostoevsky, love is essentially Christological albeit tinged with a sense of profound loss in the Western church: 'Reflecting upon the West, which a strong party in his own country would have liked Russia to take as its model, he [Dostoevsky] says: "The West has lost Christ, and that is why it is dying; that is the only reason"' (1998b: 304; 1945: 251). In his guidelines for dialogue between Christians and atheists, de Lubac draws on the riches of Dostoevsky but in a way that surpasses him (see de Lubac 1998b: 10).

Consideration of the place of spirituality and psychology in de Lubac's 'total' ecclesiology demonstrates his deep concern for the human person. Von Balthasar asserts pithily that *Méditation sur l'Église* provides 'the spirituality for the theology of *Catholicisme*' (1991: 107). There is one further point that can be alluded to briefly. Congar encouraged de Lubac to write *Catholicisme: les aspects sociaux du dogme*, which is widely regarded as one of the most important theological texts of the twentieth century. As Fergus Kerr remarks: 'Many, including Congar, Balthasar, Wojtyla and Ratzinger, regarded it as the key book of twentieth-century Catholic theology, the one indispensable text' (Kerr 2007: 71). *Catholicisme* attempted to address the problem of an extremely individualized, privatized religious sensibility among Catholics (de Lubac 1988; 2010; also 1993: 28; 2006a: 26; Komonchak 1990: 591). Acknowledging that the work was 'made up of bits and pieces that were first written independently, then stitched together, so to speak, into three parts, without any preconceived plan', de Lubac, nonetheless, points to its 'character of universality and totality best expressed by the word "catholicism"' (1993: 27; 2006a: 25). Consideration of his ecclesial spirituality leads directly to the Eucharist.

One of the most important fruits of de Lubac's contribution to *ressourcement* is *Corpus Mysticum*, a historical study of the Eucharist in the Middle Ages that played a major role in the renewal of Catholic ecclesiology and ecumenism in the twentieth century. This book is, as de Lubac remarks, 'a work of intensive concentration on two words' in which he locates his vision for the church at the heart of the Eucharistic mystery. It is also, as the subtitle suggests, a systematic treatment of the relationship between the Eucharist and the church. De Lubac's study carefully unravels the sources, meaning, and application of these terms by reference to Scripture, theology, and pure history or exegesis. He asserts that research must focus on the Latin authors of the high Middle Ages who wrote about the Eucharist, as well as on the later period, and on the Eastern authors. As we read in *Catholicisme*, 'the whole Latin Middle Ages were nourished on this teaching'. In his memoirs, de Lubac describes the purpose of *Corpus Mysticum* in a way that is illuminating for our present task: 'In *Corpus mysticum*, through the history of these two words whose surprising vicissitudes I retraced, I tried to show the depths and the complexity of the bonds that unite these two realities of the Eucharist and the Church in Christian life and doctrine; that is, in the final analysis, to define the kind of relationship that ties, in the Catholic synthesis, the most "mystical" element to the most institutional' (1993: 93; 2006a: 93).

De Lubac distinguishes three levels of meaning for *corpus mysticum*. First, *mystical body* that pertains to the sphere of ceremonial and refers to the mystical action of '*the celebration of the body*', namely, the body of Christ hidden under material or ritual appearances. Second, *mystical body* unites sacrifice and sacrament in a process of mystical signification. In this context, de Lubac makes a point of profound ecumenical significance. He asserts that the second meaning of *mystical body* may be seen more clearly if the Eucharist is viewed 'within the whole spectrum of its relationship to the sacrifices of the ancient Law and the Patriarchs' (2006b: 62; 1949: 75). His insistence on the link between the Old and New Testaments facilitates enhanced relations between Judaism and Christianity since, in bringing the sacraments of the old and new orders into relationship, he is proposing not two books or two instruments of salvation but one. '[T]he passage from one Testament to the other is understood as a *transformation of sacraments*', as de Lubac demonstrates by reference to Pseudo-Hildebert, '*No longer is a roasted lamb given to the people through Moses, but Christ is present as the lamb who suffered on the cross for us*' (2006b: 64–5; 1949: 78). Third, the *mystical body* may be understood as a process orientated towards the future and dependent on building up the church that is the effective sign of fraternal charity.

When *mystical body* passed from Eucharist to the church, it was the mystery that described the ecclesial body. De Lubac cites St Augustine for whom the Eucharist is 'far more than a symbol, because it is most truly the sacrament *by which the Church is bound together in this age* . . . It is a real presence because it makes real' (2006b: 253; 1949: 284). De Lubac's Eucharistic ecclesiology, with its reinstatement of Augustinian symbolism, is in fact deeply Augustinian throughout, as scholars have carefully demonstrated. 'For de Lubac, this Augustinian principle ["You shall not change me into yourself as bodily food, but you shall be changed into me": *Confessions*, VII, 10.16] was the key to the mystical life in all its zones of meaning. It gives us a vision of Christ, the Great Mystery, drawing close in the Eucharist to incorporate us into that great mystery and so to transform the Church into his mystical self' (Moloney 2005: 333).

One of the issues de Lubac emphasizes is the role of the Eucharist in society. The summit of all the sacraments, the Eucharist is pre-eminently 'the sacrament of unity: *sacramentum unitatis ecclesiasticae*' (1988: 88–9; 2010: 63). The Eucharist acts as a mysterious, hidden principle of unity whereby the members draw more closely to the church and to Christ. In the context of the twentieth-century return to an understanding of the church based on the Eucharist, de Lubac is credited with a highly succinct formulation of the reciprocal relationship between the church and the Eucharist. As he writes, 'Literally speaking, therefore, the Eucharist makes the Church. It makes of it an inner reality. By its hidden power, the members of the body come to unite themselves by becoming more fully members of Christ, and their unity with one another is part and parcel of their unity with the one single Head' (2006b: 88; 1949: 104; also McPartlan 2006; McPartlan 1996; Wang 2003; Moloney 2005; Le 2006). De Lubac's achievement in this domain was to reinstate the Eucharist at the centre of human society and of the world. 'Now, the Eucharist is the mystical principle, permanently at work at the heart of Christian society' (2006b: 88, 253; 1949: 103, 284). This is a point of utmost importance because it demonstrates how in de Lubac's ecclesiology the true locus for the church and the Eucharist is at the heart of the world for the construction of a civilization based on charity. '*By the food and blood of the Lord's body let all fellowship be bound together!*' (2006b: 260; 1949: 293).

In the Eucharist, the sacrament of remembrance par excellence, de Lubac identifies a 'total symbolism' which not unlike the 'total symbolism' of Scripture may be understood in a variety of ways. 'Just as the sacrifices of the ancient Law were symbolic prefigurations, the Eucharist in its entirety [*tout entière*], as the rite of the new Law, is a "sacrament of remembrance"' (2006b: 59; 1949: 71). The sacrifice of the church and the memorial of the Lord's passion cannot be separated since they are, strictly speaking, one and the same reality. 'Everything happens at the altar "in the sacrament of his precious death"' (2006b: 60; 1949: 73). By reference to what he calls the 'scriptural sphere', de Lubac seeks to gain a sound understanding of certain terms in Eucharistic vocabulary. In this context, he provides an insight into the patristic origins of his concern for 'totality'. He notes that just as the reflection of the Fathers on the Eucharist cannot be separated from their reflection on the entire Christian economy, so their reflection on Scripture moves well beyond the limits of exegesis to include 'the totality of the work of God in the world' (2006b: 65; 1949: 78). De Lubac, in a note of concordance with defenders of the 'real presence', urges scholars to study the totality of texts relative to the Eucharist in the two Testaments:

> In the texts being alluded to, it is the entire 'Eucharistic complex', if I may use such a term—action and presence, sacrifice and sacrament, tangible sign and profound reality—which is being brought into juxtaposition either with Calvary—*the sacrament of the body which hung on the tree*—or with the Mosaic rites or the sacrifices of the patriarchal era. (2006b: 65–6; 1949: 79)

De Lubac's innovative contribution to Eucharistic ecclesiology has contributed to a fertile ecumenical collaboration between East and West. As John Zizioulas comments: 'The idea that the Eucharist makes the Church represents one of the most significant developments in the ecumenical dialogue of our time, particularly with regard to the theological *rapprochement* between the Western and the Eastern Churches' (McPartlan 2006: xiii).

In de Lubac's renewed vision of the church, psychology also plays an important role. Indeed, careful study of *Méditation sur l'Église* reveals a spirituality, and a corresponding psychology. A successful revitalization in ecclesiology depends directly on its reception in the Christian community (see Congar 1972; Alberigo, Jossua, and Komonchak 1987; Lennan 2008; Richard 1993; Clifford et al. 2011), thus pointing to the importance of psychology. The elements of de Lubac's proposed psychology are as follows. First, a strong emphasis on community, the apex of which is the unity of the human family centred on the Trinity. His insistence on a *Gemeinschaft* model of human well-being, formulated in precise Christological terms against the backdrop of a deeply fragmented world, provides a response to the isolationism that has come to characterize much of modern living. 'God did not make us "to remain within the limits of nature", or for the fulfilling of a solitary destiny; on the contrary, He made us to be brought together into the heart of the life of the Trinity. Christ offered Himself in sacrifice so that we might be one in that unity of the divine Persons' (1986: 174–5; 1954: 206).

Second, the realization of the 'mystery of communion in action' is essential for a renewed ecclesiology since without engagement with the world, the church risks being closeted in a kind of spiritual lacuna (1986: 177; 1954: 208). De Lubac's communion ecclesiology attempted to respond to a growing spiritual crisis in Europe at the dawn of an era of unparalleled darkness and brutality (see Arendt 2004). The reconstruction of the church and of society would necessitate a Christian/Catholic spirit, which is none other than the spirit of European civilization and French tradition, the main characteristics of which are enshrined in the following points: 'respect for the person, openness to a spiritual community, belief in God' (de Lubac 1941: 25). The crisis in European society and civilization showed de Lubac and other like-minded Catholic intellectuals that the answer to the longings of the human heart is to be found in a profound sense of communion capable of withstanding the threat to civilized society posed by aggressive totalitarianism. Consideration of the 'mystery of communion in action' places de Lubac in the vanguard of the Catholic social renaissance of the twentieth century, the genesis of which lies in the formulation of '*Gaudium et Spes*: the Pastoral Constitution on the Church in the Modern World' at the Second Vatican Council. Moreover, it is now widely accepted that *communio* provides 'a key for the renewal of Catholic ecclesiology' (Congregation for the Doctrine of the Faith 1992: 108).

The third element of de Lubac's psychology is the love of tradition (1986: 179; 1954: 210). De Lubac is careful to avoid any hankering after past antiquity and the myths of the Golden Age. While emphasizing the presence of Christ in the church to the end of time, he shows how Scripture, tradition, and the magisterium form a 'threefold channel' for the Christian 'by which the Word of God reaches him; and he will see that, far from damaging one another or imposing limitations on one another, these three things provide mutual support, establishing order among themselves, confirming, elucidating and exalting' (1986: 181; 1954: 212). In an important corollary, he argues that such uncompromising attachment to tradition cannot destroy 'friendliness' (*la puissance d'accueil*) and is incompatible with contempt or a lack of feeling (1986: 184; 1954: 216).

The closely interrelated elements of de Lubac's psychology are inextricably connected to his spirituality. The matter may be elucidated in this way. The first and most important element of the spirituality of ecclesiology outlined in *Méditation sur l'Église* is active membership of the church. Far from a nominal or passive participation in the Body of Christ, de Lubac has in mind a transformative and dynamic spiritual vision for unity and justice. Members of the church will therefore 'be responsive to what affects other members . . . Anything that bears hard upon the body as a whole, or paralyses it, or damages it, affects him too, and he can no more be indifferent to it than he can be amused by it' (1986: 188; 1954: 220). The consequence of such affective engagement with the Christian community is the perception of the church as a spiritual mother whereby the Christian 'will have fallen in love with the beauty of the House of God; the Church will have stolen his heart. She is his spiritual native country, his "mother and his brethren" ' (1986: 178; 1954: 209, also 1982: 62). The realization of this element of de Lubac's proposed spirituality contributes to the active witness of Christians in the world, and ultimately to the strengthening of the bonds of unity and friendship between peoples. De Lubac's articulation of the spiritual motherhood of the church is, however, not without difficulty since it includes the normally controversial assertion that the Catholic Church is the 'mother and mistress of all the Churches', with its concomitant diminution of the ecumenical potential of his spirituality.

Second, service of the community is paramount. Christians must be 'wholly at the service of the great community, sharing its happiness and its trials, and taking part in its battles' (1986: 183; 1954: 214). Such service must be devoid of 'fanaticism', avoid the pull of the world, and be possessed of an instinct for the detection and avoidance of spiritual dangers. Acceptance of the noble calling of service to the Christian community also necessitates firm adherence to truth, the preservation of unity in the body of Christ, and the avoidance of 'any kind of doctrinal liberalism' (1986: 184; 1954: 216). Third, preoccupation with authenticity and 'poverty of spirit' constitutes an essential element in de Lubac's ecclesial spirituality. In the post-modern world, trust is perhaps the most damaged virtue; its rehabilitation requires a renewed engagement with gospel poverty. De Lubac's appeal to evangelical poverty provides perhaps the best antidote to the abuse of power and authority wherever it is allowed to thrive in the church. Although de Lubac sometimes depicts the church in idyllic terms (1986: 207; 1954: 239), it must be acknowledged that he recognizes, however obliquely, a place for healthy auto-critique in the church (1986: 215; 1954: 248).

CONCLUSION

This chapter has attempted to delineate the key elements of de Lubac's ecclesiology. It has focused primarily on his articulation of the organic relationship between the

Eucharist, the church, and the world. The analysis of the place of the Eucharist in his worldview points to an urgent concern to articulate a spiritual vision for civilization, one that is capable of withstanding the brutality of totalitarianism in its myriad forms, past and present. By outlining the ambiguous and paradoxical nature of the church, de Lubac showed that it is at once of God and of the world, visible and invisible, temporal and eschatological (Schnackers 1979: 160–9). The bridge between the various polarities is provided by the sacramental economy. De Lubac's emphasis on eschatology helps to distinguish between the church's temporal and eternal aspects and, by pointing to the transience of ecclesial structures, assists in deciphering the path of true reform. In the final analysis, by attempting to protect the integral faith in its totality, de Lubac advocated submission 'to the total mystery: that is the only logical attitude of faith' (2002: 122; 1994: 151).

REFERENCES

Alberigo, A., Jossua, Jean-Pierre, and Komonchak, Joseph A. (eds) (1987). *The Reception of Vatican II*. Tunbridge Wells: Burns & Oates.

Arendt, H. (2004). *The Origins of Totalitarianism*. 9th edn. New York: Schocken Books.

Aubert, R. (1954). *La Théologie Catholique au milieu du XXᵉ siècle*. Tournai: Casterman.

Boersma, H. (2009). *Nouvelle Théologie and Sacramental Ontology: A Return to Mystery*. Oxford: Oxford University Press.

Chantraine, G. (2007). *Henri de Lubac: De la naissance à la démobilisation (1896–1919)*, vol. 1, *Études lubaciennes*, vi. Paris: Cerf.

Chantraine, G. (2008). '*Catholicism*: On "Certain Ideas"'. *Communio* 35: 520–34.

Chantraine, G. (2009). *Henri de Lubac: les années de formation (1919–1929)*, vol. 2, *Études lubaciennes*, vii. Paris: Cerf.

Cholvy, B. (2011). 'Une controverse majeure: Henri de Lubac et le surnaturel'. *Gregorianum* 92: 797–827.

Clifford, C. E., et al. (2011). *Vatican II: expériences canadiennes/Canadian Experiences*. Ottawa: University of Ottawa Press.

Coffele, G. (1996). 'De Lubac and the Theological Foundation of the Missions'. Trans. Adrian Walker. *Communio* 23: 757–75.

Congar, Y. (1972). 'Reception as an Ecclesiological Reality'. Trans. John Griffiths. *Concilium* 8: 43–68.

Congregation for the Doctrine of the Faith (1992). 'Some Aspects of the Church Understood as Communion'. *Origins* 22: 108–12.

Conway, M. A. (2012). 'Maurice Blondel and *Ressourcement*'. In Gabriel Flynn and Paul D. Murray (eds), *Ressourcement: A Movement for Renewal in Twentieth Century Catholic Theology*. Oxford: Oxford University Press, 65–82.

De Lubac, H. (1938). *Catholicisme: les aspects sociaux du dogme*. 4th edn. Unam Sanctam, 3. Paris: Cerf.

De Lubac, H. (1941). *Vocation de la France*, Coll. Le Témoignage chrétien. Le Puy: Mappus.

De Lubac, H. (1944). *Corpus mysticum: l'Eucharistie et l'Église au moyen âge, Étude historique*. Théologie, 3. Paris: Aubier.

De Lubac, H. (1945). *Le Drame de l'humanisme athée*. 3rd edn. Paris: Éditions Spes.

De Lubac, H. (1946a). *Surnaturel: études historiques*. Théologie, 8. Paris: Aubier.

De Lubac, H. (1946b). *Le Fondement théologique des missions*. Paris: Seuil.

De Lubac, H. (1949). *Corpus Mysticum: L'Eucharistie et L'Église au Moyen Âge, étude historique*. 2nd edn. Théologie, 3. Paris: Aubier.

De Lubac, H. (1954). *Méditation sur l'Église*. 3rd edn. Théologie, 27. Paris: Aubier.

De Lubac, H. (1967). *Paradoxe et mystère de l'Église*. Paris: Aubier.

De Lubac, H. (1969). *The Church: Paradox and Mystery*. Trans. James R. Dunne. Shannon: Ecclesia Press: ET of de Lubac (1967).

De Lubac, H. (1982). *The Motherhood of the Church Followed by Particular Churches in the Universal Church and an Interview Conducted by Gwendoline Jarczyk*. Trans. Sergia Englund. San Francisco: Ignatius Press.

De Lubac, H. (1986). *The Splendour of the Church*, 3rd edn. London: Sheed and Ward; ET of de Lubac (1954).

De Lubac, H. (1988). *Catholicism: Christ and the Common Destiny of Man*. Trans. Lancelot C. Sheppard and Elizabeth Englund. San Francisco: Ignatius; ET of de Lubac (2010).

De Lubac, H. (1990). *Théologie dans l'histoire. I. La Lumière du Christ; II. Questiones disputées et résistance au nazisme*. Paris: Desclée de Brouwer.

De Lubac, H. (1992). 'La Question des évêques sous l'occupation', *Revue des Deux Mondes* (février): 67–82. De Lubac Papers, Jesuit Archives, Vanves, Paris, Dossier 5, 'Résistance spirituelle au nazisme, 1940–1945'.

De Lubac, H. (1993). *At the Service of the Church: Henri de Lubac Reflects on the Circumstances that Occasioned his Writings*. Trans. Anne Elizabeth Englund. San Francisco: Ignatius Press; ET of de Lubac (2006a).

De Lubac, H. (1994). *Autres paradoxes*. Namur: Culture et vérité.

De Lubac, H. (1996). *Theology in History*. Trans. Anne Englund Nash. San Francisco: Ignatius Press; ET of de Lubac (1990).

De Lubac, H. (1998a). *The Mystery of the Supernatural*. Trans. Rosemary Sheed. New York: Crossroad Publishing; ET of de Lubac (2009).

De Lubac, H. (1998b). *The Drama of Atheist Humanism*. Trans. Edith M. Riley, Anne Englund Nash, and Mark Sebanc. 2nd edn. San Francisco: Ignatius Press; ET of de Lubac (1945).

De Lubac, H. (2002). *More Paradoxes*. Trans. Anne Englund Nash. San Francisco: Ignatius Press; ET of de Lubac (1994).

De Lubac, H. (2006a). *Mémoire sur l'occasion de mes écrits*. Ed. Georges Chantraine. Œuvres complètes, xxxiii, Paris: Cerf.

De Lubac, H. (2006b). *Corpus Mysticum: The Eucharist and the Church in the Middle Ages*. Ed. Laurence Paul Hemming and Susan Frank Parsons. Trans. Gemma Simmonds, CJ with Richard Price and Christopher Stephens. London: SCM; ET of de Lubac (1949).

De Lubac, H. (2007a/1985). *Entretien autour de Vatican II: Souvenirs et Réflexions*, Théologies. 2nd edn. Paris: France Catholique/Cerf.

De Lubac, H. (2007b). *Carnets du Concile*. Ed. Loïc Figoureux. 2 vols. Paris: Cerf.

De Lubac, H. (2008). 'The Total Meaning of Man and the World'. Trans. D. C. Schindler. *Communio* 35: 613–41.

De Lubac, H. (2009). *Le Mystère du surnaturel*. Œuvres complètes, xii. Paris: Cerf.

De Lubac, H. (2010). *Catholicisme: les aspects sociaux du dogme*. Œuvres completes, vii. Paris: Cerf.

De Lubac, H. (n.d.). 'The Spiritual Testament of Fr H. de Lubac: In the Name of the Father, and of the Son, and of the Holy Spirit'. De Lubac Papers, Jesuit Archives, Vanves, Paris, Dossier 1.

Doyle, D. M. (2000). *Communion Ecclesiology: Vision and Versions*. Maryknoll, NY: Orbis Books.

Dulles, A. (28 September 1991). 'Henri de Lubac: In Appreciation'. *America* 165: 180–2.

Dupuis, J. (2001). *Toward a Christian Theology of Religious Pluralism*. 3rd edn. Maryknoll and New York: Orbis Books.

Fédou, M. (2011). 'Sources Chrétiennes: Patristique et renaissance de la théologie'. *Gregorianum* 92: 781–96.

Flynn, G. (2004). *Yves Congar's Vision of the Church in a World of Unbelief*. Aldershot and Burlington, VT: Ashgate.

Flynn, G. (2011). 'A Renaissance in Twentieth-Century Catholic Theology'. *Irish Theological Quarterly* 76: 323–38.

Fouilloux, E. (1995). *La Collection 'Sources chrétiennes': éditer les Pères de l'Église au XXᵉ siècle*. Paris: Cerf.

Garrigou-Legrance, R. (1946). 'La Nouvelle Théologie où va-t-elle'. *Angelicum* 23: 126–45.

Guelluy, R. (1986). 'Les Antécédents de l'encyclique "Humani Generis" dans les sanctions Romaines de 1942: Chenu, Charlier, Draguet'. *Revue d'histoire ecclésiastique* 81: 421–97.

Guillet, J. (1992). 'P. Henri de LUBAC 1896–1991'. *Compagnie: Courrier de la Province de France* 257: 69–73.

Kerr, F. (2002). *After Aquinas: Versions of Thomism*. Oxford: Blackwell.

Kerr, F. (2007) *Twentieth-Century Catholic Theologians: From Neoscholasticism to Nuptial Mysticism*. Oxford: Blackwell.

Komonchak, J. A. (1990). 'Theology and Culture at Mid-century: The Example of Henri de Lubac'. *Theological Studies* 51: 579–602.

Labourdette, M.-M. (1946a). 'La Théologie et ses sources'. *Revue Thomiste* 46: 353–71.

Labourdette, M.-M. (1946b). 'La Théologie, intelligence de la foi'. *Revue Thomiste* 46: 5–44.

Le, L. T. (2006). 'The Eucharist and the Church in the Thought of Henri de Lubac', *Irish Theological Quarterly* 71: 338–47.

Lennan, R. (2008). 'Roman Catholic Ecclesiology'. In Gerard Mannion and Lewis Mudge (eds), *The Routledge Companion to the Christian Church*. Oxford: Routledge, 234–50.

McDermott, J. M. (1997). 'De Lubac and Rousselot'. *Gregorianum* 78: 735–59.

McPartlan, P. (1996). 'The Eucharist, the Church and Evangelization: The Influence of Henri de Lubac'. *Communio* 23: 776–85.

McPartlan, P. (2006). *The Eucharist Makes the Church: Henri de Lubac and John Zizioulas in Dialogue*. 2nd edn. Fairfax, VA: Eastern Christian Publications.

Mayeur, J. M. (1966). *La Séparation de l'Église et de l'Etat*. Paris: Julliard.

Milbank, J. (2005). *The Suspended Middle: Henri de Lubac and the Debate concerning the Supernatural*. London: SCM.

Moloney, R. (2005). 'Henri de Lubac on Church and Eucharist'. *Irish Theological Quarterly* 70: 331–42.

Neufeld, K. H. (1988). 'In the Service of the Council: Bishops and Theologians at the Second Vatican Council'. In René Latourelle (ed.), *Vatican II: Assessment and Perspectives Twenty-Five Years After (1962–1987)*, 3 vols, vol. 1. New York: Paulist Press, 74–105.

Nichols, A. (2012). 'Henri de Lubac: Panorama and Proposal'. *New Blackfriars* 93: 3–33.

O'Sullivan, N. (2009). *Christ and Creation: Christology as the key to Interpreting the Theology of Creation in the Works of Henri de Lubac*. Religions and Discourse, 40. Oxford: Lang.

Pelchat, M. (1988). *L'Église mystère de communion: L'ecclésiologie dans l'œuvre de Henri de Lubac*. Montreal: Éditions Paulines.

Pius XII (1950). *Humani Generis*. Encyclical Letter concerning some False Opinions Threatening to Undermine the Foundations of Catholic Doctrine, *AAS* 42: 561–78; ET

(1959). *False Trends in Modern Teaching: Encyclical Letter (Humani Generis)*. Trans. Ronald A. Knox. Rev. edn. London: Catholic Truth Society.

Ratzinger, J. (1987). *Principles of Catholic Theology: Building Stones for a Fundamental Theology*. Trans. Mary Frances McCarthy. San Francisco: Ignatius.

Ravitch, N. (1990). *The Catholic Church and the French Nation 1589–1989*. London: Routledge.

Richard, L. (1993). 'Reflections on Dissent and Reception'. In P. M. Hegy (ed.), *The Church in the Nineties: Its Legacy, its Future*. Collegeville, MN: Liturgical Press, 6–14.

Russo, A. (1990). *Henri de Lubac: teologia e dogma nella storia. L'influsso di Blondel*. La Cultura 40. Rome: Edizioni Studium.

Schnackers, H. (1979). *Die Kirche als Sakrament und Mutter: Zur Ekklesiologie von Henri de Lubac*. Regensburg: Studien zur Theologie.

Tilliette, X. (1992). 'Henri de Lubac: The Legacy of a Theologian'. Trans. Mark Sebanc. *Communio* 19: 332–41.

Voderholzer, R. (2008). *Meet Henri de Lubac*. Trans. Michael J. Miller. San Francisco: Ignatius Press.

von Balthasar, H. U. (1991). *The Theology of Henri de Lubac: An Overview*. Trans. Joseph Fessio and Michael M. Waldstein. San Francisco: Ignatius Press.

Wagner, J.-P. (1997). *La Théologie fondamentale selon Henri de Lubac*. Cogitatio Fidei, 199. Paris: Cerf.

Wagner, J.-P. (2007). *Henri de Lubac*, Initiations aux théologiens. Paris: Cerf.

Walsh, C. J. (1992). 'De Lubac's Critique of the Postconciliar Church'. *Communio* 19: 404–32.

Wang, L. (2003). '*Sacramentum Unitatis Ecclesiasticae*: The Eucharistic Ecclesiology of Henri de Lubac'. *Anglican Theological Review* 85: 143–58.

SUGGESTED READING

De Lubac, H. (1946). *Surnaturel: études historiques*. Théologie, 8. Paris: Aubier.

De Lubac, H. (1969). *The Church: Paradox and Mystery*. Trans. James R. Dunne. Shannon: Ecclesia Press; ET of de Lubac (1967). *Paradoxe et mystère de l'Église*. Paris: Aubier.

De Lubac, H. (1986). *The Splendour of the Church*, 3rd edn. London: Sheed and Ward; ET of de Lubac. *Méditation sur l'Église*. 3rd edn. Théologie, 27. Paris: Aubier.

De Lubac, H. (1988). *Catholicism: Christ and the Common Destiny of Man*. Trans. Lancelot C. Sheppard and Elizabeth Englund. San Francisco: Ignatius; ET of de Lubac (2010). *Catholicisme: les aspects sociaux du dogme. OEuvres completes*, vii. Paris: Cerf.

De Lubac, H. (1993). *At the Service of the Church: Henri de Lubac Reflects on the Circumstances that Occasioned his Writings*. Trans. Anne Elizabeth Englund. San Francisco: Ignatius Press; ET of de Lubac, (2006). *Mémoire sur l'occasion de mes écrits*. Ed. Georges Chantraine. *OEuvres complètes*, xxxiii, Paris: Cerf.

De Lubac, H. (1998). *The Drama of Atheist Humanism*. Trans. Edith M. Riley, Anne Englund Nash, and Mark Sebanc. 2nd edn. San Francisco: Ignatius Press; ET of de Lubac (1945). *Le Drame de l'humanisme athée*. 3rd edn. Paris: Éditions Spes.

De Lubac, H. (2006). *Corpus Mysticum: The Eucharist and the Church in the Middle Ages*. Ed. Laurence Paul Hemming and Susan Frank Parsons. Trans. Gemma Simmonds, CJ with Richard Price and Christopher Stephens. London: SCM; ET of de Lubac (1949). *Corpus Mysticum: L'Eucharistie et L'Église au Moyen Âge, étude historique*. 2nd edn. Théologie, 3. Paris: Aubier.

De Lubac, H. (2007). *Carnets du Concile*. Ed. Loïc Figoureux. 2 vols. Paris: Cerf.

CHAPTER 19

KARL RAHNER

RICHARD LENNAN

The theology of Karl Rahner (1904–84) is a sustained engagement with the working of grace in history. Rahner was prolific as a writer and editor—his *Sämtliche Werke* fill more than thirty imposing volumes, while the English translation (*Theological Investigations* (*TI*)) of his best-known collection of essays, *Schriften zur Theologie*, runs to twenty-three volumes. The quantity of his publications may suggest that Rahner aspired to produce either a comprehensive synthesis of theology or an exhaustive study of selected topics. In fact, his purpose, which was twofold, was both broader and less obviously academic than either of those options: Rahner sought to articulate how God comes to meet us in the world of the everyday, and to promote engagement with that God. At the heart of Rahner's theology, therefore, was an exploration of grace in the life of the human person, understood not only as an individual, but as a being in communion with others and as part of history.

Rahner's project determined the preferred instrument for his work: the essay, rather than the book. Through essays that ranged over a dazzlingly broad array of topics— from laughter and genetics to the future of Europe, from poetry and old age to nuclear weapons, as well as the full spectrum of more obviously 'theological' themes—Rahner highlighted the graced dimension of human life. As a corollary, he also argued for the inextricable link between our response to God and the fulfilment of our deepest human identity, an identity inseparable from our relationships with one another and our presence in history.

Not surprisingly, then, grace is at the heart of Rahner's ecclesiology. Indeed, the church in Rahner's theology is the product of grace, the unique outcome of God's self-revelation in Jesus Christ through the Holy Spirit. Rahner's approach to every aspect of the church, to its doctrine, structure, and needed reforms, including what might enable the church to relate most fruitfully to the wider world, has its grounding in his understanding of grace. The relationship of the church to grace also accounts for Rahner's insistence that the church must engage with the challenges of history or risk a refusal to enter more deeply into relationship with God. To establish why this is so, and to prepare the way for detailing particular aspects of his ecclesiology, the first task of this chapter is to introduce the central features of Rahner's theology.

Mystery and
the Self-Communicating God

Reaction against both liberal democracy and Liberal Protestantism was a feature of the Roman Catholic Church in which Rahner grew up. The definition of papal infallibility at the First Vatican Council (1869–70), as well as the pope's disengagement from the newly united Italian state after 1870, amplified the suspicion of 'modernity' that had resounded through Pope Pius IX's *Syllabus of Errors* (1864). Reaction against liberal trends in theology produced both Pope Leo XIII's re-assertion of Thomism as essential for Roman Catholic theology (1893) and, more dramatically, Pope Pius X's rejection of Modernism (1907); it also buttressed the dominance of neo-scholasticism, which continued until the Second Vatican Council (1962–5). Taken together, the two forms of reaction resulted in a narrowing of the church's horizons, a turning away from an increasingly complex world.

In his critique of neo-scholasticism Rahner rejected its pursuit of a 'timeless' theology, one divorced from contemporary questions. As an alternative, Rahner sought a more creative approach, one that he believed did greater justice both to God and God's involvement with human history. Thus, Rahner insisted that theology was 'an endeavour of the spirit and a science which has to be of service to its own time, just as it has, or should have grown out of its own time' (*TI*, i. 2).

In addition, Rahner objected to neo-scholasticism's tendency to construe faith as 'a highly complicated system of orderly statements': for Rahner, Christian faith was 'a mysteriously simple thing of infinite fullness' (*TI*, iv. 37). For this reason, he rejected the reference of neo-scholastic theologies to 'the mysteries of faith', which such theologies presented as both multiple and 'provisional', as something that human beings were powerless to overcome in this life, but which would evaporate in light of the beatific vision, when we would come into all knowledge and understanding (*TI*, iv. 40). Rahner argued that human beings did not encounter 'mysteries', pieces of information that left us as much puzzled as enriched, but 'mystery', the reality of God. This mystery was 'primordial', ineradicable, as God would always be beyond the mastery of human beings (*TI*, iv. 40). Indeed, Rahner claimed that human beings would continue to experience God's mystery, God's incomprehensibility, even in the beatific vision, where that mystery would be 'the very object of our blissful love' (*TI*, iv. 41).

Rahner's contention was that the emphasis on 'mysteries', which had prevailed in Roman Catholic thought since the Council of Trent (1545–63) and which Vatican I had reinforced, represented an impoverished theology of revelation, one that failed to do justice to either God or the relationship between God and creation, especially humanity. In its place, Rahner advanced a starkly simple understanding of revelation: God revealed God. Revelation, then, was God's self-communication, God's self-offering. To account for this claim, Rahner described revelation in terms of God's 'quasi-formal' causality, which meant both that God was the source of all that existed and, consequently, that all existence could be a source of encounter with God—Rahner added 'quasi' to the standard vocabulary of 'formal causality' in order to highlight that he was speaking analogously, that he was preserving a distinction between God's action and other examples of formal causality (*TI*, i. 326–31). Since revelation established God as the end or fulfilment of all that existed, it was an 'uncreated grace', the very presence of God to humanity, rather than the product of efficient causality, which would have suggested that God was an artisan, bringing about something with no necessary relationship to God (*TI*, i. 330–4).

Rahner's theology of mystery, which he forged by synthesizing his patristic studies, his formation in the spiritual theology of Ignatius of Loyola, his reading of Thomas Aquinas, as well as the philosophy of Martin Heidegger (1889–1976), and his reception of the philosophical-theological method of his fellow Jesuit Joseph Maréchal (1878–1944), was a formative factor in the rethinking of the theology of revelation in the Roman Catholic tradition, which issued ultimately in Vatican II's *Dei Verbum* (1965). Rahner's approach helped to shift the emphasis from revelation as the communication of 'propositions' about God, to revelation as 'an historical dialogue between God and humanity in which something *happens* and in which the communication is related to the continuous "happening" and enterprise of God' (*TI*, i. 48; original emphasis).

While Rahner stressed that this 'happening', God's self-communication, was entirely God's initiative, he also developed a theological anthropology to illustrate how it was possible for human beings to receive God. Rahner's theology of revelation and his theological anthropology—which are linked with his theology of symbol, another of his foundational themes—are essential to his Christology and ecclesiology. Indeed, it is reasonable to argue that the key to understanding Rahner is to see him working both backwards and forwards from God's self-revelation in Christ. In other words, Rahner's theology, with its grounding in the incarnation, asks two questions: If God in Jesus Christ could become one like us, what does that say about humanity? If the saving love of God revealed in the life, death, and resurrection of Jesus Christ is permanent, victorious, and irreversible, how do human beings encounter that love in history? Rahner's theological anthropology, with grace at its centre, answered the first question; his ecclesiology answered the second. Since the two answers, like the two questions, are interconnected, a clear understanding of Rahner's ecclesiology requires that we locate his theology of 'the Church' in relation to his anthropology and Christology.

Graced Humanity
and Revelation in Christ

The key challenge for any theological anthropology is to articulate its understanding of the human person in a way that also clarifies humanity's relation to God. This must be done, however, without diminishing the sovereignty and freedom of God, but also without making humanity either independent of God or less than fully human, that is, less than free. Rahner's response to that challenge, a response developed primarily in his writings from the 1930s through to the 1950s, was to portray the human person as defined by the orientation to God, which was itself a gift of God's love: 'the capacity for the God of self-bestowing personal Love is the central and abiding existential of man as he really is' (*TI*, i. 312).

This approach enabled Rahner to characterize the relationship with God as constitutive of the human person and human freedom—it was what he named as humanity's 'supernatural existential' (*TI*, i. 312–16). Accordingly, the human person was 'a reality opened upwards' (*TI*, i. 183), one whose 'obediential potential' to be a 'hearer of the word' only God could satisfy. The fulfilment of human freedom, therefore, could not occur outside of the relationship to God: 'As human we are the beings who, as finite spirits who inquire and must inquire about being, stand before the free God, affirm our freedom in the way we raise questions of being, and must therefore take this divine freedom into account' (Rahner 1994: 76). In addition, human freedom was not an abstraction, but something realized in history: 'Spatiotemporality is our inner makeup, and properly belongs to us as human. Because matter is one of our essential components, we ourselves construct space and time as intrinsic components of our existence' (Rahner 1994: 112).

Since Rahner's construction of humanity as radically orientated to God identified God as the source of that relationship, God's freedom remained undiminished. Nonetheless, Rahner was at pains to emphasize that the divine freedom was most evident in God choosing to communicate Godself: 'God wishes to communicate himself, to pour forth the love which he himself is . . . And so God makes a creature whom he can love: he creates man. He creates him in such a way that he *can* receive this Love which is God himself, and that he can and must at the same time accept it for what it is: the ever astounding wonder, the unexpected, unexacted gift' (*TI*, i. 310; original emphasis).

Rahner's account of both God's desire to communicate divine love and humanity's God-given capacity to receive that love provided him with crucial building-blocks for both his Christology and ecclesiology. The capstone, however, was his theology of the symbol, the early seeds of which were present in his writings from the 1930s, although it did not receive its full articulation until the late 1950s.

Rahner distinguished sharply between 'sign' and 'symbol': with the former, one thing simply pointed to another; with the latter, one reality actually made the other present, such that what was symbolized was known only through the symbol (*TI*, iv. 225). Consequently, an authentic symbol, which Rahner referred to as a *Realsymbol*, existed in a 'differentiated unity' with what it symbolized (*TI*, iv. 234). For Rahner, God's self-communication was symbolic; the paradigm of that self-communication was the revelation of God in Jesus Christ.

As noted, the whole of Rahner's theology of revelation revolves around God's self-communication in Jesus Christ. Accordingly, the incarnation was not simply another instance, albeit the most significant one, of God's self-revelation, but was the key that unlocked the dynamics of God's self-communication, thereby enabling recognition of God's loving presence in the 'everyday':

[T]he incarnate word is the absolute symbol of God in the world . . . He is not merely the presence and revelation of what God is in himself. He is also the expressive presence of what—or rather, who—God wished to be, in free grace, to the world, in such a way that this divine attitude, once so expressed, can never be reversed, but is and remains final and unsurpassable. (*TI*, iv. 237)

In being the 'absolute' symbol of God, Jesus was also the fullness of humanity, the realization of humanity's highest possibility: 'The humanity is the self-disclosure of the Logos itself, so that when God, expressing himself, exteriorises himself, that very thing appears which we call the humanity of the Logos' (*TI*, iv. 239). In Jesus, the love and mercy of God became definitively present in human history. Through the death and resurrection of Jesus, the mercy of God for humanity achieved its definitive expression, which includes being both irreversible and indomitable. Since that mercy had a historical form in Jesus Christ, since it was other than a disembodied 'spiritual' reality, and also proffered an alternative to a vision of humanity as isolated individuals, its definitive and irreversible nature called out for an ongoing expression in history. Here, we have the immediate context for Rahner's theology of the church.

THE CHURCH AS SACRAMENT

Rahner approached the church as a genuinely *theological* reality, as an irreducible element of God's self-communication in Jesus Christ, and so as a means of encounter with the saving mystery of God. This does not mean, as this chapter will amplify, that he treated the church as an ahistorical reality, ignored the limitations of the church's structures, or was passive in the face of the flaws of those who presided over those structures. It does mean, however, that Rahner insisted on the need for the historical mediation of God's presence that the church represented: 'God has not left it to the free choice of human beings to decide for themselves in what concrete form and historically verifiable reality they wish to find Christ's salvation and the grace of God' (*TI*, ii. 34). Just as Rahner had relied on the theology of the symbol to articulate his Christology, he drew on that same focus for his ecclesiology:

Christ is the primal sacramental word of God, uttered in the one history of mankind, in which God made known his irrevocable mercy . . . and did this by effecting it in Christ and effected it by making it known. The Church, is the continuance, the contemporary presence of that real, eschatologically triumphant and irrevocably established presence in the world, in Christ, of God's salvific will. The Church is the abiding presence of that primal sacramental word of definitive grace, which Christ is in the world, effecting what is uttered by uttering it in sign. (Rahner 1974: 18)

In locating the church under the caption of God's symbolic self-revelation, Rahner made three significant contributions to Roman Catholic ecclesiology, each of which will be developed further herein. First, by highlighting the connection between the church and grace, the gift of the Holy Spirit, Rahner helped to broaden the Roman Catholic view of the church beyond a narrow emphasis on the 'founding' of the church in particular historical acts of Jesus. Rahner thus developed the Trinitarian dimension of ecclesiology, no less than its eschatological orientation. Secondly, by underscoring the indispensable nature of the church's 'inner' reality, the presence of the Holy Spirit expressed through the church's 'outer' reality, Rahner contributed to the liberation of Roman Catholic ecclesiology from the dominance of an all-but exclusive emphasis on the church's juridical forms, which was a corollary of the focus on Christ as 'founder' of the church and its structures. Thirdly, by identifying the church as the *Grundsakrament*, he added noteworthy depth and breadth to the Roman Catholic understanding of the ecclesial sacraments as something radically other than discrete interventions by God into human events. Each of those contributions was important to the work of the Second Vatican Council, as well as having positive implications for relations between the Roman Catholic Church and other Christian churches.

From the 1930s onwards, Rahner maintained a consistent emphasis on the sacramental identity of the church. At the heart of that portrayal was his understanding of God's self-communication in grace as the source of the church's being: 'God's holy people of the redeemed takes on the form of the Body of Christ and of the Church, which is the combined product of the interior mutual union of the redeemed by grace and of the historical, visible form of this transcendent interior union' (*TI*, ii. 122). As the work both of the Holy Spirit and humanity's 'free voluntary decision and historical action' (*TI*, ii. 123), the church's existence was inseparable from history and the dynamics of being human. For that reason, there was always room for the community of the church to grow in its relationship to the God at the heart of its life, to realize more deeply what God enabled it to be.

As sacrament, as the product of God's initiative, the church's fulfilment was also to be the product of God's action, rather than merely human achievement. Consistent with this emphasis, Rahner's focus on the church's eschatological orientation expressed his confidence that grace would have the last word in the history of the church, despite contrary indications at any given moment of that history: 'The Church is always in history, always in a one-way history, in which it never loses its legitimate past, and in this unpredictable, dark history of suffering, the Church always comes from Jesus Christ, crucified and risen' (*TI*, xix. 37).

Significantly, Rahner stressed that the church's existence as sacrament, as the 'historically and socially constituted assembly of those who have the courage to believe', did not constitute it as the equal of God (*TI*, v. 345). Nor did the church's sacramentality mean that it existed as the sole oasis of the Spirit in an otherwise godless world. Rather, the church, as the community of explicit faith, was one half of 'a relationship between a hidden reality on the one hand, which is still trying to express itself to the full in history, and on the other hand the full historical manifestation of this' (*TI*, xiv. 180)—this emphasis was foundational for one of the best-known, albeit controversial, aspects of Rahner's work: his theology of the 'anonymous Christian', through which Rahner sought to explain for his fellow Christians how every instance of self-sacrificing love in the world, including those exhibited by people of many faiths and none, could be understood as a response to the universal presence and invitation of the grace of Jesus Christ. As the 'medium' of the Spirit's grace, however, the church not only provided the social context for faith, it also passed on the message of Christ that is the doorway to the mystery of God. As a result, the church had a unique role in linking every age to God's self-communication in Jesus Christ: 'I heard about him only through the Church and not otherwise . . . Attachment to the Church is the price I pay for this historical origin' (*TI*, xx. 9).

Rahner acknowledged that the identification of the church as 'the enduring and abiding medium of faith' (*TI*, vii. 110) posed a challenge to individual believers. Indeed, he recognized that the individual was both humbled and liberated by believing with the church: humbled because the ecclesial community was a constant reminder that none of us alone could achieve the fullness of faith, but also liberated as within the community of faith each individual gained access to the full reality of what the church believes, which was always more than the faith of the individual (*TI*, v. 347). The fact that the church transcended the limits of any individual, that it had a communal profession of faith which was not at the disposal of any individual or groups of members, was for Rahner an indicator of the church's irreplaceable role in God's self-communication: 'Christianity is the religion of a demanding God who summons my subjectivity out of itself only if it confronts me in a Church which is authoritative . . .. a Church which confronts me in a mission, a mandate and a proclamation which really make the reality of salvation present for me' (Rahner 1978: 344).

As noted, the second significant contribution that Rahner's sacramental approach made to Roman Catholic ecclesiology was that it helped to free that ecclesiology from a narrow focus on the church's juridical structures. While sacramental ecclesiology could not validly ignore the church's external reality, or divorce it from any role for the Holy Spirit, it did check the danger of reducing consideration of God's presence in the church to an exclusive focus on the church's structures and their historical foundation. It did so by underscoring that 'the grace of salvation, the Holy Spirit himself, is of [the church's] essence' (*TI*, iv. 241). Indeed, in a lengthy article written in 1947 as an engagement with *Mystici Corporis Christi* (1943), the encyclical of Pope Pius XII, Rahner warned that 'ecclesiological Nestorianism' would be the primary outcome if concern with the church's juridical apparatus dominated all discussion about the church (*TI*, ii. 70). Even earlier, in 1942, Rahner had argued that ' "Church" is then, *before* being the visible social organisation—even though this is its necessary expression—the social accessibility of the historico-sacramental permanent presence of the salvation reality of Christ' (*TI*, iii. 248; original emphasis).

The third major implication of Rahner's sacramental ecclesiology was that it brought into relief the ecclesial grounding of the church's sacraments. Thus, he argued that the church's constitution in grace established it as 'truly the fundamental sacrament, the well-spring of the sacraments in the strict sense' (Rahner 1974: 18). Rahner rejected any notion that the ecclesial sacraments were discrete events of grace, unconnected to anything other than themselves. Rather, his portrayal stressed that every liturgical encounter with Christ derived from the existence of the church as the primary sacrament—*Grundsakrament*—in relation to the ecclesial sacraments: 'Christ is present in the Church through his *pneuma*. *His* presence actually is *pneuma hagion*. But precisely as such this presence of the Spirit in the Church is the "medium" which is the necessary prior condition for that further presence which is achieved precisely between Christ and the Church in the enactment of the *cult*' (*TI*, x. 74; original emphasis). The ecclesial sacraments, then, 'constitute the highest stages in the word of grace in the Church in its character as exhibitive and as event' (*TI*, xiv. 144). The richest understanding of the sacraments, then, recognized that they were 'the eschatologically efficacious word of God, as the absolute self-realization of the Church, according to its essence as the primary sacrament' (*TI*, iv. 274).

THE QUEST FOR A HOLY CHURCH

Given Rahner's emphasis on the link between God's self-communication and the identity of the church, his focus on the church's Trinitarian foundation and eschatological orientation, and his overarching insistence on the sacramental nature of the church, it might appear that Rahner would have championed a 'high' ecclesiology, one more likely to associate the church with the glory of God, rather than with the church as 'the seed and the beginning' of God's kingdom, which was Vatican II's summation of the church's 'pilgrim' status (*Lumen Gentium*, art. 5). Such, however, was not the case. Indeed, Rahner was an unfailing advocate of the need for a spirit of self-criticism in the church. His goal in so arguing was to ensure that every manifestation of the church made present the Spirit at the heart of the church.

This self-critical attitude was not the denial of the church's sacramentality, but rather the application of it: since the Spirit was at the heart of the church, there was always room for the church to become more authentically what it professed to be. As sacrament, the church, unlike Christ, was not divine, but rather 'the proclaiming bearer of the revealing word of God as God's utterance of salvation, and *at the same time*, she is the subject, harkening and believing, to whom the word of salvation of God in Christ is addressed' (*TI*, xiv. 143; original emphasis). Every dimension of the church, therefore, needed to be open to the conversion that life in Christ invited.

Far from idealizing the church, Rahner was one of the few Roman Catholic theologians in the decades before Vatican II to discuss the impact of sin on the church. This discussion too drew out an implication of the church's sacramentality: since the church expressed in a unique way the presence of Christ in history, the church was also uniquely capable of distorting that presence, of wrapping 'a shroud' around Christ (*TI*, vi. 262). While it was usual to distinguish the holy church from its sinful members, Rahner rejected that distinction, refusing to accept that 'the Church' could exist independently of those who composed it. Consequently, it followed for Rahner that the church itself was sinful (*TI*, vi. 259).

After the Second Vatican Council referred to the church as *sancta simul et semper purificanda* (*Lumen Gentium*, art. 8), Rahner revisited the relationship between the church and sin. He appreciated not only the council's willingness to address the topic, especially since it was the first time that it had found a place in the official teaching of the Roman Catholic Church, but also the document's focus on the pilgrim nature of the church. On the other hand, he also judged the council to have been timid, especially in its reluctance to speak explicitly of 'the sinful Church', rather than simply 'the Church of sinners' (*TI*, vi. 284–5).

Rahner emphasized that every member of the church, including those in positions of authority, could be responsible for 'reducing the clarity of the Church's manifestation' (*TI*, xx. 10). Thus, Rahner's focus on the church's sinfulness was less a concern with individual moral failure than with the failure of the church as a whole, particularly because of fear, to live the life of faithful witness to Christ that the Spirit enabled:

> Does the fact that the Church can never end up outside the truth of Christ mean also that she proclaims this truth with that power, in that topical and always freshly assimilated form one might hope for and which would make it truly salutary? . . . Do we not frequently (contrary to the meaning of the gospel truth) purchase the permanence of the gospel message in the Church at the price of guarding scrupulously against exposing ourselves to this 'chaos' (out of which tomorrow will be born) or, at best, by meeting it purely defensively, trying merely to preserve what we have? (*TI*, v. 339)

When fear trumped trust in the Spirit's capacity to guide the church on its pilgrimage, the church sought to distance itself from history and the surrounding world. Then, there was a danger that the church as a whole would increasingly find itself 'in the position of one who glorifies her past and looks askance at the present, in so far as she has not created it herself . . . it often loves the calm more than the storm, the old (which has proved itself) more than the new (which is bold and daring)' (*TI*, v. 16).

Rahner's discussion of the church's sinfulness was not reflective of a loss of faith in his own sacramental ecclesiology. Rahner was never less than convinced that it was 'the saints', in whom the Spirit's presence was truly effective, who best represented the church, since they witnessed to the 'miracle of pneumatic existence as the discovery of grace-given individuality in a selfless opening of the innermost kernel of the person's being towards God and so towards all spiritual persons (Rahner 1963a: 139). He underscored consistently, however, that the level of conversion in the church as a whole did not echo what the saints expressed; consequently, proclamation of the need for the church's conversion remained his priority.

Ecclesial Life
and the Challenge of Unity

Rahner's stress on the conversion needed to bring about in the church the holiness that the Spirit made possible, had its parallel in his concern to promote the unity of the church. Just as Rahner's focus on holiness reflected his conviction that a sinful church gave a counter-witness to the presence of Christ, so too his reflections on unity expressed the conviction that a divided church veiled the identity of the church as a sacrament of God's salvation offered in Christ through the Spirit. In the discussion of 'unity', Rahner's emphasis was twofold: unity within the Roman Catholic Church; unity between the divided Christian churches.

Both foci of Rahner's engagement with the unity of the church had the same grounding: the reality of ecclesial faith as a shared experience. Without denying the importance and validity of the individual experience of faith, Rahner gave priority to the communal: 'Faith does not only mean accepting what "I" as an individual believe that I have heard. It also means accepting what the Church has heard, giving my assent to the "confession" of the Church, the Church which is not only the bearer of the message of Christ which it delivers to individuals (and which then disappears again like a postman), but it is the enduring and abiding medium of faith' (*TI*, vii. 109).

The priority of communal faith reflected Rahner's awareness that individual conviction alone could not adequately express the historical reality of God's revelation in Christ. Grounded in that historical revelation, the church was not free to remake itself in every age. In fact, the church was permanently dependent on the apostolic witness: 'God, then, has a unique, qualitatively not transmissible relationship to the Church's first generation, one which God does not have in the same sense to other periods of the Church's history, or rather has to the latter only through the former' (Rahner 1964b: 45). Faithful reception of the apostolic faith was a charge for the church as a whole, but involved the church's authoritative leaders, its bishops, in a particular way. The latter fact underpinned many of the tensions in the church, tensions that always posed a challenge to the unity of the Roman Catholic Church.

When Rahner wrote about the unity of the church in relation to the exercise of authority and episcopal leadership, he did not do so as a dispassionate observer, as a detached academic. Rather, he wrote as someone who engaged actively in many issues in the life of the Roman Catholic Church that had the potential to divide the bishops from the rest of the faithful. In particular, he wrote as a theologian who had himself been subject to various forms of censorship from the church's authorities in the repressive environment in which Roman Catholic theology operated between the condemnation of Modernism and the Second Vatican Council.

His own experience of censorship notwithstanding, Rahner never wavered in his commitment to the necessity of ecclesial faith: 'Since I am a human being and a Christian, it is obvious to me that I am a Christian in the Church, an ecclesial Christian'

(*TI*, xx. 9). Nor did he waver in his conviction that episcopal authority was a graced reality, given for the unity of the church and its mission. The corollary of the latter emphasis was that there could be no justification for schism in the church: 'the will to enter into schism in this way runs counter to the eschatological hope of the Christian, who holds firm to the truth that, in spite of all, the good that God wills always finds its due place in the long run through the exercise of humility, patience, and courage' (*TI*, xii. 107). Those emphases, however, did not mean that Rahner promoted unquestioning obedience to those in authority or viewed the church as the combination of a tiny, but active, episcopate and a large, but passive, laity.

Indeed, what Rahner sought was the realization of the church as a grace-filled community of believers. This required that the laity was not passive, since such passivity could not do justice to the Spirit shared by all the baptized:

> ... in the Church to which charismatic elements belong, subordinates are not simply those who have to carry out orders from above. They have other commands as well to carry out: those of the Lord, who also guides God's Church directly and does not always in the first place convey God's commands and promptings to ordinary Christians through ecclesiastical authorities. (Rahner 1964a: 70)

The focus on the Spirit at work in the whole community required that the bishops not only recognize the limits of their authority, but understand their role as something other than protectors of an ecclesiastical system: 'The institutionalized mentality of bishops is, if one may so say it, feudal, impolite and paternalistic' (Rahner 1977: 69). Those in authority in the church, therefore, needed to avoid acting as if they alone possessed the Spirit or as if the church were 'a clerical, religiously camouflaged kind of totalitarian system' (*TI*, ii. 99).

Of central interest to Rahner was the relationship between episcopal authority and theologians. From his early years to his late writings, he appealed both for a common respect for the particular charism of each group and an acceptance of the limits of one's own gifts. For theologians, this meant that if they 'want to live in the Church with the theology they want to live with, then their theology must really be an ecclesial one, and it must have in principle an unprejudiced and positive relationship to the teaching authority' (*TI*, xxi. 107). For bishops, particularly in the period following Vatican II, the requirement was for a greater sensitivity to the pluralism of theologies, as well as to cultural pluralism, which challenged the bishops to question their tendency to 'believe that the style in which one is accustomed to think, feel and live in a clerical milieu is also valid outside it' (*TI*, xiv. 106).

Rahner offered no simple formula to preserve the unity of the church. He did, however, appeal constantly for attentiveness to the presence of the Spirit, and the need to preserve the church as an 'open' system, one that reflected developments at Vatican II, and contrasted with the 'closed' system of the Pian era, the period from Pope Pius IX to Pope Pius XII (*TI*, xii. 88–9). Above all, Rahner advocated the importance of dialogue, even on matters of faith, as 'in such a dialogue, without prejudice to the divine truth, the

Church can and must be she who learns as well, she who is capable of being led into still deeper levels of her own truth and her understanding of that truth' (*TI*, x. 105).

Rahner's emphasis on the Spirit at work to enhance the 'open' nature of the church and so promote unity within the Roman Catholic Church, was also present in his approach to ecumenism, which assumed a prominent place in his theology from the end of Vatican II until his death in 1984. The need for dialogue, which he had supported in order to enhance relations between bishops and theologians, loomed large in Rahner's approach to the possibility of increased communion between divided Christians.

Rahner's promotion of dialogue had a twofold basis: the recognition that Christians in the divided churches already shared the same Spirit; the need for the churches to work together if the gospel was to find a place in societies that had become both more pluralistic and less accustomed to the traditional forms of Christianity. On the first point, Rahner stressed that the members of the divided churches were already possessed by the one Spirit, even though, at present, they objectified their faith in different ways. Dialogue, then, expressed the conviction that 'in hope, if not in an act of recognition which can ultimately be expressed in theoretical form, we are convinced that the partners to the dialogue on both sides live in the grace of God, are truly justified by the Holy Pneuma of God, and are sharers in the divine nature' (*TI*, xiv. 249). Rahner understood a primary aim of dialogue to be the endeavour to distinguish shared truth from disagreements over theological formulations. While he discouraged any dilution of truth, Rahner was open to changes in conventional theological language—such as, for example, 'transubstantiation'—if such language became an obstacle to the realization of greater unity around deeper truths (*TI*, xi. 41).

The other basis for Rahner's commitment to 'the one Church' was his conviction that the church's authenticity depended on its response to the challenges of history. More explicitly, Rahner believed that the Christian church would be irrelevant to the contemporary world if members of the churches focused only on the controversies that derived from the Reformation. Without denying that there were important issues of theological truth in the disputes that arose in the sixteenth century, Rahner contended that those questions were not the ones that were crucial to the future of Christianity. He argued that if the Christian churches continued to sink their energy into the topics that had been historically divisive, the churches would become increasingly unable to address the contemporary world (*TI*, xi. 53). In that world, not only had pluralism and relativism become the norm, but 'God' had even become increasingly incomprehensible. Such a world, then, had little interest in sixteenth-century disputes (*TI*, xx. 168). Accordingly, Rahner's perspective was that members of the divided churches needed to work together to meet their common challenges. Such cooperation, he believed, could also provide a new context in which to address whatever contentious issues remained from the Reformation: 'If God becomes the one radical question for all Christians . . . it will simply be impossible for them any longer to feel so separated by the question of the Pope as was the case between the sixteenth and nineteenth centuries' (*TI*, xii. 214).

Rahner's conviction that the churches could develop closer relationships, without dissolving into relativism, took on concrete shape in *Unity of the Churches: An Actual*

Possibility (1983), a book he co-authored with Heinrich Fries. That book, one of Rahner's final publications, proposed a concrete model for the reconciliation of the divided Christian churches, one that took its inspiration from Vatican II's principle of the 'hierarchy of truths' (*Unitatis Redintegratio*, art. 11). Rahner and Fries encouraged the churches to seek unity by agreeing on the primary matters on Christian faith 'as they are expressed in Holy Scripture, in the Apostles' Creed, and in that of Nicaea and Constantinople' (Rahner 1985: 7). Accordingly, the churches were not to impose on each other any requirement to accept secondary points of doctrine, nor were they to reject as incompatible with Christian faith any doctrines of other churches that their own church did not accept. Rahner thus envisaged that institutional unity between the churches was possible even with a pluralism of creeds. Rahner and Fries sought a means by which the churches might reconcile differences in order to preach the gospel and witness to Christ in contemporary society. Their concern, therefore, was genuinely evangelical, rather than an appeal for the churches to work together in the hope of ensuring their survival.

Although Rahner affirmed the contribution that theological dialogue could make to the possibility of unity, he also stressed the need for those in authority in the churches to act in a way that demonstrated courageous trust in the Spirit. For his own Roman Catholic tradition, this would require a more generous and creative response to ecumenism than was usual:

> Let the Roman Curia show bold resolution and dare to hope to achieve something of which the end-result cannot be calculated in advance, thus displaying itself in its ministries of teaching and leadership in a way demanded by the whole historical situation today; let it eliminate many features of a centralist and bureaucratically administered state, seeking to decree from above more or less everything that is at all important; let the limits of the universal primacy as they arise from dogma or can be restricted by the papacy itself be more clearly defined. (*TI*, xx. 171)

A Missionary Church
in a Changing World

Rahner's focus on the church's context as a crucial factor in his approach to ecumenism was a specific application of a theme that was evident in his theology from the end of the Second World War onwards: the need for the members of the church to be aware that they no longer lived in a 'traditional' Christian culture. In the 'diaspora', which was Rahner's preferred term for the new situation of the church in a society characterized, especially in Europe, by secularization and pluralism, the urgent requirement was for creativity that went beyond 'business as usual' (*TI*, ii. 288). Rahner had no fear of that challenge, but recognized that meeting it had implications both for the internal life of the church and for the ways in which the church viewed the world.

In Rahner's analysis, the primary resource that could guide the church in its new situation was the Holy Spirit. That Spirit, 'the element of dynamic unrest', was the driving force for a church open to the future (Rahner 1963b: 79). Rahner's focus on the church as the product of grace, formed by the Spirit to be the sacrament of God's presence in the world, and as a community oriented to eschatological fullness, all suggested that the church would be denying its deepest reality if it refused to respond to new challenges. While observing the imperatives of unity and faithfulness to the apostolic tradition, the church was to be a locus of creative ferment, rather than a 'graveyard' or a community characterized by 'indifferent conformism' (*Grace in Freedom*, 35). The object of the ferment was to seek new ways of engaging the world with the gospel: 'the Church community of the future must be open to the outside world, must be ready to be shaped by individuals who obviously and whole-heartedly engage themselves in the life of the pluralistic society in general' (*TI*, xii. 208).

To that end, Rahner welcomed the priority that Vatican II accorded to 'the local Church' (*Lumen Gentium*, 26–9), the dioceses spread through the world. In those diverse communities, people gathered to celebrate the Eucharist, while being integrally connected to all other communities through the ministry of their bishop, a member of the college of bishops. That emphasis offered an alternative to the presentation of the church as a monolithic structure whose every action depended on decisions that emanated from Rome. While Rahner believed that the council had opened new possibilities in the relationship between local churches and 'the centre', his reflections on life in the church after Vatican II concluded that the relationship between the pope and the bishops remained too strongly weighted in favour of the central authority. To the end of his life, therefore, Rahner continued to advocate that the pope should take action both to limit his own authority and to give practical expression to the fact that the bishops were more than advisers to the pope (*TI*, xx. 133–42).

Beyond the need for less centralized structures, Rahner also promoted the importance of the church adopting new forms of theological engagement with the world. Thus, he was an early advocate of 'practical' theology, a discipline that could provide '*theological* illumination of the particular given situation, in which the Church must realize itself in all its dimensions' (*TI*, ix. 102; original emphasis). The rationale for such a theology was the recognition that the 'essence' of the church could not be known independently of the church's self-realization in the unique historical situations through which the Spirit led the church on its eschatological journey (*TI*, ix. 102–3). Rahner characterized practical theology as an expression of the prophetic dimension of the church's *caritas*, an act of creative imagination, born of hope, one that, through the use of 'sociology, futurology and similar sciences as its aids', sought new forms for the church's relationship to the world (*TI*, x. 352).

The aim of practical theology, however, was not to enable the church to merge seamlessly with a changing world, but to seek an authentically Christian response to the world. In being aware that 'the sphere in which salvation is achieved is identical with the sphere of human existence in general', Rahner was never less than intent on ensuring that the church did not limit itself to the sacral and cultic alone, but he also acknowledged the difference between the church and secular society (*TI*, xii. 236). That difference derived from the church's confession of God as humanity's 'absolute future', a recognition that led the church to be critical of any attitudes and projects suggesting that a lesser end could provide humanity's final satisfaction (*TI*, xii. 239). Such criticism, however, was not tantamount to the church seeking to control or abolish 'the worldliness of the world' (*TI*, vi. 60–8).

Without being naive about the extent of the challenges that the church faced in the contemporary world, Rahner evinced no doubt that the Spirit would enable the church to meet those challenges. In short, what Rahner sought from the church at large, as well as from every local expression of it, was the openness to the wider world that he regarded as characteristic of Vatican II:

> [The Church] cannot and will not continue any longer to act as an impregnable fortress with small arrow-slits in the walls from which the defenders shoot at their enemies. Now it is rather the spacious house with large windows from which one looks out upon all spheres of humanity, all of which are encompassed by the creative power of God and by [God's] compassion. (*TI*, vii. 96)

In his writings from the late 1960s to his final essays in the early 1980s, Rahner stressed not only that the church must be committed to love of neighbour, in historical and sociological tangibility, but that in so doing the church would find 'its own ground and its own potential, which is love of God' (*TI*, xx. 69). Similarly, the authentic love of neighbour, which members of the church were to practise, began with the recognition that 'the human being is, once and for all, that being which only possesses, discovers and consummates itself when it transcends itself in reaching out to that without which this being would stick fast in finitude, that being which is itself infinitely more than [the human being]' (*TI*, xiv. 306–7).

While each member of the church was obliged to love of neighbour, that activity was not subject to control by the church's officials. Indeed, Rahner stressed that it was not 'the official Church' and its hierarchy that bore primary responsibility for the church's engagement with the world (*TI*, xii. 243). Since love of neighbour needed to take place in concrete circumstances, its shape could not be determined independently of those who had the responsibility to enact it in particular circumstances (*TI*, xiv. 312). The church's teaching could appeal to the freedom of those addressed, it could promote 'orthodox practice', but it could not replace the actions of individual members of the church (*TI*, xii. 243–4).

KARL RAHNER AS ECCLESIOLOGIST AND 'MAN OF THE CHURCH'

Karl Rahner was not an ecclesiologist 'by trade'. He did not write a major treatise on ecclesiology, did not pursue the history of the discipline, and did not teach ecclesiology.

Nor would most commentators describe Rahner as an ecclesiologist, in a way that they would, unhesitatingly, apply that title to his contemporary, Yves Congar. Nonetheless, 'the church' was a constant focus of Rahner's work; indeed, a case can be made that half of his writings dealt in some way with 'the church'. The resolution of this conundrum resides in what has been the primary thesis of this chapter: Rahner locates the church as linked, inextricably, with the Trinitarian God, the self-revelation of that God in Jesus Christ and the Holy Spirit, and with the ubiquity of grace, the opportunity for encounter with God. The logic of Rahner's approach ran thus: since God is inseparable from every human experience, so, properly understood, is the church. For Rahner, such a claim had nothing to do with promoting the church's social hegemony or control over grace; it was, rather, what followed from the consistent application of his understanding of God's self-revelation as taking place sacramentally.

Whether proposing new ways in which the church might engage the wider culture or critiquing, often trenchantly, specific decisions or styles of leadership, Rahner's guiding principle was that the church exists to give particular form to the universality of grace, to be the *Grundsakrament* of God's saving love revealed in Jesus Christ. The manifold implications of that emphasis, and Rahner's willingness to engage with them, represent his profound contribution to ecclesiology. That contribution flowed not simply from his writing *about* the church, but also from his participation *in* the church, a participation that included most significantly, his involvement in the theological ferment that shaped the documents of the Second Vatican Council.

I have referred to Rahner's rejection of neo-scholasticism on the grounds that it sought a 'timeless' theology, a project that he believed severed the relationship between theology and God's presence in our changing world. Rahner, by contrast, stressed what we could call the permanent 'timeliness' of the church. That timeliness derived from the fact the church had its grounding in the constancy of the self-offering of 'that infinite, incomprehensible reality, exalted above all coming to be and perishing, which we call God' (*TI*, xx. 113). As a result of that grounding, Rahner had no doubt of the enduring necessity of the church, whatever challenges it faced: 'If this message does not perish and cannot perish, since it is the answer to humanity's infinite hope, then neither does the Church perish, being the fellowship of those who in faith and hope make this message the centre of their existence' (*TI*, xx. 113). Rahner's writings attest to the depth of his sharing in that faith and hope.

References

Works by Rahner

Rahner, K. (1961–92). *Theological Investigations*. 23 vols. London: Darton, Longman and Todd/ New York: Crossroad. [NB For all articles from *TI*, the date given is for the text's original publication. References in the body of the chapter are to *TI* by volume and page.]

TI, i. 'The Prospects for Dogmatic Theology' [1954]: 1–18.

TI, i. 'The Development of Dogma' [1954], 39–77.

TI, i. 'Current Problems in Christology' [1954], 149–200.

TI, i. 'Concerning the Relationship between Nature and Grace' [1950], 297–317.

TI, i. 'Some Implications of the Scholastic Concept of Uncreated Grace' [1939], 319–46.

TI ii. 'Membership of the Church according to the Teaching of Pius XII's Encyclical, *Mystici Corporis Christi* [1947], 1–88.

TI ii. 'Personal and Sacramental Piety' [1952], 109–33.

TI ii. 'Peaceful Reflections on the Parochial Principle' [1948], 283–318.

TI iii. 'Priestly Existence' [1942], 239–62.

TI, iv. 'The Concept of Mystery in Catholic Theology' [1959], 36–73.

TI, iv. 'The Theology of the Symbol' [1959], 221–52.

TI, iv. 'The Word and the Eucharist' [1960], 253–86.

TI, v. 'Thoughts on the Possibility of Belief Today' [1962], 3–22.

TI, v. 'Dogmatic Notes on "Ecclesiological Piety"' [1961], 336–65.

TI, vi. 'The Church of Sinners' [1947], 253–69.

TI, vi. 'The Sinful Church in the Decrees of Vatican II' [1966], 270–94.

TI, vi. 'Marxist Utopia and the Christian Future of Man' [1965], 59–68.

TI, vi. 'The Christian in his World' [1965], 88–99.

TI, vii. '"I Believe in the Church"' [1954], 100–18.

TI, ix. 'Practical Theology within the Totality of Theological Disciplines' [1967], 101–14.

TI, x. 'The Presence of the Lord in the Christian Community at Worship' [1966], 71–83.

TI, x. 'Dialogue in the Church' [1967], 103–21.

TI, x. 'Practical Theology and Social Work in the Church' [1967], 349–70.

TI, xi. 'On the Theology of Ecumenical Discussion' [1968], 24–67.

TI, xii. 'Observations on the Factor of the Charismatic in the Church' [1969], 81–97.

TI, xii. 'Schism in the Catholic Church?' [1969], 98–116.

TI, xii. 'Perspectives for the Future of the Church' [1967], 202–17.

TI, xii. 'The Function of the Church as a Critic of Society' [1969], 229–49.

TI, xiv. 'The Congregation of the Faith and the Commission of Theologians' [1970], 98–115.

TI, xiv. 'What is a Sacrament?' [1971], 136–48.

TI, xiv. 'Considerations on the Active Role of the Person in the Sacramental Event' [1970], 161–84.

TI, xiv. 'Some Problems in Contemporary Ecumenism' [1972], 245–53.

TI, xiv. 'The Church's Commission to Bring Salvation and the Humanization of the World' [1971], 295–313.

TI, xix. 'The Church's Redemptive Historical Provenance from the Death and Resurrection of Jesus' [1977], 24–38.

TI, xx. 'Courage for an Ecclesial Christianity' [1979], 3–12.

TI, xx. 'The Future of the Church and the Church of the Future' [1977], 103–14.

TI, xx. 'Dream of the Church' [1978], 133–42.

TI, xx. 'Unity of the Church—Unity of Mankind' [1978], 154–72.

TI, xx. 'Theological Justification of the Church's Development Work' [1976], 65–73.

TI, xxi. 'A Theology that We Can Live With' [1982], 99–112.

Rahner, K. (1963a). *Mission and Grace* (vol. 1). Trans. C. Hastings. New York: Sheed and Ward.

Rahner, K. (1963b). *Nature and Grace*. Trans D. Wharton. London: Sheed and Ward.

Rahner, K. (1964a). *The Dynamic Element in the Church*. Trans. W. J. O'Hara. Montreal: Palm Publishers.

Rahner, K. (1964b). *Inspiration in the Bible*. Trans. C. H. Henkey. Rev. trans. M. Palmer. New York: Herder and Herder.

Rahner, K. (1969). *Grace in Freedom*. Trans. H. Graef. New York: Herder and Herder.

Rahner, K. (1974). *The Church and the Sacraments*. Trans. W. J. O'Hara. Tunbridge Wells: Burns and Oates.

Rahner, K. (1977). *Meditations on Freedom and the Spirit*. Trans. R. Ockenden, D. Smith, and C. Bennett. London: Burns and Oates.

Rahner, K. (1978). *Foundations of Christian Faith: An Introduction to the Idea of Christianity*. Trans W. Dych. New York: Seabury.

Rahner, K. (1985). [with Heinrich Fries] *Unity of the Churches: An Actual Possibility*. Trans. R. C. L. Gritsch and E. W. Gritsch. Philadelphia: Fortress.

Rahner, K. (1994). *Hearers of the Word: Laying the Foundations for a Philosophy of Religion*. Original: 1941. Trans. J. Donceel. New York: Continuum.

Other Sources

Lennan, R. (1995). *The Ecclesiology of Karl Rahner*. Oxford: Oxford University Press.

Lennan, R. (2005). 'Faith in Context: Rahner on the Possibility of Belief'. *Philosophy and Theology* 17: 233–58.

Lennan, R. (2013). '"Narcissistic Aestheticism?" An Assessment of Karl Rahner's Sacramental Ecclesiology', *Philosophy and Theology* 25: 249–70.

Marmion, D. and Hines, M. (eds) (2005). *The Cambridge Companion to Karl Rahner*. Cambridge: Cambridge University Press.

Tanner, N. (1990). *Decrees of the Ecumenical Councils*. Vol. 2. Washington, DC. Georgetown University Press.

Vorgrimler, H. (1986). *Understanding Karl Rahner: An Introduction to his Life and Thought*. New York: Crossroad.

Suggested Reading

Conway, P. and Ryan, F. (eds) (2010). *Karl Rahner: Theologian for the Twenty-First Century*. Bern: Peter Lang.

Crowley, P. (ed.) (2007). *Rahner Beyond Rahner: A Great Theologian Encounters the Pacific Rim*. Lanham, MD: Sheed and Ward.

Ebert, H. (2016). 'The Social Nature of the *Sensus Fidei* in the Thought of Karl Rahner'. *Philosophy and Theology* 28: 493–512.

Lassalle-Klein, R. (2013). 'Ignacio Ellacuria's Rahnerian Fundamental Theology for a Global Church'. *Philosophy and Theology* 25: 275–99.

Marmion, D. (2017). 'Karl Rahner, Vatican II, and the Shape of the Church'. *Theological Studies* 78: 25–48.

CHAPTER 20

JOSEPH RATZINGER

THEODOR DIETER

As a scholar, as a theological expert (*peritus*) at the Second Vatican Council, as Cardinal and Prefect of the Congregation for the Doctrine of the Faith (CDF), and eventually as Pope Benedict XVI, Joseph Ratzinger made substantial contributions to the development of Roman Catholic ecclesiology for more than sixty years, on both a theological and a doctrinal level. His ecclesiological insights and convictions show a remarkable constancy in many of their features, from his early doctoral dissertation (1951, published 1954) to the time when he served as pope (2005–13). Certainly, new topics and types of arguments, new controversies, and different emphases appear, often related to his different positions within the church; nevertheless, the same basic lines of thought can be identified from the beginning of his career until the time of his pontificate. Thus in this chapter these lines will be described without differentiating his positions chronologically. The main sources are Ratzinger's own writings, and in a few cases also official statements for which he was responsible.

THE DISSERTATION

Joseph Ratzinger's dissertation on 'The People and House of God in Augustine's Doctrine of the Church' was located within the ecclesiological debate between the two world wars. Opposed to a centuries-old, primarily institutional, and hierarchical understanding of the church, the concept of the mystical body of Christ was favoured by many in this time in order to emphasize the spiritual character of the church as a mystery centred in Christ. Pius XII's encyclical letter *Mystici Corporis* (1943) was the high point of this development. But the concept of the body of Christ tended to be understood as 'mystical', not in the sense of 'sacramental' but as 'spiritual' and 'internal', quite in opposition to the original meaning of 'body'. It became clear that from this starting point it was not possible to develop a concept of the church that included its institutional dimension. Thus it was thought that this idea would need the concept of the 'people of God' as its corrective. Nevertheless, the two concepts stood side by side, unrelated to each other and seen as alternatives.

In this situation, it was the aim of Ratzinger's *Doktorvater* and his own hopes to clarify basic ecclesiological concepts and to overcome the tensions among them by studying Augustine's doctrine of the church. The church father's teaching was seen as authoritative also for contemporary problems. The historical study was undertaken with a clear systematic perspective so that the emphasis did not lie with a historical-critical analysis of texts of the distant past and their contexts but on their function as exemplars that would be able to help solve present challenges. Nevertheless, some forty years later, in the preface to the new edition, Ratzinger insisted that he approached the texts 'with the unconditional readiness to be led by them alone wherever they directed me' (2011: 51; my translation). In fact, the assumption of his *Doktorvater*—that 'people of God' would be the hermeneutical key for this church father's understanding of the church—was not confirmed. To his surprise, Ratzinger realized that Augustine called the church simply the 'body of Christ' (not: the *mystical* body of Christ) simply because she receives the body of Christ in the Eucharist and thus becomes the body of Christ. He concluded: the church always originates around the altar. The 'body of Christ' has turned out to be the fundamental concept of the church, but *not* as a mysterious spiritual organism; rather, it is the most concrete reality of the celebration of the Eucharist and the communion originating in it. He found that the *unus panis—unum corpus sumus multi* (one bread—we many are one body) is the centre of Augustine's concept of the church (2011: 415). 'People' is the general term while 'body of Christ' denotes the specific difference. Thus Ratzinger could say: 'The church is just the people of God existing as the body of Christ' (2011: 417). Since the body of Christ appeared as the determining element of the people of God, the tension between the two concepts was overcome. Ratzinger discovered in Augustine that ecclesiology had to be eucharistic ecclesiology. This focus on the sacrament as the centre enabled him to unite what is often seen as opposites: internal and external, spiritual and institutional.

Looking back at his dissertation in 2011, Benedict XVI stated that his study 'put me on the track of eucharistic ecclesiology and thus granted me an understanding of the reality of the Church that is in agreement with the deepest intentions of the Second Vatican Council and at the same time leads into the spiritual centre of Christian existence' (2011: 9).

THE METHOD

Augustine had developed his concept of the church through a Christological *relecture* of the Old Testament; this challenged Ratzinger to develop his own ecclesiology by reconstructing the Bible's understanding of the church by means of modern exegesis and at the same time with an orientation toward the church fathers. The way in which he does this deserves special attention. There are four approaches that he uses and combines with each other. Careful, perceptive exegesis of the biblical witnesses of the church is the first constitutive approach, precisely in line with the claim of Second Vatican Council's *Dei Verbum* that studying Scripture is 'the soul of theology'. According to Ratzinger this claim has a revolutionizing significance for the systematic structure of Catholic theology. In his ecclesiology, he tries to develop an example of a possible new structure that does not start by presenting the dogmatic tradition but starts with Scripture. Nevertheless, he reads Scripture in connection with the church fathers since for him both belong together as a word and its answering word ('Ant-wort'); the word has only continued and become effective since it has found an answer. Taking the fathers consequently into consideration is the second feature of his ecclesiology. In addition, according to him, the measure of the church is her descent, her 'decisive origin', and this is not limited to Scripture but comprises also the basic form of the early church. To speak biblically means for him to adapt to the dynamics of the historical development that the Bible has opened up to us and to receive the whole of this dynamics. Thus, early developments in the church play a systematic role in his ecclesiology (the third feature). Referring to Scripture, the fathers, and the early development of the church he develops certain principles (for example, the so-called 'We'-principle and the principle of personal responsibility) that in turn allow for understanding the logic of what those sources demonstrate; but drawing conclusions from those principles alone would not be sufficient to undergird a doctrinal statement, since for Ratzinger the decisive elements of the church are not matters of conclusions but of historical realities. Nevertheless, such principles, insofar as they interpret the historical processes, are the fourth feature of his ecclesiology.

This methodology is intimately connected with the content of his theology, especially with his understanding of the relationship between revelation, Scripture, and history. In this respect a remarkable talk that Ratzinger gave just before the solemn inauguration of the Second Vatican Council deserves attention. Addressing the German-speaking bishops, he critically examined the Preparatory Theological Commission's schema on revelation, Scripture, and tradition. This schema spoke about two sources of revelation, Scripture and tradition. Ratzinger criticized it for observing the order of knowing instead of the order of reality. 'Scripture and tradition are *for us* sources from which we know revelation, but they are not *in themselves* its sources, for revelation is itself the source of Scripture and tradition . . . revelation is not something following upon Scripture and tradition, but is instead God's speaking and acting which comes before all historical formulations of this speaking, being the one source that feeds Scripture and tradition' (Wicks 2008: 270). '[R]evelation is always more than its material principle, the Scripture, namely, that it is life living on in the Church in a way that makes Scripture a living reality and illumines its hidden depths . . . But if revelation is prior and greater, then there is no trouble in having only *one* material principle [i.e. Scripture], which even so is still not the whole, but only the material principle of the superior reality revelation, which lives in the Church' (Wicks 2008: 276). At that time, this talk contributed to a complete rewriting of the original schema. Its understanding of Scripture and revelation is precisely the background for Ratzinger's methodological approach in his ecclesiology.

Thus Ratzinger's systematic theology is based on historical investigation, and also in part on the findings of historical-critical research, while at the same time he remains critical of what he calls the ideological presuppositions of researchers and their tendency to create hypotheses and to slice texts into always smaller pieces. He instead attempts syntheses of the different witnesses in Scripture and the witnesses to Scripture in the course of church history. He is convinced that 'the base memory of the Church' can serve as 'the standard for judging what is to be considered historically and objectively accurate, as opposed to what does not come from the text of the Bible but has its source in some private way of thinking' (Ratzinger 1996: 20). Exegetical theologians and church historians who practise historical-critical methods are sometimes critical of Ratzinger's way of taking up exegetical and historical findings into a synthesis in line with the dogma, but on the other hand it is fascinating to see how intensely and comprehensively he takes those findings into account in order to make systematic use of them and to reconstruct church doctrines as a whole.

The Exegetical Basis

Certain exegetical observations, findings, and arguments recur quite often in Ratzinger's texts. Thus it is appropriate to give a short sketch of the main topics, also in order to honour his Scripture-orientated approach. Ratzinger's first exegetical step is to enquire after the will of the historical Jesus for the church. Of course, he is aware that the centre of Jesus' proclamation was the kingdom of God. Ratzinger transforms the famous saying of Loisy about the kingdom that was foretold and the church that arrived into: 'The Kingdom was promised, what came was Jesus' (1996: 23). But a kingdom cannot be without people, so Jesus' mission aims at the gathering of a new people. This is not an amorphous group but has a centre, 'the Twelve'.

> In constituting the circle of Twelve, Jesus presents himself as the patriarch of a new Israel and institutes these twelve men as its origin and foundation. There could be no clearer way of expressing the beginning of a new people, which is now no longer formed by physical descent but by 'being with Jesus', a reality that the Twelve receive from him and that he sends them to mediate to others. (1996: 25)

Calling the Twelve is one church-founding act, while Jesus' celebration of the Last Supper is the other. In the pericopes of the Lord's Supper, Jesus' death is understood in relation to the Passover, while the words of institution deal with the event of a covenant. Thus instituting the Eucharist is constituting a new people through a new covenant. This is consonant with Jesus' saying about the temple destroyed and rebuilt in three days (Mark 14:58; 15:29). 'The Body of the Lord, which is the center of the Lord's Supper, is the one new temple that joins Christians together into a much more real unity than a temple made of stone could ever do' (1996: 27). Ratzinger is emphasizing the unity of the Old and the New Testaments very strongly by referring to the covenant while perceiving the old covenant as promise, hope, and longing and the new covenant as fulfilment.

In a second step of exegetical reconstruction, Ratzinger asks how the emerging church understood herself by following the traces of two words: 'ekklēsia' and 'body of Christ'. 'Ekklēsia' denotes the people's assembly in a Greek *polis* but also the *qahal* of the Israelites. Since the people of God (Israel) was spread over the world after the destruction of the first temple, it was part of the eschatological hope that Israel would be gathered anew. By calling herself 'ekklēsia', the early church claimed to be the fulfilment of this desire to be the new people of God. The word 'people of God' is used in the New Testament nearly exclusively for Israel. Thus, if 'ekklēsia' is rendered by 'people of God' one must never forget its Christological determination. That this happened—for Ratzinger a falling back into the Old Testament—is his constant criticism with respect to developments after Vatican II.

The main source for the concept of the church as 'body of Christ' is found in 1 Cor. 10:16f.: 'The formula "the Church is the Body of Christ" thus states that the Eucharist, in which the Lord gives us his body and makes us one body, forever remains the place where the Church is generated, where the Lord himself never ceases to found her anew; in the Eucharist the Church is most compactly herself—in all places, yet one only, just as he is one only' (1996: 37). The motif of the church as bride sets another accent indicating that there is no simplistic equation of Christ himself with the body of Christ. The church is not simply Christ but remains the maiden whom he elevates as his bride.

Thirdly, the depiction of Pentecost in the Acts of the Apostles is of special ecclesiological significance, according to Ratzinger. It shows that the church is the creature of the Holy Spirit and not the product of human decisions. Many languages and cultures belong to it so that there is an interplay between plurality and unity.

> 'In this respect it can be said that we find here [in Pentecost] a preliminary sketch of a Church that lives in manifold and multiform particular Churches but that precisely in this way is the one Church. At the same time, Luke expresses with this image the fact that at the moment of her birth, the Church was already catholic, already a world Church. Luke thus rules out a conception in which a local Church first arose in Jerusalem and then became the base for the gradual establishment of other local Churches that eventually grew into a federation. Luke tells us that the reverse is true: what first exists is the one Church, the Church that speaks in all tongues—the *ecclesia universalis*; she then generates Church in the most diverse locales, which nonetheless are all always embodiments of the one and only Church. The temporal and ontological priority lies with the universal Church; a Church that was not catholic would not even have ecclesial reality . . . (1996: 44)

This understanding of Acts 2, presented in 1990, was to become part of a controversy between Cardinals Ratzinger and Kasper some years later. In any event, Luke describes the way of the church in Acts as the way of the gospel from the Jews to the Gentiles and thus as the fulfilment of Jesus' command to be witnesses to the end of the earth (1:8). This move will later play a role in the development of the primacy of Rome and its bishop.

This is, in brief, the exegetical foundation of Ratzinger's ecclesiology to which certain aspects, especially concerning the role of Peter, will be added. He often points to the fact that '*ekklēsia*' has three meanings in the New Testament: a worship gathering, a local parish, and the universal church. This semantic finding is of great theological significance for him. Worship is the event through which the people of God is ever created anew. Since there is only one worship, although performed in many different places, it is the source of unity for the whole church. Ratzinger describes the three levels with this formula: 'The one (ideal) Church—making herself appear concretely in Jerusalem, Corinth etc.—realises herself as Church in the gathering for worship' (2010a: 163 [1958]; my translation). The many local parishes together are the one church precisely because 'they altogether are the representation of a certain thought of God, the divine idea of an eschatological community of saints' (2010a: 164). 'They are one, the one representation of the eschatological idea of God just by celebrating the one Lord's Supper' (2010a: 164). It is remarkable that he calls the universal church 'the one (ideal) Church'; this understanding was to play a role in the Ratzinger–Kasper debate already mentioned. It is Ratzinger's concern to emphasize that 'One understands both meanings [of 'ecclesia': local parish and one church] only if one recognizes that the universal church is not an a-posteriori summarizing of individual parishes but rather the other way around: the idea of the universal Church is primary' (2010a: 163). Here we see how exegetical observations are systematically explained and elaborated.

EUCHARISTIC ECCLESIOLOGY

Many other features in Ratzinger's understanding of the church are developed from the Eucharistic centre of the church as the starting point. Eucharistic ecclesiology is at the same time *communio*-ecclesiology. Ratzinger develops the many different aspects of *communio* very carefully and repeatedly. *Communio* is the basic structure of the church. Eucharist is God's communion with human beings through Christ and thus at the same time their communion with all other communicants. Sin—a division whose source lies in self-centredness—is broken through the love of God when the 'We' of faith is constituted. The Eucharist is not the lonely encounter of a soul with Christ but the communication of the *caritas* of God, which creates the *caritas* of the communicants among themselves and transcends the worship and group of worshippers. Thus it becomes a sign and instrument for the unity of the whole of humanity. But the deepest ground for the 'We' of communion lies in the communion of the Holy Trinity.

Communio also exists among the local churches celebrating the Eucharist. Since Christ is the one bread that is received in many different places, there is only one body of Christ consisting of the many local congregations. There is not only a communion of communicants but also a communion of local churches. Eucharistic ecclesiology does necessarily include the plural of local churches (*communio ecclesiarum*). Local churches are churches led by a bishop. That there is one bishop in one place follows from the public character of the church—she is not a private cultic association—and from the Eucharist: God's call means that all who live in a certain place all gather in one Eucharist. The bishop represents both the unity and the public character of the local church. Thus being in communion means being in communion with the bishop. And the bishops themselves are in communion with each other. Their communion or collegiality is rooted in the sacrament of the Eucharist and is an expression of the *communio*-character of the church as such. The collegiality of the bishops presupposes brotherhood in the church and has to serve it. It plays a decisive role for the *communio ecclesiarum*. Ratzinger explains this with an interesting detail: When a person in the early church living in one local church travelled and wished to participate in the Eucharist of another local church, she brought letters of communion with her bearing the name of her bishop, so that in the other church they could see whether this person belonged to a church in communion with their own. There were lists of bishops whose churches were in communion with one another. The sign for this was the fact that the bishops were consecrated by neighbouring bishops. This makes it clear that a community cannot give itself a bishop. It must receive him, even if they choose him.

Ratzinger refers to historical developments with systematic interest. History shows that not all bishops in the early church were equal, rather there were primacies—the word 'primacy' first appeared in the plural—attributed to the 'main churches' of Rome, Antioch, and Alexandria. Antioch and Rome were directly related to Peter, Alexandria to the tradition of Mark. Rome's claim of the primacy of the primacies was founded in the conviction that Rome had remained free of heresies, that Rome had succeeded Jerusalem, and mainly because Rome was the see of Peter and Paul and the place of their martyrdom. In the course of time, the argument of the succession of Peter became more important. The bishop of Rome gained a universal responsibility, though this did not include a universal administrative responsibility. Ratzinger emphasizes that this responsibility was attached to the patriarchates, but with respect to this the three sees were equal. In his eyes, it was a mistake that Rome mixed the apostolic presidency with the primacy of ecclesial law. For the East, ecclesial law could only be conciliar law (i.e. enacted by councils), while for the West ecclesial law could be conciliar law or papal law. Thus it was tragic that Rome did not succeed in separating its apostolic task from the basically administrative idea of the patriarchate. This contributed to the alienation and conflict between East and West. In medieval times, the church of Rome incorporated the whole Latin West so that the plural *ecclesiae* disappeared. Already in 1964 Ratzinger offers the following perspective: 'Within the unity of the one Ecclesia the plural of ecclesiae must have space: Only faith is indivisible; the unity-creating function of the papacy is assigned to it. Everything else may be different' (2010b: 654; my translation). He insists that there should be a clear distinction between the original ministry of the successor of Peter and the ministry of the patriarchate.

Beside the argument of the historical development, of course, the exegetical argument for the primacy of the successor of Peter is for Ratzinger the most important. In this respect, he appeals to a few observations. A special role for Peter is mentioned in all three of the main lines of tradition in the New Testament (Paul's letters, the Synoptic

Gospels, and John). Together with the church fathers he includes Matt. 16:16 (Peter's confession of faith) in the Petrine passage (Matt. 16:16–19), even as its main part. Thus he tries to overcome the alternative stemming from Augustine as to whether Peter's profession of faith or his person is the rock of the church: Simon Peter is the rock precisely through his profession. This profession requires a bearer. Simon receives a new name (Cephas), which indicates his personal responsibility, while the name transcends the historical individual and thus becomes an institution that continues on through history, existing only through a particular person with particular responsibility. Ratzinger refers to the findings of *Formgeschichte* according to which it is clear that the Gospels report only what has not only historical but also contemporary significance. Thus the Petrine passages do not refer to Peter only as a person in history but to a contemporary ministry, too. As described herein, history shows that in the course of time the apostolic see of Rome and eventually the pope gained normative significance for identifying the true apostolic tradition.

Ratzinger also argues via principles. Since the church is communion, therefore the bearer of the witness to the word of God—the bishop—is never alone but is always in a network with other bishops, the *collegium*. But alongside this 'We'-principle, there is also the biblical principle of personal responsibility. People are called by their names. Among the many disciples of Jesus, 'the Twelve' were especially called, among them a group of three (Simon, James, John), and within them Simon, who was given a new name. Thus by different methods (historical, exegetical, consistent principles) Ratzinger shows that the primacy of the pope is well founded in Scripture and in the ongoing tradition.

Ratzinger often applies the concept of the body of Christ to the church without mentioning the Word of God; this is astonishing even though one might argue that the Word is included in the Eucharist. But he also states 'that the Church of the incarnate Word is in turn the Church of the word, and not just of the sacrament . . . sacrament *and* word are the two pillars upon which the Church stands' (2008c: 21). Since the Word of God is basically not a written word but a proclaimed word, it requires a witness and authorization of the witness in order to be a *viva vox* (living voice). Thus tradition requires succession, and succession aims at handing over the Word. Ratzinger's famous formula is: 'The succession is the form of the tradition, and the tradition is the content of the succession' (2008c: 28). He emphasizes that the 'rule of faith' served as canonical already before Scripture was established as canon; Scripture became Scripture through tradition, and the primacy of Rome played a role in it. He sees the precedence of proclamation over mere Scripture to be genuine for the New Testament, and he claims that this understanding is a defining aspect of Catholic Christendom. In this he sees a basic difference from a Christendom that defines itself with reference to the gospel (*evangelisch*), which he narrows to the *sola scriptura*. For Ratzinger, ' "apostolic succession" is by its nature the living presence of the word in the personal form of the witness. The unbroken continuity of witnesses is derived from the nature of the word as *auctoritas* and *viva vox*' (2008c: 30).

One can distinguish two lines of argument for both collegiality and primacy in Ratzinger's theology, even though they appear combined with each other: one line starting from *communio*, the other starting from *successio*. The *communio ecclesiarum* requires a network of bishops of local churches and thus their collegiality. The apostles were jointly called by Jesus, thus a bishop as the *successor of the apostles* is bishop within the *collegium* of bishops. Only the bishop of Rome is the *successor of a certain apostle*, Peter; thus primacy is rooted in Jesus' special mandate to Peter. But primacy is also seen as rooted in the communion of the church, since this communion has needed one common point of reference. Being in communion with the bishop of Rome turned out to be the criterion for belonging to the universal church. Ratzinger has always been concerned with the balance between primacy and collegiality. The unity of the church comes from the Eucharist from which the church lives, but the unity of the Eucharist has its final point of reference in the bishop of Rome. 'The theological locus of primacy is . . . the Eucharist, in which ministry *and* spirit, law *and* love have their common centre and their common starting point' (1969a: 89; my translation).

UNIVERSAL CHURCH—LOCAL CHURCHES

As mentioned, in 1990 Ratzinger used the phrase 'The temporal and ontological priority lies with the universal Church' in commenting on Acts 2 (1996: 44). In 1992, this expression occurred again in the Letter of the Congregation for the Doctrine of the Faith (CDF), 'Some Aspects of the Church Understood as Communion', under the signature of Cardinal Ratzinger: the universal church 'is a reality *ontologically and temporally* prior to every *individual* particular Church' (CDF, 1992, no. 9; italics added). Bishop (later Cardinal) Walter Kasper expressed serious concerns about the CDF document, criticizing its possible effect in strengthening Roman centralism over the local churches. Ratzinger sharply rejected this accusation, claiming that the problem discussed in that document was on another level from the division of power between the Roman curia and the local churches. In view of Ratzinger's eucharistic ecclesiology, this rejection is indeed convincing.

In speaking of the priority of the universal church, Ratzinger had two main concerns. First, he observed that in the reception of Vatican II, the concept of 'the people of God' and later the concept of the church as communion were damaged by 'an increasing emphasis on the horizontal dimension, the omission of the idea of God' (2005a: 132). For Ratzinger, there seems to be an alternative between, on the one hand, either assuming the 'ontological precedence of the Church as a whole, of the one Church and the one body, of the one bride, over the empirical and concrete realizations in the various individual parts of the Church', or, on the other, focusing on 'the empirical structure of the Church', the Church 'existing in human organizations' (2005a: 134–5). *Tertium non datur*. Thus, since Kasper denied the ontological precedence of the universal church, Ratzinger criticized him, as Kasper saw it, for assuming 'that there exist only parishes that are empirically perceptible entities and that the depth of the theological understanding of the church has got lost' (Kasper 2000: 797; my translation). Kasper rejected this as a terrible misunderstanding and even caricature of his position. He claimed that he 'consistently fought against the sociological reduction of the church to individual parishes' (2000: 797), emphasizing instead the unity of the church. Thus Kasper denied the same position as Ratzinger, but his alternative was different from Ratzinger's. That means: *Tertium datur*. In the course of the debate, Ratzinger's concern to overcome the omission of the idea of God in parts of the church passed out of mind.

Another concern of Ratzinger's in this debate was the struggle against the understanding that the universal church is the product or sum of particular churches and their union. Again, the problem seems to have been how to define the alternative. For Ratzinger, there are only two parts to these exclusive alternatives: either there is an ontological precedence of the universal church over the particular churches, or there is an ontological priority of the particular churches over the universal church. *Tertium non datur*. Thus, because the second part would be in strict contradiction to the basic Catholic assumption of the unity of the church, it is necessary to opt for the first alternative. But Ratzinger's critics have insisted that there is a third possibility: the equiprimordiality of the universal church and her particular churches. If one takes up what Ratzinger himself said about eucharistic or communion ecclesiology—the particular church can exist only within a network of communions of table fellowship— then it is not necessary to assume the ontological priority of the universal church in order to secure the conviction that communion is not external to the particular churches but is a condition of their being a church. Kasper rejected just as strongly as Ratzinger the idea that the universal church was the sum of particular churches, but his alternative to this position was different from Ratzinger's. Again, there was a third alternative.

Ratzinger argued for the ontological priority of the universal church by referring to the pre-existence of 'God's great idea, the Church' (2005a: 135) and seeing in the 'gathering of the nations under the will of God the inner goal of creation' (2005a: 134). Kasper agreed with assuming this pre-existence of the church but he claims that, together with the universal church, the particular churches in and from which she exists are also in God's saving will. Thus the allusion to the church's pre-existence does not imply the ontological priority of the universal church over the particular churches.

But what does 'ontological priority' mean? The phrase has different meanings; one meaning comes close to causality when it is said that the universal church 'gives birth to the particular churches as her daughters' (CDF 1992, no. 9). But the mother–daughter relation contradicts the relation of 'mutual interiority' of the universal church and the particular churches that is maintained at the same time. The CDF adds to the formula of Vatican II '*The church in and formed out of the churches*' (*ecclesia in et ex ecclesiis*) the further qualification '*the churches in and formed out of the church*' (*ecclesiae in et ex ecclesia*) (CDF 1992, no. 9). The two formulas seem to be symmetrical such that they express 'mutual interiority', but in fact they are not, because the word *ex* in the first formula means 'consisting of' while in the second formula it means 'originating from'. The ecumenical problem of this understanding becomes clear when the CDF states, quoting John Paul II, 'The primacy of the bishop of Rome and the episcopal college are proper elements of the universal church that are "not derived from the particularity of the churches", but are nevertheless *interior* to each particular church. Consequently, "we must see the ministry of the successor of Peter not only as a *global* service, reaching each particular church from *outside*, as it were, but as belonging already to the essence of each particular church from *within*" ' (CDF 1992, no. 13; italics added). The questions that needed to be clarified had been what the 'proper elements of the universal Church' are, and how precisely the mutuality of mutual interiority is to be understood. The debate between the two cardinals ended too soon without ever answering these questions.

SUBSISTIT

Vatican II took a huge step towards ecumenism by recognizing not only Christians but also ecclesial realities (churches and ecclesial communities) outside the Roman Catholic Church. This made it impossible to continue saying that the Catholic Church *is* (*est*) the one Mystical Body of Christ. Instead, the council stated that the church confessed in the Creed *subsists* (*subsistit*) in the (Roman) Catholic Church. In 1966, Ratzinger commented that *subsistit* is 'more open' (*weiträumiger*) than *est*, and he sees 'possibilities of a not only moral but also really theological respect of the other churches as churches' (1969c: 237; my translation). Later he preferred to derive the meaning of the much debated *subsistere* from the Christological *hypostasis*: '*Subsistere* is a special variant of *esse*. It is "being" in the form of an independent agent. That is exactly what is concerned here. The Council is trying to tell us that the Church of Jesus Christ may be encountered in this world as *a concrete agent* [special emphasis by Ratzinger] in the Catholic Church. That can happen only once, and the view that *subsistit* should be multiplied fails to do justice to the particular point intended' (2005a: 147). But are the ecclesial communities not also 'concrete agents'? What is their difference from that one agent in terms of agency? Since the council sees the paradox 'between the uniqueness and the concrete existence of the Church, on the one hand, and, on the other, the continuing existence of a concrete ecclesiastical entity outside of the one active agent' (2005a: 148), it declared that ecumenism as the search for true unity is a duty for the church in the future. It is precisely the replacement of *est* by *subsistit* that is meant 'to build the ontological bridge, so to speak, toward the existence of other Church communities' (2005b: 240). But for Catholic understanding, the institution and the spirit of the church are interwoven so that her embodiment is inherent in the church herself. Thus ecumenism proposed by the council is in strict opposition to a relativistic one that regards ecclesial communities as 'multitudinous variations upon a theme, in which all the variations are in some sense right, and all in some sense wrong' (2005a: 148), to such an extent that there would be no need to seek unity; thus ecumenism would consist 'of everyone granting each other mutual recognition in some sense, because they are all merely fragments of what Christianity is' (2005a: 148).

Ecumenism

The topic of the unity of the church runs like a golden thread through Ratzinger's work from the beginning of his career to his pontificate. He was highly interested in Protestant thinking and theology, challenged by it, received ideas and impulses from it, but also emphasized its basic difference from Catholic theology.

Ratzinger has always distinguished two different types of church division, depending on whether or not the basic structure of the church has been preserved. He finds this structure expressed in the tradition–succession principle. With respect to the Orthodox churches he states

> that, along with Scripture, the Church that came into existence from and in Scripture is also truly and irrevocably accepted, in the basic form in which she had developed before Nicaea, as a vessel of the word. It belongs to this basic form that the bishops, by virtue of their sacramental consecration and the ecclesial tradition they received with it, personify the Church's unity with her source. In other words, that basic factor that has been expressed since the second century in the concept of the *successio apostolica*, the apostolic succession, belongs intrinsically to this structure. This means, in turn, that the structural unity has not been destroyed. (1987: 194)

In this respect Ratzinger sees a big difference from the churches shaped by the Reformation. For him, there is a line of thought going back to Augustine, who distinguished between the empirically existing church and the theological entity of the church as a salvific reality. After the great Western Schism in the fourteenth and fifteenth centuries, when two and then three popes existed at the same time and excommunicated each other and their followers, many no longer felt that the church was able to offer assurance of faith. They looked for a true pledge of salvation outside the ecclesiastical institutions. According to Ratzinger, Luther must be understood against this background of experiencing the church as the adversary of salvation instead of its guarantor. In Ratzinger's perspective, Luther on the one hand reduced the concept of the church to the local community, and on the other hand he understood the church as the community of the faithful through all time whom only God knows, the institutional dimension being without theological significance. In Luther the tradition–succession structure has disappeared. For Luther, the pure gospel is set independently over against the church; this marks the true break in the concept of the church in the Reformation. 'Not ministry but the "purity of the gospel" is the criterion for the presence of church . . . Protestant theology defines church without ministry, and understands the word as autonomously corrective of the ministry, whereas Catholic theology perceives ministry as a criterion of the Word: It does not know a word that is independent from the church, so to speak a hypostatic word, but the word lives in the church as the church lives from the word—a relation of mutual dependency and relationship' (1969b: 106; my translation). As a consequence, the structure of the act of faith has changed; there is no longer the 'We' of faith but only the isolated 'I' who believes. Nevertheless, the Lutherans whom Ratzinger has mainly in mind here would generally not feel that he has understood their ecclesiology correctly.

In a famous talk that he gave in Graz (Austria) in 1976, Ratzinger made challenging prognoses and proposals for the future of ecumenism. At that time, he still was a professor in Regensburg, but he published this paper again in his *Principles of Catholic Theology* in 1982 (in German) when he was already serving as Prefect of the Congregation for the Doctrine of the Faith. With respect to the Orthodox churches, he stated that the West must 'admit that, in the Eastern church, the form and content of the Church of the Fathers is present in unbroken continuity' (1987: 196). An ecclesial unification will be viable if both sides do not make maximal demands. In this sense, Ratzinger argued 'what was possible for a thousand years is not impossible for Christians today' (1987: 198). His remarkable conclusion is that 'Rome must not [read: does not need to] require more from the East with respect to the doctrine of primacy than had been formulated and was lived in the first millennium' (1987: 199). He explained this in more detail: 'Reunion could take place in this context if, on the one hand, the East would cease to oppose as heretical the developments that took place in the West in the second millennium and would accept the Catholic Church as legitimate and orthodox in the form she had acquired in the course of that development, while, on the other hand, the West would recognize the Church of the East as orthodox and legitimate in the form she has always had' (1987: 199). This was a statement in 1976 about what is theologically possible, but Ratzinger emphasized that a reunion would require a long and deep spiritual process. He was very well aware of the serious difficulties in this respect and very cautious with any prognosis.

With respect to Roman Catholic–Protestant ecumenism, Ratzinger noted that the maximum demand from the Protestant side 'would be that the Catholic Church accept, along with the unconditional acknowledgement of all Protestant ministries, the Protestant concept of ministry and their understanding of the Church', but this would mean for the Catholics to 'renounce the apostolic and sacramental structure of the Church' and so amount to 'the conversion of Catholics to Protestantism' (1987: 197). This demand is often heard, as Ratzinger mentions, but he strictly denies it. Instead, he proposes 'a manner of thinking and acting that respects the other in his search for the true essence of Christianity; an attitude that regards unity as an urgent good that demands sacrifice, whereas separation demands justification in every single instance' (1987: 202). Thus Catholics do not wish to dissolve the Protestant confessions of faith; on the contrary, they hope for strengthening these confessions and ecclesial reality in the Protestant realm. But a 'confessionalism of separation' should be overcome by 'a hermeneutics of union that sees the confession of faith as that which unites' (1987: 202). Thus unity requires a Christianity of faith and faithfulness that is committed to a definite content and therefore is constantly looking for unity and helping the other to identify the common centre in the processes of purification and deepening.

The CDF's *Response* to the *Final Report* of the First Anglican/Roman Catholic International Commission (ARCIC I) prompted a fierce debate in 1982. Ratzinger commented on it one year later, repeating the basic features of Roman Catholic ecclesiology, in his understanding. According to him, the core problem of the dialogue was the problem of authority and tradition. For Christians, Scripture is the authority, but it needs the church as the vital environment for its witness so that it becomes a living voice. 'Who decides whether what you say is in accord with Scripture or not?' (2008a: 75). Thus 'only the whole Church can be the locus of Scripture' (2008a: 74), since the word of the universal church alone can be obligatory. For Catholics, tradition is not mainly a set of old doctrines that are handed down; rather, it is the way of coordinating the authoritative word of the Bible with the living word of the church. 'Here "tradition" means above all that the Church, living in the form of apostolic succession with the Petrine office at its center, is the place in which the Bible is lived and interpreted in a binding way. This interpretation forms a historical continuity, setting fixed standards but never itself reaching a definitive point of completion after which it is a thing of the past' (2008a: 82). Thus there is a priority of the universal church with respect to the particular churches, and an 'individual bishop has full authority as pastor of a particular Church because, and insofar as, he represents the universal Church therein' (2008a: 77). If the problem is put in this way, it is difficult for other churches to relate to this entity 'universal church'.

Here, as in other topics, one may raise the question of whether Ratzinger has changed his mind. This question was explicitly put in a letter to Ratzinger when, after *Dominus Iesus*, the Orthodox Metropolitan Damaskinos of Switzerland asked him 'whether there is any continuity between Professor Joseph Ratzinger and the Prefect of the Congregation for the Doctrine of the Faith' (Damaskinos 2005: 223). In his response, Ratzinger pointed to the difference of offices and their corresponding tasks. The prefect 'does not, as the Professor does, write texts based on his own research and findings; rather, he must see to it that the organs of the teaching Church carry on their work with a high degree of responsibility, so that in the end a text is purged of everything that is merely personal and truly becomes the common message of the Church' (Ratzinger 2005b: 230). Two changes may be identified as Ratzinger shifted from one role to the other. In 1964, Ratzinger had spoken cautiously about a new approach of the Council [*Ansatz*], about 'the idea of the unity of the churches that remain *churches* and nevertheless become *one* church' (1964: 105; emphases by Ratzinger; my translation) and also about 'the recognition that the non-Catholic Christian communities are not "the church" but truly [*in Wahrheit*] "churches"' (1964: 106). Even though he stated that strictly speaking the plural 'churches' only refers to local churches within the unity of the one church, he also argued that 'the centralistic system in which the local church of Rome, so to speak, had absorbed all other local churches' (1964: 104) contributed to the development that the plural of 'churches' spread outside the one church. Thus he saw ecumenical possibilities in regaining the understanding of the church as communion of churches. These possibilities disappear if the priority of the universal church is understood as described.

Another topic where a change in theological positions is noticeable is in Ratzinger's understanding of the Synod of Bishops. At the time of the Second Vatican Council, he perceived the synod as an expression of collegiality, attempting to offer a counterpart to

Roman centralism. In the 1980s, he defended the restricted legal structure of this synod instituted by Paul VI that was much narrower than he had originally thought. He distinguished between its theological aspect (serving the interaction between Primacy and episcopacy, strengthening collegiality) and its legal aspect (the synod is only an advisory institution). The theological emphases (*communio*) remained basically the same, but the legal aspects do not seem to correspond fully to them, since they do not sufficiently address the urgent problems of centralism. This is to a certain degree surprising, since Ratzinger has always insisted on the unity of the theological/sacramental and juridical dimensions of the ecclesial order. But he obviously felt that after the council he had to emphasize within the polarity of unity and plurality the element of unity more strongly than earlier when he advocated plurality (though of course still within unity).

In later years, Ratzinger addressed the problem that, in spite of the ecumenical dialogues, divisions between the churches have not disappeared as quickly as many had hoped. He called for leaving 'to God what is his business and his alone and to investigate then what our tasks are, in all seriousness. This sphere of our tasks includes doing and suffering, activity and patience' (2008b: 138). He also reflected on the Pauline statement 'there must be factions' (1 Cor. 11:19), assuming that there can be a divine 'must' even though divisions originated from human failure and sin. Astonishingly, he connects this with Oscar Cullmann's idea of a 'unity through plurality'. This does not mean to resign oneself to the divisions but rather to engage their challenging character if the poison of hostility can be removed. One can hope that finally diversity will become polarity without division.

In an ecumenical meeting at World Youth Day in Cologne in 2005, Benedict XVI said in an address to representatives of churches in Germany that many think that ministry remains the main obstacle between the churches after the clarification regarding the doctrine of justification. Benedict claims that this narrows the problem too much to a mainly institutional problem, while the real issue is 'the presence of the Word in the world' (Benedict 2006: 84). This is a challenging formulation, since Protestants traditionally have understood the communication of the Word of God as their main concern. Ratzinger refers to the early church that in the second century took a threefold decision: 'first, to establish the canon, thereby stressing the sovereignty of the Word'; second, to establish 'the episcopal ministry, in the awareness that the Word and the witness go together; that is, the Word is alive and present only thanks to the witness, so to speak, and receives from the witness its interpretation. But the witness is only such if he witnesses to the Word' (2006: 84); third, to use the *regula fidei* (rule of faith) as a key for interpretation. Benedict thinks that these three elements mutually penetrate each other, and that the unresolved difference between the churches lies in the shape and configuration of these elements. We could thus draw the conclusion: the church is where the word of God is a living voice, and so the Triune God is really present and effective, while our ministries, doctrines, and theologies are means and instruments of this final goal. The presence of the Word of God will be the decisive criterion for the true church and the final proof of its existence. All churches should await, self-critically and humbly, God's own judgement in this matter.

Ratzinger's Eucharistic ecclesiology is an impressive, complex synthesis integrating from its Eucharistic centre elements from Scripture, the church fathers, and church history, logically unfolding itself as *communio* ecclesiology, attempting to overcome widespread dichotomies (spiritual vs institutional, law vs love), trying to balance conflicting aspects such as unity and plurality, primacy and collegiality. But it also employs inappropriate dichotomies in sharpening its profile. Historical-critical *analysis* may cast doubts on whether the *synthesis* reflects precisely enough the elements in their respective profiles as Ratzinger integrates them into the whole. Nevertheless, Ratzinger's ecclesiology remains a significant challenge, both for Roman Catholics and for Christians of other traditions.

References

Benedict XVI (2006). *God's Revolution: World Youth Day and Other Cologne Talks*. San Francisco: Ignatius Press.

Congregation for the Doctrine of the Faith [CDF] (1992). 'Letter to the Bishops of the Catholic Church on Some Aspects of the Church Understood as Communion'. *Origins* 22: 108–12.

Kasper, Walter (2000). 'Das Verhältnis von Universalkirche und Ortskirche: Freundschaftliche Auseinandersetzung mit der Kritik von Joseph Kardinal Ratzinger'. *Stimmen der Zeit* 218: 795–804.

Metropolitan Damaskinos (2005). 'Letter to Joseph Ratzinger'. In Joseph Ratzinger, *Pilgrim Fellowship of Faith: The Church as Communion*. Ed. S. O. Horn and V. Pfnür. Trans. H. Taylor. San Francisco: Ignatius Press, 217– 28.

Ratzinger, Joseph (1964). 'Die Kirche und die Kirchen'. *Reformatio* 13: 85–108.

Ratzinger, Joseph (1969a). 'Vom Ursprung und vom Wesen der Kirche'. In Joseph Ratzinger, *Das neue Volk Gottes: Entwürfe zur Ekklesiologie*. Düsseldorf: Patmos, 75–89.

Ratzinger, Joseph (1969b). 'Das geistliche Amt und die Einheit der Kirche'. In Joseph Ratzinger, *Das neue Volk Gottes: Entwürfe zur Ekklesiologie*. Düsseldorf: Patmos, 105–20.

Ratzinger, Joseph (1969c). 'Theologische Aufgaben und Fragen bei der Begegnung lutherischer und katholischer Theologen nach dem Konzil'. In Joseph Ratzinger, *Das neue Volk Gottes: Entwürfe zur Ekklesiologie*. Düsseldorf: Patmos, 225–45.

Ratzinger, Joseph (1987). *Principles of Catholic Theology: Building Stones for a Fundamental Theology*. Trans. Sister M. F. McCarthy SND. San Francisco: Ignatius Press.

Ratzinger, Joseph (1996). 'The Origin and Essence of the Church'. In Joseph Ratzinger, *Called to Communion: Understanding the Church Today*. Trans. A. Walker. San Francisco: Ignatius Press, 13–45.

Ratzinger, Joseph (2005a). 'The Ecclesiology of the Constitution *Lumen Gentium*'. In Joseph Ratzinger, *Pilgrim Fellowship of Faith: The Church as Communion*. Ed. S. O. Horn and V. Pfnür. Trans. H. Taylor. San Francisco: Ignatius Press, 123–52.

Ratzinger, Joseph (2005b). 'Letter to Metropolitan Damaskinos'. In Joseph Ratzinger, *Pilgrim Fellowship of Faith: The Church as Communion*. Ed. S. O. Horn and V. Pfnür. Trans. H. Taylor. San Francisco: Ignatius Press, 228–41.

Ratzinger, Joseph (2008a). 'Problems and Prospects of the Anglican–Catholic Dialogue'. In Joseph Ratzinger, *Church, Ecumenism, and Politics: New Endeavors in Ecclesiology*. Trans. M. J. Miller et al. San Francisco: Ignatius Press, 69–99.

Ratzinger, Joseph (2008b). 'On the Progress of Ecumenism'. In Joseph Ratzinger, *Church, Ecumenism, and Politics: New Endeavors in Ecclesiology*. Trans. M. J. Miller et al. San Francisco: Ignatius Press, 132–38.

Ratzinger, Joseph (2008c). 'Primacy, Episcopacy, and *Successio Apostolica*'. In Joseph Ratzinger, *God's Word: Scripture-Tradition-Office*. Ed. T. Söding and P. Hünermann. Trans. H. Taylor. San Francisco: Ignatius Press, 13–39.

Ratzinger, Joseph (2010a). 'Kirche und Liturgie'. In Joseph Ratzinger, *Gesammelte Schriften 8/1: Kirche—Zeichen unter den Völkern: Schriften zur Ekklesiologie und Ökumene*. Freiburg im Breisgau: Herder, 157–77 (presentation offered in 1958).

Ratzinger, Joseph (2010b). 'Primat und Episkopat'. In Joseph Ratzinger, *Gesammelte Schriften 8/1. Kirche—Zeichen unter den Völkern: Schriften zur Ekklesiologie und Ökumene*. Freiburg im Breisgau: Herder, 629–59 (presentation offered in 1964).

Ratzinger, Joseph (2011). *Gesammelte Schriften 1: Volk und Haus Gottes in Augustins Lehre von der Kirche: Die Dissertation und weitere Studien zu Augustinus und zur Theologie der Kirchenväter*. Freiburg im Breisgau: Herder (1st edn. Munich: Karl Zink, 1954; 2nd edn. St Ottilien: EOS, 1992, new preface).

Wicks, Jared (2008). 'Six Texts by Prof. Joseph Ratzinger as *peritus* before and during Vatican Council II'. *Gregorianum* 89.2: 233–311.

SUGGESTED READING

Koch, Kurt (2010). *Das Geheimnis des Senfkorns: Grundzüge des theologischen Denkens von Papst Benedikt XVI*. Regensburg: Friedrich Pustet.

Nichols, Aidan (2007). *The Thought of Pope Benedict XVI: An Introduction to the Theology of Joseph Ratzinger*. London and New York: Burns & Oates.

Ratzinger, Joseph (1987). *Principles of Catholic Theology: Building Stones for a Fundamental Theology*. Trans. H. Taylor. San Francisco: Ignatius Press.

Ratzinger, Joseph (1996). 'The Origin and Essence of the Church'. In Joseph Ratzinger, *Called to Communion: Understanding the Church Today*. Trans. A. Walker. San Francisco: Ignatius Press, 13–45.

Ratzinger, Joseph (2005). 'The Ecclesiology of the Constitution Lumen Gentium'. In Joseph Ratzinger, *Pilgrim Fellowship of Faith: The Church as Communion*. Ed. S. O. Horn and V. Pfnür. Trans. H. Taylor. San Francisco: Ignatius Press, 123–52.

Ratzinger, Joseph (2008). 'On the Progress of Ecumenism'. In Joseph Ratzinger, *Church, Ecumenism, and Politics: New Endeavors in Ecclesiology*. Trans. M. J. Miller et al. San Francisco: Ignatius Press, 132–8.

Rowland, Tracey (2008). *Ratzinger's Faith: The Theology of Pope Benedict XVI*. Oxford: Oxford University Press.

Schaller, Christian (ed.) (2011). *Kirche-Sakrament und Gemeinschaft: Zu Ekklesiologie und Ökumene bei Joseph Ratzinger*. Regensburg: Friedrich Pustet.

Wiedenhofer, Siegfried (2016). *Die Theologie Joseph Ratzingers/Benedikts XVI.: Ein Blick auf das Ganze*. Regensburg: Friedrich Pustet.

CHAPTER 21

···

JOHN ZIZIOULAS

···

PAUL MCPARTLAN

HAILED in 1982 by the outstanding Roman Catholic ecclesiologist, Yves Congar (1904–95), as 'one of the most original and most profound theologians of our time' (Congar 1982: 88), the Orthodox theologian John Zizioulas (b. 1931; Metropolitan of Pergamon since 1986) has continued to exercise a decisive influence on the course of ecclesiological investigation, especially within an ecumenical setting, well into the twenty-first century (see, e.g., Knight 2007). Congar was reviewing Zizioulas's book *L'Être ecclésial* (1981) which, with slightly modified content, appeared soon afterwards in English as *Being as Communion* (Zizioulas 1985). As the English title in particular indicates, ecclesiology for Zizioulas is actually situated in a much broader perspective; in fact, it is profoundly linked both to Trinitarian theology and to anthropology. He developed the latter areas more fully in *Communion and Otherness* (Zizioulas 2006), which in turn was praised as 'a great book and a converting one', in fact 'a comprehensive model for the whole of Christian theology', by the then archbishop of Canterbury, Rowan Williams (Zizioulas 2006: xi–xii), whose comments further witness to the remarkable ecumenical impact of Zizioulas's thought.

INTRODUCTION

···

The year 1982 saw the publication of two crucial ecumenical texts in the production of which Zizioulas was strongly involved: the first agreed statement of the Joint International Commission for Theological Dialogue between the Roman Catholic Church and the Orthodox Church, *The Mystery of the Church and of the Eucharist in the Light of the Mystery of the Holy Trinity* (RC-O 1982; the 'Munich document'), and the Lima report of the Faith and Order Commission of the World Council of Churches, *Baptism, Eucharist and Ministry* (World Council of Churches 1982). Having been a prime architect of the 'Plan to set underway the theological dialogue between the Roman Catholic Church and the Orthodox Church' in 1980 (Borelli and Erickson 1996: 47–52), the influence of Zizioulas on all of the subsequent statements of that dialogue (except the Balamand statement of 1993 with which he was not involved) is clearly discernible, most especially in the case of the Munich document and of the 2007 'Ravenna document', *Ecclesiological and Canonical Consequences of the Sacramental Nature of the Church: Ecclesial Communion, Conciliarity and Authority* (RC-O 2007). Equally evident is his influence on the 2006 'Cyprus statement', *The Church of the Triune God* (A-O 2006), from the International Commission for Anglican–Orthodox Ecumenical Dialogue, of which he served as co-chairman for the sixteen years of work which resulted in the statement.

Also long in preparation was the 2013 convergence statement of the Faith and Order Commission, *The Church: Towards a Common Vision*, work having begun in 1989 with the benefit of Zizioulas's own suggestions for a major ecumenical study of the church (Zizioulas 1990), many of the responses from the churches regarding the Lima report also having urged such a study (World Council of Churches 2013: 43). The fact that the second of the 2013 statement's four chapters should itself be entitled 'The Church of the Triune God', and the third, 'The Church: Growing in Communion', again testifies to the reverberating influence that Zizioulas has had on ecumenical reflection on the church in recent times, all of which has been centred on the theme of communion, a theme that Zizioulas has consistently expounded since his earliest published writings in the 1960s (see bibliographies in McPartlan 2006 and Papanikolaou 2006), most notably in his books *Being as Communion* and *Communion and Otherness*.

What characterizes Zizioulas's writings on communion or *koinōnia* is threefold: first, his anchoring of the idea in a theology of the Trinity drawn principally from the Cappadocian fathers; second, his proposal that it is through the celebration of the Eucharist most of all that the church participates in the communion life of God; and third, his conviction that the structure of the church must correspond to and reflect the mystery of that divine communion. He has been one of the foremost exponents in recent times of 'Eucharistic ecclesiology'—a Eucharistic understanding of the church and, correspondingly, an ecclesial understanding of the Eucharist—described by Paul Avis as 'one of the most creative developments in Christian theology in the last half-century' (Avis 2007: 103). Eucharistic ecclesiology has gained wide adherence and has enormous ecumenical potential (see McPartlan 1986 and McPartlan 2010). The Catholic–Orthodox Munich document manifests its own espousal of such an ecclesiology in its programmatic statement: 'the eucharistic celebration makes present the Trinitarian mystery of the Church' (RC-O 1982: I, 6).

With frequent reference to *Being as Communion, Communion and Otherness*, and to *The One and the Many* (Zizioulas 2010), a valuable anthology of many of Zizioulas's writings, the three main sections of this chapter consider the three fundamental points just indicated, which lie at the heart of Zizioulas's ecclesiology: the relationships between the church and the Trinity, and between the church and the Eucharist, respectively, and then the structural consequences of those relationships for the church. Though such a distinction may be helpful for the sake of analysis, it is essential to remember throughout that these considerations are completely interwoven in his thought. The brief conclusion finally considers the purpose of the church thus conceived and structured.

CHURCH AND TRINITY

Being as Communion and *Communion and Otherness* may be said to form a diptych. The former emphasizes that all being is characterized by communion, first of all the being of God who is Father, Son, and Holy Spirit, and then likewise the being of all of creation. The latter emphasizes, complementarily, that rather than suppressing otherness, as might be imagined, communion actually releases, enables, and even requires true otherness, again primarily in God himself—Father, Son, and Spirit are totally other yet totally one—and in all that God has made. Zizioulas says that it is in the church that 'communion with the other fully reflects the relation between communion and otherness in the Holy Trinity' (Zizioulas 2006: 6). Thus, the church reflects, and indeed participates in, the communion life of the Holy Trinity: 'the ground of the church's being . . . can be no other than the Triune God'; 'the fabric of the church's being is communion' (Zizioulas 1990: 211–12). Moreover, the church has its participation in the life of God 'in Christ and in the Spirit' (Zizioulas 2006: 6).

Such a view relies on important preparatory steps in the account that Zizioulas gives, relating on the one hand to the priority of the person in the theology of God, and on the other hand to the new birth that brings about membership of the church. Zizioulas explains that ancient Greek thought espoused an 'ontological monism' (Zizioulas 1985: 16), understanding there to be 'an organic and indissoluble bond between God and the world' (Zizioulas 2006: 252). In such a view, ultimacy belonged to 'being *qua* being' (Zizioulas 2006: 220). Confronting such a view with biblical faith, the Greek fathers brought about 'two basic "leavenings"' (Zizioulas 1985: 39) in Greek thought. First of all, God was radically distinguished from the world as its creator, such that 'the being of the world became free from necessity' (Zizioulas 1985: 40), and secondly it was necessary to stress that the being of God himself was free from necessity, also. This was achieved by the Cappadocian fathers and especially by St Basil who gave real '*ontological content*' to the notion of *person* by associating the crucial ontological term, 'hypostasis', with person rather than with substance (Zizioulas 2006: 186; all emphases in quotations are original unless otherwise indicated), and maintained that 'the ontological "principle" or "cause" of the being and life of God' is '*the person of the Father*'. In other words, 'the one God is not the one substance but the Father, who is the "cause" both of the generation of the Son and of the procession of the Holy Spirit'. 'God, as Father and not as substance, perpetually confirms through "being" His *free* will to exist. And it is precisely his trinitarian existence that constitutes this confirmation: the Father out of love—that is, freely—begets the Son and brings forth the Spirit' (Zizioulas 1985: 40–1). Thus, primacy belongs to the person in ontology: the Father is 'the "ground" of God's being' and the 'ultimate reason for existence' (Zizioulas 1985: 89). Zizioulas emphasizes that only in such a view is God's absolute *freedom* secured.

Freedom is a theme of extraordinary importance for Zizioulas. Created in the image of God, human beings yearn for freedom, but are constrained by necessity. They yearn for 'a state of existence in which freedom is not a choice among many possibilities but a movement of love'. Such a state, says Zizioulas, 'obviously can only be realized from outside human existence', and then he strikingly adds: 'The whole of Christian doctrine ought to be precisely about this' (Zizioulas 2006: 237). In other words, this is precisely what constitutes salvation, which is received from God in the church by the work of Christ and the Spirit. It is received by means of a new birth in baptism which imparts a new hypostasis—in fact, true personhood—to human beings. For Zizioulas, quite simply, 'personhood is freedom' (Zizioulas 2006: 9–10), and salvation consists in the simultaneous achievement of both, in Christ and in the Spirit, through baptism (Zizioulas 1985: 19). 'Jesus Christ does not justify the title of Saviour because he brings the world a beautiful revelation, a sublime teaching about the person, but because he realizes in history *the very reality of the person* and makes it the basis and "hypostasis" of the person for every man' (Zizioulas 1985: 54). It is thus as members of the body of Christ that human beings enjoy true personhood, and 'the body of Christ' is indeed the basic understanding of the church in Zizioulas's theology—rarely does he use any other title.

Zizioulas refers to the 'ecclesial hypostasis' that is given in baptism, and contrasts it with the 'biological hypostasis' with which human beings are born. These are two quite different 'modes of human existence'. The latter, 'constituted' by 'conception and birth', is characterized by necessity: 'Who consulted me when I was brought into the world?' Its natural dynamism is self-assertion by separation and individualism, and it tends naturally towards death (Zizioulas 1985: 50–1). Sin has precipitated the death which is natural to humans as created beings: 'what is *created* naturally contains, at its heart, no power of survival.' 'What is *created* is, by nature, tragic because its existence is determined by the paradoxical synthesis of two elements which exclude one another absolutely, namely life and death, being and nothingness, all because its being had a beginning, a "starting point"' (Zizioulas 2006: 257). Notably, Zizioulas adds that 'space and time, which exclusively characterise what is created, are the very expression of this paradox'. 'By space and time, we all commune with one another in weaving together the thread of life; but it is also by time and space that we are divided from one another by the cutting edge of death' (Zizioulas 2006: 258). As will be seen, essential aspects of the communion that is enjoyed in the church are communion in space and communion in time.

Only communion with the living God can secure life for created beings, and sin breaks that vital communion. Death came to humanity 'not as a punishment in a juridical sense but as an existential consequence of the break of this communion'. 'What sin did was of deep ontological significance: it made the limitation of creaturehood show itself in the existential contrast between being and nothingness' (Zizioulas 2006: 228). Baptism imparts forgiveness. 'Every baptised person by being forgiven ceases to be identified by his or her past, and becomes a citizen of the city to come, that is, of the Kingdom' (Zizioulas 2006: 6). It is a 'new birth'; 'baptism leads to a new mode of existence, to a regeneration (1 Pet. 1:3, 23), and consequently to a new "hypostasis" ' (Zizioulas 1985: 53), namely the *ecclesial hypostasis*. Indicative of Zizioulas's profoundly existential understanding of ecclesiology, as just outlined, are the two short opening sentences of *Being as Communion*: 'The Church is not simply an institution. She is a "mode of existence", *a way of being*' (Zizioulas 1985: 15; also, Zizioulas 2010: 15). She is, in fact, 'an image or sign of the Trinity' (Zizioulas 2010: 16).

Two points need to be noted here: one with regard to the utter centrality of Christ, and the other with regard to a further refinement that leads Zizioulas to speak of a 'eucharistic hypostasis'. As has been mentioned already, Christ himself is the focal point of the work of salvation; it is his personhood that grounds the personhood of members of the church, his body. Zizioulas says that patristic Christology 'loses all meaning if it is not related to the problem of the *created* and the overcoming of death'. In that light he particularly stresses the teaching of St Paul that Christ's victory lies in his Resurrection (1 Cor. 15:14), and the teaching of the council of Chalcedon that the hypostasis or personhood of Christ is *uncreated*, being 'that of the eternal Son in the holy Trinity'. Created human nature and uncreated divine nature are united in him 'without division', but also 'without confusion', that is, in a way that is loving and life-giving, and also free (Zizioulas 2006: 259–63).

So it is that in the one Christ the many are saved, and this is a good point at which to highlight the recurrent motif of 'the one and the many' in Zizioulas's theology. In 1995, he said that the 'key concept' of communion enables 'subjects such as Christology, Pneumatology, anthropology, ecclesiology, etc.' to be interrelated (Zizioulas 2010: 382). Some years earlier, he similarly said that the one and the many is 'the mystery of Christology and Pneumatology, the mystery of the Church and, at the same time, of the Eucharist' (Zizioulas 2010: 72). It is thus clear that 'the one and the many' is, for Zizioulas, the primary form or shape of communion. This configuration does indeed repeatedly recur in different communional contexts in his theology. First of all, he explains that, with regard to God, although the familiar formula, 'one substance, three persons', tends to imply that the unity in God comes from the divine substance, in fact it comes from the person of the Father (Zizioulas 1985: 40). Hence, the 'one' with regard to God is not the divine substance, but the Father, and the 'many' are the three divine persons: 'the one God is the Father and not the divine nature or *ousia*' (Zizioulas 2010: 142). The 'one', in general, then, is not the overall reality embracing the many, but precisely one of the 'many', who stands at the centre of the many and constitutes their unity.

Such is the relational character of personhood. The one constitutes the many; the Son and the Spirit clearly cannot exist without the Father. But in an extremely important paper of 1986, entitled 'The Mystery of the Church in Orthodox Tradition', Zizioulas also stresses that 'there is no Father unless there is a Son and the Spirit'. 'There is no "one" whose identity is not conditioned by the "many" ' (Zizioulas 2010: 142). He then says: 'and if this applies to the being of God, it must be made equally to apply also to Christ'. In other words, Christ's identity itself is 'conditioned by the existence of the "many" '; he is not an *individual* but a *person*, indeed a 'corporate personality', prefigured in the Old Testament by the corporate 'Servant of God' in Isaiah and 'Son of man' in Daniel, 'simultaneously one and many' (Zizioulas 2010: 142). This happens because Christ is 'born of the Spirit' (that is why he is *Christos*; see Zizioulas 2010: 138); the Spirit is '*constitutive of the identity* of Christ', and the 'primary work' of the Spirit 'consists in opening up reality to become *relational*' (Zizioulas 2010: 141–2; compare the reference to 'the communion of the Holy Spirit' in 2 Cor. 13:13).

This makes ecclesiology an essential aspect of Christology; the latter without the former is 'inconceivable' says Zizioulas (Zizioulas 2010: 142), building on the legacy of his teacher, Georges Florovsky (1893–1979), who referred to ecclesiology as 'a vital chapter of Christology' (and who also interestingly said that 'the whole body of Orthodox belief' could be derived from the dogma of Chalcedon; McPartlan 2006: 212–13). 'What is at stake is the very identity of Christ', says Zizioulas adamantly. 'If Christ does not draw his identity from his relation with the Church', then either his situation is one of 'demonic isolationism' (Zizioulas 2010: 143; also, Zizioulas 1985: 182), or he should be understood 'only in terms of his relationship with the Father', but such a view would sever him from the church and tend in the direction of ecclesiological monophysitism. Christ's 'I' is the 'I' of the eternal Son in relation to the Father, as Chalcedon taught, but the incarnation has 'introduced into this eternal relationship another element: us, the many, the Church'. 'If the Church disappears from his identity he is no longer Christ, although he will still be the eternal Son.' 'The mystery hidden before all ages' is 'the incorporation . . . of us, or the many, into the eternal filial relationship between the Father and the Son'. This, in short, is the mystery of 'the Church' (Zizioulas 2010: 143).

Zizioulas contrasts his corporate understanding of Christ with the view of those who operate with 'an individualistic understanding of Christ' and make 'a clear-cut distinction between Christ and the Church', and he frankly says that he regards the 'deindividualisation of Christ' as 'the stumbling-block of all ecclesiological discussion in the ecumenical movement' (Zizioulas 2010: 142). It is indeed notable that even such biblical images of the church as the bride of Christ (see Eph. 5; Rev. 21–2) are absent from Zizioulas's ecclesiology, presumably because of their connotations of a distinction between Christ and the church (though he does frequently refer to the church as 'she'). His focus is always on the church as the body of Christ. Highlighting both the distinctiveness and the urgency of his view of Christ as a corporate personality constituted by the Spirit, Zizioulas says that Orthodox theology itself has 'not yet worked out the proper synthesis of Christology and Pneumatology' on which that view relies, and moreover that 'without [that] synthesis it is impossible to understand the Orthodox tradition itself or to be of any real help in the ecumenical discussion of our time' (Zizioulas 1985: 139).

It is, of course, the reality of sin that leads many to distinguish between Christ and the church, and Zizioulas's approach to this problem also is quite distinctive: sin does not give rise to a dialectic between Christ and the church; rather, the church to which he refers as conditioning the identity of Christ is the eschatological company of the saints, and sin pertains rather to the dialectic between the heavenly corporate reality of Christ and the saints and the earthy corporate reality of the bishop surrounded by his local church in the celebration of the Eucharist. The earthly church is 'an eikon of the Kingdom to come', and in every celebration of the Eucharist she is renewed in that eschatological identity: 'She is what she is by becoming again and again what she will be' (Zizioulas 2010: 144; also Zizioulas 2006: 296). While this may sound like a very 'high' notion of the church, Zizioulas notes that, in fact, the church is both 'maximalised and minimalised' in such a view. 'She is maximalised in that she will definitely survive eternally when her true identity will be revealed in the Parousia. And she is minimalised in that she has no *hypostasis* of her own but draws her identity from Christ and the Kingdom to come' (Zizioulas 2010: 144).

The reason for this fundamentally eschatological account of the church is again pneumatological. Being constituted by the Spirit has in fact a twofold consequence for Christ: he is corporate, conditioned by the many, because the Spirit makes reality relational and communional, as described above; and he is also eschatological, the 'last Adam', because when the Spirit acts in history it is 'in order to bring into history the last days, the *eschaton*' (Zizioulas 1985: 130). Thus, by being constituted in the Spirit, the person of Christ is 'automatically linked with . . . a *community*', and that community is 'the eschatological company of the "saints" that surround Christ in His Kingdom' (Zizioulas 2010: 68). Essential to this view is, of course, an understanding that the Spirit does not animate 'a Church which somehow already exists'; rather 'the Spirit makes the Church *be*'. 'Pneumatology does not refer to the well-being but to the very being of the Church' (Zizioulas 1985: 132). That is why Zizioulas always refers to the essential importance for ecclesiology of a synthesis between Christology and Pneumatology.

The fundamental relationship between the Eucharist and the church has already been mentioned. Recalling Zizioulas's distinction between the biological hypostasis with which human beings are born and the ecclesial hypostasis received in baptism, we may now note that he ponders the relationship between these two, because death in particular shows that the biological hypostasis continues to exert an effect on the baptized. He says, in fact, that 'a new ontological category' is needed to express the situation in which the baptized find themselves, because the ecclesial hypostasis is really a future, eschatological reality, experienced here on earth only as a foretaste, in the celebration of the Eucharist. So the baptized actually live in 'expectation and hope' of their ecclesial identity; they have a 'paradoxical hypostasis which has its roots in the future and its branches in the present'. Zizioulas refers this mode of existence as 'a *sacramental* or *eucharistic hypostasis*' (Zizioulas 1985: 59), and it is clear that, for him, the Eucharist is the true locus of churchly existence in this life, the lens, so to speak, through which all the light of the kingdom is mediated to this world and the essential reference point for all that is authentically ecclesial. The ecclesial hypostasis, he says, 'corresponds historically and experientially *only* to the Eucharist' (Zizioulas 1985: 60, emphasis added), and it is by being bound to the Eucharist that all of the church's actions, and especially the sacraments, are rendered 'transcendent and eschatological' (Zizioulas 1985: 61).

Church and Eucharist

The Eucharist is thus 'the heart of the Church' (Zizioulas 2006: 7), and the fact that it is a regular celebration means that it can be called a *beating* heart (McPartlan 2006: 269–74). Quite simply, it is '*the reality which makes it possible for us to exist at all*' (Zizioulas 1979: 193). Accordingly, for Zizioulas, the Christian is fundamentally 'a liturgical being, a *homo eucharisticus*' (Zizioulas 1979: 203), and the decisive importance of the Eucharist for the church is indicated, he says, by its very name of 'Communion'. All of the dimensions of communion, so essential to the church, are found in the Eucharist: 'God communicates himself to us, we enter into communion with him, the participants of the sacrament enter into communion with one another, and creation as a whole enters through man into communion with God' (Zizioulas 2006: 7).

As is evident from such statements, Zizioulas understands 'Eucharist' more widely than simply as the transformation of the bread and wine into the body and blood of Christ. The Eucharist should be 'understood primarily not as a *thing* and an objectified means of grace', he says, 'but as an *act* and a *synaxis* of the local Church' (Zizioulas 1985: 145). It is 'a communion-event' (Zizioulas 1985: 119; McPartlan 2006: 193–4), 'a gathering and a *liturgy*'.

> [T]he mystery of the transformation of the Gifts and the 'real presence' of Christ cannot be separated off and examined in isolation; it has to be examined as an organic unity with all the basic liturgical actions which make up the recapitulation of the divine Economy and the imaging of the Kingdom . . . The Spirit does not come down only 'upon these gifts here set forth' but also 'upon us' (the celebrants and the eucharistic gathering). Thus the 'real presence' of Christ is broadened to include the Head and the Body in one unity in the Holy Spirit. (Zizioulas 2011: 74–5)

There is thus not a sequential, causal passage from *holy gifts* to *holy people* in his understanding, but rather a strict simultaneity of the two (Zizioulas 2011: 75–6), and that leads him to integrate two famous principles which Henri de Lubac (1896–1991) both coined and treated sequentially: 'the Church makes the Eucharist' and 'the Eucharist makes the Church' (de Lubac 1986: 134, 152). It was in his landmark study, *Corpus Mysticum* (1944; 2nd edn, 1949), that de Lubac, the foremost pioneer of Eucharistic ecclesiology in the Catholic Church, first used the expression: 'the Eucharist makes the Church' (de Lubac 2006: 88). In the early years of his own theological research, Zizioulas read de Lubac's book, and he regularly cites it in his writings (McPartlan 2006: xv–xvi). Having done so in an important address of 1982, he made the significant integration just mentioned. 'My position', he said, 'is that *the Church constitutes the Eucharist while being constituted by it*', and he continued: 'Church and Eucharist are interdependent, they coincide, and are even in some sense identical' (Zizioulas 2010: 68). The likeness of these words to those of another Catholic exponent of Eucharistic ecclesiology, Joseph Ratzinger, subsequently Pope Benedict XVI, is striking: 'The Church is the celebration of the Eucharist;

the Eucharist is the Church; they do not simply stand side by side; they are one and the same; it is from there that everything else radiates' (McPartlan 1995: xiv).

A more significant and evident influence on Zizioulas's Eucharistic ecclesiology, however, comes from the Russian Orthodox theologian Nicholas Afanassieff (1893–1966), who actually coined the expression 'Eucharistic ecclesiology', and described its basic thesis in his important article '*Una Sancta*' (1963), as follows: 'the Church is where the eucharistic assembly is', or, more fully, 'where there is a eucharistic assembly, there is Christ, and there is the Church of God in Christ' (Afanasiev 2003: 14, 18). Afanassieff advocated such an ecclesiology in contrast to what he called 'universal ecclesiology', which he regarded as 'the predominant system in ecclesiology', both Catholic and Orthodox, according to which a local church has its ecclesiality from the union of its bishop with all the other bishops in a universal body (Afanasiev 2003: 6–8). He believed that the latter system derived from Cyprian and led to an impasse, because it implied that there could only be one true church, and both Catholics and Orthodox respectively understood their own church to be that one church, whereas Eucharistic ecclesiology opened the way to an understanding that since Catholics and Orthodox both celebrate the one Eucharist they are still actually one church (Afanasiev 2003: 22–4).

Afanassieff was a pioneer, and, while inevitably needing subsequent development and qualification, his basic principle served dramatically to refocus discussion of ecclesiology. It also had a substantial ecumenical impact. Zizioulas acknowledges that the idea that 'wherever the Eucharist is celebrated there is the Church' is 'an authentically Orthodox theological position' (Zizioulas 1980: 2), and John Meyendorff said of Afanassieff that 'his thought, both in methodology and in content, stands as perhaps the most original contribution of post-World War II Russian theology' (Meyendorff 1990: 364). Nevertheless, there is sharp criticism as well as praise in both Zizioulas's and Meyendorff's (Meyendorff 1990: 362–4) references to Afanassieff. Remarkably, the preparatory drafts of what became Vatican II's dogmatic constitution on the church, *Lumen Gentium* (1964), also demonstrated an appreciation of Afanassieff's contribution, but again with certain reservations. The drafts favourably acknowledged his emphasis on the bond between the Eucharist and the church, but indicated that it was necessary to show that the Catholic Church espouses a Eucharistic ecclesiology 'which is at the same time universal' (McPartlan 1986: 327).

While a reading of both reveals many points of similarity between Zizioulas's ecclesiology and that of Afanassieff, Zizioulas tends to emphasize the differences. He followed the complimentary comment above by complaining that Afanassieff was, however, too narrow in suggesting that it was 'sufficient to "celebrate" the Eucharist for there to be the Church' (Zizioulas 1980: 8). In his view, Afanassieff one-sidedly promoted the Eucharistic presuppositions of ecclesiology and neglected 'the ecclesiological presuppositions of the Eucharist' (Zizioulas 2010: 66), such as ecclesial communion and doctrinal orthodoxy. In '*Una Sancta*', acknowledging that his views might be seen as provocative, Afanassieff indeed went so far as to advocate the restoration of communion between the Orthodox Church and the Catholic Church 'the dogmatic divergences notwithstanding and without demanding that the catholic church renounce the doctrines that distinguish her from the orthodox church' (Afanasiev 2003: 25–6; also 24).

Zizioulas voiced his criticism of Afanassieff already in his doctoral thesis of 1965, subsequently published as *Eucharist, Bishop, Church: The Unity of the Church in the Divine Eucharist and the Bishop During the First Three Centuries* (Zizioulas 2001). Acknowledging that he did not have access to the full corpus of Afanassieff's writings in Russian but only to various articles of his in French, including 'Una Sancta' (Zizioulas 2001: 36, note 47), he nevertheless complained that the idea of the church and her unity was not fully expressed by 'a eucharistic unity *which lacks any preconditions*'. 'The Church has always felt herself to be united in *faith, love, baptism, holiness of life*, etc. And, it is certainly true that all this was incorporated very early into the Eucharist' (Zizioulas 2001: 17).

It is particularly what he regards as Afanassieff's neglect of various *structural* preconditions for the Eucharist that Zizioulas repeatedly criticizes. He insists that the Eucharist is fundamentally linked to the ministry of the bishop, who presides over the liturgy and the life of his local church, and that each local church must be in communion with the others in and through its bishop. The idea that 'wherever the eucharist is, there is the Church' risks suggesting that even a parish is 'a complete and "catholic" Church', which it is not, he says, because it doesn't gather together all the faithful and all of the ministers, especially the bishop and the presbyterium, of a given place in a true expression of 'catholicity' (Zizioulas 1985: 24). He then turns to the recurrent ecclesiological issue of the relationship between the 'local Church' and the 'universal Church', and acknowledges that Eucharistic ecclesiology is often suspected of giving priority to the local over the universal, and even of fostering 'congregationalism' (Zizioulas 1985: 133). He regards Afanassieff as one of those responsible for that misunderstanding. The latter's principle 'risks suggesting the idea that each Church could, *independently of other local Churches*, be the "one, holy, catholic and apostolic Church"' (Zizioulas 1985: 25). Looking to the early centuries of the church, Zizioulas counters that '[t]he fact that in each episcopal ordination at least two or three bishops from the neighbouring Churches ought to take part tied the episcopal office and with it the local eucharistic community in which the ordination took place with the rest of the eucharistic communities in the world in a fundamental way' (Zizioulas 1985: 155).

Whether Zizioulas's criticisms of Afanassieff are fully justified is a moot point (see e.g. Alexandrov 2009; Wooden 2010; and the interesting discussion in Bordeianu 2009). However, they serve to bring his own view into sharp focus. It may particularly be noted that he attributes the frequent and, in his view, mistaken prioritizing of the local church over the universal in Eucharistic ecclesiology to 'the lack of a proper synthesis between Christology and Pneumatology' (Zizioulas 1985: 133), and that he regards the opposite tendency, to prioritize the universal over the local, which he considers a characteristic of Catholic theology, as deriving from the same cause (Zizioulas 1985: 132). 'If Pneumatology is made constitutive of both Christology and ecclesiology' (Zizioulas 1985: 132), he says, a different view follows, one in which his key motif of the one and the many can again be discerned. 'The one Christ event takes the form of *events* (plural), which *are as primary ontologically* as the one Christ event itself. The local Churches are as primary in ecclesiology as the universal Church.' His firm conclusion is that the Eucharist indicates 'the *simultaneity* of both local and universal'. 'The dilemma "local or universal" is transcended in the eucharist, and so is any dichotomy between Christology and Pneumatology' (Zizioulas 1985: 132–3).

Two final points may be made in this section, in which some of the structural implications of Eucharistic ecclesiology have already become very evident. First, Zizioulas proposes a powerful image, again profoundly related to the motif of 'the one and the many', in order to resolve the issue of the local and the universal in ecclesiology. Local churches form not a '*unity in collectivity*', he says, such that they need to be added together as parts of a whole, but a '*unity in identity*'. Local churches are '*full circles* which cannot be added to one another but *coincide* with one another and finally with the Body of Christ and the original apostolic Church' (Zizioulas 1985: 158 n. 66). Second, Zizioulas's insistence that if local churches were to allow one of their number 'to close itself to the other communities either entirely (i.e. by creating a schism) or partially (i.e. by not allowing certain individual faithful from one community to communicate in another or by accepting to communion faithful excluded from it by their own community)' then 'they would betray *the very eucharistic character of their catholicity* and the catholic character of the eucharist' (Zizioulas 1985: 156–7) finds a significant echo in a Catholic context in the following teaching of the Congregation for the Doctrine of the Faith (CDF) when Cardinal Joseph Ratzinger was its prefect: 'it is precisely the Eucharist that renders all self-sufficiency on the part of the particular Churches impossible'. 'Indeed, the oneness and indivisibility of the Eucharistic body of the Lord implies the oneness of his mystical body, which is the one and indivisible Church. From the Eucharistic centre arises the necessary openness of every celebrating community, of every particular Church' (CDF 1992: n. 11). Once again, the ecumenical convergence enabled by Eucharistic ecclesiology is evident.

The CDF went on to propose that, since the papacy exists precisely as 'a foundation of the unity of the episcopate and of the universal Church', that ministry, also, should be understood in relation to the Eucharist: 'the existence of the Petrine ministry . . . bears a profound correspondence to the Eucharistic character of the Church' (CDF 1992: n. 11). Such a Eucharistic understanding of the papacy is a recent development in Catholic theology with considerable ecumenical implications, especially with regard to reconciliation between the Catholic Church and the Orthodox Church (see McPartlan 2016), the international dialogue between the two churches having adopted a Eucharistic ecclesiology in its statements ever since the 'Munich document' of 1982 (RC-O 1982), and the papacy being the most contentious issue between Catholics and Orthodox. Zizioulas's own espousal of the need for primacy at all levels in the life of the church, including the universal level, has been one of the most remarkable and ecumenically valuable features of his Eucharistic ecclesiology ever since the 1980s (McPartlan 2006: 205–11), opening up possibilities for constructive dialogue about that most dramatic of structural issues in ecclesiology.

Structural Consequences

As already noted, Zizioulas regards Eucharistic ecclesiology as having definite structural implications both within and among local churches (see also Zizioulas 1990: 212–13). In fact, the idea of the one and the many is the structural key to his ecclesiology, being the very shape of the communion that originates in God and is communicated to the church in and through Christ by the work of the Holy Spirit. That idea ripples through his ecclesiology, and indeed through his theology as a whole, constantly recurring. He intriguingly stresses, furthermore, that as well as having a communion in space, which gives rise to the familiar structural issues just indicated, the church, especially in its liturgy, is also characterized by a 'communion in time', transcending the 'fragmentation of time . . . which is a sign of the brokenness of our fallen existence'. Such a 'communion in time' is the proper context for the discussion of such ideas as 'apostolic succession' and 'tradition' (Zizioulas 1990: 212).

In *Being as Communion*, Zizioulas carefully explains how and why it is that the one–many structure of the church derives from the Eucharist. When he gathered his disciples together in the upper room, says Zizioulas, 'Our Lord . . . offered them a sort of "diagram" of the Kingdom', by which he presumably means that the gathering of the disciples around Jesus was an image of the heavenly gathering around the risen Lord. He continues: 'It was not one "sacrament" out of "two" or "seven" that He offered them, nor simply a memorial of Himself, but a real image of the Kingdom. . . . In the eucharist, therefore, the Church found *the structure of the Kingdom*, and it was this structure that she transferred to her own structure. In the eucharist the "many" become "one" (1 Cor 10:17)' (Zizioulas 1985: 206). As explained, this happens by the power of the Holy Spirit, who both makes reality relational and brings the last days into history, and the result is that 'ecclesial institutions are *reflections of the Kingdom*'. Zizioulas firmly adds that 'all ecclesial institutions must have some justification by reference to something ultimate and not simply to historical expedience' (Zizioulas 1985: 138; see also Zizioulas 2010: 144–5). As we shall see, it is therefore only because he believes that a truly theological case can be made for universal primacy, for instance, that Zizioulas advocates such a primacy; he considers that historical arguments count for little, if anything. As reflections of the kingdom by the power of the Spirit, ecclesial institutions, he says, 'lose . . . their self-sufficiency, their individualistic ontology, and exist *epicletically*, i.e. they depend for their efficacy constantly on prayer, the prayer of the community' (Zizioulas 1985: 138).

The influence of these ideas, first published in article form in 1975 and 1981 (see Zizioulas 1985: 261, for details), on the Roman Catholic-Orthodox 'Munich document' is very evident. That document emphasizes the dependence of the church on the Holy Spirit: '[t]he Church is continually in a state of *epiclesis*' (RC-O 1982, I: 5c). It then states that 'the church finds its model, its origin and its purpose in the mystery of God, one in three persons', and that the Eucharist 'understood in the light of the Trinitarian mystery is the criterion for [the] functioning of the life of the Church as a whole'. 'The institutional elements should be nothing but a visible reflection of the reality of the mystery' (RC-O 1982, II: 1). Later, it explicitly refers to the one and the many, and says programmatically:

> Since Christ is one for the many . . . in the church which is his body, the one and the many, the universal and local are necessarily simultaneous. Still more radically, because the one and only God is the communion of three persons, the one and only church is a communion of many communities and the local church a communion of persons. The one and unique church finds her identity in the *koinonia* of the churches. Unity and multiplicity appear so linked that one could not exist without the other. It is this relationship constitutive of the Church, that institutions make visible and, so to speak, 'historicise'. (RC-O 1982: III, 2)

'The ecclesial community is . . . called to be the outline of a human community renewed' (RC-O 1982: II, 3).

In his 1981 article, Zizioulas says that the one–many idea should replace 'all *pyramidal* notions' in ecclesiology, and he indicates how the idea applies at the universal and local levels of the church's life. 'On the universal level this means that the local Churches constitute one Church through a ministry or an institution which composes *simultaneously* a *primus* and a synod of which he is a *primus*. On the local level, this means that the head of the local Church, the bishop, is conditioned by the existence of his community and the rest of the ministries, particularly the *presbyterium*' (Zizioulas 1985: 139). The terminology of 'levels' of the church's life was subsequently adopted by the Ravenna document, which referred to *three* levels: local, regional, and universal (see RC-O 2007: nn. 17–44). In his article, Zizioulas did not directly refer to the 're-gional level', but it was by no means absent from his presentation. On the contrary, he spoke of it in some detail with reference to Apostolic Canon 34, which he introduced in order to correct mistaken Orthodox understandings of the role of the synod, which would contrast synodality as a democratic Orthodox principle of government with primacy as a monarchical Catholic principle. His point was that, properly understood, there is no synod without a primate and no primate without a synod—the one and the many again (Zizioulas 1985: 135–6).

Canon 34 from the fourth-century collection of *Apostolic Canons* has continued to play a major role in Zizioulas's ecclesiology, and has played an increasing role in Catholic–Orthodox dialogue. The Ravenna document states it as follows, in its section on the regional level of the life of the church:

> The bishops of each province (*ethnos*) must recognise the one who is first (*protos*) amongst them, and consider him to be their head (*kephale*), and not do anything important without his consent (*gnome*); each bishop may only do what concerns his own diocese (*paroikia*) and its dependent territories. But the first (*protos*) cannot do anything without the consent of all. For in this way concord (*homonoia*) will prevail, and God will be praised through the Lord in the Holy Spirit. (RC-O 2007, n. 24)

Zizioulas concluded his 1981 presentation of the canon, which he saw as perfectly expressing the pneumatologically conditioned Christology and ecclesiology that he advocates, by stating his firm view that a properly Orthodox understanding of the church requires both primacy and synodality, expressing the church's oneness and multiplicity, respectively. The church is therefore not simply 'a confederation of local Churches'; there must be a ministry of oneness. But likewise, 'the multiplicity is not to be subjected to the oneness; it is constitutive of the oneness'. Thus, there needs to be a 'first one' (*protos*) amidst the many 'heads of the local Churches', and 'oneness and multiplicity . . . must coincide' (Zizioulas 1985: 136).

With such principles and safeguards, Zizioulas believes that Orthodoxy, and the church in general, has nothing to lose and in fact much to gain by embracing primacy, also at the universal level of the church, always within the context of synodality. In a notable presentation to the Fifth World Conference on Faith and Order in Santiago de Compostela in 1993 on the conference theme of communion/*koinōnia*, Zizioulas again advocated 'a proper synthesis between Christology and Pneumatology', and 'a proper understanding of the "one" and the "many"', in order to ground a proper perception of the interrelationship of primacy and synodality. He again invoked Apostolic Canon 34, expressing the understanding of the early church, and suggested that that understanding might serve as a 'model' offering 'inspiration' to us today. Referring explicitly now to the three levels of church life—local, regional, and universal—he said that primacy was needed at all three levels in order for the church to be united and to 'speak with one voice'. He stressed, however, that primacy must be 'a truly relational ministry', and, with presumably not just the regional level of the church in mind but also the universal, he said that primacy must act only in unison with the heads of the local churches, expressing their consensus. He rather strikingly concluded: 'A primacy of this kind is both desirable and harmless in an ecclesiology of communion' (Zizioulas 2010: 55–6).

In the years since then, and especially in symposia following Pope St John Paul II's remarkable call in his 1995 encyclical letter *Ut Unum Sint* for ecumenical dialogue regarding the exercise of universal primacy, so that 'we may seek—together of course—the forms in which this ministry may accomplish a service of love recognised by all concerned' (Pope St John Paul II 1995: n. 95), Zizioulas has further elaborated his proposal for a universal primacy that truly accords with the nature and the needs of the church. Two papers stand out in this regard: 'Primacy in the Church: An Orthodox Approach' (delivered in 1996; see Zizioulas 2010: 262–73), and 'Recent Discussions on Primacy in Orthodox Theology' (delivered in 2003; see Zizioulas 2010: 274–87). In 1996, he said that at the time of the Great Schism (AD 1054) Rome was claiming a universal jurisdiction that was not recognized by the churches of the East (namely the other four patriarchates of Constantinople, Alexandria, Antioch, and Jerusalem), and that the latter 'formed their own structure and recognised the bishop of Constantinople as the first one among them . . . in the sense of canon 34 of the Apostolic Canons'. He then expressed his dissatisfaction with the phrase a 'primacy of honour', often used to describe the primacy of the patriarch of Constantinople (and, we may note, also often used by Orthodox to describe a possible universal primacy of the bishop of Rome), since 'it is not an "honorific" primacy but one that involves actual duties and responsibilities' (Zizioulas 2010: 270).

He then turned to the main issue of the primacy of the bishop of Rome, and stressed that, for him, 'the question is not an historical but a theological one'. 'The primacy of the Bishop of Rome', he said, 'has to be theologically justified or else be ignored altogether', because only a theological argument, and not historical or practical considerations, could show it to be necessary for the church's 'esse', rather than simply for her 'bene esse' (Zizioulas 2010: 270–1). He turned again to Apostolic Canon 34, the Trinitarian conclusion of which indicates its theological grounding (Zizioulas 2010: 269), and proposed that a universal primacy exercised according to 'the spirit and the provisions' of that canon, that is, in a synodical context and with no claim of jurisdiction over other local churches, whereby the primate would be president of the 'heads of churches' and 'spokesman' for decisions reached by 'consensus', would indeed be more than simply acceptable. 'A universal primus exercising his primacy in such a way is not only "useful" to the Church but an ecclesiological necessity in a unified Church' (Zizioulas 2010: 272–3).

In 2003, Zizioulas indicated that although Apostolic Canon 34 originally probably referred to a metropolitan district, its provisions could be taken as applying 'by extension [to] all forms of primacy' (Zizioulas 2010: 277), presumably including, therefore, universal primacy. He also reiterated what he called 'the simple and obvious fact that synodality cannot exist without primacy', and then gave the following very strong affirmation of the essential importance of primacy for the church: 'If, therefore, synodality exists jure divino, . . . primacy also must exist by the same right' (Zizioulas 2010: 279). He repeated, 'if synodality is an ecclesiological, that is, dogmatic, necessity, so also must be primacy', and reasoned that, since the church also exercises synodality at a universal level in ecumenical councils, a universal primate is needed. 'The logic of synodality leads to primacy, and the logic of the ecumenical council to universal primacy' (Zizioulas 2010: 284). He then indicated the applicability of Apostolic Canon 34 to the universal as well as to the regional level of the church's life by saying that that canon could be 'the golden rule of the theology of primacy', its closing words showing that its provisions derive from the fact that 'God himself is Trinity' (Zizioulas 2010: 284).

Finally, he emphasized the theological rather than biblical or historical nature of his argument, and indeed stated bluntly that he thinks that Catholics and Orthodox will never be able to agree on biblical or historical arguments for universal primacy. The only remaining option is to ask 'whether we can meet on the basis of certain fundamental theological principles'. He thinks that, especially after Vatican II and the overcoming of scholasticism in the theology of both churches, Catholics and Orthodox can indeed agree, on the basis of 'an ecclesiology of communion', and recognizing the 'ecclesial fulness' of local churches, that 'primacy at all levels is a necessary means to realize and guarantee [the] balance between the many and the one' (Zizioulas 2010: 285–7).

Zizioulas's rigorously argued advocacy of primacy in general and universal primacy in particular on the basis of principles acceptable to Orthodox theology is of truly historic significance. It has considerable implications not only for Catholic–Orthodox dialogue, and for the possibility of progress on the most contentious issue in that dialogue, namely, the papacy, but also for Orthodoxy itself. At the Synaxes of primates of the Orthodox churches held in Constantinople in 2008 and in 2014, Ecumenical Patriarch Bartholomew stressed the need for unity among the autocephalous Orthodox churches. In 2008, he specifically highlighted the danger of Orthodoxy seeming to be 'not one Church, but rather a confederation or a federation of churches' (Ecumenical Patriarch Bartholomew 2008: n. 8). As we have seen, it was precisely to avoid such a conception that, in 1981, Zizioulas stressed the importance of a ministry of oneness, a genuine primacy, within the context of synodality, both at the regional and also at the universal level of the church.

The argument that Zizioulas makes for primacy, intrinsically related to synodality, at all levels of the church is clear and impressive in its scope and power, linking as it does with fundamental theological principles of wide reach and relevance. It is a systematic argument, with a persuasive coherence and simplicity. However, significant questions of various sorts arise in its regard. First of all, as noted, Zizioulas himself acknowledges that the synthesis of Christology and Pneumatology upon which it rests, and with which the idea of the one and the many is intimately related, is rather new, unfamiliar, and challenging not just for ecumenical partners in theological dialogue in general but even for Orthodox theology. Second, while the idea of the one and the many is very clear in itself, precisely how it applies at the three levels of the church's life is not so clear. Are the many at the local level all the members of the local church? Does the bishop not relate differently to the people and to his presbyters? Are the many at the universal level all the bishops of the church or just the regional primates? And the notion that the same dynamic is to be found in the relationship between the one and the many at all three levels of the church's life also seems problematic. For example, while it may be said at the regional level that the primate can do nothing without the other bishops and they can do nothing without him, can the same be said, in the same way, about the relationship between a bishop and his people, or between the universal primate and the regional primates? Is the relationship between the one and the many at the universal level, where the primate is the first in a listing or *taxis* of major sees, the same as at the regional level where there is no such *taxis*?

Third, Zizioulas's determination to avoid biblical and historical argumentation, at least with regard to primacy at the universal level, is somewhat disconcerting. In a faith based on the Incarnation, it seems strange to make an argument abstracted from the data of Scripture and history, and the means by which the argument can then actually be verified are unclear. Is it really the case that ecumenical dialogue on this and other issues is unable to achieve a common reading of the Scriptures and of history? Fourth, is the perfect balance of the one and the many, which after all is patterned on the life of God himself, attainable in human life on earth, marked by creaturely limitation and sin? In particular, is it realistic to stipulate the full 'consensus' of the bishops/primates in order for the universal primate to speak/act? Might such conditions not constrain the church in its historical witness and action? Is it not part of the charism of primacy to take initiatives?

These are certainly not arguments against Zizioulas's case for primacy, but simply indications that his own remarkable argument still needs further clarification. His proposal is bold, visionary, and pioneering, and, as such, it is hardly surprising if it should require more elaboration and nuance. It is notable that the Ravenna document (as also the subsequent Chieti document; see RC-O 2016), while adopting the idea of three levels in the church, and presenting the case for primacy at each level, did not offer one single, unifying theological argument, a 'golden rule', for primacy across the three levels. In fact, it acknowledged, with regard to primacy at the universal level, that East and West have 'differences of understanding . . . with regard to its scriptural and theological foundations' (RC-O 2007: n. 43.2). It referred to the idea of the one and the many only once, speaking of 'unity and multiplicity, the relationship between the one Church and the many local Churches', as the 'constitutive relationship of the Church' (RC-O 2007: n. 4). It did, however, refer to the *headship* of Christ in the church and of the bishop at the local level and of the primate at the regional level (RC-O 2007: nn. 12, 13, 20, 23), and to the primate at each of the three levels—local, regional, and universal—as the '*protos*' (RC-O 2007: nn. 20, 24, 41, 42, 44; also 10); and 'head' and '*protos*' are, of course, terms which occur in Apostolic Canon 34, as we have seen. Overall, it simply, but momentously, concluded that, at all three levels of the life of the church, primacy is 'a practice firmly grounded in the canonical tradition of the Church', and that 'primacy and conciliarity are mutually interdependent', such that each must 'always' be considered in the context of the other (RC-O 2007: n. 43).

Conclusion

At the start of *Being as Communion*, as already noted, Zizioulas memorably summarized the nature and purpose of the church. 'The Church is not simply an institution. She is a "mode of existence", a way of being. The mystery of the Church, even in its institutional dimension, is deeply bound to the being of man, to the being of the world and to the very being of God.' Because of those connections, which we have investigated in this chapter, he said that 'ecclesiology assumes a marked importance, not only for all aspects of theology, but also for the existential needs of man in every age' (Zizioulas 1985: 15).

Zizioulas is acutely conscious of the need for theology and the church to respond to those existential needs. Speaking at a Faith and Order consultation with younger theologians in 1995, he said that '[a]t a time when all sciences realise that they cannot operate as closed units any longer, theology cannot afford to remain indifferent to the challenges coming from the nontheological world'. 'Questions such as the meaning of personhood or the ecological problem must be introduced into the theological problematic of, for example, Trinitarian theology, Christology, Pneumatology, or even ecclesiology' (Zizioulas 2010: 383). He draws inspiration from the fathers, both Greek and Latin, but especially, naturally, from the Greek fathers, who 'did not take simply a critical view of Hellenic culture, but entered deeply into it and established creative links with its premises'. The church today, he says, must likewise 'play a leading part in dialoguing with the prevailing culture at the deepest level'. 'By entering and sharing fully the human condition, God in the Person of Christ made it imperative that his Church constantly allow Him to enter fully into every culture' (Zizioulas 2010: 393–4).

As we have seen, Zizioulas's own ecclesiology is deeply interwoven with his theology as a whole, and it is abundantly clear that, for him, the church, most especially in the Eucharistic event in which and from which it lives, is the manifestation of the kingdom of God, for the benefit both of its members and of the world as a whole. 'This [the kingdom, in which all is gathered into one in Christ] is the image which the Church ought to show, both to itself and to the world, as it celebrates the Eucharist and composes its institutions. This is the greatest vision and the most important proclamation that the Church has to offer' (Zizioulas 2011: 73). Moreover, as the body of Christ, participating in 'the eternal life of the Trinity', the church is the means by which, thanks to the conquering of death, 'the eschatological unity of all is offered as a promise to the entire world' (Zizioulas 1985: 206). As such, the church has a 'mission . . . to perform in God's overall plan for his creation' (Zizioulas 1990: 211). Its task, so to speak, is to span between God and his creation, between this world and the next, drawing not only humanity but the whole of creation to its fulfilment. 'Ecclesial being must never separate itself from the absolute demands of the being of God—that is, its eschatological nature—nor from history. The institutional dimension of the Church must always incarnate its eschatological nature without annulling the dialectic of this age and the age to come, the uncreated and the created, the being of God and that of man and the world' (Zizioulas 1985: 20).

Emphasizing the cosmic dimension of salvation in Christ, which has led him to develop the idea of human beings as 'priests of creation', again in closest relation to the celebration of the Eucharist (Zizioulas 2011: 133–75), Zizioulas says: 'The Church exists for the entire creation and not simply for itself or humanity. In this sense, the Church does not differ from the Kingdom, since her *raison d'être* and her purpose is to be an icon of the Kingdom and to be identified with it in reality at the *eschaton*' (Zizioulas 2010: 386–7). This statement describing the church's service in the present while anchored in the future may aptly serve to summarize Zizioulas's vision, a vision which has inspired, equipped, and energized so much work in recent decades for the unity of the church to the glory of God.

References

Afanasiev, Nicolas (2003). '*Una Sancta*'. In Michael Plekon (ed.), *Tradition Alive: On the Church and the Christian Life in our Time*. Lanham, MD: Rowman & Littlefield, 3–30.
Alexandrov, Victor (2009). 'Nicholas Afanasiev's Ecclesiology and Some of its Orthodox Critics'. *Sobornost* 31.2: 45–68.
Anglican–Orthodox (A-O) (2006). *The Church of the Triune God: The Cyprus Agreed Statement of the International Commission for Anglican-Orthodox Theological Dialogue*. London: Anglican Communion Office.

Avis, Paul (2007). *The Identity of Anglicanism: Essentials of Anglican Ecclesiology*. London: T&T Clark.

Bartholomew, Ecumenical Patriarch (2008). 'Address by His All Holiness Ecumenical Patriarch Bartholomew at the Synaxis of the Heads of Orthodox Churches (Phanar, October 10, 2008)'. <http://www.ec-patr.org/docdisplay.php?lang=en&id=994&tla=en>.

Bordeianu, Radu (2009). 'Orthodox–Catholic Dialogue: Retrieving Eucharistic Ecclesiology'. *Journal of Ecumenical Studies* 44: 239–65.

Borelli, John and Erickson, John H. (ed.) (1996). *The Quest for Unity: Orthodox and Catholics in Dialogue*. Crestwood, NY: St Vladimir's Seminary Press.

Congar, Yves (1982). 'Bulletin d'ecclésiologie'. *Revue des sciences philosophiques et théologiques* 66: 87–119.

Congregation for the Doctrine of the Faith (CDF) (1992). '*Communionis Notio*: Letter to the Bishops of the Catholic Church on Some Aspects of the Church understood as Communion'. <http://www.vatican.va/roman_curia/congregations/cfaith/documents/rc_con_cfaith_doc_28051992_communionis-notio_en.html>.

De Lubac, Henri (1986). *The Splendor of the Church*. Trans. Michael Mason. San Francisco: Ignatius Press.

De Lubac, Henri (2006). *Corpus Mysticum: The Eucharist and the Church in the Middle Ages*. Trans. Gemma Simmonds CJ, with Richard Price. London: SCM Press.

John Paul II, Pope St (1995). Encyclical letter, *Ut Unum Sint*. <http://www.vatican.va/holy_father/john_paul_ii/encyclicals/documents/hf_jp-ii_enc_25051995_ut-unum-sint_en.html>.

Knight, Douglas H. (ed.) (2007). *The Theology of John Zizioulas: Personhood and the Church*. Aldershot: Ashgate.

McPartlan, Paul (1986). 'Eucharistic Ecclesiology'. *One in Christ* 22: 314–31.

McPartlan, Paul (1995). *Sacrament of Salvation: An Introduction to Eucharistic Ecclesiology*. Edinburgh: T&T Clark.

McPartlan, Paul (2006). *The Eucharist Makes the Church: Henri de Lubac and John Zizioulas in Dialogue*. New edition. Fairfax, VA: Eastern Christian Publications.

McPartlan, Paul (2010). 'The Body of Christ and the Ecumenical Potential of Eucharistic Ecclesiology'. *Ecclesiology* 6: 148–65.

McPartlan, Paul (2016). *A Service of Love: Papal Primacy, the Eucharist, and Church Unity*. Washington, DC: The Catholic University of America Press.

Meyendorff, John (1990). Review of Aidan Nichols, *Theology in the Russian Diaspora: Church, Fathers, Eucharist in Nikolai Afanas'ev (1893–1966)* (1989). *St Vladimir's Theological Quarterly* 34: 361–4.

Papanikolaou, Aristotle (2006). *Being with God: Trinity, Apophaticism, and Divine-Human Communion*. Notre Dame, IN: University of Notre Dame Press.

Roman Catholic–Orthodox (RC-O) (1982). Joint International Commission for Theological Dialogue between the Roman Catholic Church and the Orthodox Church. Agreed statement. *The Mystery of the Church and of the Eucharist in the Light of the Mystery of the Holy Trinity* (the 'Munich document'). <http://www.vatican.va/roman_curia/pontifical_councils/chrstuni/ch_orthodox_docs/rc_pc_chrstuni_doc_19820706_munich_en.html>.

Roman Catholic–Orthodox (RC-O) (2007). Joint International Commission for Theological Dialogue between the Roman Catholic Church and the Orthodox Church. Agreed statement. *Ecclesiological and Canonical Consequences of the Sacramental Nature of the Church: Ecclesial Communion, Conciliarity and Authority* (the 'Ravenna document').

<http://www.vatican.va/roman_curia/pontifical_councils/chrstuni/ch_orthodox_docs/rc_pc_chrstuni_doc_20071013_documento-ravenna_en.html>.

Roman Catholic–Orthodox (RC-O) (2016). Joint International Commission for Theological Dialogue between the Roman Catholic Church and the Orthodox Church. Agreed statement. *Synodality and Primacy During the First Millennium: Towards a Common Understanding in Service to the Unity of the Church* (the 'Chieti document'). <http://www.vatican.va/roman_curia/pontifical_councils/chrstuni/ch_orthodox_docs/rc_pc_chrstuni_doc_20160921_sinodality-primacy_en.html>.

Wooden, Anastacia (2010). 'Eucharistic Ecclesiology of Nicolas Afanasiev and its Ecumenical Significance: A New Perspective'. *Journal of Ecumenical Studies* 45: 543–60.

World Council of Churches (1982). *Baptism, Eucharist and Ministry*. Faith and Order Paper No. 111. Geneva: World Council of Churches.

World Council of Churches (2013). *The Church: Towards a Common Vision*. Faith and Order Paper No. 214. Geneva: World Council of Churches.

Zizioulas, John D. (1979). 'The Eucharistic Prayer and Life'. *Emmanuel* 85: 191–6, 201–3.

Zizioulas, John D. (1980). 'Ortodossia'. In *Enciclopedia del Novecento*. Vol. 5. Rome: Istituto della Enciclopedia Italiana, 1–18.

Zizioulas, John D. (1985). *Being as Communion: Studies in Personhood and the Church*. London: Darton, Longman and Todd.

Zizioulas, John D. (1990). 'Suggestions for a Plan of Study on Ecclesiology'. In Thomas F. Best (ed.), *Faith and Order 1985–1989: The Commission Meeting at Budapest 1989*. Faith and Order Paper No. 148. Geneva: World Council of Churches, 209–15.

Zizioulas, John D. (2001). *Eucharist, Bishop, Church: The Unity of the Church in the Divine Eucharist and the Bishop During the First Three Centuries*. Trans. Elizabeth Theokritoff. Brookline, MA: Holy Cross Orthodox Press.

Zizioulas, John D. (2006). *Communion and Otherness: Further Studies in Personhood and the Church*. Ed. Paul McPartlan. London: T&T Clark.

Zizioulas, John D. (2010). *The One and the Many: Studies on God, Man, the Church, and the World Today*. Ed. Fr Gregory Edwards. Alhambra, CA: Sebastian Press.

Zizioulas, John D. (2011). *The Eucharistic Communion and the World*. Ed. Luke Ben Tallon. London: T&T Clark.

SUGGESTED READING

Chryssavgis, John (ed.) (2016). *Primacy in the Church: The Office of Primate and the Authority of Councils*. 2 vols. Yonkers, NY: St Vladimir's Seminary Press.

Collins, Paul (2009). 'The Church and the "Other": Questions of Ecclesial and Divine Communion'. In Gesa Elsbeth Thiessen (ed.), *Ecumenical Ecclesiology: Unity, Diversity and Otherness in a Fragmented World*. London and New York: T&T Clark, 101–14.

Vgenopoulos, Maximos (2013). *Primacy in the Church from Vatican I to Vatican II: An Orthodox Perspective*. DeKalb, IL: Northern Illinois University Press.

Volf, Miroslav (1998). *After our Likeness: The Church as the Image of the Trinity*. Grand Rapids, MI: Eerdmans.

CHAPTER 22

WOLFHART PANNENBERG

FRIEDERIKE NÜSSEL

THE ecclesiology of the German Lutheran theologian Wolfhart Pannenberg (1928–2014) is part of his comprehensive approach to Systematic Theology that responds to two rather divergent modern phenomena: the secularization of Western societies on the one hand and the twentieth-century ecumenical movement among Christian churches on the other. Both phenomena led to a significant transformation of ecclesiology. Pannenberg's ecclesiology is closely related to broader developments in the doctrine of the church. This subject became a formal subdivision of Systematic Theology only in the Reformation of the sixteenth century. In the following confessional movement, the major task of ecclesiology across denominations was to explore and defend the respective denominational understanding of the church's nature and mission. This changed significantly with the rise of modern ecumenism and especially so after the Second Vatican Council. Ecumenism then stimulated many theologians to reconstruct ecclesiology with a focus on the goal of visible unity. For much of the twentieth century, Systematic Theology also focused on the more fundamental and demanding challenges of atheism, radical criticism of religion, scientism, and naturalism. In these dynamic contexts, Pannenberg constructed an ecclesiological approach that provided a relevant explanation of the Christian faith in a secularizing culture and at the same time offered theological argumentation for overcoming the church-dividing controversies and polemics in historical Christian doctrines.

In this chapter I will first give an introduction to the development of Pannenberg's ecclesiology and its role as part of his general approach to Systematic Theology. After exploring the origin, nature, and mission of the church as topics of ecclesiology in a more narrow sense, I will then present Pannenberg's doctrine of word and sacrament, his theology of sacraments and of ministry. These topics are essential for a comprehensive understanding of the church's mission and life and at the same time highly controversial in interdenominational dialogue.

The Development
of Pannenberg's Ecclesiology

Pannenberg's first public approach to ecclesiology came out of a course he taught in 1962 at Johannes-Guttenberg-University in Mainz titled 'The Theology of the Church'. With some hesitation he published a provisional manuscript in 1970 as *Theses on the Theology of the Church* (Pannenberg 1974: see Preface; no English translation). Responding to debates over a sociological approach to ecclesiology in German theology in the 1950s and 1960s (cf. Laube 2006: 32–80), Pannenberg addressed the societal and political role of the church as the general horizon of ecclesiology and defined ecclesiology's central task as being able to explain why a Christian institution such as the 'church' is necessary. In his central thesis he claimed that the societal and political role of the church must be understood in terms of the eschatological hope for God's future kingdom, which is the heart of Jesus's proclamation and the eschatological *kerygma* in the New Testament. For Pannenberg it was most important that this message of God's future kingdom would include the hope for a final fulfilment not only for individuals but also for a reconciled society of all people in God's kingdom. The particular mission of the church in history consists in representing the eschatological kingdom of God in an anticipatory and explicitly provisional way. Since sociological categories cannot integrate this anticipatory nature of the church but rather tend to glorify existing ecclesial institutions and practices, Pannenberg regarded them as insufficient to describe the societal role of the church.

Apart from the realized norms of institutional structures, the church in Pannenberg's view must give witness above all to God's law as the divine rule for humanity in the future kingdom. God himself has installed a provisional, eschatological law through the life, death, and resurrection of Jesus Christ and through this event has revealed his law as a law of love. Unlike a set of commandments or legal norms, God's law of love builds on love's creative power to respond to the other, to the challenges of life in which human beings are able to act as loving neighbours. The sovereignty of God's law means that it is open to a diversity of human needs, goes beyond requiring obedience, and culminates in undoing the hierarchy between ruler and ruled. It is this law of love, as Pannenberg claimed in his *Thesen* (*Theses*), that should shape the life of the church as a messianic community. Pannenberg believed that the church can be a sign to the world of humanity's future goal by accurately representing God's future kingdom in the public sphere and by reminding society that the common good is the central goal of political order. The church must walk a narrow path, therefore, between contemporary political orders and powers and God's ultimate kingdom. Maintaining this difficult distinction from the civil state on the one hand and the future kingdom of God on the other is constitutive for the church as a messianic community and returns the Christian community toward its ancient rituals. The church's most authentic way to be an eschatological sign is thus to worship God in its liturgical life, because through the proclamation of the gospel in word and sacrament the church points most clearly to its future goal and hope in God's kingdom.

While the first part of the *Thesen* focuses on the wider horizon of ecclesiology, the second part ('Church as a Messianic Community') concentrates on the more traditional topics of ecclesiology. It addresses the church's foundation in the work of Jesus Christ and the Holy Spirit and the institutional mediation of the community through preaching of the gospel and administering the sacraments. For Pannenberg, these topics also influence the structure of ministry and the church's contributions to formative education (*Bildung*).

As Pannenberg explained in the Preface, the larger ecclesiological approach would eventually include a third section on the history of the church in relation to the idea of divine election. For the publication of the *Theses* Pannenberg merely outlined key ideas. The elaboration of his ecclesiology would be done first in his *Systematic Theology*. Before he could attempt this major contribution, however, he needed to explore some fundamental epistemological and anthropological questions. Three years after the *Thesen*, he published the monograph *Theology and the Philosophy of Science*. A decade later his *Anthropology in Theological Perspective* followed. These two studies were important precursors to his *Systematic Theology* (Pannenberg, 1988–93; English: Pannenberg, 1991–7) and were central to the development of his ecclesiology as they explored the nature of theological propositions and the religious and social receptivity of ecclesial life.

Ecclesiology as Part of *Systematic Theology*

The ecclesiological focus in Pannenberg's *Systematic Theology* (ST) is centred on integrating ecclesial concerns into an overall defence of Christian truth-claims, not only for theologians but for the entire academy. In his view, Christian doctrine must demonstrate coherently why it is rational to hope for an eternal kingdom, in which God will realize his law of love for all humanity. Ecclesiology plays a crucial role in this rational model.

Pannenberg develops his ecclesiology in the third volume of the ST, introducing the topic with a reflection on the origin of the church and its relation to the kingdom of God (ch. 12). He then revisits the traditional areas of ecclesiology—the nature and mission of the church, the work of the Spirit through the proclamation of word and sacrament, the doctrine of ministry, and the notion of the church as the people of God—with a general focus on the interdependence of individual and communal salvation (ch. 13). After reviewing and updating his initial ecclesiological proposals from the *Thesen*, he then elaborates on his earlier reflections on history and election, describing the history of the church in light of eternal election (ST, ch. 14). In contrast to his method in the *Theses*, in the ST Pannenberg grounds his ecclesiology in a historical-critical analysis of ecclesiological witness in the New Testament. In line with Lutheran hermeneutics, he also includes patristic theology and research on the formation of the Christian church in the first centuries as an important resource for ecclesiological teaching. On this basis he develops the ecclesiological core thesis that God sent the church not only to witness to the gospel but to be 'a sign of the destiny of the human race to be renewed in the future of God's kingdom' (Pannenberg 1997: XV). For Pannenberg, this definition of the church's mission involves two major tasks of a doctrine of the church: one is to distinguish carefully the church from the future kingdom while still viewing the church as a legitimate sign of that kingdom; the other is to resolve the discrepancy between the church's role as foretaste of the eternal kingdom and the fracturing of Christian unity manifested in denominationalism and many other institutional divisions. Such divisions contradict Christian claims about the 'one, holy, catholic and apostolic church'. Therefore, the loss of Christian unity severely affects the church's credibility as a functioning symbol of God's future kingdom. In Pannenberg's view, little else obscured the truth of the gospel of Jesus Christ as much as Christian division and the way sectarianism leads ministers to seek power rather than service. Overcoming church-dividing differences on a doctrinal level was a sincere and perennial hope that Pannenberg had for his own work.

The Church and the Work of the Spirit

The Spirit's Work with the Father and the Son

Pannenberg presents ecclesiology as an aspect of pneumatology, because the church comes into existence only through the outpouring of the Holy Spirit as part of God's triune activity in the world. In line with traditional Trinitarian theology, Pannenberg emphasizes that God's activity in the world in creation, redemption, and perfection is a shared work of Father, Son, and Holy Spirit. The Spirit's unique role in this activity is to synthesize, to complete the creative activity of the Father, as the principle of all being, and of the Son, as the generative principle of all distinctiveness in creation. Through this synthesizing activity, the Spirit grants life and overcomes division not just in God's activity toward the world but also in the eternal, divine relationship between Father, Son, and Spirit in which God's being subsists. Thus, God's Trinitarian activity in his economy corresponds with his immanent Trinitarian relationship.

In this synthesizing power the Spirit also calls the church together and leads the world to its eternal goal in God's kingdom. God's Spirit is active in human redemption by teaching us to know God in Jesus of Nazareth and by moving our hearts to praise this God. The Spirit is at work at the very beginning of all creative acts, active in God's mighty breath at the origin of all movement and life. The Spirit is also active with the external Word of God. The Spirit creates faith in each individual believer and brings forth an entirely new creation in the resurrection of the dead. As the source of spontaneity and of 'spiritual' activities in nature and in human beings, the Spirit provides humanity with the epistemological resources that enable the understanding of the natural world and of all phenomena outside our own existence as individuals.

The Spirit is thus not just an external, invisible, and incomprehensible force but rather is tied to the person and life of Jesus. The Spirit empowered Jesus to fulfil the will of the Father. As Veli-Matti Kärkkäinen observed, 'Pannenberg's ecclesiological vision sees an integral, dialogical relationship between the Spirit and Son . . . Everywhere the work of the Spirit is closely related to that of the Son, from creation to salvation to the consummation of creation in the eschaton' (Kärkkäinen 2002: 121). Christology and pneumatology together define Pannenberg's ecclesiology, because the Spirit and the Son mutually indwell one another as Trinitarian persons. In the New Testament, the church is constituted through the outpouring of the Spirit (Acts 2), while Jesus Christ is called the foundation of the church (1 Cor. 3:11). The Spirit's synthesizing power moves believers into a reality outside themselves in Jesus. Jesus then works in them to bind them in fellowship with one another. The Spirit is given to believers not in certain moments but as a constant active presence with the faithful, although the Spirit never comes under the control of creatures. The Spirit rather 'indwells' believers, thereby bringing them into participation in Jesus' sonship and granting them the same freedom that Jesus had, the freedom even to call confidently upon God as 'our Father'.

The Community of the Church and Individual Salvation

Because the Spirit grants individuals an immediate relationship with God while simultaneously gathering believers together in the community of the church, the Spirit overcomes the antagonism between individual and society. The Spirit solves 'the underlying anthropological tension between society and individual freedom' (Pannenberg 1997: 130; cf. Wenz 2013: 174–86). The Spirit is constantly giving new life both to the church and to individual believers. Pannenberg therefore presents the doctrines of individual salvation and of the constitution of the church as two simultaneous effects of the Spirit's work. He addresses the Spirit's salvific work in individuals only after a general reflection on the church as the fellowship of believers. Pannenberg's soteriology therefore remains focused on how the Spirit raises individuals above their own finitude and individual needs by granting them faith and the resulting freedom to participate selflessly in the Christian community. Pannenberg insists that faith is not first received into an individual heart before he or she can turn outward toward the neighbour but that the two happen together. Although Robert Jenson, an important contemporary of Pannenberg, claimed that Pannenberg sees the church as merely mediating an individual's development of an independent relation with Jesus Christ, Pannenberg actually reconciles the idea of individual salvation with the communal and ecclesial dimensions of salvation. He describes the Spirit's power to free individuals from their self-centredness, claiming that the faith and hope that the Spirit grants does embrace the believer's own self and recreates his or her relation to fellow human beings, but only in the broad context of God's mission to redeem all of creation.

THE NATURE AND MISSION OF THE CHURCH

The Church as the Body of Christ

The outpouring of the Spirit constitutes the church in such a way that each individual believer is united with Jesus Christ and through Christ with fellow Christians. As a communion of believers, the church is the body of Christ, that is a collection of individuals participating in the one Lord. Thus the 'body of Christ' remains the most basic and also the most comprehensive image for the church. Pannenberg insists that this concept is not only a metaphor or just one of several biblical concepts for the church, but rather the most accurate description of the church. It points to the real union of believers with Christ as a community of saints and a fellowship of believers.

Christ meets believers in the church through the proclamation of his gospel in word and sacrament. Therefore, the community of the church must teach the gospel purely (*pure*) and administer the sacraments rightly (*recte*), which Pannenberg confirms in line with Article VII of the Augsburg Confession. The preaching of the gospel and administration of the sacraments form an objective basis for defining the church as the body of Christ. Through the preaching of the gospel of Jesus Christ and through the right administration of the sacraments the Holy Spirit enables people to become believers in Jesus Christ and active participants in the fellowship of believers by confessing their faith. Although confession is a definite and comprehensive expression of an individual's beliefs, authentic individual confession always points to the whole church. The ecumenical creed of Nicaea and Constantinople, therefore, is more authentic than the Apostles' Creed because it looked beyond the Christian West to the whole church and was widely received as such. Confession has a third dimension as well, an eschatological dimension. Believers transcend their individual and even communal situation and relate to the final goal of the kingdom of God.

The Church as the Mystery of Salvation in Christ

For Pannenberg the notion of the church as the body of Christ is also fundamental for explaining the particular role of the church in and for the world. Since God has revealed his plan of salvation for all humanity through the work of Jesus Christ, the church not only knows God's promises and plan of salvation but is actually elected to be the eschatological people of God, chosen to be an actual sign of reconciliation with God.

In this way the church can be described as the mystery of salvation in Christ. For an adequate understanding of this theme two clarifications are necessary. First, the church is a mystery of salvation only in and through its participation in Jesus Christ. The church itself is not Christ. Second, the church alone is not capable of transforming the world into the kingdom of God. The kingdom comes only from God himself. Therefore, the church remains a sign of the future kingdom, distinct from the efficacious person and work of Jesus Christ yet never confined only to the role of transmitting information. The church is thus a special kind of sign, one which can enact, through the working of the Holy Spirit, that which it represents: the living out of its future with God in this world through its liturgical life.

Revisiting historical Protestant criticisms, Pannenberg critiqued certain Roman Catholic formulations of the church as a sacrament, or a primary Christian sacrament ('Ursakrament'). Nevertheless, *Lumen Gentium's* explanation of the sacramental character of the church as a 'sign and tool for the most inward union with God and for the unity of all people' is not problematic because the church is in many ways a functional instrument of our unity with God and with one another. Under these terms, Pannenberg could accept the term 'sacrament' for the church, borrowing Jürgen Moltmann's phrase the 'sacrament of the kingdom' (Nüssel 2017: 58–63).

The Visibility and the Unity of the Church

A major ecclesiological controversy in twentieth-century ecumenism is whether and how we can discern the church of Jesus Christ in this world. In line with Protestant ecclesiology, Pannenberg confirms that the church is first a hidden reality that only faith can perceive. This does not, however, mean that the true church of Jesus Christ is an invisible *civitas platonica* (Platonic state). The idea of the church as an *ecclesia invisibilis*, or 'a hidden fellowship of the Spirit'—a concept defended by twentieth-century theologian Paul Tillich—is compatible neither with the biblical witness to the Spirit nor with the biblical notion of *ekklēsia*. Moreover, if the church were invisible, it could not adequately represent God's future kingdom.

Building on the ecclesiology of the Augsburg Confession, Pannenberg points out that when the pure gospel is preached and the sacraments are rightly administered, there is always 'a *manifestation* of the one church that is made holy by Jesus Christ' (Pannenberg 1997: 107; italics mine). The pure proclamation of the gospel and the right administration of the sacraments are thus constitutive of the true church. Accordingly, it is part of the Christian mission to witness to the unity of the church by sharing word and sacrament, where Christ himself promises to be present. Thus for Pannenberg, division at the Lord's Table is the most profound and visible contradiction to the unity of the church as the body of Christ, as if the Nicene Creed's description of Christian unity applied solely to our own denomination. Separation at the Lord's Table damages each church's witness to the unity of the church. He writes: 'even the Roman Catholic and Orthodox churches cannot fully and consistently uphold this verdict on other Christians' (Pannenberg 1997: 411).

In the light of such separation and division, the mission of the church includes the obligation to seek unity and to engage in ecumenism. Theology contributes to this mission by exploring ways to overcome doctrinal condemnations. Pannenberg himself did this in ecumenical work, especially as a member of the Faith and Order Commission of the World Council of Churches that prepared the convergence document *Baptism, Eucharist and Ministry* (1982). In Germany he was a member of the ecumenical Working Group of Protestant and Catholic Theologians. Both Pannenberg and Cardinal Lehmann moderated the work on the study document 'Doctrinal condemnations, church-dividing?' ('Lehrverurteilungen—kirchentrennend?') that served as a fundamental resource for the *Joint Declaration on the Doctrine of Justification* (1999). The group also achieved significant progress in overcoming doctrinal divisions between Roman Catholic and Protestant churches in the areas of sacraments and ministry.

In his ST Pannenberg built on these and other ecumenical achievements. Before addressing traditional controversies over sacraments and ministry, he attempted to overcome the opposition between, on the one hand, a purely forensic, and, on the other, an effective understanding of justification in his doctrine of individual salvation. By first explaining faith, hope, and love as works of the Spirit in the individual Christian, he was able to describe justification as the act through which God declares justification to sinners. On the methodological and hermeneutical levels, he reconsidered the term 'heresy', concluding that the term should not be used for simply any deviation from the church's norms but only for those doctrines that involve a form of 'concealed apostasy' from the faith of the church as the body of Christ. This means that doctrinal differences should be revisited to ask whether they demonstrate concealed apostasy. Only in such a case would excommunication be justified. In Pannenberg's view the experience of apostasy and division, however, should first of all remind the church and particularly the ministry of the responsibility to prevent apostasy and to serve the unity of the church.

The Essential Attributes of the Church

Pannenberg's ST includes no separate chapter on the attributes and the four marks of the church. Instead, he discussed the essential attributes of the church as confessed in the Nicene-Constantinopolitan Creed in the doctrine of ministry section, which follows the doctrine of the sacraments. Pannenberg interprets the essential attributes of the church as criteria for the eschatological role and mission of the church, where the church is called to give a *visible* witness of its essential unity, holiness, catholicity, and apostolicity through the proclamation of word and sacrament. Pannenberg emphasizes the fact that unity is the first attribute mentioned. This is no accident but theologically meaningful, he says, because unity is a central aspect of the church as a fellowship grounded in the participation of believers in the one Lord Jesus Christ, whereas the other attributes are implications of the church's unity. Holiness, catholicity, and apostolicity do not only describe the nature of the church but also indicate how the unity of the church should be preserved and renewed. Taken in this way, the attribute of *holiness* reminds us of the holiness of Jesus Christ, who has sanctified the church through his self-sacrifice and allows believers to participate in his salvation through the proclamation of the gospel and the administration of the sacraments. The holiness of the church is linked closely with *apostolicity*, the church bearing witness to the universal and definitive truth of the revelation of God in Jesus Christ. But apostolicity goes beyond conservation and in many cases must critique it. The church can be authentically apostolic only when it remains willing to alter traditional ways of thinking and remain open to constant renewal, not pandering to the *Zeitgeist* but committed to a living word that must be re-articulated for each generation's comprehension.

The apostolicity of the church in turn is connected with the *catholicity* of the church because the apostolic sending is directed toward the eschatological renewal of *all* humanity. For Pannenberg catholicity means more than a quantitative extension through space and time. He defends a qualitative understanding of catholicity that entails an openness of the church's actual fellowship in which the church can transcend particularity, specifically the boundaries of gender, race, and nationality that divide human society. Churches must keep in mind that their witness to the catholicity of the church is only provisional in relation to the eschatological fullness of the church of Jesus Christ. Pannenberg regards universalistic claims by particular churches as a perversion of true catholicity. Such a view, says Pannenberg, misses the complex relation between the universal church and local churches as it is explicitly enacted in the celebration of the Lord's Supper, where all local congregations equally depend on and share with all other congregations the promises of Christ. Local churches are not secondary to the one universal church but are themselves manifestations of the one church of Christ, and their fellowship in the unity of the one Lord is most easily recognized in the celebration of the Eucharist.

While the essential attributes of the church are not invisible in principle, it is impossible, especially in the situation of divided churches, to discern clearly the nature of the universal church in the life of local churches. Pannenberg agrees with Gerhard Ebeling and most Protestant theologians in stating that the essential attributes of the church cannot be taken as marks of the church (*notae ecclesiae*) in an external sense. In his view, the same problem applies to the criteria for the church's unity mentioned in Article VII of the Augsburg Confession. The precise content of the gospel and the very nature of right administration of the sacraments are themselves open to debate. Pannenberg, therefore, does not define the pure preaching of the gospel and the right administration of sacraments as marks of the church but as criteria for the church's witness to the unity of the church.

THE ECCLESIAL ROLE OF THE SACRAMENTS

Pannenberg interprets the sacraments as signs of the presence of Christ's salvation in the life of the church. The ecclesiological importance of the sacraments follows from the fact that they represent and provide an occasion for the accomplishment of Christ's salvation for individual believers. They also have an active function of forming the church into a community that is a sign of God's kingdom. In this way sacraments are important to Pannenberg's understanding of the relationship between individual and communal salvation.

Terminology and Institution

Pannenberg sees a special challenge existing between the churches regarding their sacramental theologies, particularly concerning the term 'sacrament', the number of sacraments, and the question of their divine institution in the light of modern biblical exegesis. Since the term *mysterion* in the New Testament does not refer to symbolic acts of the church, Pannenberg reflects on the concept of 'sacrament' only after an analysis of the two major 'significatory' acts of the church: baptism and the Lord's Supper. These were both part of the church's life before they, along with other churchly activities, came to be called 'sacraments'. It is evident, therefore, that the meaning of these actions does not depend on the term 'sacrament', the term being formalized long after the ritual reality. With Thomas Aquinas, the Reformers, and the Council of Trent, Pannenberg would call 'sacraments' only those acts that are instituted by Jesus Christ. While the claim that Jesus commanded the church to baptize all peoples in the name of Father, Son, and Holy Spirit (Matt. 28:19) is controversial in historical analysis, and while it is debated whether and in what sense Christ invited his disciples to celebrate the Lord's Supper, Pannenberg suggests that we understand the term 'institution' more broadly. He argues that both practices have their origin in the life of Jesus, since he celebrated the Last Supper in the light of previous meals and interpreted his own baptism in a way that legitimized the development of baptism in the name of the triune God in early Christian congregations.

While baptism and the Lord's Supper are most basic for the constitution and life of the church, other acts may relate to the work and person of Jesus as well, especially the proclamation of the gospel and Christian worship. These ecclesial activities have a sacramental character as a whole (Pannenberg 1997: 368). Since the criteria for discerning Christ's institution of sacramental acts are not altogether evident, it is not possible to define strictly the number of sacramental actions. Other actions such as confirmation, absolution, marriage, ordination, and unction, which are sacraments in the Roman Catholic and Orthodox churches, also have a sacramental character. Therefore, Pannenberg thinks it should be possible to overcome the divisive effects of sacramental controversies which refer to the number of sacraments.

Soteriological and Ecclesiological Meaning

Pannenberg characterizes baptism and the Eucharist as 'significatory acts'—not merely illustrations of a promise, but containing and conveying what they signify. Only by participating in the sacraments do hearers of the proclamation actually receive the promises of salvation that unite them with Christ and his church. Baptism and the Lord's Supper grant the salvific presence of God because 'with the enacting of the sign the thing signified is itself present' (Pannenberg 1997: 353).

In further interpretation of baptism and the Lord's Supper, Pannenberg elaborates the ecclesiological impact of both actions for the messianic community and the individual believer. Baptism is an 'event of regeneration' (Pannenberg 1997: 237) in which the baptized person is granted a new existence in fellowship with Jesus Christ and becomes related to the triune God concretely by participation in the filial relation Jesus has with the Father. Drawing on Martin Luther's understanding of baptism, Pannenberg describes baptism as a concrete location of justification in the life of a Christian. At the same time, baptism integrates the baptized person into the community of the church and constitutes church membership. In Pannenberg's view, baptism is a church action because those who administer baptism do so on behalf of the whole church, which gains a new member through this act.

While baptism grants new life and Christian identity to the baptized person, the celebration of the Lord's Supper offers a way to experience the gracious presence of Jesus Christ and the community of the body constituted by baptism. Celebration of the Lord's Supper not only assures individual believers of the forgiveness of sin, but as a communal meal it demonstrates Christian fellowship. In this way the Lord's Supper renews Christian fellowship by representing and repeating Christ's promise to be present in this meal. Pannenberg's ecclesiology defends the idea of the real presence of Christ as grounded in Christ's promise and made effective through the work of the Holy Spirit. Modern readings of the doctrine of transubstantiation help to overcome Lutheran criticism, but the idea of a personal presence responds to theological concerns from the Reformed tradition and helps to distinguish a proper theology of Christ's real presence from a theology that would limit Christ's presence to the elements of bread and wine. Referring to Paul and Luke, Pannenberg claims that the promise of Christ's presence is not limited to the moment of consecration but relates to the whole Eucharistic liturgy characterized by the dynamics of *anamnesis* ('reminiscence', 'recollection') and *epiclesis* ('invocation'). To celebrate the Lord's Supper as a Eucharistic expression is, therefore, the adequate way to follow Jesus in his exemplary relation to the Father. It is not human agency that actualizes Christ's presence but rather the work of the Spirit, who, through *anamnesis* and *epiclesis*, fulfils Christ's promise to be present.

Since all Christians at all times and places are members of the body of Christ, the celebration of the sacraments has a universal and catholic dimension. At each celebration of the Eucharist, all of Christianity is present (Pannenberg 1997: 103). The fact that local congregations can enact this reality on a weekly basis has ecumenical implications. When a celebration of the Supper fails to preserve fellowship with all who belong to Christ, there is an offence to the entire church that must be made right. Unlike Moltmann, who rejects any restrictions on admission to communion, Pannenberg sees the open invitation addressed to all those who desire fellowship with Jesus in his new covenant, which implies some sort of conversion to God. Pannenberg argues for baptism as a prerequisite, in order that each participant demonstrate a readiness to ground their life in the fellowship promised by Christ in the Supper. While a sense for Christ's presence is important, a theological understanding of the nature of his presence cannot be made a condition for participation. So long as the presence of Christ is sought in the meal, other Christians must take it on faith that each participant has a relationship with God.

MINISTRY IN THE SERVICE OF UNITY

Half a century of dialogue between various Christian denominations has made it clear that the topic of ministry is the most controversial of all and is, therefore, the biggest stumbling block for ecumenism. Pannenberg addresses this crucial role of ministry not only explicitly but also implicitly in the way that he develops the chapter on the doctrine of ministry (Pannenberg 1997: 370; cf. Wenz 2013: 194–200). His central thesis is that the ordained ministry must serve the public proclamation of God's gospel and is, in this way, responsible to preserve the unity of the church. Only in this way can it fulfil its mission and serve as a sign of the unity of the church. Despite the plurality of callings and charismas mentioned in the New Testament writings, Pannenberg emphasizes that all Christians are called to witness to Christ's lordship. This includes a common responsibility for the unity of the witness itself. The particular mission and character of ordained ministry can be understood only in relation to the mission of the whole church as the community of believers. Ordained ministry is distinct from the priesthood of all believers and was instituted by Christ's sending the apostles to proclaim the gospel publicly. Ordained ministry requires a certain amount of authority because the plurality of individual Christian contributions must be organized into a single witness. Thus, the authority of ordained ministry involves a particular responsibility for the unity and common mission of the church for the sake of the gospel. In their 'public charge to teach the gospel and to lead the churches', ordained ministers embody 'the total church and the mission that has come down to it from Jesus Christ by way of the apostles' (Pannenberg 1997: 391). While apostolic succession is primarily a 'succession in the teaching and faith of the apostles and only secondarily . . . a matter of succession in office' (Pannenberg 1997: 403), Pannenberg considers succession in ordination as an important sign of the apostolicity of the church. Thus only ordained ministers should 'represent the whole church of Christ and in his capacity hand down the commission that the apostles received from Jesus Christ himself' (Pannenberg 1997: 403).

Concerning the controversies around episcopal apostolic succession, Pannenberg draws on New Testament and patristic research to highlight how, after the death of the apostles, the public proclamation of the gospel became a particular responsibility of leaders of local congregations (*episkopoi*). Even though the apostles had not installed bishops, the ministry of oversight proved to be essential for preserving the unity of the church's witness, first on the local level and later on larger stages. In Pannenberg's view, the development of the episcopate into a normative reality in the church must be recognized as a divine institution because of the importance of preserving the gospel. Consequently, episcopal ordination can be regarded as an adequate and canonical sign of unity. But with regard to the original unity of the episcopal and presbyteral ministry in patristic ecclesiology, Pannenberg claims—in line with Luther and Melanchthon—that presbyteral ordination is possible in principle and that presbyteral ordination was inevitable at the time of the Reformation, when bishops denied ordination to ministers who supported the reform. Nevertheless, the Lutheran Reformation supported the idea of episcopal ordination as an external sign of apostolic succession and emphasized that the office of *episcopé* was necessary for the unity of the church. In line with Melanchthon, Pannenberg thus acknowledges such a ministry on the universal level and, looking only at historical developments, accepts the bishop of Rome in this role. But to accept him as the pope would only be possible if the Roman Catholic Church were to submit to a theological reinterpretation and practical restructuring of the papacy in order to subordinate the entire system to the primacy of the gospel. Furthermore, Pannenberg's entire argument proceeds from the fact that only Jesus Christ is the head of the church.

So while Pannenberg supports a representative model of ministry, even on the universal level, he is clear that this representation fully depends on Christ's mission and the power of the Spirit. He claims that it is never bound or limited to personal qualities other than those required for public proclamation of the gospel. The church cannot justify the exclusion of women from ordination because 'the minister is not representing the earthly man Jesus of Nazareth but the exalted Christ in whose body the distinctions of sex, as well as those of social status, nationality, and race have been overcome' (Pannenberg 1997: 389–91). Ordained ministers represent Christ and support the church's catholicity only when they remain aware of the provisional nature of the church and commit themselves to serving a truly ecumenical Christian unity rather than supporting bureaucratic structures.

In sacramental matters, Pannenberg suggests that ordination may indeed be considered a sacrament, since it is 'a concretion of the one mystery of salvation that unites Christ and his church' (Pannenberg 1997: 397). Unlike baptism, however, ordination does not change the soteriological status of the ordained. And the sacramental sign is the laying on of hands and the prayer for ministerial blessings, not the handing over of the chalice and paten as instruments for sacrifice. In the significatory act of ordination the ordained are called to proclaim the gospel publicly and to administer the sacraments. The only indelible aspect of such a call is that ordination is not limited by time, nor is it repeatable, but expresses a lifelong vocation to serve God.

THE CHURCH AS THE PEOPLE OF GOD AND THE DOCTRINE OF ELECTION

An account of the church as the 'people of God', a theme drawn from the Old Testament account of God's relationship with Israel, was rediscovered in the Reformation. It was used to describe the church without a focus on hierarchy. Pannenberg argues that the ecclesiological impact of this concept can be explored only in the light of the more fundamental notion of the body of Christ. He emphasizes that the term 'people of God' is a description that involves election. It cannot, therefore, be articulated in the plural form. This is because the 'unity of God and his kingdom . . . demands the concept of a single people of God that constitutes the object and goal of what God does in election' (Pannenberg 1997: 477). Both considerations have implications for the relation between the Christian church and Israel. Following Paul's discussion in Romans 9–11, Pannenberg confirms that God has not dissolved his covenant with the Jewish people. Pannenberg rejects the idea that the church has replaced Israel as God's elected people and claims that this theory reveals a deficient understanding of the provisional character of the church, as if 'eschatological consummation had come already in the existence of the church' (Pannenberg 1997: 476).

In view of Israel's election and the provisional character of the church, it is inappropriate for the Christian church to claim an exclusive identity as the people of God. Pannenberg critiques the traditional theological understanding of election in terms of an eternal act of God realized in the calling of individual believers. He instead emphasizes that God's election is a process in history and as such is orientated toward the future fulfilment of humanity in the kingdom of God. God reveals himself in election and demands that the elected people behave in a way that corresponds to their fellowship with him. Furthermore, election includes universal mission 'as the reverse side of the particularity of election' (Pannenberg 1997: 493). This involves 'experiences of divine assistance on the path of the elect, but also of judgment on deviation' (Pannenberg 1997: 495).

These conclusions regarding the doctrine of election are possible only through theological reflection on the history of the church. In Pannenberg's view, this is the task of the discipline of church history. Accordingly, he disapproves of the secularization of the discipline of church history and the systematic exclusion of the ideas of divine providence and divine judgement as categories for Christian historiography. Instead, he interprets all history in the light of the electing will of God which unites humanity on the basis of its reconciliation with God. The goal of all history, then, is to bring the people of God together, not for the sake of any human institution but for an 'eschatologically consummated humanity' (Pannenberg 1997: 457). The church's mission is to witness to God's will for universal fulfilment and to the 'dynamic inclusiveness' (Pannenberg 1997: 523) of God's election. Election is not for individual believers, because fellowship cannot happen in isolation. Only as members of the church, orientated outwardly toward all humanity, can we move toward a future humanity renewed in the kingdom of God.

CONCLUSION

With his comprehensive ecclesiological approach, Pannenberg contributed, at the end of the twentieth century, to the further development of modern ecclesiology in several important ways. A first and fundamental contribution consists in the way that he has explored the constitutive relation between the individual and collective dimensions of salvation. Pannenberg emphasizes that Christian hope for the salvation of the individual cannot be separated from the hope of redemption and the reconciliation of all humanity in the kingdom of God. Thus, the Spirit's work has two dimensions. Through the proclamation of the gospel in word and sacrament, the Holy Spirit calls individuals to believe in Jesus Christ and to become children of God; and at the same time the Holy Spirit incorporates believers into the body of Christ and creates the church as a *communio sanctorum,* in which Christians live and experience a community that is established by the Spirit. In this, Christians can anticipate the communal life of the children of God in God's eternal kingdom. While the older Lutheran dogmatics understood the Spirit's work primarily in the application of grace on the individual level, Friedrich Schleiermacher described the Holy Spirit as the 'Common-Spirit' ('Gemeingeist') and by doing so he focused pneumatology on the constitution of a new society of believers ('neues Gesamtleben'). Pannenberg combines both aspects in his pneumatology and makes ecclesiology an integral part of pneumatology. Kärkkäinen rightly observes that Pannenberg 'does not want to see the faith *first* received into an individual heart and *then* the church added as an afterthought' (Kärkkäinen 2002: 114; my italics). Rather, the work of the Spirit culminates in the assembling of believers in the community of the church. According to Pannenberg's pneumatological account, the Spirit lifts 'individuals above their particularity and finitude' (Pannenberg 1997: 135) and allows individuals to enter into community with God and with fellow Christians by granting them faith, love, and hope. These traditional Christian virtues are essential not only for the individual's relation with God, but also for the communal life in the church.

A second important achievement can be found in the way that Pannenberg rethinks ecclesiology in the light of the eschatological role of church. Drawing on the rise of future eschatology after the Second World War that was particularly promoted by Jürgen Moltmann's *Theology of Hope* (1964), Pannenberg points to the apocalyptic character of God's future kingdom that will be realized by God's divine power at the end of history. In light of this hope it is not the church's mission to bring about the kingdom that Jesus had proclaimed, nor to contribute to a successive growth of God's kingdom in this world, nor to gradually transform culture and society into a Christian culture. Rather, the church's mission is to be a proleptic sign of God's future kingdom through her life in *leiturgia, koinōnia, martyria*, and *diakonia*. As a sign of the kingdom, the church anticipates and supports the eschatological hope for the kingdom. In worshipping God in liturgy and prayer, and especially in celebrating the Eucharist, the communal life of the church is a foretaste of the eternal community in which all humans will be reconciled with God and among one another. It is correct to say that Pannenberg's ecclesiology builds on a sacramental spirituality (cf. Grenz 1990: 185), because the sacraments, as visible signs of God's promise in the gospel, offer experience of the creative power of God's Spirit, which will lead all creation to the future kingdom. At the same time, this experience is proleptic and anticipatory in character. The eschatological mission of the church implies that the church should always clearly distinguish itself from the future kingdom, but also from human institutions, especially from the state and political order. To explain this two-fold self-distinction in a coherent way is one of the core issues of modern ecclesiology, as Pannenberg argues. While self-distinction from the kingdom of God is constitutive for the church to be a *sign* of the kingdom, self-distinction from the state and the political order is a prerequisite for the church to 'remind democracy of its religious roots, reveal the danger of collapse that comes if secular society forgets the religiously transmitted concept of justice, and protect the basic values of freedom and equality' (Grenz 1990: 180). This potential for a productive church–state relation, however, depends on Christianity's engagement in ecumenism. If only reconciled churches can witness to the unity of the church as the body of Christ, this is also a necessary condition for 'a renewal of Christian influence in modern society' (Grenz 1990: 151).

Both ecclesiological achievements just mentioned culminate in the ecumenical argumentation of Pannenberg's ecclesiology. As we have seen, he understands the divisions and separations between churches and ecclesial communities as a contradiction of the confession of the church's unity and its universal character as the mystery of salvation. As such, the church should continue forever at all times and in all places—as Article VII of the Augsburg Confession teaches—to be open for all human beings, and should overcome human divisions. Therefore, it is a major task of ecclesiology to explore and defend the ecclesiological truth-claim by demonstrating how ecclesial controversies and divisions can be overcome. Robert Jenson finds that Pannenberg combines a Catholic line of argumentation with a Protestant concept of the church that focuses the individual relationship with God. He concludes that 'some will find in Pannenberg's ecclesiology the sharpest and most widely informed clarification of their attitude to the church. Others will find it the best possible presentation of a Protestantism which almost but not quite transcends its difference from Catholicism' (Jenson 1998). Pannenberg's intention, however, is somewhat different. While systematic theology cannot but start from a certain denominational perspective, in Pannenberg's view it has to explore the truth of the Christian faith in its universal character. This includes the task of overcoming not only individual denominational divisions, but more fundamentally denominational perspectives and all attitudes of denominational exclusivism. Pannenberg, therefore, addresses traditional controversies not with an eye on their denominational origin and profile, but with regard to the ecclesiological concerns they involve. In this way he not only addresses concerns from the Protestant and Roman Catholic traditions; in exploring the eschatological role of the church and the anticipatory character of the celebration of the liturgy and especially the Eucharist, he responds also to a major concern of Orthodox theology. Moreover, he addresses fundamental dogmatic issues such as the relation between faith and baptism, the nature of the presence of the Lord in the Lord's Supper, and the notion of election that had been discussed especially among denominations that have adopted basic ideas from the sixteenth-century Reformation. With particular regard to differences between Lutheran and Reformed teaching, Pannenberg offers substantial theological argumentation for why it was possible and adequate to overcome separation between Lutheran and Reformed churches.

Pannenberg's ecclesiology attempts to transcend denominational perspectives for the sake of a real *catholicity* and openness of the church. This openness embraces the synthesizing power of God's Spirit, who at all times and places reconciles human beings with God and with one another over and against human boundaries and discriminations. Hence, ecclesiology has to start from a reflection of the Trinitarian activity of God, the Father, who through the Son in the power of the Spirit regenerates the relationship of human beings with God and among one another and promises to fulfil the destination of all humanity in his eternal kingdom. Through word and sacrament, this future kingdom can be experienced in a proleptic way in worship, and in the spiritual and communal life of the church. This happens naturally on the level of local congregations. At the same time, through sharing the same gospel in word and sacrament, local congregations participate in the universal church of Jesus Christ. In Pannenberg's view, this church is not a *civitas platonica*, but exists in the communion between local congregations, dioceses, and regional churches. Acknowledging the universal dimension of local worship in local communities is essential for the witness to the unity and catholicity of the church, and ecclesiology has to support such a witness with theological argumentation. While in an age of secularization churches tend to be more and more concerned about their denominational identity, Pannenberg's ecclesiology demonstrates that the identity of the church is defined by its Trinitarian foundation and its eschatological mission to be a sign of hope for the future reconciliation of all humanity.

REFERENCES

Grenz, S. (1990). *Reason for Hope: The Systematic Theology of Wolfhart Pannenberg*. New York and Oxford: Oxford University Press, 149–87.
Jenson, R. (1998). 'Catholic and Evangelical?' *First Things* (Oct.): <http://www.firstthings.com/article/1998/10/001-catholic-and-evangelical>.
Kärkkäinen, V.-M. (2002). *An Introduction to Ecclesiology: Ecumenical, Historical & Global Perspectives*. Downers Grove, IL: InterVarsity Press.
Laube, Martin (2006). *Theologie und neuzeitliches Christentum. Studien zu Genese und Profil der Christentumstheorie Trutz Rendtorffs*. Tübingen: Mohr Siebeck.
Nüssel, F. (2017) 'Kirche als Zeichen und Werkzeug des Reiches Gottes. Zu Genese und Profil der Ekklesiologie Wolfhart Pannenbergs'. In G. Wenz, *Kirche und Reich Gottes: Zur Ekklesiologie Wolfhart Pannenbergs*. Göttingen: Vandenhoeck & Ruprecht, 49–66.
Pannenberg, W. (1974). *Thesen zur Theologie der Kirche*, 2, durchges. Munich: Aufl. Claudius.
Pannenberg, W. (1988). *Systematische Theologie*. Göttingen: Vandenhoeck & Ruprecht.
Pannenberg, W. (1991). *Systematic Theology*. Grand Rapids, MI: Eerdmans.
Wenz, G. (2013). *Introduction to Wolfhart Pannenberg's Systematic Theology*. Göttingen: Vandenhoeck & Ruprecht.

SUGGESTED READING

Bolos, L.-T. (2010). *Die Ekklesiologien von Dumitru Staniloae und Wolfhart Pannenberg: Ein ökumenisch-theologischer Vergleich*. Oradea: Editura Universitatii din Oradea.
Brinkman, M. E. (1978). 'De plaats van de kerk in W. Pannenbergs theologie'. *Nederlands Theologisch Tijdschrift* 32: 31–41.

Eggenberg, T. (2010). 'Kirche als Zeichen des Reiches Gottes: Eine Studie zur Bedeutung des Reiches Gottes für die Kirche in Auseinandersetzung mit Küng, Moltmann, Pannenberg und Hauerwas'. Proefschrift Evangelical Theological Faculty, Leuven.

Lee, Chien-Ju (2006). *Der Heilige Geist als Vollender: Die Pneumatologie Wolfhart Pannenbergs*. Frankfurt am Main, Berlin, Bern, Brussels, New York, Oxford, and Vienna: Peter Lang, 207–23.

Lehmann, K. and Pannenberg, W. (1986). *Lehrverurteilungen—kirchentrennend? Rechtfertigung, Sakramente und Amt im Zeitalter der Reformation und heute. Dialog der Kirchen* 4. Freiburg/Göttingen: Herder/Vandenhoeck & Ruprecht.

Madrigal Terrazas, J. S. (2000). 'La Iglesia en la teología sistemática de W. Pannenberg (I): "signo del reinado de Dios" y "Congregatio fidelium" '. *Estudios Eclesiásticos* 75: 177–233.

Madrigal Terrazas, J. S. (2000). 'La Iglesia en la teología sistemática de W. Pannenberg (II): el ministerio eclesial y el pueblo de Dios'. *Estudios Eclesiásticos* 75: 421–72.

Madrigal Terrazas, J. S. (2000). 'W. Pannenberg, intérprete del Concilio Vaticano II'. In *Ecclesia una* [FS A. González Montes], Salamanca, 89–130.

Müller, G. L. (1994). 'Pannenbergs Entwurf einer Systematischen Theologie (III)'. *Theologische Revue* 90.1: 1–10 [Münster: Aschendorf].

Noceti, S. (1998). 'Chiesa, comunità dello Spirito: note per una lettura critica della relazione chiesa-Spirito nell'opera di W. Pannenberg'. *Vivens Homo* 9: 137–51.

Noceti, S. 2005. 'La Chiesa segno del Regno di Dio: l'ecclesiologia ecumenica di Wolfhart Pannenberg'. Diss. Firenze: Facoltà Teologica dell'Italia Centrale.

Taylor, I. (2007). 'Pannenberg's Trinitarian Doctrine of the Kingdom and the Church'. In I. Taylor, *Pannenberg on the Triune God*. London and New York: T&T Clark, 137–63.

Zeuch, M. (1996). 'Zeichen des Reiches Gottes: Ekklesiologie und Sakramententheologie bei Wolfhart Pannenberg'. *Lutherische Theologie und Kirche* 20: 176–91.

CHAPTER 23

ROWAN WILLIAMS

MIKE HIGTON

ROWAN WILLIAMS (b. 1950) has moved from the university to the church and back again. Lady Margaret Professor of Divinity at the University of Oxford from 1986 to 1992, he was then elected as bishop of Monmouth, then archbishop of Wales, and eventually archbishop of Canterbury (from 2002 to 2012), before returning to university life as master of Magdalene College, Cambridge, in 2013. Yet although the academic and ec-clesial worlds might be very different, the link between the work he has done in the two contexts is very strong, not least because of the centrality of ecclesiology to his theology.

Williams's theology is not easy to summarize. He is not one given to producing sys-tematic overviews or bird's-eye guides. The vast majority of his writing is occasional—a response to particular invitations or (especially in his time as archbishop) particular challenges or opportunities. Nevertheless, it is possible to identify a broad shape that unites a good deal of his work, and it is in the context of this broad shape that it is pos-sible to speak of the centrality of ecclesiology.

THE PLACE OF ECCLESIOLOGY IN ROWAN WILLIAMS'S WORK

Williams's work has its roots in an exploration of the Christian spiritual tradition. It grows in the soil of a broadly apophatic, even ascetic account of the spiritual life—of growth in Christian faith. Yet when, in the light of that tradition, he describes the trans-formation wrought in human beings by God's love in Christ, he consistently turns the spotlight on the ongoing remaking of their relations to one another. The transformation wrought in human beings by God's grace is a transformation made visible in the ma-terial of their common life. Since Williams's theology is above all things an exploration of the difference made by God's love in Christ, at its centre is the description of this transformed sociality—and the nature of the transformation is made visible in the life of the church. The central shape, then, of Williams's theology is a move from the territory of spirituality (an account of spiritual discipline and spiritual growth) to the territory of ecclesiology (an account of the ways in which Christians are called to learn from one another, and to learn to live together). We might tentatively say that the idea of *growing up together* is the key to Williams's theology as a whole.

In Williams's descriptions, what human beings are saved *from* is clear. Human beings live, he suggests, in a world where the goods that each person pursues cannot all be realized simultaneously, and where people's desire for the good is distorted by their imagining and experience of others' desires as standing over against theirs. This is an unnatural world where competition, rivalry, and defensiveness appear to be the natural shape of our relations.

What human beings are saved *by* is equally clear. The world is loved by its maker, God, who as the one who sustains the whole world is not a competitor or rival within it. God's love is a love beyond the calculations that shape the fallen world—indeed, it is a love that overthrows those calculations. It is a love that, properly speaking, cannot be coerced, hoarded, or manipulated.

A good deal of Williams's theology describes the transformation that such love works when it impinges upon human lives—when they are opened up to the possibility that their ultimate security is granted by God's love, not by their defensive self-positioning amidst a world of rivals. And a good deal of Williams's description focuses on the challenge that such a realization creates for habits and imaginations shaped by and for the world of rivalry. For those whose habits of speech are fitted for that world, to encounter the gospel is 'to be questioned, judged, stripped naked and left speechless' (1979: 1 [all references in the main text are to works by Williams]). Allowing this love to reshape one is 'a hard and frightening task' (2002b: 33) that will involve 'pain and disorientation' because it asks one to forget that one has 'a self to be shielded, reinforced, consoled and lied to' (1982: 54). It calls one to let that old self die. As such, '[t]he Gospel frees us from fear and fantasy . . . it is the great enemy of self-indulgent fantasy' (1983a: 17).

Human beings are set free by this love to see and to accept their finitude and their materiality not as limitations on their power, but as their gift: as the existence given to them by God, as the material on which God is working, and as a medium through which God can speak to the world. They are set free to become people whose lives, by being lived differently, can speak to the world precisely of God's love beyond calculation. If they are 'stripped naked and left speechless', it is in order to become God's speech.

Yet to be made into God's speech is to be made into God's speech *to one another*. It involves people becoming words spoken to one other, and becoming hearers of the word that is spoken to them by each other. The transformation that God's love works when it impinges upon human lives takes the form of a reconstruction of human beings' relations to one another and to their world.

For Williams, the church is the crucible of that transformation. It is not by any means the only place where God's love is reshaping relationships, but it is the place where the source of that transformation in God is named, acknowledged, and pursued—however fallibly and incompletely—and where the nature of God's work precisely as a transformation of sociality is displayed. Ecclesiology is therefore absolutely central to Williams's theology because it treats how people should form a life together in response to the gospel. It is grounded in the conviction that the gospel 'makes possible new levels of belonging together in the human world' (2002a).

THE CHURCH AS THE COMMUNITY OF JESUS

At the centre of the life of the church stands Jesus of Nazareth. In his enthronement sermon as archbishop of Canterbury in 2002, Williams told the following story:

> About twelve years ago, I was visiting an Orthodox monastery, and was taken to see one of the smaller and older chapels. It was a place intensely full of the memory and reality of prayer. The monk showing me around pulled the curtain from in front of the sanctuary, and inside was a plain altar and one simple picture of Jesus, darkened and rather undistinguished. But for some reason at that moment it was as if the veil of the temple was torn in two: I saw as I had never seen the simple fact of Jesus at the heart of all our words and worship, behind the curtain of our anxieties and our theories, our struggles and our suspicion. Simply there; nothing anyone can do about it, there he is as he has promised to be till the world's end. Nothing of value happens in the Church that does not start from seeing him simply there in our midst, suffering and transforming our human disaster. (2003a)

The basic shape of Williams's theology, as described above, is visible in this anecdote. What human beings are saved from—the 'human disaster'—is a world of 'anxieties . . . struggles and . . . suspicion'. What rescues humanity from that disaster is not any human achievement or strategy but something '[s]imply there', unavoidably and faithfully—one who does not act as a player in the world of anxiety and suspicion, but stands at the heart of it (or even 'behind' it). And that transformation is seen in whatever 'of value happens in the Church', in the church's 'words and worship'. And the one who stands at the heart is the man Jesus of Nazareth.

Williams consistently declares that Jesus is the incarnation of God—the making fully present in the world of the utterly gratuitous love of God. (And this is true in both senses of the phrase 'love of God': Jesus is one who, in the power of the Spirit, lives in unfettered love for the Father, and one who, in the same power, enacts the Father's love of the world.) Though as utterly particular as the enthronement sermon's 'one simple picture of Jesus, darkened and rather undistinguished' suggests, this human life is of unlimited significance. 'Jesus is the form which God's judgment takes' (1993: 257); he is the form which God's creative action—and the form which God's people-shaping power—takes. 'I can't see any way of being a Christian', Williams says, 'that doesn't involve you at some point saying that it is in relation to Christ that human beings become as human as they are meant to be' (2000c).

Jesus is

> free from local limitation, and free from the limitation of belonging to the past: without ceasing to be a particular person in a particular place, he is capable of interpreting an unlimited range of human situations . . . and there is no place or time or condition in which he can be domesticated, in which we can say that his story and his Spirit are exhaustively defined. He is utterly unsusceptible to definition; and while we may continue to burden him with our hopes, fantasies and projections, there is an obstinate and restless dimension of unclarity which will break through and challenge sooner or later. (1982b: 82)

The 'restless dimension of unclarity' is precisely all that is not yet taken into account whenever Christians (as they must) describe and define Jesus—the excess or surplus that is ready to disrupt the church's existing patterns of thought and action. Williams does not picture this surplus as a passive hinterland, awaiting further exploration, but as an active presence, capable of breaking in as creative judgement.

If the church is, as described above, 'the place where the source of [the world's] transformation in God is named, acknowledged and pursued', then it is the place where the particular human being Jesus of Nazareth is named, his unlimited significance explored, and his active and dangerous exceeding of the church's present understanding is acknowledged and awaited.

More specifically, the church is, for Williams, the church of the Resurrection. The undefended life of God was transformatively present in the world of rivalry and suspicion in Jesus of Nazareth, but was pushed out of that world on the cross. As Jesus died, his disciples abandoned him to save their own skins, throwing in their lot with the world of defensiveness and self-protection. Yet not even direct and deliberate denial of their Lord was enough to move the disciples beyond his promised, insistent presence. Jesus returned to them and forgave them, transforming their betrayal.

Williams describes, for instance, the encounter between Peter and the risen Jesus on the shore of Galilee, describing how Jesus' questioning drives Peter to face his betrayal, and transforms the betrayer into one who will feed the people. 'Peter's fellowship with the Lord is not over, not ruined, it still exists and is alive because Jesus invites him to explore it further . . . To know that Jesus still invites is to know that he accepts, forgives, bears and absorbs the hurt done: to hear the invitation is to know oneself forgiven, and *vice versa*' (1982b: 30). The resurrection, says Williams, creates forgiven persons, in a community of the forgiven (1982b: xii). The resurrection creates the church.

THE CHURCH AS THE COMMUNITY OF WORD AND SACRAMENT

The church, in order to be the church, must constantly represent to itself the fact that its life depends upon Jesus' life. It is not accidentally but essentially *his* community, and its life demands 'steady and radical exposure to the fundamental events of Christian faith' (1987b: 7). The church acknowledges this demand in part through its involvement in sacramental action. '[A] Christian community', Williams says, 'involved in activities it calls "sacramental" is a community *describing* itself in a way that is importantly at odds with other sorts of description' (2000b: 209, Williams's italics). In the Eucharist, for instance, the church 'shows itself its source and its criterion' (1982a: 97); it is an activity in which the church is shown again and again that it is dependent upon the prior action of Jesus of Nazareth.

When Christians celebrate the Eucharist, they relinquish the bread and wine as their own possessions, and receive them back from Jesus' hands (1982b: 102–3) and so are marked out as the church. '[T]he great mark of discipleship to the risen Christ is, as the New Testament has it, that we eat and drink with him after his resurrection' (1995: ix).

> The glorified Christ, crucified and risen, is eternally active towards God the Father on our behalf, drawing us into the eternal movement of self-giving love that the Son or Word directs towards the source of all, the God Jesus calls 'Abba'. The sacrifice of the cross is, among other things, the 'transcription' into this world's terms of the Son's movement of love towards the Father in heaven. In the Eucharist, our prayer is swept into that current, and we are set free to share in the Son's self-giving. The giving of thanks over the elements renews for us the covenant made by God in Christ, and the work of God in the cross is again 'applied' to us, in word and action, in body and soul. (1995: viii)

The Eucharist is, in a sense then, the presence of Christ in the church—but

> the presence that is appropriate and intelligible in the Eucharist is neither the presence of an idea in our minds . . . nor the presence of a uniquely sacred *object* on the Table. It is the presence of an active Christ, moving in love not only towards the Father but towards us. (1995: viii–ix, Williams's italics)

In celebrating the Eucharist, the church acknowledges its existence as a community held together despite failures and betrayals by the gracious giving of God's love in Christ; it acknowledges that it is a community given the terrifying privilege of handling this gift, and passing it on, made by this gift into givers and communicators.

A church seeking 'steady and radical exposure to the fundamental events of Christian faith' will also 'necessarily accord central and decisive importance to Scripture, since Scripture is the unique witness to those events' (1987b: 7). The Bible, says Williams,

> tells us what we could not otherwise know: it tells us that God, the maker of the world, is committed to that world and desires with all his being to save it from disaster and the imprisonment of sin; that he does this by calling a people to witness to him by their prayers and their actions, in obedience to what he shows them of his will through the Law; that he brings this work to completion when God the eternal Son, the eternal Word, becomes human as Jesus of Nazareth and offers his life to destroy or to 'soak up', as you might say, the terrible consequences of our sin; and that Jesus is raised from the tomb to call a new people together in the power of the Spirit, who will

show what kind of God God is in the quality of their life together and their relation with him . . . This is the world of the Bible into which the Church has to be brought again and again. (2002c)

The Bible is the engine of the church's exposure to the gospel. It is 'the utterances and records of human beings who have been employed by God to witness to his action in the world, now given to us by God so that we may learn who he is and what he does; and the "giving" by God is by means of the resurrection of Jesus' (2003a: 33). It is a witness to God's formation of a resurrection people in the midst of the world, and it is by the witness of the Scriptures that the resurrection people is formed and sustained in the present.

The church cannot rely, however, on some existing systematic or harmonized readings of Scripture. Scripture is a bearer of the 'restless dimension of unclarity', the excess or surplus described in the section 'The Church as the Community of Jesus', and the church is therefore called to ongoing reading, to an extravagant patience with the text. The church is to be formed by prayerful and reflective reading practised intensely and devoutly over years, in a constant return to the text, in the knowledge that it will always say more than the church currently expects.

Above all, the church is formed by reading in company (2001a: ix), with each individual reading with those who read differently, and those whose readings challenge that individual to look again, look more closely, and to take more time. The church is therefore properly and inherently a community of conversation—even argument—about Scripture.

The Church as a Doctrinal Community

For Williams, doctrine too needs to be understood in relation to the church's dependence upon 'steady and radical exposure' to its source. The role of doctrine, he says, 'is to *hold us still* before Jesus' (2000a: 37, Williams's italics); its purpose is to hold open 'the possibility of preaching Jesus as a questioning and converting presence in ever more diverse cultures and periods' (1989: 17). More fully:

> The slow and difficult evolution of a doctrinal language, creeds and definitions . . . [has] to do at heart with maintaining the possibility of speaking about a God who becomes unreservedly accessible in the person of Jesus Christ and in the life of Christ's community. What is rejected is, pretty consistently, any teaching that leaves God only provisionally or partially involved in the communicating of the new life of grace and communion. (1991: 32)

This is why it is no accident that Trinity and Christology were at the heart of the formation of classical doctrine. The 'slow and difficult evolution' of Trinitarian and

Christological doctrine has to do precisely with securing at the heart of the church's life an irremovable, unsurpassable attention to Jesus of Nazareth as the one in whom God has become unreservedly accessible—and through whom God's saving and transformative judgement is heard. In the light of the discussion above, it should be no surprise to hear Williams say that 'all doctrine [is], essentially, reflection on Easter' (1982b: xiii).

> Doctrine is about our end (and our beginning); about what in our humanity is not negotiable, dispensable, vulnerable to revision according to political convenience or cultural choice and fashion ... Doctrine purports to tell us what we are for, and what the shape is of a life lived in accordance with the way things are, and how such a life becomes accessible to us, even in the middle of the corruption and unfreedom of a shadowed history. (1997: 382)

Doctrine emerges, as Williams sees it, within the worshipping life of the church—the life gathered by Word and Sacrament around Jesus. That worshipping life is characterized by an open, diverse, evolving, even playful richness of verbal and non-verbal speech. The diversity and evolution of that speech, however, unavoidably raises questions about coherence and faithfulness—about what apparently natural developments undermine the existing breadth of that speech and what differences make a shared conversation in this speech impossible. 'Only in the activity of conversation do we find what the depths and what the limits are of our common language, what it is that holds us together as sharers in one world' (1990: 283). Doctrinal reflection investigates the extent to which '[t]he openness, the "impropriety", the *play* of liturgical imagery is anchored to a specific set of commitments as to the limits and defining conditions within which the believing life is lived' and it attempts to find ways to 'characterize these defining conditions' (1987a: 236).

> Given a commitment to the truthfulness of the whole complex of practices, verbal and non-verbal, moral, imaginative, devotional, and reflective, which embody 'the church's conviction' about Jesus, dogmatic Christological definition sets out to establish the conditions for telling this truth in the most comprehensive, least conceptually extravagant and least idly mythological language. (1993: 250-1)

Heresy, by contrast, is found wherever adoption of a particular pattern of speech brings with it a 'major reduction in the range of available resources of meaning' (1983b: 16). Williams therefore puts 'heresy' in the same category as 'the deadness of bureaucratic jargon, the deadness of uplifting waffle, the deadness of acronyms and target setting'. Heresy is one of the forms of language that 'flattens out the depth' of human life, and deprives the church of a resource for bringing before the resurrected one 'the extremities of experience, obsessive passion or jealousy, adoration, despair' (2002d: 173-4).

If, for Williams, doctrine emerges within the worshipping life of the church, it does so most urgently insofar as the church is a more-than-local community. It is in the exchange between Christians in different contexts (geographically and, in a sense, temporally) that the limits of difference and evolution in the church's speech are most deeply tested, and that the defining conditions of that language are most likely to be discerned.

The very idea of 'orthodoxy' in the early church emerged, according to Williams, from the attempt of scattered Christian communities to recognize in one another a focus on the same Christ that they themselves worshipped. As Williams tells the story, through the second and third centuries a distinction arose between strands of Christianity for which communication between congregations was an ad hoc and occasional affair, and strands in which there were 'regular and significant links' to the point of 'an almost obsessional mutual interest and interchange' between congregations—interest and interchange that took the form of visits, meetings, and letters (1989: 11–12). These obsessively interconnected Christians believed that they were exploring a common heritage, that they were hearers of a common gospel—and that it therefore *mattered* that they could not yet see the unity between their differing languages. Doctrine emerged as a way of thinking the unity of a scattered church.

The irony of doctrine is, however, that the very passion to hold the church's language open against threatened closures can itself become a threat. Williams notes that the history of doctrine 'has the paradoxical character of a repeated effort of definition designed to counter the ill effects of definition itself—rather like the way in which a good poet will struggle to find a fixed form of words that will decisively avoid narrowing and lifeless fixtures or closures of meaning' (1990: 285).

When 'we begin instead to use this language to defend ourselves, to denigrate others, to control and correct ... then it becomes a problem' (2000a: 37).

> [T]he Church's dogmatic activity, its attempts to structure its public and common language in such a way that the possibilities of judgement and renewal are not buried, must constantly be chastened by the awareness that it so acts in order to give place to the freedom of God—the freedom of God from the Church's sense of itself and its power, and thus the freedom of God to renew and absolve. This is why dogmatic language becomes empty and even destructive of faith when it is isolated from a lively and converting worship and a spirituality that is not afraid of silence and powerlessness. (2000: 84)

THE CHURCH AS A COMMUNITY OF TRUTH AND UNITY

The transformation that forms the church, according to Williams, is not over in a flash. It takes time, and is worked out by repeated encounter with Jesus of Nazareth, in Word and Sacrament, steadied by doctrine. It requires, again, 'steady and radical exposure' to Christ. It is not that there is anything incomplete or unfinished in God, or in God's love for the world in the incarnation—but that God's love, decisively enacted for the world in the life, death, and resurrection of Jesus of Nazareth, is inexhaustible and always more than Christ's followers have yet grasped. So Williams can say that 'Jesus grants us a solid identity, yet refuses us the power to "seal" or finalize it, and obliges us to realize that this identity only exists in an endless responsiveness to new encounters with him in the world of unredeemed relationships' (1982b: 76).

That 'endless responsiveness' takes the form, in part, of a deep commitment on the part of members of the church to learn *from one another*—to grow up together. I spoke at the beginning of this chapter about the transformation wrought by the gospel as one in which people are made into God's speech to one another. I said that the transform-ation involves people becoming words spoken to one other, and becoming hearers of the word that is spoken to them by each other. To be drawn into the life of Christ is therefore, for Williams, to become those who communicate that life to one another. 'To belong in the apostolic community', Williams says, 'is to be involved in a complex act of giving away: to be at the disposal of God's will, to give away the life we have, so that God's life can be given through us' (1994: 257). And precisely because the journey of disciple-ship for each person is one that involves the whole messy and particular material of their unique life history being brought to the feet of the resurrected Jesus, the word that each person's life becomes will speak about Jesus differently.

I have also written of the 'restless dimension of unclarity' that characterizes encoun-ters with Jesus: the excess or surplus that is not a passive hinterland awaiting further exploration, but an active presence, capable of breaking in as creative judgement. The difference between two members of the Body of Christ is, for Williams, one of the char-acteristic places where that presence lives. That is what it means for God's life to be given through the members of the Body. Each member of the body is therefore called to be open 'to the wealth of communal life and thought' (1975: 33). No one individual, no one group of Christians already *possesses* Christ, and so does not need to receive him—and to go on receiving him—from others.

The church is therefore an ongoing conversation. That is true for Williams at the level of the local body of Christ. It is also true at the trans-local level—in the life of the Church of England, for instance, and in the life of the wider Anglican Communion. And it is true in ecumenism, and in that strange conversation in time that unites different gen-erations of the church into one tradition. The church simply *is* the conversation of the faithful at all these levels.

However, to describe the church in this way risks papering over some very wide cracks. Many of the differences that cross the church involve disagreements about what it means to be orientated towards encounter with Jesus—disagreements in which others in the church are thought to be misleading guides to the Scriptures (or to have turned their back on those Scriptures), or in which they are thought to have strayed (or gal-loped) beyond the doctrinal discipline that is supposed to hold the church together *as* a conversation. One of the central contributions of Williams's ecclesiology has been his wrestling with precisely this question—and that wrestling was itself forced deeper by his immersion in the Anglican Communions controversies, especially as regards human sexuality, during his time as archbishop of Canterbury.

Williams himself clearly has (as we have seen) a particular construal of what faithfulness to the gospel of Jesus of Nazareth involves. Just as clearly, others in the church can and do differ from him, not just in detail, but in their ways of describing what faithfulness to the gospel means. There is therefore a difference between asking whether he is trying to be faithful to the gospel in the terms in which he understands that faithfulness, and asking whether he is trying to be so in his interlocutor's terms. Yet if an interlocutor contented herself with asking whether Williams's understanding of the gospel, and of the nature of obedience to that gospel, agreed with hers, she would be insulating herself against any deep challenge or insight that his understanding might have to offer to her: she would be declaring in advance that she was right, that those who differ from her are wrong, and that she is not open to reconsidering that opinion. She would be failing to take seriously a situation in which a church is divided precisely by the diversity of its construals of 'obedience', and so each construal is rendered controversial. Clearly something more subtle is needed.

There is more than one way of striving for that greater subtlety, however. The most obvious is to make some attempt to set out the absolutely central points on which one is not willing to compromise, and to ask about someone else's agreement only with those central points—combining that adamant stance with a flexible willingness to learn on all other matters. And some such attempt to set out what is central is an inevitable part of the mix—though it has perhaps not played quite as central a role in Anglicanism as it has in other traditions where habitual reference to a detailed 'Confession' of some kind has been an important driver of theological conversation.

Williams suggests, however, that Christians should also be asking whether the claims of those who differ from them are nevertheless recognizably a contribution *to a common conversation* about obedience. That is: rather than asking a static question ('Does your position agree with mine, or does it agree with the points I have identified as central to mine?') Williams is suggesting that Christians ask a dynamic question: 'Having heard what you say, can I recognise the possibility of being called to deeper obedience to the gospel (given what I currently understand that obedience to mean) by what you say, and can I see the possibility (given what you currently understand that obedience to mean) of calling you to deeper obedience?'

'If I might put it in a formula that may sound too much like jargon,' he says,

> I suggest that what we are looking for in each other is the grammar of obedience: we watch to see if our partners take the same kind of time, sense that they are under the same sort of judgement or scrutiny, approach the issue with the same attempt to be dispossessed by the truth they are engaging with. This will not guarantee agreement; but it might explain why we should always first be hesitant and attentive to each other. Why might anyone think this might count as a gift of Christ to the Church? (2001b: 11)

Can I, Williams asks, look at that other Christian and recognize that he or she came to that disturbing conclusion on the basis of a serious and recognizable attempt to be obedient to the gospel? Can I see that he or she is recognizably reading the same

Scriptures, praying with the same seriousness, worshipping the same God? Can I see that his or her discernment is being offered as a gift to the church, an attempt to show the church more of the church's Lord and the demands that his love makes on our lives?

With a question like this in mind, a Christian might move from a picture of the world divided into those with whom he agrees versus those with whom he disagrees (whether wholesale, or on the fundamentals), to a more complex picture in which, around the brittle inner circle of agreement, there is the more unruly company of those with whom he disagrees but with whom he shares enough to sustain a serious conversation: the wider circle of a community not in possession of truthfulness but in serious pursuit of it, hoping and working for it.

Williams often uses the language of 'recognition' for this wider circle. The boundary of this wider circle of recognition is, however, inevitably much more difficult to discern than are the boundaries of truthfulness—though boundaries there certainly are. And those boundaries are not defined simply by the *forms* of obedience—by the bare fact that my opponent appeals to the same Scriptures, say, or tells a broadly recognizable salvation-historical story. Williams asks Christians whether they can 'see in one another at least some of the same habits of attention and devotion to Scripture, whatever the diversity of interpretation', but beyond that he asks whether they 'can see that the other person is trying to *listen* to God's self-communication in scripture, not just imposing an agenda' (2009a).

We can see how this emphasis coheres with Williams's wider ecclesiology by walking through a portion of an address he gave to the 2008 Lambeth Conference, in which he asked directly what 'Christian unity' might mean. '[F]irst and above all, this is union with Jesus Christ; accepting his gift of grace and forgiveness, learning from him how to speak to his Father, standing where he stands by the power of the Spirit. We are one with one another because we are called into union with the one Christ and stand *in* his unique place—stand in the Way, the Truth and the Life' (2008a). Here Williams offers a characteristic Trinitarian description of where the church stands: as recipients of forgiveness at Jesus' hands, as brought by that forgiveness into relation to the one who does not stand over us as competitor or rival, and as drawn into union with him—into lives that say what his life says—by the power of the Spirit working on each member. 'Our unity is not mutual forbearance but being summoned and drawn into the same place before the Father's throne. *That* unity is a pure gift—and something we can think of in fear and trembling as well as wordless gratitude; because to be in that place is to be in the light of absolute Truth, naked and defenceless.' This unity is not something achieved; nor is it something given at the end of the journey. Rather, just as Jesus is 'simply there', Christians are simply given each other. And note the deep connection in Williams's words between standing with each other and standing before God's transforming, freeing judgement. 'St John's gospel has been reminding us that the place of Jesus is not a place where ordinary, fallen human instinct wants to go. Yet it's where we belong, and where God the Father and Our Lord Jesus Christ want us to be, for our life, our joy and our healing.' In other words, despite all the language of strain, of difficulty, of being stripped and left speechless, this transformation is a homecoming. God's creatures belong with each other in this deep sense, and the journey deeper into God's love in Jesus Christ is a journey home. Human beings belong with God—and they belong with each other.

> That's the unity which is inseparable from truth. It's broken not when we simply disagree but when we stop being able to see in each other the same kind of conviction of being called by an authoritative voice into a place where none of us has an automatic right to stand. Christians divided in the sixteenth century, in 1930's Germany and 1980's South Africa because they concluded, painfully as well as (often) angrily, that something had been substituted for the grace of Christ—moral and ritual achievement, or racial and social pride, as if there were after all a way of securing our place before God by something other than Jesus Christ.

So there *are* limits to this unity—and they are not limits of the church's ability to paper over cracks, and to keep the show on the road or the ship afloat by any means available—but they are the limits of recognition of an orientation to God's gracious love in Christ.

> Now all this might help us to see why Christian communities express their unity in so many visible, tangible ways. They read the same Bible in public and private, and shape their words and actions in conformity with it—or at least they try to. They seek for consistent practices around the sacraments, so that the baptism or eucharist of each community can be recognised by others as directed in the same way, working under the same authority. It happens in different ways and different degrees in different Christian confessions and families of churches; but all Christian communities have some such practice.

Churches are communities of Word and Sacrament—and, we might add, doctrinal communities—precisely because those things are the concrete forms of their obedience, the tangible forms of their mutual recognizability.

It is important to stress, therefore, that this unity is not, in Williams's eyes, a matter of 'unity for unity's sake' or of 'unity at all costs'. The whole process of seeking to sustain unity is directed to the deepening of truthfulness: the deepening of obedience to the God of Jesus Christ, the deepening of exposure to and proclamation of the gospel. On the other hand, to become truthful means precisely learning 'to act in such a way that my action becomes something given into the life of the community and in such a way that what results is glory—the radiating, the visibility, of God's beauty in the world', and it means 'looking and listening for Christ in the acts of another Christian who is manifestly engaged, self-critically engaged, with the data of common belief and worship' (2001b: 7, 13). Unity and truth are inseparable.

Williams expressed similar ideas in a 2005 address to General Synod, during a debate on the Windsor Report.

> I've become very much accustomed to being accused by both sides in this debate of setting unity before truth. And my dilemma, a dilemma which I suspect is shared by

a good many people here, is that I'm not sure as a Christian that I'm wholly able to separate truth from unity. For as a Christian I believe that unity is what enables us to discover truth within the body of Christ, not simply truth according to my own preferences, my own intelligence, my own resources, but in the richness of life an understanding that is shared in the body. And part of the agony of the situation we face at the moment has to do with those two things beginning to pull apart from one another. (2005)

To be the church is, for Williams, to be held together before Christ, learning from one another. It is to participate in an ongoing journey of learning together—and as the members of the church can never have done with that learning of God's inexhaustible life, so they can never have done with one another. The gift of truth and the gift of each other are inseparable.

It is only when the recognition that enables this exchange breaks down, Williams suggests, that Christians should find themselves called to the tragic recognition that they and their opponents do not share a recognizable conversation, that those on opposing sides of whatever divide it is cannot call one another to obedience except by standing against one another, in prophetic denunciation of one kind or another.

Let me illustrate this. For Williams, appeals to Scripture in theological argument are properly *mediated* appeals. That is to say, the material gleaned from Scripture is subjected to the kind of attention and reflection where the emphasis falls on the attempt to understand the deep patterns of reasoning that move the Scriptures as a whole, and then to read particular injunctions in the light of those deep patterns, even when that means being taken beyond the plain sense. Imagine (for the sake of argument) that Williams were speaking to a Christian community that regarded 'obedience to the gospel' as quite straightforwardly defined by *un*mediated appeal to the plain sense of the Scriptures. Such a community might find that, except to the minor degree that they found the plain sense of certain Scriptures elucidated by his readings, Williams's arguments were simply *irrelevant* to their own way of doing theology—or, worse, that his arguments seemed like nothing more than sophisticated attempts to sidestep the Scriptures. They would not be able to see his arguments as, in any direct way, calling them to deeper obedience (as they currently understand obedience). And they might find in return that they simply could not call him to deeper obedience, because the means by which they might do so—pointing out once again the plain sense of the Scriptures in question—was consistently met with a 'Yes, but...'. In such a situation, we might have to conclude that there is not a common conversation about obedience. The attempt at conversation would stutter to a halt.

Where it does not fail, however, Christians will retain at least the possibility of being called out of themselves, and called more deeply into the truth, at each others' hands. At General Synod in 2009, in response to someone's comment about the proposed Anglican Covenant involving a giving up of rights, Williams said:

I don't believe that a process of shared discernment is a handing over of something that belongs to me to someone to whom it doesn't belong, because I have a rather more, excuse the word, robust doctrine of our participation in the body of Christ than that. I don't believe that when I invite someone else to share my own process of prayer and decision making I'm resigning something which I ought to be clinging on to. I believe rather than I'm trying to discover more fully who I am in Christ by inviting others who share my life in Christ into the process of making a decision. (2009d)

In other words, Williams is describing the church as a community in which not only do *I* seek *your* deeper obedience, but in which *I* also seek *your* seeking of *my* deeper obedience. I see that I can call you to deeper obedience, and I long for that, but I also see that you can call me to deeper obedience, and I long for that too. We are, in other words, talking about a community capable of sustaining an interlocking economy of desire: I desire Christ; you desire Christ; I desire your desiring of Christ; you desire my desiring of Christ; I desire your desiring of my desiring of Christ; you desire my desiring of your desiring of Christ . . . and so on. This is a process in which each is 'handed over' to the other, in which each learns to become more human, and to become more holy, through the other.

Williams holds that to be a community not in possession of truthfulness but in serious pursuit of it, hoping and working for it, requires just such commitment: it requires the safety that comes from being able to trust that you will not walk away from this conversation simply because we do not yet agree. Of course, it is not that divorce is impossible—but to walk into this marriage with a prenuptial agreement that assumes the inevitability or propriety of divorce is already to betray the commitment involved. This is a union in which the partners will have made what Williams has called 'a promise to be willing to be converted by each other' (2008b).

It is here, above all, that we can see what Williams took to be his role as archbishop of Canterbury, and it is here above all that the attempts to create some kind of Anglican Covenant that characterized his time in Canterbury are best situated. In an interview in *Time* in 2007, Williams said, 'The task I've got is to try and maintain as long as possible the space in which people can have constructive disagreements, learn from each other, and try and hold that within an agreed framework of discipline and practice' (2007). Elsewhere he described his task, and that of other Anglicans concerned about the future of their disagreement, as 'thinking about how the most life-giving kinds of exchange are made possible' (2009b). His task, as he saw it, was to hold on to unity for the sake of truth.

Williams does not, however, believe that this is simply a recipe for inertia—for the kind of structural conservatism that arises when a large community can only travel at the speed of its slowest members.

[T]o say that truth for a Christian is not discovered without unity is not to provide a simple solution to our dilemma. We all know . . . that there are some moments when the church, or parts of the church, take risks. They speak for a church which doesn't yet exist, so they believe, out of a conscience informed by scripture and revelation. At the Reformation, our church and many others took that kind of risk. and [*sic*] we have to be candid, in our decision to ordain women to the priesthood we engage in something of that sort of risk. The trouble is, that risk really is risk. You don't and you can't know yet whether it's justified. The church is capable of error and any local church is capable of error, as the Thirty-Nine Articles remind us forcibly. So if one portion of the church decides that it must take a conscientious risk, then there are inevitable results to that. There are consequences in hurt, misunderstanding, rupture and damage. It does us no good to pretend that the cost is not real. So I don't think it will quite do to say, if anyone does really say this, that a risky act ought to have or can have no consequences. (2005)

There is an attempt at a delicate balance here: an affirmation both of the possibility of risk and the reality of consequences. If the church is to be a community of gift and reception, of speech and hearing, it will often take the form of a community of prophecy and discernment—and needs both sides to remain in truth and unity.

Williams also does not believe that this attempt to hold on to unity is without serious cost. The question of the truthfulness of the church is, from Williams's point of view, the question of whether the church's members are becoming words that speak truly to each other, and speak truly to the world, of God's gracious love. The divisions amongst Christians that strike most deeply are precisely those in which each side believes that the other is heading down a path that will make such truthful speech impossible.

In a 2009 speech, Williams described the conflicts of the Anglican Communion in these terms. He spoke of those on one side who would say that 'Christian credibility is shattered by the sense of rejection and scapegoating which they experience . . . The cost they feel is often they cannot commend the Christianity that they long to believe in because they feel that they are bound up in a system and a community where scapegoating and rejection are very deeply engrained' (2009b).

For these people, the danger is that the church will cease speaking of God's love in Jesus Christ, and instead speak the language of the world of rivalry and suspicion—precisely that world from which human beings are saved. On the other hand, Williams said, there are

those for whom the credibility of Christianity is at stake in another way, those for whom the cost is felt like this: that the decisions that others have made in other parts of the world have put them in a position where they cannot commend the Christianity they long to share with their neighbours with any ease or confidence because they feel that fellow Christians have somehow undermined their witness. (2009b)

Here, the danger identified is of a failure to acknowledge that the church is a single conversation, and that what is said in one place is communicated to the whole—such that decisions taken in isolation cannot but be damaging. In the light of these two deep concerns, Williams poses the question:

How can those who share that sense of cost and that sense of profound anxiety about how to make the Gospel credible—how are they to come together at least for some recognition and respect to emerge? How are they to come together so that they can recognise the cost that the other bears, and also recognise the deep seriousness about Jesus and his Gospel that they share? (2009b)

That is the characteristic question of Williams's ecclesiology.

An Unfinished Community

In closing, it is worth emphasizing that there is no sense in Williams's work that the true unity of the church is already in the church's possession. The witness of the church in the world is not simply found in the extent to which it has arrived at this unity already and displays it. Rather, its witness is, at least in part, given by the seriousness by which it acknowledges its failure to display this unity, and the urgency with which it pursues it. This is a theme that, in different forms, has cropped up throughout Williams's writing on the church. At the 2006 General Convention of the Episcopal Church, Williams told delegates: 'Life is proclaimed not in our achievement, our splendid record of witness to God, but in our admission of helplessness and of the continuing presence and lure of death in our lives. To be able to speak this, and not to retreat in fear or throw up defences is part of true life' (2009c). Much earlier, while still pursuing an academic career (and a few years before being appointed Lady Margaret Professor), he had written:

> If we had to choose between a Church tolerably confident of what it has to say and seeking only for effective means of saying it, and a Church constantly engaged in an internal dialogue and critique of itself, an exploration to discover what is central to its being, I should say that it is the latter which is more authentic—a Church which understands that part of what it is *offering* to humanity is the possibility of living in such a mode. (1984: 12, Williams's italics)

Between these two, around the time that he was appointed as archbishop of Wales, he wrote:

> I long for the Church to be more truly itself . . . Yet I must also learn to live in and attend to the reality of the Church as it is, to do the prosaic things that can and must be done now and to work at my relations now with the people who will not listen to me or those like me—because what God asks of me is not to live in the ideal future but to live with honesty and attentiveness in the present. (2000a: 85-6)

Finally, at the end of his tenure as archbishop of Canterbury, Williams wrote an Advent letter to the Primates of the Anglican Communion.

> When we try to pretend that the holiness of Jesus is triumphantly visible in the Church, we are in danger of turning our minds away from the fact that the enduring power that sustains the Church is Christ alone, not our measures of success or coherence. But it

is still true that . . . the glory of the future can be seen from time to time in lives that are fully turned to the face of Jesus . . . We have not arrived at the end of all things, but we long for it because we have seen something of its radiance and joy in the life of the Christian community and its worship and service. In the past ten years, these things have become more and more clear to me in my involvement in the Communion's life. Our Communion has endured much suffering and confusion, and still lives with this in many ways; yet we are still privileged to see the glory of God in the face of Jesus Christ in different ways within our common life, and so are reminded by God's grace that it is still Christ who lives secretly at the heart of our fellowship, and renews it day by day. (2012)

CRITICISMS

The most common criticisms of Williams's ecclesiology circle around an idea already touched on in this chapter: that, in the end, his focus on unity overcomes his focus on truth. When he says that his task 'is to try and maintain as long as possible the space in which people can have constructive disagreements' in the church, it is clear that 'as long as possible' is a crucial qualifier—and that how long *is* possible is going to be a matter for fallible and debatable discernment, rather than for clarity and certainty. It is inevitable, then, that Williams was faced with repeated claims that he had held on *longer* than was possible—and that there can be no knock-down rejoinder to such claims, but only on-going, careful attention to the actual life of the church.

The final two quotations given in the section 'An Unfinished Community' suggest, however, a different kind of criticism that can be levelled at Williams's ecclesiology. On the one hand, he speaks of the privilege of having seen at times 'the glory of God in the face of Jesus Christ' shining in the life of the church. On the other hand, he speaks of 'the prosaic things that can and must be done now'. It is at least possible that Williams's focus on division and struggle, on painful learning across difference, on the agonistic element in the life of the church, leaves less than adequate space for the good and the ordinary, the joyful and the prosaic. If 'growing up together' is indeed the central theme of his ecclesiology, Williams's broadly apophatic and ascetic account could perhaps be supplemented by a greater focus on these other forms and contexts of growth—on routine nourishment and joyful celebration.

REFERENCES

Williams, Rowan (1975). *The Theology of Vladimir Nikolaievich Lossky: An Exposition and Critique*. D.Phil. thesis, University of Oxford.

Williams, Rowan (1979). *The Wound of Knowledge: Christian Spirituality from the New Testament to St John of the Cross*. London: Darton, Longman & Todd.

Williams, Rowan (1982a). 'Authority and the Bishop in the Church'. In Mark Santer (ed.), *Their Lord and Ours: Approaches to Authority, Community, and the Unity of the Church*. London: SPCK, 90–112.

Williams, Rowan (1982b). *Resurrection: Interpreting the Easter Gospel*. London: Darton, Longman & Todd.

Williams, Rowan (1983a). *The Truce of God: The Archbishop of Canterbury's Lent Book*. London: Collins/Fount.

Williams, Rowan (1983b). 'What is Catholic Orthodoxy?' In Rowan Williams and Kenneth Leech (eds), *Essays Catholic and Radical: A Jubilee Group Symposium for the 150th Anniversary of the Beginning of the Oxford Movement 1833–1983*. London: Bowerdean Press, 11–25.

Williams, Rowan (1984). 'Women and Ministry: A Case for Theological Seriousness'. In Monica Furlong (ed.), *Feminine in the Church*. Monica Furlong. London: SPCK, 11–27.

Williams, Rowan (1987a). *Arius: Heresy and Tradition*. London: Darton, Longman, and Todd.

Williams, Rowan (1987b). 'On Doing Theology' (with James Atkinson). In Christina Baxter (ed.), *Stepping Stones: Joint Essays on Anglican Catholic and Evangelical Unity*. London: Hodder & Stoughton, 1–20.

Williams, Rowan (1989). 'Does it Make Sense to Speak of Pre–Nicene Orthodoxy?' In Rowan Williams (ed.), *The Making of Orthodoxy: Essays in Honour of Henry Chadwick*. Cambridge: Cambridge University Press, 1–23.

Williams, Rowan (1990). 'Newman's *Arians* and the Question of Method in Doctrinal History'. In Ian Ker and Alan Hill (eds), *Newman after a Hundred Years*. Oxford: Oxford University Press, 263–86.

Williams, Rowan (1991). 'Teaching the Truth'. In Jeffrey John (ed.), *Living Tradition: Affirming Catholicism in the Anglican Church*. London: Darton, Longman & Todd, 29–43.

Williams, Rowan (1993). 'Doctrinal Criticism: Some Questions'. In Sarah Coakley and David A. Pailin (eds), *The Making and Remaking of Christian Doctrine: Essays in Honour of Maurice Wiles*. Oxford: Clarendon, 239–64.

Williams, Rowan (1994). *Open to Judgement: Sermons and Addresses*. London: Darton, Longman & Todd.

Williams, Rowan (1995). 'Foreword'. In Henry McAdoo and Kenneth Stevenson, *The Mystery of the Eucharist in the Anglican Tradition*. Norwich: Canterbury, vii–x.

Williams, Rowan (1997). 'Hooker: Philosopher, Anglican, Contemporary'. In Arthur S. McGrade (ed.), *Richard Hooker and the Construction of Christian Community*. Washington, DC: Medieval & Renaissance Texts and Studies, 369–83.

Williams, Rowan (2000a). *Christ on Trial: How the Gospel Unsettles our Judgement*. London: Fount.

Williams, Rowan (2000b). *On Christian Theology*. Oxford: Blackwell.

Williams, Rowan (2000c). 'The Lambeth Talk' (interview, Greenbelt Festival). <http://www.surefish.co.uk/news/features/2003/rowan2.htm>.

Williams, Rowan (2001a). 'Foreword'. In Mark Pryce (ed.), *Literary Companion to the Lectionary: Readings throughout the Year*. London: SPCK, ix.

Williams, Rowan (2001b). 'Making Moral Decisions'. In Robin Gill (ed.), *The Cambridge Companion to Christian Ethics*. Cambridge: Cambridge University Press, 3–15.

Williams, Rowan (2002a). Jubilee sermon, Bangor Cathedral, 11 June. <http://www.churchinwales.org.uk/sermonsr/r14/>.

Williams, Rowan (2002b). *Ponder These Things: Praying with Icons of the Virgin*. Norwich: Canterbury.

Williams, Rowan (2002c). Presidential Address at the Monmouth Diocesan Conference, 12 October. <http://www.churchinwales.org.uk/sermonsr/r18/>.

Williams, Rowan (2002d). 'Statements, Acts and Values: Spiritual and Material in the School Environment'. In Stephen Prickett and Patricia Erskine-Hill (eds), *Education! Education! Education! Managerial Ethics and the Law of Unintended Consequences*. Exeter: Imprint Academic, 167–78.

Williams, Rowan (2003a). *The Dwelling of the Light: Praying with Icons of Christ*. Norwich: Canterbury.

Williams, Rowan (2003b). Enthronement sermon, 27 February. <http://rowanwilliams.archbishopofcanterbury.org/articles.php/1624/enthronement-sermon>.

Williams, Rowan (2005). Speech in Debate on the Windsor Report, 17 February. <http://rowanwilliams.archbishopofcanterbury.org/articles.php/1680/general-synod-speech-in-debate-on-the-windsor-report>.

Williams, Rowan (2007). 'Keeping the Faith' (interview). In *Time*, 7 June. <http://www.time.com/time/magazine/article/0,9171,1630234,00.html>.

Williams, Rowan (2008a). Concluding Presidential Address to the Lambeth Conference, 3 August. <http://rowanwilliams.archbishopofcanterbury.org/articles.php/1350/concluding-presidential-address-to-the-lambeth-conference>.

Williams, Rowan (2008b). Debate on A Covenant for the Anglican Communion, 13 February. <http://rowanwilliams.archbishopofcanterbury.org/articles.php/1522/debate-on-a-covenant-for-the-anglican-communion>.

Williams, Rowan (2009a). Archbishop's Presidential Address to General Synod, 10 February. <http://rowanwilliams.archbishopofcanterbury.org/articles.php/831/the-archbishops-presidential-address-general-synod-february-2009>.

Williams, Rowan (2009b). Presidential Address to the 14th Meeting of the Anglican Consultative Council, 11 May. <http://rowanwilliams.archbishopofcanterbury.org/articles.php/1510/archbishops-presidential-address-to-the-14th-meeting-of-the-acc>.

Williams, Rowan (2009c). Sermon Preached during a Eucharist at the General Convention, 9 July. <http://rowanwilliams.archbishopofcanterbury.org/articles.php/879/sermon-preached-during-a-eucharist-at-the-general-convention>.

Williams, Rowan (2009d). 'What kind of Global Communion Do We Want to Be?', Speech to General Synod, 12 February. <http://rowanwilliams.archbishopofcanterbury.org/articles.php/828/archbishop-what-kind-of-global-communion-do-we-want-to-be>.

Williams, Rowan (2012). Advent letter to Anglican Primates, 2 December. <http://rowanwilliams.archbishopofcanterbury.org/articles.php/2732/archbishops-advent-letter-to-anglican-primates>.

SUGGESTED READING

General Studies of Rowan Williams's Ministry and Theology

Goddard, Andrew (2013). *Rowan Williams: His Legacy*. Oxford: Lion.

Gray, Brett (2016). *Jesus in the Theology of Rowan Williams*. London: Bloomsbury.

Higton, Mike (2004). *Difficult Gospel: The Theology of Rowan Williams*. London: SCM.

Myers, Ben (2012). *Christ the Stranger: The Theology of Rowan Williams*. London: T&T Clark.

Shortt, Rupert (2009). *Rowan's Rule: The Biography of the Archbishop*. London: Hodder & Stoughton.

Rowan Williams's Ecclesiology

Higton, Mike (2011). 'The Ecclesial Body's Grace: Obedience and Faithfulness in Rowan Williams' Ecclesiology'. *Ecclesiology* 7: 7–28.

Tanner, Mary (2012). 'The Ecumenical Theology of Archbishop Rowan Williams'. *Ecclesiology* 8: 163–83.

Zink, Jesse (2013). 'Patiently Living with Difference: Rowan Williams' Archiepiscopal Ecclesiology and the Proposed Anglican Covenant'. *Ecclesiology* 9: 223–41.

PART IV

CONTEMPORARY MOVEMENTS IN ECCLESIOLOGY

CHAPTER 24

FEMINIST CRITIQUES, VISIONS, AND MODELS OF THE CHURCH

ELAINE GRAHAM

THE history of the largely hidden and unacknowledged contribution of women to American religious life tells a sobering tale. It is one of hidden labour, thankless dedication, and above all an indictment of the biases and silences at work in the telling of history, whether of church or society, as Ann Braude notes:

> There could be no lone man in the pulpit without the women who fill the pews. Women raised money for churches, synagogues, temples, and mosques through bake sales, community suppers, and sewing circles. They embroidered altar cloths, taught Sunday school, prepared festival meals, played the organ, and directed the choir. Perhaps most important, they took their children to their places of worship and educated them in their beliefs. Without such women, there would be no next generation to sustain the faith. And without their material and financial support, there would be no churches, synagogues, or mosques for men to administer. There would be no clergy, no seminaries to train them, no theology to teach them, no denominations to ordain them, and no ceremonies for them to lead unless women found it worth their while to support religious organizations. But no matter how great their contributions, women have usually been asked to take a backseat to male religious leaders.
>
> (Braude 2008: 1–2)

Sadly, this picture is not restricted to one particular tradition, cultural context, or historical era and it perfectly demonstrates the frustrations and challenges facing those who wish to write women back into the history of Christianity and the church.

Introduction

Although, historically, they have invariably constituted the majority of church members, women have been and still are virtually invisible: in positions of leadership, in formal texts and traditions, in ecclesiological deliberations on the nature and mission of the church. It is a story of marginalization and exclusion. In many parts of the church today women are barred from exercising ministries of Word and Sacrament, from performing certain tasks, or even from occupying sacred space. Even within denominations that formally espouse the equality of women and men and place no official or doctrinal bar on women's ministry, there is often talk of a 'stained-glass ceiling' that prevents women from rising to senior positions (Zikmund, Lummis, and Chang 1998, cited in Ross 2002: 231).

Feminist perspectives on ecclesiology have emerged in part to challenge and refute these traditional barriers. Much of this work focuses on reclaiming a tradition free of patriarchal interpretation, in order to restore the visibility and historic legitimacy of women's ministry. This is premised on a belief that the absence and silence of women in the churches, and the oppressive power of teaching from Scripture and tradition—including, crucially, particular versions of theological anthropology—is not due to women's inherent inferiority but to ideological representations and interpretations. One focal point for feminist ecclesiological work has therefore been in historiography. 'Arguments *from tradition* that women have not played a serious role in church leadership or in worship life suffer from a highly limited idea of what involvement constitutes, as well as an ignorance of the extent of women's leadership roles' (Ross 2002: 229).

Yet the overarching task of such critique and rehabilitation has clearly been constructive in its ecclesiological intentions: to enable women to claim the right to occupy, name, and represent the sacred within the Body of Christ today and to work in a renewed community of women *and* men in the church. The undergirding vision is a community of equals that truly embodies the 'dangerous memory' of Jesus Christ (Metz 1987) and promises to transform the structures, rituals, and missionary priorities of the church.

It is not the intention of this chapter to offer a systematic 'Feminist Ecclesiology', however, partly because feminist reflections on the nature and calling of the church have often sprung from single-issue campaigns or specific issues, such as the ordination of women or gender-inclusive language. It may be the case, therefore, that feminist ecclesiological considerations are more authentically approached through studies of women's lived experiences of the church. In particular, while they have been accused of merely co-opting women into patriarchal structures, global movements for the ordination of women have nevertheless been a fulcrum on which other initiatives (in liturgy, language, and leadership styles) have rested.

In looking for testimonies and witnesses to women's true experiences of being church, then, as Susan Ross argues above, we may have to rethink what counts as evidence.

Elizabeth Schüssler Fiorenza's hermeneutic of suspicion toward the New Testament argued that attention to the *text* should not cloak the significance of *context*. Similarly, liturgical or congregational studies that work solely from official documents fail to incorporate the 'living human documents' of experience and performance. In more recent years, through the medium of ethnography, oral history, and other qualitative research, new insights on women's experiences of being the church have emerged. These focus on the lived experiences of faith and, methodologically speaking, highlight the significance of first-person (and collective) narratives of faith and spirituality. They test the rhetoric and reality of participation in traditional settings (Fulkerson 1994; Clark-King 2004), as well as exploring the concerns of those in newer, women-centred liturgical and ritual movements (Berry 2009).

But questions still remain. How far have feminist critiques and new visions really informed 'mainstream' ecclesiological thinking in the churches? The story of the World Council of Churches' programme of 'The Community of Women and Men in the Church' during the 1980s suggests that a project of women's testimony and re-visioning did little to shift deep-seated ecumenical divisions on fundamental questions of theological anthropology and authority. New perspectives on ecclesiology, even those purporting to incorporate social scientific and theological study (Ward 2012), offer disappointingly little attention to gender dynamics. Similarly, despite its post-modern, holistic sensibilities, there is little sign of a developed feminist consciousness in writings on emergent or emerging church (Carson 2005). At the same time, however, if sociological data on Western patterns of religious observance are to be believed, women are steadily abandoning institutional loyalties in favour of more individualistic, 'post-secular' forms of spirituality (Brown 2009; Woodhead 2008). It remains to be seen what the consequences will be for the future of the church as a whole.

HISTORICAL PERSPECTIVES

The philosophical and theological origins of women's exclusion are rooted in binary systems of gender that have long equated women and the feminine with nature, affect, and embodiment, and men and masculinity with culture, reason, and the spirit. In relation to gender, traditional theological anthropology, especially in Natural Law traditions, regards gender difference as ontological and complementary, derived from sexual reproduction. Hence, the essential nature of women is to be receptive and nurturing, and that of men to be active, rational, and competitive. Biblical injunctions against women's public speech and New Testament notions of headship also provide scriptural grounds for the church's refusal to admit women to ministry on an equal footing to men. Similarly, the church is the bride of Christ, its Head, and so the historical maleness of Jesus is reinforced by an ecclesiological logic that argues only men can represent Christ at the altar (Congregation for the Doctrine of the Faith 1976).

From its emergence in church and academy from the 1970s, feminist studies of religion have stressed the significance of women's active participation in their traditions. As they re-evaluated Christian history, feminist historians and theologians began to recover stories of women's ministry, from references to women disciples, deacons, and missionaries in the New Testament and early Christianity (Berger 2012; Moltmann-Wendel 1983; Torjesen 1995). Such scholarship represented the beginnings of a feminist historiography that undermined arguments against the recognition of women's ministry on the grounds of lack of historical precedent. Such work continues in more recent scholarship (Madigan and Osiek 2005; Jones, Thorpe, and Wootton 2008).

Studies of women leaders or other religious figures, such as medieval mystical theologians, pioneer missionaries, or early modern preachers (Smith 2007; Berger 2012), have done much to restore women's visibility within the history of Christianity and to reinscribe their presence back into the story of the church. They represent important role models and often remind the church of significant theological insights that formerly may have been overlooked. In addition, however, many of these rehabilitations of historical reputations serve to remind contemporary generations of the ways women have always had to negotiate the limited opportunities available to them, and the circumscribed and often precarious spaces from which their Christian vocations were exercised.

The difficulties facing the first generations of women admitted into the ordained ministry—recorded in many empirical investigations—suggest that deep-seated obstacles to their full acceptance are remarkably persistent. Lack of women in senior positions, widespread disparity in pay and conditions between women and men clergy (exacerbated if a woman minister is married to another), congregational resistance to calling women ministers, have all been well documented (Jones, Thorpe, and Wootton 2008). More encouragingly, however, there is a significant body of evidence which suggests that even those once opposed to the ordination of women can undergo a change of heart (Jones 2004).

A more identifiably feminist movement began to emerge within North American Christianity in the nineteenth century. Out of the campaign for women's suffrage in the 1840s emerged groups of middle-class women who were convinced that reform of religious traditions was an essential part of the social and political emancipation of women. Most prominent amongst these was Elizabeth Cady Stanton, editor and co-ordinator of the highly influential *The Woman's Bible* (Stanton 1898). The beginnings of campaigns for women's equal ministry accelerated around the end of the nineteenth century, as the first Protestant denominations admitted women to ordained ministry.

As well as their interest in the historical contribution of women's religious orders, feminist historians of Christianity turned their attention to lay movements and guilds which functioned as semi-autonomous spheres for women in the church, such as the Mothers' Union, altar guilds, philanthropic and charitable work (Braude 2008; Moyse 2011). Often these have provided precious autonomy for women, especially lay women, sometimes extending into global communions, within which (albeit circumscribed) degrees of independence could be exercised. Within religious communities, whilst women might have been subject to male ecclesiastical authorities, in practice they often exercised many quasi-sacramental tasks, such as hearing confession and conducting spiritual direction (Stogdon 2004).

As second-wave feminism gained prominence in the West, many women began to articulate a powerful critique of Jewish and Christian traditions. Feminist writers argued that an image of God as Father was a fundamental mainstay of the system of patriarchy, in which male power is institutionalized in social structures and ideological worldviews that perpetuate the social and symbolic subordination of women. Religious doctrines and narratives collude in binary systems whereby maleness is identified with reason, spirit, public, and divinity, and femaleness with affect, body, private, and nature. Traditional religion was thus complicit with social norms that excluded women from power, limited their ambitions, and reinforced the view that female subordination was divinely sanctioned. Moreover, due to its patriarchal nature, religion was incapable of providing women with the symbols, narratives, and rituals that might speak to their experience or nurture their self-esteem.

The origins of the various 'women-church' movements of the last quarter of the twentieth century lay in Roman Catholic and Protestant campaigns for the ordination of women and for greater liturgical autonomy. While many activists were committed to remain within their denominational traditions, many other grass-roots adherents drew influences from pre- or post-Christian sources, such as indigenous spiritualities or neo-paganism. Globally, too, different expressions of woman-centred liturgical and ritual groups were formed and flourished into the early twenty-first century (see the section 'Women-Church').

Feminist Biblical Scholarship

The pioneering work of second-wave feminist theologians such as Rosemary Radford Ruether, Katie Cannon and Letty Russell, and biblical scholars like Elizabeth Schüssler Fiorenza, did much to galvanize feminist perspectives on ecclesiology. Such scholarship did not simply expose the marginalization of women's role within Christian history. It laid bare the systematic misogyny of centuries of tradition and ecclesial practice whilst providing robust analysis of the very mechanisms of exclusion and silencing of women's voices and agency. However, such work also pointed to alternative threads of 'usable tradition' from which more inclusive and hopeful models of the church could be reconstructed. Here, I will focus on Fiorenza's ground-breaking scholarship, since it highlights her methodological contribution which, alongside that of Ruether, formed the foundations on which subsequent feminist ecclesiological work was built.

Elizabeth Schüssler Fiorenza

Elizabeth Schüssler Fiorenza's contribution rests on two main contributions: a feminist historiography of Christian origins, which retrieves women's ministry within the early church from sexist misinterpretation; and a theorizing of a renewed church as the *ekklēsia* of equals. She thus offers a rereading of early Christian history which restores women to full agency, as well as offering historical precedent for movements seeking equality of women with men in the contemporary church. She argues that the New Testament provides ample evidence for women as active and visible followers of Jesus and leaders of the first Christian communities. Furthermore, these early communities were consciously counter-cultural in their celebration of the 'dangerous memory' of Jesus as one who disrupted conventional social, ethnic, and gender divisions (Fiorenza 1983: 140–54).

Fiorenza's hermeneutical principle is 'to articulate a feminist theory of interpretation as a critical practice of freedom' (Fiorenza 1992: 9). This means a search for traces of the *ekklēsia* of women from the testimonies of history in order to construct an alternative past, present, and future. Yet there is no history uncontaminated by patriarchy. Her critical reading of the New Testament thus entails a refusal to take texts or teachings at face value, but instead to attempt to reconstruct evidence of the true *praxis* of the earliest Christians in the face of later, ideological renditions.

> Insofar as androcentric biblical texts not only reflect their patriarchal cultural environment but also continue to allow a glimpse of the early Christian movements as a discipleship of equals, the reality of women's engagement and leadership in those movements precedes the androcentric injunctions for women's role and behaviour. Women who belonged to a submerged group in antiquity could develop leadership in the emerging Christian movement which, as a discipleship of equals, stood in tension and conflict with the patriarchal ethos of the Greco-Roman world. (Fiorenza 1983: 35)

While she acknowledges her debt to Elizabeth Cady Stanton's *The Woman's Bible* (1898) as setting in train a tradition of feminist hermeneutics that exposes the androcentric nature of biblical texts, translations, and interpretations, Fiorenza argues that her task is to read 'behind' the text in order to retrieve the history of women as active participants in the events and debates to which the texts refer, albeit often ideologically. This she characterizes as a move from a 'textual-biblical' to a 'historical-biblical hermeneutics' (Fiorenza 1983: 29–30).

Although the evidence of women's leadership within the earliest Christian communities may be salvageable, Fiorenza notes the gradual reversion of post-Petrine and post-Pauline traditions into greater conformity with patriarchal conventions (Fiorenza 1983). Some of this may have been for missionary and apologetic reasons, in order to reduce hostility between the church and Graeco-Roman society and to prevent Christianity from falling into disrepute. The freedom and equality of the *ekklēsia* was superseded by a model of the church as household, which asserted the authority of the paterfamilias over subordinates such as women and slaves. By drawing a distinction between the social order of the patriarchal pagan household and the worship assembly, Christian practice and teaching worked to erase ideas of a discipleship of equals from the tradition altogether (Fiorenza 1983: 245–50).

Nevertheless, Fiorenza's paradigm of biblical revelation is not to regard canonical texts as timeless or abstract imperatives, but as contextual responses to concrete human dilemmas. The test of their enduring value is the extent to which they bear witness to models of Christian faith and community that facilitate liberation and affirm women and men as equally made in the image of God. Fiorenza assembles evidence for an egalitarian, counter-cultural 'Jesus-movement' as the paradigm of the life of the church and as the overriding hermeneutical principle for reading all Scripture, canonical or otherwise. This evidence serves not as 'archetype' but 'prototype' of a non-patriarchal Christianity, since it is not intended to be a form of 'reconstructionism' whereby the past represents a closed canon (Watson 1998: 472–4).

Fiorenza sees the prototypical vision of non-patriarchal Christianity as always already hedged around with its detractors, and still only incompletely realized in the endeavours of women-church today. Yet the spirit of women's affirmation and visibility is the underlying criterion that enables the contemporary church to articulate an ethic of equality and parity between the genders in continuity with the 'dangerous memory' of the women and men around Jesus. The following statement of Fiorenza shows the double hermeneutic at work in Fiorenza's own reconstruction of Christian origins:

> The vision of the *ekklēsia* of women focuses on the empowerment of women because women as church have been excluded from the interpretation of the world and the divine. It seeks to enable women to find their own theological voices and to become visible as church. Hence the expression '*ekklēsia* of women' has constructive *and* reconstructive aims. It seeks to recover women's heritage as church. If the oppression of a people is total because it has neither an oral nor a written history, then the reconstruction of such a history of suffering and resurrection, of struggle and survival, is an important means to empower women and other nonpersons . . . I have attempted to articulate such a feminist theological reconstruction of the discipleship of equals in the first centuries of the church as a heritage and memory for women-church. (Fiorenza 1993a: 329)

The 'hermeneutical center' of a feminist critical theology of liberation is the struggle of women in church and society for freedom, self-determination, and full humanity. This then becomes the criterion for authenticity: renewed *praxis* that embodies mutuality and justice, not just between the genders but as the paragraphs above indicate, for all those oppressed and marginalized by hierarchical social relations—what Fiorenza sometimes terms 'kyriarchy' (Fiorenza 1992: 8). There is, then, within Fiorenza's vision always an implied social ethic that embraces social justice in the world as well as parity for women in the churches.

The power of the *ekklēsia* of women is to create an oppositional discursive space from which critical renewal can emerge. Fiorenza's intentional use of *ekklēsia*, a term used in the New Testament to denote the public, civil dimensions of the community of faith, highlights the significance of rendering women visible within the public assembly. It serves to emphasize that transformation rests in 'a feminist public that seeks equality and citizenship of women by articulating, confronting and combating patriarchal divisions. It does so not by declaring itself to be a liberated space of sisterhood, but by engaging feminist theoretical and practical differences as democratic discursive practices' (Fiorenza 1993b: 346).

Rather than relying on essentialist or naturalistic constructions of women's subjectivity, feminist theologies of liberation acknowledge the heterogeneity of women's experiences, resist romanticized notions of women-church, and establish the aim of such communities of praxis as pluralistic and inclusive 'feminist counterpublics' (Fiorenza 1993b: 348).

WOMEN-CHURCH

Fiorenza develops her critical hermeneutic of Christian origins into a constructive ethic of ecclesial renewal. Her aim is to empower a feminist movement within the church that is more than a special interest-group or sectional lobby, but a vision of 'a "new church" in solidarity with the oppressed and "least" of this world, the majority of whom are women and children dependent on women' (Fiorenza 1983: 344). In other words, the retrieval and normalization of the discipleship of equals within Christian history becomes the model for today. From the 1980s on, Fiorenza's work was also influenced by the life and practices of emergent women-church movements, both in the USA and internationally, something she shared with her contemporary and compatriot, Rosemary Radford Ruether.

Rosemary Radford Ruether

Like Fiorenza, Ruether also exemplifies the twin approach of 'critique' and 'reconstruction' in her approach to feminist theology. This can be clearly traced in her work on ecclesiology. Her analysis of women's exclusion from the churches—especially from the Roman Catholic tradition—bears the marks of a Marxist-feminist interpretation. Historically, she argues, men have claimed the right of access to symbolic and sacred power that in turn grants other kinds of ecclesial and temporal authority, whilst women have been deprived, alienated even, from the right to name themselves in God's image and to claim their experience as theologically or spiritually meaningful:

If we understand clericalism as the appropriation of ministry, sacramental life, and theological education from the people, then women-church—and indeed all base Christian communities—are engaged in a revolutionary act of reappropriating to the people what has been falsely expropriated from us. We are reclaiming sacramental life as the symbol of our own entry into and mutual empowerment within the redemptive life, the authentic human life or original blessing upon which we stand naturally when freed from alienating powers. (Ruether 1985: 72)

Given the depth of women's marginalization in the church, which spans sacramental, intellectual, and ecclesial forms of leadership, it is no wonder, argues Ruether, that the advancement of alternative patterns and practices will have to be nurtured outside existing power structures. Those seeking a more inclusive church cannot wait for the institution to reform itself. There is a pressing need to address women's 'linguistic deprivation and eucharistic famine' (Ruether 1985: 4); to form primary ecclesial communities that will nurture this spiritual hunger.

We do not form new communities lightly, but only because the crisis has grown so acute and the efforts to effect change so unpromising that we often cannot even continue to communicate within these traditional church institutions unless we have an alternative community of reference that nurtures and supports our being. (Ruether 1985: 5)

A strategically separatist women-church, or 'exodus community', is therefore necessary in order that women can 'develop words and analysis for the different aspects of this system of marginalization, and . . . learn how to recognize and resist the constant messages from patriarchal culture that try to enforce their acquiescence and collaboration with it . . . Women have to withdraw from male-dominated spaces so they can gather together and [define] their own experience' (Ruether 1985: 73). This is not exile but exodus, in which the sacraments, scriptures, and symbols of patriarchal church are borne on the exodus journey and, 'empowered by [the] liberated Spirit . . . in the community of liberated sisterhood' (Ruether 1985), are cleansed and reappropriated.

It is important to see that, like Fiorenza, Ruether regards her work as one of rehabilitation of a flawed, but not redundant, tradition. In common with feminist biblical and historical retrievals of women's agency within the church, however, it is not a question of the non-existence of exceptional women, but their suppression by a male-identified tradition. She paints the history of the church as one of tension between 'spirit-filled community and historical institution' (Ruether 1985: 31)—between the forces of reform and those of institutional atrophy.

However, whilst Ruether recognizes the difficult choice inherent in choosing to remain within church structures (and thereby risking tacitly continuing to consent to its abuses of power) or abandoning the patriarchal church for new woman-centred spaces, her insistence, like that of Fiorenza, is that women 'are' church and therefore somehow 'take' church with them. The 'exodus' is thus, for Ruether, more towards new forms of para-church rather than away entirely from the institution itself; and, perhaps most significantly, this model is firmly a corporate expression which makes space for experimental forms of liturgy, hymnody, and ministry.

> As Women-Church we are not left to starve for the words of wisdom, we are not left without the bread of life. Ministry too goes with us into exodus. We learn all over again what it means to minister, not to lord over, but to minister to and with each other, to teach each other to speak the words of life. Eucharist comes with us into exodus. The waters of baptism spring up in our midst as the waters of life, and the tree of life grows in our midst with fruits and flowers. (Ruether 1985: 73)

Modelling women-church on the basic ecclesial communities of Latin America, Ruether argues that such grass-roots, informal groupings embody a more authentic apprehension of the gospel, since they are more faithful to the presence of charismatic and transformative gifts of the Spirit and to the messianic, prophetic calling of the church. The prevailing hermeneutic of community life—in its internal structure and its vocation of engagement with the wider world—is one of a preferential option for the poor and the marginalized. Such communities are 'harbingers' of God's justice and reconciliation and provide the inspiration for her constructive feminist ecclesiology.

Ruether predicts a number of stages for those who wish to resist the logic of patriarchy and move towards a new vision of the church. First, women must gather together, collectively, in order to find their voice and end their historic silencing within church and society. Ruether defends this separatism as a necessary strategy for the development of a 'critical culture' of resistance and autonomy. This is what Ruether terms women-church: 'the feminist collectivization of women's experience and the formation of a critical culture' (Ruether 1985: 61). This is a staging-post towards an ultimate goal of a mixed gender group in which empowered women and post-patriarchal men can create an inclusive and non-hierarchical community together. Women-church rests on an identifiably feminist theological anthropology and ecclesiology. Its anthropology refuses to collude with an ideological understanding of women as misbegotten and objectified. One objective of the reforming community of women-church must be its determination to cast down the 'idol' of patriarchy, or the veneration of a system that is man-made (literally) but contrary to the will of God:

> Our God and Goddess, who is mother and father, friend, lover, and helper, did not create this idol and is not represented by this idol . . . The message and mission of Jesus, the child of Mary, which is to put down the mighty from their thrones and uplift the lowly, is not served by this idol. Rather, this idol blasphemes by claiming to speak in the name of Jesus and to carry out his redemptive mission, while crushing and turning to its opposite all that he came to teach . . . The powers and principalities of rape, genocide, and war achieve their greatest daring by claiming to be Christ, to represent Christ's mission . . . As Women-Church we cry out: Horror, blasphemy, deceit, foul deed! This is not the voice of our God, the face of our Redeemer, the mission

of our Church. Our humanity is not and cannot be represented here, but it is excluded in this dream, this nightmare, of salvation. (Ruether 1985: 72)

One of the chief symptoms of institutional abuses of power, for Ruether, is clericalism, which she identifies as a tendency to confuse the conferring of function with a monopoly on the charisms of ministry. The problem has been when, historically, the institution has claimed a monopoly on interpreting the tradition, and equates its own bureaucratic authority with the workings of the Spirit. Ruether is not inimical to ecclesiastical structures per se; but the test of any church polity must always be its 'responsible transmission of the tradition, and, at the same time, of being open to new movements of the Spirit' (Ruether 1985: 34). This may explain why, throughout her career, she has consistently reminded those campaigning for the ordination of women that such a victory may not necessarily dismantle ecclesial tendencies towards clericalism. In 2011 Ruether was still asking, 'Should Women want Women Priests or Women-Church?' and whether the goal of full inclusion in ordained ministry was compatible with 'the creation of egalitarian Christian communities' (Ruether 2011: 63).

Yet one of Ruether's enduring themes is that, when it comes, women's full participation in the life of the church, including its sacramental expressions through the admission of women to the Roman Catholic priesthood, will not simply be an aping of men's conventions or even an inversion of patriarchal hierarchies. Exodus, and furthermore its return, will be transformative. What will be reborn is a totally new way of being church that is modelled on a vision of the new heaven and new earth:

> We are not waiting for a call to return to the land of slavery to serve as altar girls in the temples of patriarchy . . . We call our brothers to join us . . . in our common quest for that promised land where there will be no more war, no more burning children, no more violated women, no more discarded elderly, no more rape of the earth. (Ruether 1985: 73)

Letty Russell

The ecclesiology of Letty Russell, a North American Presbyterian, deliberately draws on a conventionally domestic image: of the kitchen table, the hospitable hub of the household of God (Russell 1993). At the heart of Russell's model is the 'Church in the Round', conceived as a non-hierarchical, open community whose practices of inclusion and justice prefigure the coming of God's reign. The 'table principle' is the defining characteristic of feminist ecclesiology, bridging the sacred and secular in its evocation of the everyday work of preparing and eating food with Eucharistic overtones. Like other feminist ecclesiologies the focus is as much on the immanent community as on the transcendent God; the work of the church—and the work of the people of God—is validated in its orthopraxis of justice and communal flourishing, of which the gathered table fellowship is a portent and sign. Its mission must be relevant to the 'situation of evil that exists in the world, not an abstract dogma or theology' (Perera 1995: 51). This is typical of feminist ecclesiology, which places relationships, non-hierarchy, and community at the heart of its vision of the church (Cannon 1995). As Mary Grey puts it, 'Solidarity, mutuality, interdependence and commitment to the on-going process of liberation are the very foundations of feminist Christian community' (Grey 1993: 129). Insofar as patriarchy is built on a hierarchical distinction between persons, and tends to foster qualities of individualism and competition, it is the antithesis of this more collaborative, relational model which is rooted in the life of the Triune God.

Whilst Russell's vision is rooted in the biblical witness to the table fellowship of Jesus and the early Christians and in a Eucharistic theology, the domestic nature of such metaphors also connects powerfully with the association of women with the home and the private realm. By using such everyday images of tables, meals, and hospitality, Russell subverts their traditional meanings to encompass an unbounded, grace-filled vision of the church as the exemplar of divine hospitality. Like Fiorenza, Russell sees the public nature of the church, and its commitment to social justice, as integral. She deliberately links the table principle, and its domestic context, with New Testament traditions of the 'household' or, extrapolating from *oikos* as domestic home to embrace the *oikoumene*, the global community or 'commonwealth' (Russell 1993: 25) of peoples in which all are unconditionally welcomed. The model of the church as an inclusive commonwealth echoes Jesus' practices of table fellowship with the marginalized and stigmatized of his day, but it is also, as Russell argues, 'a sign of the coming feast of God's mended creation, with a "guest list" that sounds very much like the announcements of the jubilee year in ancient Israel (Luke 4:12–14)' (Russell 1993: 14).

Women's voices from the global South echo the conviction that ecclesiology is not done as a discrete discipline, but is intertwined with questions of ministry, language, liturgy, and social justice (Perera 1995). Feminist writing on ecclesiology from the two-thirds world is critical not only of sexism and the marginalization of women, but of the way in which colonialism and globalization shape their visions of critique and reconstruction. Women are inhibited from exercising leadership in church structures that are hierarchical, with a clear distinction between clerical and lay. In many parts of the two-thirds world, there is a debate as to whether the introduction of Christianity has improved or hindered women's status. Western ideologies of gender complementarity and women's domesticity were imported by missionary movements into the world church. In many post-colonial situations, women's greater social and economic freedom was not matched by changes in perceptions within the churches, although women have gradually entered theological education and ordained ministry (Mombo 2008). It has sometimes been easier for women in African-instituted denominations to achieve parity of recognition than it has been in the churches of Western missionary origin (Amoah 1995). These voices add weight to the conviction that ecclesiology and mission are indivisible: unless the churches confront the inequity of their own structures and practices they cannot witness with integrity on questions of poverty, violence and abuses of power within families, government, or global capital (WCC 2013: 88–9).

THE COMMUNITY OF WOMEN
AND MEN IN THE CHURCH

The Community of Women and Men in the Church Study (1978–82; hereinafter CWMC) was a major ecumenical initiative devoted to gender relations in the churches with particular reference to biblical and theological sources of teaching about the relative roles and relations of women and men. It arose out of a resolution passed at the Fifth Assembly of the World Council of Churches (hereinafter WCC) in Nairobi in 1975, and was conceived as a global, four-year programme, beginning in local churches and culminating in an international consultation, eventually held in Sheffield, United Kingdom, in 1981 (Lazareth and von Wartenberg 1983). Its objective was 'to seek in common assembly a new vision of the community of women and men in the church: a vision that would encourage women to explore and affirm their full contribution and would encourage men to take seriously and self-critically a new relationship of the partnership between women and men' (Parvey 1983a: 2).

The study documents reflect the wide-ranging nature of discussions: the authority and interpretation of Scripture, theological anthropology, ecumenical understandings of the church, the androcentric and colonialist nature of much church history and the relationship between struggles to achieve gender equality in the churches and in wider society. It is clear from the documents themselves and the accounts from the Sheffield consultation that cross-cultural differences of understanding of all these issues dominated proceedings throughout—in particular, whether sexism was the greatest priority in cultures facing issues of poverty and racism, and how far tradition, both in church and culture, could be reinterpreted. The strongest consensus seems to have been two-fold: first, that a preoccupation with the ordination of women to the priesthood diverts attention away from the many kinds of ministry, lay and ordained, available to women and men; and secondly, that the churches' proclamation of a community of women and men in society will have no integrity if it is not embodied in the corporate life of the church itself (Parvey 1983b: 125).

The study also echoes another core feminist principle, that as women occupy positions of leadership, it is imperative that they forge new patterns of authority, rather than mimicking patriarchal relationships. Similarly, there is a conviction that the ways in which the body of Christ prays and worships are essential signs of the newly emergent community of mutuality. New images of the church as *koinōnia*, and new images of God, are essential in order to advance this vision: 'The traditional use of mostly or exclusively male images has made the churches' understanding limited and prevents the rich diversity of God's people from particularizing their own identity in relation to the community of the whole people of God as female and male, poor and rich, colorful and bland' (Parvey 1983b: 141).

The Community study was located in the WCC's Faith and Order division. This was a deliberate tactic so that consideration of gender issues would be firmly located in foundational thinking about ecclesiology. Constance Parvey records how the deliberations of the consultation, both the Sheffield meeting itself and its preparatory documents, charted a trajectory from the specifics of concrete issues towards deeper, collective thinking about the nature of the church and its mission:

> Reflection on the study has started with the 'where' of the concrete, the experience of women and men in church and society and how they have seen the churches contributing to, or helping to overcome, human inequality and injustice in many forms . . . Reflection on the church has been directed toward how structures and styles of ministry reordered could better support and enrich the churches' service and spirituality in its vocation of renewal of humankind. (Parvey 1983c: 183)

Reflecting later on the impact of the study, Janet Crawford notes that the issue of women's participation in the churches was central to the concerns of the WCC since its foundation in 1948, with an insistence that this should never be written off as a sectional or minority interest but one with a bearing on the ecumenical movement's very understanding of the nature and mission of the church. Yet despite various initiatives, work on the role of women still remains somewhat marginal. After the Community Study from 1978–82 came the Ecumenical Decade of Churches in Solidarity with Women (1988–98). Various projects, such as *Baptism, Eucharist and Ministry* (hereinafter BEM) (1982–90), CWMC itself and the 'Unity of the Church and the Renewal of Human Community' (UCRHC) (1982–90), purported to be examining fundamental questions of faith and order, but often failed to make decisive statements relating to the role of women. For example, Crawford argues that BEM did not engage with issues of the ordination of women, for fear that they were too contentious. Similarly, the report of UCRHC (1990) submerges issues of gender equality amidst wider questions of unity and cross-cultural difference, by concluding that there is 'no consensus' on the ordination of women amongst member churches and that the issue remained 'divisive'.

Crawford concludes that the WCC's progress on this issue remains unacceptably slow. CWMC and other programmes have failed to provide an ecumenical lead on an inclusive ecclesiology, despite its founders' ambitions; but perhaps this indicates how deeply gender issues touch upon fundamental theological questions, all of which shape the church's very self-understanding: authority, interpretation of Scripture, relationship between gospel and culture and understandings of the human person.

More recent evidence would also suggest that the priorities of the WCC continue to be delicately balanced between a commitment to gender justice and church unity. So, the documents for the Tenth Assembly in 2013 speak both of the 'urgent needs prevailing in many contexts to create more space for women in theological education, theological leadership and in the ministries of the church' and of the exclusionary nature of androcentric and hierarchical theological language (WCC 2013: 119, 134–5). On the other hand, they still concede that the ordination of women is a stumbling-block to dialogue with other ecumenical partners such as the Orthodox and Roman Catholic Churches for whom the ordination of women continues to be a major impediment to further unity (WCC 2013: 131).

Feminist Liturgical Communities

The history of Christian worship has been shaped by patriarchal social relations in which women's social and material subordination to men is instantiated in language, symbol, and sacred space. Within the life of the church, however, liturgy and worship has paradoxically proved also to be one of the most creative elements of feminist reimaginings of the church over the past generation. The ritual activities of women-church and other alternative feminist ecclesial movements were premised on their being sites of resistance to traditional manifestations of exclusion and spaces for alternative practices. They are therefore an important source of renewal for the church and constitute 'ecclesiologies in operation' (Beckman 2006: 145). They raise profound challenges to notions of authority, language, the nature of tradition, ideas of sacred time and space, often rooted in the specifics of women's life-cycles and rites of passage.

> Indeed, liturgy has become one of the most politicized of ecclesial sites in our time . . . For the Christian tradition in which ritual authority was the prerogative of a male priesthood, or more recently, a caste of liturgical experts, women's active claim to ritual authority is a prime example of their claim to power . . . Women have moved from liturgical consumption and reproduction to production, as they grasp ritual as a crucial site for the negotiation of faith and feminism. (Berger 2012: 532)

Berger here echoes Ruether's early diagnosis of women's exclusion within the church as not only a question of the appropriation of their (ritual) labour but the denial of their very right to name the divine, and themselves, as sacred. Berger continues to describe liturgical renewal as a form of 'border politics' (2012: 536) within the liminal space between church and world, male-dominated and woman-centred, out of which new understandings and visions of what it means to be the church may emerge. More problematic even than that, potentially, for established traditions of ecclesiological study, is the extent to which such groups do not respect the boundaries of denominational church structures. In membership, such groups span the divide between Christian, non-Christian, and post-Christian; similarly, the rituals themselves draw on a range of traditional, biblical sources as well as pre-Christian, neo-pagan, and original resources for prayer, ritual, and hymnody.

Crucially, of course, such communities are always locally based in nature, even though many of the liturgical sources and resources may draw upon a global sensibility, and trans-national networks and exchanges do occur. Berger highlights some of the 'glocalized' characteristics of various women-church networks, such as post-colonial, ex-missionary connections between communities in Peru, Korea, and Chile;

or the common causes around questions of ecology, sex trafficking, or trade justice (Berger 2012).

By the 1980s publishers were producing many women's liturgies (Swidler 1974; Morley 1988; Gjerding and Kinnamon 1984) and countless others were circulating unofficially. In many cases (e.g. St Hilda Community of London 1993) the group served as a significant catalyst for emergent liturgical writers, whose publications had an impact far beyond feminist organizations. By the 1990s Marjorie Proctor-Smith was referring to an established 'feminist liturgical tradition' (Proctor-Smith 1995; Berger 2012).

The calls for woman-centred or non-sexist liturgical communities had their roots, as I have already noted, in early second-wave feminist theologians' visions of a renewed church that could be said to be both more authentic to its counter-cultural roots and a prophetic sign of a Body of Christ embodying justice and inclusion. But the practical impetus often emerged from the gap between rhetoric and reality in most mainline denominations. For some, liturgical experiments accompanied a desire to create spaces for the exercise of women's full ministry, especially in traditions which prohibited women's ordination to the priesthood. But for many, it extended to a frustration with the clericalism of many denominations; and attention often focused on the way in which the language and ritual practice of Christian worship simply silenced women.

For example, the St Hilda Community was a London-based group that had its roots in the campaign for the ordination of women to the priesthood within the Church of England. Its initial objective was to provide a focus for the Eucharistic ministry of 'Women Lawfully Ordained Abroad', but it became much more: as one of its founding members and long-standing champion of the ordination of women, Monica Furlong, put it, 'a radical new way of being Church' (Furlong 1993: 6), a focus for inclusive liturgies. Shortly after it began a regular cycle of meetings, the community decided to name itself after Hilda of Whitby (614–80 CE), founder of several Christian communities in England and a leading figure in the Synod of Whitby (664 CE). In this respect, the community was synthesizing Ruether's feminist vision of women-church as a new, inclusive 'non-sexist' space, providing 'full space and authority to women, without apology, secrecy, or shame' (Furlong 1993: 6), with another important principle of reclaiming significant women of Christian history as role models.

Despite some negative press coverage and opposition from the local bishop, the group continued to meet into the 1990s. For its liturgies, it drew on original material from its membership as well as other sources: historical, contemporary, ecumenical. There was a close relationship between experimental liturgy and forging of a new community identity. The group wanted to create a space in which women's ministry in all its dimensions could be experienced, yet it also realized that it was pioneering new ways of being the church in which 'ministry' was truly shared. 'The women and men of St Hilda's needed to work out a pattern, as yet unimaginable in many, perhaps all, of the institutional churches of this country, of a community where women were not patronized and ignored, and where it was safe to be fully themselves' (Furlong 1993: 15).

More generally, an analysis of typical feminist liturgies is given by Diann Neu, who identifies them as reflecting three different phases of women's journey to self-determination. First, there are liturgies celebrating 'the telling of our untold stories to link our personal experiences . . . celebrated liturgically in a Litany of naming' (Neu 1996: 259). This typically involves the invocation of women role models from biblical literature, history, and participants' own lives. It breaks the silence of a patriarchal tradition that overlooks the witness of women, and retrieves such witness as a legitimate expression of faith. The second phase Neu calls 'the Laying on of Hands', or the articulation of a woman-centred spirituality. This involves a conscious use of women-centred images or actions for mediating transcendence and delivering blessing. The third phase 'is the claiming of our power to give birth to a new vision of Church and community', commemorated in a Eucharistic Meal—an acknowledgement of liberation in the midst of brokenness and oppression (Neu 1996: 267).

Insofar as such feminist liturgical communities were drawing upon 'the needs and longings of the participating women, and not . . . reflected dogmatic considerations or adherence to a specific tradition' (Beckman 2006: 144), such communities were also demonstrating how the abstractions and generalizations of 'women's experience' might be concretized in ritual practices. Often, this involved traditional forms being imbued with new content or application: anointing might be offered to a survivor of sexual assault or abuse; confession and absolution was given and received corporately; milk and honey replaced the traditional Eucharistic elements; natural cycles of the seasons or the moon might be used to structure the liturgical calendar, and so on (Berger 2012: 536–9). Many woman-centred liturgical groups drew intentionally on aspects of women's life-cycle as ritual sources for worship. These included celebrations of childbirth, menopause, and same-sex relationships, or litanies of sexual violence and injustice. Similarly, language and imagery (for humanity and God) explored new avenues, often using feminine images or metaphors from the natural world. In a rite for Palm Sunday in the St Hilda Community, for example, branches of blossom are handed around and stripped of their buds, to denote both the triumph and impending desolation of Holy Week (St Hilda Community 1993: 82). As well as being sites of significant creativity—and important places of sanctuary—for many women, these liturgical communities were also crucibles of innovation in the exercise of new styles of leadership, both liturgical and administrative, although many groups record their struggles with non-hierarchical approaches (St Hilda Community 1993).

Such woman-centred ritual groups present significant challenges for mainstream denominations, however. In many respects, they represent a return to the earliest forms of 'house church'—but is this a privatization of Christian liturgy or a reclamation, a resacralization, of domestic space for women? At a local level, such groups drew together women from across the denominational spectrum or merged Christian with post-Christian, neo-pagan, and indigenous rites and spiritualities; they were more akin to basic ecclesial communities than to mainstream churches.

Recent ethnographic studies by Nicola Slee (2004) and Jan Berry (2009) of alternative woman-centred networks demonstrate both the heterodoxy of members' religious affiliations and the diversity of the life-experiences brought to their gatherings. It is a matter of debate how readily this new generation would rally behind Ruether's hopeful

544 ELAINE GRAHAM

vision of a spirit-filled para-church, separate yet nonetheless strategically engaged with existing structures as intentional catalysts for change; for an increasing number of women, these groups are not a temporary sanctuary but a permanent home. Yet if such communities continue to run on parallel, rather than convergent lines to the mainstream churches, it is also true that many more mainstream liturgical developments of the past thirty years have absorbed identifiably feminist principles, in use of gender-inclusive language (for human and divine subjects), an explicit alignment of spirituality with social justice, openness to new patterns of leadership and presidency, and a deeper sensitivity towards the embodied, holistic dimensions of Christian worship (Slee and Burns 2010; Shakespeare 2008).

Writing Women's Lived Experience into Feminist Ecclesiology

Mary McClintock Fulkerson

Mary McClintock Fulkerson's study is concerned with 'the working of Christian traditions in the lives of non-feminist women' (Fulkerson 1994), and whether an explicitly feminist theological analysis has any bearing on these women's experiences of the church. Fulkerson's ethnographic study was anticipated by the findings of Nancy Ammerman's sociological study of a North American fundamentalist church, in which she identified a strong, formal adherence to male authority, coupled with a discourse of Christian masculinity that emphasized respect for women, familial responsibility, and marital fidelity. Whilst this remained firmly within the conventions of gender complementarity, it also created a culture of protection for women, albeit within closely circumscribed roles (Ammerman 1987). Rather than being a study into new ways of being church in the light of intentional, espoused non-sexist and feminist principles, Fulkerson's work serves as an example of how feminist theology stands in relation to those women who remain within—often quite conservative—Christian traditions. Are these women guilty of false consciousness? How can their ecclesial, ritual, and spiritual practices be embraced?

Openly committed to 'a vision of God's realm as one of justice' (Fulkerson 1994), Fulkerson's research examines the problematic heritage of 'women's experience' within feminist theology and proposes an alternative which represents a 'thicker' and more complex elaboration of how such a category might operate. For any study of gender relations in the church—and the practices by which less exclusive visions might be effected—Fulkerson's study suggests that whilst women's experience cannot be unimportant within feminist alternatives, it cannot be essentialized or self-evident.

As I have already argued, early feminist theology (including developments in ecclesiology such as women-church) rested on a generic but under-theorized evocation of 'women's experience' as both critical and reconstructive tool (Ruether 1983). As time went on, this became more contested, especially in the face of cultural and global diversity. Under the influence of post-modern and poststructuralist thinking, feminist theology became more receptive to understandings of 'experience', 'difference', and identity as themselves constructed rather than natural. In particular, poststructuralist theory argued that language could never be an entirely transparent representation of experience, which, under the influence of psychoanalytic theory, was itself portrayed as contested, unstable. This represented a challenge to types of feminist theology which purported to be disclosures of authentic truth by deriving from women's narratives and experience. Whether it was critical or reconstructive, 'experience' could only be strategic and performative: an appeal to experience is a speech-act whereby its veracity rests in its capacity to render those acts as doing or making the condition to which they point. An utterance or symbolic act serves as a pledge or promise that calls a new state of affairs into being. Fulkerson thus challenges assumptions that language reflects an objective social reality and that biblical or other canonical texts have fixed meanings. Instead, she attends to the meaning-making practices of 'ordinary' women in three conservative Christian communities in the United States: in the 'Presbyterian Women' organization; in two Pentecostal denominations; and in an independent Holiness church in Appalachia. These are congregations defined by evangelical and charismatic theologies, not least in their patterns of worship.

Fulkerson is interested in how communities of women—crucially, women who remain within traditional church contexts—inhabit a reality which may appear oppressive to those committed to the abolition of patriarchy and the realization of the 'full humanity' of women within the churches. The tenets of academic feminist theology would be alien to Pentecostal women, for example, since 'the idea that the dominance of male images is oppressive is untenable for a faith that still commends submission to men' (Fulkerson 1996: 132). Since this entails a closer and more nuanced attention to the *lived* experience of such women, Fulkerson's work, whilst purporting to displace experience (at least as a universal, reified category), actually adopts more sustained, ethnographical methods of enquiry than many of the early evocations of 'experience' had managed to achieve. Her aim is to broaden prevailing notions of 'experience' (although I am not sure she is confident that it can entirely be rehabilitated) and account for a diversity of subjectivities and locations in relation to feminist or non-sexist ambitions for a more inclusive church.

The experience of 'being church' for such women is, Fulkerson argues, a complex mix of conformity and resistance: of finding spaces of autonomy within highly circumscribed discourses of feminine subordination and compliance to convention. This is consistent with her objective of reading Christian churches 'as places where sinful orderings of social life are resisted and alternatives created' (Fulkerson 1994). Despite the hegemony of gender complementarity and male headship, these women were still able to gain independence to forge their own distinctive spheres of influence, both within church affairs and in social ministries.

For Fulkerson, anything approaching a full-blown feminist theology or ecclesiology can only ever grow in the cracks and fissures of the established canon. As such it is only ever provisional and proleptic; women's emergent theological voices and ecclesial leadership, similarly, will be constantly struggling for legitimacy. Thus, women's experiences of being the church are conditioned by 'both oppressive gender constraints and emancipatory possibilities' (Fulkerson 1994: 118). Studies such as Fulkerson's show that women's relationships with official sources of power and authority in the church may be complex, and that anything formally labelled as 'feminist' may go nowhere near adequately reflecting the strategies for empowerment, which is nevertheless evident, albeit tightly circumscribed and sometimes costly.

When the women of Fulkerson's three congregations speak, a representational model of language would 'hear' their utterances as merely conforming to patriarchal teachings about women's inferiority. Fulkerson's contention, however, is that their words must be placed in context, especially within the particular social and theological conventions by which such things 'make sense'. What emerges is a more nuanced understanding of these women's discourses in which the authority of men is usurped by the power of the Holy Spirit in the lives of sinful and sanctified believers. An apparently self-denigratory statement of worthlessness is used to testify to the workings of the Holy Spirit, and to authorize a life of testimony, service, and public ministry which trumps patriarchal sanctions. Similarly, the licence enjoyed in worship makes possible such phenomena as glossolalia, ecstatic singing and dancing, free prayer, and extravagant testifying, which are permitted as being gifts of the Spirit, even as they transgress norms of female submission and modesty.

Ellen Clark-King's interviews with working-class churchgoing women in the northeast of England (2004) paints a similar picture, of greater acceptance of traditional understandings and images of God than many feminist theologians would have predicted. The church was important to these women's self-identity, with little sense of alienation from its language or hierarchical structures. Whilst the 'horizontal' fellowship with other church members was valued, the women reported that their 'vertical' relationship with God was a more important factor in church membership. That reflects a traditional and some might say dualistic understanding of the relationship between immanence and transcendence. Nevertheless, they do seem at odds with feminist expectations, although Clark-King's informants were convinced that Christian life was this-worldly and that communion with God should lead to communion with others.

Secularization and Pluralism

I have already highlighted the contrast between women's relative lack of power and prominence in most religious traditions and their numerical majority within the membership. But in the context of secularization in many Western societies, and the gradual decline of active participation, what, if anything, can be concluded about the future of women's participation? If women's gradual withdrawal from the churches is consistent with the broad trajectories of secularization, then this will have serious implications for the future viability of the institution. One study to have addressed this is Callum Brown's account of the roots of secularization in British society (2009; first published 2001), which was exceptionally attuned to the extent to which women's changing participation in church life was responsible for institutional decline.

Brown argues that traditionally, piety was perceived as a feminine quality and that women were not only the pillars of much church life but the transmitters of Christian culture. After 1945, women's participation in the workforce contributed to their drift away from organized religion and to the decline of the churches. The fortunes of women in the church may have had as much to do, therefore, with socio-economic trends than any direct feminist dissatisfaction with institutional church life. Nevertheless, it does appear that in many Western contexts, churches are witnessing a generation gap insofar as older women continue to identify with churchgoing, but are not being succeeded by their daughters and granddaughters (Brown 2009: 196–200).

Other research into women's religious lives suggests that they constitute the overwhelming majority of adherents to new forms of spirituality, such as neo-paganism and Mind-Body-Spirit therapies. Linda Woodhead argues that this is symptomatic of a shift towards self-religions more endemically in the West, but women's enthusiastic embrace of these kinds of spirituality also shows, possibly, how far the churches have failed to match the aspirations of younger generations of women from Baby-Boomers onwards (Woodhead 2008). Women may always have been the 'backbone' of church life—as Ann Braude puts it, the essential but unseen core support—and at one time, were prepared to tolerate their relative lack of status. Now, however, increasingly women are choosing to absent themselves voluntarily, and any evaluation of the church's future has to face up to this new, and potentially more catastrophic, withdrawal.

CONCLUSION

Serene Jones sees the task of feminist theological reflection on the nature and calling of the church as a matter of practice matching doctrine: 'feminist systematic theology asks whether the church practices what it confesses . . . [and] requires that doctrinal dramas be tested in the concrete lives of women' (Jones 2000: 18). In reality, much feminist ecclesiology, whilst mindful of the gulf between the ideal and the actual, has assumed a more performative quality, in which the liturgical, missional, and symbolic practices of the faithful are held to embody new models of what it means to be the Body of Christ in the world. As Susan Ross argues, feminist ecclesiology may well emerge 'from the ground up . . . not with official definitions but with women's experiences of God, often in the most ordinary of circumstances' (Ross 2002: 235).

Women-church denies the binding or divinely sanctioned nature of androcentric texts and interpretations and seeks to establish alternative practices of reading, praying, and naming the divine, founded on the ideal of the 'full humanity of women' and the dangerous memory of Jesus as instituting an egalitarian and inclusive community of disciples. The ritual activities of women-church and other alternative feminist ecclesial movements were premised on their being sites of resistance to traditional manifestations of exclusion and spaces for alternative practices. They raise profound challenges to notions of authority, language, the nature of tradition, ideas of sacred time and space, often rooted in the specifics of women's life-cycles and rites of passage. The early visions of women-church represented an overwhelming conviction that the praxis of the gathered community, whilst remaining part of the universal church, also held the potential to become a sacrament of inclusion and transformation; not only for its own members but, prophetically and proleptically, for the whole Body. Such praxis represents 'truly the sacrament, the sign, the symbol of God's kingdom that is within us and is coming to be' (Perera 1995: 50).

At the heart of feminist ecclesiology, therefore, has been the imperative to recast the mould of traditional patterns of Christian formation and discipleship that are most relevant to women's lives and to affirm their full humanity in the image of God. Some of this critical and reconstructive work has been scholarly in nature, engaging in particular with historical and biblical sources; but some has emerged directly from the many groups and networks that have arisen to fulfil women's spiritual and theological needs. This has not been without its controversies. Some dispute that there ever was a pristine heritage of 'pure' Jesus-movement Christianity to which contemporary feminist ecclesiologies can easily return, arguing that the historical evidence is far more diverse and ambivalent. Others have concluded that the tradition has been so distorted by patriarchy that its rehabilitation is impossible. Many question what it means to reconstitute liturgical practice through appeal to a category as contested as 'women's experience', especially in the light of differences of class, race, culture, and generation. Nevertheless, commentators such as Rosemary Radford Ruether see in movements such as women-church an example of contemporary renewal within the churches, a vibrant example of ecumenism which transcends divisions of existing traditions and institutions and which is contributing to the realization of a new way of being the church from the grass-roots up.

> All the functions of church—the repentance by which we enter it, the Eucharist by which we commune with it, and the ministry by which we mutually empower it—are simply expressions of entering and developing a true human community of mutual love. (Ruether 2005: 87)

However, feminist visions of such a renewed church have always been aware of the tension between entering patriarchal spaces and offices on men's terms and casting off time-worn patterns of authority and hierarchy, which may necessarily entail the creation of safe liturgical and sacred spaces for women to exercise ministries of word and sacrament in new ways. Whether this is expressed as the choice between 'Women Priests or Women-Church' (Ruether 2011) or that of 'either leaving or staying' (Watson 2002), the decision is seldom clear-cut, but nevertheless serves to highlight the fact that strategies and visions cannot be divorced. Can the church be changed—is it worth changing? If so, how can it be changed—from the inside or the outside? What kind of models might

emerge as women take their full and rightful place alongside men as members of an inclusive Body of Christ?

References

Ammerman, N. (1987). *Bible Believers: Fundamentalists in the Modern World*. New Brunswick, NJ: Rutgers University Press.

Amoah, E. (1995). 'Theology from the Perspective of African Women'. In O. Ortega (ed.), *Women's Visions: Theological Reflection, Celebration, Action*. Geneva: World Council of Churches, 1–7.

Beckman, N. E. (2006). 'The Theology of Gathering and Sending: A Challenge from Feminist Liturgy'. *International Journal for the Study of the Christian Church* 6.2: 144–65.

Berger, T. (2012). 'Feminist Ritual Practice'. In S. Briggs and M. M. Fulkerson (eds), *The Oxford Handbook of Feminist Theology*. Oxford: Oxford University Press, 525–43.

Berry, J. (2009). *Ritual Making Women: Shaping Rites for Changing Lives*. London: Equinox.

Braude, A. (2008). *Sisters and Saints: Women and American Religion*. New York: Oxford University Press.

Brown, C. (2009). *The Death of Christian Britain*. 2nd edn. London: Routledge.

Cannon, K. G. (1995). *Katie's Canon: Womanism and the Soul of the Black Community*. New York: Continuum.

Carson, D. (2005). *Becoming Conversant with the Emerging Church*. Grand Rapids, MI: Zondervan.

Clark-King, E. (2004). *Theology by Heart: Women, the Church and God*. London: SCM.

Fiorenza, E. S. (1983). *In Memory of Her: A Feminist Theological Reconstruction of Christian Origins*. London: SCM Press.

Fiorenza, E. S. (1992). *But She Said: Feminist Practices of Biblical Interpretation*. Boston: Beacon Press.

Fiorenza, E. S. (1993a). 'Daughters of Vision and Struggle'. In E. S. Fiorenza (ed.), *Discipleship of Equals: A Critical Feminist Ekklesia-logy of Liberation*. London: SCM, 307–31.

Fiorenza, E. S. (1993b). 'Theorizing the Ekklesia of Women'. In E. S. Fiorenza (ed.), *Discipleship of Equals: A Critical Feminist Ekklesia-logy of Liberation*. London: SCM Press, 332–52.

Fiorenza, E. S. (1996). 'For Women in Men's World: A Critical Feminist Theology of Liberation'. In E. S. Fiorenza (ed.), *The Power of Naming*. Maryknoll, NY: Orbis, 3–13.

Fulkerson, M. M. (1994). *Changing the Subject: Women's Discourses and Feminist Theology*. Minneapolis: Fortress.

Fulkerson, M. M. (1996). 'Changing the Subject: Feminist Theology and Discourse'. *Literature & Theology* 10.2: 131–47.

Furlong, M. (1993). 'A "Non-Sexist" Community'. In The St Hilda Community (ed.), *Women Included*. London: SPCK, 5–15.

Gjerding, I. and Kinnamon, K. (eds) (1984). *No Longer Strangers: A Resource for Women and Worship*. Geneva: World Council of Churches.

Grey, M. (1993). *The Wisdom of Fools? Seeking Revelation for Today*. London: SPCK.

Jones, I. (2004). *Women and Priesthood in the Church of England Ten Years On*. London: Church House Publishing.

Jones, I., Thorpe, K., and Wootton, J. (eds) (2008). *Women and Ordination in the Christian Churches: International Perspectives*. London: T&T Clark.

Jones, S. (2000). *Feminist Theory and Christian Theology: Cartographies of Grace*. Minneapolis: Fortress.

Lazareth, W. H. and Von Wartenberg, B. (1983). Preface. In C. F. Parvey (ed.), *The Community of Women and Men in the Church: The Sheffield Report*. Geneva: World Council of Churches, ix–x.

Madigan, K. and Osiek, C. (eds) (2005). *Ordained Women in the Early Church: A Documentary History*. Baltimore: Johns Hopkins University Press.

Metz, J. B. (1987). 'Communicating a Dangerous Memory'. In F. Lawrence (ed.), *Communicating a Dangerous Memory: Soundings in Political Theology*. Atlanta, GA: Scholars.

Moltmann-Wendel, E. (1983). *The Women Around Jesus: Reflections on Authentic Personhood*. Trans. J. Bowden. London: SCM Press.

Mombo, E. (2008). 'The Ordination of Women in Africa: An Historical Perspective'. In I. Jones, K. Thorpe, and. J. Wootton (eds), *Women and Ordination in the Christian Churches: International Perspectives*. London: T&T Clark, 123–43.

Morley, J. (1988). *All Desires Known*. London: SPCK.

Moyse, C. (2011). *A History of the Mothers' Union*. Woodbridge: Boydell Press.

Neu, D. (1996). 'Our Name is Church: Catholic-Christian Feminist Liturgies'. In E. S. Fiorenza (ed.), *The Power of Naming*. Maryknoll, NY: Orbis, 259–72.

Parvey, C. F. (1983a). 'The Church—Women and Men in Community'. In C. F. Parvey (ed.), *The Community of Women and Men in the Church: The Sheffield Report*. Geneva: World Council of Churches, 2–18.

Parvey, C. F. (1983b). 'The Section Reports'. In C. F. Parvey (ed.), *The Community of Women and Men in the Church: The Sheffield Report*. Geneva: World Council of Churches, 102–54.

Parvey, C. F. (1983c). 'The Community of Women and Men in the Ecumenical Movement'. In C. F. Parvey (ed.), *The Community of Women and Men in the Church: The Sheffield Report*. Geneva: World Council of Churches, 156–83.

Perera, M. (1995). 'An Asian Feminist Ecclesiology'. In O. Ortega (ed.), *Women's Visions: Theological Reflection, Celebration, Action*. Geneva: World Council of Churches, 49–51.

Proctor-Smith, M. (1995). *Praying with our Eyes Open: Engendering Feminist Liturgical Prayer*. Nashville: Abingdon.

Ross, S. A. (2002). 'Church and Sacrament—Community and Worship'. In S. F. Parsons (ed.), *The Cambridge Companion to Feminist Theology*. Cambridge: Cambridge University Press, 224–42.

Ruether, R. R. (1983). *Sexism and God-Talk: Toward a Feminist Theology*. Boston: Beacon Press.

Ruether, R. R. (1985). *Women-Church: Theology and Practice of Feminist Liturgical Communities*. Boston: Beacon Press.

Ruether, R. R. (2005). *Goddesses and the Divine Feminine*. Berkeley: University of Berkeley Press.

Ruether, R. R. (2011). 'Should Women Want Women Priests or Women-Church?' *Feminist Theology* 20.1: 63–72.

Russell, L. M. (ed.) (1993). *The Church in the Round: Feminist Interpretation of the Church*. Louisville, KY: Westminster John Knox Press.

Sacred Congregation for the Doctrine of the Faith (1976). 'Declaration on the Question of Admission of Women to the Ministerial Priesthood' (*Inter Insigniores*), 15 October. Available at: <http://www.papalencyclicals.net/Paul06/p6interi.htm> [accessed 28/10/13].

St Hilda Community (1993). *Women Included: A Book of Services and Prayers*. 3rd edn. London: SPCK.

Shakespeare, S. (2008). *Prayers for an Inclusive Church*. London: Canterbury Press.

Slee, N. (2004). *Women's Faith Development: Patterns and Processes*. Aldershot: Ashgate.

Slee, N. and Burns, S. (eds) (2010). *Presiding Like a Woman: Feminist Gestures for Christian Assemblies*. London: SPCK.

Smith, S. A. (2007). *Women in Mission: From the New Testament to Today*. Maryknoll: New York: Orbis.

Stanton, E. C. (1898). *The Woman's Bible*. New York: European Publishing Company.

Stogdon, K. M. (2004). *The Risk of Surrender: Se livrer in the Life of Therese Couderc (1805–85)*. University of Manchester: Unpublished PhD thesis.

Swidler, A. (1974). *Sistercelebrations: Nine Worship Experiences*. Minneapolis: Fortress.

Torjesen, K. J. (1995). *When Women Were Priests: Women's Leadership in the Early Church and the Scandal of their Subordination in the Rise of Christianity*. San Francisco: HarperCollins.

Ward, P. (ed.) (2012). *Perspectives on Ecclesiology and Ethnography*. Grand Rapids, MI: Eerdmans.

Watson, N. K. (1998). 'Faithful Dissenters? Feminist Ecclesiologies and Dissent'. *Scottish Journal of Theology* 51.4: 464–84.

Watson, N. K. (2002). *Introducing Feminist Ecclesiology*. London: Sheffield Academic Press.

Woodhead, L. (2008). '"Because I'm Worth It": Religion and Women's Changing Lives in the West'. In K. Aune, S. Sharma, and G. Vincett (eds), *Women and Religion in the West: Challenging Secularization*. Aldershot: Ashgate, 147–64.

World Council of Churches (2013). *Resource Book 10th Assembly Busan 2013*. Geneva: World Council of Churches.

Zikmund, B. B., Lummis, A. T., and Chang, P. M. Y. (1998). *Clergy Women: An Uphill Calling*. Louisville, KY: Westminster John Knox Press.

Suggested Reading

Aune, K., Sharma, S., and Vincett, G. (eds) (2008). *Women and Religion in the West: Challenging Secularization*. Aldershot: Ashgate.

Fiorenza, E. S. (1983). *In Memory of Her: A Feminist Theological Reconstruction of Christian Origins*. London: SCM.

Fulkerson, M. M. (1994). *Changing the Subject: Women's Discourses and Feminist Theology*. Minneapolis: Fortress.

Jones, I., Thorpe, K., and Wootton, J. (eds) (2008). *Women and Ordination in the Christian Churches: International Perspectives*. London: T&T Clark.

Ruether, R. R. (1985). *Women-Church: Theology and Practice of Feminist Liturgical Communities*. Boston: Beacon Press.

Slee, N. (2004). *Women's Faith Development: Patterns and Processes*. Aldershot: Ashgate.

Watson, N. K. (2007). 'Feminist Ecclesiology'. In G. Mannion and L. S. Mudge (eds), *The Routledge Companion to the Christian Church*. London: Routledge, 461–75.

CHAPTER 25

....

SOCIAL SCIENCE AND IDEOLOGICAL CRITIQUES OF ECCLESIOLOGY

....

NEIL ORMEROD

In theological terms the emergence of the social sciences as empirical disciplines is relatively recent. While theology has long engaged philosophy as a dialogue partner, the social sciences raise a new set of issues as both theology and the social sciences reflect concretely on the human condition. Indeed historically the aspirations of the founding fathers of the social sciences were that they could eliminate the unending disputes of philosophers and theologians about the human condition through an appeal to empirical evidence. While such aspirations have proved unfulfilled, the interrelationship between theology and the social sciences remains problematic. Perhaps this is nowhere more evident than in the area of ecclesiology. Whenever ecclesiology turns from more idealistic ahistorical forms of discourse to deal with the actual context and constitution of historical communities, the role of the social sciences in providing insights into those contexts and constitutions becomes difficult to deny. This present contribution will seek to map out some of the history of the engagement with the social sciences by ecclesiologists and the challenges that this engagement poses. Underlying this debate are profound theological issues concerning grace and nature. While not seeking to resolve all these issues, I hope that by the end the reader will have some grasp of the complexity of the issue and some appreciation of what a social science perspective might bring to the study of the church.

ECCLESIOLOGY AND THE TURN TO HISTORY

Ecclesiology, the theological study of the church as a distinct object of enquiry, is relatively recent in the history of Christianity. Generally those who wrote about the church in their theological endeavours did so within some other context. The existence and nature of the church was something of an unquestioned given, an environment within which theological discourse could take place rather than an object of focus in itself. Things changed radically with the Reformation when the great reformers began to use New Testament accounts of the church as a measure or standard against which to evaluate the church of their day. Then theological reflection on the nature of the church began in earnest, though the context was largely polemical. Both sides of the Reformation debates sought to establish the true 'marks' of the church—one, holy, catholic, and apostolic; or where the gospel is preached and the sacraments properly administered—in ways that favoured their ecclesial stance over against their opponents. Questions of the being and well-being of the church, of church order and ministry, the range and number of the sacraments, and so on all came to the fore. Theological reflection on the church was necessary to establish criteria for the identity of the one true church.

This brief excursus reveals two important aspects which continue to shape all ecclesiological debate and discussion. The first is the distinction between the empirical reality of the church and its normative identity. The lived reality of the church never lives up to all that is implied by the theological implications of what it means to be church. What then is the object of theological investigation, the concrete reality or its normative form? If we focus on the concrete reality we may distort our theology; if we focus on the normative form the result will be a pleasing enough abstraction, but not relate to the church that people actually live in. Worse still, we run the risk of conflating the two, allowing us to pretend that somehow the concrete reality fulfils all that is implied in the normative form. There is also the question of how we identify exactly what the normative form is. Is it to be excavated from a close reading of the New Testament? What role is to be given to the emerging structures and developing traditions of the church in constructing a norm? In raising these questions we can identity a fundamental difference between ecclesiology and, say, the theology of the Trinity. Our reflections on the Trinity make no difference to the structure of the Trinity itself; God remains forever exactly what God is, the triune God of Christian faith. The church on the other hand is very different. Our reflections on the nature of the church always have a practical dimension. They concern not just what is, but what should be, with practical consequences in terms of church structures, ministries, and disciplines. In terms we shall spell out more fully below, ecclesiology is not just concerned with the cognitive function of meaning (concerned with what can truthfully be said), but also with the constitutive and effective functions of meaning, constituting the present reality of the church or effecting a new reality in the church through our ecclesiological reflections.

The second important aspect that emerges is the constitutive role of history in ecclesiology. Broadly speaking, in the debates of the Reformation the Reformers appealed to the pristine state of the early church, a particular historical reality accessible through a reading of the New Testament and the church fathers. The Catholic Church on the other hand appealed to unwritten apostolic and post-apostolic traditions to justify its position. Both appealed to a set of historical data, one to establish discontinuity between past practice and present reality; the other to establish a larger sense of continuity.

Underlying both is the issue of historical development within the life of the church. What developments if any are legitimate? What developments if any would delegitimate the claims of a community genuinely to be the church established by Jesus Christ (however one might understand the claim to such establishment)? Church communities span millennia or at least centuries. They are subject to significant historical forces, existing as they do within a larger 'secular' history not of their own making, which nonetheless impacts upon them. Change is a fact of historical existence, but not all change will be a genuine development. How then do we assess trajectories of change across historical time frames? What constitute genuine developments and what are corruptions? These are issues that John Henry Newman sought to address in his ground-breaking essay on doctrinal development (Newman 1992). Again we must deal with the issue of normativity, of the discernment of genuine development from mere change.

In the present stage of cultural development any attempt to deal with concrete historical data in a coherent and systematic fashion must turn its attention to the potential contribution of the social sciences. The goal of the social sciences is to seek to understand human communities, both in their internal structures, institutions, and power relations (synchronically) and in the patterns of their longer-term trajectories of change (diachronically). If ecclesiology is concerned with understanding the church in its concrete historical manifestations, then at the very least engagement with the social sciences is a necessary prerequisite.

EXAMPLES OF ENGAGEMENT OF SOCIAL SCIENCES IN ECCLESIOLOGY

Dietrich Bonhoeffer

A number of theologians have taken up the challenges offered by question of the relationship between theology and the social sciences. One of the first was Dietrich Bonhoeffer whose doctoral thesis, written in 1930 and published as *Sanctorum Communio: A Theological Study of the Sociology of the Church* (Bonhoeffer 1998), was a ground-breaking attempt to place ecclesiology in dialogue with sociological theory. Bonhoeffer begins his study with a serious engagement with various authors within the German school of sociology. He introduces a significant distinction between social philosophy which 'deals with fundamental social relationships that are presupposed by all knowledge of, and will for, empirical community' and sociology as 'the study of the structures of empirical communities' (28–30). He argues that social philosophy provides a normative component to sociology. For Bonhoeffer both these disciplines belong to the humanities rather than the natural sciences. He carefully distinguishes a 'sociology of religion' which might study the church from an external perspective and a genuine ecclesiology which takes sociological insights into its core and 'can only be understood from within . . . never by nonparticipants' (33). Drawing on the writings of Tönnies, he introduces a typological distinction between 'community' (*Gemeinschaft*) and 'society' (*Gesellschaft*) based on the directional determination of the wills of their members either towards communal formation (community) or towards a willed goal (society) (86–9). While he clearly favours the former over the latter as an explanatory type for the church, in the end he concludes that the church 'transcends the activities characteristic of both community and society and combines both' (263). It combines both a will to unity and a will to embrace God's purpose. In this seminal work Bonhoeffer has provided a significant contribution to the use of the social sciences to ecclesiology. As Richard Roberts notes, of the variety of approaches to be found in this area, 'it is Bonhoeffer who, despite the archaism of his sociological appropriations, offers most inspiration, even if his insights into social science are extremely dated' (Roberts 2002: 212).

Edward Schillebeeckx

Edward Schillebeeckx made a significant contribution with his theological and sociological study of ministry in the church (Schillebeeckx 1985). He attacks a dualism which would attempt to separate sociological and historical insights from theological considerations. While he concurs that it would be wrong to reduce ministry to its sociological and historical analysis, he argues that 'there is also such a thing as theological reductionism, which puts the character of ministry as grace alongside and above its socio-historical reality' (5). For Schillebeeckx theological reflection on ministry in a particular era cannot be separated from the concrete social practice of ministry in that era. In particular dominant theologies justify and promote a particular practice of ministry. Utilizing a conflictualist social theory, Schillebeeckx then reads the history of emerging structures of ministry with a hermeneutic of suspicion, considering the institutionalization of ministry in terms of consolidation of power relations. Rather than a theological distinction leading to different offices, he seeks to uncover 'a gradually increasing theological legitimation of relationships of subjection and power which are essentially contrary to the gospel' (69). The theological legitimization of the distinction comes after a process of the centralizing of power, and designates a ranking of that power, which is increasingly focused in the monarchical bishop. For Schillebeeckx, the theological distinction between differing orders of ministry is little more than an ideological superstructure.

David Bosch

David Bosch drew upon the theory of paradigm shifts by Thomas Kuhn, as developed further by Hans Küng and others (Küng and Tracy 1989), to identify major paradigms for understanding the church's mission as they operated in different historical periods (Bosch 1991). In order to control the vast historical data Bosch draws on suggestions of

Hans Küng to divide the history of Christianity into six eras characterized by distinct 'paradigms' (Küng 1995). Whereas Küng suggests that each of these periods has its own distinctive understanding of Christian faith, Bosch adds that each also offers a distinctive understanding of the church's mission. These paradigms provide overarching thought-forms or metaphors for analysing and evaluating these eras. The six paradigms are:

- The apocalyptic paradigm of primitive Christianity: the dominant feature of this paradigm is the sense of the imminent, apocalyptic end of history and the dawning of the kingdom. There is a sense of urgency to the preaching of the church, which witnessed to the power of the Spirit through ecstatic phenomena such as speaking in tongues. The overall outlook is still largely Jewish, while the entry of the Gentiles into the church is a sign of the gathering of the nations prior to the last days.
- The Hellenistic paradigm of the patristic period: initiated by Paul, the shift to this paradigm is marked by the movement from the largely Jewish setting towards the Hellenistic culture of the Roman Empire. Gentiles begin to dominate the church numerically, making Greek the language of the church, and Rome the increasingly powerful centre, over Jerusalem. There is a growing institutionalization of church life and a move to inculturate Christianity into its new cultural setting.
- The medieval Roman Catholic paradigm: this shift is initiated by the conversion of Constantine and the Christianization of the Roman Empire. With the collapse of the Empire, the church becomes a powerful social and cultural force, especially through the office of the pope, which became increasingly monarchical. It is the era of Christendom, where the church has a role in all aspects of people's lives.
- The Protestant (Reformation) paradigm: the Reformers reacted against the world-liness of the powerful Catholic institutions, and offered a return to the simplicity of the Scriptures, and the primacy of faith as the ground of justification. The article of 'justification by faith alone' is that by which the church stands or falls. It is the measure of all church doctrines and practices. The emphasis on the priesthood of all believers also tended to relativize church office which was seen as of human rather than divine institution, basically for the sake of good order.
- The modern Enlightenment paradigm: the Enlightenment was marked by a renewed humanism and rationalism. This was the Age of Reason whose creed was progress through scientific discovery and the elimination of prejudice and superstition. Religion tends to a non-historical deism—belief in an all-powerful God, but not a historical revelation—or an inward pietism, as the world becomes increasingly hostile to the appearance of religion in the public sphere.
- The emerging ecumenical paradigm: as Bosch identifies it, this is an emerging paradigm, so its features are to some extent speculative and anticipatory. It is a paradigm for a post-modern era, one less concerned with dogma and more concerned with shared praxis. Its context is global, no longer Europe; its goal is inculturation of the gospel, not the exporting of Western culture. The lines between salvation and socio-political liberation are no longer clear, as the churches work together for social justice as the basis for their witness to Jesus Christ.

While it is an interesting exercise in historical periodization Bosch's use of paradigm theory renders it incapable of providing any form of normativity to his missiological and ecclesial observations. Changes in paradigm occur but of themselves such changes are neither good nor bad.

Roger Haight

Most ambitiously, Roger Haight has produced a three-volume ecclesiology which seeks to incorporate a sociological imagination in its handling of the historical movement of the church from its inception to the present day (Haight 2004, 2005, 2008). Like Schillebeeckx, Haight envisages a historical form of ecclesiology, one which takes the historical data of the church into the heart of his theological method. Moreover Haight's work is significantly more comprehensive than that of Schillebeeckx, seeking to develop an account of the whole of the history of the Christian church from its origins to the present day. In this respect his work represents a major achievement. And as with the work of Schillebeeckx, Haight recognizes the need to engage with the social sciences in order to write his historical ecclesiology.

From the outset Haight is clear that 'the primary object of the study of ecclesiology is the empirical church' (Haight 2004: 35), and that the church is 'not only an empirical and human reality, it is also a historical reality' (37). He eschews any attempted 'theological reductionism' which would neglect or deny this and turn ecclesiology into some idealized form. Haight then sets up his ecclesiological problematic in the following terms. 'The church is simultaneously a human, historical, social reality on the one hand and a theological reality on the other hand. These two dimensions of the church are quite distinct …' (38). Drawing on the work of Schillebeeckx he argues that 'the church is a single reality in history, but one that must be understood in two irreducible languages' (39), a theological language relating the church to God and a critical, historical sociological language to deal with the human dimension of the church. Nonetheless he insists that 'these are two dimensions of one reality; there are not two churches. We need a theological method that respects these two dimensions of the one church, that does not hold them in balance over and against each other but integrates them into a single understanding' (39).

Assessment

Whatever one might think of the success or failure of these attempts they do raise basic questions about the relationship between ecclesiology and the social sciences. It is by no means obvious how one might go about bringing these into constructive relationship and mutual dialogue. For the theologian coming to the social sciences for the first time, one must deal with the fact that the social sciences are not a united discipline with a uniform methodology. There are different schools of thought, some with strongly positivist leanings and others more hermeneutical in approach. The choice of methodology can play a large part in the outcome of the process. And so, when Schillebeeckx makes the methodological decision to adopt a conflictualist approach, it determines the outcome of his investigation that structures of ministry reflect power relations and conflicts. If he had adopted a more functionalist approach the outcome would have been very different. What then is the theological justification for the choice of approach?

There is then the difficulty of how these two approaches can be brought into relationship. The most common way of doing so is some method of correlation, whereby the theological tradition is correlated with a context whose description is provided by a non-theological approach such as sociology. However this situation becomes problematic if one recognizes that the context is already theological and so no non-theological account of it will be adequate (Ormerod 1996). For example, it is not difficult to identify concerns with Haight's approach discussed here. Initially he speaks of a human, historical, social reality and a theological reality. So already we are speaking of two realities. The language then shifts to 'two dimensions' of the one reality. Nonetheless these two dimensions require 'two irreducible languages' to give expression to them, which again gives the impression of two distinct realities. Further if one of these languages is already theological, why do we need a further theological method to bring these two dimensions into some further integration? If we already have a theological language to describe the relationship of the church to God, then what does the critical historical sociological language add to that? Is not the church that is in relationship to God the same as the historical church? Certainly we need a single understanding of the church, but it will not be achieved in the fashion that Haight spells out.

This is not the place to resolve such difficulties. Our aim here is more to set out the issues that arise as ecclesiology moves more towards the concrete historical data of the life of the church and then seeks to draw upon the social sciences in a theologically justifiable and responsible manner.

A THEOLOGICAL PERSPECTIVE ON THE SOCIAL SCIENCES

There have been other difficulties in the relationship between theology and the social sciences. No one has been more vocal in relation to these difficulties than John Milbank (Milbank 1991). Milbank's work is a theological critique of the social sciences themselves, claiming that in one way or another they represent heterodox forms of Christian belief. Focusing on functionalist and conflictualist accounts of social theory, Milbank argues that the functionalist stance masks a metaphysics which is basically a will to power; while the conflictualist account represents an ontology of primordial violence. Such a conflictual view is basically pagan, not Christian, which promotes the ontological priority of peace. Milbank is suspicious of any 'dialectic method' since it represents the constant temptation to violence in the name of dialectic 'benefits' which only encourage further violence. Drawing on post-modern emphases on particularity and narrativity, Milbank views ecclesiology as a form of Christian social theory, a theory which is embedded in the social practice of the church. From Milbank's post-modern perspective, there are no 'societies' in general, only concrete communities and their histories, so there can be no general 'theory' of society. On the other hand, Christianity is itself an embodied social reality with its own history, the history of the church, not as a hypostatized idea, but in the concrete lives of Christian communities. Milbank contends that Christianity is a distinctive ethical practice which requires its own distinctive social theory. Talk of a 'Christian sociology' makes sense precisely because there is no universal sociology, only the narratives of particular societies such as the church.

> The theory [i.e. the Christian theory of society], therefore, is first and foremost an *ecclesiology*, and only an account of other human societies to the extent that the Church defines itself, in its practice, as in continuity and discontinuity with these societies. As the Church is *already*, necessarily, by virtue of its institution, a 'reading' of other human societies, it becomes possible to consider ecclesiology as also a 'sociology'. (Milbank 1991: 380)

The significant insight in Milbank's work is that the question of the relationship between ecclesiology and the social sciences maps onto one's more general understanding of the relationship between grace and nature. The more pessimistic one's anthropology (Augustinian) the more likely one is to discount the contribution that might come from the use of reason (for example the social sciences) as tainted by sin and corruption; the more optimistic (Thomistic), the more likely one is to see the use of reason as part of the mix in dealing with the question. And so the more Augustinian approach of Milbank will be suspicious of the outcomes of the social sciences, not just as applied to ecclesiology, but in their ability to offer any genuine insight into the human condition.

We can clarify this theological ambiguity of the social sciences by asking the disarming question, what is the goal of the social sciences? If we answer as we did above that this goal consists in seeking to understand human communities, both in their internal structures, institutions, and power relations (synchronically), and in the patterns of their longer-term trajectories of change (diachronically), and if we wish to maintain that this human realm is constituted at least in part by human acts of meaning and value, of acts of understanding, judgement, and decision, then understanding that human realm inevitably raises questions of human anthropology, particularly the nature of human freedom. Different theological and philosophical stances on human freedom will impact on how we will construct a systematic understanding of the social realm. For example, if we take a broadly Thomistic stance that human freedom is orientated to the good and human decisions are intelligible inasmuch as they are motivated by terminal values, considered as an objective structure of the good to be achieved, then attempts to separate out questions of fact and value to construct a 'value free' social science, often associated with the work of Max Weber, are inherently flawed. Purely positivist constructions of the social sciences, which gather data and seek to let the facts speaks for themselves, would then be invalid. They would not actually be understanding the social realm, but producing a truncated and distorted account of that realm.

On the other hand, working within this same Thomistic framework, decisions may fail to embody terminal values, or may in some way distort the social good, and so are inherently unintelligible. Such actions are theologically described as sinful and would be objectively unintelligible. One might think, for example, of the multiple human decisions which led to the creation of Apartheid in South Africa. These decisions created a state which embodied objective falsehood, that one race is superior to another. With regard to such a possibility Alasdair MacIntyre concisely argues, 'Unintelligible actions are failed candidates for the status of intelligible action; and to lump unintelligible actions and intelligible actions together in a single class of actions and then characterise actions in terms of what items of both sets have in common is to make the mistake of ignoring this' (MacIntyre 1984: 209). A form of social science which fails to recognize this distinction between intelligible actions (properly ordered to terminal values) and unintelligible actions will in fact not be properly scientific.

Finally, from a theological perspective our social situation is not simply the outcome of an orientation to the good (nature), and of our failures to embody that good (sin), but also of the divine initiative to redeem our human sinfulness and turn around our social and historical decline (grace). Inasmuch as the social realm is also constituted by grace, a form of the social sciences which fails to recognize this element cannot comprehend the full reality of that social realm. From this one might conclude with Bernard Lonergan that the only proper form of the social sciences is theological (Lonergan 1993: 130). Nevertheless, in this perspective theology does not replace the genuine insights of the social sciences but adds a further dimension to them. As Lonergan notes, 'Grace perfects nature, both in the sense that it adds a perfection beyond nature and in the sense that it confers on nature the effective freedom to attain its own perfection. But grace is not a substitute for nature, and theology is not a substitute for empirical human science' (Lonergan 1992: 767). Of course such claims are far from being accepted within the general community of social scientists.

All this is predicated however on a particular theological option. As Milbank's work demonstrates, a different theological option will lead to significantly different conclusions. A more Augustinian stance built upon a grace–sin dialectic might tend to deny a natural orientation to the good, viewing it as destroyed by the effects of original sin, to conclude that the social realm has no natural intelligibility but becomes intelligible only through its relationship to divine grace. In that case the only true social realm is one constituted by the communication of grace, that is, the church, and ecclesiology is the only true form of social science.

All of which can lead us to conclude that the relationship of the social sciences to ecclesiology can never be theologically neutral. Different theological and metaphysical options underlie quite different forms of social science. Indeed this is why we can find such a variety of approaches within the social sciences, such as positivist, functionalist, conflictualist, and symbolic interactionist (Winter 1966; Baum 1974; Ormerod 2005a).

And so, as we have noted, Schillebeeckx's choice of a conflictualist approach to the emergence of structures of ministry inevitably leads to a conclusion that such a process is ideologically driven. Similarly, a functionalist reading of Paul's evocation of the symbol for the church as the Body of Christ will differ significantly from a conflictualist reading (Ormerod 2005a: 825–6). Any attempt to appropriate the social sciences within ecclesiology must be aware of these difficulties.

TYPES OF INCORPORATION OF SOCIAL SCIENCES INTO THEOLOGY

The history of such attempts to incorporate the social sciences into theology has had what can best be described as mixed results. Writing from the perspective of liberation theology, Clodovis Boff has proved a fivefold typology of the various strategies that theologians have utilized in incorporating the social sciences (Boff 1987: 20–9):

1. Empiricism, or absence of mediation: this approach assumes some direct access to social reality unmediated by social theory. It simply lets the social facts 'speak for themselves'. In place of a critical reading that social theory might provide, it substitutes its own naive, uncritical stance which is adopted as normative.
2. Methodological purism, or exclusion of mediation: this position holds to the self-sufficiency of faith and revelation for all theorizing. It has no need to use other disciplines. Boff notes that such purism does not work in classical areas such as Christology and Trinity. One adopts either critical philosophical assumptions or uncritical ones. The same is true in theologies which engage social and historical realities. Perhaps the clearest exponent of methodological purism is Karl Barth.
3. Theologism, or substitution for mediation: this pushes purism further by arguing that theology is itself a mediation, so that 'theology pretends to find everything it needs to express the political in its own walls' (Boff 1987: 26). The outcome of this approach is a 'religio-political rhetoric'. Boff refers to it as 'supernaturalism', and it is present in the ideologies of 'Christendom', apoliticism, and 'faith without ideology'. One would argue that Milbank's work falls within this strategy.
4. Semantic mix, or faulty articulation of mediation: this position makes use of the language of the social sciences, but results in a mixed discourse, drawing on the resources of two distinct realms of knowledge. The social mediation is generally uncritical and not properly assimilated. Boff argues that one side of the mix tends to dominate: 'the mixture is always organised under the domination of the logic of one of the languages in question' (Boff 1987: 28). Boff claims that church social teaching documents tend to this mix.
5. Bilingualism, or unarticulated mediation: this consists of 'practicing two readings of the real', juxtaposing 'socio-analytic discourse and theological discourse' (Boff

1987: 29). One could argue that Haight's attempts to incorporate the social sciences within ecclesiology adopt such a strategy.

In the end Boff judges each of these strategies to be defective and seeks to develop a further approach in which the social science provides theology with a non-theological reading of the social realm which is then appropriated within theology. 'The text of a theological reading with respect to the political is prepared and furnished by the sciences of the social. Theology receives its text from these sciences, and practices upon it a reading in conformity with its own proper code, in such a way as to extract from it a characteristically, properly theological meaning' (Boff 1987: 31). It is not that the 'political *turns* theological, *becomes* theological by absorption, but by enrichment' (Boff 1987: 33). Still Boff's position is built on an assumption of the theological automony and neutrality of the social sciences, which on the above analysis may be questioned.

Drawing on a more thorough familiarity with recent trends in the social sciences Richard Roberts provides a different fivefold typology of the various strategies:

> First, the fundamentalist option involves the repudiation of modernity and concomitant patterns of regression; second, theology can tend towards reductive absorption into the social scientific perspective (Ernst Troeltsch); third, the theologian may draw upon and use sociological categories as part of his or her essentially theological project (Dietrich Bonhoeffer, H. R. Niebuhr); fourth, theological and sociological categories can be regarded as coinherent aspects of an integral 'form of life', 'life-world' or 'phenomenology of tradition' (Edward Farley) [an approach] which subsists at a remove from the question of modernity; fifth, the theologian may repudiate sociology as heretical secular thought and posit the persuasive option of commitment to the Christian cultural-linguistic practice (John Milbank). (Roberts 2002: 194)

Roberts acknowledges that 'This depiction of possible ways of configuring the relation of theology and the social sciences is in no way exhaustive, but it is representative of a range of possible strategies in a fraught borderland.'

In the face of the inadequacies of these approaches, Roberts develops his own tentative agenda for relating theology to the social sciences. The final goal will require a far-reaching transformation of theology. 'It will therefore require thoroughgoing methodological renewal within theology (rather than occasional intellectual transfers by unusually energetic theologians) before the disjunctions between theology, the sociology of religion, and mainline social theory are better understood and more well-founded working relationships are established' (Roberts 2002: 209). In the meantime Roberts's suggestion is one of constructive and pragmatic engagement. 'The theologian should be an organic intellectual, a risk-taker, an entrepreneur of the mind and heart who is willing to withstand the systemic marginality that afflicts all those who are willing to cross boundaries in the borderlands that are normative in the contemporary human condition' (213).

Roberts's conclusion is perhaps the best statement of where theology at present sits in relation to its engagement with the social sciences. Various approaches have been adopted, different proposals have been made, but none demands assent, nor constitutes a common currency among ecclesiologists. In general one could conclude that 'the engagement with social sciences by ecclesiologists has been eclectic, sporadic, intermittent and secondary to what they view as their primary task' (Ormerod 2005a: 816).

The Ambiguity of the Social Sciences and their Use in Ecclesiology

Positive Phase and Normative Phase

Roberts mentions the need for a 'thoroughgoing methodological renewal within theology' in order to bring the social sciences into a constructive relationship with theology. Given the discussion herein, one could also argue for the need for a thoroughgoing methodological renewal within the social sciences. Within theology there have been various discussions around questions of theological method, the most substantive proposal being that of Bernard Lonergan (Lonergan 1972). According to Lonergan's approach, theological method consists of two distinct phases, a positive phase which seeks to recover that which has been handed down from the past and a normative phase which having learnt from the past seeks to mediate the normative meanings and values of the tradition into the future. Each of these phases is further divided into four functional specialities. The positive phase embraces research, interpretation, history, and dialectics, while the normative phase comprises foundations, doctrines, systematics, and communications. The hinge which links these two phases is the question of conversion which Lonergan unpacks in terms of religious, moral, and intellectual conversions. The formalism of this proposal allows us to clarify some of the issues that arise in the use of the social sciences in ecclesiology, especially how that use will differ in the two phases, positive and normative.

In the positive phase ecclesiology is concerned with the historical data of the life of the church, not the history that is written, but the history that is written about. This process involves gathering, sorting, and establishing the data (research); interpreting that data using appropriate hermeneutical tools (interpretation); constructing a critical narrative of the life of the church (history); and analysing the divergent narratives which various scholars have produced in undertaking these same tasks (dialectics). It is not difficult to see how the social sciences might and indeed have contributed to these various functional specialities.

For example the social sciences have provided scriptural exegetes with a variety of insights in the *interpretation* of the biblical text. One might think of ground-breaking works such as those of Philip Esler (Esler 1987) and Wayne Meeks (Meeks 1983). Both of these authors pioneered the use of the social sciences to bring to light the life of the early Christian community and the ways in which those insights could assist in understanding the biblical text. The use of the social sciences in the interpretation of Scripture is now well established (Osiek 1992) and similar tools may be used for the interpretation of documents from any era of the church. The social sciences have also been used to clarify the dynamics of social changes in *history*, subjecting them to empirical verification. Here the work of Rodney Stark (Stark 1996) has been most valuable in bringing social science methodology, particularly rational choice theory, to assist in mapping out the growth of the early church and the reasons for that growth. In a more recent setting the use of social theories of secularization (Taylor 2007) have proved fruitful in analysing the contemporary situation of the church and the best options for responding to this situation (Paas 2011). Further liberation and feminist theologies have helped to uncover the *dialectic* divergences, utilizing a hermeneutic of suspicion to identify the presence of ideologies within the life of the church which marginalize the poor (Boff 1985) and women (Schüssler Fiorenza 1994). And as we have already noted, Edward Schillebeeckx uses social theories of power to provide an ideological critique of the emergence of structures of ministry in the early church (Schillebeeckx 1985).

More broadly, in the growing area of what might be called 'practical ecclesiology', the use of social sciences in the form of ethnographic studies and statistical surveys is becoming more widespread. A pioneer in the use of ethnographic work in the study of ecclesial communities was Don Browning (Browning 1991). Browning's work established a discipline of practical theology which sought to bring the insights of the social sciences to bear on the practical issues of church communities and their struggles. Ethnographic methods are now well established in ecclesiological researches (Ward 2012). In terms of large-scale empirical statistical work there is the long-term work of the National Church Life Survey in Australia (<http://www.ncls.org.au/>) which has been gathering data from a range of Christian denominations every five years or so since 1991. These surveys cover areas of church life, belief, and practice, starting with 312,000 attendees from 6,700 congregations in 1991 to over 500,000 attendees in 2012. This data is invaluable in terms of tracing trends and providing church leaders with information about the well-being of their church communities so as to assist in future planning.

Foundational Issues

Laudable as these efforts are, they largely prescind from the issue of how the social sciences may contribute to the normative phase of ecclesiological studies. In the first instance there are the *foundational* issues which raise questions about whether or in what ways insights from the social sciences might shape our handing on of the past. Just as the early church was caught up in debates about the use of philosophical categories in formulating the doctrine of the Trinity, so now we must ask about the suitability of sociological categories in formulating the doctrine of the church. It is to his credit that John

Milbank (Milbank 1991) brought this question to the serious attention of theologians, even if one might disagree with his conclusions.

A counter-voice to that of Milbank has been the long-term advocacy of the foundational role of the social sciences in ecclesiology by Joseph Komonchak (Komonchak 1995). He argues that, 'just as one cannot construct a theology without an at least implicit philosophy, so one cannot construct an ecclesiology without an implicit social theory; and without making the implicit explicit and securing its foundations neither constructions can be considered critical' (64). Coming to grips with social theory is necessary if theology is to move beyond description and move into explanation, to move beyond common sense and into a realm of theory. The church is a social and historical reality, so it is essential to a systematic understanding of the church to employ tools developed for a systematic understanding of social and historical realities. 'How can one work out a systematic ecclesiology without working out first such terms as "individual," "community," "society," "meaning," "change," "structure," "institution," "relationship," and so on, and the various relationships, or at least types of relationships, that can obtain among these those terms?' (69–70). Komonchak is aware of the difficulties involved, in particular 'the ecclesiologist who attempts it will not find himself before a unified body of social theory' (73), though he is less explicit on the theological dimension of social theory itself. As we have already indicated this debate is part of a larger and more profound theological debate over questions of grace and nature.

Implications for Doctrine

If indeed one accepts a positive role for the social sciences within theological foundations, the next question concerns their impact on our stance towards traditional ecclesiological *doctrines*. One gets a hint of this as far back as John Henry Newman. In his account of the development of doctrine, Newman identifies five distinct trajectories of historical development in general, one of which he calls 'political' (Newman 1992: 76–84; Ormerod 2010: 614–20). When he seeks to illustrate how doctrinal development may take different trajectories, he specifies 'the Episcopate as taught by St Ignatius . . . [as] an instance of political development' (Newman 1992: 85). This intriguing and understated suggestion seems to propose both the historical development of the office and the doctrinal legitimacy of its claims to divine authority as a genuine doctrinal development. This stands in some contrast to the claims of Schillebeeckx that the emergence of ministerial office should be read through the lens of a hermeneutic of suspicion (Schillebeeckx 1985). Indeed one's willingness to affirm a doctrine of the divine origins of structures of ministry may depend on one's evaluation of social processes of institutionalization in general and questions of the legitimacy of authority, where the social scientific account on both these issues is largely dominated by the work of Max Weber (Weber 1947). A *foundational* engagement with Weber's work and its appropriate reorientation may lead one to conclude both a form of historical development of the structures of ministry and their doctrinal status as 'divinely instituted' and authoritative (Ormerod 2007: 2012). In this way one can see that one's appropriation of the social sciences in theology may affect what doctrines one is willing to affirm and what doctrines one may seek to pass over in silence or outright reject.

Systematic Ecclesiology

Further we may consider the task of a systematic ecclesiology which takes the historical data of the church as its starting point. If the goal of the social sciences is to seek to understand human communities, both in their internal structures, institutions, and power relations (synchronically) and in the patterns of their longer-term trajectories of change (diachronically), then we may define the goal of a systematic ecclesiology as seeking to understand the church, both in its internal structures, institutions, and power relations (synchronically) and in the patterns of its longer-term trajectories of change (diachronically). This would involve the large-scale understanding of the church in its historical movements and events—for example the emergence of structures of ministry, the emergence of Christendom, the collapse of Christendom, and the Reformations—within the structure of an overarching and reorientated social scientific framework. Such a desideratum is far from being achieved, but one can grasp something of an anticipation of such a project in Schillebeeckx (1985), Haight (2004, 2005, 2008), and Bosch (1991). The goal of such a project is to produce an ecclesiology which is empirical, historical, critical, normative, and perhaps even practical as it works its way into the task of *communications* (Ormerod 2002).

This distinction between the positive and normative phases of theology at the least helps to delineate the different concerns that arise and ways of approaching the task of utilizing the social sciences in ecclesiology.

CONVERSION, SOCIAL SCIENCE, AND THEOLOGY

As noted, the hinge on which the two phases hang together is conversion. While we may readily expect a high degree of religious conversion among ecclesiologists, questions of moral and intellectual conversion are also pertinent as they impact on how one conceives of the social sciences and of their relationship to theology. We have argued that a truly scientific account of the social order must take into account questions of terminal values, as the intelligible ground of human decisions. Immediately this raises questions about the orientation of both the social scientist and the ecclesiologist to terminal values. Do we think of values as matters of arbitrary choice, as an unintelligible realm, or as a mere fiction with no objective reality, or simply social convention? Social sciences that attempt to exclude questions of value will not only be of little value theologically, they will truncate and distort our understanding of the social order. Social sciences that are more attuned to questions of value, particularly those that engage in ideology critiques, may still view values as a product of arbitrary choice, reducing the social order to a realm of power and domination. Nonetheless such ideology critiques can help attune us to particular values which we have failed to properly appreciate, as with Feminist and Liberationist approaches. In this way they can assist in attuning us to a proper scale of terminal values.

These are often issues that relate to what Lonergan calls intellectual conversion as well. To speak of values as objective is to raise questions about the nature of reality, of what constitutes objectivity, and how we can come to know these. These issues lie at the heart of intellectual conversion. An empiricist will never be convinced of the reality or objectivity of values while an idealist may be convinced of their objectivity but not their reality, depending on whether they are Platonic or Kantian in orientation. Divisions between positivist (empiricist), functionalist (Platonic), and conflictualist (Kantian) approaches to the social sciences are as much the result of underlying epistemologies and metaphysics as anything else and until such issues are properly addressed through something like intellectual conversion we cannot expect the social sciences to produce a methodologically well-grounded approach.

Ecclesiologists too must address such epistemological and metaphysical questions. In his well-known debate with then Cardinal Joseph Ratzinger over the relationship between the local and the universal church, Walter Kasper stated that their differences lay in different philosophical starting points. 'The conflict is between theological opinions and underlying philosophical assumptions. One side [Ratzinger] proceeds by Plato's method; its starting point is the primacy of an ideal that is a universal concept. The other side [Kasper] follows Aristotle's approach and sees the universal as existing in a concrete reality' (Kasper 2001). Significantly these differences also lie behind the tensions within the grace–nature debate discussed herein where Augustinian (Platonic) and Thomistic (Aristotelian) approaches lead to different conclusions on the relationship between theology and the social sciences.

All of which leads one to conclude that there is a significant amount of *foundational* work still to be done as a consequence of questions of conversion in sorting out where an ecclesiologist is to stand in relation to quite fundamental questions in ecclesiology, not least being the needed reorientation of the social sciences required before they can be fruitfully engaged in helping us understand that particular human community we call the church.

Effective, Constitutive, and Cognitive Meaning— Ecclesiology as 'Ideological'

At the beginning of this chapter I noted the difference between ecclesiology and, say, theology of the Trinity. This difference would be immediately clear to a social scientist who would identify ecclesiology itself as a form of discourse which attempts not just to understand its theological object but to shape that object in various ways. From the perspective of the social sciences we can view ecclesiology as a form of 'social engineering' or 'political discourse'. Indeed when we consider the period in which ecclesiology emerged as a distinct theological theme, the Reformation, it is easy to recognize that it functioned largely as a form of political or ideological discourse which sought to justify the validity of the competing ecclesial commitments of the various participants. Whether it be Robert Bellarmine's insistence that the church be 'as visible and palpable as the assembly of Romans, or the Kingdom of France, or the Republic of Venice' (Haight 2005: 283) or the Reformers' determination that the church is the place where the 'Gospel be preached in conformity with a pure understanding of it and the sacraments be administered in accordance with the divine word' (Tappert 1959: 32), ecclesiological discourse is as much concerned with an author's judgement as to what the church *should be* as to what it actually *is*. Ecclesiologists are always, either explicitly or implicitly, seeking to shape the ecclesial reality according to their theological insights.

We can clarify this distinction between descriptive and prescriptive aspects of theology by referring to Lonergan's 'effective', 'constitutive', and 'cognitive' functions of meaning (Lonergan 1972: 81–5). *Constitutive* meaning recognizes the fact that our human world is a world of meaning, that our institutions and cultures are in fact constituted by meaning. Through shared meanings we create community, including the community we call the church. The *effective* function of meaning seeks to bring about a new reality in the world constituted and mediated by meaning. Effective meaning motivates and challenges us, through envisaging new elements in that world of meaning. The *cognitive* function of meaning seeks to understand and affirm truth, what is in fact the case. In fact much ecclesiological discourse is more concerned with the constitutive and effective functions of meaning than with the cognitive function. It is concerned with reinforcing the central meanings of the church as church (constitutive meaning) and/or with reshaping aspects of the church (effective meaning) according to the ecclesiologist's vision of church. For this reason much current ecclesiological discourse remains at a descriptive and often symbolic or metaphorical level.

These observations concerning effective and constitutive meaning are particularly pertinent when ecclesial authorities make statements about the constitution and nature of the church. In the Roman Catholic tradition, the 1985 Synod of Bishops declared that the notion of *communio* was 'the central and fundamental idea of the Council's documents'. Such a statement must be seen against a backdrop of various competing claims concerning the central ecclesiological insights of the council, notably the ecclesiology of the church as the pilgrim People of God. This latter position was seen as risking reducing the church to a sociological or political reality, losing the essentially theological dimension which *communio* adds, as a participation in the unity of the Trinitarian persons. However, from a sociological perspective the notion of *communio* fits firmly into a functionalist sociological stance with key values of social harmony and stability. To challenge the status quo or to question the existing social order is then viewed as a threat which must be eliminated. And so when the Australian bishop William Morris was deposed as bishop of his diocese of Toowoomba because of statements he had made concerning the ordination of women, he was told that he had broken ecclesial communion. From a conflictualist perspective one may ask who defines what constitutes *communio*. Inevitably there are questions about power and authority within the ecclesial context, and the ways in which differing stances operate effectively and constitutively. None of which should be taken to suggest that there is no place for genuine authority in the ecclesial community (Ormerod 2005b) or that the authority exercised in the case above was not genuine, but it does illustrate that any ecclesiological discourse is never simply cognitive in its meaning, but always has elements of constitutive and effective meaning. In sociological terms one can say it has an ideological intent.

Of course one should not think that it is possible to eliminate this aspect in ecclesiology. Nonetheless the primacy focus of ecclesiology as a theological discipline should be the cognitive function of meaning, what we can truly affirm and understand of the nature of the church. Here one may concur with the conclusion of Komonchak mentioned in the subsection 'Foundational Issues', 'How can one work out a systematic ecclesiology without working out first such terms as "individual," "community," "society," "meaning," "change," "structure," "institution," "relationship," and so on, and the various relationships, or at least types of relationships, that can obtain among these those terms?' (Komonchak 1995: 69–70). In such a task the social sciences have an irreplaceable role to play. To move in this direction is to move beyond descriptive and symbolic language into explanatory language, not merely a satisfying flow of image and affect, but hopefully to promote genuine understanding.

CONCLUSION

Because of its potential to effect genuine change in ecclesial communities, ecclesiology faces particular challenges in the present context where churches are dealing with many problems that require theological and practical resolution. Ecumenically speaking, questions of church order, the validity of different forms of ministry, notions of authority, and the relationship between the universal and the local church have a pressing urgency. Any lasting resolution to such questions must rest on theological positions which have genuine explanatory power. It is difficult to see how this can be achieved without some input from the social sciences, though this might require considerable reorientation of those sciences as they are currently constituted. The challenges are formidable, requiring, as Roberts notes, that an ecclesiologist become an 'organic intellectual, a risk-taker, an entrepreneur of the mind and heart who is willing to withstand the systemic marginality that afflicts all those who are willing to cross boundaries in the borderlands that are normative in the contemporary human condition' (Roberts 2002: 213).

REFERENCES

Baum, G. (1974). *Sociology and Theology: Church as Institution*. New York: Herder and Herder.

Boff, C. (1987). *Theology and Praxis: Epistemological Foundations*. Maryknoll, NY: Orbis.

Boff, L. (1985). *Church, Charism and Power: Liberation Theology and the Institutional Church*. New York: Crossroad.

Bonhoeffer, D. (1998). *Sanctorum Communio: A Theological Study of the Sociology of the Church*. Minneapolis: Augsburg Fortress.

Bosch, D. (1991). *Transforming Mission: Paradigm Shifts in Theology of Mission*. Maryknoll, NY: Orbis.

Browning, D. S. (1991). *A Fundamental Practical Theology: Descriptive and Strategic Proposals*. Minneapolis: Fortress.

Esler, P. F. (1987). *Community and Gospel in Luke–Acts: The Social and Political Motivations of Lucan Theology*. Cambridge: Cambridge University Press.

Haight, R. (2004). *Historical Ecclesiology*. New York: Continuum.

Haight, R. (2005). *Comparative Ecclesiology*. New York: Continuum.

Haight, R. (2008). *Ecclesial Existence*. New York: Continuum.

Kasper, W. (2001). 'A Friendly Reply to Cardinal Ratzinger on the Church'. *America* 184 (23–30 April): 8–14.

Komonchak, J. (1995). *Foundations in Ecclesiology*. Boston: Boston College.

Küng, H. (1995). *Christianity: The Religious Situation of our Time*. London: SCM.

Küng, H. and Tracy, D. (1989). *Paradigm Change in Theology: A Symposium for the Future*. New York: Crossroad.

Lonergan, B. J. F. (1972). *Method in Theology*. London: Darton, Longman & Todd.

Lonergan, B. J. F. (1992). *Insight: A Study of Human Understanding*. Toronto: University of Toronto Press.

Lonergan, B. J. F. (1993). 'Theology and Understanding'. In F. E. Crowe and R. M. Doran (eds), *Collection*. Toronto: University of Toronto Press.

MacIntyre, A. (1984). *After Virtue: A Study in Moral Theory*. Notre Dame, IN: University of Notre Dame Press.

Meeks, W. A. (1983). *The First Urban Christians: The Social World of the Apostle Paul*. New Haven: Yale University Press.

Milbank, J. (1991). *Theology and Social Theory: Beyond Secular Reason*. Cambridge, MA: Blackwell.

Newman, J. H. (1992). *Conscience, Consensus, and the Development of Doctrine*. New York: Image Books.

Ormerod, N. (1996). 'Quarrels with the Method of Correlation'. *Theological Studies* 57: 707–19.

Ormerod, N. (2002). 'The Structure of a Systematic Ecclesiology'. *Theological Studies* 63: 3–30.

Ormerod, N. (2005a). 'A Dialectic Engagement with the Social Sciences in an Ecclesiological Context'. *Theological Studies* 66: 815–40.

Ormerod, N. (2005b). 'Power and Authority—A Response to Bishop Cullinane'. *Australasian Catholic Record* 82: 154–62.

Ormerod, N. (2007). 'On the Divine Institution of the Three-fold Ministry'. *Ecclesiology* 4: 38–51.

Ormerod, N. (2010). 'Vatican II—Continuity or Discontinuity? Toward an Ontology of Meaning'. *Theological Studies* 71: 609–36.

Ormerod, N. (2012). 'Ecclesiology and Exclusion: Setting Boundaries for the Church'. In D. Doyle, P. Bazzell, and T. Furry (eds), *Ecclesiology and Exclusion: Boundaries of Being and Belonging in Postmodern Times*. Maryknoll, NY: Orbis.

Osiek, C. (1992). *What are they Saying about the Social Setting of the New Testament?* New York: Paulist Press.

Paas, S. (2011). 'Post-Christian, Post-Christendom, and Post-Modern Europe: Towards the Interaction of Missiology and the Social Sciences'. *Mission Studies* 28: 3–25.

Roberts, R. H. (2002). *Religion, Theology, and the Human Sciences*. Cambridge: Cambridge University Press.

Schillebeeckx, E. (1985). *The Church with a Human Face: A New and Expanded Theology of Ministry*. New York: Crossroad.

Schüssler Fiorenza, E. (1994). *In Memory of Her: A Feminist Theological Reconstruction of Christian Origins*. New York: Crossroad.

Stark, R. (1996). *The Rise of Christianity: A Sociologist Reconsiders History*. Princeton: Princeton University Press.

Tappert, T. G. (1959). *The Book of Concord: The Confessions of the Evangelical Lutheran Church*. Philadelphia: Mühlenberg Press.

Taylor, C. (2007). *A Secular Age*. Cambridge, MA: Belknap Press.

Ward, P. (2012). *Perspectives on Ecclesiology and Ethnography*. Grand Rapids, MI: Eerdmans.

Weber, M. (1947). *The Theory of Social and Economic Oranization*. New York: Free Press.

Winter, G. (1966). *Elements for a Social Ethic: Scientific and Ethical Perspectives on Social Process*. New York: Macmillan.

Suggested Reading

Bonhoeffer, D. (1998). *Sanctorum Communio: A Theological Study of the Sociology of the Church*. Minneapolis: Augsburg Fortress.

Haight, R. (1987). 'Historical Ecclesiology: An Essay on Method in the Study of the Church'. *Science et Esprit* 39: 345–74.

Komonchak, J. (1995). *Foundations in Ecclesiology*. Boston: Boston College.

Ormerod, N. (2005). 'A Dialectic Engagement with the Social Sciences in an Ecclesiological Context'. *Theological Studies* 66: 815–40.

Ormerod, N. (2009). 'Ecclesiology and the Social Sciences'. In G. Mannion and L. Mudge (eds), *The Routledge Companion to the Christian Church*. New York: Routledge.

Ormerod, N. (2014). *Re-Visioning the Church: An Experiment in Systematic-Historical Ecclesiology*. Minneapolis: Fortress Press.

Roberts, R. H. (2002). *Religion, Theology, and the Human Sciences*. Cambridge: Cambridge University Press.

CHAPTER 26

LIBERATION ECCLESIOLOGIES WITH SPECIAL REFERENCE TO LATIN AMERICA

MICHELLE A. GONZALEZ

To speak of contemporary ecclesiology is to speak of the current issues that shape Christian understandings of the church, as well as the challenges that it faces in the contemporary globalized world. Ecclesiology is always grounded in the New Testament witness of the first Christians as well as the historical events and theological developments that shaped the historical church. However, contemporary Christians and theologians read the history and the New Testament witness through the eyes of the modern church (and for Roman Catholics, through the eyes of Vatican II). This reading is also shaped by critical theory, literary analysis, the social sciences, and an awareness of power that defines these documentary and historical witnesses. While knowledge of the diverse ways that Christian churches have understood themselves historically informs contemporary ecclesiologies, overwhelmingly theologians today begin with the contemporary world and the manner in which the issues raised by this context shape ecclesial self-understandings.

Within these analyses of contemporary Christian churches there is increasing recognition that modern Christian academic theology has an unhealthy emphasis on Euro-American communities in North American and European churches. Christian theologians overwhelmingly emerge from these regions and backgrounds and their insights on the church are shaped by their context. This gives a false impression of the contemporary globalized church that finds its centres more likely in Latin America and Africa than in Europe and in the United States more likely among Latino/as than Euro-Americans. In addition to this regional and racial-ethnic bias, for decades US minority and Third World theologians have offered a methodological shift in the manner in which theology should be construed broadly and ecclesiology in particular. Many of the contributions by these academics fall under the heading of liberation theology.

LIBERATION THEOLOGIES

Liberation theologians offer a new way of being the church, one that they root in the gospel message, where the church should be part of both denouncing and transforming unjust social structures. Liberation theologians argue that these movements are rooted in grass-roots churches. Liberation theologies emerge from the underside of history and argue that the oppressed and the marginalized must be the starting point and centre of theological reflection. They offer a methodological and epistemological shift within theology. Theology has a new interlocutor, the non-person. As Peruvian liberation theologian Gustavo Gutiérrez passionately argues:

> What we have said from the very beginning—and it is being more and more accepted today—is that the theology of liberation has a different 'interlocutor' from other contemporary theologies, be they Catholic or Protestant, 'postconciliar' or 'progressive.' The best thing about these later theologies is their attempt to deal seriously with the challenges of the modern spirit and liberal ideology . . . 'Progressive' theology seeks to answer the questions of the *nonbeliever*; liberation theology confront the challenge of the *nonperson*. The spirit of modernity, typically skeptical, or even frankly nonbelieving, where religion is concerned, calls the faith into question by challenging the meaning of religion for human life . . . To be sure, when we say 'nonperson' or 'nonhuman being', we are not using these terms in an ontological sense. We do not mean that the interlocutor of liberation is actually a nonentity. We are using this term to denote those human beings who are considered less than human by society, because that society is based on privileges arrogated by a minority. (Gutiérrez 1993: 91–2)

Liberation theologies have dramatically challenged Christian churches' self-understandings. 'The church, by representing the values of the kingdom of God, subverts institutions which hold human freedom and dignity captive; the church is dedicated to liberation where and in the exact measure that social institutions suppress human freedom from flourishing' (Haight 2005: 413). This chapter examines the contribution of liberation theologies to contemporary ecclesiologies through an examination of Latin American liberation theologies. This emphasis on Latin America is not to detract from the strong impact of other liberation ecclesiologies, rather serving as an entry point into a broader movement within academic theologies and churches.

Perhaps the most recognized of all liberationist discourses is Latin American liberation theology. This is due, in great part, to two factors: the involvement and consequent martyrdom of clergy, women religious, and catechists in the face of the unjust treatment of the Latin American poor and the Vatican's consistent vilification of the pastoral and academic incarnations of this theology. In addition to its widespread notoriety,

Latin American liberation theology is significant for the development of both Black and Latino/a theologies in the United States. Black theologians have remained in constant dialogue and debate with their Latin American colleagues since the 1970s, primarily through the Ecumenical Association of Third World Theologians (EATWOT). The EATWOT was founded in 1976 to continue the development of Third World theologies. The first meeting was held when twenty-one theologians gathered in Dar es Salaam in August 1976 for an ecumenical dialogue. EATWOT is committed to fostering new theological models and emphasizes the irrelevance of Western European theology in their contexts. Third World, in EATWOT, is understood not as a geographical reality but instead as a quality of life or social condition; thus US minorities are included in EATWOT. EATWOT theologians do theology from the vantage point of the poor and oppressed. EATWOT publications abound and demonstrate the level of dialogue that occurs between the various liberation theologies represented in this organization.

Latin American liberation theology speaks of God's manifestation in the victims of history. More specifically, this theology is characterized by reflection on God's grace and action amongst the poor in history. As defined by Gustavo Gutiérrez, in his monumental work *A Theology of Liberation*, for the Latin American liberation theologian, theology is 'critical reflection on Christian praxis in the light of the Word' (Gutiérrez 1988b: 11). This definition highlights the critical and praxiological emphasis of the theological task. With its emphasis on the poor, Latin American liberation theology offers a revolutionary shift in theological method, radically departing from the traditional interlocutor of contemporary theologies. Within the institutional Roman Catholic Church, the conferences of Latin American bishops both at Medellín (1968) and at Puebla (1979) are significant moments in the development of Latin American liberation theology, where the institutional church articulated a commitment to the struggles of the poor.

The poor and marginalized challenge dominant understandings of church today, 'Beyond this they feel that general descriptions of "the church today" exclude their own experience. They expect therefore that more attention will be given to their economic, political, social, cultural, and religious experiences. Their spokespersons reject an abstract conceptualization of God made outside their own historical struggle for liberation' (Fahey 1991: 11). Pluralism and an awareness of the globalized church marks ecclesiology today. The ecumenical movement also marks contemporary churches with the establishment of the World Council of Churches (1948) and EATWOT.

Latin American liberationist ecclesiologies began among Roman Catholic scholars who were profoundly impacted by the Vatican II Council in the 1960s. Vatican II had many significant insights that shifted the manner in which theology is approached and written. In the case of ecclesiology, three are of special note. Vatican II emphasized the fullness of the local church as the church of Christ (not just part of a whole). The council empowered local churches and local theologians to understand their churches as part of the sacramental life of the church. Second, Vatican II taught that 'The church exists for the world' (Haight 2005: 398). This call to engage the modern context and address the pressing issues of our time led many Latin American liberation theologians and church leaders to engage the overwhelming poverty and injustice of the region. Third, Vatican II presented an ecclesiology of the church as the people of God. This will become a recurrent theme within liberation theologies, examining the contributions of the laity at the grass-roots level.

Liberation ecclesiologies examine a variety of topics that are shaped by their contexts. African liberation ecclesiologies emphasize the need to construct an African church that is inculturated as authentically African. African liberation theologies recognize the legacy of European colonialism on the continent and the religious pluralism and diversity of the African context. In some sectors, SCCs (small Christian communities) created a space for the involvement and engagement of grass-roots Christians to the life of the church. Among Asian liberation theologians the diversity of the Asian context does not allow for a set Asian ecclesiology. Issues of inculturation and injustice mark their theological writings. In the United States, minority theologians raise issues of culture, race, poverty, and justice in their theological writings. All of these ecclesiologies share in their critique of the manner in which academic theology has offered a narrow and de-historicized vision of the church, arguing for an alternative vision that takes the concrete church in all its diversity seriously.

This historical consciousness leads to a variety of issues that are discussed within liberation theologies. They all share in an ecclesiological principle of the preferential option for the marginalized, though the manner in which the marginalized are described can vary from region to region. For some an emphasis on economic injustice prevails, while for others issues of colonialism, racism, and ethnocentrism dominate. For feminist theologians across the globe the category of gender becomes a central theme. Feminist theology is a truly global liberation theology, found in every region and throughout the diversity of Christian churches. Feminist theologians raise the historical marginalization of women in Christianity, the manner in which patriarchy has distorted the Christian message, and offer a new vision of Christianity informed by their critical analysis.

While liberation theologians highlight the concrete particularity of their local churches, they argue that this does not undermine the unity of Christianity. Instead, they argue, one can have unity within diversity. Homogeneity does not create unity. Instead, it is through the recognition of the diversity of Christianity that one has to enter into its unity. Linked to this are the themes of inculturation, globalization, and interdependence. It is in the spirit of this unity in diversity that we enter into one particular liberation theology, Latin American, in order to explore its ecclesiological contributions. The section 'Contact and Conquest' offers a brief overview of Latin American Christianity. This is followed by a thematic analysis of the major contributions of Latin American liberation theology. The chapter concludes with an analysis of the future of liberation theologies within Christianity today.

CONTACT AND CONQUEST

The world that the Spanish, French, and Portuguese encountered through Central America, South America, and the Caribbean varied tremendously based on geographic region. Whether it was the tribal society of the Taínos in the Caribbean or the extensive empire of the Aztecs, Europeans encountered religious worldviews in the Americas that varied dramatically from their Christian sensibilities. In some respects indigenous religions are not religious in the traditional sense of the word; many are non-hierarchical, and religion permeated their lives in manners that contemporary definitions of religion in the academy do not address. The contemporary distinction between the sacred and the profane is not operative. Indigenous religions are marked by themes of reciprocity and mutual dependence between humans, the divine, and the natural world.

In spite of the bloody battles between the Aztecs and the Spanish or the virtual extinction of the indigenous due to forced labour and disease in the Caribbean, indigenous religions and populations continue to leave their mark on the Latin American religious landscape. Indigenous rituals and imagery have come to shape Christianity throughout Latin America. This is perhaps most clearly seen in devotion to Our Lady of Guadalupe, the patroness of the Americas. Our Lady of Guadalupe appeared in 1531 on the mountain of Tepeyac to the indigenous man Juan Diego. Juan Diego, a convert to Christianity, was walking to mass early on a Saturday morning when he heard some beautiful music. He then heard a voice calling him. He walked up the hillside, drawn to the voice. At the top of the hill, he encountered a beautiful lady, radiant with love and compassion. She identified herself as the Mother of God, mother of creation, who had come in response to the cries of those in the Americas who called to her in their suffering. She then ordered Juan Diego to go to the bishop to request that a shrine be built in her honour on the site of her apparition. Juan Diego protests, claiming he is a nothing, unworthy of the bishop's attention or this important message. Guadalupe assures him that he is the one chosen for this task. The bishop, as Juan Diego predicted, does not believe him, and the next day he returns and reports his failure to her. She sends him back to the bishop, who remains unconvinced and demands a sign as proof.

Juan Diego tries to avoid encountering Guadalupe again. He has failed in his task and his uncle is also very ill. However, he cannot avoid her. Guadalupe assures him that his uncle will be healed, and then instructs Juan Diego to go gather roses on the hillside as proof of her apparition. Since this is winter in the desert, these flowers truly are a miracle. Juan Diego gathers the flowers in his cloak and goes to the bishop. The bishop's servants recognize Juan Diego from his earlier visit and attempt to block his entry. However, the intoxicating smell of the roses convinces them to allow Juan Diego to enter and see the bishop. In order to present the flowers to him, Juan Diego opens his cloak and as the flowers fall to the floor the image of Guadalupe miraculously appears on his cloak. This is the image that hangs in her basilica outside Mexico City.

The narrative of Guadalupe's apparition raises various important themes that are fundamental for understanding the Latin American church. In the narrative, she appears to Juan Diego, a self-proclaimed 'lowly' indigenous man who sees little worth in himself. This apparition occurred during the bloodiest moment in Mexican history, the conquest. In the midst of the bloodshed and trauma of an indigenous community that is having its entire universe overturned, there is a story about Mary's preferential option for the marginalized. Surely if Guadalupe wanted her shrine built immediately, the most efficient and appropriate means to communicate this would have been to appear before the bishop. He is, after all, the one who has official authority in transmitting the gospel. However, in this story Guadalupe empowers Juan Diego with the gospel message. It is he, the indigenous man, who brings Mary's message of love to the bishop. In a moment when the Catholic Church is imposing the forced conversion of thousands of indigenous men, women, and children, we find an indigenous man converting the bishop to Mary's message. He becomes the bearer of the gospel. In 1999 John Paul II named her patroness of the Americas in his apostolic exhortation *Ecclesia in America*. Her significance does not allow the indigenous of the continent to be forgotten.

COLONIAL PERIOD

One cannot separate the conquest of the Americas from Christian evangelization. 'The spread of Christianity was a major feature of Spanish imperial policy for legitimizing its empire' (Schwaller 2009: 51). A primary goal of Columbus' voyages was to convert the people of the New World to Catholicism, spreading the church's power and geographic scope. The church served as spiritual and intellectual arm of the Conquest. This evangelization must be contextualized in light of the Reconquista and the Reformation. The church saw its evangelization efforts in the Americas as connected to their combating of Protestantism, Judaism, and Islam in Europe.

The first Franciscan missionaries arrived in 1524 beginning the wave of clergy members whose goal was conversion of the natives. The clergy first learned the native languages and then set upon the task of translating Christian doctrine into their language. A significant figure in this endeavour was Bernardino de Sahagún. It was his belief that the conversion of the indigenous would be facilitated by learning their languages and customs. His twelve-volume *Florentine Codex* was an encyclopedia of Nahua culture. His work was critiqued for it was interpreted as undermining evangelization by preserving native cultures. Sahagún and the controversies surrounding his work demonstrate the tensions within Christianity as it attempted to spread its message to native people in a manner that was translatable to them yet at the same time wanting to eliminate traces of indigenous religious worldviews.

In spite of Spanish efforts to eliminate indigenous religions, their rites and practices were inculturated into Christian practices. 'The diversity in local ways of embracing and accommodating Christian practices led to a hybrid set of religious practices that could be termed "indigenous Christianities"' (Tavárez and Chuchiak 2009: 78). In addition, it is important to understand that the Catholicism that came to the Americas was syncretic, influenced by the presence of Judaism and Islam on the Iberian peninsula. The Catholicism that came to the Americas was a folk Catholicism marked by devotion to saints and Mary, processions, and medieval passion plays.

Throughout the colonial period Catholicism dominated the religious life of Latin America. Roman Catholicism was the official religion. Refusal to adhere to Catholicism led to punishment, the Inquisition. This period is also marked by hybridization. The issue of the conversion of the indigenous became a contentious issue during the infamous Valladolid debate. In 1550 King Carlos V of Spain arranged a debate between Bartalomé de las Casas, who argued that indigenous people had souls and should be converted to Christianity peacefully, and Juan Ginés de Sepúlveda, who argued for the forced conversion of natives. There was no definitive conclusion to this debate. Las Casas, known as the great liberator of the indigenous, was extremely critical of the *encomienda* system throughout the Spanish colonies. This system of cheap labour gave the conquistador control over the native populations by requiring them to pay tribute from their lands. The natives often rendered personal services as well. In return the grantee was theoretically obligated to protect his wards, to instruct them in the Christian faith, and to defend their right to use the land for their own subsistence. This rarely happened. Las Casas was sickened by the unjust deaths of the Indians in Hispaniola and also during the evangelization in Cuba. He came to dedicate his priesthood to the liberation of the Indians. He believed that Jesus came to save all humanity, and this included the indigenous. His ambiguous position on slavery makes him a controversial figure in Latin American history, though he later recanted his support of the transatlantic slave trade.

Yet the indigenous are not the sole community that suffered at the hands of European colonizers. As the indigenous population dwindled the Spanish turned their eyes to Africa for a source of labour. The transatlantic slave trade resulted in the suffering and death of millions of Africans both on the continent and during the horrific Middle Passage across the Atlantic. Slaves were forced to convert to Christianity and were subject to brutal conditions. Yet the waters of Christian baptism did not erase the beliefs and practices of African populations in the Americas, who maintained their religious beliefs and rituals in secret, often masking them behind the imagery of Roman Catholicism. In addition, slaves did not receive the same missionary attention as the indigenous. 'Evangelization of enslaved Africans was not a priority of the Catholic Church in Spain and Spanish America. . . . Africans played almost no role in the Spanish theory of American empire, although in practice, African labor, religion, and culture shaped both Spanish and Portuguese holdings in the Americas' (Von Germeten and Villa-Flores 2009: 85). Missionaries were primarily focused on converting the indigenous. Notable exceptions exist, for example Peter Claver's (1581–1654) missionary work in Cartagena. He is said to have converted 300,000 Africans.

The colonial church also created spaces, albeit unknowingly, for the preservation of African religious traditions. During the early and mid-nineteenth century, no institution plays a stronger role in the preservation of African religion, culture, and language in Cuba, for example, than the *cabildos*. The urban population of slaves, some of whom were able to buy their freedom, was able to gather in *cabildos*. These brotherhoods of Africans date to as early as 1598 (Nuestra Señora de los Remedios in Havana). Their predecessors are the Andulasian brotherhoods known as *cofradías*. Cuban ethnographer Fernando Ortiz traces the formation of *cabildos* of Africans to the fourteenth century in Seville, long before the conquest of the Americas. It is this structure that the Spanish bring to the Americas. In Andalusia, the term *cabildo* often referred to a religious brotherhood; throughout the rest of Spain it referred to a city council (Ortiz 1992: 4). *Cabildos* were associations of Africans (men and women) from the same tribe in a city, a representative body of a particular nation. They were social societies and were very active on religious feast days (Ortiz 1992: 1). In Havana they were also known as *reinados*, for during festivals one woman was made queen of the *cabildo*. The elder of the community was known as the king of the *cabildo*. 'Although cabildos often restricted participation in their associations along ethnic lines, they also recognized commonalities with larger cultural groups common to areas of the slave trade.' Some groups recognized their larger cultural association, yet divided their cabildos along ethnic lines (Childs 2006: 221). Depending on if you were *mulatto* or Cuban-born you might be excluded from *cabildo* membership. In this lengthy quote Philip A. Howard highlights the role of the *cabildo* within the Afro-Cuban community.

> After arriving in Cuba, Africans, particularly those in the principal cities and towns of the island, established mutual aid societies known as *cabildos de naciones de afrocubanos*. As early as the middle of the sixteenth century, these voluntary associations were created in order to mitigate the psychological and cultural shock of transplantation from the familiar context of traditional African societies to the uncertainties of life in the Americas as slave laborers. In the countryside, plantation owners with government approval, even permitted their slaves to gather on days of rest or holidays to allay their sense of alienation. These reunions were spontaneous affairs without structure, however, and consisted only of recreational activities. But in the towns and cities of the island, individuals who spoke to the same or related languages—such as Yoruba, Mandinga, Arará, and Carabalí—came to form and employ their mutual aid societies to promote the maintenance of African languages, customs, and heritage. The associations also provided assistance to sick members and assured them a decent funeral and burial when they died. Thus, these language- and group-based associations not only provided a sense of community to members and cushioned them from the blow of cultural dislocation, but they also provided a forum for the transmission of African cultures in Cuba. (Howard 1998: xii–xiv)

Cabildos were not directly connected to the Catholic Church and were instead headquartered in members' households. This distance from the institutional church allowed members to enjoy more freedoms, including using the *cabildo* as a site for political resistance. While women did not have leadership roles in *cabildos* they did participate in their activities (including ceremonial roles). 'It was the cabildos rather than the parish churches which were the principal organizations for the religious life of urban Afro-Cubans up until the twentieth century. . . . Not much is known now about the internal organization of the cabildos beyond the fact that membership was by election and that the cabildos each elected a person called *el rey* (the king) or *capataz* (boss or overseer) who mediated between the cabildo and both the church and the police. . . . By the nineteenth century at least fourteen African nations had their own cabildos' (Brandon 1993: 71). *Cabildos* thus play a central role in the preservation of African culture, religion, and identity.

Perhaps two figures that best summarize the colonial church in Latin America are St Martín de Porres and Sor Juana Inés de la Cruz. St Martín (1579–1639) was born in Lima, Peru. His father, Don Juan de Porres, was Spanish, and his mother, Ana Velázquez, was a freed black slave. His father, while not acknowledging his son (thus rendering him illegitimate), set him up with an apprenticeship with barber Dr Marcelo de Ribero of Lima. Martín learned the medical arts and at the age of 11 became a *donado* (a lay helper who received room and board) with the Dominican friars in the Convento del Santo Rosario. In 1603, against social convention, he became a lay brother. St Martín became known for his healing powers and his work with marginalized peoples. In addition he was recognized for his social work among widows, orphans, and prostitutes; his founding of hospitals and orphanages; his work with the indigenous, blacks, mestizos, and mulatto poor of the city; and for his love of animals. Throughout his lifetime he established an orphanage, a children's hospital, and an animal shelter. For many he is known as the 'St Francis of the Americas'. In spite of his recognition, it took the Roman Catholic Church over 300 years to recognize him as a saint. He was the first bi-racial saint to be canonized in 1962. St Martín's life and ministry is indicative of the ambiguity of racial identity in the institutional church, yet also shows us that ministry was not exclusive to the ecclesial elites. In addition, he reminds us that solidarity with the marginalized was present within the colonial church and is not a twentieth-century interpretation of Christianity.

Sor Juana Inés de la Cruz is a compelling seventeenth-century Mexican figure. Scholars who study her religious writings consider her to be the first female theologian of the Americas. Her poetry and dramas offer a theological voice through the medium of literature. Juana Ramirez de Asbaje y Santillana was born in the town of Nepantla, Mexico, between 1648 and 1651. The daughter of unwed parents, her mother was a *criolla* (American of Spanish descent) and her father a Spanish military officer. Around the age of 13 Sor Juana went to live in the court of the viceroy of New Spain (colonial Mexico) as a lady-in-waiting. She stayed there for three years. In 1667 she entered into the ascetic, cloistered Order of Discalced Carmelites, which she left after a short time. Two years later she joined the order of the Hieronymites.

Sor Juana was an avid reader, primarily self-taught, and by her mid-teens was recognized as the most erudite woman in Mexico. Her reputation as a scholar was a crucial factor in her gaining a position in the viceregal court. Her desire for a life of scholarship and study was perhaps a significant factor in her decision to enter cloistered life. Sor Juana hesitated to take the veil, fearing that life there would impede her studies. Sor Juana is not the only woman to enter into convent life in colonial Latin America. Nor is she the only woman writing. However, the intellectual astuteness of her corpus sets her apart from other cloistered women in her era.

After enjoying a very public life as a writer and intellectual, in 1690 Sor Juana's situation took a dramatic turn. In this year Sor Juana's critique of a male theologian's analysis of Christ's greatest demonstration of love entitled *La Carta Atenagorica* was circulated without her authorization. Accompanying her critique was a letter written under the pseudonym Sor Filotea criticizing Sor Juana's intellectual pursuits. Her response to that publication, *La Respuesta*, an autobiographical defence of women's right to intellectual pursuits, was completed the following year. Within four years of the production of *La Respuesta*, Sor Juana renounced her public life. Two years after her renunciation, Sor Juana died from an illness she contracted while caring for the sick in her convent.

All three volumes of Sor Juana's works were published in Madrid between the years 1689 and 1700. Her writings incorporate an eclectic mixture of colonial Mexican philosophy and theology, including Thomism, Neoplatonism, and Hermeticism. A child of the Americas, Sor Juana incorporates indigenous and African sources and voices throughout her corpus. One of her most significant contributions to Christian theology is her defence of indigenous peoples and her understanding of indigenous religions as prefigurations of Christianity. Sor Juana's life and struggles are indiciative of a church that sought to control the intellectual life of Latin American society and was threatened by the prominence of a female intellectual. When independence movements begin to burgeon in the eighteenth century, the Roman Catholic Church will have new challenges to face as it confronts its role historically as the religious arm of colonialism.

INDEPENDENCE PERIOD

The formation of nation states in Latin America spans the nineteenth century. Once independence from Spain was gained many nations removed the privileged status of Roman Catholicism as the official religion. The church was connected to Spanish colonialism and had sided with Spain in struggles for independence. For newly independent nations there was a wariness of this legacy. This weakened the institution of the church and led to greater diversity within Catholicism and also the religious landscape of Latin America as a whole. Anticlericalism was a widespread phenomenon in post-independence Latin America. It should be noted that a shortage of clerics has always marked the Roman Catholic Church in the region, and in this era it becomes more pronounced. The church was seen as an obstacle to progress and democracy. Tensions are high between *criollos* (born in Latin America, though of European descent) and *peninsulares* (European-born residents of the Americas). Latin American liberal *criollos* saw Protestantism as a means to open up society. The independence period is marked by the Roman Catholic Church's isolation in Latin American societies as well as the introduction of Protestant churches.

During the colonial period non-Catholic immigrants were banned from the Spanish and Portuguese colonies, though this was far from effective. 'Most of these non-Catholics did not practice their religions openly, however, and many lived as "new Christians," or *conversos*, for fear of the Inquisition and other penalties' (Peterson and Vásquez 2008: 159). Protestants became allies in a sense and an alternative to the royalist Catholic Church and also emphasized democratic values that were sympathetic to independence movements. Immigration was a key factor in the arrival of Protestantism in Latin America, though this was quickly followed by intentional evangelization efforts.

With the arrival of Protestant missionaries in the late nineteenth and early twentieth centuries came the arrival or Protestant schools, missions, and clinics. Nonetheless, it is not until the mid-twentieth century that Protestantantism becomes a rooted presence in Latin America. The infrastructure that Protestants provided did not at first lead to evangelization. In the mid-twentieth century mainline US churches established national mission boards, making these national churches autonomous (Garrard-Burnett 2009: 193). This leads to the secure establishment of Protestantism throughout the region.

Independence did not give power to all the inhabitants of the region. A *criollo* elite comes to control these newly independent nations. Nonetheless, blacks and indigenous people struggle to claim the space and preserve their identities. African Diaspora religions are able to acquire a more public role in culture and society, though with some resistance from the controlling Christian ethos. *Cabildos* slowly transform into worship houses in people's homes. In spite of efforts to maintain the religious practices of these subalterns, they continue to struggle against a dominant Christian ethos.

LATIN AMERICAN LIBERATION ECCLESIOLOGY

Twenty-first-century Christianity in Latin America inherited a legacy of colonial Catholicism that was linked to the oppressive regime of the Spanish empire and its conquest of the Americas. As a result of this history, once Latin American countries gained independence from Spain the church was faced with liberal governments that promoted staunch anticlericalism, and it was forced to align itself with conservative factions in the nineteenth and early twentieth centuries. Also of note is the historical lack of indigenous clergy within Latin American countries, whose priests and women religious were predominantly foreign-born. In addition, a shortage of priests throughout Latin America led to a population that was well schooled in popular Catholicism and religiosity yet was not thoroughly instructed in dogmatic theological teachings. A distinctive Latin American Catholicism emerged, constituted by a mixture of indigenous and African religions with Catholic elements that was due, in part, to the lack of a strong clerical presence. The nature of the Catholic Church's presence as a dominant religious and political force, coupled with the absence of the ecclesial church in the daily lives of many Latin Americans, also left fertile ground for the growth of Protestantism.

Roman Catholic lay movements were born in Latin America in the early twentieth century. Their purpose was threefold: to defend Catholicism in the face of anti-Catholic governments, to encourage Catholic culture, and to promote social justice. Movements such as Catholic Action emerged from an apologetic Catholicism with an eye towards promoting Catholic social teachings. Catholic Action sought to promote lay leadership in the church globally and was very active in Latin America. The intention was for lay people to influence the secular realm with Catholic values. Catholic Action utilized a 'see-judge-act' methodology that encouraged adherents to describe the world around them, assess this in light of Catholic principles, and respond with concrete action. Catholic Action was an essential dimension of twentieth-century Latin American Catholicism.

Perhaps no other dimension of the Latin American church in the twentieth century is better known than Base Christian Communities. The birth of Base Christian Communities (or BCCs) may be traced to 1963 when North American priest Leo Mahon led a group of priests from Chicago to Panama City to run an adult ministry programme. This became a focal point for BCCs and hundreds of clergy, women religious, and laity came to explore and model this community effort. The 'base' of base Christian communities refers to both the socio-economic and internal structure of BCCs (Levine 1992: 10). BCCs are also referred to as CEBs (*comunidades eclesiales de base*). They are small religious groups typically consisting of friends and neighbours; most often they were initiated by members of the institutional church (priests, lay leaders). BCCs combine religiosity such as Bible study and prayer with community activism. While many understand these communities as entirely geared towards leftist political activism, the theological and political bent of base communities varies significantly (Levine 1992: 13). They also vary dramatically in light of the parish structure and priest with which they coexist.

BCCs represent a new experience of the church and of community. They are a lay movement that emerged, in part, from a shortage of clergy in Latin America. This is a key point: BCCs are not distinct from the institutional church but instead a natural development within it. 'We are not dealing with the expansion of an existing ecclesial system, rotating on a sacramental, clerical axis, but with the emergence of another form of being church, rotating on the axis of the word and the laity' (Boff 1986: 2) Base communities are not rival churches. Members of these communities have not left the church. They emphasize the gospel, liberation and conscientization, de-clericalization, and a preferential option for the poor. Part of the appeal and success of BCCs is that due to their small size these communities have a stronger spirit of communitarianism and a lack of institutionalization. Institutionalization, in fact, would lead to the death of the communitarian spirit. For BCCs church is not limited to the institutionalized mass but occurs when the community gathers in discipleship to celebrate Jesus Christ. BCCs constitute church despite the absence of clergy and Eucharist within them. 'It is not that this absence is not felt, is not painful. It is, rather, that these ministers do not exist in sufficient numbers. The historical situation does not cause the church to disappear. The church abides in the people of God as they continue to come together, convoked by the word and discipleship of Jesus Christ. Something *is* new under the sun: the new church of Christ' (Boff 1986: 13). BCCs, however, are not in conflict or competition with the institutional church. The communitarian aspect of BCCs is instead a source of institutional renewal. The two, communitarian and institutional, must coexist together. Ultimately, liberation theologians argue, BCCs represent the true church of the poor. 'Thus, we are no longer speaking of the Church *for* the poor but rather a Church *of* and *with* the poor' (Boff 1985: 10) The grass-roots nature of BCCs as the church of the masses reveals them as constituted by and in solidarity with poor Latin Americans.

The contributions of BCCs are significant, albeit at times saturated with a romanticization and idealization that perhaps led to their downfall in academic circles. This is seem both in the description of the base communities themselves and the exaggeration of their numbers. Also, not all scholarship on BCCs paints the extensive and favourable picture given by most liberation theologians. While early liberation theologians depicted BCCs in a utopian manner, social scientists have painted a different picture. 'To begin with, in contrast to liberationism, the authors of the new social science research generally interpreted the CEBs not as simple carriers of popular aspirations but as products of institutional church initiative—as oriented to social change but in ways sanctioned by the official goals of the church' (Hewitt 1998: 174). In other words, BCCs were much more intimately linked to the institutional church than many liberation theologians implied. The widespread nature of BCCs has been contested, with some studies stating that both liberation theology and BCCs affected less than 5 per cent of the Catholic population in Latin America. Their presence, success, and/or failure must be studied at the regional level, for the influence varied significantly depending on country and region.

One cannot understand the rise of Latin American liberation theology without noting the impact of Medellín (1968) and Puebla (1979). Vatican II called the church to engage the modern world. Medellín took this impulse to interpret the world through a sociological framework. It interpreted the church as the church of the poor, where the church of the poor is a sign of the kingdom of God and the church must be at the service of the kingdom of God. The meetings also promoted the notion of the church as the sacrament of liberation within human history as salvation history.

Perhaps no other thinker has shaped the foundational call for transformation that marks Latin American liberation ecclesiologies more than Peruvian-born priest Gustavo Gutiérrez, who calls for 'A radical revision of what the Church has been and what it now is has become necessary'(Gutiérrez 1988b: 141). Gutiérrez traces the impulse behind this renovation to the council, though he argues that in Latin America it has now taken on a life of its own. This calls for a new ecclesial consciousness that is not only in the world but part of the world. 'As a sign of the liberation of humankind and history, the Church itself ought to be a place of liberation' (Gutiérrez 1988b: 147). The work of the church must focus on the salvation history here in human history, yet salvific action cannot be reduced exclusively to the church.

Gutiérrez and other liberation theologians emphasize the image of the church as sacrament emerging from Vatican II. 'In the sacrament the salvific plan is fulfilled and revealed; that is, it is made present among humans and for humans. But at the same time, it is through the sacrament that humans encounter God. This is an encounter *in* history, not because God comes *from* history, but because history comes from God' (Gutiérrez 1988b: 146). The church must exist for others, not for its own self-preservation. It must focus on service not survival. The fellowship of the Eucharist demands fellowship and denounces exploitation. Without a commitment to the struggle against oppression and marginalization the Eucharist is empty. 'Within this framework the Latin American Church must make the prophetic *denunciation* of every dehumanizing situation, which is contrary to fellowship, justice, and liberty. At the same time it must criticize every sacralization of oppressive structures which the Church itself might have contributed' (Gutiérrez 1988b: 152). The church must be critical of the contemporary social order, and as part of this order must also be self-critical. For Latin American liberation theologians the church is a sacrament of liberation, of the liberation of the community, not just the individual. It is a salvation that must be realized in the here and now in concrete social transformation. The church must emerge from, be an advocate for, and make an option for the oppressed. The church is just a sacrament, however, and cannot be equated with the kingdom of God.

Latin American liberation ecclesiologies call for a renewal of the church, arguing that the emphasis on the poor is not new to the self-understanding of the church. Liberation ecclesiologists argue that, 'For the first time in history, since this is what our epoch requires, the church has addressed the challenge of identifying with the poor and of walking with them along the road to liberation, to sociohistorical transformation. And this is seen in the privileged way of bringing into history the liberation of the gospel of Jesus' (Quiroz Magaña 1993: 196). Liberation ecclesiologies emerge from the unjust and inhumane situation of the marginalized, and that liberation is part of God's plan. This is grounded in the irruption of the poor that leads to the evangelization by the poor. 'This new model would respond to concrete situations of oppression and to the steps already beginning to be taken in the direction of liberation' (Quiroz Magaña 1993: 199). The prophetic dimension of the gospel calls the church to be the church of the poor.

Latin American liberation theologians also recognize that the history of Christianity in the region cannot be reduced to the institutional church. 'It is clear that as Christianity established itself in Latin America, it was not limited to the official church and its teachings or even to the religious practices and devotions recommended to the laity by the clergy but actually combined in a variety of ways with other religious practices and beliefs' (González and González 2008: 7). For liberation theology the church is the people of God; the church is an event.

Liberation theologians depict Jesus as the Messiah of the poor, marginalized, oppressed, and crucified. Jesus today is incarnate among the poor and marginalized. The church must open itself to the reality of the crucified Christ today, which is best exemplified in the martyrdom of the suffering. 'They are Yahweh's suffering servant, who bears the sin of the world and of the Church. They are the crucified Christ' (Sobrino 2003: 138). The church of the poor is the church in solidarity with the poor committed to make the kingdom of God a reality in the here and now. It is not an alternative to the institutional church but a realization of the true vocation of the church. Liberation theologians also consistently emphasize that liberation is in the here and now, not just in the eschatological future. Such a vision of the church empowers the poor to evangelize the church.

Connected to martyrdom is the image of the poor and suffering as crucified peoples. '*Crucified peoples* is useful and necessary language at the real level of fact, because *cross* means death, and death is what the Latin American people are subjected to in thousands of ways . . . Crucified peoples exist. It is necessary and urgent to see our world this way' (Sobrino 2003: 157). The crucified peoples are the suffering servant today. This is connected to the emphasis on martyrdom in liberationist thought. This is most clearly witnessed in the life and murder of Oscar Romero.

Oscar Romero was born in Ciudad Barrios, San Miguel, El Salvador, on 15 August 1917. He was ordained in Rome on 4 April 1942. In 1967 he was selected Secretary General of the Salvadoran bishops' conference; in 1974 he was appointed bishop of Santiago de María; and in 1977 he was appointed archbishop by Paul VI. Romero was originally conservative and his appointment was anticipated to be a stabilizing force amidst growing conflicts between poor Salvadorans and the oligarchy. He had good relations with the elite class. Romero initially understood the gospel as a message of peace and reconciliation, not social justice and liberation. He interpreted liberationist readings as leading to conflict and threatening church unity, and was troubled by the teachings of Medellín. After being named archbishop, the repression of the rural poor escalated, and Romero was profoundly affected by their suffering.

Romero was confronted with the inability to remain neutral. He was moved to compassion, for he saw the people as a source of grace. He was profoundly impacted by the murder of his friend, the Jesuit Rutilio Grande. Grande had denounced wealthy landowners and defended peasant rights. After Grande's assassination Romero came to see the preferential option for the poor as the defending of life itself. Romero's sympathy towards the poor and oppressed grew, and he began to openly criticize injustice and violence. He saw the church that encompasses the passion of Christ in the passion of oppressed peoples. He was assassinated on 24 March 1980, while saying mass. Archbishop Oscar Romero insisted that the church 'Is one, holy, catholic, and apostolic by union with Christ and its accompaniment of the poor, by its fidelity to the Gospel proclaimed as good news to the poor, by its mission of evangelization to defend the life of the poor and to promote justice, and by the testimony of its martyrs to bear witness to God's love' (Dennis et al. 2001: 46). Romero highlighted that the church was flawed and it never represented these marks in their fullness. The church must therefore convert to the poor as both a vessel of and in need of salvation.

Latin American liberationist ecclesiologies emphasize that the church must be incarnate in the world as it exists today, a world full of injustice and suffering. We must always remember that God is greater than the church. When the church makes an option for the poor it enters into conflict with power structures in this world. The church becomes persecuted. Thus a church on the side of the poor is a church in conflict. 'It must make an option: either service to the God of life and against the idols of death, or the contrary' (Sobrino 1989: 145). Medellín called members of the church to evangelical poverty as a witness to the poverty crippling the Latin American continent.

It is not surprising that given its critical analysis of the church Latin American liberation theology has had a rocky relationship with the Vatican. In 1977 the International Theological Commission published an ambiguous dossier that both celebrated liberation theology yet highlighted a perceived tension in the relationship between salvation history and human works in this theology. In 1984 the Congregation for the Doctrine of the Faith published *Instruction on Certain Aspects of the Theology of Liberation*. This document criticized Latin American liberation theology's use of Marxist social analysis. The two major critiques that emerge from this document are: the use of Marxist ideology and the creation of a popular church outside of the official church (Gibellini 1987: 46). These two critiques surface repeatedly throughout various Christian sectors. The term popular church was dropped by liberationists in response to Vatican pressure and critique.

At the core of Latin American liberation ecclesiologies is the notion that the poor must evangelize the church. The church must arise from the uninvited. 'These downtrodden, marginalized people are the *uninvited*, who are called to the Kingdom. They are called because they are poor, not necessarily because they are good' (Gutiérrez 1988a: 119). The poor and the kingdom of God are connected: God's gratuitous love is revealed in them. As a strong summation of liberation ecclesiologies, Leonardo Boff outlines thirteen characteristics of the church rooted in the oppressed: church as the people of God (people as oppressed class); church of the poor; church of the despoiled; church of the lay people; church as a community of power (not of just one person); Diaspora church (church within society); church of liberation; church that sacramentalizes liberation; church of Tradition (rooted in Jesus and his followers); church in communion with the church (not two churches); church that builds unity; the church as the concrete embodiment of its universality; church as apostolic; church as building new type of holiness (Boff 1988: 122–4). This vision of the church is rooted in the New Testament witness. 'The church is the people of the oppressed which finds in Jesus Christ its hope of full liberation—liberation as true human beings, worthy and free— and it receives from the Holy Spirit the strength and courage to struggle for this liberation. This is the figure of the church that is closest to the biblical teaching and to the manner of the early church' (Comblin 2004: 47). In this sense, Latin American liberation theologians call Christian churches to return to their biblical roots of prophetic denouncement of oppression.

LIBERATION ECCLESIOLOGIES TODAY

Two major trends mark Latin American Christianity in the second half of the twentieth century to the present: the growth of Protestantism and the impact of the Second Vatican Council. The increasing marginalization of the Roman Catholic Church leads to evangelization efforts at the grass-roots level with the heavy involvement of the laity. While academic studies of the explosion of Pentecostalism abound, there has been a strong religious revival in the leadership in the Catholic Church in recent history. Afro-Brazilian Catholicism has seen a growth in 'Inculturated masses' that integrate African elements with Catholicism. Bishop Samuel Ruiz in Chiapas created an extensive programme of indigenous catechists and deacons chosen by the community. Ruiz advocated a new model of evangelization and the rights of the indigenous community and helped broker a ceasefire between the Mexican army and the Zapatistas which led to the San Andrés Accords in 1996. These are but two examples of the growing inculturation of Roman Catholicism throughout the region.

In addition, church membership for Latin Americans is much more fluid than academic scholarship suggests. This is not to downplay the growth of evangelical Protestantism in the region. By the late 1960s Protestant churches were overwhelmingly controlled by local leadership. A local Protestant church began to emerge throughout the region. Today many evangelical churches claim their origins in Latin America. 'Most church growth in Latin America since the 1960s has occurred not in established, historic denominations, but in smaller splinter churches that have minimal or no ties at all to traditional Protestant denominations' (Garrard-Burnett 2009: 197). They are overwhelmingly Pentecostal. 'Nearly 40% of the world's Pentecostals are estimated to live in Latin America. The vast majority of them had been Catholic' (Cleary 2009: 1). Even though not all churches are self-named as Pentecostal, many have been influenced by the worship style and leadership of Pentecostal churches.

Pentecostalism began in rural areas throughout Latin America and then moved to urban centres. Within Pentecostalism there is an emphasis on personal conversion, not political agendas. 'Pentecostals are far more concerned with strengthening their churches and working on the politics of the personal than in transforming society wholesale' (Peterson and Vásquez 2008: 166). Neo-Pentecostalism builds on Pentecostalism with its own distinctive character, for example the prosperity gospel. Today scholars outline five types of Pentecostalism: classical Pentecostalism with denominations such as Assemblies of God; indigenous Pentecostalism not connected to the USA (i.e. the Universal Church of the Kingdom of God founded in Rio de Janeiro and with networks across the world); independent neo-Pentecostal churches often led by charismatic pastors and market driven; Catholic Charismatic Renewal Movement; proto-Charismatic traditions that look Pentecostal but don't identify as Pentecostal (Miller and Yamamori 2007: 26–8). Pentecostalism appeals to the religious impulses found among indigenous and African peoples. It is heavily inculturated. Pentecostalism understands itself as a church where one encounters the Spirit of God, a spirit-filled community grounded in the theology of the early church.

Catholic Charismatic Renewal (CCR) emerged among US university students in 1967 as a response to the increasing secularism. The centre of Charismatic Catholicism is the encounter with the Holy Spirit both individually and in the worshipping body of the church. Charismatic Catholicism maintains that the Spirit can work spontaneously. It is this openness to the workings of the Spirit in ways that might be regarded as 'enthusiastic' as well as mundane that marks out the charismatic spiritual tradition (Cartledge 2007: 19). The roots of the twentieth-century Charismatic movement in Catholicism is found in Pentecostalism, which has come to influence Christianity well beyond the confines of Pentecostal churches.

Concluding Comments

Christianity in Latin America has had a tumultuous history and stands today at a crossroads. The legacy of a colonial church that was the spiritual arm of the crusade continues to haunt its presence throughout the region. Yet liberation theologians offer an alternative Christian narrative. Their ecclesiological vision is one of a church in solidarity with the marginalized, a church that takes the side of the oppressed in a world defined by struggle. Yet this vision of the church is being challenged today by an increasingly diverse religious landscape. 'Religion matters in Latin America. And it matters even more in its increasing and astounding variety. The traditional binary confrontation between the secular state and the Roman Catholic Church is now being displaced by an array of multiple relations among religiosities of assorted theological and ritual configurations' (Rivera-Pagán 2008: 207). This religious pluralism is not only found in the diversity of religious practices throughout the region, but also within Christianity itself.

Academic liberation theology, admittedly, has become increasingly detached from the everyday lives of ecclesial Christians. In addition, the explosion of Pentecostalism in Central and South America, as well as in the Caribbean, offers an alternative ecclesial model contrary to the church of the poor celebrated by liberation theologians which emphasizes political and social engagement. Nonetheless, the notion that the era of liberation theology is past and its effectiveness undermined is untrue. Such critiques emerge from a detached academy that is disconnected from the life of grass-roots communities within the Latin American church.

The growth of evangelical Christianity within Latin America challenges liberation theologians to recast how they understand the faith of the poor. One characteristic of Pentecostalism and Charismatic Catholicism is a stronger emphasis on everyday life and spirituality versus broader social issues. In many ways this creates some core questions for liberation theologians. 'One of the major differences between Liberation Theology and Pentecostalism is that Pentecostalism is saddled with an eschatology that foresees the imminent return of Christ, which militates against long-term social and economic struggle' (Miller and Yamamori 2007: 182). How will liberation theologians' theologies be transformed if they write about Christians who do not see an automatic connection between their faith and broader social structures? Will liberation theologians ignore those Christians and only write about those Christian communities that embody the academic principles of theologians? What kind of Christianity is truly liberative?

Progressive Christianity as a whole is at a crossroads in Latin America. While adherents have managed to spread their programmes and concerns throughout Latin America, they have failed to become strongly institutionalized. New social movements are rising that deal with more contextual, local issues. 'These movements press the state for a decentralization of power and also challenge traditional opposition actors such as trade unions, leftist political parties and the Catholic Church . . . Many new social movements retain strong religious bases, but their affiliations are likely to be diverse, encompassing not only Catholicism but also Pentecostal Protestantism and African-based religions, among others' (Peterson et al. 2001: 5). This move towards more localized social movements is increasingly the new face of religious activism in the region, one which liberation theology must draw from as a resource.

Critiques from within the church and in the academy have led to the premature proclamations of the death of liberation theology. These premature obituaries are based on a misunderstanding of the nature of liberation theology. Liberationist discourse has at times remained alien to the worldview of poor people and has often been paternalistic. In a similar vein, liberation theology's heavy emphasis on social action in contrast to ritual and prayer has been foreign to the religiosity of the poor. This emphasis on the political has been at the expense of valuing daily life. What need to be laid to rest are the inflated hopes for the accomplishments of liberation theology. 'What needs to be buried is not liberation theology itself, but rather the exaggerated expectations and myths surrounding it. Liberation theology has neither created protest and revolution (the myth of the Right), nor does it represent, much less organize, overwhelming popular majorities (the myth of the Left). With expectations of this magnitude, it is no wonder that hopes are disappointed: no one could fill this bill' (Tombs 2001: 128). Linked to the high expectations placed on liberation theologians is unfamiliarity with the diversity and complexity that constitutes Latin American liberationist discourse. In spite of these critiques the core teachings of liberation theologians and their vision of the church remain a challenge for Christians today to define Christian life through the eyes of and in solidarity with the disenfranchised.

References

Boff, Leonardo (1985). *Church: Charism and Power: Liberation Theology and the Institutional Church*. New York: Crossroad.

Boff, Leonardo (1986). *Ecclesiogenesis: The Base Communities Reinvent the Church*. Maryknoll, NY: Orbis Books.

Boff, Leonardo (1988). 'Theological Characteristics of a Grassroots Church'. In Sergio Torres and John Eagleson (eds), *The Challenge of Basic Christian Communities*. Maryknoll, NY: Orbis Books, 124–44.

Brandon, George (1993). *Santería from Africa to the New World: The Dead Sell Memories*. Bloomington, IN: Indiana University Press.

Cartledge, Mark (2007). *Encountering the Spirit: The Charismatic Tradition*. Maryknoll, NY: Orbis Books.

Childs, Matt D. (2006). '"The Defects of Being a Black Creole": The Degrees of African Identity in the Cuban *Cabildos de Nación*, 1790–1820'. In Jane G. Landers and Barry M. Robinson (eds), *Slaves, Subjects, and Subversives: Blacks in Colonial Latin America*. Albuquerque, NM: University of New Mexico Press.

Cleary, Edward (2009). *How Latin America Saved the Soul of the Catholic Church*. New York: Paulist Press, 2009.

Comblin, Jose (1998). *Called for Freedom: The Changing Context of Liberation Theology*. Maryknoll, NY: Orbis Books.

Comblin, Jose (2004). *People Of God*. Maryknoll, NY: Orbis Books.

Dennis, Marie et al. (2001). *Oscar Romero: Reflections on his Life and Writings*. Maryknoll, NY: Orbis Books, 2001.

Fahey, Michael (1991). 'Church'. In Francis Schüssler Fiorenza and John P. Galvin (eds), *Systematic Theology: Roman Catholic Perspectives*. Vol. 2. Minneapolis: Fortress Press.

Garrard-Burnett, Virginia (2009). '"Like a Mighty Rushing Wind": The Growth of Protestantism in Contemporary Latin America'. In Lee M. Penyak and Walter J. Perry (eds), *Religion and Society in Latin America: Interpretive Essays from Conquest to Present*. Maryknoll, NY: Orbis Books.

Gibellini, Rosini (1987). *The Liberation Theology Debate*. Maryknoll, NY: Orbis Books.

González, Ondina and González, Justo (2008). *Christianity in Latin America: A History*. New York: Cambridge University Press.

Gutiérrez, Gustavo (1988a). 'The Irruption of the Poor in Latin America and the Christian Communities of the Common People'. In Sergio Torres and John Eagleson (eds), *The Challenge of Basic Christian Communities*. Maryknoll, NY: Orbis Books.

Gutiérrez, Gustavo (1988b). *A Theology of Liberation: History, Politics, and Salvation*. Maryknoll, NY: Orbis Books.

Gutiérrez, Gustavo (1993). *The Power of the Poor in History*. Maryknoll, NY: Orbis Books.

Haight, Roger D. (2005). *Christian Community in History*, vol. 2: *Comparative Ecclesiology*. New York: Continuum Press.

Hewitt, W. E. (1998). 'From Defenders of the People to Defenders of the Faith: A 1984–1993 Retrospective of CEB Activity in São Paulo'. *Latin American Perspectives* 98: 25.

Howard, Philip E. (1998). *Changing History: Afro-Cuban Cabildos and Societies of Color in the Nineteenth Century*. Baton Rouge, LA: Louisiana State University Press.

Levine, Daniel H. (1992). *Popular Voices in Latin American Catholicism*. Princeton: Princeton University Press.

Miller, Donald E. and Yamamori, Tetsunao (2007). *Global Pentecostalism: The New Face of Christian Social Engagement*. Berkeley: University of California Press.

Ortiz, Fernando (1992; 1921). *Los cabildos y la fiesta afrocubanos del Dia de los Reyes*. Havana: Editorial de Ciencias Sociales.

Peterson, Anna, et al. (2001). *Christianity, Social Change, and Globalization in the Americas*. New Brunswick, NJ: Rutgers University Press.

Peterson, Anna and Vásquez, Manuel A. (2008). *Latin American Religions: Histories and Documents in Context*. New York: New York University Press.

Quiroz Magaña, Alvaro (1993). 'Ecclesiology in the Theology of Liberation'. In Ignacio Ellacuría SJ and Jon Sobrino SJ (eds), *Mysterium Liberationis: Fundamental Concepts of Liberation Theology*. Maryknoll, NY: Orbis.

Rivera-Pagán, Luis N. (2008). 'Pentecostal Transformation in Latin America'. In Mary Farrell Bednarowski (ed.), *Twentieth-Century Global Christianity*. Minneapolis: Fortress Press.

Schwaller, John F. (2009) 'Friars' Accounts of the Native Peoples of the Americas'. In Lee M. Penyak and Walter J. Perry (eds), *Religion and Society in Latin America: Interpretive Essays from Conquest to Present*. Maryknoll, NY: Orbis Books.

Sobrino, Jon (1989). *Spirituality of Liberation: Toward Political Holiness*. Maryknoll, NY: Orbis Books.

Sobrino, Jon (2003). *Witness to the Kingdom: The Martyrs of El Salvador and the Crucified Peoples*. Maryknoll, NY: Orbis Books.

Tavárez, David and Chuchiak, John F. (2009). 'Conversion and the Spiritual Conquest'. In Lee M. Penyak and Walter J. Perry (eds), *Religion and Society in Latin America: Interpretive Essays from Conquest to Present*. Maryknoll, NY: Orbis Books.

Tombs, David (2001). 'Latin American Liberation Theology Faces the Future'. In Michael Hayes (ed.), *Faith in the Millennium*. Sheffield: Sheffield Academic Press.

Von Germeten, Nicole and Villa-Flores, Javier (2009). 'Afro-Latin Americans and Christianity'. In Lee M. Penyak and Walter J. Perry (eds), *Religion and Society in Latin America: Interpretive Essays from Conquest to Present*. Maryknoll, NY: Orbis Books.

SUGGESTED READING

Allacuria, Ignacio and Sobrino, Jon (1993). *Mysterium Liberationis: Fundamental Concepts of Liberation Theology*. Maryknoll, NY: Orbis Books.

Boff, Leonardo and Boff, Clodovis (1987). *Introducing Liberation Theology*. Maryknoll, NY: Orbis Books.

Fabella, Virginia and Torres, Sergio (1983). *Irruption of the Third World: Challenge to Theology*. Maryknoll, NY: Orbis Books, 1983.

Penyak, Lee M. and Perry, Walter J. (2009). *Religion and Society in Latin America: Interpretive Essays from Conquest to Present*. Maryknoll, NY: Orbis Books.

Smith, Christian (1991). *The Emergence of Liberation Theology: Radical Religion*. Chicago: University of Chicago Press.

CHAPTER 27

....

ASIAN ECCLESIOLOGIES

....

SIMON CHAN

THIS chapter focuses mainly on the grass-roots contribution to ecclesiology in Asia. A grass-roots approach assumes that theology arises as much from how being the church is practised as how it is understood. Adopting this approach opens up a fascinating and largely unexplored field (Lian 2010). By contrast, much of ecumenical discussion tends to be confined to what theologians are saying about the church, and over the years what they are saying has become quite predictable. My account of the latter therefore will be brief. The study will draw mostly from South and East Asia as materials from these regions are more readily available. But they exemplify broad patterns found in other regions such as South-East Asia (Poon 2010).

FROM ECUMENICAL
TO GRASS-ROOTS PERSPECTIVES

Ecumenical discussions on ecclesiology in Asia, both Roman Catholic and mainline Protestant, are almost exclusively confined to questions relating to liberation, inculturation, and dialogue (Tagle 2000). This is perhaps best summed up at the First Bishops' Institute for Missionary Apostolate of the (Roman Catholic) Federation of Asian Bishops' Conferences in 1979. It spells out what each of these three concerns entails. Liberation from poverty and oppression calls for the church to be on the side of the poor, not to create 'a confrontation between rich and poor' but to bring 'them together in love, in sharing, in service' (FABC Papers, no. 19: 7). Dialogue is not opposed to evangelization since 'the ideal form of dialogue is also the ideal form of evangelization, for it carries on the dialogue of salvation in which God speaks His word in the world'. Nor does dialogue impugn the uniqueness of Christ since it presupposes the presence of the 'Cosmic Christ in whom the uniqueness of Jesus of Nazareth is fully and finally manifested' (8). Inculturation is not merely an anthropological and sociological matter, but 'a truly theological issue'. It not only 'brings the Good News into the heart of people in the concrete life-situation in which they are' but also 'challenges people to a change of heart' (9). The church engages in liberation and inculturation through a 'triple dialogue' with 'cultures and traditions', 'religions and spiritualities', and 'people in need of liberation from poverty and oppression' (5).

Subsequent papers show that these three concerns continue to occupy the FABC to this day with dialogue as the means to engaging the other concerns. In the early formulation of the church's mission (FABC Papers, no. 69: 5) an intricate balance is sought between the church as what the Second Vatican Council called the 'sacrament of Christ' in *Lumen Gentium* and as 'sacrament of mankind' in *Gaudium et Spes*. This balance appears to have been maintained in the landmark document *Ecclesia in Asia* (John Paul II 1999). But in some subsequent FABC papers the focus seems to have shifted to the latter. One result is a significant shift from the church's universal, hierarchical, and institutional life to 'basic ecclesial communities' or 'the local church' (e.g. FABC Papers, no. 57b) and from an ecclesially centred to a culturally centred mission as seen in the Asian Synod in 1998 (Phan 2002). These shifts are by no means uniform and seem to reflect the theological tensions within the Asian churches.

In mainline Protestantism, the ontological nature of the church as seen in *Lumen Gentium* is almost totally absent. This could be readily borne out by an examination of the documents from the Ecumenical Association of Third World Theologians (EATWOT). What we see is the church defined mostly in functional terms. Further, of the three concerns that define the mission of the church which mainline Protestantism shares with Catholicism, the Asian theologians in EATWOT seem to focus almost exclusively on the liberation motif (Abraham 1990). Even when a subject is Christian spirituality (Fabella, Lee, and Suh 1992) or indigenous peoples, it is understood largely in socio-political terms (EATWOT 2010). In short, the ecumenical perspective on ecclesiology is largely reduced to what the church does in the world. From such a perspective, Tagle's conclusion is hardly surprising: 'Apart from the ecumenical perspectives arising from dialogue between mainline Christian groups, there is not much "ecumenical ecclesiology" in Asia' (Tagle 2000: 76).

One wonders if the paucity of ecumenical reflection on ecclesiology might not be due to an elitist approach which is increasingly recognized to be unsatisfactory because it not only fails to assess grass-roots Christianity on its own terms but also tends to ignore its rich, implicit theologies. For example, studies of popular Christian movements in South-East Asia have shown that they are capable of ingenious ways of inculturation even if they do not theorize about it (Poon 2010: 113–14). This new awareness has resulted in a gradual shift in theological methodology, as seen in minjung theology (Chung, Kim, and Kärkkäinen 2007). Minjung theology originated in Korea and shares similar concerns with liberation theology in Latin America such as the focus on the poor as the victims of structural evils. A number of Pentecostal scholars have questioned the minjung theologians' claim to speak for the people. They argue that the minjung are, in fact, better represented by the Pentecostals, whose implicit theologies are more readily received by ordinary people (Yoo 1988: 206; Yun 2007: 100). The different approaches exemplified by traditional minjung theology and Korean Pentecostalism could be seen in other places as well, such as Latin America (Lehmann 2003: 122–38). The outcome there is similar. As one Latin American theologian admits, 'Liberation theology opted for the poor at the same time that the poor were opting for Pentecostalism' (cited by Miller and Yamamori 2007: 215; FABC Papers, no. 119: 30).

THE CHURCH AND OTHER RELIGIOUS COMMUNITIES

Asia is the continent of the great world religions with their comprehensive visions, integrating the 'cosmic' (this-worldly) and 'metacosmic' (other-worldly) dimensions of existence (Pieris 1988: 74–81). It is hardly surprising, therefore, to find that the major ecclesiological issue revolves around the church's relation to these religions. The problem arising from this relationship is complicated by the fact that Christianity differs significantly from other Asian religions with respect to the nature of religious communities.

In Asia, the primary locus of religious life is the home. In Confucianism, the family 'has always been the centre of Confucian life and ethics'. Even the ruler–subject relationship is modelled after the family (Ching 1978: 96–8). In Hinduism too, much of its ritual expressions occur daily at home. Unlike the church, worship in the Hindu temple is not congregational. Devotees go there only on special occasions such as on the feast day of a particular deity (Parrinder 1961: 47–50) Thus, in Asia, religion blends seamlessly with family and social life. This close relationship reflects the value that Asians place on traditional family structure and corporate life. It also forms a solid substructure of many an Asian church. For example, many urban churches in South-East Asia have developed strong family-friendly ministries both within and outside the church (Poon 2010: 108–10). It also explains why denominational churches in Asia with their inherited beliefs and practices tend to be more conservative than their parent bodies. The gay issue that splits the Anglican Communion is a poignant illustration of this: Global South Anglicans generally see it as a serious challenge to the basic structure of the family.

Beyond the family, Christianity also sees the church as essentially eschatological (*Gaudium et Spes*, n. 45; *Lumen Gentium*, ch. 7). It exists not only as 'the historical community of Christ', but also as 'the eschatological creation of the Spirit' which transcends history and points to the new creation (Moltmann 1977: 33–5). Thus entrance into the new community may at times require severing natural family ties (Matt. 10:34–7; Luke 14:26). This is why the chief marks of the church are baptism, which incorporates one into the new community, and the Eucharist, the eschatological family meal. While early Christians worshipped in homes, their worship enacts a new reality that transcends home and social relations. As Schmemann puts it, the church is formed in the liturgical gathering around word and sacrament which begins with Christians leaving the world to 'go to church' or to 'become church' (1973: 26–7). The new community created by the

Spirit distinguishes itself from the social and familial bonds that have shaped Asian religions for millennia. Frequently it detaches Christians from their kin and loosens familial and social bonds. This does not mean that the church is merely a collectivity of individuals; rather, it brings families within a new network of relationship (Hauerwas 1986). The existence of such a community is both a threat and a promise. For some, chafing under the iron law of karma, it is the promise of a new beginning; for others, it threatens to undo cherished institutions that have been built from time immemorial. Such is the nature of the church. While Christianity's Western trappings may pose a problem for the church in Asia, the greater problem by far is Christianity's eschatological orientation. It explains why Christianity appears so foreign to a world where the (extended) family forms the basic structure of society and where religion is co-opted to support it. The various ecclesiological reconfigurations in Asia are ways of addressing the tension that Christianity's eschatological vision inevitably creates.

In response, some theologians have sought to develop a church with porous boundaries; others, however, believe that precisely because of the challenge posed by another religion, the church needs to present a clear witness to its essential identity. This is well illustrated in the exchanges between M. M. Thomas and Lesslie Newbigin (Thomas and Newbigin 1972). The debate occurred in India in the 1970s, but the issues they raised are still relevant today. Thomas wants to create a church that is part of the larger Hindu community. Thomas's strategy is understandable given the history of Christianity, especially in the colonial period when it was perceived not only as a foreign religion but a tool of imperialism. Thomas argues that there is a 'new humanity' which is larger than the church. There are two places where this new humanity can be found. First, it is found in 'struggles of societies for a secular human fellowship' which goes beyond ideologies.

> There are some struggles in which the men involved have come to realise the frustration of the path of self-righteousness of principle, law and ideology, and are looking for a new path beyond it, and open themselves up to the reality of transcendent forgiveness in the secular experience of mutual forgiveness which makes love and community real at the I–Thou level. (Thomas and Newbigin 1972: 72)

In this secular fellowship, Thomas observes, there may not be 'the full acknowledgement of Christ as Person' but 'a partial but real acknowledgement' (72). The second place where the new humanity is found is in the 'churchless Christianity' represented by people like Keshub Chander Sen and Subba Rao. In these communities, Christ is explicitly acknowledged, but they stop short of identifying themselves with the existing institutional churches through baptism. The problem with churches is that they are perceived as 'socio-political-religious' communities tending towards separation from the larger Hindu community. Thomas is open to the idea of a 'church' of word and sacrament 'linked explicitly and decisively with Jesus but remaining religiously, culturally and socially part of the Hindu community' (74). For Thomas the 'minimum' at which a fellowship can be considered in historic continuity with the church is when it acknowledges 'the centrality of the Person of Jesus Christ for the individual and social life of mankind' (74).

Newbigin, however, questions what we may call Thomas's *docetic* fellowship which is 'explicitly linked to Jesus Christ' yet remaining '"culturally and socially part of the Hindu community"' (Thomas and Newbigin 1972: 78). Historically, Newbigin argues, the church's very existence necessarily involves a break with the socio-cultural-religious element which challenges the lordship of Christ. For Newbigin, the issue is not whether the Christian faith can exist without a community with its 'forms, structures, practices, beliefs' (it cannot); rather, it is whether the community's structures are 'congruous with the Lordship of Jesus Christ' (80). Newbigin believes that if the church is to bear witness in a secular society, it does so not so much as a corporate entity, but by its members being faithful in their witness and suffering in the world. To do so, the church needs to strengthen its religious life through worship, prayer, word, and sacrament. This could only happen by maintaining strong ecclesial communities.

Thomas's second context in which the 'new humanity' is found poses less of a problem than the first. Since Thomas acknowledges that it is still open to further development into the plentitude of Christ, it could be understood as an example of *praeparatio evangelica* (McDermott 2007). The problem is with the first locus of the new humanity, namely, the 'struggles of societies for a secular human fellowship'. Where there is no explicit acknowledgement of Christ, according to Newbigin, it is difficult to see how Thomas could avoid reducing Christ to a christic principle (82). The problem is exacerbated by the fact that Thomas does not sufficiently clarify the substantial difference between the two *loci* with respect to the person of Christ. The first acknowledges Christ only implicitly, while the second does so explicitly.

In his response to Newbigin, Thomas explains his preference for the Christian fellowship remaining within the Hindu religious community: only in this way could the Hindu community be transformed from within. Newbigin, however, questions the viability of such a 'fellowship' as it would require 'disowning the existing churches and starting something wholly new'. One ends up creating another sect. Newbigin's warning of how Thomas's ecclesial programme might end up a century down the road could well be prophetic:

> It would be very easy to envisage—round about the year 2,100 A.D.—a litter of small Indian sects embodying in a fossilised form the particular ideas about secularisation, dialogue, etc., which happen to be fashionable just at the moment, comparable to the litter of American sects which are the fossilised reminders of the living religious ideas of the mid-19th century. (Thomas and Newbigin 1972: 81)

Churchless Christianity

Leaving aside Thomas's idea of the secular fellowship, his proposal of a 'Christ-centred fellowship' deserves further consideration since it constitutes a significant form of Christian expression in India and elsewhere commonly known as 'churchless Christianity'. The phrase is used to describe a range of phenomena from individual practices to more organized movements. It sounds like a contradiction in terms that a study on ecclesiology should include a phenomenon distinguished by the explicit repudiation of the church. The reason for its inclusion is that churchless Christianity, however amorphous it may be, coheres around a number of discernible characteristics and acknowledged leaders, so that, phenomenologically, it could be considered a kind of church. Hoefer calls such Christians 'non-baptized believers in Christ' (NBBC) (Hoefer 1991). He estimated that there could be as many as 200,000 NBBCs in the city of Madras (Chennai) alone in the 1980s. They are mostly educated but poor. The majority are women, for whom, not surprisingly, the place of greatest significance is the home. They have a personal relationship with Jesus Christ but do not belong to any Christian church. Many came to experience Jesus personally through answered prayer and miraculous healing (13), but they want to remain within a Hindu or Muslim cultural setting. A common reason given is that baptism would disrupt the harmony in the family and certain family religious practices like the *puja* (daily acts of worship). Since, in Hinduism, one is free to worship a god of one's choice, for the NBBCs, Jesus is their chosen God. Usually the God who answers prayer is the God to be served (14).

In Japan a movement with a wide following stemming from similar impulses is the No-Church (*Mukyokai*) movement founded by Kanzō Uchimura. Mullins calls it 'the fountainhead of Japanese Christianity' as it was the major inspiration for other indigenous churches that followed (1998b: 54–67). Uchimura is strongly opposed to institutional Christianity which he accuses of trivializing the faith by keeping to a form without content. The No-Church movement should be better termed 'non-churchism' (Jennings 1958) since *Mukyokai* is not opposed to church as such, but to church being dominated by its organizational life, formal assent to doctrines, rituals, etc. Joining a church often means being isolated from family and community. *Mukyokai* seeks to cultivate in the individual the essence of Christianity without isolating him or her from the community: 'Christianity is God's grace appropriated by man's faith' which provides the inner power to enable a person to keep the law—something that heathen religion could not provide. 'Christianity is Christ, and Christ is a living person'; more precisely, it is Christ crucified:

> When, as at present, many things pass for Christianity, which are not Christianity— such for instance as Social Service, Ethical Evangelism and International Thinking— it is very desirable that we should call Christianity by a new name. I propose Crucifixianity as such; and when it too shall have been abused and vulgarized by new theologians, I will coin another. (Cited by Jennings 1958: 47–9)

Mukyokai is decidedly non-sacramental in its worship since it is institutional Christianity expressed in certain rites and ceremonies in a church that is seen as opposed to Japanese religion and its rituals found in the home (Jennings 1958: 77; Howe 2007). The Christian content of *Mukyokai* could be described as strongly evangelical, with strong affinities to Quakerism in its anti-institutional stance and to Anabaptism in its Bible-centred emphasis, but at the same time open to learning from Buddhism and Confucianism (Mullins 1998b: 59, 61).

An Assessment

Churchless Christianity has other problems besides the ones that Newbigin highlighted. Wingate notes that compared to baptized believers, NBBCs do not last very long in their faith (1999: 204). Attempts to create loose fellowships of unbaptized believers such as the Hindu Church of Jesus Christ or *Natu Sabai* and the movement inspired by Subba Rao have no grass-roots appeal. Both churchless Christianity in India and *Mukyokai* in Japan require a level of intellectual sophistication not normally found among the masses (Wingate 1999: 194; Mullins 1998b: 95–6). But they also fail theologically: the church is not only a new community of the Spirit, it is also a community of the Incarnation, finding expression in a visible structure. Churchless Christians may relish a spiritual experience with Jesus, but in repudiating the incarnational dimension of the Christian faith, they fall short of its fullness (Wingate 1999: 205).

INDIGENOUS CHURCHES

Churchless Christianity is not the only alternative to institutional Christianity. As Wingate notes, there are Pentecostal churches which appeal to the masses while making a clear distinction between Christianity and Hinduism (Wingate 1999: 194). They exemplify a way of being church which is replicated in many indigenous churches throughout Asia.

In India alone, it is estimated that there are more than a hundred indigenous denominations (Hiebert 2004: 332). Unlike churchless or non-church Christianity, indigenous church movements recognize the need for church structure and organization. They reflect the serious attempt to live out the Christian faith in a particular context; at the same time, however, they seek to be identified with the church universal. Theologically, they do not differ greatly from denominational churches; what distinguish them are a combination of emphases reflecting their peculiar context and their strongly independent character stemming from their charismatic founders. An example is the Mukti Church founded by Pandita Ramabai (1858–1922) which combines Pentecostal fervour with outreach to abused women and children (Hedlund 2004: 375–7).

There are usually some distinctive features that set indigenous churches apart. The Ceylon Pentecostal Mission (CPM; later named the Pentecostal Mission) was formed in 1924 by two leaders, Paul Ramankutty, a Dalit, and Alwin R. de Alwis, a college teacher. It insists that their ministers embrace celibacy and wear white. Their outfit not only comports with Buddhist practice in Sri Lanka, but is also believed to come from Scripture: Ecclesiastes 9:8 (KJV): 'Let thy garments be always white' (Somaratna 1996).

Another unique feature is the founding of 'faith homes'. These are places for worship and training but also serve as communal homes for CPM's pastors and church workers. Possessions are held in common and hospitality is extended to all especially the destitute (35–6). Indigenous churches reflect in various degrees the eschatological orientation of Christianity. Needless to say, CPM teachings are much more so (Hedlund 2004: 377). Hiebert notes that while indigenous churches maintain a strong Indian identity and character, their links with the global church are weak. This has tended to result in suspicion, leading to the charge of syncretism (Hiebert 2004: 333). However, among the Indian initiated churches are Pentecostal groups which are clearly Indian in identity but their Pentecostal faith at once links them to the worldwide Pentecostal movement (Hedlund 2005). Among them, the CPM again stands out. Not only is it international in reach, it manifests a rare ecumenical ethos. It has 848 branches in nineteen countries with 3,984 full-time ministers. Pulikottil describes it as 'the first Dalit Pentecostal denomination in India . . . which integrated Dalit and non-Dalits in its membership and leadership' (Pulikottil 2005: 246). In the South Asian context, its ability to transcend caste, race, and social status is quite unprecedented when compared with other churches (Somaratna 1996: 36). Another remarkable achievement is that it suffered no major division for nearly eighty years (Pulikottil 2005: 246). Paul Ramankutty was very much influenced by the Ezhava reformer Sri Naryana Guru (1854–1928) who 'created an alternative public sphere' for the low-caste Ezhavas. The Pentecostal Mission too was an alternative public to those created by missionaries and Christians from the higher castes (Pulikottil 2005: 253–5).

In Japan, while the earlier indigenous movements such as *Mukyokai* and the Christ Heart Church founded by Kawai Shinsui (1867–1962) appeal largely to the elite, there are several others that started in the 1930s and 1940s which appeal more to the masses. They address the folk religionists' concerns like ancestral veneration and the world of spirits by developing a theology of the dead and appropriate Christian rituals to honour them. In so doing, they challenge mainstream Christianity's culturally restricted interpretations (Mullins 1998a). For instance, Mullins notes that the JICM (Japanese Indigenous Christian Movement) interpretation of salvation beyond the grave may provide fresh insights into the phrase 'descent into hell' in the Apostles' Creed and neglected passages of Scripture like 1 Pet. 3:18–22; 4:6. It is perhaps not coincidental that some of the founders of JICMs like Murai Jun of the Spirit of Jesus Church (1941) were Pentecostal, and their movements still retain distinctively classical Pentecostal doctrines like Spirit-baptism and glossolalia (Mullins 1990; 1998b: 97–8).

Mullins further observes that while the rites following from JICM belief, such as evangelism of the departed and prayer and baptism for them, may strike traditional Christians as novel, yet underlying them is a basically orthodox Christian belief that salvation for all could only come from a personal encounter with Jesus Christ (1998: 60). It is precisely because of their strong conviction of the necessity of salvation through Christ that a major concern (namely, ancestors who did not know Christ while they were on earth) needs to be adequately addressed. In terms of contemporary theologies of religion, the JICM approach could be seen as a specific form of the post-mortem theory of salvation—a view to which some Catholics and evangelicals are favourably disposed (DiNoia 1992: 107; Bloesch 1987: 227). The main difference between JICMs and other Christians is that the former have devised appropriate rites to address their peculiar concerns. This is important because in a Confucian culture, as in many other traditional Asian societies, proper rites or *li* are crucial in embodying the Confucian Way (Ching 1993: 59–60; cf. Zahniser 1997). Further, the response of JICMs to ancestral veneration challenges Protestants to take a fresh look at the doctrine of the communion of saints transcending space and time.

THE CHURCH AS A CONTRAST COMMUNITY

If some indigenous churches like the JICMs seek to establish continuity between gospel and culture, there are others which seek to maintain discontinuity. If the former show the need to start with what is good and true in culture (e.g. filial piety) the latter show the need for the church to stand its ground against what is false. They envision the church as a contrast community. Two examples will be considered.

Wang Ming Dao (1900–1991)

Though not a theologian, Wang was nevertheless deeply conscious of the vast implications of the gospel for the church. And within the peculiar historical situation that he found himself in, he sought to create a contrast community that would indirectly pose a challenge to the absolutist claims of a totalitarian regime. Wang Ming Dao, the name he took after his conversion, means understanding the truth. Wang did not write theology, but in his many sermons there is a consistent theological ethics. Wang lived in a period of Chinese history when China was going through vast changes socially and politically. The impact of Western science and technology on China led to radical rethinking and self-questioning among the Chinese intellectuals beginning with the May Fourth Movement in 1919. Such soul-searching led to the question of the role that religions had played in Chinese society. Inevitably Christianity came up for questioning. The Western-educated elite saw Christianity as a superstition and a hindrance to progress. Many Chinese Christian apologists rose up to defend the faith. But Wang was seemingly unconcerned about these developments. This has led some scholars to regard him as an escapist who was concerned only with spiritual matters (Lam 1983: 22–3, 75–6). But this is really to misunderstand Wang. Part of the problem is that Wang has been evaluated by a particular theory of social engagement—what Hauerwas calls the 'Constantinian' model (1989)—where the only recognizable form of social engagement is one which subsumes the church within a supposedly larger public sphere. Wang's approach is far more subtle, less direct, but no less threatening to a totalitarian regime (Harvey 2002: 36–7).

Wang was primarily concerned about the church and what it ought to be. He directed his messages to and at the church, but always with an eye on the way the church would affect the world. Even in his earlier sermons, when conflict with the Three Self Patriotic Movement was not on the horizon, Wang was consciously seeking to mould the church into a contrast community. In 'Dangers of the Present-Day Church' he warns of the enemies inside the church, namely, the worship of wealth, conformity to the world, and toleration of sin. His idea of holiness was not formed by the typical Holiness list of dos and don'ts; rather, he castigated social evils that had crept into the church, such as 'mammon worship' and money politics (1983a: 39).

His call to the church became even clearer between 1949 and 1955, the year when he was imprisoned. In sermon after sermon he spoke out against compromise and for the need to be faithful and obedient to God. In 'Nitty Gritty Faithfulness' based on Luke 16: 10a, he warned of the danger of making small compromises which, in the long term, undermined one's integrity and made one completely powerless. This is obviously a reference to the leaders of the Three Self Patriotic Movement (1983b: 18).

Wang's implicit hermeneutics is quite post-modern; it is a process of indwelling the gospel story. This is a feature he shares with many other Asian preachers. Their sermons are mostly taken from biblical narratives, especially the Gospels, and filled with anecdotes and testimonies. The truth is not an abstract principle but a concrete reality which is either confirmed in the daily lives of Christians or repudiated by unbelievers. For example, when Wang challenged his congregation to obey God rather than 'men' in the face of the pressure of the Three Self Patriotic Movement (TSPM) to capitulate to the Chinese Communist Party, he did not launch into a discussion of ethical principles, dilemmas, or casuistry. In a sermon 'Obey God or Men', the example of Peter before the Sanhedrin clinched the argument (1983b: 23–8). For him, the biblical story has the ring of truth that ought to shape the story of the present-day church (Harvey 2002: 74). The underlying 'narrative theology' of Wang carries vast socio-political implications. As Harvey has pointed out, 'This was a war to decide whose rhetoric, drama, and sacred text would define the church in China: the ideology of the state or the dramatic narrative of the Bible' (2002: 77–8).

Wang knew what was really at stake: the line must be clearly drawn between truth and falsehood, between the church and the world. The choice between God and the world always comes as an either/or: 'Anyone who works for God should make an irrevocable decision whether he intends to please God or to please men. There is only one choice—a person cannot have it both ways' (1983b: 68–9). Only by remaining a contrast community can the church maintain integrity in the midst of incessant assaults from a godless ideology.

Vishal Mangalwadi (1949–)

Vishal Mangalwadi is an Indian Christian and founder-director of the Association for Comprehensive Rural Assistance (ACRA), an organization dedicated to helping the poor villagers who are often the victims of exploitation and injustice perpetrated by their high-caste landlords with the connivance of a corrupt bureaucracy. Mangalwadi discovered early in his work among the poor that the problem of poverty is not a matter of backwardness in technology; it was part of a system of ordering society based on religious sanctions going back thousands of years. When the rich and high-caste believe that it is their right to be rich and powerful and the poor and oppressed also believe that it is their lot to live in poverty and servitude because the all-pervading law of karma so dictates, the only way to change this unjust structure is by changing the basic outlook of people. Mangalwadi sees three possible options. First, one could minimize the injustices inherent in the caste system by enacting laws; but this will not fundamentally change the structure of a caste-based society. Or, one could try to change people at the top, that is, by removing those who are responsible for the injustices. Again, this will not do in India where the perpetrators of oppression of the lower castes number in the hundreds of thousands. The only option is the third, which requires a two-pronged approach: first, 'to change the oppressed' by freeing them 'from mental or ideological slavery' through gospel proclamation, and second, having them 'opt out of the socio-religious systems' by joining a community that practises the gospel (Mangalwadi 1989: 36–7).

Common to Mangalwadi and Wang is the central place they give to the church. Both see the church as a counter-culture. But Mangalwadi is more explicit. He describes the church as a 'power structure' that provides the antidote to structural evil (106–23). Structural evil can only be effectively dealt with by a counter-structure which is the church that Christ built against which the gates of Hades will not prevail (109). Mangalwadi chides modern theologians who 'dismiss the very concept of the church as irrelevant to the struggle against injustice and the struggle for the weak' (101). For him, evangelism and church planting must go together: the church is 'an inseparable part of the Good News' (107). His concern for the church reminds us of what D. T. Niles, the Sri Lankan ecumenist, once said: 'The answer to the problems of the world is the answer that Jesus Christ provided, which is the Church' (Niles 1966: 50).

The Church as Universal and Local: Watchman Nee

While Watchman Nee could be considered as belonging to the tradition of building contrast communities, his unique contribution to ecclesiology is that he not only successfully implemented a peculiar indigenous church principle throughout China and among diaspora Chinese, but also developed one of the most elaborate theologies of the church as its basis. His concept of the 'local church' will remain controversial, but there is no denying that it was based on a well-thought-out ecclesiology. For this reason his theology of the church merits more extended treatment. To understand Nee's radical ecclesiology, we need to appreciate the profound impact that the Christian faith had on him. Grace May notes that Nee's spiritual experience freed him to do very uncon-ventional things in defiance of deeply rooted Chinese traditions as long as the actions were biblical (May 2000: 101, 102). He was as equally prepared on the same basis to part ways with those he deeply respected, such as the Plymouth Brethren, whose teaching on closed communion he could not accept (May 2000: 100).

The Corporate Christ

Central to Nee's ecclesiology is his concept of the church as a spiritual reality. Using typological interpretation, he argues that just as Eve was 'the constituent of Adam', so the church was a constituent part of Christ. 'Only that which is out of Christ can be the church' (Nee 1993b: 27). And just as 'Eve was not made from clay but from Adam' the 'material' of the church is Christ (29). The church has its beginning even before cre-ation: it exists as God's plan from eternity (Nee 1993b: 32, 40–1). The church is not so much going to heaven as made in heaven: 'Heaven is both the origin and abode of the Church, but not her destination' (Nee 1993c: 164); it is 'perfect beyond any possibility of improvement' (165). 'To see eternal reality in Christ is to cease to differentiate between what the Church is potentially and actually' (166). The church is so linked to Christ that it could be called the 'corporate Christ'.

> In the New Testament there are two ways to look at Christ. On the one hand, He is Jesus Christ the Nazarene—this is the individual Christ. On the other hand, He is Christ plus the church—the corporate Christ . . . There is only one thing in a Christian that forms a part of the church—Christ. The church is the corporate Christ. In the church there is only Christ. During the bread-breaking meeting, the portion that we break off from the whole still signifies the Body of Christ, the church. The church is not what is added to Christ but what issues out from Christ. (Nee 1993d: 787; cf. 1993b: 29–33)

Nee's strong emphasis on the church leads naturally to an equally strong emphasis on corporate spirituality. Christian living is essentially living in the Body of Christ (1993d: 808). This corporate spirituality is expressed in bearing the cross. To live in the Body means to carry the Cross, die to the natural life so that the life of Christ might be revealed. Practically, bearing the cross in the Body requires one to be limited by the weaknesses of other members (805). In the Body there is no 'direct communion with another'. Fellowship must always be through the Head, without which fellowship turns into little cliques (1993d: 812).

The Lord's Supper

The central act of the church that expresses this corporate life is the Lord's Supper. For Nee, the 'breaking of bread' was no mere ritual but a profound religious experience (May 2000: 100). The Chinese have a deep appreciation of the family meal. Just as the family meal epitomizes the traditional Chinese family, the Lord's Supper for Nee is the spiritual family meal of the church. Nee regarded the Supper even more highly than preaching since church membership is based on the number of persons breaking bread, which is the first action in the assembly. Thus Nee prefers the Supper to be observed in the evening service where a smaller group of committed Christians come together (May: 334–5). Nee is no sacramentalist, but his understanding of the Lord's Supper resonates generally with traditional teachings: the meal itself declares the death of Christ by presenting the bread (body) and wine (blood) as separate. It is also the meal that binds Christians together in table fellowship (1 Cor. 10). Nee is open to having Christians from anywhere participate at the Table (1993e: 261–72).

The 'Local Church'

One of the most controversial teachings of Nee is his doctrine of the local church. Critics regard it as exclusive, authoritarian, and incompatible with his earlier doctrine of the universal church (Roberts 1980: 131–8). The local church, however, cannot be properly understood apart from his doctrine of the eternal church. The church eternal is concretely realized in the local church. The local church is where the real action of the Body of Christ is taking place. This gives rise to a concept of the church as a divine-humanity: 'The church is partly heavenly and partly on earth. The heavenly part concerns the authority of the Holy Spirit; the earthly part concerns the boundary of locality.' One is just as necessary as the other: 'the church absolutely belongs to a locality' (Nee 1974: 19).

Historically, Nee notes, the churches are distinguished by time, place of origin, personality, and doctrine, but the only valid distinction is the locality or city (1993e: 94). There can only be one true church in one locality (1974: 20–3). The church cannot be smaller or bigger than the locality and must be named after the locality, not after a person, doctrine, system, place of origin, for example Church of England (1974: 96).

The actualization of the eternal church in the local church is brought about by the Holy Spirit. Nee's pneumatology develops directly out of his doctrine of the corporate Christ. Reading Psalm 133 typologically and correlating it with Ephesians 4, Nee believes that just as Christ is anointed by the Spirit, the same anointing extends to the whole Body. Christ is the Anointed One; we as members of his Body are 'little anointed ones'. We are not anointed individually but only 'in Christ' (1993d: 816). The anointing of the Spirit links the Body to the Head and to one another. Again and again, Nee brings out the spiritual implications of his teaching. The anointing is translated into an 'inner feeling of life' which must guide our action. Without the anointing everything becomes dead letter, mere doctrine (1993d: 816–20). Our part is to 'consecrate and yield ourselves [so] that the authority of the Holy Spirit might come out continuously' (1974: 17).

Authority

Nee is no bleary-eyed idealist. He knows all too well that for a church to function effectively, it has to address the issue of authority. Here again, it is hard to gainsay Nee's concept of ecclesiastical authority. The problem with denominations, according to Nee, is that they have substituted human authority for the authority of the Holy Spirit (which is the mark of the eternal church). Leaders are selected based on social status and natural abilities rather than on vital faith and relationship with God (1993d: 822). 'In the Body of Christ authority is a matter of life, not of position' (825). This is a further reason why denominational churches cannot be the true church. All church authorities are derived from the Head. Apostles, prophets, and so on do not have authority in themselves; they represent Christ's authority on earth. Leaders who are given Christ's authority will be *recognized* as leaders by the people rather than ratified by the people through an election. An elder of the church cannot be *made* an elder by the people any more than a father can be made a father. A father is one by virtue of having a son (825–7).

This is the context in which Nee understands the practice of the laying on of hands. At baptism, the 'representative authority established by God', such as an apostle, lays his hand on the candidate, signifying that the person is joined to the Body of Christ and the blessing of God is transmitted to him. It also means that the person is now under the authority of Christ the Head. The laying on of hands ensures that the blessing of God's anointing on the Head continues to flow to each member of the Body on whom hands are laid (1993e: 99–111).

It is easy to see Nee's insistence on male headship as reflecting an authoritarianism derived from Chinese culture (Lee 2005). Two things must be said by way of qualification. First, we have noted that Nee is a thoroughgoing biblicist who is prepared to jettison anything from culture which he deems unbiblical. Second, he has a theology of authority which is seldom appreciated, namely, authority is to be exercised in mutual dependence between leaders and people. Mutuality is the character of the Body of Christ (1993d: 805). The pulpit needs the help of the congregation just as the congregation needs the help of the pulpit (806). Mutuality is needed even in the matter of elders anointing the sick (Jas. 5:14–16). Nee believes that the sickness here is no ordinary sickness, but is brought on by the sin of breaking away from the body of Christ (1 Cor. 11:29–30). Mutual confession between the elders and the sick is needed. The sick person confesses to having broken fellowship, while the elders confess that they have failed in love and watchfulness (833). Mutual confession is followed by mutual prayer: the elders praying for the sick and the sick for the elders (833). But beyond the biblical horizon lies the Confucian principle of reciprocity. Nee's local church may look like a macrocosm of the Confucian family (Lee 2005: 76), but underlying it is a rather sophisticated theology of ecclesial authority.

An Assessment

Nee is often accused of sectarianism, but theologically, Nee's ecclesiology is no more exclusive than the Roman Catholic Church's claim that the true church 'subsists' in the Catholic Church (*Lumen Gentium* no. 8). What Nee has done is to transfer the Roman Catholic exclusiveness to the 'local church' (in his sense). But unlike the Roman Catholic understanding, the charge of sectarianism will not go away as long as Nee questions the legitimacy of non-local churches. Yet, for all the problems that Nee's local church doctrine entails, it has several advantages. First, it encourages the development of strong indigenous churches which are not dependent on foreign support. Nee was a master strategist, using the same methods as the communists to establish many indigenous churches in even the remotest parts of China (Lee 2005). His method involves encouraging several families to migrate to a new area to form a local church (Chua 2009). Secondly, it encourages strong corporate life at the local church level. Over and over again, Nee spoke in the strongest possible terms against individualism: 'Therefore, even though we have God's life within us, we still need God to work upon us to break our individualism. God must break down the thought that I myself am enough. We need to be one with all the rest of God's children . . . [God] must crush us day after day until we come to know the life of the Body' (1993b: 32). 'Individualism is hateful in the sight of God . . . I must allow the other members of the Body to minister to my needs. We must avail ourselves constantly of the fellowship of the Body, for it is our very life' (1993d: 801). Thirdly, it encourages local churches to be kept at a reasonable size. It should be big enough for the full complement of ministries to be exercised, but small enough for discipline to be maintained and meaningful fellowship to be realized especially at the Lord's Table (May 2000: 329).

Nee's theological vision of the church is far more traditional and 'catholic' than perhaps he himself realized. His concepts of the corporate Christ and the distinction between the Body and the Bride bear close resemblance to the Catholic idea of *totus Christus* seen in Pope Pius XII's encyclical *Mystici Corporis Christi* and other Roman Catholic writers (Mersch 1951; 1962). His understanding of authority as a reciprocal relationship between the elders and people is not very different from that of Orthodoxy (Afanasiev 2007; Schmemann 1987). Even the laying on of hands is surprisingly close to the traditional understanding of the sacrament of confirmation.

Nevertheless, Nee's vision of the universal church when juxtaposed to his rather exclusive concept of the local church at first seems quite baffling. But there is an underlying logic that runs from one to the other. For Nee, doctrines are not abstract ideas but truths that have far-reaching implications for living. The doctrine of the corporate Christ is 'a reality and not a doctrine or a theory' and entails a spirituality of cross-bearing and self-abnegation (1993d: 805–8). Nee probably derives this peculiar understanding of spirituality from Keswick sources. Basic to Keswick spirituality is the belief that all that is possible for Christian living has already been accomplished by Christ. What Christians need to do is appropriate the reality through a process of self-surrender and 'reckoning' that it is so (Smith 1970: 44; Nee 1993a: 41–56). Nee's understanding of the church as both an eternal reality and a human reality lived out in the local church conforms to this Keswick pattern.

CONCLUDING OBSERVATIONS

The chief ecclesiological issue in Asia is how to be the church in the midst of more ancient family-based religious communities. The 'faith homes' of the Ceylon Pentecostal Mission, the family-orientated megachurches in Singapore, and the family-based 'local church' of Watchman Nee could be understood as indigenous responses to this basic problematic. Beyond this, the diversity of contexts of Asia accounts for further differentiation in ecclesiological expressions.

Churchless Christianity in India and Japan arises from a situation where the person of Christ is often warmly received, but the church as a visible community is disregarded. The problem is how to accommodate these believers within an existing church structure. The problem is perhaps more acute for established church bodies. The issues that churchless Christianity raises are not merely practical but theological: what is the nature of the ecclesial community into which a believer is baptized? Can the church be a 'religious' community without being a socio-cultural community? Churchless Christianity fits well within societies where religious practices are undertaken primarily in the home. But can Christianity exist without the church? Putting it theologically, what would the church be like without its eschatological orientation? These questions concern not only the function, but the ontology of the church. The exchanges between M. M. Thomas and Lesslie Newbigin highlight these issues that are still being contested.

In contrast to churchless Christianity, indigenous churches are various attempts at being visible ecclesial communities in this complex situation. Pentecostal churches seem to have done better than the established churches. They seek to be contrast communities; at the same time their adaptation to the primal religious worldview (Cox 1995) allows them to respond more adequately to popular religiosity compared to elitist approaches. Their fluid structure is better equipped to address the concerns of NBBCs (Hoefer 1991: 246). For instance, they are less enamoured of issues like the nature of baptism, but more concerned with building vibrant, worshipping communities. Also, their peculiar emphasis on miracles, healing, and exorcism appears to coincide with the felt needs of many NBBCs. In short, a Hindu believer in Christ is less likely to feel out of place in a Pentecostal church. At the same time, Pentecostal churches are less likely to compromise on what they regard as essential. They are quite prepared to break with whatever they perceive as un-Christian practices (e.g. the CPM's attitude towards caste). They tend to encourage the building of contrast communities. It is noteworthy that in recent times the Roman Catholic Church in Asia has been taking notice of Pentecostal adaptability (FABC Papers, nos 81, 119). The JICMs have shown that, where bold steps are taken to find appropriate Christian ritual expressions of ancestral veneration, fresh theological insights have emerged. Against this backdrop, the ecclesiology of Watchman Nee stands out as quite unusual by its sustained reflection that juxtaposes the universal and the local church. The result is an ecclesiology which is surprisingly traditional, closer perhaps to Catholicism and Orthodoxy than to Protestantism, but at the same time well suited to a context where family life is highly valued (Chua 2009). Looking at Asian ecclesiologies from a grass-roots perspective reveals new possibilities that go beyond what is typically found in ecumenical discussions.

REFERENCES

Note: For Chinese and Korean names, the traditional form is retained: surname followed by given names.

Abraham, K. C. (ed.) (1990). *Third World Theologies: Commonalities and Divergences*. Maryknoll, NY: Orbis.

Afanasiev, Nicholas (2007). *The Church of the Holy Spirit*. Notre Dame, IN: University of Notre Dame Press.

Bloesch, Donald (1987). *Essentials of Evangelical Theology*, vol. 2. San Francisco: Harper and Row [1978].

Ching, Julia (1978). *Confucianism and Christianity: A Comparative Study*. New York and Tokyo: Kodansha International.

Ching, Julia (1993). *Chinese Religions*. Maryknoll, NY: Orbis.

Chua Wee Hian (2009). 'Evangelization of Whole Families'. In Ralph D. Winter (ed.), *Perspective on the World Christian Movement: A Reader*. Pasadena, CA: William Carey Library, 653–6.

Chung, Paul S., Kim Kyoung-Jae, and Kärkkäinen, Veli-Matti (eds) (2007). *Asian Contextual Theology for the Third Millennium: A Theology of Minjung in Fourth-Eye Formation*. Eugene, OR: Pickwick Publications.

Cox, Harvey (1995). *Fire from Heaven: The Rise of Pentecostal Spirituality and the Reshaping of Religion in the Twenty-first Century*. New York: Addison-Wesley.

Dinoia, J. A. (1992). *The Diversity of Religion: A Christian Perspective*. Washington: Catholic University of America Press.

EATWOT (2010). 'Indigenous Peoples' Struggle for Justice and Liberation in Asia'. Asia Theological Conference VII. Ecumenical Association of Third World Theologians. <http://www.eatwot.org/index.php?option=com_content&task=view&id=33&Itemid=42>. Accessed 12 March 2012.

FABC Papers. <http://www.fabc.org/offices/csec/ocsec_fabc_papers.html>. Accessed 12 March 2012.

Fabella, Virginia, Lee, Peter K. H., and Suh, David Kwang-Sun (1992). *Asian Christian Spirituality: Reclaiming Traditions*. Maryknoll, NY: Orbis.

Harvey, Thomas Alan (2002). *Acquainted with Grief: Wang Mingdao's Stand for the Persecuted Church in China*. Grand Rapids, MI: Brazos.

Hauerwas, Stanley (1986). *A Community of Character: Toward a Constructive Christian Social Ethic*. Notre Dame, IN: University of Notre Dame Press.

Hauerwas, Stanley and Willimon, William H. (1989). *Resident Aliens*. Nashville: Abingdon.

Hedlund, Roger E. (2004). 'Indigenous Christianity'. In Roger E. Hedlund and Paul Joshua Bhakiaraj (eds), *Missiology for the 21st Century: South Indian Perspectives*. Madras: ISPCK, 369–83.

Hedlund, Roger E. (2005). 'Indigenous Pentecostalism in India'. In Allan Anderson and Edmond Tang (eds), *Asian and Pentecostal: The Charismatic Face of Christianity in Asia*. Oxford: Regnum, 215–44.

Hiebert, Paul G. (2004). 'The Christian Response to Hinduism'. In Roger E. Hedlund and Paul Joshua Bhakiaraj (eds), *Missiology for the 21st Century: South Indian Perspectives*. Madras: ISPCK, 324–35.

Hoefer, Herbert E. (1991). *Churchless Christianity*. Madras: Asian Program for Advancement of Training and Studies India.

Howes, John F. (2007). 'Christian Prophecy in Japan: Uchimura Kanzō'. *Japanese Journal Of Religious Studies* 34.1: 127–50. *ATLA Religion Database with ATLASerials*, EBSCOhost. Accessed 1 February 2012.

Jennings, Raymond P. (1958). *Jesus, Japan, and Kanzo Uchimura*. Tokyo: Kyo Bun Kwan Christian Literature Society.

John Paul II (1999). *Church in Asia: Ecclesia in Asia*. Reprint Catholic Bishops' Conference of Malaysia-Singapore-Brunei.

Lam Wing Hung (1983). *Chinese Theology in Construction*. Pasadena, CA: William Carey Library.

Lee, Joseph Tse-Hei (2005). 'Watchman Nee and the Little Flock Movement in Maoist China'. *Church History* 74.1: 68–96.

Lehmann, David (2003). 'Dissidence and Conformism in Religious Movements: What Difference Separates the Catholic Charismatic Renewal and Pentecostal Churches?' *Concilium* 3: 122–38.

McDermott, Gerald R. (2007). *God's Rivals: Why Has God Allowed Different Religions? Insights From the Bible and the Early Church*. Downers Grove, IL: InterVarsity Press.

Mangalwadi, Vishal (1989). *Truth and Social Reform*. London: Spire Books.

May, Grace Y. (2000). 'Watchman Nee and the Breaking of Bread: The Missiological and Spiritual Forces that Contributed to an Indigenous Chinese eEcclesiology'. D.Th. diss., Boston University School of Theology.

Mersch, Emile (1951). *The Theology of the Mystical Body*. St Louis, MO: B. Herder.

Mersch, Emile (1962). *The Whole Christ: The Historical Development of the Doctrine of the Mystical Body in Scripture and Tradition*. London: Dennis Dobson.

Miller, Donald E. and Yamamori, Tetsunao (2007). *Global Pentecostalism: The New Face of Christian Social Engagement*. Berkeley: University of California Press.

Moltmann, Jürgen (1977). *The Church in the Power of the Spirit*. New York: Harper and Row.

Mullins, Mark R. (1990). 'Japanese Pentecostalism and the World of the Dead: A Study of Cultural Adaptation in Iesu no Mitama Kyōkai'. *Japanese Journal of Religious Studies* 17.4: 354–74.

Mullins, Mark R. (1998a). 'What about the Ancestors? Some Japanese Christian Responses to Protestant Individualism'. *Studies in World Christianity* 4.1: 41–64.

Mullins, Mark R. (1998b). *Christianity Made in Japan: A Study of Indigenous Movements*. Honolulu: University of Hawaii Press.

Nee, Watchman (1974). *Further Talks on the Church*. Los Angeles: The Stream Publishers.

Nee, Watchman (1993a). *The Normal Christian Life. The Collected Works of Watchman Nee*, vol. 33. Anaheim, CA: Living Stream Ministry.

Nee, Watchman (1993b). *The Glorious Church. Collected Works*, vol. 34.

Nee, Watchman (1993c). *What Shall This Man Do? Collected Works*, vol. 40.

Nee, Watchman (1993d). *Conferences, Messages, and Fellowship (4). Collected Works*, vol. 44.

Nee, Watchman (1993e). *Messages for Building Up New Believers (1). Collected Works*, vol. 48.

Niles, D. T. (1966). *The Message and its Messengers*. Nashville: Abingdon.

Parrinder, Geoffrey (1961). *Worship in the World's Religions*. London: Faber & Faber.

Phan, Peter C. (ed.) (2002). *The Asian Synod: Texts and Commentaries*. Maryknoll, NY: Orbis.

Pieris, Aloysius (1988). *An Asian Theology of Liberation*. Maryknoll, NY: Orbis.

Poon, Michael Nai-Chiu (ed.) (2010). *Christian Movements in Southeast Asia: A Theological Exploration*. Singapore: Genesis Books.

Pulikottil, Paulson (2005). 'Ramankutty Paul: A Dalit Contribution to Pentecostalism'. In Allan Anderson and Edmond Tang (eds), *Asian and Pentecostal: The Charismatic Face of Christianity in Asia*. Oxford: Regnum, 245–57.

Roberts, Dana (1980). *Understanding Watchman Nee*. Plainfield, NJ: Haven Books.

Schmemann, Alexander (1973). *For the Life of the World: Sacraments and Orthodoxy*. Crestwood, NY: St Vladimir Seminary Press.

Schmemann, Alexander (1987). *The Eucharist*. Crestwood, NY: St Vladimir Seminary Press.

Smith, Hannah W. (1970). *The Christian's Secret of a Happy Life*. Old Tappen, NJ: Fleming H. Revell.

Somaratna, G. P. V. (1996). *Origins of the Pentecostal Mission in Sri Lanka*. Mirihana-Nugegoda, Sri Lanka: Margaya Fellowship of Sri Lanka.

Tagle, Luis Anthony G. (2000). 'Ecclesiology: Asian'. In Virginia Fabella and R. S. Sugirtharajah (eds), *Dictionary of Third World Theologies*. Maryknoll, NY: Orbis.

Thomas, M. M. and Newbigin, Lesslie (1972). 'Baptism, the Church, and Koinonia'. *Religion and Society* 19.1: 69–90.

Vatican II (1966). *Documents of Vatican II*. Ed. Walter M. Abbot. New York: Guild Press.

Wang Ming Dao (1983a). 'Dangers in the Present-Day Church'. In *Spiritual Food*. Southampton: Mayflower Christian Books.

Wang Ming Dao (1983b). *A Call to the Church*. Trans. Theodore Choy; ed. Leona F. Choy. Fort Washington, PA: Christian Literature Crusade.

Wingate, Andrew (1999). *The Church and Conversion: A Study of Recent Conversions to and from Christianity in the Tamil Area of South India*. Delhi: ISPCK.

Xi Lian (2010). *Redeemed by Fire: The Rise of Popular Christianity in Modern China*. New Haven: Yale University Press.

Yoo Boo-Woong (1988). *Korean Pentecostalism: Its History and Theology*. Frankfurt: Peter Lang.

Yun Koo D. (2007). 'Minjung and Asian Pentecostals'. In Paul S. Chung, Kim Kyoung-Jae, and Veli-Matti Kärkkäinen (eds), *Asian Contextual Theology for the Third Millennium: A Theology of Minjung in Fourth-Eye Formation*. Eugene, OR: Pickwick, 87–100.

Zahniser, Mathias A. H. (1997). *Symbol and Ceremony: Making Disciples Across Cultures*. Monrovia, CA: World Vision.

Suggested Reading

Borgall, Saheb John (2016). *The Emergence of Christ Groups in India: The Case of Karnataka State*. Oxford: Regnum.

Cao Nanlai (2011). *Constructing China's Jerusalem: Christians, Power, and Place in Contemporary Wenzhou*. Stanford, CA: Stanford University Press.

Chee Nan Pin (2016). *The Search for the Identity of the Chinese Christian Church: Ecclesiological Responses of the Chinese Church in 1949–1958 to the Political Changes*. Hong Kong: WEC International.

Dyrness, William A. (2016). *Insider Jesus: Theological Reflections on New Christian Movements*. Downers Grove, IL: IVP Academic.

Maggay, Melba Padilla (ed.) (2013). *The Gospel in Culture: Contextualization Issues Through Asian Eyes*. Manila: OMF Literature.

Ruokanen, Miikka and Huang, Paulos (eds) (2010). *Christianity and Chinese Culture*. Grand Rapids, MI: Eerdmans.

Synan, Vinson and Yong, Amos (eds) (2016). *Global Renewal Christianity, Vol. 1: Asia and Oceania*. Lake Mary, FL: Charisma House.

CHAPTER 28

AFRICAN ECCLESIOLOGIES

STAN CHU ILO

THIS chapter examines the key issues in scholarship on the identity and mission of the church in Africa. While identifying the main features of different ecclesiologies in African Christianity, this chapter will also explore in depth the identity of the Roman Catholic Church in Africa. This approach will be developed in three ways. First, I will explore the methodological question in scholarship in this area while highlighting the types and models of African ecclesiology in general. Second, I will historicize the narrative of the church in Africa, showing the theological trajectories of scholarship on *ecclesia in Africa* in the Roman Catholic tradition. Finally, I will briefly survey the key themes being developed in African Catholic ecclesiology from the Second Vatican Council (1962–5) to the Second African Synod (2009). I will conclude with a thematic account of how the priorities and practices of the church of Christ are being enacted in the mission of the church in Africa with regard to the challenges facing the Christian faith there. The chapter will end with some indications of the gift of the church in Africa to the world church, while proposing the future directions of scholarship in this area.

THE POPE'S VISIT TO AFRICA (1969)

On 31 July 1969 Pope Paul VI became the first modern pontiff to make a pastoral visit to Africa. The visit was significant because of the pope's definitive invitation to African Catholics to embrace a specific African brand of Christianity when he said, 'You may, and you must, have an African Christianity' (AAS 61: 575). Many African Roman Catholic theologians refer to this famous speech as a mandate from the institutional church of Rome to African Christians to embrace a distinctive African Catholic ecclesiology in the spirit of Vatican II. This gesture was also seen as recognition of an emerging church which is truly African and truly Catholic. Even though the emergence of a church is not the fruit of the mandate given by the pope to a particular church, however, such gestures from a pope proved to be decisive in promoting creativity and innovation in African

Roman Catholicism. All Christians believe, however, that the emergence and growth of any church is not the result of simple human efforts. The church emerges and grows through the action of the Holy Spirit. Vatican II affirms with clarity that the church takes her origin and unity from Trinitarian communion (*Lumen Gentium* 4). However, ecclesiology is not simply the account of the history of the church, the lay–clerical relationship or how particular communities of faith embody and transmit the doctrines and dogmas of the church and her structures. Ecclesiology is a theological reflection on the faith, life, and context of a community of God's people gathered in the name of the Lord Jesus. It is a judgement on what is moving forward in the life of churches and their members as the Christian faith crosses different cultural and spiritual frontiers. It is also an account of how particular contexts of faith and life are enacting in history the eschatological fruits of God's kingdom revealed in the words and deeds of the Lord Jesus Christ. This is true not only of the church in Africa but in the life of every Christian community of faith in their self-constituting mission and vocation (Lonergan 1999: 364).

In the Roman Catholic tradition, the pre-Vatican II ecclesiology was heavily institutional in nature with a post-Tridentine ecclesial spirit which emphasized ecclesial visibilism, juridicism, clericalism, and the pyramidal structure of power. This sometimes gave the impression that the church was more an institutional archetype, a blueprint (Mannion 2007: 63) and a bastion (Balthasar: 1993) which Catholics have to construct as guided by Rome. The Roman church presented herself as the moderator of cultural traditions, rather than a cultural mediation of the mission of God. This kind of ecclesiology gave the impression that the church was a transcendental reality which Roman Catholics must defend, and something they are obliged to bring to the ends of the earth as a neatly packaged cargo to be reproduced in all contexts as a true replica of the church of Rome. This notion of the church did not sufficiently take into account the fact that the church is the initiative of the Trinity which should be received with a spirit of humility, reverence, freedom, and creativity. It also neglected a total ecclesiology of the whole people of God. Most studies on the nature of the Roman Catholic Church or her ecclesial life before the Second Vatican Council concentrated on the efficacy of the structures of authority in the church, the solidity of her institutional claims and official teaching, and the coherence of the particular churches to these structural elements with a strong emphasis on centralization, the powers of the pope, hierarchical prerogatives, and obedience to the church of Rome. The pope's visit was a post-Vatican II gift to Africa which affirmed the place of the African church in world Catholicism. This visit was preceded by the publication of an important encyclical in 1967 directed specifically to Africa, *Africae Terrarum*, where Pope Paul VI affirmed the uniqueness and richness of African religiocultural and spiritual traditions. African Catholic ecclesiology grew out of the emergence of distinctive post-Vatican II African theological conversations in Africa on the unique identity of African Christianity and the need to embrace Africa's versions and types of Christianity in world Christianity. Within the African Protestant traditions, there was a strong push in the early 1970s for a truly indigenous African ecclesiology. The post-independence cultural and political assertion of African identity gave birth to uniquely African exuberant spiritual celebrations of the Christian faith and the direct harvesting of the transformative presence of the Lordship of Jesus Christ by African Christians through diverse appeals to their cultural and religious traditions. Africa was not simply a *terra incognita* when it came to Christian faith. African theologians were beginning to develop theologies of the church, culture, social mission, eschatology, and mission premised on the realization beyond the restrictive narrative of Africa's past by Western missionaries and anthropologists, that Africa is the land of Christian faith, a land of hope, and the land of light and life.

APPROACHES TO ROMAN CATHOLIC ECCLESIOLOGY IN AFRICA

Theological understanding of how Africans embrace the Christian faith and how they have lived and reflected on *Ecclesia in Africa* have been approached in three ways by African theologians—sociologico-historical studies and theologico-ecclesiological studies. In some cases, some scholars mix both methods focusing on missional cultural hermeneutical method in terms of how the mission of God is being realized through Africa's appropriation of the faith in multiple contexts of ecclesial and cultural life. These are emerging paradigms which do not necessarily lend themselves to a homogeneous methodological template. However, they display a certain pattern and relationship in their respective starting points and points of arrival.

Sociologico-historical Approaches

Such scholars as Lamin Sanneh, John Baur, Elizabeth Isichei, Eugene Uzukwu, Laurenti Magesa, J. N. K Mugambi, Tinyiko Maluleke, Agbonkhianmegher Orobator, Philomena Mwaura, Douglas W. Waruta, Emmanuel Katongole, Alward Shorter, F. Eboussi Boulaga, Elias Bongmba, Ezra Chitando, Jean Mac Ela, Engelvert Mveng are in some cases historians, experts in religious studies, or theologians. They adopt tools from critical social theories, historical approaches to religious studies, and post-colonial social analysis with a liberationist approach to the study of African ecclesiology. African ecclesiology is presented in the writings of these scholars as a type of religious system in African religious history and world Christianity. These scholars apply historical tools in examining the phenomena intrinsic to and manifested in African churches in relation to Christian expansion and religious conversion in Africa and Africa's challenging social context. They also engage with such questions as post-colonial theologies, church, and politics in Africa, ecumenical relations in African Christianity, popular religious practices, Pentecostalism, the impact of Bible translation in Africa's types and models of Christian life and faith. These scholars are developing ecclesiologies of hope and transformation as the churches in Africa confront the pressing questions emerging from the social context of Africans. They reject predominant transcendental ecclesiology especially in the Roman Catholic tradition, while prioritizing the narrative of faith from the margins of history. They seek not only to give a descriptive account of African Catholic ecclesiologies, but also to give explanatory, critical, constructive, and creative accounts, while courageously re-imagining the present and future relevance of African ecclesiology to new questions emerging from the daily lives of Africans.

Theologico-ecclesial Approaches

The second group of scholars are theologians and biblical scholars (Charles Nyamiti, Teresa Okure, Efoe Julien Penoukou, Justin S. Ukpong, Chantal Nsongisa, Paul Bere, Patrick Ryan, Nicholas Fogliacco, Cecil McGarry, Cedric Mayrargue, Adrian Hastings, John Mary Waligo, Musa W. Dube, Clement Majawa, Paulinus Odozor) who are reflecting on the lived faith of African Christians. Their methodological approach is biblical and theological. Scholars in this group harvest the stories of God's dealings with Africans from the daily narratives of living faith in conversation with biblical revelation, church doctrines, and dogmas on the church developed in Western theologies. Furthermore, they seek a link between God's dealings with humanity as revealed in biblical narratives and the spiritual and moral traditions of Africa. These theologians— without being locked in the dualism of ecclesiology from above or from below—chart the cultural self-understanding of Africa's unique map of the universe, worldviews, and cultural grammar in conversation with trends and shifts in World Christianity. While searching for how the Christian faith could be incarnated in Africa, they give greater accent to grounding and appropriating biblical and received Roman Catholic traditions, for example in African ecclesiologies of hope, questions about the place of African women in the church, ecology, social transformation, and abundant life. They take seriously how the faith in Africa is inculturated in worship and moral traditions, as well as the spiritual practices of hope and transcendence mediated through the instrumentality of the church in her personnel, structures, teaching authority, theological systems, catechetical models, pastoral life, and social engagements.

There are those scholars who could be categorized as missional-historical in their study of the church in Africa and who mix the two preceding methods. These scholars—Sidbe Sempore, F. Kabasele Lumbala, A. Nasimiyu-Wasike, Francis Oborji, Leonard Santedi Kinkupu, Oliver Onwubiko, Stan Chu Ilo, Meinrad Hebga—combine a theological and historical approach with a missional focus that is concerned with identifying the movement of the spirit in African Christian history. In their critical and creative engagement with the structures of the church and Catholic beliefs, practices, and social teaching, they examine the continuities and discontinuities between Western type Roman Catholicism, for instance, and African Catholicism. These scholars are more analytical than synthetic in their narrative, and seek to stretch the history of God's mission in Africa beyond any restrictive embodiment of this mission simply as Western ecclesiological incarnations in African soil. These scholars are also concerned with how the eschatological fruits of God's kingdom in concrete ecclesial acts and the manner in which the church is structured and run in Africa embody transformative praxis for African Christians. This is particularly related to the response of churches in Africa to the urgent questions and challenges of the mission of God in Africa which translates to the African religio-cultural tradition of abundant life— human and cosmic flourishing.

Despite the diversity of approaches to African ecclesiology, these scholars are all inspired in their writings by the momentum of Christian expansion in African Christianity. They are all searching for new language, new structures, and new narrative of being church in Africa which can bring about authentic and integral human and cosmic flourishing in Africa. These African scholars are all seeking for how the reign of God can become embodied in concrete life-transforming praxis for ordinary African Christians in their deepest hunger for God and their search for meaning and hope in a complex world.

UNDERSTANDING AFRICAN ECCLESIOLOGY

One cannot define an African ecclesiology. What I will do here is to describe the nature of churches in Africa and show how they are distinct from other forms of the church outside Africa (for example Ilo 2014; Orobator 2015; Nyamiti 2007 and 2008). Writing in his post-synodal apostolic exhortation *Africae Munus* (2010), Pope Benedict XVI proclaimed, 'A precious treasure is to be found in the soul of Africa, where I perceive a "spiritual 'lung' for a humanity that appears to be in a crisis of faith and hope", on account of the extraordinary human and spiritual riches of its children, its variegated cultures, its soil and sub-soil of abundant resources' (Benedict XVI 2011: 13). In a similar vein, Pope John Paul II in his 1994 post-synodal exhortation *Ecclesia in Africa* extolled African Christianity in these words: 'Indeed, this continent is today experiencing what we call a sign of the times, an acceptable time, a day of salvation. It seems that the "hour of Africa" has come, a favorable time' (John Paul II 1994: 6). These expressions—'spiritual lungs', 'new center of gravity of World Christianity', 'historical moment of grace', 'a sign of the times', 'an acceptable time', 'creative Africa', 'rich Africa', 'new home for Christ', and 'hour of Africa'—indicate the conviction that the church in Africa has not only come of age but is becoming a strong spiritual force within world Christianity in what has been called 'the fourth great age of Christian expansion' (Isichei 1995: 1). According to the *Statistical Overview of the World's 2.2 Billion Christians and their Activities*, the population of Christians in Africa has already exceeded 447 million. Specifically with regard to Roman Catholicism in Africa, the Pew Forum (2013) using the data from *World Population Database* (2013) reports that the percentage of Roman Catholics living in Africa grew from 1 per cent in 1910 to 21 per cent in 2010. Many studies have concluded that sub-Saharan Africa is experiencing the fastest church growth than any other region in the world (Kalu 2008: 77).

However, in spite of this growth in numbers, African Christianity and African theologies have not been accorded their rightful place in world Christianity. The challenge for theology in African Christianity is how to listen to what God is saying to Africa in the current Christian expansion in sub-Saharan Africa. Added to this is to discover how to valorize the agency of African Christians in their buoyant religio-cultural spirituality in bringing about an ecclesial life which meets the spiritual and material hunger of Africans. The ecclesiological images—church-as-family of God (First African Synod), the church in Africa as Salt and Light (Second African Synod), church-as-ancestral initiatory family models of eucharistic communion (Nyamiti), a listening church of Trinitarian Communion in Africa (Elochukwu E. Uzukwu), ecclesiology of Christ as Proto-Ancestor of the New Tribal community (Bujo), the African clan as the true model of the African church (John Mary Waliggo), the family as an African metaphor for Trinity and church (Nicholas Fogliacco)—these images are being developed through translation of biblical images and appropriation of African cultural knowledge, symbols, and artefacts in conversation with African social contexts. These ecclesiological models aim at helping Africans celebrate the Christian faith as a gift, while at the same time using the liberating force and transformative grace of the gospel in Africa's march toward modernity.

The church in Africa is both evolving and dynamic; it is very ancient in nature, going back to the first centuries of church history, and remains contemporary. It appropriates within itself elements of African cultures, religions, and spiritualities, and is influenced by Western Christian traditions and structures. It is also being enriched every day by the shifting and multiple spiritual traditions that are emerging in African Christianity outside the conventional Roman-type and Vatican-approved brand of Roman Catholic faith and life. It is giving birth to an ecclesiology that is deeply biblical, but reflects Africa's translation of biblical images and metaphors into local idioms and spiritual practices. It is appropriating into the liturgy diverse beliefs and practices that are emerging spontaneously in African Pentecostalism and African Initiatives in Christianity (AICs) with a rich evangelical flavour. The African Christian religious experience is filled with stories of encounters with the 'holy' in personal and faith communities, and personal spiritual experiences of healing, reconciliation, exorcism, and wholeness. The African churches are flourishing with a gradual but challenging adoption of specific African approaches to addressing limit situations like sudden death, childlessness, ancestral curse, epidemic outbreaks, and personal and communal tragedies. It is also becoming a strong social capital, and a vibrant driver of civil society and political activism. Many churches from all denominations in Africa cooperate as partners in many instances with social agencies in the fight against poverty, illiteracy, and diseases, and continue to help in conflict-resolution in Africa in order to put an end to civil and ethnic conflicts, and wars among nations and within nations, as well as in the resettlement of refugees, and homeless migrants. The Roman Catholic Church in Africa is one of the biggest NGOs in Africa (e.g. Ilo 2014; Calderisi 2013). In Ghana for instance, Catholics make up about 30 per cent of the population but control more hospitals than any other private agency in the country. In Africa the Roman Catholic Church works in 16,178 health centres, including

1,074 hospitals, 5,373 out-patient clinics, 186 leper colonies, 753 homes for the elderly and physically and mentally less able brothers and sisters, 979 orphanages, 1,997 kindergartens, 1,590 marriage counselling centres, 2,947 social re-education centres, and 1,279 other various centres. There are 12,496 nursery schools with 1,266,444 registered children, 33,263 primary schools with 14,061,000 pupils, and 9,838 high schools with 3,738,238 students. Some 54,362 students are enrolled in higher institutes, of which 11,011 are pursuing ecclesiastical studies. In Africa there are 53 national chapters of Caritas, 34 national commissions of justice and peace, and 12 institutes and centres promoting the social doctrine of the church (Ilo 2014: 250). But beyond this descriptive account of the church in Africa lies a deeper ecclesiological question of identity in African Catholicism which I will explore by looking at the contested terminology, 'African church' or 'the church in Africa'.

African Church or
the Church in Africa?

These are two important distinctions in understanding the contested question in African theology on the identity of the churches in Africa which identify themselves with the church of Rome whose visible head is the pope. For centrist Roman Catholic theologians and canonists, the description 'African church' is unacceptable because it could mean that such a church is independent and self-governing and that her communion with the Roman centre is not definitive in terms of mission, form, structure, and pastoral priorities. For others, the designation categorizes as a single reality an ecclesial experience which is as diverse as the multiple languages and cultural and spiritual traditions of millions of African Christians. The Second Vatican Council's Dogmatic Constitution on the Church, *Lumen Gentium* (23), teaches that there is an intimate, inseparable, and mutual relation between the universal church and the local churches. The question then is how does this play out concretely in the relationship between Rome and the dioceses, national episcopal conferences, religious and lay Roman Catholic movements, and institutes of consecrated life in Africa?

In his homily to the bishops of Africa in Kampala, which we have referred to in the introduction, Pope Paul VI used the term 'African church' seven times. 'African church' was a term used to designate the specific and unique African way of living and celebrating the Christian faith. It also resonated with the post-independence renaissance in African culture, arts, and religious traditions and with a renewed sense of African identity. It is this conviction of the uniqueness of the African church that made African bishops pursue the following pastoral actions before and immediately after the Second Vatican Council: (a) A proposal for a pan-African Episcopal Conference which would address pastoral issues common to African peoples. Rome granted this assembly of African Episcopal Conferences only the status of a 'symposium' (Symposium of

Episcopal Conferences of Africa and Madagascar) which means that it is 'a talking shop' that has no juridical or legislative power. An enquiry that I made from the secretariat of SECAM (October 2014) revealed that most national Episcopal Conferences in Africa have better equipped administrative structures than SECAM. This is because Rome has no provision for continental Episcopal bodies like SECAM. (b) The retired archbishop of Bangui, Joachim N'Dayen, reported that in 1969 the regional conference of the bishops of Central Africa and Cameroun had drawn up a motion in favour of a married clergy in the Roman Catholic Church in Africa. He also noted that many African bishops felt strongly that the current pastoral approach to African Christians and practitioners of African traditional religion (ATR) who lived in polygamous marriages based on Western bias against polygamy should be addressed (N'Dayen 1977: 61–3). (c) The development of pastoral institutes in Africa (e.g. the Pastoral Institute at Gaba in 1967) (Hastings 1996: 319) as centres of theological and pastoral planning for contextual ministries and for the creation and dissemination of catechetical texts (e.g. the foundation of the first English-speaking journal of African church and life, *African Ecclesial Review* in 1959) and pastoral formation resources designed to meet the challenges of faith-formation and faith praxis in Africa. (d) The formation of basic Christian communities which started in Africa with the decision of the Sixth plenary assembly of the Zairean Episcopal Conference from 20 November to 2 December 1961 to promote 'living Christian communities'. Today there are over 110,000 small Christian communities in the African Roman Catholic Church (Healey 2012: 1–3). (e) The commitment of African bishops after the Second Vatican Council, under the inspiration of Cardinal Malula and theologians like Engelbert Mveng, Elochukwu Uzukwu, Brookman-Amissah, and Mutiso Mbinda, to convoke an African council in Africa. This council was expected to formulate the shape of a post-Vatican II African church with its own vision, pastoral programmes, and inculturation agenda at all levels of church life (e.g. Mveng 1992: 112–28).

However, the term 'African church' used as the identifier for the Roman Catholic Church in Africa until the 1980s was considered by Rome to be very imprecise and confusing because it could not answer the question: which church? What is the relationship between the 'African church' and the Protestant churches in Africa or the Orthodox churches, both the Eastern and the Ethiopic, the Coptic church, or the African initiatives in Christianity? Is it possible to have a distinctive African Catholicism which is in communion with the church of Rome on equal terms as partners? Particularly within Catholicism, the strong centrist emphasis of Pope John Paul II permanently stamped out such designations within Roman Catholicism through the worldwide continental synods which he called in preparation for the Great Jubilee 2000 which led to the writing of *Ecclesia in Africa* (1995), *Ecclesia in America* (1999), *Ecclesia in Asia* (1999), *Ecclesia in Oceania* (2001), and *Ecclesia in Europa* (2003).

In African Protestantism, the term 'African church' has multiple applications—designating individual denominations, or national, regional, or continental ecclesial associations—as an identifier of the uniqueness and context of African ecclesial life in local communities. The formation of the All Africa Conference of Churches in 1963, as

the single largest organization of African churches, reflected the intention of these ecclesial communities to work together in finding common grounds for promoting the
kingdom of God in Africa and furthering the unity of the Christian peoples. The same
also applies to the Organization of African Instituted Churches which was formed in
1978, representing more than 1,000 African churches formed without any direct influence from the West. The concern over 'the church in Africa' and 'African churches'
is Roman Catholic in nature because it reflects a wider concern about whether the
Roman church has universal primacy over particular churches which are in communion with the church of Rome. But for thousands of African initiated churches and
Pentecostal churches, their very birth, existence, and sustenance is the gift of the Holy
Spirit. Their mission is not understood as a universalizing ideal similar to the agenda of
Christendom. Quite to the contrary, they see their mission as the summons of the Holy
Spirit to offer pastoral care which caters to the immediate needs of particular communi-
ties in their search for abundant life.

In practice, this designation—church in Africa—promoted a more centrist ecclesiology which made African churches more dependent on Rome. As a result, African
Catholicism has embraced a strong emphasis on the primacy of the pope and Vatican
officials in directing the churches in Africa. Furthermore, Rome controls the shape, texture, character, and identity of African Catholicism in such areas as inculturation, liturgy, the ministries of bishops, priests, and religious in Africa, and the pastoral life of
local churches. One reason often given for this is because in the Roman Catholic tradition, churches in Africa are under the 'protection' of Propaganda Fide, meaning that
they are still regarded as being dependent—materially, spiritually, theologically, and
pastorally—on the Western churches and the Roman centre. As a result, there is a reluctance to seek authentic and contextual African approaches to some of the burning questions in African Catholicism: married priests, the place of African women in the church,
and integrating African answers and responses to the fight against HIV/AIDS, etc. The
same reluctance to apply African contextual approaches is evident with regard to such
important aspects of the mission of the church as the integration of African priorities,
theological methods, and contextual curricula in the education of the clergy and religious, as well as Roman Catholic education in general and the principles and practices
for Roman Catholic social services and the church's involvement in politics in Africa.
The distinction between 'African church' and 'the church in Africa' is very important for
understanding the challenges that African Roman Catholics face in their desire to live
fully the faith which they have received from the Lord Jesus and their openness to the
surprises of the Holy Spirit.

THE CHURCH IN AFRICA: YOUNG BUT OLD

The emergence of systematic theologies of the church in Africa is a very recent development, emerging especially since Vatican II; but the history of the church in Africa

is very old, going back to the time of the flight of Jesus to Egypt. We are concerned in this section with the *history of ecclesiology* in Africa and not with *church history*. This distinction is significant in many ways for understanding the nature and identity of the churches in Africa. There is a clear methodological distinction between what Hubert Jedin calls 'historians of the church as institution' and 'historians of ecclesiology' (O'Malley 2005: 246–7). In the first case, one writes ecclesiology as an account of what is going on in the history of the church, beginning from biblical times and continuing with the development of the shape and structure of the early Christian communities in the West and continuing to the era of Western Christian mission to Africa, Asia, and the Americas, etc. This account is given in terms of the development of the structures and mission of the church and its expansion from the West to non-Western cultures. Furthermore, the historian concentrates on how this institutional account defines the reality of faith for non-Western cultures by concentrating on such theological issues as faith and culture, faith and politics, ecumenical initiatives, church councils, sacramental life, hierarchical structures, and inter-faith relations among others. This is the classical approach to ecclesiology which is presented in most Roman Catholic seminaries and theological faculties in Africa. It is a closed-system approach.

Justo Gonzales's distinction between *mission history* and *church history* is helpful in offering the open-system approach being employed here in historicizing African ecclesiology. The mission of God in history, mediated in part through the church, is irreducible to its concretion in any particular context of ecclesial life. What it means is that the mission of God, in particular and diverse historical contexts, in most cases defies categorization or specification along the limiting cultural axis of predominant and established Euro-centric ecclesial structures, liturgies, laws, and canons, as well as the structure of belief and worldviews. The mission of God in history and the mission of the church in history are not coterminous; hence the assumption that the concrete realization of the church in the West can serve as the prototype for the development of the church in a non-Western context is problematic. Gonzales holds that this problem was introduced into ecclesiological studies by Eusebius when he asserted that 'the church is not a historical fact, but is supra-historical, transcendent and strictly eschatological from its very beginning, without any possibility of historical mutation' (Gonzales 2002: 107). Gonzales argues that, beginning from Eusebius, the study of church history always concentrated on the growth of the Western church—with the influence of the Roman Empire, the Greek and Roman traditions—through its replication in other non-Western contexts. Mission history gave an account of how this replication of Western Christianity in a non-Western context took place, but church history was not concerned with the cultural realities of the non-Western contexts which do not fit into this design of God represented in the Western map. Gonzales argues thus:

> Church history studied how Justin Martyr interpreted Christianity in dialogue with Greco-Roman culture, but the issue of polygamy in some African cultures and how African Christians struggled with it are part of the history of the missions . . . Indeed, if African Christians or Native American Christians somehow allowed their

traditions to color their understanding and their practice of the faith, the specter of syncretism immediately arose, thus implying not only that their Christianity was not really part of the history of the church but even that it was not part of the church at all. (Gonzales 2002: 105)

This defensive attitude limited the narrative of the diverse mission of God cross-culturally specified by the movement of the Spirit in history. Another drawback of this institutional approach is that it supports denominationalism. Particularly in African ecclesiology, Ogbu Kalu argues that institutional approaches 'make it difficult for Africans to see themselves as Africans instead of products of warring confessional groups in Europe' (Ogbu Kalu 2007: 13).

The approach of *history of ecclesiology* which we adopt here studies the history of ecclesial communities from a more comprehensive narrative, leveraging multiple voices of where God is at work in the stories from the daily realities of Christians and faith communities in history. It goes beyond a clerical and hierarchical Western account of church history to the stories of living faiths in the encounter of peoples and cultures with Christ in their daily lives. It involves the lives of the whole people of God—clergy and laity. It embodies the stories of the stress and strains, glories and triumphs of the cultural life of the whole people of God—African communities, many unsung heroes and martyrs of the faith in Africa, Western cultures, etc., and the histories of God's dealing with all people—in biblical and non-biblical texts. It gives an account of the faith of African mothers and fathers who may not be among the patriarchs, saints, and doctors of the church in Western church history, but whose lives, sacrifices, proverbs, and words of wisdom continue to be models which reflect the virtues and values taught by the Lord Jesus Christ. This is an empirical and open-structured approach which privileges the narrative of living-faith-in-action of ordinary, everyday Christians at the multiple frontiers of proclamation, witness, martyrdom, worship, and service.

This history of ecclesiology approach takes as its starting point and organizing principle the biblical statement that 'where two or three are gathered in my name' there God is found (Matt. 18:20). While not narrowing its concerns to fragmented ecclesial communities, ecclesiology is understood here as more than theological reflection on the acts of bishops, or the teachings of the pope or clerical top-down culture broadly conceived. Rather, following the tradition of the Acts of the Apostles, there is a strong emphasis on a narrative of both/and. This means broadening the content of ecclesiological studies beyond the institutional mission of the Roman Catholic Church and the teaching of the magisterium, to embrace the actual enactment of the mission of God through the church in the multiple forms of the daily faith and life of the people. This seems to me to be an entirely valid methodological starting point if one is to give a true account of the ecclesiology of the church in Africa as an evolving theological narrative of the mission of God in Africa. This approach will include other mediations of Christ in Christianity outside the traditional Western churches (Roman Catholic, Anglican, Methodist, Presbyterian, etc.), which may still be considered Christian, even though the practices and beliefs may not find any echo in any Western Christian category or description of faith and life. The mission of God assumes different forms as it crosses diverse and unknown cultural and spiritual spaces in Africa, which may confound many in African and non-African contexts, but which only reflects the surprises of the Holy Spirit who lifts up the lowly and brings down the mighty.

Scholars of African ecclesiology identify five stages in the history of the church in Africa (de Gruchy and Chirongoma 2010: 291–2). (i) The period of the early church reaching to the fifth century, marked by the strong presence of the Roman church in Africa, with centres in Carthage, Alexandria, and Numidia. (ii) The period of great conversion, expansion, and division within worldwide Roman Catholicism resulting in the East–West Schism in 1054; and the emergence of the Holy Roman Empire under Charlemagne, and the Gregorian reforms. During this second phase, there was the rise of Islam which wiped away Catholicism in Northern Africa–Numidia and the entire Maghrib, with the remnants of the Coptic church being the only surviving churches along with the Ethiopian churches. Dead also were the flourishing churches and catechetical schools in Alexandria and Hippo. The Christian decline in this period also weakened the foundation of Christianity in Nubia with its eventual collapse and disappearance less than ten centuries later (O'Malley 2001: 186–7). By 1073/6, Pope Gregory VII could not find the required three bishops in the whole of Northern Africa for the consecration of any African bishop (Baur 2009: 29). (iii) Western contacts with Africa through the failed Christian mission (fifteenth–sixteenth century), European trade missions and the transatlantic slave trade (seventeen–nineteenth centuries). The first Western missionary enterprise in the fifteenth and sixteenth centuries started when Pope Alexander (1492–1603) sent the first missionaries to the New World of Asia and Africa, dividing the New World between Spain and Portugal. This missionary project was judged to be largely unsuccessful, even though it established missionary posts and churches in Benin, São Tomé, Angola, Congo, Mozambique, and Madagascar. Two significant historical facts, however, are worth remembering. The first is that Don Henrique was consecrated the first native black bishop of Africa in 1518 by Pope Leo X in Rome (*Ecclesia in Africa*: 32). The second is the significance of African agency and initiatives in the Christian mission in Africa which are often neglected in scholarly debates on the success and failures of missionary work in Africa (Gray 2012). This was also the period of the Reformation and the crisis and divisions in the Western churches which unfortunately defined the doctrinal and denominational conflicts and rivalry which characterized missionary work in Africa which still affect ecumenical initiatives in African Christianity. (iv) The revival of Christian missionary trips to Africa, post-slavery era from the Berlin African Conference (1884–5), colonialism and the successful Christian missionary enterprise (led by many Western European missionaries: Society of Missionaries of Africa, Jesuits, Holy Ghost Fathers, Dominicans, Cistercian Monks, Vincentian fathers and brothers, Oblates of Mary Immaculate, Capuchins, and African clerics like Ajayi Crowther, Wader Harris, etc.) (O'Malley 2001: 120) to the end of the Second Vatican Council (1965). (v) The present stage: from the end of Vatican II (1965) to the Second African Synod of 2009 (*Ecclesia in Africa*: 30–4).

There are three points among many which could be identified in scholarship with regard to the impact of this history on the shape of the church in Africa. The first point is that African ecclesiology is developing as a strong conversation with an African history which harks back to the first century when the Lord Jesus walked the African soil; and even further back to the ancestral past when God spoke to our fathers and mothers in many signs and languages and in shadows and images which pointed to the full revelation of God in Christ (e.g. *Ecclesia in Africa*, 32). In doing this, African ecclesiology, like African Christianity, combats the often negative characterization of any form of religiosity in Africa as pagan, primitive, or syncretistic.

From the foregoing, it is evident that the Christian faith in Africa has a rich past. According to Lamin Sanneh, the Christian faith in Africa should be seen as 'a legitimate tributary of the general stream of Christian history' (Sanneh 1983: xvii). Thomas Oden argues in the same vein when he writes:

> Some scholars of African culture have regrettably acquired a persistent habit of assuming that Christianity began in Africa only a couple of centuries ago, strictly imported from 'the West' or 'the North'. They appear to view Africa as only two or three centuries deep, not two or three millennia. This false start is repeated frequently in some well-intended African theological literature. Even the best of African theologians have been tempted to fall into the stereotypes that Christianity came from Europe. This is a narrow, modern view of history, ignoring Christianity's first millennium, when African thought shaped and conditioned virtually every diocese in Christianity worldwide. (Oden 2007: 25)

Early African Christianity, according to Oden, influenced Western Christianity in seven ways: in the development of modern university education; in the maturing of the exegesis of Scripture; in shaping early Christian dogma; in modelling the conciliar patterns for dialogue in the church; in stimulating early monasticism; in developing Neoplatonism; and in refining the rhetorical and dialectical skills of Christian apologetics and catechetical pedagogy (e.g. Oden 2007: 42–59). Oden notes that in Ethiopia for instance, the apostolic tradition is about 1,650 years old, harking back to the tradition that narrates how the king travelled to the Nile Delta, sat under Athanasius of Alexandria, and became himself the first bishop of Ethiopia. According to Oden, Christians of northern Africa—of Coptic, Berber, Ethiopian, Arabic, and Moorish descent—are treasured as part of the whole multicultural matrix of African Christianity. African Christianity produced so many popes (Victor I, Melchiades, and Gelasius I), many saints and church divines (Monica, Thecla, Perpetua and Felicitas, Paul, Antony, Fulgentius of Ruspe, Abba Salama, Pachomius, Cyprian), and many theologians who helped shape the doctrines of the church (Augustine, Tertullian, Athanasius, Origen, Cyril, and the school of Alexandria) (*Ecclesia in Africa* 30–2). Pope Benedict XVI also spoke in the same light when he said: 'In Jesus, some two thousand years ago, God himself brought salt and light to Africa. From that time on, the seed of his presence was buried deep within the hearts of the people of this dear continent, and it has blossomed gradually, beyond and within the vicissitudes of its human history' (Pope Benedict XVI, AAS 101: 310).

The second consequence of this rich historical treasure of the church in Africa is the question of the identity of African ecclesiology. Are there elements of this history which offer African Christians strong resources for retrieval of a renewed and 'progressive self-constituting' narrative today? Are there, as Oden argues, some original liturgical, exegetical, and theological practices which were retained in Africa during the Dark Ages in Europe (fifth–tenth centuries) which could serve in the construction of the kind of church which Africans want today? Are there some writings of African theologians like Augustine, Cyprian, or the synodal traditions and consultative and participatory shared faith life in the church of Carthage under the leadership of Cyprian (e.g. Mushete and Alberigo 1992: 1–13) which can be appropriated in meeting the challenges of leadership facing African churches today? The object of future research should be how to retrieve Africa's Christian past in a way that does justice to the transitions and differentiates the levels of meaning without being enthusiastically simplistic in imagining a happy, unadulterated African past or being reductionistic and normative in the account of the African Christian past (e.g. Maluleke in Kalu 2007: 415).

Eboussi Boulaga, for instance, privileges the retrieval of the first stage of church history in Africa (the first three centuries), which, he believes, will help bring about in Africa a Christianity without cultural accretions (or what he calls 'fetishes') from Europe; a recapture of what is truly Christian; a return to the true source excluding those dominant cultural narratives that have been imposed as normative for the rest of Christianity (Boulaga 1984: 9). As Metena Nteba argues, 'For Eboussi, this concept of restatement includes the taking over, by Africa, of the "original" (the memory of Jesus Christ) and the "foundations" (the inaugural acts of Christianity) by including them in Africa's own schemes and languages' (Mushete and Alberigo 1992: 136). It needs to be noted, in conversation with Boulaga, that the African church of the first five centuries was not a pristine church. There was no regnant, single narrative of this past which could be assigned a homological description—there were doctrinal and pastoral problems, like the Novatian Schism, which grew out of Decian persecution, and Donatism which grew out of the Diocletian persecution (303–13) (Isichei: 36–7). There were also other divisive doctrinal battles over Pelagianism, Monophysitism, and Nestorianism, all of which challenged the churches of North Africa and in many cases created permanent divisions in the African churches of the first five centuries (Baur 2009: 25). Therefore, restatement or retrieval must discern the horizons of differences in the appropriation of the faith across these diverse cultural, spiritual, and historical moments.

The third and most important consequence of this history for African Catholic ecclesiology is the question of historiography and how African ecclesiology is written and documented. This raises the question whether the theologies of church being developed and taught in the African academy reflect the true reality and faces of faith and life in Africa. Who determines what is included and what is left out in the narrative of ecclesial life? How does one delineate and map the new frontiers of faith in Africa without employing the wrong theological navigational equipment, borrowed from the West, which could lead the African faithful away from the eschatological fulfilment of African history?

There is also the question of conversion which is an ongoing theological challenge in African Christianity. How successful was the conversion of Africans by Portuguese missionaries in the kingdoms of Benin, Warri (mid-western Nigeria), Kongo, and Angola? What is the meaning of conversion in African Christianity today and how is it different from conversion for instance during the colonial period? Is there a new conversion taking place today in African Christianity—Africa's own version of *ressourcement* and *aggiornamento*—which is distancing itself from the European-type Romanism and re-discovering an inculturated Christianity rich in biblical images and brewed in autochthonous African religio-cultural traditions which go back to the earliest centuries of church history? Is there an African version of modernity being enacted through the Christian expansion in Africa?

In most cases, African ecclesiology has been an attempt to extricate African Christianity—Catholic or Protestant—from its northern epistemological and doctrinal captivity. One significant result of Western Catholic missions in Africa which has continued today in African churches is the strong emphasis on education, social justice, social mission, and healthcare services. However, modern Catholicism in Africa was born in the late nineteenth century from missionaries who were forged in the furnace of a normative Roman Catholicism with its elaborate claim on universalizing Eurocentric Roman Catholic faith and morals as a single sociological unit without cultural or spiritual differentiation. This quest for a synchronizing ecclesiology and a unitary method of enquiry into truth, and the presupposition of a *theologia perennis* and of the church as a perfect society, were the foundations on which Catholicism was built in Africa. It is one of the greatest challenges facing African ecclesiology. Despite the reform of Catholic ecclesiology at Vatican II with recognition of the ecclesial status of local churches, there is in African Catholicism today a strong rebuttal of any attempt to introduce diversity or dialogue in any of the doctrinal issues at the heart of what mainline Catholicism regards as unchangeable and unchanging rule of faith. In this regard, it seems that constructing Roman Catholic ecclesiology is, properly speaking, the task of rewriting African Christian religious history. Such an account will privilege the mission of God in African history, the riches and limitations of African traditional religio-cultural spiritual traditions and worldviews, and African initiatives in the missionary and post-missionary movements. It will also embrace a praxis of faith and hope to meet the challenges of the social context in re-imagining the mission of the church in Africa.

The Future of African Ecclesiology: Inculturation

One major challenge facing the church in Africa today is inculturation. Most scholars believe that the presence of 'double conscience', 'schizoid faith', 'swinging faith', and 'permeable religious affinity' among many African Christians raises fundamental questions about the nature of conversion in African Christianity. What are Africans converting from and what kind of faith and ecclesial life and structures are they embracing? What is the before and the after of conversion from ATRs to Christianity in Africa. This is particularly with regard to the loose and experimental religious affinity in limit situations in the daily life and faith of many African Christians. Particularly in the Roman Catholic tradition, the challenge of inculturation in Africa is about how to address the tension between the official/received teaching, beliefs, and practices of the magisterium of the Roman Catholic Church, and the actual living faith experience of African Catholics.

Karl Rahner first drew attention to this problem in Roman Catholic systematic theology when he noted that 'most Christians believe explicitly much less than what is explicitly present in the doctrine of the magisterium' (Rahner in Mannion 2003: 305). The question then is how can the actual faith of African Catholics, for instance, which has 'a normative significance for the official faith of the Church', find accommodation in the teaching of the authoritative magisterium 'that is in principle, normative for the faith of the individual' (Rahner: 307)? The actual faith is similar to popular piety which Pope Benedict XVI referred to as 'a precious treasure of the Catholic Church' (Pope Benedict XVI, AAS 90, 2007: 446). However, in societies like that of Africa, where the mysterious ways of God and spontaneous faith expressions are not ensconced in any written dogma or liturgical manual but are alive in non-literal cultural texts, memorial traditions, cultural behaviours and artefacts, can one affirm these manifestations of actual African Christian faith as an expression of the *consensus fidelium*?

Actual faith in African Christianity and particularly in Roman Catholicism is much more than popular piety, with its Marian devotions, novenas, spiritual sodalities, Charismatic prayer meetings, healing sessions, exorcism, and perpetual adorations, etc. It refers to the cultural grammar of assent of most African Catholics, their worldviews, their map of the universe, and their understanding of the presence of God in the person of the Lord Jesus Christ in every aspect of life. This is markedly different from a sacred–secular dualism in Western theologies and worldview. The typical African Catholic believes in the sacramental economy of the Roman Catholic Church, but holds to the actual faith that God does intervene in their lives through other forms of mediation outside of the sacramental system. An African ecclesiology which works from this actual faith presupposes that the religious experiences which imbue the worship and practices in African Catholicism are in themselves an African appropriation—inculturated formally or informally—of the way of being the church which is at home with Africans and acceptable as a form of divine revelation in history. While they are in themselves manifestations of the divine and share a family trait with Catholicism in other contexts, they have a lot in common with other expressions of Christianity and religiosity in Africa. This kind of African Christian religious experience abhors denominationalism. It thus overlaps in both categorization and classification with other ways of being the church and living the Christian faith in Africa which are not Roman Catholic. This actual faith has its own internal plausibility structures and logic and is alive and constantly evolving beyond the restrictive sacramental systems and defined boundaries of what is spiritual or profane, or what is orthodox or syncretistic, outside the normative canon of Roman Catholic faith.

Some typical instances in the daily lives of African Catholics which validate the presence of this actual faith in Africa are the strong ties of most African Catholics to ancestral beliefs, unique appeal to ATRs in dealing with limit situations, traditional funeral rites and traditions which are preferred to the Western Christian type, the question of the immortality of the soul and the afterlife, childless marriage, polygamy, rites of passage, initiatory rites at different stages of liminality, among others. In most of these instances, many African Roman Catholics may hold some beliefs and practices and embrace some rituals which may not fit into the received canons of orthodoxy in the Catholic Church.

A reflection of this actual faith in the emergence of unique African narratives of the Christian faith is the strong presence and influence of Pentecostalism and African Initiatives in Christianity (AICs). The growing influence of African Pentecostalism and its variant in the African Catholic Charismatic movement reflect the mining of the powers of the Holy Spirit by Africans while bringing African cultural grammar and social conditions into Christian experience. African Pentecostalism is offering most African Christians a new experience of the Trinity through a powerful experience of the manifestations of the fruits and gifts of the Holy Spirit. It is also giving them new ecclesial images as they link the symbols of the Trinity with cultural categories and experiential faith acts which provide answers to the most pressing questions of the times. Cedric Mayrargue argues that it is not enough to dismiss African Pentecostals as 'local religious entrepreneurs'; rather there is a need to see them as Africa's unique contextualization of the faith and a reflection of the diffused centres of influence in World Christianity (Mayrargue 2004: 100). There are four important points here in scholarship on how African Pentecostalism has been presented. The first is that they represent an attempt to respond to the challenges posed by the insertion of ATRs into Christianity in sub-Saharan Africa. The second is that they are the fruits of a growing rejection among African Christians of aspects of Western Christianity and its Latinized and Gregorian liturgies; in a sense it is a protest against the normalization of Western Christianity in Africa and a religious variant of Africa's contestations with the currents of modernity. The third is that they use the resources of the Christian heritage to address the challenging social context of suffering, poverty, political instability, diseases, ancestral curse, witchcraft, wars, and deaths which have characterized African history for more than a century. Most of these issues are not addressed in any official teaching of the church. They offer some narratives of hope. Finally, depending on the type of African initiatives being considered (messianic, AIC, etc.), African Pentecostalism has been criticized as watered down Christianity and its leaders as merchants of a prosperity gospel, without any theology and praxis of hope (e.g. Kalu 2008: 103–47). However, the deep Christological and pneumatological retrieval of biblical and patristic spirituality in African Pentecostalism reveals a Trinitarian foundation to this movement in African Christian consciousness. It goes beyond a simplistic claim that they are merely sectarian, chiliastic, and syncretistic movements, purveying watered-down spiritual antidotes to soothe the troubled social and spiritual world of many gullible and vulnerable African poor. A theology of African Pentecostalism should emerge from and accompany the experience of African Christians, rather than being an abstract guide, developed as a prioristic negative judgement of this complex and evolving force which is redefining the Christian spiritual landscape in Africa.

The First African Synod, conscious of the challenges posed to the Christian faith in Africa by the gulf between official faith and actual faith, identified five aspects of the mission of the church in Africa as the family of God moving into the new millennium: evangelization, inculturation, dialogue, pastoral care to meet the challenges of evangelization, and the means of social communication (Pope John Paul II, EA, 1994: 16). However, of all these goals, inculturation is what has been central in theological and ecclesial discussion about the future of the church in Africa. *Ecclesia in Africa* (no. 59) defines inculturation as having two dimensions, 'the ultimate transformation of authentic cultural values through their integration in Christianity' and 'the insertion of Christianity in the various human cultures'. The Synod noted (EA, 59) that inculturation is an urgent task. African Catholic bishops at the Synod also committed themselves to building the church in Africa into self-sufficient (EA, 104) communities of faith, and to promoting the cause of justice and peace (EA 112–14). But most importantly with regard to addressing the challenges of the actual faith and the official faith, the Synod embraced the message of 'respecting, preserving and fostering the particular values and riches of Africa' on one hand, while 'bringing Christ into the very center of African life and of lifting African life to Christ' because, as Pope Paul VI proclaimed, 'Christianity is not only relevant to Africa, but Christ, in the members of his Body, is himself African' (EA, 127).

There are many theological judgements among African scholars on how inculturation has been carried out in the church in Africa (e.g. Magesa 2004, 2013). However, F. Kabisele Lumbala's proposals (Lumbala 2002: 351–64; cf. Kalilombe 2004: 38–48; McGarry and Ryan 2001) on the way forward for inculturated African Catholic ecclesiology is a fitting summary of the key issues in terms of the future of inculturation in Roman Catholic ecclesiology in Africa. (i) An integrated evangelization which addresses authentic and integral human and cultural development in Africa which requires respectful encounter and dialogue with African Traditional Religions. (ii) The Africanization and contextualization of the hierarchical, clerical, and religious life in Africa, which should include not only the indigenization of the clergy and the inclusion of women, but a pastoral formation and education that is brewed in an African pot. (iii) The greater involvement and promotion of small Christian communities in Africa; and greater research and a wholehearted embrace of liturgical reform in Africa, similar and even more profound than the Zairean Rome Rite (Lumbala 2002: 358). The church in Africa needs an African liturgical rite and an African canon law which could be developed in conversation with the actual faith of the people. (iv) Inculturation should also profoundly lead to the transformation of the structure, charism, identity, and mission of religious orders and congregations, ecclesial movements, and lay formation. (v) Particularly to be noted is the need for social ministries and pastoral life which address the cry of the poor in Africa, especially the continued subordination of women in the Roman Catholic Church in Africa. At the same time inculturation should be intrinsically and intimately connected with conversion, social transformation, liberation, and the creation of a new Africa. There is also the need to create more centres of research and African Christian academies that will advance, articulate, and promote relevant research on African culture, African theology, and African Christian mission. The outcomes of such research should guide the church leadership and the lay faithful in inculturating the faith in Africa.

Conclusion: Reverse Conversion and Reverse Mission

There are two important conclusions which one can draw from the discussion of Roman Catholic ecclesiology in terms of research into the future and Africa's contribution to the world church. The first is the question of the identity of the African church and the second is the relevance of these ecclesial images and identity for realizing the mission of God in Africa. The Second African Synod proposed that the church in Africa should become salt and light to both Africa and the world. Since the end of the Second Vatican Council, many popes (especially Paul VI and John Paul II) have called on African Christians to become missionaries to Africa and the world. There are two movements in African Catholicism which will become more significant in the years to come as the church in Africa responds to this double missionary vocation.

The first movement is *a reverse conversion* from the received missionary faith and beliefs and practices defined by Western categories to a deepening of the Christian faith in Africa. This begins with a gospel-based recovery of authentic African spiritual and moral traditions of abundant life and community. This is a reverse movement of rediscovering the inner enrichment of African Christian values in the enthusiastic attachment of Africans to Christ and the church. Methodologically, this can be achieved by scholars through an ethnographic mapping of the cultural universe of Africans as it is presently being shaped by their embrace of the Christian faith. Attention ought to be given to the structures of meaning which shape people's faith and choices today in Africa and harvesting the narratives of faith through the socio-cultural portraiture of African peoples. This will lead to an ecclesiology which will be defined by African priorities and grounded in African religio-cultural spiritual grammar, and which reflects the actual faith of African Christians as they seek the realization of the reign of God in history. This will be a slow process of digging deeper into the historical faith narratives from the past, going beyond an enchanted African Christianity to experimentation with new approaches and new forms of ecclesial life which may require embracing a positive syncretism and a theology of the in-between. This is already emerging gradually in the faith life of many African Christians. It can be seen reflected in the increasing influence of priest and lay healers in African churches, in dynamic liturgies and para-liturgies with their emphasis on direct spiritual experiences and harvesting of the power of God.

There are also some emerging trends in African churches which should occupy the attention of African ecclesiologists. These trends include the strong emergence of African women as new voices in theologies and pastoral ministries, the practical ecumenical initiatives of ordinary African Christians, and the emphasis given in much church teaching to the social mission of the church to the poor and those on the margins and the heroic witness of many nuns in Africa such as Sr Rosemary Nyirumbe and Sr Namaika, among many, in creating communities of hope in hidden corners in Uganda and Congo-Kinshasa.

This reverse movement will gradually weaken the entrenched clericalism and authoritarian hierarchical structures in African Roman Catholicism. It will also bring about the birth of new forms of pastoral practices, faith formation, spiritual movements, lay sodalities, and greater attention to accountability in the church with regard to the gifts which God has given to the whole people of God in Africa. This will be a long process of retrieval, reform, renewal, transformation, and rebirth. It will also be a missionary movement because it will be driven by the desire to give birth to African churches which fully embody the local realization of the mission of God in the life of the church. At the same time, such freedom of the Spirit reflected in the structures of the church will lead African Christian churches away from absolute and sometimes 'magical' attachment to devotionalism, pious activities, and multiplication of prayers characteristic of an enchanted Christianity. What will emerge will be an ecclesiology from the margins and from the narratives of faith in daily life and an ecclesial praxis of hope for the enactment in present history of the reign of God for the transformation of Africa and the liberation of her peoples.

The second movement is *a reverse mission* from Africa to the West. Bigard memorial Seminary in Enugu in eastern Nigeria with over 1,000 seminarians is the largest seminary in the Roman Catholic world. With the dearth in vocation to religious and priestly life in the West, many African priests and nuns are not only becoming missionaries to the West and Asia; they are also taking leadership and teaching positions in Western churches and universities. What this means is that there will be a significant but gradual impact in world Christianity of an African brand of religiosity and spirituality and African theologies of family, sexuality, gender, and ecology against the Western *ratio* which still dominate discourse in World Christianity. This is already happening in the Anglican Communion with the emergence of a strong Anglican Global South movement (GAFCON and GFCA) since 2008 led by African primates opposed to the stand of Western Anglican churches on same-sex relations, women's ordination, etc.

The enthusiasm for God and the centrality of the Christian faith in African history is a strong rebuttal of the secular and post-modern thinking in the West which claims that Christianity might become a cultural relic in history. This is not the story in Africa because Christianity is alive, young, and ever new in the hearts and homes of Africans. The pathway of Africa's march towards modernity will pass through a contextualized African ecclesial life; it does not have to be a reproduction of the same pathway and cultural dynamic dictated by the West. The central question, however, is: Can African types and models of church become influential for the revival of the faith in the West if African churches are still dependent financially on Western churches? What images of the church can Africans present to world Christianity as her 'success stories' in dealing with the challenges of ethnocentric and clannish sentiments in African churches or the troubling authoritarianism, marginalization of women, and the highly clerical culture which is still dominant in African churches? What message will churches in Africa offer to world Christianity on how they are dealing with ecumenical and inter-faith relations? What are specific African Christian approaches to religious persecution of African Christians in African countries with a predominant Muslim population, and how should Christianity relate to other cultural subjects, faith traditions, and people on the margins in diverse societies to promote human and cosmic flourishing and the reign of God?

The second concern for scholarship is about the social context of Africa. How can the images of the church current in African Christianity help bring about the realization of God's mission for Africa? The two African synods spoke strongly of the need for African Christianity to give hope to Africans by embracing an option for the poor (EA, 44, 52, 68–9, 70, 113, 139; *Africe Munus*, 25, 27, 29, 30, 84, 88–90). Jean-Mac Ela and Gustavo Gutiérrez all argue that Vatican II opened the church not only to the world, but above all to recognizing the contradiction and pain in the world for the poor of the Lord (Guttiérez 1987: 171–93; Ela 1996: 55: Orobator 2013: 284–300). Pope Francis placed the service of the poor as central to the mission of the church and as the hermeneutical key for understanding his papacy. In a continent where the majority of the people are holding on to God, and finding courage and hope through the Christian faith, the church in Africa must become a poor church for the poor and the voice of the voiceless. She must find pastoral models and strategies which will offer the people the personal and communal conditions for realizing their hope in their daily life (e.g. Ashworth 2014). In a continent wounded by ethnocentricism, seen, for example, in the post-Rwandan genocide, African ecclesiology must show the African faithful the reason to believe that the waters of baptism are stronger than the blood of ethnicity.

The greatest pastoral challenge facing the churches in Africa today in the complex social context of Africa is how to proclaim and enact the praxis of hope to the poor by being a poor church for the poor in Africa. This is particularly so with regard to *accountability to God* for the gift of the church to Africa, and *accompaniment of the churches in Africa with the people of Africa*, especially those on the margins, by being fully immersed in the social condition of the poor, while speaking from the chaos of their lives. The decisiveness of this will be reflected in theologies of the church which grow from the living faith of the people and are being translated into pastoral actions, performance, and praxis of social transformation for Africa. How this identity of the poor church for the poor is embodied in the theologies of church in Africa will most certainly define the relevance of the church in Africa in the coming years. It will also be a significant contribution of African churches in the search in world Christianity for a new image for the church and Christianity which points to the poor man of Galilee.

REFERENCES

Allen, John (2009). *The Future Church: How Ten Trends are Revolutionizing the Catholic Church*. New York: Doubleday.

Ashworth, John (2014). *The Voice of the Voiceless: The Role of the Church in the Sudanese Civil War*. Nairobi: Paulines Publications Africa.

Balthasar, Hans Urs von (1992). *Razing the Bastions*. Trans. Brian McNeil. San Francisco: Communio Books.

Baur, John (2009). *2000 Years of Christianity in Africa: An African Church History*. Nairobi: Paulines Publications Africa.

Benedict XVI (2011). *Africae Munus: Post-Synodal Apostolic Exhortation*. Nairobi: Paulines Publications Africa.

Bonk, Jonathan (2009). 'Africa and the Christian Mission'. *International Bulletin of Missionary Research* 33.2: 58.

Bujo, Benezet (1996). 'On the Road Toward an African Ecclesiology'. In Maura Browne (ed.), *The African Synod: Documents, Reflections, Perspectives*. Maryknoll, NY: Orbis, 139–51.

Bujo, Benezet (2007). *Plea for Change of Models for Marriage*. Nairobi: Paulines Publications Africa.

Bulaga, F. Eboussi (1984). *Christianity Without Fetishes: An African Critique and Recapture of Christianity*. Trans. Robert R. Barr. Maryknoll, NY: Orbis.

Calderisi, Robert (2013). *Earthly Mission: The Catholic Church and World Development*. New Haven: Yale University Press.

De Gruchy, John and Chirongoma, Sophie (2010). 'Earth, Water, Fire and Wind: Elements of African Ecclesiologies'. In Gerard Mannion and Lewis S. Mudge (eds), *The Routledge Companion to the Christian Church*. New York: Routledge.

Ela, Jean-Marc (1986). *African Cry*. Trans. Robert J. Barr. Maryknoll, NY: Orbis.

Fogliacco, Nicholas (2001). 'The Family: An African Metaphor for Trinity and Church'. In Cecil McGarry and Patrick Ryan (eds), *Inculturating the Church in Africa: Theological and Practical Perspectives*. Nairobi: Paulines Publications Africa, 120–58.

Gonzales, Justo (2002). *The Changing Shape of Church History*. St Louis, MO: Chalice.

Gray, Richard (2012). *Christianity, The Papacy and Mission in Africa*. Ed. Lamin Sanneh. Maryknoll, NY: Orbis.

Guttiérez, Gustavo (1987). 'The Church and the Poor: A Latin American Perspective'. Trans. Matthew J. O'Connell. In Giuseppe Alberigo, Jean-Pierre Jossua, and Joseph Komoncha (eds), *The Reception of Vatican II*. Washington, DC: The Catholic University of America Press, 171–93.

Hastings, Adrian (1986). 'The Council Came to Africa'. In Alderic Stacpoole (ed.), *Vatican II by Those Who Were There*. London: Geoffrey Chapman.

Hastings, Adrian (1989). *African Catholicism: Essays in Discovery*. London: SCM.

Healey, Joseph G. (2012). *Building the Church as Family of God: Evaluation of Small Christian Communities in Eastern Africa*. Nairobi: AMECEA Gaba Publications-CUEA Press.

Ilo, Stan Chu (2014a). 'Method and Models of African Theology'. In Agbonkhianmeghe E. Orobator (ed.), *Theological Reimaginations: Conversations on Church, Religion, and Society in Africa*. Nairobi: Paulines Publications, 115–30.

Ilo, Stan Chu (2014b). *The Church and Development in Africa: Aid and Development from the Perspective of Catholic Social Teaching*. 2nd edn. Eugene, OR: Pickwick.

Ilo, Stan Chu et al. (eds) (2011). *The Church as Salt and Light: Path to an African Ecclesiology of Abundant Life*. Eugene, OR: Pickwick.

Isichei, Elizabeth (1995). *A History of Christianity in Africa: From Antiquity to Present*. Grand Rapids, MI: Eerdmans.

John Paul II (1994). *Ecclesia in Africa*. Nairobi: Paulines Publications Africa.

Kalilombe, Patrick A. (1991). 'The Effects of the Council on World Catholicism'. In Adrian Hastings (ed.), *Modern Catholicism: Vatican II and After*. New York: Oxford University Press, 313–15.

Kalilombe, Patrick, A. (2004). 'Praxis and Methods of Inculturation in Africa: Some Background Reflections'. In Patrick Ryan (ed.), *Theology of Inculturation in Africa Today: Methods, Praxis and Mission*. Nairobi: Catholic University of Eastern Africa Press, 38–48.

Lonergan, Bernard (1999). *Method in Theology*. Toronto: University of Toronto Press.

Lumbala, F. Kabasele (2002). 'L'Inculturation et les églises d'Afrique entre Vatican II et le Synod Africain'. In M. Lamberigts and L. Kenis (eds), *Vatican II and its Legacy*. Leuven: Leuven University Press, 351–64.

Magesa, Laurenti (2004). *Anatomy of Inculturation: Transforming the Church in Africa*. Maryknoll, NY: Orbis.

Mannion, Gerard (ed.) (2003). *Readings in Church Authority: Gifts and Challenges for Contemporary Catholicism*. Aldershot: Ashgate.

Mayrargue, Cedric (2004). 'Trajectoires et enjeux contemporains du Pentecostism en Afrique de l'Ouest'. *Critique internationale* 22 (January): 100.

Mveng, Engelbert (1992). 'The African Synod: Prologomena for an African Council'. In Giuseppe Alberigo and Alphonse N. Mushete (eds), *Towards the African Synod. Concilium* 1992/1: 112–28.

N'Dayen, Joachim (1977). 'Relations of the Local Churches with Rome and the Function of the Episcopal Conference of Black Africa'. In Claude Geffre and Bertrand Luneau (eds), *The Churches of Africa: Future Prospects*. New York: Seabury, 60–8.

Nteba, M. (1992). 'Inculturation in the "Third Church": God's Pentecost or Cultural Revenge'. In Giuseppe Alberigo and Alphonse N. Mushete (eds), *Towards the African Synod. Concilium* 1992/1: 129–46.

Nyamiti, Charles (2007). *Studies in African Christian Theology: Some Contemporary Models of African Ecclesiology. A Critical Assessment in the Light of Biblical and Church Teaching*. Vol. 3. Nairobi: CUEA.

Nyamiti, Charles (2010). *Studies in African Christian Theology: Christ's Ancestral Mediation Through the Church Understood as God's Family: An Essay on African Ecclesiology*. Vol. 4. Nairobi: CUEA.

Oden, Thomas (2007). *How Africa Shaped the Christian Mind: Rediscovering the African Seedbed of Western Christianity*. Downers Grove, IL: IVP.

Ogbu, Kalu (ed.) (2007). *African Christianity: An African Story*. Trenton, NJ: Africa World Press.

Ogbu, Kalu (2008). *African Pentecostalism: An Introduction*. Oxford: Oxford University Press.

Ogbu, Kalu and Low, Alaine (eds) (2008). *Interpreting Contemporary Christianity: Global Processes and Local Identities*. Grand Rapids, MI: Eerdmans.

O'Malley, John, W. (2005). 'Yves Congar as Historian of Ecclesiology'. In Gabriel Flynn (ed.), *Yves Congar: Theologian of the Church*. Grand Rapids, MI: Eerdmans, 246–7.

O'Malley, Vincent, J. (2001). *Saints of Africa*. Huntington, IN: Our Sunday Visitor.

Opongo, Elias, O. and Kaulemu, David (eds) (2014). *Catholic Church Leadership in Peace Building in Africa*. Nairobi: Paulines Publications Africa.

Orobator, Agbonkhianmeghe E. (ed.) (2007). *From Crisis to Kairos: The Mission of the Church in the Time of HIV/AIDS, Refugees and Poverty*. Nairobi: Paulines Publications Africa.

Orobator, Agbonkhianmeghe E. (ed.) (2011). *Reconciliation, Justice, and Peace: The Second African Synod*. Maryknoll, NY: Orbis.

Orobator, Agbonkhianmeghe E. (2013). 'After all, Africa is Largely a Non Literate Continent'. *Theological Studies* 74: 284–300.

Paul VI, Pope (1969). 'Address to the Symposium of Episcopal Conferences of Africa and Madagascar'. Kampala: AAS, 61, 575.

Sanneh, Lamin (1983). *West African Christianity: The Religious Impact*. Maryknoll, NY: Orbis.

Sempore, Sidbe (1977). 'The Churches in Africa Between Past and Future'. In Claude Geffre and Bertrand Luneau (eds), *The Churches of Africa: Future Prospects*. New York: Seabury.

Uzukwu, Elochukwu (1996). *A Listening Church: Autonomy and Communion in African Churches*. Maryknoll, NY: Orbis.

Suggested Reading

Baur, John (2009). *2000 Years of Christianity in Africa: An African Church History*. Nairobi: Paulines Publications Africa.

Healey, Joseph G. (2012). *Building the Church as Family of God: Evaluation of Small Christian Communities in Eastern Africa*. Nairobi: AMECEA Gaba Publications-CUEA.

Ilo, Stan Chu (2014). *The Church and Development in Africa: Aid and Development from the Perspectives of Catholic Social Ethics*. Eugene, OR: Pickwick.

Magesa, Laurenti (2004). *Anatomy of Inculturation: Transforming the Church in Africa*. Maryknoll, NY: Orbis.

Mugambi, Jesse (ed.) (1990). *The Church in African Christianity: Innovative Essays in Ecclesiology*. Nairobi: Initiatives Ltd.

Orobator, Agbonkhianmeghe E. (ed.) (2016). *The Church We Want: African Christians look Toward Vatican III*. Maryknoll, NY: Orbis.

Ryan, Patrick (ed.) (2001). *Inculturating the Church in Africa: Theological and Practical Perspectives*. Nairobi: Paulines Publications Africa.

Uzukwu, Elochukwu (1996). *A Listening Church: Autonomy and Communion in African Churches*. Maryknoll, NY: Orbis.

Index of Names

Note: Names of authors referred to in roundbracketed references in the text or listed in the bibliographies or who receive brief passing mention are not all noted here.

Abelard, Peter 206–7
Abravanel 42
Adam, Karl 274, 280
Afanasiev/Afanassieff, Nikolai 196, 475–6
Ainsworth, Henry 303, 305–6
Alexander III *Pope* 202
Alexander V *Pope* 212
Alexander VI *Pope* 215
Ambrose *Bishop, Saint* 174, 176, 278
Ammerman, Nancy 544
Anderson, Allan 337
Andrewes, Lancelot *Bishop* 247, 251
Anselm *Archbishop, Saint* 252
Aquinas, Thomas *see* Thomas Aquinas
Aristotle 207, 568
Arnold, Matthew 297
Asbury, Francis *Bishop* 326
Athanasius *Bishop, Saint* 147, 176
Augustine of Canterbury *Archbishop, Saint* 178, 247
Augustine of Hippo *Bishop, Saint* 77, 171, 175–6, 414, 449–50, 460, 560–1
Aurelian *Emperor* 170
Avis, Paul (P. D. L.) 240, 468

Balthasar, Hans Urs von 411, 415, 421
Bancroft, Richard *Archbishop* 244
Banks, Robert 127–8, 135, 138
Barrett, C. K. 59
Barrow, Henry 299, 303
Bartalomé de las Casas *Bishop* 579
Barth, Karl 1, 7, 361–82, 390, 562
Bartholomew *Ecumenical Patriarch* 482
Basil the Great *Bishop, Saint* 5–6, 469
Baur, F. C. 256

Bayne, Stephen *Bishop* 240
Becket, Thomas *Archbishop, Martyr* 202
Behr, John 196
Bellarmine, Robert S. J. *Archbishop, Cardinal, Saint* 266–7, 270, 273, 275, 277, 282, 569
Benedict XIII *Pope* 213
Benedict XV *Pope* 272
Benedict XVI *Pope* 25, 283–4, 413, 449–65, 474–5, 477, 568, 619, 627–8, 630
Benigni, Umberto 272
Bennett, Dennis 338
Berger, Teresa 541
Bernardino de Sahagún 578
Berry, Jan 543
Beza, Theodore 244
Billot, Louis, S. J. 279
Blandina *Martyr* 186–8
Blondel, Maurice 272, 411–12
Boersma, Hans 156
Boff, Clodovis 562
Boff, Leonardo 588
Bonhoeffer, Dietrich 555–6
Boniface VIII *Pope* 6, 202, 204, 208–9, 211
Borromeo, Charles *Archbishop, Cardinal, Saint* 266
Bosch, David 13, 556–8
Bouillard, Henri, S. J. 413
Boulaga, Eboussi 628
Bradford, William 296, 309
Bradshaw, William 306
Bramhall, John *Archbishop* 253
Branick, V. 137
Braude, Ann 527, 547
Brown, Callum 547
Brown, Raymond E. 257

INDEX OF NAMES

Browne, Robert 299, 304–5
Browning, Don 565
Bucer (Butzer), Martin 231, 309
Bullinger, Heinrich 307
Bultmann, Rudolf 365
Bunyan, John 311

Caecilian *Bishop* 171
Callistus *Bishop* 166–8
Callixtus II *Pope* 201
Calvin, John (Jean) (Calvinism) 6, 151,
    176, 217–36, 242, 244–5, 297, 299, 304,
    307, 309
Campbell, R. A. 131–2
Cartwright, Thomas 244
Catherine of Siena *Saint* 205, 212
Celestine *Pope* 176
Cerfaux, Lucien 277–8
Cerularius, *Patriarch* 200
Charlemagne *Emperor* 178
Charles I *King, Martyr* 245, 250–1
Charles II *King* 245
Chenu, Marie-Dominique, O. P. 275, 386
Childs, Brevard 36–7
Chrysostom, John *Archbishop, Saint* 52
Clare of Assisi *Saint* 205
Clark King, Ellen 546
Claver, Peter *Saint* 579
Clement V *Pope* 210–11
Clement VII *Pope* 212
Clement of Rome *Bishop, Saint* 164
Coakley, Sarah 15
Coke, Thomas *Bishop* 325–6
Coleridge, Samuel Taylor 50
Columbus, Christopher 578
Combes, Émile 409
Congar, Yves, O. P. 275, 280–1, 285, 383–407,
    446, 467
Connolly, Robert 167
Constantine I *Emperor, Saint* 6, 171, 194, 557
Cornelius *Bishop* 169–70
Cosin, John *Bishop* 242
Cranmer, Thomas *Archbishop, Martyr* 7, 247,
    251, 256
Crawford, Janet 540
Cromwell, Oliver 245
Cullmann, Oscar 278, 463

Cyprian *Bishop, Martyr, Saint* 168–70, 175,
    475, 628
Cyril of Alexandria *Bishop, Saint* 176
Cyril of Jerusalem *Bishop, Saint* 176

Damaskinos, Papandreou *Metropolitan* 462
Dante Alighieri 205, 215
Darwin, Charles 268
de Chardin, Teilhard, S. J. 281, 416
de Lubac, Henri, S. J. *Cardinal* 7, 156, 275–6,
    278–83, 386, 409–29, 474
Denck, Hans 307
Diego, Juan *Saint* 577
Diocletian *Emperor* 171
Dionysius (of Alexandria) *Bishop* 170
Dionysius (of Rome) *Bishop* 170
Dominic *Saint* 205
Donatus (Donatism) 171
Dostoevsky, Fyodor 421
Drey, Johann Sebastian 268
Dulles, Avery, S. J. *Cardinal* 283, 391, 411
Dunn, J. D. G. 126, 136, 138
Dupuis, Jacques, S. J. 414
Durandus, William 6

Ebeling, Gerhard 495
Edward VI *King* 246
Ela, Jean Mac 635
Eleutherus *Bishop* 166
Eliot, T. S. 5
Elizabeth I *Queen* 242, 248, 303
Elphinstone, William *Bishop* 215
Ephrem the Syrian 187–8
Esler, Philip 564
Eugenius IV *Pope* 213–14
Eusebius (of Caesarea) *Bishop* 166, 194, 624
Eutyches 177

Faggioli, Massimo 283
Fawcett, John 299
Felix of Abthungi *Bishop* 170–1
Field, Richard 245, 251
Fiorenza, Elizabeth Schüssler 529, 531–5
Fitz, Robert 303
Florovsky, Georges 192–3, 472
Foliot, Gilbert *Bishop* 202
Fouilloux, Étienne 387

Foxe, John 309
Francis *Pope* 17, 283–4, 635
Francis of Assisi *Saint* 205
Franzelin, Johannes Baptist, S. J. 270
Frederick II *Emperor* 203
Freud, Sigmund 268
Fries, Heinrich 443
Friessen, S. J. 124
Frings, Joseph *Archbishop, Cardinal* 419
Froude, Richard Hurrell 248
Fulkerson, Mary McClintock 544–6
Furlong, Monica 542

Garrigou-Lagrange, Réginald,
    O. P. 276, 386, 412
Gehring, B. 130
Gelasius *Pope* 177
Gill, John 297
Glanville, Joseph 249
Goldingay, John 35–6
Gonzales, Justo 624–5
Gore, Charles *Bishop* 257
Graham, Elaine 15
Grande, Rutilio, S. J. *Martyr* 587
Gratian 208
Greenwood, John 303, 305
Gregory I *Pope* 178, 247
Gregory VII (Hildebrand) *Pope* 178,
    199–201, 203
Gregory IX *Pope* 209
Gregory XI *Pope* 212
Gregory XII *Pope* 213
Grey, Mary 15, 538
Grosseteste, Robert *Bishop* 203–4, 210
Guardini, Romano 274, 280, 415
Gutiérrez, Gustavo, O. P. 574–5, 585–6, 635

Haight, Roger, S. J. 11–12, 558–9, 563
Hales, John 242
Hamer, Jérôme 279
Hanson, Paul 35
Harnack, A. von 256, 365
Hatch, Edwin 257
Hauerwas, Stanley 603
Hawkins, Robert 304
Hazony, Yoram 42
Heidegger, Martin 433

Héloise 206
Helwys, Thomas 294, 296, 298, 307, 310
Henry II *King* 202
Henry V *Emperor* 201
Henry VIII *King* 241, 246–7
Herbert, George 249, 251
Hilary of Poitiers *Bishop, Saint* 174, 415
Hilda of Whitby *Saint* 542
Himes, Michael 264
Hippolytus *Martyr* 167–8
Hofman, Melchior 307
Hollenweger, Walter 337
Honorius III *Pope* 209
Hooker, Richard 7, 246–7, 251, 257, 296
Horrell, D. 139
Howard, Philip A. 580
Hubmaier, Balthasar 307
Humbert *Cardinal* 200
Hus, John *Martyr* 206–7, 213
Hut, Hans 307

Ignatius of Antioch *Bishop, Martyr, Saint* 5,
    188, 256, 300
Ignatius of Loyola *Saint* 433
Innocent III *Pope* 203–4
Innocent IV *Pope* 203–4, 211
Irenaeus of Lyon *Bishop, Martyr, Saint* 165–6,
    186, 256, 413

Jacob, Henry 296
James I (VI) *King* 242, 244, 248
James II *King* 250
Jedin, Hubert 624
Jenson, Robert 491, 502
Jerome *Saint* 174
Jewel, John *Bishop* 245, 251
Jewett, R. 139
John *King* 203
John XXIII *Pope* (15th century) 212–13
John XXIII *Pope, Saint* (20th century) 279,
    390, 415–16
John Paul II *Pope, Saint* 279, 283–4, 419, 458,
    480, 578, 596, 619, 622, 632–3
Johnson, Francis 299, 303, 305–6
Johnson, L. T. 82, 130
Jones, Serene 547
Joseph of Arimathea *Saint* 247

642 INDEX OF NAMES

Juan Ginés de Sepúlveda 579
Juana Inés de la Cruz 581–2
Juliana of Liège *Saint* 210
Julius II *Pope* 214
Justin Martyr *Martyr* 165
Justinian I *Emperor, Saint* 177

Kalu, Ogbu 625
Kärkkäinen, Veli-Matti 491, 501
Kasper, Walter *Bishop, Cardinal* 14, 25, 241,
    453–4, 457–9, 568
Keach, Benjamin 297–8
Keach, Elias 298
Keble, John 248
Kerr, Fergus, O. P. 421
Khomiakov, Alexei 189–91
Kilby, Karen 15
King, Peter 325
Kleutgen, Joseph, S. J. 270–1
Knox, Alexander 253
Komonchak, Joseph 270, 280, 566, 570
Koster, Mannes Dominikus, O. P. 276–7
Kuhn, Thomas 556–7
Küng, Hans 3, 279–80, 283, 556–7

Last, R. 140
Laud, William *Archbishop, Martyr* 245, 250–1
Lefebvre, Marcel *Archbishop* 419
Lehmann, Karl *Cardinal* 494
Lennan, Richard 283
Leo I (The Great) *Pope* 177–8
Leo IX *Pope* 200
Leo XIII *Pope* 267, 271, 276
Lightfoot, J. B. *Bishop* 257
Lindbeck, George 37–9
Loades, Anne 15
Locke, Kenneth 242
Loisy, Alfred 56, 271–2, 452
Lombard, Peter 6
Lonergan, Bernard, S. J. 561, 564, 568–9
Lossky, Vladimir 192
Louis IX *King, Saint* 208–9
Louis XII *King* 214
Lull, Raymond 205
Lumbala, F. Kabisele 632–3
Luther, Martin 5–6, 149, 214, 217–36, 402, 460
Luz, Ulrich 74–6

McAdoo, Henry *Archbishop* 239
MacDonald, M. Y. 120, 131, 137
MacIntyre, Alasdair 561
McMichael, Ralph 249
Mahon, Leo 584
Mangalwadi, Vishal 604–5
Mann, Thomas 22
Mannion, Gerard 11
Manson, T. W. 61, 94–5
Maréchal, Joseph, S. J. 433
Marpeck, Pilgram 307
Martin V *Pope* 213
Martín de Porres *Saint* 581
Mary, Blessed Virgin *Saint* 78, 184–8,
    243, 577–8
Mary I ('Tudor') *Queen* 309
Mary of Oignies *Saint* 209–10
Matthew Paris 209
Maurice, Frederick Denison 248–50
Maximos the Confessor *Saint* 189–90
Mayrargue, Cedric 631
Mechtild (Mechthild) of Magdeburg 210
Meeks, Wayne 121, 124, 564
Meggitt, J. J. 124
Melanchthon, Philipp 6, 217–36
Menenius Agrippa 127–8
Mensurius *Bishop* 171
Mersch, Émile, S. J. 276
Meyendorff, John 475
Michelangelo 215
Milbank, John 559–62, 565–6
Miltiades *Bishop* 170–1, 175
Milton, Anthony 242
Milton, John 21
Minear, Paul 56–7
Möhler, Johann Adam 268–70, 274–6,
    278, 396
Moltmann, Jürgen 493, 501
Morris, William *Bishop* 570
Murphy O'Connor, J. 138–9
Murray, Paul 15

Nautin, Pierre 166
N'Dayen, Joachim *Archbishop* 622
Nee, Watchman 605–10
Neu, Diann 542–3
Neufeld, Karl Heinz, S. J. 281

INDEX OF NAMES 643

Newbigin, Lesslie 598–9
Newman, John Henry *Blessed* 21, 151, 175, 248, 269, 555, 566
Nicholas V *Pope* 214
Nichols, Aidan, O. P. 411
Niles, D. T. *Bishop* 605
Novatian *Bishop* 169–71
Nteba, Metena 628
Nuttall, Geoffrey 296

Oakes, P. 139
Oden, Thomas 627–8
Oecolampadius 307
O'Malley, John W., S. J. 265, 282
Optatus of Milevis *Saint* 174–5
Origen 76, 148, 188
Ortiz, Fernando 579
Ottaviani, Alfredo *Cardinal* 416, 419
Outler, Albert 321

Palladius *Bishop* 176
Pannenberg, Wolfhart 487–504
Parente, Pietro *Archbishop, Cardinal* 412
Parker, Matthew *Archbishop* 247
Parker, Robert 306
Parmenianus *Bishop* 175
Passaglia, Carlo, S. J. 270
Patrick, Simon *Bishop* 249
Paul III *Pope* 264
Paul VI *Pope* 397, 419, 463, 587, 615, 621, 632–3
Paul of Samosata *Bishop* 170
Payne, E. A. (Ernest) 309
Péguy, Charles 273
Pelagius 176
Perkins, William 299
Perrone, Giovanni, S. J. 270
Peter *Apostle, Martyr, Saint* 75–8, 150–1, 204, 257, 455–6, 459, 462, 508
Philip IV ('le Bel', 'The Fair') *King* 204, 211
Philip Augustus *King* 203
Philips, Dietrich 306, 308
Philips, Gérard 281, 392, 418
Phillips, George 269
Pius II *Pope* 214
Pius IV *Pope* 265–6
Pius IX, *Pope* 270–1, 432, 441
Pius X *Pope* 271–2, 432

Pius XII *Pope* 276–7, 412–13, 437, 441, 449, 609
Plato 568
Pliny 151, 164
Polycarp *Martyr, Bishop, Saint* 256
Polycrates *Bishop* 166
Porete, Margarete 210
Pottmeyer, Hermann 283
Proctor Smith, Marjorie 542
Pusey, Edward Bouverie 248

Radner, Ephraim 38–9
Rahner, Karl, S. J. 26, 277–8, 282, 431–48, 630
Ramabai, Pandita 601
Ramankutty, Paul 601–2
Ramsey, A. M. (Michael) *Archbishop* 239, 247
Ratzinger, Joseph *Cardinal see* Benedict XVI *Pope*
Rendtorff, Trutz 365
Ricoeur, Paul 37
Riedemann, Peter 308
Robert of Pont l'Evêque *Archbishop* 202
Roberts, Richard 556, 563–4, 570
Robinson, Gene *Bishop* 255
Romero, Oscar *Archbishop, Martyr* 587
Ross, Susan 528, 547
Ruether, Rosemary Radford 531, 534–7, 541, 543–4, 548
Ruiz, Samuel *Bishop* 588–9
Runcie, Robert *Archbishop* 240
Russell, Lettie 537–8

Sanneh, Lamin 627
Sattler, Michael 307
Savanarola, Girolamo *Martyr* 215
Scheeben, Matthias Joseph 270
Scheffczyk, Leo *Cardinal* 281
Scheler, Max 274
Schillebeeckx, Edward 278, 556, 558–9, 562, 565–6
Schleiermacher, F. D. E. 364, 501
Schmemann, Alexander 597
Schnackenburg, Rudolf 55, 75
Scholer, John 154
Schrader, Clemens, S. J. 270
Schweizer, Eduard 75
Semmelroth, Otto, S. J. 278
Sergii *Metropolitan* 196

644 INDEX OF NAMES

Sigismund *Emperor* 212
Silvester *Bishop* 171
Sixtus IV *Pope* 215
Slee, Nicola 543
Smyth, John 294–7, 306, 308–12
Soskice, Janet Martin 15
Stanton, Elizabeth Cady 530, 532
Stark, Rodney 565
Stephen (of Rome) *Bishop* 170
Stillingfleet, Edward *Bishop* 325
Suárez, Emmanuel, O. P. 386
Suenens, Leon-Joseph *Archbishop, Cardinal* 418
Sullivan, Francis, S. J. 257
Sykes, S. W. (Stephen) *Bishop* 240

Tardini, Domenico *Cardinal* 415
Taylor, Jeremy *Bishop* 253
Tertullian 52, 168, 256
Theodoric *Emperor* 177
Theodosius II *Emperor* 177
Thomas, M. M. 598–9
Thomas Aquinas *Saint* 6, 207, 271, 560–1
Thurneysen, Eduard 362
Tillich, Paul 272, 365, 493
Tilliette, X. 411
Troelsch, Ernst 310–11
Tromp, Sebastian, S. J. 276, 279, 416
Turner, Daniel 298, 301, 311
Tyconius 176
Tyrrell, George, S. J. 272

Uchimura, Kanzō 600–1
Urban IV *Pope* 210

Urban V *Pope* 212
Urban VI *Pope* 212
Ussher, James *Archbishop* 253

Van Dusen, Henry Pitt 338
Victor *Bishop* 166
Visser't Hooft, W. A. 400
Vonier, Anscar, O. S. B. 277
von Rad, Gerhard 40, 49

Waldeck Rousseau, Pierre 409
Wang Ming Dao 603–5
Watkins, Clare 19
Watson, Francis 41
Watson, Natalie 15
Weber, Max 560, 566
Wesley, Charles 320
Wesley, John 317–34
White, B. R. 297, 309
Whitgift, John *Archbishop* 244, 251
William of Ockham 207
William of Orange (William III) *King* 250
Williams, Rowan *Archbishop* 467, 505–23
Wingate, Andrew 601
Witherington, B., III 137
Wittstadt, Klaus 393
Woodhead, Linda 547
Wright, Christopher 40
Wyclif, John 206–7, 213

Zephyrinus *Bishop* 167–8
Zizioulas, John *Metropolitan* 196, 423–4, 467–86
Zosimus *Pope* 176
Zwingli, Huldrych 307

Index of Subjects

Note: 'church', 'ecclesiology', 'God', and 'theology' are not indexed because the whole book is devoted to those subjects.

African ecclesiology 342, 538, 615–38
African Instituted Churches 342, 623
Aggiornamento 280, 285, 629
Anabaptists 293, 306–15, 376, 600–1; *see also* Radical Reformation
Anglican Communion Covenant 254–5
Anglican Consultative Council (ACC) 254
Anglican–Methodist Covenant 243
Anglican–Roman Catholic International Commission (ARCIC) 241, 256, 461–2
Anglicanism, Anglican ecclesiology 239–62, 461–2, 512–21
anticlericalism 383, 583–4
Apartheid 561
apologetics 3–4, 627
apostles 63, 71, 74, 86–90, 256–7
Apostolic Fathers 5
apostolicity, apostolic succession 193–4, 240, 246, 325
Archbishop of Canterbury 254
architecture 324
Arles, Council of (AD 314) 171
Asian ecclesiology 595–614
atheism 421
Augsburg Confession 318, 321, 492–3, 495, 502
authority 330, 462, 608–9
autocephalous Orthodox churches 195
Avignon papacy 211–12
Azusa Street revival 337–9, 342

baptism 8, 112, 134–5, 147, 150, 178, 328, 496–8; *see also* sacraments
Baptism, Eucharist and Ministry 256, 321, 494, 540
Baptist ecclesiology 293–315
Baptist Union of Great Britain 299

Baptist World Alliance 293, 299
base/basic Christian Communities 384–5, 622
Basel, Council of (1431–7) 199, 213, 215
Beguines 209–10
belief 103–5; *see also* creed, creeds
Bible, Scripture 4, 8–9, 33–160, 321, 450–1, 509–10, 532–4; *see also* Word of God
Black Death 205
Black theology 575
body of Christ, Mystical Body 6, 276, 421–4, 449–53, 459, 470, 492, 513, 547–8; *see also* images of the church
Bolshevism 196

Cambridge Camden Society 3
canon (biblical), canonical criticism 36–37, 53
canon law *see* law
Canterbury, See of, Cathedral 202, 254
Catholic Action 383–4
catholicity 191–2, 324, 494–5
Chalcedon, Council of (AD 451) 177–8, 472
charismatic movement/churches 335–57; *see also* Pentecostalism
Chaucer, Geoffrey 215
Chinese churches 342–3
Christology 15–16
church and state 194–6, 250–1, 307, 310, 409, 502
church as sacrament 278, 329, 435–8, 446, 493
churchless Christianity 599–601
colonialism 578–82, 626
communion ecclesiology (*koinōnia, communio*) 14, 90–1, 254, 278–9, 284, 396–8, 409–29, 454–7, 467–86, 569–70

646 INDEX OF SUBJECTS

communion of saints, *sanctorum communio* 3, 191–2, 555–6
Conciliar Movement, conciliarity, conciliarists, synodality 6–7, 199, 212–14, 258, 265–6, 479–83
Concordat of Worms 201
connexionalism 322–3
Constance, Council of (1414–18) 199, 212–13, 265
Constantinople (city) 177, 195, 199, 215
Constantinople, Council of (AD 381) 190
contingency 8–10
conversion 122, 388, 438–40, 564–8, 629–33
Councils (general) 6, 193, 248; *see also Councils by name and date*
covenant 293–7
creation 484
creed, creeds 5, 11, 22–3, 177, 183, 190–1, 248, 323, 443, 492
Critical Theory 17; *see also* Frankfurt School

Dead Sea Scrolls 95
development (of doctrine) 8, 21, 566
diaconate 327
dialogue 442
discipleship 62–71, 73–5, 80–1, 86–7, 108–9
discipline (excommunication) 232–3, 294, 308
division, disunity, schism 22–4
doctrine 510–12
Donation of Constantine 178
Donatism 175–6, 628
Dort, Synod of 242

Eastern Orthodox Churches 5, 183–98, 213–14, 240, 254, 256, 273, 419, 460–1, 467–8
Ecclesiological Investigations International Research Network 11
Ecclesiology (journal) 11
Ecumenical Association of Third World Theologians (EATWOT) 575, 596
ecumenism, Ecumenical Movement 2, 13–16, 22–4, 399–400, 419, 493–4, 595–6; *see also* unity, World Council of Churches (WCC)
Edinburgh International Missionary Conference (1910) 2

ekklēsia, ecclēsia 2–3, 33, 55–7, 70, 87–8, 100, 125–7, 147, 453, 493, 533–4
election *see* predestination, election
Elvira, Council of (early 4th century AD) 171
Enlightenment 557
episcopacy *see* ministry
eschatology, *eschaton* 23–4, 67, 72–3, 80–2, 83–6, 472–3, 597–8
ethics, morals 148–9
ethnography 18–19, 565, 633
Eucharist, Holy Communion, Last Supper, Lord's Supper 8, 22, 24, 48, 68–9, 90, 112, 135–6, 147, 156–7, 174, 190–1, 248, 278–9, 298, 327–8, 409–29, 421–4, 452–3, 493–4, 496–8, 537–8, 543, 606–7
Eucharistic Ecclesiology 196, 278–9, 329, 421–4, 450–64, 468
evangelization, evangelism 13

Faith and Order, faith and order 2, 4, 14
family 105–6, 127, 597–8
Federation of Asian Bishops' Conferences (FABC) 595–6
feminist ecclesiology/theology 15–16, 527–51, 576
Florence, Council of (1437–9) 195, 213–14
foundation of the church 19–21, 93–5
Frankfurt School 17
Free Church 310–11
friars, orders of 204–5

Gallicanism 265, 268
gender 527–51
Global Anglican Future Conference (GAFCON) 634
globalisation 557, 573
glossolalia 86, 341, 345–6, 602
gospel *see* Word of God
grace 431–48
Great Schism (between East and West, 1054) 199–200, 480
Great Schism (of the West, 1378–1417) 6, 212–14, 460
Gregorian Reform 199

Hampton Court Conference 244
Hermas, Shepherd of 164–5, 184–5
HIV/AIDS 623

holiness of the Church 191–2, 438–9, 494–5

Holy Spirit, pneumatology 9, 59–62, 82, 85–7, 103, 109–10, 112–13, 220, 268–9, 275, 318, 324, 327, 335–7, 371–2, 436–7, 444, 453, 471–3, 490–1, 589, 607–8

household, housechurches 120–141, 344

identity 3–4, 7, 9, 15, 99, 103–5

ideology 12, 553–72

images of the church 106–7, 127–30, 152, 184–8, 394–6; *see also* body of Christ, Mystical Body

inculturation 557, 576, 578, 588–9, 598–9, 624, 630–3

Independents 293, 310

indigenous Asian churches 601–3

infallibility 282

institutions 19–20, 130–1, 266, 441, 471, 584–5, 600, 616, 625

Instruments of Communion 254–5; *see also* Anglican Consultative Council (ACC), Archbishop of Canterbury, Lambeth Conference

International Theological Commission 587–8

investiture controversy 201–2

Jews, Judaism, ancient Israel 33–53, 66, 79, 100, 148, 349–50, 369, 453, 500

Joint Declaration on the Doctrine of Justification 329, 463, 494

Keswick Convention 609–10

Kingdom/Reign of God 19–20, 59–67, 71–2, 79–80, 83–91, 478, 484, 488–90, 493, 589

laity 200, 275, 398–9, 418, 441, 583–4

Lambeth Conference 240, 252, 254

Lateran, Fourth Council of (1215) 203

Lateran, Fifth Council of (1512–17) 214

Latin America 573–93

law, canon law 206, 247, 375

lay presidency (at the Eucharist) 327

leadership *see* ministry

Liberation(ist) Theology 573–93

liturgy *see* worship

local and universal church 24–5, 467–86, 605–10, 621

love 113–15

Lyons, Council of (1245) 204

magisterium 284, 630

Magna Carta 203, 252

Marxism 588

meeting(s) 136–41

Meissen Agreement 243

Methodist ecclesiology 317–34

middle way (*via media*) 249

ministry (bishops, priests, deacons, elders, pastors) 8, 88–9, 131–4, 147, 150, 153, 163–4, 167–8, 194–5, 217–36, 255–6, 300–1, 325–8, 331–2, 339–41, 376–7, 398–9, 476, 498–9, 530, 540, 556

minjung theology 596–7

mission, missiology 3–4, 13, 91–2, 101–3, 284, 331, 378–9, 443–5, 493–4, 626, 632

Modernism (Roman Catholic) 271–2, 276, 280, 412, 432

monasticism, monasteries, religious life 246, 248

mystery 5, 281–2, 414, 418, 432–3, 493

Mystical Body *see* body of Christ, Mystical Body

Nazism (National Socialism) 274, 411

Nicaea, Council of (AD 325), Creed of 177

No-Church movement 600–1

Non-Jurors 257

nouvelle théologie 273–6, 386, 412–13

Orthodox Churches *see* Eastern Orthodox Churches

Oxford Movement, Tractarian/s/ism 247–8, 257, 326

papacy 6, 202, 211–12, 218, 225, 257, 271, 455–7, 477–83; *see also* Rome

paradigm shifts 556–7

Pastoral Theology 17

patriarchates 194–5

patriarchy 531

Pauline churches 119–46

Pentecostalism, Pentecostal ecclesiology, Pentecostal churches 13, 335–57, 588–9, 596–7, 610–11, 631–2

648   INDEX OF SUBJECTS

People of God 277, 569; *see also* images of
  the church
periti, peritus 280-1, 416-17, 449
persecution 90, 150-1, 168-9, 171
personhood, personalism 470-1
Pisa, Council of (1511) 214
Platonism 9
pluralism 546
polity, governance 130-4, 244, 257, 321,
  339-41; *see also* ministry
Pontifical Council for Promoting Christian
  Unity 14
poor, oppressed 573-93, 635-6
Porvoo Agreement 243
power 10
practice, practical ecclesiology 17-19, 444
praxis 573-93
Prayer Book(s) (Book of Common Prayer,
  1662) 245, 256, 318, 328
predestination, election 232, 499-500
Presbyterianism 244, 257, 310
priesthood of all believers *see* royal
  priesthood
primacy 479-83
Protestantism 217-36, 241-5, 264-5, 460-1,
  582-3, 596, 622-3
psychoanalysis 545
Puritanism 243-5, 293, 299, 309-10, 324, 328

Quakerism 600

Radical Orthodoxy 2
Radical Reformation 25, 225-6; *see also*
  Anabaptists
Receptive Ecumenism 14-15
reform, renewal 10-11, 217-36, 253, 282,
  352-3, 400-2
Reformation, Reformers 6-7, 151, 217-36,
  241-2, 250, 257, 264-5, 307, 376, 442, 460,
  499, 502, 554, 557, 569
regula fidei (rule of faith) 463
religions, Asian 595-614
Renaissance 214, 246
renewal (movements) 272-3
ressourcement 273-6, 280, 285, 383-7,
  412-13, 629
revelation 432-3, 451

ritual(s) 134, 248
Roman Catholic Church 2, 7, 75, 241, 245,
  256-7, 263-92, 297, 363-4, 383-465,
  467-8, 554, 573-93, 610-11, 615-38;
  see also papacy
Rome, See of, city of 163-76, 177, 199,
  202, 214-15
royal priesthood (priesthood of all
  believers) 151-2, 222-4, 326, 380

sacraments 8, 112, 134-6, 147, 149, 174-5,
  217-36, 318-19, 322, 340-1, 350-1, 376,
  492, 496-8, 508-10; *see also* baptism,
  church as sacrament, Eucharist
saints 192
Sardica (Serdica), Eastern Council of
  (AD 343) 176
Scripture *see* Bible
secularisation 378, 409, 546
*sensus fidelium, consensus fidelium, sensus
  fidei* 269, 276, 282-4, 330, 630
Separatists (English) 293-315
sexuality, homosexuality 254-5, 597
sin in/of the church 9, 21-2, 438-9, 472-3
slavery 579
social science 12, 121-3, 553-72, 617-18
societas perfecta 267, 270, 277, 279, 629
Society of St Pius X 419
Sociology of Knowledge 17
St Hilda Community 542-3
symbol(ism) 434-5
Symposium of Episcopal Conferences
  of Africa and Madagascar
  (SECAM) 621-2
Synod of Bishops 283, 397, 462-3

Thirty-nine Articles of Religion 246, 249, 318
Three Self Patriotic Movement 342, 604
toleration 311
Tractarian/s/ism *see* Oxford Movement
tradition 461-2
Trent, Council of (1545-63) 199, 246, 248,
  264-8, 280, 397, 432
Trinity 341, 469-70, 490-1

ultramontanism 268, 270
United Methodist Church 321-2, 326, 332

unity 170, 189–91, 224, 243, 268–9, 273, 279–80, 323, 331–2, 440–3, 459–63, 494–5, 512–20; *see also* ecumenism, Ecumenical Movement

universities 206–8

Vatican I (First Vatican Council, 1869–70) 199, 267–8, 270–1, 276, 432

Vatican II (Second Vatican Council, 1962–5) 2, 7, 11–12, 19, 151, 199, 240, 267, 273–4, 279–85, 322, 379, 383–407, 409–29, 432–48, 449–65, 615–38

Vienne, Council of (1311) 210

vocation 26, 61, 320

Windsor Report, The 255, 516

witness 115–16

Word of God, preaching, proclamation 64, 80–3, 89, 217–36, 318–19, 321, 456, 463, 492, 508–10; *see also* Bible, Scripture

World Council of Churches (WCC) 2, 14, 372, 529, 539–40; *see also* ecumenism, Ecumenical Movement, unity

World Methodist Council 321–2, 329

worship 110–11, 153–5, 246, 474, 541–4

Printed in the USA/Agawam, MA
May 2, 2024